COLLEGES
WORTH
YOUR MONEY

COLLEGES WORTH YOUR MONEY

A Guide to What America's Top Schools Can Do for You

Andrew Belasco, Dave Bergman, & Michael Trivette

ROWMAN & LITTLEFIELD

Lanham • Boulder • New York • London

Published by Rowman & Littlefield
An imprint of The Rowman & Littlefield Publishing Group, Inc.
4501 Forbes Boulevard, Suite 200, Lanham, Maryland 20706
www.rowman.com

6 Tinworth Street, London, SE11 5AL, United Kingdom

British Library Cataloguing in Publication Information Available

Library of Congress Cataloging-in-Publication Data

Names: Belasco, Andrew, author. | Bergman, Dave, author. | Trivette, Michael, author.
Title: Colleges worth your money : a guide to what America's top schools can do for you / Andrew Belasco, Dave Bergman, Michael Trivette.
Description: 2nd edition. | Lanham, Maryland : Rowman & Littlefield, [2021] | Includes bibliographical references. | Summary: "Unlike existing college guidebooks, which contain easy-to-Google admissions statistics and anecdotal generalizations about campus life, Colleges Worth Your Money reveals where graduates work, salaries, grad school acceptances, internships and research opportunities, career services ratings, and data-rich, school-specific admissions strategies."—Provided by publisher.
Identifiers: LCCN 2021005812 (print) | LCCN 2021005813 (ebook) | ISBN 9781475859638 (paperback) | ISBN 9781475859645 (epub)
Subjects: LCSH: College choice—United States—Directories. | College costs—United States—Directories. | College graduates—United States—Finance, Personal. | Universities and colleges—United States—Directories.
Classification: LCC LB2350.5 .B429 2021 (print) | LCC LB2350.5 (ebook) | DDC 378.1/61—dc23
LC record available at https://lccn.loc.gov/2021005812
LC ebook record available at https://lccn.loc.gov/2021005813

♾️™ The paper used in this publication meets the minimum requirements of American National Standard for Information Sciences—Permanence of Paper for Printed Library Materials, ANSI/NISO Z39.48-1992.

Andrew Belasco, Ph.D., a graduate of Georgetown University and Harvard University, is a higher education researcher, counselor, and CEO of College Transitions, an educational consulting firm. His work has been published in the nation's top higher education journals and featured in dozens of media outlets, including *The New York Times*, *Washington Post*, *Time*, *Boston Globe, Forbes*, *The Chronicle of Higher Education*, and NPR, among others. Andrew is also the co-author of *The Enlightened College Applicant: A New Approach to the Search and Admissions Process* (Rowman & Littlefield, 2016).

Dave Bergman, Ed.D., earned his doctoral degree from Temple University and has fifteen years of professional experience that includes work as a teacher, high school administrator, adjunct professor, researcher, and independent educational consultant. As a co-founder of College Transitions, Dave oversees the collegetransitions. com blog and Dataverse, reaching an audience in excess of two million readers annually. Dave is also the co-author of *The Enlightened College Applicant: A New Approach to the Search and Admission Process* (Rowman & Littlefield, 2016).

Michael Trivette, Ph.D., a graduate of the University of Georgia Institute of Higher Education, has over fifteen years of experience in the higher-education field, including college admissions, enrollment management, intercollegiate athletics, student support services, and student life. A co-founder of College Transitions, he also has experience working within the University of North Carolina System and the University System of Georgia. His research has been published in *Educational Policy*, *Review of Higher Education*, *The Journal of Higher Education*, and the *Journal of Education Finance*.

Contents

Introduction & Methodology

Before the birth of the modern internet, savvy teens seeking information on prospective colleges cracked open the latest Yellow Pages-thick college guidebook, eager to soak in school-specific admissions data that felt like classified information. Possessors of such guidebooks were the true insiders of the day, privy to admissions statistics that simply could not be found within the glossy brochures delivered to the masses via snail mail. By 2021, those oversized volumes have been rendered far less essential. Basic admissions data such as SAT ranges, grade point averages, tuition costs, and acceptance rates are available via fast and free Google searches. Everyone is now—at least in 1980s or '90s terms—an insider.

The formula for these annual editions is simple. Easy-to-find admissions and tuition data points are complemented by blocks of heavily anecdotal text designed to reveal something about the campus milieu: the quality of the food, the architectural style of the buildings, the political leanings of the student body, and the subjective like. While these books all serve as useful starting points for your college search (we read them ourselves each year), they fail to acknowledge the seismic shift taking place in the national conversation about higher education—the idea that students should stop obsessing over gaining admission into the most prestigious schools that will accept them and instead ask, "What can a given college do for me?" If students/parents are going to pony up $200,000 or more in tuition alone, they should first demand to see outcomes data, return on investment (ROI) figures, and a statistically backed account of unique opportunities for undergraduates. That's where the college guide you're holding comes into play.

Why do I need this guide?

There are two main reasons:

(1) Given the absurd cost of a college education, finding a school that will provide an acceptable ROI has never been more challenging.

(2) Your prospective colleges are likely to be more selective than they were only a few years ago; greater information gathering/strategic planning will be required to successfully gain admission.

Let's begin with the issue of price. As we get older, it's easy to fall into a nostalgic trap on the subject of how much things cost. For example, "When I was a boy, you could feed a family of four for a Buffalo nickel." Yet when it comes to lamenting rising college expenses, there is actual data to back up the sticker shock. In 1950, the University of Pennsylvania charged $600 per year to attend—roughly $6,000 in 2021 money. Today, Penn's annual cost of attendance is over $79,000. By 1960, most private institutions charged an annual fee of $1,500–$2,000 that equates to $12,000–$16,000 today. In the current marketplace, a $50,000 annual tuition is considered "reasonable." This is hardly just a private school phenomenon. The University of North Carolina at Chapel Hill's current in-state tuition cost of $9k is one of the best bargains in all of higher education. Of course, that pales in comparison to the in-state tuition of thirty years ago—only $504 per year. (No, that's *not* a typo).

Turning to the matter of increased selectivity, you don't need to look back to the '50s, '60s, or even '70s to find a college admissions landscape vastly different from today's hyper-competitive environment. In 1980, nearly half of all applicants were accepted into prestigious Swarthmore College while the Class of 2023 had a 9 percent acceptance rate. As recently as the 1990s, the University of Chicago accepted 60–70 percent of those who applied, but for applicants to the Class of 2023, only 6 percent were successful. Less drastic but still significant changes have proliferated as the overwhelming majority of desirable public and private schools have grown more selective in recent years. As of the publication of this book, many of the most prestigious schools in the country boast single-digit acceptance rates, including all the Ivy League schools (except Cornell University, which is a fraction over 10 percent) as well as Stanford University, Johns Hopkins University, Duke University, Bowdoin College, Pomona College, Northwestern University, Vanderbilt University, Rice University, and the Massachusetts Institute of Technology. Other elite schools including Williams College, Amherst College, and the University of Southern California all have inched closer to the single-digit club and will likely join it soon.

The reasons for this increased level of selectivity include an influx of highly-qualified foreign students applying to US colleges, the Common App making it easier for top students to apply to as many elite schools as they wish, and a greater number of applicants paying for services, such as private SAT tutors, that ultimately enhance their academic profiles.

How to use this guide:

We hope the above statistics have convinced you that the college selection and admissions process has never been more of a high-stakes game. Parents/students who are about to essentially take out another mortgage to finance their own or their teens' college education should, at the very least, first perform the equivalent of a home inspection. Just as it is easy to fall in love with a house based on a Zillow photo, many select a college based on surface observations such as the campus is pretty, the school colors would look nice on a bumper sticker, or you've heard good things from other parents in your social circle. Think of this guidebook as an inspection report with no crawlspace left unexplored.

Each profile includes six statistically rich narrative sections and two tables containing in excess of seventy additional data points. The following is a brief overview of the information included for each school and why it is important for prospective college students (and their parents) to know.

Inside the Classroom

We begin each profile by discussing what makes a given institution academically unique. Some schools have a core curriculum that dictates three semesters of study; others have an entirely open curriculum. Some mandate foreign language, physical education, a freshman seminar or two, and a senior thesis; others have no such requirements. Statistics on class size, undergraduate research opportunities, study abroad participation and—when possible—institutional survey data regarding professor availability and the quality of classroom instruction are included. In this section, we also highlight particular programs/departments that have standout reputations as well as how seniors fare in landing nationally competitive postgraduate scholarships.

Outside the Classroom

Words such as "vibe," "feel," and "atmosphere" may sound like flaky reasons to pick one college over another, yet when formulating college lists, future applicants absolutely should be mindful of their fit at a given school. The key is to properly size up the vibe/feel/atmosphere through more than merely a brief and heavily sanitized campus tour.

Some traits of a given school are easy to spot, and the contrast between institutions can be stark. For example, attending a small liberal arts school is going to be a wholly different social experience than attending a flagship state university with ten times the enrollment. However, there are many small liberal arts schools with high percentages of student-athletes where Greek life dominates the social scene. While this section is certainly our most anecdotal, we use statistics to dig beyond mere generalizations wherever possible.

For instance, if—like at Wake Forest University—85 percent of the student body participates in National Collegiate Athletic Association (NCAA), club, or intramural sports, and you hate sports, that information may help you cross the school off your list. If you are dead set on joining a fraternity or sorority, Bucknell University's 35-40 percent rate of participation in Greek life will be more attractive than the 4 percent pledge rate at Wesleyan University. If volunteer work is important to you, you may wish to target a school filled with kindred spirits, such as the College of William & Mary, where thousands perform community service every year. If a cappella is an essential creative outlet for you, a school such as Amherst, where one can barely count the number of established singing groups on two hands, may be appealing.

Undoubtedly, any personality type can find at least a few like-minded souls at any of the 3,000 four-year colleges in the United States, but it's important that teens find schools where they can develop a true sense of belonging. Research has consistently demonstrated that college students who feel connected to their school experience far greater academic success than those who do not.

Career Services

In an effort to entice applicants, college brochures are usually filled with group shots of smiling students on picturesque quads, amenities such as Olympic-size pools and rock-climbing walls, and dining halls that look like five-star restaurants. Those images are usually accompanied by some hollow catchphrase such as "Where leaders are born." Yet you likely won't find much (if any) information about the career services offerings—one of the most overlooked but important offices within a university. In reality, the professionals who provide individual career counseling, arrange internships, engage in corporate recruiting, and plan job fairs will do far more for your future than that towering rock climbing wall.

We answer the questions that students should ask when they evaluate their prospective colleges: What is the student-to-counselor ratio? What percent of students engage with career services? Does this happen in freshman year or does counseling only get utilized by seniors? We'll provide information on job fairs, networking events, corporate recruiting on campus, and how helpful staff are with arranging internships. In utilizing this section, you will discover which schools actually give rise to tomorrow's leaders vs. those whose public relations departments merely thought up an empty marketing slogan. And, yes, on occasion we will briefly note rock climbing walls or exceptionally delicious cuisine because, well, those things are nice to know as long as they aren't one of the top reasons you pick School A over School B.

Professional Outcomes

We'll look at how recent graduating classes are faring six months after graduation. In examining the list of companies that hire the most alumni, you'll see which schools serve as a pipeline to many of the nation's premier employers. Geographic information will allow you to see where the largest pockets of alumni settle—a factor that may assist your networking efforts. You'll also be able to identify which undergraduate institutions send large numbers of students to elite graduate and professional schools. Universities that have notable success preparing their students for admission into law and medical schools are highlighted.

Admissions

As wonderful as many high school guidance counselors are, even the best are pulled in a million different directions over the course of the day. To quantify that phenomenon, counselors in public high schools report spending only 22 percent of their time on college-related counseling while their private school counterparts spend a far healthier 55 percent. In either setting, given their breadth of responsibilities, even knowledgeable counselors may not be able to keep track of the latest admissions-related news at every one of the top postsecondary institutions in the country.

Given the aforementioned escalation in selectivity over the last few years, schools that may have been considered *safety schools* when you were a freshman may now be closer to *reach schools*. A multitude of applicants to the University of California's branch campuses discovered that reality the hard way just a few short years ago. It's important to consider the way a given school is trending from a selectivity standpoint, which is why we include our unique "five-year admissions trend" metric that shows the degree to which the school has become more/less competitive in recent years. Further analysis of that number will reveal whether the decreasing acceptance rate is simply the result of an influx of borderline applicants or whether the profile of the average accepted student is actually shifting. We also will identify whether an admissions edge can be gained by applying early, the impact of legacy status, and the factors each admissions office values most.

Worth Your Money?

The worth of a college degree is almost always context-dependent. Plenty of students attend unspectacular universities and go on to incredible levels of success; conversely, plenty of young people have attended prestigious institutions and struggled in their careers. A school that may be an incredible value for an in-state electrical engineering major may be a terrible choice for out-of-state students concentrating in sociology.

The intent of this section is to (a) give you an overview of how generous (or stingy) particular schools are with financial aid; (b) inform you about cost of attendance, in-state vs. out-of-state tuition rates, and the amount of debt students graduate with; and (c) give an assessment of the circumstances in which one might want to be wary of paying the full sticker price for a given school. Think of this as an introductory counseling session that will get you thinking about whether a school's cost makes sense for *you*.

Data Tables

In addition to the data-heavy narrative section, each profile is accompanied by two tables brimming with useful and often under appreciated statistical information.

But first, a quick note on missing data points

Missing data points fall into one of three different categories: Not Applicable, Not Offered, or Not Reported

Not Applicable – Used when the data point in question is not applicable to this specific institution. For example, the admission rate for men at a women's only college will be listed as "Not Applicable."

Not Offered – Used when an institution does not offer the admission plan or activity listed. For example, if an institution does not offer an Early Action application plan, "Not Offered" is indicated.

Not Reported or NR – Used when the institution does not make the data point available to the public.

Now, let's get to the data! The following data points are included for each of the 175 institutions listed in this guide:

Admissions Data

Admission Rate
The overall percentage of the total application pool that is offered admission.

Admission Rate (Men)
The overall percentage of male applicants that are offered admission.

Admission Rate (Women)
The overall percentage of the female applicants that are offered admission.

Early Action Admission Rate
The percentage of applicants admitted during the early action (EA) or single-choice early action (SCEA) rounds.

Early Decsion Admission Rate
The percentage of applicants admitted during the early decision (ED) round.

Early Decision Admits as a Percentage of Total Admits
The percentage of total admits that come by way of early decision (ED).

Admission Rate (five-year trend)
This is the percentage change in the acceptance rate from five years ago. For example, if a school's acceptance rate was 32 percent in 2014 and 27 percent in 2019, the five-year trend would be -5 percent.

Percent of Admits Attending (yield rate)
A school's yield rate is the percentage of accepted students who ultimately elect to enroll in the freshman class divided by the number of accepted applicants. For example, if 5,000 students were accepted and 1,000 chose to enroll, the yield rate would be 20 percent.

Transfer Admission Rate
The overall percentage of the total transfer applicant pool that is offered admission.

SAT Reading/Writing (middle 50 percent)
The 25th-and 75th-percentile reading/writing SAT scores for first-year students.

SAT Math (middle 50 percent)
The 25th-and 75th-percentile SAT math scores for first-year students.

ACT Composite (middle 50 percent)
The 25th-and 75th-percentile composite ACT scores for first-year students.

Percent in Top 10 percent, 25 percent, and 50 percent of High School Class
Among enrolled freshmen who reported their class ranks, the percent that finished in the top tenth, quarter, and half of their graduating classes.

Demonstrated Interest
Whether an applicant's demonstrated interest is considered in the admissions process.

Legacy Status
Whether an applicant's familial ties to the institution is considered in the admissions process.

Interview
Whether a college offers an alumni, on-campus or virtual admissions interview.

Enrollment Data

Total Undergraduate Enrollment
The number of undergraduate students attending the institution.

Percent Part-Time
The percentage of undergraduates taking fewer than twelve credits per semester.

Percent Male/Female
The percentage of males and percent of females that comprise the undergraduate student body.

Percent Out of State
The percentage of domestic (U.S.) students who are not residents of the state in which the college is located.

Percent Fraternity/Sorority
The percentage of undergraduates who are members of Greek organizations.

Percent on Campus (Freshmen)
The percentage of freshmen who live on campus.

Percent on Campus (All Undergraduates)
The percentage of all undergraduates living on campus.

Ethnic/Racial Demographics
The percentage of undergraduate students who identify as African American, Asian, Hispanic, and white. Categories are also provided for "other" and "race or ethnicity unknown."

Percent International
The number of foreign students enrolled at an American university who are studying through a temporary visa divided by the undergraduate population.

Percent Low-Income
The number of students who meet the US Department of Education standard for "low income" (for a family of four, that figure is $39,300 per year) divided by the undergraduate population.

Academics

Student-to-Faculty Ratio
The number of undergraduate students divided by the number of full-time faculty members.

Percent of Classes under Twenty Students
The number of undergraduate course sections with an enrollment under 20 divided by the number of undergraduate course sections.

Percent of Classes between Twenty and Forty-Nine Students
The number of undergraduate course sections with an enrollment between 20 and 49 divided by the number of undergraduate course sections.

Percent of Classes with Fifty Students or More
The number of undergraduate course sections with an enrollment of 50 or more divided by the number of undergraduate course sections.

Percent of Full-Time Faculty
The percentage of faculty members who are full-time professors at a given institution.

Percent of Full-Time Faculty with Terminal Degree
The percentage of full-time professors who possess the highest possible degree in their field (typically PhD).

Top Programs
This is not purely a list of the most popular majors by volume. While that is factored into our algorithm, so are other metrics including selectivity, student-to-faculty ratio, class size, peer assessment, graduate earnings (by major), and PhD productivity. (More details are included later in this section.)

Retention Rate
The percentage of freshmen who return to the same institution the following fall to begin their sophomore year.

Four-Year Graduation Rate
The percentage of enrolled undergraduate students who graduate in four years or fewer.

Six-Year Graduation Rate
The percentage of enrolled undergraduate students who graduate in six years or fewer.

Curricular Flexibility

Many colleges have a "core curriculum" and "distributional requirements" that dictate what specific courses and/or general categories of courses all undergraduates must complete in order to graduate. We awarded schools one of three grades: Very Flexible, Somewhat Flexible, or Less Flexible, depending on the extent and specificity of their curricular mandates.

Academic Rating

To construct an academic rating for each college, we rely on ten different indicators of academic quality, namely the average SAT/ACT composite of incoming students, the percentage of incoming students ranked in the top 10 percent of their high school class, student-to-faculty ratio, class size, the percentage of faculty who are full-time employees, the percentage of faculty with terminal degrees, mean faculty salary, freshman retention rate, six year-graduation rate, and graduation performance. This last variable compares an institution's actual graduation rate with its predicted graduation rate, after controlling for the high school class rank and SAT/ACT scores of incoming students as well as the percentage of undergraduates receiving a Pell Grant, a grant primarily given to low-income students.

After collecting data, we normalize and subsequently sum values across all ten indicators, assigning each institution a total score, and by extension, its academic rating. Academic ratings range from one to five stars (institutions receiving a rating of lower than three stars are not featured in this book), with a rating of five stars assigned to colleges and universities receiving the highest total scores. We opted to use a discrete variable (a "star" rating) instead of each college's total numerical score, because incorporating the latter would presume that our assessment is precise. It is not. An institution's academic environment and offerings can never be captured by a single number. That said, we do believe the ratings assigned can prove useful when comparing the academic climates and offerings of the colleges featured in this book.

Financial

Institutional Type

Indicates whether the school is a public or private institution.

In-State Tuition

For public schools, the annual cost of full-time tuition for one academic year charged to state residents. For private schools, we list the general tuition here.

Out-of-State Tuition

For public schools, the annual cost of full-time tuition for one academic year charged to state residents. For private schools, we list the general tuition here.

Room & Board

The annual cost for university-owned housing and meal plans.

Required Fees

Mandatory fees charged by the school for things such as technology, the library, athletics, laboratory experiences, and transportation.

Books and Supplies

The average figure students pay for one academic year's worth of books purchased through the university bookstore.

Average Need-Based Grant

Of students who qualified for need-based aid, the average dollar amount the institution awarded.

Average Percent of Need Met
Of students who qualified for need-based aid, the average percentage of the demonstrated need that the institution met.

Average Merit-Based Award
Among incoming freshmen without financial need who received a merit-based award, the average annual award that was granted.

Percentage Receiving Merit-Based Awards – All Freshmen
The percentage of incoming freshmen who received merit aid.

Percent Receiving Merit-Based Awards – Freshmen without Need
The percentage of incoming freshmen who received some degree of non-need-based aid.

Average Cumulative Debt
Among students who took out loans to pay for a given college, the average cumulative debt owed upon graduation.

Percentage of Students Borrowing
The percentage of students who are taking out loans in order to fund a portion of their educational expenses.

Career

Who Recruits
A list of high-profile companies that regularly recruit on campus.

Notable Internships
Collected from institutional data sources, this is a list of employers who regularly provide meaningful internships to undergraduate students.

Top Industries
According to LinkedIn data, a list of the sectors where the highest number of recent graduates find employment.

Top Employers
According to LinkedIn data, the companies/organizations that employ the largest number of graduates.

Where Alumni Work
According to LinkedIn data, the cities where the largest concentration of alumni currently live.

Earnings
In an effort to give you the most complete picture of alumni earning possible, we include three data points. They are as follows:

College Scorecard: This number is the median earnings of students who received federal financial aid ten years after entering a given college.

PayScale (Early Career): The median salary of individuals with 0-5 years of work experience, based on the responses of 3.5 million survey respondents.

PayScale (Mid-Career): The median salary of individuals with 10+ years of work experience based on millions of survey respondents. This figure tends to be higher than the other two because it includes professionals in mid-to-late career, when earnings are typically highest.

Rankings

Money Ranking
A college's ranking by *Money*, which is determined via the following formula: six-year graduation rate (30 percent), value-added graduation rate (30 percent), peer quality (10 percent), instructor quality (10 percent), financial troubles (15 percent), and Pell Grant recipient outcomes (5 percent).

US News & World Report Ranking
A college's ranking by *US News & World Report (US News)*, which is determined via the following formula: outcomes (35 percent), faculty resources (20 percent), expert opinion (20 percent), financial resources (10 percent), student excellence (10 percent), and alumni giving (5 percent).

Wall Street Journal/Times Higher Education Ranking
A college's ranking by *The Wall Street Journal/Times Higher Education (THE)*, which is determined via the following formula: resources (30 percent), engagement (20 percent), outcomes (40 percent), and environment (10 percent).

Washington Monthly Ranking
A college's ranking by *Washington Monthly*, which is determined via the following formula: social mobility (33.3 percent), research (33.3 percent), and community and national service (33.3 percent).

Overlaps

Five schools with which a particular college shares applicants and important institutional characteristics, such as selectivity, academic quality, location, and majors/programs of strength and emphasis

Where did this data come from?

Admissions Data

Our primary source for SAT and ACT middle-50 percent ranges is the Common Data Set (CDS), a collaborative effort of data providers in the higher-education community in which most institutions participate. We gathered superscoring policies from institutional websites and, in the many cases where nothing was listed publicly, from direct contact with admissions offices. We also gathered regular and early decision (ED) acceptance rates and waitlist statistics from a combination of the CDS and institutional websites.

Enrollment Data

We took enrollment and demographic data directly from each school's CDS. If the school did not publish a CDS, we collected that information from alternative institutional reports.

Academics Data

We pulled class sizes, student-to-faculty ratios, and graduation/retention rates from the CDS or other available institutional publications.

Top Programs Within Colleges

Our methodology for determining each college's top academic programs incorporated the following four factors:

1. Major Emphasis
Indicates the number of students at an institution studying a specific major. If a high percentage of students at a particular college are studying a major, it is likely that the major attracts a relatively large portion of the institution's resources. To measure major emphasis, we relied on data collected by the National Center for Education Statistics as reported by The Integrated Postsecondary Education Data System (IPEDS).

2. Student-to-Faculty Ratio and Class Size
Research consistently shows that class size as well as student–faculty interaction and collaboration leads to better learning and career-related outcomes. We collected data for these indicators from the US Department of Education, institutional websites, and surveys of college administrators.

3. Peer Assessment
To derive a peer assessment score, we relied on questionnaires distributed to both college admission experts (including school counselors, independent education consultants, and college admission officers) and higher education administrators, and then compared responses with "strong programs" data published by U.S. News & World Report, Niche, and other reputable sources that rank colleges within a specific discipline (e.g. *CSRankings.org* for Computer Science, *The Hollywood Reporter* for Film, *Foreign Policy* for International Relations, etc.) Alone, peer assessment surveys are subject to a fair amount of bias. However, when evaluated in sum and considered along with more objective data—such as that examining major emphasis and class size—they can provide more complete and corroborative insight into the strength of a particular program/major.

4. PhD Productivity
While most undergraduates have no intent to pursue a doctoral degree, the rate at which a department/program produces Ph.D. recipients arguably reflects how well the program promotes academic rigor and prepares students to tackle advanced coursework. When available, we used data provided by the National Science Foundation in order to assess which programs graduated the highest percentage of students who later completed a PhD degree.

Top Programs Across Colleges ("Top Colleges for America's Top Majors")

When choosing which majors to feature in section, we considered both professional prospects (i.e., which majors results in high salaries and ample job opportunities) and popularity of discipline (i.e., how many students pursue the major). In order to identify the top colleges for each major, we relied on the same variables used to select the top programs within each college, as well as three additional variables, namely those for institutional selectivity, major share, and graduate earnings (see descriptions of variables below). It is also important to note that for some areas of study (e.g., Actuarial Science, Information Systems), we list colleges that do not offer a formal major, but that possess offerings (within a minor or informal concentration) so strong that they warrant inclusion.

1. Institutional Selectivity
Though selectivity is not a perfect proxy for college or major/program quality, it is highly correlated with student ability/achievement and institutional expenditures per student, which both contribute significantly to the undergraduate learning experience. We looked to a college's freshman admission rate and average SAT/ACT score (as reported by each institution's CDS) to measure selectivity.

2. Major Share
If a college enrolls a relatively high percentage of all students in the United States studying a particular major, it is likely that the college has been identified by prospective students, employers, and other stakeholders as a leader in that subject area. Though this assumption may result in bias against smaller institutions or programs, it is important to account for the fact that larger programs often have the ability to attract more tuition revenue, meet fixed costs, and reinvest the major's offerings. To measure major share we relied on data collected by the National Center for Education Statistics as reported by IPEDS.

3. Graduate Earnings

To measure graduate earnings, we relied on salary data provided by College Score Card, PayScale, and the Equality of Opportunity Project, all of which indicate both early-career and mid-career wages of students by college. We analyzed both early-career and mid-career wages because the former is typically an indicator of how employers perceive the quality of a particular major/program, while the latter indicates how well a major/program may have prepared students for work.

In addition, when able, we used data indicating graduate earnings by field of study, as doing so provides a more accurate measure of the relationship between a specific academic program and graduate earnings. For example, PayScale provides salary data for a student attending Boston University and majoring in engineering, which is different from salary data for students attending Boston University and majoring in business.

Financial Data

Financial data is taken directly from each school's CDS. If the school did not publish a CDS, we collected this information from alternative institutional reports.

Career/Salary Data

There are two main sources for information related to the most popular industries and the companies at which alumni have the most representation. LinkedIn is an excellent resource for gathering data on how many alumni of all ages are working for a particular employer. Reports the colleges produce for each recent graduating class—often called "First Destination Surveys"—receive high response rates and offer a glimpse into where the Class of 2019 is headed. If your aim is to work at a relatively new mega-company such as SpaceX, Uber, or Airbnb, it may be more helpful to know where recent graduates have landed. Where possible, we included this data in the narrative sections of the profiles.

No one source of salary data is perfect, so we sought to give you as many data points as possible for each college. As previously mentioned, the salary figures provided in each data table come from College Scorecard, PayScale, and the Equality of Opportunity project. We also included First Destination Survey data in instances where reliable institutional data could be reported. This sometimes offers a glimpse at average or median starting salaries for a school's recent graduates; certain universities provide a breakdown of starting salary by major.

Rankings

Taken at face value, a school's rank in a given publication can be unhelpful or even misleading to your unique college search. For instance, the fact that the 2021 *US News & World Report* rankings list Emory University 21st and Tufts University as 30th doesn't mean that one school is superior to the other; Emory and Tufts happen to be two of the finest schools in the country, and assigning any value to a fraction of a point in a ranking algorithm would just be plain silly. However, when considered in proper context and across several different rankings systems utilizing different algorithms, one can get a general idea of a school's reputation in the eyes of graduate schools and top employers. Collectively, we believe that these rankings can provide a degree of insight as you ponder your postsecondary future.

Why some colleges made the cut and others did not.

We wish to be fully transparent about an important issue: There is no definitive algorithm that would determine the dollar-for-dollar "best colleges for your money." Sure, you could base your rankings solely on return-on-investment figures and just list the top 175 schools in terms of median salaries. However, doing so would pretty much produce a list of the colleges that produce the greatest percentage of business, computer science, and engineering grads because those fields generally pay the best. You could also concoct a pseudoscientific formula with dozens of inputs that would spew out a concrete score that would serve as a defense as to why one school made the 175 and others were left out in the cold.

In truth, selecting these schools was as much art as science. In aiming to create a useful college guide, we drew on our collective experience of having guided thousands of students through the application process over the past decade. In seeking quantifiable evidence of value, we also examined every available report on earnings, social mobility, academic rankings, and school-specific outcomes. In the end, we were genuinely surprised by some of the lesser-known schools that stood out by those metrics and were equally surprised by some big-name schools that fared poorer than expected. Ultimately, we are extremely confident that every institution included in this book does admirable work on behalf of its undergraduates.

On the other hand, there are *not* only 175 schools that are, in our professional opinion, "Worth Your Money." So before alums or representatives from omitted schools start penning nasty emails to us, this book is not being intentionally exclusionary—175 is an arbitrary cutoff because—well—you have to have an arbitrary cutoff. Depending on one's circumstances, (again, all higher education value is context-dependent), there may be hundreds more schools that could serve as fine postsecondary destinations from which to springboard into a successful career/life. Our hope is that this book will help give the tools and mindset to evaluate any prospective institution, whether or not you find that college in the pages that follow.

Final Thoughts

Before you turn to the profiles section of this book, consider the following startling facts:

- Barely half of current college students can provide an accurate estimate of their freshman year cost of attendance.
- Only 60 percent of undergraduates nationwide finish their degree within six years.
- For those who do graduate, the average debt load is roughly $30,000.
- Studies estimate that as many as 43 percent of college grads end up working in jobs that do not require a college degree.
- Fifty-one percent of college grads ultimately wish they had chosen a different school, degree program, or major.

If picking the right college was easy, the numbers above wouldn't be nearly so bleak. Selecting a school that will put you on the right side of those unfortunate statistics takes a great deal of hard work and planning. Applicants are often so swept up in the quest to gain admission into a given school that they fail to stop and consider exactly why their dream school became their dream in the first place.

A dream college—or to be less hyperbolic, a good-fit college—should check boxes in terms of the availability and quality of academic programs of interest, the extracurricular opportunities and aspects of campus life that will promote a sense of connectedness, the level of career services you will need to get on the path to the right career/graduate school, a demonstrated history of positive outcomes for graduates, and a school where you have a genuine chance of being accepted.

Whether you are a parent or high school student, rest assured that by carefully examining the profiles that follow you are about to become a more knowledgeable college consumer than your adult or teenage peers. Ideally, you will enter the pages that follow with an open mind and be willing to consider disconfirming data about a school you previously thought was perfect for you as well as new, unexpected information about a school you would never have considered before. While the college search and admissions process is rife with challenges and stressors, eschewing the cacophony of unhelpful voices in favor of data will result in increased confidence and focus as you make this extremely important life decision.

Enjoy the journey ahead!

American University

Washington, District of Columbia | 202-885-6000

Located in the heart of our nation's capital, American University's highly desirable location and access to an abundance of government/corporate internships and networking opportunities has contributed to the university becoming far more selective than it was a decade ago. AU presently plays host to 8,500 undergraduate students as well as over 5,700 graduate and law students. Campus is a genuinely diverse place with an undergraduate population comprised 25 percent of underrepresented minorities and another 16 percent of international students. There are sixty-seven undergraduate degrees for students to choose from at AU across six colleges: the College of Arts & Sciences, the Kogod School of Business, the School of Communication, the School of Education, the School of International Service, and the School of Public Affairs.

Inside the Classroom

All undergrads are exposed to a recently-adopted core curriculum that focuses on enhancing students' metacognitive abilities. Requirements include more than thirty credits of study in courses such as Complex Problems, Quantitative Literacy, Ethical Reasoning, Creative-Aesthetic Inquiry, and Written Communication. As the school itself explains, the "AU Core general education program offers a four-year, inquiry-based liberal arts education, beginning with a Complex Problems seminar (small, nineteen-person seminars that include cocurricular experiences), bridging to essential habits of mind and integrating these skills and habits with the student's major, and culminating in a capstone." The American University Experience Program is designed to provide first-years with the advising and experiences that help students adjust to the academic rigors and social challenges that arise with the transition to college.

A low 11:1 student-to-faculty ratio allows 55 percent of offered courses to be capped at nineteen students; the average undergraduate class size is 24. Undergraduate research opportunities are taken advantage of by 50 percent of first-year students and 40 percent of seniors. For the last twelve years AU has hosted an Undergraduate Research Symposium at the end of each year where students can present their research. Students here are not afraid to hop on a plane and pursue a semester's worth of education in a foreign land. A substantial 54 percent of undergrads take a semester abroad with the most popular destination points being the United Kingdom, Italy, Spain, Kenya, and Belgium.

American's School of International Service (SIS) is one of the top-ranked programs in the country—its Public Affairs program also receives universally high marks. In terms of sheer popularity, the most commonly conferred degrees are in the social sciences (38 percent), business (16 percent), communication/journalism (11 percent), and the visual and performing arts (5 percent). Graduates fare quite well in securing service-oriented awards and scholarships. Among medium-sized universities, AU is the number one producer of Peace Corps volunteers in the country. It also boasts the second most Boren Scholars, awarded to students who wish to study language for the purpose of national security. AU saw thirty-seven undergraduates win Fulbright Scholarships from 2013-18; 11 alumni captured Fulbrights in 2020.

Outside the Classroom

This ninety-acre campus receives accolades as one of the most beautiful urban campuses in the country. Off campus, Northwest DC is a happening place, containing a number of other large schools (Georgetown, GW, Howard, and Catholic) and Capital One Arena, home to the Wizards, Capitals, and countless concerts. All of the dining, cultural, and museum experiences the District of Columbia offers can be accessed car-free via the Metro. For a flat fee, students receive a University Pass entitling them to unlimited Metro rides. The undergraduate population is 61 percent female, which certainly influences social life on campus. Fraternities attract 14 percent of men and sororities draw 16 percent of women. The Eagles play Division I sports in the Patriot League (except for wrestling) and boast six men's teams and eight women's teams. Another twenty-five club teams provide opportunities for athletic participation. For the less athletically inclined, 250 student organizations are available including student government, political clubs, charitable groups, and those dedicated purely to recreational pursuits. Facilities for student use include three gymnasiums, an aquatic center featuring two eight-lane pools, a two-mile fitness trail, and a beautiful outdoor athletic complex with basketball and tennis courts.

Career Services

The AU Career Center is staffed by 26 full-time professional employees who serve as career counselors, employer relations specialists, merit awards program coordinators, and alumni career coordinators. That works out to a phenomenal student-to-advisor ratio of 328:1, among the best of any midsize institution included in this book. It's no wonder that 99 percent of surveyed undergraduates are happy with the school's career advising services.

AU does an exceptional job hooking up students with internship opportunities; 91 percent of grads had such an experience. Being located in DC is a boon to internship opportunities as the leading host agencies include the Department of Education, State, Homeland Security, DC Public Schools, and the Public Defender Service for the District of Columbia. The Employer-in-Residence program brings organizations including Deloitte, the CIA, CNN, and Google on campus for one-one-one networking opportunities with undergrads. Student-Alumni Networking Receptions in areas such as human security, public health, education, and energy, the environment, and sustainability allow current students to network with alumni working in their area of interest. In the 2018-19 academic year, 504 employers recruited at AU, 238 hiring organizations attended career fairs, and 523 on-campus interviews were conducted. Among the employers that recruited on campus in that same time were the CIA, Politico, Booz Allen Hamilton, the Washington Nationals, the US Department of Defense, EY, Bloomberg, and Yelp.

Professional Outcomes

Within six months of graduation, 92 percent of AU grads have found employment, are enrolled in grad school, or both. There is a 60/40 split on landing jobs in the private sector versus finding employment in nonprofit/government arena. A healthy percentage of grads are attracted to public service in the form of Teach for America and the Peace Corps as both organizations are among the top five employers of recent grads. Ernst & Young, Deloitte, and the US Army round out the list. Across all graduating years, more than one hundred alumni presently work for the US House of Representatives, the US Department of State, Booz Allen Hamilton, Google, EY, IBM, PwC, and Accenture. With a heavy concentration of grads flowing into the public sector, starting salaries are not eye-popping—39 percent start above $50k, and 76 percent start above $40k. Many remain in DC but many others flock to New York City, Boston, San Francisco, Los Angeles, and Philly in substantial numbers.

Many of the most popular grad school destinations are only a Metro stop away. George Washington, Georgetown, Johns Hopkins, and American itself head the list. Seventeen percent of those who graduate from the School of Arts Sciences and the School of Public Affairs go straight into graduate school (including those working and going to grad school). Far lower concentrations of graduates from other schools within the university dive right into continuing their education. Fewer than fifty graduates apply to medical school each year, but some have had success in recent years gaining acceptance into schools including the Georgetown University School of Medicine, the University of Massachusetts Medical School, and Upstate Medical University. Recent grads pursuing a legal education have done so at the University of Pennsylvania, the University of Miami, Villanova University and, of course, American's own Washington College of Law.

Admission

American University had a 46 percent acceptance rate in 2014, hit an all-time low of 26 percent in 2016, and accepted 32 percent of applicants seeking a place in the Class of 2022. It ticked up a touch to 33 percent for the Class of 2023. While acceptance rates have plummeted at AU in recent years, the profile of the average attending student hasn't changed commensurately. The ACT middle-50 percent range five years ago was 27-31, identical to the range today, and the SAT ranges have remained fairly constant as well at 1220-1380. The average GPA for an entering member of the Class of 2023 was 3.69. In previous years, 40 percent possessed high school GPAs above a 3.75, 16 percent earned under a 3.25, giving hope to those with more B's than A's on their transcript.

Additionally, it is important to note that American is test-optional, having been one of the earlier competitive institutions to jettison test scores almost a decade ago. The strongest emphasis is placed on the rigor of one's course load, GPA and, most interestingly, applicant's interest. Since AU is a popular backup, the school very much wants to know if it is one of your top choices. This idea is supported by the school's early decision acceptance rate. In 2020-21, the school accepted 833 of 983 ED applicants, an overwhelming 85 percent. American is a quality institution situated in a city that is a highly desirable destination for young people. AU remains accessible to good but not top-of-the-class students who view the school as their number one choice.

Worth Your Money?

Spending big money on tuition to attend American University can be a wise decision, but it really depends on your financial circumstances and academic area of interest. The annual cost of attendance is $66k, but approximately 40 percent of undergraduates qualify for an average aid award of $29k. Unfortunately, American is not terribly generous with merit aid, awarding scholarships to only one-quarter of students, for a low average sum of $4,168. Yet, if you want a school that opens doors to jobs in politics, government, and major consulting firms, AU may be worth the expense.

FINANCIAL
Institutional Type: Private
In-State Tuition: $50,542
Out-of-State Tuition: $50,542
Room & Board: $14,980
Required Fees: $793
Books & Supplies: $800

Avg. Need-Based Grant: $38,820
Avg. % of Need Met: 74%

Avg. Merit-Based Award: $12,899
% Receiving (All Freshmen): 22%
% Receiving (Freshmen w/o Need): 13%

Avg. Cumulative Debt: $35,889
% of Students Borrowing: 63%

CAREER
Who Recruits
1. Central Intelligence Agency
2. Politico
3. Yelp
4. Government Accoutability Office
5. AARP

Notable Internships
1. United States Senate
2. Smithsonian
3. American Foreign Service Association

Top Industries
1. Business
2. Education
3. Media
4. Social Services
5. Operations

Top Employers
1. U.S. State Department
2. Deloitte
3. Booz Allen Hamilton
4. U.S. House of Representatives
5. IBM

Where Alumni Work
1. Washington DC
2. New York City
3. Boston
4. Philadelphia
5. San Francisco

Median Earnings
College Scorecard (Early Career): $61,000
PayScale (Early Career): $58,100
PayScale (Mid-Career): $116,200

RANKINGS
Money: 569
U.S. News: 76 (T), National Universities
Wall Street Journal/THE: 139
Washington Monthly: 114, National Universities

COLLEGE OVERLAPS
Boston College
Boston University
Georgetown University
George Washington University
Northeastern University

Amherst College

Amherst, Massachusetts | 413-542-2328

ADMISSION
Admission Rate: 11%
Admission Rate - Men: 12%
Admission Rate - Women: 11%
EA Admission Rate: Not Offered
ED Admission Rate: 36%
ED Admits as % of Total Admits: 16%
Admission Rate (5-Year Trend): -3%
% of Admits Attending (Yield): 39%
Transfer Admission Rate: 8%

SAT Reading/Writing (Middle 50%): 690-760
SAT Math (Middle 50%): 720-790
ACT Composite (Middle 50%): 31-34

% Graduated in Top 10% of HS Class: 88%
% Graduated in Top 25% of HS Class: 98%
% Graduated in Top 50% of HS Class: 100%

Demonstrated Interest: Not Considered
Legacy Status: Considered
Admission Interview Offered: No

ENROLLMENT
Total Undergraduate Enrollment: 1,839
% Part-Time: 0%
% Male: 50%
% Female: 50%
% Out-of-State: 86%
% Fraternity: Not Offered
% Sorority: Not Offered
% On-Campus (Freshman): 100%
% On-Campus (All Undergraduate): 98%

% African-American: 10%
% Asian: 15%
% Hispanic: 13%
% White: 43%
% Other: 7%
% Race or Ethnicity Unknown: 3%
% International: 9%
% Low-Income: 24%

ACADEMICS
Student-to-Faculty Ratio: 7 to 1
% of Classes Under 20: 71%
% of Classes 20-49: 27%
% of Classes 50 or More: 2%
% Full-Time Faculty: 79%
% Full-Time Faculty w/ Terminal Degree: 95%

Top Programs
Biochemistry and Biophysics
Computer Science
Economics
English
History
Law, Jurisprudence, and Social Thought
Mathematics
Statistics

Retention Rate: 97%
4-Year Graduation Rate: 88%
6-Year Graduation Rate: 95%

Curricular Flexibility: Very Flexible
Academic Rating: ★★★★★

#CollegesWorthYourMoney

One of the premier liberal arts colleges in the country—and one the most selective—Amherst College is an Ivy-equivalent institution that offers its brilliant student body a one-of-a-kind academic experience. A mere 1,839 undergraduates grace this picturesque rural campus located seventy-five miles west of Boston. Yet, a small town location is not at all indicative of an isolated existence. If the forty majors and 850 course offerings on campus aren't enough, Amherst belongs to the Five College Consortium that allows students to take any course offered at Mount Holyoke, Smith, Hampshire College, or UMass-Amherst.

Inside the Classroom
Similar to Brown's "Open Curriculum," Amherst operates its "New Curriculum" that requires no specific courses or distribution of credits. Students have the flexibility to pursue their areas of passion and interest from the very start of their collegiate experience. With no burdensome requirements, double majoring is commonplace with over 30 percent of the student body electing to study at least one additional discipline. The college encourages students to "take full responsibility for their intellectual growth, in the same way they will take responsibility for important choices later in life."

If you crave facetime with your professors, Amherst delivers. A 7-to-1 student-to-faculty ratio allows for 71 percent of courses to have fewer than twenty students and 32 percent to have single-digit enrollments. That level of intimacy pays off with the forging of student-faculty relationships. By senior year, 98 percent of seniors report feeling close enough to a faculty member to ask for a letter of recommendation. The eight-to-ten-week Summer Science Undergraduate Research Program is available for students as are plenty of grants aimed at funding original student research projects. A sizable number of students study abroad, 45 percent to be precise, in just about any country you can name from Namibia to Trinidad. The school's student body has become increasingly diverse in recent years, now boasting double-digit percentages of African American, Latino, and first-generation students.

A true liberal arts college, Amherst possesses strong offerings across the board, most notably in economics, English, history, mathematics, and law (through its one-of-a-kind major in Law, Jurisprudence and Social Thought). Amherst also boasts one of the most esteemed (and highest paid) liberal arts faculties in the country. The social sciences account for 20 percent of degrees conferred, 13 percent are in mathematics, and 7 percent are in computer science. Students are always competitive for postgraduate awards and fellowships. The college has been recognized as one of the top producers of Fulbright Scholars for over a decade; it had eight winners in 2019 and had more Watson Fellows in 2017 than any other institution in the country.

Outside the Classroom
Amherst is the rare school where 98 percent of undergraduates reside in school-owned housing. There are no Greek organizations, but a colossal 35-38 percent of Amherst students are rostered on one of the college's twenty-seven NCAA Division III sports teams, which means that many are dedicating a good portion of their time to athletics. For everyone else, over 150 student organizations are operating on campus. The school's six a cappella groups and four-ensemble Choral Society play a notable enough role to have earned the school the nickname "The Singing College." Membership in the Five College Consortium opens the door to a variety of other clubs and activities within close proximity. However, it is important to note that the other four campuses are not adjoining—UMass and Hampshire are about a ten-minute drive, and Smith and Mount Holyoke take twenty minutes to reach by car. Guest speakers are regularly on campus. Each year, the Amherst Leads organization brings up to twenty-five well known athletes, business leaders, and writers/journalists to speak on campus. Dorms, food, and other amenities generally receive positive reviews. For students who want to be in touch with nature, a 500-acre wildlife preserve is located on campus, and it can be freely hiked and explored.

Career Services
Unlike at just about every other institution of higher education, the vast majority of the Amherst student body actually takes advantage of the Career Center's offerings. In fact, the Loeb Center for Career Exploration and Planning advises more than 1,400 students and alumni each year for a total of more than 6,000 sessions. That prodigious output comes from the office's fifteen full-time staff members who focus on either career advising or employer relations. Loeb's 123:1 student-to-advisor ratio is among the best of any school featured in this guide.

Amherst does a superb job recruiting companies to campus with more than 175 visiting per year and close to 450 interviews taking place on campus, which is roughly the size of the graduating class. There were fifty-nine days in the 2017-18 school year on which interviews were taking place on campus. Other programs, such as Career

Treks, involve organized trips to Boston, New York City, and Los Angeles. Those trips allow students the chance to meet with alumni in the areas of finance, government, entertainment, education, and philanthropy. The Pathways program facilitates hundreds of additional mentoring relationships between alumni and current students each year. Nearly one-quarter of freshmen are enrolled in the Amherst Select Internship Program, which allows first-year students to jump directly into a hands-on learning opportunity.

Professional Outcomes

Whether you are interested in going directly into the workforce or continuing into graduate school, Amherst's reputation and connected alumni network will open doors. Six months after graduation, 95 percent of the Class of 2019 had already found its way into the world of employment, graduate school, or a volunteer organization. The highest number of recent grads went into education (21 percent), with finance (21 percent) and healthcare (13 percent) next in popularity. Recent graduates found jobs everywhere from Bain Capital to the United Talent Agency to the US Department of State. By sheer volume, the largest employers of Amherst grads comprise a high-end list including Google, Deloitte, Morgan Stanley, and Goldman Sachs. The average starting salary for Amherst graduates is around $60k, making them among the highest-paid liberal arts grads in the country. That is even more impressive when you consider that Amherst doesn't even have an engineering program, the profession that usually bolsters starting salary figures.

Amherst grads fare well at gaining acceptance to elite schools. It regularly sees 50 percent or more of applicants get into law schools like those at Georgetown, Columbia, Harvard, Berkeley, and Stanford, more than twice those schools' overall acceptance rates. In total, the schools where the highest number of Amherst grads can be found pursuing advanced degrees includes University of Cambridge (UK), MIT, Dartmouth, and the University of Pennsylvania. Fifty to sixty Amherst grads apply to medical school each year, and the acceptance rate hovers around 75-80 percent. As with law schools, students attend many of the finest medical institutions in the world. In order, the greatest number of alumni settle in New York City, Boston, San Francisco, and Washington, DC.

Admission

Amherst accepted under 11 percent of applicants to the Class of 2023. This cohort had a gaudy mid-50 percent standardized test score range of 1420-1530 on the SAT and 31-34 on the ACT. However, this incredible degree of selectivity is nothing new as Amherst has long been one of the most selective liberal arts schools in the country, so the landscape hasn't changed all that much. The college has had an acceptance rate of under 16 percent for more than a decade. Unsurprisingly, a high percentage of admitted students finished in the top 10 percent of their high school class—88 percent at last count; an impressive 20 percent were valedictorians.

The admissions office lists a whopping nine categories as having the highest level of influence on admissions decisions. That list includes talent/ability, character/personal qualities, recommendations, and first-generation status. While the process is holistic and genuinely committed to increasing the underrepresented minority and first-generation presence on campus, Amherst remains one of the most selective liberal arts colleges in the United States.

If Amherst is your top choice, applying ED can give you a slight edge; 36 percent of the 2019-20 freshman class were accepted via the ED round, versus 10 percent in the regular round; roughly 20 percent of those admitted via the early round are children of alumni. Many of Amherst's varsity athletes are also admitted early; the school claims that fewer than seventy admitted athletes per year are given preferential admissions treatment, a figure that equates to a sizable 15 percent of the class. Successful applicants will be near (or at) the top of their high school class, have earned standardized test scores in the top 1-2 percent, and possess unique gifts/intangibles that help separate them from a mass of similarly qualified peers.

Worth Your Money?

Close to half of Amherst students will pay the full $82k+ cost of attendance, a four-year sum of well over $300,000. This is because the college does not award merit aid, only need-based. For the 56 percent who qualify for financial aid, Amherst does meet 100 percent of their demonstrated need, which works out to an average of $59k per year, making the school quite affordable. The majority of the students paying full freight come from families in the top income percentiles, rendering the impact of the huge bill minimal. Amherst is an Ivy-level school that is worth attending for most as it will legitimately play a role in opening any and all employment or graduate schools dreams you could conjure up.

FINANCIAL
Institutional Type: Private
In-State Tuition: $57,640
Out-of-State Tuition: $57,640
Room & Board: $15,310
Required Fees: $1,000
Books & Supplies: $1,000

Avg. Need-Based Grant: $58,697
Avg. % of Need Met: 100%

Avg. Merit-Based Award: $0
% Receiving (All Freshmen): 0%
% Receiving (Freshmen w/o Need): 0%

Avg. Cumulative Debt: $22,629
% of Students Borrowing: 28%

CAREER
Who Recruits
1. Hulu
2. FiscalNote
3. T. Rowe Price
4. RBC Capital
5. Fox Sports

Notable Internships
1. National Center for Health Research
2. U.S. House of Representatives
3. NY State Division of Human Rights

Top Industries
1. Business
2. Education
3. Research
4. Media
5. Legal

Top Employers
1. Google
2. Goldman Sachs
3. JP Morgan
4. Massachusetts General Hospital
5. Citi

Where Alumni Work
1. New York City
2. Boston
3. San Francisco
4. Washington DC
5. Springfield, MA

Median Earnings
College Scorecard (Early Career): $65,000
PayScale (Early Career): $68,100
PayScale (Mid-Career): $139,800

RANKINGS
Money: 80
U.S. News: 2, Liberal Arts Colleges
Wall Street Journal/THE: 21 (T)
Washington Monthly: 1, Liberal Arts Colleges

COLLEGE OVERLAPS
Brown University
Dartmouth College
Harvard University
Princeton University
Williams College

Arizona State University

Tempe, Arizona | 480-965-7788

It may be surprising to see one of the largest universities in the country—one which sports an 85 percent acceptance rate—included in this guidebook. Yet, Arizona State University has flourished across its five desert locations (including the ASU Colleges at Lake Havasu City), enhancing its offerings and academic quality in recent years. Serving over 44,000 students at its Tempe campus, ASU offers a staggering 350 academic majors. The renowned Barrett Honors College enrolls an incredible 7,400 students compared to the average honors college size of 1,200. Barrett attracts a talented bunch, enrolling more National Merit Scholars than Duke, Stanford, or MIT.

Inside the Classroom
All students must complete a minimum of twenty-nine credits in General Studies courses. Courses can be used to meet more than one requirement at a time but, ultimately, boxes must be checked in the areas of literacy and critical inquiry; mathematical studies; humanities, arts and design; social-behavioral sciences; and the natural sciences. Three "awareness areas" also must be satisfied: Cultural Diversity in the United States, Global Awareness, and Historical Awareness.

The faculty-to-student ratio is a fairly high 20:1, but not all classes call for stadium seating. In fact, 35 percent of course sections seat fewer than twenty students. You'll find classes of over fifty students 18 percent of the time, not unreasonable for a university of this unmatched size. There are plenty of opportunities for experiential learning as 49 percent of students engage in research, land an internship, or have a practicum experience as part of their academic program. The school also has above-average study abroad rates, ranking in the top ten in the nation by sending approximately 2,500 students to 250 programs in sixty-five countries each year.

Business is the concentration in which over one-quarter (27 percent) of total bachelor's degrees are conferred. Engineering (13 percent), the social sciences (8 percent), and biology (9 percent) are the next three most popular. The WP Carey School of Business offers many highly ranked programs as does the Fulton Schools of Engineering. In the last decade, the number of Sun Devils winning competitive national fellowships has skyrocketed. ASU produced an outstanding twenty-one Fulbright Scholars in 2019. It also is becoming a regular producer of Marshall, Gates-Cambridge, Truman, Goldwater, Udall, and Boren Scholarships. Over the past five years 117 graduates have been awarded National Science Foundation Graduate Research Fellowships.

Outside the Classroom
Young people don't typically come to ASU to live a hermetic existence. While the university has begun to shed its "party school" label in recent years, it remains a vibrant, extremely connected campus. Athletics are popular with ten NCCA Division I men's teams and fourteen women's teams. Sun Devil football stadium plays host to 71,000 raucous fans on game days. In addition, ASU fields forty club teams and at least 6,000 additional students take place in competitive intramural sports leagues. Greek life attracts 10 percent of men and 16 percent of women, giving it substantial influence on the social scene. There are more than 1,000 clubs operating across the five campuses with the ASU Outdoors Club and the school's seven identity-based student coalitions drawing large memberships. Interestingly, only 27 percent of the undergraduate student body lives on campus—however, 76 percent of freshmen do opt for that experience. Due to large numbers of students renting apartments/houses in surrounding neighborhoods, ASU hosts an Off-Campus Housing Fair and provides free advice to undergrads seeking a place to reside. In addition to living in the surrounding communities, Sun Devils like to get involved in volunteer work. Collectively, the student body contributes 1.8 million hours of community service each year. There is plenty to do in the cities of Phoenix, Tempe, Mesa, and Scottsdale, all a short drive from one another.

Career Services
ASU's Career and Professional Development Services (CPDS) has offices on its Tempe, Downtown, Polytechnic, and West locations. When you boast 59,000 undergraduate students across your four metropolitan campuses, things can only be so personalized, but ASU does a solid job making services available on a mass scale. Amazingly, it claims 95,000+ annual interactions with students through job fairs, workshops, and networking events.

Nearly 60,000 jobs are posted each year on Handshake, and the school has been selected as a top choice for recruiting talent by more than one hundred companies including Marriot International, Microsoft, General Mills, Charles Schwab, Geico, Ford, FedEx, and Yelp. For such a behemoth of an institution, ASU has a fairly impressive level of internship participation. Around 50 percent of undergraduates have at least one internship, and 44 percent of those are paid opportunities. In total, more than 13,000 internships are posted each year. Having an alumni base of over half a million Sun Devils is great for networking. It is an active and proud bunch that presently has over

100,000 members who donate annually to the university. Thanks to this strong alumni base, wealth of employer partnerships, and strong internship participation rate, the CPDS succeeds in helping the great majority of its graduates swiftly arrive at their next destination soon after receiving diplomas.

Professional Outcomes

A healthy 89 percent of 2019 ASU graduates were employed or in graduate school within six months of earning their degrees. As you would expect from a large school offering 350 majors, the most prolific employers of Sun Devils represent a broad array of corporations and nonprofit entities. Among the school's top fifty employers are Amazon, Apple, Intel, The Vanguard Group, Walt Disney Company, a number of local school districts, and Arizona-based government organizations. In total, the five industries most frequently entered by alumni are banking and finance, technology and engineering, health care, and public and human services. Arizona also ranks thirteenth in the nation among large universities for graduates entering the Peace Corps. The median salary for a member of the Class of 2019 was $54,000. The majority (55 percent) of newly minted grads were working in Arizona with California (13 percent) next in popularity.

Approximately one-fifth of recent grads enrolled in graduate school. Similar to employment, the size and scope of the university leads to many graduate pathways. Many grads continue at ASU itself, but some continue at various prestigious institutions. For example, Yale Law School typically claims at least one ASU alum in its 1L class. From 2010-14, ASU sent 375 graduates to medical school; today, over 350 apply each year. The school's Mayo Medical Scholars program exclusively offered to Barrett Honors College students can open doors for future doctors. While the majority of ASU grads continuing their education do not enter prestigious graduate or professional programs, getting strong grades at ASU absolutely puts them in a position to be strong applicants at any university in the country, including the elites.

Admission

While ASU's reputation for academics has been climbing in recent years, the school is still only slightly selective, accepting 86 percent of those who apply. Considering that friendly acceptance rate, the academic profile of the typical Sun Devil may surprise you. The median freshman SAT score was 1230 and the average GPA was a 3.5. Thirty-one percent of Class of 2023 freshmen ranked in the top 10 percent of their high school class while 61 percent were in the top quartile, and 88 percent were in the top half. Among the students presently enrolled in the superb Barrett Honors College, the average SAT score was 1370 and the average unweighted GPA is 3.8. Only a decade ago, the 75th percentile SAT score was 1210, meaning that despite the high acceptance rate, ASU is attracting a more academically superior crop than in the past.

As you might expect at one of the nation's largest universities, admissions officers will not be agonizing over every detail of your application, carefully weighing the merits of your essay, recommendations, and extracurricular resume. In fact, none of those factors are even considered at ASU. Grades, class rank, and test scores are considered "most important," and the rigor of your secondary school record is "important." Conveniently for those entering the admissions process now, the university began accepting the Common Application in 2018. Getting into Arizona State is a straightforward proposition; those who bring a solid transcript and test scores to the table will be invited to join this thriving institution. Admission into the Honors College requires another level of achievement.

Worth Your Money?

Competitively priced for both in-state and out-of-state students, it's no wonder students from around the globe flock to Arizona State. Those from the Grand Canyon State pay close to $30,000 per year cost of attendance while nonresidents cough up $49,000, not that much more than the in-state rate for many public schools on the East Coast. Further, ASU awards merit aid to 46 percent of undergraduates; the average amount is $10k, and the average need-based grant is $14k. Thanks to those extremely reasonable prices (we don't utter that phrase often without major qualifiers), this university produces graduates that carry a below-average debt load relative to their peers. Whether you're a local majoring in American Indian Studies or an out-of-stater learning cybersecurity, your tuition dollar goes far at ASU.

FINANCIAL
Institutional Type: Public
In-State Tuition: $10,710
Out-of-State Tuition: $28,800
Room & Board: $13,164
Required Fees: $628
Books & Supplies: $1,171

Avg. Need-Based Grant: $13,988
Avg. % of Need Met: 71%

Avg. Merit-Based Award: $10,158
% Receiving (All Freshmen): 46%
% Receiving (Freshmen w/o Need): 37%

Avg. Cumulative Debt: $23,711
% of Students Borrowing: 29%

CAREER
Who Recruits
1. Amazon
2. Aetna
3. ExxonMobil
4. Ticketmaster
5. General Motors

Notable Internships
1. Intel
2. Geico
3. Phoenix Suns

Top Industries
1. Business
2. Operations
3. Education
4. Sales
5. Engineering

Top Employers
1. Intel
2. Wells Fargo
3. Amazon
4. American Express
5. Apple

Where Alumni Work
1. Phoenix
2. Los Angeles
3. San Francisco
4. New York City
5. Seattle

Median Earnings
College Scorecard (Early Career): $47,700
PayScale (Early Career): $57,400
PayScale (Mid-Career): $106,000

RANKINGS
Money: 123
U.S. News: 103 (T), National Universities
Wall Street Journal/THE: 196 (T)
Washington Monthly: 58, National Universities

COLLEGE OVERLAPS
Michigan State University
San Diego State University
University of Arizona
University of California, Santa Barbara
University of Oregon

Babson College

Babson Park, Massachusetts | 781-239-5522

With an unmatched entrepreneurial ethos, tiny but powerful Babson College in Wellesley, Massachusetts, only has one offering on the menu, a BS in business administration, but it is expertly prepared. Instead of offering a smorgasbord of majors, Babson students pick from twenty-seven areas of concentration including business analytics, global business management, and statistical modeling that offer more curricular flexibility than a traditional major. Babson was an all-male college until 1969, but it has completely transformed as women now comprise close to 50 percent of the school's 2,386 undergraduate population. Of equal interest is the college's status as one the best schools for international students; over one-quarter of the population hails from outside the United States.

Inside the Classroom
The Babson experience kicks off with a one-credit first-year seminar designed to help you "better understand your identity, your classmates' identities, and what it takes for all of you to be successful students in the diverse Babson community." While you'll unavoidably spend a good portion of your time swimming in business-related curriculum, roughly half of the courses you will take will be in the liberal arts on engaging subjects such as Art and Ecology; Imagining Nature, Imagining Ourselves; Sports and Literature; Literature and Philosophy of Madness; Constructing and Performing the Self; and Global Pop. One of the many unique experiences at Babson is Foundations of Management and Entrepreneurship, a freshman requirement. Students are given $3,000 in start-up money to launch and run an actual business. They concurrently take part in the Coaching for Teamwork and Leadership Program, working with staff and alumni coaches to enhance personal development, problem-solving skills, and ethical decision-making.

This school's exceptionally interactive and hands-on approach to undergraduate education is evident from the moment students step foot on campus. While a fair number of courses are large—half have more than thirty students—the nature of the instruction is highly interactive with professors and with peers. It is simply not possible to be an anonymous student at Babson. Around one-half of the undergraduate population spends time studying abroad in one of the college's 104 programs spread across forty-one countries. While Babson is more about doing than spending time in the ivory tower, students are encouraged to assist with faculty-led research or propose an independent research study of their own (for credit).

It's little surprise that a business school like Babson has done an excellent job of branding. It is regularly ranked at the top of any list of best colleges for entrepreneurship and business. Babson also ends up toward the top of any list that looks at return on investment as its graduates fare well on the job market. This institution usually produces one or two Fulbright Scholars per year, but the vast majority of graduates are champing at the bit to enter the workforce.

Outside the Classroom
Babson's classrooms are filled with entrepreneurial spirits, and that obsession doesn't disappear when students leave the academic setting. Of the one hundred or so clubs and activities at the college, a large number have the words "investment," "business," or "banking" somewhere in their titles. The school does run twenty-two varsity sports teams, but it does not offer athletic-based scholarships, so while its men's soccer and basketball teams have captured NCAA Division III titles in recent years, sports hardly dominate life at Babson. Roughly 18% percent of Babson students partake in Greek life, and the number of sorority and fraternity members has grown in recent years. Close to 80 percent of students live in one of the eighteen on-campus residence halls, and some socialize in the surrounding suburb of Wellesley, but with Boston a short T ride away, jaunts into the city are commonplace. The demographic makeup of the student body continues to grow more and more diverse as one-quarter of all students are international, coming from forty-three countries, and 45 percent of US students are nonwhite.

Career Services
The Career Development Services Center at Babson is dedicated solely to the college's undergraduates; a separate career services office exists for MBA students. With twelve full-time, professional staff members, Babson operates with a 199:1 student-to-advisor ratio, far better than the average school featured in this guide. The career center facilitates a number of corporate sponsorships with major companies including PEPSICO, Boston Scientific, EY, and PwC. Events sponsored by the office occur frequently, at least once per week, and are well attended by the student body. Those include regular Industry Spotlights where corporate guests present to and network with students as well as Career Expos.

Babson College

E-mail: ugradadmission@babson.edu | Website: www.babson.edu

A global alumni network of more than 40,000 graduates spread across 115 countries and all fifty US states and the Babson Connector, an online resource, help connect current students with alumni. As a result of this type of engagement, a staggering 90 percent of all Babson students embark on at least one internship during their four years of study. Further, thanks to the diligent, hands-on work of this career services office, less than 1 percent of graduates are still looking for employment/grad school within six months of graduating. Considering its well-staffed office and excellent track record for helping graduates find internships and high-paying employment options, Babson's career services is worthy of a great deal of praise.

Professional Outcomes

Babson students are a group of young people with exceptional drive and direction. Within six months of graduation, 99 percent are already employed or in graduate school. The largest numbers flock to finance, technology, and accounting with the highest concentration of recent graduates ending up at EY, PwC, Dell, and Wayfair. Many alumni also work at Fidelity Investment, IBM, Deloitte, Google, Amazon, Siemens, and Accenture. Keeping with the entrepreneurial philosophy of the college, 5 percent of Babson grads start their own businesses soon after graduation. Starting salaries are strong at approximately $61k. The highest average salaries await those entering the oil, financial services, and accounting industries while the lowest average salaries go to those in the sports/entertainment, staffing, and media/publishing fields. Even though only 16 percent of undergrads hail from Massachusetts, many put down roots nearby after graduation, and over 11,000 alumni are clustered in the Boston area.

While many pursue MBAs down the road, only 5 percent enter a program right out of undergrad. Babson students typically enter excellent institutions once they do decide to pursue a graduate or professional track. Recent grads have entered law school at the likes of Harvard, Tulane, Boston University, UVA, and UC-San Diego. Alumni going the MBA route have attended top programs including at the London Business School, Yale, Columbia, Boston College, USC, and Northwestern.

Admission

Babson is a school whose national and international reputation is on the rise, and with that has come shrinking acceptance rates. As recently as five years ago, 40 percent of applicants were accepted. For students entering in the 2020-21 academic year that number was only 27 percent. Women fared better than men, gaining acceptance 34 percent of the time versus 22 percent for their male counterparts. The caliber of student admitted has risen with the school's selectivity. For those offered a place in the Class of 2024, the mid-50 percent SAT range was 1340-1490 and 30-33 on the ACT. Five years back, a 30 on the ACT would have placed you in the 75th percentile of attending students.

Successful Babson applicants do not have to have perfect grades, but they need to have performed at the B+/A- range within a rigorous high school program. Interviews are not required but are evaluative in nature and would be a good idea for any applicant with borderline statistics. The process is genuinely holistic as admissions staff want to see evidence of leadership and extracurricular involvement during your high school career. Those committing to Babson via early decision were admitted 35 percent of the time into the Class of 2023, making ED a wise choice, particularly for those on the admissions bubble. In general, Babson is undoubtedly getting more selective year by year, but students with excellent grades, strong standardized test scores, and a burning passion for business should still fare well in the application process.

Worth Your Money?

With business being the dominant area of focus in the classroom, the $75,000 annual cost of attendance is not as terrifying as it might otherwise be. The school also offers students the chance to apply for various merit scholarships ranging from the Weissman Scholarship that covers full tuition to a Dean's Scholarship worth $5,000 per year. If you're committed to a career in business, Babson is worth your money thanks to its distinctive brand of education, industry connections, and solid starting salaries that would allow students to comfortably pay back some level of student loans.

FINANCIAL
Institutional Type: Private
In-State Tuition: $54,144
Out-of-State Tuition: $54,144
Room & Board: $17,668
Required Fees: $0
Books & Supplies: $1,178

Avg. Need-Based Grant: $40,042
Avg. % of Need Met: 100%

Avg. Merit-Based Award: $20,636
% Receiving (All Freshmen): 7%
% Receiving (Freshmen w/o Need): 3%

Avg. Cumulative Debt: $37,444
% of Students Borrowing: 42%

CAREER
Who Recruits
1. Boston Scientific
2. AXA Advisors
3. RxAdvance
4. Applause
5. PepsiCo

Notable Internships
1. Mid-Market Securities
2. CoreAxis Consulting
3. PepsiCo

Top Industries
1. Business
2. Finance
3. Operations
4. Sales
5. Marketing

Top Employers
1. Fidelity Investments
2. PwC
3. EY
4. Dell
5. IBM

Where Alumni Work
1. Boston
2. New York City
3. Sao Paulo, Brazil
4. San Francisco
5. United Kingdom

Median Earnings
College Scorecard (Early Career): $96,100
PayScale (Early Career): $73,900
PayScale (Mid-Career): $153,200

RANKINGS
Money: 132
U.S. News: Not Ranked
Wall Street Journal/THE: 124 (T)
Washington Monthly: Not Ranked

COLLEGE OVERLAPS
Bentley University
Bryant University
Boston College
Boston University
Northeastern University

Barnard College

New York, New York | 212-854-2014

ADMISSION
Admission Rate: 12%
Admission Rate - Men: Not Applicable
Admission Rate - Women: 12%
EA Admission Rate: Not Offered
ED Admission Rate: 24%
ED Admits as % of Total Admits: 27%
Admission Rate (5-Year Trend): -9%
% of Admits Attending (Yield): 58%
Transfer Admission Rate: 22%

SAT Reading/Writing (Middle 50%): 670-750
SAT Math (Middle 50%): 670-770
ACT Composite (Middle 50%): 31-34

% Graduated in Top 10% of HS Class: 84%
% Graduated in Top 25% of HS Class: 99%
% Graduated in Top 50% of HS Class: 100%

Demonstrated Interest: Considered
Legacy Status: Considered
Admission Interview Offered: Yes

ENROLLMENT
Total Undergraduate Enrollment: 2,631
% Part-Time: 2%
% Male: 0%
% Female: 100%
% Out-of-State: 71%
% Fraternity: Not Offered
% Sorority: 20%
% On-Campus (Freshman): 91%
% On-Campus (All Undergraduate): 91%

% African-American: 5%
% Asian: 15%
% Hispanic: 11%
% White: 50%
% Other: 6%
% Race or Ethnicity Unknown: 0%
% International: 11%
% Low-Income: 21%

ACADEMICS
Student-to-Faculty Ratio: 9 to 1
% of Classes Under 20: 79%
% of Classes 20-49: 15%
% of Classes 50 or More: 6%
% Full-Time Faculty: 70%
% Full-Time Faculty w/ Terminal Degree: 100%

Top Programs
Area Studies
Art History
Dance
Economics
English
Neuroscience and Behavior
Political Science
Psychology

Retention Rate: 95%
4-Year Graduation Rate: 84%
6-Year Graduation Rate: 92%

Curricular Flexibility: Somewhat Flexible
Academic Rating: ★★★★★

#CollegesWorthYourMoney

Affiliated with Columbia University, this all-women's college serves 2,600+ accomplished young women in the heart of Manhattan's Upper West Side. The institution's cosmopolitan locale is appropriately populated by a diverse student body—39 percent of the Class of 2023 identify as women of color, and 12 percent are first-generation college students. Roughly fifty majors are offered, including crossover programs with Columbia such as the 3:2 engineering program or five-year programs that lead to a BA plus a Master of International Affairs or Master of Public Administration. Barnard also has partnerships with The Jewish Theological Seminary and the Julliard School.

Inside the Classroom

The newly-adopted Foundations curriculum has refined an already rigorous educational tradition at the college. Freshmen must tackle a first-year writing course and a first-year seminar that emphasizes persuasive writing/speaking. In subsequent years, students must fulfill six Modes of Thinking courses that focus on local NYC history, global inquiry, social difference, historical perspective, quantitative and empirical knowledge, and technological thinking. Distributional requirements in a foreign language, arts/humanities, social sciences, and the hard sciences also must be fulfilled. Regardless of major, seniors must complete a semester or year-long thesis/project that is publicly presented or displayed.

All of this unfolds in an academic environment in which students will work closely with professors. Barnard has a 9:1 student-faculty ratio, and a sensational 79 percent of courses are capped at nineteen or fewer students; 29 percent have fewer than ten. Many get the chance to engage in research alongside a professor as 197 undergraduates were granted such an opportunity through the Summer Research Institute in 2018-19. Many students also take advantage of the more than 150 study abroad programs spread over sixty-five countries. Roughly one-third of students elect to take a semester in a foreign country.

Barnard's most popular majors, by number of degrees conferred, are economics, English, political science, history, psychology, biology, neuroscience, computer science, urban studies, and art history. The dance program is notably strong and often places near the top of national rankings. With a strong emphasis on global perspective and public service, it makes sense that the school produces a disproportionately high percentage of Fulbright and Truman Scholars. In 2019, four graduates won Fulbright Scholarships, and three students captured Critical Language Scholarships. Additionally, four Barnard grads were named National Science Foundation fellows in 2018.

Outside the Classroom

Outside the classroom is where Barnard's affiliation with Columbia really comes into play. The school doesn't have its own athletic teams, so Barnard students are recruited to play for Columbia's NCAA Division I teams. Barnard has seventy clubs of its own, mostly of a fairly serious nature (pre-professional and performance-oriented), but the bulk of opportunities for campus engagement come from Columbia's more than 500 student organizations that are open to Barnard students. Parts of dorm life are also a shared experience. For the 91 percent of students who decide to live on campus, two buildings serve as co-ed dorms where Barnard students are mixed with Columbia students, and meal plans for all dorm residents can be utilized at either school's cafeterias. Of course, being located in the heart of New York City, opportunities for fun and excitement are hardly limited to the Barnard and Columbia campuses. Within a single mile of their dorm rooms, students can enjoy multiple parks, theaters, music venues, diners, and countless other attractions.

Career Services

Barnard has ten professionals, a number of peer advisors, and a handful of administrative assistants working in the offices of Beyond Barnard, the recently reorganized/renamed career services center. In past years complaints about the lack of hands-on assistance from the career services office were voiced by the student government and school newspaper. The college responded by beefing up its offerings, and the work being done today is impressive by any quantifiable measure. Beyond Barnard's 263:1 student-to-advisor ratio is superior to many other colleges featured in this guide, and it puts that staffing to good use. In 2018-19, they conducted 4,424 one-on-one appointments, hosted 350+ events, and served 2,500 individuals in some capacity.

The school hosts career and internship fairs in the fall and spring. Fairs are attended by 1,000 students and approximately fifty employers including Brown Brothers Harriman, Uber, and Hearst Magazines. Those sessions also are open to Columbia students, and there is some degree of reciprocity with Barnard students being allowed to attend a good number of Columbia-hosted events. The New York Network mentoring program saw 140 alumni work in person with current students, and an additional seventy individuals participated in a Virtual Mentoring program. Beyond Barnard helps fund internships offering summer stipends of $4,000; it funded 425 internships last year alone. Students interned at exciting locations including the New York Times, the US House of Representatives, Comedy Central, and Christie's.

Professional Outcomes

Six months after graduation, 90 percent of 2019 Barnard grads had found employment or were enrolled in a graduate program. The school is known for producing women with a wide array of interests, so it makes sense that grads disperse into many different fields. Finance and banking led the way, albeit only representing 11 percent of graduates. JP Morgan, Goldman Sachs, Blackrock, Citibank, and Morgan Stanley all appear on the list of the top fifteen employers of Barnard alumni. The journalism, government, and education sectors are next in popularity. Across all fields, companies employing twenty-five or more Barnard alums include the NYC Department of Education, Google, IBM, Accenture, and the Metropolitan Museum of Art.. By leaps and bounds, New York City remains home to alumni with small clusters of graduates forming in San Francisco, Boston, Los Angeles, DC, and Philadelphia.

It is rare for a student to call it an academic career after finishing her bachelor's. Within ten years of graduation, over 80 percent of Barnard alums eventually enroll in graduate school. Those entering graduate school flock to a number of other nearby institutions with Columbia, Yeshiva, Rutgers, Fordham, NYU, and Hunter College (CUNY) among the ten most commonly attended schools. Boston University, Georgetown, and Harvard also have a strong representation of Barnard grads in their graduate/professional programs. Medical Schools where recent grads enrolled include St. Louis University School of Medicine, Icahn School of Medicine, and Jefferson College of Health. Barnard typically sports a medical school admissions rate of 60-75 percent.

Admission

The last six years have seen the admission rate at Barnard fall from 24 percent (2014) to an all-time low of 12 percent for those entering the Class of 2023. The middle-50 percent SAT range of attending students is 1360-1500; for the ACT it's 31-34. In 2014, the 25th percentile was a far friendlier 1240 SAT/28 ACT. Therefore, it is safe to conclude that Barnard is trending in a more selective direction.

The average weighted high school GPA of a Barnard student was over 4.0, and 84 percent finished in the top 10 percent of their high school class. That aligns with the school's stated beliefs that rigor of secondary record and GPA are among the admissions committees' strongest considerations. Also making this list are more holistic factors including the essay, recommendations, and character/personal qualities. The early decision acceptance rate is 24 percent compared to 10 percent in the regular round, so that may be an avenue worth exploring for those dead-set on attending this fine institution. Additionally, transfer students fare well at Barnard, especially relative to other highly selective liberal arts schools. In 2019, there were 179 applicants accepted as transfers— 22 percent of the transfer applicant pool. As at many selective colleges, gaining acceptance into Barnard is more difficult than ever. Sterling grades, solid test scores, and winning personal attributes are the right combination to receive serious consideration at one of, if not the best women's college in existence.

Worth Your Money?

Close to half of Barnard students come from families that fall in the top 5 percent of income-earners in the United States. Those individuals will almost always be asked to pay the full $78,000 cost of attendance as merit aid is nonexistent at this school. Those on the lower end of the income scale see 100 percent of their demonstrated need paid for by the college through an annual grant of almost $51k. Thanks to this equitable process, the average debt carried by a Barnard graduate is far less than the average college graduate. In addition to its generous financial aid, Barnard is worth the price for the incredible employment and graduate school networks it will open for you post-graduation.

FINANCIAL
Institutional Type: Private
In-State Tuition: $57,668
Out-of-State Tuition: $57,668
Room & Board: $17,856
Required Fees: $0
Books & Supplies: $1,150

Avg. Need-Based Grant: $50,835
Avg. % of Need Met: 100%

Avg. Merit-Based Award: $0
% Receiving (All Freshmen): 0%
% Receiving (Freshmen w/o Need): 0%

Avg. Cumulative Debt: $23,927
% of Students Borrowing: 42%

CAREER
Who Recruits
1. Harlem Arts Alliance
2. 826NYC
3. Bank of America
4. Mastercard
5. Hospital for Special Surgery

Notable Internships
1. U.S. Embassy
2. MacMillan Publishers
3. Prudential

Top Industries
1. Business
2. Education
3. Media
4. Social Services
5. Healthcare

Top Employers
1. NYC Department of Education
2. Google
3. JPMorgan Chase
4. Citi
5. IBM

Where Alumni Work
1. New York City
2. San Francisco
3. Boston
4. Los Angeles
5. Washington DC

Median Earnings
College Scorecard (Early Career): $57,900
PayScale (Early Career): $62,400
PayScale (Mid-Career): $123,200

RANKINGS
Money: 147
U.S. News: 22 (T), Liberal Arts Colleges
Wall Street Journal/THE: 52
Washington Monthly: 24, Liberal Arts Colleges

COLLEGE OVERLAPS
Brown University
Bryn Mawr College
Columbia University
New York University
Wellesley College

ADMISSION
Admission Rate: 43%
Admission Rate - Men: 43%
Admission Rate - Women: 44%
EA Admission Rate: Not Offered
ED Admission Rate: Not Offered
ED Admits as % of Total Admits: Not Offered
Admission Rate (5-Year Trend): +16%
% of Admits Attending (Yield): 26%
Transfer Admission Rate: 53%

SAT Reading/Writing (Middle 50%): 550-640
SAT Math (Middle 50%): 580-690
ACT Composite (Middle 50%): NR

% Graduated in Top 10% of HS Class: 41%
% Graduated in Top 25% of HS Class: 74%
% Graduated in Top 50% of HS Class: 92%

Demonstrated Interest: Not Considered
Legacy Status: Not Considered
Admission Interview Offered: No

ENROLLMENT
Total Undergraduate Enrollment: 15,482
% Part-Time: 22%
% Male: 53%
% Female: 47%
% Out-of-State: 3%
% Fraternity: Not Offered
% Sorority: Not Offered
% On-Campus (Freshman): 9%
% On-Campus (All Undergraduate): 2%

% African-American: 9%
% Asian: 33%
% Hispanic: 25%
% White: 21%
% Other: 2%
% Race or Ethnicity Unknown: 0%
% International: 10%
% Low-Income: 45%

ACADEMICS
Student-to-Faculty Ratio: 19 to 1
% of Classes Under 20: 67%
% of Classes 20-49: 17%
% of Classes 50 or More: 16%
% Full-Time Faculty: 45%
% Full-Time Faculty w/ Terminal Degree: 94%

Top Programs
Accounting
Business Administration
Computer Information Systems
Corporate Communication
Finance
Real Estate

Retention Rate: 89%
4-Year Graduation Rate: 44%
6-Year Graduation Rate: 70%

Curricular Flexibility: Less Flexible
Academic Rating: ★★★

#CollegesWorthYourMoney

Locating a certifiable commuter school with a highly selective admissions process and an outstanding academic reputation sounds about as realistic as stumbling upon a unicorn on your way to the grocery store. Amazingly, there may be only one institution in the country that perfectly fits that description. Baruch College, a gem within the CUNY system, shines bright in the eyes of employers, even those New York City juggernauts with a taste for Ivy League grads. Of course, not every commuter school is situated in Midtown Manhattan, a primo location for high-level internships and flourishing corporate connections. Baruch students take full advantage; of the three undergraduate schools within the college, the Zicklin School of Business attracts a mind-boggling 75 percent of the student population.

Inside the Classroom

All students at Baruch have to complete a forty-five-credit sequence of required courses, but there is some choice within the broad boxes that need to be checked. The nonnegotiable courses are Writing I & Writing II, Speech Communication, Mathematics, and Foreign Language. Students also need to choose classes that fulfill requirements in fine and performing arts, history, literature, philosophy, natural sciences, anthropology/sociology, economics, politics and government, and psychology. Those who are part of the Honors Program complete an honors thesis as a culminating academic experience during their senior year.

With a 19:1 student-to-faculty ratio and more part-time than full-time faculty, one-on-one bonding time with your professors is at a premium. Single-digit classes are a rarity, and only 16 percent of courses have twenty or fewer enrolled students. That being said, Baruch does offer many courses in the twenty- to thirty-student range; 42 percent of sections fall in that span. Tapping into undergraduate research projects is tough at a business-oriented commuter school. Procuring those opportunities requires initiative, but it can be accomplished through connecting with individual faculty members. Those who do make such a connection eventually share their research at the college's Creative Inquiry Day. Studying abroad is an option at any of the CUNY system's 166 programs in fifty-one countries.

Zicklin is not only a great business school for the money, it's a great business school period. Popular majors within this well-respected and well-connected institution include accounting, finance, marketing, and business communication and, as we will cover later, leading companies in those fields have a strong affection for Baruch graduates. With so many entering the job market postgraduation, prestigious scholarships and fellowships are an afterthought, but the school does produce an occasional Fulbright winner.

Outside the Classroom

Only 2 percent of undergraduate students live on campus, and no—that is not a typo—it is simply a reality for this school of 15,000 set on three Manhattan acres. Baruch is not going to provide a typical college campus experience, and for some that's not a bad thing, but it's just important to go in with the right expectations. The surrounding area is not a college town in any way, shape, or form. As a result, the typical student is there for one purpose—to earn a degree. This "nose to the grindstone" ethos shapes campus life. There are no Greek organizations, although there are thirteen NCAA Division III sports teams that play as the Bearcats. While most time spent on campus is time spent in the classrooms themselves, there are ways to get involved through 130+ clubs and activities. The weekly newspaper, The Ticker, and the student-run radio station, WBMB, have lengthy histories. Most clubs meet at specific times during the early afternoon while people are actually on campus, and most of those meetings are held in the Newman Vertical Campus, a seventeen-floor architectural wonder that was erected in 2003 for $327 million dollars. (For a CUNY school, Baruch has some very wealthy donors.)

Career Services

The Starr Career Development Center (SCDC) employs sixteen professional staff as well as four part-time staff members. Full-timers play roles such as career counselor, internship coordinator, and employer relations director. Including full-time and adjunct career coaches, Baruch sports a half-decent 942:1 student-to-advisor ratio, but the service delivery exceeds expectations.

More than eighty companies traveled to Baruch's campus for recruiting purposes in 2017-18 (most recent data available) including KPMG, Amazon, Moody's, HarperCollins Publishers, and Colgate-Palmolive. In excess of 2,900 students attended those events. Overall, 46 percent of Baruch students land at least one internship; the average student who found employment within six months had 1.5 such experiences. Five or more 2018 graduates interned at each of KPMG, EY, Citi, Deloitte, and JP Morgan. The SCDC provided 3,480 career consultations in

2017-18; for perspective, that is similar to the number of total graduates annually. It also conducted over 2,700 resume reviews, posted 6,600+ jobs online, and facilitated 1,271 on-campus interviews with employers. The online system, cleverly named Starr Search, is utilized by 84 percent of the undergraduate student body, and it offers countless opportunities for those aggressive and motivated enough to follow leads.

Professional Outcomes

Within six months of graduation, 80 percent of the Class of 2019 were already employed or in full-time graduate programs. Given that over three-quarters of graduates possess business-related degrees, most first jobs are in the realms of accounting, finance, real estate, management, and marketing. Baruch is one of the few accessible public institutions that is a direct feeder to many of Wall Street's top banks. In fact, the top employers of Class of 2019 members were JP Morgan (23 grads), PwC (12), EY (11), Bank of America (9) and Citi (8). Goldman Sachs, Morgan Stanley, Deloitte, and KPMG were other companies scooping up six or more 2019 graduates. The average salary for Arts & Sciences grads was $48,000 while Zicklin School of Business grads earned $54,000. Just about everyone graduating from this college remains in New York City, although some alumni head to Miami, DC, San Francisco, or Los Angeles, but only in dribs and drabs.

Graduate studies are not usually the immediate step after receiving one's diploma from Baruch—only 10 percent of those finishing their bachelor's go right into another degree program. There are few students majoring in the hard sciences at this school, so you don't see a ton on the premed path, but sophomores do have the option of applying for early admission to the Icahn School of Medicine at Mount Sinai through the FlexMed program. Of the alumni who decide to go the law school route, even if they do so years later, many attend local NYC schools like Pace or Brooklyn Law School, but a handful of recent grads have been welcomed to the law schools of the University of Michigan, Tufts, Fordham, and Cornell.

Admission

Baruch admitted 47 percent of the 20,673 students who applied for admission into the Class of 2023; that is significantly higher than the 23 percent acceptance rate the college registered a decade prior. Part of the change is that the school's enrollment has grown during that same period, increasing by a few thousand undergraduates even though admissions standards have become more rigid. Today, 41 percent of entering freshman are top 10 percent finishers at their respective high schools; in 2009, only 32 percent held that distinction. Further, the 75th percentile SAT score from ten years ago is close to the 25th percentile score today. The 2019-20 freshmen had an average score of 1287 on the SAT, the test submitted 94 percent of the time by applicants.

The Baruch College Admissions Office considers GPA, standardized test scores, and rigor of curriculum above all else. Recommendation letters and essays sit alone in the next rung of important categories. This is a school that can be forgiving of a bad grade or two. In fact, 42 percent earned under a 3.5 in high school, and 7 percent had under a 3.0. It's hard to find a school as exceptional as Baruch that is willing to accept late-bloomers and, in some cases, bright AP/honors kids who earned B's and C's throughout high school.

Worth Your Money?

New Yorkers pay under $7,500 in tuition for a school with an alumni network with deep ties to a number of major Wall Street players. This school is unequivocally worth every cent for Big Apple denizens. Outsiders pay a reasonable $19,100 per year in tuition—of course, there is the small matter of finding an affordable place to live. Once again, that's about as likely as spotting that unicorn.

FINANCIAL
Institutional Type: Public
In-State Tuition: $7,461
Out-of-State Tuition: $19,131
Room & Board: $15,499
Required Fees: $0
Books & Supplies: $1,364

Avg. Need-Based Grant: NR
Avg. % of Need Met: NR

Avg. Merit-Based Award: $2,459
% Receiving (All Freshmen): NR
% Receiving (Freshmen w/o Need): NR

Avg. Cumulative Debt: $10,510
% of Students Borrowing: 11%

CAREER
Who Recruits
1. BBC Worldwide Americas
2. FDM Group
3. Home Advisor
4. NYS Department of Civil Service
5. Yelp

Notable Internships
1. PwC
2. RBC Capital Markets
3. Atlantic Records

Top Industries
1. Business
2. Finance
3. Accounting
4. Operations
5. Sales

Top Employers
1. JPMorgan Chase
2. Citi
3. NYC Department of Education
4. Morgan Stanley
5. EY

Where Alumni Work
1. New York City
2. Miami
3. Washington DC
4. Los Angeles
5. San Francisco

Median Earnings
College Scorecard (Early Career): $57,200
PayScale (Early Career): $60,000
PayScale (Mid-Career): $114,600

RANKINGS
Money: 33
U.S. News: 16, Regional Universities North
Wall Street Journal/THE: 248 (T)
Washington Monthly: 48, Master's Universities

COLLEGE OVERLAPS
Binghamton University (SUNY)
Brooklyn College (CUNY)
Hunter College (CUNY)
Queens College (CUNY)
Stony Brook University (SUNY)

Bates College

Lewiston, Maine | 207-786-6000

The nation's second adopter (1984) of a test-optional admissions policy, Bates College has always prided itself on a commitment to egalitarian education—even back to its official founding in the middle of the Civil War when it proudly admitted students regardless of race, religion, or sex. Today, the school is once again on the cutting edge of higher education, advocating a curriculum that honors the liberal arts tradition but also prepares students for "purposeful work" that is both personally meaningful and societally relevant.

Inside the Classroom

Toward those aims Bates students are required to complete (a) three "writing-attentive" courses; (b) three courses focused on scientific reasoning, lab experience, and quantitative literacy; and (c) two four-course concentrations revolving around a particular issue or area of inquiry. General education at Bates is intended to ensure "depth of knowledge" and a "comparative appreciation of how the several disciplines function and what they can teach us." Distinctive features include a mandatory first-year seminar, senior thesis requirement, and a Short Term at the end of the academic year that provides students the opportunity to focus exclusively on one course, field project, internship, or study abroad opportunity. For those wishing to save money and/or fast-track their undergraduate education, the college offers a three-year option that allows students to graduate in three years, provided they register for five courses (as opposed to four) each semester and one course during each Short Term.

Thirty-eight percent of courses at Bates have a single-digit enrollment, and 69 percent of classrooms contain nineteen or fewer students, allowing for this process to unfold in an intimate academic atmosphere. Additionally, the student-to-faculty ratio is 10:1, and not a single graduate student is present to vacuum up professorial attention. Students interested in research will find opportunities across all disciplines, many of which culminate with a presentation at the Mount David Summit, an annual campus-wide celebration of undergraduate research and creative works. Bates has one of the highest percentages of study abroad participation of any college in the country, typically sending over two-thirds of each class to one of 200+ global destinations.

Thirty-one percent of all degrees earned at Bates are in the social sciences and biology (14 percent), psychology (11 percent), English (10 percent), and the visual and performing arts (8 percent) are next in popularity. Though strong across many disciplines, Bates boasts exemplary programs in political science, art, philosophy, economics, and psychology. The college has produced more than seventy Fulbright Scholars in the last five years and is recognized as a top recipient of prestigious academic fellowships, even among highly selective institutions. In 2020 alone, Bates produced 24 Fulbright Scholars, more than any other undergraduate-only liberal arts college in the United States.

Outside the Classroom

Outside the classroom Bates places a particularly strong emphasis on community and civic engagement, facilitating numerous volunteer and civic leadership opportunities, primarily through the Harward Center. More than half of all Bates students participate in community-engaged learning (for academic credit). Aside from community service, Bates offers more than 110 officially recognized student organizations, including a nationally ranked debate team and an active investment club. Athletic opportunities also abound at the Division III varsity level and within the college's extensive intramural program that encompasses club sports ranging from equestrian to rugby. There are no fraternities or sororities at Bates, and 95 percent of students live in one of the dorms or school-owned Victorian homes that accommodate ten to thirty students each. Lewistown is the state's second most populous city, yet that isn't saying much in Maine because Lewistown is a post-industrial town with only 60,000 residents. Portland, the state's largest city, can be reached in about forty minutes by car.

Career Services

The Bates Career Development Center (BDCD) features eleven full-time staff and a student-to-advisor ratio of 165:1, a superior level of support when compared to most other institutions included in this book. Services offered by the center include career/interest assessment, interview preparation, and a guest lecture series. The BDCD hosts an annual graduate and professional school fair (with Bowdoin and Colby), as well as a number of its own networking events throughout the year, one example being a presentation from Google/Pinterest on tech careers for liberal arts majors. Organizations such as The Beacon Group, Analysis Group, Barclays, and the CIA have recruited on campus in recent years. Over 350 interviews are conducted on campus by sixty-five companies in a single academic year.

The Career Discovery Program in Practice, in existence since 1978, affords undergrads the opportunity to job shadow a Bates alum in a field of interest. Roughly 250 Bobcats take advantage of that program each year. The Purposeful Work Internship Program helps fund living expenses of students interning more than 300 summer hours. Despite Bates' location in Maine, internship opportunities are plentiful, particularly in Boston and smaller cities throughout the New England region. This past summer Bates students worked in over 130 companies and organizations throughout the United States and internationally, including at JP Morgan, the Institute of Infectious Diseases, the Conservation Law Foundation, Amazon, and the Sloan Kettering Cancer Center.

Professional Outcomes

Within six months of graduation, 99 percent of the Class of 2019 were either employed, enrolled in graduate school, or otherwise meaningfully engaged in a fellowship or internship. The most frequently entered fields were education (21 percent), healthcare (13 percent), finance/banking (10 percent), and technology (8 percent). Popular employers included Accenture, Fidelity Investments, Google, Wayfair, and Liberty Mutual Insurance whereas common employment destinations of Bates graduates were concentrated primarily in the Northeast, namely Boston, New York, and Portland, Maine. However, sizable numbers of Bates alumni also can be found working in the Washington, DC, and San Francisco areas.

According to the Bates Career Development Center, within ten years of graduation approximately 13 percent of Bates graduates are in, or have completed, law school whereas 7 percent enroll in medical school. In 2019, every single law school applicant was accepted into at least one school. Students from the same cohort were accepted into med school at the UNC School of Medicine, Chicago Medical School, and Tulane University School of Medicine. In addition, Bates is currently among the top producers of graduates who eventually go on to enroll in PhD programs in the social sciences, especially economics and sociology. By midcareer, Bates alumni are most frequently found working in the professional fields of business development, education, and community and social services.

Admission

From 2014 to 2018, Bates experienced a hefty 52 percent increase in applications and, during the same period, the school's acceptance rate fell from 24 percent to 18 percent. By the time the school set about constructing the Class of 2023, just 12% were accepted. The mid-50 percent standardized test score ranges are approximately 1280-1460 on the SAT and 29-33 on the ACT. Students typically ranked high in their graduating high school class with 71 percent in the top 10 percent and 90 percent in the top quartile.

Aside from grades, class rank, and course rigor, Bates places significant emphasis on an applicant's essay, letters of recommendation, extracurricular profile, talent/ability, and character/personal qualities. Demonstrated interest also plays a considerable role. Of course, the ultimate declaration of love is the submission of an early decision application. Those who go the binding ED route enjoy an acceptance rate three times higher than those who apply in the regular cycle (42 percent vs. 9 percent). A massive 70 percent of the 2019-20 freshman class was admitted via early decision, making it a wise strategic maneuver for anyone serious about attending Bates.

Worth Your Money?

Upper-income families will likely pay the full $77,000+ annual cost of attendance. For the 41 percent of students who do qualify for need-based financial aid, Bates delivers in a big way. The college meets 100 percent of the demonstrated need for every qualifying student with grants averaging $47,569 each year. Not only do Bates grads generally find solid-paying jobs after graduation, they also have far less debt, on average, than their peers receiving diplomas from other institutions.

FINANCIAL
Institutional Type: Private
In-State Tuition: $55,683
Out-of-State Tuition: $55,683
Room & Board: $15,705
Required Fees: NR
Books & Supplies: $900

Avg. Need-Based Grant: $47,569
Avg. % of Need Met: 100%

Avg. Merit-Based Award: $0
% Receiving (All Freshmen): 0%
% Receiving (Freshmen w/o Need): 0%

Avg. Cumulative Debt: $23,383
% of Students Borrowing: 33%

CAREER
Who Recruits
1. Chevron
2. Hulu
3. Oppenheimer & Co.
4. athenaHealth
5. Owl Cybersecurity

Notable Internships
1. CNN
2. United States Senate
3. Morgan Stanley

Top Industries
1. Business
2. Education
3. Operations
4. Social Services
5. Research

Top Employers
1. Fidelity Investments
2. Massachusetts General Hospital
3. Liberty Mutual Insurance
4. Google
5. Amazon

Where Alumni Work
1. Boston
2. New York City
3. Portland, ME
4. Lewiston, ME
5. Washington DC

Median Earnings
College Scorecard (Early Career): $59,200
PayScale (Early Career): $61,700
PayScale (Mid-Career): $130,100

RANKINGS
Money: 71
U.S. News: 22 (T), Liberal Arts Colleges
Wall Street Journal/THE: 63
Washington Monthly: 21, Liberal Arts Colleges

COLLEGE OVERLAPS
Bowdoin College
Colby College
Dartmouth College
Middlebury College
Tufts University

Baylor University

Waco, Texas | 254-710-3435

ADMISSION
Admission Rate: 45%
Admission Rate - Men: 52%
Admission Rate - Women: 41%
EA Admission Rate: Not Offered
ED Admission Rate: 88%
ED Admits as % of Total Admits: 3%
Admission Rate (5-Year Trend): -10%
% of Admits Attending (Yield): 21%
Transfer Admission Rate: 85%

SAT Reading/Writing (Middle 50%): 600-680
SAT Math (Middle 50%): 600-700
ACT Composite (Middle 50%): 26-32

% Graduated in Top 10% of HS Class: 44%
% Graduated in Top 25% of HS Class: 76%
% Graduated in Top 50% of HS Class: 96%

Demonstrated Interest: Considered
Legacy Status: Considered
Admission Interview Offered: Yes

ENROLLMENT
Total Undergraduate Enrollment: 14,108
% Part-Time: 1%
% Male: 40%
% Female: 60%
% Out-of-State: 33%
% Fraternity: 20%
% Sorority: 34%
% On-Campus (Freshman): 99%
% On-Campus (All Undergraduate): 34%

% African-American: 5%
% Asian: 7%
% Hispanic: 16%
% White: 61%
% Other: 5%
% Race or Ethnicity Unknown: 0%
% International: 5%
% Low-Income: 20%

ACADEMICS
Student-to-Faculty Ratio: 13 to 1
% of Classes Under 20: 53%
% of Classes 20-49: 38%
% of Classes 50 or More: 9%
% Full-Time Faculty: 79%
% Full-Time Faculty w/ Terminal Degree: 85%

Top Programs
Accounting
Biology
Communication
Design
Entrepreneurship
Exercise Physiology
Finance

Retention Rate: 88%
4-Year Graduation Rate: 63%
6-Year Graduation Rate: 78%

Curricular Flexibility: Less Flexible
Academic Rating: ★★★

#CollegesWorthYourMoney

A private Christian university in Waco, Texas, the "mission of Baylor University is to educate men and women for worldwide leadership and service by integrating academic excellence and Christian commitment within a caring community." The oldest continually operating university in the state of Texas has 14,000 undergraduates along with another 3,900 graduate/professional students. In offering 125+ majors and minors, the school captures high marks for everything from undergraduate teaching to hands-on research opportunities, and applicants have taken notice. Baylor is a far more selective school than it was in the first decade of the millennium when four fifths of applicants got in. Today, only 45 percent make the cut.

Inside the Classroom
Structured freshman experiences at Baylor have received national attention for their inside-the-classroom offerings like New Student Experience courses that help give students tools and support to have a successful first year. The core curriculum, revamped in 2019, includes the following required courses: Chapel, Creative Arts Experience, American Literary Cultures, The United States in Global Perspective, The US Constitution, Christian Scriptures, and Christian Heritage. There are also distributional requirements one must fill in the areas of communication and media literacy, contemporary social issues, fine arts, foreign language and culture, and scientific methods, among others. All told, those requirements can account for up to 56 credits toward a Baylor degree, a sizable chunk of one's overall coursework.

Class sizes at Baylor generally range from small to medium, with 53 percent of sections containing fewer than 20 students and 78 percent enrolling fewer than 29. The student-to-faculty ratio is 13:1. This solid level of support enables the school to truly encourage undergraduates to collaborate with professors on research "as early as the first semester of their freshman year." The Undergraduate Research and Scholarly Achievement (URSA) office does a superb job connecting students with a research opportunity in their field of interest. The school also pushes overseas experiences in the form of an internship, academic semester, or mission trip. Baylor offers signature programs in Scotland, the Netherlands, and Ireland.

Almost double as many Bears major in business/marketing (29 percent) than the second place finisher, health professions (15 percent). Other popular academic pursuits are biology (10 percent) and communication/ journalism (7 percent), both of which are very strong. The Hankamer School of Business is highly respected across the country, particularly for accounting, entrepreneurship, and finance. Baylor, as a whole, does well capturing prestigious scholarships and fellowships. Nine Bears took home Fulbrights in 2019, and two seniors received National Science Foundation Graduate Research Fellowships that same year.

Outside the Classroom
Almost every single freshman at Baylor lives on campus, but the same is true of only one third of the total undergraduate population. There are 12 residence halls that each seek to establish a cohesive community for first-year students. Greek life draws in a large percentage of the student body, with one fifth of men joining fraternities and 34 percent of women entering sorority life. Overall, there are 40 national and local Greek organizations and 330 other clubs and activities. The spirit of volunteerism is strong as the undergraduate student body contributes a collective 150,000 hours of community service each year. There are 19 varsity sports teams that compete at the Division I level within the Big 12 Conference. School spirit is strong at this university, even on non-game days. Perhaps this is best exemplified by the fact that there are actually two live bears on campus! Other traditions include a well-attended Family Weekend, weekly Dr. Pepper Hours (the soft drink was invented in Waco), epic Christmas celebrations, and two mandatory trips per week to Chapel, a gathering where spiritual and philosophical issues can be discussed in depth. Waco is not the most celebrated college town, but it is situated 1.5 hours south of Dallas and roughly the same distance from Austin for those seeking big-city adventure on the weekends.

Career Services
The Career Center at Baylor University is staffed by 26 professional staff members who serve in various capacities including, most notably, as career success professionals who advise students within a particular academic discipline. The Career Center's student-to-advisor ratio of 538:1 is within the average range when compared to other colleges selected for inclusion in this guidebook. Simply by looking at a random week's career services programming, one learns a great deal about how hard this office works on behalf of students. For example, in one single day in September 2020, the office presented a workshop on standing out as a graduate school applicant, a Q&A with professionals in the consulting field, a JPMorgan Chase information session, a Google resume workshop, a seminar on the career of financial advising, and four additional events.

Major companies recruit and interview on Baylor's campus with great frequency and are eager to attend Baylor's two campus-wide career fairs every fall and spring. The office goes to great effort to engage freshmen and sophomores in beginning the process of career exploration early in their academic careers. They encourage students to meet with them every single year in a 1:1 capacity to utilize career discovery tools and seek assistance with lining up internships and alumni connections. The mix of Baylor's personal touch and wide network of employer connections leads to very positive postgraduate results for its undergraduates.

Professional Outcomes

At the 90-day postgraduation point, those who earned their diplomas from Baylor in 2019 and 2020 had entered the world of full-time employment at a 43 percent clip, and 24 percent had entered a graduate or professional degree program. At this three-month juncture, 18 percent of graduates were still seeking employment. Large numbers of grads were scooped up by many of the most desirable employers in the country. KPMG employed 105 Bears from these two cohorts, with Deloitte (70), PwC (68), EY (62), Dell (40), Oracle (40), and Accenture (35) also recruiting 35 or more Bears into their corporate families. Remaining in Texas after graduation is a popular choice with Dallas, Houston, Waco, Austin, and San Antonio containing the greatest number of alumni.

Among the classes of 2019 and 2020, the most commonly attended graduate school was Baylor itself (366), followed by UT Dallas (26), Southern Methodist University (25), UT Austin (23), and the University of Houston (21). Substantial numbers also matriculated into elite institutions such as USC (10), NYU (7), Duke (6), Notre Dame (6), Emory (5), and Georgetown (5). Baylor produced 335 applicants to medical schools during 2019-20; among those who completed the first-destination survey, 117 individuals are presently enrolled in MD programs and another 23 in DO programs. Nineteen members of the last two classes are presently students at the renowned Baylor College of Medicine while others entered the Saint Louis University School of Medicine, the Long School of Medicine, and the UT Southwestern Medical Center. Of the 99 individuals in the survey who entered law school, 12 did so at Baylor while others entered their legal training at the likes of Texas Tech, Washington and Lee, and Tulane.

Admission

Baylor received 34,582 applications for its Class of 2023; 45 percent were accepted, a significant departure from the 80+ percent acceptance rates back in the aughts. Freshmen entering the university in fall 2019 possessed a middle-50 percent SAT score of 1210-1370 and an ACT range of 26-32. Forty-four percent of this group finished in the top 10 percent of their high school class while over three-quarters finished in the top 25 percent. Sixty percent of those in this group resided in the state of Texas. Other states sending a significant number of students to Baylor were California (324), Colorado (115), and Illinois (89).

The admissions committee gives preference to the hard facts of an application granting "very important" status to the rigor of one's course load, class rank, and standardized test scores. Only GPA sits in the "important" column, and soft factors like essays, recommendations, extracurricular factors, legacy status, work experience, talent/ability, character/personal qualities, and demonstrated interest are "considered." Borderline candidates who do not have much financial need should strongly consider applying early decision. Last year, the ED acceptance rate was 88 percent, close to double the overall rate. Having a familial connection can also be beneficial as 28 percent of incoming freshmen in 2020 had an alum in their family.

Worth Your Money?

The estimated cost of attendance for a student living on campus is $65,500 with $42,842 coming in the form of annual tuition. The university does cover 68 percent of the demonstrated financial need for qualifying students and awards average merit aid packages totaling $18k annually. However, the school does not fare well when it comes to average debt load that students carry with them after graduation. For the 51 percent of students who borrow, the average amount of debt is just shy of $50k, about $20k more than the national average. Like many schools included in our book, Baylor is only worth your money if you are taking advantage of one of its premier programs like finance or accounting, and have a clear pathway to a solid starting salary. We would not recommend selecting Baylor if you have a significant level of financial need and are uncertain about your academic/professional pathway.

FINANCIAL
Institutional Type: Private
In-State Tuition: $44,544
Out-of-State Tuition: $44,544
Room & Board: $14,324
Required Fees: $4,702
Books & Supplies: $1,284

Avg. Need-Based Grant: $26,522
Avg. % of Need Met: 68%

Avg. Merit-Based Award: $18,255
% Receiving (All Freshmen): 91%
% Receiving (Freshmen w/o Need): 39%

Avg. Cumulative Debt: $49,610
% of Students Borrowing: 51%

CAREER
Who Recruits
1. Goldman Sachs
2. Oracle
3. Bank of America
4. Hershey
5. Allstate

Notable Internships
1. Texas Legislature
2. Methodist Healthcare System
3. MTV

Top Industries
1. Business
2. Education
3. Healthcare
4. Operations
5. Sales

Top Employers
1. US Army
2. Baylor Scott & White Health
3. EY
4. AT&T
5. PwC

Where Alumni Work
1. Dallas
2. Houston
3. Waco
4. Austin
5. San Antonio

Median Earnings
College Scorecard (Early Career): $51,600
PayScale (Early Career): $58,200
PayScale (Mid-Career): $110,100

RANKINGS
Money: 452
U.S. News: 76 (T), National Universities
Wall Street Journal/THE: 175 (T)
Washington Monthly: 336, National Universities

COLLEGE OVERLAPS
Southern Methodist University
Texas A&M University - College Station
Texas Christian University
Texas Tech University
University of Texas at Austin

Bentley University

Waltham, Massachusetts | 781-891-2244

Situated just west of Boston, Bentley University is one of the premier business-focused institutions in the country. Rival Babson College is only ten miles away geographically, but the two schools used to be a much greater distance apart in reputation and prestige. That gap has closed quickly in recent years. The school's 4,200 undergraduate students traversing this attractive 163-acre Waltham, Massachusetts, campus are, somewhat surprisingly, exposed to a top-notch liberal arts education while working toward a BA or BS in a business-related field.

Inside the Classroom

Of the twenty-five majors and thirty-six minors to choose from, a handful are non-business concentrations such as English, philosophy, and history. These students typically supplement their education with a healthy number of business courses. The majority take the opposite path, majoring in business and supplementing their studies with liberal arts courses. Always innovating, the school recently started three cutting-edge majors in data analytics, professional sales, and creative industries. Regardless of one's major, the core curriculum consisting of sixteen mandatory courses must be tackled. That includes a first-year seminar, information technology and computer system concepts, a sequence of two expository writing classes as well as courses in math, the hard sciences, government, and history.

Earning a Bentley degree is far from a passive experience. The average undergraduate class is comprised of twenty-six students, and academics are intense. Twenty percent of the student body is double majoring, tacking the liberal studies major on to their business concentration. Roughly half of Bentley students elect to study abroad in one of eighty programs spread across twenty-five countries. Just about everyone lands an internship; the majority of students complete two. Undergraduate research participation has increased in recent years as the school has joined The Council on Undergraduate Research. While not a focal point of the school, it is possible to land a position assisting a faculty member with a research project at some point during your four years on campus.

Bentley is a school on the rise. Having just celebrated its one-hundred-year anniversary, it has become a highly-respected name in the corporate world and possesses an international reach. The most popular majors are all within the business domain and include finance, business, management, marketing, accounting, and poetry—just kidding on that last one. Bentley is a one-trick pony, and that's not a bad thing when you examine the outcomes data for recent graduates (more ahead).

Outside the Classroom

A bastion for extraverts, 90 percent of Bentley undergrads belong to at least one student organization; one-third consider themselves "highly involved." Over one hundred clubs and activities are available with a multitude of options in the academic, cultural, religious, arts and media, and recreational realms. Participation in athletics is high. The Falcons compete in eleven men's and ten women's sports in NCAA Division II (men's ice hockey is the lone Division I team). Intramural and club sports are popular, including ultimate Frisbee, sailing, rugby, and equestrian. More than 1,700 students participate in an intramural sport each year. With 78 percent of students living in school-owned housing, most social events are centered on campus. Fraternity and sorority life attract a significant but not dominant 17 percent of undergraduates. Additionally, some students live in defined communities—residential housing for those passionate about areas such as women's leadership, social justice, or service learning. Waltham, also home to Brandeis University, is a historic and pretty New England town with plenty of bars, restaurants, and other attractions. The university is only thirteen miles from downtown Boston, and the school provides free public transportation to-and-from Harvard Square.

Career Services

TThe Career Services Office at Bentley has ten professional staff members who work with the college's undergraduates. That equates to a 423:1 student-to-advisor ratio, placing the university in the average range compared to other schools featured in this guide. Career services may be average in this category, but it is exceptional by just about every other metric. For example, the staff does an incredible job facilitating meaningful internships. Of the 92 percent of Bentley students who had an internship (71 percent complete more than one) as part of their undergraduate education, 37 percent landed their first job directly through this experience. On-campus recruiting events led another 18 percent of employed graduates to their first employment destination, and a sizable number of students also found their way through alumni networking, school-organized career fairs, and referrals from the school. The school has developed close corporate partnerships with companies including Dell, Fidelity Investments, Liberty Mutual, and United Technologies, all of whom hire their fair share of graduates each year.

ADMISSION
Admission Rate: 47%
Admission Rate - Men: 42%
Admission Rate - Women: 54%
EA Admission Rate: Not Offered
ED Admission Rate: 67%
ED Admits as % of Total Admits: 5%
Admission Rate (5-Year Trend): +5%
% of Admits Attending (Yield): 22%
Transfer Admission Rate: 44%

SAT Reading/Writing (Middle 50%): 600-680
SAT Math (Middle 50%): 630-730
ACT Composite (Middle 50%): 27-31

% Graduated in Top 10% of HS Class: 37%
% Graduated in Top 25% of HS Class: 73%
% Graduated in Top 50% of HS Class: 97%

Demonstrated Interest: Important
Legacy Status: Considered
Admission Interview Offered: Yes

ENROLLMENT
Total Undergraduate Enrollment: 4,228
% Part-Time: 1%
% Male: 59%
% Female: 41%
% Out-of-State: 58%
% Fraternity: 5%
% Sorority: 10%
% On-Campus (Freshman): 97%
% On-Campus (All Undergraduate): 78%

% African-American: 4%
% Asian: 9%
% Hispanic: 7%
% White: 58%
% Other: 3%
% Race or Ethnicity Unknown: 4%
% International: 15%
% Low-Income: 14%

ACADEMICS
Student-to-Faculty Ratio: 11 to 1
% of Classes Under 20: 73%
% of Classes 20-49: 27%
% of Classes 50 or More: 0%
% Full-Time Faculty: 63%
% Full-Time Faculty w/ Terminal Degree: 83%

Top Programs
Accounting
Data Analytics
Finance
Management
Managerial Economics
Marketing
Professional Sales

Retention Rate: 92%
4-Year Graduation Rate: 85%
6-Year Graduation Rate: 90%

Curricular Flexibility: Less Flexible
Academic Rating: ★★★★

#CollegesWorthYourMoney

Offerings include career development seminars that begin freshman year; 97 percent of first-years sign up for the introductory class. Those seminars are part of the school's larger Hire Education Program that helps students formulate career goals, hone job-readiness skills, and build professional networks. The Mentor Marketplace is an online tool that helps connect current students with alumni who work in a relevant field to serve as a career resource. In addition to the full internships taken advantage of by the bulk of the student body, Bentley also offers micro-internships in which alumni can bring in undergraduates to work on short-term, impactful projects within their company. Taking into account the breadth and quality of its services as well as the stellar outcomes achieved by its graduates, Bentley has as high quality of a Career Services Office as you will find anywhere in the country.

Professional Outcomes

A superb 99 percent of recent Bentley grads were employed or in graduate school six months after receiving their diplomas. The financial services and technology sectors each account for 22 percent of new hires. Most job functions are in the areas of finance, sales, accounting, analytics, marketing, consulting, and operations/logistics. A hub of entrepreneurship, the school saw 7 percent of its graduating class start their own businesses right out of college. Companies employing the highest number of alumni include Fidelity Investments, PwC, EY, Dell EMC, and Wayfair. The median starting salary for graduates is $60,000, a strong figure compared to other universities of its ilk. By midcareer, Bentley grads have a median income similar to Harvard and Tufts alumni.

Bentley does not see a high number of graduates directly enter graduate school—roughly 10 percent in any given year. While many pursue MBAs or other advanced business degrees later in their careers, those in this field typically gain work experience prior to attending graduate school. Recent graduates have ended up in advanced degree programs at elite business schools like Wharton (Penn), Stern (NYU), Columbia Business School, Yale School of Management, Sloane School of Management (MIT), and the Tuck School of Business (Dartmouth). Whether entering graduate school or chasing their first job, the vast majority of Falcons stay in the Boston area.

Admission

In the 2019-20 admissions cycle Bentley accepted 47 percent of the 9,017 who applied. Members of the Class of 2023 averaged 1316 on the SAT and 29 on the ACT. For perspective, in 2011 the acceptance rate was a nearly identical 46 percent, but the 75th percentile on the SAT was a 1300. The percent of students ranking in the top 10 percent (37 percent) and 25 percent (73 percent) of their high school classes has risen sharply in that same time. Therefore, we can deduce that while acceptance rates have stayed relatively similar at Bentley in recent years, the standardized test scores and grades needed to gain acceptance have risen significantly.

Test scores, grades (including an emphasis on senior year grades), two letters of recommendation, and an on-campus interview are all important components of the admissions process. While the interviews are not mandatory, they can be an excellent opportunity to highlight interpersonal skills and intangible attributes that a top business school like Bentley is seeking. With a relatively low yield of 22 percent, Bentley is competing with many other rival institutions for the same pool of students. Thus, it makes sense that the school accepts 67 percent of applicants through its binding early decision program. Bentley is a competitive business school and is a notch easier to gain admission into than comparable Babson.

Worth Your Money?

Among Bentley's undergraduates who qualify for financial aid, 89 percent of demonstrated need is met by the university. The average annual grant is for just under $35k, helping to alleviate the pain of the $72,000 per year cost of attendance. Even at that high cost, Bentley is worth the money for most applicants. The school rates very well in terms of pure salary—both starting and midcareer—and it rates well for social mobility, allowing those from poor-to-modest backgrounds to climb the economic ladder.

FINANCIAL
Institutional Type: Private
In-State Tuition: $53,790
Out-of-State Tuition: $5,370
Room & Board: $17,620
Required Fees: $0
Books & Supplies: $1,325

Avg. Need-Based Grant: $34,669
Avg. % of Need Met: 89%

Avg. Merit-Based Award: $18,366
% Receiving (All Freshmen): 36%
% Receiving (Freshmen w/o Need): 27%

Avg. Cumulative Debt: $35,187
% of Students Borrowing: 55%

CAREER
Who Recruits
1. Cognex Corporation
2. Boston Scientific
3. Grant Thornton LLP
4. P&G Gillette
5. Lincoln Financial Group

Notable Internships
1. Liberty Mutual Investments
2. KPMG
3. L'Oreal

Top Industries
1. Business
2. Finance
3. Accounting
4. Sales
5. Operations

Top Employers
1. Fidelity Investments
2. PwC
3. Liberty Mutual Insurance
4. EY
5. State Street

Where Alumni Work
1. Boston
2. New York City
3. Hartford
4. San Francisco
5. Providence

Median Earnings
College Scorecard (Early Career): $86,900
PayScale (Early Career): $69,800
PayScale (Mid-Career): $125,000

RANKINGS
Money: 139
U.S. News: 1 (T), Regional Universities North
Wall Street Journal/THE: 133 (T)
Washington Monthly: 34, Master's Universities

COLLEGE OVERLAPS
Babson College
Boston College
Bryant University
Fordham University
Villanova University

Binghamton University (SUNY)

Binghamton, New York | 607-777-2171

ADMISSION
Admission Rate: 41%
Admission Rate - Men: 40%
Admission Rate - Women: 41%
EA Admission Rate: 64%
ED Admission Rate: Not Offered
ED Admits as % of Total Admits: Not Offered
Admission Rate (5-Year Trend): -1%
% of Admits Attending (Yield): 19%
Transfer Admission Rate: 41%

SAT Reading/Writing (Middle 50%): 630-700
SAT Math (Middle 50%): 650-740
ACT Composite (Middle 50%): 29-32

% Graduated in Top 10% of HS Class: 55%
% Graduated in Top 25% of HS Class: 89%
% Graduated in Top 50% of HS Class: 98%

Demonstrated Interest: Considered
Legacy Status: Considered
Admission Interview Offered: No

ENROLLMENT
Total Undergraduate Enrollment: 14,165
% Part-Time: 2%
% Male: 50%
% Female: 50%
% Out-of-State: 6%
% Fraternity: 16%
% Sorority: 16%
% On-Campus (Freshman): 98%
% On-Campus (All Undergraduate): 50%

% African-American: 5%
% Asian: 15%
% Hispanic: 12%
% White: 58%
% Other: 3%
% Race or Ethnicity Unknown: 1%
% International: 6%
% Low-Income: NR

ACADEMICS
Student-to-Faculty Ratio: 19 to 1
% of Classes Under 20: 48%
% of Classes 20-49: 40%
% of Classes 50 or More: 13%
% Full-Time Faculty: 72%
% Full-Time Faculty w/ Terminal Degree: 94%

Top Programs
Accounting
Chemistry
Industrial and Systems Engineering
Integrative Neuroscience
Nursing
Political Science
Psychology

Retention Rate: 90%
4-Year Graduation Rate: 71%
6-Year Graduation Rate: 81%

Curricular Flexibility: Somewhat Flexible
Academic Rating: ★★★✔

#CollegesWorthYourMoney

Created in the GI Bill era to accommodate the influx of returning soldiers entering college, SUNY Binghamton (a.k.a., Binghamton University) is the shining star of the State University System of New York. Considered a "Public Ivy," the 14,000+ undergraduates are an accomplished bunch (average SAT is 1350), and the excellence of the academic offerings is commensurate with the student body. It's no wonder that 92 percent of freshmen return to campus the next fall, a retention rate that is unparalleled among non-flagship public institutions.

Inside the Classroom

The university offers over 130 areas of concentration across its five undergraduate schools: the Harpur College of Arts and Sciences, the College of Community and Public Affairs, the Decker School of Nursing, the School of Management, and the Thomas J. Watson School of Engineering and Applied Science. General education requirements include foreign language (except for engineering majors), creating a global vision, the liberal arts (aesthetics, humanities, laboratory sciences, social sciences, and mathematics), and a series of physical activity and wellness classes. Unlike many state universities there is no long list of required courses awaiting you. Rather, the mandated categories of coursework are broad enough that you'll have plenty of room for exploration.

The student-to-faculty ratio is on the high side at 19:1, but class sizes are reasonably small with 48 percent of sections containing fewer than twenty students. Only 13 percent of courses are held in large lecture halls with 50+ students. Research opportunities are available with the Freshman Research Immersion program being one shining example. This program welcomes students to college with a year-long authentic research experience in the sciences and engineering. The Office of Undergraduate Research is adept at connecting students in all fields, not just STEM, to research opportunities alongside faculty members. The school's own undergraduate research journal, Alpenglow, gives students the chance to publish scholarly, as well as original creative works. Study abroad opportunities are available at over fifty worldwide locations, and roughly one-fifth of undergraduates spend a semester in a foreign country.

In the spring of 2019, Binghamton awarded the greatest number of degrees in the social sciences (17 percent), biology (16 percent), business (14 percent), engineering (10 percent), and psychology (8 percent). The School of Management is renowned for its accounting program and is well known by NYC-based companies. Programs in chemistry, psychology, and nursing are also well respected. The university's graduates are somewhat competitive in procuring prestigious postgraduate fellowships, and between 2017 and 2019, the school produced seventeen Fulbright Scholars.

Outside the Classroom

Just over half of undergrads reside on campus in dorms or in residential college communities designed for 200 to 1,000 students each, and all have their own distinct personalities. Most off-campus apartment dwellers reside in the city's West Side neighborhood, but some end up in small towns a ten- to twenty-minute drive away. With fifty-six fraternities and sororities and thousands of participants, you might think that Greek life would be a dominant presence, yet only 14 percent of men and 11 percent of women pledge, leaving the majority to carve out their own social scene. The Binghamton Bearcats field twenty-one varsity sports teams in NCCA Division I. However, with no football team, the university is not a sports-centered campus. There is much to do within the university's 930 acres of grounds that includes a 190-acre nature preserve, a 156,000-square-foot multipurpose center, two fully equipped gyms, two pools, twenty-six tennis courts, and a 1,200-seat theater for art/speaking/musical events. Over 2,000 students participate in forty-two recreational and club athletic teams, and another 3,000 play intramural sports. There are 300 other clubs and activities. From their high-achieving speech and debate squad to a plethora of political, cultural, academic, and religious clubs, all 14,000 undergrads can find some way to connect. There are also eighty-five organizations focused on community service and volunteer work. Green initiatives are popular on campus, including energy efficiency, local food sources, recycling, and the bike-share program.

Career Services

The Fleishman Center for Career and Professional Development is not your average state school career services office. Consisting of nineteen professional employees and fifty peer assistants and interns, the 746:1 student-to-advisor ratio (only counting the professionals) is more supportive than it appears. In a single year Fleischman staff conducted 7,246 1:1 counseling sessions. The 740 career programs hosted by career services personnel drew 27,500 attendees. About 10,000 unique students connected directly with career services, a sizable portion of the undergraduate population.

Recruiting on campus is a regular occurrence with over 2,700 on-site interviews conducted each year. The hireBing platform (run by Handshake) sees 7,000 job and internship postings annually. SUNY Binghamton's Fall Job Fair attracts more than 120 corporate, government, and nonprofit employers including Teach for America, Geico, Wayfair, and Raytheon Company. The school's recently launched Washington, DC, Employer Site Visit Program complements its successful New York City Site Visits Program. Having increased its staffing, outreach, and technological capabilities in recent years, Binghamton's career services is on the rise.

Professional Outcomes

The Class of 2019 saw 77 percent of job-seeking graduates land their first professional job within six months of commencement. Those entering the technology/computing fields found homes at companies like Facebook, IBM, Apple, and Microsoft in large numbers. Graduates entering finance careers were successful in finding employment at firms like Morgan Stanley, JPMorgan, Goldman Sachs, and CitiGroup. In the accounting/consulting realm the most popular employers of Binghamton grads were EY, PwC, Deloitte, and KPMG. The average starting salary procured was nearly $60,938, well above the national average for college grads. New York City is, by far, the most common landing spot for Binghamton graduates, but many also remain in Upstate New York or travel to Washington, DC; Boston; San Francisco; Philadelphia; and Los Angeles.

Of the Binghamton grads seeking to transition directly into graduate studies, 93 percent were already enrolled in a program six months after graduation. Many SUNY branch campuses were among the most popular graduate school destinations, but many prestigious universities also graced this list including Harvard, Dartmouth, Georgetown, Columbia, Stanford, Penn, and the University of Michigan. SUNY Binghamton's reputation also helped open the doors to law school as it enjoyed an 84 percent acceptance rate. The school's early admission med school program (during sophomore year) creates a pipeline into SUNY Upstate Medical University. In the 2018-19 academic year, 196 seniors applied to medical school and were accepted at a rate 14 percent higher than the national average.

Admission

SUNY Binghamton received 37,516 applications in 2019 and accepted 41 percent. That acceptance rate was similar to acceptance rates at this selective state university over the past decade, but the profile of the average enrolling freshman indicates that the school is becoming significantly more competitive. Entering freshmen in 2019-20 had an average weighted GPA of 4.0. The mid-50 percent range on the SAT for the previous year's freshmen was 1295-1430 and 29-32 for the ACT. Ten years ago, the SAT range was 1190-1350. Even with SAT score inflation, it is safe to say that the average student at this school today is a higher achiever than the average student of a decade ago.

The factors that are considered above all others in admissions decisions are grades, test scores, and rigor of secondary curriculum. Class rank, the essay, recommendations, and extracurricular activities make up the second tier of important considerations. With such a massive applicant pool, interviews are not offered. SUNY Binghamton is a special value, especially by the standards of today's higher education marketplace. With an annual in-state tuition of just over $10,000, this excellent public research university continues to draw more and more qualified applicants each year. The admission formula falls far short of rocket science. Strong test scores and solid grades in AP/honors classes rule the day.

Worth Your Money?

You simply won't find a better combination of quality and price anywhere on the East Coast than Binghamton University. With a total annual cost of attendance of $27,670 (much lower for those who commute) for an in-state student, this SUNY school is worth anyone's money, no matter your major or career path. More than half of students qualify for financial aid and receive an average grant package of almost $10k, making an already affordable school nothing less than a ridiculous bargain.

FINANCIAL
Institutional Type: Public
In-State Tuition: $10,201
Out-of-State Tuition: $27,791
Room & Board: $16,068
Required Fees: $0
Books & Supplies: $1,000

Avg. Need-Based Grant: $9,918
Avg. % of Need Met: 70%

Avg. Merit-Based Award: $8,331
% Receiving (All Freshmen): 12%
% Receiving (Freshmen w/o Need): 4%

Avg. Cumulative Debt: $27,679
% of Students Borrowing: 49%

CAREER
Who Recruits
1. AMETEK Aerospace and Defense
2. NYS Department of Transportation
3. Dick's Sporting Goods
4. AXA Advisors
5. Mirabito Energy Products

Notable Internships
1. United Health Services
2. Cushman & Wakefield
3. Deloitte

Top Industries
1. Business
2. Education
3. Engineering
4. Operations
5. Information Technology

Top Employers
1. IBM
2. EY
3. JPMorgan Chase
4. PwC
5. Morgan Stanley

Where Alumni Work
1. New York City
2. Ithaca, NY
3. Washington DC
4. Boston
5. San Francisco

Median Earnings
College Scorecard (Early Career): $61,600
PayScale (Early Career): $64,100
PayScale (Mid-Career): $120,600

RANKINGS
Money: 73
U.S. News: 88 (T), National Universities
Wall Street Journal/THE: 158 (T)
Washington Monthly: 93, National Universities

COLLEGE OVERLAPS
Boston University
Cornell University
New York University
Stony Brook University (SUNY)
University at Buffalo (SUNY)

Boston College

Chestnut Hill, Massachusetts | 617-552-3100

Along with Notre Dame, Georgetown, and Villanova, Boston College, home to 9,370 undergrads, is among the most academically renowned Catholic universities in the world. The college offers fifty-eight majors across four schools that award undergraduate degrees: the School of Management, the School of Education, the School of Nursing, and the Morrissey College of Arts & Sciences. Certain majors that one takes for granted as being offered at a large research institution, such as engineering, do not yet exist at BC. However, the school is breaking ground on a new $150 million science facility that will offer a full spectrum of engineering degrees in the not-too-distant future.

Inside the Classroom

The core curriculum lays out an extensive series of academic requirements that includes two courses in the natural sciences, social sciences, history, philosophy, and theology as well as one course in the arts, cultural diversity, math, and writing. All told, the core curriculum accounts for three full semesters of coursework. The breadth of the requirements is far from accidental—BC's program is designed to expand students' intellectual horizons and build character at the same time.

This odyssey unfolds in a caring and personal atmosphere. Approximately half of the college's sections contain nineteen or fewer students; there are some larger lecture hall classes, but those are fairly rare. Working closely with their professors pays off for students. In their own self-assessment, 95 percent of graduates reported learning how to think critically at BC, and 93 percent said they learned how to write clearly and effectively. Fifty percent of BC grads pursued a semester abroad in one of 200+ locations around the globe, and 90 percent cited the experience as a source of personal growth.

BC offers highly respected programs in communications, psychology, and business through the renowned Carroll School of Management. Other popular and well-regarded majors include economics, biology, and chemistry. Graduates fare decently in procuring prestigious awards, especially in the realm of fellowships to study abroad. Sixteen members of the Class of 2018 won Fulbright Scholarships, and BC holds the distinction as one of the top twenty Fulbright-producing research universities over the past decade.

Outside the Classroom

Unlike at Boston University, BC is not located in the heart of its namesake city. Fortunately, downtown Boston is only six miles away and easily accessible from the Chestnut Hill section of Newton where BC's main campus is located. With 70 percent of students identifying as Catholic, it is little surprise that religion and spirituality are a big part of campus life. Clubs in this arena are well represented among the 273 student organizations on campus, but there are a multitude of pre-professional, special interest, performing arts, and political offerings as well. There are no Greek houses at BC, a void that is filled by tightly knit groups with common interests. One such galvanizing force is the school's athletic teams. The Eagles compete in thirty-one NCAA Division I and forty-four intramural sports. The men's ice hockey team is always in the national spotlight, regularly appearing in the Frozen Four. For those seeking charitable opportunity, the Volunteer & Service Learning Center connects students with a plethora of organizations all over the country. One of the most popular of those experiences is the Appalachia Volunteers Program that sends around 500 students each year on spring break to forty impoverished cities and towns in the United States.

Career Services

The Career Center is manned by eighteen professionals whose specialty areas include career counseling, exploration, and employer engagement. Not counting the five graduate assistants and nine peer coaches who also are available to work with undergraduate students, this calculates to a student-to-advisor ratio of 521:1, about average when compared to the pool of institutions included in this book.

The better news is that the office is effective at what is most important—helping students achieve positive career and graduate school outcomes. In fact, five of the top six resources cited by job-holding recent grads as being most helpful in landing employment had to do with the Career Center—EagleLink interviews, BC career fairs, networking through BC, EagleLink listings, and internships. Over 200 companies recruit on campus each year with most offering in-person interviews. Career fairs occur throughout the year; some events are general while others cater to specific areas of interest including public accounting, government, and sports and entertainment. The Career Center regularly offers job shadowing opportunities, networking nights, Career Treks, workshops covering a host of topics, and the Eagle Intern Fellowship that provides a $3,500 stipend to selected students pursuing unpaid internships. The alumni network is 180,000 strong and is generally very active and willing to help current students.

Professional Outcomes

Within six months of graduation, 95 percent of the Class of 2019 had landed at their next destination, whether that was employment, graduate school, a fellowship, or a volunteer position. The most favored industries were finance/accounting/real estate (22 percent), health care/science (16 percent), business/consulting (13 percent), and technology/engineering (9 percent). More than forty newly minted alumni found employment at both Ernst & Young and PricewaterhouseCoopers. Notable numbers also flocked to Oracle, Citi, Mass General, and KPMG. Across all graduating years, more than 150 alumni also work at Deloitte, Google, Morgan Stanley, and Goldman Sachs. The median starting salary for a BC grad is $60,000. By a wide margin, the locale where the must alumni settle is the university's home state of Massachusetts; New York City also draws a sizable number of BC grads.

Eighteen percent of the Class of 2019 entered graduate schools including Brown, Columbia, the University of Chicago, and Yale. Examining the last five years of graduate data, enrollment in graduate, medical, or law school is a choice made by 18-23 percent of graduates. Of that higher-education-minded cohort, the greatest number are pursuing master's degrees in education or business. Law school was next in popularity at 12 percent followed by a PhD or applied doctorate at 10 percent and medical school at 8 percent. Of the law school attendees, a dozen continued in BC's own program. BC was also, by far, the most common graduate choice for those pursuing advanced degrees in education and business. Tufts was the No. 1 target for medical school and the natural sciences. Graduates also enjoyed acceptances into other elite medical schools including Georgetown, Duke, and Boston University.

Admission

Boston College received more than 35,000 applications for the Class of 2023. The acceptance rate fell to 27 percent in 2019; it was 28 percent in 2018. However, this level of selectivity is nothing new for BC. A decade ago, acceptance rates were in the 26-27 percent range. What is changing is the academic profile of the average student being offered a spot at this high-end Catholic university. The mid-50 percent SAT score for the Class of 2023 was 1370-1490; fifteen years ago that 1370 would have had you above the 75th percentile. Over 80% of freshmen in the 2019-20 academic year placed in the top decile of their high school graduating class, and 93 percent hailed from the top quartile.

The school introduced an Early Decision admission plan this past fall and 37 percent were accepted compared to just 24 percent in the earlier round. No matter when you apply, BC places a high value on writing ability and requires completion of the Boston College Writing Supplement. There are no interviews as part of the admissions process. BC attracts some of the most gifted Catholic students in the country as well as a fair number of non-Catholics. SAT scores in the 1400s and A/A- grades in a rigorous curriculum will put applicants on solid footing.

Worth Your Money?

In 1990, Boston College had an annual cost of attendance of around $15,000. Today, you will owe $75,000+ per year for the privilege of attending this fine institution. While this jump in price far outpaces the rate of inflation, so goes the entire higher education marketplace. The good news is that BC awards healthy amounts of financial aid to those unable to pay full freight as eligible undergraduates receive close to $44,000 per year, making the cost far more palatable. The university meets 100% of demonstrated need. If you were in a situation where you had to take on massive loans to study at BC, it would likely be a good investment if you planned on going the finance or consulting route but less so if you planned to study education.

FINANCIAL
Institutional Type: Private
In-State Tuition: $60,202
Out-of-State Tuition: $60,202
Room & Board: $15,220
Required Fees: $0
Books & Supplies: $1,250

Avg. Need-Based Grant: $43,953
Avg. % of Need Met: 100%

Avg. Merit-Based Award: $24,843
% Receiving (All Freshmen): 2%
% Receiving (Freshmen w/o Need): 1%

Avg. Cumulative Debt: $23,136
% of Students Borrowing: 45%

CAREER
Who Recruits
1. MullenLowe Mediahub
2. Oracle
3. Epsilon
4. Liberty Mutual
5. Accenture

Notable Internships
1. NBC Sports Boston
2. Pfizer
3. IBM

Top Industries
1. Business
2. Education
3. Finance
4. Operations
5. Sales

Top Employers
1. PwC
2. EY
3. Deloitte
4. Morgan Stanley
5. Citi

Where Alumni Work
1. Boston
2. New York City
3. Washington DC
4. San Francisco
5. Los Angeles

Median Earnings
College Scorecard (Early Career): $72,500
PayScale (Early Career): $66,700
PayScale (Mid-Career): $124,400

RANKINGS
Money: 85
U.S. News: 35 (T), National Universities
Wall Street Journal/THE: 55
Washington Monthly: 51, National Universities

COLLEGE OVERLAPS
Boston University
Georgetown University
New York University
Notre Dame University
Villanova University

Boston University

Boston, Massachusetts | 617-353-2300

Growing more selective each year, Boston University is a private research institution playing host to just under 18,000 undergrads as well as an additional 15,000 graduate students. It's hard to imagine a more dynamic locale than BU's sprawling campus that shares a neighborhood with Fenway Park, the Museum of Fine Arts, MIT, and countless culinary and cultural enticements. In total, the university offers more than 250 programs of study, about half of which are distinct undergraduate degrees spread across ten schools/colleges.

Inside the Classroom
Unique programs include the Kilachand Honors College that welcomes 150 new students each year and offers a unique, original, integrated four-year curriculum thematically centered on global challenges and practical solutions. Not shockingly, it's tough to pin down course requirements with so many colleges within the larger university. College of Arts & Sciences students must satisfy basic requirements in foreign language, mathematics, and writing as part of their 128 credits. Engineering students, on the other hand, must complete sixteen credits in mathematics and twelve in the natural sciences. First-year experience courses are available but not required.

Many classes at BU are reasonably small—62 percent contain fewer than twenty students; only 17 percent contain more than forty. The student–to–faculty ratio is 10:1, quite an achievement for a school of its size. BU's Undergraduate Research Opportunities Program (UROP) funded 650 students in 2018-19, and many additional students participate in BU's research for credit, volunteer, work study, and other independent opportunities. More than ninety study abroad sites in twenty-five countries are available for those seeking a global experience. Participation is relatively high—40 percent of arts and sciences students complete a semester on a foreign campus.

The greatest number of degrees are conferred in business/marketing (18 percent) communications and journalism (16 percent), social sciences (15 percent), biology (9 percent), engineering (8 percent), and health professions/related sciences (7 percent). The Questrom School of Business and the College of Engineering are highly regarded as well as the university's College of Communication and College of Health & Rehabilitation Services. Over the last five years, BU has produced at least five Fulbright Scholars annually. In 2019, grads took home ten Fulbright Scholarships, four Goldwater Scholarships, two Critical Language Scholarships, a Boren Scholarship, and a Truman Scholarship.

Outside the Classroom
Three-quarters of the undergraduate student body reside on campus. Greek life has a modest presence at BU—roughly 10 percent elect to pledge one of the school's eight frats and twelve sororities. Nicknamed the Terriers, BU is represented by twenty-three teams (13 women's, 10 men's) in NCAA Division I, highlighted by its perennially stellar men's ice hockey team. In an odd move for a school of its size, BU dissolved its football program in 1997. The basketball team makes an occasional appearance in March Madness. For those a bit less serious about/skilled at sports, 7,000 students participate in intramural athletics. With close to 500 student organizations and offerings from improv to synchronized swimming, just about everyone can find their niche. The student-run Daily Free Press is recognized as one of the tops in the country and claims the fourth highest circulation of any paper in Boston. Volunteer spirit runs rampant at BU—the Community Service Center has a volunteer base of over 1,500 students and contributes 75,000 hours of service to the Boston-area community each year. Being located in the heart of Boston, students have limitless choices for nightlife and culture and can conveniently hop aboard the Green Line to explore the farthest reaches of the city.

Career Services
Twenty counselors, recruiters, and outreach coordinators comprise the BU Center for Career Development (CCD). That equates to a student-to-advisor ratio of 899:1, below average when compared to the pool of institutions included in this book. Despite limited personnel for a school so large, the office is successful at working with those who engage with them. In fact, students who regularly utilized the career center reported 22 percent higher earnings than their peers. Last year, staff conducted 2,437 one-on-one advising sessions. Remarkably for a school of BU's size, the CCD helps 90 percent of students complete at least one internship over their four years of study.

Every spring and fall, the CCD organizes an All-Majors Career Fair with over one-hundred guest employers; individual colleges within BU also host discipline-specific career fairs in business, engineering, nonprofit leadership, and public health. In total, 725 employers attended BU fairs, and 770 recruited on campus in 2018-19. That led to 600+ on-campus interviews being facilitated by the CCD. Freshmen are encouraged to attend a seminar called

Boston University

E-mail: admissions@bu.edu | Website: www.bu.edu

Career Directions: Starting Your Journey that gives tips on how to maximize one's educational experience with an eye on life beyond college. Through the Career Advisory Network, the CCD also works to connect students with over 6,000 participating alumni who are employed in a wide spectrum of fields. Even with a less-than-ideal number of counselors, BU's career services staff works hard to reach students through seminars, job fairs, and online resources.

Professional Outcomes

Six months after graduation, 94 percent of BU grads have found their way into the world of employment or full-time graduate study. A recent survey of corporate recruiters with international companies revealed that Boston University alums have the sixth highest employability ranking, directly behind the likes of MIT, Caltech, Harvard, and Stanford. Recent graduating classes have seen more than ten graduates join employers like EY, PwC, Deloitte, and TJX Companies. Healthy numbers of engineering grads found their way to Amazon, IBM, Lockheed Martin, and Pfizer. Across all graduating years, companies employing more than 250 BU alums include Google, Oracle, Accenture, and Wayfair. Starting salary data is highly dependent on which school within BU one attended. For the Class of 2019, grads of the Questrom School of Business earned a starting salary of roughly $62k, College of Engineering grads averaged $71k, and Arts & Sciences students came in just shy of $53k.

Respect for the BU degree comes from more than just the corporate world. Of the 23 percent of 2019 grads who moved directly into graduate school, many were welcomed onto the campuses of elite graduate programs. For example, engineering students found new academic homes at MIT, Stanford, Carnegie Mellon, and Columbia. Most top law schools have some level of representation from BU alumni including BU Law itself, a top twenty-five institution that accepts a significant number of its own undergraduates. Those aiming to become medical doctors can apply for the Seven-Year Liberal Arts/Medical Education Program that leads directly to study at the BU School of Medicine. Overall, the university saw 300 undergraduates apply to med school in 2020 alone. Whether attending grad school or starting their careers, the greatest number of BU grads remain in Boston with New York City, San Francisco, Los Angeles, DC, and Philadelphia next in popularity.

Admission

Over 64,000 applications rolled into BU for spots in the Class of 2023, and 19 percent gained acceptance. For historical context, 46 percent of applicants were accepted in 2012 and close to three quarters in 2005. The average member of the Class of 2023 finished with a 3.72 GPA and earned a 1415 SAT score. Back in 2012, the 75th percentile on the SAT was 1390, an indicator that gaining acceptance into BU is considerably more difficult than in the not-too-distant past. Most BU students finished in the upper echelon of their high school classes—64 percent were in the top 10 percent, and 92 percent were in the top 25 percent. On a 4.0 scale, 87 percent had unweighted GPAs of 3.5 or higher.

The only two admissions criteria rated as "very important" for all applicants are the rigor of one's high school course load and talent/ability. Factors in the second run of importance are class rank, GPA, standardized test scores, recommendations, essays, extracurricular activities, alumni relation (legacy), and the level of an applicant's interest. Those who demonstrate the most fervent interest and commitment by applying early decision receive a slight boost, gaining acceptance at a 30 percent clip. It is critical to remember that this isn't your mother's or father's BU—it's not even your older sibling's BU. Far more highly selective than even a few years ago, Boston University hopefuls need to bring top-tier credentials in order to be offered admission at this fine private research institution.

Worth Your Money?

At $74,000, Boston University has a hefty list price cost of attendance, a sum made slightly more manageable for undergraduates who receive an annual merit-based award of $26k or some level of need-based financial aid. BU does award need-based aid to approximately two-fifths of its undergraduates, but it fails to meet 100 percent of all demonstrated need for all students. Still, the average annual award to qualifying students is $47k, which cuts the overall costs considerably. Boston University graduates end up with an average debt load of $40,300, a figure that is higher than the national average. If you were in the position that attending BU would necessitate taking out large loans, your decision should come down to whether you intend to major in a field with a high enough starting salary so you could comfortably make monthly payments.

FINANCIAL
Institutional Type: Private
In-State Tuition: $54,720
Out-of-State Tuition: $54,720
Room & Board: $16,160
Required Fees: $1,172
Books & Supplies: $1,000

Avg. Need-Based Grant: $47,141
Avg. % of Need Met: 93%

Avg. Merit-Based Award: $26,153
% Receiving (All Freshmen): 14%
% Receiving (Freshmen w/o Need): 5%

Avg. Cumulative Debt: $40,349
% of Students Borrowing: 46%

CAREER
Who Recruits
1. Marriott
2. Turner Broadcasting System
3. TJX
4. General Electric
5. Bloomberg LP

Notable Internships
1. Amazon
2. Boston Scientific
3. BuzzFeed

Top Industries
1. Business
2. Education
3. Operations
4. Media
5. Information Technology

Top Employers
1. IBM
2. Google
3. Amazon
4. Microsoft
5. Oracle

Where Alumni Work
1. Boston
2. New York City
3. San Francisco
4. Los Angeles
5. Washington DC

Median Earnings
College Scorecard (Early Career): $65,300
PayScale (Early Career): $64,100
PayScale (Mid-Career): $126,300

RANKINGS
Money: 144
U.S. News: 42 (T), National Universities
Wall Street Journal/THE: 40 (T)
Washington Monthly: 110, National Universities

COLLEGE OVERLAPS
Cornell University
New York University
Northeastern University
Tufts University
University of Michigan

Bowdoin College

Brunswick, Maine | 207-725-3100

Set on 215 lush acres in the quaint town of Brunswick, Maine, Bowdoin College serves just over 1,800 undergraduate students. This quintessential, elite New England liberal arts college is steeped in history and tradition; its oldest buildings date to the late eighteenth century, and the curriculum is guided by a poem, "The Offer of College," penned by the school's president in 1906. Does it get any more New England liberal-artsy than that?

Inside the Classroom

Among its core beliefs, Bowdoin offers a flexible and broad liberal arts education. Polar Bears can choose from one of thirty-three academic programs or get more creative through an interdisciplinary or student-designed major. One-size-fits-all requirements are minimal. All must take a freshman seminar in an area of interest such as Women of Color in Politics, Intro to Documentary Film Studies, or Food and Foodways in China: A Cultural History. Bowdoin students are required to take one course from each of five distribution areas: (1) mathematical, computational, or statistical reasoning; (2) inquiry in the natural sciences; (3) exploring social difference; (4) international perspectives; and (5) visual and performing arts.

Class sizes are small—68 percent contain fewer than twenty students—and more than one- quarter have fewer than ten students. The student-faculty ratio is 9:1, which leads to ample and meaningful interaction and guidance in and out of the classroom. More than half of Bowdoin undergrads report interacting with a professor outside of regular class time at least once per week. Professors have a reputation for being extremely dedicated to their teaching. Students also enjoy a plethora of study abroad opportunities with over 50 percent electing to spend a semester learning in a foreign locale.

The greatest percentage of degrees are conferred in the social sciences (31 percent), biology (11 percent), area/ethnic/gender studies (10 percent), and mathematics (8 percent). Economics and government and legal studies are two of the more popular majors within the social sciences. Bowdoin is one of the strongest in the country for those on a pre-med track. The school is also a prolific producer of fellowship/scholarship winners. In 2020 alone, twenty-two graduates and alumni were named Fulbright Scholars—the second highest total from any one school. Graduates also routinely win other prestigious awards including National Science Foundation Graduate Research Fellowships, Boren Scholarships, Watson Fellowships, and Critical Language Scholarships awarded by the US State Department.

Outside the Classroom

By sheer numbers, athletics are a driving force of life outside the classroom. An insanely high 43 percent of undergrads are varsity athletes who compete on one of thirty NCAA Division III teams. And that doesn't include those who play on one of the six club teams or participate in one of ten intramural sports, each of which has an A, B, and C level. Over one hundred non-sports clubs are also active, including the Outing Club, which boasts over 400 members and takes over 150 nature-themed excursions per year. Greek life was disbanded around the turn of the new millennium and replaced with a system of eight college houses that serve as the backbone of the campus residential experience. Each house has its own student government and hosts special events throughout the year. The dining halls are known to prepare extravagant meals that receive rave reviews across the board. Eighty-nine percent of students live on campus, and certain annual events like the Gala and Ivies concert bring together the whole student body. Among the most favored off-campus destinations is Portland, Maine's largest city, which is less than half an hour away.

Career Services

Bowdoin Career Planning is staffed by six full-time career counselors and one employer relations professional. That works out to a student-to-advisor ratio of 304:1, lower than the average institution included in this book. Students are always welcome to schedule a one-on-one counseling session or mock interview or drop by between noon and 2 p.m. each weekday, unannounced, with a quick question. In a single year, the office planned 204 programs with over 5,200 attendees, more than two-and-half times the size of the student body. Incredibly, the staff managed to work, in some capacity, with 80 percent of students and 99 percent of the senior class.

The school combines some events with Colby and Bates; the Graduate & Professional School Fair that is held every October, and the annual Maine Employers Career Fair are two examples. The school's outreach efforts pay off with additional companies recruiting on campus each year. In 2017, it added HSBC, Jefferies Group, Wayfair, and LogMeln to an already long list. Bowdoin also distributes close to a quarter of a million dollars in grants to support unpaid internships each year. Two-thirds of graduates complete some type of internship. To provide further assistance in carving out career pathways, 200 alumni and parents of current students come to campus to help students with career exploration and networking

Professional Outcomes

An examination of five years' worth of outcomes data (2012-2016) reveals that by the fall after graduation between 70 and 78 percent of recent grads have found full-time employment, and between 15 and 20 percent have gone directly into graduate school. Only 2-4 percent are still seeking employment. Prominent corporations across all sectors love Bowdoin grads. Recent alumni have found positions at Apple, IBM, Goldman Sachs, Google, HBO, and Microsoft. Other companies that employ more than a dozen alumni are Fidelity Investments, Morgan Stanley, Amazon, UBS, Facebook, and Barclays. The cities attracting the greatest numbers of graduates are (in order) Boston; New York City; Portland, Maine; San Francisco; DC; and Los Angeles.

Of those entering graduate school, 20 percent were enrolled in PhD programs, 15 percent were in med school, 8 percent in law school, and 41 percent were in master's programs. The top twenty graduate schools attended, by volume, in the last five years make an exclusive list including six Ivies along with Duke, MIT, Johns Hopkins, Northwestern, and Stanford. Boston University is also one the largest recipients of Bowdoin grads. Those aiming for medical school fare exceptionally well with 90 percent typically earning acceptance into at least one institution. Recent grads are presently studying medicine at Tufts, Harvard, Boston University, NYU, and the University of Michigan.

Admission

Already a highly selective school, Bowdoin has become even more difficult to get into in recent years. The acceptance rate for applicants to the Class of 2023 was a paltry 9 percent compared to 10% percent the previous year and 20 percent back in 2012. An examination of the middle-50 percent ranges on standardized tests for attending students suggests there is little evidence that the school is accepting a higher caliber of student than it was just a handful of years ago. In 2013-14, Bowdoin freshmen scored 1360-1510 on the SAT and 30-33 on the ACT. In 2019-20, those SAT figures were slightly lower at 1340-1512 while the ACT range was slightly higher at 31-34. Bowdoin is famous for becoming the first test-optional school in the country (1969). Nevertheless, 59 percent of the Class of 2023 submitted SAT scores, and 45 percent shared ACT scores. Those numbers add up to more than 100 percent because a decent number of students submitted results from both tests, so it is fair to conclude that the vast majority of successful applicants elected to submit standardized test scores.

Being in the top 10 percent of your high school class is almost required—85 percent of freshmen held that distinction, and 97 percent were in the top 25 percent. The school also ranks essays, recommendations, talent/ability, personal qualities, and extracurricular activities as "very important" in the admissions process. Although Bowdoin is, technically, a test-optional school, it pays to have high SAT/ACTs. The acceptance rate may be shrinking, but the average student profile has held relatively steady. Those with the best chance of acceptance will be near the top of their high school class and possess standardized test scores above the 95th percentile. Applying early decision also will provide a great boost for your prospects; 23 percent of ED applicants are accepted compared to only 7% percent in the regular round.

Worth Your Money?

Bowdoin's annual cost of attendance is $73,800, and merit aid awards are practically nonexistent. Fortunately, the school is generous with need-based aid, meeting 100 percent of the demonstrated need for qualifying students. At present, undergraduates that can demonstrate need receive an average annual grant of $48,856. If you come from a family making an income in the top 5 percent nationwide—it is estimated that nearly half of all Bowdoin students do--you can expect to pay full price. In the end, the average graduate borrower takes out approximately $27,000 in loans, which isn't bad for the privilege to attend one of the nation's most elite institutions.

FINANCIAL
Institutional Type: Private
In-State Tuition: $55,822
Out-of-State Tuition: $55,822
Room & Board: $15,360
Required Fees: $528
Books & Supplies: $840

Avg. Need-Based Grant: $51,131
Avg. % of Need Met: 100%

Avg. Merit-Based Award: $1,000
% Receiving (All Freshmen): 2%
% Receiving (Freshmen w/o Need): 2%

Avg. Cumulative Debt: $26,775
% of Students Borrowing: 28%

CAREER
Who Recruits
1. Barclay's
2. Deutsche Bank
3. Prudential
4. Cornerstone Research
5. Teach for America

Notable Internships
1. Athena Global Advisors
2. eBay
3. CBS News

Top Industries
1. Business
2. Education
3. Research
4. Operations
5. Social Services

Top Employers
1. Unum
2. Fidelity Investments
3. Massachusetts General Hospital
4. Google
5. Morgan Stanley

Where Alumni Work
1. Boston
2. New York City
3. Portland, ME
4. San Francisco
5. Washington DC

Median Earnings
College Scorecard (Early Career): $65,500
PayScale (Early Career): $65,200
PayScale (Mid-Career): $134,600

RANKINGS
Money: 92
U.S. News: 6 (T), Liberal Arts Colleges
Wall Street Journal/THE: 42
Washington Monthly: 11, Liberal Arts Colleges

COLLEGE OVERLAPS
Brown University
Colby College
Carleton College
Dartmouth College
Yale University

Brandeis University

Waltham, Massachusetts | 781-736-3500

ADMISSION
Admission Rate: 30%
Admission Rate - Men: 27%
Admission Rate - Women: 32%
EA Admission Rate: Not Offered
ED Admission Rate: 37%
ED Admits as % of Total Admits: 11%
Admission Rate (5-Year Trend): -7%
% of Admits Attending (Yield): 25%
Transfer Admission Rate: 20%

SAT Reading/Writing (Middle 50%): 660-730
SAT Math (Middle 50%): 690-790
ACT Composite (Middle 50%): 30-33

% Graduated in Top 10% of HS Class: 56%
% Graduated in Top 25% of HS Class: 83%
% Graduated in Top 50% of HS Class: 97%

Demonstrated Interest: Considered
Legacy Status: Considered
Admission Interview Offered: Yes

ENROLLMENT
Total Undergraduate Enrollment: 3,688
% Part-Time: 0%
% Male: 39%
% Female: 61%
% Out-of-State: 70%
% Fraternity: Not Offered
% Sorority: Not Offered
% On-Campus (Freshman): 99%
% On-Campus (All Undergraduate): 76%

% African-American: 5%
% Asian: 14%
% Hispanic: 8%
% White: 46%
% Other: 4%
% Race or Ethnicity Unknown: 3%
% International: 20%
% Low-Income: 22%

ACADEMICS
Student-to-Faculty Ratio: 10 to 1
% of Classes Under 20: 58%
% of Classes 20-49: 32%
% of Classes 50 or More: 11%
% Full-Time Faculty: 69%
% Full-Time Faculty w/ Terminal Degree: 94%

Top Programs
Biology
Chemistry
Economics
Health: Science, Society, and Policy
History
International Studies
Neuroscience
Sociology

Retention Rate: 93%
4-Year Graduation Rate: 81%
6-Year Graduation Rate: 87%

Curricular Flexibility: Somewhat Flexible
Academic Rating: ★★★★

#CollegesWorthYourMoney

Unlike many other elite Boston-area universities, this institution does not have 300-400 years of history and tradition. Founded in 1948 by a group of Jewish donors only a few weeks before the modern State of Israel was established, Brandeis has been a nonsectarian university open to talented students of all backgrounds and faiths. Home to 3,600 undergraduates with a female-heavy split (61/39), Brandeis offers forty-four majors, the most popular of which are the social sciences (21 percent), biology (15 percent), business (9 percent), psychology (7 percent), and computer science (7 percent).

Inside the Classroom
An ethos of high academic standards and intellectual curiosity permeates this Waltham, Massachusetts, campus. An awe-inspiring 54 percent of Brandeis undergraduates double major, and 40 percent elect to study abroad in one of over 350 approved programs across the globe. Core requirements for all students include a university writing seminar; one qualitative reasoning course; one diversity, equity, and inclusion course; one difference and justice in the world course; three semesters of a foreign language; and at least one class within each of the schools of humanities, science, social science, and creative arts.

Professors at Brandeis are committed to undergraduate education and will interact with you in close enough quarters that you can rest assured they will learn your name. The student-faculty ratio is 10:1, and 58 percent of courses contain nineteen or fewer students. Invitations to assist faculty members with academic research is common, even for undergraduates. In the Chemistry Department alone, 260 undergrads have coauthored and published papers with their professors in the last fifteen years. International experiences also abound, whether you are interacting with the 20 percent of the student body who are citizens of another country or decide to travel abroad for a semester, which 40 percent of undergraduates do.

Departments with a particularly strong national reputation include economics, international studies, and sociology as well as all of the traditional premed pathways including biology, chemistry, and the health: science, society, and policy program. More than 200 students work each year with the school's Office of Academic Fellowships to pursue sponsored opportunities to pursue their intellectual passions after graduation. Many have successfully landed Fulbright, Boren, and Critical Language Scholarships, among others.

Outside the Classroom
With over 260 student organizations, the club scene plays a prominent role at Brandeis. A cappella, Jewish groups, intramural sports, and theater are among the most popular. Opportunities to volunteer in the local community abound, and many take advantage; sixty-four members of the Class of 2019 accrued more than 300 service hours over their four years. Fraternities and sororities do operate on campus and have a genuine presence, although they are unrecognized by the university. The Brandeis Judges (the school is named for famed Supreme Court Justice Louis Brandeis) compete in NCAA Division III and field nineteen teams (10 for women, 9 for men). The school also has nineteen club teams that include Brazilian Jiu-Jitsu, archery, and sailing. With a plethora of activities in which to participate and a generally active social scene, you don't need to venture off campus in order to fill your days with excitement. Of course, with Boston less than ten miles away, many do stray away from Waltham on the weekends. For the 76 percent of undergrads (and 100 percent of freshmen) who choose to live on campus, Brandeis' nineteen dorms are often ranked highly on lists of best collegiate housing.

Career Services
The Hiatt Career Center is staffed by fifteen professionals with expertise in career counseling, giving it a 240:1 student-to-advisor ratio, which is better than average compared to other schools featured in this guide. It deploys its resources effectively, connecting annually with over 50 percent of each class through counseling appointments, workshops, or job fairs. One-on-one counseling is available to all students as often as once per week, and the center encourages developing a relationship with one particular counselor over your four years of study.

Specialized counseling is available for those considering pursuing an MD or other health-care-related position after undergrad. Walk-in hours are more generous than most universities and can be utilized for quick questions that require fifteen minutes or less of interaction. Career Services connects students with internship/employment opportunities by a variety of means. Industry Meetups bring Brandeis alumni to campus from a host of fields. Brandeis Networking Nights are held over winter break each year in Washington, DC, and New York City. It also hosts area-specific fairs for students concentrating in computer science, careers with a social impact, or volunteer and internship opportunities. On-site interviews are conducted at fall and spring career fairs. As an additional aid, 19,000 jobs and internships are posted each year on Handshake. This adds up to almost all graduates finding their next destination within months of leaving the university.

Professional Outcomes

Within six months of graduation, 98 percent of the Class of 2019 had found their way to employment (65 percent), graduate school (28 percent), or another full-time activity like travel or volunteer work (5 percent). The most common industries entered by Brandeis grads are (in order) health care, scientific research, education, computer science, finance/banking, and consulting. Three of the four largest employers of recent grads are in the health-care sector: Boston Children's Hospital, Massachusetts General Hospital, and the Dana Farber Cancer Institute. Nonprofits such as Teach for America, City Year, and the Peace Corps are also well represented. The greatest number of graduates remains in Boston but many flock to New York City, DC, San Francisco, Los Angeles, and Philadelphia.

A large contingent of grads elect to continue at Brandeis for graduate school. The next most commonly attended graduate/professional schools over a recent three-year period were (in order) BU, Columbia, NYU, Harvard, and Tufts. That list is a good indication that Brandeis' reputation for academic excellence leads to positive outcomes for those applying to elite graduate schools. Those applying to medical school are remarkably successful, gaining acceptance between 65 and 75 percent annually, 20-30 points higher than the national average.

Admission

Brandeis is one of the rare, elite New England liberal arts schools that has not experienced an admissions rate freefall over the past decade. Typically, 33-35 percent of applicants find success, the same range as five years ago, although the Class of 2023 faced a slightly harsher 30 percent. The average SAT and ACT scores of accepted students have increased, but that is likely more a result of the school going test-optional in 2013 than an indicator that the applicant pool has become more competitive. We should note that Brandeis is test-optional, but with an asterisk. Students must submit one of the following: SAT/ACT scores; 3 AP/SAT Subject Tests, including a math/science and an English/social science discipline; or one graded analytical writing sample as well as an additional recommendation from an eleventh or twelfth grade course. Those who submitted traditional standardized test scores generally earned high scores. The average SAT score earned by a member of the Class of 2023 was 1420 and the average composite ACT score was 32.

Excellent performance in the classroom is valued most strongly by the admissions committee with 83 percent of Brandeis undergrads in the top 25 percent of their high school class and 56 percent in the top 10 percent. The other categories that qualify as "very important" to the committee are class rank, character, personal qualities, and the rigor of one's high school curriculum. The rate of acceptance for early decision is only nine points higher than during the regular cycle (37 percent vs. 29 percent), which means that ED may only offer a slight admissions edge.

Worth Your Money?

Given the annual cost of attendance of $73k, you may be pleasantly surprised to learn that Brandies is known for being quite generous, meeting 97 percent of demonstrated need. The school does prioritize enrolling an economically diverse student body, awarding need-based grants of $44,000 to qualifying undergraduates. Due to that generosity, many lower-to-middle income students have the opportunity to attend this school. However, graduates do hold slightly more debt than the average college graduate in the United States. With solid financial aid offerings (as well as bit of merit aid) and positive graduate outcomes, Brandeis University is typically worth its net price.

FINANCIAL
Institutional Type: Private
In-State Tuition: $55,340
Out-of-State Tuition: $55,340
Room & Board: $15,890
Required Fees: $2,275
Books & Supplies: $1,000

Avg. Need-Based Grant: $44,006
Avg. % of Need Met: 97%

Avg. Merit-Based Award: $14,542
% Receiving (All Freshmen): 22%
% Receiving (Freshmen w/o Need): 17%

Avg. Cumulative Debt: $32,158
% of Students Borrowing: 46%

CAREER
Who Recruits
1. TIBCO
2. Analysis Group
3. John Hancock
4. Sun Life Financial
5. Kayak

Notable Internships
1. Uber
2. Symantec
3. Goldman Sachs

Top Industries
1. Business
2. Education
3. Research
4. Healthcare
5. Social Services

Top Employers
1. Dell
2. Google
3. IBM
4. Morgan Stanley
5. Amazon

Where Alumni Work
1. Boston
2. New York City
3. Washington DC
4. San Francisco
5. Los Angeles

Median Earnings
College Scorecard (Early Career): $57,900
PayScale (Early Career): $63,400
PayScale (Mid-Career): $128,100

RANKINGS
Money: 350
U.S. News: 42 (T), National Universities
Wall Street Journal/THE: 114 (T)
Washington Monthly: 107, National Universities

COLLEGE OVERLAPS
Boston University
Brown University
Cornell University
New York University
Tufts University

Brigham Young University

Provo, Utah | 801-422-2507

An almost exclusively Mormon student body of more than 31,000 undergraduates occupy Brigham Young's high-altitude campus in the mountainous and breathtaking area of Provo, Utah. In addition to living by a strict honor code guided by the LDS Church (more on this later), students come to BYU for its more than 200 programs and reputation for academic excellence.

Inside the Classroom

Required coursework for BYU undergraduates includes a number of courses in the Mormon faith including Teachings & Doctrine of the Book of Mormon, Christ and the Everlasting Gospel, Foundations of the Restoration, and The Eternal Family. Mandatory courses in American heritage, global and cultural awareness, first-year writing, advanced oral and written communication, foreign language, and the social, biological, and physical sciences are all part of the core curriculum that supports BYU's larger mission "to provide an education that is (1) spiritually strengthening, (2) intellectually enlarging, and (3) character building, leading to (4) lifelong learning and service."

A 20:1 student-to-faculty ratio translates to some undergraduate sections being a bit large. Roughly 12 percent of sections contain more than fifty students. However, those lecture hall courses are balanced with classes of more modest size; 46 percent of courses have nineteen or fewer students. Despite the size of the university and some classes, the school does an excellent job getting undergraduate students involved in hands-on research. In the Department of Chemistry and Biochemistry, 88 percent of students worked with a faculty mentor on a research project. Additionally, the school offers 206 approved study abroad programs in seventy-five countries, and 17 percent of undergrads participate.

The ten most popular majors at BYU are exercise science, elementary education, psychology, management, English, public health, computer science, family life (a major unique to BYU), chemical engineering, and communications. The programs with the strongest national reputations are those within the Marriott School of Business and, to a slightly lesser extent, the Ira A. Fulton College of Engineering. Brigham Young alumni do occasionally win highly competitive post-graduation recognition, but in 2017 the National Scholarships, Fellowships, and Programs office was shut down, and those duties now fall under the purview of the Honors College. Students can still apply, but this is certainly a program in transition.

Outside the Classroom

While not a requirement, most freshmen (63 percent) live in on-campus dorms. In total, only 16 percent live on campus, but over 23,000 students live in BYU-contracted housing in the immediate area. There is no Greek life; rather, the LDS Church is at the center of much of student life outside the classroom. The school is governed by an Honor Code that includes clauses about facial hair, foul language, chastity, and abstaining from the consumption of caffeinated beverages. A good number of recognized student organizations are related to religion, volunteer work, or professional associations. One of the more recognizable and typical elements of BYU college life is the passion displayed for the school's sports teams. The Cougars send twenty-one athletic squads into high-level competition in NCAA Division I and have seen ten NCAA titles, a Heisman Trophy winner, and over 1,000 All-Americans. Football games draw 56,000 fans to LaVell Edwards Stadium. Over 12,000 students participate in intramural sports each year on this extremely athletically-inclined campus. Outdoor activities are also emphasized and are aided by the overwhelming natural beauty surrounding the school's 550+ acre campus situated at the edge of the Rocky Mountains.

Career Services

Brigham Young's University Career Services Office employs twenty-three professionals (not including office managers) who are responsible for career development and counseling. That works out to a counselor-to-student ratio of 1,360:1. BYU's Career Services staff believes that a career is more than just a job; it is a calling to which one is deeply dedicated. To help students find their path, the office offers free assessments such as the Myers-Briggs, the Strong Interest Inventory, and TypeFocus. The university even offers a credited course called Career Exploration intended to help undergrads learn their strengths, define their interests, and begin seriously thinking about a vocation.

A recent career fair was attended by 126 companies and 1,919 students. Fifteen of those employers conducted 189 interviews. A larger operation, the STEM Career Fair, drew 246 companies to campus and was visited by 5,346 students. All students are able to utilize Handshake accounts that allow them to connect with potential employers for jobs and internships. One of the school's greatest career services strengths is the tightknit network of alumni who are always willing to help a fellow Cougar. While this office is understaffed, it does excel in the areas of graduate school placement and career development that is uniquely tailored to this mostly LDS-affiliated population.

Professional Outcomes

In 2019, the average age of a BYU graduate was nearly twenty-five, a result of the eighteen months to two years of missionary work members of the LDS Church are required to complete. The most popular fields entered are business management, education, operations, engineering, sales, and information technology. By a wide margin, the two largest employers of BYU alums are the university itself and the LDS Church. However, there are hundreds of Cougars working at major corporations including Adobe, Google, Microsoft, and Goldman Sachs. The median salary of a 2019 grad was $54,000. Unsurprisingly, Provo and the Greater Salt Lake area see the highest concentrations of BYU alumni. Major cities outside of Utah with significant numbers of graduates include San Francisco, Phoenix, LA, and Seattle.

Brigham Young is in the same league with Berkeley, Cornell, the University of Michigan, and the University of Wisconsin in terms of producing future PhDs. Over the past decade, more than 3,000 alumni have gone on to earn doctoral degrees. Many grads pursuing advanced degrees do so at BYU, yet plenty of others relocate to pursue educational opportunities at institutions such as MIT, Harvard, and the University of North Carolina. (In 2005, two-thirds of the UNC PhD in accounting candidates were BYU alums.) Each year, approximately 500 BYU students apply to medical school; 67 percent are accepted, a far better mark than the national average. Those who attend law school flock to BYU's own well-regarded Rueben Clark Law School, but many attend other elite law schools. Harvard Law and Yale Law have BYU representation in just about every one of their entering 1L classes.

Admission

Despite a 67 percent acceptance rate, gaining admission to BYU requires a strong academic profile. The high rate of acceptance is attributable to the school's uniquely self-selecting applicant pool. Unless you are a member of the Church of Jesus Christ of Latter-day Saints, you likely aren't placing the university on your college wish list. Most students who apply favor the ACT over the SAT, and among 2019-20 freshmen, the middle-50 percent ACT range was 26-31. Those who submit SAT scores have a middle-50 percent band of 1220-1410. A narrow majority, 54 percent, also finished in the top 10 percent of their high school class; 85 percent placed in the top 25 percent. On a 4.0 scale, 82 percent had a GPA of 3.75 or higher.

Even with roughly 10,500 applications to read, BYU employs a holistic review of each one. It values eleven factors as being "very important" in influencing admissions decisions. In addition to the usual factors of rigor of curriculum, grades, recommendations, essays, and test scores, the university also places great importance on religious affiliation, volunteer work, work experience, character/personal qualities, talent/ability, and extracurricular involvement. High-achieving LDS teenagers frequently see BYU as their top or, perhaps, even their only choice for postsecondary education. Those who fit the mold will gain acceptance. Only rarely do non-Mormon individuals attend BYU; they comprise less than 2 percent of the student body.

Worth Your Money?

Similar to an in-state and out-of-state rate, BYU charges different tuition to Latter-day Saints than it does to non-Latter-day Saints. Members of the LDS Church pay an annual tuition of only $5,970, an unheard amount in the third decade of the twenty-first century. The total annual cost of attendance is under $20k, and the majority also receive some type of merit aid with the average award being over $4,000. Close to half also receive need-based aid that averages out to the full price of tuition. For members of the LDS Church, BYU is an amazing fit and worth every penny. For the limited numbers of non-LDS members who apply, Brigham Young University is still an exceptional value, even at a higher cost.

FINANCIAL
Institutional Type: Private
In-State Tuition: $5,970
Out-of-State Tuition: $11,940
Room & Board: $7,808
Required Fees: $0
Books & Supplies: $896

Avg. Need-Based Grant: $5,545
Avg. % of Need Met: 32%

Avg. Merit-Based Award: $4,310
% Receiving (All Freshmen): 58%
% Receiving (Freshmen w/o Need): 37%

Avg. Cumulative Debt: $14,672
% of Students Borrowing: 24%

CAREER
Who Recruits
1. Podium
2. Qualtrics
3. Domo, Inc.
4. Pluralsight
5. Lucid

Notable Internships
1. Adobe
2. Bain Capital
3. Utah Jazz

Top Industries
1. Business
2. Education
3. Operations
4. Engineering
5. Sales

Top Employers
1. LDS Church
2. Intermountain Healthcare
3. Qualtrics
4. Adobe
5. Vivint Smart Home

Where Alumni Work
1. Provo, UT
2. Salt Lake City, UT
3. Phoenix
4. San Francisco
5. Los Angeles

Median Earnings
College Scorecard (Early Career): $59,700
PayScale (Early Career): $63,200
PayScale (Mid-Career): $123,800

RANKINGS
Money: 104
U.S. News: 80 (T), National Universities
Wall Street Journal/THE: 129 (T)
Washington Monthly: 32, National Universities

COLLEGE OVERLAPS
Arizona State University
Brigham Young University - Hawaii
Brigham Young University - Idaho
University of Utah
Utah State University

Brown University

Providence, Rhode Island | 401-863-2378

ADMISSION
Admission Rate: 7%
Admission Rate - Men: 9%
Admission Rate - Women: 6%
EA Admission Rate: Not Offered
ED Admission Rate: 18%
ED Admits as % of Total Admits: 28%
Admission Rate (5-Year Trend): -2%
% of Admits Attending (Yield): 44%
Transfer Admission Rate: 6%

SAT Reading/Writing (Middle 50%): 700-770
SAT Math (Middle 50%): 740-800
ACT Composite (Middle 50%): 33-35

% Graduated in Top 10% of HS Class: 94%
% Graduated in Top 25% of HS Class: 98%
% Graduated in Top 50% of HS Class: 100%

Demonstrated Interest: Not Considered
Legacy Status: Considered
Admission Interview Offered: Yes

ENROLLMENT
Total Undergraduate Enrollment: 7,160
% Part-Time: 5%
% Male: 47%
% Female: 53%
% Out-of-State: 95%
% Fraternity: 11%
% Sorority: 12%
% On-Campus (Freshman): 100%
% On-Campus (All Undergraduate): 72%

% African-American: 7%
% Asian: 16%
% Hispanic: 11%
% White: 41%
% Other: 6%
% Race or Ethnicity Unknown: 6%
% International: 13%
% Low-Income: 17%

ACADEMICS
Student-to-Faculty Ratio: 6 to 1
% of Classes Under 20: 69%
% of Classes 20-49: 20%
% of Classes 50 or More: 11%
% Full-Time Faculty: 92%
% Full-Time Faculty w/ Terminal Degree: 95%

Top Programs
Applied Mathematics
Computer Science
Economics
Engineering
English
Geology
History
Neuroscience

Retention Rate: 98%
4-Year Graduation Rate: 83%
6-Year Graduation Rate: 96%

Curricular Flexibility: Very Flexible
Academic Rating: ★★★★★

#CollegesWorthYourMoney

Founded in 1764, Brown University holds the distinction as one of the oldest colleges in the United States and, of course, as a member of the vaunted Ivy League. Yet, much like its Rhode Island home, Brown possesses an uncommon blend of tradition and extraordinary commitment to the celebration of individuality. Toward that aim, Brown's Open Curriculum has long been the guiding academic force at the university, perfectly capturing its spirit and core values. The 7,100+ undergraduates who choose (and were chosen by) Brown fit the school's ethos and relish the chance to be the architects of their own educational journey.

Inside the Classroom
Students must choose one "concentration program," but there are no required courses. In essence, the guiding philosophy is that students should take control of their learning, pursue knowledge in areas that they are truly passionate about, and learn to integrate and synthesize information across disciplines. Specialized programs include the Brown/RISD five-year Dual Degree program that leads to a bachelor's from Brown as well as a BFA from the famed Rhode Island School of Design. Teens committed to the medical field even before exiting high school can apply for entry into the program in Liberal Medical Education that allows them to graduate in eight years with an MD from Brown's Warren Alpert Medical School.

This one-of-a-kind experience transpires with a student-faculty ratio of only 6:1, and 100 percent of faculty members spend time teaching the undergraduate population of just over 7,100. Class sizes tend to be small— 69 percent have fewer than twenty students—and 36 percent are comprised of nine or fewer students. Student surveys reveal an unsurpassed level of satisfaction with the quality of instruction and professor availability. Undergraduates give favorable reviews in those areas at an overwhelming 92-97 percent clip. Undergraduate research is a big part of the Brown experience for many students; 54 percent conduct research alongside a faculty member or work on an independent project with supervision. As is typical in the Ivy League, the majority of students stay grounded on (or near) campus for all four years. The number of students choosing to study abroad has declined in recent years and presently sits at approximately 500 per year.

Biology, economics, computer science, mathematics, and engineering are among the most popular areas of concentration at Brown; however, it is hard to distinguish any one program, because Brown possesses out-standing offerings across so many disciplines. Computer science is a growing department, conferring 10 percent of the school's degrees in 2019; applied math and English are notably strong. Graduates are a scholarly lot and experience high levels of success at procuring prestigious academic fellowships. In 2019 alone, the school produced thirty-eight Fulbright Scholars and, in 2018, graduates and alumni earned thirty National Science Foundation Graduate Research Fellowships. Brown has produced the seventh most Rhodes Scholars of any institution in history.

Outside the Classroom
The Main Green, surrounded by iconic buildings and located at the heart of campus, is almost always a lively hub of activity. There are more than 300 clubs and activities available to what tends to be a highly involved student body. Performance-based groups such as a cappella, improv, music, and theater draw large numbers of participants. A thriving student-run media scene includes the Brown Daily Herald, the nation's second oldest collegiate daily, and two award-winning campus radio stations. Brown fields an unusually large number of varsity athletic teams, thirty-eight, which compete in NCAA Division I. The Brown Bears claim twenty-one women's teams, the largest number of any school in the country. Greek life plays a moderate role on campus with about a 12 percent participation rate for women and an 11 percent rate for men. Ninety-five percent of students (97 percent of freshmen) live on campus in one of forty-nine residence halls as old as 1822 and as new as 2012. Off-campus housing and a multitude of cultural and entertainment options exist in Providence, including the bustling Thayer Street that runs through campus.

Career Services
The CareerLAB ("LAB" stands for Life After Brown) has thirteen full-time staff members who focus on career advising, pre-professional advising, employer relations, marketing, and BrownConnect, which connects current students with alumni. The 551:1 student-to-advisor ratio is slightly higher than the ratio for other schools featured in this guide. However, the LAB is extremely effective at outreach and has a measurable impact on student success.

In the 2018-19 academic year, career services staff counseled 3,237 students and brought 251 employers to campus, leading to 950 job interviews. Freshmen engaged at an extremely high rate, 68 percent, which has been an institutional goal. Keeping busy, Brown manages to put on more than one hundred career programs and one hundred employer information sessions per year. Its career fairs, alumni events, and workshops drew almost 13,000. If you can name a corporation, chances are it will be visiting Providence at some point this upcoming year. Help finding internships is always available as the school provides 600+ funded opportunities per year. The CareerLAB deploys its resources well in order to meet the needs of its talented population, and it receives high praise from our staff.

Professional Outcomes

Soon after receiving their Brown diplomas, 70 percent of graduates enter the world of employment. The university has placed significant numbers of recent graduates in the top companies within the following fields: the arts (CAA, Lincoln Center), consulting (every major firm), finance (every major investment house), government (United Nations, Federal Reserve Board), technology (Amazon, all major tech companies), and the list goes on and on. Companies employing the most Brown alums all time are Google, Microsoft, Facebook, Goldman Sachs, Amazon, Morgan Stanley, Apple, McKinsey & Company, and Bain & Company. New York, Boston, Providence, San Francisco, and DC are the five cities attracting the greatest number of Brown alumni. That makes sense given that the two most popular areas of employment are in technology and finance, and many such firms are based in those urban areas.

The Class of 2019 saw slightly more than one-fifth of graduates go directly into graduate/professional school. Right out of undergrad, Brown boasted an exceptional 92 percent admission rate to med school (the national average was 43 percent) and a 91 percent admission rate to law school (national average was 75 percent). A decade after graduating, 80 percent of Brown alumni have earned an advanced degree. Frequently attended institutions include all of the Ivies plus Stanford, Duke, Carnegie Mellon, the London School of Economics, Oxford, Johns Hopkins, Berkeley, UCLA, and UVA. In sum, you can rest assured that if you do well at Brown, there are few graduate or professional schools on the planet that will not welcome you with open arms.

Admission

In 2019, Brown accepted only 7 percent of applicants, and 94 percent of those who went on to enroll were in the top 10 percent of their high school class. A decade earlier, the admit rate was just shy of 16 percent, but it has been in the single digits since 2014. Back in 2014, the middle 25th-75th percentile range for Brown freshmen was 1330-1550 compared to the current range of 1440-1550. Even with a degree of SAT score inflation, those numbers indicate that the university has become even more competitive in recent years. Eighty-five percent of freshmen in the Class of 2023 scored better than a 1400 on the SAT.

The admissions office lists eight areas that are considered most important in determining admission: rigor of courses, grades, class rank, recommendations, essays, test scores, talent/ability, and character/personal qualities. In a typical year, close to half of admitted students were either the valedictorian or salutatorian of their high school class. Those applying early are accepted at a much higher rate than in the regular round. The Class of 2023 saw 769 seats filled through ED with an acceptance rate of 18 percent compared to a 6 percent acceptance rate in the regular cycle. The 769 admits account for roughly 64 percent of the total class. In short, those looking to come to Providence should be individuals at the top of their class who are intellectually curious, open-minded, and who possess intangible qualities that would allow them to flourish in Brown's unique academic program.

Worth Your Money?

With a $80,448 annual cost of attendance, Brown University will cost a great deal for anyone who does not qualify for financial aid. For the current students who receive need-based grants, 100 percent of their demonstrated need will be covered. That equates to an average grant of almost $53,000 per year. Despite the cost, Brown is the type of school worth its hefty price tag. Not only will the Ivy League credentials benefit you in graduate/professional school admissions and the world of employment, but the quality of the educational experience, the flexibility of your coursework, and the chance to take many small, seminar-style classes with distinguished faculty are of incredible value.

FINANCIAL
Institutional Type: Private
In-State Tuition: $59,254
Out-of-State Tuition: $59,254
Room & Board: $15,908
Required Fees: $1,342
Books & Supplies: $1,642

Avg. Need-Based Grant: $52,881
Avg. % of Need Met: 100%

Avg. Merit-Based Award: $0
% Receiving (All Freshmen): 0%
% Receiving (Freshmen w/o Need): 0%

Avg. Cumulative Debt: $24,304
% of Students Borrowing: 31%

CAREER
Who Recruits
1. Boston Consulting Group
2. Oracle
3. Millenium Management
4. BlackRock
5. Teach for America

Notable Internships
1. Google
2. Etsy
3. Apple

Top Industries
1. Business
2. Education
3. Research
4. Media
5. Engineering

Top Employers
1. Google
2. Microsoft
3. Facebook
4. Goldman Sachs
5. Amazon

Where Alumni Work
1. New York City
2. Providence
3. Boston
4. San Francisco
5. Washington DC

Median Earnings
College Scorecard (Early Career): $67,500
PayScale (Early Career): $71,700
PayScale (Mid-Career): $144,800

RANKINGS
Money: 77
U.S. News: 14 (T), National Universities
Wall Street Journal/THE: 5 (T)
Washington Monthly: 37, National Universities

COLLEGE OVERLAPS
Columbia University
Cornell University
Duke University
Harvard University
University of Pennsylvania

Bryn Mawr College

Bryn Mawr, Pennsylvania | 610-526-5152

ADMISSION
Admission Rate: 33%
Admission Rate - Men: Not Applicable
Admission Rate - Women: 33%
EA Admission Rate: Not Offered
ED Admission Rate: 52%
ED Admits as % of Total Admits: 16%
Admission Rate (5-Year Trend): -7%
% of Admits Attending (Yield): 34%
Transfer Admission Rate: 22%

SAT Reading/Writing (Middle 50%): 640-740
SAT Math (Middle 50%): 650-770
ACT Composite (Middle 50%): 29-33

% Graduated in Top 10% of HS Class: 67%
% Graduated in Top 25% of HS Class: 95%
% Graduated in Top 50% of HS Class: 99%

Demonstrated Interest: Not Considered
Legacy Status: Considered
Admission Interview Offered: Yes

ENROLLMENT
Total Undergraduate Enrollment: 1,384
% Part-Time: 1%
% Male: 0%
% Female: 100%
% Out-of-State: 85%
% Fraternity: Not Offered
% Sorority: Not Offered
% On-Campus (Freshman): 100%
% On-Campus (All Undergraduate): 92%

% African-American: 5%
% Asian: 11%
% Hispanic: 10%
% White: 43%
% Other: 5%
% Race or Ethnicity Unknown: 5%
% International: 21%
% Low-Income: 13%

ACADEMICS
Student-to-Faculty Ratio: 9 to 1
% of Classes Under 20: 72%
% of Classes 20-49: 28%
% of Classes 50 or More: 0%
% Full-Time Faculty: 80%
% Full-Time Faculty w/ Terminal Degree: 96%

Top Programs
Biology
English
Growth and Structure of Cities
History of Art
Mathematics
Physics
Psychology

Retention Rate: 90%
4-Year Graduation Rate: 77%
6-Year Graduation Rate: 84%

Curricular Flexibility: Somewhat Flexible
Academic Rating: ★★★★

#CollegesWorthYourMoney

Eleven miles west of Philadelphia and situated on the swanky Main Line rests an immaculate, 135-acre campus that serves as the educational home to more than 1,300 brilliant, politically active, and fiercely independent young women. Bryn Mawr College, still an all-female institution, used to serve as the sister school to Haverford College, which was all male until the late 1970s. The two schools still retain a degree of partnership. In fact, Bryn Mawr, Haverford, and Swarthmore (collectively known as the Tri-Co) all run on the same academic calendar so students can take courses at all three schools. Additionally, Bryn Mawr undergraduates can opt to take up to two courses at Penn each semester. There are more than 3,000 cross-registrations exercised each year.

Inside the Classroom
On the home campus, undergraduates can choose from thirty-six majors and forty-six minors. Roughly 30 percent of the student body earns degrees in the natural sciences or mathematics, a figure four times the national average for women. However, as a true liberal arts school, all students must take courses in each of Bryn Mawr's four "approaches": critical interpretation, cross-cultural analysis, inquiry into the past, and scientific investigation. Additional courses in quantitative reasoning and a full year studying one of ten foreign languages round out the mandated coursework. The college does point out that "within this structure, variety abounds," noting that students averse to the hard sciences can fulfill their scientific investigation requirement through the likes of anthropology or psychology.

A 9:1 student-to-faculty ratio leads to small class sizes with 72 percent of sections having fewer than twenty students, and 23 percent of sections enrolling nine students or fewer. This type of academic setting leads to close mentoring from professors. Over 500 undergraduates collaborate on research and independent projects with faculty each year. Those electing to study abroad have more than seventy programs to choose from and, in recent years, students have spent a semester in thirty countries across six continents.

This elite liberal arts school offers a number of excellent academic programs that receive national recognition from employers and graduate schools. By volume, the most popular majors are mathematics, psychology, sociology, English, and biology. Nationally competitive fellowship/scholarship programs also look favorably upon Bryn Mawr alumni. Recent graduates have been successful in procuring Boren, Fulbright, and Watson Fellowships.

Outside the Classroom
Bryn Mawr's breathtakingly beautiful and historic campus is where 88 percent of freshmen and 85 percent of the overall student body reside. Sororities are not permitted at Bryn Mawr as the college prefers participation in the 150 nonexclusive student organizations presently active. Clubs in music/performing arts and community service are among the most popular. Student government is also strong as elected members are dedicated to carrying out the institution's Honor Code. This is a tradition-rich school with events such as Parade Night, Lantern Night, and May Day all taken seriously by the student population. The Owls participate in twelve NCAA Division III sports, and casual athletic participation is always an option as the school boasts a 50,000-square-foot gymnasium, Olympic-size swimming pool, and outdoor tennis courts. While there is plenty to do on campus, nearby Haverford College, Swarthmore, and Villanova University provide Bryn Mawr undergrads with additional social scenes to explore. The college's proximity to Philadelphia means that restaurants, concerts, sporting events, museums, and theater are only a short drive away.

Career Services
The Career and Civic Engagement Center is staffed by seventeen professionals who specialize in areas like career counseling, pre-law advising, and employer relations. With an eye-popping 81:1 student-to-advisor ratio, Bryn Mawr rates well above average compared to other colleges featured in this guide. That provides undergraduates with ample opportunity to work closely with a career counselor on resume development, internship hunting, and networking.

In terms of employer relations, rather than hosting their own events the college tends to rely more on partnerships with other Seven Sisters schools and the Tri-College Consortium (TCC) with Haverford and Swarthmore. The Fall Policy & Government Career Fair is held at the University of Pennsylvania and is open to members of the TCC. Spring events held at Haverford College include the Tri-College STEM Recruiting Day and the Philadelphia Career Connection that attracts forty employers. Students can find internship and job opportunities online through

E-mail: admissions@brynmawr.edu | Website: www.brynmawr.edu

Handshake or via the Selective Liberal Arts Consortium that can facilitate off-campus interviews. Bryn Mawr has a low student-to-counselor ratio and has an excellent track record for helping its students gain acceptance into top graduate schools. However, its alumni salary figures lag behind its peers, and its on-campus recruiting opportunities are somewhat limited.

Professional Outcomes

One year after receiving their diplomas, 60 percent of Bryn Mawr graduates have found employment and a robust 32 percent have already entered graduate school. Among those who are employed, the five most popular fields are business, education, health/medicine, science, and communications/media. With graduating classes of under 400 students there are no massive numbers of alumni clustered in particular companies as is the case at many larger institutions. Most of the organizations employing the greatest number of alumni are universities and hospital systems although Google, Accenture, JPMorgan Chase, and Vanguard do employ a fair number of Bryn Mawr graduates. Median mid-career salaries are on the low side by elite college standards, in part due to the heavy concentration of students pursing lengthy graduate programs.

Of those pursuing further education, 63 percent were in master's programs, 10 percent in medical school, 2 percent in law school, and 13 percent were already working on their PhD. Again, due to the minuscule class sizes, it's rare that multiple graduates flock to particular institutions for graduate school. However, to get a sense of the prestigious programs accepting Bryn Mawr alumni one can simply examine the higher education destinations of members of the Class of 2019. Those included Brown University, MIT, Stanford University, Oxford University, and Yale University.

Admission

Bryn Mawr accepts 33 percent of those who apply, making it more selective than Mount Holyoke, comparable to Smith, and a touch less selective than Barnard and Wellesley. Freshmen at Bryn Mawr possessed middle-50 percent SAT scores of 1290-1510 and 29-33 on the ACT. A healthy 67 percent finished in the top 10 percent of their high school class; 95 percent were in the top quarter. In terms of class rank/GPA, the average accepted applicant looks similar to those from five years ago. Yet, the SAT scores of admitted applicants has risen rather dramatically. In 2013, the middle-SAT range for the freshman class was 1190-1420.

The admissions office places the greatest emphasis on the rigor of an applicant's high school curriculum and recommendation letters. Grades, essays, extracurricular activities, and character/personal qualities are next. While Bryn Mawr is a test-optional school, 61 percent submitted SAT results, and 32 percent submitted ACT scores, so tests do still play a role in shaping the overall admissions picture. Early decision is the right choice for those who have the school atop their college list. Bryn Mawr fills 48 percent of its freshman class in the early round and accepts 52 percent of those who apply. A highly selective destination point for high-achieving young women, this member of the Seven-Sisters Colleges is tougher to get into than its acceptance rate would imply. Known as a supportive, collaborative, and academically excellent school, Bryn Mawr draws brilliant and accomplished applicants from around the globe. An impressive resume is needed, and applying early can give you an edge.

Worth Your Money?

Despite a list price above $73,000, Bryn Mawr is generous with aid, leading to graduates who possess lower-than-average debt. Unusual for a school of its ilk, 21 percent of current students receive an annual merit award averaging $19k in value. A healthy 48 percent of students are found eligible for need-based aid, and 100 percent of their demonstrated need is met by the college. The average annual value of these grants is close to $44,000, helping to make Bryn Mawr more accessible to those of varying socioeconomic backgrounds.

FINANCIAL
Institutional Type: Private
In-State Tuition: $56,610
Out-of-State Tuition: $56,610
Room & Board: $17,720
Required Fees: $0
Books & Supplies: $1,000

Avg. Need-Based Grant: $43,829
Avg. % of Need Met: 100%

Avg. Merit-Based Award: $19,046
% Receiving (All Freshmen): 29%
% Receiving (Freshmen w/o Need): 21%

Avg. Cumulative Debt: $28,772
% of Students Borrowing: 52%

CAREER
Who Recruits
1. FDIC
2. Moody's Corporation
3. Philadelphia Museum of Art
4. Vanguard
5. Northwestern Mutual

Notable Internships
1. Whitney Museum of Art
2. JetBlue
3. Citi

Top Industries
1. Education
2. Business
3. Healthcare
4. Social Services
5. Media

Top Employers
1. Penn Medicine
2. Children's Hospital of Philadelphia
3. Vanguard
4. Accenture
5. Google

Where Alumni Work
1. Philadelphia
2. New York City
3. Washington DC
4. Boston
5. San Francisco

Median Earnings
College Scorecard (Early Career): $54,600
PayScale (Early Career): $59,200
PayScale (Mid-Career): $112,800

RANKINGS
Money: 496
U.S. News: 28 (T), Liberal Arts Colleges
Wall Street Journal/THE: 66 (T)
Washington Monthly: 17, Liberal Arts Colleges

COLLEGE OVERLAPS
Barnard College
Brown University
Haverford College
Mount Holyoke College
Smith College

Bucknell University

Lewisburg, Pennsylvania | 570-577-3000

ADMISSION
Admission Rate: 34%
Admission Rate - Men: 31%
Admission Rate - Women: 37%
EA Admission Rate: Not Offered
ED Admission Rate: 64%
ED Admits as % of Total Admits: 13%
Admission Rate (5-Year Trend): +5%
% of Admits Attending (Yield): 29%
Transfer Admission Rate: 32%

SAT Reading/Writing (Middle 50%): 620-700
SAT Math (Middle 50%): 635-730
ACT Composite (Middle 50%): 28-32

% Graduated in Top 10% of HS Class: 58%
% Graduated in Top 25% of HS Class: 83%
% Graduated in Top 50% of HS Class: 98%

Demonstrated Interest: Not Considered
Legacy Status: Considered
Admission Interview Offered: No

ENROLLMENT
Total Undergraduate Enrollment: 3,627
% Part-Time: 1%
% Male: 49%
% Female: 51%
% Out-of-State: 79%
% Fraternity: 35%
% Sorority: 42%
% On-Campus (Freshman): 100%
% On-Campus (All Undergraduate): 91%

% African-American: 3%
% Asian: 5%
% Hispanic: 6%
% White: 74%
% Other: 4%
% Race or Ethnicity Unknown: 0%
% International: 6%
% Low-Income: 10%

ACADEMICS
Student-to-Faculty Ratio: 9 to 1
% of Classes Under 20: 55%
% of Classes 20-49: 44%
% of Classes 50 or More: 1%
% Full-Time Faculty: 90%
% Full-Time Faculty w/ Terminal Degree: 95%

Top Programs
Accounting
Biology
Computer Science
Economics
Engineering
Finance
Political Science

Retention Rate: 92%
4-Year Graduation Rate: 86%
6-Year Graduation Rate: 90%

Curricular Flexibility: Somewhat Flexible
Academic Rating: ★★★★✓

#CollegesWorthYourMoney

Approximately 3,700 undergraduate students grace this gorgeous, 450-acre campus in bucolic Lewisburg, Pennsylvania. While technically a "university," the number of graduate students is nominal and, academically, the school functions more as a liberal arts college with a strong engineering program. Socially, with its focus on athletics and Greek life, the "university" label may start to feel more apt.

Inside the Classroom
Over fifty majors and sixty-five minors are on tap across three undergraduate schools: the College of Arts & Sciences, Freeman College of Management, and the College of Engineering. Required core curriculum coursework for A&S and Freeman is identical and must include multiple classes under the umbrella categories of intellectual skills, disciplinary perspectives, tools for critical engagement, and a culminating experience that involves research and/ or independent study. The College of Engineering keeps the vast majority of its requirements concentrated in the areas of math, science, and engineering. Before classes even commence, all first-year students attend a five-day new student orientation centered around scholarship and community. Further, all freshmen take a foundation seminar course, and that instructor serves as the faculty adviser until the student declares a major in the sopho- more year. That supportive environment helps the school maintain a superb 92 percent retention rate.

Getting well-acquainted with your professors is easy with a 9:1 student-faculty ratio, and class sizes are reasonably small. Slightly more than half of courses at Bucknell unfold in a classroom of no more than nineteen students, and 88 percent of all sections enroll fewer than twenty-nine students. All of Bucknell's 350 full-time professors spend some of their time teaching undergraduates. Last year, almost 300 students took advantage of summer research opportunities on campus. An additional 175 typically engage in research for academic credit during the regular school year. Study abroad semesters are available at over 130 sites across six continents, and 45 percent of the student body takes advantage of that.

The greatest number of degrees are conferred in the areas of the social sciences (24 percent), engineering (15 percent), business (15 percent), biology (10 percent), and psychology (7 percent). The Freeman College of Management and College of Engineering have the most prominent national reputations, but Bucknell is a well-regarded institution across the board. With a career-focused student body, this is a not a college that produces a sizable number of postgraduate fellows or scholars, but three Class of 2020 Bucknell grads were awarded Fulbright Scholarships, and the school has averaged one Goldwater Scholar per year over the last five years.

Outside the Classroom
The vast majority of the student body, 79 percent, reside in university housing on campus. Many join the school's thriving Greek life with 35 percent of men and 42 percent of women becoming members of one of the school's eight fraternity or ten sorority chapters. For a university of Bucknell's modest size, athletics are massive in scale. The school fields twenty-seven teams that play in the Patriot League of NCAA Division I. On top of that, intramural and club sports attract a high level of participation. Over 150 student clubs run on campus and enjoy small but loyal followings, thanks to the energy pouring into fraternities and athletics. Many Bucknell students also make time for volunteer work; three-quarters perform some degree of community service over the course of their four years. With no major city within a quick driving distance, students seeking some semblance of nightlife settle for Main Street in quiet Lewisburg. Central Pennsylvania does offer limitless opportunity for those who love the great outdoors with camping, hiking, kayaking, and similar activities available in abundance.

Career Services
Manned by fifteen full-time professionals with expertise in career counseling, internship coordination, and company recruitment, the Career Development Center (CDC) offers a 242:1 student-to-advisor ratio, which is better than average compared to other schools featured in this guide. Each year, the CDC hosts a fall Job Expo attended by up to one hundred employers and 750 students. Attendees include corporations like Deloitte, Coca Cola, and Hershey Entertainment & Resorts. Additionally, it organizes a separate internship/job fair in the spring, the Health & Law School Fair, Engineering Career Network Event, and several off-campus events in New York and DC to afford Bucknell students the chance to meet with additional companies in the finance and government realms. More than 200 employers attend school-sponsored career fairs each year.

E-mail: admissions@bucknell.edu | Website: www.bucknell.edu

Corporations, including the likes of ExxonMobil and Proctor & Gamble, appear regularly on campus to conduct job interviews. In a single year, 670 on-campus interviews were conducted with Bucknell seniors. Annually, the CDC helps over 500 students secure summer internships, which was cited by grads as frequently leading to their maiden jobs. Approximately 70% of graduates complete at least one internship. With generous staffing and a track record of helping students, Bucknell's career services does a strong job preparing its undergraduates for the real world.

Professional Outcomes

Nine months after graduation, 95 percent of the Class of 2019 had launched their careers or entered graduate school. Financial services is the most common sector for Bucknell grads to enter, attracting almost one-quarter of alumni. The largest concentration of recent grads can be found working at Accenture, Sloan Kettering Cancer Center, PwC, Amazon Robotics, Yelp, and Axis Group. Across all graduating years more than fifty Bucknellians are presently working at Goldman Sachs, Google, Merck, JPMorgan Chase & Co., IBM, and Johnson & Johnson. Starting salaries for recent grads are solid but highly dependent on the field of study. The mean salary for an engineering student is $70k while an Arts & Sciences graduate earned $54k. Across all disciplines, the mean salary for a Class of 2019 grad was $60k.

The Class of 2019 saw 17 percent of diploma recipients go directly into an advanced degree program. Bison alumni heading to graduate school predominantly pursue degrees in the medical field, social sciences, or engineering. Recent graduates have found their way into top med schools (e.g., Columbia, Duke, and Johns Hopkins) and to top engineering schools (e.g., Carnegie Mellon, Princeton, Stanford). Eight percent of this group decided to pursue a legal education. Law schools attended by recent grads include Boston University, George Washington, and UC San Diego. Geographically, most Bucknell grads remain concentrated in Pennsylvania, New York, New Jersey, and the DC metro area.

Admission

Bucknell admitted 34 percent of the 9,845 applicants into the Class of 2023. Surprisingly, the university received more applications four years prior and had a significantly lower acceptance rate of 24.8 percent. Admission into the well-regarded engineering programs is far more difficult than it is for the College of Arts & Humanities. The middle 50 percent SAT range for the Class of 2023 was 1280-1410; the ACT range was 28-32. A hefty 58 percent finished in the top 10 percent of their high school class, and 83 percent were in the top quarter. The average unweighted GPA was a 3.58, and one-third of attending students earned better than a 3.75.

Rigor of classes, GPA, test scores, and essays headline the most important factors for acceptance into Bucknell. Admissions staff members have stated that they keep a six-minute timer on their desks while they examine each application as a team. Thus, we know that your measurable achievements need to be within range in order for your intangibles/outside-the-classroom activities to become serious factors in admission. Those who apply early decision enjoy a major edge; last year, 64 percent of ED applicants were accepted compared to 32 percent in the regular round. Being a legacy also gives you an admissions boost. The school regularly hosts events for children (or grandchildren) of alumni, and legacy students comprise 6-9 percent of the average freshman cohort.

Worth Your Money?

A $72,600 list price cost of attendance is made slightly less onerous by the $14,000 (on average) annual merit aid package that goes to 6 percent of undergraduates as well as the $33,700 (on average) need-based aid package that is awarded to 43 percent of current students. However, Bucknell's clientele tends to include many— an estimated 60 percent of current undergraduates come from families in the top 20 percent income-wise. Those falling in between—not qualifying for aid but not well-off enough to pay full freight—will need to consider whether their intended major/future career is likely to make loan payments worth the cost. If you were on a budget and studying to be a teacher, Bucknell may not prove a wise choice. If you were in the same financial boat but studying engineering or business, attending this school absolutely could be worth your money.

FINANCIAL
Institutional Type: Private
In-State Tuition: $57,882
Out-of-State Tuition: $57,882
Room & Board: $14,670
Required Fees: $320
Books & Supplies: $900

Avg. Need-Based Grant: $33,700
Avg. % of Need Met: 92%

Avg. Merit-Based Award: $14,024
% Receiving (All Freshmen): 20%
% Receiving (Freshmen w/o Need): 6%

Avg. Cumulative Debt: $31,000
% of Students Borrowing: 46%

CAREER
Who Recruits
1. Exelon
2. Horizon Media
3. Nielsen
4. Ralph Lauren
5. Southwest Airlines

Notable Internships
1. NBCUniversal
2. CBRE
3. Bloomberg LP

Top Industries
1. Business
2. Education
3. Operations
4. Finance
5. Sales

Top Employers
1. PwC
2. Deloitte
3. Morgan Stanley
4. IBM
5. Merck

Where Alumni Work
1. New York City
2. Philadelphia
3. Washington DC
4. Boston
5. Williamsport, PA

Median Earnings
College Scorecard (Early Career): $70,800
PayScale (Early Career): $69,500
PayScale (Mid-Career): $143,000

RANKINGS
Money: 188
U.S. News: 34 (T), Liberal Arts Colleges
Wall Street Journal/THE: 77 (T)
Washington Monthly: 43, Liberal Arts Colleges

COLLEGE OVERLAPS
Colgate University
Lafayette College
Lehigh University
Pennsylvania State University - University Park
Villanova University

California Institute of Technology

Pasadena, California | 626-395-6341

ADMISSION
Admission Rate: 6%
Admission Rate - Men: 5%
Admission Rate - Women: 11%
EA Admission Rate: NR
ED Admission Rate: Not Offered
ED Admits as % of Total Admits: Not Offered
Admission Rate (5-Year Trend): -4%
% of Admits Attending (Yield): 44%
Transfer Admission Rate: 6%

SAT Reading/Writing (Middle 50%): 740-760
SAT Math (Middle 50%): 790-800
ACT Composite (Middle 50%): 35-36

% Graduated in Top 10% of HS Class: 99%
% Graduated in Top 25% of HS Class: 100%
% Graduated in Top 50% of HS Class: 100%

Demonstrated Interest: Not Considered
Legacy Status: Not Considered
Admission Interview Offered: No

ENROLLMENT
Total Undergraduate Enrollment: 938
% Part-Time: 0%
% Male: 55%
% Female: 45%
% Out-of-State: 64%
% Fraternity: Not Offered
% Sorority: Not Offered
% On-Campus (Freshman): 100%
% On-Campus (All Undergraduate): 94%

% African-American: 2%
% Asian: 37%
% Hispanic: 17%
% White: 27%
% Other: 9%
% Race or Ethnicity Unknown: 0%
% International: 8%
% Low-Income: 8%

ACADEMICS
Student-to-Faculty Ratio: 3 to 1
% of Classes Under 20: 69%
% of Classes 20-49: 23%
% of Classes 50 or More: 8%
% Full-Time Faculty: 92%
% Full-Time Faculty w/ Terminal Degree: 98%

Top Programs
Biology
Chemistry
Computer Science
Engineering
Geological and Planetary Sciences
Physics
Mathematics

Retention Rate: 98%
4-Year Graduation Rate: 84%
6-Year Graduation Rate: 94%

Curricular Flexibility: Somewhat Flexible
Academic Rating: ★★★★★

#CollegesWorthYourMoney

The setting of television's *Big Bang Theory*, the California Institute of Technology is, as suggested by the show's focus on a group of socially-awkward physicists, a collection of some of the most brilliant science and engineering minds in the world. Situated in gorgeous Pasadena, California, Caltech enrolls a mere 938 undergraduates, affectionately known as "Techers," very few of whom got a single question wrong on the math portion of the SAT. As tough as it is to gain admission, coursework at the school is perhaps an even more rigorous and consuming process.

Inside the Classroom
The university's common core is, not surprisingly, STEM-heavy with requirements that includes Freshman Mathematics, Freshman Physics, Freshman Chemistry, and Freshman Biology. However, students also must conquer 36 units of the humanities and social sciences, nine units of physical education, and one course in scientific communication in which undergrads write a paper for submission to a peer-reviewed academic journal. There are six academic divisions: biology and biological engineering; chemistry and chemical engineering; engineering and applied science; geological and planetary sciences; the humanities and social sciences; and physics, mathematics, and astronomy, each with more options for specialized concentrations. Across all divisions, there are thirty-two distinct majors.

Possessing an absurdly favorable 3:1 student-to-faculty ratio, plenty of individualized attention is up for grabs. Class sizes are not quite as tiny as the student-to-faculty ratio might suggest, but 69 percent of courses enroll fewer than twenty students, and 37 percent enroll fewer than ten. Summer Undergraduate Research Fellowships (SURF) enjoy wide participation with 80 percent of undergraduates partaking, and 20 percent of that group going on to publish their results. Six approved study abroad programs are available at Cambridge University, University College London, University of Edinburgh, Copenhagen University, the University of Melbourne, and Ecole Polytechnique in France.

Engineering is the most popular major, accounting for 35 percent of all degrees conferred. Computer and information science (27 percent), the physical sciences (22 percent), and mathematics (10 percent) also have strong representation. Grads find a high level of success in obtaining prestigious scholarships for graduate study including Watson, Fulbright, and Hertz Fellowships. The school also sees an incredible number of students win National Science Foundation Fellowships (the head of the organization received her PhD from Caltech). An astounding twenty-seven 2018 graduates won NSF Graduate Research Fellowships.

Outside the Classroom
Given its small undergraduate population, campus is a spacious 124 acres, and 64 percent elect to live in one of the university's eleven residences; freshmen are required to do so. Greek life was long ago banished in favor of a coeducational residential house system. Each house has its own vibe and traditions, and students go through a two-week rotation period (in place of a pledging process) to find the best fit. On the athletics front, the Beavers field nine men's and nine women's teams to compete in intercollegiate sports, mostly at the NCAA Division III level, although they are more noted for insanely long losing streaks than anything else (the baseball team once lost 228 straight games). Four-fifths of undergrads participate in some kind of organized athletics, and the high rate of involvement isn't limited to sports. Roughly 65 percent of students also play a musical instrument, and many join one of the more than one hundred student-run organizations on campus. There are plenty of pre-professional and tech-oriented club options as well as groups like Magic: The Gathering Club or the Anime Society. While students generally report that academic pursuits plus a club or two generally take up 100 percent of their waking hours at Caltech, gorgeous Pasadena and nearby downtown Los Angeles provide limitless opportunities for those seeking some degree of socialization.

Career Services
The Caltech Career Development Center has four full-time professional staff members working on career counseling, internship coordination, and employer recruiting. That equates to a 235:1 student-to-advisor ratio, which is among the best of any university featured in this guide. Caltech hosts two large career fairs per year, one in October and one in January. Anywhere from 150-200 companies attend those fairs, which is a massive number when considering the school has fewer than 1,000 undergraduates. Small events take place pretty much weekly, and samples of those regular offerings include visits from the likes of Harvard Business School, Bain & Company, Yahoo, and the Google Women's Focus Group.

Caltech students have little trouble procuring summer internships in engineering, computer science, or business/finance. Unlike most schools where undergrads compete for internships at top companies, the top companies typically have to compete to attract Caltech students. (Its website offers advice for companies in that regard.) Similarly, on-campus recruiting is strong with companies constantly visiting campus to try to snag young talent. That list includes NASA, Facebook, Goldman Sachs, Oracle, and SpaceX. Based on its low student-to-counselor ratio, prodigious on-campus recruiting efforts, placement of more math/science PhD candidates than any university in the country, and unmatched starting salaries for graduates, Caltech's Career Development Center easily earns the highest praise from the College Transitions staff.

Professional Outcomes

Caltech is a rare school that sees six-figure average starting salaries for its graduates; the Class of 2017 (most recent available) figure was $106,000. Over 60 percent of recent grads go directly into the workforce and find homes at tech giants such as Google, Intel, Microsoft, Apple, and Facebook. Engineering students are routinely courted by the likes of Boeing, Lockheed Martin, SpaceX, and Northrup Grumman. The school also has a strong alumni representation at NASA. Those who go the academic/research route ultimately end up on the faculty at schools such as Stanford, MIT, USC, and Caltech itself. Networking as a Caltech alum is a dream. The university has 22,000 alumni, many of whom are leaders in the tech world including seventeen living Nobel Prize winners and countless founders/execs of major corporations.

Not surprisingly, the largest number of alumni remain in California, settling into careers in Silicon Valley. A healthy 35 percent of those receiving their diplomas continue directly on the higher education path, immediately entering graduate school. Caltech is the number one producer of math/science PhDs in the country. Many continue their education at Caltech or other elite STEM graduate programs. After attaining graduate degrees, careers in research and higher education are popular pursuits. While engineering is where the largest number of grads eventually land, higher education is a close second.

Admission

With an acceptance rate of 6.4 percent, Caltech occupies the same uber-selective air as MIT. Sporting a middle 50 percent SAT range of 1530-1570 and near-perfect ACT range of 35-36, it is next to impossible to gain admission without acing your standardized tests. In fact, 94 percent of accepted applicants possess a 700 or higher on the reading section of the SAT; 100 percent have a 700 or higher on the math portion of the exam. SAT subject test scores, once an integral component of the admissions process, will no longer be considered as of 2020.

Directly from the admissions office, five factors carry the heaviest weight in the process: rigor of secondary curriculum, standardized test scores, essay, recommendations, and character/personal qualities. Caltech does not offer early decision, but its nonbinding early action round does offer better odds of gaining acceptance. In previous cycles, the regular round saw 5 percent admitted, but 10 percent of those who applied by Nov. 1 found success. Caltech is among the most competitive universities in the world and is a top choice for many of the most brilliant young minds seeking to study computer science, the hard sciences, and engineering. Flawless standardized test scores are necessary but not sufficient for admissions consideration; those whose intangibles shine brightest gain an edge in this highly competitive process.

Worth Your Money?

Anything beyond a simple "Yes" here feels superfluous but, nevertheless, we'll offer a few statistics to back up the claim. While the school does not offer merit aid, the majority of students do not pay anything close to the almost $75,000 annual cost of attendance. Need-based aid is awarded to 57 percent of the undergraduate population and carries a mean value of $49,618. Regardless of what you have to pay to attend this institution, it will be well worth the cost. As we highlighted previously in the profile, students' average starting salaries right out of Caltech are in the six figures.

FINANCIAL
Institutional Type: Private
In-State Tuition: $56,862
Out-of-State Tuition: $56,862
Room & Board: $17,337
Required Fees: $0
Books & Supplies: $1,428

Avg. Need-Based Grant: $49,618
Avg. % of Need Met: 100%

Avg. Merit-Based Award: $0
% Receiving (All Freshmen): 0%
% Receiving (Freshmen w/o Need): 0%

Avg. Cumulative Debt: $20,192
% of Students Borrowing: 30%

CAREER
Who Recruits
1. Goldman Sachs
2. Southern California Edison
3. Amazon
4. Facebook
5. Intel

Notable Internships
1. Facebook
2. Adobe
3. Apple

Top Industries
1. Engineering
2. Business
3. Research
4. Education
5. Information Technology

Top Employers
1. Northrop Grumman
2. Google
3. Boeing
4. NASA Jet Propulsion Laboratory
5. Apple

Where Alumni Work
1. Los Angeles
2. San Francisco
3. New York City
4. Boston
5. San Diego

Median Earnings
College Scorecard (Early Career): $85,900
PayScale (Early Career): $93,200
PayScale (Mid-Career): $159,900

RANKINGS
Money: 25
U.S. News: 9 (T), National Universities
Wall Street Journal/THE: 7 (T)
Washington Monthly: 57, National Universities

COLLEGE OVERLAPS
Harvard University
Massachusetts Institute of Technology
Princeton University
Stanford University
University of California, Berkeley

ADMISSION

Admission Rate: 28%
Admission Rate - Men: 25%
Admission Rate - Women: 32%
EA Admission Rate: Not Offered
ED Admission Rate: Not Offered
ED Admits as % of Total Admits: Not Offered
Admission Rate (5-Year Trend): -6%
% of Admits Attending (Yield): 30%
Transfer Admission Rate: 15%

SAT Reading/Writing (Middle 50%): 620-700
SAT Math (Middle 50%): 620-740
ACT Composite (Middle 50%): 26-32

% Graduated in Top 10% of HS Class: 54%
% Graduated in Top 25% of HS Class: 85%
% Graduated in Top 50% of HS Class: 98%

Demonstrated Interest: Not Considered
Legacy Status: Not Considered
Admission Interview Offered: No

ENROLLMENT

Total Undergraduate Enrollment: 20,454
% Part-Time: 4%
% Male: 52%
% Female: 48%
% Out-of-State: 15%
% Fraternity: 6%
% Sorority: 10%
% On-Campus (Freshman): 100%
% On-Campus (All Undergraduate): 35%

% African-American: 1%
% Asian: 14%
% Hispanic: 18%
% White: 54%
% Other: 8%
% Race or Ethnicity Unknown: 4%
% International: 2%
% Low-Income: 18%

ACADEMICS

Student-to-Faculty Ratio: 18 to 1
% of Classes Under 20: 72%
% of Classes 20-49: 16%
% of Classes 50 or More: 12%
% Full-Time Faculty: 66%
% Full-Time Faculty w/ Terminal Degree: 75%

Top Programs
Agricultural Business
Biological Sciences
Civil Engineering
Computer Science
Electrical Engineering
Industrial Engineering
Mechanical Engineering

Retention Rate: 94%
4-Year Graduation Rate: 51%
6-Year Graduation Rate: 83%

Curricular Flexibility: Less Flexible
Academic Rating: ★★★

#CollegesWorthYourMoney

Nestled between San Francisco and Los Angeles, California Polytechnic State University-San Luis Obispo is the more competitive of the state's two public polytechnic schools, Pomona being the less selective branch. Home to more than 20,400 undergraduate students, Cal Poly churns out a jaw-dropping number of engineers each year, but it is far from a unidimensional university.

Inside the Classroom

Cal Poly is comprised of six undergraduate schools: the College of Agriculture, Food & Environmental Sciences, College of Architecture & Environmental Design, College of Engineering, College of Liberal Arts, College of Science & Mathematics, and the Orfalea College of Business. Across all divisions there are sixty-three majors and eighty-four minors offered. While academic requirements vary by college and program, there are a number of general graduation must-haves that apply to all Mustangs. They include seventy-two units of general education, demonstration of writing competency, and the completion of a senior project.

You won't find many small, liberal-arts-style learning spaces—only 4 percent of classes have a single-digit enrollment. Yet you also won't find many classes that enroll one hundred or more students; only 4 percent do. The majority of courses, 58 percent, fall between twenty and forty students. Cal Poly's student-to-faculty ratio is a high 18:1, but such is the cost of an uber-affordable STEM degree from an excellent institution. Still, faculty receive extremely favorable reviews for their accessibility, and opportunities to work intimately with professors are built into the curriculum in many programs. For example, all students in the College of Science & Mathematics are required to participate in faculty-directed research and complete a senior project in order to graduate. One-quarter of students take advantage of the school's robust study abroad program that offers learning opportunities in over seventy-five countries.

The School of Engineering is the university's crown jewel. Over one-quarter of all degrees conferred (27 percent) are in engineering, and Cal Poly gets recognition in many specialty areas of the field including industrial engineering, mechanical engineering, aerospace engineering, computer engineering, and civil engineering. The Orfalea College of Business also receives strong national recognition and is recognized as one of the better ROI business degrees one can find; 13 percent of undergrads earn a business degree. Other popular majors include agriculture (12 percent), biology (6 percent), architecture (5 percent), and the social sciences (5 percent).

Outside the Classroom

While more students are living on campus than ever—the university has added 5,600 beds since 2003—only 15 percent of undergraduates presently reside on campus. Ten percent of women and 6 percent of men sign up for Greek life. However, thirty-six of the school's sororities and fraternities were suspended in the spring of 2018 for racial insensitivity, leaving the future of Cal Poly Greek life in question. With twenty-one NCAA Division I sports on tap, there is always an opportunity to cheer on the Mustangs. Across all men's and women's sports, Cal Poly squads have captured fifty Big West Conference championships. Twenty-seven club sports, from rodeo to surfing, are available, and massive intramural program attracts 10,000 participants each year. There are an additional 300 student-run clubs, including a heavy dose of pre-professional organizations. San Luis Obispo is known as "The Happiest City in America" for a reason. Located on the coast, students have access to the beach and the natural beauty of Big Falls Trail. Outdoor concerts, an art museum, and the Thursday night farmer's market offer a taste of the effervescence of the surrounding town known as SLO Cal.

Career Services

The Cal Poly Career Services Office has twenty full-time professional staff members working on career counseling, employer relations, and employer recruiting. That includes two counselors—the Freshman Focus Team—who are dedicated solely to first-year students. Overall, the school's 1,022:1 student-to-advisor ratio does not fare well against other colleges featured in this guide. In spite of the high student-to-counselor ratio, the office does accomplish impressive things on behalf of students. Each year Cal Poly hosts ten major career fairs, including three large, non-major-specific events in the fall, winter, and spring that draw 150+ employers each. Additional fairs cover fields that include teaching, architecture and environmental design, computing, and construction management.

California Polytechnic State University, San Luis Obispo

E-mail: admissions@calpoly.edu | Website: www.calpoly.edu

A survey of recent graduates revealed that among those already employed, 43 percent attributed obtaining employment directly to the Career Services Office. An additional 22 percent cited MustangJOBS, the office's online database of employment opportunities, and 9 percent were offered employment after an internship experience while in undergrad. An impressive 97 percent of graduates ended up in jobs related to their major. Such success is not merely a byproduct of producing highly employable STEM graduates. Amazingly, the Freshman Focus Team engaged 100 percent of the 4,451 first-year students in over 6,000 counseling sessions. Further, the office has forged official employer/university partnerships with 334 companies, creating excellent networks for current undergrads to lean on while pursuing employment.

Professional Outcomes

Within nine months of graduating, 93 percent are "positively engaged" in their next life activity. Top employers of Cal Poly grads include many of the top tech/consulting/engineering/financial firms in the country such as Google, Deloitte, KPMG, Microsoft, Northrup Grumman, Adobe, EY, and Apple. Overall, grads enjoy a median starting salary of $65,000. Engineering majors lead the way at $75,000 while liberal arts grads bring in a median income of only $45,000. Given that the in-state tuition is only $10k per year, this makes the university one of the best ROI schools in the country. An overwhelming majority, 83 percent, remain in California upon graduation. Washington, Colorado, and Texas are next three most popular destinations.

Of the 13 percent of alumni who directly enter graduate school, the six most commonly attended schools are all in California. By far the greatest number continue their studies at Cal Poly. UC Davis, USC, UC San Diego, San Jose State, and Berkeley also draw more than a handful of graduates each year. Many graduates of the Orfalea College of Business pursue master's degrees in accounting. The highest number of engineering students pursued MBAs or master's degrees in specific branches of engineering. Pursuing a legal education is a frequent choice of liberal arts graduates, and the University of San Diego, USC, and UCLA are the most commonly attended law schools.

Admission

Cal Poly accepted 28 percent of the 54,072 freshmen applicants who applied for membership in the Class of 2023. Like many California public universities, Cal Poly has become more competitive in recent years. While acceptance rates have remained steady, other indicators strongly suggest this trend. A startling 10,000 students with 4.0 GPAs (or higher) were denied entry to the Class of 2023. For 2019-20 freshmen, the mid-50 percent standardized test scores were 1250-1420 on the SAT and 26-32 on the ACT. Fifty-three percent of freshmen entering in 2019-20 claimed a spot in the top 10 percent of their high school class, and 85 percent were in the top quartile. Five years ago, those numbers were all significantly lower.

Freshman applicants apply to one of six colleges within the university, and some are more competitive than others. For example, the acceptance rate into the College of Engineering is 31 percent, and the SAT range is 1350-1520. Those aiming for the School of Agriculture, Food & Environmental Sciences enjoy a 43 percent acceptance rate and average a significantly lower 1230-1430 range on the SAT. No matter the college to which you apply, Cal Poly is mainly interested in three factors when making admissions decisions: the rigor of your secondary curriculum, GPA, and standardized test scores. Things like extracurricular activities, work experience, and first-generation status also carry a small amount of weight. Getting into Cal Poly is a straightforward, albeit increasingly challenging proposition. Candidates with a sparkling transcript and SATs north of 1350 should fare well. Those aiming to study engineering, business, or science and mathematics will need stronger credentials than those applying to other colleges.

Worth Your Money?

Annual in-state tuition and fees to attend Cal Poly remain just a hair above five figures, an astounding value in today's higher education marketplace. Including room, board, and all other expenses, the cost of attendance for California residents sits at $28,926. Out-of-staters pay an annual COA of under $43,000, not at all an unreasonable sum for the quality of education one will receive at this university. The school does not award large sums of need-based or merit-based aid; however, the net price most students pay still remains relatively low given the school's modest sticker price.

FINANCIAL
Institutional Type: Public
In-State Tuition: $5,742
Out-of-State Tuition: $264 per unit
Room & Board: $14,209
Required Fees: $4,206
Books & Supplies: $1,941

Avg. Need-Based Grant: $2,451
Avg. % of Need Met: 56%

Avg. Merit-Based Award: $1,505
% Receiving (All Freshmen): 28%
% Receiving (Freshmen w/o Need): 13%

Avg. Cumulative Debt: $22,411
% of Students Borrowing: 41%

CAREER
Who Recruits
1. Lockheed Martin
2. NBCUniversal
3. Greystar
4. The Raymond Group
5. Cushman & Wakefield

Notable Internships
1. Nike
2. EY
3. Oracle

Top Industries
1. Business
2. Engineering
3. Operations
4. Education
5. Sales

Top Employers
1. Apple
2. Google
3. Cisco
4. Oracle
5. Amazon

Where Alumni Work
1. San Francisco
2. San Luis Obispo, CA
3. Los Angeles
4. San Diego
5. Orange County, CA

Median Earnings
College Scorecard (Early Career): $66,900
PayScale (Early Career): $67,900
PayScale (Mid-Career): $127,000

RANKINGS
Money: 51
U.S. News: 3, Regional Universities West
Wall Street Journal/THE: 201 (T)
Washington Monthly: 26, Master's Universities

COLLEGE OVERLAPS
Cal Poly, Pomona
San Diego State University
University of California, Davis
University of California, Irvine
University of California, San Diego

Carleton College

Northfield, Minnesota | 507-222-4190

ADMISSION
Admission Rate: 19%
Admission Rate - Men: 19%
Admission Rate - Women: 19%
EA Admission Rate: Not Offered
ED Admission Rate: 26%
ED Admits as % of Total Admits: 18%
Admission Rate (5-Year Trend): -2%
% of Admits Attending (Yield): 38%
Transfer Admission Rate: 8%

SAT Reading/Writing (Middle 50%): 670-750
SAT Math (Middle 50%): 690-790
ACT Composite (Middle 50%): 31-34

% Graduated in Top 10% of HS Class: 71%
% Graduated in Top 25% of HS Class: 93%
% Graduated in Top 50% of HS Class: 100%

Demonstrated Interest: Not Considered
Legacy Status: Considered
Admission Interview Offered: Yes

ENROLLMENT
Total Undergraduate Enrollment: 2,119
% Part-Time: 1%
% Male: 49%
% Female: 51%
% Out-of-State: 83%
% Fraternity: Not Offered
% Sorority: Not Offered
% On-Campus (Freshman): 100%
% On-Campus (All Undergraduate): 96%

% African-American: 5%
% Asian: 9%
% Hispanic: 8%
% White: 58%
% Other: 7%
% Race or Ethnicity Unknown: 2%
% International: 11%
% Low-Income: 14%

ACADEMICS
Student-to-Faculty Ratio: 9 to 1
% of Classes Under 20: 69%
% of Classes 20-49: 31%
% of Classes 50 or More: 0%
% Full-Time Faculty: 82%
% Full-Time Faculty w/ Terminal Degree: 94%

Top Programs
Biology
Chemistry
Computer Science
Economics
Geology
History
Mathematics
Political Science

Retention Rate: 95%
4-Year Graduation Rate: 88%
6-Year Graduation Rate: 92%

Curricular Flexibility: Somewhat Flexible
Academic Rating: ★★★★⁄

#CollegesWorthYourMoney

One of the top liberal arts schools (if not the top) in the Midwest, Carleton has the reputation as a destination point for studious young people who love to learn for learning's sake. Located in fairly remote Northfield, Minnesota, the college still manages to be a magnet for the academically gifted and intellectually curious from coast to coast. Carleton is a small institution of just over 2,100 undergraduate students. It offers thirty-four majors, the most popular of which are within the disciplines of the social sciences (20 percent), physical science (14 percent) computer science (10 percent), biology (9 percent), visual and performing arts (9 percent), and psychology (8 percent).

Inside the Classroom

Mandated coursework is extensive and includes an argument and inquiry seminar for first-year students, a global citizenship requirement, a class in international studies as well as domestic studies, and three writing-intensive courses. Undergrads also must take a stroll through the usual liberal arts categories of humanistic inquiry, literary/artistic analysis, the arts, science, statistics, and social inquiry. All of this is done via three ten-week terms per academic year during which most students take only three courses per term.

Students work closely with their professors, and the college is routinely rated atop lists of best undergraduate teaching institutions. Small classes are the norm with the average being only sixteen students; in 17 percent of your classes you will be surrounded by no more than nine of your peers. Faculty-mentored research is embedded into many courses, independent study opportunities abound, and full-time supervised research is available during summer and winter break. Over three-quarters of the student body elect to study abroad in one of 130 programs offered in sixty countries. Furthermore, 100 percent of students in the Class of 2019 majoring in a foreign language, art history, environmental studies, and women's and gender studies spent a semester studying in another part of the globe.

All academic programs at this elite liberal arts school are well regarded, particularly by other universities where an exceptional percentage of Carleton grads later pursue doctoral degrees (more on this below). Consistently named a top producer of Fulbright Scholars, the college enjoyed five award recipients in 2020. The Peace Corps also ranked Carleton thirteenth on its list of Top Volunteer-Producing (small) Colleges.

Outside the Classroom

With 83 percent of students living on campus and no Greek life at Carleton, the dorms take on the role as the preferred social setting. Fourteen theme houses also play a big role on campus, allowing people with aligned interests to live communally. Those include the WHOA House for campus activists, the Culinary House for those committed to gastronomic pursuits, and the Q&A House for the LBGTQA community. Over 200 student-run clubs offer a multitude of niche activities to suit this fairly eclectic student body. The Ravens' eighteen varsity athletic teams are split evenly between men and women, and they all compete in NCAA Division III. Club and intramural sports are popular with ultimate Frisbee in the lead by a wide margin. Northfield is a small town, but it has its share of social/cultural offerings as well as neighboring St. Olaf's College, which opens additional social opportunities. Those looking for more action than Northfield can provide will be pleased to find the bustle of Minneapolis and St. Paul, both less than fifty miles away. Students seeking natural beauty do not have to look any further than the on-campus Cowling Arboretum, a 900-acre wooded area perfect for hiking or cross-country skiing.

Career Services

The Career Center is staffed by ten full-time professionals, just about all of whom have director, assistant director, or manager in their title. However, at such a small school most of these individuals do work directly with students in some capacity, and that results in a student-to-advisor ratio of 212:1, significantly better than the average institution included in this book.

The major career/internship/graduate school fairs that are open to Carleton students are joint efforts with other Minnesota-based universities, yet many companies, nonprofits, and government entities do make the trip to Northfield to directly recruit this talented cohort of undergraduates. Those companies include Amazon, Ernst & Young, Facebook, Google, and Microsoft. The 30 Minutes Program brings current students face-to-face with alums who work in a field of interest for quick (hence the name) informational/networking sessions. Externships with alumni allow students to shadow alumni in their place of employment for one to three weeks. Alumni remain extremely engaged with the school as evidenced by an extremely high percentage who donate. The area in which the career services office truly excels is advising students on graduate school pathways, an area we will explore further in a moment.

Carleton College

E-mail: admissions@carleton.edu | Website: www.carleton.edu

Professional Outcomes

Carleton does not track the activities of every graduating class, but when it last administered a senior survey in 2016, nearly three-quarters of soon-to-be grads were headed into the workforce with the most common job functions being business analyst, project manager, research assistant/associate, software engineer, and medical scribe. There are thirty-five companies that employ more than ten Carleton alums. Many are prestigious academic institutions including the University of Chicago, the University of Michigan, Colombia, Stanford, Northwestern, and Penn; the University of Minnesota is the largest employer of Knights with over 150 alumni in its ranks. Target, Epic Systems, UnitedHealth Group, Wells Fargo, Amazon, 3M, and Facebook all employ more than twenty-five alumni. Geographically, the greatest number of students remain in the Minneapolis-St. Paul area, but many also head to New York City, San Francisco, Chicago, DC, Boston, Seattle, and Los Angeles.

Carleton is a breeding ground for future scholars as a ridiculously high number of graduates go on to earn PhDs. In fact, by percentage, Carleton is one of the top ten producers of any college or university in the country of PhDs in economics, math, political science, sociology, chemistry, physics, biology, and history. In recent years 20-25 percent of graduates immediately entered graduate school; within ten years, 75 percent of graduates have enrolled in or completed an advanced degree program.

Admission

The 7,382 applications submitted for the Class of 2023 doesn't sound like an overwhelming number, but for tiny Carleton, that figure is more than double the number of applications received at the turn of the millennium. Only 19 percent of those applicants received an offer of admission. That was only a slight decrease from the admit rates of the previous five years. Those presently enrolled at Carleton almost exclusively finished near the top of their high school classes; 71 percent of those admitted into the 2019-20 freshman class were in the top 10 percent, and the school typically attracts around fifty National Merit Scholars each cycle. The 25th percentile SAT score was 1380, and the 75th percentile marker was 1520. A larger number of applicants submitted ACT scores to Carleton with a middle-50 percent range of 31-34. Most Carleton admits were active in their high school communities; 58 percent played varsity sports, 43 percent studied music, and an overwhelming 83 percent participated in some type of volunteer work.

The college lists three factors as the most significant in the admissions process: rigor of secondary curriculum, GPA, and class rank. Yet, excellent standardized test scores seem to be a prerequisite as 85 percent of enrolling students possess an ACT above 30, and 75 percent scored better than a 700 on the math section of the SAT. With such a low number of applications, those from remote areas of the country may particularly benefit from the quest for geographic diversity; five states sent zero students in the Class of 2023. Early decision can also provide a major advantage to those targeting the college as their number one choice. With two rounds of early decision offered, in a typical year Carleton fills 47 percent of its incoming class via ED. Yet, the acceptance rate isn't all that encouraging, as they admitted only 26 percent of ED students in 2019. Carleton is among the most highly selective liberal arts colleges not located on the East or West coasts. Its remote location keeps application numbers in check, but the applicant pool tends to be self-selecting.

Worth Your Money?

With little merit aid and a $74,500 estimated annual cost of attendance, there are many Carleton students who will be paying $298,000 for their bachelor's degree. The good news is that current undergraduates with demonstrated financial need see 100 percent of that need met, which averages to a $47,243 grant. Forty-four percent of the student body comes from families without need, and most of those families will pay the sticker price, as Carleton offers little in the way of merit aid. While Carleton's excellence isn't directly reflected in the early-to-mid career salaries of its graduates, the tiny classes, professor quality, extensive career services, and preparation for those aiming for prestigious graduate schools make this school very much worth your money.

FINANCIAL
Institutional Type: Private
In-State Tuition: $59,352
Out-of-State Tuition: $59,352
Room & Board: $14,658
Required Fees: $15,147
Books & Supplies: $901

Avg. Need-Based Grant: $47,243
Avg. % of Need Met: 100%

Avg. Merit-Based Award: $2,042
% Receiving (All Freshmen): 11%
% Receiving (Freshmen w/o Need): 2%

Avg. Cumulative Debt: $19,405
% of Students Borrowing: 40%

CAREER
Who Recruits
1. U.S. Bank
2. Anderson Corporation
3. Lewin Group
4. SPS Commerce
5. UnitedHealth Group

Notable Internships
1. Moody's Analytics
2. Smithsonian
3. Federal Rserve Bank of St. Louis

Top Industries
1. Education
2. Business
3. Research
4. Social Services
5. Media

Top Employers
1. Google
2. Epic
3. UnitedHealth Group
4. Target
5. Wells Fargo

Where Alumni Work
1. Minneapolis
2. New York City
3. San Francisco
4. Chicago
5. Washington DC

Median Earnings
College Scorecard (Early Career): $54,200
PayScale (Early Career): $61,000
PayScale (Mid-Career): $128,000

RANKINGS
Money: 208
U.S. News: 9 (T), Liberal Arts Colleges
Wall Street Journal/THE: 36
Washington Monthly: 19, Liberal Arts Colleges

COLLEGE OVERLAPS
Brown University
Bowdoin College
Grinnell College
Macalester College
Pomona College

ADMISSION

Admission Rate: 15%
Admission Rate - Men: 12%
Admission Rate - Women: 21%
EA Admission Rate: Not Offered
ED Admission Rate: 19%
ED Admits as % of Total Admits: 8%
Admission Rate (5-Year Trend): -10%
% of Admits Attending (Yield): 37%
Transfer Admission Rate: 6%

SAT Reading/Writing (Middle 50%): 700-760
SAT Math (Middle 50%): 760-800
ACT Composite (Middle 50%): 33-35

% Graduated in Top 10% of HS Class: 88%
% Graduated in Top 25% of HS Class: 96%
% Graduated in Top 50% of HS Class: 99%

Demonstrated Interest: Not Considered
Legacy Status: Important
Admission Interview Offered: Yes

ENROLLMENT

Total Undergraduate Enrollment: 7,022
% Part-Time: 3%
% Male: 50%
% Female: 50%
% Out-of-State: 86%
% Fraternity: 7%
% Sorority: 5%
% On-Campus (Freshman): 100%
% On-Campus (All Undergraduate): 56%

% African-American: 4%
% Asian: 31%
% Hispanic: 9%
% White: 25%
% Other: 4%
% Race or Ethnicity Unknown: 6%
% International: 22%
% Low-Income: 13%

ACADEMICS

Student-to-Faculty Ratio: 7 to 1
% of Classes Under 20: 66%
% of Classes 20-49: 22%
% of Classes 50 or More: 12%
% Full-Time Faculty: 91%
% Full-Time Faculty w/ Terminal Degree: 93%

Top Programs
Artificial Intelligence
Business Administration
Computer Science
Economics
Engineering
Information Systems
Mathematical Sciences
Statistics

Retention Rate: 97%
4-Year Graduation Rate: 76%
6-Year Graduation Rate: 90%

Curricular Flexibility: Somewhat Flexible
Academic Rating: ★★★★★

#CollegesWorthYourMoney

Founded by steel baron Andrew Carnegie in 1900 as an eponymous technical school, CMU's rise to its present position as one of the best research universities in the country is as much a Horatio Alger story as that of its original namesake. Despite its humble roots and gradual ascension into a regional powerhouse, Carnegie Mellon today is home to 7,022 brilliant undergrads and an additional 7,777 graduate students who come from all over the world to reap the benefits of a top-notch educational experience.

Inside the Classroom

Carnegie Mellon is unique in a number of ways; it is both highly segmented by area of study and, at the same time, interdisciplinary. Students are admitted to one of six colleges: the College of Engineering, College of Fine Arts, Dietrich College of Humanities and Social Science (which houses the popular information systems program), Mellon College of Science, Tepper School of Business, and the School of Computer Science. There are a combined ninety undergraduate majors available across the six schools, but young people simply do not come to CMU as "undecided." CMU students are expected to be well-rounded, and that philosophy is reflected in departmental requirements. For example, Dietrich students are required to take courses on data and computer science as freshmen, and students in the College of Engineering must take courses in writing and expression and foreign language.

Impressive, particularly for a school with more graduate students than undergrads, CMU boasts a 7:1 student-to-faculty ratio and class sizes are small with 31 percent containing single digits and two-thirds having an enrollment of nineteen or fewer. In the 2018-19 school year, 823 undergraduates conducted research through the University Research Office, and many others participated through various outside arrangements. Between 500-600 students study abroad for a semester each year in such countries as Japan, China, and Germany.

The most commonly conferred degrees are in engineering (27 percent), computer science (12 percent), business (10 percent), mathematics (10 percent), and visual and performing arts (9 percent). CMU boasts a number of programs that have a stellar worldwide reputation. In fact, it's hard to think of a university that accrues such high praise across such a broad spectrum of disciplines. The School of Computer Science is one of the best in the country, perennially ranked right next to (or above) the likes of MIT, Caltech, and Stanford. Also of note, it enrolls women at two or three times the national average. Tepper is recognized as one of the top undergraduate business schools by corporations around the globe. The drama program is a constant producer of top talent and, amazingly, in 2016, seven alumni were nominated for Tony Awards. The School of Engineering and the information technology program are also regulars in any top ten list. In the last five years, CMU students also have captured thirty Fulbright Scholarships, six Goldwater Scholarships, and two Churchill Scholarships.

Outside the Classroom

CMU undergrads are known for being so consumed with academics that some might ask, "What life outside the classroom?" Yet, there is plenty of activity, both on campus and in the surrounding Oakland section of Pittsburgh. All freshmen, and 56 percent of the entire student body, live on campus. There are over 280 student organizations including the famed Scotch'n'Soda, one of the oldest student theater groups in the country. It regularly puts on professional quality plays and musicals. More than sixty of the clubs on campus are pre-professional in focus, such as the popular Society of Women Engineers, but there are plenty of options in the LGBTQ, spiritual, tech-hobby realms as well. Fraternities and sororities have twenty-three chapters on campus, and a substantial but not overwhelming 7 percent of men and 5 percent of women participate in Greek life. Star speakers from all walks of life can frequently be heard on CMU's campus. Attending sports events is not among the most favored CMU pastimes, but the Tartans do compete in eight men's and nine women's sports in NCAA Division III. Plenty of club sports are available as well including badminton, cricket, and Alpine skiing.

Career Services

The Career and Professional Development Center at Carnegie Mellon produces enviable results for its students. A fantastically high number of graduates find their first jobs through internships (26 percent), career fairs (14 percent) Handshake (12 percent), or directly through their career advisor (11 percent). The university pours ample resources into career services, employing twenty-four full-time consultants, experiential learning coordinators, and employee relations specialists. That equates to a student-to-advisor ratio of 293:1, which is better than average when compared to the other institutions included in this book.

Carnegie Mellon University

E-mail: admission@andrew.cmu.edu | Website: www.cmu.edu

The office does a strong job of engaging with students, whether in person or virtually. Over three-quarters of undergrads login to Handshake to view the roughly 12,000 job and 5,000 internship postings. Many job search-related events focus on specific sectors such as the Civil & Environmental Engineering Career Fair, Energy Industry Career Fair, or Tepper Meetup (for business students). Multiple members of each class intern at companies that include Amazon, Deloitte, and JP Morgan Chase. In 2018-19, an impressive 488 companies recruited at the university and conducted 5,900 on-campus interviews. Close to 80 percent of undergraduates complete at least one internship. Possessing a heavy arsenal of industry connections and hands-on offerings, CMU's Career and Professional Development Center provides exemplary service to its undergraduates.

Professional Outcomes

By the end of the calendar year in which they received their diplomas, 61 percent of 2019 grads were employed, and 27 percent were continuing to graduate school. The companies that have routinely scooped up CMU grads include Google, Facebook, Microsoft, Uber, Apple, Disney Research, McKinsey, and Deloitte as well as Pittsburgh-based PNC Bank. Starting salaries for CMU grads are exceptionally high, due in part, of course, to the high number of engineering and computer science diplomas it awards, yet all Tartans tend to do well financially. With an average starting salary of over $90,000, CMU grads outpace the average starting salary for a college grad nationally ($51k) by a wide margin. Some majors offer even better remuneration, such as computer science ($118k), electrical and computer engineering ($112k), information systems ($100k), and business ($81k). While some do remain in Pittsburgh, graduates flock in large numbers to San Francisco, New York, and DC.

Of those pursuing graduate education, around 20 percent typically enroll immediately in PhD programs. A perusal of the schools where recent grads have decided to continue their education is a who's who of the Ivy League and includes MIT, Caltech, and Stanford as well as Carnegie Mellon itself (a popular choice). In 2018-19, there were fifty-nine CMU applicants to medical school. Recent grads have gone on to medical institutions at Harvard, Rutgers, Temple, UMass, and SUNY Downstate Medical Center. Those entering law school are currently studying at elite schools including UVA, Columbia, Penn, Yale, and Georgetown.

Admission

Carnegie Mellon received 27,634 applications in 2019, roughly double the number that applied a decade ago. The overall acceptance rate for the Class of 2023 was 15 percent, however, since applicants apply to one of the six schools within the university, it's essential to examine a school-specific breakdown. Further, those applying to the College of Fine Arts (CFA) must indicate their intended area of study from six choices. Acceptance rates vary greatly from program to program. For example, in 2019-20 only 7 percent of applicants were accepted into the School of Computer Science (SCS) while 26 percent were accepted into the Dietrich College of Humanities and Social Sciences (DC). Within the DC, School of Architecture applicants enjoyed a robust 34 percent admit rate while among School of Drama applicants, the percent admitted was an infinitesimal 4 percent. You can apply to more than one program at CMU, but you must fill out separate applications, pay the fee for each, and meet the unique requirements for every school you apply to.

The 50 percent SAT range for students admitted into the CFA was 1340-1520; for the SCS it as a markedly more competitive 1570-1580. The average GPA ranges from 3.77-3.92 on a 4.0 scale. Successful applicants to CMU have taken the most rigorous high school schedules available to them, and the school also lists work experience, volunteer work, and extracurriculars among the most important factors for admission. Additionally, it is worth highlighting the fact that women fared much better than their male counterparts, being admitted at a 21 percent rate versus less than 12 percent for men.

Worth Your Money?

A Carnegie Mellon education carries an annual cost of attendance of $76,874 that, for most attendees (except fine arts and many humanities students), will be less than their starting salary when they graduate. While it does not meet 100 percent of the demonstrated financial aid for all qualifying students, the 43 percent of students who receive financial aid see grants averaging $47k. With few exceptions, a degree from Carnegie Mellon is worth taking on a bit of debt. The average amount owed by graduates is $31,000, right around the average college debt nationwide.

FINANCIAL
Institutional Type: Private
In-State Tuition: $57,560
Out-of-State Tuition: $57,560
Room & Board: $15,550
Required Fees: $1,364
Books & Supplies: $2,400

Avg. Need-Based Grant: $43,599
Avg. % of Need Met: 99%

Avg. Merit-Based Award: $12,151
% Receiving (All Freshmen): 16%
% Receiving (Freshmen w/o Need): 2%

Avg. Cumulative Debt: $31,342
% of Students Borrowing: 52%

CAREER
Who Recruits
1. PNC
2. Uber
3. Epic
4. Google
5. Goldman Sachs

Notable Internships
1. GoDaddy
2. Microsoft
3. Chicago Trading Company

Top Industries
1. Engineering
2. Business
3. Education
4. Information Technology
5. Research

Top Employers
1. Google
2. Microsoft
3. Facebook
4. Amazon
5. Apple

Where Alumni Work
1. Pittsburgh
2. San Francisco
3. New York City
4. Washington DC
5. Boston

Median Earnings
College Scorecard (Early Career): $83,600
PayScale (Early Career): $80,800
PayScale (Mid-Career): $144,500

RANKINGS
Money: 117
U.S. News: 26 (T), National Universities
Wall Street Journal/THE: 20
Washington Monthly: 79, National Universities

COLLEGE OVERLAPS
Cornell University
Massachusetts Institute of Technology
Princeton University
University of California, Berkeley
University of Michigan

Case Western Reserve University

Cleveland, Ohio | 216-368-4450

ADMISSION
Admission Rate: 27%
Admission Rate - Men: 26%
Admission Rate - Women: 28%
EA Admission Rate: 32%
ED Admission Rate: 39%
ED Admits as % of Total Admits: 3%
Admission Rate (5-Year Trend): -15%
% of Admits Attending (Yield): 17%
Transfer Admission Rate: 25%

SAT Reading/Writing (Middle 50%): 640-720
SAT Math (Middle 50%): 700-790
ACT Composite (Middle 50%): 30-34

% Graduated in Top 10% of HS Class: 70%
% Graduated in Top 25% of HS Class: 92%
% Graduated in Top 50% of HS Class: 99%

Demonstrated Interest: Considered
Legacy Status: Considered
Admission Interview Offered: Yes

ENROLLMENT
Total Undergraduate Enrollment: 5,383
% Part-Time: 3%
% Male: 54%
% Female: 46%
% Out-of-State: 72%
% Fraternity: 36%
% Sorority: 34%
% On-Campus (Freshman): 97%
% On-Campus (All Undergraduate): 80%

% African-American: 5%
% Asian: 21%
% Hispanic: 9%
% White: 45%
% Other: 5%
% Race or Ethnicity Unknown: 1%
% International: 14%
% Low-Income: 19%

ACADEMICS
Student-to-Faculty Ratio: 11 to 1
% of Classes Under 20: 50%
% of Classes 20-49: 37%
% of Classes 50 or More: 14%
% Full-Time Faculty: 78%
% Full-Time Faculty w/ Terminal Degree: 91%

Top Programs
Accounting
Biochemistry
Biology
Biomedical Engineering
Business Management
Electrical Engineering
Nursing

Retention Rate: 93%
4-Year Graduation Rate: 68%
6-Year Graduation Rate: 84%

Curricular Flexibility: Somewhat Flexible
Academic Rating: ★★★★

#CollegesWorthYourMoney

A private, midsize institution in Cleveland, Ohio, Case Western Reserve University (CWRU) is a school whose reputation and selectivity are among the fastest risers in the nation. Long an engineering powerhouse with a rich history of technical education, there has been a recent, sharp rise in the caliber of students clamoring to join this undergraduate student body of almost 5,400. In fact, the university granted acceptance to close to three-quarters of applicants a mere decade ago; today, that figure is sliding toward one-quarter.

Inside the Classroom
Unlike many schools of its ilk, CWRU has a single-door admission policy. Those accepted into the broader university are free to pursue any of the nearly one hundred areas of concentration. All students must complete four seminars called SAGEs (one first-year seminar, two university seminars, and one in the major), and two semesters of physical education. From there, most requirements are school/major specific. In their final year, students must conquer the senior capstone, which can take many forms, but it must be designed in consultation with a faculty member.

Sporting an 11:1 faculty-to-student ratio, the university does a nice job keeping classes on the small side with 50 percent of course sections capped at nineteen and only 14 percent of courses having fifty students or more. An exceptional 81 percent of students have the opportunity to participate in undergraduate research as the school places heavy emphasis on experiential learning. The same goes for international experiences. Case Western has a high rate of undergraduates who elect to study abroad; just under half spend a semester in a foreign land.

The Weatherhead School of Management and the Case School of Engineering have stellar reputations within the worlds of employment and academia. Engineering is the most commonly conferred undergraduate degree at 31 percent followed by the social sciences (11 percent), biology (10 percent), business (10 percent), and computer science (8 percent). In a typical year, Case Western produces between two and four Fulbright Scholars as well as Churchill Scholars and NSF Fellowship recipients. The school counts sixteen Nobel Prize winners among its alumni and faculty, past and present.

Outside the Classroom
The main campus covers 155 acres, not including a verdant 389-acre, university-owned farm located only ten miles away. Freshmen and sophomores are required to live on campus and almost three-quarters of the overall undergraduate student body reside on the university's grounds. First-year students live in one of four residential colleges designed to foster a sense of community and belonging. Greek life is thriving with twenty-seven fraternities and sororities attracting 36 percent of men and 34 percent of women. An academically focused student body does not pay a ton of attention to the school's nineteen NCAA Division III sports teams. There are over 200 student-run groups, including plenty of opportunities for intramural athletics, volunteer work, and faith-based connections. CWRUbotix, the school's robotics team, has placed near the top of various national competitions in recent years. Case Western's proximity to downtown Cleveland makes off-campus excursions popular even though the immediate surroundings of East Cleveland are less than ideal. An endless array of restaurants, museums, concerts, and professional sporting events are easily within reach for those willing to take an occasional break from studying.

Career Services
The Career Center at CWRU includes fourteen full-time staff members, equating to a student-to-advisor ratio of 385:1, similar to the average institution included in this book. The office is guided by a Four-Phase Plan designed to cultivate career-oriented thinking from freshman through senior year. CWRU has implemented the Student Success Initiative in which each freshman is assigned to a "navigator," a single staff person who remains the student's contact throughout the student's time at the school. Workshops are regularly offered on basic topics such as resume development, internship search strategies, interviewing, and graduate school preparation. Two major career fairs take place each year: the University Career Fair held in October and the Get Experienced! Internship & Career Fair held in February.

Case Western Reserve University

E-mail: admission@case.edu | Website: www.case.edu

Annually, more than 300 employers, from global corporations to start-ups, conduct on-campus interviews with undergraduates. Case Western has fifteen official career center partners including IBM Watson Health, GE, Progressive Insurance, and Yelp. A healthy 81 percent of those landing jobs did so in an area relevant to their college major. Thanks to a strong emphasis on hands-on education, 98 percent of graduates report having the opportunity to engage in some type of experiential learning. Those opportunities include both traditional internships and more structured 560-hour practicums. Two-thirds of students complete at least one internship during their undergraduate years. In a given year, more than a handful of Case Western students land internships at organizations including NASA, Proctor & Gamble, Amazon, and Deloitte.

Professional Outcomes

Fifty-four percent of 2019 CWRU graduates head into the world of professional employment upon receiving their diplomas; only 6 percent were still looking for work six months after leaving the university. Members of the Class of 2019 enjoyed a median salary range of $65,999-$69,999. The employers of the greatest number of graduates included the Cleveland Clinic, University Hospitals, Accenture, Microsoft, Deloitte, and Google. Many alumni also presently work for IBM, Medtronic, EY, and PwC. Nearly 40 percent work in the engineering field, 11 percent enter nursing, and 10 percent find employment in the research realm. A good number of alumni stay in the Cleveland area, but San Francisco and New York are other common destinations.

Of the 37 percent of graduates who decide to enroll in an advanced degree program after completing their undergraduate work, many are accepted by elite graduate schools. In 2019, five or more grads were accepted to continue their studies at the likes of Boston University, Columbia University, Johns Hopkins University, the University of Chicago, and Penn. However, the most popular option is to continue studying at Case Western as 44 percent of those going on to graduate school elect to stay on the CWRU campus. Of those going directly into graduate/professional studies, between 13 and 23 percent have gone on to medical school in recent years. Only 4 percent of those going to graduate school chose to pursue a law degree.

Admission

Case Western received a record 28,786 applications for admittance into its Class of 2023 and accepted an all-time low of 27 percent. For comparison, only a decade ago Case Western received a little over 7,300 applications and accepted 73 percent of those students. SAT/ACT scores in the 75th percentile for incoming freshmen back then would barely crack the 25th percentile now. Freshmen in 2019-20 boasted a middle-50 percent SAT of 1360-1480 and a 30-34 on the ACT. Seventy percent of successful applicants finished in the top 10 percent of their high school classes and 92 percent placed in the top 25 percent.

This increasingly selective admissions committee ranks five factors as "very important": rigor of secondary school record, class rank, GPA, standardized test scores, and extracurricular activities. Essays, recommendation letters, interviews, volunteer work, ethnic status, talent/ability, and personal qualities comprise the second tier of considerations. Case Western offers an early action as well as ED I & ED II rounds. Those applying early find success at close to twice the rate of regular round applicants—39 percent versus 23 percent in applications for the Class of 2023. We often see schools make massive jumps in selectivity over the course of a generation where a warning of "This isn't your mother's/father's fill-in-the-blank university" would be apt. Yet, with CWSU, "This isn't your older sibling's Case Western" is a far more accurate statement. Exponential leaps in the profile of the average accepted student have created an extremely competitive environment, so applying prior to the regular cycle is a much-needed admissions edge.

Worth Your Money?

A Case Western degree will cost you $72k per year if you do not qualify for any need-based or merit aid. Fortunately, there aren't many students who fail to qualify for some sort of tuition reduction. Need-based aid is awarded to 56 percent of students, and the average award is over $37k; the majority of those eligible see 100 percent of their demonstrated need met by the university. When all is said and done, graduates possess reasonable levels of postsecondary debt relative to the national average. Higher-than-average starting salaries make repaying those loans a doable task.

FINANCIAL
Institutional Type: Private
In-State Tuition: $52,448
Out-of-State Tuition: $52,448
Room & Board: $16,080
Required Fees: $598
Books & Supplies: $1,200

Avg. Need-Based Grant: $37,456
Avg. % of Need Met: 100%

Avg. Merit-Based Award: $23,188
% Receiving (All Freshmen): 54%
% Receiving (Freshmen w/o Need): 36%

Avg. Cumulative Debt: $33,946
% of Students Borrowing: 44%

CAREER
Who Recruits
1. Progressive Insurance
2. Lubrizol Corporation
3. Rockwell Automation
4. Amazon
5. The MetroHealth System

Notable Internships
1. Merck
2. Deloitte
3. MITRE

Top Industries
1. Business
2. Healthcare
3. Education
4. Engineering
5. Research

Top Employers
1. Cleveland Clinic
2. University Hospitals
3. Rockwell Automation
4. IBM
5. Microsoft

Where Alumni Work
1. Cleveland
2. New York City
3. San Francisco
4. Washington DC
5. Chicago

Median Earnings
College Scorecard (Early Career): $74,600
PayScale (Early Career): $69,700
PayScale (Mid-Career): $127,000

RANKINGS
Money: 236
U.S. News: 42 (T), National Universities
Wall Street Journal/THE: 48
Washington Monthly: 132, National Universities

COLLEGE OVERLAPS
Carnegie Mellon University
Ohio State University - Columbus
Purdue University - West Lafayette
University of Michigan
University of Rochester

Claremont McKenna College

Claremont, California | 909-621-8088

ADMISSION
Admission Rate: 10%
Admission Rate - Men: 10%
Admission Rate - Women: 10%
EA Admission Rate: Not Offered
ED Admission Rate: 28%
ED Admits as % of Total Admits: 31%
Admission Rate (5-Year Trend): -1%
% of Admits Attending (Yield): 52%
Transfer Admission Rate: 10%

SAT Reading/Writing (Middle 50%): 670-730
SAT Math (Middle 50%): 690-780
ACT Composite (Middle 50%): 31-34

% Graduated in Top 10% of HS Class: 83%
% Graduated in Top 25% of HS Class: 100%
% Graduated in Top 50% of HS Class: 100%

Demonstrated Interest: Not Considered
Legacy Status: Considered
Admission Interview Offered: Yes

ENROLLMENT
Total Undergraduate Enrollment: 1,343
% Part-Time: 0%
% Male: 51%
% Female: 49%
% Out-of-State: 55%
% Fraternity: Not Offered
% Sorority: Not Offered
% On-Campus (Freshman): 100%
% On-Campus (All Undergraduate): 96%

% African-American: 4%
% Asian: 11%
% Hispanic: 15%
% White: 41%
% Other: 7%
% Race or Ethnicity Unknown: 5%
% International: 16%
% Low-Income: 16%

ACADEMICS
Student-to-Faculty Ratio: 8 to 1
% of Classes Under 20: 83%
% of Classes 20-49: 16%
% of Classes 50 or More: 2%
% Full-Time Faculty: 87%
% Full-Time Faculty w/ Terminal Degree: 99%

Top Programs
Accounting
Economics
Environment, Economics, and Politics (EEP)
Government
History
International Relations
Philosophy, Politics, and Economics
Psychology

Retention Rate: 95%
4-Year Graduation Rate: 84%
6-Year Graduation Rate: 91%

Curricular Flexibility: Very Flexible
Academic Rating: ★★★★★

#CollegesWorthYourMoney

Start with your average elite liberal arts college in the Northeast, cut the size of the student body in half, replace stuffy Gothic edifices with a modern California feel, and physically connect the campus to four other elite schools whose premier offerings can all be shared communally. That's the recipe for Claremont McKenna College (CMC), a liberal arts school that is home to 1,343 bright and motivated undergraduates and is a founding member of the Claremont Consortium that is comprised of four additional undergraduate institutions: Pomona, Pitzer, Scripps, and Harvey Mudd.

Inside the Classroom
CMC offers thirty-two majors and eleven "sequences," series of courses that can be completed across the neighboring schools in addition to one's major. Registering for courses in one or more of the other Claremont Colleges is a staple of academic life at CMC; 99 percent of undergrads do so. An academically focused group, 32 percent of the student population ends up completing a double major. No matter your academic pursuit, required courses will include a first-year writing seminar, a humanities seminar, multiple semesters of a foreign language, a laboratory science, a math or computer science course, physical education and—of most significance—a senior thesis.

The college boasts an average class size of eighteen, and 83 percent of course sections have fewer than twenty students. With an 8:1 student-to-faculty ratio and only one graduate program offered (an MA in finance), undergrads benefit from ample professor attention. In the 2018-19 school year an incredible 75 percent of CMC students had the chance to conduct research with a faculty member, and the school has eleven partner research institutes and centers that provide graduate-level research experiences. Studying abroad is another popular pursuit as CMC offers approved programs on each of the world's six populated continents. Thirty-nine percent of undergrads spend time at one of 115 approved programs in forty countries.

Economics, government, international relations, and psychology are the most popular majors, and among the strongest. Interdisciplinary majors such as Environment, Economics, and Politics (EEP) and Philosophy, Politics and Economics (PPE) also carry outstanding reputations. Claremont graduates annually have representation of Fulbright, US Department of State Critical Language, and Luce Scholarships. Per capita, it is often among the top ten in Fulbright production, boasting five winners in 2019.

Outside the Classroom
Academically, students attending any of the Claremont Colleges are used to crossing campuses to take courses at one of the other schools. Those permeable borders apply to life outside the classroom as well. Pomona, Pitzer, Scripps, Harvey Mudd, and CMC are all located on the same 560-acre property, and many activities are joint efforts between members of the consortium. Even Claremont McKenna's twenty-one NCAA athletic teams are combined squads with Harvey Mudd and Scripps student-athletes; it has won over 300 conference championships since its founding in 1958. Not everything is a shared-venture; there are seventy CMC-exclusive student- run organizations of the academic, identity-based, service, sports, or music/arts nature. The Model UN team has won the world championship four of the last five years. An endless flow of public speakers grace the stage at the Marian Miner Cook Athenaeum that presents guest lectures four nights per week. With 96 percent of CMC students electing to live on campus and no fraternities or sororities, campus life is an open and vibrant experience. Most facilities are shared among the members of the consortium, including the eight-lane pool; Roberts Pavilion, which includes a 2,200 seat arena and a state-of-the-art fitness center; and the Collins Dining Hall, which garners solid culinary reviews. Situated thirty-five miles east of Los Angeles, all of the culture and excitement you could want is never more than a relatively quick car ride away. The SoCal beaches are about an hour drive as is Disneyland and Joshua Tree National Park.

Career Services
The Claremont McKenna Career Services Office has nine full-time professional staff members working on grad school/career advising and employer relations and internship procurement. That equates to a 150:1 student-to-advisor ratio, which is superior to just about every college featured in our guidebook. The college aims to provide individualized career coaching to all of its students and begins that process freshman year. It even has a counselor solely dedicated to the school's 350 first-year students, and that counselor met with 93 percent of the class that entered last year. Annual fall career expos attract representatives from more than one hundred top employers. Events like company information sessions, two-to-five-day networking treks, and job shadowing experiences take place frequently throughout the year.

Employers recruiting at CMC include Google, Deloitte, Bain, the CIA, NASA, Goldman Sachs, and the National Football League. A phenomenal 94 percent of students participate in at least one internship. Many of those are financially supported by the Sponsored Internship Experiences Program that provided between $500 and $8,000 grants for 340 students in 2018. In a single school year, staff conducted 3,000 one-on-one counseling appointments, enticed forty-four employers into recruiting on campus, and facilitated 581 on-campus interviews, more than one per member of the senior class. Thanks to that focus on hands-on experience, strong employer relations, and ample resources (including personnel), Claremont McKenna's career services easily earns the highest praise from the College Transitions' staff.

Professional Outcomes

Eighty five percent of graduates have found employment within six months of graduation, and only 4 percent are still looking for work. Financial services/accounting, consulting, and technology are the most frequently entered sectors. Companies employing the highest number of graduates include Accenture, Ernst & Young, Goldman Sachs, Amazon, Deloitte, and JP Morgan. The median starting salary for a Claremont grad is $67,000, a particularly impressive figure for a liberal arts college.

You name the prestigious graduate/professional program and, chances are, a recent CMC grad (or two or three) is presently studying there. Since 2004, many alumni have enrolled at USC (81), UCLA (77), Stanford (55), and Columbia (53). In the last four years, students have been accepted to medical schools at Stanford, Emory, Harvard, Johns Hopkins, and Penn. Students also have enjoyed law school acceptances at institutions including Columbia, NYU, Berkeley, the University of Chicago, and Yale. The list of MBA and other graduate programs attended by alumni is similarly eye-popping. Ten years out, 15 percent of the total alumni have earned a law degree, 5 percent a PhD, 4 percent a medical degree, and 10 percent have completed an MBA.

Admission

CMC's acceptance rate dipped into the single digits each of the past two cycles but climbed back up to 10.3 percent for the Class of 2023. The mid-50 percent test scores of freshmen entering in 2019-20 were a 1380-1490 on the SAT and a 31-34 on the ACT. The vast majority, 83 percent, placed in the top 10 percent of their high school class, and 100 percent landed in the top quartile. Claremont McKenna has trended in the more selective direction in recent years. A handful of years ago, the acceptance rate was a slightly higher 12 percent, median test scores were 1410/31, and fewer students placed in the top 10 percent of their graduating classes.

The process is a holistic one with seven factors deemed "very important" by the admissions committee: rigor of secondary coursework, class rank, GPA, standardized test scores, recommendations, extracurricular activities, and character/personal qualities. First-generation status is listed as a factor that is merely "considered," yet 21 percent of the Class of 2023 met that criterion. Applying early decision is a worthwhile strategic maneuver as the ED acceptance rate tends to be up to four times that of the regular cycle; in 2019, it was 28 percent versus 8 percent in the regular round. To gain admission into CMC applicants should bring exceptional credentials, as expected at any highly selective liberal arts college. There are sometimes surprise decisions here. For example, in looking at the freshman class of 2019-20, just 1.7 percent possessed an SAT score below 1200. However, in general, students should be closer to the mean to have a genuine chance at being granted admission.

Worth Your Money?

Over two-fifths of CMC undergrads qualify for need-based financial aid, taking home an annual grant averaging $56,137, helping make the $76,475 sticker price a bit more manageable. Those who can pay full price at Claremont McKenna likely will, and there are plenty of students capable of handling the bill. Tax return data estimates that nearly 50 percent come from families with incomes in the top 5 percent nationally. Whether you're a full-paying student or the recipient of generous aid, CMC's strong academics, sterling reputation and incredible career service offerings will more than justify your investment in this top-notch liberal arts school.

FINANCIAL
Institutional Type: Private
In-State Tuition: $56,475
Out-of-State Tuition: $56,475
Room & Board: $17,300
Required Fees: $0
Books & Supplies: $0

Avg. Need-Based Grant: $56,137
Avg. % of Need Met: 100%

Avg. Merit-Based Award: $24,447
% Receiving (All Freshmen): 19%
% Receiving (Freshmen w/o Need): 2%

Avg. Cumulative Debt: $21,450
% of Students Borrowing: 36%

CAREER
Who Recruits
1. Cloudfare, Inc.
2. United Talent Agency
3. Whittier Trust Company
4. Boston Pharmaceuticals
5. Morgan Stanley

Notable Internships
1. BlackRock
2. Adidas
3. House of Representatives

Top Industries
1. Business
2. Education
3. Finance
4. Operations
5. Research

Top Employers
1. Deloitte
2. Google
3. Microsoft
4. EY
5. Accenture

Where Alumni Work
1. Los Angeles
2. San Francisco
3. New York City
4. Seattle
5. Orange County, CA

Median Earnings
College Scorecard (Early Career): $72,900
PayScale (Early Career): $73,800
PayScale (Mid-Career): $150,000

RANKINGS
Money: 82
U.S. News: 6 (T), Liberal Arts Colleges
Wall Street Journal/THE: 35
Washington Monthly: 9, Liberal Arts Colleges

COLLEGE OVERLAPS
Georgetown University
Pomona College
University of California, Berkeley
University of California, Los Angeles
University of Southern California

Clark University

Worcester, Massachusetts | 508-793-8821

Founded as a graduate-only institution in 1887, Clark has been a cutting-edge undergraduate institution for the last 117 years, from hosting a series of lectures by Sigmund Freud to being at the forefront of AIDS research to starting the first PhD program in Holocaust and Genocide Studies. Today, Clark University continues to beat its own drum, with a unique liberal arts program focused on experiential learning, community service, and the pursuit of a meaningful life's work. With an undergraduate enrollment of just 2,349, this school offers the intimacy of a liberal arts college with the research emphasis of a university.

Inside the Classroom
Freshmen must begin their collegiate experience with a First Year Intensive (FYI) course capped at 16 students and designed to forge close relationships with students and a professor with similar academic interests to your own. This FYI professor then becomes your academic advisor for the rest of your time at Clark. All students complete eight Program of Liberal Studies courses over their four years and must take one course (each) categorized as verbal expression, formal analysis, aesthetic perspective, global comparative perspective, historical perspective, language and culture perspective, natural scientific perspective, and values perspective. As seniors, students will complete a capstone project that "addresses a significant issue, problem, or theme" in their field of study.

Class sizes are fairly small with 15 percent containing fewer than 10 students and 54 percent having an enrollment of under 20. The average undergraduate class size is exactly 20 students. As a result, strong working relationships with faculty routinely develop. An impressive 67 percent of students participate in undergraduate research at some point in their four years of study. Study abroad opportunities are seized upon by 30 percent of students who travel to one of 50 available programs in 20+ countries.

Psychology and geography are two standout departments at Clark, and psychology (18 percent) is actually the school's most commonly conferred degree. Biology (10 percent), visual and performing arts (8 percent) and management (6 percent) are next in popularity. Clark's reputation with employers and grad schools is solid, and alumni tend to also fare well in the procurement of prestigious postgraduate scholarships and fellowships. In 2019, four Clark grads landed Fulbright Scholarships. The university also produced an astonishing nine Gilman Scholars in 2018.

Outside the Classroom
Almost two-thirds of undergrads at Clark live off campus, however, among first-year students, 98 percent reside in university-owned housing. The university does not allow fraternities or sororities on campus, which leads to a less-cliquish, fairly cohesive student body. Clark undergrads crack many lists of "happiest students" and tend to be, in general, an extroverted and liberally inclined bunch. With 17 (7 men's, 10 women's) NCAA Division III sports teams (the Cougars) and 130 student-run organizations, most Clarkies are involved in some type of extracurricular activity. The volunteering spirit is huge at Clark; 20 student groups based on volunteering as well as the school's own Community Engagement Office help connect undergrads to charitable efforts in the Worcester area. The Worcester area, previously a deterrent to many college applicants, now provides a surprising number of recreational opportunities—Shrewsbury Street is lined with more than 40 restaurants offering any type of cuisine imaginable. The CitySquare area just received a $500 million transformation and is now brimming with retail and dining options. For those up for a longer trip, downtown Boston is just an hour away, and New York City is about a three-hour car ride from campus.

Career Services
The Liberal Arts & Effective Practice (LEEP) Center is staffed by nine professional staff members who specialize in advising students in the various majors; one counselor works with students applying to prestigious scholarships or fellowship programs. This student-to-advisor ratio of 249:1 is lower than the average institution included in this book. Individualized support is offered in the form of career advising sessions, resume development, interest inventories, and networking assistance. Beyond these traditional career services offerings, LEEP is guided by its stated mission to provide students with experiential learning opportunities in an effort to help them parlay their academic studies into "a meaningful life and career."

LEEP's annual Fall Career and Internship Fair is on the small side, with roughly 25 employers attending, including notables such as the FBI, Booz Allen Hamilton, and Fidelity Investments. It also hosts the On-Campus Job & Internship Fair each February with approximately 35 organizations in attendance. Clark students are also encouraged to attend off-campus job fairs such as the career fair at Worcester State University. Overall, career center staff engage with over 250 employers per year. The reported number of academic internships during the fall and spring semesters, 125 per year, represents a fairly low percentage of the overall student body. However, many additional students pursue internships during the summer term.

Professional Outcomes

Six months after graduation, 98 percent of Cougars have clawed their way into gainful employment or full-time graduate programs. The companies/organizations that employ the largest number of Clark grads include Amazon, the Clinton Foundation, Google, IBM, Microsoft, National Geographic, and Fidelity Investments. Sectors employing the greatest number of alumni are business development, education, and information technology. At age 34, alumni salaries are comparable to those from other Bay State institutions such as Simmons, Mount Holyoke, and UMASS but significantly lower than elite liberal arts schools like Tufts, Amherst, or Brandeis. The bulk of Clark diploma-holders stay in the Greater Boston area. New York City and Washington, DC, are next in popularity.

Of the 44 percent of freshly minted alumni who enrolled in graduate school, a good number continued their education at Clark or at nearby universities such as UMASS-Amherst, Boston College, and Boston University. Recent grads also found homes in highly selective graduate programs such as Brown University, NYU, Penn, USC, and the University of Cambridge. Clark does not produce a large number of students who go on to prestigious law schools, however, recent grads have earned acceptances into UNC's and Notre Dame's law programs. Those applying to medical school do have a strong track record of finding a home—Clark claims an acceptance rate 50 percent better than the national average.

Admission

Clark received approximately 7,600 applications for a place in the Class of 2023 and accepted 53 percent of applicants. A test-optional university, freshmen who submitted standardized test scores had a middle-50th percentile range of 1180-1370 on the SAT and a 27-31 on the ACT. Perfect grades and being positioned at the top of your high school class are not prerequisites at Clark—just 27 percent ranked in the top decile, 67 percent in the top quartile, and 94 percent in the top half. The mean GPA for the Class of 2023 was 3.66. The school attracted students from 40 US states and 27 countries into this group. The largest numbers of students came from Massachusetts followed by New York, Connecticut, California, and Maine.

Clark assigns the most weight to three factors: rigor of coursework, GPA, and letters of recommendation. The next tier of factors in terms of importance are essays, extracurricular activities, talent/ability, character/personal qualities, and volunteer work. Early decision and early action are both options for those with a strong interest in the university, however, the acceptance rate for those early rounds is typically comparable to the regular cycle. A realistic landing spot for those with a B average in a rigorous high school course load, Clark's test-optional status makes it an attainable destination for solid, but less-than-perfect, applicants.

Worth Your Money?

Clark's list price cost of attendance (COA) is $58,402, but 85 percent of students receive some type of institutional aid. The university awards merit scholarships at four different levels with annual values of $10k, $15k, $20k, and full COA. Even the full sticker price is equal to the tuition alone at many private schools in the state of Massachusetts, making it a relative bargain. With 98 percent of graduates finding their next stop very quickly, it is no shock that the loan default rate for Clark alumni is less than half of the national average. With some level of institutional aid, the cost of attending Clark can be well worth it for the small class sizes, undergraduate research opportunities, and personalized career services offerings.

FINANCIAL
Institutional Type: Private
In-State Tuition: $48,250
Out-of-State Tuition: $48,250
Room & Board: $9,800
Required Fees: $352
Books & Supplies: $800

Avg. Need-Based Grant: $28,463
Avg. % of Need Met: 92%

Avg. Merit-Based Award: $18,034
% Receiving (All Freshmen): 46%
% Receiving (Freshmen w/o Need): 32%

Avg. Cumulative Debt: $34,390
% of Students Borrowing: 61%

CAREER
Who Recruits
1. Reliant Medical Group
2. Eaton Vance
3. Microsoft
4. Fidelity
5. Dana-Farber Cancer Institute

Notable Internships
1. American Red Cross
2. Mountain Health
3. IBM

Top Industries
1. Business
2. Education
3. Infromation Technology
4. Operations
5. Social Services

Top Employers
1. Fidelity Investments
2. UMass Medical School
3. Public Consulting Group
4. Dell EMC
5. IBM

Where Alumni Work
1. Boston
2. New York City
3. Washington DC
4. San Francisco
5. Poland (Europe)

Median Earnings
College Scorecard (Early Career): $49,100
PayScale (Early Career): $56,000
PayScale (Mid-Career): $119,500

RANKINGS
Money: 377
U.S. News: 103 (T), National Universities
Wall Street Journal/THE: 208 (T)
Washington Monthly: 164, National Universities

COLLEGE OVERLAPS
American University
Boston University
Northeastern University
University of Massachusetts Amherst
University of Vermont

ADMISSION
Admission Rate: 75%
Admission Rate - Men: 76%
Admission Rate - Women: 72%
EA Admission Rate: Not Offered
ED Admission Rate: 83%
ED Admits as % of Total Admits: 2%
Admission Rate (5-Year Trend): +11%
% of Admits Attending (Yield): 16%
Transfer Admission Rate: 80%

SAT Reading/Writing (Middle 50%): 560-660
SAT Math (Middle 50%): 600-690
ACT Composite (Middle 50%): 23-30

% Graduated in Top 10% of HS Class: 37%
% Graduated in Top 25% of HS Class: 69%
% Graduated in Top 50% of HS Class: 94%

Demonstrated Interest: Considered
Legacy Status: Considered
Admission Interview Offered: Yes

ENROLLMENT
Total Undergraduate Enrollment: 3,081
% Part-Time: <1%
% Male: 69%
% Female: 31%
% Out-of-State: 31%
% Fraternity: 14%
% Sorority: 11%
% On-Campus (Freshman): 94%
% On-Campus (All Undergraduate): 82%

% African-American: 3%
% Asian: 4%
% Hispanic: 5%
% White: 79%
% Other: 4%
% Race or Ethnicity Unknown: 2%
% International: 3%
% Low-Income: 24%

ACADEMICS
Student-to-Faculty Ratio: 14 to 1
% of Classes Under 20: 53%
% of Classes 20-49: 30%
% of Classes 50 or More: 17%
% Full-Time Faculty: 71%
% Full-Time Faculty w/ Terminal Degree: 84%

Top Programs
Biology
Civil Engineering
Environmental Engineering
Environmental Science and Policy
Global Supply Chain Management
Innovation and Entrepreneurship
Mechanical Engineering

Retention Rate: 91%
4-Year Graduation Rate: 63%
6-Year Graduation Rate: 81%

Curricular Flexibility: Somewhat Flexible
Academic Rating: ★★★

#CollegesWorthYourMoney

Among the lesser-known of the Upstate New York schools, Clarkson University is even further north than Syracuse, Rochester, or Buffalo. For perspective, it would take a six-hour drive to reach Potsdam from New York City. The good news is that Clarkson's remote location makes getting in much easier than at comparable small, engineering-heavy schools like Lehigh University, Lafayette College, or Union College. The student body is comprised of close to 3,100 undergraduate students pursuing more than fifty programs in engineering, business, the arts, education, and sciences and health professions.

Inside the Classroom
All Golden Knights are required to complete the Common Experience Curriculum that includes a First-Year Experience course on adjustment to college life, the Clarkson Seminar, which is an introduction to college-level thinking and writing, and five courses that adequately cover the six broad areas of knowledge: cultures and societies; contemporary and global issues; imaginative arts; science, technology, and society; economics and organizations; and individual and group behavior. The four common threads in all of the introductory coursework are communication, diversity, ethics, and recognizing how technology can better serve humanity. Students in the business and engineering schools have a fairly rigid schedule of courses the first two years of study. For instance, all business students take Principles of Microeconomics their first semester and Principles of Macroeconomics second semester.

A student-to-faculty ratio of 14:1 translates to reasonable undergraduate class sizes. Fifty-three percent of sections enroll fewer than twenty students, but there are a mix of fifty or more or even one hundred or more student sections for some introductory courses. Undergraduate research is embedded in the Honors Program that admits forty to fifty students each year. Everyone else can apply to programs like the Research Experience for Undergrads (REU) that offers a ten-week apprenticeship funded by the National Science Foundation. Within the Biology Department, for example, all students are strongly encouraged to engage in research during their four years via the REU program, departmental connection, or by completing a senior thesis and presenting the findings at the Clarkson Symposium for Undergraduate Research. The school also offers thirty-seven study abroad programs in twenty countries but, as at most engineering-focused schools, the participation is low, approaching 10 percent.

An overwhelming 54 percent of undergrads are studying in the Coulter School of Engineering, 25 percent in the business school, and 21 percent in the School of Arts and Sciences. Overshadowed in most ranking systems by large research institutions, the School of Engineering is, nevertheless, a stud whose quality is fully recognized by big-time employers well outside the region. The National Science Foundation awarded two engineering undergrads and one biology student their prestigious Graduate Research Fellowship in 2019.

Outside the Classroom
Clarkson students tend to be proud nerds. As the admissions office states, "If the idea of working all night on an animated video for physics class sounds more like fun than work, you'll fit right in at Clarkson." This school has a 69 percent male, 31 percent female student body, which impacts the make-up of the social scene. The presence of SUNY Potsdam and its 58 percent female student body does help even the town's gender divide a bit. Four in five undergrads live on campus in one of eight dorm buildings or in one of the four apartment complexes. Additional Living-Learning Communities bring together students with common interests in areas like robotics, gaming, or women in engineering/business. There are nine fraternities and four sororities that, together, attract 11-14 percent of students. The school's 225 intramural teams draw an incredible 80 percent of the student body into recreational athletics. NCAA Division I ice hockey is huge as this tiny powerhouse has produced approximately thirty NHL players in its history; the other ten teams participate in Division III. Overall, there are 250 student-run clubs and activities from which to choose. Like the woods? If so, you're in luck. Not only do you get to enjoy the 640 wooded acres on which the campus is set, but the grounds are adjacent to Adirondack Park that adds another six million acres (not a typo). Like to spend time in a major metropolitan area? You're not so lucky on that front—Ottawa and Montreal, Canada (both around a two-hour drive), are closer to Clarkson than any major American city.

Career Services
The Clarkson Career Center (CCC) is staffed by seven professionals with expertise in career coaching, employer relations, and graduate school advising. That works out to a 440:1 student-to-advisor ratio, which is in the average range compared to other schools in the guidebook. Despite its distance from major American cities, the CCC

still manages to entice companies to campus with regularity, and 200 come to the annual career fairs. Even more impressive are the office's efforts in arranging internship and co-op experiences; the rate of participation is near 100 percent, and many undergrads procure two or more placements. It's no wonder 95 percent of Clarkson grads end up finding a job directly related to their area of study.

A proactive office, the Clarkson Career Center has a reputation for seeking to connect personally with every student. Whether you are a freshman or a senior, staffers are equally happy to have you stop by to take a personality assessment, discuss career options one-on-one, work on your resume, or arrange an employer site visit. Golden Knights have a powerful alumni base to tap when it comes time for the job hunt. According to the university, among its 42,000 alumni, "One in five is already a CEO, senior executive, or owner of a company." Thanks to a thriving internship/co-op network that leads to fantastic employment/salary results for grads, the CCC gets high marks as an efficient and effective career services office.

Professional Outcomes

Within six months of graduation the Class of 2019 enjoyed a job/grad school placement rate of 97 percent and an average starting salary of $62,756. Annually, 170+ employers snatch up Clarkson seniors. Top employers of recent grads include BAE Systems, Amazon, IBM, General Electric, Lockheed Martin, and Pratt & Whitney. Other companies that historically hire large numbers of Golden Knights include GlobalFoundries, Corning Incorporated, Xerox, Siemens, Accenture, and Intel. While a fair number of graduates stay in Upstate New York—Utica, Syracuse, Albany, and Rochester rank as the third through sixth most popular cities—the Greater New York and Boston areas are the most common alumni destinations.

Only 15 percent of Class of 2019 members were pursuing advanced degrees immediately after completing their undergraduate education. Students from that cohort were admitted into graduate school at institutions including Duke, Georgia Tech, the University of Rochester, and Rochester Polytechnic Institute. Medical school is usually the direction of choice for around ten graduates each year. Medical school-bound students often attend SUNY schools, including SUNY Upstate Medical University, SUNY Stonybrook Medical School, and SUNY Buffalo Medical School. Recent grads also have landed at Dartmouth, Johns Hopkins, and Penn State. Remaining at Clarkson for graduate study is an option many also pursue, and the school offers approximately forty advanced degree programs.

Admission

In evaluating applicants for membership in the Class of 2023, Clarkson ultimately admitted 75 percent of the pool, pretty nice considering that your average engineering school of this quality typically possesses an admit rate that is a mere fraction of those generous figures. Still, many top students choose Clarkson as 37 percent of freshmen hailed from the top decile of their high school class, and almost 70 percent finished in the top 25 percent. The average high school GPA was 3.7, and the average test scores were 1255 on the SAT and 26 on the ACT. The admissions standards have toughened in recent years. Back in 2012, the university admitted 80 percent of those who applied, and the SAT range was 1100-1270, significantly lower than the 2018-19 freshman class, even when accounting for recent SAT inflation.

Two factors reign supreme in the minds of admissions officials—GPA and a rigorous high school curriculum. Factors on the next rung of importance include standardized test scores, class rank, extracurricular activities, recommendations, and volunteer work. The early decision acceptance rate is even friendlier than the regular round as 83 percent of ED applicants were admitted during the last cycle. A personal visit to Potsdam as well as a face-to-face informational interview with an admissions counselor is highly recommended. Clarkson remains a rare, strong engineering school that is open to B students with less-than-perfect test scores.

Worth Your Money?

The focus on engineering unsurprisingly raises starting salaries into a higher stratosphere than most schools of Clarkson's size. The list price of this university is roughly $69,000, including room and board, but merit and need-based aid are distributed generously; nine of ten students receive financial aid. Middle-class families can expect to pay closer to $30-35k per year in total costs which, depending on one's academic track, can lead to a terrific return on investment.

FINANCIAL
Institutional Type: Private
In-State Tuition: $52,724
Out-of-State Tuition: $52,724
Room & Board: $15,786
Required Fees: $0
Books & Supplies: $1,446

Avg. Need-Based Grant: $38,195
Avg. % of Need Met: 90%

Avg. Merit-Based Award: $32,143
% Receiving (All Freshmen): 33%
% Receiving (Freshmen w/o Need): 16%

Avg. Cumulative Debt: $29,000
% of Students Borrowing: 79%

CAREER
Who Recruits
1. Procter & Gamble
2. General Dynamics
3. Tecnica Group
4. Whiting-Turner
5. Novelis

Notable Internships
1. Salesforce
2. Siemens
3. Hewlett Packard

Top Industries
1. Engineering
2. Operations
3. Business
4. Information Technology
5. Sales

Top Employers
1. IBM
2. Lockheed Martin
3. GLOBALFOUNDRIES
4. Corning Incorporated
5. GE

Where Alumni Work
1. New York City
2. Boston
3. Utica, NY
4. Albany, NY
5. Syracuse, NY

Median Earnings
College Scorecard (Early Career): $72,000
PayScale (Early Career): $68,700
PayScale (Mid-Career): $139,600

RANKINGS
Money: 218
U.S. News: 124 (T), National Universities
Wall Street Journal/THE: 200
Washington Monthly: 90, National Universities

COLLEGE OVERLAPS
Rensselaer Polytechnic Institute
Rochester Institute of Technology
St. Lawrence University
Syracuse University
Worcester Polytechnic Institute

Clemson University

Clemson, South Carolina | 864-656-2287

Championship-caliber sports teams, thriving Greek life, and a passionate and generally happy undergraduate population of over 20,000 young people define the Clemson experience—not to leave out the strong academic reputation, which becomes more pronounced with each passing year. A highly selective school for out-of-staters, Clemson caters to those residing within its home state of South Carolina. Nearly two-thirds of the student body are South Carolina born and bred, and locals enjoy more relaxed entry requirements (not to mention one-third the tuition costs) of those from out of state.

Inside the Classroom
There are seven undergraduate colleges within the larger university: the College of Forestry and Life Sciences; the College of Architecture, Arts, and Humanities; the College of Business; the College of Engineering, Computing and Applied Sciences; the College of Education; the College of Science; and the College of Behavioral, Social, and Health Sciences. All Tigers, regardless of their academic program, must tackle thirty-three hours of required coursework that includes six credits in communications, ten in mathematical, scientific, and technical literacy, six in arts and humanities, six in social science, three in cross-cultural awareness, and three in science and technology in society. Most degree programs also require coursework in a foreign language.

Class sizes are mixed, and many sections are smaller than you would expect for such a large university where the student-to-faculty ratio is 16:1. Nineteen percent of classes have single-digit enrollments, and 53 percent contain fewer than twenty students; 14 percent of courses are larger, playing host to fifty or more undergraduates. More than half of Clemson students participate in some type of undergraduate research, a strong percentage given the size of the school. Each year over 1,400 students elect to study abroad in one of Clemson's own programs or one offered by a third party.

Business and engineering are the two programs with the highest profiles, and the university's highly selective Clemson University Honors College (formerly named Calhoun Honors College) regularly draws national attention and praise. Business and engineering also are the most popular majors with a 19 percent and 21 percent market share of diplomas, respectively. The next most frequently conferred degrees are in biology (10 percent), health professions (7 percent), and the social sciences (6 percent). With such an emphasis on professional career tracks there is not a strong emphasis on winning prestigious postgraduate fellowships. In 2018, two graduates received Boren Fellowships and one captured a Fulbright; Clemson had six Fulbright Scholars in 2020.

Outside the Classroom
Only 33 percent of undergrads, mostly underclassmen, reside on Clemson's 1,400-acre campus. Yet, that figure is not indicative of a dull social scene. Athletics are a galvanizing force as the Tigers compete in eight men's and nine women's NCCA Division I sports. Over 81,000 pack Memorial Stadium, nicknamed "Death Valley," on Saturdays to watch their highly ranked football squad; Clemson won the national title in 2016 and again in 2019. Other sports draw large audiences as well. Greek life is almost as big a tradition here as 31 percent of women join a sorority and 16 percent of men are fraternity affiliated. As at many Greek-heavy institutions, there has been increased scrutiny of those organizations in the wake of some incidents of sexual assault and hazing. Other opportunities for involvement abound as Clemson has over 500 student-run organizations. The school's thirty-four club sports attract widespread participation as does the intramural program. The town of Clemson offers plenty of enjoyable bars and restaurants within walking distance. Hiking trails and botanical gardens offer nature lovers everything they could ask for. Greenville, only forty minutes away, provides a more exciting downtown feel.

Career Services
Clemson's Center for Career and Professional Development employs thirty full-time staff members who function as counselors, recruiters, and internship coordinators. That equates to a student-to-advisor ratio of 673:1, above average compared to the other institutions included in this book. Despite a less-than-ideal ratio, Clemson's staff garners much-deserved praise for its dedication to student success through the sheer scope of their offerings. Fall and spring career fairs attract more than 600 employers and more than 5,500 students annually. The school's online database features up to 9,000 job and internship postings each year. The center has forged corporate partnerships with twenty-four large corporations including Home Depot, Vanguard, Bosch, and General Electric.

Even more impressively, the CCPD personally reaches a massive number of students, claiming more than 33,600 engagements per school year. Fifty-six percent of those engagements were made at workshops, job fairs, and information sessions while the other 44 percent were made via one-on-one counseling sessions. An astonishing

E-mail: cuadmissions@clemson.edu | Website: www.clemson.edu

99 percent of those attending information sessions or individualized career counseling rated the experience favorably. Staff also does an exceptional job hooking students up with hands-on learning experiences; 78 percent of graduates had one experiential learning opportunity and 62 percent partook in two. Just under 900 students participated in the University Professional Co-op/Internship Program with the school's 450 employer partners. An additional 1,400 participated in other co-op placements, and 95 percent reported being satisfied with the experience. As a result, 93 percent of those receiving diplomas believe their resumes demonstrate marketable skills.

Professional Outcomes

Within six months of graduation 90 percent of Clemson alumni have entered the working world or are pursuing a graduate degree. The top employers of newly-minted diploma holders include Michelin, Amazon, Vanguard, and Wells Fargo. Including all alumni, the most frequent employers include Bank of America, GE Power, Deloitte, IBM, and Microsoft. Recent graduates of the College of Engineering, Computing and Applied Sciences reported a median starting salary of $63,000. College of Business graduates enjoyed median earnings of $49,000. Graduates of the College of Architecture, Arts, and Humanities averaged $47k while those completing degrees in the College of Education brought in a university-low $37k per year. Forty-four percent of graduates remain in South Carolina, and most stay in the Southern United States with North Carolina, Georgia, Texas, and Florida being the next most popular destinations.

Of the 21 percent of 2019 graduates directly entering graduate or professional school, the largest number retained their Tiger stripes by continuing their studies at Clemson. The next most frequently attended institutions were the Medical University of South Carolina, the University of South Carolina, UNC, the University of Georgia, and Wake Forest University. Clemson grads also enjoyed three or more acceptances to prestigious graduate schools including Duke, Penn, Emory, Vanderbilt, and the University of Virginia. Among all alumni pursuing advanced degrees, 15 percent were in PhD programs, and a robust 33 percent were pursuing professional degrees in law or medicine.

Admission

The number of applicants to Clemson has rapidly risen in the past decade as 29,070 students applied in 2019-20 compared with 15,542 in 2008. In that time, the average SAT score of attending students has climbed from 1221 to 1318; the ACT mid-50 percent range was 27-32. Most successful applicants—87 percent—finished in the top 25 percent of their high school class, and 56 percent were in the top 10 percent. The average high school GPA for entering students was 4.43, and 90 percent earned a 3.75 or higher. Those applying to the Honors College need to be even stronger. On average, admitted honors students have a 1480/32 and are ranked in the top 4 percent of their class.

A healthy 60 percent of first-year students accepted are from South Carolina, but including transfers, home-state students comprise an even larger percentage of the student body. Being a South Carolina resident is listed among the five most important criteria for admission along with rigor of secondary coursework, GPA, class rank, and standardized test scores. Soft factors like essays, recommendations, and extracurricular activities comprise a distant second tier. Legacy status is also considered at Clemson. There is no early admission round at Clemson, but those who apply by the priority deadline of December 1 will receive an answer by February 15. This desirable Southern public university is friendlier toward in-state applicants than outsiders. Applicants not from South Carolina will need to bring above average standardized test scores and strong grades in honors and AP courses to gain acceptance.

Worth Your Money?

The cost of attendance for South Carolina residents is under $35,000 per year, making Clemson a fantastic bargain for them. For nonresidents, the price is over $57k, not a fortune relative to the out-of-control higher education marketplace at large, but not the steal that it is for those from the Palmetto State. Forty-two percent of current students are recipients of need-based aid awards that average $10,838 per year. In-state, attending Clemson is worth your money no matter what you are studying. If you hail from outside the state, a little bit of financial aid can keep the university affordable and a strong educational investment.

FINANCIAL
Institutional Type: Public
In-State Tuition: $15,120
Out-of-State Tuition: $38,112
Room & Board: $11,414
Required Fees: $0
Books & Supplies: $1,436

Avg. Need-Based Grant: $10,838
Avg. % of Need Met: 52%

Avg. Merit-Based Award: $5,126
% Receiving (All Freshmen): 69%
% Receiving (Freshmen w/o Need): 27%

Avg. Cumulative Debt: $32,510
% of Students Borrowing: 47%

CAREER
Who Recruits
1. Bank of America
2. ScribeAmerica
3. Global Lending Services LLC
4. Insight Global
5. TD Bank

Notable Internships
1. BMW
2. Booz Allen Hamilton
3. Capital One

Top Industries
1. Business
2. Operations
3. Engineering
4. Education
5. Sales

Top Employers
1. Michelin
2. Fluor Corporation
3. Bank of America
4. Wells Fargo
5. Amazon

Where Alumni Work
1. Greenville, SC
2. Charlotte
3. Charleston, SC
4. Atlanta
5. Columbia, SC

Median Earnings
College Scorecard (Early Career): $52,400
PayScale (Early Career): $60,200
PayScale (Mid-Career): $110,500

RANKINGS
Money: 67
U.S. News: 74 (T), National Universities
Wall Street Journal/THE: 189 (T)
Washington Monthly: 161, National Universities

COLLEGE OVERLAPS
Auburn University
College of Charleston
North Carolina State University
University of Georgia
University of North Carolina at Chapel Hill

Colby College

Waterville, Maine | 207-859-4828

Situated within the natural splendor of Waterville, Maine, Colby College's location may be remote, but the alluring sheen of this liberal arts gem is spotted each year by a growing number of top students from around the globe. Over the past decade, applications to Colby have tripled, and the school has become commensurately more selective. The 2,003 undergraduates presently on campus are, by far, the highest-achieving group the school has seen in its 206 years.

Inside the Classroom
Offering fifty-eight majors and thirty-five minors, Colby provides a classic liberal arts education with a high degree of flexibility and room for independent intellectual pursuits. Dual engineering degrees with Dartmouth and Columbia, independent majors of your own creation, and a strong premed track are among the bevy of options. Academic requirements for all Colby undergraduates include a freshman writing seminar, three semesters of a foreign language, two natural science courses (including one lab science), two courses dealing with diversity, and one course each in historical studies, literature, quantitative reasoning, history, and social sciences.

A 9:1 student-to-faculty ratio is put to good instructional use as 73 percent of courses have fewer than nineteen students. The school's "Jan Plan" tacks on a truncated semester during which students can conduct research alongside faculty, pursue internships, or take an accelerated course; 90 percent of undergraduates participate. An exceptionally high 67 percent of students study abroad at some point during their four years at Colby. The college runs three of its own off-campus study programs and allows participation in hundreds of programs around the globe.

Being a true liberal arts school, Colby has strengths across many disciplines, but biology, economics, and global studies draw especially high praise. These programs along with government and environmental science—both of which are also very strong—attract the highest number of students as well. Unlike many of its elite Northeastern liberal arts counterparts, Colby does not produce a significant number of fellowship/scholarship winners, but in 2018 three graduates were named Fulbright Scholars. Bates and Bowdoin routinely produce in excess of twenty winners per year. In 2019, Colby also had a Davis Projects for Peace and Watson Fellowship winner.

Outside the Classroom
The vast majority of students—96 percent—live on campus with a smattering of undergraduates living off campus in the surrounding town of Waterville. Colby ditched fraternities and sororities in the 1980s, but underground Greek-like organizations still exist. The Colby Mules field thirty-two NCAA Division III athletic teams (16 men's, 15 women's, 1 co-ed) as well as extensive intramural and club sports programs. An incredible one-third of undergraduates are members of a varsity athletic team. Of the one hundred student-run clubs and activities, the Colby Outing Club has the largest membership, catering to an outdoorsy student body. Wildlife trails and a pond perfect for ice skating are only two of the many natural treasures found on the school's 714-acre campus. In fact, the outdoor life is impossible to avoid as all freshmen participate in an outdoor bonding experience prior to the start of the fall semester. Manmade features of note include three libraries, the Colby College Art Museum that features more than 6,000 works, and an Olympic-size pool. Getting to major cities from Colby will require the use of planes, trains, or automobiles. Portland, Maine, is seventy-eight miles from the college, Boston is 180 miles away, and New York City is a lengthy 390-mile trip.

Career Services
DavisConnects, the office that provides Colby students with career counseling, internship procurement, and facilitates employer recruiting features nine full-time professional staff members and a student-to-advisor ratio of 223:1. That figure is significantly better than average compared to the other institutions included in this book. Career services staff members do an excellent job of directly engaging the undergraduate population, reaching roughly 1,200 students per year in more than 3,300 counseling sessions. The office also runs a job shadowing program, hosts an interview boot camp, and the CampusTap program that hooks undergraduate students up with alumni-parent mentors in their fields of interest.

Colby College

E-mail: admissions@colby.edu | Website: www.colby.edu

Due to its small size and remote location, Colby hosts an annual joint career fair with fellow elite Maine-based schools Bowdoin and Bates. However, many companies do host information sessions directly with Colby undergrads, and those employers include Google, Prudential, Epic, and Citigroup. DavisConnects has increased its number of credited internship opportunities in recent years, now facilitating close to 300 summer/winter experiences at Lockheed Martin, Goldman Sachs, Citigroup, Time, Massachusetts General Hospital, and others. Organizations that have formal partnerships with DavisConnects include PwC, Goldman Sachs, Accenture, Hearst Magazines, the US Department of State, and IBM. Overall, with strong graduate school advising, employer relations, and job placement rates, Colby's career services receive high marks from our staff.

Professional Outcomes

More than 55 percent of graduates have already secured gainful employment by the time they receive their diplomas. Within six months of graduation 95 percent have either obtained jobs or are enrolled full-time in a graduate program. Over one-quarter of graduates enter the financial industry, 19 percent start careers in education, with government/nonprofit, STEM, and health- care work next in popularity. Organizations hiring recent Colby grads were an eclectic bunch that included Teach for America, Barclays, Harvard Medical School, HBO, Deutsch Bank, and the United States Olympic Committee. The median income for a Colby graduate by age thirty-four is $59,000, which places it slightly behind Bowdoin and slightly ahead of Bates in the Maine liberal arts pecking order.

Medical school results have fluctuated over the past five years with acceptance rates between 48 percent and 81 percent. In that time multiple graduates have enrolled at prestigious medical schools including Tufts University School of Medicine, Emory University School of Medicine, Dartmouth Medical School, and University of Michigan Medical School. Overall, the five-year average for the medical school acceptance rate is double the national average. Over 80 percent of law school applicants also find success. Law schools where multiple recent alumni have studied include the University of Pennsylvania, Georgetown University, Boston College, and Cornell University.

Admission

In 2019, the number of applicants to Colby hit 13,584, an all-time high. Such has been the pattern at Colby in recent years. A decade ago, Colby attracted fewer than 5,000 applicants and had an acceptance rate greater than 30 percent. The Class of 2014 enjoyed a 28 percent acceptance rate. In stark contrast, those seeking a place in the Class of 2023 were accepted at a paltry 10 percent clip. The average standardized test scores of this cohort were a 1435 SAT with a 32 ACT, and 68 percent of students graduated in the top 10 percent of their high school class. Just four years ago, a 1435 SAT/32 ACT would have placed you in the 75th percentile of attending students.

Among the factors rated as most important by the admissions committee are rigor of secondary curriculum, grades, recommendations, and character/personal qualities. In the fall of 2018, Colby announced it would become a test-optional institution. Serious applicants should strongly consider early decision as the ED rounds usually allow more generous acceptance rates, often more than three times as high as the regular round. The Class of 2023 was comprised of 51 percent ED-round applicants, and the acceptance rate was 38 percent versus 11 percent for those in the regular cycle. Colby has become exponentially more competitive in recent years and shows no sign of slowing down. Applicants that would have been accepted a mere five years ago may quickly end up on the rejection pile. Those dead-set on Colby should apply early to gain a much-needed edge in this now hypercompetitive admissions process.

Worth Your Money?

While priced at the level one would expect for a premier New England liberal arts school—the current cost of attendance is over $77,000—Colby College is generous when it comes to need-based financial aid. In fact, all undergraduates with demonstrated financial need—approximately 46 percent of Colby's student body-- have the full amount of their need met, with the annual grant averaging more than $55,000. Those grants are balanced by the many wealthy families who send their children to the college and pay full price for the pleasure. It is estimated that slightly more than half of the student body comes from families placing in the top 5 percent of incomes. That makes possible the school's new policy that says, "Families with a total household income of $60,000 or less and typical assets may expect a parent or guardian contribution of $0." Overall, given its excellent reputation and generous need-based aid, Colby proves a sound investment for most.

FINANCIAL
Institutional Type: Private
In-State Tuition: $56,930
Out-of-State Tuition: $56,930
Room & Board: $15,295
Required Fees: $2,500
Books & Supplies: $850

Avg. Need-Based Grant: $55,650
Avg. % of Need Met: 100%

Avg. Merit-Based Award: $0
% Receiving (All Freshmen): 0%
% Receiving (Freshmen w/o Need): 0%

Avg. Cumulative Debt: $24,380
% of Students Borrowing: 60%

CAREER
Who Recruits
1. CGI
2. Market Axess
3. Analysis Group
4. Ocean Spray
5. Boston Medical

Notable Internships
1. Morgan Stanley
2. Boston Red Sox
3. Vertex Pharaceuticals

Top Industries
1. Business
2. Education
3. Operations
4. Research
5. Social Services

Top Employers
1. Fidelity Investments
2. Morgan Stanley
3. Goldman Sachs
4. Massachusetts General Hospital
5. Google

Where Alumni Work
1. Boston
2. New York City
3. Lewiston, ME
4. Portland, ME
5. Washington DC

Median Earnings
College Scorecard (Early Career): $58,100
PayScale (Early Career): $63,300
PayScale (Mid-Career): $114,100

RANKINGS
Money: 50
U.S. News: 15 (T), Liberal Arts Colleges
Wall Street Journal/THE: Not Ranked
Washington Monthly: 33, Liberal Arts Colleges

COLLEGE OVERLAPS
Bates College
Bowdoin College
Brown University
Dartmouth College
Middlebury College

Colgate University

Hamilton, New York | 315-228-7401

ADMISSION
Admission Rate: 23%
Admission Rate - Men: 20%
Admission Rate - Women: 25%
EA Admission Rate: Not Offered
ED Admission Rate: 46%
ED Admits as % of Total Admits: 19%
Admission Rate (5-Year Trend): -4%
% of Admits Attending (Yield): 35%
Transfer Admission Rate: 21%

SAT Reading/Writing (Middle 50%): 660-730
SAT Math (Middle 50%): 670-770
ACT Composite (Middle 50%): 31-34

% Graduated in Top 10% of HS Class: 69%
% Graduated in Top 25% of HS Class: 92%
% Graduated in Top 50% of HS Class: 100%

Demonstrated Interest: Not Considered
Legacy Status: Considered
Admission Interview Offered: Yes

ENROLLMENT
Total Undergraduate Enrollment: 2,980
% Part-Time: 0%
% Male: 45%
% Female: 55%
% Out-of-State: 74%
% Fraternity: 11%
% Sorority: 19%
% On-Campus (Freshman): 100%
% On-Campus (All Undergraduate): NR

% African-American: 4%
% Asian: 5%
% Hispanic: 9%
% White: 65%
% Other: 4%
% Race or Ethnicity Unknown: 3%
% International: 10%
% Low-Income: 10%

ACADEMICS
Student-to-Faculty Ratio: 9 to 1
% of Classes Under 20: 70%
% of Classes 20-49: 29%
% of Classes 50 or More: 1%
% Full-Time Faculty: 94%
% Full-Time Faculty w/ Terminal Degree: 95%

Top Programs
Economics
English
Education Studies
History
International Relations
Neuroscience
Philosophy
Political Science

Retention Rate: 95%
4-Year Graduation Rate: 88%
6-Year Graduation Rate: 91%

Curricular Flexibility: Less Flexible
Academic Rating: ★★★★✓

#CollegesWorthYourMoney

When the sons of toothpaste/soap magnate William Colgate bailed out the penniless, struggling seminary/college known as Madison University in the late 1800s, the school had no idea that, from that point on, it would bear the family's name and rise to become one of the most respected liberal arts colleges in the country. Today, Colgate University is just that—one of the finest schools of its kind and home to approximately 2,980 high achievers in the rustic, hilly town of Hamilton, New York.

Inside the Classroom
Fifty-six majors are on tap at Colgate, including all of the expected liberal arts concentrations. No matter your discipline, students must work through the extensive core curriculum. The requirements start with five classes that everyone must complete by the end of sophomore year: Legacies of the Ancient World, Challenges of Modernity, Communities and Identities, Scientific Perspectives on the World, and Global Engagements. An additional six courses from a range of the usual disciplines round out the mandated components of the curriculum as well as foreign language and physical education requirements.

With a student-faculty ratio of 9:1 and an average class size of seventeen, Colgate undergraduates work intimately with their instructors. Undoubtedly, the resulting connections help to explain the school's sterling 94-95 percent freshman retention rate. It is commonplace for Colgate students to research alongside professors. Each summer the school funds over 200 undergraduates who assist with research projects and, year-round, it maintains a useful database of professors who are seeking research across all disciplines. Raiders study abroad in overwhelming numbers with a 72 percent participation rate in one hundred programs that operate in fifty countries.

The social sciences account for 33 percent of all degrees conferred and, within that umbrella, economics, political science, and English are among the most popular and most well-regarded majors. International relations and neuroscience are also very strong. Other commonly issued degrees include biology (12 percent), psychology (6 percent), physical sciences (6 percent), and computer science (5 percent). Compared to other elite liberal arts schools, Colgate grads do not pursue competitive fellowships at a high rate. The university produces an occasional Fulbright, Gilman, Watson, Goldwater, or Critical Language Scholarship recipient, but not on the scale of many in its peer group.

Outside the Classroom
Rural Hamilton is not exactly a hotbed of activity, leading many to spend a great deal of time within the bubble of the university's grounds. Fortunately, those grounds happen to be a lush, 575-acre paradise that often receives accolades as one of the most beautiful colleges in the country. The university's eight Greek organizations, dating as far back as 1856, attract 21 percent of males and 31% of females and play a leading role in defining the university milieu. Like many other colleges in frigid Central/Upstate New York, Colgate has, not unfairly, earned a "party school" label. The sports tradition at Colgate is rich as the Raiders field twenty-five teams that compete in NCAA Division I. The ice hockey team is particularly exceptional and has produced many NHL players. Also competing are club teams in forty sports including Aikido, juggling, and Nordic skiing. Including those who play in varsity, club, and intramural sports, a majority of undergraduates find themselves involved in some level of athletic competition. For everyone else, there are 190+ student-run organizations with a fair representation of environment-oriented clubs. That aligns with the university's status as one of the more eco-friendly campuses as it runs almost exclusively on hydroelectric power and places a strong emphasis on organic food, sustainable energy, and increasing the use of bicycles on campus.

Career Services
The Center for Career Services (CCS) is comprised of twelve professionals with expertise in career advising, employer relations, and alumni engagement. That works out to a 248:1 student-to-advisor ratio, which is better than average compared to other schools featured in this guide. Further, this staff deploys its ample resources effectively, engaging with 90 percent of students each academic year, including 93 percent of seniors and 88 percent of freshmen.

The CCS holds over 10,800 individual meetings with more than 3,000 current students and recent alumni per year. On-campus workshops and programs attract over 11,000 attendees. The office also excels in employer relations, having forged formal recruiting partnerships with 177 companies/hiring institutions, which leads to roughly 600 on-campus interviews per year (close to one per senior). Premier employers include many of the top banking, accounting, and consulting firms in the country. The university supplies generous funding to students who wish to take low-paying or nonpaying internships, financially supporting close to 200 students per year. Job shadowing opportunities with alumni are arranged for more than 300 undergrads and 4,500 jobs and internships are posted exclusively for Colgate students each year. Displaying proficiency in undergraduate engagement, recruiting, and generating positive graduate outcomes, Colgate's career services rates among the best anywhere in the country.

Professional Outcomes

Nine months after graduation only a few Colgate alumni are still looking for work; in 2019, that group represented less than 1 percent of the graduating class. A substantial 85 percent had already landed full-time jobs. Business, education, sales, and finance are the most commonly entered sectors, in that order. Employers hiring the most Colgate grads included Bank of America Merrill Lynch, IBM, EY, Sloan Kettering Cancer Center, Massachusetts General Hospital, and the NIH. Including alumni of all ages, the strongest concentrations of Raiders can be found roaming the corporate offices of Google, Goldman Sachs, JPMorgan Chase & Co., Deloitte, Citi, UBS, PwC, and Amazon. A sizable portion of alumni set up shop in the Greater New York City area. Boston and DC are the next most popular locales.

According to the most recent data available, 85 percent of law school applicants were accepted into one of their target institutions. The medical school numbers were even more impressive with 100 percent of graduating seniors (who were recommended by the school) gaining acceptance into at least one med school. The other most commonly pursued areas of graduate study are biology, business, engineering, public affairs and policy, and the social and behavioral sciences. Over the last four years the most frequently attended graduate schools were primarily elite institutions that included Boston College, Boston University, Columbia, Cornell, Georgetown, NYU, Northeastern, and the University of Pennsylvania.

Admission

Colgate hit an all-time high in the number of applications received in 2019 with 9,951. The acceptance rate for a spot in the Class of 2023 was 23 percent, down from 28 percent two years prior. The average standardized test scores of enrolled students in the Class of 2023 were 1408 on the SAT and 32 on the ACT. The average unweighted GPA was 3.72. Among freshmen in the 2019-20 school year, 69 percent finished in the top 10 percent of their high school class while 92 percent were in the top 25 percent.

The admissions office ranks only three factors as being "very important": rigor of coursework, GPA, and class rank. Standardized test scores are included in the next tier of factors, however students who gain acceptance tend to score well. Though Colgate claims that demonstrated interest is not a factor, 56 percent of the Class of 2023 was admitted through early decision, so the school does "want you to want them." Those who applied early in 2019 got in at a far more generous 46 percent acceptance rate than those who applied in the regular cycle (20 percent). Children of alumni, so-called legacies, obtained an even more favorable 51 percent. Over the past decade Colgate's admit rate has held fairly steady, but on the metrics of class rank and standardized tests scores, the average admitted student possesses superior credentials to Raiders of the recent past.

Worth Your Money?

Tax return data suggests that, along with schools such as Colorado College, Trinity College, and Washington University in St. Louis, Colgate enrolls the highest percentage of students from the "top 1 percent." It's no wonder the average amount of debt accrued by its graduates is lower than the national average. While the majority of students come from upper-income homes, those from less-fortunate backgrounds are showered with need-based aid. The 29 percent of undergraduates who qualify receive $55k per year, meeting 100 percent of their demonstrated need. One way or another, people are pleased with their decision to invest their time and money in Colgate University.

FINANCIAL
Institutional Type: Private
In-State Tuition: $60,015
Out-of-State Tuition: $60,015
Room & Board: $15,035
Required Fees: $0
Books & Supplies: $1,050

Avg. Need-Based Grant: $55,553
Avg. % of Need Met: 100%

Avg. Merit-Based Award: $0
% Receiving (All Freshmen): 0%
% Receiving (Freshmen w/o Need): 0%

Avg. Cumulative Debt: $25,044
% of Students Borrowing: 37%

CAREER
Who Recruits
1. NYU Langhorne Medical Center
2. Revlon
3. Guidepoint Global
4. AlphaSights
5. Zipcar

Notable Internships
1. ESPN
2. Wells Fargo
3. Barclay's

Top Industries
1. Business
2. Education
3. Operations
4. Finance
5. Sales

Top Employers
1. EY
2. Morgan Stanley
3. Google
4. Goldman Sachs
5. JPMorgan Chase

Where Alumni Work
1. New York City
2. Boston
3. Washington DC
4. San Francisco
5. Syracuse, NY

Median Earnings
College Scorecard (Early Career): $63,600
PayScale (Early Career): $70,000
PayScale (Mid-Career): $145,600

RANKINGS
Money: 84
U.S. News: 20 (T), Liberal Arts Colleges
Wall Street Journal/THE: 50
Washington Monthly: 22, Liberal Arts Colleges

COLLEGE OVERLAPS
Boston College
Brown University
Cornell University
Hamilton College
Tufts University

The College of New Jersey

Ewing, New Jersey | 609-771-2131

Let's lead off with a telling factoid: The freshman-to-sophomore retention rate at the College of New Jersey is 94 percent, better than at the majority of selective private schools. As one of only six public colleges in the country to maintain a four-year graduation rate above 70 percent, the school is in the esteemed company of such institutions as UVA, Michigan, and UNC-Chapel Hill. Central Jersey may not draw a flood of applicants from the far reaches of the globe (only 7 percent of the student population comes from out of state), but the TCNJ, a midsize state school with close to 7,200 undergraduate students, is simply one the best bargains you can find in the Northeastern United States.

Inside the Classroom

There are more than fifty majors, but whether you're studying art history or computer science, there are an identical series of general requirements known as Liberal Learning awaiting you, beginning as a freshman. As part of the Intellectual and Scholarly Growth phase of your education, new arrivals participate in a First-Year Program, a seminar-style course centered on one of seventy engaging topics. Students also complete an online, not-for-credit course on Information Literacy. A second language requirement exists for the School of Humanities and Social Sciences and selected programs with the arts and sciences, business, and science schools. While you can test out of the introductory course, three writing-intensive classes are on the menu, including a senior capstone. Additionally, you must choose a collective eight courses that fulfill your breadth requirements in the areas of the arts and humanities, social sciences and history, and natural science and quantitative reasoning.

TCNJ sports a 13:1 student-to-faculty ratio, an average class size of twenty-one, and 86 percent of sections contain fewer than thirty students. While you won't find many seminar-style courses with single-digit enrollments, there are plenty of ways to personally connect with faculty thanks to the school's serious commitment to facilitating undergraduate research. In fact, the Council on Undergraduate Research awarded TCNJ its signature honor, the Campus-Wide Award for Undergraduate Research Accomplishment. In addition to plenty of research opportunities in the hard sciences, this school has invested in specialized facilities that include twenty psychology research labs, a digital humanities lab, and a fully equipped quantitative studies lab for criminology and sociology students. The College of New Jersey may not attract many from outside its state borders, but it certainly helps its own expand their global horizons as 30 percent of undergrads participate in one of 500 study abroad programs.

Twenty-percent of degrees conferred are in education as many attend TCNJ to become teachers. The School of Education is widely considered the finest in the state. Next in popularity are business/marketing (22 percent), education (15 percent), health professions (8 percent), the social sciences (6 percent) and engineering (6 percent). Jersey- and New York-based employers think highly of the school that also has strong programs in biology, criminology, accounting, and nursing. Recent TCNJ students have won or placed as finalists for Fulbright, Marshall, Gates, and Truman awards. Two 2019 graduates won Goldwater Scholarships, and five 2018 graduates were awarded National Science Foundation Graduate Research Fellowships.

Outside the Classroom

While only 53 percent of the undergraduate student body reside on the 289-acre, well-maintained grounds of this suburban campus in Ewing, The College of New Jersey's fourteen residence halls do accommodate 92 percent of freshmen; housing is guaranteed for a student's first two years only. Greek life does have a noticeable presence on campus with 15 percent of men pledging fraternities and 11 percent of women entering sororities. Aikido, knitting, and broadcasting on WTSR 91.3 are only three of the diverse 150+ active clubs available. A strong Division III athletics program features nine men's and nine women's teams that, since 1979, have captured forty team and forty-nine individual NCAA championships. The Student Recreation Center features an indoor track, tennis courts, and a dance studio for those wanting to stay in shape, and there are plenty of intramural sports on tap at that same location. TCNJ is only five miles from the state capital of Trenton, ten miles from Princeton, and an hour's drive from Philly or New York City.

Career Services

A small office, the Career Center at the College of New Jersey employs only five full-time professional staff, not counting secretaries, office assistants, interns, or peer career educators who assist with things like resume reviews and career fair organization. The student-to-counselor ratio of 1,440:1 isn't terribly strong, but it's clearly enough staffing to make plenty of positive things happen for the school's undergraduates.

Over 400 employers recruit on campus, a phenomenal number given that there are only 7,200 undergrads. A solid 67 percent of surveyed graduates reported having at least one internship with 70 percent of that group having procured a paid internship. In large part due to the efforts of the Career Center, 30 percent of graduates say the school did an excellent job in preparing them for entering the workforce, 44 percent rate the center's efforts as "above average," and fewer than 5 percent of respondents gave a mark of "below average." The large presence of graduates, recent and otherwise, in the offices of many top companies and banks around the country speaks to the superb employer engagement efforts of this school.

Professional Outcomes

Checking in with TCNJ grads one year after receiving their degrees, a near-perfect 97.2 percent had entered the working world or started an advanced degree. The list of companies employing significant numbers of Class of 2019 alumni includes Johnson and Johnson, JP Morgan Chase & Co., Bank of America, Bloomberg LP, MetLife, EY, and PricewaterhouseCoopers. Factoring in all alumni, the school also has a huge presence within Verizon, Merrill Lynch, Merck, and Bristol-Meyers Squibb. The starting salary after exiting the College of New Jersey was an impressive $57,500, more than the national average for college grads. School of Arts & Communication grads earned $47,500 while School of Business degree-holders took home $62,500. The most popular geographic destinations were New Jersey (63 percent), New York (21 percent), and Pennsylvania (7 percent).

The most frequently attended graduate schools by members of the Class of 2019 included Boston University, Columbia University, NYU, UNC Chapel Hill, and the University of Pennsylvania. Recent graduates entered law schools including William & Mary, Hofstra, Penn State, and Rutgers. Young alums have also attended an array of excellent medical schools including Johns Hopkins, the Icahn School of Medicine at Mt. Sanai, NYU, Drexel, and Penn State University. Many also attend Rutgers via the 7-Year Combined BS/MD Program with Rutgers New Jersey Medical School. Overall, undergraduates enjoy a 65 percent medical school acceptance rate, more than 20 points higher than the national average.

Admission

The College of New Jersey is a rare school that isn't terribly hard to get into—the acceptance rate for 2019-20 freshman was 49 percent—but it provides a superior and supportive academic experience to its undergraduates. Thirty-six percent of the Class of 2023 placed in the top 10 percent of their high school class, 71 percent were in the top 25 percent, and 97 percent were in the top 50 percent. The mid-50 percent standardized test score ranges were 25-30 on the ACT and 1160-1360 on the SAT. In a higher education world where many schools have experienced massive spikes in selectivity in recent years, TCNJ remains fairly steady; the profile of an accepted student five years ago is similar to today's freshman.

At the top of the list of "very important" admissions factors sits participation in a rigorous course load, class rank, standardized test scores, extracurricular activities and, most interestingly, volunteer work. The essay, teacher recommendations, talent/ability, character/personal qualities, and state residency are all in the next tier of "important" factors. However, given that the overwhelming majority of TCNJ students come from inside New Jersey, out-of-state applicants should enjoy a slight advantage. This is reality is made more evident by the fact that TCNJ offers an application fee waiver to all students applying from out of state. Finally, applying early decision may also offer a very slight edge--of the 864 submitting ED applications in 2019, fifty-four percent were accepted. Those accepted through early decision comprised 27 percent of the entire freshman class.

Worth Your Money?

Garden State residents will pay around $18,000 per year in tuition and fees, and while the school isn't as cheap as it used to be (what is?), TCNJ represents an exceptional bargain for an East Coast public school with a tremendously successful alumni base. Few out-of-state students seek out this college, but the price is not unreasonable, particularly for those wishing to study business or a STEM field.

FINANCIAL
Institutional Type: Public
In-State Tuition: $16,923
Out-of-State Tuition: $28,901
Room & Board: $14,048
Required Fees: $0
Books & Supplies: $1,200

Avg. Need-Based Grant: $12,781
Avg. % of Need Met: 38%

Avg. Merit-Based Award: $4,972
% Receiving (All Freshmen): 34%
% Receiving (Freshmen w/o Need): 12%

Avg. Cumulative Debt: $37,937
% of Students Borrowing: 62%

CAREER
Who Recruits
1. Target
2. withum
3. NJM Insurance Group
4. Cenlar
5. Johnson & Johnson

Notable Internships
1. U.S. Department of Education
2. Prudential Financial
3. Lockheed Martin

Top Industries
1. Education
2. Business
3. Operations
4. Healthcare
5. Sales

Top Employers
1. Johnson & Johnson
2. Merrill Lynch
3. Bristol-Myers Squibb
4. Merck
5. Prudential Financial

Where Alumni Work
1. New York City
2. Philadelphia
3. Washington DC
4. Boston
5. Los Angeles

Median Earnings
College Scorecard (Early Career): $58,500
PayScale (Early Career): $62,100
PayScale (Mid-Career): $109,400

RANKINGS
Money: 68
U.S. News: 5, Regional Universities North
Wall Street Journal/THE: 262 (T)
Washington Monthly: 20, Master's Universities

COLLEGE OVERLAPS
Pennsylvania State University - University Park
Rutgers University - New Brunswick
University of Delaware
University of Maryland, College Park
Villanova University

College of the Holy Cross

Worcester, Massachusetts | 508-793-2443

The oldest Catholic college in all of New England, the College of the Holy Cross in Worcester, Massachusetts, offers an exceptional liberal arts education with a strong Jesuit influence that permeates the service-oriented undergraduate student body of 3,174. The college offers thirty traditional majors as well as additional subjects in which one can pursue a student-designed major. Hands-on learning, interdisciplinary connections, a genuine quest for meaning and value, and faculty guidance that extends beyond the classroom are all staples of academic life for all Crusaders.

Inside the Classroom
So-called "common requirements" that must be fulfilled by all undergraduate students is a comprehensive but straightforward list. Mandatory areas of study include one course each in religion, philosophical studies, arts, literature, history, and cross-cultural studies. Two courses are required in language studies, social science, and natural and mathematical sciences. All freshmen complete a year-long seminar called Montserrat that is centered on an interdisciplinary topic and designed to help students "develop broad foundational skills, including critical thinking, strong writing, and effective communication."

The average class size is a manageable nineteen students, and 59 percent of courses have enrollments lower than that. An undergraduate-only institution, Holy Cross offers ample individualized attention and guidance from faculty. Each year, one hundred students participate in the intensive Weiss Summer Research Program that offers STEM majors the opportunity for one-on-one mentorship from a professor. Across all disciplines, research apprenticeships are available to undergrads as early as the sophomore year. Study abroad figures are relatively modest as roughly 300 students travel each year to one of fifty approved locales.

There are no majors that undergrads flock to in overwhelming numbers, but the most popular are economics (14 percent), psychology (13 percent), political science (10 percent), and English (8 percent). All of those popular departments also rank well nationally. Biology and chemistry are very strong as well. Highly competitive postgraduate fellowships are frequently pursued by seniors. In fact, Holy Cross is one of the nation's top Fulbright producers with ninety-three such scholars named since 2005, and seven students and alums took home the award in 2019 alone.

Outside the Classroom
Thanks to a campus regularly voted as one of the country's most beautiful, few undergraduates wish to flee the grounds. Guaranteed housing is available for all four years in one of eleven residence halls, and 90 percent of students elect to live in college-owned housing. The nine campus eateries also receive acclaim and leave students with little reason to seek off-campus dining options. Those seeking the typical university experience of Greek parties and big-time athletics will find themselves batting .500. There are no fraternities or sororities on campus, but with twenty-seven Division I squads, twenty-two club teams, and eleven intramural sports on the menu it seems like most of the student body participates in some form of athletic competition. The Hart Center is replete with amenities including a six-lane swimming pool, ice rink, and a 2,800-square-foot facility dedicated to cardiovascular and strength training. There are 103 student organizations, including a healthy dose of clubs in the performing arts, service, and multicultural realms. While Worcester isn't a town that teems with alluring activities, recent investment in the city's downtown area has provided an increasing number of dining and entertainment options. In addition, the college is located only forty-four miles west of Boston and sixty-one miles northeast of Hartford.

Career Services
The Center for Career Development (CCD) is staffed by nine professional employees (not counting office assistants), resulting in a 353:1 student-to-advisor ratio that is in the average range when compared with other schools featured in this guide. The CCD believes in a "three-stage model of career development: self-assessment, exploration, and implementation." Individualized attention is available to undergraduates at each stage of their education, whether it involves discussing the results of an interest inventory, preparing a resume, engaging in a mock interview, or applying to graduate/professional school.

Fall and spring career fairs attract approximately sixty employers and 300 students. Well-known employers such as City Year, GE, EY, PepsiCo, and the FBI are regular attendees. The office excels in coordinating student internships as an impressive 73 percent of graduates end up with at least one such experience. A few years ago, the school ponied up $209,000 to help defray costs of eighty-two undergrads completing unpaid summer intern-ships. Students who completed internships enjoyed better job placement rates and higher starting salaries than those who did not. Through the Career Advisor Network current students can link up to alumni in fields of interest to arrange a job-shadowing experience or to receive career advice. Thanks to a high level of student engagement and strong employment/graduate school results (more on this in a moment), the Center for Career Development is performing admirably on behalf of its undergraduates.

Professional Outcomes

Six months after moving their tassels to the left, 68 percent of the Class of 2019 were employed, 14 percent were in graduate school, 6 percent were engaged in volunteer work, and only 2 percent were still seeking full-time employment; the overall success rate was 93 percent. The industries drawing the most Holy Cross grads were financial services (17 percent), health care (12 percent), technology (12 percent), government/politics/law (12 percent), and education (7 percent). Organizations employing more than one recent graduate include Fidelity Investments, JP Morgan, Goldman Sachs, Massachusetts General Hospital, Deloitte, EY, PwC, Oracle, and Dell. Large numbers of alumni also can be found at State Street, Morgan Stanley, and the Dana Farber Cancer Institute. The median salary for graduates is $55,000 and varies greatly by industry. Those in finance enjoyed median starting salaries of $70,000 while those entering health care, government, or education took home $39-44k. New England is the most popular home, keeping 56 percent of grads in the area with the Mid-Atlantic region soaking up an additional 30 percent. Boston and New York City are the two most common destinations.

Among those enrolled in graduate school, 14 percent were in law school, 17 percent were pursuing degrees in a health profession, and 17 percent were in PhD programs. Boston College and Fordham are among the most frequently attended law schools. Recent graduates have earned spots in medical schools such as Tufts and acceptances into dental school at the University of Pennsylvania and Boston University. Overall, Holy Cross gradu-ates enjoy 90 percent acceptance rates to both law and medical schools. Grads have been accepted into masters and doctoral programs at elite schools including Georgetown, Johns Hopkins, Princeton, Harvard, the University of Chicago, and Columbia.

Admission

A competitive pool of more than 7,200 applicants for a place in the Holy Cross Class of 2023 encountered a 34 percent acceptance rate. This is in the same ballpark as the acceptance rates over the last five years. Holy Cross is test-optional and, unlike many other highly selective test- optional schools, attending freshmen actually submitted test-free applications. Of the Class of 2023, only 44 percent submitted SAT scores, and 21 percent submitted ACT scores. Given that a fair number of applicants are likely to have submitted both, it is reasonable to assume that a healthy percentage of the class were admitted sans standardized tests scores. Among those that did submit scores, the mid-50 percent range on the SAT was 1280-1410 and 28-32 on the ACT. Crusaders finished in the top 10 percent of their high school class at a 53 percent clip, and 86 percent fell within the top quarter.

According to the admissions committee, six factors rise above the rest when evaluating applicants: rigor of secondary school record, GPA, essays, recommendations, the interview, and character/personal qualities. Extracurricular activities and talent/ability are the only other factors labeled as being "important." Those dead-set on attending this school shouldn't think twice about applying early decision as the ED acceptance rate climbed as high as 83 percent last cycle. (The regular round acceptance rate was 31 percent.) Early decision admits comprised 50 percent of the Class of 2023. The two most notable items related to admissions at the College of the Holy Cross are its test-optional admissions and incredibly generous ED acceptance rate. Serious applicants are advised to strongly consider the latter.

Worth Your Money?

Holy Cross helps to mitigate the impact of its $70k sticker price by meeting 100 percent of demonstrated need for every single student who qualifies for financial aid. All told, 57 percent of students qualify for an average grant of $42k, making the overall cost sting a bit less. Merit aid is awarded to only a sliver of the student body, so if you don't obtain need-based aid, you're likely to be paying a large portion of the $300k four-year bill. Holy Cross is an excellent school, but you won't get a huge income boost from attending (median salaries are right around average), so you may not want to go deep into debt to afford a full-price tab, especially if you're considering a lower-paying field.

FINANCIAL
Institutional Type: Private
In-State Tuition: $55,800
Out-of-State Tuition: $55,800
Room & Board: $15,560
Required Fees: $720
Books & Supplies: $1,000

Avg. Need-Based Grant: $42,069
Avg. % of Need Met: 100%

Avg. Merit-Based Award: $16,357
% Receiving (All Freshmen): 22%
% Receiving (Freshmen w/o Need): 7%

Avg. Cumulative Debt: $26,258
% of Students Borrowing: 52%

CAREER
Who Recruits
1. Dell
2. General Electric
3. Peace Corps
4. Wayfair
5. Deloitte

Notable Internships
1. National Football League
2. McCann
3. MetLife

Top Industries
1. Business
2. Education
3. Finance
4. Operations
5. Sales

Top Employers
1. Fidelity Investments
2. PwC
3. Deloitte
4. EY
5. Morgan Stanley

Where Alumni Work
1. Boston
2. New York City
3. India
4. Washington DC
5. United Kingdom

Median Earnings
College Scorecard (Early Career): $71,000
PayScale (Early Career): $64,000
PayScale (Mid-Career): $126,200

RANKINGS
Money: 112
U.S. News: 36 (T), Liberal Arts Colleges
Wall Street Journal/THE: 117
Washington Monthly: 18, Liberal Arts Colleges

COLLEGE OVERLAPS
Boston College
Fordham University
Providence College
University of Notre Dame
Villanova University

College of William & Mary

ADMISSION

Admission Rate: 38%
Admission Rate - Men: 43%
Admission Rate - Women: 34%
EA Admission Rate: Not Offered
ED Admission Rate: 49%
ED Admits as % of Total Admits: 10%
Admission Rate (5-Year Trend): +4%
% of Admits Attending (Yield): 33%
Transfer Admission Rate: 51%

SAT Reading/Writing (Middle 50%): 660-740
SAT Math (Middle 50%): 660-770
ACT Composite (Middle 50%): 30-34

% Graduated in Top 10% of HS Class: 75%
% Graduated in Top 25% of HS Class: 97%
% Graduated in Top 50% of HS Class: 99%

Demonstrated Interest: Considered
Legacy Status: Considered
Admission Interview Offered: Yes

ENROLLMENT

Total Undergraduate Enrollment: 6,256
% Part-Time: 1%
% Male: 42%
% Female: 58%
% Out-of-State: 31%
% Fraternity: 31%
% Sorority: 29%
% On-Campus (Freshman): 99%
% On-Campus (All Undergraduate): 70%

% African-American: 7%
% Asian: 8%
% Hispanic: 10%
% White: 58%
% Other: 6%
% Race or Ethnicity Unknown: 5%
% International: 6%
% Low-Income: 10%

ACADEMICS

Student-to-Faculty Ratio: 11 to 1
% of Classes Under 20: 53%
% of Classes 20-49: 41%
% of Classes 50 or More: 6%
% Full-Time Faculty: 69%
% Full-Time Faculty w/ Terminal Degree: 96%

Top Programs
Accounting
Business
Biology
Chemistry
Government
History
International Relations
Public Policy

Retention Rate: 95%
4-Year Graduation Rate: 85%
6-Year Graduation Rate: 91%

Curricular Flexibility: Somewhat Flexible
Academic Rating: ★★★★⸍

#CollegesWorthYourMoney

Brimming with tradition, the College of William & Mary is one of the oldest public institutions in the country (some contend the oldest), the alma mater of three US presidents, and a school that has long been a member of the "Public Ivy" club. Roughly two-thirds of the 6,200+ undergraduates on this spectacularly beautiful Williamsburg campus hail from in-state, and members of the student body known as "the Tribe" tend to be an intellectual and passionate lot who adore their school. Of W&M's nearly 100,000 living alumni, you'll rarely meet one who doesn't have a strong affinity for their school.

Inside the Classroom

Forty undergraduate programs are available with the most popular being business, psychology, economics, biology, and government. All undergraduates must work through the College Curriculum, the school's liberal arts core including two first-year seminars, four COLL 200 courses covering a variety of topics, COLL 300 (that often involves studying abroad), and COLL 400 as a senior, which requires the production of original research. Additional requirements include taking courses in three "knowledge domains" and demonstrating proficiency in mathematics and foreign language.

William & Mary has an 11:1 student-to-faculty ratio. Class sizes are rarely tiny seminars, but 53 percent do enroll fewer than twenty students, and only 6 percent contain more than fifty. An extremely high percentage of undergrads study abroad for a semester; by graduation, roughly half of the class has done so, traveling to one of more than sixty countries. Undergraduate research opportunities are widely available. In the Chemistry Department, for example, 80-90 percent of students complete independent/professor-assisted research with many becoming coauthors of studies alongside faculty. Across the college, an average 85 percent of undergraduates participate in research each year.

Among the college's most notable academic programs are (1) government and (2) international relations, both of which serve as pipelines to Washington, DC, employers. The Mason School of Business is highly regarded in the corporate world. With a notable service-minded ethos, William & Mary is the top producer of Peace Corps volunteers among midsize universities. In 2018, the college had seven Fulbright Scholarship winners. However, the school doesn't take home other prestigious scholarships in large numbers.

Outside the Classroom

The campus is large and lush with over 1,200 acres, including an amphitheater, Lake Matoaka, and College Woods, the latter two of which can be freely enjoyed by nature-loving students. William and Mary's grounds easily make any list of the most beautiful college campuses in the country. Seventy percent of students live on campus, which includes a sizable number of Greek houses. Greek life first appeared at W&M in 1776, and the tradition is still alive and well today. Presently, 29-31 percent of undergrads participate with higher numbers in the school's sororities than fraternities. More than 450 student clubs in every area imaginable are available with volunteer organizations drawing large numbers—3,500+ each year. That spirit of involvement carries over into athletics as well with an 85 percent participation rate when including the school's twenty-three NCAA Division I teams and thriving intramural and club sports. Nightlife in the surrounding Williamsburg area is generally pretty tame unless you happen to be a colonial-era history buff. Most students enjoy a social life more centered around campus activities and dorm life.

Career Services

The Cohen Career Center (CCC) employs fifteen full-time staff members, not counting graduate assistants or administrative assistants, giving it a student-to-advisor ratio of 413:1, which is slightly higher than the average school profiled in this guide. The CCC does arrange several well-attended job fairs each year including the Government & Nonprofit Career Expo that features ninety employers as well as large-scale career and internship fairs in the fall and spring that are attended by as many as 1,000 undergrads. All told, 397 employers attended William & Mary career fairs in 2018-19.

In a typical year the office conducts over 900 mock interviews, one hundred workshops, and information sessions with 125 employers. In the 2018-19 academic year, 2,344 one-on-one counseling sessions were conducted with undergraduates. For those interested in graduate school, representatives from more than one hundred programs across the academic spectrum attend the annual Graduate & Professional Fair. Partnerships with Deloitte, PwC, KPMG, EY, and Accenture lead to on-campus recruiting and interviewing with those giants of the accounting and consulting fields. Close to 1,000 on-campus interviews are arranged each year with W&M seniors. A respectable 61 percent of grads participated in at least one internship, externship, or research project. The office does a solid job guiding undergraduates toward meaningful work as 91 percent found first jobs that aligned to some degree with their career goals.

Professional Outcomes

The Class of 2018 (the most recent class for which data is available) saw 74 percent of its cohort join the work-force, and 15 percent enter graduate school within six months of graduation. Over 500 employers snatched up at least one member of the Tribe. Companies hiring the highest number of 2018 grads included Accenture, Booz Allen Hamilton, KPMG, and IBM. More than fifty alumni across all graduating years can be found in the corporate offices of Capital One, PwC, Microsoft, Google, Amazon, and Deloitte. Starting salaries varied significantly by industry. The average salary for those entering the world of IT/computing was over $70k, financial services was $58k, and health care was $39k, The vast majority of alumni remain in the Mid-Atlantic region; the Northeast is a distant second.

Many of those opting for immediate entry into graduate school stayed at their alma mater, with 24 continuing their studies at William & Mary. The next most frequented universities were UVA (11), Virginia Commonwealth University (8), Columbia (5), and Old Dominion University (4). Twenty-four grads were pursuing PhDs, fifteen were studying to be MDs, and twenty-two headed to law school. In previous years, a greater number of alumni have entered JD or PhD programs. Most impressively, William & Mary graduates gain acceptance into medical school at a rate twice the national average.

Admission

Of the 14,680 applicants vying for a seat in W&M's Class of 2023, just over 5,500 received the proverbial thick envelope. That calculates to an acceptance rate of 38 percent. Like UNC-Chapel Hill, but not to nearly as extreme a degree, in-state applicants have an easier pathway to acceptance at William & Mary. The acceptance rate for out-of-state students was 32% while in-staters enjoyed a 48 percent acceptance rate. Of those who enrolled in the Class of 2023 the SAT middle-50 percent range was 1320-1510, and the ACT range was 30-34. (A far greater number of applicants submit SAT scores.) Three-quarters of enrolled freshmen hail from the top 10 percent of their high school class, and 97 percent placed in the top quartile.

The admissions office ranks a dozen factors as being most important in the admissions process. In addition to the obvious factors of grades, test scores, and class rank, the college also prioritizes state residency status, volunteer work, work experience, character/personal qualities, and talent/ability. Applying early decision can work to your advantage as over 49 percent of ED applicants get positive results, and ED admits comprised 31 percent of the 2019-20 freshman class. The regular round acceptance rate is only 37 percent. William & Mary is a highly selective school, but even more so for non-Virginia residents. The school maintains a 65/35 split of in-state versus out-of-state students.

Worth Your Money?

High-achieving residents of Virginia are lucky to have two Ivy-level public schools at their disposal. Like UVA, William & Mary comes at a bargain price for those living in Virginia. The cost of attendance is roughly $40,000 in state and $63,000 out of state. The 38 percent who receive need-based aid rarely see 100 percent of their need met, but the average grant amount of $18,657 certainly helps, particularly for those paying the in-state rate. The average amount of debt for a W&M graduate is slightly less than the national average. For in-state students attending this school is a no-brainer. Prospective out-of-state students have to factor in the amount of loans you would need and the starting salaries typical of the field you eventually wish to enter.

FINANCIAL
Institutional Type: Public
In-State Tuition: $17,168
Out-of-State Tuition: $40,089
Room & Board: $13,356
Required Fees: $6,194
Books & Supplies: $1,000

Avg. Need-Based Grant: $18,657
Avg. % of Need Met: 84%

Avg. Merit-Based Award: $17,835
% Receiving (All Freshmen): 16%
% Receiving (Freshmen w/o Need): 1%

Avg. Cumulative Debt: $28,895
% of Students Borrowing: 33%

CAREER
Who Recruits
1. Central Intelligence Agency
2. National Institutes of Health
3. The Carlyle Group
4. Aldi
5. Navigant Consulting

Notable Internships
1. Booz Allen Hamilton
2. Vanguard
3. NFL Films

Top Industries
1. Business
2. Education
3. Operations
4. Social Services
5. Research

Top Employers
1. Capital One
2. Booz Allen Hamilton
3. Deloitte
4. EY
5. IBM

Where Alumni Work
1. Washington DC
2. Norfolk, VA
3. New York City
4. Richmond, VA
5. Boston

Median Earnings
College Scorecard (Early Career): $58,500
PayScale (Early Career): $62,100
PayScale (Mid-Career): $123,300

RANKINGS
Money: 31
U.S. News: 39 (T), National Universities
Wall Street Journal/THE: 73
Washington Monthly: 43, National Universities

COLLEGE OVERLAPS
Georgetown University
James Madison University
University of North Carolina at Chapel Hill
University of Virginia
Virginia Tech

Colorado College

Colorado Springs, Colorado | 719-389-6344

ADMISSION
Admission Rate: 14%
Admission Rate - Men: 14%
Admission Rate - Women: 13%
EA Admission Rate: 19%
ED Admission Rate: 27%
ED Admits as % of Total Admits: 25%
Admission Rate (5-Year Trend): -9%
% of Admits Attending (Yield): 29%
Transfer Admission Rate: 13%

SAT Reading/Writing (Middle 50%): 650-730
SAT Math (Middle 50%): 650-750
ACT Composite (Middle 50%): 29-33

% Graduated in Top 10% of HS Class: 82%
% Graduated in Top 25% of HS Class: 98%
% Graduated in Top 50% of HS Class: 100%

Demonstrated Interest: Considered
Legacy Status: Considered
Admission Interview Offered: Yes

ENROLLMENT
Total Undergraduate Enrollment: 2,099
% Part-Time: 0%
% Male: 45%
% Female: 55%
% Out-of-State: 83%
% Fraternity: 11%
% Sorority: 11%
% On-Campus (Freshman): 100%
% On-Campus (All Undergraduate): 83%

% African-American: 3%
% Asian: 5%
% Hispanic: 9%
% White: 65%
% Other: 8%
% Race or Ethnicity Unknown: 2%
% International: 8%
% Low-Income: 11%

ACADEMICS
Student-to-Faculty Ratio: 10 to 1
% of Classes Under 20: 75%
% of Classes 20-49: 25%
% of Classes 50 or More: 0%
% Full-Time Faculty: 85%
% Full-Time Faculty w/ Terminal Degree: 98%

Top Programs
Art
Economics and Business
Environmental Studies
International Political Economy
Organismal Biology and Ecology
Political Science
Sociology

Retention Rate: 96%
4-Year Graduation Rate: 80%
6-Year Graduation Rate: 83%

Curricular Flexibility: Very Flexible
Academic Rating: ★★★★⤍

#CollegesWorthYourMoney

With the Rocky Mountains visible from Colorado College's ninety-acre campus, the school's 2,099 undergraduates find themselves in rarefied air—in more ways than one. A magnet for high-achieving, civic-minded, and generally liberally inclined young people, CC is ideally located seventy miles south of Denver and within a reasonable car ride of seven national parks and ten ski resorts. The student body is geographically diverse with about one-quarter hailing from the Northeast, one-quarter from the West Coast, and a sizable representation from the Midwest and the South.

Inside the Classroom

Rather than the typical semester schedule, Colorado College operates on the "block plan," a series of eight three-and-half-week periods during which students take only one course. Requirements are broad, affording undergraduates the opportunity to chart their own course. That course, however, must stay within some boundaries that include a first-year seminar, a foreign language, as well as courses fitting under the umbrellas of global cultures, social inequality, quantitative reasoning, and scientific investigation of the natural world.

You won't find a more intimate liberal arts college than CC. Classes have a cap of twenty-five students, and no more than a handful of courses exceed that figure. The average class consists of sixteen students, and 32 percent of offerings have single-digit enrollments. Face time with your professors is a certainty as the school boasts a 10:1 student-faculty ratio. Although it does offer master's programs for teachers, this is a teaching college that focuses on undergraduate education. In faculty-wide surveys, the vast majority of professors report that quality of instruction is properly factored into their evaluations. Research opportunities are built into the academic program as 20 percent of CC classes involve some degree of undergraduate research. Another 6 percent of students receive stipends to conduct research. Tigers appear unafraid to go into the world and immerse themselves in other cultures as a healthy 81 percent study abroad.

Regularly ranked among the top liberal arts schools in the country, Colorado College has an excellent reputation. Environmental studies, art, and sociology are considered very strong, but CC doesn't necessarily offer programs that clearly stand above the rest. In its own words, "The most popular majors at CC are those that are popular nationally." In terms of sheer volume, most degrees are conferred in the social sciences (27 percent), biology (18 percent), natural resources and conservation (7 percent), and the visual and performing arts (6 percent). This institution is a regular producer of Watson and Fulbright Scholarship winners. It also ranks seventh in the nation for the number of Peace Corps volunteers produced, which is especially impressive given the modest size of each graduating class.

Outside the Classroom

Every freshman lives on Colorado College's campus, and 83 percent of the total undergraduate student body remains in school-owned housing. There is a Greek presence, but it in no way dominates the social scene. Only 11 percent of men join fraternities and an identical 11 percent of women enter a sorority. More than 135 student clubs and organizations are available, the most popular being the Outdoor Recreation Committee. That makes sense given the natural splendor surrounding campus that is conducive to hiking, skiing, cycling, and the like. Students have the dual benefit of attending what is, technically, an urban campus situated in Colorado Springs that is, by area, the largest city in the state. Dorms, food, and campus facilities all receive generally favorable reviews from the student body. Community service projects are inclusive with an 80 percent undergraduate participation rate. While no one would mistake CC for a jock school, it does have sixteen total men's and women's sports teams competing in NCAA Division III, except for the highly competitive Division I ice hockey squad.

Career Services

The Career Center has seven full-time staff members who focus on either career advising or employer relations. Titles include career coach, health professions advisor, and pre-law advisor. The 300:1 student-to-advisor ratio is superior to many schools featured in this guide. The center puts its personnel to excellent use, having conducted a remarkable 1,700 one-on-one counseling sessions in the 2018-19 academic year.

Colorado College is a member of the nine-school Selective Liberal Arts Consortium that is comprised mostly of elite schools on the East Coast such as Vassar and Haverford College. This organization hosts off-campus interview days based in New York City and DC as well as video interviewing days with a host of high-caliber employers. The Career Center also arranges so-called "Tiger Treks" in which current students travel to a major city to meet with alumni in a variety of job settings. On-campus recruiting and interviewing is not a regular occurrence; only twenty-two companies recruited on campus last year. Internship opportunities are available, but assistance in landing one is limited. Roughly 57 percent of graduating seniors report having participated in at least one internship.

Professional Outcomes

Being a small school, Colorado College does not send massive numbers of graduates to any one company or organization, but there are employers that have wrangled their fair share of Tigers. That list includes Microsoft, Wells Fargo, Amazon, Google, and Charles Schwab. The largest number of graduates who pursue employment end up in the fields of education, technology, health care, the arts, and government. Ten years after entering college, CC alumni have lower average salary figures than one might expect. Again, this is attributable to many graduates pursuing careers in nonprofit sectors and the relatively low number of STEM majors. Further, as we will discuss in a minute, seemingly all graduates of this school continue their educational journeys, a choice that typically delays financial rewards. Roughly one-quarter of grads stay in the state of Colorado while the majority migrate to major cities across the United States with San Francisco, New York, Seattle, and Los Angeles among the most popular destinations.

The bachelor's degree earned at Colorado College is unlikely to be the last degree a graduate will earn. Five years after graduation the typical cohort sees 70-90 percent of its members having either completed or finishing an advanced degree. Over half of that group are in PhD or professional programs with an average of 25 percent going to medical school. Recent graduates pursuing legal training have matriculated at a wide range of law schools including UVA, Columbia, NYU, Fordham, the University of Colorado, Temple, and Vermont Law School.

Admission

With an acceptance rate of only 14 percent, Colorado College unquestionably qualifies as a highly selective school. That figure has been sliced in half over the past five years as the number of applicants continues to soar. The good news is that the profile of the average admitted student has remained fairly steady. An SAT score in the mid-1300s (or an ACT around 30-31) will put you on solid ground if accompanied by a strong academic transcript. The mid-50 percent on standardized tests for those entering the Class of 2023 was 1320-1460 on the SAT and 29-33 on the ACT.

Colorado College's testing policy used to be as unique as its academic calendar. However, starting in 2020, the school made the shift from test-flexible to full-blown test-optional. Superb grades in a challenging high school curriculum are a must as "rigor of secondary school record" is the sole category rated by the admissions staff as "very important." The data suggests that the school means what it says: 13 members of the Class of 2023 were the valedictorians of their graduating class; 82 percent finished in the top 10 percent. Applying via early action or early decision can have a profound impact on your chances of gaining admission. Last year, those applying nonbinding early action were accepted 19 percent of the time, ED applicants 27 percent of the time, and regular applicants at only a 5 percent clip. Early decision applicants alone made up 59 percent of the incoming freshman class. In short, Colorado College is an institution with a low acceptance rate but a clear idea of what type of applicants it is looking for. While highly selective, those who performed at the top of their high school class can expect to be welcomed here, even if they didn't score perfectly on the SAT/ACT.

Worth Your Money?

The affluent make up a sizable portion of the undergraduate population at Colorado College, rendering the $78,080 annual cost of attendance of little concern to many considering the school. For those who are concerned about the price tag, Colorado College comes through strong for qualifying applicants, meeting 100 percent of demonstrated need for every financial aid recipient. The average annual value of those grants is roughly $54,000, helping make the school a worthy investment to students coming from more modest economic backgrounds. Students coming from families who make too much to qualify for significant need-based aid, but who make too little to comfortably cover CC's hefty price tag, are encouraged to consider their career and/or graduate school plans before committing.

FINANCIAL
Institutional Type: Private
In-State Tuition: $60,864
Out-of-State Tuition: $60,864
Room & Board: $13,392
Required Fees: $0
Books & Supplies: $1,240

Avg. Need-Based Grant: $53,720
Avg. % of Need Met: 100%

Avg. Merit-Based Award: $8,718
% Receiving (All Freshmen): 8%
% Receiving (Freshmen w/o Need): 6%

Avg. Cumulative Debt: $23,579
% of Students Borrowing: 33%

CAREER
Who Recruits
1. US Olympic Committee
2. El Pomar Foundation
3. Accenture
4. SunShare Community Solar
5. Amazon

Notable Internships
1. National Science Foundation
2. Late Show with Stephen Colbert
3. Accenture

Top Industries
1. Business
2. Education
3. Operations
4. Social Services
5. Media

Top Employers
1. Denver Public Schools
2. Microsoft
3. Amazon
4. Google
5. Charles Schwab

Where Alumni Work
1. Denver
2. Cororado Springs, CO
3. San Francisco
4. New York City
5. Seattle

Median Earnings
College Scorecard (Early Career): $45,400
PayScale (Early Career): $57,500
PayScale (Mid-Career): $107,600

RANKINGS
Money: 300
U.S. News: 25 (T), Liberal Arts Colleges
Wall Street Journal/THE: 102 (T)
Washington Monthly: 86, Liberal Arts Colleges

COLLEGE OVERLAPS
Colby College
Lewis & Clark College
Middlebury College
University of Colorado Boulder
University of Denver

Colorado School of Mines

Golden, Colorado | 303-273-3200

ADMISSION
Admission Rate: 53%
Admission Rate - Men: 47%
Admission Rate - Women: 67%
EA Admission Rate: Not Offered
ED Admission Rate: Not Offered
ED Admits as % of Total Admits: Not Offered
Admission Rate (5-Year Trend): +17%
% of Admits Attending (Yield): 21%
Transfer Admission Rate: 60%

SAT Reading/Writing (Middle 50%): 620-710
SAT Math (Middle 50%): 640-750
ACT Composite (Middle 50%): 27-33

% Graduated in Top 10% of HS Class: 50%
% Graduated in Top 25% of HS Class: 81%
% Graduated in Top 50% of HS Class: 98%

Demonstrated Interest: Considered
Legacy Status: Considered
Admission Interview Offered: No

ENROLLMENT
Total Undergraduate Enrollment: 5,154
% Part-Time: 4%
% Male: 69%
% Female: 31%
% Out-of-State: 42%
% Fraternity: 15%
% Sorority: 22%
% On-Campus (Freshman): 100%
% On-Campus (All Undergraduate): 11%

% African-American: 1%
% Asian: 5%
% Hispanic: 11%
% White: 70%
% Other: 5%
% Race or Ethnicity Unknown: 3%
% International: 6%
% Low-Income: 14%

ACADEMICS
Student-to-Faculty Ratio: 15 to 1
% of Classes Under 20: 49%
% of Classes 20-49: 29%
% of Classes 50 or More: 21%
% Full-Time Faculty: 53%
% Full-Time Faculty w/ Terminal Degree: 92%

Top Programs
Computer Science
Civil Engineering
Engineering Physics
Environmental Engineering
Geological Engineering
Metallurgical and Materials Engineering
Petroleum Engineering

Retention Rate: 92%
4-Year Graduation Rate: 62%
6-Year Graduation Rate: 83%

Curricular Flexibility: Less Flexible
Academic Rating: ★★★✓

#CollegesWorthYourMoney

Less than a half hour ride from Denver and a neighbor of the Coors factory, the Colorado School of Mines, commonly referred to as "Mines," is a public technical institute with an ever-increasing undergraduate enrollment of nearly 5,200, over 1,000 more students than a decade ago. The majority of students are Coloradans taking advantage of the reasonable $17,000 in-state tuition. However, the school is becoming more of a draw for out-of-staters and international students. Presently, there are representatives from all fifty states and eighty countries on campus.

Inside the Classroom
There are sixteen bachelor of science degree options to choose from as well as additional areas of specialization. The vast majority of undergraduates are pursuing engineering degrees in areas such as petroleum engineering, mining, mining engineering, geological engineering, mechanical engineering, and chemical engineering. In short, you don't come to Mines to read Tolstoy or intensively study Picasso's Blue Period. That being said, the university does demand that all undergrads complete its core curriculum that does include a smidgeon of work in the humanities and social sciences with an emphasis on "fundamental technical, mathematical, and writing skills.."

Classes are rarely small as Mines possesses a student to faculty ratio of 15:1. The average class has thirty-four students, and only 29 percent of sections have an enrollment under twenty. Yet, that does not translate into a lack of hands-on opportunities. All Mines students must take a two-semester sequence of courses called EPICS (Engineering Practices Introductory Course Sequence) in which they tackle an open-ended design problem as part of a small team. Freshmen also take Cornerstone Design in which teams of students must solve real-world design problems. In a given year, roughly 125 students are awarded Mines Undergraduate Research Fellowships and work as research assistants on faculty-led projects.

The largest number of degrees are conferred in mechanical engineering and petroleum engineering. To be precise, 85 percent of all earned degrees are classified under the engineering umbrella. However, any degree from the Colorado School of Mines, thanks to its terrific academic reputation and extensive alumni base, will open doors in the world of industry. Nine percent major in computer science, 3 percent in math, 2 percent in the physical sciences, and 1 percent in the social sciences. Prestigious postgraduate fellowships are within reach even though they are not pursued in large numbers; ten Mines students and alumni were awarded National Science Foundation Graduate Research Fellowships in 2019.

Outside the Classroom
The 373-acre campus is populated by mostly modern, recently-renovated buildings, but only five residence halls that mostly house freshmen who are required to live on campus. Just about everyone else lives off campus in apartments in Golden, nearby Lakewood, or in Greek houses. Greek life is prevalent, but not overbearing, with seven fraternities and three sororities attracting 15 percent of men and 22 percent of women. The Orediggers compete in eighteen NCAA Division II sports and generally place well within the Rocky Mountain Athletic Conference. Club and intramural programs enjoy widespread participation. There are 220 registered student clubs and endless opportunities for outdoor recreation. The school's official Outdoor Recreation Center lends equipment for hiking, biking, or rock climbing. A practice rock climbing wall prepares students for organized climbing trips to the Rockies. "E-Days" are campus-uniting events held multiple times per year that feature activities like carnivals, boat races, concerts, and fireworks shows. Golden, Colorado, which many know only through beer commercials "brewed in Golden, Colorado"—is a place of natural beauty where the Great Plains meet the Rocky Mountains. In addition to natural splendor and ample outdoor recreational opportunities, Golden has a nice downtown replete with shops, restaurants, and cafes. Denver is only a quick fifteen-mile car ride away, making Mines' location anything but remote.

Career Services
The Colorado School of Mines Career Center has six full-time professional staff members working on career counseling and employer relations. That equates to an 867:1 student-to-advisor ratio that is higher than many schools featured in this guide. Yet, that statistic is not at all telling of the level of career services the school provides. For a moderately sized institution, Mines' career fairs draw an exceptional number of companies to campus. In 2018, the Fall Career Day event drew 356 companies. The 2018-19 school year saw 214 companies visit the school to conduct 3,165 job interviews with undergraduate students on campus.

A commendable 75% of students engaged with the career center during the 2018-19 academic year. Over sixty small-group workshops are held on topics related to career skill acquisition and job and internship search strategies. A fantastic 76 percent of 2019 graduates had at least one hands-on internship or co-op experience. In total, 1,320 organizations recruited or hired at Mines.

Professional Outcomes

Members of the Class of 2019 landed industry jobs or full-time graduate school positions at a clip of 95 percent. The largest number of students entered the oil and natural gas industry; aerospace/defense/transportation, information technology, and construction were next in line. Companies employing massive numbers of Mines' grads include Lockheed Martin, BP, ExxonMobil, Halliburton, Chevron, and Shell. Those finding employment enjoyed an average starting salary of $73,000. Petroleum engineering majors averaged $92k and had offers as high as $130k. After graduating, 51 percent of Mines Class of 2023 grads remained in Colorado. Texas and California were the next most popular destinations.

Twenty-one percent of freshly printed diploma-holders directly enter graduate school, and the most popular institution is Mines itself, which is the choice of 84 percent of those pursuing advanced degrees. Other universities attended by recent graduates include Baylor College of Medicine, Boston University, Carnegie Mellon, Columbia University, Imperial College London, Kyoto University, Rice University, and Stanford University.

Admission

Accepting 53 percent of the 11,756 who applied for a spot in the Class of 2023, Mines may not sound as highly selective as it actually is. Acceptance rates can fluctuate greatly at this school from year to year. Two years ago, it was friendlier—56 percent of applicants were admitted—but in 2015 only 38 percent were. Freshmen in 2019-20 sported ACT middle-50 percent ranges of 27-33 (59 percent of applicants submit ACT results) and 1260-1450 on the SAT. Fifty percent finished in the top 10 percent of their high school classes and 81 percent were in the top 25 percent. The profile of the average freshman today is similar to previous years, whether 56 percent or 38 percent of applicants were admitted.

There is nothing complicated about the admissions process at Mines. The committee considers four cut-and-dried factors to be "very important" in evaluating applicants: rigor of secondary school record, class rank, GPA, and standardized test scores. There are no factors considered "important." Criteria including recommendations, essays, and extracurricular activities are "considered." With 69 percent of the student body being male, being a qualified female applicant can yield a significant admissions edge. The acceptance rate for women is 67 percent compared to 47 percent for men. Almost three-fifths of the student body hail from the Rocky Mountain State, and being a resident can give you a slight boost. No early round is offered, but students should aim for the priority deadline of November 1 to maximize their chances. Mines uses about as straightforward a formula as you will find to make its admissions decisions. That makes self-assessment of one's chances for admission simple. Strong grades in rigorous courses + standardized test scores in the 90th percentile = probable acceptance.

Worth Your Money?

With the annual cost of attendance under $38,000 for Colorado residents and under $58,000 for out-of-staters, Mines is a good value for everyone, especially given that the average starting salary is over $70k. The news only gets sunnier when you look at the fact that 50 percent of undergraduates receive an annual need-based grant with a mean value of $6,126. Whether you live in the Centennial State or not, the Colorado School of Mines is a wonderful place to study engineering or computer science. You will have no trouble finding well-compensated work after you earn your diploma.

FINANCIAL
Institutional Type: Public
In-State Tuition: $16,650
Out-of-State Tuition: $37,350
Room & Board: $14,211
Required Fees: $2,412
Books & Supplies: $1,500

Avg. Need-Based Grant: $6,126
Avg. % of Need Met: 61%

Avg. Merit-Based Award: $8,896
% Receiving (All Freshmen): 78%
% Receiving (Freshmen w/o Need): 36%

Avg. Cumulative Debt: $32,736
% of Students Borrowing: 50%

CAREER
Who Recruits
1. Rio Tinto
2. Chevron
3. Phillips 66
4. Procter & Gamble
5. Occidental Petroleum

Notable Internships
1. ExxonMobil
2. Cigna
3. Chevron

Top Industries
1. Engineering
2. Operations
3. Business
4. Research
5. Education

Top Employers
1. Lockheed Martin
2. Chevron
3. Aramco
4. BP
5. National Renewable Energy Laboratory

Where Alumni Work
1. Denver
2. Houston
3. San Francisco
4. Colorado Springs, CO
5. Dallas

Median Earnings
College Scorecard (Early Career): $84,900
PayScale (Early Career): $76,800
PayScale (Mid-Career): $144,800

RANKINGS
Money: 137
U.S. News: 88 (T), National Universities
Wall Street Journal/THE: 183 (T)
Washington Monthly: 78, National Universities

COLLEGE OVERLAPS
Colorado State University
Purdue University - West Lafayette
Texas A&M University - College Station
University of Colorado Boulder
The University of Texas at Austin

Columbia University

New York, New York | 212-854-2522

ADMISSION
Admission Rate: 5%
Admission Rate - Men: 6%
Admission Rate - Women: 5%
EA Admission Rate: Not Offered
ED Admission Rate: 16%
ED Admits as % of Total Admits: 32%
Admission Rate (5-Year Trend): -1%
% of Admits Attending (Yield): 62%
Transfer Admission Rate: 6%

SAT Reading/Writing (Middle 50%): 710-770
SAT Math (Middle 50%): 740-800
ACT Composite (Middle 50%): 32-35

% Graduated in Top 10% of HS Class: 96%
% Graduated in Top 25% of HS Class: 100%
% Graduated in Top 50% of HS Class: 100%

Demonstrated Interest: Not Considered
Legacy Status: Considered
Admission Interview Offered: Yes

ENROLLMENT
Total Undergraduate Enrollment: 6,298
% Part-Time: 0%
% Male: 50%
% Female: 50%
% Out-of-State: 79%
% Fraternity: 20%
% Sorority: 14%
% On-Campus (Freshman): 100%
% On-Campus (All Undergraduate): 92%

% African-American: 9%
% Asian: 21%
% Hispanic: 13%
% White: 33%
% Other: 4%
% Race or Ethnicity Unknown: 2%
% International: 17%
% Low-Income: 32%

ACADEMICS
Student-to-Faculty Ratio: 6 to 1
% of Classes Under 20: 82%
% of Classes 20-49: 9%
% of Classes 50 or More: 9%
% Full-Time Faculty: 88%
% Full-Time Faculty w/ Terminal Degree: 100%

Top Programs
Chemistry
Computer Science
Economics
Engineering
English
History
Mathematics
Political Science

Retention Rate: 99%
4-Year Graduation Rate: 87%
6-Year Graduation Rate: 96%

Curricular Flexibility: Less Flexible
Academic Rating: ★★★★★

#CollegesWorthYourMoney

Attending an Ivy League school that also happens to be located in Manhattan is, for many, an opportunity to have your cake and eat it too. It's no wonder that this particular "cake," Columbia University, is one of the most selective schools in the country. It's also one of the most rigorous in the classroom. The 6,298 exceptional students who make it through a treacherous admissions gauntlet are spread across two schools: Columbia College and the Fu Foundation School of Engineering & Applied Sciences. Combined, those schools offer ninety-six unique areas of study as well as a number of pre-professional and accelerated graduate programs.

Inside the Classroom
The academic experience at Columbia is driven by the famed core curriculum that lays out an extensive to-do list that includes highly specified courses rather than categorical requirements. Those courses include Introduction to Contemporary Civilization in the West, Masterpieces of Western Art, Masterpieces of Western Literature & Philosophy, Frontiers of Science, University Writing, and Music Humanities. Additional science, global core, foreign language, and physical education mandates add seven courses to the core as well as two activities (for phys ed). School of Engineering & Applied Science students only tackle approximately half of the core curriculum (depending on your major). Columbia College students will spend roughly a year and a half slogging through this considerable scholarly workload.

Class sizes are small with 82 percent containing fewer than twenty students. The student-faculty ratio is 6:1, but you are likely to be instructed by a few graduate students as you work through the core. Fortunately, only full-time professors lead classes within each major. More than 500 students per year participate in the Columbia Overseas Program. A little over one-quarter of the students leave Manhattan for a foreign country during their four years of study. Undergraduate research is taken seriously by the university, which offers multiple avenues through which students can work side-by-side with faculty on their projects or pursue funding for their own original research ideas. Recent student projects included the following: "Analyzing Sediment Levels in New York Harbor to Examine Urban Growth" and "Examining Chemical Pathways in Stimulating Ovarian Follicle Stem Cell Renewal." Those who participate in a ten-week Summer Undergraduate Research Fellowship present their findings the following spring at a school-run symposium and can publish their work in a number of undergraduate academic journals affiliated with the university.

The greatest number of degrees are conferred in the social sciences (21 percent), engineering (15 percent), computer science (11 percent), and biology (6 percent). The Engineering School as a whole can be found near the top of most national rankings, along with nearly every other department and program. Fewer students pursue prestigious postgraduate fellowships at Columbia than at its Ivy-League brethren; Dartmouth produces double the number of Fulbright Scholars, Brown closer to triple. Yet, if earning a Clarendon, Gates Cambridge, Schwarzman, US State Department Critical Language, or Truman Scholarship is your aim, it can certainly be done at Columbia.

Outside the Classroom
Morningside Heights is a quiet, relatively safe section of New York City, and while Columbia is not situated in the traditional heart of the city like NYU, there are plenty of restaurants and cultural experiences within the immediate vicinity of campus. Unusual for an NYC university, 92 percent of the student body lives in college-owned housing. (Try to rent a place in Manhattan at your own risk—or your wallet's.) A decade ago, Greek life was flatlining with a minimal number of participants, but in recent years it has undergone a rebirth, and now nearly one in every five undergrads joins a fraternity or sorority. The Lions field thirty-one NCAA Division I teams and an additional forty+ club squads, including a number of recent strong performers. Columbia has won seventeen Ivy League titles in the last five years. A full cornucopia of opportunities await through the school's more than 500 student-run organizations. With thirteen a cappella groups, twenty-three dance troupes, thirty-one student run media outlets/publications, and forty political organizations, everyone can find a place to explore their passions at Columbia. The volunteer spirit is also strong with the Community Impact organization attracting more than 900 members who work in twenty-seven community service programs throughout New York City.

Career Services
The Columbia Center for Career Education (CCE) has twenty-seven professional staff members who are dedicated to undergraduate counseling, employer relations, and other functions related to undergraduate career/graduate school exploration. That 233:1 student-to-advisor ratio is better than average compared to other schools featured

in this guide. The CCE is a well-oiled machine that provides meaningful guidance and experiential opportunities from freshman year through graduation. In 2018-19, staff engaged in 8,233 one-on-one counseling sessions (98 percent of students reported those as helpful), facilitated 3,065 on-campus interviews, and posted more than 77,000 jobs and internships on the LionSHARE database. Hosting over 400 events that attracted 8,503 students, the CCE is dedicated to bringing a range of large-scale career fairs as well as industry showcases where students with targeted interests can learn from professionals in fields such as book publishing, fashion, sports marketing, and health-care technology.

Columbia does an excellent job with outreach, but its internship numbers are, perhaps, even more impressive. A staggering 85 percent of undergraduates complete at least one internship. In part, that phenomenal participation rate is due to Columbia's relationships with hundreds of major employers. Thanks to its high level of undergraduate engagement and superb employer relations efforts, the Center for Career Education receives high praise overall from our staff.

Professional Outcomes

Examining the most recent graduates from Columbia College and the Fu Foundation School of Engineering & Applied Science, 74 percent had found employment within six months, and 17 percent had entered graduate school. Investment banking, internet & software, and consulting were the three most favored industries. The companies hiring the largest number of Lions are among the most desirable employers in the world including IBM, Goldman Sachs, Morgan Stanley, Google, Citigroup, and Credit Suisse. The median starting salary for graduates of Columbia College/Columbia Engineering is above $70,000.

Those moving on to graduate/professional school were welcomed in large numbers into other universities of Columbia's ilk. In addition to remaining at Columbia (the most popular choice), top ten institutions attended were Stanford, Harvard, NYU, Yale, Carnegie Mellon, Cambridge, Oxford, Icahn School of Medicine, and Cornell. A significant number of students from each graduating class also generally secure spots at elite law and medical schools that include the university's own top five law school and the esteemed Vagelos College of Physicians & Surgeons.

Admission

As with the rest of the Ivy League, Columbia received a record number of applications for entry into the Class of 2023. Of the 42,569 hopefuls, only 2,245 were offered admission, which works out to a 5 percent acceptance rate, a shade below Princeton. Infinitesimal chances at admission is not a new phenomenon here—the acceptance rate hasn't been in the double-digits since 2011. The profile of the average accepted student is impressive. Entering 2019-20 freshmen had a middle-50 percent SAT of 1450-1570, and the ACT range was 33-35. Ninety-six percent were in the top 10 percent of their high school class.

Straight from the admissions office, there are six main factors that are given primary importance as part of the university's holistic process: curriculum and grades, context (family circumstances), extracurricular activities, character, fit, and recommendations. Columbia is definitely a school where it is advantageous to apply early decision as ED admit rates are typically at least four times higher than in the regular round; it was 18 percent for the Class of 2023. The university fills close to 52 percent of its freshman class through the early round. Among the Ivies, only Penn scoops up a higher percentage of its entering class through ED. Even by Ivy League standards, gaining acceptance into Columbia is an intimidating proposition. The aforementioned admitted student bona fides should give you an idea if you have a puncher's chance at success, but no one is a sure thing when only one of every twenty high school superstars is welcomed aboard.

Worth Your Money?

All qualifying students at Columbia receive an aid package that meets 100 percent of their demonstrated need and averages almost $57,000. Columbia does not offer any degree of merit aid, so those without financial need will end up paying the full annual cost of attendance of $80k+ per year. While $320,000 for a bachelor's degree sounds (and probably is) insane, Columbia certainly has a number of degree programs that will lead you into a high-paying job right out of college. It's also hard to undervalue the social capital accrued by spending four years at Columbia, which makes spending a massive amount of money on undergraduate tuition a less onerous proposition.

FINANCIAL
Institutional Type: Private
In-State Tuition: $62,430
Out-of-State Tuition: $62,430
Room & Board: $14,490
Required Fees: $0
Books & Supplies: NR

Avg. Need-Based Grant: $56,829
Avg. % of Need Met: 100%

Avg. Merit-Based Award: $0
% Receiving (All Freshmen): 0%
% Receiving (Freshmen w/o Need): 0%

Avg. Cumulative Debt: $27,595
% of Students Borrowing: 21%

CAREER
Who Recruits
1. eBay
2. Memorial Sloan Kettering
3. Boeing
4. Calgene
5. Arup

Notable Internships
1. Mount Sinai Hospital
2. Google
3. Glassdoor

Top Industries
1. Business
2. Education
3. Research
4. Media
5. Engineering

Top Employers
1. Google
2. Morgan Stanley
3. Citi
4. Goldman Sachs
5. JPMorgan Chase

Where Alumni Work
1. New York City
2. San Francisco
3. Los Angeles
4. Washington DC
5. Boston

Median Earnings
College Scorecard (Early Career): $83,300
PayScale (Early Career): $76,100
PayScale (Mid-Career): $140,800

RANKINGS
Money: 44
U.S. News: 3, National Universities
Wall Street Journal/THE: 15 (T)
Washington Monthly: 14, National Universities

COLLEGE OVERLAPS
Cornell University
Harvard University
Princeton University
Stanford University
Yale University

Connecticut College

New London, Connecticut | 860-439-2200

Founded as a school for women in the early twentieth century, Connecticut College, known affectionately as Conn College, went co-ed in 1969 and operates today as a unique liberal arts school in the sleepy seaport town of New London. Conn College Camels can pick from an academic menu consisting of forty-one majors, most of which are available as minors as well. There are 1,861 undergraduates on campus, but there is not a single graduate student to be found, which means that, beginning freshman year, the full resources of this school are already at your disposal.

Inside the Classroom

In typical liberal arts fashion, students are required to complete one course in every major discipline: physical and biological sciences, mathematics, social sciences, literature, creative arts, philosophy/religion, and history. There are also requirements in foreign language, writing, and technology. For a laid-back group there is no shortage of academic ambitions as over one-quarter of undergrads complete a double major. Many also complete a thematic minor that is offered in distinct areas including Modern Greece and Its Background, Non-Violence, or Psychoanalysis: Theories of the Unconscious.

The student-faculty ratio is an inviting 9:1, and 75 percent of classes contain fewer than twenty students; 26 percent contain fewer than ten. Conn College's faculty has a reputation for being wholly committed to teaching and forging meaningful relationships with students. Evidence of a personalized experience can be found in the numbers—84 percent of seniors complete a capstone project, 30 percent engage in an individual study with a professor's guidance, and roughly the same number report giving a public presentation or performance during their undergraduate career. Slightly more than half of students elect to study abroad in forty countries, with Denmark, Italy, and the United Kingdom being the most common destinations.

Consistently named a "top producer" of Fulbright Scholars, Conn College saw five students win the prestigious award in 2020. Many recent Fulbright winners majored in the school's strong programs in international relations or region-specific programs (e.g., Hispanic Studies, Slavic Studies). Other well-regarded majors include neuroscience, psychology, English, dance, and theatre. In terms of the most frequently conferred degrees, the social sciences at large lead the way (26 percent), followed by biology (18 percent), visual and performing arts (12 percent), psychology (10 percent), and area/ethnic/gender studies (6 percent).

Outside the Classroom

This gorgeous 750-acre campus is wedged between two large bodies of water and features its own hiking trails and arboretum. The gender breakdown still skews strongly in one direction; men make up only 38 percent of the undergraduate population. Three-quarters of the student body participate in competitive sports. For a tiny school it manages to field twenty-eight intercollegiate sports teams (NCAA Division III) as well as a number of intramural squads. Outside of athletic clubs there are roughly seventy student organizations on campus highlighted by six popular a cappella groups. There are no fraternities or sororities at Conn College, but 99 percent of the student body lives on campus in one of twenty-three residence houses. A close-knit community, Camels come together for some notable campus-wide events like Floralia, Harvestfest, or the massive Seinfeld-inspired Festivus celebration. Public transportation options are plentiful, and the campus and surrounding area are easily bikeable. Even with the relatively close proximity to bigger cities like Boston, New York, and Providence, the school itself estimates that 80 percent of its students stay put on the weekends, making campus a vibrant place seven days a week.

Career Services

The Office of Career Professional Development has eight full-time staff members who specialize in employer relations, general advising, pre-law advising, and connecting students with internships. With a 233:1 student-to-advisor ratio, Conn College sports a higher level of support than many other schools featured in this guide. Its four-year career program assures that the only interaction with the office isn't a harried and panicked "What do I do now?" conversation right before graduation. Advisors visit the required first-year seminar courses and begin to engage students right away, encouraging them to keep in touch via one-on-one advising sessions as well as by attending sponsored events like Sundays with Alumni, workshops, and joint career fairs such as the Liberal Arts Recruiting Connection in Boston that features on-site interviews with more than thirty companies.

E-mail: admission@conncoll.edu | Website: www.conncoll.edu

Rising seniors are eligible to spend their summers in a school-funded internship. That's right— all students are guaranteed $3,000 to help fund an internship experience anywhere in the world. Plenty are advertised on Camel-Link, but advisers will also work individually with students to unearth additional opportunities. It's a testament to the career services staff that nearly 80 percent of alumni reported that their first job out of school put them on their permanent career path.

Professional Outcomes

One year after graduating, 69 percent of the Class of 2018 (most recent data available) were engaged in full-time employment, 13 percent were in graduate school, 5 percent were employed part time, and 4 percent were still searching for jobs. Connecticut College produces an interesting blend of career pathways. A solid 20 percent recent grads entered the finance industry, but a large swath also veered toward education (17 percent); art, design, and entertainment (11 percent); and health care (11 percent). Those in banking frequently find homes at Bank of America, JPMorgan Chase & Co., and Morgan Stanley. On the public service/health side, three of the largest employers are AmeriCorps, Fulbright, and Sloan Kettering Cancer Center. Other companies employing twenty or more alumni include Pfizer, Massachusetts General Hospital, Deloitte, and UBS. Camels end up working predominately in New York (33 percent) and Massachusetts (22 percent), but London/Norwich, Connecticut; DC, San Francisco, and Hartford claim sizable pockets as well.

Conn College students are known for being grad school ready as a surprising (given the small size of the school) twenty-seven alumni earn their doctoral degrees each year. Examining the graduate school attendees from recent graduating classes, it is common for multiple students to land at prestigious schools such as NYU, Columbia, and Yale as well as nearby state schools like UMass and UConn. In recent years graduates have earned spots at just about every top law school in the country including Harvard, Emory, Columbia, Penn, Duke, and Northwestern. Those pursuing medical and dental degrees do so at the likes of Tufts University School of Medicine, NYU School of Medicine, and the University of Texas School of Medicine.

Admission

The school admitted 37 percent of applicants in the 2019 admissions cycle. Over the last five years its acceptance rate has hovered in the 35-40 percent range; its low ebb was 32 percent in 2010. Conn College is test-optional, and unlike most test-optional colleges, the majority of accepted applicants elected not to submit a standardized test score as part of their applications. For those who did, the middle 50 percent range for attending students is 1330-1430 on the SAT and 30-33 on the ACT.

While test scores occupy the "considered" category for the Conn College admissions staff, rigor of coursework, grades, class rank, and character/personal qualities are deemed "most important." Academic performance needs to be strong, but you don't need to be perfect to be considered as 81 percent are in the top 20 percent of their high school class and 45 percent cracked the top 10 percent. Legacy students have an edge and have access to special Admission 101 sessions hosted by the college while they are still in high school. The Class of 2022 had the largest number of legacy students of any class in the school's history. Conn College offers two rounds of early decision, and for those who consider it a top choice, it would be wise to consider partaking. A healthy 58 percent of early applicants were accepted in 2019, accounting for 53 percent of the 2019-20 freshman class. In essence, this is not a school with a strict formula for admission. It tends to attract a distinguished applicant pool but does not require Ivy-level qualifications for acceptance. Those who apply early face the best odds.

Worth Your Money?

For a very sizable 58 percent of the student population, 100 percent of financial need is met to the tune of almost $45,000 per year, making attending Conn College possible for lower- and middle-income students. This is a school that the rich pay close to full price to attend, and the not-rich get generous aid packages. Still, the average debt load carried by alumni is higher than the national average. Therefore, middle- to upper-income students without a solid financial aid offer should carefully consider their future plans before investing in the school.

FINANCIAL
Institutional Type: Private
In-State Tuition: $59,025
Out-of-State Tuition: $59,025
Room & Board: $16,290
Required Fees: $0
Books & Supplies: $1,000

Avg. Need-Based Grant: $44,953
Avg. % of Need Met: 100%

Avg. Merit-Based Award: $15,662
% Receiving (All Freshmen): 46%
% Receiving (Freshmen w/o Need): 36%

Avg. Cumulative Debt: $37,817
% of Students Borrowing: 54%

CAREER
Who Recruits
1. Amazon
2. JLL
3. Morgan Stanley
4. Deloitte
5. UBS

Notable Internships
1. Sony Music Entertainment
2. Smithsonian
3. J. Crew

Top Industries
1. Business
2. Education
3. Social Services
4. Operations
5. Media

Top Employers
1. Pfizer
2. Google
3. Fidelity Investments
4. JPMorgan Chase
5. Bank of America

Where Alumni Work
1. New York City
2. Boston
3. Norwich, CT
4. Washington DC
5. San Francisco

Median Earnings
College Scorecard (Early Career): $54,900
PayScale (Early Career): $60,900
PayScale (Mid-Career): $112,700

RANKINGS
Money: 293
U.S. News: 51, Liberal Arts Colleges
Wall Street Journal/THE: 106 (T)
Washington Monthly: 27, Liberal Arts Colleges

COLLEGE OVERLAPS
Bates College
Colby College
Hamilton College
Skidmore College
Trinity College

Cooper Union for the Advancement of Science and Art

New York, New York | 212-353-4120

ADMISSION
Admission Rate: 16%
Admission Rate - Men: 17%
Admission Rate - Women: 15%
EA Admission Rate: Not Offered
ED Admission Rate: 26%
ED Admits as % of Total Admits: 15%
Admission Rate (5-Year Trend): NR
% of Admits Attending (Yield): 50%
Transfer Admission Rate: 7%

SAT Reading/Writing (Middle 50%): 650-740
SAT Math (Middle 50%): 660-790
ACT Composite (Middle 50%): 30-35

% Graduated in Top 10% of HS Class: 51%
% Graduated in Top 25% of HS Class: 85%
% Graduated in Top 50% of HS Class: 99%

Demonstrated Interest: Important
Legacy Status: Considered
Admission Interview Offered: Yes

ENROLLMENT
Total Undergraduate Enrollment: 857
% Part-Time: <1%
% Male: 59%
% Female: 41%
% Out-of-State: 44%
% Fraternity: 4%
% Sorority: 0%
% On-Campus (Freshman): 80%
% On-Campus (All Undergraduate): 20%

% African-American: 5%
% Asian: 24%
% Hispanic: 12%
% White: 32%
% Other: 4%
% Race or Ethnicity Unknown: 8%
% International: 16%
% Low-Income: 28%

ACADEMICS
Student-to-Faculty Ratio: 8 to 1
% of Classes Under 20: 74%
% of Classes 20-49: 25%
% of Classes 50 or More: 1%
% Full-Time Faculty: 28%
% Full-Time Faculty w/ Terminal Degree: 75%

Top Programs
Architecture
Art
Civil Engineering
Electrical Engineering
Mechanical Engineering

Retention Rate: 93%
4-Year Graduation Rate: 69%
6-Year Graduation Rate: 88%

Curricular Flexibility: Less Flexible
Academic Rating: ★★★✦

#CollegesWorthYourMoney

Tuition-free from its founding in 1859 until 2013, The Cooper Union is home to under 900 talented undergraduate students concentrating in art, architecture, and engineering. While tuition has returned (at least until 2029), CU remains an immensely popular destination for its unique programmatic offerings and world-class faculty; hence, it has an intimidating acceptance rate of 16 percent.

Inside the Classroom
The Irwin S. Chanin School of Architecture offers a five-year bachelor's program. The School of Art offers a Bachelor of Fine Arts degree with concentrations in painting, sculpture, drawing, film and video, graphic design, photography, and printmaking. The Albert Nerken School of Engineering offers Bachelor of Engineering degrees in chemical, civil, electrical, and mechanical engineering. All undergraduates must pursue a core curriculum consistent with founder Peter Cooper's insistence on not ignoring the humanities and social sciences in the pursuit of a practical education. As such, a four-semester sequence is required of all students that includes a freshman seminar that focuses on poetry and drama, and three history/sociology courses that follow a chronological sequence from the 1500s to modern day.

No matter your area of study at CU, students report receiving a high degree of attention and mentorship from faculty. With nearly three-quarters of class sections containing fewer than twenty students, learning is an intimate endeavor. Roughly 20 percent elect to study abroad through one of the school's six- to eight-week summer offerings. Engineering students can travel to Spain, Iceland, or Germany while art students have additional options in The Netherlands, France, England, and Sweden. Undergraduate research opportunities are most common in the School of Engineering where all students must complete a senior project.

Accounting for 50 percent of the student body, engineering is the subject in which the largest number of degrees are conferred followed by visual arts and then architecture. All three schools shine in the eyes of employers as well as other institutions of higher education. Graduates of The Cooper Union obtain prestigious fellowships and scholarships at impressive rates. CU has enjoyed thirty-nine Fulbright scholars since 2001, thirteen National Science Foundation Graduate Research Fellowships since 2004, and typically sweeps all four annual Royal Society of Arts-Architecture Student Design Awards.

Outside the Classroom
Most of campus is located in three large buildings: The Foundation Building, 41 Cooper Square, and one freshman-only residence hall where 20 percent of undergraduates reside. Yet, being located in the heart of the East Village, your "campus" is really all of New York City. When they aren't up all night working on projects, students can enjoy the array of restaurants, shops, theaters, and museums within easy walking distance of the school or hop one of the nearby subway stops for access to Midtown Manhattan as well as the outer boroughs. CU does have five club sports teams—men's and women's basketball, men's and women's volleyball, and a coed soccer squad. Two fraternities and one sorority have local chapters, but they fall well short of being a dominant force in the social sphere. Over eighty student-run organizations are active on campus including music and drama troupes, a student newspaper, cultural clubs, and professional societies that participate in intercollegiate competitions.

Career Services
The Center for Career Development employs three full-time professional staff members, equating to a 286:1 student-to-advisor ratio that allows for plentiful personalized attention. Undergraduates are always free to book forty-five-minute one-on-one sessions focusing on areas including résumé and cover letter writing, portfolio development, job and internship search strategies, interview preparation, grad school applications, and applications to competitive fellowship and scholarship programs. Current students and alumni can utilize Handshake for a wealth of job postings. Employers attend the fall and spring career fairs and stop by campus for recruiting sessions and on-campus interviews.

The office organizes a multitude of targeted information sessions and networking opportunities for CU students. Recent examples include a roundtable discussion with gallerists and curators, a graduate school information session with Carnegie Mellon, and lunch with alumni. Opportunities for experiential learning are facilitated by career services staff. For instance, art students can partake in the Professional Internship Program for Art that provides undergraduates with a stipend to work at one of a dozen partner NYC-based museums and galleries. Thanks to a full calendar of intimate events catering to art, architecture, and engineering, The Cooper Union's Center for Career Development serves its students admirably.

Cooper Union for the Advancement of Science and Art

E-mail: admissions@cooper.edu | Website: www.cooper.edu

Professional Outcomes

Due to the exceptionally low numbers of graduates from Cooper Union each year, it is hard to say that large numbers of alumni cluster in any particular company. However, it is fair to state that CU graduates regularly find their way into the most desirable firms within their respective disciplines. Recent graduates of the School of Architecture found homes at many of the world's largest architecture firms such as AECOM, Gensler, Perkins Eastman, and HOK as well as any desirable boutique firm one can name. School of Art alumni can be found at every great museum of art in the county, including the MoMA and the Met, and at prestigious media outlets such as The New Yorker and the New York Times. Engineering grads waltz into an endless list of top companies including Deloitte, ExxonMobil, Google, Goldman Sachs, IBM, and SpaceX.

Forty percent of CU graduates continue their education at top-ranked graduate programs. In the last few years Cooper Union diploma-holders have gone on to advanced study in architecture at Columbia, Harvard, MIT, Princeton, the Rhode Island School of Design, MIT, Penn, and Yale. Art students have been accepted to US-based programs at Cornell, Georgetown, NYU, and Pratt and internationally at The Glasgow School of Art; Oslo Academy of Art; and Goldsmiths, University of London. Engineering students pursuing master's and doctorate degrees have landed spots at Carnegie Mellon, Johns Hopkins, Stanford, Berkeley, and Vanderbilt.

Admission

Among those seeking a spot in the Class of 2023, only 369 of the 2,326 applicants to The Cooper Union gained acceptance, a 16 percent acceptance rate which was higher than the 13% acceptance rate the previous year. This is a self-selecting group of students, many of whom have slotted CU as their number one choice, a fact affirmed by the school's solid 50 percent yield rate. The profile of the average accepted student varies greatly by program. Based on the most recent data available, freshmen in the School of Engineering possessed middle-50 percent SAT scores between 1460 and 1540 and ACT composite scores between 33 and 34. Architecture students scored a significantly lower 1190-1410 (26-32 on the ACT). Freshmen studying art held the lowest standardized test scores with middle-50 percent SAT scores between 1080 and 1330 and 24-30 on the ACT. Successful applicants to all three programs generally had A/A- averages. The five categories rated as "most important" to one's admissions prospects at CU are test scores, GPA, rigor of courses, talent/ability, and the level of an applicant's interest.

The admissions office recommends that all applicants "take a well-rounded high school program, preferably in advanced coursework." Program-specific recommendations include that "engineering students should also be well prepared in calculus, chemistry, and physics. Art and architecture applicants should take visual art classes" and that architecture applicants should take pre-calculus in high school. Additional application components are required by the various programs. Engineering applicants are encouraged to submit two SAT subject tests, one in math and one in physics or chemistry as well as a writing supplement. School of Art students must complete a Hometest and submit a portfolio. Those applying to the School of Architecture must complete a studio test. While standardized test scores differ greatly across the three schools, all successful applicants to Cooper Union boast solid academic credentials along with demonstrated gifts in their area of interest. Those seeking to study art or architecture will face a holistic review process; those applying to study engineering will be judged more heavily by their test scores.

Worth Your Money?

After over one hundred years of providing a tuition-free education to undergraduate students, Cooper Union controversially decided, in light of a depleted endowment, to begin charging tuition. While plans exist to progressively reduce tuition over the next decade before returning to a tuition-free policy, those entering the school now encounter an annual cost of attendance of almost $53k per year. However, the school does remain extremely generous with aid, awarding every admitted student a half-tuition scholarship valued at $22,275 per year. While it's not as great as receiving a world-class education gratis, Cooper Union remains worth every dollar and is, undoubtedly, worth your money.

FINANCIAL
Institutional Type: Private
In-State Tuition: $46,820
Out-of-State Tuition: $46,820
Room & Board: $13,410
Required Fees: $0
Books & Supplies: $1,800

Avg. Need-Based Grant: $44,734
Avg. % of Need Met: 99%

Avg. Merit-Based Award: $24,160
% Receiving (All Freshmen): 92%
% Receiving (Freshmen w/o Need): 43%

Avg. Cumulative Debt: $19,483
% of Students Borrowing: 30%

CAREER
Who Recruits
1. AECOM
2. Bloomberg
3. General Motors
4. AT&T
5. Credit Suisse

Notable Internships
1. Con Edison
2. Bloomberg LP
3. PepsiCo

Top Industries
1. Arts & Design
2. Business
3. Engineering
4. Education
5. Operations

Top Employers
1. Con Edison
2. Google
3. Bloomberg LP
4. IBM
5. Amazon

Where Alumni Work
1. New York City
2. San Francisco
3. Los Angeles
4. Boston
5. Philadelphia

Median Earnings
College Scorecard (Early Career): $64,900
PayScale (Early Career): $73,600
PayScale (Mid-Career): $143,100

RANKINGS
Money: 39
U.S. News: 2, Regional Colleges North
Wall Street Journal/THE: Not Ranked
Washington Monthly: 2, Bachelor's Colleges

COLLEGE OVERLAPS
Carnegie Mellon University
Cornell University
Georgia Institute of Technology
New York University
Rhode Island School of Design

Cornell University

Ithaca, New York | 607-255-5241

By a wide margin, Cornell boasts the largest undergraduate enrollment of any school in the Ivy League at 15,043 students, roughly 5,000 more than the next largest school, the University of Pennsylvania. Located in Ithaca, a certifiable college town in the Finger Lakes region of Upstate New York, Cornell's campus is a seemingly endless 745 acres, and that is not including the adjacent Botanic Gardens owned by the university. A diverse array of academic programs includes ninety majors and 125 minors spread across the university's seven schools/colleges: the College of Agriculture and Life Sciences; College of Architecture, Art and Planning; College of Arts and Sciences; SC Johnson College of Business; College of Engineering; College of Human Ecology; and School of Industrial and Labor Relations.

Inside the Classroom
Most degrees conferred in 2019 were in engineering (15 percent), business (15 percent), agriculture (12 percent), computer science (12 percent), and the social sciences (8 percent). Beginning with the Class of 2023, required courses within the College of Arts & Sciences included two first-year writing seminars, mastery of a foreign language, and ten distributional requirements. While that sounds like a substantial number of mandated classes, the school does allow certain courses to simultaneously fill more than one distributional requirement.

Classes are a bit larger at Cornell than at many other elite institutions. Still, 56 percent of sections have fewer than twenty students. Introductory courses sometimes take place in larger lecture halls, so 23 percent of courses have an enrollment of more than forty students. Undergraduates do give their professors generally high marks: 93 percent report being satisfied with the instruction they have received, 71 percent report participating in class discussions, 48 percent report completing a thesis/research project, and 62 percent plan on or already have conducted research with a faculty member. Members of Big Red can choose from study abroad opportunities in more than forty countries, and roughly one-third participate.

The SC Johnson College of Business houses two undergraduate schools, both of which have phenomenal reputations. The Cornell School of Hotel Administration is one of the finest such programs in the world, and the Charles H. Dyson School of Applied Economics and Management cracks most lists of the top 10 business programs in the United States. The School of Engineering offers fourteen areas of specialization and is held in high regard by employers and prestigious graduate schools. Highly-desired postgraduate scholarships are procured by Cornell grads at a steady rate. The university has twenty-nine Rhodes Scholars to its credit as well as a regular flow of Fulbright, Schwarzman, Goldwater, and Truman Scholarship award winners.

Outside the Classroom
Ithaca has as much Upstate New York natural splendor as you can handle, from Lake Cayuga to parks to the many breathtaking ravines and gorges. (You've likely seen the "Ithaca is Gorges" T-shirt.) Yet, thanks to frigid weather and the absence of a major metropolis nearby, campus itself and the nearby neighborhoods are where the action is. With a roughly 25 percent participation rate across the fifty-five fraternity and sorority chapters on campus, Greek life dominates much of the social scene. Freshmen are required to live in university housing, although a substantial 48 percent of undergrads live off campus. Student-run organizations can be found for almost anything your mind can fathom. Over 1,000 clubs are active. The Cornell Concert works to bring major acts to campus that suit a variety of tastes from Bob Dylan to Ke$ha. The university also succeeds in luring a fair share of impressive guest speakers to campus each year. The Cornell Daily Sun, founded in 1880, is one of the finest student papers in the country, and the dining hall cuisine and libraries (Hogwarts-esque Uris in particular) receive high marks. Athletics feature eighteen men's and nineteen women's teams competing against NCAA Division I competition as well countless club and intramural opportunities.

Career Services
The Career Services Department has fifty-five full-time staff members, excluding office assistants, who are spread across the various colleges within the university. Those individuals serve as career counselors, internship co-op coordinators, recruiting coordinators, and graduate school advisors in specified disciplines. The 274:1 student-to-advisor ratio is better than average compared to other schools featured in this guide. Among large universities, Cornell's level of support is unparalleled.

Career fairs at Cornell are two-day affairs involving hundreds of Fortune 500, government, and nonprofit employers. In recent years, the fall University Career Fair Days have drawn over 6,000 students and 260 employers. Of the Class of 2019, 13 percent found their jobs through on-campus recruiting, 8 percent through career fairs, and 17 percent through an internship or volunteer experience. In an average year, students make over 16,000 advising appointments, and more than 15,000 students attend programs and presentations. Over 500 students take advantage of job-shadowing opportunities offered during winter and spring breaks. Most importantly, 90 percent of students have completed, or plan to complete, an internship/practicum.

Professional Outcomes

Breaking down the graduates of the College of Arts and Sciences, the largest school at Cornell, 62 percent entered the workforce, 28 percent entered graduate school, 5 percent pursued other endeavors such as travel or volunteer work, and the remaining 4 percent were still seeking employment six months after receiving their diplomas. The top sectors attracting campus-wide graduates in 2019 were technology (18 percent), financial services (17 percent), consulting (13 percent), and education (11 percent). Starting salary data varies greatly across schools as well as by major. For example, the average Dyson graduate earns $77,000 while the average College of Agriculture and Life Sciences graduate starts at $63k. College of Engineering students enjoy an average starting salary of $80k+ with a heavy representation at Google, Amazon, Microsoft, and Goldman Sachs. Across all schools, the median starting salary was a healthy $66,000.

Of the students from A&S going on to graduate school, 15 percent were pursuing JDs, 12 percent MDs, 8 percent computer science degrees, and 7 percent physics degrees. Popular destinations included staying at Cornell (especially computer science majors), other Ivies, Stanford, MIT, universities in the UC system, or abroad at Oxford, Cambridge, University of Toronto, or University of St. Andrews. Harvard was the No. 1 destination for biology majors, and Stanford attracted the highest number of chemistry graduates. The ten most frequently attended law schools by Big Red alumni include Columbia, UCLA, Penn, Harvard, and Yale. Those entering medical school typically stay nearby as every one of the five most popular medical schools was located within the states of New York, New Jersey, or Pennsylvania.

Admission

The deluge of over 49,114 applications for the Class of 2023 was actually slightly down from last year's all-time high. The acceptance rate of 10.8 percent was up by a fraction over the prior year's result. For further comparison, Class of 2016 applicants gained acceptance at a 16 percent rate. At Cornell, applicants must apply to one of the eight colleges or schools (counting Dyson and the Hotel School separately), and acceptance rates vary among schools. For example, in the 2018-19 admissions cycle, only 8 percent of applicants were accepted into the Dyson School of Applied Economics and Management while the College of Human Ecology admitted 23 percent.

Most (83 percent) Cornell freshmen in 2019-20 placed in the top 10 percent of their high school class. The Class of 2023 entered with mid-50 percent ranges were 1420-1540 on the SAT and 32-35 on the ACT. Children of alumni comprised 22 percent of the class, and legacy students are believed to have a significant edge, although the school has not been willing to release any statistics in that area. The eight criteria deemed most important by the admissions office are rigor of coursework, grades, test scores, recommendations, essays, extracurriculars, talent/ability, and character/personal qualities. While technically the "easiest" Ivy to get into, that qualifier doesn't mean much these days. Only a fraction away from joining the other seven Ivy League institutions with single-digit acceptance rates, becoming part of Big Red is only a possibility for the crème de la crème of college applicants.

Worth Your Money?

Graduates emerge from their four years of study with an average debt load of just under $30,000, right around the national average. Like many other elite universities, Cornell does not award any merit aid, instead focusing its generosity on students who could not otherwise afford the school. As a result, the $78,000 annual cost of attendance is greatly reduced for students who demonstrate financial need. These students have 100 percent of their need met to the tune of a $44,000 grant. Alumni enjoy starting salaries far superior to those from your average college, making Cornell a phenomenal investment, even if you need to take out sizable loans to attend.

FINANCIAL
Institutional Type: Private
In-State Tuition: $58,586
Out-of-State Tuition: $58,586
Room & Board: $15,846
Required Fees: $730
Books & Supplies: $990

Avg. Need-Based Grant: $44,767
Avg. % of Need Met: 100%

Avg. Merit-Based Award: $0
% Receiving (All Freshmen): 0%
% Receiving (Freshmen w/o Need): 0%

Avg. Cumulative Debt: $27,094
% of Students Borrowing: 40%

CAREER
Who Recruits
1. Four Seasons Hotel and Resorts
2. WeWork
3. Uber
4. Accor
5. Hilton

Notable Internships
1. American Express
2. Lyft
3. PayPal

Top Industries
1. Business
2. Education
3. Operations
4. Research
5. Engineering

Top Employers
1. Google
2. Amazon
3. Microsoft
4. IBM
5. Facebook

Where Alumni Work
1. New York City
2. San Francisco
3. Boston
4. Washington DC
5. Los Angeles

Median Earnings
College Scorecard (Early Career): $77,200
PayScale (Early Career): $74,600
PayScale (Mid-Career): $140,200

RANKINGS
Money: 49
U.S. News: 18, National Universities
Wall Street Journal/THE: 9
Washington Monthly: 25, National Universities

COLLEGE OVERLAPS
Brown University
Columbia University
Princeton University
University of Pennsylvania
University of Michigan

Dartmouth College

Hanover, New Hampshire | 603-646-2875

The smallest school in the Ivy League, Dartmouth plays home to 4,459 undergraduate students on its remote, 237-acre New Hampshire campus. Dartmouth has long wrestled with its reputation as one of the most conservative of the Ivy League universities as well as one of the top party schools. Regardless, there are few arguments against the academic superiority of the college that sports sixty majors and a stunning breadth of course selections for an institution of its size.

Inside the Classroom
Dartmouth offers a unique year-round academic calendar with four ten-week terms that allow students maximum flexibility as they pursue internships, paid work, research opportunities, or travel abroad. Undergraduates design their own individual "D-Plan." Needing thirty-five credits for graduation, individuals are free to take anywhere from two to four courses per term. (Most students take three.) Typically, students are expected to spend twelve of the fifteen terms during their natural four-year period on campus, including Sophomore Summer, a mandatory term for rising juniors. All freshmen must take a writing requirement and a first-year seminar course, both designed as intensive workshops to elevate student writing to Dartmouth's high standards.

The learning environment at Dartmouth is extraordinarily intimate. Not only do 64 percent of course sections have under twenty students, but 20 percent have single-digit enrollments. The student-to-faculty ratio is an outstanding 7:1. Undergraduate research opportunities abound with 58 percent of students participating at some point. Further, 88 percent of those participants report having a satisfying experience working with a faculty member in that capacity. The rate of satisfaction is hardly surprising as Dartmouth's faculty consistently rates at the top of rankings/surveys regarding quality of instruction. An extensive study abroad program offers dozens of Dartmouth faculty-led academic experiences around the world, and around half of all students partake.

Top programs offered by Big Green include biology, economics, neuroscience, and government. The social sciences are the most popular, accounting for 35 percent of degrees conferred, followed by engineering (9 percent), biology (8 percent), computer science (7 percent), and mathematics (6 percent). In recent years, an average of fifteen Dartmouth grads have been offered Fulbright Scholarships annually. With sixty-two Rhodes Scholars to its credit, Dartmouth is the sixth highest producer in the history of the award. The Truman Foundation lists Dartmouth as one of its Honor Institutions as many grads have been awarded its $30,000 prize to pursue graduate study in a public service field.

Outside the Classroom
The presence of Greek life at Dartmouth is powerful with over half of the student population belonging to fraternities and sororities. In fact, the school sports one of the highest percentages of Greek-affiliated undergraduates in the entire Northeast; female upperclassmen join sororities at a 43 percent clip and 37 percent of men sign-up for fraternity life. Over thirty intercollegiate Division I sports are on tap along with two dozen intramural sports and over thirty-five club sports. Roughly three-quarters of Dartmouth men and women participate in some form of athletics. Other highlights include The Dartmouth, America's oldest school newspaper, 170 student-run clubs and organizations, and the Dartmouth Outing Club, the largest collegiate outdoor recreation club in the country. The college owns over 30,000 acres of New Hampshire land that can be enjoyed by students for camping, skiing, hiking, and similar activities. Eighty-five percent of the student body and 100 percent of freshmen live on campus. Dorms earn rave reviews from students, and all are supervised by full-time, live-in community directors. Big Green is living up to its nickname as a green campus with a number of sustainability ventures including transportation, eco-friendly energy options, and its own organic farm/student-operated farmer's market. If you come from an urban environment, the remote feel of Hanover may induce some culture shock, yet Boston is only a two-hour drive away.

Career Services
The Center for Career Development has seven full-time staff members who focus on either career advising or employer relations. The 637:1 student-to-advisor ratio is slightly higher than other schools featured in this guide. However, also available to advise students are the thousands of alumni who volunteer their time as members of the Dartmouth Career Network. Employer Connection Fairs draw over 1,000 students and feature a strong corporate presence. The fall 2019 Engineering Career Fair attracted fifty-one companies including Microsoft, DraftKings, Mastercard, and Wayfair. Students are given a DartBoard account that allows them to access event notifications, on-campus recruiting opportunities, and thousands of internships.

In part because of its unique academic calendar, Dartmouth does an exceptional job facilitating undergraduate internships. Eighty-seven percent of the Class of 2019 participated in at least one internship experience. Many major corporations have elected to become employer partners with the college, a designation that includes, among other things, annual recruiting on campus. Many of those are financial institutions that also grace the list of top employers of Dartmouth grads. (Please see "Professional Outcomes" below.) This alignment of on-campus recruiting and offers of employment at Dartmouth is most impressive.

Professional Outcomes

A great reputation along with a passionate alumni network that is 80,000 strong leads Dartmouth grads to successful transitions into career and graduate school. At the time of receiving their diplomas, 2019 grads had already found employment at a 72 percent clip while 14 percent were headed to graduate school and 11 percent were still weighing their options. Finance is a popular arena for graduates with 24 percent of the Class of 2019 going in that direction. Thus, it is little surprise that included in the top ten employers of Dartmouth grads are a number of investment banks including Goldman Sachs, Morgan Stanley, Bain & Company, Citibank, and Deutsche Bank. Another 21 percent enter the world of consulting. While many start in finance and consulting, a large number of grads plan to enter academia or a career in government down the road. Dartmouth grads will not struggle financially. The median income for Dartmouth grads with ten or more years of professional experience is $152,500, thirteenth best of any college in the United States. Upon graduation the majority of the student body migrates to major cities with notably high concentrations in Chicago, DC, New York, Seattle, San Francisco, and Mountain View, California.

Those pursuing graduate and professional degrees often trade one Ivy for another. Harvard, Columbia, and Princeton are three of the most frequent landing spots for Dartmouth grads. Many others continue their studies in one of Dartmouth's own graduate programs or head to other top institutions such as the University of Cambridge, Duke, Carnegie Mellon, or UC Berkeley. Among the Class of 2019, 21 percent of graduates intended to obtain a medical degree, 10 percent were chasing a law degree, and 13 percent enrolled in PhD programs.

Admission

Like many highly selective schools, Dartmouth's popularity is at an all-time high. The college's yield—the percentage of accepted students who choose to attend—reached a record of 64 percent in 2019-20. Due to that sky-high yield rate, the number of accepted students fell to only 1,875, one of the lowest totals since the early 1990s. In 2019, Dartmouth shed its double-digit acceptance rate for the second year in a row at 7.9 percent. Five years ago, the admit rate was 12 percent; a decade ago, it was over 18 percent.

The mean SAT is up to 1486 and the mean ACT is 33. Finishing at the top of your class is a must; 95 percent hail from the top 10 percent of their high school graduating class. Legacy students have a fairly strong but not overwhelming presence on campus, comprising 8-9 percent of the student body. Fifteen percent of students are the first in their family to attend college. Alumni interviews are offered but not required. Essays and recommendations are rated as "very important" by the admissions staff. Bottom line: many pine to be part of this Ivy League institution, but earning a spot on the bucolic Hanover campus has never been tougher. Those who wish to experience its renowned teaching faculty and intimate learning environment, rich with hands-on opportunities, will need to bring stellar credentials to the table.

Worth Your Money?

An average annual grant of $54k is delivered to the 2,113 qualifying students, a figure that meets 100 percent of every single student's demonstrated financial need. Most other students will pay the full cost of attendance—$79,525—as there is no merit aid offered at Dartmouth. Big Green is unlikely to cost you large amounts of green unless you can comfortably afford it. For that reason, coupled with the stellar postgraduate outcomes you would expect from an Ivy, Dartmouth is, without question, worth the price.

FINANCIAL
Institutional Type: Private
In-State Tuition: $57,796
Out-of-State Tuition: $57,796
Room & Board: $17,022
Required Fees: $1,662
Books & Supplies: $1,005

Avg. Need-Based Grant: $57,562
Avg. % of Need Met: 100%

Avg. Merit-Based Award: $0
% Receiving (All Freshmen): 0%
% Receiving (Freshmen w/o Need): 0%

Avg. Cumulative Debt: $25,071
% of Students Borrowing: 40%

CAREER
Who Recruits
1. Partenon
2. Nomura
3. Oliver Wyman
4. Bridgewater
5. Trinity Partners

Notable Internships
1. PNC
2. Bain & Company
3. ICM

Top Industries
1. Business
2. Education
3. Research
4. Finance
5. Operations

Top Employers
1. Google
2. Goldman Sachs
3. Amazon
4. Morgan Stanley
5. Facebook

Where Alumni Work
1. Boston
2. New York City
3. San Francisco
4. Washington DC
5. Los Angeles

Median Earnings
College Scorecard (Early Career): $75,500
PayScale (Early Career): $75,500
PayScale (Mid-Career): $152,500

RANKINGS
Money: 63
U.S. News: 13, National Universities
Wall Street Journal/THE: 12
Washington Monthly: 33, National Universities

COLLEGE OVERLAPS
Brown University
Cornell University
Duke University
Princeton University
Yale University

Davidson College

Davidson, North Carolina | 704-894-2230

Strolling around Davidson's lush campus, taking in the historic buildings and intellectually engaged student body, it's easy to forget that you are situated about twenty miles north of Charlotte, North Carolina, and not in the heart of New England. The 1,837 students who grace this undergrad-only institution are high achievers who take academics and their school's more-than-just-lip-service Honor Code seriously.

Inside the Classroom

With its small size, the impressive part of the college is the exceptional quality of its offerings, not the breadth of them, as only twenty-nine majors are available. Additional interdisciplinary majors also can be accessed for those seeking another pathway. However, the majority of students stick to traditional areas of concentration with economics, biology, political science, and psychology being the most popular. Required courses include eight classes under the umbrella category of Ways of Knowing that feature, among others, history, rhetoric, quantitative thought, and the visual performing arts. Additional mandated coursework in foreign language, writing, diversity, justice/equality, and physical education must be completed by all students, regardless of major.

The student-to-faculty ratio is 9:1, which allows the college to ensure that 69 percent have fewer than twenty students and 27 percent have enrollments you can count on two hands. Overall, the average number of students per class is only fifteen. Study abroad is encouraged, and more than three-quarters of students elect to study in one of 110 programs around the globe. Undergrads working side-by-side with their professors is commonplace as over 60 percent of faculty have published with student coauthors at some point.

Top programs at Davidson include political science, chemistry, and English. However, any degree from Davidson is a credential from one of the most respected liberal arts colleges in the country. In fact, it regularly cracks top ten lists of best liberal arts schools and best teaching faculty. Students are no strangers to accolades either; six students were awarded Fulbright Scholarships in 2019. In recent years, others have won Boren, Truman, Watson, and Princeton in Africa fellowships/scholarships. In addition, twenty-three alumni have won Rhodes Scholarships.

Outside the Classroom

"Typical" is not a word that applies to any facet of campus life at Davidson. For example, team sports participation is required at the varsity, club, or intramural level. The ten men's and nine women's varsity teams compete in NCAA Division I with the successful men's basketball team atop the popularity charts. Davidson's fourteen Greek houses are all under the purview of one entity, Patterson Court, which ensures that fraternities, sororities, and eating houses all have a social/charitable mission and abide by a common set of rules. Participation is extremely high as 30 percent of male students and 49 percent of females join a Patterson Court house. Students also run over 200 clubs, including Davidson Outdoors, which organizes kayaking, hiking, and climbing trips around the globe as well as in the school's own backyard. The Lake Norman campus, a 110-acre waterfront property only seven miles from the main campus, is reserved for exclusive use by Davidson students. The college's Union Board, the largest student organization, puts on well-attended events including concerts, trivia nights, and movie screenings on a regular basis. The surrounding town of Davidson features many attractions such as an array of student-friendly coffee shops and restaurants as well as a local farmer's market. Those seeking off-campus nightlife and cultural experiences can make that easy twenty-minute drive south to Charlotte.

Career Services

The Center for Career Development (CCD) is staffed by twelve full-time staff members. That works out to a student-to-advisor ratio of 153:1, much lower (i.e., better) than the average institution included in this book. Despite the administrative titles, all members of the staff get hands-on with career counseling. In the 2019-20 school year 96 percent of undergrads engaged with the CCD, including 2,111 one-on-one advising appointments. Over 250 employers recruited on campus including Amazon, Google, Bain, IBM, Deloitte, and Cigna.

One nice aspect of the CCD is its systematic four-year development model that outlines recommended activities for students at all phases of their undergraduate education. As freshmen, Davidson students are encouraged to get comfortable with Handshake and get one-on-one assistance with resume writing. From there, students receive career coaching, help locating an internship, and can participate in the Senior Bootcamp. Close to 150 students per year participate in the school's job-shadowing program, and 98 percent reported that the experience was helpful. Eight-five percent of 2019 grads had at least one internship experience. The newly launched Insider Series brings professionals in a host of fields (e.g., sports marketing, advertising, and writing careers) to campus to impart career advice. Participation in Career Treks and group visits to corporations and nonprofit agencies has increased significantly in recent years.

Professional Outcomes

Looking at the Class of 2019 outcomes data, 76 percent of graduates landed jobs within six months of graduation, 18 percent were enrolled in a graduate program, and 4 percent were still seeking employment. Remaining in North Carolina after graduation is a popular choice, but many grads migrate to New York and DC as well. The top four industries favored by graduates are (in order) education, health care, STEM, and financial services. Employers of the largest number of Davidson grads include Carolina Healthcare System, Teach for America, the NIH, Wells Fargo, and Bank of America.

Of those who attended grad school, the highest number were in health-care-related programs (including MDs), law school, and laboratory sciences. Significant numbers of students pursue advanced degrees at other Southern gems including Vanderbilt, Emory, Duke, Wake Forest, and UNC. In fact, over a five-year period the college sent more law school-bound alumni to UNC Law School (22), Duke (10), and Emory (7) than any other institution. There is also a fair showing of Ivy League acceptances in all graduate disciplines among Wildcat alumni.

Admission

In 2019, Davidson received a modest but all-time high of 5,982 applications, but it accepted an all-time low 18 percent into the Class of 2023. For perspective, in 2013, the school accepted 26 percent of applicants, so the school has become a bit more selective in recent years. On standardized tests, enrolled students have a middle 50 percent of 1320-1470 on the SAT and 30-33 on the ACT. The two tests are submitted with equal frequency by Davidson applicants. Davidson students being admitted today do possess slightly higher test scores than students did five years ago. The average GPA of an enrolled student is 3.84, and 72 percent finished in the top 10 percent of their class; 95 percent finished in the top quartile.

The college has a unique set of admissions criteria atop its list. According to the admissions office, it places the most weight on rigor of coursework, recommendations, volunteer work, and character/personal qualities. Test scores are among the criteria viewed as being next in importance followed by the merely "considered" factors of class rank, GPA, and legacy status. Applying via binding early decision greatly improves your odds. Class of 2023 members who applied ED were accepted at a 49 percent rate compared to only 14 percent in the regular round. Almost two-thirds of the incoming class was filled through the early round, one of the highest figures you will find at any school. One of the most selective liberal arts schools in the South, Davidson's high yield rate (how many accepted students enroll) of 49 percent suggests the applicant pool is self-selecting as well as frequently applying through ED. Those offered admission typically sport excellent grades/test scores, although components of the process are genuinely holistic.

Worth Your Money?

Half of Davidson undergraduates qualify for need-based aid, an area in which the university is notably generous. Almost every student who qualifies for financial aid sees 100 percent of demonstrated need met, and the average annual grant is for over $47,000. At $70,225 in annual cost of attendance, Davidson's list price is a touch lower than many other schools of its ilk and, even better, most of those students do not pay the full amount. An estimated 50 percent of undergrads have parents who are top 5 percent income-earners, and pretty much everyone else gets a steep discount. With a record of solid graduate outcomes to boot, Davidson is absolutely worth your money.

FINANCIAL
Institutional Type: Private
In-State Tuition: $54,520
Out-of-State Tuition: $54,520
Room & Board: $15,225
Required Fees: $540
Books & Supplies: $1,000

Avg. Need-Based Grant: $47,531
Avg. % of Need Met: 100%

Avg. Merit-Based Award: $17,526
% Receiving (All Freshmen): 26%
% Receiving (Freshmen w/o Need): 3%

Avg. Cumulative Debt: $23,535
% of Students Borrowing: 30%

CAREER
Who Recruits
1. ESPN
2. Barings
3. Deloitte
4. EY
5. BlackArch Partners

Notable Internships
1. Cancer Treatment Centers of America
2. U.S. House of Representatives
3. POLITICO

Top Industries
1. Business
2. Education
3. Social Services
4. Healthcare
5. Operations

Top Employers
1. Wells Fargo
2. Bank of America
3. University of North Carolina
4. US Army
5. Deloitte

Where Alumni Work
1. Charlotte
2. New York City
3. Washington DC
4. Atlanta
5. Raleigh-Durham, NC

Median Earnings
College Scorecard (Early Career): $58,900
PayScale (Early Career): $61,700
PayScale (Mid-Career): $127,400

RANKINGS
Money: 81
U.S. News: 15 (T), Liberal Arts Colleges
Wall Street Journal/THE: 59 (T)
Washington Monthly: 36, Liberal Arts Colleges

COLLEGE OVERLAPS
Duke University
Emory University
University of North Carolina at Chapel Hill
University of Virginia
Vanderbilt University

Denison University

Granville, Ohio | 740-587-6276

ADMISSION
Admission Rate: 29%
Admission Rate - Men: 31%
Admission Rate - Women: 28%
EA Admission Rate: Not Offered
ED Admission Rate: 57%
ED Admits as % of Total Admits: 13%
Admission Rate (5-Year Trend): -19%
% of Admits Attending (Yield): 24%
Transfer Admission Rate: 34%

SAT Reading/Writing (Middle 50%): 590-680
SAT Math (Middle 50%): 610-730
ACT Composite (Middle 50%): 27-31

% Graduated in Top 10% of HS Class: 70%
% Graduated in Top 25% of HS Class: 84%
% Graduated in Top 50% of HS Class: 100%

Demonstrated Interest: Considered
Legacy Status: Considered
Admission Interview Offered: Yes

ENROLLMENT
Total Undergraduate Enrollment: 2,293
% Part-Time: 1%
% Male: 47%
% Female: 53%
% Out-of-State: 74%
% Fraternity: 26%
% Sorority: 42%
% On-Campus (Freshman): 100%
% On-Campus (All Undergraduate): 99%

% African-American: 6%
% Asian: 4%
% Hispanic: 8%
% White: 62%
% Other: 3%
% Race or Ethnicity Unknown: 3%
% International: 14%
% Low-Income: 18%

ACADEMICS
Student-to-Faculty Ratio: 9 to 1
% of Classes Under 20: 65%
% of Classes 20-49: 35%
% of Classes 50 or More: 0%
% Full-Time Faculty: 77%
% Full-Time Faculty w/ Terminal Degree: 99%

Top Programs
Biology
Communication
Economics
History
International Studies
Political Science
Psychology

Retention Rate: 90%
4-Year Graduation Rate: 81%
6-Year Graduation Rate: 85%

Curricular Flexibility: Less Flexible
Academic Rating: ★★★★

#CollegesWorthYourMoney

Ohio is loaded with top-notch liberal arts schools with the two most famous undoubtedly being Kenyon and Oberlin. Those two cast long shadows, often stealing some of the light from another stellar college of 2,300 undergraduates located in the quiet village of Granville, 35 miles east of the state capital of Columbus. Parents of college-bound teens who were somewhat familiar with Denison back in their own college search days, will remember a school that, in the 1990s, received roughly 2,000 applications per year and had an acceptance rate of 85 percent. The number of applications has since quadrupled, and the acceptance rate hit an all-time low of 29 percent for the Class of 2023.

Inside the Classroom
As you would expect from a liberal arts college, the General Education Program at this school is full of competencies and divisional requirements that students must address. This is not a university where foreign language can be evaded; rather, students must complete the third semester of their chosen language. Courses within general areas like the fine arts, the sciences (including lab), the humanities, and social sciences must be checked off as well as more specific mandates in areas such as power and justice and two writing-intensive courses.

Boasting a 9:1 student-to-faculty ratio, face time with your professors is never hard to come by. In fact, roughly 70 percent of sections contain fewer than 20 students. All students have the opportunity to engage in undergraduate research, such as through the Summer Scholar Independent Research Program, which has 130 student participants each year. Off-campus opportunities, including those in the study abroad realm, are pursued by 80 percent of the student body at some point during their four undergraduate years.

You won't find business or engineering among the most popular majors for a very solid reason—the school doesn't offer them. However, Denison's outstanding economics department does offer a financial economics concentration as well as Bloomberg Module Certification (BMC), a key credential for students pursuing jobs and internships in the financial industry. The greatest number of degrees are conferred in the social sciences (25 percent), biology (12 percent), communication/journalism (11 percent), psychology (8 percent), and English (7 percent). Denison students apply in droves for competitive national scholarships. The school was named a Top Fulbright Producer having an astonishing 10 winners in 2020—a truly remarkable number given the size of the university. In the last seven years, students and alumni also have received 19 National Science Foundation Graduate Research Fellowships, 13 Critical Language Scholarships, and five Boren Scholarships.

Outside the Classroom
This 931-acre campus offers university-owned housing to all undergraduates; 99 percent live on campus all four years. For a liberal arts school, Greek life is surprisingly prevalent, with over 20 total fraternities/sororities that attract approximately 30 percent of the population. Denison offers 160+ clubs and student organizations, 40+ intramural sports, and 24 NCAA DIII varsity sports teams. More than 600 campus leadership positions in various endeavors are available. With an annual student government budget of one million dollars, anything is possible. Despite the massive spread of the grounds, the buildings are all within walking distance of one another. Highlights of the campus include a 350-acre biological reserve and the Denison Golf Club, one of the finest public courses in the Midwest. The Campus Series of lectures, performances, and exhibitions bring fascinating people to campus from Yo-Yo Ma to Madeline Albright to Robert Ballard, the discoverer of the Titanic wreckage. Rural Ohio may not be a hotbed of excitement, but the on-campus life is more than lively enough to keep most students sufficiently entertained. Stir-crazy individuals can get to Columbus in half an hour by car; Cleveland and Cincinnati are both over two hours away.

Career Services
With 17 professional employees working at the Knowlton Center for Career Exploration, Denison has been able to assemble one of the most supportive career guidance programs in the country with a 135:1 counselor-to-student ratio. It has multiple staff members working in employer relations and as career coaches, including in discipline-specific advising roles such as a prelaw advisor.

Denison University

E-mail: admission@denison.edu | Website: admission@denison.edu

Professional success and living a fulfilling life can be two very separate achievements, but not at Denison. According to alumni, 94 percent feel that Denison prepared them for professional success after college, and 89 percent feel that the school helped them toward a rich and fulfilling life, professionally, personally, and civically. Part of the Knowlton Center helps facilitate the type of self-discovery that leads to such phenomenal postgraduate outcomes during freshman year. For example, in September of one's first semester, the office hosts a First-Year Pre-Medicine meeting to give an overview of how to become a quality med school applicant over the next four years. For those more toward the end of their undergraduate journey, career center staff put on separate graduate school fairs for a variety of subjects, including social work, psychology, computer science, education, and environmental science. Whatever your aims may be, the Knowlton Center for Career Exploration almost certainly offers relevant programming for you.

Professional Outcomes

Denison does an excellent job tracking the long-term outcomes for its graduates, something many schools do not even attempt. Through this process, it can say with certainty that five years after graduating 99 percent of alumni are currently employed or in graduate school. Ninety-two percent of grads achieve this successful result within six months of leaving the university. More than 25 alums have held jobs at companies such as JPMorgan Chase, Morgan Stanley, UBS, PNC, Deloitte, Wells Fargo, IBM, and Microsoft. Some graduates stay somewhat local in the Columbus, Cleveland, or Cincinnati areas, but large clusters of alumni can be found in New York City; Chicago; Washington, DC; Boston; and San Francisco. When last tabulated in 2016, the median salary earned by Denison grads five years after finishing their degree was $56,720, and 69 percent of this group earned more than $50k.

Within five years of receiving their bachelor's degree, over three fifths of Denison alumni have already earned an advanced degree or are presently in a graduate program. Those applying to Doctor of Osteopathic Medicine programs fared phenomenally well in 2018 as three quarters of those applying gained acceptance. Medical schools attended by 2017-2019 graduates included Harvard Medical School, the University of Michigan Medical School, and the David Geffen School of Medicine at UCLA. In that same time frame, those seeking a legal education have entered law schools such as Ohio State, Fordham, and Temple University.

Admission

At just a 29 percent acceptance rate, Denison hit a record low for the incoming freshman class of 2019-20. Eighty-two percent of these students came from outside the state of Ohio, and members of the cohort hailed from all 50 US states and 56 countries. The SAT middle-50 percent scores were 1200-1410, and the ACT range was 27-31. Students at this university tend to have finished in at least the top quarter of their high school class; 84 percent have earned this distinction while 70 percent placed in the top 10 percent. Over one third reported GPAs of 3.75 or higher.

Denison is "seeking students who have demonstrated a seriousness toward their academic life and who, in addition, would bring a variety of interests, characteristics, and personal qualities to our dynamic campus community." The committee places the heaviest emphasis on an applicant's GPA, rigor of coursework, recommendations, and essays. An interview, extracurricular participation, and talent/ability are rated as "important." Standardized test scores are "considered" if submitted, but the school has been test-optional for 15 years. Applying via early decision will give you a massive edge at this institution. In the 2019-20 admissions cycle, ED applicants were accepted at a 57 percent clip compared to just 27 percent for regular decision applicants. If you are on the fence about applying, the lack of an application fee may just entice you.

Worth Your Money?

Including an allowance for personal expenses and books, the estimated cost of attendance at Denison for the 2020-21 school year is $72,900. Don't have that kind of change lying around? No problem. This school meets 100 percent of demonstrated need, which translates to an average need-based grant of $32,405. The average merit scholarship is in the amount of $22,548. However, the high sticker price does lead to an average debt load of $33,500+, more than the national average. With the majority of students graduating with liberal arts or social science degrees, prospective attendees should engage in proper financial planning to make sure they are not biting off more than they can chew.

FINANCIAL
Institutional Type: Private
In-State Tuition: $55,420
Out-of-State Tuition: $55,420
Room & Board: $13,720
Required Fees: $1,260
Books & Supplies: $1,000

Avg. Need-Based Grant: $32,405
Avg. % of Need Met: 100%

Avg. Merit-Based Award: $22,528
% Receiving (All Freshmen): 54%
% Receiving (Freshmen w/o Need): 44%

Avg. Cumulative Debt: $33,548
% of Students Borrowing: 48%

CAREER
Who Recruits
1. DreamWorks
2. JPMorganChase
3. Cisco
4. Pitney Bowes
5. Orix

Notable Internships
1. Vector Marketing
2. John Hancock
3. Epic

Top Industries
1. Business
2. Education
3. Sales
4. Operations
5. Social Services

Top Employers
1. JPMorgan Chase
2. Ohio State University
3. Morgan Stanley
4. UBS
5. Deloitte

Where Alumni Work
1. Columbus, OH
2. New York City
3. Chicago
4. Washington DC
5. Boston

Median Earnings
College Scorecard (Early Career): $48,800
PayScale (Early Career): $57,200
PayScale (Mid-Career): $119,500

RANKINGS
Money: 240
U.S. News: 44 (T), Liberal Arts Colleges
Wall Street Journal/THE: 114 (T)
Washington Monthly: 49, Liberal Arts Colleges

COLLEGE OVERLAPS
The College of Wooster
Dickinson College
Kenyon College
Lafayette College
Miami University

Dickinson College

Carlisle, Pennsylvania | 717-245-1231

ADMISSION
Admission Rate: 40%
Admission Rate - Men: 38%
Admission Rate - Women: 41%
EA Admission Rate: Not Offered
ED Admission Rate: 62%
ED Admits as % of Total Admits: 8%
Admission Rate (5-Year Trend): -4%
% of Admits Attending (Yield): 18%
Transfer Admission Rate: 36%

SAT Reading/Writing (Middle 50%): 620-700
SAT Math (Middle 50%): 620-710
ACT Composite (Middle 50%): 28-32

% Graduated in Top 10% of HS Class: 42%
% Graduated in Top 25% of HS Class: 72%
% Graduated in Top 50% of HS Class: 96%

Demonstrated Interest: Very Important
Legacy Status: Important
Admission Interview Offered: Yes

ENROLLMENT
Total Undergraduate Enrollment: 2,133
% Part-Time: 1%
% Male: 43%
% Female: 57%
% Out-of-State: 75%
% Fraternity: 5%
% Sorority: 25%
% On-Campus (Freshman): 100%
% On-Campus (All Undergraduate): 100%

% African-American: 5%
% Asian: 4%
% Hispanic: 9%
% White: 63%
% Other: 4%
% Race or Ethnicity Unknown: 1%
% International: 14%
% Low-Income: 11%

ACADEMICS
Student-to-Faculty Ratio: 8 to 1
% of Classes Under 20: 80%
% of Classes 20-49: 20%
% of Classes 50 or More: 0%
% Full-Time Faculty: 80%
% Full-Time Faculty w/ Terminal Degree: 94%

Top Programs
Bioloy
Economics
Environmental Studies
Foreign Languages
History
International Business and Management
International Studies

Retention Rate: 87%
4-Year Graduation Rate: 80%
6-Year Graduation Rate: 83%

Curricular Flexibility: Somewhat Flexible
Academic Rating: ★★★✓

#CollegesWorthYourMoney

Set in the small town of Carlisle, Pennsylvania, Dickinson College is a liberal arts school with a strong academic reputation that dates back to the earliest days of the United States. In fact, it was founded the same week the United States signed the Treaty of Paris that ended the Revolutionary War. Today, the 2,133 undergraduate students who call Dickinson home are an increasingly diverse group, both in terms of academic/career interests and demographically. In recent years the school has doubled its rate of international students to 13 percent and raised the presence of underrepresented minorities from 15 percent in 2013 to 22 percent in 2019. The school does have a notable gender gap to the tune of a 57/43 split in favor of women.

Inside the Classroom

Freshmen are matched with a professor-advisor and engage in a mandatory first-year seminar intended to hone critical thinking, analysis, and research skills. From there, students must embark on an extensive trek through required coursework in quantitative reasoning, the humanities and arts, the social sciences, laboratory science, foreign language, and four physical education blocks. There are additional boxes to check in the areas of US diversity, global diversity, and a sustainability course.

As students immerse themselves in one of forty-four areas of concentration, Dickinson supports them with an 8:1 student-to-faculty ratio and average class size of fifteen with 80 percent of classes being capped at nineteen students. This type of intimacy allows the school to advertise that: "Not only will you have the opportunity to conduct advanced research as an undergraduate that most wouldn't experience until graduate school, you'll also have the chance to work alongside faculty in the process." The majority of students also elect to venture to other continents as part of their undergraduate experience. Offering study abroad opportunities in thirty-nine locations in twenty-four countries across six continents, Dickinson enjoys a 70 percent participation rate.

By discipline, the greatest number of degrees are conferred in the social sciences (25 percent); business (11 percent); biology (10 percent); and area, ethnic, and foreign language (8 percent). The college's foreign language program that features thirteen offerings—including Arabic, Hebrew, and Portuguese—is recognized as one of the top programs in the country. International studies, history, and environmental studies also have particularly strong reputations. Dickinson students are known as a globetrotting and service-oriented bunch. Thus, it is fitting that the college is a leading producer of Fulbright scholars (13 in 2020 alone) and Peace Corps volunteers.

Outside the Classroom

Dickinson is located in central Pennsylvania about twenty miles from the state capital of Harrisburg. Carlisle may be a small town, yet there are a reasonable number of nearby shopping/dining options, including dozens of restaurants within walking distance. The school's small town location means that a good deal of social life takes place on campus where literally 100 percent of students reside in college-owned housing. Greek life has a strong but not dominant presence with only 5 percent of men joining fraternities but 25 percent of women joining sororities. More than one hundred student clubs exist with the highest concentrations in the performing arts and club sports. For those serious about athletics, the Red Devils compete in NCAA Division III in eleven men's and twelve women's sports. Environmental sustainability is important to the administration and students alike, and with its own organic farm and pledge to be climate neutral, the college is regularly ranked as one of the top eco-friendly colleges in the country.

Career Services

The Career Center has twelve professional employees who play advising, pre-professional counseling, and employer relations roles. That works out to a 178:1 student-to-advisor ratio, which is significantly better than average when compared to other schools featured in this guide. One counselor is dedicated to pre-health advising and another guides pre-law students.

Dickinson does not host its own career fairs but does endorse two nearby gatherings, the Capital Region Internship Fair at Penn State Harrisburg and the Not-for-Profit Networking Fair in Philadelphia. However, there are other areas where this office excels. For example, a tremendous 94 percent of 2019 grads completed an internship, service-learning, or research apprenticeship at some point over their four years of study. In the summer of 2019, more than 400 students completed internships and summer research experiences in thirty states and twenty-one countries. In 2016, the college also launched an externship program in which students can spend between two and ten days over winter break shadowing alums in their workplaces. In short, it is hard to go through Dickinson without completing relevant, hands-on learning opportunities that lead to successful postgraduate outcomes.

Professional Outcomes

One year after graduating, 93 percent of Dickinsonians have found jobs, full-time volunteer work, or have enrolled in graduate school. The most popular industries are, in order, business and industry, education, health and medical services, and nonprofits. Red Devils head to a wide range of organizations/employers with multiple 2019 grads headed to the US Army, the Peace Corps, Teach for America and, on the other end of the spectrum, the Vanguard Group. Many other well-known financial, pharmaceutical, and consulting companies are represented on the list of 2019 graduate destinations as are a host of other nonprofit organizations. Across all graduating years, companies employing more than twenty-five Dickinson alumni include Deloitte, IBM, Morgan Stanley, JPMorgan Chase & Co., Merck, EY, PNC, PwC, Google, and Amazon. The median salary for a Dickinson alum five years into their career, is $58,600. It's interesting that more alumni can be found in New York City than in Pennsylvania.

Within five years of receiving their diplomas, 55-60 percent of recent grads have entered or finished graduate school. For the Class of 2019, the majority of graduate school-bound new alums found homes in state universities; however, a fair number of prestigious acceptances were sprinkled in including Georgetown, Carnegie Mellon (computer science), Johns Hopkins, Columbia, Brown, and USC. Law school applicants are accepted at a rate of 94 percent with some applicants finding success at the Boston University School of Law, Penn State Dickinson School of Law, and New York Law School. Of students recommended for medical school by the college, 75 percent were accepted into at least one institution.

Admission

The admit rate in 2019 was 40 percent, down from 49 percent in 2018. Standardized test scores for admitted students have remained fairly constant over the years, and the majority do submit them (52 percent submit SATs and 23 percent submit ACTs) even though the school went test-optional a long time ago. The mid-50 percent range on the ACT is 28-32 and 1260-1390 on the SAT. In terms of class rank, 42 percent of freshmen hail from the top 10 percent of their high school cohort, and 72 percent finish in the top 25 percent; only 4 percent of this group did not finish in the top half of their class.

Dickinson shows love to students who love them. Sixty-two percent of early decision applicants were offered admission in 2019, which was a reduction from the previous year. It is unusual for a college to include "demonstrated interest" as one of the most important factors in admissions decisions, but Dickinson does exactly that. With a yield rate of only 18 percent, the vast majority of those accepted into the college elect to attend another institution. A handful of other soft factors also sit atop the list: volunteer work, talent/ability, and character/personal qualities. Despite its status as a highly selective institution, intelligent students with a blemish still have a chance to find a home here. With its test-optional policy, those who exceled in the classroom but struggled on Saturday mornings with a No. 2 pencil in their hand are still in the running as are those with the opposite imperfection—strong SAT-takers who bloomed late as serious-minded students.

Worth Your Money?

An impressively high 66 percent of Dickinson students are awarded some level of need-based aid. While not all see 100 percent of their demonstrated need met, the majority do, and the average annual grant is $41,571. An additional 19 percent of undergraduates receive annual merit aid awards of $12,796, helping to reduce the total cost of attendance that is estimated at over $74k+ per year. Thanks to that assistance, the amount of debt incurred by the average Dickinson student is less than that of the average college student in the United States. If you were borrowing $100k+ to study the liberal arts, we would caution against selecting this school without first exploring more cost-effective options. However, for those taking on modest amounts of student loans, this is a college worth attending for the intimate class environment and solid graduate outcomes.

FINANCIAL
Institutional Type: Private
In-State Tuition: $55,948
Out-of-State Tuition: $55,948
Room & Board: $14,672
Required Fees: $575
Books & Supplies: $1,290

Avg. Need-Based Grant: $41,571
Avg. % of Need Met: 99%

Avg. Merit-Based Award: $12,796
% Receiving (All Freshmen): 19%
% Receiving (Freshmen w/o Need): 15%

Avg. Cumulative Debt: $27,030
% of Students Borrowing: 55%

CAREER
Who Recruits
1. Gartner
2. Amazon
3. Booz Allen Hamilton
4. PwC
5. PNC

Notable Internships
1. BlackRock
2. IBM
3. Cushman & Wakefield

Top Industries
1. Business
2. Education
3. Operations
4. Social Services
5. Sales

Top Employers
1. US Army
2. Deloitte
3. IBM
4. Morgan Stanley
5. JPMorgan Chase

Where Alumni Work
1. New York City
2. Philadelphia
3. Washington DC
4. Boston
5. Harrisburg, PA

Median Earnings
College Scorecard (Early Career): $57,400
PayScale (Early Career): $58,600
PayScale (Mid-Career): $108,500

RANKINGS
Money: 233
U.S. News: 47 (T), Liberal Arts Colleges
Wall Street Journal/THE: 93
Washington Monthly: 28, Liberal Arts Colleges

COLLEGE OVERLAPS
Bucknell University
Franklin & Marshall College
Gettysburg College
Lafayette College
Lehigh University

Drexel University

Philadelphia, Pennsylvania | 215-895-2400

ADMISSION
Admission Rate: 75%
Admission Rate - Men: 74%
Admission Rate - Women: 75%
EA Admission Rate: 92%
ED Admission Rate: 82%
ED Admits as % of Total Admits: 1%
Admission Rate (5-Year Trend): -7%
% of Admits Attending (Yield): 13%
Transfer Admission Rate: 49%

SAT Reading/Writing (Middle 50%): 590-680
SAT Math (Middle 50%): 600-710
ACT Composite (Middle 50%): 25-31

% Graduated in Top 10% of HS Class: 35%
% Graduated in Top 25% of HS Class: 67%
% Graduated in Top 50% of HS Class: 92%

Demonstrated Interest: Considered
Legacy Status: Considered
Admission Interview Offered: No

ENROLLMENT
Total Undergraduate Enrollment: 15,346
% Part-Time: 10%
% Male: 52%
% Female: 48%
% Out-of-State: 51%
% Fraternity: 11%
% Sorority: 10%
% On-Campus (Freshman): 88%
% On-Campus (All Undergraduate): 22%

% African-American: 7%
% Asian: 20%
% Hispanic: 7%
% White: 50%
% Other: 4%
% Race or Ethnicity Unknown: 2%
% International: 10%
% Low-Income: 20%

ACADEMICS
Student-to-Faculty Ratio: 11 to 1
% of Classes Under 20: 52%
% of Classes 20-49: 39%
% of Classes 50 or More: 10%
% Full-Time Faculty: 56%
% Full-Time Faculty w/ Terminal Degree: 84%

Top Programs
Biomedical Engineering
Civil Engineering
Design
Information Systems
Mechanical Engineering
Nursing
Public Health

Retention Rate: 89%
4-Year Graduation Rate: NR
6-Year Graduation Rate: 69%

Curricular Flexibility: Somewhat Flexible
Academic Rating: ★★★

#CollegesWorthYourMoney

Building your campus adjacent to an Ivy League school like the University of Pennsylvania is a solid recipe to end up a higher education afterthought. Yet Drexel, established in 1891, has carved out its own solid reputation as a private research university specializing in engineering, business, and nursing, all bolstered by a groundbreaking and distinctive co-op program that just celebrated its one hundredth anniversary. Drexel Dragons come to the university for its rigorous programs as well as the emphasis placed on experiential learning. They leave, by and large, with well-paying jobs in their area of interest. Practical, career-minded teens find a good partner institution in Drexel University.

Inside the Classroom
There are eighty-plus undergraduate majors to choose from at Drexel, and the academic culture lets you get down to brass tacks quickly. Other than a Composition & Rhetoric course and introductory classes that provide an overview of university life and the co-op experience, most students dive right into their major-specific course-work as freshmen. Business students take courses like Foundations of Economics, Principles of Economics, and Introduction to Analysis. Engineering students are plopped right into Chemistry, Calculus, and Introduction to Engineering Design and Data Analysis. The robust co-op program sees just about every single undergraduate participate. Students can choose between a five-year plan that includes three co-op experiences or a traditional four-year pathway that allows for one co-op placement. The school runs year-round on a quarter calendar to accommodate students on co-ops.

Drexel offers a reasonable 11:1 student-to-faculty ratio with commensurately reasonable class sizes. Fifty-two percent of sections contain nineteen or fewer students, and just a sliver under 10 percent of sections contain fifty or more. Drexel students are encouraged to begin seeking undergraduate research opportunities "as early as the freshman year." An array of research-oriented co-ops exist at local hospitals, museums, and pharmaceutical companies as well. With the emphasis on co-op education, it can be difficult to carve out time to study abroad while at Drexel. Last year, roughly 900 students managed to study internationally at one of sixty locations. Co-ops in foreign countries are another way to access the benefits of this type of experience.

Looking at the number of degrees conferred by discipline, the big three at Drexel are business (22 percent), health professions (22 percent), and engineering (20 percent). Visual and performing arts (10 percent), computer science (5 percent), and biology (4 percent) round out the list of majors with a sizable representation. The Westphal College of Media Arts & Design has a growing reputation, as do programs in engineering. Also on the rise is Drexel's number of winners of prestigious postgraduate fellowships. In 2019, four undergraduates won Fulbright Scholarships and six former Drexel undergrads took home National Science Foundation Graduate Research Fellowships.

Outside the Classroom
Set on a ninety-six-acre urban campus in University City, the section of Philadelphia that also includes the University of Pennsylvania, Drexel has 88 percent of freshmen residing in university-owned housing, but only 22 percent of the overall student body live on campus. Greek life draws 11 percent of males and 10 percent of female students. There are eighteen NCAA Division I sports teams that compete in the Colonial Athletic Association. Club and intramural sports are huge with over 9,000 participants each year. The Drexel Recreation Center is an 18,000-square-foot facility with all of the fitness amenities one could desire. There are 300 active student organizations on campus and a ton more opportunities for fun in the surrounding area. Drexel students get in free at the Academy of Natural Sciences, the oldest museum of its kind in the country, and can just as easily walk to World Café Live and catch a free concert with a big-name artist every Friday afternoon. Famed art museums, major sporting events, and an excellent food and bar scene are all within a short distance of campus. Student groups like the Campus Activities Board organize group trips to amusement parks, Broadway plays, and host block parties and other special events on campus.

Career Services
The Steinbright Career Development Center is staffed by sixteen full-time staff members who serve as career counselors, pre-law/pre-health advisors, and employer relations specialists. However, there are twenty-six additional professional employees dedicated to the co-op program, bringing the total to forty-two staff members who work with undergraduates on career-related matters. That works out to a 365:1 ratio, a respectable figure for a university of Drexel's size and scope. Its three annual career fairs are well attended by employers, but student attendance is lower than one would expect. A recent Fall Career Fair drew 228 employers and 1,678 students, the Spring Career Fair attracted 109 companies/organizations and 923 students, and the Engineering Career Fair saw 135 employers and 625 students in attendance.

Drexel University

E-mail: enroll@drexel.edu | Website: www.drexel.edu

When it comes to career services at Drexel the co-op experiences are, to quote Philadelphia-area native Reggie Jackson, "The straw that stirs the drink." Among surveyed graduates, 88 percent had a co-op experience that was relevant to their current job, and 92 were satisfied with their positions. More importantly, 48 percent of students received a job offer from one of their co-op employers. Placements are available in thirty-one states and thirty-eight countries, and partner organizations include major players like Goldman Sachs, Lockheed Martin, and Exelon. The strength of this one-of-a-kind co-op program combined with strong employment statistics earns the Steinbright Career Development Center high marks from our staff.

Professional Outcomes

One year after graduating, 97 percent of the Class of 2018 (most recent year available) had arrived at their next destination; 85 percent were employed, and 12 percent had matriculated into graduate or professional school. The largest employers of Drexel alumni are Comcast, Merck, Vanguard, and Johnson & Johnson. There are also at least one hundred Dragons within GlaxoSmithKline, JP Morgan Chase, SAP (software), Amazon, Microsoft, IBM, Accenture, Deloitte, Google, and EY. Six times as many graduates remain in Philadelphia as go to the second most popular post-graduation destination of New York City. The average starting salary for Drexel grads with a full-time job was $60,843

The predominately career-driven group that attends the university does not immediately move on to graduate schools in large numbers. However, those who do have produced some solid results, particularly those applying to medical and law school. Drexel's medical school acceptance rate was 60 percent, roughly 20 points higher than the national average. It offers an accelerated BS/MD program with its own Drexel University College of Medicine. Eighty-four percent of law school applicants ultimately found a home for their legal education. Recent grads have landed at prestigious law schools at Harvard, the University of Michigan, Vanderbilt, and the University of Pennsylvania as well as a number of local options including Drexel's own law school that opened in 2006.

Admission

Drexel's 31,824 applicants for a place in the freshman class of 2019-20 overwhelmingly received favorable admissions news—75 percent were accepted. That healthy percentage is the norm at Drexel as acceptance rates have been in the 70-80 percent range for some time. Its yield rate, the number of accepted students who actually enroll, is around 13 percent. This is because, for many, Drexel is not their first choice. Still, those who end up attending have a strong academic profile. Freshmen in 2019-20 possessed a mid-50 percent SAT of 1200-1380 and an ACT of 25-31. Thirty-five percent placed within the top 10 percent of their high school class, and 67 percent were in the top quartile; 51 percent of students sported a GPA of 3.75 or higher and, on the other end, 4 percent had a GPA under 3.0.

Admissions decisions are made in a manner consistent with Drexel's STEM-focus—the hard numbers are of utmost importance. GPA, class rank, and the rigor of one's high school coursework are deemed "very important" while soft factors like recommendations, essays, and character/personal qualities join standardized test scores in the second tier. With such a low yield rate, the university looks favorably upon those who will commit to it through binding early decision. The ED acceptance rate in 2019 was 82 percent. In short, Drexel is a rare school with a pre-professional focus that is not terribly difficult to get into. Those with standardized test scores around the 80th percentile and solid but imperfect grades should find a welcome home here.

Worth Your Money?

Drexel graduates earn 18.5 percent above the national average which, even given the focus on business, engineering, and nursing is still an impressive achievement. That salary boost is needed thanks to the $72,000+ annual cost of attendance, although students receiving merit aid do receive an average annual grant of $33k. Fortunately, the co-op experience is top notch and frequently leads to gainful employment in one's area of study. Students do not pay tuition during their co-op year and, in fact, are paid a median six-month salary of over $18k. This college is unique and connected enough to be worth the high price tag, particularly for students pursing more pre-professional majors.

FINANCIAL
Institutional Type: Private
In-State Tuition: $56,238
Out-of-State Tuition: $56,238
Room & Board: $16,009
Required Fees: $0
Books & Supplies: $1,700

Avg. Need-Based Grant: $33,379
Avg. % of Need Met: 80%

Avg. Merit-Based Award: $16,014
% Receiving (All Freshmen): 35%
% Receiving (Freshmen w/o Need): 24%

Avg. Cumulative Debt: $72,883
% of Students Borrowing: 67%

CAREER
Who Recruits
1. Seer Interactive
2. Bentley Systems
3. Johnson & Johnson
4. Spark Therapeutics
5. Lockheed Martin

Notable Internships
1. KPMG
2. Anthropologie
3. Delancy Street Partners

Top Industries
1. Business
2. Engineering
3. Operations
4. Education
5. Healthcare

Top Employers
1. Lockheed Martin
2. Comcast
3. Merck
4. Vanguard
5. Johnson & Johnson

Where Alumni Work
1. Philadelphia
2. New York City
3. Washington DC
4. San Francisco
5. Baltimore

Median Earnings
College Scorecard (Early Career): $68,800
PayScale (Early Career): $64,700
PayScale (Mid-Career): $118,500

RANKINGS
Money: 431
U.S. News: 133 (T), National Universities
Wall Street Journal/THE: 106 (T)
Washington Monthly: 134, National Universities

COLLEGE OVERLAPS
Pennsylvania State University - University Park
Rutgers University - New Brunswick
Rochester Institute of Technology
Temple University
University of Pittsburgh

Duke University

Durham, North Carolina | 919-684-3214

Duke is a place where students can be, at once, fanatical, face-painted members of the Cameron Crazies as well as studious, career-minded young people in an Ivy League-caliber academic environment. In fact, Duke is now more selective than several Ivies, which is no surprise given the university's unique combination of academic prestige and extracurricular excitement. Close to 6,700 undergrads are joined by more than 9,900 graduate students on this picturesque, 8,800-acre campus in Durham, North Carolina.

Inside the Classroom
The academic offerings at Duke include fifty-three majors, fifty-two minors, and twenty-six interdisciplinary certificates. More than 4,000 undergraduate courses run each semester in the College of Arts & Sciences alone. Rarely do students concentrate solely on one major—83 percent either double major, add a minor, or pursue an additional certificate. Undergraduates encounter a good number of unique academic requirements. All freshmen in the Trinity College of Arts & Sciences must take a first-year seminar and first-year writing course. Before graduation, each individual must take two small group learning experiences that can involve an independent study and/or constructing a thesis. Foreign language and multiple courses under the umbrellas of Areas of Knowledge and Modes of Inquiry also must be tackled.

Class sizes are on the small side—70 percent are nineteen or fewer, and more than one-quarter are less than ten. A stellar 6:1 student-to-faculty ratio helps keep classes so reasonable even while catering to almost five-figures of graduate students. The Undergraduate Research Support Office does great work connecting students with opportunities to conduct research, either over the summer or during the regular school year. All told, more than half of undergraduates conduct research. More than any other top-ten research institution, Duke students pursue a semester abroad—47 percent of 2020 grads elected to venture off to one of the school's 300 partner programs scattered around the world.

Duke has a sterling reputation for academics across the board. The Department of Biology is world class and a leading producer of successful medical school applicants. Programs in economics, English, and public policy consistently earn top ranking as well. Nineteen percent go on to earn degrees in the social sciences followed by engineering (15 percent), biology (14 percent), public administration and social services (9 percent), and psychology (7 percent). Blue Devils win prestigious postgraduate fellowships on a regular basis. Named a top producer of Fulbright Scholars for the last thirteen years, Duke churned out eighteen winners in 2020. The university has produced an incredible fifty Rhodes Scholars in its illustrious history, more than Emory and Vanderbilt combined.

Outside the Classroom
When you enter campus through Duke Gardens, it can feel like you're strolling through a perfectly manicured Disney theme park; everything is pristine and aesthetically pleasing. Thus, no one is anxious to live anywhere other than the university's grounds and 100 percent of freshmen and 85 percent of the entire student body live on campus. With thirty-nine recognized Greek chapters, fraternities and sororities play a major role in social life at Duke. Forty-two percent of women and 29 percent of men become Greek affiliated. Those who occupy dorms are generally pleased, and the food at Duke is universally praised. Big-time sports is a staple of life on campus as the Blue Devils compete in twenty-three sports in NCAA Division I's vaunted Atlantic Coast Conference. Since the beloved Coach K took over in 1980, the men's basketball squad has made the Final Four a dozen times and has won five national championships. One of the most popular non-sports-related, campus-wide events is the annual Last Day of Classes (LDOC) celebration that draws a large percentage of the student body for activities, beverages, and music. More than 400 student organizations run on campus, including a high-performing mock trial team and The Chronicle, an award-winning student newspaper with a seven-figure budget. The culture of volunteering is strong with an 80 percent participation rate as Blue Devils perform community service in the city of Durham in programs like Engineers Without Borders.

Career Services
The Career Center at Duke is staffed by eight undergraduate career advisors and ten employer relations specialists and event coordinators, calculating to a student-to-advisor ratio of 369:1, which is in the average range when compared to other schools in its weight class. Yet, this "mediocrity" is not indicative of anything less than outstanding career services offerings. This assessment can be delivered by one quick fact: An astounding 95 percent of graduating seniors who had lined up their first jobs were hired by companies that work in some capacity with the Duke Career Center.

Undergrads each have their own assigned career counselor, and the school recommends establishing a relationship as a freshman. Two-thirds of graduates reported meeting with a career center staff member at least once over their four years of study. Regular events held include Practice Interview Day, Ignite Your Internship Search, and the Fall Career Fair that includes over one hundred top companies, many of which recruit and offer interviews on campus. Bottom line—the Career Center at Duke is among the best in the country at preparing students for high-paying employment and admission into prestigious graduate/professional programs.

Professional Outcomes

At graduation, 71 percent of surveyed seniors in 2018 (most recent year available) were set to enter the world of work, 20 percent were continuing into graduate schools, and 2 percent were starting their own businesses. The industries that attract the largest percentage of Blue Devils are finance, IT, health care, business and consulting, and science/research. Companies employing a minimum of three Class of 2018 Duke grads include Google, Capital One, Facebook, Amazon, Microsoft, Oracle, Goldman Sachs, Morgan Stanley, Accenture, and a host of other top-shelf corporations in the areas of technology, finance, and consulting. Thirty-four percent of Duke alumni elect to stay in North Carolina. New York, California, DC, and Massachusetts follow in popularity. The top foreign destinations for employment are the United Kingdom and China. Duke students, on average, do exceptionally well financially, bringing home the eleventh highest salary by age thirty-four of any school in the country, ahead of schools like Georgetown, Stanford, and Caltech.

Of the 20 percent headed into graduate school, a hefty 22 percent are attending medical school, 18 percent are in PhD programs, and 12 percent are entering law school. The med school acceptance rate is 85 percent, more than twice the national average. Eventually, 84 percent of Duke undergraduates will go on to earn an advanced degree. A typical graduating class sees around 150 members apply to law school, scoring an average of 165 on the LSAT, among the highest in the country. Those applicants find their way into just about every top-ranked law school in existence. In the last few years, Blue Devils have pursued a JD at Stanford Law School, University of Chicago Law School, and Harvard Law School, among others.

Admission

Getting into Duke is an Ivy League-level, single-digit proposition. The application pool vying for a place in the Class of 2023 saw only 8 percent gain acceptance. That isn't a new trend. Rather, Duke has had an admit rate under 10 percent for the last six years. Among freshmen in 2019-20, 72 percent submitted ACT scores and had a 50th percentile range of 33-35; the SAT range was 1480-1570. An intimidating 95 percent of Blue Devils graduated in the top 10 percent of their high school class, and 98 percent were in the top quartile.

Early decision applicants saw a far more favorable acceptance rate, 18.4 percent versus the regular round rate of 6.4 percent; a sizable 41 percent of the freshman class is cemented during this early round. However, it is worth keeping in mind that athletes and legacy students are typically admitted in the early round, which certainly helps prop up the acceptance rate. Additionally, legacy students comprise 10-13 percent of the student body in any given year, and they typically apply ED. The Duke Admissions Committee considers eight factors as "very important" in admissions decisions: rigor of classes, grades, test scores, essays, recommendations, extracurricular activities, talent/ability, and character/personal qualities. Like the Ivies, Duke routinely rejects valedictorians and teens with perfect standardized test scores. Successful applicants will have exceptional academic credentials, attention-grabbing essays, and special talents that set them apart from a crowded field of aspiring Blue Devils.

Worth Your Money?

Duke's annual cost of attendance is a hair below $79,000, but 52 percent pay less than that amount. Members of the undergraduate student body who qualify for need-based financial aid receive annual grants of $53,400 per year, meeting 100 percent of their demonstrated need. The university has the fourteenth largest endowment in the United States ($7 billion), and it puts it to good use, making Duke affordable to those from non-wealthy families. Essentially, the approximately 45 percent of students who come from wealthy families (top 5 percent income) pay the bulk of the sticker price while those from lower-to-middle income homes get significant tuition reductions. Even if you had to take on a lot of debt to attend Duke, this is one school that will almost certainly pay you back many times over; alumni salaries and employment prospects are that strong.

FINANCIAL
Institutional Type: Private
In-State Tuition: $58,085
Out-of-State Tuition: $58,085
Room & Board: $16,026
Required Fees: $2,159
Books & Supplies: $1,434

Avg. Need-Based Grant: $53,400
Avg. % of Need Met: 100%

Avg. Merit-Based Award: $76,181
% Receiving (All Freshmen): 9%
% Receiving (Freshmen w/o Need): 1%

Avg. Cumulative Debt: $22,203
% of Students Borrowing: 33%

CAREER
Who Recruits
1. 4170 Trading LLC
2. Cornerstone Advisors LLC
3. National Security Agency
4. Xerox
5. Qualtrics

Notable Internships
1. Carlyle Group
2. CNBC
3. Instagram

Top Industries
1. Business
2. Education
3. Research
4. Operations
5. Engineering

Top Employers
1. Google
2. Amazon
3. Microsoft
4. Facebook
5. Goldman Sachs

Where Alumni Work
1. Raleigh-Durham, NC
2. New York City
3. Washington DC
4. San Francisco
5. Boston

Median Earnings
College Scorecard (Early Career): $84,400
PayScale (Early Career): $75,400
PayScale (Mid-Career): $145,400

RANKINGS
Money: 5
U.S. News: 12, National Universities
Wall Street Journal/THE: 5 (T)
Washington Monthly: 6, National Universities

COLLEGE OVERLAPS
Cornell University
Northwestern University
Princeton University
University of North Carolina at Chapel Hill
University of Pennsylvania

Elon University

Elon, North Carolina | 336-278-3566

Nestled in the centralized Piedmont region of North Carolina, Elon University is home to 6,277 undergraduates and is—most fittingly for a school whose mascot is the Phoenix—a school on the rise. Not yet an uber-selective school (over three-quarters of applicants get in), this modestly sized university is known for its quality undergraduate teaching, experiential learning opportunities, and unparalleled study abroad program. Individualized attention is available at every turn, particularly from a well-staffed and highly effective Career Services Department.

Inside the Classroom
Students choose from sixty majors and can add a number of interesting minors like adventure –based learning, coaching, and multimedia authoring. Regardless of one's area of concentration, all Elon undergrads must work through an extensive core curriculum that is made up of six interrelated parts: two first-year foundations courses focused on developing writing and critical thinking skills; an experiential learning component that requires studying abroad, interning, or conducting independent research; foreign language (can be exempted through AP tests); a total of thirty-two credits in the arts and sciences; eight credit hours of advanced coursework outside one's major; and a capstone seminar as a senior. Ninety-eight percent of students elect to take a one-credit freshman course entitled Elon 101 that, among other things, helps new students map out a graduation plan.

Elon's 12:1 student-to-faculty ratio leads to an average class size of twenty students; 52 percent of sections contain fewer than twenty students. A whopping 78 percent elect to study abroad, the highest participation rate in the country among master's-granting institutions. There are limitless options for overseas study including official Elon Centers Abroad in Shanghai, Dunedin, London, and Florence. Chances for working closely with faculty on research projects are also plentiful; 23 percent of students participate in faculty-mentored research.

Though Elon possesses solid offerings in many disciplines, programs in finance, communication, exercise science, and the performing arts receive the most praise. The areas in which the greatest number of degrees are conferred are business (33 percent), journalism/communication (19 percent), social services (7 percent), parks and recreation (6 percent), and psychology (6 percent). Elon is recognized as a top producer of Fulbright Scholars seeing ten fellowship winners in 2020; it had forty-five winners between 2013 and 2018. Recent graduates also have received a Truman Scholarship, a Goldwater Scholarship, and grants from the National Science Foundation.

Outside the Classroom
Sixty-four percent of undergrads live on the school's 656-acre grounds. Greek life is a dominant force on the Elon social scene with 39 percent of women joining sororities and 20 percent of men signing up for fraternity life. The 60/40 gender breakdown in favor of women is certainly a factor in social life. It also should be noted that Elon has been rated as one of the LGBTQ-friendlier schools in the country. An athletically inclined student body participates in seventeen NCAA Division I sports as well as twenty-one intercollegiate club teams and eighteen intramural sports. Elon students are known for being involved in their college community as nearly 90 percent contribute some level of volunteer service, and 49 percent hold some type of leadership role in a student organization. There are 250 student-run clubs, including a student-run television station and an award-winning weekly newspaper, The Pendulum. The Elon Speakers Series sees an incredible list of notable figures visit campus each year. In the last few years, it has welcomed David Cameron, Anita Hill, and Bob Woodward. The town of Elon is not the world's most exciting place, but those with access to a car are no more than an hour from the larger cities of Durham, Raleigh, and Winston-Salem.

Career Services
The Student Professional Development Center (SPDC) at Elon University has twenty-two professional employees (not counting a number of graduate fellows and apprentices) who play advising, pre-professional counseling, and employer relations roles. That works out to a 285:1 student-to-advisor ratio, which is better-than-average when compared to other schools featured in this guide. This office has sufficient resources to offer individualized services and coordinate large events such as fall and spring job fairs that attract over ninety employers and over 1,000 students. The center also regularly offers smaller events, such as the Accounting Meet and Greet, which attract fifteen firms and 120 undergraduate students. Its Graduate & Professional School Fair brings representatives from fifty institutions to campus each October. In total, 250+ employers attend career fairs during a given academic year.

Thanks to efforts of the Student Professional Development Center, 87 percent of Elon students complete an internship during their four undergraduate years and 62 percent of those internships led directly to a job offer. Members of the Class of 2019 interned at a range of employers including Red Hat, Boeing, the Kennedy Center, KMPG, and C-SPAN. Companies known to recruit at Elon and/or offer on-campus interviews include Walt Disney Co., ESPN, Oracle, Credit Suisse, EY, PwC, Goldman Sachs, and ABC News. The SPDC facilitates more than 5,600 one-on-one advising appointments per year, an absolutely remarkable number given the modest size of the school.

Professional Outcomes

Results of a survey administered nine months after graduation found that 95 percent of the Class of 2019 had found employment, a graduate school, or an internship. That is a significant improvement from six years ago when only 83 percent of graduates had found their next postsecondary or employment home nine months after receiving their diplomas. Of those accepting employment, a magnificent 92 percent reported that their job directly related to their area of study. Top employers of recent Elon graduates include Bloomberg, Deloitte, EY, Google, Goldman Sachs, Red Ventures, and Wells Fargo. Geographically, alumni are dispersed all over the map. A mere 20 percent of graduates remained in the Tar Heel State while 19 percent migrated to New York and 12 percent to Massachusetts. The average starting salary for an Elon graduate is over $45,000.

Just under one-quarter of 2019 grads gained acceptance into graduate/professional school. Many remain at Elon or continue at other Carolina-based schools such as UNC-Chapel Hill, Duke, Wake Forest, East Carolina University, or North Carolina State. Class of 2018 members gained acceptance into prestigious graduate schools such as Boston University, Columbia, NYU, Penn, and Georgetown. Applicants to medical school typically gain acceptance at the same rate as the national average, around 40 percent. However, in recent years, Elon students enjoyed a better than 50 percent acceptance rate. That group of students earned average MCAT scores that placed them in the 75th percentile. Few graduates in recent years have been accepted into the top medical schools in the country.

Admission

Elon admitted 78 percent of the 10,500 applicants for a place in the 2019-20 freshman class. First-year students possessed an average SAT score of 1241 and ACT of 27. Only 25 percent of admitted students finished in the top 10 percent of their high school class, and 56 percent finished in the top quartile. Interestingly, a decade ago, the acceptance rate was a much stingier 42 percent, but the credentials of accepted students were roughly the same. In that time the quality of applicants has remained consistent, but the school's yield rate has declined from 33 percent to 20 percent, leading to more offers of acceptance in order to meet enrollment goals.

The admissions committee rates five factors as of the greatest importance: rigor of secondary curriculum, GPA, standardized test scores, essays, and recommendations. Attributes such as talent/ability as well as work experience, extracurricular activities, and legacy status round out the next tier of considered factors. Applying early decision offers a sizable advantage as 88 percent were accepted in the early round. ED admits account for one-quarter of the freshman class. A school whose reputation is ascending, Elon, for now, remains a welcoming landing spot for teens with solid but unspectacular transcripts. Applying early further increases your odds but may be unnecessary as an admissions strategy unless you are a borderline applicant.

Worth Your Money?

As far as private universities go, a list price of $51,000 (COA) isn't outlandish. Roughly one-third of the undergraduate student body receives need-based aid averaging $15k per recipient. Elon isn't a bargain for most students, but it is a solid deal for a school that provides ample individualized attention and has largely positive student outcomes.

FINANCIAL
Institutional Type: Private
In-State Tuition: $36,082
Out-of-State Tuition: $36,082
Room & Board: $12,685
Required Fees: $489
Books & Supplies: $900

Avg. Need-Based Grant: $15,187
Avg. % of Need Met: 58%

Avg. Merit-Based Award: $6,603
% Receiving (All Freshmen): 53%
% Receiving (Freshmen w/o Need): 30%

Avg. Cumulative Debt: $32,028
% of Students Borrowing: 34%

CAREER
Who Recruits
1. Walt Disney Company
2. SAS
3. Oracle
4. Net Suite
5. Vanguard

Notable Internships
1. ABC's The View
2. Aflac
3. Merrill Lynch

Top Industries
1. Business
2. Education
3. Sales
4. Operations
5. Media

Top Employers
1. Wells Fargo
2. Bank of America
3. EY
4. PwC
5. IBM

Where Alumni Work
1. Winston-Salem, NC
2. New York City
3. Raleigh-Durham, NC
4. Washington DC
5. Charlotte

Median Earnings
College Scorecard (Early Career): $51,900
PayScale (Early Career): $56,000
PayScale (Mid-Career): $99,200

RANKINGS
Money: 395
U.S. News: 88 (T), National Universities
Wall Street Journal/THE: 146
Washington Monthly: 146, National Universities

COLLEGE OVERLAPS
Clemson University
James Madison University
University of North Carolina at Chapel Hill
University of Richmond
University of South Carolina

Emerson College

Boston, Massachusetts | 617-824-8600

Positioned in Boston's historic Theater District, Emerson College is a school of approximately 3,900 undergraduate students, all united in their desire to make a mark in a creative field like film, television, or marketing/advertising. All 23 majors offered by the school have some element of performance or artistry and include highly unique academic concentrations such as comedic arts, sports communication, and musical theater. Like many other schools situated in downtown Boston, Emerson has become a more popular destination in recent years and, thus, the credentials needed to earn an invitation to this East Coast paradise for creative minds have been raised.

Inside the Classroom
No matter what artistic or performance-based field one is attending Emerson for, exposure to a broad liberal arts core is assured through the series of mandatory courses all students must embark upon. Freshmen take foundations courses in oral and written communication. In subsequent years, students must complete courses classified as aesthetics, global diversity, US diversity, ethics and values, history and politics, interdisciplinary, literary, scientific, social and psychological, and quantitative reasoning. Those in the school's Honors Program can add a senior thesis and a number of small seminar courses to the checklist of graduation requirements.

Emerson has a 13:1 student-to-faculty ratio and average class sizes in the 20-25 student range. Professors are generally accessible as evidenced by 83 percent of seniors rating their interactions with faculty as being "satisfactory" or "very satisfactory." Overall, 81 percent were "satisfied" or "very satisfied" with their educational experience at the college. Opportunities to study in other cities, both foreign and domestic, can be had through Emerson-sponsored external programs in Los Angeles, DC, The Netherlands, Prague, Spain, Beijing and Shanghai, Ireland, Mexico, Austria, Greece, and France.

The Journalism and Communications Studies programs rank among the top in the country. Emerson's various degree offerings in the film/television realm will open doors thanks to the school's LA affiliations and connected alumni network. By sheer popularity, the most popular majors are media arts production (38 percent), journalism (11 percent), marketing (7 percent), theater and performance (5 percent), and creative writing (5 percent). Seniors will, on occasion, win a prestigious national scholarship/fellowship, but very few apply, as Emerson grads enter the workforce in overwhelming numbers.

Outside the Classroom
Undergrads are fairly evenly divided between living in one of the school's five residential spaces and off-campus housing. While finding a cheap dwelling in Beantown is impossible (studio apartments start at $2k per month), the college offers resources to help students find the most reasonably priced options available. Despite the school's 61 percent women, 39 percent men gender breakdown, there are actually more fraternities at Emerson than sororities. Yet, Greek life is anything but a dominant part of the social scene. United more by their creative passions than official affiliations, the 90+ student-run clubs tend to be more a draw, especially the student publications—highlighted by Ploughshares, a literary journal—film groups, theater, comedy troupes, Emerson TV, and WERS FM, the acclaimed campus radio station. Close to 200 undergrads participate in the school's 14 NCAA Division III sports teams known as the Lions, but sports are a secondary interest for the bulk of the student body. Perhaps the best part about Emerson's campus is that it's located in the heart of downtown Boston. Everything you could ever want is within a short walk or T-ride of the college. This list includes the Museum of Fine Arts, Loews Theater (which offers free film screenings to students), Fenway Park, Boston Common, as well as countless restaurants, cafes, and bars.

Career Services
Emerson's Career Development Center (CDC) has eight professional employees who work in advising and employer engagement capacities. This works out to a 485:1 student-to-advisor ratio, which is fairly average when compared to many of the other small-to-midsize colleges featured in this guide. The office places an emphasis on helping students carve out Career Design Pathways which, beginning freshman year, help connect on-campus events and opportunities to "students' long-term planning and professional development." Some components of this program take place online, but face-to-face counseling is also encouraged.

Internship fairs are hosted by the college each fall and spring and draw representatives from an impressive array of arts and media employers such as the Boston Globe, the Boston Ballet, Converse (for advertising/marketing), and a number of Boston-area media companies/stations. The CDC's emphasis on helping students find internships pays off, with 90 percent of undergraduates landing at least one internship experience; the majority actually completed more than one. Of those in this category, 93 percent found their internships helpful in preparing them for their eventual first post-college job. Further, one third of interns were offered a job with their host employer. Overall, a survey of recent graduates found that 79 percent of graduates found the Career Development Center helpful.

Professional Outcomes

Within six months of leaving Emerson, 75 percent of Class of 2019 members were employed, 4 percent are enrolled in graduate school, and 21 percent are still seeking their next landing spot. The arts and entertainment sector is the area employing the largest number of alumni (20 percent), followed by media production (12 percent), marketing (10 percent), publishing (6 percent), education (5 percent), and journalism (5 percent). Top employers of the Class of 2019 include Apple, ICM Partners, the Walt Disney Company, and NBCUniversal. Many members of the alumni network can be found working at Netflix and at a number of local radio and television stations throughout the New England region.

The majority of graduates remain in the state of Massachusetts, with California, New York, Connecticut, and Texas attracting most of those electing to relocate. The average full-time salary for employed members of the Class of 2019 was $52,432. This figure is impressive when you consider the school's lack of a STEM program and emphasis on preparing students for careers in more creative and, generally, lower-paying jobs. Upon completing their undergraduate education, only about 1-in-20 students decide to immediately begin pursuing an advanced degree. Obviously, if you want to be a scientist or medical doctor, Emerson doesn't offer the right academic programs. Of those entering a master's program, the bulk stay put, pursuing a master's at Emerson in an area like writing for film and television, creative writing, or journalism.

Admission

A more selective school than it was just a few short years ago, Emerson admitted only 33 percent of its 15,354 applicants seeking a spot in the Class of 2023. In 2015, there were only 8,618 applicants, and 49 percent were accepted. Emerson shares an applicant pool with many other Boston-based schools, many of whom may rank higher on applicants' lists. As a result, the yield rate is only 18 percent, but—unusual for a school in this boat— no binding early decision option exists.

The admissions committee wants to see "how students have challenged themselves academically, balancing hard work with extracurricular activities." This is reflected in the average freshman's unweighted GPA of 3.72. In terms of class rank, 28 percent of freshmen finished in the top 10 percent of their high school class, and 69 percent were in the top quarter. As of 2017, Emerson implemented a test-optional policy. Those not submitting scores must either include in the application an additional essay or a creative sample/portfolio related to their major. While Emerson, like just about every other school in downtown Boston, is growing increasingly more difficult to get into, it will still open its door to students not at the very top of their class. Strong students with solid grades in rigorous courses and standardized test scores in the 85th-90th percentile will find success, particularly those with a nice extracurricular resume and portfolio.

Worth Your Money?

Emerson's 2020-21 tuition is $50,240, and room and board will set you back another $18,768. The school does award some level of financial aid to 84 percent of those who seek it. The average award for those receiving need-based aid is right around $20k; merit aid is awarded to 13 percent of undergrads who do not demonstrate any financial need with an average gift of $13,850. An Emerson education is unlikely to come cheap but, for those entering fields in performing arts or film, the training you will receive and connections you will make will definitely make this school worth the high cost.

FINANCIAL
Institutional Type: Private
In-State Tuition: $51,148
Out-of-State Tuition: $51,148
Room & Board: $18,768
Required Fees: $0
Books & Supplies: $1,150

Avg. Need-Based Grant: $23,198
Avg. % of Need Met: 55%

Avg. Merit-Based Award: $14,634
% Receiving (All Freshmen): 29%
% Receiving (Freshmen w/o Need): 21%

Avg. Cumulative Debt: $24,193
% of Students Borrowing: 61%

CAREER
Who Recruits
1. CNN
2. Penguin Random House
3. United Talent Agency
4. Spotify
5. The Daily Beast

Notable Internships
1. The Boston Globe
2. Vogue China
3. Discovery Studios

Top Industries
1. Media
2. Business
3. Arts and Design
4. Education
5. Operations

Top Employers
1. NBC Universal
2. Netflix
3. Northeastern University
4. MIT
5. Apple

Where Alumni Work
1. Boston
2. New York City
3. Los Angeles
4. San Francisco
5. Washington DC

Median Earnings
College Scorecard (Early Career): $46,600
PayScale (Early Career): $52,200
PayScale (Mid-Career): $102,200

RANKINGS
Money: 654
U.S. News: 9 (T), Regional Universities North
Wall Street Journal/THE: 501-600
Washington Monthly: 417, Master's Universities

COLLEGE OVERLAPS
Boston University
Fordham University
Ithaca College
New York University
Syracuse University

Emory University

Atlanta, Georgia | 404-727-6036

Widely viewed as a "Southern Ivy," Emory University hosts 7,118 elite undergraduates on its Atlanta-based campus. To be more geographically precise, the prestigious school, which boasts the sixteenth largest endowment of any university in the United States, is located in the Druid Hills section of Atlanta, home to the Centers for Disease Control as well as one of the wealthiest neighborhoods in the entire state of Georgia. This midsize university offers a diverse array of majors (70+) and minors (50+), and more than half of Emory students pursue more than one area of study.

Inside the Classroom

All freshmen must complete a first-year seminar in which they are tasked with stretching their critical thinking and research skills as they explore one of a series of fascinating topics in an intimate setting with a faculty member. The immersion and support don't stop there; all freshmen also must take a one-credit advising program called PACE (Pre-Major Advising Connections at Emory) in which they work with a faculty advisor and peer mentor to explore academic pathways. Ultimately, the greatest number of students go on to earn degrees in the social sciences (16 percent), business (15 percent), biology (14 percent), mathematics (7 percent), and psychology (5 percent).

One unique feature of Emory is that one of its undergraduate divisions, Oxford College, about forty-five minutes away, functions as a small liberal arts college for freshmen and sophomores. Oxford students knock out many of their lower-level courses before declaring a major and attending upper-level courses at Emory. No matter which school you attend, hands-on learning opportunities abound. A healthy 56 percent of Emory's student body works directly with a faculty member on academic research. Also noteworthy is the fact that 62 percent of courses have class sizes of under twenty students, a number comparable to many smaller liberal arts colleges. Studying abroad is a fairly common feature of an Emory education, with 40 percent of students traveling to one of 100 international destinations.

Emory is notable for its renowned Woodruff School of Nursing and Goizueta School of Business. It also routinely rates well in biology, neuroscience, creative writing, and political science. Undergrads at Emory have a strong history of winning national awards; the school boasted fourteen Fulbright Scholars in 2020 alone and has produced twenty Rhodes Scholars in its history. Further, Emory churns out more Teach for America candidates than any other midsize school in the United States, and it is also a leading producer of students who join the Peace Corps upon graduation.

Outside the Classroom

One-hundred percent of freshmen and 63 percent of all undergraduates reside in university-owned housing. Many also live in Greek houses as 23 percent of men pledge fraternities and 22 percent of women join sororities. Emory claims over 550 student-run clubs and sports teams, and Oxford College adds another eighty to that diverse list. Volunteer Emory organizes twenty to thirty service trips per week, and over 80 percent of students participate in one or more of the opportunities for community service each year. If you are looking for top-of-the-line collegiate athletics, Emory may not be a great fit. Despite the absence of nationally televised football games, roughly 400 non-scholarship athletes compete in a variety of Division III athletic competitions. Another 600+ students compete in one or more of Emory's club sports, which include everything from flag football to golf to swimming. Impressive amenities, such as two Olympic-size swimming pools and a rock climbing arena, also are available for recreational use. Notable campus-wide events include Wonderful Wednesdays, a weekly open-invite celebration that can include anything from a petting zoo to a volunteer fair and an annual town hall with former President Jimmy Carter. Off campus there is something for everyone with Atlanta's nightlife and natural beauty (a nature trail begins on Oxford's campus) right in your backyard.

Career Services

The Career Center at Emory is staffed by fourteen full-time professional employees as well as six additional full-time staff members who exclusively serve business majors at Goizueta. That equates to a student-to-advisor ratio of 356:1, slightly below average compared to the other institutions included in this book. Spring and fall job fairs are well attended (over 1,000 students each), and approximately 200 companies recruit on campus each year. Each year, more than 12,000 jobs and internships are posted on Handshake, 350+ events are held, and 1,500 one-on-one counseling sessions take place.

ADMISSION
Admission Rate: 16%
Admission Rate - Men: 17%
Admission Rate - Women: 15%
EA Admission Rate: Not Offered
ED Admission Rate: 23%
ED Admits as % of Total Admits: 15%
Admission Rate (5-Year Trend): -8%
% of Admits Attending (Yield): 29%
Transfer Admission Rate: 23%

SAT Reading/Writing (Middle 50%): 670-740
SAT Math (Middle 50%): 690-790
ACT Composite (Middle 50%): 31-34

% Graduated in Top 10% of HS Class: 84%
% Graduated in Top 25% of HS Class: 97%
% Graduated in Top 50% of HS Class: 100%

Demonstrated Interest: Not Considered
Legacy Status: Considered
Admission Interview Offered: Yes

ENROLLMENT
Total Undergraduate Enrollment: 7,118
% Part-Time: 1%
% Male: 40%
% Female: 60%
% Out-of-State: 80%
% Fraternity: 23%
% Sorority: 22%
% On-Campus (Freshman): 100%
% On-Campus (All Undergraduate): 63%

% African-American: 8%
% Asian: 21%
% Hispanic: 11%
% White: 39%
% Other: 4%
% Race or Ethnicity Unknown: 1%
% International: 16%
% Low-Income: 20%

ACADEMICS
Student-to-Faculty Ratio: 9 to 1
% of Classes Under 20: 62%
% of Classes 20-49: 25%
% of Classes 50 or More: 13%
% Full-Time Faculty: 88%
% Full-Time Faculty w/ Terminal Degree: 96%

Top Programs
Biology
Business Administration
Chemistry
English
Film and Media
International Studies
Neuroscience and Behavioral Biology
Philosophy

Retention Rate: 95%
4-Year Graduation Rate: 82%
6-Year Graduation Rate: 90%

Curricular Flexibility: Somewhat Flexible
Academic Rating: ★★★★✦

#CollegesWorthYourMoney

Typical career-prep services are available to undergraduate students. Resumes, cover letters, and personal statements can be submitted online for editing by a staff member with fairly quick turnaround times. High Five networking events are held at least once a year for ten career categories including legal, data science, green, STEM, and government and public policy. A full slate of guests, many of whom are Emory alums, discuss their careers with undergraduate attendees. At any time, students can access alumni as well as internship opportunities through their Handshake account. Emory Connects: Career Discovery Days provides students with job- shadowing opportunities in the Atlanta area.

Professional Outcomes

Within three months of graduation, 52 percent of Emory grads are already employed, and 92 percent have arrived at their next destination. The top ten employers of Emory's Class of 2019 include Ernst & Young, Triage Consulting Group, Google, Goldman Sachs, BlackRock, and Accenture. Past graduating classes have had a significant numbers of Eagles (the schools lesser-known mascot) land at Deloitte, PwC, the Home Depot, Facebook, and the Coca-Cola Company. Teach for America is the largest employer of the previous three graduating classes. While a healthy number of Emory grads found employment in Georgia, the top destinations for the Class of 2019 included non-Southern locales New York City, DC, LA, Chicago, and Philadelphia. Graduates of the Goizueta Business School found strong starting salaries with an average of $69k. The vast majority of Woodruff School of Nursing found employment within three months at an average salary of $54k. The average salary across all schools in 2019 was $53k.

A healthy number of Emory grads pursue further education upon graduation. In the last few years, multiple Emory grads/alums received acceptance letters from the following top law schools: Columbia, Berkeley, Michigan, Northwestern, and Georgetown. Med school acceptances included Duke, Johns Hopkins, Vanderbilt, and USC. Overall, the most commonly attended graduate schools included Emory itself, Columbia, Duke, University of Chicago, NYU, Penn, Harvard, and Stanford.

Admission

Emory received a record number of applications in 2019—30,017; only 4,682 were accepted, an overall acceptance rate of 15.6 percent, down from a 25 percent acceptance rate only three years ago. Enrolled students in the Class of 2023 applicant pool had a mean SAT score of 1442. The mid-50 percent ACT range was 31-34. The average GPA on a 4.0 scale was 3.8, and fewer than 2 percent of students possessed a GPA under a 3.5.

While high test scores and near-perfect grades (84 percent were in the top 10 percent of their high school classes) are close to prerequisites, Emory does employ a holistic review process that carefully considers letters of recommendations, essays, and how you spent your time outside the classroom. It is a fairly common strategy for students to submit applications to both Emory and Oxford. The latter is slightly less selective with a 19 percent acceptance rate (vs. a 15 percent acceptance rate at Emory College). It is also important to note that 51 percent of first-year students at Emory were admitted through early decision, and the ED acceptance rate was eight points higher than the regular round rate. Thus, if Emory is your first choice, applying early may be a good idea. In sum, Emory is a highly selective, elite school where competition for a spot-on campus is growing more difficult every year. Nothing short of straight A's in a rigorous selection of courses, along with a 1400+ SAT score, puts you in good standing to earn a place in one of the South's most prestigious universities.

Worth Your Money?

Almost all Emory students who qualify for financial aid see 100 percent of their demonstrated need met by the university. That translates to 42 percent of the undergraduate student body receiving an average grant of $48,738 per year. Other students pay the full $73k annual cost of attendance. Emory does a tremendous job of opening its doors to students from every socioeconomic background as the median family income for current students (estimated by tax return data) is much lower than many other private institutions of its ilk. Given that grads enjoy top-shelf employment prospects and generous financial aid, Emory is likely to be worth every dollar it will cost you.

FINANCIAL
Institutional Type: Private
In-State Tuition: $55,200
Out-of-State Tuition: $55,200
Room & Board: $15,572
Required Fees: $798
Books & Supplies: $1,224

Avg. Need-Based Grant: $48,738
Avg. % of Need Met: 100%

Avg. Merit-Based Award: $19,225
% Receiving (All Freshmen): 20%
% Receiving (Freshmen w/o Need): 4%

Avg. Cumulative Debt: $24,889
% of Students Borrowing: 35%

CAREER
Who Recruits
1. American Express
2. SunTrust
3. Turner Construction
4. Macy's
5. BNP Paribas

Notable Internships
1. ExxonMobil
2. Booz Allen Hamilton
3. BlackRock

Top Industries
1. Business
2. Healthcare
3. Education
4. Research
5. Social Services

Top Employers
1. Centers for Disease Control
2. Deloitte
3. EY
4. PwC
5. Google

Where Alumni Work
1. Atlanta
2. New York City
3. Washington DC
4. San Francisco
5. Boston

Median Earnings
College Scorecard (Early Career): $66,000
PayScale (Early Career): $66,400
PayScale (Mid-Career): $126,600

RANKINGS
Money: 108
U.S. News: 21, National Universities
Wall Street Journal/THE: 24 (T)
Washington Monthly: 63, National Universities

COLLEGE OVERLAPS
Duke University
Johns Hopkins University
New York University
University of Pennsylvania
Vanderbilt University

Fairfield University

Fairfield, Connecticut | 203-254-4100

ADMISSION
Admission Rate: 57%
Admission Rate - Men: 57%
Admission Rate - Women: 57%
EA Admission Rate: 59%
ED Admission Rate: 78%
ED Admits as % of Total Admits: 3%
Admission Rate (5-Year Trend): -13%
% of Admits Attending (Yield): 17%
Transfer Admission Rate: 28%

SAT Reading/Writing (Middle 50%): 610-670
SAT Math (Middle 50%): 600-680
ACT Composite (Middle 50%): 26-30

% Graduated in Top 10% of HS Class: 41%
% Graduated in Top 25% of HS Class: 73%
% Graduated in Top 50% of HS Class: 97%

Demonstrated Interest: Important
Legacy Status: Considered
Admission Interview Offered: Yes

ENROLLMENT
Total Undergraduate Enrollment: 4,303
% Part-Time: 3%
% Male: 41%
% Female: 59%
% Out-of-State: 73%
% Fraternity: Not Offered
% Sorority: Not Offered
% On-Campus (Freshman): 95%
% On-Campus (All Undergraduate): 73%

% African-American: 2%
% Asian: 3%
% Hispanic: 7%
% White: 76%
% Other: 2%
% Race or Ethnicity Unknown: 6%
% International: 4%
% Low-Income: 15%

ACADEMICS
Student-to-Faculty Ratio: 12 to 1
% of Classes Under 20: 60%
% of Classes 20-49: 39%
% of Classes 50 or More: 2%
% Full-Time Faculty: 47%
% Full-Time Faculty w/ Terminal Degree: 91%

Top Programs
Accounting
Communication
English
Finance
Marketing
Nursing
Politics

Retention Rate: 90%
4-Year Graduation Rate: 80%
6-Year Graduation Rate: 83%

Curricular Flexibility: Less Flexible
Academic Rating: ★★★

#CollegesWorthYourMoney

If you're seeking a high-caliber Catholic/Jesuit institution and don't have the grades and test scores for Georgetown, Holy Cross, Boston College, or Fordham, say hello to a new friend named Fairfield University. This school may not have the national name recognition of its Jesuit brethren but, rest assured, this Connecticut university of 4,303 undergraduates has its share of stellar students and no shortage of connections to the nearby corporate world of New York City, including many of Wall Street's premier firms.

Inside the Classroom
No matter which of the forty-seven majors you happen to be pursuing, a significant amount of time will be spent fulfilling the required Magis Core Curriculum, beginning with the Class of 2023. Totaling forty-five credits (15 courses), students must complete Introduction to Rhetoric and Composition and Introduction to Philosophy as well as coursework in math, history, religious studies, modern or classical language, and additional forays into the behavioral and social sciences, literature, natural sciences, and visual and performing arts. Business majors, of which there are many (stats to follow), take a whole extra set of mandated coursework including Calculus, Introduction to Microeconomics, and Introduction to Macroeconomics.

A 12:1 student-to-faculty ratio is fully felt in the classroom as courses average only twenty students per section. While 39 percent come in under that marker and only a smattering of sections contain forty+ students, the greatest number of courses have enrollments in the twenty to twenty-nine range. Each year 300+ faculty-directed undergraduate research projects are completed and shown-off at the university's Annual Research and Creative Accomplishments Symposium. Study abroad programs have a 30 percent participation rate, and opportunities are available to travel to sixty sites across forty countries on five continents.

Fairfield is primarily known for its business program, which serves as a pipeline to many of the top financial/accounting/consulting firms in the country. A whopping 38 percent of degrees conferred are from the highly respected Dolan School of Business. Next in popularity are majors within the health professions (14 percent) and communication (11 percent)—both areas also receive high marks at Fairfield. Fulbright winners have trailed off in recent years, but the school has had as many as nine in a single year in the not-too-distant past. However, landing fellowships is rarely the postgraduate goal of this business-minded group.

Outside the Classroom
Housing is guaranteed for all four years, but just below three-quarters of students elect to live on the school's 200-acres campus. Demographically, two things at Fairfield stand out. One, the lack of ethnic diversity is real—76 percent of current undergrads identify as white, and secondly, women make up 59 percent of the undergraduate population. As at many Jesuit institutions, Greek life doesn't exist here, but there are plenty of social opportunities around; for many years Fairfield made appearances on top party school lists, but today it cracks prominent lists measuring schools with the happiest students and best quality of life. With twenty NCAA Division I teams boasting a combined forty-two NCAA tournament appearances in school history, Fairfield certainly has plenty of sports to offer. While the Stags' fan base is quiet compared to a place like fellow Jesuit school Boston College, it is still significant that 10 percent of the student body are Division I athletes. There are over one hundred clubs and activities to enjoy, including twenty intramural sports and twenty-five club teams. Being just sixty miles from NYC is an advantage not only for networking but for weekend trips. Campus itself cannot unreasonably be assigned adjectives like "idyllic" and "stunning." It's location on the Connecticut coast turns the nearby beach into an extension of campus; in fact, 400 seniors each year live in beachfront homes and apartments.

Career Services
The Career, Leadership, and Professional Development (CLPD) staff at Fairfield is comprised of nine full-time employees who work in employer development, recruitment, and experiential learning and internship coordination. The 478:1 student-to-advisor ratio is only average compared to the schools featured in this guidebook, but that does not appear to prevent the CLPD staff from directly touching the lives of almost every student. The office hosts four career fairs per year, including general expos in the fall and spring and smaller affairs specific to nursing and law school. One recent Fall Career Fair was attended by 123 employers and 745 students. Companies in attendance included EY, KPMG, Morgan Stanley, and Epsilon.

Fairfield University

E-mail: admis@fairfield.edu | Website: www.fairfield.edu

Events including mock interviews, job shadowing, industry nights, resume-writing workshops, and employer presentations occur on a regular basis. The Stags4Hire platform connects students with job opportunities and can help book on-campus interviews. An impressive 47 percent of Class of 2019 members reported that they found their first job through on-campus recruiting/interviewing opportunities during their senior year. Among that same cohort, 605 individuals participated in internships and 23 percent of 2019 grads cited that experience as directly leading to their first full-time employment opportunity. Taking full advantage of their proximity to NYC, Fairfield's CLPD provides all of the internship and employment opportunities one could hope for.

Professional Outcomes

Fairfield's Class of 2019 found its next destination within six months of graduating at a hard-to-beat 98 percent clip. Healthcare/Nursing was the most commonly entered industry (21 percent), followed by financial services (19 percent), communications/marketing (16 percent), and consumer products (10 percent). Many major investment banks, accounting firms, and consulting companies employ large numbers of Fairfield alumni. For example, PwC, Deloitte, Morgan Stanley, JP Morgan & Chase Co., EY, UBS, and Merrill Lynch all employ one hundred or more Stags, and Fairfield grads also have strong representation at IBM, Goldman Sachs, Citi, and Prudential. Thus, it's no wonder that the average starting salary is a healthy $58,830, not including bonuses. Connecticut is not the primary destination for graduates. Rather, New York City attracts the greatest number of alumni with Boston second and Hartford a distant third.

Twenty-three percent of 2019 grads enrolled directly in graduate or professional school. The breakdown of programs was as follows: business (46 percent), education (17 percent), arts and sciences (12 percent), health care (10 percent), and law (6 percent). The university produces roughly thirty graduates per year that go on to earn their degrees in medicine and dentistry. Medical schools where recent grads have been admitted include Johns Hopkins, Georgetown, and the Albert Einstein College of Medicine. Those headed to law school do so at a range of institutions that includes elite schools Fordham, Boston College, and Cornell. Graduate schools pursued and attended by Stag alumni run the gamut of selectivity, but those with high GPAs are in the running for a place in elite graduate institutions.

Admission

Applications to the Class of 2023 set a record for the school as over 12,315 lined up for the chance to become a Stag; 57 percent were admitted, still an unintimidating acceptance rate despite the school's rising reputation. Fairfield is a test-optional school, but the vast majority of the 2019-20 freshman class did submit test scores with the SAT being the people's choice. The mid-50 percent SAT range was 1220-1340 and the ACT range was 26-30. Forty percent finished in the top 10 percent of their high school class, 73 percent were in the top quartile, but 4 percent did not land in the top half, giving hope to late bloomers with some blemishes on their transcripts. The average GPA was 3.64, but plenty of students with lower GPAs received acceptance letters; in fact, 18 percent of accepted students had lower than a 3.25.

The four factors the committee lists as being of supreme importance are rigor of curriculum, GPA, recommendations, and the essay. On the next tier of still "important" factors are an interview, extracurricular activities, first-generation status, character/personal qualities, talent/ability, work experience, volunteer work, and demonstrated interest. It's definitely a good idea to visit campus and interview in order to let the university know you are serious about attending. Fairfield only has a 17 percent yield rate, meaning that 83 percent of those accepted into the school do not ultimately enroll. Applying early decision is a good way to punch your ticket to campus as those going the ED route enjoyed an 78 percent acceptance rate.

Worth Your Money?

On the surface, Fairfield, being a not terribly selective, high-priced private school is an unlikely candidate for this guide. Yet, Fairfield succeeds where many others in its class fail. For one, thanks to generous merit and need-based aid, even parents in high-income brackets can expect to pay an average annual COA of $40k, which is more than $25k less than the sticker price. Parents in lower-income brackets receive commensurate discounts (90 percent of students receive some type of aid) and, with strong graduate outcomes and connections to major corporations, this university could make financial sense for students of all income levels, especially if they have business-related aspirations. However, it is worth noting that the average cumulative debt for Fairfield grads is almost $10k higher than the national average.

FINANCIAL
Institutional Type: Private
In-State Tuition: $49,080
Out-of-State Tuition: $49,080
Room & Board: $15,150
Required Fees: $750
Books & Supplies: $1,150

Avg. Need-Based Grant: $32,441
Avg. % of Need Met: 89%

Avg. Merit-Based Award: $17,066
% Receiving (All Freshmen): 91%
% Receiving (Freshmen w/o Need): 50%

Avg. Cumulative Debt: $39,214
% of Students Borrowing: 61%

CAREER
Who Recruits
1. FBI
2. Deloitte
3. Ipsos
4. McIntyre Group
5. TEKsystems

Notable Internships
1. Major League Baseball
2. PwC
3. Deutsche Bank

Top Industries
1. Business
2. Education
3. Finance
4. Sales
5. Operations

Top Employers
1. PwC
2. Deloitte
3. Morgan Stanley
4. UBS
5. EY

Where Alumni Work
1. New York City
2. Boston
3. Hartford, CT
4. Philadelphia
5. Washington DC

Median Earnings
College Scorecard (Early Career): $72,100
PayScale (Early Career): $65,100
PayScale (Mid-Career): $128,100

RANKINGS
Money: 361
U.S. News: 3, Regional Universities North
Wall Street Journal/THE: 195
Washington Monthly: 39, Master's Universities

COLLEGE OVERLAPS
Boston College
Fordham University
Loyola University Maryland
Providence College
Quinnipiac University

Florida State University

Tallahassee, Florida | 850-644-6200

Founded in 1851, FSU is one of the state's oldest institutions of higher education as well as one of the nation's finest public research universities. A wide range of baccalaureate degrees—104 to be precise—are available to the school's 33,270 undergraduate students, a group possessing increasingly impressive academic credentials with every passing year. Bound by excellent academics and athletics, FSU's student body and alumni are, with good reason, proud to call themselves Seminoles.

Inside the Classroom
The greater university is comprised of sixteen distinct colleges, and all except the College of Law and College of Medicine offer undergraduate degree programs. All students must meet a number of state and university requirements as they progress through their four years of study. Regardless of academic concentration, thirty-six semester hours of coursework are mandated in the areas of quantitative and logical thinking, English composition, natural sciences, social sciences/history, humanities, and cultural practices/ethics, and two semesters of foreign language.

The student-to-faculty is a rather high 21:1, which translates into larger class sizes. Ten percent of sections contain more than fifty students, and 5 percent have more than one hundred. However, that is balanced by the 60 percent of sections that contain fewer than twenty students. Out-of-class undergraduate research is taken advantage of by one-quarter of students, and the school plans to greatly expand such offerings. An abundance of study abroad choices include special summer programs in Panama, Florence, London, and Valencia, Spain. FSU has sixty academic programs available in twenty locations throughout the world; one in five students elects to participate.

FSU boasts a number of standout academic programs including those in the College of Motion Picture Arts, the premier film school in the region. The College of Business is extremely well regarded in the corporate world as its real estate, marketing, accounting, management, and insurance programs are all highly ranked. Twenty-two percent of degrees conferred fall under the business umbrella. The social sciences (17 percent), psychology (8 percent), biology (7 percent) and homeland security (6 percent) are next in popularity. More Seminoles have landed prestigious postgraduate fellowships in recent years than ever. Nine graduates took home Fulbright Scholarships in 2020 and 28 captured Gilman Scholarships in 2019.

Outside the Classroom
Florida State could easily be called Extrovert U—95 percent of undergrads participate in at least one on-campus activity. Just about everyone cheers on the Seminole football team as well as seventeen other NCAA Division I teams competing in the esteemed Atlantic Coast Conference (ACC). Forty sports clubs and a thriving intramural program draw widespread participation. The Bobby E. Leach center offers students recreational amenities including a sixteen-lane pool and indoor track, and all of the exercise equipment one could ever desire. While campus is a sizable 477 acres, only 20 percent of undergrads live on site, almost exclusively freshmen. Greek life is a driving force on campus despite a temporary ban in 2017 after a tragic hazing death. The school has a 22 percent participation rate across its twenty-six sororities and a 13 percent participation in its fraternities. Those seeking non-Greek, non-sports activities can pick from one of more than 650 recognized student organizations. Approximately 2,000 students become engaged in community service projects each year. Club Downunder, a student-run venue in town, brings notable comedy and musical acts to Tallahassee on a regular basis. The Student Life Cinema plays free movies for students six night a week. Tallahassee offers plenty of nightlife and cultural opportunities and can be easily accessed via public transit.

Career Services
The Career Center at Florida State University employs forty-two full-time staff members (not including office assistants) who work in career advising, employer relations, and experiential learning. This student-to-advisor ratio of 792:1 is below average compared to the other institutions included in this book. Of course, the size and scope of the operation is massive, and FSU's Career Center does a solid job of reaching a healthy number of the 30,000 undergraduate students through a variety of means.

The university puts on twenty job fairs per year that attract close to 1,450 employers and 11,500 students. Annually, the office puts on 1,200+ programs/workshops drawing a total audience of greater than 40,000. Florida State's internship participation rate was 66 percent for the Class of 2019. An impressive 7,700+ students obtain internship/co-op positions, and close to 8,600 students find other opportunities for experiential learning. Over 40 percent of graduates who found employment credited the Career Center with providing them the lead. Many big-time corporations recruit on campus including PepsiCo, KPMG, and PricewaterhouseCoopers. Close to 5,000 on-campus interviews are conducted each year. Despite a high student-to-counselor ratio, Florida State's Career Center deploys its resources efficiently, reaching an extremely high percentage of the student body.

Professional Outcomes

Seventy-three percent of 2019 FSU grads already had a job offer in hand when they threw their caps toward the sky in celebration. Within six months of graduation, 87 percent of Seminoles achieve positive outcomes; 69 percent were employed full time. The top five sectors employing Seminoles are (in order) education, technology, retail, financial, and health. Employers hiring the greatest number of FSU alumni include Apple, Northrup Grumman, EY, General Motors, and Deloitte. The average starting salary for graduates is a shade over $50k. Among ACC schools, FSU ranks toward the bottom in terms of median salary by midcareer, coming in at thirteenth of fourteen, behind Pitt and slightly ahead of the University of Louisville with alumni, by some measures, making roughly half as much as Duke graduates. Geographically, the greatest number of alumni remain in Florida but large numbers also relocate to Massachusetts, Georgia, Texas, Washington State, and California.

Roughly one-quarter of Florida State grads elect to immediately pursue admission into an advanced degree program; 75 percent of those who apply receive at least one acceptance. A typical graduating class sees over one hundred students accepted into medical schools and over 200 accepted into law schools. Students enjoy graduate school acceptances at a wide range of state and private universities with some recent alumni landing at prestigious institutions including Emory, Johns Hopkins, MIT, Northwestern, Georgetown, Vanderbilt, and the University of Chicago.

Admission

The acceptance rate into Florida State's Class of 2023 dipped below 40 percent for the second time, hitting 36 percent as the university received a record 58,936 applications. Only five years ago, the university received fewer than 30,000 applications and accepted more than half. Enrolled freshmen possessed middle-50 percent SAT scores of 1220-1330 and ACT scores of 26-30. For perspective, a decade ago, the ranges were 1090-1270 and 23-28, indicating a notable increase in the academic caliber of the average first-year student. A solid 47 percent of FSU freshmen finished in the top 10 percent of their high school class; 73 percent were in the top quarter. A GPA of 3.75 or higher was possessed by 83 percent of first-year students in 2019-20 and the average GPA was a 4.07.

The admissions committee ranks the rigor of an applicant's secondary school record above all other factors but also strongly weights GPA, standardized test scores (the ACT is the more commonly submitted test), talent/ability, and state residency (out-of-state applicants face tougher prospects and were admitted at a rate of 20 percent). Class rank, extracurricular activities, and essays are merely "considered." Due to the immense volume of applicants, the university does not offer admissions interviews. While FSU does not offer a binding early decision option, it does have two deadlines—one in November and one in February. The November deadline is preferable as this early round typically sees acceptance rates close to 60 percent. Over 80 percent of attendees are residents of the Sunshine State, and admissions standards are more lax for residents than outsiders. With draws like elite sports, beautiful weather, and an excellent academic reputation, the number of applicants to FSU is likely to continue to rise. Candidates should be mindful of the increasingly selective admissions process and the need to post strong ACT/SAT scores and grades, above all else.

Worth Your Money?

An in-state cost of attendance of just over $23,000 puts places like FSU in the "absurd bargain" category. While the school rarely meets full demonstrated need, it does give average awards to qualifying undergrads of $13,401. Even for the 20 percent of students who do not have residency status, the out-of-state COA is a reasonable $37k. Attending Florida State and paying $37k per year is especially appealing if you are entering a field in which grads enjoy high average starting salaries like computer science ($66k), engineering ($68k), or math and sciences ($64k).

FINANCIAL
Institutional Type: Public
In-State Tuition: $6,517
Out-of-State Tuition: $21,683
Room & Board: $11,088
Required Fees: $0
Books & Supplies: $1,000

Avg. Need-Based Grant: $13,401
Avg. % of Need Met: 95%

Avg. Merit-Based Award: $7,875
% Receiving (All Freshmen): 84%
% Receiving (Freshmen w/o Need): 10%

Avg. Cumulative Debt: $25,013
% of Students Borrowing: 42%

CAREER
Who Recruits
1. Grant Thorton LLC
2. Enterprise
3. Aldi
4. Northrop Grumman
5. KPMG

Notable Internships
1. Equifax
2. Walt Disney Company
3. Royal Carribean Cruises

Top Industries
1. Business
2. Education
3. Operations
4. Sales
5. Social Services

Top Employers
1. IBM
2. Raymond James
3. JPMorgan Chase
4. Amazon
5. Microsoft

Where Alumni Work
1. Tallahassee, FL
2. Miami
3. Tampa, FL
4. Orlando, FL
5. Atlanta

Median Earnings
College Scorecard (Early Career): $46,400
PayScale (Early Career): $53,700
PayScale (Mid-Career): $99,900

RANKINGS
Money: 96
U.S. News: 58 (T), National Universities
Wall Street Journal/THE: 187 (T)
Washington Monthly: 73, National Universities

COLLEGE OVERLAPS
University of Alabama
University of Central Florida
University of Florida
University of Miami
University of South Florida

Fordham University

Bronx, New York | 718-817-4000

ADMISSION
Admission Rate: 46%
Admission Rate - Men: 45%
Admission Rate - Women: 47%
EA Admission Rate: 54%
ED Admission Rate: 52%
ED Admits as % of Total Admits: 1%
Admission Rate (5-Year Trend): -1%
% of Admits Attending (Yield): 10%
Transfer Admission Rate: 50%

SAT Reading/Writing (Middle 50%): 620-710
SAT Math (Middle 50%): 620-740
ACT Composite (Middle 50%): 28-32

% Graduated in Top 10% of HS Class: 46%
% Graduated in Top 25% of HS Class: 80%
% Graduated in Top 50% of HS Class: 97%

Demonstrated Interest: Considered
Legacy Status: Considered
Admission Interview Offered: No

ENROLLMENT
Total Undergraduate Enrollment: 9,767
% Part-Time: 6%
% Male: 43%
% Female: 57%
% Out-of-State: 58%
% Fraternity: Not Offered
% Sorority: Not Offered
% On-Campus (Freshman): 76%
% On-Campus (All Undergraduate): 49%

% African-American: 4%
% Asian: 11%
% Hispanic: 16%
% White: 55%
% Other: 4%
% Race or Ethnicity Unknown: 1%
% International: 9%
% Low-Income: 19%

ACADEMICS
Student-to-Faculty Ratio: 13 to 1
% of Classes Under 20: 52%
% of Classes 20-49: 48%
% of Classes 50 or More: 1%
% Full-Time Faculty: 40%
% Full-Time Faculty w/ Terminal Degree: 94%

Top Programs
Communication and Culture
English
Finance
Global Business
International Studies
Performing Arts
Psychology

Retention Rate: 91%
4-Year Graduation Rate: 78%
6-Year Graduation Rate: 83%

Curricular Flexibility: Somewhat Flexible
Academic Rating: ★★★↙

#CollegesWorthYourMoney

With campuses in both Manhattan and the Bronx, Fordham University, a private Jesuit school with 175 years of tradition, has hit new heights of popularity and prestige in recent years; it shows no signs of slowing down. As one of the top twenty-five most expensive schools in the United States, paying for Fordham may be even more challenging than getting accepted. Yet, for those who can afford it, this is a wonderful place to live and learn for four years. Of course, paying back loans becomes easier when you enter a high-paying field like business, which accounts for 28 percent of all degrees conferred.

Inside the Classroom
The university offers more than seventy majors, minors, and pre-professional programs. Regardless of concentration area, on their way to earning 124 credits all Rams (minus many pursuing a Bachelor of Science) are required to tackle from one to four semesters of foreign language. Freshmen must complete an advanced composition course, Computational Reasoning, Philosophy of Human Nature, Faith and Critical Reason, and one seminar course that focuses on enhancing students' written and oral communication ability. As students progress to sophomore, junior, and senior year they are required to tackle additional courses in philosophy, literature, life science, theology, the performing arts, natural science, and ethics.

Fordham's 13:1 student-to-faculty ratio leads to average class sizes of twenty-two. Some classes will be on the smaller side as 52 percent of sections contain nineteen or fewer students. Rarely will an undergrad end up in a classroom of more than forty students. A substantial 45 percent of the student body spend a semester abroad at one of the school's 110 programs in fifty-two countries. The undergraduate research program has awarded 1.5 million dollars to students over the last decade and recently saw thirty-eight undergrads obtain coauthor status on professor-published work in a single year.

The university's theater and dance programs are world-renowned for sending countless alumni to Broadway and Hollywood. Gabelli is a top-rated business program with standout programs in international business and finance and serves as a pipeline to many large firms. Other popular areas of study include the social sciences (19 percent), journalism (9 percent), and psychology (6 percent). Another point of pride is the phenomenal number of graduates who earn competitive national scholarships and fellowships. Fordham has produced 130+ Fulbright scholarships since 2003. Grads also regularly win Beinecke, Gates-Cambridge Harriman, and Truman Scholarships/Fellowships.

Outside the Classroom
The undergraduate experience will differ depending on whether you attend the Rose Hill Campus in the Bronx or the Lincoln Center campus in Manhattan. At Lincoln Center there are two large high-rises that offer every convenience imaginable. Of course, Manhattan has all of the culture, shopping, dining, and entertainment you could ever dream of. The Bronx campus offers fourteen residential buildings and is near the New York Botanical Garden, the Bronx Zoo, Yankee Stadium, and Little Italy. Between the two sites, roughly half of the student body lives on campus. Greek Life at Fordham is a complete non-factor—the university does not have any fraternities or sororities. Instead, 160 student-run organizations provide opportunities for social bonding. Athletics are popular as the Rams field twenty-three teams in NCCA Division I and also run twenty-four club and intramural sports. Over 4,000 students participate in community service each year, contributing over one million collective hours. The school's newspaper, The Observer, enjoys a loyal readership and has garnered widespread praise. Yet, no feature of campus life will play a bigger role in the Fordham experience than its Big Apple location, which opens the doors to limitless possibilities on a daily basis.

Career Services
The Career Services office at Fordham is staffed by thirteen professional employees who specialize in areas that include undergraduate counseling and employer relations. That 751:1 student-to-advisor ratio is significantly higher than many of the other schools featured in this guide. In order to reach the masses, the office puts on four career fairs in the fall and two in the spring. Some are specific to areas like finance, STEM, or government while others are more general. The school attempts to engage with students beginning in their freshman year, encouraging first-years to meet one-on-one with an advisor, attend a resume/cover letter workshop, and take personality assessments.

Fordham University

E-mail: enroll@fordham.edu | Website: www.fordham.edu

A phenomenal 81 percent of 2019 graduates completed at least one internship during their undergraduate years. An examination of how recent graduates found their jobs reveals the following breakdown: internships (16 percent), Handshake/Career Services (11 percent), and the alumni network (1 percent). The vast majority found employment primarily through non-school resources. Yet plenty of opportunities exist to expand one's contacts by taking advantage of a Ram alumni network of over 175,000 individuals embedded in top companies across the globe. Despite a less-than-ideal student-to-counselor ratio and a low percentage of students attributing their job acquisition to the direct efforts of career services, Fordham grads do enjoy better-than-average employment and graduate school outcomes.

Professional Outcomes

Class of 2019 graduates found employment, graduate school, or other meaningful activities at a 93 percent clip within six months of receiving their degrees. Three-fifths of this group landed employment and enjoyed an average salary of $59,593, higher than the national average. Financial services was, by a large margin, the most common industry followed by advertising, media and communications, health care, and accounting. Significant numbers of 2019 grads found homes at major companies including JP Morgan Chase & Co. (27), PwC (24), Ernst & Young (23), KMPG (19), and Deloitte (18). A sizable number of graduates also moved into working for nonprofit organizations such as the Jesuit Volunteer Corps, AmeriCorps, or the Peace Corps.

Those aiming for graduate school found homes at a variety of excellent institutions. The greatest number of 2019 graduates landed at Fordham (160), NYU (29), and Columbia (26). Some also gained acceptance into Penn, Georgetown, Boston University, and George Washington. Law school applicants were successful 95 percent of the time, a rate 17 percent higher than the national average. In recent years, Fordham alumni have gone on to Harvard Law School, University of Pennsylvania Law School, Cornell Law School, and Northwestern University School of Law. Those applying to professional health programs, including medical school, gained acceptance at a 76 percent rate compared to the national average of 45 percent.

Admission

Fordham offered admission to 46 percent of the 47,930 applicants vying for a place in the Class of 2023. Those who ultimately enrolled possessed a mean test score of 1340 and a mean high school GPA of 3.64 on a 4.0 scale. In 2014, a 1350 would have placed in the 75th percentile of all Fordham freshmen. Last year, the mid-50 percent standardized test score ranges were 1240-1450 Forty-six percent of freshmen finished in the top 10 percent of their high school cohort, and 80 percent placed in the top quarter; three percent did not place in the top half. While 72 percent of entering freshmen in 2019-20 possessed better than a 3.75 GPA, 3 percent did earn a 3.25 or under in high school.

The admissions committee prioritizes the usual factors of rigor of coursework and GPA. In part because it serves as a safety school for many elite students aiming for Ivies or Ivy equivalents, Fordham has an exceptionally low yield rate—around 10 percent of admitted students actually enroll. Therefore, demonstrating your genuine interest in attending and applying early decision are strategic moves that serious applicants should consider. ED applications to the university are surprisingly low, but acceptance rates are higher than during the regular cycle (54 percent versus 40 percent). Like many schools in Manhattan, Fordham's rising popularity can be best summed up by the real estate cliché of location, location, location. Always a school that required students to have reasonably strong credentials, Fordham is entering a new strata and is now a viable option for very accomplished students.

Worth Your Money?

An annual total cost of attendance exceeding $79,000 sounds prohibitive, but a good number of students do obtain aid, either need based or merit. Fifty-nine percent of students qualify for grants that average over $32k and a whopping 84 percent receive merit aid awards averaging $20k. Unfortunately, only a small number see 100 percent of their need covered by the university. The average graduate owes more than $37k in loans, but starting salaries tend to be solid, making it worth incurring a moderate amount of debt, particularly for students pursuing study within Fordham's strongest programs, most notably business.

FINANCIAL
Institutional Type: Private
In-State Tuition: $54,730
Out-of-State Tuition: $54,730
Room & Board: $19,066
Required Fees: $1,058
Books & Supplies: $1,040

Avg. Need-Based Grant: $31,873
Avg. % of Need Met: 79%

Avg. Merit-Based Award: $20,363
% Receiving (All Freshmen): 41%
% Receiving (Freshmen w/o Need): 27%

Avg. Cumulative Debt: $37,283
% of Students Borrowing: 57%

CAREER
Who Recruits
1. EY
2. Teach for America
3. Standard Motor Products
4. Enterprise
5. Northwestern Mutual

Notable Internships
1. The Philadelphia Zoo
2. NBCUniversal
3. Spotify

Top Industries
1. Business
2. Education
3. Social Services
4. Operations
5. Finance

Top Employers
1. NYC Department of Education
2. Teach for America
3. NBCUniversal
4. JPMorgan Chase
5. US Army

Where Alumni Work
1. New York City
2. Washington DC
3. Boston
4. Los Angeles
5. Philadelphia

Median Earnings
College Scorecard (Early Career): $59,200
PayScale (Early Career): $61,800
PayScale (Mid-Career): $121,600

RANKINGS
Money: 407
U.S. News: 66 (T), National Universities
Wall Street Journal/THE: 183 (T)
Washington Monthly: 267, National Universities

COLLEGE OVERLAPS
Binghamton University (SUNY)
Boston College
Boston University
New York University
Villanova University

Franklin & Marshall College

Lancaster, Pennsylvania | 717-358-3953

Situated on the pastoral hills of Lancaster County, Pennsylvania, most famous for its large Amish community, Franklin & Marshall has carved out its own stellar reputation ever since its two namesake colleges merged in 1853. An undergraduate population of 2,315 gets to choose from a generous liberal arts menu that features fifty-nine academic programs. Never content to rest on its laurels, F&M is in the middle of a $200 million fundraising campaign entitled "Now to Next" that is designed to take this already excellent school to even greater heights.

Inside the Classroom
The educational experience at F&M is guided by its "Connections" curriculum, a series of requirements divided into three phases: Introduction, Exploration, and Concentration. Freshmen must take two small, intensive seminar classes that immerse them in the world of intellectual discourse, academic writing, and the art of oral presentation. Next, students tackle courses in the arts, humanities, social and natural sciences, foreign language, and non-Western cultures. As a culminating experience, students complete a capstone project that may involve research alongside a professor.

Franklin & Marshall's student-faculty ratio is 9:1, and 65 percent of classes have fewer than twenty students enrolled; 31 percent are in the twenty to twenty-nine range. The average classroom contains eighteen students. Juniors are encouraged to spend a semester abroad, and 55 percent oblige, jetting off to locations from Argentina to Vietnam. Grants through the Hackman Scholars program allow approximately seventy-five students to conduct research with faculty each summer. Many more Diplomats research with faculty through other means during the academic year and, by graduation, 35 percent of students have engaged in a research experience.

The greatest number of degrees conferred at the college are in the social sciences (26 percent), interdisciplinary studies (22 percent). Programs in public health and environmental science receive high marks, as does F&M's interdisciplinary major in Business, Organizations and Society (BOS). In addition, students in the official pre-med program and related majors have experienced a high degree of success in earning acceptances into medical school. F&M students also find success when it comes to securing prestigious fellowships--eight earned Fulbright Scholarships in 2020 while other recent graduates were recently awarded fellowships from Public Policy and International Affairs, Princeton in Asia, and Princeton in Africa.

Outside the Classroom
Lancaster, Pennsylvania, may be notable primarily for its Amish population, but there is a surprisingly large downtown area replete with a full array of shopping, eating, and entertainment options. Those seeking the excitement of a bigger city will have a bit of a car ride ahead of them—Philly is eighty miles away. Being in a relatively remote locale, the center of social life at F&M is on campus where 98 percent of the student population resides. Greek life is a big part of the Franklin and Marshall tradition, dating back to the school's founding, and it enjoys a robust participation rate of 13 percent for men and 19 percent for women. Participation in athletics is also central to campus life. Being a small school and fielding twenty-seven sports teams, mostly in NCAA Division III, translates to over 30 percent of the student body being comprised of varsity athletes. Outside of sports and frats/sororities, there are roughly one hundred active, student-run organizations that cover everything from a cappella to seven student-run publications. The vast majority of incoming freshmen performed community service in high school, and that practice continues while at F&M through numerous volunteer groups as well as through Greek organizations.

Career Services
The Office of Student and Post Graduate Development (OSPGD), a mouthful to say, is staffed by nine full-time professionals. That works out to a 257:1 student-to-advisor ratio, which is better than average compared to other schools featured in this guide. Noteworthy for a small liberal arts school, F&M employs expert advisors who specialize in health care professions and law school advising so that undergrads on those tracks can receive specialized guidance. In the 2018-19 academic year an impressive 2,540 (more than one per student) one-on-one advising sessions were conducted.

Students seeking a personal touch in advising will appreciate the OPSGD's availability to meet one-on-one to discuss internship opportunities, professional pathways, or graduate school planning. A commendable 80 percent of the student body engages with the office each year. Annual Job and Internship Fairs, draw roughly eighty employers, and 100+ employers recruit at some point on campus during a single year. The office puts on about 150 events each year with a total attendance of over 3,200. Other career-oriented offerings include Life After F&M, a handy feature that allows current Diplomats to view the types of jobs held by graduates of every major offered at the college. With each student's Handshake account, they also can access a database of 800+ alumni and parent mentors more than happy to dispense career advice. With a high level of engagement and positive graduate outcomes, the OSPGD receives a positive rating from our staff.

Professional Outcomes

Shortly after graduation, 99 percent of 2019 F&M grads are either employed or continuing their educational journey. The most frequently pursued industries are education (18 percent), finance and insurance (14 percent), healthcare (8 percent), and consulting (8 percent). Students find work at a cornucopia of interesting companies and organizations from HBO to the Selective Mutism Research Institute to Sotheby's. Across all graduating years the companies with the greatest number of Diplomats on staff are Morgan Stanley, Deloitte, Vanguard, EY, Merrill Lynch, IBM, Wells Fargo, and Citi. Sixty-five percent of graduates stay in the Northeast, and 19 percent head down South. There are more alumni living in New York City than in Philadelphia.

F&M boasts excellent results for premed students. Over a three-year period, 89 percent of students with at least a 3.3 GPA and an MCAT score in the 67th percentile or better were accepted into medical school. That includes admissions into schools of medicine at Harvard, Yale, Johns Hopkins, Penn, and Georgetown. Those seeking a legal education head to universities such as Villanova, Harvard, William & Mary, NYU, Yale, Tulane, and UC Berkeley. Of the 18 percent of graduates furthering their education, there is a genuine mix of prestigious and less prestigious graduate programs, but it is fair to say that excelling at F&M at least puts you in the running for a spot at a top graduate school.

Admission

Applications to F&M surged to record levels as 9,502 poured in for a place in the Class of 2023, and 30 percent were accepted. The implementation of a full-blown test-optional strategy could be behind the massive spike. In 2018, Franklin & Marshall admitted 35 percent of more than 6,500 applicants. The Class of 2023 possessed mid-50 percent standardized test scores of 1290-1418 on the SAT and 28 to 32 on the ACT. F&M continues to place the highest value on rigor of coursework, GPA, class rank, and character/personal qualities. On that last factor, it particularly values athletic participation/leadership; an insanely high percentage of incoming students played a varsity sport in high school. Seventy-one percent of freshmen in the 2019-20 academic year finished in the top 10 percent of their high school cohort; 88 percent were in the top 25 percent.

F&M faces stiff competition for students as it must compete with a high number of other excellent liberal arts schools in PA and the surrounding states. Its yield rate (the percentage of accepted students who enroll) is only 22 percent, which means the admissions staff is particularly interested in qualified applicants for whom F&M is a top choice. Thus, it is no surprise that the early decision acceptance rate is 69 percent, far more favorable than that of the regular round; 64 percent of the 2019-20 freshman cohort came through the ED round. Not a school with a formulaic admissions algorithm, F&M students do typically share two common traits—excellent high school grades and strong interest in attending the college.

Worth Your Money?

Attending Franklin & Marshall will cost you $75k+ per year unless you are among the 54 percent of undergraduates who demonstrate financial need, in which case you see 100 percent of your financial need met. The average grant is for more than $51,000. Merit-based aid is not offered. Overall, F&M does an admirable job of making the school affordable for those from a wide range of socioeconomic backgrounds. However, middle-to-upper income students who cannot comfortably afford F&M's price and who fail to qualify for significant need-based aid should consider their desired path after college before committing. For everyone else, investing in an F&M degree is likely worth the money.

FINANCIAL
Institutional Type: Private
In-State Tuition: $58,615
Out-of-State Tuition: $58,615
Room & Board: $14,450
Required Fees: $185
Books & Supplies: $1,200

Avg. Need-Based Grant: $51,407
Avg. % of Need Met: 100%

Avg. Merit-Based Award: $0
% Receiving (All Freshmen): 0%
% Receiving (Freshmen w/o Need): 0%

Avg. Cumulative Debt: $27,928
% of Students Borrowing: 54%

CAREER
Who Recruits
1. W.B. Mason
2. The JDK Group
3. Travelers
4. ScribeAmerica
5. S&T Bank

Notable Internships
1. New Jersey Office of the Governor
2. Acacia Finance
3. Audible

Top Industries
1. Business
2. Education
3. Operations
4. Finance
5. Sales

Top Employers
1. Morgan Stanley
2. Deloitte
3. UBS
4. Vanguard
5. EY

Where Alumni Work
1. New York City
2. Philadelphia
3. Lancaster, PA
4. Washington DC
5. Boston

Median Earnings
College Scorecard (Early Career): $58,900
PayScale (Early Career): $61,100
PayScale (Mid-Career): $130,100

RANKINGS
Money: 124
U.S. News: 43, Liberal Arts Colleges
Wall Street Journal/THE: 76
Washington Monthly: 25, Liberal Arts Colleges

COLLEGE OVERLAPS
Bucknell University
Dickinson College
Gettysburg College
Lafayette College
Lehigh University

Needham, Massachusetts | 781-292-2222

Perhaps the most highly-regarded school of its size in the entire United States, The Franklin W. Olin College of Engineering was founded in the early 2000s as an experimental, cutting-edge training ground for budding engineers. Today, this Boston-area institution has an undergraduate enrollment of 386 students who are every bit as brilliant as the talent at Caltech or MIT. Academically, there is only one item on the menu here but, boy, is it delicious. Every single degree conferred at Olin has "engineering" in its name: electrical and computer engineering, mechanical engineering, or general engineering with a concentration area such as bioengineering, computing, or design and robotics.

Inside the Classroom
No matter one's major, all students most take a collection of core courses that the college deems essential to its mission, giving its students the engineering toolkit needed to "have a positive impact in the real world." Those required classes are tied to three interconnected themes: Design and Entrepreneurship, Modeling and Analysis, and Systems and Control. Students also work through a concentration in either the arts and humanities or entrepreneurship that can be completed at partner colleges Brandeis, Wellesley, or Babson. Unlike most engineering schools where students knock out a laundry list of math and science requirements before taking a deep dive into their engineering-specific coursework, Olin students take three such courses in their first semester.

Many classes are taught in a studio environment to encourage collaboration, and a number of courses are co-taught by professors from different disciplines. Classes are generally reasonably small; 50 percent of class sections contain fewer than twenty students. The school's 8:1 student- to-faculty ratio translates into an enormous amount of individualized attention and invitations to participate in research. Students can easily track down current research projects and contact information on the school's website and can obtain funding for their efforts via the Undergraduate Research Fund. Additionally, students can elect to take advantage of study abroad programs in thirty-five foreign locations. Half of students ultimately do spend a semester in a foreign country, a notably high percentage for an engineering school.

As chronicled in more detail in our "Professional Outcomes" section, the Franklin W. Olin College of Engineering may not be a household name for the average American, but employers and elite graduate schools adore its graduates every bit as much as those from Stanford or Carnegie Mellon. For such an incredibly small school, Olin graduates annually take home a number of prestigious awards. In fact, the school has already produced 17 Fulbright winners in its short history. Eight recent grads were named Grand Challenge Scholars by the National Academy of Engineers.

Outside the Classroom
Not far from Wellesley and Babson, Olin College of Engineering's Needham locale places it only eighteen miles outside of Boston. It features a seventy-acre campus lined with buildings as new as the college itself. Nearly all students reside on campus in one of two residence halls. No frats or sororities operate at this institution. There are no NCCA sports because it would be interesting to field teams from a pool of 386 engineering geniuses. However, thanks to agreements forged with nearby schools, Olin students can participate in intra-mural leagues at Babson or Wellesley. Additionally, Olin does field its own intercollegiate soccer and ultimate Frisbee teams. Fans of the outdoors can connect with hiking trails on campus and all around Needham and the town of Wellesley. There are plenty of student-run clubs with an engineering/innovation emphasis, including the Olin robotic sailing team that competes in global competitions, Olin Baja—a vehicle design competition, and AERO—a drone and plane designing team. Historic Needham is a safe suburb with plenty of restaurants, shops, museums, and cultural events.

Career Services
The Office of Postgraduate Planning consists of three professional employees, equating to a superior student-to-advisor ratio of 129:1, among the best of any school in the country. The office's mission is aligned to that of the school's—to assist future engineers in finding meaningful opportunities for hands-on training. This mission is accomplished to the tune of 100 percent of those graduating in 2020 having had a technical internship or research experience; 91 percent had more than one such experience. The Fall Career Fair is attended by more than fifty top companies. Given that this works out to about one company for every two seniors, this attendance is extraordinary and speaks to how desirable Olin students are in the eyes of employers.

Franklin W. Olin College of Engineering

E-mail: info@olin.edu | Website: www.olin.edu

With only fourteen years' worth of graduates, the total alumni base has barely crossed the 1,000 mark—but the industry connections made via the school's Corporate Partners Program open countless doors. In the past year undergrads landed internships at organizations including Tesla, Bose, GE, Microsoft, and Google. Thanks to a focus on experiential learning, ample industry connections, and exceptional starting salaries for grads, Olin's career services is held in high esteem by our staff.

Professional Outcomes

For a school exclusively graduating engineers, it isn't a surprise that alumni tend to find good-paying jobs. The average starting salary for recent graduates is in excess of $88,000. Electrical and computer engineers have averaged over $91k while mechanical engineers are at the "low" end with $76k in compensation. Over the past decade, the companies employing the greatest number of alumni are Google, Microsoft, athenahealth, Apple, and Amazon. In 2020, Epic, Tesla, and Facebook all hired more than one Olin graduate. While a majority of graduates find work in Massachusetts, a large number also migrate to California where Silicon Valley welcomes them with open arms.

Olin College of Engineering undergrads have gone on to prestigious graduate engineering programs in impressive numbers. Since 2006 more than twenty graduates have gone to Stanford, MIT, and Harvard. The school also has sent double-digit numbers of alumni to Carnegie Mellon, Cornell, and Berkeley. Perusing the lists of graduate school acceptances, it is rare that anyone attends anything less than one of the world's most prestigious institutions. The majority of those hopping right into advanced studies are pursuing PhDs.

Admission

The 85 freshmen in the Class of 2023 are an impressive group, no matter the metric. With an average unweighted GPA of 3.9 and middle 50 percent standardized test scores of 1450-1540 on the SAT and 34-35 on the ACT, Olin students are nothing shy of Ivy caliber. In 2019, the school's acceptance rate was 16 percent, but it has dipped as low as 13 percent in recent years.

Applicants can rest assured that they will be viewed in three dimensions as a number of factors beyond grades and test scores are considered "very important" to the admissions committee. Those include essays, recommendations, interview, extracurricular activities, talent/ability, character/personal qualities, and level of demonstrated interest in the college. In fact, those considerations all rate ahead of standardized test results. Yet, consideration of those traditional factors is only half of the acceptance process. Each year, roughly 225-250 applicants are selected by Olin College of Engineering to visit during a Candidates' Weekend—a process closer to how most schools hire faculty than select their undergraduates. The prospective students are put through a design challenge, an individual interview, and group exercise to help evaluate which students would bring the most to and benefit the most from the Olin College of Engineering. Getting into Olin is a marathon; it is not a school you even apply to unless you are 100 percent committed to attending. Elite academic prowess is only one of many prerequisites for consideration to join this small but potent engineering juggernaut.

Worth Your Money?

The total annual cost of attendance at Franklin W. Olin is a hair below $77,000. Thankfully, 54 percent of the undergraduate population receives need-based aid averaging $52k per year, and merit awards with an average yearly value of $25k are distributed generously. Even if you didn't receive any aid, you're always safe investing in a college where the average starting salary exceeds the annual cost of attending. Olin is such a school, and with engineering being the only pathway, you are just about guaranteed a solid return on your educational investment.

FINANCIAL
Institutional Type: Private
In-State Tuition: $53,990
Out-of-State Tuition: $53,990
Room & Board: $17,460
Required Fees: $3,366
Books & Supplies: $200

Avg. Need-Based Grant: $52,376
Avg. % of Need Met: 99%

Avg. Merit-Based Award: $26,159
% Receiving (All Freshmen): 100%
% Receiving (Freshmen w/o Need): 46%

Avg. Cumulative Debt: $13,480
% of Students Borrowing: 28%

CAREER
Who Recruits
1. Cognex Corporation
2. Ford Motor Company
3. General Electric
4. Watts
5. Tableau

Notable Internships
1. Ford Motor Company
2. Raytheon
3. Tableau Software

Top Industries
1. Engineering
2. Education
3. Research
4. Information Technology
5. Business

Top Employers
1. Google
2. Microsoft
3. Apple
4. athenahealth
5. Skydio

Where Alumni Work
1. Boston
2. San Francisco
3. Seattle
4. New York City
5. Los Angeles

Median Earnings
College Scorecard (Early Career): NR
PayScale (Early Career): NR
PayScale (Mid-Career): NR

RANKINGS
Money: Not Ranked
U.S. News: Not Ranked
Wall Street Journal/THE: Not Ranked
Washington Monthly: Not Ranked

COLLEGE OVERLAPS
Cornell University
Georgia Institute of Technology
Harvey Mudd College
Massachusetts Institute of Technology
University of California, Berkeley

Furman University

Greenville, South Carolina | 864-294-2034

Young people from 48 states and 22 countries are among the 2,700 undergraduates presently enrolled at Furman University in Greenville, South Carolina, the state's oldest private university. What draws such a diverse group of people to the foothills of the Blue Ridge Mountains is an immensely personal in-class educational opportunity with an equal focus on experiential learning and near-universal student involvement outside of the classroom. Make no mistake; this school has a "university" label, but it hosts only 100 graduate students. Furman is a top-notch, yet not uber-exclusive, Southern liberal arts school with a litany of impressive statistics from its freshman retention rate to its tremendous postgraduate outcomes.

Inside the Classroom

At Furman, undergrads have the choice of 60 academic programs, all in the liberal arts and sciences realm. General education requirements are fairly extensive, but they also allow room for flexibility within certain umbrella categories. All undergrads most complete two writing courses, two global awareness courses, and 11 core courses. The core includes forays into the natural world, human behavior, historical analysis, interpreting texts, mathematical and formal reasoning, the visual and performing arts, and the completion of a foreign language through the 201 level. (Where you start depends on placement tests.)

The vast majority of courses at Furman take place in an intimate classroom environment. A 10:1 student-to-faculty ratio and very few graduate students lead to an average class size of just 15 students. One quarter of sections have only a single-digit enrollment, and 98 percent of courses enroll fewer than 29; giant lecture halls don't even exist at this university. The school is consistently rated highly for professor accessibility and under-graduate teaching. Ninety percent of the Class of 2019 participated in at least one of what the university calls a "high impact practice," which includes a research experience, an internship, or a term studying abroad.

Standout programs at this school include business, public health, and politics and international affairs. The social sciences are the area in which most degrees are conferred (16 percent), followed by business (13 percent), health professions (9 percent), communication/journalism (8 percent), and the visual and performing arts (7 percent). Furman is a prolific producer of Fulbright Scholars having seen six members of the Class of 2020 capture the award. In the school's history, it has produced 52 Fulbright Scholars and six Rhodes Scholars.

Outside the Classroom

Pretty much everyone lives on campus, either in the dorms or Greek houses; 98 percent of freshmen reside in school-run housing, and 88 percent of the entire undergraduate student body does the same. Women join sororities at an astonishing 61 percent clip; men go Greek at around half that rate. Furman's 18 Division I athletic teams, 20+ club teams, and ample intramural leagues ensure that just about everyone is involved in some recreational activity. The 96,000- square-foot Trone Student Center serves as a hub for the school's 150+ student organizations. The school features everything from a notably active student government to a 50-member Super Smash Bros. video game club. However, the largest organization is the Heller Service Corps, which facilitates community service participation for over 1,800 students each year. Furman's beautifully designed 750-acre campus is among the nation's most admired. On-campus features include a lake, a 16,000-seat football stadium, an 18-hole golf course, a pool, and a newly renovated science complex that features a planetarium. The city of Greenville (population 71,000) also receives high grades for its affordable housing, "foodie" reputation, and endless opportunities for outdoor recreation.

Career Services

The Malone Center for Career Engagement has seven professional employees who work in advising and employer engagement capacities. This works out to a 393:1 student-to-advisor ratio, which is very solid compared against similarly sized institutions featured in this guide. As such, the staff are able to genuinely encourage each student to stop by to explore careers or grad programs, and the center offers almost daily events. In one week in September 2020 alone, the center hosted a prelaw workshop on how to apply to law school during COVID-19, an alumni chat on careers in consulting, and a seminar on pitching yourself to startups.

Furman University

E-mail: admissions@furman.edu | Website: www.furman.edu

Thanks in part to the fact it provides 1:1 assistance in the internship search, a solid 72 percent of the Class of 2019 completed at least one such experience during their four years. The Malone Center's ability to facilitate so many meaningful internships yields dividends in terms of future employment satisfaction. The Class of 2019 boasted a 93 percent satisfaction rate in terms of their postgraduate employment plans, and 95 percent of those continuing their education were pleased with those plans. Paladins also enjoy helping other Paladins, and an alumni network of 30,000+ active members can assist current students as they search for ways to get a foot in the door of just about any industry/company.

Professional Outcomes

The first-destination survey for the Class of 2019 reveals some highly encouraging results, starting with the fact that 99 percent of grads quickly achieved positive outcomes with 53 percent employed, 37 percent continuing their education, 5 percent working and attending graduate school, 2 percent engaged in volunteer work, 2 percent joining the military, and only 1 percent still seeking employment. The greatest number of students entered the education/nonprofit sector (17 percent), followed by accounting/finance (12 percent), arts/media (12 percent) marketing/sales (12 percent), and business/consulting (11 percent). Companies that employ a large number of Paladin alums include Wells Fargo, EY, Deloitte, Bank of America, Michelin, and PwC. Recent grads have also found their way to SpaceX, the PGA Tour, and the US Department of Commerce. Furman alumni can be found in large numbers in the Greenville, South Carolina, area, as well as Atlanta; Charlotte; Washington, DC; and New York City. According to PayScale, the median salary for a Furman graduate with 0-5 years of work experience is $54k; those entering mid-career enjoy a median income of $106k.

Furman graduates tend to pursue an advanced or professional degree very quickly after earning their bachelor's degree. Among the Class of 2019, 47 students were studying in a health-related field, 26 were in a science and engineering program, 18 were pursuing a business degree, and 18 were in law school. Over the past decade, medical school applicants from the university with at least a 3.5 GPA have been accepted into at least one program at a 79 percent clip, almost double the national average. Since 2006, the school has seen alumni matriculate at elite medical schools including Columbia, Duke, Harvard, Johns Hopkins, and Yale. Prelaw students have found similar success, enjoying a 90 percent acceptance rate and beginning their legal training at the likes of UVA, Berkeley, and Duke.

Admission

Out of 5,258 applications received for a place in the Class of 2023, Furman offered 2,987 students an invitation to join the 2019-20 freshman class. Only 22 percent of accepted students went on to enroll. Middle-50 percent SAT reading scores were 630-710, and the math section range was 610-710; the composite ACT middle-50 percent range was 28-32. The middle 50th percentile unweighted GPA was 3.4-3.9. An impressive 55 percent of last year's freshmen hailed from the top decile of their high school class, and 75 percent placed in the top quartile.

Furman places the greatest emphasis on the rigor of one's secondary school record, followed by class rank, GPA, essays, extracurricular activities, and character/personal qualities. Furman is a test-optional institution but will consider any submitted scores (40 percent of attending students submitted SATs, and 50 percent submitted ACTs). Additional factors that will be considered by the admissions committee are recommendations, an interview, talent/ability, legacy, first-generation status, racial/ethnic status, volunteer work, work experience, and the level of an applicant's interest. Applying early decision is one way to communicate that you are passionate about becoming a Paladin, and it pays off—85 percent of ED applicants gain acceptance. If your devotion isn't quite at ED-level, applying early action is a wise move; 59 percent of the Class of 2023 went that route.

Worth Your Money?

Furman's total cost of attendance for the 2020-21 academic year, including tuition, room and board, books, transportation, and personal expenses is an estimated $68,952. Forty-one percent of the entering 2019-20 freshman class borrowed money to pay tuition, and the average cumulative debt for graduates is $30k, right around the national average. We would not recommend borrowing more than that to attend Furman unless you were majoring in business or had a clear plan that would lead to a high enough starting salary to make debt repayment manageable. Fortunately, the school does provide average merit awards of $18k and need-based awards of $35k, making Furman a more affordable choice for some.

FINANCIAL
Institutional Type: Private
In-State Tuition: $51,712
Out-of-State Tuition: $51,712
Room & Board: $13,362
Required Fees: $380
Books & Supplies: $810

Avg. Need-Based Grant: $35,154
Avg. % of Need Met: 79%

Avg. Merit-Based Award: $17,963
% Receiving (All Freshmen): 57%
% Receiving (Freshmen w/o Need): 34%

Avg. Cumulative Debt: $30,388
% of Students Borrowing: 41%

CAREER
Who Recruits
1. Wells Fargo
2. Merrill Lynch
3. S&P Global
4. Prisma Health
5. PwC

Notable Internships
1. Manhattan Institute
2. W.W. Norton
3. Salesforce

Top Industries
1. Business
2. Education
3. Operations
4. Sales
5. Social Services

Top Employers
1. Greenville County Schools
2. Wells Fargo
3. US Army
4. Prisma Health
5. Clemson University

Where Alumni Work
1. Atlanta
2. Charlotte
3. Washington DC
4. New York City
5. Columbia, SC

Median Earnings
College Scorecard (Early Career): $51,200
PayScale (Early Career): $55,400
PayScale (Mid-Career): $107,900

RANKINGS
Money: 331
U.S. News: 52 (T), Liberal Arts Colleges
Wall Street Journal/THE: 135 (T)
Washington Monthly: 102, Liberal Arts Colleges

COLLEGE OVERLAPS
Clemson University
Elon University
University of South Carolina
Wake Forest University
Wofford College

George Mason University

Fairfax, Virginia | 703-993-2400

ADMISSION
Admission Rate: 87%
Admission Rate - Men: 84%
Admission Rate - Women: 89%
EA Admission Rate: 92%
ED Admission Rate: Not Offered
ED Admits as % of Total Admits: Not Offered
Admission Rate (5-Year Trend): +25%
% of Admits Attending (Yield): 22%
Transfer Admission Rate: 84%

SAT Reading/Writing (Middle 50%): 560-660
SAT Math (Middle 50%): 550-660
ACT Composite (Middle 50%): 24-30

% Graduated in Top 10% of HS Class: 15%
% Graduated in Top 25% of HS Class: 44%
% Graduated in Top 50% of HS Class: 81%

Demonstrated Interest: Considered
Legacy Status: Considered
Admission Interview Offered: No

ENROLLMENT
Total Undergraduate Enrollment: 26,662
% Part-Time: 19%
% Male: 51%
% Female: 49%
% Out-of-State: 10%
% Fraternity: 5%
% Sorority: 6%
% On-Campus (Freshman): 62%
% On-Campus (All Undergraduate): 21%

% African-American: 11%
% Asian: 21%
% Hispanic: 15%
% White: 38%
% Other: 5%
% Race or Ethnicity Unknown: 3%
% International: 6%
% Low-Income: 24%

ACADEMICS
Student-to-Faculty Ratio: 17 to 1
% of Classes Under 20: 31%
% of Classes 20-49: 56%
% of Classes 50 or More: 14%
% Full-Time Faculty: 48%
% Full-Time Faculty w/ Terminal Degree: 91%

Top Programs
Accounting
Criminology, Law and Society
Computer Science
Economics
Government and International Politics
History
Information Technology

Retention Rate: 86%
4-Year Graduation Rate: 47%
6-Year Graduation Rate: 70%

Curricular Flexibility: Less Flexible
Academic Rating: ★★★

#CollegesWorthYourMoney

If you had to describe George Mason University in five adjectives or less, large, public, affordable, career-focused, and politically conservative (the Koch brothers are/were major donors) would be apt selections. Outsiders sometimes find the number of GMU students surprising; there are 37,000+ of them, nearly 27,000 of whom are undergraduates. The high numbers of commuters can hide the actual scope of the university that features ten undergraduate schools and colleges and approximately seventy distinct academic programs. You can get a sense of the pre-professional feel of the student body simply by examining the areas where the greatest number of degrees are conferred. Business (18 percent) is followed by the social sciences (10 percent), health professions (10 percent), computer and information sciences (10 percent), and engineering (6 percent).

Inside the Classroom

Mason aims to make every one of its graduates an "engaged citizen and well-rounded scholar who is prepared to act." Toward that goal it requires a journey through the "Mason Core," a forty-three-credit collection of foundation, exploration, and integration requirements. Among the mandatory topics one must tackle are written communication, oral communication, quantitative reasoning and information technology, literature, arts, natural sciences, and other liberal arts staples. That trek will take you the equivalent of three full semesters. The Honors College requires twelve additional credits.

As a result of a 17:1 student-to-faculty ratio and over 11,000 graduate students, class sizes at GMU are rarely small, but it tends to be a mixed bag, and many sections do feature relatively modest numbers. Thirty-one percent of sections enroll nineteen or fewer students, 26 percent have forty or more students, and the remaining sections lie in between. More intimate educational experiences can be sought in the form of undergraduate research, which roughly half of all students ultimately engage in. There are plenty of summer research opportunities, but you can also take courses designated as Discovery of Scholarship, Scholarly Inquiry, or Research & Scholarship Intensive that offer built-in supervised research. Presently, only ten percent of GMU students study abroad, but the school does sponsor 140+ programs, including travel to the school's own international campus in South Korea.

The Volgenau College of Engineering, which houses a top-tier Information Technology Department, and the School of Business are both extremely reputable in the eyes of prospective employers, and the school's Northern Virginia location allows many connections with industry to be forged via internships and face-to-face recruiting opportunities. Recent grads have also captured a growing number of prestigious fellowships and scholarships. In 2018, five students won Boren Awards, and in 2019, the school produced a Truman Scholarship winner and has boasted a handful of Fulbright Scholars in recent years.

Outside the Classroom

Only 62 percent of freshmen and 21 percent of the overall undergraduate population reside in on-campus housing. There are many students who commute and/or live in (sometimes) cheaper off-campus housing in Arlington, Falls Church, Annandale, or Manassas. Because 85 percent of GMU students are Virginia residents, they are usually in fairly close proximity to their families. Greek life exists but doesn't dominate; 5 percent of men join frats, and 6 percent of women join sororities. While DC isn't exactly in your backyard at Mason, it is like having a beautiful park right down the street. The heart of the city is only fifteen miles from campus. Meanwhile, the 677 wooded acres that comprise the school's grounds are home to 500+ student-run clubs. There are hundreds of events to attend for free at the Center for the Arts, organic gardens that can be fully utilized by students, two pools, and loads of intramural and club sports. On the more serious athletic front, the Patriots' 462 student-athletes compete in twenty-two NCAA Division I sports with a men's basketball team good enough to have made a Final Four run this millennium. The Hub Student Center is another place where a student body with a large contingent of commuters can coalesce and mingle, but surveys indicate that, at present, the social scene at Mason has room for improvement. Seniors offer much lower ratings of indicators like "sense of belonging" and "involvement in campus activities" than the quality of academic instruction they received.

Career Services

George Mason University Career Services employs twenty-five professionals (not including office assistants, the webmaster, or peer advisors). Roles include employer outreach, industry advisor, career counselor, and career fair manager. That works out to a 1,066:1 student-to-advisor ratio, poorer than the average ratio when compared to other institutions included in this guidebook but not altogether unusual for a school of Mason's size. The career services staff still manages to help more than 20,000 unique students each year, close to 80 percent of all undergraduate students, which is impressive.

This level of outreach helps to explain why, among employed Class of 2019 members, 87 percent were in jobs that aligned with their career goals. Some connections are made through fall and spring career fairs that draw 150 employers and 1,500+ students each semester. The internship outlook is aided by the prime location of the university as well as cultivated relationships with many companies. There are fifteen Fortune 500 Companies and, of course, every government agency within a stone's throw. Within the Civil Engineering Department, over 90 percent of undergrads complete at least one internship. Over 100,000 Mason alumni, who are mainly concentrated in the Beltway area, also greatly aid the job and internship hunt.

Professional Outcomes

Six months after receiving their degrees, 83 percent of the class of 2019 had accepted a job offer or started work in a graduate program. The most commonly entered industries were education (25 percent), government (12 percent), technology (12 percent), and health (9 percent). GMU grads flow into major consulting firms like Booz Allen Hamilton, Deloitte, and Accenture, financial institutions like Capital One and Freddie Mac, and engineering/tech firms like General Dynamics, IBM, and Microsoft. Class of 2019 graduates also secured employment at Lockheed Martin, the Smithsonian, the Department of Homeland Security, MITRE, and the U.S. Senate. The vast majority of recent grads stay in the area as 92 percent work in DC, Virginia, or Maryland. New York City and San Francisco also have sizable numbers of Mason alumni. Including bonuses, the average first year salary for a GMU grad is $71,000.

George Mason is presently conducting a feasibility study for creating its own medical college. In the meantime, it offers two guaranteed admissions, joint-degree programs with Virginia Commonwealth University and George Washington University. George Mason does have its own institution for legal education—the Antonin Scalia Law School—and it offers a 3+3 bachelor's/JD program. Across all disciplines Mason graduates tend to pursue advanced degrees either at Mason itself or at other area schools including George Washington, American University, or the University of Maryland.

Admission

At 87 percent George Mason has one the highest acceptance rates of any school featured in this guide, making it an excellent choice for someone with less-than-stellar credentials but a desire to attend a school with tremendous resources. The school is test-optional for those with a strong GPA (It cites a mid-50 percent mark as 3.3-3.9, a record of honors and AP courses, and an impressive list of extracurricular activities that demonstrate leadership). Most applicants end up submitting standardized test scores—72 percent of the Class of 2023 submitted SAT scores, and 8 percent produced ACT results. The mid-50 percent ranges were 1120-1300 on the SAT and 24-30 on the ACT. Only 15 percent of 2019-20 freshman placed in the top 10 percent of their high school class, 44 percent were in the top quartile, and 81 percent were in the top 50 percent. The average GPA was 3.65, but 30 percent were below 3.5, giving hope to those who may have hit some bumps along their academic road.

GMU values the rigor of one's high school courses and the GPA earned above all else. Class rank, standardized test scores, and intangibles like talent/ability and character/personal qualities come next. There are no interviews offered as part of the process, nor is there an option for binding early decision. An early action deadline of November 1 will get students a decision by December 15. Entry to Mason is competitive, but compared to many other schools of its class, the bar is easier to clear.

Worth Your Money?

As a state resident George Mason is an unequivocal steal at under $10,000 in tuition. Out-of-staters will pay more than three times as much, making it a question of (a) will Mason provide me with significantly better academics/job prospects than public universities in my own state, and (b) will my potential area of study warrant the extra cost? For example, an applicant from Pennsylvania intent on majoring in education would be unlikely to get a solid return on investment depending, of course, on the degree of merit and need-based aid.

FINANCIAL
Institutional Type: Public
In-State Tuition: $9,060
Out-of-State Tuition: $32,520
Room & Board: $11,705
Required Fees: $3,504
Books & Supplies: $1,278

Avg. Need-Based Grant: $7,507
Avg. % of Need Met: 61%

Avg. Merit-Based Award: $7,565
% Receiving (All Freshmen): 40%
% Receiving (Freshmen w/o Need): 16%

Avg. Cumulative Debt: $33,362
% of Students Borrowing: 58%

CAREER
Who Recruits
1. CoStar
2. BAE Systems
3. Andersen Tax
4. Boeing
5. Black Horse

Notable Internships
1. Verizon
2. Cisco
3. BAE Systems

Top Industries
1. Business
2. Education
3. Infromation Technology
4. Operations
5. Engineering

Top Employers
1. Booz Allen Hamilton
2. Deloitte
3. Northrop Grumman
4. Capital One
5. Freddie Mac

Where Alumni Work
1. Washington DC
2. New York City
3. Richmond, VA
4. San Francisco
5. Baltimore

Median Earnings
College Scorecard (Early Career): $59,900
PayScale (Early Career): $60,700
PayScale (Mid-Career): $114,500

RANKINGS
Money: 105
U.S. News: 143 (T), National Universities
Wall Street Journal/THE: 178 (T)
Washington Monthly: 61, National Universities

COLLEGE OVERLAPS
James Madison University
University of Maryland
University of Virginia
Virginia Commonwealth University
Virginia Tech

George Washington University

Washington, District of Columbia | 202-994-6040

ADMISSION
Admission Rate: 41%
Admission Rate - Men: 41%
Admission Rate - Women: 41%
EA Admission Rate: Not Offered
ED Admission Rate: 71%
ED Admits as % of Total Admits: 8%
Admission Rate (5-Year Trend): -5%
% of Admits Attending (Yield): 24%
Transfer Admission Rate: 39%

SAT Reading/Writing (Middle 50%): 630-720
SAT Math (Middle 50%): 650-750
ACT Composite (Middle 50%): 29-33

% Graduated in Top 10% of HS Class: 53%
% Graduated in Top 25% of HS Class: 83%
% Graduated in Top 50% of HS Class: 96%

Demonstrated Interest: Considered
Legacy Status: Considered
Admission Interview Offered: No

ENROLLMENT
Total Undergraduate Enrollment: 12,484
% Part-Time: 11%
% Male: 38%
% Female: 62%
% Out-of-State: 96%
% Fraternity: 5%
% Sorority: 9%
% On-Campus (Freshman): 97%
% On-Campus (All Undergraduate): 58%

% African-American: 8%
% Asian: 11%
% Hispanic: 11%
% White: 49%
% Other: 4%
% Race or Ethnicity Unknown: 5%
% International: 12%
% Low-Income: 14%

ACADEMICS
Student-to-Faculty Ratio: 13 to 1
% of Classes Under 20: 52%
% of Classes 20-49: 38%
% of Classes 50 or More: 10%
% Full-Time Faculty: 44%
% Full-Time Faculty w/ Terminal Degree: 94%

Top Programs
Communication
Finance
History
International Affairs
International Business
Political Science
Public Health
Public Policy

Retention Rate: 92%
4-Year Graduation Rate: 76%
6-Year Graduation Rate: 82%

Curricular Flexibility: Somewhat Flexible
Academic Rating: ★★★✓

#CollegesWorthYourMoney

Appropriately located only four blocks from the White House, the university named after our nation's first president educates 12,484 undergraduate students and an additional 15,000+ graduate students. One of the pricier schools in the United States, George Washington University, nevertheless, has rarely been in higher demand since its founding in 1821. Thanks to the popularity of DC as a college setting and a number of highly regarded academic programs, GW has become increasingly selective, catering to a more talented group of students today than it did at the turn of the millennium.

Inside the Classroom
GW undergraduates choose from seventy majors spread across nine colleges: the Columbian College of Arts & Sciences, Corcoran School of the Arts & Design, School of Business, School of Engineering & Applied Science, Elliot School of International Affairs, School of Media & Public Affairs, School of Medicine & Health Sciences, School of Nursing, and the Milken Institute School of Public Health. All GW students must complete one course in mathematics or statistics, one course in natural and/or physical laboratory sciences, two courses in social sciences, one course in humanities, and two writing-intensive courses. From there, another set of college/major-specific requirements follow, but general education requirements tend not to be overly restrictive.

The school's 13:1 student-to-faculty ratio translates to a mix of small, medium, and large undergraduate sections. Ten percent of courses have single-digit enrollments, 10 percent have over fifty students, and the majority fall in the ten to thirty range. In recent years, the university has invested in increasing the number of undergraduate research experiences available to its students through the GW Center for Undergraduate Research and Fellowships. The efforts are paying off as a record 430 undergrads were slated to present at the 2020 GW Research Days, a two-day event held in April that was, unfortunately, canceled by the pandemic. Close to half of Colonials study abroad for one semester in Europe (65 percent), Asia (10 percent), Latin America (8 percent), Africa (7 percent), or Australia (6 percent).

Standout programs at GW include political science, international affairs, communications, and public health. Any degree earned from the university will serve students well when they vie for positions at top companies and elite graduate schools. The social sciences (34 percent) are the area in which the greatest number of degrees are awarded followed by health professions (16 percent), business (15 percent), engineering (6 percent), and communications/journalism (5 percent). A service-oriented institution, GW is proudly the number one producer of Peace Corps volunteers among midsize universities, and it also churns out Teach for America members at one of the highest rates in the country. Eleven students were named Fulbright Scholars in 2019 and they sported a higher Fulbright acceptance rate than Harvard, Princeton, or Columbia in recent years.

Outside the Classroom
Freshmen and sophomores are required to live in one of twenty-six residence halls situated on the university's two campuses. Three-quarters of freshmen reside at the main Foggy Bottom Campus, and the other 25 percent of first-years live at the Mount Vernon Campus that is three miles away in Northwest DC. Only 5 percent of men and 9 percent of women are Greek affiliated, making fraternities and sororities only modestly powerful social forces at GW. The school's robust sports program includes twenty-seven NCAA Division I teams. An additional 1,000 students participate in club sports, and the intramural programs scoop up the rest of the athletically inclined undergrads. The 475 registered student organizations collectively offer 1,200 leadership positions, and 87 percent of undergraduates are involved with at least one group. Noteworthy guest speakers appear with regularity through the GW Speaker Series. Of course, what's on campus is only the first layer of recreational opportunities at George Washington. The Foggy Bottom campus is only a few miles from the National Mall and many of the best museums in the country. As a bridge between the school and outside city, GW's flexible meal plans allow you to visit ninety partner restaurants, cafes, and grocery stores around DC. At GW, your life outside the classroom can involve every corner of the District of Columbia.

Career Services

The Center for Career Services is staffed by twenty-two full-time employees, including eight individuals with the title of career coach as well as other professionals focusing on employer relations and graduate school advising. That calculates to a student-advisor ratio of 567:1, within the average range of institutions profiled in this guide. Personalized career coaching is readily available. The office received high marks from students who exited in 2019 as 95 percent agreed that career programs had helped enhance their career development. In the 2018-19 school year, more than 800 employers engaged with current GW students and more than 35,000 global connections were available within the GW Alumni LinkedIn group.

Internships are completed by 68 percent of undergraduates and 54 percent are either paid or awarded a stipend for their work. Thanks to the university's far-reaching connections and prime location, internships are procured at thousands of different companies/organizations each year, from the US Congress to the Smithsonian to the NFL Players Association. The school also enjoys an alumni base of over 250,000 that leads to ample opportunities for networking. In sum, the Center for Career Services does a solid job facilitating internships and utilizing its DC locale and huge, well-connected alumni base to produce decent outcomes for its graduates.

Professional Outcomes

Within six months of leaving GW, 90 percent of the Class of 2019 had found their way to gainful employment or graduate school while 13 percent were still job hunting. Of the 66 percent of grads already in the workplace, 64 percent were in a for-profit industry, 28 percent had entered a nonprofit position, and 8 percent were working in government. Forty percent of grads earned a starting salary in excess of $60k, while an additional 46 percent earned between $40k and $60k. Over four-fifths of recent grads remained in the Mid-Atlantic region with the West and Mountain regions a distant second.

A healthy 22 percent of those earning their diplomas in 2019 immediately turned their attention to earning an advanced degree. Among that group were 67 percent seeking master's degrees, 19 percent entering law school, 7 percent entering a doctoral program, and 5 percent pursuing a medical degree. Looking at recent grads over a four year period, 488 students have continued their studies at George Washington. The next most commonly attended institutions were Columbia University (48), Georgetown (42), Johns Hopkins (37), and NYU (31).

Admission

Of 26,978 Class of 2023 hopefuls, GW admitted 11,109 for an acceptance rate of 41 percent. That number has shown volatility over current attendees' lifetimes, hitting as low as 32 percent in 2010 and as high as 80 percent in 1998 when today's seniors were still years away from being born. Freshmen during the 2019-20 school year earned excellent grades in high school as 53 percent finished in the top 10 percent of their class, and 83 percent landed in the top 25 percent. Of those submitting standardized test results the middle 50 percent of SAT scores were 1310-1440 and 29-33 on the ACT.

The admissions committee rates two factors—rigor of secondary school record and GPA—as carrying the greatest weight in the process. The next tier of factors includes the essay, volunteer work, recommendations, talent/ability, and extracurricular activities. GW has been test-optional since 2015, and a fair number of applicants do actually forgo submitting standardized test scores. Over the past two decades GW has grown into a highly selective and sought-after university in one of the country's hottest cities. Still, this institution is in a dogfight for top students and rewards those who apply early, typically accepting 71 percent through ED versus 39 percent in the regular cycle.

Worth Your Money?

Attending a private college in the fifth most expensive US city isn't going to come cheap. GW will set you back $87k per year for the total cost of attendance. For the 44 percent of undergrads who qualify for need-based financial aid, an average annual award of $37,000 puts a dent in the total costs, but the school does not meet 100 percent of the demonstrated need for the majority of eligible students. George Washington grads emerge with higher-than-average debt loads, thus prospective students need to carefully determine whether this school is a good financial fit for them, given their individual circumstances. Students pursuing study in the areas of business, communication, politics and policy enjoy better prospects for a strong ROI.

FINANCIAL
Institutional Type: Private
In-State Tuition: $58,550
Out-of-State Tuition: $58,550
Room & Board: $14,711
Required Fees: $90
Books & Supplies: $1,400

Avg. Need-Based Grant: $37,439
Avg. % of Need Met: 89%

Avg. Merit-Based Award: $22,863
% Receiving (All Freshmen): 57%
% Receiving (Freshmen w/o Need): 28%

Avg. Cumulative Debt: $34,768
% of Students Borrowing: 45%

CAREER
Who Recruits
1. Becton, Dickinson and Co.
2. Consumer Financial Protection Bureau
3. Westat
4. Turner Construction
5. Gunnison Consulting

Notable Internships
1. United States Senate
2. NBC News
3. Macy's

Top Industries
1. Business
2. Education
3. Operations
4. Social Services
5. information Technology

Top Employers
1. Booz Allen Hamilton
2. Deloitte
3. IBM
4. U.S. House of Representatives
5. Capital One

Where Alumni Work
1. Washington DC
2. New Yor City
3. San Francisco
4. Boston
5. Philadelphia

Median Earnings
College Scorecard (Early Career): $69,600
PayScale (Early Career): $63,800
PayScale (Mid-Career): $131,300

RANKINGS
Money: 349
U.S. News: 66 (T), National Universities
Wall Street Journal/THE: 70
Washington Monthly: 44, National Universities

COLLEGE OVERLAPS
American University
Boston University
Georgetown University
New York University
Northeastern University

Georgetown University

Washington, District of Columbia | 202-687-3600

The nation's oldest Catholic and Jesuit university also happens to be one of the best institutions in the country and one of the premier training grounds for future political bigwigs. Spired campus buildings, cobblestone walkways, and tree-lined streets give Georgetown an elegant aesthetic and an air of sophistication that perfectly matches the rigorous educational experience and conservative/traditional campus vibe.

Inside the Classroom

The university's 7,513 undergraduates and 12,080 graduate students are divided among nine schools/colleges, but only four are open to undergrads. Applicants to Georgetown must select one of these four schools: Georgetown College, McDonough School of Business, the Walsh School of Foreign Service, or the School of Nursing & Health Studies. Core requirements vary by school but are fairly extensive. For example, Georgetown College requires one course in the humanities and writing and two courses per discipline in theology, philosophy, math/science, social science, foreign language, and diversity for a total of fourteen required courses. There are forty-four majors within Georgetown College, seven business-oriented majors within McDonough, four tracks in the nursing school, and eight majors within the Walsh School of Foreign Service.

For a large university with a heavy presence of graduate students, Georgetown maintains a personalized and intimate learning environment. The student-faculty ratio is 11:1, and 60 percent of classes enroll fewer than twenty students. While some classes are a bit larger, only 6 percent cross the fifty-student threshold. There are many ways that students can seek funding for independent research projects or become an assistant to faculty members via the Georgetown Undergraduate Research Opportunities Program. Summer research can lead to the completion of a senior thesis that can be presented at the College Academic Council Research Colloquium every spring. Each year, almost 1,000 Hoya undergrads participate in one of the schools 213 study abroad programs that are spread across 57 countries.

Those desiring to join the world of politics or diplomacy are in the right place. The Government and International Affairs programs are among the best in the country. For those with their eyes on a finance career, McDonough is one of the most esteemed business schools one can find. The greatest number of degrees are conferred in the social sciences (33 percent) followed by business (26 percent), interdisciplinary studies (7 percent), and psychology (4 percent). Georgetown is regularly a top producer of distinguished fellowship winners. In 2020, it produced 45 Fulbright Scholars, placing it first in the nation. It typically also sees multiple Truman, Boren, Gilman International, and Marshall Scholars from each graduating class.

Outside the Classroom

The scenic and safe Georgetown area of DC is littered with high-end restaurants and shops. Only a short Metro ride away, the opportunities for museums, live music, fine cuisine, sporting events, and a pulsating nightlife are endless. A touch over three-quarters of undergrads live on campus. The twenty-three NCAA Division I sports teams are part of the fabric of Hoya life, particularly the men's basketball team. More than 2,500 students participate in intramural sports, utilizing the school's superb facilities that include Yates Field House. Due to the clash of values between the Jesuits and Greek life, fraternities and sororities are not recognized by the school, but they have enjoyed a recent rise in popularity despite their unofficial status. Religion is a guiding force at the university as more than half of the student body identify as Catholic. The campus ministry is popular, and many students are part of faith-based or secular volunteer organizations. In total, there are 250 active student organizations that offer an array of clubs focused on spirituality, culture, academics, and the arts. The Georgetown University Lecture Fund brings an incredible lineup of luminaries from the realms of politics, entertainment, business, media, and social activism to speak on campus.

Career Services

The Cawley Career Education Center is manned by thirteen professionals (not counting office managers and administrative assistants). That gives it a student-to-advisor ratio of 578:1, below average compared to the pool of institutions included in this book. Yet, that does not translate to a poor delivery of services. In fact, the staff boasts over 13,000 interactions with undergraduate students each year, almost twice the population of the student body; by graduation, over 90 percent have engaged with the career center. In a given year, counselors spend approximately 800 collective hours meeting one-on-one with students to discuss professional pathways and dole out career/graduate school advice.

Georgetown University

E-mail: guadmiss@georgetown.edu | Website: www.georgetown.edu

In a single school year, Georgetown arranged for 2,460 interviews on campus and attracted more than 1,800 attendees at both its fall and spring career expos. Over 200 corporations, government, and nonprofit employers met with students at those events. Additionally, sixty-five companies visited campus to host information sessions with undergraduates. With a strong and active alumni base, the Hoya Career Connection sees roughly 15,000 internship/employment opportunities posted per year. Despite not having an elite student-advisor ratio, Cawley's extensive counseling offerings/events, proficiency with facilitating on-campus recruiting by top-level employers, and tremendous student outcomes earned it top grades from our staff.

Professional Outcomes

Within six months of graduating, 77 percent of members of the Class of 2019 entered the workforce, 15 percent went directly into a graduate or professional program of study, and 5 percent were still seeking employment. In past years, the number of fresh alums entering grad school has been significantly greater—as high as 24 percent. The Class of 2019 sent massive numbers of graduates to a number of major corporations including JPMorgan Chase (28), Deloitte (24), EY (24), PricewaterhouseCoopers (16), Citi (15), and Accenture (14), and a number of other international financial institutions. As one might ascertain from this list of companies, three of the most popular industries were investment banking (16 percent), consulting (12 percent), and internet and software (8 percent). By far, New York and remaining in DC are the two most popular postgraduate destinations, although a fair number also migrate to Virginia, California, Massachusetts, and Maryland. The financial picture for Georgetown graduates is rosy. They enjoy an average starting salary of $63,631, well above the national average.

Over the past seven years, medicine and law have been the top two graduate fields chosen by Hoya alumni. Each year, roughly forty to fifty-five grads entered law school, and another forty to fifty-five entered med school. An incredibly high percentage elect to remain at Georgetown—68 members of the Class of 2019 entered graduate school at their alma mater. The number two choice was Columbia with 13 students. In fact, since 2007 Georgetown and Columbia have been the two most frequently attended graduate schools. The other schools on that list are almost exclusively elite institutions including Harvard, Yale, Duke, Northwestern, USC, NYU, Tufts, and the University of Chicago.

Admission

Like many other prestigious universities, Georgetown registered its all-time high in applications received and all-time low acceptance rate for the Class of 2023. Of the almost 23,000 applications, 3,269 were admitted for an acceptance rate of 14 percent. For enrolled freshmen in 2019-20, the mid-50 percent range was 1370-1530 on the SAT and 31-35 on the ACT. Grades must be equally exceptional for serious consideration; 85 percent of enrolled students finished in the top 10 percent of their high school class. The profile of students admitted today has much in common with those admitted five years ago.

Georgetown does not have an early decision option but does offer nonbinding early action. However, applying early yields little advantage as the university's early round acceptance rates tend to be lower than in the regular round. Also noteworthy, the university does not allow Score Choice, the option that permits applicants to select which standardized scores are reported to prospective schools and which are not. The admissions office rates nine factors as being "very important," most notably first-generation status, a consideration weighted this heavily by few other schools. In the 2019-20 academic year 12 percent of admitted students were the first in their family to attend college. The most selective school in the DC Metro area, Georgetown attracts growing lines of extremely well-qualified candidates each year. There are few admissions surprises here. Test scores around the 97th percentile and near-perfect grades in an AP-heavy course load are virtually required.

Worth Your Money?

A year at Georgetown will cost you approximately $75,000 (tuition + room & board) if you do not receive any financial aid. Like many similarly elite institutions, it is more focused on providing sizable grants to those with true financial need. For the 45 percent of current students who qualify for financial aid, Georgetown meets 100 percent of their demonstrated need, which works out to an average annual amount of $45,509. Unless you plan to enter a low-paying field and need to take on an excessive amount of debt, this school is well worth paying for as the Georgetown name will open doors for you well into adulthood.

FINANCIAL
Institutional Type: Private
In-State Tuition: $57,384
Out-of-State Tuition: $57,384
Room & Board: $17,578
Required Fees: $544
Books & Supplies: NR

Avg. Need-Based Grant: $45,509
Avg. % of Need Met: 100%

Avg. Merit-Based Award: $0
% Receiving (All Freshmen): 0%
% Receiving (Freshmen w/o Need): 0%

Avg. Cumulative Debt: $26,759
% of Students Borrowing: 36%

CAREER
Who Recruits
1. BMO Capital Markets
2. AlphaSights
3. RBC Capital Markets
4. Capital One
5. Charles River Associates

Notable Internships
1. U.S. Securities and Exchange Commission
2. Vanguard
3. Goldman Sachs

Top Industries
1. Business
2. Education
3. Social Services
4. Operations
5. Media

Top Employers
1. Deloitte
2. Google
3. PwC
4. Citi
5. Goldman Sachs

Where Alumni Work
1. Washington DC
2. New York City
3. San Francisco
4. Boston
5. Los Angeles

Median Earnings
College Scorecard (Early Career): $93,500
PayScale (Early Career): $69,400
PayScale (Mid-Career): $148,900

RANKINGS
Money: 83
U.S. News: 23, National Universities
Wall Street Journal/THE: 32
Washington Monthly: 8, National Universities

COLLEGE OVERLAPS
Cornell University
Duke University
Northwestern University
University of Pennsylvania
University of Notre Dame

Georgia Institute of Technology

Atlanta, Georgia | 404-894-4154

ADMISSION
Admission Rate: 21%
Admission Rate - Men: 17%
Admission Rate - Women: 28%
EA Admission Rate: 20%
ED Admission Rate: Not Offered
ED Admits as % of Total Admits: Not Offered
Admission Rate (5-Year Trend): -21%
% of Admits Attending (Yield): 41%
Transfer Admission Rate: 27%

SAT Reading/Writing (Middle 50%): 630-730
SAT Math (Middle 50%): 670-780
ACT Composite (Middle 50%): 29-34

% Graduated in Top 10% of HS Class: 90%
% Graduated in Top 25% of HS Class: 98%
% Graduated in Top 50% of HS Class: 99%

Demonstrated Interest: Considered
Legacy Status: Considered
Admission Interview Offered: No

ENROLLMENT
Total Undergraduate Enrollment: 16,159
% Part-Time: 10%
% Male: 61%
% Female: 39%
% Out-of-State: 30%
% Fraternity: 22%
% Sorority: 26%
% On-Campus (Freshman): 97%
% On-Campus (All Undergraduate): 50%

% African-American: 7%
% Asian: 23%
% Hispanic: 7%
% White: 46%
% Other: 4%
% Race or Ethnicity Unknown: 3%
% International: 10%
% Low-Income: 20%

ACADEMICS
Student-to-Faculty Ratio: 19 to 1
% of Classes Under 20: 44%
% of Classes 20-49: 34%
% of Classes 50 or More: 22%
% Full-Time Faculty: 86%
% Full-Time Faculty w/ Terminal Degree: 88%

Top Programs
Architecture
Business
Chemistry
Computer Science
Engineering
Industrial Design
Mathematics
Physics

Retention Rate: 97%
4-Year Graduation Rate: 46%
6-Year Graduation Rate: 90%

Curricular Flexibility: Less Flexible
Academic Rating: ★★★★

#CollegesWorthYourMoney

Downtown Atlanta is home to one of the world's undisputed best public technological institutes. The Georgia Institute of Technology, more commonly referred to as Georgia Tech, educates 16,159 undergraduates as well as another 20,000+ graduate students who are on track to be the next generation of leaders in the engineering, computer science, and related fields. While still catering to locals (70 percent are Georgia residents), Tech has managed to grow its national reputation in recent years and has blossomed from a top public tech university to simply a top tech university.

Inside the Classroom
Georgia Tech is divided into six colleges: the College of Design, the College of Computing, the College of Engineering, the College of Sciences, Ivan Allen College of Liberal Arts, and Scheller College of Business. Altogether, more than 115 majors and minors are available to undergraduates; all students are held to a stringent list of core requirements that is partially governed by the state. Must-take courses include Constitution & History, Communication Outcomes, Quantitative Outcomes, and Introduction to Computing as well as requirements in humanities/fine arts/ethics, social sciences, and wellness (physical education).

Being a large research university, the student-to-faculty ratio is a less-than-ideal 19:1, leading to some larger undergraduate class sections. In fact, 52 percent of courses had enrollments of more than thirty students in 2019-20. On the other end of the spectrum, 20 percent of sections had single-digit enrollments. While not all of your professors will know you by name, there are plenty of ways that motivated students can strike up meaningful faculty-student relationships. For example, 30 percent of aerospace engineering majors collaborate on research with their professors. In the School of Chemical and Biomolecular Engineering that figure rises to 60 percent. Over half of Tech students have gone abroad by the time they graduate, with a growing number electing to complete internships in a foreign land rather than academic coursework. In a given year, 130+ undergraduate students participated in a global internship.

Georgia Tech's engineering and computer science programs are at the top of any "best programs" list. The Scheller College of Business boasts top programs in management information systems, production/operation management, quantitative analysis, and supply chain management/logistics. The architecture school also receives national recognition. In terms of total number of degrees conferred, the most popular areas of study are engineering (59 percent), computer science (17 percent), and business (10 percent). Those pursuing prestigious fellowships/scholarships have done well in recent years. In 2019, four students won Fulbright Scholarships. Others have succeeded at taking home Astronaut, Udall, Truman, and Marshall Scholarships. Two undergrads from one major—electrical engineering—won National Science Fellowships in 2018.

Outside the Classroom
Georgia Tech's 400-acre, wooded campus contains the vast majority of freshmen (97 percent), but only 50 percent of the overall student body lives in the school's forty residence halls. The rest find apartments or housing in surrounding neighborhoods like Buckhead, Home Park, Westside, or Atlantic Station. The Yellow Jackets field seventeen varsity intercollegiate athletic teams. The school's nine men's and eight women's teams participate in the Atlantic Coast Conference (ACC). Add twenty intramural sports, forty-three sports clubs, and one of the largest outdoor recreation programs around, and the result is an extremely athletically-inclined student body. Those who aren't involved with sports typically find another place to connect, whether it's in one of the more than 400 student organizations or fifty Greek organizations. Tech is a Greek-heavy school with 22 percent of men and 26 percent of women belonging to a fraternity or sorority. Campus provides plenty of chances for social engagement, but those seeking more can enjoy all that Atlanta has to offer.

Career Services
The Georgia Tech Center for Career Discovery and Development, cleverly nicknamed C2D2, employs twenty-two full-time staff members (not counting IT professionals and office assistants). That collection of career advisors, employee relations specialists, and graduate school counselors works out to a student-to-counselor ratio of 735:1, below average compared to the pool of institutions included in this book. Despite this unremarkable number, C2D2 is able to put on impressive, large-scale events that enhance student outcomes. The Fall Career Fair is the school's largest, featuring over 400 employers including Accenture, Capital One, GM, and Intel, and 7,000 students attend each year. The school also forges formal corporate partnerships with big-time companies including Google, Airbnb, Qualcomm, Northrup Grumman, and ConocoPhillips. Corporations routinely host information sessions on campus.

Georgia Institute of Technology

E-mail: admission@gatech.edu | Website: www.gatech.edu

Internships and co-op programs receive some of the highest marks in the country. Thirty-five percent of undergrads choose to enter the school's three-semester co-op program, which leads to a five-year degree, while many others complete a one- or two-semester internship. In an average year, C2D2 places over 1,000 students in internships and another 1,300+ in co-op programs. Individualized appointments are encouraged as early as freshman year to begin planning potential career and graduate school pathways. Overall, Georgia Tech's career services does a fantastic job of funneling undergraduates into the world's premier employers at high starting salaries.

Professional Outcomes

Graduates in the Class of 2019 procured employment at a rate of 78 percent by the time they were handed their diplomas. The median salary reported by that group was $74,000. The highest median salaries went to graduates of the School of Computer Science. By midcareer, Georgia Tech alumni enjoy the third highest salary of all public university alumni in the country. You will find graduates at every major technology company in the world. Just examining those who have LinkedIn profiles, massive numbers of Yellow Jackets work at Google, Microsoft, Amazon, IBM, Apple, Facebook, and Uber. The bulk of graduates remain in the Atlanta metro area. The next three most popular destinations are San Francisco, New York City, and Washington, DC.

At the time of their exit surveys, roughly 20 percent of grads planned on pursuing an advanced degree within the next year. Many remain on campus to earn advanced engineering degrees through Georgia Tech, but the school's reputation is such that gaining admission into other top programs including MIT, Carnegie Mellon, Berkeley, Stanford, and Caltech is an achievable feat. Those same schools are institutions where Tech alumni have gone on to work as professors and researchers.

Admission

Only 21 percent of applicants to the Class of 2023 were admitted, a slight decrease from the 22 percent who were admitted the prior year. Freshmen during the 2019-20 school year possessed middle-50 percent scores of 1310-1480 on the SAT and 29-34 on the ACT, and 95 percent had a GPA of over 3.75. A staggering 90 percent of first-year students hailed from the top 10 percent of their high school classes; 98 percent were in the top 25 percent. Only a decade ago, the university admitted 63 percent of applicants, and the 75th percentile of test-takers placed close to the Class of 2023's 25th percentile. Clearly, this school is infinitely more difficult to get into than it was only a short time ago.

Three factors can give you an advantage in your quest to gain acceptance at Tech: (1) if you are from Georgia and (2) if you are female. In 2019, the acceptance rate for Peach State residents was 40 percent, more than double the out-of-state figure (17 percent). The acceptance rate for female applicants was 28 percent versus only 17 percent for male applicants. The early action acceptance rate was 20 percent versus 21 percent for the general pool. For all applicants, the admissions committee places the most emphasis on the rigor of one's high school coursework, GPA, and extracurricular activities. Test scores, essays, talent/ability, character, and personal qualities, volunteer work, and work experience are among the factors in the next tier. Getting into Georgia Tech has become a harrowing enterprise and is a wholly different experience than for previous generations.

Worth Your Money?

Georgia residents are looking at an annual cost of attendance of $29k which, when you consider that the median starting salary is well over two times that amount, makes Georgia Tech an exceptional bargain. Even better, merit aid is generously distributed with qualifying undergrads landing, on average, $11,867 award each year. That includes the Stamps President's Scholars Program that gives a free ride to forty highly qualified applicants each year. Need-based aid is granted to 36 percent of students with the average amount in the range of $14,500. Only a small percentage of aid recipients see 100 percent of their demonstrated need met. Even if you received limited aid and/or were paying out-of-state tuition, which brings the COA to $50k, Tech would still prove a worthwhile investment of your time and money.

FINANCIAL
Institutional Type: Public
In-State Tuition: $10,258
Out-of-State Tuition: $31,370
Room & Board: $14,830
Required Fees: $2,424
Books & Supplies: $800

Avg. Need-Based Grant: $14,533
Avg. % of Need Met: 65%

Avg. Merit-Based Award: $11,867
% Receiving (All Freshmen): 58%
% Receiving (Freshmen w/o Need): 31%

Avg. Cumulative Debt: $31,545
% of Students Borrowing: 40%

CAREER
Who Recruits
1. SunTrust Bank
2. Caterpillar
3. The Chlorox Company
4. Equifax
5. Rockwell Automation

Notable Internships
1. NASA
2. Procter & Gamble
3. Uber

Top Industries
1. Engineering
2. Business
3. Operations
4. Information Technology
5. Research

Top Employers
1. Google
2. Microsoft
3. Amazon
4. Home Depot
5. Apple

Where Alumni Work
1. Atlanta
2. San Francisco
3. New York City
4. Washington DC
5. Seattle

Median Earnings
College Scorecard (Early Career): $79,100
PayScale (Early Career): $75,800
PayScale (Mid-Career): $141,800

RANKINGS
Money: 21
U.S. News: 35 (T), National Universities
Wall Street Journal/THE: 71 (T)
Washington Monthly: 60, National Universities

COLLEGE OVERLAPS
Carnegie Mellon University
Cornell University
University of California, Berkeley
University of Georgia
University of Michigan

Gettysburg College

Gettysburg, Pennsylvania | 717-337-6100

The oldest existing Lutheran College in the US, Gettysburg College was already 31 years old when President Lincoln delivered his now famous address from the newly opened Soldiers' National Cemetery. Much like the address itself, the college has garnered more admiration through the passage of time. (Lincoln's speech was widely panned at the time.) In fact, another distinguished president, Dwight Eisenhower, actually served on the school's board of trustees, greatly raising the national profile of the school during his tenure. Today, Gettysburg College offers 40 majors and 40 minors to almost 2,400 undergraduates.

Inside the Classroom
The goals of the Gettysburg curriculum emphasize inquiries and integrations over the mere checking of boxes in a host of academic disciplines. All undergrads are expected to engage in inquiries within the humanities (1 course), the arts (1 course), the social sciences (1 course), and natural sciences (2 courses). While completing these courses, the college wants each student to demonstrate (1) integrative thinking, (2) communication skills, and (3) informed citizenship. Freshmen start their postsecondary careers in a first-year seminar and conclude their experience with a capstone course within their major. Additional requirements include two diversity courses and at least two courses in a second language.

If you want to learn in a large group setting at Gettysburg, you'll have to join a battlefield tour. A student-to-faculty ratio of 9:1 allows for incredibly small class sizes; the average is 17, and 70 percent of sections enroll fewer than 20 students. Undergraduate research opportunities are accessible to students in all academic departments. Overall, 55 percent of students get a chance to work on academic/laboratory research with one of their professors. A nearly identical 56 percent of Gettysburgians elect to study abroad for a semester or longer. The school has formal partnerships in countries like China, Tanzania, and Senegal.

By a substantial margin, the social sciences are the most common choice of major at Gettysburg, accounting for 27 percent of all degrees conferred. Other frequently selected disciplines include biology (14 percent), business/marketing (9 percent), psychology (7 percent), English (6 percent), and the visual and performing arts (5 percent). This is not a school with one or two standout departments, but one with many solid academic programs. Prestigious scholarship organizations typically pluck at least a few Gettysburg grads each year—the Class of 2019 produced four Fulbrights and three Goldwater Scholars.

Outside the Classroom
Just about every single undergraduate resides in on-campus housing at the college, and 100 percent of freshmen live in dorms while 95 percent of the student population stays on the grounds for all four years. Greek life has an equally massive presence for both men and women as fraternities and sororities attract one third of all undergrads. Gettysburg sponsors 24 varsity sports, a dozen for men and a dozen for women that play at the Division III level. Additionally, there are nine club teams, and the college has a reputation as a school where just about everyone plays intramural sports. The school has over 100 student-run clubs. While campus is a hub of activity, the town itself can be a bit slow except, of course, for Civil War history buffs. The greatest number of students hail from within a few hours of campus—Pennsylvania, New Jersey, New York, Maryland, and Connecticut. Trips home or other excursions are always within reasonable driving distance. Baltimore is 55 miles from campus, Washington, DC, can be reached in an hour and a half, Philadelphia in two hours, and New York City in three and a half hours.

Career Services
The Center for Career Engagement (CCE) is staffed by eight professional staff members who specialize in career mentoring, direct counseling, and employer relations. The CCE's student-to-advisor ratio of 296:1 is lower than the average institution included in this book. This terrific level of support results in the office working "with every student from the moment they step on campus to graduation." Utilizing a four-year career framework, the CCE helps students discover, create, experience, and connect their way to a satisfying postgraduate outcome.

A wealth of real-world experience is at the fingertips of Gettysburg undergrads including internships, 3-5-day externships, job shadowing, and multiday career treks and immersion trips. Close to 80 percent of students complete at least one full-blown internship. The alumni network includes over 30,000 individuals who are known for their willingness to help current students and recent grads. The CCE hosts one large Job & Internship Fair each fall, but employer meet and greets, workshops, virtual events, and on-campus interviews take place year-round. Thanks to the multitude of available opportunities for career exploration and networking, just about all newly minted graduates quickly find their place in life.

Gettysburg College

E-mail: admiss@gettysburg.edu | Website: www.gettysburg.edu

Professional Outcomes

One year after receiving their diplomas, 98 percent of all graduates from 2015-2018 had landed their first job or had enrolled in graduate/professional school. The crop of 2019 grads posted an identical success rate. Large numbers of Gettysburg alumni are employed by major corporations and financial institutions like Vanguard, Morgan Stanley, Wells Fargo, Deloitte, Merrill Lynch, JPMorgan Chase, Google, Accenture, Pfizer, and UBS. Even though the college is closer to Philadelphia, New York City is actually the number one destination for alums. Philly is second. Next most common destinations are Washington, DC; Baltimore; Boston; Harrisburg; and San Francisco. According to PayScale, the school ranks 27th of all liberal arts schools in the country for early-career and mid-career salaries.

Five years after graduation, 36 percent of surveyed Gettysburg grads had earned an advanced degree, and another 17 percent were presently enrolled in a graduate program. The college has produced an impressive (for its size) 285 doctoral-degree earners since 2006. Medical school applicants from 2002-2017 possessing at least a 3.5 GPA and an MCAT above 510 enjoyed an 88 percent acceptance rate. Prelaw students have found law school homes at the likes of NYU, Temple University, Villanova University, Penn, and Georgetown University.

Admission

The school receives close to 6,000 applications per year and rejects slightly more prospective students than it accepts; the most recent acceptance rate was 48 percent. The average freshman had an excellent high school career, as 60 percent finished in the top 10 percent and 85 percent placed in the top quartile. Those who did elect to submit standardized test scores performed well; the middle-50 percent ACT score was 27-31, and on the SAT, students ranged from 630-700 on the reading and writing section and 620-700 on the math section.

Gettysburg was fairly early to the test-optional party, making standardized testing optional for all domestic applicants in 2006. Its holistic review process places the most stock in the rigor of each applicant's secondary school record, GPA, essay, and recommendations. Factors considered "important" include class rank, test scores, an interview, extracurricular activities, talent/ability, character/personal qualities, and volunteer work. The school does not consider religious affiliation or state residency in the admissions process. In the school's own words, the admissions office is "Very interested in individuals of character who will make positive contributions to the campus community and beyond. In estimating such qualities, we rely on what students say about themselves through essays, along with the recommendations from secondary school counselors and teachers. In-depth involvement in extracurricular and community service activities both inside and outside of school is favorably considered in the admissions process."

Worth Your Money?

The small class sizes and oodles of individual attention offered by the college do come at a cost—tuition alone is $58,500, and the full annual cost of attendance is over $72k. Fortunately, Gettysburg did give out a total of $72 million in merit and need-based grants in 2019-20; 65 percent of the student body received a portion of this money. Of those receiving need-based aid, the average amount is $43,235; the average merit aid award is for $18,140. While the mean debt load at graduation of almost $35,000 is above the national average, Gettysburg does offer enough financial aid to make this school accessible to less-than-wealthy students. That being said, those planning on borrowing $35k+ should be pursuing a major that will see quick financial returns. Otherwise, a less pricey option may fit better into your life plan.

FINANCIAL
Institutional Type: Private
In-State Tuition: $58,500
Out-of-State Tuition: $58,500
Room & Board: $13,960
Required Fees: $0
Books & Supplies: $1,000

Avg. Need-Based Grant: $43,235
Avg. % of Need Met: 90%

Avg. Merit-Based Award: $18,140
% Receiving (All Freshmen): 63%
% Receiving (Freshmen w/o Need): 38%

Avg. Cumulative Debt: $34,630
% of Students Borrowing: 60%

CAREER
Who Recruits
1. Vanguard
2. Morgan Stanley
3. T. Rowe Price
4. Deloitte
5. Accenture

Notable Internships
1. Deloitte
2. Bank of America
3. U.S. House of Representatives

Top Industries
1. Business
2. Education
3. Sales
4. Operations
5. Social Services

Top Employers
1. Vanguard
2. Morgan Stanley
3. Wells Fargo
4. Deloitte
5. Merrill Lynch

Where Alumni Work
1. New York City
2. Philadelphia
3. Washington DC
4. Baltimore
5. Boston

Median Earnings
College Scorecard (Early Career): $56,100
PayScale (Early Career): $60,400
PayScale (Mid-Career): $123,000

RANKINGS
Money: 185
U.S. News: 54 (T), Liberal Arts Colleges
Wall Street Journal/THE: 102 (T)
Washington Monthly: 50, Liberal Arts Colleges

COLLEGE OVERLAPS
Bucknell University
Dickinson College
Franklin & Marshall College
Lafayette College
Muhlenberg College

Gonzaga University

Spokane, Washington | 509-313-6572

ADMISSION
Admission Rate: 62%
Admission Rate - Men: 62%
Admission Rate - Women: 62%
EA Admission Rate: Not Offered
ED Admission Rate: Not Offered
ED Admits as % of Total Admits: Not Offered
Admission Rate (5-Year Trend): -11%
% of Admits Attending (Yield): 13%
Transfer Admission Rate: 63%

SAT Reading/Writing (Middle 50%): 600-670
SAT Math (Middle 50%): 600-690
ACT Composite (Middle 50%): 25-30

% Graduated in Top 10% of HS Class: 40%
% Graduated in Top 25% of HS Class: 75%
% Graduated in Top 50% of HS Class: 95%

Demonstrated Interest: Considered
Legacy Status: Considered
Admission Interview Offered: Yes

ENROLLMENT
Total Undergraduate Enrollment: 5,238
% Part-Time: 2%
% Male: 47%
% Female: 53%
% Out-of-State: 52%
% Fraternity: Not Offered
% Sorority: Not Offered
% On-Campus (Freshman): 97%
% On-Campus (All Undergraduate): 51%

% African-American: 1%
% Asian: 6%
% Hispanic: 11%
% White: 70%
% Other: 7%
% Race or Ethnicity Unknown: 3%
% International: 1%
% Low-Income: 17%

ACADEMICS
Student-to-Faculty Ratio: 11 to 1
% of Classes Under 20: 62%
% of Classes 20-49: 38%
% of Classes 50 or More: 1%
% Full-Time Faculty: 54%
% Full-Time Faculty w/ Terminal Degree: 87%

Top Programs
Accounting
Biology
Business Administration
Engineering
Kinesiology and Physical Education
Nursing
Public Relations

Retention Rate: 94%
4-Year Graduation Rate: 75%
6-Year Graduation Rate: 85%

Curricular Flexibility: Less Flexible
Academic Rating: ★★★✔

#CollegesWorthYourMoney

Thanks to its success on the basketball court over the past two decades, most Americans have heard the name Gonzaga. However, if you ask them where the school is located, very few will correctly answer "Spokane, Washington." Over 5,200 undergraduates attend this midsize Jesuit university that offers 49 undergraduate majors and 58 minors. This school caters to strong students (the average unweighted high school GPA is 3.71), but it is not overly exclusive as more than three fifths of applicants gain acceptance. For anyone seeking the benefits of a Jesuit education, there is much to like about what Gonzaga University has to offer.

Inside the Classroom
The school's core curriculum is guided by the question, "As students of a Catholic, Jesuit, and Humanistic University, how do we educate ourselves to become women and men for a more just and humane global community?" In year one, students also take courses covering the categories of writing, reasoning, communication and speech, scientific inquiry, and mathematics. Sophomores take classes on Christianity/Catholicism and philosophy, and juniors delve into ethics and comparative religion. Two new additions to the school's mandated courses are a first-year seminar and a core integration seminar taken toward the end of a student's undergraduate experience.

An enviable 11:1 student-to-faculty ratio leads to average class sizes of 24 students, and the school rates well in surveys of undergraduate instructional quality. Less than 1 percent of course sections enroll more than 50 students. The Center for Undergraduate Research & Creative Inquiry was launched in 2016 to facilitate an increased number of student-faculty collaborations. Opportunities for research exist not only in the natural sciences but also in the arts, humanities, and social sciences. Over half of Zags choose to study abroad during their college experience— about 700 students each year—including at the university's flagship program in Florence, Italy.

Business/marketing is the area of study that attracts the most Zag undergrads; 28 percent earn degrees in that discipline. The next most common areas of degree conferment are engineering (12 percent), social sciences (12 percent), biology (10 percent), communication/journalism (7 percent), and psychology (7 percent). The School of Engineering & Applied Science is rated extremely high among nondoctoral, degree-granting institutions, and the School of Business Administration has a solid national reputation. The university does not produce a large number of competitive postgraduate scholarship winners but does usually see at least two Fulbrights awarded to seniors each year.

Outside the Classroom
The 152-acre campus is located right along the Spokane River less than one mile from the downtown business district. Ninety-seven percent of freshmen reside in university-owned housing, and roughly half of the undergraduate population, as a whole, do the same. As is typical at Jesuit institutions, there are no Greek organizations on campus. The 18 intercollegiate sports teams are a point of pride, particularly the men's basketball team that has reached the Sweet Sixteen eight times. Intramural athletics are also huge with 58 percent of undergraduates participating in thirty different sports; another 700 students are members of club teams. There are also more than 150 student-initiated clubs including 30 academic honor societies, 30 pre-professional clubs, 20 political groups, 15 cultural clubs, and 11 volunteer organizations. So-termed "SpikeNites" occur every Saturday night, offering events such as movie night, ice skating, bingo, and bubble soccer. GU Outdoors offers students the chance to engage in skiing, snowboarding, hiking, backpacking, fishing, rock climbing, and kayaking in the beautiful natural areas that surround Gonzaga's campus. A student newspaper is published 28 times during each academic year, and iZAG internet radio runs 24/7. Being located in the heart of Washington's second largest city while also being surrounded by endless natural beauty presents enough opportunity for fun on its own. Add in Gonzaga's above-average sense of school spirit and student community, and the result is a generally happy bunch.

Career Services
Nine professional employees make up the Career and Professional Development Office at Gonzaga University, working in areas such as alumni engagement, employer relations, and in various advising capacities. This equates to a 578:1 student-to-counselor ratio, which is a fairly standard figure for a midsized university. Zags are treated to five on-site career fairs each year: the Accounting Career Fair, Post Graduate Service Fair, All Majors Career & Internship Fair, Engineering & Computer Science Career & Internship Fair, and the FUSE Career Fair.

A total of 364 employers recruited on campus during the 2018-19 school year. Companies visiting Gonzaga included Adidas, CBRE Group, HP, JPMorgan, McKinstry, PepsiCo, and Salesforce. The Gonzaga Alumni Mentoring Program (GAMP) matches current students with mentors based on geographical locations and career interests. This organization also arranges TREKS to New York, the Bay Area, Seattle, and Portland each year to meet with alumni who work at 30 of those areas' top corporations. The university has placed great emphasis on increasing the number of undergraduates who participate in at least one internship during their four years of study. In 2008, just 34 percent of students did so; today, the overwhelming majority of undergrads land internships. All of these efforts leave Gonzaga alumni enjoying the best employment rate of any school in the state.

Professional Outcomes

The Class of 2019 enjoyed a largely gentle landing as they left their Spokane campus home and flew on to their next destination. Seventy-one percent of those surveyed found full-time employment within six months, with the largest number of grads getting hired by Providence Health & Services (23), the US Armed Forces (22), Boeing (18), Teach for America (13) and Seattle Children's Hospital (18). Additional companies that employ large numbers of Zag alumni include Amazon, Microsoft, Starbucks, Nike, Deloitte, and Nordstrom. The average starting salary for 2019 grads was $54,348. The most popular cities for newly minted grads are Seattle and Spokane followed by Portland, San Francisco, and Los Angeles.

Of the 17 percent of 2019 grads who entered a graduate/professional degree program, the most popular institutions were Gonzaga (87), the University of Washington (8), Washington State University (6), the University of Notre Dame (4), Eastern Washington University (3), Seattle University (3), and the University of San Diego (3). Recent grads pursuing a legal education have matriculated into law school at the University of Minnesota, Villanova University, and UCLA. Gonzaga saw 56 students apply to medical schools in the 2019-20 school year. While the university does not have its own medical school, it does have a partnership with the UW School of Medicine.

Admission

Gonzaga is certainly a selective school but not one that should send shivers down the spines of prospective applicants. Of the 9,279 applicants vying for a place in the Class of 2023, a healthy 62 percent received invitations to join the university. Only 22 percent of this group actually went on to enroll in the university. The freshman class of 2019-20 brought with it an impressive set of high school credentials, with an average GPA of 3.82 and two fifths earning a place in the top decile of their graduating cohort. The middle 50 percent ACT composite score was 25-30. On the SAT, the range was 600-670 on the EBRW section and 600-690 on the math section.

Four factors sit atop the list in terms of how the Gonzaga committee evaluates applicants: rigor of secondary school record, GPA, first-generation status, and character/personal qualities. Standardized test scores, essays, recommendation letters, extracurricular activities, and talent/ability are deemed "important" when making admissions decisions. This school definitely looks favorably upon applicants who demonstrate significant interest in the university. With a relatively low yield rate (the 22 percent mentioned a moment ago), and no early action or early decision options, Gonzaga is anxious to admit any students who have indicated a likelihood of enrolling.

Worth Your Money?

The sticker price of a Gonzaga education is less than many other Jesuit schools featured in our guide (e.g., Boston College, Fairfield University, Santa Clara University). The $46,000 annual tuition and projected annual cost (including personal expenses, transportation, etc.) is under $65k. Including both need and merit-based aid, the average package handed out by the school is around $30,500; in total, the school meets 78 percent of eligible students' needs. The average level of indebtedness is right around $30k, close to the national average. Those seeking the perks of a private college can get what they are looking for at Gonzaga, and the school can provide value, particularly for those who are career oriented and will jump into a solid starting salary.

FINANCIAL
Institutional Type: Private
In-State Tuition: $46,060
Out-of-State Tuition: $46,060
Room & Board: $12,951
Required Fees: $860
Books & Supplies: $1,196

Avg. Need-Based Grant: $8,432
Avg. % of Need Met: 78%

Avg. Merit-Based Award: $16,782
% Receiving (All Freshmen): 99%
% Receiving (Freshmen w/o Need): 37%

Avg. Cumulative Debt: $29,685
% of Students Borrowing: 54%

CAREER
Who Recruits
1. EY
2. Booz Allen Hamilton
3. CALIBRE
4. CIA
5. American Continental Group

Notable Internships
1. Seattle Seahawks
2. KPMG
3. Columbia Records

Top Industries
1. Business
2. Education
3. Operations
4. Healthcare
5. Social Services

Top Employers
1. Boeing
2. Amazon
3. Microsoft
4. US Army
5. Nike

Where Alumni Work
1. Seattle
2. Spokane
3. Portland
4. San Francisco
5. Canada

Median Earnings
College Scorecard (Early Career): $56,100
PayScale (Early Career): $61,200
PayScale (Mid-Career): $117,000

RANKINGS
Money: 325
U.S. News: 80 (T), National Universities
Wall Street Journal/THE: 211
Washington Monthly: 186, National Universities

COLLEGE OVERLAPS
Loyola Marymount University
Santa Clara University
Seattle University
University of Portland
University of Washington

Grinnell College

Grinnell, Iowa | 641-269-3600

ADMISSION
Admission Rate: 23%
Admission Rate - Men: 22%
Admission Rate - Women: 24%
EA Admission Rate: Not Offered
ED Admission Rate: 57%
ED Admits as % of Total Admits: 11%
Admission Rate (5-Year Trend): -12%
% of Admits Attending (Yield): 25%
Transfer Admission Rate: 3%

SAT Reading/Writing (Middle 50%): 670-740
SAT Math (Middle 50%): 700-790
ACT Composite (Middle 50%): 31-34

% Graduated in Top 10% of HS Class: 62%
% Graduated in Top 25% of HS Class: 87%
% Graduated in Top 50% of HS Class: 98%

Demonstrated Interest: Considered
Legacy Status: Considered
Admission Interview Offered: Yes

ENROLLMENT
Total Undergraduate Enrollment: 1,733
% Part-Time: 2%
% Male: 47%
% Female: 53%
% Out-of-State: 91%
% Fraternity: Not Offered
% Sorority: Not Offered
% On-Campus (Freshman): 100%
% On-Campus (All Undergraduate): 88%

% African-American: 5%
% Asian: 8%
% Hispanic: 8%
% White: 48%
% Other: 4%
% Race or Ethnicity Unknown: 6%
% International: 20%
% Low-Income: 25%

ACADEMICS
Student-to-Faculty Ratio: 9 to 1
% of Classes Under 20: 64%
% of Classes 20-49: 36%
% of Classes 50 or More: 0%
% Full-Time Faculty: 80%
% Full-Time Faculty w/ Terminal Degree: 99%

Top Programs
Biology
Biological Chemistry
Chemistry
Economics
History
Physics
Political Science
Sociology

Retention Rate: 94%
4-Year Graduation Rate: 85%
6-Year Graduation Rate: 89%

Curricular Flexibility: Very Flexible
Academic Rating: ★★★★⫟

#CollegesWorthYourMoney

Long a bastion of progressive, free-thinking liberal arts education, Grinnell College, set in remote Iowa, has never been a more popular destination in its more than 170-year history than it is today. Rising numbers of applications and shrinking acceptance rates have raised the caliber of the 1,733 young people who currently occupy campus.

Inside the Classroom
Grinnell offers twenty-seven distinct bachelor's degrees and over 500 courses each semester, and students have an immense deal of autonomy with course selection. In fact, nothing better epitomizes the school's philosophy than its list of graduation requirements that are more a list of the maximum number of courses a student can take in any one area rather than a list of minimal expectations. The only required course is the First-Year Tutorial, a ten- to fourteen-student, writing-intensive seminar with topics ranging from the artist Kendrick Lamar to the comic strip Calvin & Hobbes. Outside of that one course, your education is personally crafted through the college's Individually-Advised Curriculum that sees students working closely with a faculty advisor to make the most of their educational journey.

Thanks to a 9:1 student/faculty ratio and no competition from graduate students, nearly two-thirds of classes have fewer than twenty students, and roughly one-quarter of sections have single-digit student enrollments. Participating in research is a normal part of an undergraduate education at Grinnell. Overall, 43 percent of Grinnell undergrads participate in one on- or off-campus research experience that was not simply built into their coursework. Mentor Advanced Projects, which see faculty closely work with students on scholarly or creative works, were participated in by 71 percent of the subset who had some type of research experience. Thirty percent of that group conducted research at another location such as Duke University, Georgetown University, or Carnegie Mellon University. International study is also a fairly common part of a Grinnell education with 50 percent of students studying abroad. The Grinnell-in-London program is a popular option, offering a semester's worth of courses on English politics, history, and theater.

A top producer of PhDs in both the sciences and the social sciences, Grinnell has strong offerings across the board, with programs in biology, chemistry, physics, economics, and history receiving particularly high praise. The largest number of degrees are conferred in English, foreign languages, biology, and computer science. A fast riser, the computer science program now graduates seventy students per year versus only fifteen four years ago. Grinnell students fare extraordinarily well at obtaining competitive scholarships. Graduates in the Class of 2019 captured Watson, Fulbright, and Marshall fellowships/scholarships. Grinnell is one of the top Fulbright-producing institutions in the country with five recipients in 2019 and as many as ten in recent years.

Outside the Classroom
Eighty-five percent of students live on campus in small residence halls that house between fifty and sixty students. Grinnell has a long tradition of being fraternity and sorority free, instead favoring an "inclusive and open-minded" social scene. One-third of students engage in varsity athletics; the school fields twenty NCAA Division III teams that compete in the Midwest Conference. Intramurals draw heavy participation with soccer, volleyball, flag football, and basketball being among the most popular. Two-thirds of students participate in community service projects, and opportunities include teaching at a local prison, a buddies program for nearby children, and Alternative Breaks at impoverished areas around the United States. There are more than one hundred student organizations as silly and relaxed as the Zombie Movie Club or as serious as the local chapter of the Roosevelt Institute Campus Network. With its remote location amidst the cornfields of Iowa, there's not much to explore in the surrounding area. Fortunately, campus itself is a nurturing and lively place.

Career Services
For a school of just over 1,700, the Center for Careers, Life, and Service (CLS) employs an astounding twenty-three full-time staff members that includes those specializing in career advising (14), employer relations, internships, and fellowships and awards. That equates to a student-to-advisor ratio of 75:1, better than every school except Wellesley that is featured in this guide. The personalized attention that staffing level affords enables the CLS to adhere to its core belief that "one's impact, satisfaction, and sense of purpose are maximized when one is able to align their values, strengths, and curiosities." To that aim, students are assigned a CLS exploratory advisor before they even set foot on campus. In the 2018-19 academic year the office had 4,469 one-one-one advising contacts with students, which works out to more than two per student!

While its somewhat remote location and small student body makes it tough to host a large-scale career fair, the school compensates by hosting/facilitating over 180 smaller events each year including career treks, workshops, alumni panels, and networking receptions. Seventy-seven companies recruited on campus in the last academic year. Grinnell does a solid job facilitating internship experiences with a 61 percent participation rate among 2019 graduates. Internships were procured around the globe including stops at BMW China, Amazon Japan, the White House, the United Nations, Facebook, IBM, and Twitter. Thirty-eight percent of the employed members of the Class of 2019 stated that their first job was exactly what they wanted to be doing, and 49 percent viewed their position as a "good stepping stone." Grinnell's CLS offers unparalleled support and has an excellent track record of helping students secure valuable internships, meaningful first jobs, and graduate school acceptances.

Professional Outcomes

Upon graduation 57 percent of the Class of 2019 headed into the workforce, 27 percent to graduate school, 6 percent to postgraduate service, and 3 percent earned fellowships. Multiple recent grads accepted positions with JPMorgan, Epic, and Google while others were hired by desirable organizations that included the Federal Reserve Board, Deloitte, the Brookings Institute, Goldman Sachs, and the Centers for Disease Control. The most commonly entered fields were IT/computing (23 percent), research/science (18 percent), education (10 percent), business (7 percent), and. The mean salary of those employed was roughly $52,650, and the median was $47,258. Illinois attracted the highest number of graduates, slightly more than Iowa itself. California, New York, and Minnesota were the next most popular locations for Grinnell grads.

Close to 40 percent of those entering graduate school in 2019 were pursuing PhDs or master's degrees in the hard sciences, 7 percent were headed to law school, and 3 percent were bound for medical school. Recent law school acceptances included top-tier institutions like Harvard, University of Chicago, and Johns Hopkins University School of Medicine. Others were admitted to various advanced degree programs at Cambridge, Yale, Carnegie Mellon, and Cornell University. Overall, 86 percent of law school applicants received at least one acceptance, and 43 percent of medical school applicants were successful, which was right around the national average.

Admission

The acceptance rate has jumped around in the last few years between 20 and 29 percent, landing at 23 percent during the last admissions cycle. That is far more selective than Grinnell was only a short time ago. For example, in the 2010-11 cycle Grinnell accepted 43 percent of applicants. That year it received only 2,969 applications, but it received 8,004 for a place in the Class of 2023. Standardized test scores of attending freshmen are higher as well—the mid-50 percent SAT score is 1370-1530 and 31-34 on the ACT. Sixty-two percent of Grinnell students hail from the top 10 percent of their high school classes.

Admissions factors rated by the committee as being "very important" are rigor of secondary curriculum, GPA, class rank, and recommendations. The four categories that fall under "important" are standardized test scores, extracurricular activities, and talent/ability. Most members of the Class of 2023 were deeply involved during high school with 68 percent participating in community service, 67 percent in the fine arts, 62 percent in athletics, and 53 percent held jobs. Applying through early decision yields a major advantage as 57 percent of applicants receive positive news, far higher than the regular rate (22 percent). Early decision applicants comprise 43 percent of the incoming class, meaning that a large number of spots are already filled by the time the regular cycle rolls around. Even with Grinnell's transformation into a highly sought-after liberal arts college, the process remains holistic. Grades and test scores certainly matter, but unique talents and high school involvement play a major role as well. We can't stress enough how advantageous applying early is for students dead-set on studying at this now-elite Iowa school.

Worth Your Money?

The cost of attendance at Grinnell College is $70,544, but one-third of students receive a merit award averaging $21k. More encouragingly, those who qualify receive need-based grants with an annual value of roughly $46,000. Further, Grinnell manages to meet the full-demonstrated need of 100 percent of aid-eligible students. Starting salaries are generally on the lower side coming out of this college, which is perhaps attributed to the many Grinnellians in the academic and non-profit sectors; however, that isn't a big deal for most, thanks to the generosity of the aid packages being distributed. The average graduate comes out of Grinnell with only $20,000 of debt, a very manageable sum.

FINANCIAL
Institutional Type: Private
In-State Tuition: $56,188
Out-of-State Tuition: $56,188
Room & Board: $13,864
Required Fees: $492
Books & Supplies: NR

Avg. Need-Based Grant: $46,609
Avg. % of Need Met: 100%

Avg. Merit-Based Award: $20,984
% Receiving (All Freshmen): 32%
% Receiving (Freshmen w/o Need): 21%

Avg. Cumulative Debt: $20,093
% of Students Borrowing: 61%

CAREER
Who Recruits
1. Epic Systems
2. Morningstar
3. Nationwide
4. Teach for America
5. Google

Notable Internships
1. U.S. Forest Service
2. MasterCard
3. Resorative Justice Project

Top Industries
1. Education
2. Business
3. Research
4. Social Services
5. Media

Top Employers
1. Google
2. Amazon
3. Epic
4. U.S. State Department
5. Wells Fargo

Where Alumni Work
1. Des Mones, IA
2. Chicago
3. New York City
4. Washington DC
5. Minneapolis

Median Earnings
College Scorecard (Early Career): $49,100
PayScale (Early Career): $58,100
PayScale (Mid-Career): $115,000

RANKINGS
Money: 319
U.S. News: 13 (T), Liberal Arts Colleges
Wall Street Journal/THE: 68 (T)
Washington Monthly: 14, Liberal Arts Colleges

COLLEGE OVERLAPS
Carleton College
Kenyon College
Macalester College
Oberlin College
Vassar College

Hamilton College

Clinton, New York | 315-859-4421

ADMISSION
Admission Rate: 16%
Admission Rate - Men: 17%
Admission Rate - Women: 16%
EA Admission Rate: Not Offered
ED Admission Rate: 41%
ED Admits as % of Total Admits: 18%
Admission Rate (5-Year Trend): -11%
% of Admits Attending (Yield): 35%
Transfer Admission Rate: 23%

SAT Reading/Writing (Middle 50%): 670-740
SAT Math (Middle 50%): 700-780
ACT Composite (Middle 50%): 32-34

% Graduated in Top 10% of HS Class: 83%
% Graduated in Top 25% of HS Class: 96%
% Graduated in Top 50% of HS Class: 100%

Demonstrated Interest: Considered
Legacy Status: Considered
Admission Interview Offered: Yes

ENROLLMENT
Total Undergraduate Enrollment: 1,924
% Part-Time: 0%
% Male: 48%
% Female: 52%
% Out-of-State: 72%
% Fraternity: 21%
% Sorority: 15%
% On-Campus (Freshman): 100%
% On-Campus (All Undergraduate): 100%

% African-American: 4%
% Asian: 7%
% Hispanic: 9%
% White: 64%
% Other: 5%
% Race or Ethnicity Unknown: 4%
% International: 7%
% Low-Income: 15%

ACADEMICS
Student-to-Faculty Ratio: 9 to 1
% of Classes Under 20: 78%
% of Classes 20-49: 22%
% of Classes 50 or More: 0%
% Full-Time Faculty: 83%
% Full-Time Faculty w/ Terminal Degree: 96%

Top Programs
Biology
Economics
English
Environmental Studies
Government
Mathematics and Statistics
Public Policy
World Politics

Retention Rate: 94%
4-Year Graduation Rate: 89%
6-Year Graduation Rate: 93%

Curricular Flexibility: Very Flexible
Academic Rating: ★★★★★

#CollegesWorthYourMoney

Recent years have been kind to Alexander Hamilton. His legacy has sparked a mega-hit Broadway musical, a Pulitzer Prize-winning biography, and the liberal arts college in Clinton, New York, that bears his name—Hamilton College—has achieved new heights of prestige, claiming a place among the best liberal arts schools in the United States.

Inside the Classroom
More than 1,900 undergraduate students can choose from forty-three areas of concentration, but education at Hamilton is about so much more than merely choosing a major. The unique open curriculum is immensely flexible and caters to student passions and curiosity over a rigid list of required courses. While there are no distributional requirements, certain skill areas must be addressed as you work your way through the thirty-two courses needed for graduation. That includes three writing-intensive courses, one quantitative/symbolic reasoning course, one physical education course, and an area of concentration that includes a senior project.

The student-to-faculty ratio is 9:1, and without any pesky graduate students to get in the way, face time with professors is a regular occurrence. In fact, 36 percent of all classes have nine or fewer students; 78 percent have nineteen or fewer. Each summer more than 140 students engage in high-level undergraduate research with a faculty member. Two-thirds of Hamilton students study off campus for a semester, although those locations are not always foreign countries. Many participate in domestic study programs in NYC, DC, or Boston while others take advantage of international opportunities like the school's own renowned Chinese language program in Beijing or one of one hundred other approved programs around the globe.

Economics, government, and biology are among the strongest and most popular majors; other standout programs include public policy, mathematics, and environmental studies. Hamilton students fare extremely well in competition for prestigious national fellowships, capturing a shocking number when considering the small size of each graduating class. The Class of 2019 won seven Fulbright Scholarships, a Critical Language Scholarship, a National Science Foundation Graduate Research Fellowship, and a Watson Fellowship; six juniors also won Gilman Scholarships last year.

Outside the Classroom
Just about everyone lives in university housing—100 percent in 2019-20 to be precise—leading to a cohesive atmosphere on the college's 1,350-acre campus. Greek life is strange in that it is nonresidential following a series of reforms over the past decade. While many Hamilton students belong to a fraternity (21 percent) or sorority (15 percent), those organizations do not play nearly as prominent a role on campus as they once did. The school's twenty-nine teams (15 women's, 14 men's) compete as the Colonials in the New England Small College Athletic Conference (NESCAC) with other elite liberal arts schools Amherst, Bates, Bowdoin, Middlebury, Tufts, Wesleyan, and Williams. There are 550 student-athletes donning the buff-and-blue colors, accounting for 30 percent of the total student body. Add that total to the seventeen club and twelve intramural teams and it can feel like just about everyone is, technically, an athlete. Yet, with almost 200 active student organizations, there are plenty of ways to get involved outside of competitive team sports. The Hamilton Association for Volunteering, Outreach, and Charity (HAVOC) attracts hundreds of civic-minded students each year. The Hamilton Outing Club is the largest club on campus and organizes weekend camping/hiking/skiing trips to the Adirondacks as well as more exotic locations around the world. Amazing speakers come to town as part of the Sacerdote Great Names Series. In recent years Hamilton has hosted David Cameron, Bill and Hillary Clinton, Desmond Tutu, Jon Stewart, Colin Powell, and Jimmy Carter.

Career Services
The Maurice Horowitch Career Center is staffed by twelve professionals with expertise in career development, employer development, and health professions advising. That works out to a 160:1 student-to-advisor ratio, which is significantly stronger than most schools featured in this guide. Each student is assigned a career advisor who works with that student throughout the four-year journey. On the job-finding front, the center assists "students in developing skills in self-assessment, career exploration, resume preparation, interviewing, and uncovering job leads that will empower them to proactively manage their own careers." Yet, that is all steeped in the belief that career planning is a developmental process that unfolds over a lifetime.

E-mail: admission@hamilton.edu | Website: www.hamilton.edu

The college does not host any large-scale career expos, but numerous employers do visit campus each year to host informational sessions or to recruit/interview candidates. Hamilton's Career Center does a superb job assisting students with finding opportunities for experiential learning. Nine in ten members of the Class of 2019 had at least one internship over the course of the four years, and an incredible 70 percent had two. Alumni are highly supportive of current students and are willing to present on campus or offer job-shadowing experiences; 75 percent of alumni in a recent survey stated they would be happy to supply current students with career advice. Hamilton's 22,500 alumni rank in the top 1 percent when measured by the percentage that donate to their alma mater. Students can join Handshake to find internship and career possibilities and My Hamilton to network with alumni. Despite not hosting a notable career fair, the individualized attention and care that Hamilton shows its undergrads results in tremendously overall positive postgraduate and career outcomes.

Professional Outcomes

Examining the 492 graduates in Hamilton's Class of 2019, an enviable 97 percent wasted no time landing jobs, graduate school acceptances, or fellowships. The most commonly entered industries were business (14 percent), science and technology (13 percent), education (12 percent), and finance (10 percent). Among the employers welcoming multiple recent graduates aboard were Wayfair, Goldman Sachs, Teach for America, Dana Farber Cancer Institute, Kantar Consulting, and Deutsch Bank. New York City, Boston, and DC were the most popular destinations.

Only 13 percent of 2019 graduates went directly into an advanced degree program. Of that group, 44 percent were studying a STEM field, 21 percent health care, and 2 percent went to law school. Law school acceptances over the past three years have included Georgetown, the University of Virginia, NYU, Penn, Yeshiva University, Washington University, Boston College, and Boston University. Medical school/veterinary school acceptances in that same period have included Columbia University, Penn, Temple, Tufts, SUNY, the University of Rochester, and Boston University. Other Hamilton graduates have been accepted into master's programs at Stanford, Cornell, USC, the University of Chicago, Vanderbilt, and others. Clearly, a degree from Hamilton opens doors to some of the world's top graduate/professional programs.

Admission

Hamilton saw 8,339 applicants for a coveted spot in the Class of 2023, but only 16 percent of that group made the cut, a decrease of five percentage points from the previous cycle. Most applicants provide SAT or ACT scores, but this institution is test-flexible and allows three AP/IB/SAT subject tests to be submitted in lieu of the SAT/ACT. The mid-50 percent range on the SAT was 1410-1510 and 32-34 on the ACT. The vast majority of students finished near the top of their high school class; 83 percent were in the top decile and 96 percent placed in the top quartile. Hamilton's admissions statistics have remained highly consistent over the past decade, so the level of selectivity should not come as a surprise to anyone.

The admissions committee's top priorities are an applicant's GPA, class rank, and the rigor of their coursework. Standardized test scores, essays, recommendations, character/personal qualities, and an interview comprise the second tier of key factors. Because Hamilton is competing for applicants with a host of other elite liberal arts schools, it favors those willing to commit via binding early decision; the acceptance rate for early applicants is more than double that (41 percent) of those in the regular pool (15 percent). Further, early acceptances make up 51 percent of the freshman class, leaving only a limited number of seats in the spring. To be a competitive applicant you should be in the top 10 percent of your graduating class and have standardized test scores in the 95th percentile or higher. If you're on the cusp and Hamilton is your top choice, definitely apply ED.

Worth Your Money?

If you have a genuine need for financial aid to make your education possible, Hamilton will usually answer the bell. In the 2019-20 academic year the college awarded over half of its undergraduates an average grant of $50k, taking some of the sting out of the $73,370 sticker price for full cost of attendance. In 2008, Hamilton ceased offering merit aid to admitted applicants, a rare and admirable practice in the world of higher education. With 100 percent of its focus on making college affordable to lower- and middle-class students, higher-earning families can expect to pay full freight. Still, this school, with its minuscule class sizes, truly exceptional academics, and powerful network is, in the end, worth the money for most teens.

FINANCIAL
Institutional Type: Private
In-State Tuition: $55,970
Out-of-State Tuition: $55,970
Room & Board: $14,360
Required Fees: $560
Books & Supplies: $1,000

Avg. Need-Based Grant: $50,238
Avg. % of Need Met: 100%

Avg. Merit-Based Award: $0
% Receiving (All Freshmen): 0%
% Receiving (Freshmen w/o Need): 0%

Avg. Cumulative Debt: $17,292
% of Students Borrowing: 44%

CAREER
Who Recruits
1. Merrill Lynch
2. NERA Economic Consulting
3. Isaacson Miller, Inc.
4. Teach for America
5. Kantar Consulting

Notable Internships
1. Credit Suisse
2. CNBC
3. UBS

Top Industries
1. Business
2. Education
3. Operations
4. Media
5. Finance

Top Employers
1. Morgan Stanley
2. Goldman Sachs
3. Google
4. Wayfair
5. Citi

Where Alumni Work
1. New York City
2. Boston
3. Washington DC
4. San Francisco
5. United Kingdom

Median Earnings
College Scorecard (Early Career): $60,200
PayScale (Early Career): $64,900
PayScale (Mid-Career): $119,700

RANKINGS
Money: 54
U.S. News: 9 (T), Liberal Arts Colleges
Wall Street Journal/THE: 56 (T)
Washington Monthly: 16, Liberal Arts Colleges

COLLEGE OVERLAPS
Bowdoin College
Colby College
Colgate University
Cornell University
Middlebury College

Harvard University

Cambridge, Massachusetts | 617-495-1551

The oldest university in the United States, founded 140 years before the United States itself was even a concept, it is also the most iconic and, in many ways, revered institution of higher learning. Worldwide, Harvard is the envy of other universities and the dream destination for countless teenage geniuses and overachievers. For 6,755 young people, the Ivy League university in Cambridge, Massachusetts, is their reality, and learning from Nobel Laureates, Pulitzer Prize winners, and global leaders in every field is an everyday occurrence.

Inside the Classroom

There are fifty undergraduate fields of study referred to as concentrations; many are interdisciplinary. Nearly 3,900 courses are on the menu, so learning options are extensive. Core requirements are minimal outside of expository writing, which all freshmen must conquer, proficiency in a foreign language (which must be achieved by the end of sophomore year), and a trek through the program in general education. The latter requirement ensures that undergrads are exposed to four main areas: aesthetics and culture, ethics and civics; histories, societies, and individuals; and science and technology in society. Roughly half of students complete some type of senior thesis, but there are no requirements in that area.

Even with a graduate population of over 14,000 to cater to, undergraduate class sizes still tend to be on the smaller side with 43 percent of sections having single-digit enrollments and 74 percent being capped at nineteen. Graduates report an 82 percent satisfaction rate with the experience within their academic concentration. Summer research experiences are taken advantage of by 38 percent of the student body. Approximately 55 percent of students study abroad at a number of locations in South America, Africa, Europe, or Asia.

Economics, government, and computer science are the three most popular areas of concentration at Harvard. Those programs, along with ones in biology, chemistry, physics, math, statistics, sociology, history, English, and psychology all sit atop most departmental ranking lists. The university also occupies the top position in the all-time Rhodes Scholar rankings with 375 to its credit, more than the combined total from Stanford, Penn, Dartmouth, Brown, MIT, Cornell, and Columbia. Other prestigious postgraduate fellowships are awarded to Harvard students with regularity including the Fulbright, which was captured by eighteen members of the Class of 2019. The list of all-time alumni accolades could go on forever and includes ninety-six Nobel Laureates and eight US presidents.

Outside the Classroom

Possessing a bottomless endowment, the school never needs to cut corners on any programs, campus infrastructure, or amenities—and it shows. Freshmen live together at a centralized campus location adjacent to the famed Harvard Yard and then, as sophomores, move into one of twelve stately, upper-class houses, each with its own set of traditions and sense of community. Greek life, once thriving, has taken a dip in recent years after university officials enacted new regulations to deter membership in single-sex clubs. Students who participate forfeit eligibility for leadership positions in athletics or student government and will not be recommended for prestigious scholarships. Fortunately, a bevy of other social clubs exist in the form of 450 student-run organizations including the history-rich Hasty Pudding Club and the Phillips Brooks House Association that runs eighty-six volunteer organizations. Of course, studying is also a popular "hobby," and the Harvard Library is the largest academic library in the world and boasts a staff of nearly 800. The Harvard Crimson is a premier college newspaper with a long and storied history—Franklin Roosevelt and John F. Kennedy are among its alums—and The Harvard Lampoon is one of the world's oldest humor magazines, one that has helped launch talents ranging from John Updike to Conan O'Brien. Athletics also play a prominent role in Harvard's culture, both past and present, as the school fields forty NCAA Division I sports teams, evenly split between men's and women's squads. Cambridge itself is a bustling hub of culture, nightlife, and entertainment. Downtown Boston is only a twelve-minute ride away on the city's easily accessible public transit system.

Career Services

The Center for Career Development (CCD) has twenty-seven professional staff members (excluding students, assistants, and IT staff) who are dedicated to tasks including employer relations, career counseling, and summer funding opportunities. The 250:1 student-to-advisor ratio is superior when compared to other schools featured in this guide. And, the closer you look into Harvard's career services, locating any feature that is less than superior is a nearly impossible task.

ADMISSION
Admission Rate: 5%
Admission Rate - Men: 5%
Admission Rate - Women: 5%
EA Admission Rate: 13%
ED Admission Rate: Not Offered
ED Admits as % of Total Admits: Not Offered
Admission Rate (5-Year Trend): -1%
% of Admits Attending (Yield): 82%
Transfer Admission Rate: 1%

SAT Reading/Writing (Middle 50%): 710-770
SAT Math (Middle 50%): 750-800
ACT Composite (Middle 50%): 33-35

% Graduated in Top 10% of HS Class: 93%
% Graduated in Top 25% of HS Class: 98%
% Graduated in Top 50% of HS Class: 100%

Demonstrated Interest: Not Considered
Legacy Status: Considered
Admission Interview Offered: Yes

ENROLLMENT
Total Undergraduate Enrollment: 6,755
% Part-Time: 0%
% Male: 51%
% Female: 49%
% Out-of-State: 84%
% Fraternity: Not Offered
% Sorority: Not Offered
% On-Campus (Freshman): 100%
% On-Campus (All Undergraduate): 98%

% African-American: 9%
% Asian: 21%
% Hispanic: 11%
% White: 37%
% Other: 8%
% Race or Ethnicity Unknown: 1%
% International: 13%
% Low-Income: 17%

ACADEMICS
Student-to-Faculty Ratio: 6 to 1
% of Classes Under 20: 74%
% of Classes 20-49: 15%
% of Classes 50 or More: 11%
% Full-Time Faculty: 84%
% Full-Time Faculty w/ Terminal Degree: 85%

Top Programs
Biology
Chemistry
Economics
Government
Mathematics
Physics
Psychology
Statistics

Retention Rate: 97%
4-Year Graduation Rate: 85%
6-Year Graduation Rate: 97%

Curricular Flexibility: Somewhat Flexible
Academic Rating: ★★★★★

#CollegesWorthYourMoney

E-mail: college@fas.harvard.edu | Website: www.college.harvard.edu

In 2018-19, the CCD hosted 343 events that were attended by 12,351 students. It also organizes twenty independent career fairs, each targeting a particular sector that attracts more than 6,000 net attendees. The OCS logs 6,600 advising appointments per year and manages to engage with 70 percent of the total undergraduate student body. Crimson Careers, the office's online database, posts almost 9,000 jobs/internships from thousands of unique employers. On-campus recruiting occurred on a regular basis with 143 employers, including just about any big-name company you can think of, conducting over 3,500 interviews on site in Cambridge. More than three-quarters of students participate in a summer internship during their four years of study. In short, career services are what you would expect from America's preeminent university—exceptional.

Professional Outcomes

The Crimson Class of 2019 saw 16 percent of students head directly into graduate/professional school. Of the graduates entering the world of work (virtually everyone else), 13 percent were employed in the financial services industry, technology/engineering attracted 12 percent, and 10 percent were entering the consulting field. Over 1,000 Harvard alumni presently work for Google and over 500 for Microsoft, McKinsey & Company, and Goldman Sachs. More than 250 are employed at Amazon, Facebook, and Bain & Company. Post-graduation, Harvard students tend to cluster in three main states—New York, California, and Massachusetts. Those three states collectively reel in 57 percent of newly minted alumni. Remuneration is excellent with 53 percent of graduates reporting starting salaries over $70k and 12 percent taking home $110k+ in base pay. By midcareer, grads have the third highest median salaries in the Ivy League.

Turning our attention to those moving on to graduate school, Harvard grads with at least a 3.5 GPA typically enjoy acceptance rates into medical school of 90 percent or greater, demolishing the national average. Harvard grads tend to trade one high prestige school for another when pursuing an advanced degree. Many also stay close to home—Harvard Medical School (HMS), Harvard Law School, and the Graduate School of Arts & Sciences all accept more Harvard College graduates than those from any other single institution. It is estimated that approximately one-fifth of the HMS student body already spent four years in Cambridge as an undergraduate.

Admission

Harvard's admission rate for the Class of 2023 was 4.6 percent, an identical mark to last year's all-time low. Applicants fare better in the early action round that sports a 13 percent acceptance rate; the regular round rate is an almost comically low 3 percent. For historical context, at the turn of the millennium, 12 percent of applicants were welcomed aboard. The average SAT score for enrolled freshmen in 2019-20 was 1510; over 82 percent of students scored above a 700 on each portion of the exam. It's not shocking that 93 percent of students admitted earned a place in their high school class's top decile. An insanely high number—82 percent—of admitted students elect to enroll. In other words, Harvard is second choice for few students.

The admissions staff does not rank any factor as being "very important" or even "important." All of the usual factors—grades, SATs, essays, and so on—are "considered." Demonstrated interest is not considered, which is unsurprising in light of the aforementioned yield rate. Legacy students comprise roughly one-third of the student body and enjoy an acceptance rate five times that of non-legacy applicants. For information about the role of race in admissions at Harvard, simply consult any newspaper. Getting into Harvard is the subject of plenty of (mostly awful) movies for a reason—it is a mammoth task set against harrowing odds. Even valedictorians with perfect test scores are not immune from rejection. However, impeccable credentials of that nature will at least allow you the opportunity to roll the dice with a realistic chance of success.

Worth Your Money?

Asking if Harvard is worth the money is a bit like John C. Reilly's character in Stepbrothers, Dale Doback, asking if bonito fish are big. Yes, Dale, bonito fish are big, and Harvard is worth the $72,391 annual cost of attendance. Merit aid does not exist at the university but, thanks to a $38 billion endowment, the 56 percent of the undergraduate population that is eligible for financial aid sees 100 percent of its need met; the total annual value is an extremely generous $58,643. Harvard is one of the rare schools where the average graduate's salary exceeds the annual cost of attendance, so even if you did have to take out loans to attend, it would be more than worth the expense.

FINANCIAL
Institutional Type: Private
In-State Tuition: $49,353
Out-of-State Tuition: $49,353
Room & Board: $18,389
Required Fees: $4,349
Books & Supplies: $1,000

Avg. Need-Based Grant: $58,643
Avg. % of Need Met: 100%

Avg. Merit-Based Award: $0
% Receiving (All Freshmen): 0%
% Receiving (Freshmen w/o Need): 0%

Avg. Cumulative Debt: $6,170
% of Students Borrowing: 7%

CAREER
Who Recruits
1. Putnam Investments
2. Akuna Capital
3. Atlantic Media
4. Vertica
5. Environmental Defense Fund

Notable Internships
1. McKinsey & Company
2. NASA Jet Propulsion Laboratory
3. Jane Street Capital

Top Industries
1. Business
2. Education
3. Research
4. Operations
5. Media

Top Employers
1. Google
2. Microsoft
3. Goldman Sachs
4. McKinsey & Company
5. IBM

Where Alumni Work
1. Boston
2. New York City
3. San Francisco
4. Washington DC
5. Los Angeles

Median Earnings
College Scorecard (Early Career): $89,700
PayScale (Early Career): $80,100
PayScale (Mid-Career): $159,400

RANKINGS
Money: 14
U.S. News: 2, National Universities
Wall Street Journal/THE: 1
Washington Monthly: 2, National Universities

COLLEGE OVERLAPS
Columbia University
Massachusetts Institute of Technology
Princeton University
Yale University
Stanford University

Harvey Mudd College

Claremont, California | 909-621-8011

ADMISSION
Admission Rate: 14%
Admission Rate - Men: 9%
Admission Rate - Women: 24%
EA Admission Rate: Not Offered
ED Admission Rate: 19%
ED Admits as % of Total Admits: 15%
Admission Rate (5-Year Trend): -5%
% of Admits Attending (Yield): 41%
Transfer Admission Rate: 7%

SAT Reading/Writing (Middle 50%): 710-770
SAT Math (Middle 50%): 780-800
ACT Composite (Middle 50%): 33-35

% Graduated in Top 10% of HS Class: 90%
% Graduated in Top 25% of HS Class: 100%
% Graduated in Top 50% of HS Class: 100%

Demonstrated Interest: Not Considered
Legacy Status: Considered
Admission Interview Offered: Yes

ENROLLMENT
Total Undergraduate Enrollment: 895
% Part-Time: 0%
% Male: 50%
% Female: 50%
% Out-of-State: 54%
% Fraternity: Not Offered
% Sorority: Not Offered
% On-Campus (Freshman): 100%
% On-Campus (All Undergraduate): 99%

% African-American: 4%
% Asian: 20%
% Hispanic: 20%
% White: 31%
% Other: 12%
% Race or Ethnicity Unknown: 7%
% International: 8%
% Low-Income: 13%

ACADEMICS
Student-to-Faculty Ratio: 8 to 1
% of Classes Under 20: 57%
% of Classes 20-49: 39%
% of Classes 50 or More: 5%
% Full-Time Faculty: 89%
% Full-Time Faculty w/ Terminal Degree: 98%

Top Programs
Biology
Chemistry
Computer Science
Engineering
Mathematical and Computational Biology
Mathematics and Statistics
Physics

Retention Rate: 97%
4-Year Graduation Rate: 86%
6-Year Graduation Rate: 92%

Curricular Flexibility: Somewhat Flexible
Academic Rating: ★★★★★

#CollegesWorthYourMoney

To the average college-bound teen, Harvey Mudd may not have the name recognition that other schools of its caliber enjoy. While it may sound a bit like a Depression-era comic strip, the smallest of the colleges within the illustrious Claremont Consortium (Pomona, Claremont McKenna, Scripps, and Pitzer are the others) is routinely rated one of the best liberal arts colleges in the entire country and one of the top STEM institutions in the world.

Inside the Classroom
A touch under 900 undergraduate students occupy this tiny 33-acre campus; however, it is surrounded by the aforementioned affiliated colleges, giving the experience a less claustrophobic feel. Only six majors are offered: biology, chemistry, computer science, engineering, mathematics, and physics. All are incredibly strong. Students also have the option to combine certain disciplines into what amounts to a double major. In preparing a small army of future engineers and scientists, Harvey Mudd has been at the forefront of preaching a balanced education. The school requires a significant amount of coursework in the humanities, backing up its stated belief that "technology divorced from humanity is worse than no technology at all."

Class sizes are not always as small as the school itself. While 57 percent of courses have an enrollment under twenty, another 34 percent enroll between twenty and thirty-nine students. Regardless, Mudd prides itself on offering graduate-level research opportunities and experiential learning to all undergrads. The college backs up its philosophical stance with cold, hard cash, allocating three million dollars annually to facilitate student-faculty research. Students can participate during the school year or during the Summer Undergraduate Research Program that entails ten weeks of full-time laboratory work. The Clinic Program groups juniors and seniors and lets them work on a real-world problem for corporate or agency sponsors for 1,200 to 1,500 hours over the course of one year. It is not uncommon for participants to end up with their name on a patent.

The college routinely produces winners of scholarships from the National Science Foundation, the Astronaut Scholarship Foundation, the Department of Energy, the Department of Defense, the Watson Fellowship, and the Mindlin Prize for Innovative Ideas in Science. The faculty also regularly receive accolades for their teaching. The National Science Foundation recognized the Chemistry Department as the top per capita producer of chemistry PhDs in the country.

Outside the Classroom
Campus life at Mudd is, in part, defined by the fact that you are not confined to one campus. After all, Pomona, Pitzer, Scripps, and CMC all share the same 560 acres of land, not to mention a whole lot else. For athletics, Harvey Mudd, Claremont, and Scripps combine forces to compete in twenty-one NCAA Division III men's and women's sports. Club and intramural sports from Ultimate Frisbee, equestrian, and roller hockey to water polo are available as well. Both cross-consortium and Mudd-only clubs and activities are plentiful and diverse, ranging from a poker club to a lettuce-eating competition (seriously). With Los Angeles just a half-hour drive away, Claremont is located in close proximity to all of the restaurants, museums, theaters, and even Disneyland, if you so desire. Mudd's dorms are known for having district personalities, but one common thread is that the college is known, in general, to be a friendly and accepting place.

Career Services
HMC's Career Services Office has four full-time professional staff members working on grad school/career advising and employer recruitment. That equates to a 224:1 student-to-advisor ratio, which is among the best of any college featured in this guide. Career Services is highly accessible to students, and it even offers walk-in hours from 1 to 4 p.m. each weekday. Staff members are more than happy to offer one-on-one attention, and students take advantage as the office holds roughly 900 sessions per year, just over one per student.

Harvey Mudd hosts a Fall Software Fair, a Fall General STEM Fair, and a Spring Fair that can be attended by all members of the consortium, which can draw as many as 160+ employers per year. The three fairs draw almost 2,000 student participants per year. Companies that recruit on campus comprise a who's who of tech royalty: Google, Microsoft, Facebook, Space X, and Uber. In fact, many of those companies, along with other major corporations, conducted interviews on HMC's campus. Undergrads routinely land summer internships at an equally impressive array of technology companies. In examining the breakdown of where Mudd grads end up receiving job offers, there is a clear correlation with the employer relations efforts of the Career Services Office. Overall, HMC's career services earns top grades from the College Transitions staff.

Professional Outcomes

The highest number of recent Harvey Mudd graduates are scooped up by the following companies (in order of representation): Google, Facebook, Microsoft, and Northrup Grumman. Across all graduating years, significant numbers of alumni also can be found at Apple, Raytheon, Intel, Boeing, and the NASA Jet Propulsion Laboratory. Software and technology is, by far, the career field of choice with aerospace a distant second. HMC grads end up in high-paying jobs that are directly related to their major as the 95 percent of seniors who report landing a job related to their college major confirms. The most common job titles held immediately out of college are software engineer, industrial engineer, and electrical engineer. Graduates average an impressive $87,500 starting salary, a phenomenal number even when accounting for the preponderance of STEM majors. By some measures, that is the highest graduate starting salary of any institution in the United States.

Many Harvey Mudd grads—close to one-quarter percent—go directly into graduate school programs. The highest number of recent grads pursued advanced degrees at the following institutions: Stanford, Cornell, USC, UC-Santa Barbara, Columbia, and the University of Washington. Others attended Harvard, Carnegie Mellon, Caltech, and Johns Hopkins. The most pursued graduate field of study at those elite schools are computer science, mathematics, physics, and engineering. A healthy 72 percent of those attending grad school are presently working toward a PhD.

Admission

A decade ago, over 30 percent of applicants to Harvey Mudd were accepted; five years ago, that number fell to 20 percent. In recent years HMC's admit rate has hovered in the 13 to 15 percent range; it was 14 percent for applicants aspiring to join the Class of 2023. However, it is important to note that the profile of the average accepted student has not changed significantly and, unlike many other elite colleges across the United States, the number of applicants has not skyrocketed in the past few years. Early decision applicants made up 38 percent of the 2019-20 freshman class, which means applying early may be a good idea if Mudd is your top choice. The ED rate was 19 percent, which was a touch better than the 13 percent encountered during the regular application round.

An overwhelming 90 percent of accepted applicants finished in the top 10 percent of their high school class, and every single student placed at least in the top 25 percent. Valedictorians and salutatorians make up approximately 40 percent of the student body. Standardized test scores need to be high to garner serious consideration. The mid-50 percent range on standardized tests for freshmen in 2019-20 was 1490-1550 on the SAT and 33-35 on the ACT. The school lists essays and recommendations as being "very important" factors in admissions decisions. In sum, Harvey Mudd is not a school that you add to your college list on a whim. It is an institution for those with a proven track record within the realm of science and engineering. Excellent grades in AP/IB course work, along with standardized test scores well above the 95th percentile, are just about prerequisites for serious consideration.

Worth Your Money?

At almost $80,000 per year, a degree from Harvey Mudd won't come cheap, but the majority of undergraduates do not pay the full cost. On the merit aid front, the college awards an average of $8k to 37 percent of the student body. Even better, 52 percent of attendees see 100 percent of their financial need met, which averages out to $48k in aid each year, knocking the total cost down closer to state school levels. As a result, HMC helps many students from lower- and middle-income families attend the school. While that does result in a $29k postgraduate debt load (about average), alumni enjoy such strong job prospects that paying back loans will not be overly worrisome. No matter your circumstances, if you have a chance to go to Mudd, start packing your bags.

FINANCIAL
Institutional Type: Private
In-State Tuition: $58,359
Out-of-State Tuition: $58,359
Room & Board: $18,679
Required Fees: $301
Books & Supplies: $800

Avg. Need-Based Grant: $48,474
Avg. % of Need Met: 100%

Avg. Merit-Based Award: $8,164
% Receiving (All Freshmen): 37%
% Receiving (Freshmen w/o Need): 17%

Avg. Cumulative Debt: $29,139
% of Students Borrowing: 47%

CAREER
Who Recruits
1. Palantir
2. The Aerospace Corporation
3. Oracle
4. Boeing
5. Farmers Insurance

Notable Internships
1. Google
2. Salesforce
3. PayPal

Top Industries
1. Engineering
2. Research
3. Business
4. Education
5. information Technology

Top Employers
1. Google
2. Microsoft
3. Apple
4. Northrop Grumman
5. Facebook

Where Alumni Work
1. Los Angeles
2. San Francisco
3. Seattle
4. San Diego
5. New York City

Median Earnings
College Scorecard (Early Career): $88,800
PayScale (Early Career): $93,100
PayScale (Mid-Career): $160,600

RANKINGS
Money: 200
U.S. News: 25 (T), Liberal Arts Colleges
Wall Street Journal/THE: Not Ranked
Washington Monthly: 5, Liberal Arts Colleges

COLLEGE OVERLAPS
California Institute of Technology
Carnegie Mellon University
Massachusetts Institute of Technology
Stanford University
University of California, Berkeley

Haverford College

Haverford, Pennsylvania | 610-896-1350

Serving 1,317 remarkably accomplished undergraduate students, Haverford College, situated on Philly's ritzy Main Line, has 187 years of history and a reputation as one of the best liberal arts colleges in the country. Affectionately known as "The Ford," the college is part of the Tri-College Consortium with nearby Bryn Mawr and Swarthmore, which also happen to be among the crème de la crème of liberal arts schools. Students can take courses at those two schools as well through Penn's Wharton School of Business via an additional alliance known as the Quaker Consortium.

Inside the Classroom
Haverford offers twenty-nine majors, thirty-one minors, thirteen concentrations, and eleven consortium programs—areas of study that can be pursued at partner campuses. All students must fulfill a first-year writing requirement, a two-course language requirement, and a quantitative or symbolic reasoning requirement, and students need to take an uncredited physical education course prior to their junior year. Every student produces a senior thesis, a work of original research/scholarship under the close supervision of a faculty member. Teens seeking a relatively open curriculum that encourages exploration and the pursuit of one's unique passions will adore Haverford.

The school's 9:1 student-to-faculty ratio and exclusive emphasis on undergraduate education leads to exceptionally intimate classes, 29 percent of which have fewer than ten students, and 73 percent have fewer than twenty. Plenty of summer research opportunities exist in which students can work alongside faculty, and some STEM students conduct and present original research through the Undergraduate Science Research Symposium. The study abroad program has a 49 percent participation rate, and students can choose from seventy-six programs in thirty-four countries.

The most popular areas of study at Haverford include the social sciences (28 percent), physical sciences (15 percent), biology (9 percent), foreign language (9 percent), psychology (7 percent) and computer science (7 percent). All majors are highly respected in the eyes of graduate institutions and potential employers, but programs in English, physics, and political science receive especially high marks. Science majors and those on a premed track gain acceptance to prestigious PhD programs and medical schools at an eye-popping rate (95 percent). Graduates are also no strangers to competitive national awards/fellowships. In the school's history, it claims twenty Rhodes Scholars and in 2020 alone, the Haverford seniors and alumni captured five Fulbright Scholarships and 11 National Science Foundation Fellowships.

Outside the Classroom
Ninety-eight percent of students live on this stunningly beautiful 216-acre campus; first-years are assigned to one of four residence halls. There are no fraternities or sororities at Haverford. Even with such a tiny student body, Haverford fields twenty-three varsity sports teams that compete in NCAA Division III. Combined with the seven club sports teams, 53 percent of undergrads participate in athletics. The college's 145 student-run organizations include an array of pre-professional and service-oriented groups as well as plenty of recreational/performance options such as the Martial Arts Alliance, contemporary dance, and a number of a cappella groups. HAVOC is an outdoor adventure group that has a strong membership. The mock trial team placed second in the nation in 2017. Fellow Tri-Co member schools Bryn Mawr and Swarthmore offer plenty of additional chances for social connection, both formal and informal. All that the city of Philadelphia has to offer is only eight miles away. The Main Line area itself offers plenty of dining, cultural, and entertainment choices. The college's Honor Code and governing Honor Council are central to the life at Haverford. Tenets of the code include un-proctored exams, no RAs in dorms, and tolerance of people of all backgrounds and orientations.

Career Services
The Center for Career & Professional Advising (CCPA) employs five individuals who specialize in career counseling, pre-law advising, and health professions advising; another four staff members are part time. With a 263:1 student-to-advisor ratio, Haverford compares favorably against most of the other colleges featured in this guide. The resources are deployed efficiently as in a given year the CCPA engages in 1,500+ advising sessions, reaches 84 percent of the student body in some capacity, and makes a great effort to reach first-year students. In fact, 88 percent of freshmen report engaging with the office. The level of personalized advising is also evident by the annual number of resume critiques, 550+.

Haverford College

In hosting 150 information sessions and workshops per year, there are almost daily opportunities for students to sharpen their pre-professional skills and connect with potential employers. Large- scale career fairs are typically a joint effort of the Tri-College Consortium, along with Bryn Mawr and Swarthmore. Haverford alone draws more than one hundred employers to campus for its career fairs. The CCPA funds more than 140 internships per year and helps facilitate 190 on-campus interviews. Additionally, the college has more than 1,000 alumni association volunteers who provide hundreds of job-shadowing and externship experiences to current students. The CCPA delivers ample personalized attention to undergraduates and does an unsurpassed job assisting students with acceptance into top graduate schools.

Professional Outcomes

Six months after leaving Haverford, 64 percent of the Class of 2019 had found employment, 14 percent had enrolled in graduate school, and 10 percent were still job hunting. Among the employed, education was the most common industry (15 percent), followed by health care (12 percent), business (10 percent), and the social sciences (10 percent). Employers hiring multiple recent Haverford grads include Google, The Vanguard Group, IBM, Booz Allen Hamilton, Amazon, the National Institutes of Health, and the Children's Hospital of Philadelphia. Midcareer salaries are comparable to other elite liberal arts schools such as Wesleyan, Colby, Swarthmore, and staying in the Philly metro area is the number one choice of alumni. New York City, various international destinations, Boston, and DC are next in popularity.

In 2019, only 14 percent of Haverford grads entered advanced degree programs right out of undergrad. The most commonly entered fields of study were STEM (57 percent), medicine (19 percent), the social sciences (8 percent), and arts and humanities (8 percent). Graduate schools accepting the highest number of recent alumni include Yale, Columbia, the University of Chicago, Penn, Harvard, Johns Hopkins, and the University of North Carolina at Chapel Hill. Those applying to medical school have extraordinary success as the college's 90 percent rate of acceptance from 2015-18 more than doubles the national average. Haverford undergrads average MCAT scores in the 85th percentile of all test takers. In the last three years, 100 percent of those applying to law school received at least one letter of acceptance. Of that cohort, 32 percent were accepted into a top fifteen law school, and 94 percent had found homes at a top one hundred law school.

Admission

Admissions for a place in the Class of 2023 was the most selective round in the school's history; a record 4,963 applications were received, and only 16 percent were accepted. A staggering 92 percent of enrolled freshmen earned a place in the top 10 percent of their high school class and sported a mid-50 percent test score of 1400-1520 on the SAT and 32-34 on the ACT. A handful of years ago, the acceptance rate was a slightly higher 22 percent, but the academic profile of the average admitted applicant was similar to that of a 2019-20 freshman.

According to the admissions committee the most important factors in the decision-making process are rigor of coursework, GPA, essays, recommendations, extracurricular activities, and character/personal qualities. Class rank, standardized test scores, talent/ability, work experience, and volunteer work make up the second rung of considered data points. Items like the interview, first-generation status, or legacy status are given a lesser degree of consideration. Applying early decision can be a significant advantage. In the most recent cycle ED applicants were accepted at a far more generous 43 percent clip and comprised 56 percent of that year's incoming freshmen. Even with a self-selecting applicant pool that results in modest application numbers, Haverford is an exceptionally difficult school to gain acceptance into. The 16 percent acceptance rate is almost misleadingly encouraging, and applicants sizing up their chances will be better informed by the high level of academic achievement displayed by successful applicants. Applying ED should be given serious consideration if Haverford is among your top choices.

Worth Your Money?

Haverford's annual cost of attendance is among the highest in the country at $76,000, but, on the positive end, it meets 100 percent of demonstrated need for those who qualify. The total average annual grant is over $51,000, helping make the school affordable for those not in the highest income brackets. If you can afford the upfront costs, or if you receive a sufficiently sized financial aid award, becoming part of this elite institution will likely prove worth the investment in the long run.

FINANCIAL
Institutional Type: Private
In-State Tuition: $58,402
Out-of-State Tuition: $58,402
Room & Board: $17,066
Required Fees: $498
Books & Supplies: $1,194

Avg. Need-Based Grant: $21,262
Avg. % of Need Met: 100%

Avg. Merit-Based Award: $0
% Receiving (All Freshmen): 0%
% Receiving (Freshmen w/o Need): 0%

Avg. Cumulative Debt: $17,146
% of Students Borrowing: 27%

CAREER
Who Recruits
1. Chatham Financial
2. FDIC
3. Janney Montgomery Scott
4. Boston Consulting Group
5. Analysis Group

Notable Internships
1. Boston Consulting Group
2. Spotify
3. U.S. House of Representatives

Top Industries
1. Education
2. Business
3. Research
4. Healthcare
5. Media

Top Employers
1. Google
2. Children's Hospital of Philadelphia
3. Facebook
4. US State Department
5. Deloitte

Where Alumni Work
1. New York City
2. Philadelphia
3. Washington DC
4. Boston
5. San Francisco

Median Earnings
College Scorecard (Early Career): $60,700
PayScale (Early Career): $63,700
PayScale (Mid-Career): $141,900

RANKINGS
Money: 125
U.S. News: 15 (T), Liberal Arts Colleges
Wall Street Journal/THE: 40 (T)
Washington Monthly: 12, Liberal Arts Colleges

COLLEGE OVERLAPS
Amherst College
Brown University
Swarthmore College
University of Pennsylvania
Wesleyan University

Hofstra University

Hempstead, New York | 516-463-6700

ADMISSION
Admission Rate: 68%
Admission Rate - Men: 64%
Admission Rate - Women: 72%
EA Admission Rate: 77%
ED Admission Rate: Not Offered
ED Admits as % of Total Admits: Not Offered
Admission Rate (5-Year Trend): +7%
% of Admits Attending (Yield): 9%
Transfer Admission Rate: 61%

SAT Reading/Writing (Middle 50%): 580-660
SAT Math (Middle 50%): 580-680
ACT Composite (Middle 50%): 25-30

% Graduated in Top 10% of HS Class: 32%
% Graduated in Top 25% of HS Class: 51%
% Graduated in Top 50% of HS Class: 60%

Demonstrated Interest: Considered
Legacy Status: Considered
Admission Interview Offered: Yes

ENROLLMENT
Total Undergraduate Enrollment: 6,498
% Part-Time: 5%
% Male: 45%
% Female: 55%
% Out-of-State: 37%
% Fraternity: 8%
% Sorority: 12%
% On-Campus (Freshman): 67%
% On-Campus (All Undergraduate): 43%

% African-American: 9%
% Asian: 12%
% Hispanic: 13%
% White: 54%
% Other: 3%
% Race or Ethnicity Unknown: 2%
% International: 6%
% Low-Income: 25%

ACADEMICS
Student-to-Faculty Ratio: 13 to 1
% of Classes Under 20: 47%
% of Classes 20-49: 51%
% of Classes 50 or More: 2%
% Full-Time Faculty: 39%
% Full-Time Faculty w/ Terminal Degree: 92%

Top Programs
Accounting
Criminology
Finance
Journalism
Performing Arts
Public Relations
Radio, Television & Film

Retention Rate: 83%
4-Year Graduation Rate: 55%
6-Year Graduation Rate: 65%

Curricular Flexibility: Somewhat Flexible
Academic Rating: ★★★

#CollegesWorthYourMoney

Looking at Hofstra University today, one sees a private university of 6,498 undergraduate students spread across a gorgeous and imposing Long Island campus. Its roots as a commuter school for Long Island residents have long since faded from view as the student body is now comprised of over 40 percent out-of-state and international students. While still a common safety school choice for high-achieving Northeasterners aiming for schools like Fordham and Boston University, Hofstra's national reputation is undoubtedly on the rise. It remains an excellent academic institution with tremendous resources to help students find their way to a successful career. Even better, it also is accessible to students with imperfect academic profiles—at least for now.

Inside the Classroom
There are 160 programs for undergraduates spread across the various colleges housing liberal arts, engineering, business, communications, and nursing/health professions. While the core curriculum varies from school to school, most Hofstra students are required to complete coursework in the humanities, natural sciences, history, philosophy, foreign language, quantitative reasoning, two introductory writing courses, and two advanced writing courses. In total there are thirty-three credits worth of distributional requirements for students in the College of Liberal Arts and Sciences. First-year seminars are courses reserved for freshmen that enroll nineteen or fewer students, focus on a specific topic of interest, and help new students acclimate to college-level work.

The average undergraduate class size is twenty, and the student-faculty ratio is a favorable 13-to-1. The great bulk of courses enroll between eleven and twenty-nine students; 13 percent are single-digit enrollment courses, and only 2 percent of sections contain more than fifty students. Opportunities to participate in undergraduate research are managed by each department separately. Students in the Honors College have an easier time procuring opportunities as supervised independent research is built into the program. Full-length study abroad opportunities are offered in locations that include Amsterdam, China, Florence, Rome, and Ireland. Many students prefer short-term international sessions offered in January (three weeks) or summer (five weeks).

The Zarb School of Business draws almost a quarter of the student body for good reason; it is a well-regarded business school with strong connections to many major banks and consulting firms. It also boasts one of the nation's best simulated trading rooms. The Lawrence Herbert School of Communication is widely known in the media industry, and Hofstra students enter in large numbers—15 percent of the total degrees conferred are in communication/journalism. Health professions, social sciences, and psychology are third, fourth, and fifth in popularity, respectively. Winning national postgraduate fellowships is not a major focus of Hofstra seniors. They have won an occasional Fulbright Scholarship, Critical Language Scholarship, and Gilman Scholarship in recent years.

Outside the Classroom
Only 67 percent of freshmen and roughly 43 percent of the overall undergraduate student body live on campus in one of thirty-five residence halls. There are traditional dorms as well as high-rise options that, collectively, offer single, double, triple, quad, and suite-style living options. Within the limits of the 240-acre campus are eighteen eateries, six theaters, an arboretum, bird sanctuary, and an art museum that houses 5,000 works and artifacts. Hofstra's gorgeous, tree-lined grounds are deservedly included on many "most beautiful campus" lists. The twenty-nine fraternities and sororities attract 8 percent of men and 12 percent of women, creating an atmosphere with a noticeable Greek presence, but not a suffocating one. The sports teams, for many years known as the Flying Dutchmen, now compete as the Pride at the NCAA Division I level in the Colonial Athletic Association. There are twenty-one varsity sports—ten men's and eleven women's teams. There are 200+ student-run clubs at Hofstra, including plenty of performance, cultural, or pre-professional options and a big-time collegiate radio station, WRHU, which also serves as the radio home of the National Hockey League's New York Islanders. Hempstead is not the safest area or most desirable part of town, but this is made up for by having an amenity-filled campus and being only a twenty-five-minute drive from famed Jones Beach in Long Island and, of course, being only a forty- to fifty-minute trip from all that New York City has to offer.

Career Services
Hofstra's Career Center is manned by eight professionals with expertise in career coaching, corporate outreach, and diversity and inclusion initiatives. That works out to an 812:1 student-to-advisor ratio, which is higher than the average school in this guide but not awful when compared to other midsize universities. The Fall Career and Internship Fair was attended by 130+ employers, and the center routinely offers in-person and online workshops, field trips to companies, networking events, and on-campus interview days with employers.

Hofstra University

E-mail: admission@hofstra.edu | Website: www.hofstra.edu

Drawing employers to campus and placing current students with big-name organizations is aided by the school's location and the tight connections that the Career Center has forged with New York City employers. Hofstra's internship numbers for undergraduates are particularly strong. With the help of career services staff members, 77 percent of Hofstra students participate in at least one internship, and the average student completes 2.52 such experiences. Recent grads interned at hundreds of organizations including Berkshire Hathaway, Last Week Tonight with John Oliver, ABC News, and the Securities and Exchange Commission. Current students can also benefit from connecting with the 140,000 living alumni, 1,000 of whom are active volunteers for the school and more than willing to assist with career exploration and the job search.

Professional Outcomes

Within six months of exiting with their diplomas, 93 percent of Class of 2019 grads had found employment or a graduate school destination; with 83 percent employed and 30 percent pursuing an advanced degree, which includes some overlap as many individuals were doing both. Northwell Health, the largest health care provider in New York State, is also the largest employer of Hofstra alumni. Other companies employing more than one hundred Flying Dutchmen/Pride alums include JPMorgan Chase, Citi, PwC, Morgan Stanley, EY, Deloitte, Estee Lauder, and NBC Universal. Among the Class of 2019, grads went on to a number of interesting careers with professional sports teams, major media outlets, and political groups. The median starting salary was $50,000 with 34 percent of the class bringing home less than $40k and 24 percent making over $60k. Just about everyone stays in the Greater New York City area with Boston, Philly, and DC picking up the crumbs.

Grad school is a common next step for those receiving their Hofstra degree as 30 percent enrolled within months of receiving their bachelor's degree. Class of 2019 members matriculated into a wide array of graduate and professional schools including every SUNY and CUNY institution as well as many elite universities like Harvard, Yale, Carnegie Mellon, Northwestern, Rice, MIT, and Stanford. The school offers its undergraduates a 4+4 BS/MD option in conjunction with its own Zucker School of Medicine. Other medical schools attended by recent grads include the Albert Einstein College of Medicine, Icahn School of Medicine, and SUNY Downstate.

Admission

Sixty-eight percent of the 24,425 applicants for a spot in the Class of 2023 were accepted, but a minuscule 9 percent of those accepted actually enrolled in the university. Of those that became 2019-20 freshmen, 92 percent had over a 3.0 GPA, 32 percent were in top 10 percent of their high school class, and 60 percent were in top 25 percent. The average SAT score was 1248, and the average ACT score was 27. The university's degree of selectivity has remained constant in recent years. Acceptance rates and grades from the early 2010s are comparable to those today. Standardized test scores have risen, but much of that can be attributed to going test-optional (more on that in a moment).

The five factors viewed as the most important by the admissions committee are GPA, class rank, rigor of secondary school record, recommendations, and the essay. Hofstra went test-optional in 2014 but, presently, three-quarters of applicants still submit standardized test scores. Interviews are listed as "important" but are not a required part of the process. Extracurricular activities, talent/ability, and character/personal qualities also play a major factor in the process. For a school that has such a low yield rate (the percent of accepted students that enroll), it is surprising that it does not offer a binding early decision option, but it does offer early action. Hofstra remains a realistic option for B students who take some advanced coursework in high school.

Worth Your Money?

Hofstra is an expensive school, registering a $65,758 annual cost of attendance, but it is generous with both need-based and merit aid as the average grants in both areas are approximately $23k. The Long Island location can make this school worth the money for those with a clear plan of how to take advantage of the school's New York City connections. Students without a preprofessional focus and for whom costs are a concern should also consider more affordable options.

FINANCIAL
Institutional Type: Private
In-State Tuition: $46,450
Out-of-State Tuition: $46,450
Room & Board: $16,428
Required Fees: $1,060
Books & Supplies: $1,000

Avg. Need-Based Grant: $23,883
Avg. % of Need Met: 71%

Avg. Merit-Based Award: $23,143
% Receiving (All Freshmen): 45%
% Receiving (Freshmen w/o Need): 24%

Avg. Cumulative Debt: NR
% of Students Borrowing: 60%

CAREER
Who Recruits
1. Cox Media Group
2. Stanley Black & Decker
3. Raytheon
4. Partners Healtcare
5. Boston Children's Hospital

Notable Internships
1. The Tonight Show
2. The Carlyle Group
3. CNN NY News Bureau

Top Industries
1. Business
2. Education
3. Operations
4. Sales
5. Finance

Top Employers
1. Northwell Health
2. JPMorgan Chase
3. Citi
4. Morgan Stanley
5. PwC

Where Alumni Work
1. New York City
2. Boston
3. Philadelphia
4. Washington DC
5. Los Angeles

Median Earnings
College Scorecard (Early Career): $53,100
PayScale (Early Career): $58,500
PayScale (Mid-Career): $120,200

RANKINGS
Money: 643
U.S. News: 160 (T), National Universities
Wall Street Journal/THE: 220 (T)
Washington Monthly: 374, National Universities

COLLEGE OVERLAPS
Boston University
Drexel University
Fordham University
Pennsylvania State University - University Park
Stony Brook University (SUNY)

Illinois Institute of Technology

Chicago, Illinois | 312-567-3025

A rare school that educates more advanced degree-seekers than undergraduate students, the Illinois Institute of Technology—traditionally referred to as IIT but rebranded in 2001 as Illinois Tech—is a private research university with 3,144 undergrads and 40+ undergraduate majors, mostly in the realms of engineering, business, computer science, and architecture. Located on Chicago's South Side, this school has a large international presence with forty-eight countries represented as well as a phenomenally high number of Pell Grant recipients as 30 percent of undergraduates present with serious financial need. This is significant because Illinois Tech has a reputation not just for producing grads who earn excellent salaries but for facilitating social and economic mobility as well.

Inside the Classroom
Undergraduates study in one of six undergraduate divisions: the Armour College of Engineering, the College of Architecture, the College of Science, the Lewis College of Human Sciences, the School of Applied Technology, or the Stuart School of Business. The university has four learning goals associated with its core curriculum: (1) commitment to positive change in their communities, nations, and the world; (2) the ability to think critically and viewing problems as opportunities for innovation; (3) the ability to collaborate professionally and ethically; and (4) communicate effectively. Toward those aims, one must take three courses in the humanities, three in the social or behavioral sciences, three in science or engineering, one computer science course, and complete thirty-six hours of coursework with a substantial focus on oral or written communication. A 600 SAT reading score will get you out of introductory writing.

The student-to-faculty ratio is 12:1, but with so many graduate students to serve, undergraduate course sections are not small across the board; rather, they vary from 22 percent of sections that boast a single-digit enrollment to the 17 percent of courses that enroll more than forty students. Yet, an Illinois Tech education provides many opportunities for students to have close contact with faculty. For example, the Interprofessional Projects (IPRO) Program features "teams of students from a variety of majors that develop solutions to real-world problems using design-centered methodology and innovative thinking." Completing two IPROs is a graduation requirement. The Elevate program connects students with undergraduate research and other experiential learning opportunities as early as freshman year. There are 42 study abroad programs in which IIT students can participate, although as with most technical institutions, the bulk of undergrads remain on campus for all four years.

The most popular major is computer science followed by architecture and mechanical engineering. Overall, 52 percent of the degrees conferred are in engineering, 21 percent in computer science, and 9 percent in architecture. The School of Applied Technology offers one of the most respected information technology programs in the country and serves as a pipeline to many top tech companies. The College of Architecture has a similarly sterling national reputation. Programs in engineering and computer science are also strong.

Outside the Classroom
Illinois Tech's 120-acre urban campus is home to only 43 percent of the undergraduate population; the majority of students live in university-owned housing and are graduate students. Freshmen and sophomores are required to live on campus, but commuters who live with their parents and transfers are often granted exemptions. There are two traditional dormitories and two "villages" that are collections of smaller residence halls. S.R. Crown Hall and the McCormick Tribune Campus Center are architecturally unique, and the campus as a whole sometimes cracks "most beautiful" lists. Many students self-identify as "nerds," and the rigorous academics and male-heavy population (only 37 percent of students are female) can limit social life. Greek life has a moderate presence on campus drawing 7-8% of the student body. There are seventeen varsity intercollegiate sports teams—nine men's and eight women's—many of which compete in NCAA Division III. More than 150 student-run organizations are available, and the BOG serves as a popular hub thanks to its free, eight-lane bowling alley and abundance of arcade games. Campus is only three miles south of downtown Chicago and about one mile from Guaranteed Rate Field where the Chicago White Sox play baseball. Plenty of bars, jazz clubs, museums, zoos, and an aquarium are a short distance from campus.

Career Services
The main Career Services Office at IIT consists of seven professional employees, but the Stuart School of Business has its own separate office with three full-time employees bringing the school's total to eight career services professionals. That works out to a student-advisor ratio of 314:1, within the average range of schools profiled

in the book. Freshmen are encouraged to begin working with a career counselor during their first semester. In addition to the professional staff members, eight peer counselors also are available to those looking to get the jump on vocational exploration.

Staff members are always willing to assist with "résumé and cover letter writing, networking advice, company research assistance, mock interviews, (and) dinner/business etiquette workshops." Two-day career fairs are held on campus each semester, and more than 150 employers attend, including industry giants Amazon, Goldman Sachs, NBCUniversal, and Grainger. The school claims 83,125 living alumni, many of whom are concentrated in tech companies in Chicago, making networking conditions favorable. That can come in handy when pursuing for-credit internships or co-ops during the school year or during the summer term. However, the school does not release information about what percentage of students complete one or more internships or what percentage of the undergraduate student body is serviced by the office in any capacity in a given year.

Professional Outcomes

Eight-six percent of Illinois Tech grads have already enjoyed a positive career/grad school outcome within six months of earning their degree. Alumni can be found in sizable numbers within major corporations including Motorola, Amazon, Microsoft, Google, Apple, Accenture, JPMorgan Chase, IBM, EY, and Cisco. The Greater Chicago area plays home to more than half of IIT alumni with San Francisco, New York City, Seattle, and Los Angeles and international destinations including India, Brazil, and Spain all attracting fairly large numbers of Scarlet Hawks. Starting salaries as well as midcareer compensation figures are the strongest in the state of Illinois and among the highest anywhere when compared to other highly selective private universities; the median first job salary is $60k. The school also ranks high for social mobility, lifting more students whose families fall in the bottom 20 percent income bracket into the top 20 percent than any other school in the state.

Those continuing to graduate school often stay at Illinois Tech, which offers degrees in engineering, science, architecture, business, design, human sciences, applied technology, and law. For premed students, the medical school acceptance rate is "often above the national average." A dual degree program is offered in partnership with Midwestern University's Chicago College of Osteopathic Medicine. Recent students have earned a place at top medical schools like the Northwestern University Feinberg School of Medicine, New York University School of Medicine, and the University of Michigan Medical School.

Admission

With an acceptance rate of 60 percent, the Illinois Institute of Technology is not looking to shut the door on those with imperfect credentials, yet some of that hefty number is attributed to self-selection. The mid-50 percent SAT range of 2019-20 freshmen is 1285-1370 and the ACT range is 29-32. The GPA range is 4.00-4.36. Close to half of freshmen earned a place in the top 10 percent of their respective high school class, 80 percent were in the top quartile, and 97 percent were in the top 50 percent. All of those numbers, including the overall acceptance rate, are similar to those from five years ago, despite a spike in the total number of applications.

Like most engineering-focused schools, the hard numbers are paramount when it comes to making admissions decisions. Standardized test scores, GPA, and the level of rigor of one's coursework are of the utmost importance while factors such as class rank and recommendations are also given weight by the committee. Female applicants enjoy slightly better admissions prospects with an acceptance rate of 64 percent compared to men at just under 59 percent. There is no early decision process at Illinois Tech, rather, applications are accepted on a rolling basis beginning on October 1 with a priority deadline of December 1. Applying on the early side is your best bet regardless of whether IIT is your number one choice or one of many irons in the fire.

Worth Your Money?

On paper, the cost of attendance at IIT is greater than $65,000 per year. However, 98 percent of students receive some type of aid, and even families with an income above $135,000 receive an average scholarship and grant combo adding up to $32,000 annually. As a result, the school is a worthy investment for most as solid-paying tech, finance, and architecture jobs in the Chicago area await your arrival post-graduation.

FINANCIAL
Institutional Type: Private
In-State Tuition: $50,490
Out-of-State Tuition: $50,490
Room & Board: $15,328
Required Fees: $0
Books & Supplies: $1,250

Avg. Need-Based Grant: $38,466
Avg. % of Need Met: 85%

Avg. Merit-Based Award: $27,314
% Receiving (All Freshmen): 36%
% Receiving (Freshmen w/o Need): 25%

Avg. Cumulative Debt: $29,594
% of Students Borrowing: 51%

CAREER
Who Recruits
1. Webber, LLC
2. Wise Equation Solutions
3. W.W. Grainger
4. AVG Automation
5. CCC Information Services

Notable Internships
1. BMW
2. Salesforce
3. Motorola

Top Industries
1. Engineering
2. Business
3. Infromation Technology
4. Operations
5. Education

Top Employers
1. Amazon
2. Motorola
3. Google
4. Microsoft
5. Apple

Where Alumni Work
1. Chicago
2. San Francisco
3. India
4. New York City
5. Seattle

Median Earnings
College Scorecard (Early Career): $69,100
PayScale (Early Career): $68,600
PayScale (Mid-Career): $127,100

RANKINGS
Money: 443
U.S. News: 124 (T), National Universities
Wall Street Journal/THE: 118
Washington Monthly: 74, National Universities

COLLEGE OVERLAPS
DePaul University
Loyola University Chicago
Marquette University
University of Illinois at Chicago
University of Illinois at Urbana-Champaign

Indiana University Bloomington

Bloomington, Indiana | 812-855-0661

From coast to coast, flagship public universities have seen their admissions standards skyrocket in recent years. Students for whom the University of Maryland, the University of Wisconsin, or any school within the University of California system would have been a safety school a decade ago now find themselves sweating out admissions decisions each spring. Fortunately, this is not so at Indiana's famed Bloomington campus where more than three-quarters of applicants who apply still receive a friendly Midwestern welcome, and both the quality and price of the education that await are exceptionally solid. That combination of accessibility, quality, and variety—IU offers 200+ majors—draws more out-of-state and international students than you might expect. Only 64 percent of IU undergraduates are from in state, and 8 percent of the student body are international students hailing from 120+ countries.

Inside the Classroom
Unlike many large universities made up of numerous schools and colleges, Indiana is not overeager to assign and confine you to a particular program. Upon entering IU, freshmen are housed within the University Division, and they remain there for one or two years in order to figure out their academic direction. This gives all freshmen time to begin wrestling with the Common Ground Curriculum that involves completing courses in six areas: English composition, mathematical modeling, arts and humanities, social and historical studies, natural and mathematical sciences, and world languages and cultures. Of note for any foreign language averse students, there are ways to fill the latter requirement without learning another language. Students who are members of the Hutton Honors College also typically need to complete a senior thesis within their academic departments.

The university's 16:1 student-to-faculty ratio is not bad for a school of Indiana's size, and it does make an effort to keep undergraduate classes on the small side. While there are a number of introductory courses that transpire in giant lecture halls, 46 percent of all sections contain no more than nineteen students. Experiential learning opportunities are available to those who seize them; 27 percent of arts and sciences students completed research with a faculty member. On the study abroad front, 26 percent of A&S graduates spent a semester in a foreign country. In total, the school offers 360 programs in sixty-five countries and twenty languages.

Business/marketing is the most popular major accounting for 25 percent of the total degrees conferred. Kelley is an acclaimed business school that draws immense national respect, ranking up there in prestige with Goizueta (Emory), McDonough (Georgetown), and its neighbor to the north, Mendoza (Notre Dame). Indiana, notably, did not offer an engineering program until recently, likely making Purdue a better local public option for anyone entering that field of study. However, IU's computer science degree program has tight ties to top tech companies, and it is the school's second most frequently conferred degree at 9 percent. The other degrees most commonly awarded are in social services (8 percent), parks & recreation (8 percent), journalism (7 percent), and biology (7 percent). Plenty of students from all academic backgrounds capture competitive postgraduate scholarships. In 2019, the school's haul included eleven Critical Language Scholarships, ten Fulbrights, and a Churchill Scholarship. The previous year undergraduates won a hard-to-fathom twenty-one Fulbright Scholarships.

Outside the Classroom
The university houses 98 percent of freshmen but only 33 percent of the overall undergraduate student body on its sprawling 1,936-acre campus. Living options include thirteen residence halls, eleven apartment complexes, and more than twenty residential thematic communities. For everyone else, there are plenty of affordable off-campus apartments within close proximity. Fraternities and sororities play an enormous role in social life as 24 percent of men and 19 percent of women join Greek organizations; there are seventy to choose from. There are twenty-four varsity sports, and many boast Big Ten championships, yet one shines above the rest as Hoosier hoops is nothing short of a religion in Bloomington, and you'll never find one of the 17,222 seats within Assembly Hall unfilled during men's basketball games. For those looking for lower-key athletics, there are more than seventy club and intramural sports at your disposal. Overall, Indiana University is home to more than 750 student organizations featuring clubs ranging from calligraphy to bass fishing. Bloomington gets high marks as a safe and enjoyable college town, and there are always events going on whether it's a free show at the spectacular Musical Arts Center or a community service opportunity—students donate a total of 225,000 hours per year. Indianapolis is a fifty-mile highway drive away, making it an option for a quick weekend getaway.

Career Services
The university has a main Career Development Center for those who enter undecided as well as discipline-specific career services offices housed within each undergraduate college. There are eighty-six full-time staff members

dedicated to career advising, experiential education, and employer relations. The university's overall 385:1 student-to-counselor ratio is one of the best for a public institution of Indiana's immense size. This staff's output is astounding whether measured by its 23,000+ one-on-one counseling sessions per year or its large-scale efforts that include booking almost 1,800 companies to attend the school's many career fairs.

Last year alone, 78 percent of grads completed at least one internship. Over 2,000 employers recruit at Bloomington including EY, PwC, Deloitte, Oracle, JPMorgan Chase & Co., Microsoft Corporation, Anheuser-Busch, Epic Systems, Procter & Gamble, and Grainger, Inc. Just a quick glance at the university calendar reveals a frenetic pace of career fairs taking place in the fall of 2019, including targeted events for those interested in business, media, social services, finance, public health, internships, the creative arts, and the hard sciences. Any way you measure it, the IU career services staff's output is prodigious and helps set undergraduates up for successful postgraduation transition.

Professional Outcomes

Indiana University tracks the postgraduate outcomes from each undergraduate school. Looking at the College of Arts & Sciences, by far the largest group of students, Class of 2019 grads reached their next employment or graduate school destination at a 93 percent rate within six months of receiving their degrees. Sixty percent had procured their first jobs, and one-quarter of students were in grad school; only 4 percent of those looking for jobs were unable to land one in that time. The most frequently entered industries (from A&S) were arts & entertainment, healthcare, and technology. The median starting salary for A&S grads was $40,000. In the Kelley School of Business, 96 percent were placed successfully within six months, and the median starting salary was $62,500. School of Informatics, Computing & Engineering grads had comparable starting salaries and a similar 95 percent success rate. Among the largest employers of Hoosier alumni are local pharmaceutical giant Eli Lilly, EY, Amazon, PwC, Salesforce, Deloitte, IBM, Oracle, Microsoft, Accenture, and Google. Indianapolis, Chicago, Bloomington, and New York City are the locales where you can find the greatest concentration of Indiana graduates.

Among the most frequently attended graduate schools by recent grads include Indiana Bloomington (including its own law and medical schools), Purdue, Loyola Chicago, Northwestern, and Columbia. Indiana is a premed factory with 275 applicants to med school in 2018-19 alone; that is the thirteenth highest in the nation. Impressively, the well-regarded Indiana University School of Medicine was the second most frequently attended graduate school overall. That was aided by the fact that the in-state acceptance rate at this medical school is 48 percent, six times higher than the out-of-state rate. The university also operates two separate law schools, one in Indianapolis and one in Bloomington, and both draw large numbers of IU undergraduates. A combined BA/JD program can be completed in six years.

Admission

Of all the flagship universities profiled in this book, Indiana has the most relaxed admissions standards as 78 percent of those who applied for a place in the Class of 2023 were welcomed aboard. The average SAT score was a 1255 and the average ACT composite was 27. The school became test-optional in 2020. The average GPA for an entering 2019-20 freshman was 3.7 and 35 percent finished in the top 10 percent of their high school class. More encouragingly for less-than-perfect applicants is the fact that 31 percent of undergrads did not place in the top quartile of their graduating cohort, and one-quarter of students possessed cumulative GPAs under 3.5.

With roughly 43,000 applications to wade through, the admissions committee must first rely on the easy-to-assess credentials of class rank, GPA, standardized test scores, and level of academic rigor. The application essay is "important," but factors like extracurricular activities, recommendations, and volunteer work are merely "considered." While there is no binding early decision option available, IU does offer an early action round with a deadline of November 1, also the deadline for the most complete scholarship consideration.

Worth Your Money?

Indiana residents enjoy not only a reasonable tuition cost that is a touch under $10,000 but also a modest room-and-board price as well when compared to other schools of roughly the same quality. For comparison, room and board alone at Notre Dame would cost an extra $20,000 over four years. Nonresidents should consider their aid package and program of study (business-related fields are your best bet) before packing off to Bloomington, as out-of-state rates are approaching that of many private colleges. Hoosiers cannot go wrong heading to Bloomington for their bachelor's degree, no matter what field of interest they plan to study.

FINANCIAL
Institutional Type: Public
In-State Tuition: $9,575
Out-of-State Tuition: $35,140
Room & Board: $10,830
Required Fees: $1,372
Books & Supplies: $1,110

Avg. Need-Based Grant: $12,490
Avg. % of Need Met: 71%

Avg. Merit-Based Award: $7,338
% Receiving (All Freshmen): 46%
% Receiving (Freshmen w/o Need): 35%

Avg. Cumulative Debt: $27,555
% of Students Borrowing: 44%

CAREER
Who Recruits
1. Macy's
2. Anheuser-Busch
3. Grant Thornton LLC
4. Oracle
5. Insight Global

Notable Internships
1. The Economist
2. Grant Thornton LLP
3. Bain & Company

Top Industries
1. Business
2. Education
3. Operations
4. Sales
5. Social Services

Top Employers
1. Eli Lily and Company
2. EY
3. Amazon
4. PwC
5. Salesforce

Where Alumni Work
1. Indianapolis
2. Chicago
3. Bloomington, IN
4. New York City
5. Washington DC

Median Earnings
College Scorecard (Early Career): $47,700
PayScale (Early Career): $56,100
PayScale (Mid-Career): $104,400

RANKINGS
Money: 58
U.S. News: 76 (T), National Universities
Wall Street Journal/THE: 104 (T)
Washington Monthly: 59, National Universities

COLLEGE OVERLAPS
Ohio State University - Columbus
Pennsylvania State University - University Park
Purdue University - West Lafayette
University of Illinois at Urbana-Champaign
University of Michigan

#CollegesWorthYourMoney

ADMISSION
Admission Rate: 77%
Admission Rate - Men: 71%
Admission Rate - Women: 80%
EA Admission Rate: 68%
ED Admission Rate: Not Offered
ED Admits as % of Total Admits: Not Offered
Admission Rate (5-Year Trend): +4%
% of Admits Attending (Yield): 25%
Transfer Admission Rate: 67%

SAT Reading/Writing (Middle 50%): 570-650
SAT Math (Middle 50%): 550-640
ACT Composite (Middle 50%): 23-28

% Graduated in Top 10% of HS Class: 18%
% Graduated in Top 25% of HS Class: 33%
% Graduated in Top 50% of HS Class: 90%

Demonstrated Interest: Not Considered
Legacy Status: Considered
Admission Interview Offered: No

ENROLLMENT
Total Undergraduate Enrollment: 19,895
% Part-Time: 6%
% Male: 42%
% Female: 58%
% Out-of-State: 22%
% Fraternity: 4%
% Sorority: 7%
% On-Campus (Freshman): 98%
% On-Campus (All Undergraduate): 32%

% African-American: 5%
% Asian: 5%
% Hispanic: 7%
% White: 75%
% Other: 5%
% Race or Ethnicity Unknown: 2%
% International: 2%
% Low-Income: 13%

ACADEMICS
Student-to-Faculty Ratio: 16 to 1
% of Classes Under 20: 34%
% of Classes 20-49: 55%
% of Classes 50 or More: 12%
% Full-Time Faculty: 67%
% Full-Time Faculty w/ Terminal Degree: 76%

Top Programs
Accounting
Communication Studies
Finance
Health Services Administration
International Affairs
Public Policy and Administration
Sport and Recreation Management

Retention Rate: 89%
4-Year Graduation Rate: 69%
6-Year Graduation Rate: 84%

Curricular Flexibility: Somewhat Flexible
Academic Rating: ★★★

Eighty years ago, before adopting the namesake of our nation's fourth president, the college went by the slightly less memorable handle, "The State Normal and Industrial School for Women." Men were actually not enrolled until after World War II, and the school still has a 42/58 gender split today. More than three-quarters of James Madison University's almost 20,000 undergraduates are Virginia natives, yet, this well-regarded public institution draws plenty of out-of-staters to its often-praised, beautiful Shenandoah Valley campus. Unquestionably a university with a rising national reputation as well as the distinction as one of the top public schools in the region, JMU offers 76 undergraduate degrees to a very happy student population; surveyed undergrads report a stunning 96 percent satisfaction rate.

Inside the Classroom
General Education: The Human Community, JMU's core curriculum, requires students to complete 41 credit hours in coursework covering five "clusters." The clusters are (1) Skills for the 21st Century, (2) Arts & Humanities, (3) The Natural World, (4) Social and Cultural Processes, and (5) Individuals in the Human Community. Many majors require students to demonstrate proficiency of foreign language at the intermediate level. This can entail taking between 2-4 courses, but teens who took advanced foreign language coursework in high school can test out of the requirement. All told, a minimum of one math and two science classes are needed to meet graduation requirements.

A 16:1 student-to-faculty does not fully capture how generally modest class sizes tend to be at the university. Over one-third of sections enroll fewer than 19 students. On the other end of the spectrum, there are some larger lecture-hall size courses; 19 percent of sections contained 40 or more students. Therefore, it's no shock that every measure of professor quality at JMU reveals high levels of student satisfaction. Students in the Honors College are guaranteed a research experience alongside faculty, and the school does publish its own peer-reviewed undergraduate research journal. For decades, JMU has also been a leader in study abroad participation, with some of the highest numbers of participants of any college in the country. In fact, it presently ranks second among all master's-granting institutions with almost 1,500 participants annually.

A quality nursing program leads to JMU conferring a large number of health degrees. Overall, 20 percent of all degrees awarded are in this area. Next in popularity are business/marketing (16 percent), communication/journalism (9 percent), and parks and recreation (5 percent)—majors within each discipline are strong. James Madison is the most prolific producer of Fulbright Scholars of any master's-level university in the entire country. In 2020, there were 15 recent alumni studying abroad on Fulbrights. Dukes also captured multiple National Graduate Research Fellowships, Goldwater Scholarships, and Boren Fellowships this past year.

Outside the Classroom
Not only is the campus typically found on any "most beautiful" list, JMU also ranks high for housing, food, Greek Life, and the party scene. While it sounds trite, it is accurate to say that the average student at this school can be described as "happy." Purple and gold colors can be spotted all around campus as this passionate student body supports its school's 6 men's and 11 women's varsity sports teams. Teams compete at the NCAA Division I level, with the exception of football, where the Dukes participate in the Football Championship Subdivision. Greek life is fairly pervasive, drawing in approximately 20 percent of the undergraduate student body (4,200 total students) to the 31 fraternity and sorority chapters. Ninety-eight percent of freshmen reside on campus, but the majority of upperclassmen—68 percent of the total population—reside in off-campus housing. The school offers an Off-Campus Housing Service to help students locate safe and affordable apartments and houses. More than 450 student-run clubs translates to there being something for just about everyone. There are plenty of community service, faith-based, a cappella, and intramural sports options. Harrisonburg is situated about a two-hour drive from both Washington, DC, and Richmond. To help students without a car get home on breaks, JMU offers a shuttle service to and from the Charlottesville airport, Amtrak station, and Greyhound bus station.

Career Services
There are 14 professional employees engaged in career service-related duties at the Career and Academic Planning Office. Other members of the staff focus more on academic advising. This works out to a fairly weak 1,428:1 student-to-counselor ratio, much higher than the average school featured in this guide. Still, face-to-face (or phone/Zoom) meetings with career counselors are available to current students and recent grads. Resume development is the most common focus of counseling sessions. There are a number of other less personalized

resources that Dukes have access to. In 2018, the university adopted Handshake, giving students access to 250,000 employers. Plenty of webinars and online resources are also available for major exploration and preparing for job/internship searches.

In addition to a larger two-day general career fair, JMU also hosts career-specific fairs in the areas of accounting, science and engineering, nursing, teaching, and media arts and design. For those considering extending their educational journey beyond a bachelor's, the school also hosts a Graduate & Professional School Fair that features 120 programs. The university has a good number of local and national corporate partners that leads to quality connections for internship and job leads. For example, Verizon, MITRE, AT&T, and Intuit all have some type of affiliation with JMU. A gigantic alumni association with more than 140,000 members can also help to complement the services of this relatively understaffed career services department.

Professional Outcomes

Within six months of graduating, two thirds of the Class of 2018 had obtained full-time employment, 24 percent were continuing their education, and just 3 percent were still figuring out their next step. More than 20 members of that cohort were hired by each of Accenture and Booz Allen Hamilton, 15+ went to work for Deloitte, KPMG, Capitol One, and Fannie Mae, and 10+ found employment at EY, IBM, and Northrop Grumman. Fifty-four percent remained in Virginia, 32 percent dispersed to other US states, and 12 percent settled in Washington, DC. Overall, Dukes found employment at 1,681 organizations across 42 states and 28 countries.

Among the almost one quarter of 2018 grads who matriculated directly into a graduate school program, the most popular location was JMU itself. Over 400 stayed put at their alma mater. More than 20 students attended George Mason and Virginia Commonwealth, and 10+ were accepted at UVA, George Washington, and Virginia Tech. Others were accepted into elite graduate programs at Duke, Emory, William & Mary, and Yale. Sixty-two members of the Class of 2019 applied to medical school and, while current acceptance rates are unavailable, past applicants were accepted at a 44 percent clip, which is right around the national average. Past prelaw students found success in gaining acceptance to colleges of law three-quarters of the time, attending schools such as American, Georgetown, and Washington and Lee.

Admission

This is one of the best schools you can find that accepts over three quarters of those who apply. Applicants for a place in the Class of 2023 found success in 78 percent of cases. Transfers actually faced a harsher cycle, gaining acceptance just 62 percent of the time. James Madison is a test-optional institution, yet 85 percent of accepted applicants still do include an SAT or ACT score. The mid-50th percentile scores for 2019-20 freshmen were 1130-1280 on the SAT and 23-28 on the ACT. Just 2.4 percent of those admitted had an SAT composite score of under 1000; 4.7 percent possessed a score above 1400. This is one school where you don't need perfect grades in order to gain admission. Only 18 percent of the Class of 2023 ranked in the top 10 percent of their high school cohort, roughly one third placed in the top quartile, and 90 percent finished in the top half.

Academic GPA and the rigor of one's secondary school record were the only two factors rated as "very important" by the JMU committee. No factors were ranked as being "important," and "considered" elements of the application included standardized test scores, application essay, talent/ability, recommendation letters, extracurricular activities, first-generation status, legacy status, state residency, geographical residence, volunteer work, and paid work experience. There is no binding early decision policy at JMU; however, there is an early action option that does not provide any notable edge in the admissions process. In sum, the application process here is very straightforward and "focuses primarily on high school courses and grades."

Worth Your Money?

The in-state tuition at JMU of $7,250 is among the best values in the entire country. The total in-state cost allows you to get an undergraduate degree for under $100k without any financial aid, which in today's higher education world, qualifies as an exceptional deal. JMU wisely keeps out-of-state costs within reason; the list price COA for a nonresident is a very fair $40,818. This makes the university a very attractive option for large numbers of students from outside Old Dominion. No matter your intended major or residency status, JMU is a school that will be worth the money for most graduates.

FINANCIAL
Institutional Type: Public
In-State Tuition: $7,250
Out-of-State Tuition: $24,150
Room & Board: $10,500
Required Fees: $4,956
Books & Supplies: $1,056

Avg. Need-Based Grant: $8,341
Avg. % of Need Met: 35%

Avg. Merit-Based Award: $7,105
% Receiving (All Freshmen): 6%
% Receiving (Freshmen w/o Need): 2%

Avg. Cumulative Debt: $28,554
% of Students Borrowing: 51%

CAREER
Who Recruits
1. KPMG
2. GGV Capital
3. Freddie Max
4. Ethos Group
5. Verizon

Notable Internships
1. Smithsonian
2. Carmax
3. Baltimore Orioles

Top Industries
1. Business
2. Education
3. Operations
4. Sales
5. Social Services

Top Employers
1. Capital One
2. Booz Allen Hamilton
3. Deloitte
4. EY
5. Accenture

Where Alumni Work
1. Washington DC
2. Charlottesville, VA
3. Richmond, VA
4. New York City
5. Norfolk, VA

Median Earnings
College Scorecard (Early Career): $56,600
PayScale (Early Career): $59,100
PayScale (Mid-Career): $109,700

RANKINGS
Money: 40
U.S. News: 3, Regional Universities South
Wall Street Journal/THE: 281 (T)
Washington Monthly: 8, Master's Universities

COLLEGE OVERLAPS
George Mason University
Pennsylvania State University - University Park
University of Delaware
University of Virginia
Virginia Tech

Johns Hopkins University

Baltimore, Maryland | 410-516-8171

ADMISSION
Admission Rate: 10%
Admission Rate - Men: 10%
Admission Rate - Women: 10%
EA Admission Rate: Not Offered
ED Admission Rate: 31%
ED Admits as % of Total Admits: 22%
Admission Rate (5-Year Trend): -4%
% of Admits Attending (Yield): 46%
Transfer Admission Rate: 11%

SAT Reading/Writing (Middle 50%): 710-770
SAT Math (Middle 50%): 760-800
ACT Composite (Middle 50%): 33-36

% Graduated in Top 10% of HS Class: 98%
% Graduated in Top 25% of HS Class: 99%
% Graduated in Top 50% of HS Class: 100%

Demonstrated Interest: Not Considered
Legacy Status: Not Considered
Admission Interview Offered: No

ENROLLMENT
Total Undergraduate Enrollment: 5,534
% Part-Time: <1%
% Male: 48%
% Female: 52%
% Out-of-State: 89%
% Fraternity: 24%
% Sorority: 35%
% On-Campus (Freshman): 99%
% On-Campus (All Undergraduate): 51%

% African-American: 8%
% Asian: 27%
% Hispanic: 16%
% White: 28%
% Other: 6%
% Race or Ethnicity Unknown: 5%
% International: 11%
% Low-Income: 15%

ACADEMICS
Student-to-Faculty Ratio: 7 to 1
% of Classes Under 20: 77%
% of Classes 20-49: 15%
% of Classes 50 or More: 9%
% Full-Time Faculty: 96%
% Full-Time Faculty w/ Terminal Degree: 96%

Top Programs
Biology
Biomedical Engineering
Chemistry
English
International Studies
Mathematics
Physics
Public Health Studies

Retention Rate: 98%
4-Year Graduation Rate: 88%
6-Year Graduation Rate: 94%

Curricular Flexibility: Somewhat Flexible
Academic Rating: ★★★★★

#CollegesWorthYourMoney

High schoolers who dream of entering the medical profession look to North Baltimore as their Mecca—more specifically, to Johns Hopkins University, Charm City's prestigious, midsized research institution. Yet, four years at Johns Hopkins is so much more than merely a prelude to seven years of medical school. With fifty-two majors as well as forty-seven minors, JHU excels in everything from its bread-and-butter medical-related majors to international relations and dance. Of the five undergraduate schools within the university, the vast majority of students reside in either the Krieger School of Arts and Sciences or the Whiting School of Engineering. However, the Carey School of Business, School of Education, and Peabody Institute also award bachelor's degrees.

Inside the Classroom
All Hopkins bachelor's-seekers must meet distributional requirements covering the basics: humanities, natural sciences, social and behavioral sciences, quantitative and mathematical sciences, and engineering. Writing-intensive courses also are mandated regardless of one's major. Students are encouraged to broaden their horizons by double majoring or selecting a minor, and 70 percent do so. First-year experience courses help to transition students to the school and second-year experience courses assist with community-building and career planning.

Boasting an enviable 7:1 student-to-faculty ratio and with 77 percent of course sections possessing an enrollment under twenty, face time with professors is a reality. That presents a phenomenal opportunity to learn directly from a group that includes four Nobel Laureates, four Medal of Science winners, and two recipients of the Presidential Medal of Freedom. Fittingly for America's first research university, 80 percent of JHU undergraduates complete a research experience while working closely with a faculty member. Each year, hundreds of students receive significant funding for independent projects through the Hopkins Office for Undergraduate Research.

Universally respected by employers and graduate schools alike, many departments carry a high level of clout, including biology, chemistry, English, and international studies. Biomedical engineering, public health, and nursing, which happen to be the three most popular majors, can also be found at the top of the national rankings. In 2019, there were twenty-two Fulbright Scholars named from the university. Johns Hopkins grads also are competitive in landing Luce, Truman, Marshall, Goldwater, and National Science Foundation Graduate Research Fellowships.

Outside the Classroom
The 140-acre Homewood campus located in North Baltimore is the site of the School of Engineering and the School of Arts & Sciences. The dorms located at Homewood house most underclassmen and feature dining halls that garner generally high praise. Despite the excellent chow, upperclassmen tend to outgrow university-owned housing; a slight majority of students, 51 percent, live on campus. The twenty-two Greek organizations each have their own charitable focus and attract more than one-quarter of the undergraduate student body. Nicknamed the Blue Jays, athletes compete in twelve men's and ten women's sports in NCCA Division III. Over 400 student organizations are active at JHU. Groups centered on community service tend to be the most popular. The Center for Social Concern connects students with over seventy-five local organizations. For those interested in a medical career, you'll have the chance to volunteer in one of fifteen local hospitals, including Johns Hopkins' own facilities. Popular traditions include the three-day Spring Fair, the nation's largest student-run fair. Famous guest speakers from all walks of life regularly visit campus and draw engaged audiences. Homewood is only a few miles from the bustle of Baltimore's Inner Harbor so, even though the area immediately surrounding campus isn't the most inviting, culture and nightlife can easily be found.

Career Services
The newly-renamed Life Design Center at Homewood is staffed by twenty-five full-time professional employees that work with and on behalf of undergraduates in the areas of career development, employer engagement, internship coordination, and event planning. This figure does not include administrative assistants, IT, graduate advisors, or marketing professionals. Possessing a student-to-advisor ratio of 221:1, JHU is superior to many of the institutions included in this book.

In 2018-19 (most recent data available), the Life Design Center engaged 1,999 undergraduates in one-to-one career coach appointments. More than ninety employers, including many Fortune 1000 companies, conducted 716 interviews on campus. Over 15,000 jobs and internship opportunities were available on Handshake. Homewood hosts three major career fairs each year: the flagship Fall Career Fair with more than 150 employers, the STEM

& Innovation Career Fair with forty targeted companies attending, and the spring Nonprofit Career Fair that also focuses on internship procurement. All told, 170 companies attended career fairs at JHU, and 247 companies recruited on campus. The university also provides a number of internships that are built-in to each academic department. Those include credit-bearing options in orthopedic surgery, film and media studies, business, and computational biology. An exceptional 85 percent of undergraduates complete one internship over their four years of study; it is not unusual to complete two.

Professional Outcomes

The Class of 2019 saw 97 percent of graduates successfully land at their next destination within six months of exiting the university; 59 percent of graduates entered the world of employment and a robust 33 percent went directly to graduate/professional school. Of those entering the workforce, the most popular industries were research, consulting, engineering, finance, and health care. Johns Hopkins University and its affiliated medical institutions were the largest employer of recent graduates, scooping up 29 Class of 2019 members. Other prominent companies landing more than a handful of fresh JHU alums were Deloitte, Accenture, Booz Allen Hamilton, Morgan Stanley, and ScribeAmerica. Across all graduating years you'll find hundreds of Hopkins grads working for IBM, Google, Microsoft, Facebook, and Apple. The median starting salary across all majors was $64,500.

Johns Hopkins' sterling reputation also helps land its undergrads at premier graduate schools. Engineering is the most popular graduate field with 26 percent of 2019 graduates going in that direction. Medical school was the second most common endeavor at 16 percent. The overall admit rate to medical schools was a healthy 79 percent. Law school grads also found homes at an above-average 90 percent clip. Johns Hopkins itself is the most frequently attended graduate school, and it's not even close, with over 150 Class of 2019 grads continuing their educations in Baltimore. The next five most frequently attended institutions were Harvard, Penn, Columbia, Princeton, and the University of Chicago.

Admission

If Johns Hopkins' aim in 2019 was to become one of a dozen or so elite universities with a single-digit admissions rate, it only missed that goal by a matter of percentage points. Rounding up, 10 percent of undergraduates were admitted into the Class of 2023. That follows a pattern of declining acceptance rates over the past few years. For historical context, the school admitted one-quarter of applicants only a decade ago. The SAT middle 50 percent range in 2008 was 1320-1480; today it is 1480-1550. Given that the former 75th percentile SAT score is now the 25th percentile score, it's pretty clear that Johns Hopkins has grown increasingly competitive in recent years. For those taking the ACT, the mid-50 percent is 33-35.

Current students landed in the top 10 percent of their high school classes at a 98 percent clip, so impeccable grades in the most competitive curriculum available is pretty much a prerequisite for consideration. The average unweighted GPA for 2019-20 freshman was 3.9, meaning that more than one or two imperfections on a transcript can be a disqualifier. Leadership qualities and community service are also highly valued. In the university's own words, it is "looking for students who can think beyond their limits, who don't see 'impossible' as a roadblock, and who will not only elevate themselves but also those around them." Early decision applicants will see improved odds as their acceptance rate is more than three times that of the regular round. Further, 47 percent of the Class of 2023 was accepted via ED. Always a highly selective school, Johns Hopkins is now in the upper-upper tier of selectivity along with the Ivies, Stanford, and a small cadre of elite liberal arts colleges. Only those with first-rate test scores and transcripts need apply.

Worth Your Money?

If your family is a lower-to-mid tier income bracket, Johns Hopkins will provide you with every dollar of financial aid you need to attend the university. Presently, nearly half of the undergraduate population benefits from that generosity with an average need-based grant of $46k. The annual cost of attendance is approaching $75,000, and of those families making more than $200k per year can expect to pay close to full price. Even for those taking out loans to attend, JHU is the type of school that it is almost always OK to pay up for. With fantastic job and professional school prospects down the road, the $300,000 investment will be well worth it in the long run.

FINANCIAL
Institutional Type: Private
In-State Tuition: $57,510
Out-of-State Tuition: $57,510
Room & Board: $16,800
Required Fees: $0
Books & Supplies: $1,250

Avg. Need-Based Grant: $45,836
Avg. % of Need Met: 100%

Avg. Merit-Based Award: $10,602
% Receiving (All Freshmen): 10%
% Receiving (Freshmen w/o Need): 1%

Avg. Cumulative Debt: $24,107
% of Students Borrowing: 41%

CAREER
Who Recruits
1. Dean & Company
2. Bloomberg
3. Lockheed Martin
4. Bain & Company
5. McKinsey & Co.

Notable Internships
1. Twitter
2. NASA Jet Propulsion Laboratory
3. National Institutes of Health

Top Industries
1. Business
2. Education
3. Research
4. Engineering
5. Healthcare

Top Employers
1. Booz Allen Hamilton
2. Google
3. Deloitte
4. IBM
5. Microsoft

Where Alumni Work
1. Baltimore
2. Washington DC
3. New York City
4. San Francisco
5. Boston

Median Earnings
College Scorecard (Early Career): $73,200
PayScale (Early Career): $72,800
PayScale (Mid-Career): $129,200

RANKINGS
Money: 91
U.S. News: 9 (T), National Universities
Wall Street Journal/THE: 11
Washington Monthly: 54, National Universities

COLLEGE OVERLAPS
Cornell University
Duke University
Princeton University
University of California, Berkeley
University of Pennsylvania

Kenyon College

Gambier, Ohio | 740-427-5776

ADMISSION
Admission Rate: 34%
Admission Rate - Men: 31%
Admission Rate - Women: 37%
EA Admission Rate: Not Offered
ED Admission Rate: 62%
ED Admits as % of Total Admits: 11%
Admission Rate (5-Year Trend): -4%
% of Admits Attending (Yield): 21%
Transfer Admission Rate: 49%

SAT Reading/Writing (Middle 50%): 640-720
SAT Math (Middle 50%): 630-740
ACT Composite (Middle 50%): 29-33

% Graduated in Top 10% of HS Class: 57%
% Graduated in Top 25% of HS Class: 79%
% Graduated in Top 50% of HS Class: 98%

Demonstrated Interest: Important
Legacy Status: Considered
Admission Interview Offered: Yes

ENROLLMENT
Total Undergraduate Enrollment: 1,747
% Part-Time: 1%
% Male: 45%
% Female: 55%
% Out-of-State: 86%
% Fraternity: 19%
% Sorority: 14%
% On-Campus (Freshman): 100%
% On-Campus (All Undergraduate): 99%

% African-American: 3%
% Asian: 4%
% Hispanic: 7%
% White: 70%
% Other: 5%
% Race or Ethnicity Unknown: 2%
% International: 9%
% Low-Income: 8%

ACADEMICS
Student-to-Faculty Ratio: 9 to 1
% of Classes Under 20: 75%
% of Classes 20-49: 24%
% of Classes 50 or More: 1%
% Full-Time Faculty: 81%
% Full-Time Faculty w/ Terminal Degree: 88%

Top Programs
English
History
International Studies
Neuroscience
Performing Arts
Political Science
Sociology

Retention Rate: 89%
4-Year Graduation Rate: 86%
6-Year Graduation Rate: 89%

Curricular Flexibility: Very Flexible
Academic Rating: ★★★★

#CollegesWorthYourMoney

When your list of notable alumni includes Paul Newman, National Humanities Medal recipient E.L. Doctorow, and largely forgotten US President Rutherford B. Hayes, it's clear that your college is a unique and special place. Kenyon College in rural Gambier, Ohio, has a history of excellence in drama, English, and across the broader liberal arts that produces passionate and talented alumni who are ready, willing, and able to carve out their legacies within their chosen disciplines.

Inside the Classroom

Kenyon offers thirty-three majors and an additional thirteen concentrations that allow students to complete their education with few non-departmental core requirements. All undergrads must demonstrate proficiency in a foreign language (AP opt-out is available) and take a quantitative reasoning course, but other than that, a Kenyon education is open and flexible. A senior capstone awaits all would-be graduates and can take many forms, but the project must demonstrate a student's skills in writing, speaking, collaborating and "distinguish the essential from the trivial." This latter requirement epitomizes Kenyon's emphasis on critical thought throughout one's four years of study.

The student-faculty ratio is 9-to-1, and the most common class size is fifteen. Thirty-four percent of classes are even more intimate, offering single-digit enrollments. Close relationships develop with faculty and often lead to opportunities to engage in undergraduate research. Summer research programs available to students include the Kenyon Summer Scholars Program, a joint program with Ohio State, and the Summer Science Program that sees more than thirty student-professor pairs collaborate on research for an eight- to ten-week period. Roughly half of each junior class packs up its bags and heads off to a distant land for a semester abroad. Students choose from more than 190 programs in fifty countries across Africa, Asia, Australia, Europe, and the Americas; the school also sponsors programs in England and in Rome.

English, economics, psychology, political science, and the visual and performing arts are the school's four most popular majors. As alluded to earlier, the drama program is one of the country's finest and has a lengthy alumni list of recognizable actors and performers. It's rare to identify an institution's English program as having an elevated reputation in the minds of employers and graduate schools, but Kenyon's would be one of the exceptions. For a relatively small school, Kenyon graduates procure nationally competitive scholarships and fellowships at an exceptional clip. In 2020, the college had five Fulbright winners and three Goldwater recipients. It has been a top Fulbright producer for the last decade.

Outside the Classroom

Kenyon's 1,000-acre campus is located forty-five miles from bustling Columbus and includes a 500-acre nature preserve. All students live on campus, and freshmen are clustered in special residence halls near the Gund Commons. Facilities receive rave reviews from students including the Kenyon Athletic Center that includes tennis courts, a pool, and an indoor track. Nineteen percent of male Kenyon undergraduates are involved in Greek life as are 14 percent of women, but, uniquely, fraternities and sororities are situated within residence halls, leading to a more integrated experience. Close to one-third of students are on the roster of one of the school's twenty NCAA Division III athletic teams (ten men's and ten women's). Plenty of club and intramural sports are available for those seeking a less formal sports pursuit. Intramurals include offbeat games like cornhole and capture the flag. Beyond Greek organizations and sports teams, there are 120 student organizations to consider including five a cappella groups, numerous community service opportunities, and the Kenyon College Dance & Dramatics Club that puts on high-quality student productions. Nature lovers can hike the six miles of trails in the school's own preserve along the Kokosing River or join the Outdoors Club that takes backpacking and whitewater rafting trips to more adventurous locations such as the Monongahela National Forest of West Virginia.

Career Services

The Career Development Office (CDO) employs six professional staff members who work in career development or graduate school advising. With a 291:1 student-to-advisor ratio, Kenyon provides a higher-than-average level of support when compared against the other institutions in this guidebook. While it doesn't host a large-scale career fair, it does offer employer/graduate school information sessions at a rate of fifteen to twenty per month. The CDO's strengths lie in its willingness to give individualized attention to students and its involved alumni network. The online Kenyon Career Network helps link current students to alumni working in their field of interest; there

Kenyon College

are 8,000 alumni willing to offer their advice and assistance. Job-shadowing opportunities are plentiful, and experiences have included trips to the New York Times, Random House, and the Federal Reserve Bank of Chicago. The office is adept at helping students find internships, and recent grads have had stints with organizations such as the Museum of Modern Art, the San Diego Padres, and the Library of Congress. In recent years 65-70 percent of employed graduates reported that their jobs were related to their desired career path. Only 68 percent of 2019 graduates reported that Kenyon was effective at preparing them for the work of employment. Those indicators suggest that not all graduates are fully satisfied with the career services delivered at this school.

Professional Outcomes

Popular fields for Kenyon grads include education, health care, marketing, nonprofit management, research, and writing and editing. Due to Kenyon's small size and the diversity of its academic programs, it lacks dense concentrations of alumni at particular companies. Economics majors often land as financial analysts or advisors at firms including BlackRock, Wells Fargo, JP Morgan, or Goldman Sachs. English and journalism majors end up at a diverse array of publishing houses, talent agencies, news organizations, and consulting companies. New York City, DC, Columbus, Chicago, and Boston are the five cities drawing the greatest numbers of Kenyon alumni. Early career salaries for Kenyon grads are modest, but that can partially be explained by the fact that many alumni pursue lengthy graduate/professional programs that typically pay financial dividends later in life. Other comparable schools including Vassar, Carleton, and Occidental rank similarly.

Within five years of completing their undergraduate education at Kenyon, 50 percent have already finished an advanced degree program and 70 percent are enrolled in one. Law and business school applicants find success at a 99 percent clip and, among medical school candidates with a minimum GPA of 3.7, the acceptance rate is a phenomenal 92 percent. Recent grads have been welcomed into the top law schools at Yale, NYU, Berkeley, Stanford, UVA, Michigan, and the University of Chicago. Future doctors are currently training at prestigious medical schools including Johns Hopkins, Duke, Harvard, Tufts, Vanderbilt, and Northwestern. A successful undergraduate career at Kenyon will make possible admission into the finest graduate and professional schools in the world. Across all disciplines, 98 percent of those applying to an advanced degree program are accepted by one of their top three choices.

Admission

A rarity among elite liberal arts schools, Kenyon's acceptance rate has risen in recent years. The class of 2019 acceptance rate hit an all-time low of 24 percent, but the Class of 2023 rate was a significantly friendlier 34 percent. The latest incoming freshman class possessed an average GPA of 3.9, a 1360 on the SAT, and a 31 on the ACT. Three years ago, when the acceptance rate was a dozen points lower, the SAT range was 1240-1420; the average GPA was the same. Therefore, one can conclude that the profile of the average Kenyon student has not changed much in recent years.

The admissions committee values four factors above all others: rigor of courses, GPA, recommendations, and essays. Test scores, class rank, the interview, talent/ability, extracurricular activities, character/personal qualities, and the level of an applicant's interest make up the next rung of important considerations. Facing stiff competition from other elite liberal arts schools, Kenyon very much wants to know if you truly want to go there. Applying early decision is the ultimate sign of devotion, and that act is rewarded. Almost 62 percent of ED applicants were accepted, and they comprise a good portion of each incoming class; 52 percent of the Class of 2023 was admitted via ED. Kenyon is looking for academically curious and talented students who are actively involved in their schools/communities. Excellent grades are a must, and demonstrating interest is more valuable here than at your average college. If your heart is set on Kenyon, strongly consider demonstrating your loyalty by applying early.

Worth Your Money?

Current Kenyon students who qualify for financial aid receive grants averaging $45,000 per year; the college meets 100 percent of student need. To help lower the $74k cost of attendance, it also offers annual awards of $14k in merit aid to one-quarter of the freshman class. This school is definitely worth your money but, as when considering any institution, we would caution against taking on an excessive amount of debt if you are pursuing a major that is unlikely to lead to fiscal stability upon graduation.

FINANCIAL
Institutional Type: Private
In-State Tuition: $60,800
Out-of-State Tuition: $60,800
Room & Board: $12,830
Required Fees: $300
Books & Supplies: $1,900

Avg. Need-Based Grant: $45,078
Avg. % of Need Met: 100%

Avg. Merit-Based Award: $13,843
% Receiving (All Freshmen): 44%
% Receiving (Freshmen w/o Need): 26%

Avg. Cumulative Debt: $26,865
% of Students Borrowing: 39%

CAREER
Who Recruits
1. GBQ Partners
2. DHL Supply Chain
3. Skylight Financial Group
4. TEKsystems
5. Verizon

Notable Internships
1. Penguin Random House
2. Guggenheim Museum
3. Morgan Stanley

Top Industries
1. Business
2. Education
3. Media
4. Operations
5. Social Services

Top Employers
1. JPMorgan Chase
2. Cleveland Clinic
3. Google
4. Amazon
5. US State Department

Where Alumni Work
1. New York City
2. Washington DC
3. Columbus, OH
4. Chicago
5. Boston

Median Earnings
College Scorecard (Early Career): $48,700
PayScale (Early Career): $58,000
PayScale (Mid-Career): $119,700

RANKINGS
Money: 178
U.S. News: 28 (T), Liberal Arts Colleges
Wall Street Journal/THE: 94 (T)
Washington Monthly: 66, Liberal Arts Colleges

COLLEGE OVERLAPS
Grinnell College
Hamilton College
Middlebury College
Oberlin College
Vassar College

Lafayette College

Easton, Pennsylvania | 610-330-5100

ADMISSION
Admission Rate: 31%
Admission Rate - Men: 28%
Admission Rate - Women: 36%
EA Admission Rate: Not Offered
ED Admission Rate: 51%
ED Admits as % of Total Admits: 14%
Admission Rate (5-Year Trend): -3%
% of Admits Attending (Yield): 26%
Transfer Admission Rate: 29%

SAT Reading/Writing (Middle 50%): 620-700
SAT Math (Middle 50%): 630-740
ACT Composite (Middle 50%): 28-33

% Graduated in Top 10% of HS Class: 54%
% Graduated in Top 25% of HS Class: 81%
% Graduated in Top 50% of HS Class: 97%

Demonstrated Interest: Considered
Legacy Status: Considered
Admission Interview Offered: Yes

ENROLLMENT
Total Undergraduate Enrollment: 2,662
% Part-Time: 1%
% Male: 49%
% Female: 51%
% Out-of-State: 81%
% Fraternity: 26%
% Sorority: 33%
% On-Campus (Freshman): 100%
% On-Campus (All Undergraduate): 93%

% African-American: 5%
% Asian: 4%
% Hispanic: 7%
% White: 65%
% Other: 3%
% Race or Ethnicity Unknown: 5%
% International: 10%
% Low-Income: 11%

ACADEMICS
Student-to-Faculty Ratio: 10 to 1
% of Classes Under 20: 59%
% of Classes 20-49: 40%
% of Classes 50 or More: 2%
% Full-Time Faculty: 82%
% Full-Time Faculty w/ Terminal Degree: 99%

Top Programs
Economics
Engineering
English
Film and Media Studies
Government and Law
International Affairs
Psychology

Retention Rate: 94%
4-Year Graduation Rate: 84%
6-Year Graduation Rate: 88%

Curricular Flexibility: Somewhat Flexible
Academic Rating: ★★★★✦

#CollegesWorthYourMoney

Nearing its 200th birthday, this elite liberal arts school named after the Revolutionary War hero the Marquis de Lafayette, offers a rare blend of an intimate academic experience mixed with big- time sports and prominent Greek life. Roughly 2,600 students comprise the student body at this undergraduate-only liberal arts school in quiet Easton, Pennsylvania. Undergrads are a high-caliber lot, possessing academic credentials equal to those of archrival Lehigh University.

Inside the Classroom
Lafayette offers fifty-one areas over four academic divisions: engineering, humanities, natural sciences, and the social sciences. It also allows for self-designed majors such as behavioral economics, environmental issues and policy, or nanoscience. All undergrads delve into a first- year seminar during fall of their freshman year, a course designed to strengthen writing, thinking, and speaking abilities. Other required components of the school's common course of study include a year of foreign language, a quantitative reasoning course, two classes under the umbrella of global and multiculturalism, and at least a singular foray into each of the college's academic divisions.

One-on-one attention from professors is a reality at Lafayette, thanks to a 10:1 student-to-faculty ratio and no graduate students to compete with. A solid 59 percent of sections contain fewer than twenty students; 10 percent enroll nine or fewer. By the time senior year is nearing its completion, 52 percent of students have completed a research experience with a faculty member. The school invests almost half a million dollars annually in funding undergraduate research. A majority of students also have studied for a semester in a foreign country as 60 percent of graduates elect to study abroad in one of fifty locations. In addition to semester-long options, Lafayette offers truncated study abroad opportunities during semester breaks.

Of the degrees conferred in 2019, social sciences (33 percent) and engineering (18 percent) were the disciplines in which the largest number of degrees were earned. The engineering program is one of the best in the country among non-doctoral granting institutions. Economics was the next most commonly conferred degree and is also one of Lafayette's strongest. Other popular and well-regarded programs include psychology, international affairs, and film studies. On the whole, Lafayette students fare well with employers and top graduate schools but also experience success when applying for prestigious fellowships. Named a top Fulbright producer, Lafayette had five winners in 2020. In recent years, it has had graduates land Gilman, Goldwater, and Udall Scholarships.

Outside the Classroom
In sleepy Easton, 93 percent of undergrads lay their heads at night inside college-owned housing. Greek life, which was under a microscope after a 2012 hazing death, has survived and thrived, still drawing 26-33 percent of the student body into fraternities and sororities. Athletics are also a central part of the Lafayette experience as the Leopards compete in twenty-three NCAA Division I sports as well as in more than fifty club and intramural programs. Games against rival Lehigh garner a high level of interest. Over 200 student-run organizations are active. For those interested in the performing arts, twenty-four such clubs are on the menu. There are forty-three cultural and/or service organizations that help contribute a collective 20,000 annual hours of charitable engagement. Nature lovers aren't far from the Pocono Mountains that offer all of the hiking, snowboarding, skiing, tubing, and fishing you can handle. Almost equidistant (in terms of travel time) between New York City and Philadelphia, big-city fun is only a car ride away. Easton is a small town with plenty of history and some nice eateries, but campus is the hub of the social experience.

Career Services
The recently renamed Gateway Career Center is staffed by thirteen professional employees (not counting office assistants) who work in career counseling, employer relations, internship coordination, or graduate school advising. That 205:1 student-to-advisor ratio is better-than-average when compared to other schools featured in this guide. Thanks to such generous staffing, counselors can offer distinct services to students at every phase of their college education, beginning with career exploration activities during freshman year. Mock interviews, resume development, internship/externship discovery, or individualized career/grad school counseling is available at any time.

Large-scale events, such as the Fall Career Fair, attract more than sixty employers including Goldman Sachs, ExxonMobil, and Fidelity Investments. The Gateway Career Center does an excellent job guiding students into internships and other meaningful opportunities for hands-on learning. By senior year, close to 80 percent of Lafayette undergrads have completed an internship, externship, or other field experience. A robust 40 percent of recent grads found their jobs directly through campus recruiting and/or the alumni network. On-campus interviews take place October-November and again from February-April. With a high level of personalized offerings and excellent career and graduate school outcomes, the Gateway Career Center accomplishes its mission on behalf of its undergraduates.

Professional Outcomes

Within six months of graduation, a stellar 96 percent of the Class of 2019 had already landed full-time jobs or were enrolled in graduate/professional school. The most commonly procured jobs are in business development, education, operations, engineering, sales, finance, and research. Companies employing large numbers of Lafayette alumni include Merck, IBM, Morgan Stanley, Citi, Merrill Lynch, JP Morgan Chase Co., Deloitte, and EY. Despite being a Pennsylvania institution, Philadelphia is the second most popular landing spot for alumni; New York City attracts nearly three times as many Leopards. Large pockets of alumni also can be found in DC, Boston, and San Francisco.

Those attending graduate school frequently land at some of the top programs in the country within their respective disciplines. Recent economics majors have entered business/econ programs at Stanford, the University of Chicago, and Yale. Government majors have gone on to study at Penn, Harvard, and GW. Chemistry majors go on to pursue PhDs at institutions such as Tulane, Princeton, and Emory. Medical school applicants with a 3.6 GPA or above enjoy a 74 percent acceptance rate, and dental school candidates find homes at a 90 percent clip. Recent graduates have matriculated into medical schools at Georgetown, UVA, Brown, Dartmouth, and Boston University. Law school applicants found homes at a perfect 100 percent rate, and those acceptances included many top law schools.

Admission

The 8,521 students jostling for a spot in the Lafayette Class of 2023 were granted acceptance at a 31 percent rate; the Class of 2022 was admitted at a 29 percent clip. The Class of 2023 possessed an average SAT score of 1341, ACT of 30, and average GPA of 3.5. In a typical year, over 20 incoming freshmen were the valedictorian or salutatorian of their high school classes; 54 percent hailed from the top 10 percent, and 81 percent from the top quarter. A decade ago, Lafayette was a touch easier to get into. The acceptance rate in 2008-09 was 37 percent, and the 75th percentile SAT score was 1370, a figure closer to the average SAT score held by today's freshmen. However, students' class rank from that year shows that 65 percent placed in the top 10 percent of their high school classes, and 93 percent were in the top quarter. Taken together, those figures paint a muddled picture of whether Lafayette is more or less difficult to gain acceptance into than it was a decade ago.

In the eyes of the admissions committee at Lafayette, two factors receive the highest level of consideration— rigor of coursework and GPA. The next tier of factors includes test scores, class rank, essays, recommendations, extracurricular activities, the interview, character/personal qualities, and talent/ability. Those applying early decision were accepted at a 51 percent clip and accounted for more than half of entering freshmen in the 2019-20 academic year. Lafayette is a competitive institution but not out of reach for students with SAT scores in the 1300s and/or a less-than-pristine transcript. Applying early yields a strong advantage in the admissions process as the acceptance rate is higher, and a large chunk of the spots in the freshman class are already occupied by the time applicants enter the regular round.

Worth Your Money?

The annual bill to attend Lafayette exceeds $72,000. Eleven percent of undergrads do receive merit aid averaging $28k. Only a little over one-third of undergraduates currently attending Lafayette receive any aid at all. The good news is that those who are awarded a grant see 100 percent of their need met, and the average total is over $47,000. The school's excellent offerings in engineering and strong networks in Philly and NYC lead to generally high starting salaries, making it possible for most to pay their student loans without too much economic pain.

FINANCIAL
Institutional Type: Private
In-State Tuition: $56,556
Out-of-State Tuition: $56,556
Room & Board: $16,874
Required Fees: $1,246
Books & Supplies: $1,000

Avg. Need-Based Grant: $47,148
Avg. % of Need Met: 100%

Avg. Merit-Based Award: $27,765
% Receiving (All Freshmen): 11%
% Receiving (Freshmen w/o Need): 5%

Avg. Cumulative Debt: $30,863
% of Students Borrowing: 39%

CAREER
Who Recruits
1. Gilbane Building
2. Crayola
3. SMC Partners
4. MarketAxess
5. Whiting-Turner Contracting

Notable Internships
1. Disney Streaming Services
2. RCA Records
3. Cisco

Top Industries
1. Business
2. Education
3. Operations
4. Engineering
5. Sales

Top Employers
1. Merck
2. IBM
3. Morgan Stanley
4. Citi
5. Deloitte

Where Alumni Work
1. New York City
2. Philadelphia
3. Allentown, PA
4. Boston
5. Washington DC

Median Earnings
College Scorecard (Early Career): $68,600
PayScale (Early Career): $70,400
PayScale (Mid-Career): $137,500

RANKINGS
Money: 97
U.S. News: 40 (T), Liberal Arts Colleges
Wall Street Journal/THE: 74 (T)
Washington Monthly: 26, Liberal Arts Colleges

COLLEGE OVERLAPS
Bucknell University
Colgate University
Franklin & Marshall College
Gettysburg College
Villanova University

Lawrence University

Appleton, Wisconsin | 920-832-6500

ADMISSION
Admission Rate: 62%
Admission Rate - Men: 57%
Admission Rate - Women: 67%
EA Admission Rate: 86%
ED Admission Rate: 71%
ED Admits as % of Total Admits: 2%
Admission Rate (5-Year Trend): -11%
% of Admits Attending (Yield): 18%
Transfer Admission Rate: 41%

SAT Reading/Writing (Middle 50%): 600-700
SAT Math (Middle 50%): 600-730
ACT Composite (Middle 50%): 25-32

% Graduated in Top 10% of HS Class: 39%
% Graduated in Top 25% of HS Class: 77%
% Graduated in Top 50% of HS Class: 98%

Demonstrated Interest: Considered
Legacy Status: Considered
Admission Interview Offered: Yes

ENROLLMENT
Total Undergraduate Enrollment: 1,445
% Part-Time: 3%
% Male: 46%
% Female: 54%
% Out-of-State: 75%
% Fraternity: 9%
% Sorority: 13%
% On-Campus (Freshman): 100%
% On-Campus (All Undergraduate): 95%

% African-American: 6%
% Asian: 6%
% Hispanic: 10%
% White: 60%
% Other: 4%
% Race or Ethnicity Unknown: 1%
% International: 12%
% Low-Income: 18%

ACADEMICS
Student-to-Faculty Ratio: 8 to 1
% of Classes Under 20: 79%
% of Classes 20-49: 19%
% of Classes 50 or More: 2%
% Full-Time Faculty: 89%
% Full-Time Faculty w/ Terminal Degree: 92%

Top Programs
Biology
Economics
English
Environmental Studies
Government
Music
Physics

Retention Rate: 87%
4-Year Graduation Rate: 62%
6-Year Graduation Rate: 79%

Curricular Flexibility: Somewhat Flexible
Academic Rating: ★★★✦

#CollegesWorthYourMoney

The history of Lawrence University, a tiny liberal arts school in Appleton, Wisconsin, is as unique as its present-day educational offerings. One of the earliest (ninth, to be precise) coeducational colleges in the United States and one of the top music conservatories anywhere, the 1,445 undergraduates on campus today enjoy an intimate academic environment in which the largest number of degrees conferred are in the performing arts. It is the only school in the nation whose college of arts and sciences and music conservatory are both 100 percent populated by undergraduates. There are thirty-five distinct majors as well as the option to complete a five-year double major from both the conservatory and A&S; like we said, LU is unique.

Inside the Classroom
Operating on a trimester calendar, the academic year is comprised of ten-week fall, winter, and spring sessions. For more than seventy years, part of the LU core curriculum has been a yearlong Freshman Studies program that in a small, seminar-style classroom explores questions like "What is the best sort of life for human beings? Are there limits to human knowledge? How should we respond to injustice and suffering?" From there, Lawrence undergrads encounter a dose of humanities, natural science, social science, and fine arts offerings and must show competency in a foreign language, quantitative reasoning, and a writing/speaking-intensive course. Every graduate completes a Senior Experience that can take the form of a paper, performance, portfolio, or exhibition.

An 8:1 student/faculty ratio allows for extremely small class sizes—the majority of sections contain only two to nineteen students, and many independent study/1:1 music instruction courses also are available. With Lawrence being a "university" in name only, undergraduate research opportunities are wide open. Professors are expected to allow undergraduates access to their research studies; for example, every member of the Chemistry Department has to run an active research group. The Lawrence University Research Fellows (LURF) program offers a stipend during ten-week, research-focused terms. All told, close to two-thirds of LU students gain hands-on research experience at some point during their four years of study. The college strongly encourages students to study abroad, and roughly 40 percent take the plunge. Sponsored opportunities include the London Lawrence Center or the Francophile Seminar in Dakar, Senegal.

The visual and performing arts (23 percent), the social sciences (15 percent), and biology (14 percent) comprise the most popular areas of study at LU. The world-renowned Conservatory of Music enrolls approximately 350 undergraduates. Extremely strong natural science programs allow the university to be a top producer of future STEM PhDs. It is also a top producer of Fulbright Scholars, with five to its credit in 2019. Other prestigious fellowships won by recent students include a Watson Fellowship and a Goldwater Scholarship.

Outside the Classroom
Lawrence's 88-acre campus houses 100 percent of freshmen and 95 percent of the undergraduate student body in five residence halls. The Greek presence is minimal with 9 percent of men affiliated with frats and 13 percent of women members of sororities. One-quarter of the population are NCAA Division III varsity athletes competing on one of the ten men's or nine women's squads known as the Vikings. Non-sports events that draw many participants include Fall Festival, Winter Carnival, and the Great Midwest Trivia Contest, a fifty-hour marathon that has drawn national media attention. There are over one hundred clubs and activities, and virtually every student on campus is involved in at least one. Volunteer organizations are popular, and students give a collective 10,000 hours per year. Three or four times per year campus will close for an hour while everyone flocks to Memorial Chapel for convocation where a famous speaker like Maya Angelou or David Sedaris will address the student body. If the Appleton campus that overlooks the Fox River doesn't provide enough natural beauty for you, the college also owns 425+ acres on the shores of Lake Michigan that can be utilized for hiking, ice skating, and camping. Appleton is a safe and enjoyable small town with a population around 70,000 that contains ample bars, restaurants, and shops. The town is only about a thirty-minute drive from Green Bay and about ninety minutes from Milwaukee.

Career Services
The Center for Career, Life and Community Engagement employs seven full-time staff members in employer and alumni relations, career advising, and pre-professional advising and major fellowships. That student-to-advisor ratio of 206:1 is strong when compared to other colleges featured in this guide, and it allows the career services staff to carve out time even for freshmen. All first-years are encouraged to come in for at least a fifteen- or twenty-minute counseling session. The center's stated mission is "preparing students for lives of achievement, responsible and meaningful citizenship, lifelong learning, and personal fulfillment," and it offers ample one-on-one counseling toward those aims.

Many students pursue internships with nonprofit institutions, charitable organizations, and museums, although several recent undergrads have landed positions at Apple, Google, and JPMorgan Chase. In part due to the school's small size and location, recruiting or on-campus interviewing visits from major employers are not frequent occurrences, and the school does not host a major job fair. Unfortunately, LU does not publicize data such as the percentage of students who land an internship, the number of in-person counseling sessions per year, or information about employers visiting campus. In the absence of such information and given the low starting salaries of recent graduates, it appears that some improvement may be needed in those areas.

Professional Outcomes

Of the 328 graduates in the Class of 2018 (most recent year available), an impressive 99 percent had already reached their next employment or postsecondary destination. Among the 59 percent of that group who had landed their first jobs, business/finance, social services/nonprofit, the arts, health care/pharmaceutical, and media/communications were the most popular industries. Companies presently employing more than a dozen Lawrence alumni include Deloitte, Epic Systems, Wells Fargo, Northwestern Mutual, US Bank, and UnitedHealth Group. Most students continue to reside in the Midwest after graduating. Greater Chicago; Oshkosh, Wisconsin; Greater Minneapolis-St. Paul; and Greater Milwaukee boast the greatest number of alums.

Over the last few years graduates have gone on to master's and doctoral programs at a wide range of universities on the prestige spectrum. Highlighting that list are elite schools Carnegie Mellon, Duke, Dartmouth, Emory, Georgetown, University of Pennsylvania, and Washington University in St. Louis. Medical school acceptance rates fluctuate between 67 and 75 percent, significantly higher than the national average, even in down years. Recent graduates have matriculated into medical schools at Johns Hopkins, the University of Chicago, Northwestern, Boston University, and the University of Wisconsin. According to the National Science Foundation, Lawrence produces the fourteenth most future science and engineering PhDs among liberal arts colleges.

Admission

t's hard to find a school of better quality that has a greater acceptance rate than Lawrence's 62 percent. The university is trending in a more selective direction as the admit rate was an even more generous 70+ percent five years ago, but chances remain strong, even for less-than-perfect high schoolers. While 39 percent did place in the top 10 percent of their graduating class and 38 percent possessed a GPA of greater than 3.75, many others brought more middling credentials to the table. The average GPA for admitted students is 3.52, and 23 percent did not land in the top 25 percent of their high school cohort. This school does not require SATs or ACTs but, among those who elected to submit scores anyway, the mid-50 percent range was 1230-1400 on the SAT and 25-32 on the ACT.

Lawrence was early to the test-optional party, jettisoning mandatory standardized test submission in 2006. As a result, GPA, rigor of coursework, class rank, talent/ability, and character/personal qualities are perched atop the list of most important factors. The admissions essay, recommendations, extracurricular activities, and an interview, which is recommended but not required, make up the second rung of "important factors." Few apply early decision; only forty-nine did so in 2019, and thirty-five were accepted. A safety school for many applying to even more prestigious Midwestern liberal arts institutions, only 18 percent of those admitted actually enroll. Thus, it is advantageous to communicate your genuine interest in attending throughout the application process.

Worth Your Money?

The sticker price (including room and board and all fees) at Lawrence is $61,935, but few receive an annual bill for that amount. Just under two-thirds of undergraduates receive need-based aid for an average of $39,000, and the university meets 94 percent of demonstrated need. Because the most commonly studied fields at LU are not among the highest paying, students need to adjust the value of loans they are willing to take out accordingly. That said, this school provides an amazing educational experience, particularly for those interested in performance and academia, and it typically provides enough financial aid to make a Lawrence degree affordable.

FINANCIAL
Institutional Type: Private
In-State Tuition: $50,958
Out-of-State Tuition: $50,958
Room & Board: $10,977
Required Fees: $0
Books & Supplies: $900

Avg. Need-Based Grant: $38,805
Avg. % of Need Met: 94%

Avg. Merit-Based Award: $27,671
% Receiving (All Freshmen): 49%
% Receiving (Freshmen w/o Need): 35%

Avg. Cumulative Debt: $28,828
% of Students Borrowing: 53%

CAREER
Who Recruits
1. M3 Insurance
2. Enterprise Holdings
3. Hauser Advertising
4. McAdam Financial
5. Air Wisconsin Airlines, LLC

Notable Internships
1. American Museum of Natural History
2. Uber
3. EY

Top Industries
1. Education
2. Business
3. Operations
4. Arts & Design
5. Social Services

Top Employers
1. US Bank
2. Epic
3. Northwestern Mutual
4. Target
5. Wells Fargo

Where Alumni Work
1. Chicago
2. Oshkosh, WI
3. Minneapolis
4. Milwaukee
5. New York City

Median Earnings
College Scorecard (Early Career): $44,100
PayScale (Early Career): $54,800
PayScale (Mid-Career): $112,600

RANKINGS
Money: 275
U.S. News: 63 (T), Liberal Arts Colleges
Wall Street Journal/THE: 167
Washington Monthly: 143, Liberal Arts Colleges

COLLEGE OVERLAPS
Beloit College
Grinnell College
Macalester College
Oberlin College
St. Olaf College

Lehigh University

Bethlehem, Pennsylvania | 610-758-3100

ADMISSION
Admission Rate: 32%
Admission Rate - Men: 29%
Admission Rate - Women: 36%
EA Admission Rate: Not Offered
ED Admission Rate: 66%
ED Admits as % of Total Admits: 15%
Admission Rate (5-Year Trend): -2%
% of Admits Attending (Yield): 28%
Transfer Admission Rate: 23%

SAT Reading/Writing (Middle 50%): 620-690
SAT Math (Middle 50%): 660-760
ACT Composite (Middle 50%): 29-33

% Graduated in Top 10% of HS Class: 58%
% Graduated in Top 25% of HS Class: 85%
% Graduated in Top 50% of HS Class: 97%

Demonstrated Interest: Important
Legacy Status: Considered
Admission Interview Offered: Yes

ENROLLMENT
Total Undergraduate Enrollment: 5,178
% Part-Time: 1%
% Male: 54%
% Female: 46%
% Out-of-State: 73%
% Fraternity: 26%
% Sorority: 37%
% On-Campus (Freshman): 99%
% On-Campus (All Undergraduate): 61%

% African-American: 4%
% Asian: 8%
% Hispanic: 9%
% White: 62%
% Other: 4%
% Race or Ethnicity Unknown: 4%
% International: 9%
% Low-Income: 14%

ACADEMICS
Student-to-Faculty Ratio: 9 to 1
% of Classes Under 20: 51%
% of Classes 20-49: 39%
% of Classes 50 or More: 10%
% Full-Time Faculty: 77%
% Full-Time Faculty w/ Terminal Degree: 95%

Top Programs
Accounting
Computer Science
Earth and Environmental Sciences
Engineering
Finance
International Relations
Psychology

Retention Rate: 93%
4-Year Graduation Rate: 80%
6-Year Graduation Rate: 90%

Curricular Flexibility: Somewhat Flexible
Academic Rating: ★★★★✓

#CollegesWorthYourMoney

Emblematic of the American economy as a whole, the once great industrial town of Bethlehem, Pennsylvania, is now highlighted by a research university known for preparing the next generation of problem-solving engineers. Lehigh University is a research powerhouse that caters to only 5,178 undergraduate students, allowing for lots of individualized attention from expert faculty in world-class facilities. There are three colleges within the larger university: the College of Arts & Sciences, the College of Business & Economics, and the prestigious Rossin College of Engineering and Applied Sciences.

Inside the Classroom
Despite its modest size, Lehigh offers more than one hundred undergraduate degree programs and runs 2,300+ courses each school year. Academic requirements vary by school but, notably, none possess a foreign language mandate. In the College of Arts & Sciences students must complete two semesters of Composition & Literature, First-Year Seminar, one math course, and eight credits in each of the humanities, natural sciences, and social sciences. The core curricula in the College of Business & Economics includes foundational courses in decision-making and business principles as well as introductory coursework in accounting, economics, marketing, management, and finance (no matter which of those concentrations you choose). Lastly, all business students must complete a senior capstone project. Within the Rossin College of Engineering and Applied Science undergrads must knock out ten credits of English and economics and thirteen credits in the humanities. There are also two innovative programs that require a foray into other disciplines—the Integrated Business & Engineering Honors Program (IBE) and the Integrated Degree Engineering, Arts & Sciences Honors Programs (IDEAS).

Lehigh has a 9:1 student-to-faculty ratio, but classes aren't as tiny as one might expect with such favorable staffing numbers. The average class size is twenty-nine but, on the plus side, 51 percent of courses have enrollments of nineteen or fewer. Undergraduate research is commonplace, particularly within the engineering school. Each year, 40 percent of engineering students gain faculty-led research experience. Additionally, 43 percent of graduates engage in some type of international experience, whether it's a semester of academic study abroad or a foreign-based internship. Roughly half of those students took courses in one of 250 study abroad programs approved by the university.

With a highly ranked engineering school, it's easy to view Lehigh as primarily a techie haven. Surprisingly, the majority of students pursue other programs, with Lehigh's well-regarded business school drawing the most majors (34 percent). Competitive fellowship and scholarship programs look favorably upon the university. Twenty-one undergrads and alumni were awarded Gilman Scholarships in 2020, and multiple students win National Science Foundation Fellowships in a given year.

Outside the Classroom
Lehigh's three contiguous campuses account for 1,600 picturesque acres. Only 65 percent of students live on campus, and most of those are underclassmen who are required to reside in college-owned housing. The school plans to add 1,000 undergraduate students by 2026 and is presently building additional on-campus housing to accommodate the increased student population. Even with 35 percent of students living off campus, this is an incredibly involved student body with 99 percent involved in some type of extracurricular activity. Greek life is a powerful force with 37 percent of women joining sororities and 26 percent of men pledging a fraternity. On the athletics front, the Mountain Hawks compete in twenty-five intercollegiate sports, mostly in the NCAA Division I Patriot League. An additional forty-three intramural and club teams claim another 2,900 participants annually. On the non-sports front there are 200+ student organizations at Lehigh and over 250 art events on campus annually. Service-oriented clubs are popular and account for 65,000 collective hours of community service per year. Bethlehem is known more for its industrial history as a hub of steel production than for a thrilling nightlife, but students with a car can get to Philly in an hour and a half or New York City in a little over two hours.

Career Services
The Center for Career and Professional Development (CCPD) is staffed by thirteen professional employees (not counting student interns) who work in career counseling, employer engagement, or graduate school advising. That 398:1 student-to-advisor ratio is within the average range of universities profiled in this guide. Yet, by almost any metric, the level of support offered to the school's undergraduates is of superior quality.

The CCPD entices more than 6,900 attendees to its events (more than the entire undergraduate population). The fall and spring career expos draw large student crowds and are attended by as many as 140 employers, including many major corporations. Counselors hold almost 2,500 one-on-one advising sessions and achieve 12,000+ total engagements through in-person and online interaction. Perhaps most impressive is the number of on-campus interviews conducted per year—2,700+—more than double the number of graduating seniors. Lehigh's career services staff also does a superb job facilitating internships and other valuable immersive experiences. An exceptional 94 percent of Class of 2019 members completed at least one internship or externship. Lehigh's Center for Career and Professional Development provides a top-notch level of service to its undergraduate clientele, and those efforts translate into stellar employment and graduate school outcome.

Professional Outcomes

The Class of 2019 quickly found its way toward the next productive step in their lives with 95 percent landing jobs or grad school placements within six months of leaving Lehigh. Among graduates of the School of Business and Economics, the top industries entered by graduates were financial services, accounting, consulting, and marketing. Top employers of recent business degree earners include Amazon, CitiGroup, Deloitte, EY, KPMG, Morgan Stanley, and PwC. Rossin College of Engineering and Applied Science graduates flocked to companies such as ExxonMobil, GE, Google, IBM, Lockheed Martin, Merck, and Microsoft. Arts & Sciences graduates secured employment at places like CBS, People Magazine, and the National Institutes of Health. Across all three schools, the average starting salary was $67,000 with computer science majors on the high end at $88k and math and natural sciences majors on the low end at $53k.

Among recent diploma-earners heading straight to graduate/professional school, 31 percent were studying engineering, 24 percent were pursuing business degrees, 10 percent were training for health professions, and 4 percent had entered law school. In a typical year, a phenomenal 90+ percent of medical school applicants earn at least one acceptance. That cohort possessed an average GPA of 3.7 and MCAT scores in the 85th percentile. Recent med school acceptances included Boston University School of Medicine, Harvard School of Dental Medicine, and Johns Hopkins School of Medicine. Over the past three years, law school applicants were successful 93 percent of the time and were welcomed by institutions such as the University of Pennsylvania, Tulane, Temple, and Villanova. Those pursuing a master's or a PhD from the Class of 2019 did so at Columbia, Duke, Stanford, Berkeley, Brown, Johns Hopkins, and a number of other first-class universities.

Admission

Lehigh had an all-time low 22 percent acceptance rate for those jockeying for a spot in the Class of 2022. Fortunately, for prospective students, this rose up to 32 percent for the Class of 2023. Freshmen entering Lehigh for the 2019-20 school year possessed middle-50 percent scores of 1300-1430 on the SAT and 29-33 on the ACT. Fifty-eight percent of entering freshmen in 2019-20 placed in the top decile of their high school class, and 85 percent were in the top quartile.

Six factors sit perched atop the list of criteria considered by the Lehigh admissions committee: rigor of courses, class rank, GPA, recommendations, talent/ability, and character/personal qualities. The next rung of factors deemed "important" include standardized test scores, essays, extracurricular activities, volunteer work, and demonstrated interest. On the subject of demonstrated interest, Lehigh places high value on an applicant's level of commitment to attending the university. To quantify that importance, early decision applicants are admitted at a rate of 66 percent, more than double the acceptance rate during the regular cycle. Early decision applicants comprised 54 percent of the incoming class. Women face slightly better odds, sporting an acceptance rate 7 percent higher than male applicants.

Worth Your Money?

Those who don't qualify for financial aid will not receive much help from Lehigh—fewer than 10 percent of attendees receive merit aid. Fortunately, the $72k annual cost of attendance is knocked down significantly for undergraduates who qualify for need-based aid; many see 100 percent of their demonstrated need met by the university, and the average annual grant is for $48k. With extremely high starting salaries, this school is likely to pay you back, particularly if you major in the business/engineering realm.

FINANCIAL
Institutional Type: Private
In-State Tuition: $55,260
Out-of-State Tuition: $55,260
Room & Board: $14,740
Required Fees: $0
Books & Supplies: $1,000

Avg. Need-Based Grant: $48,666
Avg. % of Need Met: 98%

Avg. Merit-Based Award: $9,909
% Receiving (All Freshmen): 10%
% Receiving (Freshmen w/o Need): 4%

Avg. Cumulative Debt: $39,609
% of Students Borrowing: 50%

CAREER
Who Recruits
1. Knowles Corporation
2. Mineral Technologies Inc.
3. SIG
4. Tge LiRo Group
5. Crayola

Notable Internships
1. Prudenial Financial
2. Barclays
3. Visa

Top Industries
1. Business
2. Engineering
3. Education
4. Operations
5. Research

Top Employers
1. Merck
2. EY
3. PwC
4. IBM
5. Deloitte

Where Alumni Work
1. New York City
2. Allentown, PA
3. Philadelphia
4. Boston
5. Washington DC

Median Earnings
College Scorecard (Early Career): $81,900
PayScale (Early Career): $72,300
PayScale (Mid-Career): $144,500

RANKINGS
Money: 110
U.S. News: 49 (T), National Universities
Wall Street Journal/THE: 58
Washington Monthly: 65, National Universities

COLLEGE OVERLAPS
Cornell University
Bucknell University
Lafayette College
Pennsylvania State University - University Park
University of Michigan

Loyola Marymount University

Los Angeles, California | 310-338-2750

ADMISSION
Admission Rate: 44%
Admission Rate - Men: 45%
Admission Rate - Women: 43%
EA Admission Rate: 62%
ED Admission Rate: 44%
ED Admits as % of Total Admits: 2%
Admission Rate (5-Year Trend): -9%
% of Admits Attending (Yield): 18%
Transfer Admission Rate: 36%

SAT Reading/Writing (Middle 50%): 620-700
SAT Math (Middle 50%): 610-710
ACT Composite (Middle 50%): 27-31

% Graduated in Top 10% of HS Class: 47%
% Graduated in Top 25% of HS Class: 79%
% Graduated in Top 50% of HS Class: 98%

Demonstrated Interest: Not Considered
Legacy Status: Considered
Admission Interview Offered: Yes

ENROLLMENT
Total Undergraduate Enrollment: 6,778
% Part-Time: 3%
% Male: 45%
% Female: 55%
% Out-of-State: 33%
% Fraternity: 20%
% Sorority: 26%
% On-Campus (Freshman): 94%
% On-Campus (All Undergraduate): 47%

% African-American: 7%
% Asian: 10%
% Hispanic: 23%
% White: 43%
% Other: 7%
% Race or Ethnicity Unknown: 0%
% International: 11%
% Low-Income: 19%

ACADEMICS
Student-to-Faculty Ratio: 10 to 1
% of Classes Under 20: 55%
% of Classes 20-49: 45%
% of Classes 50 or More: 1%
% Full-Time Faculty: 50%
% Full-Time Faculty w/ Terminal Degree: 96%

Top Programs
Film and Television Production
Engineering
Entrepreneurship
Finance
Marketing
Screenwriting
Theatre Arts

Retention Rate: 89%
4-Year Graduation Rate: 73%
6-Year Graduation Rate: 80%

Curricular Flexibility: Less Flexible
Academic Rating: ★★★↓

#CollegesWorthYourMoney

If you encounter a map of all of the four-year colleges and universities in the United States (possibly on your counselor's wall, next to the "Hang in there" cat poster), you'll notice that the Greater Los Angeles area is blown up in its own special window; there are simply too many excellent schools concentrated in this area to label them all without first zooming in. Given this reality, Loyola Marymount University, a midsize Jesuit school of roughly 6,800 undergraduate students, sometimes fails to get the acclaim it deserves. In reality, those immersed in LMU's 60 majors and 55 minors are doing so at an institution that is rising in the rankings.

Inside the Classroom
There are six undergraduate schools and colleges within the larger university: the Bellarmine College of Liberal Arts, the Frank R. Seaver College of Science and Engineering, the College of Communication & Fine Arts, the School of Film & Television, the College of Business Administration, and the School of Education. All Lions are required to take the same 13 courses that comprise the school's core. This includes First-Year Seminar, as well as a march through such areas as Rhetorical Arts; Quantitative Reasoning; Creative Experience; Faith and Reason; and Nature of Science, Technology, and Mathematics.

Faculty here are heralded for their warmth and accessibility, a sentiment backed by a 10:1 faculty-to-student ratio. Approximately 55 percent of courses enroll 19 or fewer students, and 99 percent enroll fewer than 39 individuals. Science laboratories are a noted point of pride, and research opportunities, in STEM as well as the humanities, are abundant. There are four programs through which students can access on-campus research opportunities, including the Summer Undergraduate Research Program. Each year, a healthy number of undergrads (usually 500+) elect to study abroad in more than 20 different countries including Ghana, the Netherlands, and New Zealand.

The greatest number of degrees conferred in 2019 were in the area of business/marketing (25 percent), followed by visual and performing arts (14 percent), communication/journalism (10 percent), psychology (8 percent), and engineering (5 percent). Programs in Film and Television, Theatre Arts, and Business typically receive the highest praise. LMU undergrads have begun to capture more prestigious national fellowships in recent years, taking home Goldwater and Gilman Scholarships in 2020 as well as Gates, Cambridge, and Fulbright Scholarships in 2019. A steady flow of seniors is also accepted into Teach for America each year.

Outside the Classroom
If you want a traditional, campus-centric college experience, then LMU is your place. A whopping 93 percent of undergraduate students reside on school grounds. There are 201 active student-run organizations, including many in the realm of community service. The school's Jesuit influence places strong emphasis on volunteering, and the student body contributes 200,000 service hours annually. Naturally, being such a strong school for film and television, ROAR, the school's television network, is an award winner. The school is also one of the more eco-friendly around, regularly cited by environmental organizations for its commitment in areas such as recycling and solar rooftops. Loyola Marymount athletics features 21 men's and women's Division I sports teams that compete within the West Coast Conference. Greek life is quite popular, attracting 20 percent of men and 26 percent of women; there are 23 total combined frats and sororities. No one complains about the university's location in the Westside area of Los Angeles, overlooking the picturesque Playa Vista. The 142-acre grounds easily place on just about every list you can find of "Most Beautiful Campuses." Lovely Manhattan Beach is only 5-15 minutes away from the dorms.

Career Services
With 13 professional employees in its Career and Professional Development (CPD) office, Loyola Marymount offers a 521:1 counselor-to-student ratio, within the average range compared to other midsize universities featured in this guide. There are an additional 10+ peer advisors and seven graduate assistants that make regular one-on-one connections a genuine possibility. Staff are always happy to help with career exploration, resume development, internship assistance, interview prep, and more. The office affords students access to over 500,000 companies via Handshake and offers a number of special events like Career Chats, Pathways in Entertainment, Seaver Connect, and a Gradate Summit for those interested in pursuing a career in academia.

In general, more than two thirds of LMU students land internships, which many take for credit. An impressive, 74 percent of the Class of 2019 completed one or more such experiences. The school's location near Silicon Beach gives prime access to tech giants as well as over 500 start-ups. The annual Career Expo draws 100+ employers to campus, including the LA Clippers, Warner Music Group, Wells Fargo, Honda, and PlayStation. Motivated students can also embark on Career Treks through New York, Seattle, and the Bay Area. An involved alumni network, 30,000 strong, is available to help with mentorship, internships, or just an informal career exploration session. Thanks to its connected alumni, employer outreach, and strong internship coordination, the CPD appears to be doing its job in launching successful grads.

Professional Outcomes

Just 3 percent of Loyola graduates were still looking for work six months after completing their degrees. Seventy-six percent had procured employment, 17 percent were in graduate school, and four percent were engaged in some type of service program. By sector, 83 percent entered for-profit companies, 7 percent joined nonprofit organizations, and 5 percent were hired by government agencies. Many of the top tech, accounting, and entertainment companies presently employ more than 50 Lions. These include Northrop Grumman, Google, Netflix, Amazon, NBCUniversal Media, Apple, PwC, Sony Pictures Entertainment, Facebook, EY, and Salesforce. It's no wonder that the most common income bracket for grads to find themselves in is 60k+. Roughly 60 percent of alumni remain in the Greater Los Angeles area. The next most popular destinations are San Francisco, Orange County, San Diego, and New York.

Recent alumni have gone on to further their education in a range of disciplines at the University of Chicago, Stanford University, NYU, and Georgetown University. In the last three years, premed students have been admitted into medical schools such as Duke University School of Medicine, the David Geffen School of Medicine at UCLA, Saint Louis University School of Medicine, and Harvard Medical School, along with countless other top institutions. From 2015-2019, a healthy 72 percent of applicants with a committee letter ultimately matriculated into medical school. Those on a prelaw track have found homes at law schools such as Boston College, UC-Davis, and the University of Southern California, as well as Loyola's own well-regarded legal training ground.

Admission

With an acceptance rate of 44 percent, LMU rejected more applicants than it accepted for the second straight admissions cycle. This group sported an average GPA of 3.9, and 47 percent of those enrolled in the Class of 2023 placed in the top decile of their high school class; 79 percent were in the top quartile, and 98 percent were in the top half. On standardized tests, this cohort possessed mid-50th percentile scores of 1250-1400 on the SAT and 27-31 on the ACT. Nearly 45 percent of ACT test takers earned a composite score of 30 or above. For perspective, five years ago, the freshman class had a significantly lower SAT range of 1100-1300. At that time, only 36 percent of the entering class placed in the top decile of their high school cohort.

Academic GPA is the lone factor rated as "very important" in rendering admissions decisions. Coming in as "important" were the rigor of an applicant's coursework, standardized test scores, application essay, talent/ ability, and character/personal qualities. Class rank, recommendation letters, extracurricular activities, first-generation status, legacy status (134 of incoming Lions in 2019-20 were legacies), volunteer work, and paid work experience are "considered." Students have the option to apply via the Common App, Coalition App, or directly through the LMU Online App. Seniors have the option to apply by November 1, either as an early action or early decision applicant. Somewhat surprisingly, there was little advantage to applying early for a place in the Class of 2023; just 44 percent were accepted, identical to the overall applicant pool.

Worth Your Money?

An LMU education won't come cheap for many as the estimated COA for the 2020-21 school year was $72,186. Fortunately, thanks to strong financial aid support, families making under $75,000 rarely pay more than half of that total. Strong starting salaries for the majority of graduates also help to ensure positive financial outcomes postgraduation. Only 1.8 percent of alumni end up defaulting on their loans compared to 10.1 percent nationally, a positive indicator that the school's grads are succeeding in the real world. For those entering business, a tech field, or the film/television industry, LMU is very likely to be worth the cost of attendance.

FINANCIAL
Institutional Type: Private
In-State Tuition: $51,820
Out-of-State Tuition: $51,820
Room & Board: $15,485
Required Fees: $1,157
Books & Supplies: $1,080

Avg. Need-Based Grant: $23,161
Avg. % of Need Met: 68%

Avg. Merit-Based Award: $11,045
% Receiving (All Freshmen): 50%
% Receiving (Freshmen w/o Need): 40%

Avg. Cumulative Debt: $33,742
% of Students Borrowing: 49%

CAREER
Who Recruits
1. Disney
2. Kaiser Permanente
3. Morgan Stanley
4. AT&T
5. Epson

Notable Internships
1. Tesla
2. 3M
3. LucasFilm

Top Industries
1. Business
2. Education
3. Operations
4. Media
5. Sales

Top Employers
1. LA Unified School District
2. Teach for America
3. Northrop Grumman
4. Google
5. Amazon

Where Alumni Work
1. Los Angeles
2. San Francisco
3. Orange County, CA
4. San Diego
5. New York City

Median Earnings
College Scorecard (Early Career): $61,300
PayScale (Early Career): $60,800
PayScale (Mid-Career): $127,100

RANKINGS
Money: 340
U.S. News: 66 (T), National Universities
Wall Street Journal/THE: 89 (T)
Washington Monthly: 285, National Universities

COLLEGE OVERLAPS
Chapman University
Santa Clara University
University of California, San Diego
University of California, Santa Barbara
University of San Diego

Baltimore, Maryland | 410-617-5012

ADMISSION
Admission Rate: 80%
Admission Rate - Men: 78%
Admission Rate - Women: 82%
EA Admission Rate: NR
ED Admission Rate: Not Offered
ED Admits as % of Total Admits: Not Offered
Admission Rate (5-Year Trend): +19%
% of Admits Attending (Yield): 13%
Transfer Admission Rate: 47%

SAT Reading/Writing (Middle 50%): 580-660
SAT Math (Middle 50%): 560-660
ACT Composite (Middle 50%): 25-30

% Graduated in Top 10% of HS Class: 30%
% Graduated in Top 25% of HS Class: 60%
% Graduated in Top 50% of HS Class: 91%

Demonstrated Interest: Considered
Legacy Status: Considered
Admission Interview Offered: No

ENROLLMENT
Total Undergraduate Enrollment: 3,925
% Part-Time: 1%
% Male: 42%
% Female: 58%
% Out-of-State: 80%
% Fraternity: Not Offered
% Sorority: Not Offered
% On-Campus (Freshman): 97%
% On-Campus (All Undergraduate): 81%

% African-American: 5%
% Asian: 3%
% Hispanic: 12%
% White: 76%
% Other: 3%
% Race or Ethnicity Unknown: 0%
% International: 1%
% Low-Income: 14%

ACADEMICS
Student-to-Faculty Ratio: 12 to 1
% of Classes Under 20: 51%
% of Classes 20-49: 48%
% of Classes 50 or More: 1%
% Full-Time Faculty: 75%
% Full-Time Faculty w/ Terminal Degree: 78%

Top Programs
Accounting
Communication
Education
Finance
Management
Speech-Language-Hearing Sciences

Retention Rate: 87%
4-Year Graduation Rate: 79%
6-Year Graduation Rate: 82%

Curricular Flexibility: Less Flexible
Academic Rating: ★★★

#CollegesWorthYourMoney

College consumers can sometimes find the Loyola brand hard to grasp. After all, there is Loyola University Chicago, Loyola University New Orleans, Loyola Marymount University in Los Angeles, and the school we are profiling here—Loyola University Maryland—and none of the schools is affiliated in any way with the others. While all honor St. Ignatius, the Jesuit founder, Loyola University Maryland is its own distinct entity and is a rare school where the acceptance rate and four-year graduation rate both hover around 80 percent. Offering thirty-five undergraduate programs through its three schools, Loyola College (arts and sciences), the Sellinger School of Business and Management, and the School of Education, Loyola services an undergraduate population of 3,925, only 20 percent of whom are Maryland residents.

Inside the Classroom
Consistent with the Jesuit ideology of cura personalis, Loyola has created a liberal arts curriculum designed to help develop the whole person and produce well-rounded citizens. This extensive seventeen-course set of requirements includes writing, history, literature, foreign language, social sciences, fine arts, mathematics, theology, philosophy, ethics, and diversity. Students in the small-but-excellent Honors Program follow an identical path but complete their core curriculum within honors-only sections.

A 12:1 student-to-faculty ratio leads to average class sizes of only twenty students. The vast majority of courses enroll between ten and twenty-nine students, 10 percent have a single-digit enrollment, and of 866 total sections only eleven contained forty or more undergraduates. Students are encouraged to apply for undergraduate research opportunities such as the Hauber Summer Research Fellowship Program which, in 2019, gave fourteen students in the natural and applied sciences fields a chance to conduct ten weeks of independent research. Biology majors can enroll in two courses that facilitate experiential research opportunities. Those with wanderlust will find plenty of kindred spirits and no shortage of options; there are twenty countries that students can choose from as study abroad options, and the participation rate exceeds 60 percent, one of the highest figures of any master's-granting school in the nation.

Two-fifths of the degrees conferred are in the area of business/marketing, making it, by far, the school's most popular area of concentration. Next are communication/journalism (11 percent), the social sciences (9 percent), psychology (7 percent), and biology (7 percent). The Sellinger School of Business and Management has a solid reputation beyond the immediate region, and the Department of Communication has an excellent record of placing students within media organizations. The school's push for international study translated to a record number of Fulbright Scholars in 2019 with eight winners. Additionally, three current students captured Gilman Scholarships.

Outside the Classroom
If you are looking for a school where just about everyone lives in a tightknit community on campus, then the Loyola Maryland experience is for you. Freshmen occupy university-owned dorms at a 97 percent clip, and 81 percent of the total student body resides on this 81-acre wooded campus that isn't what you'd expect to find in the middle of Baltimore. Loyola's seventeen residence halls are some of the best-rated college accommodations in the entire country. As is the case at many Jesuit institutions, there are no sororities or fraternities at this school, but there are 200+ clubs, including seventeen community service organizations, fourteen dance groups, and twelve honors societies. Service is popular as 80 percent of the student body engages in some type of charitable endeavor. Religion plays a major role as students are predominately Catholic—27 percent attended Catholic high schools. The gender split on campus is approaching 60/40 in favor of women. Loyola has a strong athletics program that features eighteen NCAA Division I teams that play in the Patriot League. Johns Hopkins is its biggest rival, and the annual lacrosse showdown is a big deal. There are also twenty-six club teams, and 20 percent of students participate in intramural leagues. Recreational amenities include a ten-lane pool, rock climbing wall, and indoor track. Not known as a big party school, there are plenty of safe commercial pockets in the city of Baltimore worth exploring, and DC is only an hour away for weekend trips.

Career Services
The Career Center at Loyola Maryland is manned by nine professionals with expertise in career counseling and employer outreach. That works out to a 436:1 student-to-advisor ratio, which is within the average range of colleges featured in this guide. This office keeps careful track of its own statistics that paint a picture of a supportive and highly available career services staff offering ample opportunity to connect with relevant employers.

Loyola University Maryland

E-mail: admissions@loyola.edu | Website: www.loyola.edu

In the 2018-19 school year the office held 1,927 counseling appointments, and attracted 2,096 students to networking events, workshops, career fairs, and information sessions. For a small university, it's highly impressive that over 100 companies and organizations interviewed seniors on campus. In total, 158 unique employers visited campus. A helpful alumni base 60,000+ strong is also willing to lend a hand to those about to launch their careers. If you're looking to land a position far from Baltimore, Loyola Marymount's Career Center has reciprocity with twenty-eight other Jesuit institution's career centers around the country. The school also has forged many strong internship partners. For example, within the Department of Writing, partners include nine publications and ten nonprofits that regularly take Loyola interns. Career fairs enjoyed official sponsors such as Bank of America, Dixon Hughes Goodman (the largest accounting firm in the South), and CareFirst BlueCross BlueShield. In sum, the Loyola Career Center directly connects with more than half of the undergraduate student body each year and facilitates a solid number of industry connections, making it a highly useful resource for all current students.

Professional Outcomes

Members of the Class of 2019 found their way to their next employment, volunteer, or grad school home within six months of receiving their diplomas at a stellar 98 percent clip. Major companies and organizations employing members of this cohort include Accenture, Booz Allen Hamilton, Bloomberg, Goldman Sachs, NASA, the National Institutes of Health, the New York Giants (NFL), Sony/ATV Music Publishing, and Walt Disney Company. Employers of the overall greatest number of alumni include T. Rowe Price, Northrup Grumman, Morgan Stanley, JPMorgan Chase, PwC, EY, Black & Decker, and Deloitte. The average starting salary for a Loyola graduate is $54,150 with humanities majors bringing home a mean salary of $44k and degree-earners in the natural and applied sciences averaging $64k. Baltimore, New York City, DC, Philly, and Boston woo the most Greyhound alumni.

Twenty-two percent of the members of the Class of 2019 immediately enrolled in graduate or professional school after completing their undergraduate work at Loyola Maryland. Some members earned a spot at elite graduate institutions like Brown, Columbia, Duke, Northwestern, and the University of Pennsylvania. Over the last decade, the percentage of successful law school applicants has vacillated between 77 percent and 93 percent, and Loyola grads are currently pursuing their legal education at Villanova, George Washington, UC Berkeley, and the University of Maryland. From 2015-2019 medical school applicants who obtained a committee letter supporting their candidacy enjoyed a 72 percent acceptance rate. Recent acceptances include some of the top medical schools in the country such as Boston University, Tufts, Harvard, and Georgetown.

Admission

Getting into Loyola is not a harrowing process, even if you hit a few bumps along your academic road. The acceptance rate for a place in the Class of 2023 was an unintimidating 80 percent, and that doesn't show any signs of falling as the school has only a 13 percent yield rate; in other terms, 87 percent of those who are accepted ultimately enroll at another institution. Loyola is test-optional, but most 2019-20 freshman submitted scores—63 percent included SATs and 25 percent included ACTs as part of their applications. The mid-50 percent scores were 25-30 on the ACT and 1150-1320 on the SAT. The average high school GPA earned by entering members of this class was 3.62, and while 30 percent ranked in the top decile of their graduating class and 60 percent were in the top quartile, 9 percent did not even rank in the top 50 percent.

This committee means what it says when it declares that it does "not use a formula or have strict cutoffs. Instead, the admission office's goal is to conduct a balanced and individual review, taking a number of factors into account." At the top of that list are GPA, rigor of secondary school record, recommendations, the essay, and character/personal qualities. Extracurricular activities, volunteer work, and talent/ability also receive strong consideration. Loyola is a school where bright but perhaps late-blooming teens can find a welcoming institution that will offer a top-notch Jesuit education.

Worth Your Money?

Living on campus brings the total annual sticker price to a more than $65,000, a steep price to pay for any school. At that cost, it is hard to justify attending Loyola University Maryland if you are in a situation where you will need to take out large loans; the average Greyhound's debt is over $41,000. However, it is worth applying to see what kind of aid package you receive. Freshmen in 2019-20 who qualified for some type of aid averaged a package north of $20,000. If the total cost of attendance is comparable to other institutions to which you are accepted, a degree from this university can certainly make it worth your money.

FINANCIAL
Institutional Type: Private
In-State Tuition: $49,700
Out-of-State Tuition: $49,700
Room & Board: $15,820
Required Fees: $1,565
Books & Supplies: $1,250

Avg. Need-Based Grant: $17,382
Avg. % of Need Met: 85%

Avg. Merit-Based Award: $20,008
% Receiving (All Freshmen): 72%
% Receiving (Freshmen w/o Need): 33%

Avg. Cumulative Debt: $41,443
% of Students Borrowing: 63%

CAREER
Who Recruits
1. Legg Mason
2. Baltimore Orioles
3. T. Rowe Price
4. Cisco
5. Stanley Black & Decker

Notable Internships
1. LGT Capital Partners
2. National Bank of Canada
3. Fidelity Investments

Top Industries
1. Business
2. Education
3. Operations
4. Finance
5. Sales

Top Employers
1. T. Rowe Price
2. Northrop Grumman
3. Morgan Stanley
4. JPMorgan Chase
5. PwC

Where Alumni Work
1. Baltimore
2. New York City
3. Washington DC
4. Philadelphia
5. Boston

Median Earnings
College Scorecard (Early Career): $68,100
PayScale (Early Career): $61,500
PayScale (Mid-Career): $122,800

RANKINGS
Money: 365
U.S. News: 4, Regional Universities North
Wall Street Journal/THE: 220 (T)
Washington Monthly: 16, Master's Universities

COLLEGE OVERLAPS
Fairfield University
Fordham University
Providence College
University of Maryland, College Park
Villanova University

Macalester College

St. Paul, Minnesota | 651-696-6357

One might expect a small liberal arts school in Minnesota to be set in a remote tundra, its own little universe surrounded by a stark landscape and frigid air. In the case of Macalester College, the frigid air would be accurate, but this collection of 2,098 undergraduate students is a rarity in the liberal arts world—it is situated in the metropolis of St. Paul on the border of Minneapolis. While typically lagging slightly behind rival Carleton College in most rankings, Macalester is every bit in the same league, boasting a strong reputation for rigorous academics that draw 81 percent of the school's student body from outside Minnesota and a stunning 15 percent from ninety foreign countries.

Inside the Classroom
International students aren't flocking to Mac for the weather or Great Plains scenery; they are here for the academic reputation. Students can choose from thirty-nine majors and over 800 courses that are offered each academic year. Requirements for all students are fairly straightforward and include a first-year course that is a small, writing-intensive seminar, courses in each of the schools four divisions—Fine Arts, Humanities, Social Studies, and Natural Science and Mathematics, and courses in multiculturalism and internationalism. Perhaps the most notable mandate is in foreign language where proficiency equivalent to four semesters of study must be demonstrated.

Being an undergraduate-only institution, Macalester students enjoy the full benefits of the school's 10:1 student-to-faculty ratio. The average class size is only sixteen students, and 17 percent of class sections have single-digit enrollments. Only 1 percent of the overall courses contain more than forty students, so the chances are high that you will never be in a course where the professor does not know your name. That level of intimacy leads to plentiful chances for being part of faculty-led research, including through the Collaborative Summer Research Program that provides stipends for student-faculty research ventures. In total, 54 percent of students participate in some form of undergraduate research. Study abroad opportunities, typically twelve weeks in length, are taken advantage of by 60 percent of Macalester undergrads.

As an elite liberal arts institution with no attached graduate schools, Macalester possesses strong offerings across many different disciplines. Programs in economics, international studies, and mathematics are among the best anywhere. In addition, science majors of all varieties benefit from the school's strong reputation for premed and preparing future PhD scientists. Prestigious postgraduate fellowships are routinely awarded to Mac seniors. In the last decade, grads have walked away with 60+ Fulbright Scholarships, including seven such awards in 2020 alone. In that same time, students and alumni have procured a Rhodes Scholar, 40+ National Science Foundation Fellowships, as well as a number of Watson Fellowships, Goldwater Scholarships, and Truman Scholarships.

Outside the Classroom
Due to limited availability of college-owned housing, only 62 percent of Macalester students live on campus. However, 100 percent of freshmen live in one of four residence halls for first-years; sophomores, who are also required to live on campus, have their own dorms as well. There is no Greek life here, so undergrads find other ways to forge deep bonds. With twenty-one sports teams and roughly 400 student-athletes, one-quarter of the student population dons a Scots jersey as they compete in NCAA Division III. Intramurals and club teams also draw heavy participation, leading to a majority of Mac students being involved in some type of formalized athletics. There are also ninety-nine student-run organizations, including eleven musical ensembles, student theater groups with 125 participants, three student publications, including the popular Mac Weekly, and a campus radio station, WMCN. The LGBTQ+ population on campus is notably large—25 percent identify in that category. This cozy 53-acre campus provides ample activity, but access to the city nightlife is quite easy by car. The Mall of America is less than a fifteen-minute drive from the college, and students also enjoy Minnesota's pro sports scene, museums, restaurants, and nightlife.

Career Services
The Career Development Center is staffed by eleven professionals, equating to a student-to-advisor ratio of 191:1, significantly better than the average college included in this book. That level of support allows the CDC to implement its four-phase process of "explore, design, connect, launch" that ultimately results in favorable outcomes for graduates. Events such as the fall and spring career fairs are small in scale—the fall 2018 Career Fair was attended by thirty-five employers. In the 2018-19 school year, it held 1,918 one-on-one advising appointments and enticed 103 employers to recruit on campus.

Macalester College

E-mail: admissions@macalester.edu | Website: www.macalester.edu

Internships and/or mentored research experiences are enjoyed by 72 percent of Macalester undergraduates. Internships, specifically, are obtained and completed by 60 percent of students. In a given year, almost 400 students engage in credit-bearing internships at organizations as varied as the US Department of State, EY, Minnesota Public Radio, the New York University School of Medicine, and Lockheed Martin. This strong internship program sets up students for a successful transition into a meaningful first job. Among 2019 grads who found employment within six months of leaving, 92 percent said their first job was congruent with their interests. While Macalester grads do not all go on to earn high starting salaries, they do find fulfilling jobs aligned with their interests and have success entering and completing top graduate/professional degree programs.

Professional Outcomes

Six months after graduating, 93 percent of the Macalester Class of 2019 had found employment, graduate school, or a fellowship. Sixty-one percent of those finding employment landed with for-profit corporations, 17 percent with nonprofit organizations, 14 percent with educational institutions, and 8 percent with federal, state, or local government. Employers of recent grads include ABC News, Google, Goldman Sachs, Dow Chemical Company, McKinsey & Company, the ACLU, the National Cancer Institute, and National Geographic. Across all sectors, the average starting salary was $53,000. Geographically, 46 percent of grads elected to stay in the North Star State while many others migrated to the East Coast (16 percent), West Coast (12 percent) or overseas (8 percent).

Graduates from 2012-2017 most frequently attended graduate schools such as the University of Washington – Seattle, University of Wisconsin – Madison, Harvard, Georgetown, NYU, and Johns Hopkins. In those same years, 100 percent of Macalester grads who applied to graduate school received at least one acceptance. From 2007-2016 the college ranked fourteenth among liberal arts schools with the most grads who went on to earn PhDs. Among students with at least a 3.5 GPA and decent MCAT scores, 90 percent were admitted to at least one medical school. Recent medical school acceptances include Tufts University, Northwestern, Brown, and Washington University in St. Louis. The most popular medical school attended by alumni is the University of Minnesota – Twin Cities.

Admission

Macalester received just under 6,000 applications for admission into the Class of 2023, and it admitted 32 percent (down 9 percent from the previous year); of that group, 24 percent went on to enroll in the school. The profile of the average freshman who enrolls is a bit more down to earth with 64 percent in the top 10 percent of their high school class and a 33 ACT representing the 75th percentile. The mid-50 percent SAT range is 1330-1460.

The admissions committee ranks the rigor of one's secondary programming and GPA earned as the two most critical factors in the process. The second rung of still "important" factors is comprised of SAT/ACT scores, recommendations, essays, extracurricular activities, and character/personal qualities. Macalester insists that it does not consider demonstrated interest in the admissions process, an unusual move for a school with a relatively low yield rate (the percent of accepted students who go on to enroll). That being said, applying via early decision is a wise choice for those committed to attending the college as the ED acceptance rate is 58 percent. Attracting students from all fifty states and ninety countries, this school's Minnesota locale draws talented applicants from around the world. Lots of AP courses and excellent grades should set up candidates for success.

Worth Your Money?

Sixty-five percent of the Macalester student population receives need-based aid for an average grant of $44k per year. Unfortunately, if you don't qualify for need-based aid, do not expect much in the way of merit aid—most likely you'll be paying close to the full annual cost of attendance of $71,562. With so many graduates pursuing advanced degrees, average early career earnings aren't spectacular, but Mac is still a school with phenomenal long-term career outcomes, and a very wise investment for students who can afford the price without racking up higher-than-average debt.

FINANCIAL
Institutional Type: Private
In-State Tuition: $56,062
Out-of-State Tuition: $56,062
Room & Board: $12,592
Required Fees: $230
Books & Supplies: $1,191

Avg. Need-Based Grant: $43,693
Avg. % of Need Met: 100%

Avg. Merit-Based Award: $14,436
% Receiving (All Freshmen): 27%
% Receiving (Freshmen w/o Need): 20%

Avg. Cumulative Debt: $23,060
% of Students Borrowing: 59%

CAREER
Who Recruits
1. ScribeAmerica
2. ESRI
3. BMO Capital Markets
4. Twin Cities Public Television
5. Airbnb

Notable Internships
1. Minnesota Wild
2. U.S. Bank
3. U.S. House of Representatives

Top Industries
1. Business
2. Education
3. Social Services
4. Research
5. Operations

Top Employers
1. Wells Fargo
2. UnitedHealth Group
3. Target
4. Epic
5. 3M

Where Alumni Work
1. Minneapolis
2. New York City
3. San Francisco
4. Washington DC
5. Chicago

Median Earnings
College Scorecard (Early Career): $47,600
PayScale (Early Career): $56,700
PayScale (Mid-Career): $106,800

RANKINGS
Money: 235
U.S. News: 27, Liberal Arts Colleges
Wall Street Journal/THE: 77 (T)
Washington Monthly: 47, Liberal Arts Colleges

COLLEGE OVERLAPS
Brown University
Carleton College
Grinnell College
University of Chicago
Wesleyan University

Marist College

Poughkeepsie, New York | 845-575-3226

Competing for attention in the world of New York State institutions of higher education must feel like raising your hand to volunteer while surrounded by equally eager-to-contribute NBA centers. As a school serving 5,824 undergraduates, Marist College is overshadowed by smaller and more selective options that include Hamilton, Colgate, Vassar, and Skidmore as well as the more famous larger universities Cornell, Rochester, and Syracuse—and that's not even considering schools in New York City. Yet, there are many reasons you should get to know Marist, an accessible school for solid-but-imperfect high schoolers that succeeds in providing a world-class education to undergraduates who go on to land enviable internships with regularity, study abroad at exceptional rates and, as a whole, experience tremendous postgraduate success.

Inside the Classroom
Marist offers forty-seven distinct bachelor's programs but is ultimately a true liberal arts institution that requires its undergrads to complete a core curriculum. As freshmen, students engage in a first-year seminar and a course called Writing for College, both of which incorporate themes related to "Cultural Diversity, Nature & the Environment, Civic Engagement, and/or Quantitative Reasoning." There are thirty-six credits worth of distributional courses of study including ethics and justice, fine arts, history, literature, mathematics, natural science, philosophy, and social science. Additionally, although this can overlap with distributional requirements, students must also tackle a four-course "Pathway," choosing from twenty-three courses including African Diaspora Studies, Gender Studies, and Public Health Studies.

Marist has average class sizes in the eighteen to twenty-six range and a 16:1 student-to-faculty ratio—few sections are single-digit seminars or large lectures. On the less-than-ideal side, the majority of Marist's professors are adjuncts. On the plus side, undergrads enjoy the real-world knowledge brought by those non-tenure-track professors, and few complain about availability outside the classroom. Marist is supportive of undergraduate research, particularly in the hard sciences where completion of a research project is often a graduation requirement. Marist sees 50 percent of its students study abroad as part of the college's robust international program that is rated among the best in the country.

The School of Management and the School of Communication are quite popular as business and communication are, by far, Marist's two most commonly conferred degrees. They are also among Marist's strongest. It is also noteworthy that the School of Mathematics and Computer Science has had a joint study program with IBM for more than three decades. This intensive collaboration frequently leads to employment at IBM after graduation. With many grads entering corporate America, applications to prestigious national fellowship programs are sparse, but thirteen grads have won Fulbright Scholarships in the past five years; three students won in 2019.

Outside the Classroom
Two-thirds of the undergraduate population at Marist live on campus in a combination of corridor, suite, apartment, and townhouse-style residences. The 150+ acre campus is spectacularly set on the shores of the Hudson River. On the border of what arguably qualifies as "Upstate" New York, Poughkeepsie is about an hour and half drive from the heart of New York City. On campus, there are three fraternities and four sororities with around 300 members, giving Greek life a modest presence of roughly 3 percent of the undergraduate population. Playing in NCAA Division I, the Red Foxes field twenty-three varsity sports teams. For less serious athletes there are eleven club teams as well as an extensive intramural program that draws an incredible 65 percent of students. Overall, there are more than eighty student-run clubs and organizations. The Hudson Valley offers plenty worth exploring, from the ample natural beauty ripe for hiking and canoeing to the commerce of the popular Poughkeepsie Galleria Mall. While the school's Catholic origins are no longer officially linked to the school, the largest student group at Marist is the Campus Ministry that has a membership of 1,300 students. At 58 percent female, there is a noticeable gender gap at this school.

Career Services
The Center for Career Services (CCS) at Marist is staffed by five professionals with expertise in career coaching, employer relations, and graduate school advising. That works out to a 1,165:1 student-to-advisor ratio that is much higher than the average school in this guide. We do, however, take it as a positive sign that the Student Services Department (which includes the CCS) received a thumbs-up from 96 percent of grads. As the CCS states, "It's never too early to begin the process of learning how your interests and passions turn into long-term career aspirations." To back up that ideal, the CCS offers daily walk-in hours, scheduled one-on-one career counseling appointments, and weekly workshops on topics like resumes, cover letters, interviewing, and building a personal brand online.

Large events take place regularly, including the two annual Career and Internship Fairs. The fall 2018-19 fairs attracted 110 employers and 1,200+ students. An annual Graduate School Forum brings forty graduate and professional schools to campus to meet with prospective students. The CCS also maintains an active Alumni Career Network of former students in a variety of fields who are willing to volunteer their time to mentor. Efforts such as those lead to an extremely healthy 83 percent internship participation rate for Marist undergrads. In 2019, over 1,100 internships were completed at organizations including the Brooklyn Nets (NBA), CBS, Goldman Sachs, HBO, Morgan Stanley, Seventeen Magazine, and Madison Square Garden. Success in helping its students secure experiential and networking opportunities ends up leading to positive career and graduate school outcomes for the vast majority of students.

Professional Outcomes

Red Foxes strutting across the graduation stage in 2018 went on to find employment or a graduate school home at a terrific 98 percent rate by the time they filled out their first-destination survey. Major employers of Marist alums include IBM, which presently employees over 700 individuals, as well as JP Morgan Chase, EY, Macy's, Citi, Morgan Stanley, Deloitte, and NBC Universal Media. Members of the Class of 2019 headed to a number of media powerhouses including CNN, NBC Sports, and MSNBC as well as other major companies Adidas, Coach, Lockheed Martin, Northrup Grumman, and Moody's. The Greater New York City area draws approximately two-thirds of grads; Boston, Atlanta, Albany, and Hartford attract their own slivers of each graduating class. Midcareer median salaries are in the same range as other excellent schools in this guide such as UC Santa Barbara, Texas A&M, Colby, and American University.

The percent of Class of 2019 members pursuing graduate/professional degrees varied greatly across disciplines. Thirty-six percent of those in the School of Social & Behavioral Sciences enrolled in graduate school followed by the School of Science (20 percent), the School of Computer Science & Mathematics (7 percent), and the School of Liberal Arts (16 percent). In terms of selectivity, a wide range of institutions were attended including elite universities Cornell, Penn, Harvard, Columbia, and Oxford. Over the last decade, 70 percent of medical school applicants were accepted to at least one institution, a figure that is more than twenty-five points higher than the national average. Acceptances have included Georgetown Medical School, Albany Medical College, New York Medical College, SUNY Upstate Medical Center at Syracuse, Medical College of Virginia, and the Albert Einstein School of Medicine. Recent law school acceptances have included William & Mary, the University of Texas, and Northeastern University.

Admission

In 2019, Marist received over 11,000 applications, accepted 49 percent, and saw one-quarter of those accepted ultimately go on to enroll. The Class of 2023 possessed an average SAT score of 1236 and a 27 on the ACT. In the classroom, this cohort earned an average high school GPA of 3.3, and only 23 percent of its members placed in the top decile of their high school class. Not only can students gain acceptance into Marist without a pristine transcript, but the college also became test-optional back in 2011. In the years since it went test-optional, the average scores have predictably gone up a bit because those with lower scores simply do not submit. The other qualifications, such as GPA and class rank, have remained fairly constant over the last decade.

According to the admissions office Marist applicants "should rank in the top half of their graduating class and hold a recalculated average of 3.3 or better." The school also likes to see some honors and/or Advanced Placement courses on an applicant's transcript. Evidence of leadership and extracurricular participation are valued by the committee as well. With lots of liberal arts competition both Upstate and around New York City, Marist finds itself fighting for quality freshmen each year. Thus, committing to the school via early decision gives you a massive edge in the admissions game; in 2019, the college accepted an overwhelming 86 percent of ED applicants.

Worth Your Money?

Tuition fees plus room and board bring the total sticker price to over $58,000, making a four-year degree a $200,000+ venture. Fortunately, through a combination of merit and need-based aid, the net price ends up under $40k per year, even for families in the top income brackets. While not cheap by any means, Marist has the type of NYC corporate connections that can eventually open doors to lucrative and interesting careers that will likely return your investment.

FINANCIAL
Institutional Type: Private
In-State Tuition: $45,530
Out-of-State Tuition: $45,530
Room & Board: $16,380
Required Fees: $0
Books & Supplies: $1,125

Avg. Need-Based Grant: $24,087
Avg. % of Need Met: 75%

Avg. Merit-Based Award: $12,677
% Receiving (All Freshmen): 36%
% Receiving (Freshmen w/o Need): 28%

Avg. Cumulative Debt: $40,007
% of Students Borrowing: 65%

CAREER
Who Recruits
1. IBM
2. EY
3. KPMG
4. UBS
5. The Met

Notable Internships
1. ESPN
2. Sony Music Entertainment
3. American Red Cross

Top Industries
1. Business
2. Sales
3. Operations
4. Education
5. information Technology

Top Employers
1. IBM
2. JPMorgan Chase
3. EY
4. Macy's
5. Citi

Where Alumni Work
1. New York City
2. Boston
3. Atlanta
4. New York City
5. Hartford, CT

Median Earnings
College Scorecard (Early Career): $56,900
PayScale (Early Career): $58,100
PayScale (Mid-Career): $107,500

RANKINGS
Money: 329
U.S. News: 11, Regional Universities North
Wall Street Journal/THE: 401-500
Washington Monthly: 311, Master's Universities

COLLEGE OVERLAPS
Fairfield University
Fordham University
Loyola University Maryland
Syracuse University
University of Connecticut

Massachusetts Institute of Technology

Cambridge, Massachusetts | 617-253-3400

A beacon of egalitarianism and meritocracy, the Massachusetts Institute of Technology is less about legacy and more about the future. MIT doesn't care who your grandfather was or how far you can throw a football; it is seeking the world's sharpest and most innovative minds in engineering, the sciences, mathematics, and related fields who, one day, will create the world the rest of us will merely inhabit. Graduate students account for the majority of students enrolled at MIT, but the 4,530 undergraduates pursue one of fifty-three majors and fifty-eight minors in this world-class research institution that continues to be one of the world's most magnetic destinations for math and science geniuses.

Inside the Classroom

There are five separate schools within MIT: the School of Architecture and Planning; the School of Engineering; the School of Humanities, Arts, and the Social Sciences; the Sloan School of Management; and the School of Science. There are a number of broad academic requirements across all five schools including an eight-subject humanities, arts, and social sciences requirement and a six-subject science requirement that includes two terms of calculus, two terms of physics, one term of chemistry, and one term of biology. Additionally, students must complete two courses under the designation of "restricted electives" in science and technology, a laboratory requirement, and a physical education course.

The student-to-faculty ratio is an astonishing 3-to-1, and even with a substantial focus on graduate programs, the class sizes are intimate. Over two-fifths of all class sections have single-digit enrollments, and 71 percent of courses contain fewer than twenty students. MIT is known for having one of the best formalized undergraduate research programs in the country. The Undergraduate Research Opportunities Program (UROP) operates year-round and helps connect 90+ percent of undergrads to a research experience with an MIT faculty member. Studying abroad is strongly encouraged, and the school offers some fantastic opportunities through programs such as MIT Madrid, Imperial College Exchanges (London), and departmental exchange programs in South Africa, France, and Japan; 57 percent participate.

The highest numbers of degrees conferred in 2019 were in the following majors: computer science and engineering (31 percent), mechanical engineering (14 percent), mathematics (8 percent), and physics (6 percent). Just about every program at MIT sits at or near the top of any rankings. The most sought after employers and grad schools aggressively recruit alumni. Graduates win nationally competitive fellowships and scholarships on a routine basis. In 2019, five students were awarded Marshall Scholarships; in 2020, thirteen of the forty-one finalists for Hertz Fellowships were MIT grads.

Outside the Classroom

The campus' 166 acres include twenty-six acres of playing fields, twenty acres of green spaces and gardens, and eighteen student residences that house the 92 percent of students who live on campus, a requirement for freshmen. It may be a bit of a surprise that the school's thirty-seven fraternities, sororities, and living groups attract 45 percent of male students and 25 percent of females. Around half live in frat/sorority/living group housing, and the other half reside in dorms. Falling victim to stereotypes, one might not immediately assume that MIT would have an athletically-inclined student body. However, the school fields thirty-three varsity sports teams (16 women's, 15 men's, 2 co-ed), most of which compete in NCAA Division III against other New England colleges. The intramural program is bursting at the seams with over 4,000 participants annually. Another 800 students are members of thirty-three club teams. Plenty of culture/creativity can be found on campus in one of MIT's twelve museums and galleries (The MIT Museum draws 150,000 visitors each year). There are also more than sixty arts, dance, music, and writing organizations for students. The school is devoted to environmental sustainability, and the campus and surrounding area are designed for a car-free lifestyle that remains highly convenient. With forty-four bike-sharing stations, six subway stations, and twenty-nine bus routes in the surrounding area, students can navigate Cambridge with ease. Harvard's campus is less than one mile away, and downtown Boston is easy to reach. For reference, Fenway Park is less than two miles from campus.

Career Services

MIT Career Advising and Professional Development (CAPD) has twenty-three professional staff members who are directly involved in employer relations, career counseling, and graduate school advising. That 197:1 student-to-advisor ratio is far better than many other schools featured in this guide. The office provides top-notch individualized counseling and also puts on phenomenal large-scale events. The MIT Fall Career Fair is an unmatched event that sees around 450 companies and 5,000 students attend. If you can think of a desirable tech/finance company, chances are it has a booth at the event. Even the less-epic Spring Career Fair attracts seventy employers including Northrup Grumman, Wayfair, Bank of America, the Walt Disney Company, Cisco, and Twitter.

With assistance from the CAPD, 87 percent of MIT undergraduates complete at least one internship. Almost one-quarter of those participating in internships received a full-time job offer from that same organization. The CAPD played a direct role in helping many others land jobs through various means as 43 percent found employment through career fairs, 31 percent through CAPD, and 22 percent through faculty members. In a single year, the CAPD hosted 130 different employers, which led to a collective 2,609 interviews held on campus. An additional 1,072 employers posted 2,595 unique jobs online in an effort to lure MIT seniors. MIT students sell themselves, so career services staff have a role akin to managing the '27 Yankees. Still, the office does a world-class job of setting up its highly desired undergrads with premium opportunities.

Professional Outcomes

The Class of 2020 saw 51 percent of its members enter the world of employment and 39 percent continue on their educational paths. By industry, the highest percentage of graduates found jobs in information technology (31 percent), scientific services (20 percent), finance (14 percent), and healthcare (17 percent). The top employers included Accenture, Facebook, Amazon, Microsoft, Goldman Sachs, Google, General Motors, the US Navy, Apple, Bain & Company, and McKinsey. The mean starting salary for an MIT bachelor's degree holder was $95,000, and the median was $90,000.

The most frequently attended graduate schools are a who's who of elite institutions including MIT itself, Stanford, Caltech, Harvard, and the University of Oxford. Also making the list were Princeton, Columbia, Northwestern, University of Chicago, University of California at Berkeley, and University of Michigan. The most common degree being pursued was a master's of engineering (39 percent) and the second most common degree was a PhD (38 percent). Only 6 percent were entering medical/dental/veterinary school, and 1 percent were headed to law school. Medical school acceptance rates typically land in the 80-95 percent range for grads/alumni, more than double the national average.

Admission

Applicants for a place in the Class of 2023 encountered a murderous 7 percent acceptance rate. Freshmen entering MIT in the fall of 2019 possessed SATs with an average SAT score of 1532 and average ACT of 35. Students were almost unanimously from the top 10 percent of their high school classes—95 percent boasted that achievement. MIT offers a nonbinding early action option with a November 1 deadline, but it yields little in the way of an admissions edge. The acceptance rate for the early round is usually almost identical to that of the regular round.

The MIT admissions committee rates character/personal qualities as "very important," and just about everything else—rigor of courses, GPA, test scores, essays, recommendations, interview, extracurricular activities—in the next tier of importance. While a nice nod to the importance of character, every one of the aforementioned factors ranked as merely "important" have to be close to perfect for it to even enter the equation. Legacy status is not considered at MIT, a rarity among elite universities, meaning that the alumni connection of your mother, grandfather, or brother plays zero role in helping you gain admission. Despite a large intercollegiate sports program, athletic prowess plays a minimal role in admissions decisions as well. MIT is as close to a true meritocracy as you can find in the world of higher education. The most brilliant and innovative minds from around the globe are admitted regardless of family name or lacrosse skills. Rather, a sparkling academic record, near-perfect test scores, and impressive STEM-focused experiences/accomplishments outside the classroom will rule the day.

Worth Your Money?

Yes . . . Need more? Going to MIT is punching your ticket to any number of lucrative careers. If you need financial assistance, this school will meet 100 percent of your demonstrated need; the average grant is for roughly $54,000. The full cost of attendance is $73,160.

FINANCIAL
Institutional Type: Private
In-State Tuition: $53,450
Out-of-State Tuition: $53,450
Room & Board: $17,320
Required Fees: $0
Books & Supplies: $820

Avg. Need-Based Grant: NR
Avg. % of Need Met: NR

Avg. Merit-Based Award: $0
% Receiving (All Freshmen): $0
% Receiving (Freshmen w/o Need): $0

Avg. Cumulative Debt: $23,517
% of Students Borrowing: 23%

CAREER
Who Recruits
1. Hudson River Trading
2. Nvidia
3. Five Rings Technology
4. Stripe
5. AB InBev

Notable Internships
1. Jane Street Capital
2. Airbnb
3. Shell

Top Industries
1. Business
2. Engineering
3. Education
4. Research
5. Operations

Top Employers
1. Google
2. Apple
3. Microsoft
4. Amazon
5. IBM

Where Alumni Work
1. Boston
2. San Francisco
3. New York City
4. India
5. Washington DC

Median Earnings
College Scorecard (Early Career): $104,700
PayScale (Early Career): $92,300
PayScale (Mid-Career): $163,900

RANKINGS
Money: 1
U.S. News: 4 (T), National Universities
Wall Street Journal/THE: 2
Washington Monthly: 3, National Universities

COLLEGE OVERLAPS
Columbia University
California Institute of Technology
Harvard University
Princeton University
Stanford University

Miami University

Oxford, Ohio | 513-529-2531

ADMISSION
Admission Rate: 80%
Admission Rate - Men: 79%
Admission Rate - Women: 81%
EA Admission Rate: 91%
ED Admission Rate: 87%
ED Admits as % of Total Admits: 2%
Admission Rate (5-Year Trend): +15%
% of Admits Attending (Yield): 19%
Transfer Admission Rate: 61%

SAT Reading/Writing (Middle 50%): 600-680
SAT Math (Middle 50%): 610-730
ACT Composite (Middle 50%): 26-31

% Graduated in Top 10% of HS Class: 32%
% Graduated in Top 25% of HS Class: 62%
% Graduated in Top 50% of HS Class: 91%

Demonstrated Interest: Not Considered
Legacy Status: Considered
Admission Interview Offered: No

ENROLLMENT
Total Undergraduate Enrollment: 17,246
% Part-Time: 3%
% Male: 50%
% Female: 50%
% Out-of-State: 34%
% Fraternity: 25%
% Sorority: 40%
% On-Campus (Freshman): 98%
% On-Campus (All Undergraduate): 31%

% African-American: 4%
% Asian: 2%
% Hispanic: 5%
% White: 72%
% Other: 4%
% Race or Ethnicity Unknown: 0%
% International: 13%
% Low-Income: 10%

ACADEMICS
Student-to-Faculty Ratio: 17 to 1
% of Classes Under 20: 31%
% of Classes 20-49: 57%
% of Classes 50 or More: 12%
% Full-Time Faculty: 77%
% Full-Time Faculty w/ Terminal Degree: 84%

Top Programs
Accounting
Architecture
Engineering
Finance
Kinesiology
Sport Leadership and Management
Strategic Communication

Retention Rate: 90%
4-Year Graduation Rate: 71%
6-Year Graduation Rate: 82%

Curricular Flexibility: Less Flexible
Academic Rating: ★★★

#CollegesWorthYourMoney

Unless you are from Ohio, telling someone that you attend Miami University will likely lead to images of palm trees, gorgeous white sand beaches, and world-famous nightclubs. Such is the fate of this excellent public university located in southwestern Ohio. The town of Oxford may not be South Beach, but it provides a home to over 17,000 undergraduates and boasts a No. 1 ranking among Ohio-based public universities for both return on investment and four-year graduation rate.

Inside the Classroom
The Global Miami Plan appears to be, at first glance, a labyrinthine set of requirements that involves foundational courses, thematic sequences, intercultural perspectives, experiential learning, and a capstone. Despite the categorical overload, the core curriculum at Miami is actually fairly straightforward and allows for a good deal of flexibility within a series of umbrella categories. Students in all 100 of the school's majors tackle 27 credits worth of foundational courses in English, the humanities, natural sciences, STEM, and global perspectives. The experiential learning and capstone requirements help ensure that Miami grads engage in activities like service learning, research, or portfolio projects.

A freshman retention rate of 90 percent is excellent for a public university, and the strength of undergraduate teaching gets high marks. In part, this is made possible from a reasonable 17:1 student-to-faculty ratio, lower than Ohio State. As at most publics, classes certainly aren't tiny, but Miami U. keeps the majority of courses—two thirds, to be precise—at an enrollment of 29 or fewer. Each year, more than 2,800 undergrads work with professors on research, and some become coauthors of academic papers and/or find themselves presenting at academic conferences. The school also ranks in the top five among public institutions for the percent of students who elect to study abroad; a phenomenal 55 percent of undergrads elect to study away from Oxford.

Almost one quarter of Miami University graduates earn a degree in business/marketing, making it, by far, the most popular area of academic concentration. Other commonly pursued majors include the social sciences (10 percent), communication/journalism (9 percent), health professions (7 percent), biology (6 percent), engineering (6 percent), parks and recreation (6 percent), and education (6 percent). The Farmer School of Business and the College of Engineering and Computing both have terrific national reputations. The university also offers standout programs in architecture, sports management, and kinesiology. The school's overall profile is also on the rise in the eyes of prestigious scholarship-granting organizations; in 2020, ten RedHawks were selected as Fulbright Scholars, bringing the total number of awards since 2000 to 69. The school also recently produced multiple winners of Astronaut Scholarships, Boren Scholarships, Critical Language Scholarships, Gilman Scholarships, and Goldwater Scholarships.

Outside the Classroom
Set on 2,100 rural acres, Miami is a school that houses just about all of its freshmen (98 percent) on campus and sees pretty much everyone else live in off-campus housing. Greek life soaks up a massive percentage of the population, with 40 percent of women joining sororities and one quarter of men affiliated with a fraternity. Just about every student in Oxford laces up athletic sneakers, cleats, or skates to participate in one of 18 Division I sports, 50+ club teams, or 600 intramural teams with 3,000 total annual participants. Facilities for these endeavors are top notch and include the Recreational Sports Center with two swimming pools and an indoor jogging track (70 percent of students participate in Rec Center programming), the Goggin Ice Center, which contains two ice rinks, and the Outdoor Pursuit Center, which offers hiking, canoeing, camping, and rafting opportunities. Oxford may be a small town a full hour away from Cincinnati, but few students complain thanks to an.

Career Services
The Center for Career Exploration & Success (CCES) employs 29 professional employees with roles in the areas of career counseling (by academic discipline), employer relations, and event coordination. This figure includes advisors who are housed within the Farmer School of Business and, in total, works out to a 593:1 counselor-to-student ratio. This wealth of resources Miami devotes to career assistance led to the office putting on 308 career programs in the 2018-19 school year compared to 263 the previous year. An impressive 3,326 members of the Class of 2022 engaged with the CCES in their freshman year.

Seven out of every ten Class of 2019 graduates completed an internship (or other field experience) during their time on campus. Students participated in 870 live mock interviews, and 14,396 logged onto Handshake. An astounding 592 companies came to Oxford to recruit and conducted a grand total of 4,043 on-campus interviews. Undoubtedly a result of all of this hard work, a solid 78 percent of recent grads are employed in their field of study, and 93 percent are employed in a position that requires a college degree.

Professional Outcomes

The overall success rate for the Class of 2019 was 96 percent, roughly the same as for the Class of 2018 (95.8 percent). This exceeds the national average of 85.7 percent. Two thirds of Miami grads were employed and secured an average salary of $53,792. Staying in Ohio is a common postgraduate choice with 44 percent of grads doing so, but Chicago; New York City; Washington, DC; and Denver are also popular landing spots. The companies attracting the greatest number of RedHawk alumni are Proctor & Gamble, EY, Fifth Third Bank, JPMorgan Chase, Deloitte, PNC, PwC, and Amazon.

Twenty-four percent of Class of 2019 grads elected to continue their education in graduate or professional school. Miami boasts a strong premed program that resulted in 60 percent of medical school applicants gaining acceptance over the last four years. Those with a 3.5 GPA and no less than the 50th percentile score on any section of the MCAT had an even more favorable 80 percent acceptance rate. Recent medical school acceptances include the University of Michigan Medical School, the University of Cincinnati College of Medicine, and Case Western Reserve University School of Medicine. Miami seniors are accepted into law schools at a 95 percent clip, above the national average, and have recently matriculated at schools like Boston College, Wake Forest, and Ohio State University.

Admission

Miami University saw 28,920 applications roll in during the 2019-20 admissions cycle and accepted 80 percent from this pool. Many of those accepted were using the university as a safety school as under 20 percent of this group actually went on to enroll. Those who did enroll in the freshman class of 2019-20 possessed a middle-50th percentile ACT score of 26-31 and SAT score of 1220-1400. Just over half of attending students earned SAT scores above 1300; 81 percent scored above 1200. The middle-50th percentile weighted GPA band was 3.57-4.15. Roughly one third placed inside the top 10 percent of their high school class, and 62 percent were in the top quartile. This public university actually attracts a greater number of out-of-state students (57 percent) than in-state students (43 percent).

Utilizing a holistic admissions process, Miami University considers seven factors as being "very important": rigor of secondary school record, class rank, GPA, standardized test scores, application essay, recommendations, talent/ability, and character/personal qualities. "Considered" factors include extracurricular activities, first-generation status, legacy status (12.8 percent of admitted students were sons, daughters, or siblings of alumni), geographical residence, state residency, volunteer work, and paid work experience. If you are a borderline applicant, applying early decision can be an effective strategy as 87 percent of ED applicants are admitted. However, if you possess credentials around the median figures, this move is not necessary as Miami University is very likely to accept you in the regular round.

Worth Your Money?

Miami University is not a public school that offers dirt-cheap (relatively speaking) tuition prices. In fact, the tuition will cost you around $5,000 more a year than at Ohio State. With housing and meals, the annual cost of attendance rises to almost $31k for residents and $51k for out-of-staters. The average debt load for graduates is just shy of $30k, about average by national standards and just a couple thousand more than the total for alumni of the aforementioned Ohio State. The school only meets 59 percent of demonstrated need, but it is fairly generous with merit aid, offering an average scholarship of $12,770 to those with excellent academic credentials. In sum, this school is reasonably priced for in-state students, but for nonresidents who are on a budget, heading to Oxford may only make sense if you are planning on pursuing a business degree.

FINANCIAL
Institutional Type: Public
In-State Tuition: $15,909
Out-of-State Tuition: $35,935
Room & Board: $14,125
Required Fees: $0
Books & Supplies: $1,240

Avg. Need-Based Grant: $13,182
Avg. % of Need Met: 59%

Avg. Merit-Based Award: $12,770
% Receiving (All Freshmen): 48%
% Receiving (Freshmen w/o Need): 40%

Avg. Cumulative Debt: $29,652
% of Students Borrowing: 45%

CAREER
Who Recruits
1. Textron
2. Deloitte
3. EY
4. Oracle
5. Fifth Third Bank

Notable Internships
1. Wells Fargo
2. E&J Gallo
3. Cleveland Clinic

Top Industries
1. Business
2. Education
3. Operations
4. Sales
5. Finance

Top Employers
1. Procter & Gamble
2. EY
3. Fifth Third Bank
4. JPMorgan Chase
5. Deloitte

Where Alumni Work
1. Cincinnati
2. Chicago
3. Columbus, OH
4. Cleveland
5. New York City

Median Earnings
College Scorecard (Early Career): $47,100
PayScale (Early Career): $58,900
PayScale (Mid-Career): $115,200

RANKINGS
Money: 268
U.S. News: 103 (T), National Universities
Wall Street Journal/THE: 229 (T)
Washington Monthly: 232, National Universities

COLLEGE OVERLAPS
Indiana University Bloomington
Ohio State University - Columbus
Ohio University
Pennsylvania State University - University Park
University of Wisconsin - Madison

Michigan State University

East Lansing, Michigan | 517-355-8332

Established in 1855, the Agricultural College of the State of Michigan was the prototype for the original land-grant institutions that forever changed the college landscape in the United States. Since then, it has been through six iterations, five of which saw the inclusion of the word "agriculture" in the school's name; the last—Michigan State University— was adopted in 1964. Today, this highly regarded state institution boasts over 200 programs—undergraduate, graduate, and professional—across 17 degree-granting colleges. Even better, it remains accessible to solid, but not elite-level applicants, accepting greater than 70 percent of those who apply.

Inside the Classroom
In addition to many school-specific requirements within its individual colleges, all Spartans must complete a mathematics course, two writing-intensive courses (Tier 1 and 2), and 24 credits worth of integrative studies courses. This includes a lower and upper level humanities course, a sequence within the social, behavioral, or economic sciences, and eight credits worth of lab-based biological or physical science. Some majors require students to become proficient in a foreign language while others do not have a language requirement. Over 4,000 students are admitted to the MSU Honors College, which offers a more flexible curriculum, smaller classes, and increased interaction with faculty.

A 16:1 student-to-faculty ratio rates in the average range for public universities of MSU's size and scope. Class sizes are a genuine mix of small seminars and giant lecture halls. Fifty-six percent of undergraduate course sections contain fewer than 30 students; just shy of one quarter enroll more than 50. Undergraduate research opportunities do exist for those bold enough to pursue them; 36 percent of 2019 grads completed one such experience. A similar number—37 percent—studied abroad at one of 275 programs located in 60+ countries.

A strong business program attracts the greatest number of undergrads; 18 percent of the degrees conferred in 2019 were in the business/marketing category. The next most common degrees were earned in biology (12 percent), communication/journalism (12 percent), and engineering (9 percent). Those academic departments all rank well nationally as well. In the university's history, it has produced 47 Goldwater Scholars, 20 Rhodes Scholars, 18 Churchill Scholars, and 16 Udall and Truman Scholars. MSU also produced seven Fulbright Scholars in the 2018-19 academic year.

Outside the Classroom
Three miles from the state capital of Lansing, MSU's campus is a seemingly never-ending 5,300-acre property, populated by 563 buildings. The 27 residence halls are occupied by 39 percent of the overall student body; 95 percent of freshmen live on campus. There are more than 900 student groups from which to choose, including a widely circulated student newspaper, the State News, and the popular Impact 89FM radio station that broadcasts to the wider Lansing community. There are 50+ Greek-letter organizations, but they do not dominate the social scene. All told, 11 percent of men join fraternities, and 12 percent of women join sororities. Athletics at Michigan State are a huge focal point as the Spartans field 25 varsity squads (12 men's and 13 women's), including a stellar basketball team that has made 22 straight March Madness appearances and has earned ten trips to the Final Four. East Lansing, as a college town, rates among the very best in the country. Among the cultural jewels on campus are the Wharton Center for Performing Arts, the MSU Museum, the Broad Art Museum, the Abrams Planetarium, the Breslin Student Events Center, and the 7.5 acres of horticultural gardens. School spirit is plentiful, sports are celebrated, and there is no shortage of ways to connect with peers.

Career Services
Michigan State's Career Services Network has 39 professional employees who work as discipline-specific career consultants, employer-relations specialists, and internship coordinators. This works out to 1,004:1 student-to-advisor ratio, which is higher than the average university featured in this guide, but it is not unusual for a school of MSU's size. The office hosts more than a dozen career fairs per year with massive numbers of employers attending. Even the relatively niche School of Hospitality Business Fair attracted 80 employers in 2019. The office is also glad to provide virtual or one-on-one assistance with career exploration, resume and cover letter writing, creating a LinkedIn profile, or honing your interview skills.

A commendable 77 percent of Class of 2019 members completed at least one internship while attending MSU. Many are able to find internships or their first jobs through MSU Connect, which helps undergrads locate mentors from the 500,000-member network of Spartan alumni. Workshops hosted or coordinated by the Career Services Network are available on an almost daily basis, even during the summer months and during the COVID-19 pandemic, when students could participate in virtual sessions with a variety of employers, learn about internship opportunities, or work on skills related to the nuts and bolts of the job search process. In sum, MSU is able to provide solid career services offerings and, even with minimal hand-holding, internship and post-graduation outcome numbers suggest it is producing very strong results.

Professional Outcomes

Within months of strutting across the graduation stage, 65 percent of Class of 2019 members had landed full-time employment, 24 percent were pursuing advanced degrees, and only 2 percent were still looking for a job. The top employers of this group included big names like General Motors, Ford Motor Company, Deloitte, Quicken Loans, Target, PepsiCo Frito-Lay, Accenture, and EY. The median starting salary earned was $57,000. Sixty-three percent of fresh alumni remained in Michigan; 11 percent situated in Illinois, and New York, Texas, and Florida each attracted around 2 percent of graduates.

Of the nearly one quarter of 2019 graduates who continued their education, the most popular choice was to stay in Lansing and continue at Michigan State. The next most commonly attended schools were the University of Michigan, Wayne State University, Boston University, and New York University. Michigan State ranks as the undergraduate institution with the 20th highest number of applicants to medical school in the 2019-20 cycle. Law schools attended by recent grads include the likes of Cornell, Northeastern, Notre Dame, Boston College, and the University of Michigan. Plenty of undergraduates on the premed and prelaw tracks end up attending Michigan State University College of Osteopathic Medicine and Michigan State University College of Law.

Admission

The university received 44,322 applications for a place in the Class of 2023 and admitted 71 percent of all who applied. Over one quarter of those who were admitted ended up becoming Spartans. The mid-50 percent standardized test ranges were 1120-1310 on the SAT and 23-29 on the ACT. Twenty-eight percent of 2019-20 freshmen placed in the top 10 percent of their high school class, 65 percent earned a spot in the top quartile, and 93 percent landed in the top half. The average GPA was an impressive 3.75, and 24 percent of those entering the university possessed a 4.0 or better.

The three most heavily weighted factors in admissions decisions are academic GPA, standardized test scores, and the application essay. The rigor of one's secondary school record registers as "important," and a litany of other variables are "considered" including class rank, recommendations, interviews, extracurricular activities, talent/ability, character/personal qualities, first-generation status, alumni relation, geographical residence, state residency, volunteer and paid work, and the level of an applicant's interest. The school does not offer a binding early decision option but does have an early action deadline of November 1. According to the school, applying EA "does not make it easier to gain admission to MSU, and the Office of Admissions promises no special privileges to early action candidates in the admissions review, such as giving your application a higher priority or a more lenient review."

Worth Your Money?

Residents of the Great Lake State face a reasonable annual cost of attendance of $25k, meaning that a bachelor's degree can be obtained at list price for right around $100k. Even at full price, this presents an affordable option by the standards of today's postsecondary market. However, the good news is that 69 percent of students receive some form of financial aid; the school awarded 1.1 billion total dollars in the 2018-19 school year (need-based plus merit aid). The close to one quarter of undergraduates from outside the state pay a COA that is almost exactly double this amount. At $200k, MSU may not be the most cost-effective option, and nonresidents would likely be better off seeking out public options within their home state.

FINANCIAL
Institutional Type: Public
In-State Tuition: $14,460
Out-of-State Tuition: $39,766
Room & Board: $10,522
Required Fees: $0
Books & Supplies: $1,134

Avg. Need-Based Grant: $12,069
Avg. % of Need Met: 53%

Avg. Merit-Based Award: $9,780
% Receiving (All Freshmen): 35%
% Receiving (Freshmen w/o Need): 11%

Avg. Cumulative Debt: $31,393
% of Students Borrowing: 51%

CAREER
Who Recruits
1. Ford Motor Company
2. Neogen Corporation
3. Nexient
4. Proctor & Gamble
5. DTE Energy

Notable Internships
1. The Detroit News
2. UFC
3. Ralph Lauren

Top Industries
1. Business
2. Operations
3. Education
4. Sales
5. Engineering

Top Employers
1. General Motors
2. Ford Motor Company
3. FCA Fiat Chrysler
4. Quicken Loans
5. Amazon

Where Alumni Work
1. Detroit
2. Chicago
3. Grand Rapids, MI
4. New York City
5. San Francisco

Median Earnings
College Scorecard (Early Career): $53,600
PayScale (Early Career): $57,900
PayScale (Mid-Career): $106,600

RANKINGS
Money: 55
U.S. News: 80 (T), National Universities
Wall Street Journal/THE: 82
Washington Monthly: 45, National Universities

COLLEGE OVERLAPS
Indiana University Bloomington
Purdue University - West Lafayette
University of Illinois at Urbana-Champaign
University of Michigan
University of Wisconsin - Madison

Middlebury College

Middlebury, Vermont | 802-443-3000

Located between the Green Mountains and the Adirondacks, Middlebury College is heading toward the summit of Northeastern liberal arts colleges. In the same conversation as (although always ranked just behind) Williams and Amherst, Middlebury's 2,580 undergraduate students are an exceptionally accomplished crew. Even the frigid Vermont winters do little to take away from the beauty of the college's historic 350-acre campus or the natural grandeur of the surrounding area. A quintessential New England liberal arts college aesthetically, "Midd" also plays that role when it comes to the classroom experience.

ADMISSION
Admission Rate: 15%
Admission Rate - Men: 16%
Admission Rate - Women: 15%
EA Admission Rate: Not Offered
ED Admission Rate: 45%
ED Admits as % of Total Admits: 25%
Admission Rate (5-Year Trend): -2%
% of Admits Attending (Yield): 40%
Transfer Admission Rate: 13%

SAT Reading/Writing (Middle 50%): 670-750
SAT Math (Middle 50%): 690-780
ACT Composite (Middle 50%): 32-34

% Graduated in Top 10% of HS Class: 79%
% Graduated in Top 25% of HS Class: 96%
% Graduated in Top 50% of HS Class: 99%

Demonstrated Interest: Considered
Legacy Status: Considered
Admission Interview Offered: Yes

ENROLLMENT
Total Undergraduate Enrollment: 2,580
% Part-Time: 1%
% Male: 47%
% Female: 53%
% Out-of-State: 95%
% Fraternity: Not Offered
% Sorority: Not Offered
% On-Campus (Freshman): 100%
% On-Campus (All Undergraduate): 95%

% African-American: 4%
% Asian: 7%
% Hispanic: 10%
% White: 62%
% Other: 5%
% Race or Ethnicity Unknown: 1%
% International: 11%
% Low-Income: 16%

ACADEMICS
Student-to-Faculty Ratio: 8 to 1
% of Classes Under 20: 66%
% of Classes 20-49: 33%
% of Classes 50 or More: 2%
% Full-Time Faculty: 88%
% Full-Time Faculty w/ Terminal Degree: 96%

Top Programs
Economics
English
Environmental Studies
History
International & Global Studies
Neuroscience
Performing Arts
Political Science

Retention Rate: 94%
4-Year Graduation Rate: 85%
6-Year Graduation Rate: 93%

Curricular Flexibility: Somewhat Flexible
Academic Rating: ★★★★★

#CollegesWorthYourMoney

Inside the Classroom
Offering forty-seven departments and programs in which to major and minor, the college requires all students to complete one course in seven of the following eight categories: literature, the arts, philosophical and religious studies, historical studies, physical and life sciences, deductive reasoning and analytical processes, social analysis, and foreign language. Undergrads also must complete four additional courses that meet the cultures and civilization requirement. Mandatory writing-intensive seminars must be tackled—one as a freshman and the second by the end of the sophomore year.

The school's 8:1 student-faculty ratio allows 100 percent of courses to be taught by professors, not graduate assistants. Most classes are small; the mean class size is nineteen, and 20 percent of sections contain fewer than ten students. The Summer Research at Middlebury program funds 130 students annually to work alongside faculty in a variety of disciplines. Each year, more than 50 percent of juniors take a semester abroad in one of ninety programs in forty countries. The college's robust international program includes Middlebury Schools Abroad in Argentina, Brazil, Cameroon, Chile, China, France, Germany, India, Israel, Italy, Japan, Jordan, Morocco, Russia, Spain, the United Kingdom, and Uruguay.

Middlebury is renowned for its Language Department as well as its programs in economics and international studies. Graduate schools know the value of a Middlebury education (see med school acceptance rates below). The college also produces a large number of national fellowship/scholarship winners. In 2020, graduates/alumni took home six National Science Foundation Graduate Research Fellowships, twelve Fulbright Scholarships, and a host of other prestigious honors.

Outside the Classroom
Implementing the Oxford/Cambridge system of residential housing, all Middlebury undergraduates are required to live in one of more than sixty on-campus buildings. First-year students are assigned to one of five larger Commons where they will reside until the end of their sophomore year. More than thirty faculty/staff members regularly eat in the Commons allowing for classroom discussions to continue over a meal. That leaves no room for Greek life, which vanished two decades ago (limited "social houses" do remain). With thirty-one varsity sports teams competing in the NCAA New England Small College Athletic Conference, the Middlebury Panthers put a sizable portion of its undergraduate population in uniform. Less committed athletes can enjoy a full array of club and intramural sports as well as the school's eighteen-hole golf course, 3.5-mile jogging trail, 2,200-seat ice hockey rink, or six-lane indoor track. Midd offers more than 170 student-run organizations with options in all the usual realms—performing arts, spiritual, social, student government, and more. Outdoor activity clubs that engage in climbing, hiking, kayaking, skiing, and camping are among the most popular groups. Student theater productions are also well attended. The town of Middlebury is tiny and quiet, so some students make the just-under-an-hour drive to Burlington. Montreal, Canada, is the closest cosmopolitan destination with Boston and New York more than three hours away.

Career Services
The Center for Careers and Internships is staffed by seventeen full-time staff members who specialize in areas such as employer relations, career advising, heath professions and STEM advising, and internships and early engagement. Its 152:1 student-to-advisor ratio places it among the most supportive career services offices of any college profiled in this guide. Middlebury's career counselors are almost always found actively engaging undergraduates in career/grad school planning. In a given year, they coordinate 240 events and workshops, and advisors hold 2,700 individual student sessions.

Middlebury College

E-mail: admissions@middlebury.edu | Website: www.middlebury.edu

For a school of modest size, Middlebury brought an impressive ninety employers to campus to host information sessions and facilitated 750 on-campus interviews in 2019. They helped Class of 2019 members find internships at a 75 percent clip and contribute $750,000 to help fund unpaid summer work experiences. More than 22,000 opportunities for jobs and internships are posted online. Further, a generous alumni base is more than willing to assist current Panthers—more than 3,600 alums in a range of professions wait to connect on Midd2Mid. In sum, Middlebury gets extremely high marks from our team, as grads regularly find their way to careers they find meaningful and fulfilling, including many at some of the country's best companies.

Professional Outcomes

Six months after graduating, 79 percent of the Class of 2019 had landed jobs, 11 percent were in graduate school, and 6 percent were still searching for employment. That was an improvement over the classes of 2017 and 2018 that saw greater numbers of alumni still hunting for jobs in the same timeframe. The most commonly held jobs fell under the category of financial services (15 percent), consulting (12 percent), technology (12 percent), education (12 percent), and arts, media, and communications (12 percent). Interestingly, the number of Middlebury grads entering tech-related fields has grown by over 50 percent in the last few years. Google is now one of the leading employers of alumni alongside Morgan Stanley, Goldman Sachs, Deloitte, Amazon, and JP Morgan.

Middlebury students with solid grades will be viewed favorably by graduate and professional schools should they wish to continue their education. Graduate schools attended by recent alumni include Columbia, Georgia Tech, Harvard Law School, Oxford, Stanford, and Yale. Members of the Class of 2019 who applied to medical school sported an average GPA of 3.7, a median MCAT score in the 90th percentile, and were accepted at a 94 percent clip (the 2017 figure was 83 percent). Over the last eight years, the most frequently attended medical schools include Tufts, Boston University, Geisel (Dartmouth), and NYU.

Admission

Middlebury College admitted 15 percent of the 9,754 applicants for a place in the Class of 2023. Of those receiving an acceptance letter, 40 percent went on to enroll at the college. The middle-50 percent standardized tests scores of those who enrolled were 1330-1500 on the SAT and 31-34 on the ACT. There is a relatively even split between those submitting scores from each exam. Formerly one of the rare test-flexible institutions, Middlebury shifted to a full-blown test-optional policy in 2020.

Six factors sit atop the pecking order of most important as applicants are being evaluated by the admissions committee: rigor of secondary coursework, GPA, class rank, extracurricular activities, talent/ability, and character/ personal qualities. Test scores, recommendations, essays, and racial/ethnic status comprise the second tier of "important" factors. Those who commit to the college through binding early decision are rewarded with a 45 percent acceptance rate, more than three times that of the regular cycle. The college continues to use a genuinely holistic approach in the admissions process, and the test-optional policy can be useful for a certain type of applicant. Even when considering the "special" students being accepted via the early round, ED still provides borderline applicants with an increased chance at getting in.

Worth Your Money?

Middlebury's list price is about the going rate for elite liberal arts institutions with a total annual cost of attendance of $75k. However, if you qualify for need-based aid, the college will meet your full level of need; the average award is $52k. As with most schools that meet a student's full demonstrated need, there isn't much, if any, merit aid money to go around. A school of superior quality, Middlebury rates as a rare liberal arts school that will pay you back multiple times over the course of your life, even if the upfront costs are steep.

FINANCIAL
Institutional Type: Private
In-State Tuition: $58,316
Out-of-State Tuition: $58,316
Room & Board: $16,630
Required Fees: $0
Books & Supplies: $1,000

Avg. Need-Based Grant: $49,740
Avg. % of Need Met: 100%

Avg. Merit-Based Award: $0
% Receiving (All Freshmen): 0%
% Receiving (Freshmen w/o Need): 0%

Avg. Cumulative Debt: $19,838
% of Students Borrowing: 50%

CAREER
Who Recruits
1. Analysis Group
2. Goldman Sachs
3. Oak Hill Advisors
4. ScribeAmerica
5. CIA

Notable Internships
1. Tesla
2. Bain & Company
3. Merrill Lynch

Top Industries
1. Business
2. Education
3. Media
4. Social Services
5. Operations

Top Employers
1. Google
2. Goldman Sachs
3. Morgan Stanley
4. Amazon
5. Deloitte

Where Alumni Work
1. New York City
2. Boston
3. Washington DC
4. San Francisco
5. Glen Falls, NY

Median Earnings
College Scorecard (Early Career): $58,200
PayScale (Early Career): $64,200
PayScale (Mid-Career): $126,800

RANKINGS
Money: 179
U.S. News: 9 (T), Liberal Arts Colleges
Wall Street Journal/THE: 37
Washington Monthly: 8, Liberal Arts Colleges

COLLEGE OVERLAPS
Amherst College
Brown University
Dartmouth College
Tufts University
Williams College

Mount Holyoke College

South Hadley, Massachusetts | 413-538-2023

ADMISSION
Admission Rate: 38%
Admission Rate - Men: Not Applicable
Admission Rate - Women: 38%
EA Admission Rate: Not Offered
ED Admission Rate: 57%
ED Admits as % of Total Admits: 15%
Admission Rate (5-Year Trend): -9%
% of Admits Attending (Yield): 33%
Transfer Admission Rate: 39%

SAT Reading/Writing (Middle 50%): 630-720
SAT Math (Middle 50%): 640-770
ACT Composite (Middle 50%): 27-32

% Graduated in Top 10% of HS Class: 52%
% Graduated in Top 25% of HS Class: 82%
% Graduated in Top 50% of HS Class: 97%

Demonstrated Interest: Considered
Legacy Status: Considered
Admission Interview Offered: Yes

ENROLLMENT
Total Undergraduate Enrollment: 2,190
% Part-Time: 2%
% Male: 0%
% Female: 100%
% Out-of-State: 81%
% Fraternity: Not Offered
% Sorority: Not Offered
% On-Campus (Freshman): 99%
% On-Campus (All Undergraduate): 96%

% African-American: 5%
% Asian: 8%
% Hispanic: 7%
% White: 47%
% Other: 4%
% Race or Ethnicity Unknown: 2%
% International: 27%
% Low-Income: 16%

ACADEMICS
Student-to-Faculty Ratio: 9 to 1
% of Classes Under 20: 75%
% of Classes 20-49: 24%
% of Classes 50 or More: 1%
% Full-Time Faculty: 77%
% Full-Time Faculty w/ Terminal Degree: 96%

Top Programs
Area Studies
Biology
Computer Science
English
Environmental Studies
International Relations
Psychology

Retention Rate: 93%
4-Year Graduation Rate: 79%
6-Year Graduation Rate: 83%

Curricular Flexibility: Somewhat Flexible
Academic Rating: ★★★★

#CollegesWorthYourMoney

Stately, majestic, and Hogwarts-esque are three of the most common adjectives used to describe the grounds of Mount Holyoke College, an exclusively female liberal arts school located in South Hadley, Massachusetts. Situated ninety miles west of Boston, MHC is home to 2,190 undergraduates and is part of the Five College Consortium with nearby Amherst, Smith, Hampshire, and UMass-Amherst. With fifty departmental and interdepartmental majors as well as the option to design your own major, MHC students, nicknamed "Lyons" after the college's founder, are free to follow their academic passions, an attribute that helps explain the incredible percentage of alumni that go on to earn PhDs.

Inside the Classroom

By liberal arts college standards Mount Holyoke requires a minimal amount of core coursework. While working toward the completion of the 128 credits needed for graduation, students must complete one class in each of the humanities, sciences, social sciences, and mathematics. A freshman seminar focused on sharpening writing skills is mandatory as is one semester of foreign language study, one course focused on multicultural perspectives, and physical education. Thanks to membership in the Five College Consortium, undergrads can take a good number of courses at one of the other institutions but must complete two of their final three years of study on the MHC campus.

Professors are known for their accessibility and commitment to undergraduate education. Thanks to a 9-to-1 student-to-faculty ratio, three-quarters of sections contain fewer than twenty students; 11 percent are single-digit seminar classes. Opportunities to research and publish alongside faculty are definitely available, and many 200- and 300-level courses have independent research baked-in as a requirement. Across all disciplines, more ambitious students can arrange summer research internships with professors. More than one hundred study abroad options are on the table, but preferred MHC-affiliated programs are definitely worth considering. Those targeted college-run programs include Globalization, Development, and Environment in Costa Rica; Economic Transformation and Business in Shanghai; and the Associated Kyoto Program that allows students to attend a full academic year of classes in Japan.

MHC isn't a school where one or two programs are more popular and/or more respected than the rest. Rather, strong programs are found across a variety of fields—for example, in biology, English, and international relations. Among undergrads, the greatest number of degrees are awarded in the social sciences (26 percent), biology (9 percent), and computer science (8 percent). Fellowships award season is usually kind to Mount Holyoke grads. In 2020, MHC students took home nine Fulbright Scholarships, one Davis Projects for Peace awards, and two Boren Awards.

Outside the Classroom

Ninety-six percent of undergraduates live on campus in one of eighteen residential halls. The last time sororities existed on campus was 1910 when they were dissolved for being "undemocratic." The college's thirteen sports teams compete in NCAA Division III, including a stellar equestrian program. Of the over one hundred student organizations, a cappella and glee are among the most popular along with volunteerism in many forms. Each year over half of MHC students volunteer at local schools, hospitals, YMCAs, and other community organizations. Speakers, including many authors, appear frequently on campus to give well-attended talks. Thanks again to membership in the Five College Consortium, social opportunities are expanded to include those offered at Smith, UMass, Amherst, and Hampshire. Campus, which is almost always cited as one the nation's prettiest, is a spacious 800 acres that features notable man-made highlights such as the MHC Art Museum, a fitness center that is less than a decade old, and an eighteen-hole golf course in addition to natural highlights such as two lakes and several hiking trails. South Hadley is a small town exploding with quaint New England charm. Those seeking more adventure can make the two-hour trip to Boston.

Career Services

The Career Development Center (CDC) is staffed by eleven professionals (not counting admin assistants) who work directly with, or on behalf of, students in the following capacities: career counseling, internships, experiential learning, and external relations. That 199:1 student-to-advisor ratio is superior to the majority of schools featured in this guidebook. Ample individualized attention is at the fingertips of undergraduates—thirty-minute advising sessions are available as often as once per week for current students or three times per year for recent graduates. The CDC does not host many large events itself; rather, it takes advantage of the school's geographic location and takes part in events such as the Smith College Life Sciences & Technology Fair, the UMASS Amherst Computer Science & Engineering Fair, and the MIT Asian Career Fair.

Through an approach dubbed the "Lynk," Mt. Holyoke strives to systematically assist students in connecting their curriculum to their future career. That goal is accomplished through the offering of experiential learning opportunities, internship connections (funding is guaranteed), industry site visits, and networking with past students who have entered fields of interest. In 2019-20, the office engaged with 80 percent of the student body and 52 percent met one-on-one with a career advisor. Over 9,600 employers posted opportunities on Handshake, a 43 percent increase from the previous year. An impressive 1,150 students participated in summer internships, research, or shadowing experiences, in the 19-20 academic year. Overall, the CDC excels in helping young women find their next destination as evidenced by a low percentage of students still seeking employment six months out and the strength of its graduate school preparation (more in a moment). Even with salaries on the lower end and a dearth of on-campus recruiting, the Mount Holyoke Career Development Center works hard to connect its students to fulfilling and relevant career paths.

Professional Outcomes

Six months after commencement, 66 percent of 2019 grads had found employment, 23 percent had entered graduate/professional school, 6 percent had landed fellowships/internships, and only 2 percent were still searching for jobs. Education was the most frequently entered field (19 percent). It was followed by healthcare (17 percent), technology, science, and engineering (11 percent), and business (10 percent). The top Lyon employers of 2019 included Bank of America, BlackRock, the National Institutes of Health, and Boston Children's Hospital. Microsoft, IBM, Harvard University, and Amazon also employ a healthy number of Lyons. Given the number of grads entering the public sector or pursuing graduate degrees, it isn't shocking that average salary statistics for alumni tend to be on the low side. Plenty of alumni also can be found in New York, California, or international locales.

Ten years after graduation, 75 percent of alumni have enrolled in graduate or professional school. The college produces an exceptional number of future STEM PhDs. Between 2004-2013 it saw 171 of its graduates go on to earn doctorates in hard sciences. In recent years the law school acceptance rate has fluctuated between 75 percent and 100 percent. Recent acceptances include Harvard Law School, Boston College, University of Michigan, and Stanford. Medical school acceptance rates tend to be above average, and recent graduates have attended Johns Hopkins, Tufts, Emory, Columbia, UVA, and Washington University. Across all disciplines, the graduate schools accepting the most recent alumni included Yale, Cornell, NYU, and Duke. Massachusetts-based Simmons, UMASS-Amherst, and Mt. Holyoke itself also cracked the list.

Admission

The 3,908 applicants for membership in the Class of 2023 were accepted at a 38 percent, a steep decline from the generous 51 percent for the Class of 2022. One-third of those who were accepted ultimately enrolled in the college. The profile of the typical Mt. Holyoke student is quite different than your average college that has seen a 50 percent acceptance rate in recent years. The middle-50 percent range for SATs was 1320-1450, and 52 percent of those attending placed in the top decile of their high school class; 82 percent were in the top quartile. Just under two-thirds of students earned GPAs of 3.75 or higher.

Four factors reign supreme in the eyes of the admissions committee: rigor of coursework, GPA, recommendations, and essays. Factors such as class rank, the interview, extracurricular activities, talent/ability, character/personal qualities, volunteer work, and work experience also are deemed "important" in the evaluation process. Missing from this list are standardized test scores because Mount Holyoke is a test-optional school. A self-selecting applicant pool leads to a deceptively high(ish) acceptance rate. Yet, the women who are offered admission at Mount Holyoke tend to be high achieving with impressive high school transcripts to their names. Those sure that this is the Seven Sisters school for them can gain a significant advantage by applying early—57 percent of 2019 ED applicants were admitted.

Worth Your Money?

Mt. Holyoke has an annual cost of attendance approaching the $73,000 mark, yet thanks to the generosity of its aid offers, many pay far less. In fact, 63 percent of the undergraduates at the college qualify for need-based aid, and the average grant is $40k, a figure that covers 100 percent of demonstrated need for every single recipient. Further, the school is not stingy with merit aid either, dishing out an average package of $21k per year to 27 percent of the student population. While many graduates don't immediately land high-paying jobs, the swarms of alumni earning advanced degrees do just fine financially in the long run.

FINANCIAL
Institutional Type: Private
In-State Tuition: $54,400
Out-of-State Tuition: $54,400
Room & Board: $16,020
Required Fees: $218
Books & Supplies: $2,000

Avg. Need-Based Grant: $40,492
Avg. % of Need Met: 100%

Avg. Merit-Based Award: $20,643
% Receiving (All Freshmen): 27%
% Receiving (Freshmen w/o Need): 17%

Avg. Cumulative Debt: $25,811
% of Students Borrowing: 67%

CAREER
Who Recruits
1. ESPN
2. Life Technologies
3. Forester Capital, LLC
4. NERA Economic Consulting
5. Analysis Group

Notable Internships
1. United States Senate
2. Nike
3. The Coca-Cola Company

Top Industries
1. Education
2. Business
3. Social Services
4. Media
5. Research

Top Employers
1. Google
2. MassMutual
3. Microsoft
4. Amazon
5. Goldman Sachs

Where Alumni Work
1. New York City
2. Boston
3. Springfield, MA
4. Washington DC
5. San Francisco

Median Earnings
College Scorecard (Early Career): $48,600
PayScale (Early Career): $56,700
PayScale (Mid-Career): $104,400

RANKINGS
Money: 370
U.S. News: 34 (T), Liberal Arts Colleges
Wall Street Journal/THE: 54
Washington Monthly: 42, Liberal Arts Colleges

COLLEGE OVERLAPS
Barnard College
Bryn Mawr College
Smith College
Vassar College
Wellesley College

New York University

New York, New York | 212-998-4500

ADMISSION
Admission Rate: 16%
Admission Rate - Men: 16%
Admission Rate - Women: 16%
EA Admission Rate: Not Offered
ED Admission Rate: 28%
ED Admits as % of Total Admits: 30%
Admission Rate (5-Year Trend): -16%
% of Admits Attending (Yield): 45%
Transfer Admission Rate: 22%

SAT Reading/Writing (Middle 50%): 660-740
SAT Math (Middle 50%): 690-790
ACT Composite (Middle 50%): 30-34

% Graduated in Top 10% of HS Class: 79%
% Graduated in Top 25% of HS Class: 100%
% Graduated in Top 50% of HS Class: 100%

Demonstrated Interest: Considered
Legacy Status: Considered
Admission Interview Offered: No

ENROLLMENT
Total Undergraduate Enrollment: 26,981
% Part-Time: 4%
% Male: 42%
% Female: 58%
% Out-of-State: 67%
% Fraternity: 3%
% Sorority: 7%
% On-Campus (Freshman): 89%
% On-Campus (All Undergraduate): 44%

% African-American: 8%
% Asian: 18%
% Hispanic: 16%
% White: 26%
% Other: 4%
% Race or Ethnicity Unknown: 6%
% International: 22%
% Low-Income: 22%

ACADEMICS
Student-to-Faculty Ratio: 9 to 1
% of Classes Under 20: 60%
% of Classes 20-49: 30%
% of Classes 50 or More: 10%
% Full-Time Faculty: 45%
% Full-Time Faculty w/ Terminal Degree: 94%

Top Programs
Business and Political Economy
Computer Science
Film and Television
Finance
Global Public Health
Journalism
Mathematics
Performing Arts

Retention Rate: 94%
4-Year Graduation Rate: 76%
6-Year Graduation Rate: 85%

Curricular Flexibility: Somewhat Flexible
Academic Rating: ★★★★

#CollegesWorthYourMoney

A genuine melting pot, even by the standards of the city in which it is located, New York University's campus is graced by talented young people of every ethnicity, from every socio-economic status, and from every corner of the globe. All told, there are almost 53,000 students presently enrolled at NYU, just over half of whom are undergraduates. With more than 230 areas of undergraduate study, the talents and passions of this student body are as diverse as its demographic makeup.

Inside the Classroom
NYU is divided into a number of smaller (but still quite large) colleges organized by discipline. Schools with undergraduate programs include the College of Arts & Sciences; Tisch School of the Arts; Tandon School of Engineering, Steinhardt School of Culture, Education, and Human Development; Silver School of Social Work; Rory Meyers College of Nursing; Stern School of Business; College of Global Public Health; and the Gallatin School of Individualized Study where students can create their own liberal arts course of study. There are five parts to NYU's core curriculum that must be tackled by all arts and sciences students. Within other colleges, alterations are made in some areas. The core is comprised of (1) a research- and writing-focused first-year seminar capped at eighteen students, (2) a course in expository writing, (3) two years of language study, (4) Foundations of Contemporary Culture, and (5) Foundations of Scientific Inquiry.

With over 25,000 graduate students and a similar number of undergrads, you might expect undergraduate courses to be held in large lecture halls, even with a 9:1 student-to-faculty ratio. However, NYU manages to run a commendable 60 percent of its classes with an enrollment under twenty students; only 10 percent of courses contain more than fifty students. The school puts a great deal of money into undergraduate research, and it has been running an Undergraduate Research Conference for over forty years. Summer research opportunities are plentiful, including through the School of Engineering's ten-week summer research program for rising juniors and seniors. With more than 4,400 students studying in foreign countries each year, NYU sends more undergrads abroad than any other US university.

While all schools within NYU have solid reputations that will open doors to top corporations and grad schools alike, Stern holds the distinction as one of the top undergraduate business programs in the country. For those entering film, dance, drama, or other performing arts, Tisch is as prestigious a place as you can find to study, and the alumni list is full of Hollywood legends. In recent years, NYU has seen an increase in the number of students winning highly competitive postgraduate scholarships. In 2019, Fulbright Scholarships were awarded to fourteen exiting seniors. The school has seen more than one Rhodes Scholar named each of the last three years with the Abu Dhabi campus producing more Rhodes winners than any other school in the country.

Outside the Classroom
Campus life at NYU is best described in one word: diverse. The make-up of the student body is 22 percent international, the highest percentage of any US school, as its students hail from 115 countries. With sizable Asian, Latino, and African American populations, only about one-fifth of the students are classified as white. Life outside the classroom is every bit as diverse as the demographics as NYU truly has something for everyone. The school's twenty-two dorms provide housing for 12,000 students (including some graduate students); overall, 44 percent of undergrads live on campus. With eleven men's and ten women's varsity teams competing in NCAA Division III sports as well as an extensive club and intramural program, NYU has enough opportunity to satisfy the athletically-inclined but is far from a "sports school." Greek life is also available but tempered with single-digit participation rates in sororities and fraternities. There are 300 student organizations open to all students as well as hundreds more school-specific clubs (e.g., Stern-only, Tandon-only). Performance-based groups abound and often sport incredible alumni lists such as those from the Hammerkatz sketch comedy, Tisch New Theater, and WNYU radio. Plenty of quirky, niche options also are available such as the uber-popular Milk and Cookies Club. The university's Greenwich Village location means all that New York City has to offer is at your fingertips. International cuisine, Broadway shows, world-renowned museums, top musical and comedy acts, and shopping can all be part of your daily existence.

Career Services
The Wasserman Center for Career Development has fifty professional staff members who work in areas such as career counseling, recruitment, and student employment. That 540:1 student-to-advisor ratio is a bit higher than the average school featured in this guide. Catering to the career services needs of 26,981 undergrads is a massive task. Fortunately, NYU's staff is up to it, hosting large-scale events such as the Fall Job & Internship Fair as well as other industry-specific events throughout the year including real estate, nursing, government, and hospitality and tourism.

Of the employed members of the Class of 2019, 64 percent landed their jobs through an NYU resource. Among the resources rated "most helpful" by job/internship seekers were NYU CareerNet, NYU Connections, and the NYU On-Campus Recruiting Program. Those landing summer jobs and internships along the way also attributed their procurement of positions directly to Wasserman at a similar 54 percent clip. The top summer internship destinations include PwC, EY, Credit Suisse, Accenture, Barclay's, Bank of America, and Wells Fargo. Thirteen percent of employed graduates were the recipients of promotions stemming from summer internships. A solid 60 percent of employed 2019 grads received job offers prior to commencement. More than half a million alumni are situated in companies and organizations around the world, leaving no shortage of networking opportunities.

Professional Outcomes

Within six months of graduating, 95 percent of NYU Class of 2019 graduates had successfully landed at their next destination. Of that group, 84 percent were employed and 15 percent were in graduate school. Over half of grads received more than one job offer. The top industries for employment were entertainment/media (14 percent), financial services/banking (14 percent), education (12 percent), healthcare (9 percent), and computer science (7 percent). Large numbers of alumni can be found at major corporations such as Google, Deloitte, Morgan Stanley, Goldman Sachs, IBM, JP Morgan Chase, Citi, and Amazon. The mean starting salary is $65k with a mean signing bonus of almost $9k. New York is (by more than ten times) the most popular destination over number two choice California. New Jersey, DC, and Massachusetts were next in attracting the highest numbers of recent alumni.

Of the 13 percent of the Class of 2019 attending graduate school, 15 percent were seeking degrees in arts/humanities/social sciences, 8 percent were in medical school, and 11 percent were in law school. Elite graduate and professional schools are very much within the grasp of an NYU alum, including the university's own top-ranked Stern School of Business, School of Law at New York University, and the School of Medicine at New York University (Langone). Even though the number of students directly matriculating into graduate school is relatively small, 42 percent stated that they planned to continue their education within the next five years.

Admission

Acceptance rates at NYU have experienced a rapid decline in recent years. In 2013, a solid 35 percent of applicants were accepted; in 2018, that figure dipped to 20 percent before plummeting to 16 percent in 2019. In total, the university received over 79,000 applications for a place in the Class of 2023. This cohort boasted a mid-50 percent SAT score of 1370-1510, an all-time high for an incoming class at NYU; the ACT mid-50 percent range was 30-34. The average GPA was 3.69, and 42 percent of freshmen possessed a 3.75 or higher. Close to 80 percent of entering freshmen placed in the top decile of their high school class, and every single individual was at least in the top quartile.

The overwhelming volume of applicants makes an in-depth, personalized admissions process unfeasible. Rather, the committee relies primarily on hard numbers like GPA, class rank, and standardized test scores. Participation in a highly rigorous course load is also a must, and special talents/abilities are given serious consideration. NYU does offer an early decision round that yields more favorable acceptance rates than those in the regular round. ED applicants to the Class of 2023 were successful 28 percent of the time versus 14 percent in the regular cycle. Warning: This is a school where high school guidance counselors, thinking of NYU-bound students they worked with a few years ago, may not be aware of the increased selectivity demonstrated by the university in the last few years.

Worth Your Money?

NYU is not nearly as generous with financial aid as many other elite schools that strive to meet 100 percent of demonstrated student need. In fact, the university is downright stingy—only a small percentage of those who qualify for aid see all of their need met and the average annual grant for those found eligible is $37k. The overall cost of attendance is $78,742, and merit aid awards are extremely uncommon and typically for very low amounts. The university is an exceptional place to learn, but for $315k+ in total costs you'll need to weigh your expected future salary (based on the field you intend to enter) versus the amount of debt you are willing to take on. Of course, if you are aiming to study at any New York City school, the living costs will be on the high side, but the benefits may be great.

FINANCIAL
Institutional Type: Private
In-State Tuition: $52,205
Out-of-State Tuition: $52,205
Room & Board: $19,245
Required Fees: $2,676
Books & Supplies: $718

Avg. Need-Based Grant: $37,080
Avg. % of Need Met: 71%

Avg. Merit-Based Award: $4,816
% Receiving (All Freshmen): 7%
% Receiving (Freshmen w/o Need): 4%

Avg. Cumulative Debt: $29,242
% of Students Borrowing: 39%

CAREER
Who Recruits
1. Infosys
2. BNP
3. Netflix
4. PayPal
5. Eileen Fisher

Notable Internships
1. United Nations
2. Credit Suisse
3. NYU Langone Health

Top Industries
1. Business
2. Education
3. Media
4. Arts & Design
5. Operations

Top Employers
1. Google
2. JPMorgan Chase
3. Citi
4. Morgan Stanley
5. Amazon

Where Alumni Work
1. New York City
2. Los Angeles
3. San Francisco
4. Washington DC
5. Boston

Median Earnings
College Scorecard (Early Career): $61,900
PayScale (Early Career): $65,600
PayScale (Mid-Career): $129,100

RANKINGS
Money: 281
U.S. News: 30 (T), National Universities
Wall Street Journal/THE: 27
Washington Monthly: 109, National Universities

COLLEGE OVERLAPS
Boston University
Cornell University
University of California, Berkeley
University of Michigan
University of Pennsylvania

North Carolina State University

Raleigh, North Carolina | 919-515-2434

Of the University of North Carolina System's seventeen campuses, UNC-Chapel Hill, the flagship, understandably has the highest national profile by a wide margin. Yet, those in the know are aware that North Carolina State University (NC State) has emerged as a highly competitive and elite academic institution in its own right. Located in the state capital of Raleigh, NC State is at the heart of the Research Triangle—in fact, the school is one of its vertices, with the aforementioned UNC-Chapel Hill and Duke University accounting for the others. Some would be surprised to learn that among entering freshmen in 2019-20, the median SAT score was 1340 and that the group included 230 valedictorians and salutatorians.

Inside the Classroom
The general education program requires all students to conquer thirty-nine credits of mandated coursework in the following areas: mathematical science, natural sciences, humanities, social sciences, health and exercise studies, US diversity, interdisciplinary studies, global studies, and technology fluency. Everyone also engages with an Introduction to Writing class and the demonstration of foreign language proficiency, but it's extremely easy to opt out of a foreign language if you choose, as long as you took two years of courses in the same language in high school.

Thanks to a reasonable 14:1 student-to-faculty ratio, you won't exclusively have classes in enormous lecture halls. Rather, NC State offers its undergraduates a mix of experiences with 65 percent of sections enrolling twenty-nine or fewer students and 16 percent enrolling fifty or more. The Office of Undergraduate Research works diligently to connect star students to faculty research projects, which leads to over 600 student presentations at spring/summer poster sessions. The "Speed-Data-ing" program brings together 250 underclassmen to learn about current research being conducted by NC State professors. The university has put a good deal of emphasis on raising its study abroad participation rate in recent years, and those efforts have been fruitful; 22 percent of undergraduates now study abroad, and there has been a 75 percent increase in participation by underrepresented students over the past seven years.

Engineering is the most popular area of concentration as 27 percent of Class of 2019 graduates earned a degree in that field. Business/marketing comes in second at 15 percent followed by biology (9 percent) and agriculture (7 percent). NC State has an exceptional regional reputation and an expanding national one with the College of Engineering now found near the top of many rankings. Programs in design, architecture, and animal science are also very strong. Wolfpack members also are gaining the attention of the most prestigious postgraduate fellowship organizations. In 2019, National Science Foundation Graduate Research Fellowships went to fourteen NC State students. Another four students won Goldwater Scholarships, four captured Fulbright Scholarships, and thirteen were awarded Gilman Scholarships.

Outside the Classroom
Freshmen overwhelmingly reside on campus as they are required to do; 97 percent of all first-year students live in university-run housing. Among all undergraduates, 37 percent live on campus in one of twenty residence halls that are a mix of suite, hotel, and traditional buildings. Greek houses draw their fair share of the population with 16 percent of women joining sororities and 12 percent of men pledging fraternities. More than 550 athletes participate as part of the twenty-three varsity athletic teams that have combined to capture four national championships, including the legendary 1983 NCAA champion men's basketball team. Wolfpack fans are a rabid bunch, and they rank in the top ten for hoops attendance in the United States. The Talley Student Union, built in 2015, is the central hub for 700+ student organizations including a daily newspaper, a popular college radio station, and plenty of cultural, performance-based, political, and pre-professional organizations. The school's 2,110-acre campus is within a few miles of many of Raleigh's finest attractions including North Carolina's state art, natural history, and history museums; multiple parks and arboretums; and the beautiful Lake Johnson Park.

Career Services
The NCSU Career Development Center employs seventeen professionals who function as career identity coaches, career counselors, employer relations specialists, and pre-professional advisors. There are numerous other departments within individual colleges that employ another five career services staff members to bring the total of full-time, professional employees to twenty-two, which works out to a 1,527:1 student-to-advisor ratio, higher than the average school featured in this guidebook.

Still, 50 percent of Class of 2019 members had received counseling in the Career Development Center, and the vast majority found the experience to be a positive one. A solid two-thirds of employed Class of 2019 members stated that their job was "directly related" to their major, a sign that career counseling staff are pointing students in the right direction. The greatest number of students reported that their internship/externship had been most helpful in their job search (43 percent) followed by a career fair at NC State (29 percent). In the Poole College of Management, the co-op/internship completion rate was 85 percent. Co-op participation is encouraged, and students can complete up to three alternating semesters of paid work experience. NC State offers 1,000 different work rotations, making it one of the largest university co-op programs in the country. Major employers are regular visitors to campus, and career expos such as the Engineering Career Fair, Poole College of Management Career & Internship Fair, and the Ag & Sciences Career Expo collectively draw hundreds of top hiring organizations to Raleigh. Being situated in the Triangle means that many big-time companies are nearby and loaded with Wolfpack alumni.

Professional Outcomes

Approximately 75 percent of students graduating in May 2019 reported that they planned to pursue employment after receiving their diplomas, and half had already secured a job offer. Members of that class obtaining a full-time job reported an average starting salary of $54,734 (with a slightly higher median). Of that cohort, 71 percent were remaining in the state of North Carolina for work with a large percentage situated in the Research Triangle area of Raleigh, Durham, and Chapel Hill. San Francisco, DC, New York City, and Atlanta also attracted a fair number of graduates. Including all graduating years, the companies employing the largest number of Wolfpack alumni are Cisco, Red Hat and SAS (major NC-based software companies), IBM, Lenovo, Amazon, Microsoft, Intel, Google, Deloitte, Facebook, and Salesforce. Many recent graduates also work for the university itself and for the Wake County Public School System.

Upon graduation, one-fourth of Class of 2019 members indicated that their plan was to attend graduate/professional school. Forty-six percent of that group planned to continue their educational journey at NC State, and 70 percent planned to attend a school in North Carolina. An encouraging 88 percent stated that they were attending their first-choice institution. The most commonly pursued degree was a master's (67 percent) followed by a professional degree (18 percent) and a doctoral degree (15 percent). Each year roughly 300 NC State students apply to medical school and another 150 to dental school. Recent med school acceptances include prestigious programs at Duke, UNC-Chapel Hill, UVA, Wake Forest, and Emory. Between 75 and 80 percent of those recommended by the Health Professions Advising Center are accepted into at least one medical school. Law candidates find similar positive results, and schools like Yale, Duke, UNC-Chapel Hill, and Washington & Lee regularly visit NC State to recruit.

Admission

The present iteration of NC State is highly selective, which may come as a shock even to an older relative who attended the university. In fact, the 25th percentile SAT score of attending freshmen in 2019-20 is close to the 75th percentile figure from a decade prior. The acceptance rate is now 47 percent, and the applicant pool is more competitive than ever. Those attending possess impressive mid-50 percent standardized test ranges of 27-32 on the ACT and 1270-1410 on the SAT with an even number of students submitting results from both exams. They also earned the grades to match those test scores with an average unweighted GPA of 3.8. A solid 50 percent hailed from the top 10 percent of their high school class, and 86 percent placed in the top quartile.

With more than 30,000 applicants annually, NC State admissions officers rely heavily on factors like SAT scores, GPA, class rank, and the rigor of one's course load. All other factors are mere considerations, unlikely to exert significant influence on the decision. There are no early action or early decision options at NC State, but we recommend that every serious applicant submit by the Nov. 1 priority deadline rather than waiting until mid-January. Thirty-four percent of those accepted ultimately enroll in the school compared with over 50 percent in 2000 when the school drew one-third as many applicants. Despite the lower yield rate, it is fair to say that NC State is a more desirable landing spot than ever for high-achieving North Carolina residents.

Worth Your Money?

When an annual tuition bill is in the four-figures it instantly qualifies as an absurd bargain. NC State's tuition is actually around one-sixth the cost of North Carolina private schools like Duke, Davidson, or Wake Forest. For the 9 percent of Wolfpack members not from in state, thanks to low housing costs, the total cost of attendance is not obscene, coming in at under $45k. Therefore, the value of this degree for a nonresident would be context dependent—engineering, computer science, and design students are more than likely to see favorable returns. For a resident, it's a no-brainer investment.

FINANCIAL
Institutional Type: Public
In-State Tuition: $6,535
Out-of-State Tuition: $26,654
Room & Board: $11,601
Required Fees: $2,566
Books & Supplies: $1,082

Avg. Need-Based Grant: $10,812
Avg. % of Need Met: 76%

Avg. Merit-Based Award: $6,653
% Receiving (All Freshmen): 12%
% Receiving (Freshmen w/o Need): 4%

Avg. Cumulative Debt: $25,893
% of Students Borrowing: 50%

CAREER
Who Recruits
1. John Deere
2. Smithfield
3. GSK
4. Allstate
5. SAS

Notable Internships
1. Barclays
2. Red Hat
3. Cisco

Top Industries
1. Business
2. Engineering
3. Operations
4. Education
5. Research

Top Employers
1. Cisco
2. SAS
3. IBM
4. Lenovo
5. Red Hat

Where Alumni Work
1. Raleigh-Durham, NC
2. Charlotte
3. Winston-Salem, NC
4. Washington DC
5. San Francisco

Median Earnings
College Scorecard (Early Career): $52,500
PayScale (Early Career): $60,200
PayScale (Mid-Career): $113,200

RANKINGS
Money: 35
U.S. News: 80 (T), National Universities
Wall Street Journal/THE: 112
Washington Monthly: 89, National Universities

COLLEGE OVERLAPS
Clemson University
Pennsylvania State University - University Park
University of North Carolina at Chapel Hill
University of South Carolina
Virginia Tech

Northeastern University

Boston, Massachusetts | 617-373-2200

ADMISSION
Admission Rate: 18%
Admission Rate - Men: 18%
Admission Rate - Women: 18%
EA Admission Rate: NR
ED Admission Rate: 37%
ED Admits as % of Total Admits: 5%
Admission Rate (5-Year Trend): -14%
% of Admits Attending (Yield): 26%
Transfer Admission Rate: 16%

SAT Reading/Writing (Middle 50%): 680-750
SAT Math (Middle 50%): 710-790
ACT Composite (Middle 50%): 32-35

% Graduated in Top 10% of HS Class: 75%
% Graduated in Top 25% of HS Class: 93%
% Graduated in Top 50% of HS Class: 99%

Demonstrated Interest: Considered
Legacy Status: Not Considered
Admission Interview Offered: No

ENROLLMENT
Total Undergraduate Enrollment: 18,359
% Part-Time: 0%
% Male: 49%
% Female: 51%
% Out-of-State: 73%
% Fraternity: 10%
% Sorority: 17%
% On-Campus (Freshman): 99%
% On-Campus (All Undergraduate): 47%

% African-American: 4%
% Asian: 14%
% Hispanic: 8%
% White: 45%
% Other: 5%
% Race or Ethnicity Unknown: 6%
% International: 17%
% Low-Income: 11%

ACADEMICS
Student-to-Faculty Ratio: 14 to 1
% of Classes Under 20: 68%
% of Classes 20-49: 26%
% of Classes 50 or More: 6%
% Full-Time Faculty: 74%
% Full-Time Faculty w/ Terminal Degree: 94%

Top Programs
Communication Studies
Computer Science
Criminal Justice
Engineering
Health Science
International Affairs
International Business
Nursing

Retention Rate: 96%
4-Year Graduation Rate: NR
6-Year Graduation Rate: 89%

Curricular Flexibility: Somewhat Flexible
Academic Rating: ★★★★✦

#CollegesWorthYourMoney

If Northeastern University was a middle-aged person headed to a twentieth high school reunion, it would easily earn the distinction as the least recognized individual in the room. Few institutions have undergone such a substantial metamorphosis in such a short time. Beginning in the 1990s NU decided to reverse-engineer the US News rankings and make a grab for increased prestige. At the time, the school was ranked the 162nd best university in the nation. By 2020, it had cracked the top fifty. Today, the average undergraduate student possesses a 4.2 GPA and a 1455 on the SAT, literally 400+ higher than two decades ago. You read that correctly—400 points!

Inside the Classroom
On the menu for this suddenly top-flight breed of undergrads are all the trappings of a major research university, including 130 majors and 195 combined majors available at Northeastern's seven undergraduate schools. All students are required to walk the NUpath, the school's core curriculum that is "built around essential, broad-based knowledge and skills—such as understanding societies and analyzing data—integrated with specific content areas and disciplines." There are eleven components to the NUpath that involve forays into the natural and designed world, creative expression and innovation, culture, formal and quantitative reasoning, societies and institutions, analyzing data, differences and diversity, ethical reasoning, writing across audiences, integrating knowledge and skills through experience, and a capstone course as you near completion of your chosen major(s).

More than two-thirds of Husky classrooms contain nineteen or fewer students, and 12 percent have single-digit enrollments. Large lecture hall courses crammed with undergrads are rare at this school—only 6 percent of sections sport a student enrollment of fifty or more. A 14:1 student-to-faculty ratio makes these cozy class sizes possible. Since 2006, Northeastern has added an incredible 650 tenured and tenure-track faculty members. Undergraduate research opportunities exist in all departments, and experiential learning of some type is had by virtually all graduates, thanks to the school's illustrious and robust co-op program. NU students have not only become more accomplished but also more worldly. In a given year, 3,800+ students have a global experience in one of eighty-eight countries, and 500+ students participate in a co-op program overseas.

The D'Amore-McKim School of Business is a top-ranked school and offers one of the best international business programs anywhere, and the both the College of Engineering and College of Computer Science are highly respected as well. Criminal justice, architecture, and nursing are three other majors that rate near the top nationally. Business/marketing (25 percent) and engineering (20 percent) account for the largest percentages of degrees conferred. The social sciences (10 percent), health-related professions (10 percent), and biology (8 percent) round out the list of most popular majors. In 2019, Northeastern grads fared better than ever in procuring nationally competitive scholarships. Nine took home Fulbright Scholarships, five were awarded Gilman Scholarships, and two won Truman Scholarships.

Outside the Classroom
Northeastern is split down the middle in terms of those who live in on-campus housing and those who do not. All freshmen and sophomores are required to live in the dorms, and most have at least one or two roommates. Campus offers six large quad areas and twenty eateries. Greek life is fairly strong with 10 percent of men and 17 percent of women joining frats and sororities. The 73-acre urban campus is situated in the true heart of downtown Boston and within one mile of Fenway Park, Newbury Street, and the Museum of Fine Arts. With such a premier location, the beloved city of Boston is truly an extension of your campus, but there are also plenty of university-sponsored activities to keep you busy. Over 480 student clubs and organizations and the Northeastern University Hus-skiers and Outing Club (NUHOC), student government, and forty club sports teams are among the most popular. In total, 3,000 students participate in club and intramural sports. Spectator sports are not a focal point of NU life—the football program was dissolved in 2009—but of the sixteen existing NCAA Division I squads, the Huskies hockey team reigns supreme. The spirit of volunteerism is huge at NU as students have contributed a collective 1.4 million hours since 2006.

Career Services
Thirty-two counselors, employer relations specialists, and experiential learning coordinators comprise the NU Employer Engagement and Career Design Office (EECD), which doesn't count admin assistants or IT professionals. Working out to a student-to-advisor ratio of 574:1, NU offers a high level of support for an institution with more than 18,000 undergraduates. Northeastern University has long held a reputation as one of the premier career services providers in the nation, and it's not hard to see why.

E-mail: admissions@northeastern.edu | Website: www.northeastern.edu

Career counselors received incredibly high reviews from students as 96 percent report progress on their career goals after only one session; 100 percent felt it was worth their time to return for a follow-up. The EECD has forged relationships with over 3,000 employers and, through its employer-in-residence program, representatives from those organizations spend up to one day per week for an entire year interacting with students, making personal connections, and offering career tips. A typical Fall Career Fair is attended by 260 employers and the Spring Engineering and Technology Career Fair usually draws 4,000+ students and 140 companies. Perhaps the most impactful role of this office is to facilitate co-op placements. Ninety-seven percent of NU graduates spend at least one semester in a co-op placement, and 50 percent of students receive a job offer from their co-op partner; 3,000+ employers participate each year.

Professional Outcomes

Nine months after leaving Northeastern, 98 percent of students have landed at their next employment or graduate school destination. Huskies entering the job market are quickly rounded up by the likes of State Street, Fidelity Investments, IBM, and Amazon, all of whom employ 500+ Northeastern alums. Between 200 and 500 employees at Wayfair, Google, Amazon, Oracle, IBM, and Apple have an NU lineage. Whether or not they originally hailed from New England, the vast majority of graduates remain in the Greater Boston area. Next in popularity are New York City, San Francisco, DC, Los Angeles, Philadelphia, and Seattle. Starting salaries are above average, in part due to the stellar co-op program, and compensation is in the same range as other highly selective schools including Fordham and Boston University.

The five graduate schools most frequently attended by NU grads are: Boston University, Columbia University, Harvard, NYU, and Northeastern University itself. The highly ranked Northeastern University School of Law also takes a large number of its own undergraduates. More than one alum is currently enrolled at such law schools as Suffolk, Harvard, Fordham, and Boston College. While Northeastern does not have its own medical college, many graduates go on to attend top institutions. Multiple recent grads are currently attending such medical schools as UMass, Harvard, UConn, and Tufts. The medical school acceptance rate was 73 percent in 2019, significantly better than the national average.

Admission

Only 18 percent of the 62,263 applicants for a place in the 2019-20 freshman class received a letter of acceptance. The average SAT score was a 1455 and the average ACT score was a 33. Three-quarters of those enrolled placed in the top 10 percent of their high school class. A decade ago, the school received only 34,000 applications, and a far less menacing 41 percent were let through the door. Freshmen in 2009-10 possessed middle 50 percent SAT scores of 1200-1370. Any way you measure it, the level of selectivity is far greater than even in the most recent past.

An applicant's GPA, rigor of courses, standardized test scores, essay, and recommendation letters are all categorized as "very important" admissions factors by this committee. Admissions officers at Northeastern place soft factors such as extracurricular activities, talent/ability, character, personal qualities, volunteer work, and work experience on the next rung of "important" categories. Northeastern's desirability and prestige have risen at a lightning pace, making it exactly the type of school that even a well-intentioned school counselor or parent can easily misjudge in terms of the current odds of gaining admission. This is a school that generally only accepts students with standardized test scores in the top 3 percent and who have virtually flawless transcripts. Applying via binding early decision is definitely a serious consideration. Of the 1,478 who did so last year, 37 percent were successful.

Worth Your Money?

Northeastern has a list price cost of attendance in excess of $73,000 per year, and the need-based aid situation is less than ideal. Only two-thirds of those applying for financial aid received an award, but over half of Northeastern students receive a merit aid award averaging $19,500, at least bringing the total four-year costs closer to $200,000. In short, this school is worth your money if you are aiming to enter a high-paying field and/or have parents who can afford the hefty tuition payments. Then the connections the school provides are worth a substantial amount. However, middle-class students set on entering public service would likely not see their investment returned and could accumulate a good deal of debt along the way.

FINANCIAL
Institutional Type: Private
In-State Tuition: $52,420
Out-of-State Tuition: $52,420
Room & Board: $16,930
Required Fees: $1,086
Books & Supplies: $1,000

Avg. Need-Based Grant: $35,299
Avg. % of Need Met: 100%

Avg. Merit-Based Award: $19,488
% Receiving (All Freshmen): 51%
% Receiving (Freshmen w/o Need): 32%

Avg. Cumulative Debt: NR
% of Students Borrowing: NR

CAREER
Who Recruits
1. IBM
2. Siemens
3. Staples
4. Coleman
5. Northwestern Mutual

Notable Internships
1. Wayfair
2. Vogue
3. Tesla

Top Industries
1. Business
2. Engineering
3. Operations
4. Education
5. information Technology

Top Employers
1. State Street
2. Fidelity Investments
3. Amazon
4. IBM
5. Wayfair

Where Alumni Work
1. Boston
2. New York City
3. San Francisco
4. Washington DC
5. Los Angeles

Median Earnings
College Scorecard (Early Career): $67,400
PayScale (Early Career): $66,200
PayScale (Mid-Career): $113,500

RANKINGS
Money: 155
U.S. News: 49 (T), National Universities
Wall Street Journal/THE: 86 (T)
Washington Monthly: 128, National Universities

COLLEGE OVERLAPS
Boston University
George Washington University
Cornell University
New York University
University of Michigan

ADMISSION
Admission Rate: 9%
Admission Rate - Men: 9%
Admission Rate - Women: 9%
EA Admission Rate: Not Offered
ED Admission Rate: 25%
ED Admits as % of Total Admits: 30%
Admission Rate (5-Year Trend): -5%
% of Admits Attending (Yield): 55%
Transfer Admission Rate: 16%

SAT Reading/Writing (Middle 50%): 700-760
SAT Math (Middle 50%): 740-790
ACT Composite (Middle 50%): 33-35

% Graduated in Top 10% of HS Class: 92%
% Graduated in Top 25% of HS Class: 98%
% Graduated in Top 50% of HS Class: 100%

Demonstrated Interest: Considered
Legacy Status: Considered
Admission Interview Offered: Yes

ENROLLMENT
Total Undergraduate Enrollment: 8,327
% Part-Time: 2%
% Male: 49%
% Female: 51%
% Out-of-State: 69%
% Fraternity: 27%
% Sorority: 34%
% On-Campus (Freshman): 100%
% On-Campus (All Undergraduate): 60%

% African-American: 6%
% Asian: 18%
% Hispanic: 12%
% White: 44%
% Other: 6%
% Race or Ethnicity Unknown: 3%
% International: 10%
% Low-Income: 15%

ACADEMICS
Student-to-Faculty Ratio: 6 to 1
% of Classes Under 20: 77%
% of Classes 20-49: 18%
% of Classes 50 or More: 5%
% Full-Time Faculty: 87%
% Full-Time Faculty w/ Terminal Degree: 100%

Top Programs
Biology
Communication Studies
Economics
Engineering
Journalism
Performing Arts
Political Science
Social Policy

Retention Rate: 98%
4-Year Graduation Rate: 84%
6-Year Graduation Rate: 94%

Curricular Flexibility: Somewhat Flexible
Academic Rating: ★★★★★

#CollegesWorthYourMoney

Like the neighboring University of Chicago, Northwestern University is a highly selective academic institution that operates on a quarter system and is located in Illinois, but the similarities end there. Where the UChicago has a reputation as a breeding ground for future academics/researchers, Northwestern's vibe is more pre-professional, athletic, and Greek-inclined, but the 8,327 undergraduates who attend must bring equally flawless academic credentials to the table—otherwise, they will find themselves among the 91 percent of applicants left outside the gates.

Inside the Classroom

Northwestern is home to six undergraduate schools: Weinberg College of Arts and Sciences; McCormick School of Engineering and Applied Science; School of Education and Social Policy; School of Communication; Medill School of Journalism, Media, Integrated Marketing Communications; and Bienen School of Music. Academic requirements vary by school. Weinberg, which enrolls half of all Wildcats, requires two first-year seminars, the demonstration of proficiency in a foreign language and in writing as well as two courses each in six intellectual divisions. Overall, coursework requirements are extensive but do allow for choice.

The quarter system allows students to take four courses at a time rather than the typical five. Even so, the academic demands are intense, and Northwestern students work hard for their grades. Fortunately, the academic experience is far from an anonymous endeavor. The university has a phenomenal 6:1 student-faculty ratio, and a spectacular 42 percent of class sections have nine or fewer students enrolled; 77 percent have fewer than twenty enrollees. Faculty receive generally favorable reviews from undergraduate students with 93 percent either "very satisfied" or "generally satisfied" with the quality of instruction; 92 percent awarded one of those two positive ratings when asked about the availability of their professors. Close to 60 percent of Northwestern students have the chance to conduct research with a faculty member at some point during their undergraduate years.

The social sciences account for the greatest numbers of degrees conferred (22 percent), followed by communications/journalism (13 percent), engineering (13 percent), biology (8 percent), visual and performing arts (8 percent), and psychology (7 percent). Medill is widely regarded as one of the country's best journalism schools. The McCormick School of Engineering also achieves top rankings, along with programs in economics, social policy, and theatre. Students from all majors bring home prestigious postgraduate fellowships at an enviable rate. In 2020 alone, the school produced twenty Fulbright Scholars and thirty-two National Science Foundation Research Fellowships. In total, the Class of 2020 took home a ridiculous 200+ competitive national/global scholarships.

Outside the Classroom

Northwestern, like its elite peers Duke, Stanford, and USC, offers top-level academics without sacrificing any of the major college frills like football and frat parties. With forty-six Greek organizations drawing 27 percent of men and 34 percent of women, fraternities and sororities exert a significant degree of influence over the social scene. Athletics are also a strong part of the university's culture with eight men's and eleven women's teams competing in NCAA Division I. The Wildcats are the lone private school competing in the Big Ten Conference, which is otherwise made up of athletic powerhouses like Penn State, Ohio State, and Michigan. NU undergrads report that over 90 percent are "deeply involved" with a student organization or athletic team. Nearly half the student population reported that same level of involvement with a community service project. Of the school's 350 student-run clubs, pre-professional organizations, service-oriented groups, and the Daily Northwestern—named the nation's top student paper by the Society of Professional Journalists—are among the most popular. Evanston is roughly thirty to forty-five minutes from downtown Chicago (depending on traffic). One of the famous North Shore suburbs of Chicago, Evanston is an affluent city with plenty of high-end restaurants and coffee shops. Natural beauty is easy to find as the school owns a lakefront beach that is on campus. Approximately 60 percent of students (and 99.9 percent of freshmen) elect to live in on-campus housing that is highlighted by thirteen residence halls, each accommodating anywhere from 25-500 students.

Career Services

Northwestern Career Advancement (NCA) employs eighteen full-time professionals who work directly with or on behalf of undergraduate students. That includes career counselors, career advisors, and employer relations staff but does not include graduate advisors, interns, or IT specialists. The student-to-advisor ratio of 463:1 puts NU in the average range compared to other institutions included in this book. Career counselors keep extensive walk-in hours and arrange a number of career-related events, large and small, from the two-day Fall Internship and Job Fair with over 150 employers to more intimate workshops and employer information sessions that are held throughout the year.

A phenomenal 92 percent of graduates reported they engaged in at least one experiential learning opportunity. When looking specifically at internships, 73 percent reported landing at least one summer of paid or unpaid experience. The Northwestern Network Mentorship Program now has 5,000 alumni across ninety industries and sixty-six countries ready and willing to help current students with their career planning. The NCA has corporate partnerships with a host of top-notch companies including Accenture, Deloitte, PwC, Capital One, and JP Morgan.

Professional Outcomes

Six months after graduating, 72 percent of the Class of 2019 had found employment, 22 percent were in graduate school, and only 3 percent were still looking for work. The four professional fields attracting more than 10 percent of Wildcat alumni were business/finance (20 percent), consulting (15 percent), communications/marketing/media (14 percent), and engineering (11 percent). Employers included an impressive group of media outlets including the BBC, NBC News, the Washington Post, and NPR. Across all other industries Wildcats had strong representation at all of the usual corporate giants including Boeing, Google, IBM, Deloitte, PepsiCo, Northrup Grumman, and Goldman Sachs. More than 50 percent of graduates remained in the Midwest. Across all majors the average starting salary was $62k while engineering and applied sciences students averaged $76k with the lowest income belonging to communications students who earned $51k.

Of the recent alums headed straight to graduate school, 18 percent were pursuing medical degrees, 13 percent were beginning PhD programs, and 6 percent were entering law school. Engineering, medicine, and business were the three most popular graduate areas of concentration. Members of the Class of 2019 pursued advanced degrees at seven of the eight Ivy League Schools—Stanford, MIT, Carnegie Mellon, UChicago, and Oxford— among a host of other elite institutions. Northwestern is a prolific producer of future MDs; 258 applied in the 2019-20 school year alone.

Admission

After nine straight years of declining acceptance rates, the Northwestern Class of 2023 stabilized at 9 percent. The profile of the average freshman in the 2019-20 school year was a mid-50 percent SAT of 1450-1540 and an ACT of 33-35. A decade ago, when 26 percent of applicants were accepted, the ACT range was a significantly lower 30-32. The percent of freshmen in the top 10 percent of their high school class also has increased during that time, jumping from 85 percent to 92 percent.

According to the admissions office, rigor of courses, GPA, class rank, and standardized test scores are the only four factors that are "very important" in the admissions process. Last year, early decision applicants comprised 55 percent of the incoming classes and enjoyed increased chances of getting in. The regular decision acceptance rate in 2019 was only 7 percent compared to 25 percent in the ED round. Northwestern has always been a highly selective school, but the bar has been raised even higher in recent years. Those who wish to find a home on this picturesque North Shore campus next fall must bring excellent credentials to the table and should strongly consider applying early decision.

Worth Your Money?

The average Northwestern graduate who took out loans owes $36k, which is a tad more than the national average. This is to be expected at a school that costs over $79k per year and does not award much merit aid. Yet, for the 46 percent of undergrads who qualify for need-based aid, the school could not be more generous. It met 100 percent of every student's demonstrated financial need with an average grant of $54k per year. With very few exceptions, this is a school worth paying for. Even in programs such as journalism that do not generally lead to high-paying first jobs, the networks you will gain at Northwestern are likely to end up paying career dividends many decades down the road.

FINANCIAL
Institutional Type: Private
In-State Tuition: $58,701
Out-of-State Tuition: $58,701
Room & Board: $17,616
Required Fees: $0
Books & Supplies: $1,662

Avg. Need-Based Grant: $54,303
Avg. % of Need Met: 100%

Avg. Merit-Based Award: $5,401
% Receiving (All Freshmen): 5%
% Receiving (Freshmen w/o Need): 5%

Avg. Cumulative Debt: $36,350
% of Students Borrowing: 34%

CAREER
Who Recruits
1. Nielsen
2. Aldi
3. AQR
4. Roland Berger
5. Flow Traders

Notable Internships
1. Brookings Institute
2. HSBC
3. BlackRock

Top Industries
1. Business
2. Education
3. Media
4. Operations
5. Research

Top Employers
1. Google
2. Accenture
3. Amazon
4. Microsoft
5. Deloitte

Where Alumni Work
1. Chicago
2. New York City
3. San Francisco
4. Los Angeles
5. Washington DC

Median Earnings
College Scorecard (Early Career): $69,000
PayScale (Early Career): $67,000
PayScale (Mid-Career): $128,900

RANKINGS
Money: 53
U.S. News: 9 (T), National Universities
Wall Street Journal/THE: 10
Washington Monthly: 30, National Universities

COLLEGE OVERLAPS
Cornell University
Duke University
University of Chicago
University of Michigan
University of Pennsylvania

Oberlin College

Oberlin, Ohio | 440-775-8411

ADMISSION
Admission Rate: 36%
Admission Rate - Men: 35%
Admission Rate - Women: 37%
EA Admission Rate: Not Offered
ED Admission Rate: 52%
ED Admits as % of Total Admits: 9%
Admission Rate (5-Year Trend): +6%
% of Admits Attending (Yield): 28%
Transfer Admission Rate: 26%

SAT Reading/Writing (Middle 50%): 650-730
SAT Math (Middle 50%): 630-750
ACT Composite (Middle 50%): 29-33

% Graduated in Top 10% of HS Class: 54%
% Graduated in Top 25% of HS Class: 84%
% Graduated in Top 50% of HS Class: 98%

Demonstrated Interest: Considered
Legacy Status: Important
Admission Interview Offered: Yes

ENROLLMENT
Total Undergraduate Enrollment: 2,846
% Part-Time: 1%
% Male: 42%
% Female: 58%
% Out-of-State: 93%
% Fraternity: Not Offered
% Sorority: Not Offered
% On-Campus (Freshman): 99%
% On-Campus (All Undergraduate): 85%

% African-American: 5%
% Asian: 4%
% Hispanic: 8%
% White: 61%
% Other: 8%
% Race or Ethnicity Unknown: 1%
% International: 12%
% Low-Income: 9%

ACADEMICS
Student-to-Faculty Ratio: 10 to 1
% of Classes Under 20: 78%
% of Classes 20-49: 21%
% of Classes 50 or More: 1%
% Full-Time Faculty: 92%
% Full-Time Faculty w/ Terminal Degree: 93%

Top Programs
Biology
Chemistry
Cinema Studies
English
Environmental Studies
History
Musical Studies
Politics

Retention Rate: 91%
4-Year Graduation Rate: 76%
6-Year Graduation Rate: 86%

Curricular Flexibility: Somewhat Flexible
Academic Rating: ★★★★

#CollegesWorthYourMoney

A Midwestern version of Oregon's Reed College in terms of the originality and progressive leanings of the student body, Oberlin College in Ohio is an extremely strong provider of a liberal arts education. Known primarily for its top-ranked Conservatory of Music and as a factory for future PhDs, particularly in the hard sciences, Oberlin enrolls 2,846 undergraduates. Boasting fifty majors and an additional forty-three minors and concentrations, the college provides an educational setting where professors in just about all of your classes will not only know your name but, amazingly, perhaps even your goals and interests.

Inside the Classroom
As part of the curriculum exploration requirement, two courses each are required in each of the college's three divisions: Arts & Humanities, Mathematics & Natural Sciences, and the Social Sciences. Two of the thirty-two total courses taken must be classified as writing and another two as meeting the Quantitative & Formal Reasoning requirement. Three additional courses must have a Cultural Diversity designation. Students are encouraged—but not required—to become proficient in a foreign language. Overall, Oberlin's mandated coursework is not cumbersome, especially compared to many liberal arts schools of its ilk.

Thanks to its almost entirely undergraduate student population, the effects of Oberlin's 9:1 student-to-faculty ratio are fully felt. Of all the courses at the college, 78 percent had nineteen or fewer students enrolled, and 46 percent contained fewer than ten students. Professors are generous with their time in an academic environment conducive to the formation of mentorships. Undergraduate research opportunities are not hard to locate. In fact, according to the school, "Many students coauthor articles with faculty, which are published in scholarly journals and presented at national meetings." The Office of Study Away helps arrange for roughly 40 percent of graduates to study in a foreign land. School-run opportunities such as Oberlin-in-London are on the table as are ninety affiliated programs.

In terms of sheer volume, the greatest number of degrees conferred in 2019 were in history (55), politics (51), biology (48), English (46), and economics (45). The Conservatory of Music has a worldwide reputation as one or more of its representative alumni are in every major ensemble in the United States. Programs in the natural sciences have sterling reputations, leading to remarkable medical school acceptance rates and the aforementioned number of future PhD scientists and researchers. Highly competitive postgraduate fellowship-granting organizations adore Oberlin grads. In 2020, seven grads and alumni were named Fulbright Scholars, and the school routinely produces Gilman, Critical Language, Goldwater, and Marshall winners as well.

Outside the Classroom
If you understand Oberlin's vibe it will not surprise you that there are no frats or sororities on campus. Instead, Oberlin requires students to live in either college-owned housing or student-run co-ops all the way through graduation. Some co-ops offer "theme living" centered on commonalities such as an obsession with sci-fi, disability status, sustainability/environmental concerns, or a love of ancient Mediterranean culture. With more than 175 clubs and organizations, twenty-one varsity teams, and thirty-one intramural and club sports, just about every one of Oberlin's undergraduate students is involved in something. The Yeoman and Yeowomen compete within NCAA Division III with 350 athletes competing at that level. If you happen to like live classical music you're in luck—the school's conservatory puts on hundreds of concerts each year. Guest speakers, often intellectuals and authors, regularly attract large crowds at Oberlin. There are a wealth of organizations catering to political/social causes and musical/theatrical performance as well as seven student-run publications. To generalize, most Oberlin students are politically liberal and enjoy challenging social norms. Most students stick around campus, and the small town of Oberlin's quaintness is best exemplified by its claim of having one of the last single-screen movie theaters in the country. For those with access to a car, Cleveland is only a forty-minute drive away.

Career Services
The Career Development Center employs five professional staff members who work in career development or graduate school advising (not counting technical support or administrative assistants). With a 569:1 student-to-advisor ratio, Oberlin provides a lower-than-average level of career services support than many comparable liberal arts schools featured in this guide. While the office does encourage one-on-one appointments and walk-ins, large-scale events like career fairs are lacking, and on-campus recruiting by major employers is not a routine occurrence.

Oberlin College

E-mail: college.admissions@oberlin.edu | Website: www.oberlin.edu

Beginning in 2019, Oberlin began hosting Career Communities covering nine sectors (e.g., entrepreneurship and innovation, professions in music, and science and technology). Up to thirty juniors and seniors can join each community, which includes a guaranteed summer internship and a set of industry-specific mentors. Each community meets as a group six times per semester. Oberlin helps to arrange summer and winter term internships for all interested students, primarily through the use of its online resources. The Oberlin Alumni Database is a platform from which current students can seek job advice from alumni. The office also recommends connecting with 7,000 alumni via LinkedIn. New programs such as the Career Communities show Oberlin's commitment to expanding its career services offerings.

Professional Outcomes

The Class of 2019 saw 74 percent of graduates find employment within six months of graduating; 17 percent enrolled in graduate school, and just 5 percent were still seeking employment. Multiple 2019 grads were hired by Google, Netflix, and Sony Pictures. In part because so many students go on to enter careers in research and academia, median salaries are quite low in the early career stage of life. However, it is important to note that many Oberlin graduates do go on to remunerative careers. New York is home to the highest number of alumni followed by San Francisco, Cleveland, DC, and Boston.

Over the last few years multiple students have gone on to pursue advanced degrees at Harvard, Stanford, MIT, Brown, Columbia, Princeton, and the University of Michigan. Graduates fare well in gaining acceptance into med school, sporting an 80 percent success rate, nearly double the national average. Recent grads have enrolled in medical school at the University of Pennsylvania, Baylor College of Medicine, and SUNY Upstate Medical University. Law school applicants have enjoyed an 83 percent acceptance rate and have found homes at the likes of Yale, Indiana, and Wake Forest. Oberlin also has a reputation for churning out future PhDs and, in fact, is among the top fifteen schools across all disciplines in producing graduates who go on to earn their doctoral degrees.

Admission

Thirty-six percent of the 7,708 applicants for a place in the Class of 2023 were successful, but that number doesn't fully tell the story of how competitive the Oberlin admissions process really is. Twenty-eight percent of those accepted went on to enroll in the college. Of those who joined the college, the median SAT score is 1400, the median ACT is 31, and 54 percent placed in the top decile of their graduating class.

GPA, class rank, and the rigor of one's secondary school record are the four factors weighted most heavily in the process. Secondary factors include standardized test scores (the school is presently test-optional through 2023), essays, recommendations, talent/ability, character/personal qualities, and the seemingly polar opposite categories of legacy and first-generation applicants. Those who apply via early decision enjoy a 49 percent acceptance rate and account for roughly one-third of each incoming class. Oberlin is definitely a college where the self-selecting applicant pool results in a deceptively high acceptance rate. Make no mistake—you need to bring extremely strong grades to the table (only 5 percent of enrolled high school freshmen possessed GPAs under 3.25). Applying early is a worthwhile maneuver for those clamoring to spend the next four years in rural Ohio at this liberal arts gem.

Worth Your Money?

Oberlin is one of the exclusive club of colleges that meets 100 percent of all undergraduates' demonstrated need. Half of all students receive an average annual aid package that exceeds $42,000. Equally encouraging is the fact that 75 percent of students net merit aid; the average award is approximately $19,000. With an annual cost of attendance of $75,888, those "discounts" are most appreciated, especially because many graduates pursue careers that are not among the most lucrative and/or require many additional years of education beyond the bachelor's degree. Admitted students should consider their future plans before committing. However, Oberlin's top-notch academics and generous aid make it a worthy investment for most.

FINANCIAL
Institutional Type: Private
In-State Tuition: $55,976
Out-of-State Tuition: $55,976
Room & Board: $16,826
Required Fees: $842
Books & Supplies: $1,908

Avg. Need-Based Grant: $42,718
Avg. % of Need Met: 100%

Avg. Merit-Based Award: $19,690
% Receiving (All Freshmen): 75%
% Receiving (Freshmen w/o Need): 26%

Avg. Cumulative Debt: $26,175
% of Students Borrowing: 45%

CAREER
Who Recruits
1. Cleveland Clinic
2. Sony Pictures
3. City Year
4. Epic
5. Microsoft

Notable Internships
1. Gotham Group
2. Colgate-Palmolive
3. Fidelity Investments

Top Industries
1. Education
2. Business
3. Media
4. Arts & Design
5. Social Services

Top Employers
1. Google
2. Apple
3. Amazon
4. Microsoft
5. IBM

Where Alumni Work
1. New York City
2. San Francisco
3. Cleveland
4. Boston
5. Washington DC

Median Earnings
College Scorecard (Early Career): $40,800
PayScale (Early Career): $56,400
PayScale (Mid-Career): $105,400

RANKINGS
Money: 559
U.S. News: 36 (T), Liberal Arts Colleges
Wall Street Journal/THE: 106 (T)
Washington Monthly: 134, Liberal Arts Colleges

COLLEGE OVERLAPS
Grinnell College
Kenyon College
Macalester College
Wesleyan University
Vassar College

Occidental College

Los Angeles, California | 323-259-2700

A rare liberal arts dynamo in an urban setting, Occidental College, one of the oldest schools on the West Coast, is home to 2,081 undergraduate students. Situated only eight miles from downtown Los Angeles, Occidental attracts a diverse set of talented and community-oriented young people. Non higher-education aficionados may have first heard of the college when Barack Obama burst onto the political scene; he attended the school through sophomore year before transferring to Columbia University. Along with the Claremont colleges, the school known affectionately as Oxy is among the best liberal arts institutions west of the Mississippi.

Inside the Classroom
Thirty-four majors are on tap, but all students must plow through the Oxy Core Program that is designed to "encourage critical thinking, problem-solving, effective communication and productive engagement with issues of difference, diversity and community." Before students even arrive on campus they must complete a summer reading assignment centered on an annual theme. Once class commences, students engage in the Cultural Studies Program, two small seminar courses intended to introduce students to collegiate-level writing and discourse.

Oxy offers an enviable 9.5:1 student-to-faculty ratio and an average class size of eighteen students. Only one class contained over fifty students, and almost 90 percent enrolled fewer than thirty. The Undergraduate Research Center facilitates a plethora of hands-on experiences including a ten-week mentored summer program and limitless chances to pursue independent and course-based academic research during the regular school year. At the end of the summer, 120+ students present their research findings. Over two-thirds of undergraduates become global citizens during their time at Occidental through international internships and fellowships or through participation in the study abroad program. Faculty-led programs are available at a variety of destinations around the globe including Italy, Costa Rica, China, the Czech Republic, and Austria. Its partnership with the United Nations provides a one-of-a-kind opportunity for a cohort of students to live in New York, intern at the UN, and take courses with Occidental professors at the same time.

The most popular degree programs at Oxy, all of which carry strong reputations with employers and top-tier graduate schools, are economics, biology, sociology, psychology, diplomacy and world affairs, mathematics, and urban and environmental policy. Prestigious postgraduate scholarship programs look kindly on those with a degree from Oxy. Ten Rhodes Scholars graduated from the school that has been a top ten producer of Fulbright Fellowships for the last decade; nine seniors took home Fulbrights in 2019 alone.

Outside the Classroom
Hardly your typical urban campus, Occidental's 120 acres are among the most notably beautiful higher education homes in the entire country. Countless Hollywood productions (e.g., Clueless, 90210) have selected Occidental as a filming location. The amenities are more in line with a private resort than a typical college. It features a 25,000-square-foot facility only for tennis, a thirty-four-meter deep pool only for water polo, and dining services that serve restaurant-quality cuisine. Just over four-fifths of the student population reside in one the school's thirteen residence halls, and there are seven Greek organizations that attract a modest membership. Roughly 25 percent of undergrads compete on one of twenty-one NCAA Division III sports teams. Tigers also have the option of joining eight club sports teams or any number of intramural athletic leagues. A full array of student organizations exist as well—115 in total—with everything from Oxy TV to a microfinance club. Wandering off campus and into the Eagle Rock and Highland Park sections of Northeast Los Angeles provides easily accessible entertainment, and downtown LA is only a short drive away, which is relevant because 60 percent of Oxy students bring a car to school. In addition, destinations including Venice Beach and Disneyland are less than an hour away.

Career Services
The Hameetman Career Center (HCC) has six full-time professional staff members working in career advising, pre-health advising, and national/international fellowship application guidance. The CDO's 347:1 student-to-advisor ratio is better than average when compared to other colleges featured in our guidebook. Additionally, the center trains four career peer advisors to assist their fellow undergrads. The six core services provided by the office are "(1) career education and career advice; (2) access to internships; (3) pre-law advice; (4) employer, alumni, and parent engagement; (5) job search; and (6) employer recruiting events." It conducts 1,650 one-on-one advising appointments per year.

Occidental College

E-mail: admission@oxy.edu | Website: www.oxy.edu

One recent Oxy Career Fair was attended by sixty-three employers and 380 students. Hosting more than 200 events each year, the HCC also brings 120 employers to campus each year for recruiting purposes. Including all events and individual counseling appointments, it interacts with 2,500 students annually. Internships hosting Oxy students in recent years include Mercedes Benz Shanghai, the Office of the Mayor of Los Angeles, the *Los Angeles Times*, and the NASA Jet Propulsion Laboratory. This office aims to reach students in their freshman year and first presents their services to incoming students at orientation with an eye toward preparing them for a productive first summer experience. Impressive employment and graduate enrollment statistics indicate that its approach works, earning Occidental's Hameetman Career Center praise from current and former students alike.

Professional Outcomes

One year after graduation, 94 percent of Occidental alumni are employed, pursuing graduate studies, or engaged in both simultaneously. By sector, the largest numbers of grads enter community service/education (25 percent), STEM (23 percent), and business (20 percent). Among the largest employers of Oxy alumni are the Los Angeles Unified School District, Kaiser Permanente, Microsoft, NASA Jet Propulsion Laboratory, Google, Morgan Stanley, and Amazon. Also on the list are a number of universities that employ Occidental grads after they earn advanced degrees. Most Tigers remain on the prowl in California—mainly LA or San Fran, although there are large alumni clusters on the East Coast, especially in New York City and DC. Midcareer average salaries are in the six figures and among the highest of any institution in the country. According to PayScale, recent graduates earn an average of $56,800 and, by midcareer, bring home $118,800.

Close to three-quarters of Oxy alumni eventually earn one or more advanced degrees. Recent graduates have gone on to continue their educations at Harvard, Stanford, NYU, University of Chicago, UCLA, USC, and UC Berkeley. Those pursuing law degrees have done so at Stanford, USC, UCLA, University of Pennsylvania, Yale, Columbia, Vanderbilt, and Emory. Each year Occidental sees roughly twenty graduates and alumni accepted into medical school, including many of the finest universities in the country. In short, graduate and professional schools respect the college's reputation and know that those who post an impressive undergraduate GPA have fully earned it.

Admission

Of the 7,501 applicants vying for a place in Occidental College's 2019-20 freshman class, 37 percent were admitted, and 562 ultimately enrolled. Members of the Class of 2023 held a median unweighted GPA of 3.7, SAT score of 1390, and an ACT score of 30. Students were generally active outside the classroom as 52 percent of freshmen played a sport in high school, 75 percent volunteered in their community, and 28 percent played a musical instrument. Fifty-three percent placed within the top decile of their high school graduating class; 87 percent landed in the top quarter.

An admissions review from the Occidental staff is a genuinely holistic process. As the committee states, "Creative, soulful, funny, introspective—all words to describe some of our most memorable applicants, but the common thread is always authenticity." That philosophy is supported by GPA, rigor of secondary school record, and the application essay as the triumvirate of admissions factors designated as "most important." Men may receive a slight edge in the admissions process as they make up 43 percent of the student body, but the admit rate for men and women is generally comparable. Those applying early decision received a "Yes" 49 percent of the time. The college has an fairly low yield rate of 20 percent, which means that it is always on the lookout for students who demonstrate interest and view the school as their number one choice.

Worth Your Money?

An education at Occidental is a phenomenal and highly personalized experience. Of course, providing such an intimate and supportive learning environment costs money. As a result, the annual cost of attendance is $73,176. Fortunately, those with significant financial need will see 100 percent of their need met by the school. That translates to 58 percent of current undergraduates receiving grants of over $45k, helping to make the Occidental experience far more affordable and a worth investment. Middle-income students without a significant financial aid offer should consider their career plans before agreeing to attend.

FINANCIAL
Institutional Type: Private
In-State Tuition: $55,980
Out-of-State Tuition: $55,980
Room & Board: $16,034
Required Fees: $596
Books & Supplies: $1,240

Avg. Need-Based Grant: $45,568
Avg. % of Need Met: 100%

Avg. Merit-Based Award: $14,509
% Receiving (All Freshmen): 46%
% Receiving (Freshmen w/o Need): 14%

Avg. Cumulative Debt: $29,306
% of Students Borrowing: 59%

CAREER
Who Recruits
1. NASA Jet Propulsion Laboratory
2. Northwestern Mutual
3. Aflac
4. Bank of America
5. Teach for America

Notable Internships
1. Calvin Klein
2. Paramount Pictures
3. Pfizer

Top Industries
1. Business
2. Education
3. Operations
4. Media
5. Social Services

Top Employers
1. Kaiser Permanente
2. Google
3. NASA Jet Propulsion Laboratory
4. Microsoft
5. Amazon

Where Alumni Work
1. Los Angeles
2. San Francisco
3. New York City
4. Seattle
5. Orange County, CA

Median Earnings
College Scorecard (Early Career): $50,600
PayScale (Early Career): $58,700
PayScale (Mid-Career): $124,000

RANKINGS
Money: 416
U.S. News: 40 (T), Liberal Arts Colleges
Wall Street Journal/THE: 100 (T)
Washington Monthly: 83, Liberal Arts Colleges

COLLEGE OVERLAPS
Colorado College
Macalester College
Pitzer College
Pomona College
Whitman College

The Ohio State University — Columbus

Columbus, Ohio | 614-292-3980

Anyone who has ever seen a college football game, even a flicker of one while flipping channels on a Saturday afternoon, will immediately associate the name Ohio State with gray football helmets covered in buckeye leaves. Yet, football is hardly the only draw at the great state of Ohio's flagship university, one of the top public research institutions anywhere. Over 46,000 undergraduate students now grace the Columbus campus, 75 percent of whom are Ohio natives, 19 percent of whom are from out of state, and 8 percent of whom are international students. As you will see in the "Admissions" section below, if you want to gain access to the 2021 version of OSU, you'd better be one of the best students in your high school graduating class.

Inside the Classroom

With 200+ undergraduate majors and eighteen schools and colleges housed within OSU, there are a number of curricular requirements that vary among the many academic programs. However, all Buckeyes must take a liberal arts core that includes writing, quantitative skills, natural science, literature, visual and performing arts, history, social science, and a foreign language. From there it's all about completing your major, but students can find electives in just about anything you can imagine because the university offers 12,000+ courses.

A 19-to-1 student-to-faculty ratio leads to fairly large classes as only 32 percent of sections enroll fewer than twenty students, so expect a fair number of courses in a large lecture hall setting. In fact, 31 percent of courses contain forty or more undergraduate students. Still, aggressive students can find opportunities to work closely with faculty. The Office of Undergraduate Research & Inquiry helps 800 students participate in annual Denman Undergraduate Research Forum and fifty+ students receive funding from OSU for summer research. All told, approximately 20 percent of students gain research experience. The same percentage of undergraduates elect to study abroad in one of 200 programs spread across seventy countries, the highest figure of any Big Ten university.

Business saw the greatest percentage of degrees conferred at 20 percent followed by engineering (15 percent), health professions (9 percent), and the social sciences (9 percent). It makes sense that so many flock to the business and engineering schools as they are among the highest rated undergraduate programs in their respective disciplines. Top companies adore new Buckeye grads, and hundreds of alums can be found at some of the top tech companies, banks, and accounting firms in the United States. In recent years, the university has produced between five and eleven Fulbright Scholars annually and as many as six Boren Scholars, thirteen Gilman Scholars, four Goldwater Scholars, and eleven National Science Foundation Graduate Research Fellowship honorable mentions.

Outside the Classroom

There's a little something for everyone on this anything-but-little 1,665-acre campus that ranks third largest in the United States in sheer size. If you are seeking Greek life, you can find it—11 percent of women join sororities and 7 percent of men enter fraternities. The sports scene is epic in scope whether you are a casual athlete wanting to join one of the sixty+ club teams and numerous intramural leagues or one of the 1,000+ big-time athletes on the Buckeyes' thirty-six varsity teams. Football Saturdays are kind of a big deal as more than 102,000 fans of the Scarlet and Gray pack Ohio Stadium. In total, 1,300 student organizations are awaiting your participation on the Columbus campus alone. Only 33 percent of students live in university-owned housing so, for many, sports and club activities are a way to stay connected. Many aspects of OSU campus life receive rave reviews in surveys—from the food to general happiness to LGBTQ friendliness, the university gets a giant thumbs up from its own students. Ohio's capital city is almost equidistant from Cincinnati and Cleveland, about a two-hour car ride. However, Columbus itself has much to offer, recently being ranking by several publications, including U.S. News and Time, as among the best places to live in the United States. For those craving nature, skiing, camping, and hiking opportunities can be found less than an hour away.

Career Services

Buckeye Careers is a university-wide office staffed by four professionals, yet the bulk of the counseling takes place within discipline-specific career services offices housed within individual colleges. Including career coaches and other professional staff from the College of Arts & Sciences (14), College of Engineering (9), Fisher School of Business (6), and smaller undergraduate schools, there are forty-two professional members on the OSU career services team. The university's overall 1,115:1 student-to-counselor ratio is poor compared to many other schools in this guide, but there are myriad facts and figures that suggest the university is preparing students for successful post-graduation outcomes.

A recent Career and Internship Fair was attended by over 200 employers and more than 4,000 students, 93 percent of whom rated the event as helpful. The Fisher School of Business has its own career fair that brings 185 companies to campus in the fall and another 130 in the spring. In a typical year, an eye-popping thirty-six career fairs are held. A solid 71 percent of Ohio State graduates completed at least one internship, and those students have been 2.8 times more likely to receive a job offer prior to graduation than their peers who did not complete an internship. Within the Fisher School of Business, 95 percent of graduates participated in an internship or other intensive work experience; Fisher also conducts over 1,100 mock interviews per year. Three-quarters of grads believe the university prepared them well for the job market. Despite less-than-desirable staffing levels, Ohio State University's career services is well-run and manages to have a positive impact on students' lives.

Professional Outcomes

Class of 2019 graduates were primarily entering the world of employment (71 percent) while 26 percent were already accepted into graduate or professional school. Hordes of Buckeyes can be found in the offices of many of the nation's leading companies. More than 2,000 alumni work for JPMorgan Chase, more than 1,000 are employed by Cardinal Health and Nationwide, and at least 300 OSU grads inhabit the halls of Amazon, Oracle, IBM, Microsoft, Google, and Apple. Roughly half of graduates settle in for the long haul in the Columbus area, and many others remain in the state, residing in Cleveland or Cincinnati. New York, Chicago, DC, and San Francisco also attract a fair number of alumni. Overall, the average starting salary for a recent graduate is $54,627, a figure buoyed by the high number of business and engineering grads the school produces.

Of the more than one-quarter of recent grads directly matriculating into graduate or professional school, many continue in one of OSU's own ninety-four doctoral programs, ninety-seven master's programs, or excellent law and medical schools. In the last few years law school-bound graduates have earned admission at universities including UVA, Penn, Fordham, Harvard, George Washington, Georgetown, Case Western, and Cornell. Over 500 graduates apply to medical school each year, and some have gone on to prestigious medical institutions like Harvard Medical School, Duke University School of Medicine, and Johns Hopkins School of Medicine. In sum, Ohio State grads attend a wide variety of graduate schools, and they can absolutely earn their way into some of the best institutions in the world.

Admission

Fifty-four percent of the 47,703 applicants for a place in the Class of 2023 gained acceptance, but that figure hardly tells the whole story of just how selective the flagship Columbus campus has become. The ACT is, by far, the more commonly submitted test, and members of the 2019-20 freshman class possessed a mid-50 percent ACT composite score of 28-32; the SAT range was 1300-1420. Even more shocking is the fact that 60 percent of enrolled students finished in the top 10 percent of their high school classes; 93 percent were in the top quartile. Ohio State has become significantly more competitive in recent years. A decade ago, it received fewer than half as many applications as it does today, admitted 62 percent of the pool, and the ACT range was far lower than today at 25-30; the average ACT score today is 29.3.

The OSU admissions staff promises a holistic review of each application but does rank the concrete factors of class rank, standardized test scores, GPA, a rigor of curriculum as "very important" in the process. Essays, extracurricular activities, talent/ability, first-generation status (few schools give this factor so much weight), volunteer work, and work experience get second billing. In a broad sense, OSU seeks individuals who are "not only smart but willing to lead; who see strength in diversity of people and ideas; who seek collaboration when solving problems; and who make use of all opportunities to figure out what kind of impact they want to have in the world." An influx of out-of-staters and international students has caused the school to make huge jumps in selectivity. As a result, Buckeye state residents need to be A/A- students with standardized test scores in at least the 90th percentile to be on solid footing.

Worth Your Money?

Ohio residents have a cost of attendance of $28,000+ per year, making the cost of a four-year degree from a well-respected university very reasonable. The out-of-state cost of attendance is over $51,000 per year. Thirty-four percent of undergrads receive a small merit aid award, but as is typical at public institutions, the need-based aid tends to be a bit more substantial. Close to half of current students receive some level of grant with an average award of $13,174. In state, OSU is an easy choice and a spectacular value; out of state it may be worth paying for certain top programs, particularly those that lead to careers with above-average starting salaries.

FINANCIAL
Institutional Type: Public
In-State Tuition: $11,084
Out-of-State Tuition: $32,061
Room & Board: $12,708
Required Fees: $0
Books & Supplies: $1,082

Avg. Need-Based Grant: $13,174
Avg. % of Need Met: 74%

Avg. Merit-Based Award: $6,825
% Receiving (All Freshmen): 34%
% Receiving (Freshmen w/o Need): 30%

Avg. Cumulative Debt: $27,242
% of Students Borrowing: 50%

CAREER
Who Recruits
1. Abercrombie & Fitch
2. Cargill
3. Nestle
4. Sherwin-Williams
5. Marriott International

Notable Internships
1. Sun National Bank
2. Walt Disney World
3. U.S. Department of State

Top Industries
1. Business
2. Education
3. Operations
4. Healthcare
5. Sales

Top Employers
1. JPMorgan Chase
2. Nationwide
3. Cardinal Health
4. Amazon
5. IBM

Where Alumni Work
1. Columbus, OH
2. Cleveland
3. Cincinnati
4. New York City
5. Chicago

Median Earnings
College Scorecard (Early Career): $46,100
PayScale (Early Career): $58,200
PayScale (Mid-Career): $103,200

RANKINGS
Money: 102
U.S. News: 53 (T), National Universities
Wall Street Journal/THE: 100 (T)
Washington Monthly: 98, National Universities

COLLEGE OVERLAPS
Indiana University Bloomington
Miami University
Pennsylvania State University - University Park
Purdue University -- West Lafayette
University of Michigan

University Park, Pennsylvania | 814-865-5471

ADMISSION
Admission Rate: 49%
Admission Rate - Men: 46%
Admission Rate - Women: 52%
EA Admission Rate: NR
ED Admission Rate: Not Offered
ED Admits as % of Total Admits: Not Offered
Admission Rate (5-Year Trend): -6%
% of Admits Attending (Yield): 24%
Transfer Admission Rate: 43%

SAT Reading/Writing (Middle 50%): 580-670
SAT Math (Middle 50%): 580-700
ACT Composite (Middle 50%): 25-30

% Graduated in Top 10% of HS Class: 35%
% Graduated in Top 25% of HS Class: 73%
% Graduated in Top 50% of HS Class: 96%

Demonstrated Interest: Not Considered
Legacy Status: Considered
Admission Interview Offered: No

ENROLLMENT
Total Undergraduate Enrollment: 40,639
% Part-Time: 3%
% Male: 53%
% Female: 47%
% Out-of-State: 34%
% Fraternity: 17%
% Sorority: 20%
% On-Campus (Freshman): NR
% On-Campus (All Undergraduate): 36%

% African-American: 4%
% Asian: 6%
% Hispanic: 7%
% White: 64%
% Other: 3%
% Race or Ethnicity Unknown: 2%
% International: 12%
% Low-Income: 14%

ACADEMICS
Student-to-Faculty Ratio: 15 to 1
% of Classes Under 20: 29%
% of Classes 20-49: 54%
% of Classes 50 or More: 17%
% Full-Time Faculty: 89%
% Full-Time Faculty w/ Terminal Degree: 75%

Top Programs
Architecture
Business
Criminal Justice
Earth Sciences
Economics
Engineering
Information Sciences and Technology
Kinesiology

Retention Rate: 94%
4-Year Graduation Rate: 66%
6-Year Graduation Rate: 85%

Curricular Flexibility: Less Flexible
Academic Rating: ★★★

#CollegesWorthYourMoney

"We are Penn State," the signature slogan of Pennsylvania State University, is one of the more recognizable chants echoing across any college campus in the United States. More than 40,000 undergraduates reside in State College, nicknamed Happy Valley, a moniker that has weathered scandal and continues to be a destination point for Pennsylvanians as well as many out-of-staters and international students who make up 46 percent of today's student population. Not only does PSU have one the world's largest and most passionate alumni bases, it also possesses as diverse an academic menu as you will find anywhere with its 275 majors and a number of top-ranked programs in a host of disciplines.

Inside the Classroom
There are forty-five credits worth of general education requirements that you'll need to fulfill whether you are studying turfgrass science, toxicology, or telecommunications—all actual majors at PSU. Fifteen of those credits will come through introductory courses in writing, speaking, and quantification, and thirty will come via explorations of the humanities, natural sciences, social and behavioral sciences, the arts, and health and well-ness. First-year engagement courses help students hone study and research skills and introduce freshmen to resources around campus. Students also must take courses that satisfy the categories of writing across the curriculum, United States cultures, and international cultures, but those can overlap with the aforementioned forty-five credits worth of distributional mandates.

Unlike some public research universities that can have student-to-faculty ratios greater than 20:1, PSU boasts a solid 15:1 ratio. That level of support allows 60 percent of classes to have an enrollment below thirty students. Still, you will take some intro courses in massive lecture halls, and 17 percent of sections enroll more than fifty undergraduates. Even at such a large institution, it is possible to get involved in undergraduate research. Eberly College of Science professors are running upwards of 3,000 research projects per year, and the school has a well-maintained and up-to-date database of undergraduate research positions. All told, 20 percent of graduates report having engaged in undergraduate research. Twenty-three percent of Penn Staters avail themselves of study abroad opportunities in one of 300 programs in fifty countries.

Penn State University's College of Engineering is rated exceptionally well on a national scale, cracking the top twenty-five on just about everyone's list, and even hits the top ten in some sub- disciplines such as industrial and biological engineering. It's no wonder that engineering is the most popular field of study at the university, accounting for 17 percent of the degrees conferred. The Smeal College of Business is equally well regarded, also earning high rankings in everything from supply chain management to accounting to marketing. This school not only ranks among top undergraduate public business colleges in the United States but among all colleges, and it attracts 15 percent of total degree-seekers. In addition to gaining positive attention from the engineering and business communities, PSU is viewed favorably by prestigious national fellowship organizations. In 2019, ten graduates captured Fulbright Scholarships as well as one or more Boren, Critical Language, Astronaut, Marshall, and Goldwater Scholarships in the last two years.

Outside the Classroom
Only 36 percent of Nittany Lions technically live in university-owned housing, but that doesn't quite capture the cohesive spirit of the PSU community. Greek life is a major social force at the school as 17 percent of men join frats and 20 percent of women become members of sororities. A tragic hazing death a few years back led to a shutdown of one fraternity and increased administrative scrutiny of the practices of others. Unfortunately, the school is no stranger to national controversy. Yet, even after the infamous Sandusky scandal, Penn State football is a tradition like no other as 106,000 pack into Beaver Stadium to watch the Lions battle with Big Ten rivals like Ohio State, Michigan, and Nebraska. Thon, an annual charity dance marathon, is one of the grandest and most impressive events on campus, raising over $10 million to fight childhood cancer in 2019. With over 1,000 clubs and activities to choose from, it's hard not to find your niche at Penn State. Campus itself covers almost 8,000 acres and contains its own arboretum, the Palmer Art Museum, and the famous (and delicious) Penn State Creamery. State College may be in the middle of nowhere, but it truly is the ultimate college town, walkable and brimming with terrific restaurants, bars, and shop.

Career Services
Not counting graduate assistants and office managers, there are thirty full-time employees occupying the Bank of America Career Services Center at University Park. However, there are additional offices that serve specialty groups such as the Career Resources & Employer Relations department housed within the College of Engineering that is staffed by seven professionals, the Smeal College of Business that has nine career services employees, and eleven other staff members are spread across campus in other departments. Based on this grand total of

Pennsylvania State University — University Park

E-mail: admissions@psu.edu | Website: www.psu.edu

fifty-seven career counselors, internship coordinators, employer relations specialists, and related positions, the student-to-counselor ratio is 713:1, higher than most of the schools featured in this guide, but not at all bad for a school of PSU's size.

Career fairs, such as the major one held each fall, are massive undertakings, some featuring 300+ companies. The Fall Career Fair is four days in length, and that time is divided to cover technical jobs, nontechnical jobs, internships, and interviews. It also offers many smaller (but still large) targeted fairs in areas such as nursing, education, graduate school, small business and startups, and impact (nonprofits). The majority of graduates, 63 percent, report participating in at least one internship while at University Park. More than one recent graduate held an internship position at companies like Amazon, Pfizer, and Xerox. Within the first week of students returning to school for the 2019-20 school year, Microsoft and Lockheed Martin were already actively recruiting on campus. PSU does not publish statistics on how many students take advantage of career services offerings, but it is clear that this staff facilitates powerful, door-opening opportunities for those proactive enough to seek them out.

Professional Outcomes

By the day of graduation, 72 percent of Nittany Lions have found their next employment or graduate school home; within some of the universities many colleges, that rate is even higher. Three months after receiving their diplomas, 91 percent of Smeal College of Business Class of 2019 grads already had their next step lined up. They flock in large numbers to some of the nation's best finance, accounting, consulting, and technology firms. More than 500 PSU alumni are currently working at each of IBM, Deloitte, PwC, Amazon, EY, JPMorgan Chase, Microsoft, Google, and Oracle. Hundreds more work at Citi, Salesforce, and Facebook. Philadelphia, New York City, Pittsburgh, DC, San Francisco, Boston, and Los Angeles all have a strong PSU alumni presence. The median salary for Penn State grads ten years after arriving at the school averages $50,000. Of course, salaries vary greatly by academic discipline; business graduates' salaries start at $65,000 while engineering students start at over $70,000.

Medical school acceptance rates for PSU graduates hover around 60 percent, well above the national average, an impressive figure when considering that over 300 students applied in 2019. Seventy percent of those accepted into medical school enroll at Pennsylvania-based institutions including the Penn State College of Medicine. Overall, presently PSU alumni are enrolled in sixty medical schools throughout the country. Likewise, many prelaw students go on to pursue legal educations at one of the university's two law schools (Penn State Law and Dickinson Law), other strong local options like Temple or Villanova, or prestigious national universities like the University of North Carolina, Stanford, Cornell, or Wake Forest.

Admission

The 71,903 Nittany Lion hopefuls seeking a place in the Class of 2023 were accepted at a 49 percent rate, a figure that somewhat undersells how competitive gaining admission right out of high school truly is (transferring later is easier). For some, Penn State is a clear number one choice and often a family tradition, for other Pennsylvania students it occupies mere safety status. Overall, the yield rate—the percentage of accepted students who go on to enroll—is 24 percent. Freshmen who entered the university in 2019-20 possessed median SAT/ACT scores of 1240 and 28, respectively. With 35 percent of freshmen having earned a place in the top ten percent of their high school class and 73 percent in the top quartile, most Penn State admits sport strong grades, generally a mix of A's and B's in at least some AP and honors courses.

The only two "very important" factors in the admissions process are GPA and standardized test scores. The rigor of one's high school coursework sits alone in the next tier of still "important" factors. Soft factors like essays, extracurricular activities, work experience, talent/ability, character/personal qualities as well as state residency status and ethnicity are "considered" in candidate evaluation. An early option allows students to submit an application by November 1. After that admission is rolling, but you should absolutely meet the priority date of November 30.

Worth Your Money?

PSU's in-state tuition cost of roughly $18,500 and total cost of attendance of $32,000+ isn't as cheap as, for example, schools in New York's SUNY system that have a COA approximately $10k cheaper. A non-Keystone State resident would pay a COA of over $50,000, which would not make sense in most circumstances. Denizens of Pennsylvania will generally reap the benefits of this flagship institution's strong reputation and incomprehensibly vast alumni network.

FINANCIAL
Institutional Type: Public
In-State Tuition: $17,416
Out-of-State Tuition: $34,480
Room & Board: $11,884
Required Fees: $1,034
Books & Supplies: $1,840

Avg. Need-Based Grant: $6,517
Avg. % of Need Met: 64%

Avg. Merit-Based Award: $5,695
% Receiving (All Freshmen): 34%
% Receiving (Freshmen w/o Need): 7%

Avg. Cumulative Debt: $40,128
% of Students Borrowing: 52%

CAREER
Who Recruits
1. Google
2. Grant Thorton LLP
3. Oracle
4. PNC
5. Accenture

Notable Internships
1. Anheuser-Busch
2. Morgan Stanley
3. Aramark

Top Industries
1. Business
2. Operations
3. Education
4. Engineering
5. Sales

Top Employers
1. IBM
2. PwC
3. Amazon
4. Johnson & Johnson
5. EY

Where Alumni Work
1. Philadelphia
2. New York City
3. Pittsburgh
4. State College, PA
5. Washington DC

Median Earnings
College Scorecard (Early Career): $50,100
PayScale (Early Career): $61,500
PayScale (Mid-Career): $110,800

RANKINGS
Money: 278
U.S. News: 63 (T), National Universities
Wall Street Journal/THE: 109 (T)
Washington Monthly: 108, National Universities

COLLEGE OVERLAPS
Ohio State University - Columbus
Purdue University - West Lafayette
University of Maryland
University of Michigan
University of Pittsburgh

Pepperdine University

Malibu, California | 310-506-4392

ADMISSION
Admission Rate: 32%
Admission Rate - Men: 35%
Admission Rate - Women: 30%
EA Admission Rate: NR
ED Admission Rate: Not Offered
ED Admits as % of Total Admits: Not Offered
Admission Rate (5-Year Trend): -4%
% of Admits Attending (Yield): 18%
Transfer Admission Rate: 36%

SAT Reading/Writing (Middle 50%): 610-700
SAT Math (Middle 50%): 620-750
ACT Composite (Middle 50%): 27-32

% Graduated in Top 10% of HS Class: 46%
% Graduated in Top 25% of HS Class: 77%
% Graduated in Top 50% of HS Class: 97%

Demonstrated Interest: Not Considered
Legacy Status: Considered
Admission Interview Offered: No

ENROLLMENT
Total Undergraduate Enrollment: 3,583
% Part-Time: 7%
% Male: 42%
% Female: 58%
% Out-of-State: 45%
% Fraternity: 18%
% Sorority: 27%
% On-Campus (Freshman): 99%
% On-Campus (All Undergraduate): 60%

% African-American: 5%
% Asian: 11%
% Hispanic: 14%
% White: 49%
% Other: 7%
% Race or Ethnicity Unknown: 2%
% International: 12%
% Low-Income: 20%

ACADEMICS
Student-to-Faculty Ratio: 13 to 1
% of Classes Under 20: 69%
% of Classes 20-49: 29%
% of Classes 50 or More: 2%
% Full-Time Faculty: 50%
% Full-Time Faculty w/ Terminal Degree: 86%

Top Programs
Advertising
Business Administration
Communication
International Studies
Psychology
Public Relations
Sports Medicine
Theatre

Retention Rate: 91%
4-Year Graduation Rate: 79%
6-Year Graduation Rate: 86%

Curricular Flexibility: Less Flexible
Academic Rating: ★★★✦

#CollegesWorthYourMoney

The incongruity of a resort-like university located in Malibu that only lifted its ban on dancing in the late 1980s is hard to reconcile. Maybe the most beautiful campus in the world, Pepperdine is also a bastion of evangelical Christianity and largely conservative politically. On the academic menu for the 3,583 undergrads at Seaver College (the school's undergraduate wing) are forty-five majors and forty minors with the most commonly conferred degrees being in business/marketing (32 percent), communication/journalism (20 percent), general social sciences 9 percent), psychology (7 percent), and parks and recreation (7 percent). Only 2 percent pursue degrees in religion, but its influence is interwoven into the fabric of both the academic experience and the social scene.

Inside the Classroom
Among the nineteen courses that constitute Pepperdine's general education requirements for all undergraduates are three classes under the umbrella of Christianity and Culture. Other mandated areas of study include the American experience, Western cultures, human institutions and behavior, world civilizations, fine arts, mathematics, laboratory science, and speech and rhetoric. First-year seminars are intended to sharpen skills in the areas of communication, critical thinking and learning how to "apply the university's Christian mission." Those seminars tackle big-picture topics that include science and religion, the nature of conscience, and the pain of betrayal. Students must continually update a writing portfolio that is formally evaluated as the junior writing portfolio when students reach their third year of study.

A 13:1 student-to-faculty ratio is solid, and faculty are fully deployed with the aim of creating an intimate liberal arts classroom setting. The average class contains nineteen students, and close to one-quarter of courses will contain fewer than ten students. There are three formal programs for undergraduate research: the Summer Undergraduate Research Program, the Cross-disciplinary/Interdisciplinary Undergraduate Research Program, and Academic Year Undergraduate Research Initiative. Close to two-thirds of Seaver students study abroad and build global experience in locations such as Buenos Aires, Florence, London, and Shanghai.

The Graziadio Business School has a strong reputation that penetrates far beyond the school's home state. The Communication Division also registers on many national ranking lists. Thanks in part to the school's focus on international experience, six 2019 graduates won Fulbright Scholarships. Recent grads also have, on occasion, been awarded Gilman, Boren, and National Science Foundation fellowships.

Outside the Classroom
The university's 835-acre grounds can be found in the number one or two position in just about any nationwide ranking of "most beautiful campuses." Given its size and luxurious feel, it's a bit strange that under 60 percent of the undergraduate population lives on campus, however 98 percent of freshmen do reside in university-owned housing. Dorms and on-campus apartments are single-sex, and overnight visitors of the opposite sex are prohibited. The alcohol policies are also enforced more than at your average college. Gender-wise, Seaver has a 58/42 split in favor of women, 27 percent of whom join sororities while 18 percent of men join fraternities. A relatively athletic undergraduate student body participates on seventeen NCAA Division I sports teams (the Waves) that have produced an impressive fifty-two Olympians in the school's history. There are plenty of intramural and club teams as well as four fitness centers and an Olympic-size swimming pool. One hundred and ten student organizations are active, and more than 1,000 on-campus events are hosted each semester. A focus on service leads three-fifths of students to engage in volunteer work with over 80,000 hours contributed each year. Pepperdine is nestled in the Santa Monica Mountains only minutes from some of the world's premier surfing beaches. As another bonus, campus is only thirty miles west of Los Angeles, so Hollywood is only a short car ride away.

Career Services
Pepperdine Career Services employs five full-time professional staff members (not counting office managers) working as counselors, industry specialists, events managers, and employer relations coordinators. That works out to a 717:1 student-to-counselor ratio, within the high-average range of institutions profiled in this book. This department offers a solid blend of one-on-one counseling and large-scale events such as industry-specific career fairs in business, health and sciences, nonprofit and government, and arts/entertainment/media. There is also a more generalized Spring Career Expo attended by fifty+ employers and graduate schools.

Pepperdine University

E-mail: admission-seaver@pepperdine.edu | Website: www.pepperdine.edu

A phenomenal 94 percent of Class of 2018 grads had at least one internship, work experience, or formal undergraduate research experience. Career Services posted 8,750 internships last year and facilitated 125 job shadowing opportunities. Each year, 150+ employers recruit on site at Pepperdine, conducting information sessions as well as on-campus interviews. The alumni network is always happy to be involved in assisting current students. Over 500 alumni volunteer to work with undergraduates directly, and 110,000 living alumni can be found around the globe. A formalized Career Coaching Program has set up 350 students with alumni mentors who have guided them through each stage of the career exploration and development process since its inception in 2001. An above-average level of next-step support and reasonably successful student outcomes makes Pepperdine Career Services a strong performing outfit.

Professional Outcomes

Members of the Seaver Class of 2018 (most recent year available) landed at their next destination within six months of graduating at a 93 percent clip with 69 percent employed full time, 18 percent admitted to graduate school, 3 percent volunteering, and 11 percent seeking their first job or a graduate school home. Of those entering the world of work, 86 percent were in the for-profit sector, 9 percent with nonprofit/government entities, and 5 percent pursuing entrepreneurial ventures. Disney, Morgan Stanley, Northrop Grumman, and Wells Fargo have hired the most recent graduates. Other companies employing fifty or more alumni include Kaiser Permanente, Apple, Google, and Amazon. Many graduates remain in California as Los Angeles and Orange County are the two most common landing spots. Other West Coast locales including San Diego, San Francisco, and Seattle also sport sizable numbers of alums.

Class of 2018 graduates were admitted to graduate/professional school at a 90 percent rate. Training in a medical field was the choice of 17 percent of that group, and 14 percent matriculated into law school. In a typical year, twenty to thirty grads apply to medical school, and 70-80 percent are successful. Recent students have gained acceptance to medical schools at Georgetown; Emory; USC; University of California, San Diego; and Washington University in St. Louis. Those going the law school route study at many fine institutions including Pepperdine's own law school. In the last few years, others have been admitted to Harvard Law School, UCLA School of Law, and NYU School of Law. No matter your postgraduate pursuit, a solid transcript and a Pepperdine degree will leave you with many strong graduate/professional school options.

Admission

In the 2019 admission cycle, the university admitted 32 percent of 12,764 applicants. Applicants who accepted a place in the freshman class had a 27-32 ACT range, a 1250-1430 SAT range, and an average GPA of 3.67. "Only" 46 percent of that cohort placed in the top 10 percent of their high school class, a low figure compared to many other elite universities. Further, 23 percent did not place in the top quartile, so there is some leeway here for students with imperfect academic transcripts.

There are seven factors rated as "very important" by the admissions committee, most notably religious affiliation because Pepperdine, as noted earlier, is a Christian school. The other more common critical factors are: rigor of coursework, GPA, application essay, extracurricular activities, talent/ability, and character/personal qualities. Standardized tests, recommendations, and volunteer work make-up the second rung of still "important" factors. The yield rate (percent of those accepted who actually enroll) is only 18 percent, which means that Pepperdine is definitely interested to know if you are a student who truly places the university at the top of your college list. Since it offers only early action and does not have a binding early decision program, demonstrating interest is a good idea if you are serious about this school. Admissions standards at Pepperdine today are almost identical to those of five years ago. It remains a niche institution for devout Christians with strong academic credentials.

Worth Your Money?

Pepperdine's annual cost of attendance is approaching $78,000, making it one of the most expensive colleges in the country. The average need-based grant amount is over $37,000, just about slicing the COA in half. Roughly one-quarter of current students receive an average merit aid grant of $20k. There aren't exactly dozens of academically competitive, conservative Christian universities with a beachfront view; so, if that's the description of your ideal school, Pepperdine will likely be worth your money, especially if you have plans to enter the fields of business or communication.

FINANCIAL
Institutional Type: Private
In-State Tuition: $57,750
Out-of-State Tuition: $57,750
Room & Board: $16,160
Required Fees: $252
Books & Supplies: $1,250

Avg. Need-Based Grant: $37,678
Avg. % of Need Met: 77%

Avg. Merit-Based Award: $19,506
% Receiving (All Freshmen): 25%
% Receiving (Freshmen w/o Need): 25%

Avg. Cumulative Debt: $34,711
% of Students Borrowing: 52%

CAREER
Who Recruits
1. PennyMac
2. Disney
3. Universalizer
4. Sony Pictures Entertainment
5. REX-Real Estate Exchange Inc.

Notable Internships
1. United Nations
2. U.S. Securities and Exchange Commission
3. Farmers Insurance

Top Industries
1. Business
2. Education
3. Operations
4. Sales
5. Healthcare

Top Employers
1. Boeing
2. Kaiser Permanente
3. Wells Fargo
4. Walt Disney
5. Amazon

Where Alumni Work
1. Los Angeles
2. Orange County, CA
3. San Francisco
4. San Diego
5. New York City

Median Earnings
College Scorecard (Early Career): $65,500
PayScale (Early Career): $61,400
PayScale (Mid-Career): $109,500

RANKINGS
Money: 414
U.S. News: 49 (T), National Universities
Wall Street Journal/THE: 168
Washington Monthly: 197, National Universities

COLLEGE OVERLAPS
Loyola Marymount University
Southern Methodist University
University of California, San Diego
University of California, Santa Barbara
University of San Diego

Pitzer College

Claremont, California | 909-621-8129

ADMISSION
Admission Rate: 14%
Admission Rate - Men: 17%
Admission Rate - Women: 12%
EA Admission Rate: Not Offered
ED Admission Rate: 34%
ED Admits as % of Total Admits: 27%
Admission Rate (5-Year Trend): -1%
% of Admits Attending (Yield): 46%
Transfer Admission Rate: 19%

SAT Reading/Writing (Middle 50%): 670-730
SAT Math (Middle 50%): 680-750
ACT Composite (Middle 50%): 30-33

% Graduated in Top 10% of HS Class: 59%
% Graduated in Top 25% of HS Class: 82%
% Graduated in Top 50% of HS Class: 100%

Demonstrated Interest: Considered
Legacy Status: Considered
Admission Interview Offered: Yes

ENROLLMENT
Total Undergraduate Enrollment: 1,119
% Part-Time: 2%
% Male: 43%
% Female: 57%
% Out-of-State: 56%
% Fraternity: Not Offered
% Sorority: Not Offered
% On-Campus (Freshman): 99%
% On-Campus (All Undergraduate): 75%

% African-American: 6%
% Asian: 8%
% Hispanic: 14%
% White: 47%
% Other: 9%
% Race or Ethnicity Unknown: 5%
% International: 11%
% Low-Income: 16%

ACADEMICS
Student-to-Faculty Ratio: 10 to 1
% of Classes Under 20: 72%
% of Classes 20-49: 28%
% of Classes 50 or More: 0%
% Full-Time Faculty: 79%
% Full-Time Faculty w/ Terminal Degree: 97%

Top Programs
Environmental Analysis
Human Biology
Media Studies
Organizational Studies
Political Studies
Psychology
Sociology

Retention Rate: 93%
4-Year Graduation Rate: 78%
6-Year Graduation Rate: 85%

Curricular Flexibility: Somewhat Flexible
Academic Rating: ★★★★

#CollegesWorthYourMoney

Every member school within the Claremont Consortium has its own distinct personality—Harvey Mudd is for engineering geniuses, Scripps is a highly selective women's college, Pomona and CMC are premier liberal arts colleges that battle East Coast schools Swarthmore, Amherst, and Williams for the top spot in the national rankings. Then there is Pitzer College, a liberal arts powerhouse in its own right with an emphasis on service learning and global engagement that has experienced logarithmic leaps in selectivity itself since the dawn of the new millennium. Cozy in size, hosting a mere 1,119 students, Pitzer still manages to offer forty+ majors and twenty minors and, as a bonus, students are free to take more than 2,000 courses across the consortium.

Inside the Classroom
Graduating from Pitzer involves the completion of thirty-two courses including a minimum of eleven required courses that are part of meeting the college's education objectives. That involves two courses in the humanities and fine arts, two in the behavioral and social sciences, and one each in written expression, quantitative reasoning, and the natural sciences. Sequences covering social justice/social responsibility and intercultural understanding global/local also must be completed. The class on social justice requires active community engagement. First-year experience courses are taught on a variety of topics, and are capped at fifteen students.

A 10:1 student-to-faculty ratio and no graduate student presence leads to an average class size of fifteen students, and 72 percent of sections enroll nineteen or fewer students. In 2019-20, not one single course section was larger than thirty-nine students. Finding mentorship is doable in this atmosphere and can lead to undergraduate research opportunities such as those at the Keck Science Department, which also services CMC and Scripps students. Those opportunities can occur in the summer or during senior year while completing a required thesis. With one of the highest study abroad percentages of any school at 75 percent, Pitzer runs eight foreign programs and offers access to thirty-two international exchange programs.

The most popular majors at Pitzer are in the social sciences (18 percent), interdisciplinary studies (11 percent), natural resources/conservation (10 percent), and business (9 percent). Nearly all programs have the full admiration of graduate/professional schools as well as prestigious scholarship programs, but majors within the social and behavioral sciences (e.g. psychology and sociology) typically draw the most praise. In 2019, ten seniors and recent alumni captured Fulbrights, three were named Napier Fellows, and two students won Gilman Scholarships. Students also captured one Goldwater Scholarship, a National Science Foundation Graduate Research Fellowship, a Princeton in Asia Fellowship, and a Davis Project for Peace Award. Not bad for a school with fewer than 250 graduates per year.

Outside the Classroom
Every single Pitzer freshman and 75 percent of all students live in six dorms on the school's thirty-one-acre campus. Dorms receive glowing reviews as environmentally responsible housing and their farm-to-table program that is ranked as one of the best in the country. From those two facts you're likely picking up on the school's ethos and can guess that it does not have fraternities or sororities. Pitzer does have a joint athletics department with Pomona College that features twenty-one NCAA Division III varsity sports teams known as the Sagehens. There are 250+ clubs students can join, many of which are of the cross-college variety. Every single member of the Pitzer community gives back through service. In total, students, faculty, and staff commit approximately 100,000 hours to community-based projects each year. Activism carries over to student government, which is consistently passionate and vocal whether the issue is undergraduate housing costs or a recent ban on study abroad in Israel. Pitzer Outdoor Adventure (POA) is also immensely popular and regularly leads its large membership on hiking, cycling, climbing, camping, and surfing trips. Those seeking big-city fun will relish in the fact the City of Angels can be reached in less than an hour.

Career Services
Career Services at Pitzer has only four full-time professional staff members, yet being such a small college, that number still works out to a solid 280:1 student-to-advisor ratio, slightly better than the average college featured in our guidebook. For such a tiny operation, the level of outreach is spectacular as 85 percent of freshmen engage with career services. Overall, approximately two-thirds of the student body utilize career services, and 33 percent take advantage of walk-in counseling appointments each year. It hosts roughly ninety events per year that attract almost 800 student participants. Of the 378 students that received one-on-one counseling last year, 96 percent had a positive experience. The office also put on 63 workshops that drew 630 student participants.

Being part of the Claremont Consortium has as many advantages with regard to career development as it is does with regard to academics. Over 300 companies recruit annually at the 5Cs, and Pitzer students enjoy full access to networking and on-campus interviews. The office also does an excellent job financially supporting students' job-exploration endeavors. Roughly fifty students per year receive financial assistance from the Pitzer Internship Fund, which enables students to complete unpaid or low-paid experiential learning opportunities. Roughly fifty students engage in a job-shadowing experience with an alum over winter break. Overall, this is an accessible office that greatly benefits from its affiliation with its neighbor schools.

Professional Outcomes

Upon receiving their degrees, 57 percent of 2019 Pitzer graduates had already found full-time employers, 15 percent were headed to graduate school, and 7 percent were entering fellowship, internship, or service programs. Among those employed, the most popular industries were finance/business (26 percent), tech/engineering (20 percent), education (17 percent), entertainment/arts (14 percent), and education (6 percent). Employers presently issuing paychecks to more than ten Pitzer alumni include Google, Kaiser Permanente, the Los Angeles Unified School District, and Accenture. Graduates tend to be a globetrotting bunch, and the 11,000 living alumni can be found all over the map, although roughly half settle in Los Angeles or San Francisco. Median salaries, even ten years after graduation, are on the lower end of selective colleges. While plenty of Pitzer grads go on to pursue high-paying finance and tech jobs, many others choose PhD programs, medical school, or fellowship programs abroad that can delay financial returns.

Members of the Class of 2019 headed to prestigious graduate schools including Vanderbilt, Oxford, Emory, Columbia, Georgetown, NYU, and Cornell. For premed students, the college offers a Joint Medical Program with the Western University of Health Sciences admitting up to six students each year. The W.M. Keck Science Department services Scripps, Claremont McKenna, and Pitzer, so all students have access to an excellent premed curriculum and facility. Those heading to law school in recent years have matriculated into a wide range of institutions that includes Notre Dame, UC Berkeley, Georgetown, Santa Clara, and Loyola Marymount University.

Admission

Applicants to the Class of 2023 were admitted at only a 14 percent clip, a rate similar to five years ago but far below that of 2005 when the admit rate was 39 percent. Even that 39 percent figure represented a sharp decline from a more forgiving admissions era in the 1990s. An early adopter of test-optional policies, Pitzer stopped requiring SAT or ACT scores in 2003, and more applicants take advantage of that option here than at most other test-optional institutions. Unsurprisingly, the test scores of freshmen who divulged them tended to be strong; the mid-50 percent range was a 1350-1460 on the SAT and a 30-33 on the ACT. It's within the realm of high school performance that successful Pitzer applicants set themselves apart. Fifty-nine percent placed within the top 10 percent of their graduating class, and 82 percent were in the top quartile. The average GPA for an entering member of the Class of 2023 was 3.89.

The admissions process at Pitzer is highly personalized, and each application receives a lengthy review. A rigorous high school course load, a high GPA, a strong essay, and the demonstration of solid and unique character/personal qualities are at the forefront of the decision-making process. Recommendations, volunteer work, talent/ability, and extracurricular activities are also important factors. If you are a borderline applicant who is serious about getting in, applying early decision may be the way to go; 34 percent of applicants were accepted—162 students—59 percent of the freshman class.

Worth Your Money?

Pitzer has notably generous financial aid as roughly 47 percent of undergraduates received an average annual package of $43,482. That assistance helps greatly lessen the blow of a $56k list tuition price and $65k+ cost of attendance. While median salaries are on the low side, being part of the world-renowned Claremont Consortium allows access to premier facilities and professors and opens doors to the most competitive grad schools, fellowships and, should you choose, major corporations. You wouldn't want to pay $300,000 for a humanities degree without a clear plan for how to pay back those loans. Again, thanks to merit aid and need-based awards from the school, you are unlikely to be asked to pay anything approaching the full sticker price.

FINANCIAL
Institutional Type: Private
In-State Tuition: $57,104
Out-of-State Tuition: $57,104
Room & Board: $17,082
Required Fees: $0
Books & Supplies: $1,100

Avg. Need-Based Grant: $49,150
Avg. % of Need Met: 100%

Avg. Merit-Based Award: $5,000
% Receiving (All Freshmen): 3%
% Receiving (Freshmen w/o Need): 2%

Avg. Cumulative Debt: $26,489
% of Students Borrowing: 37%

CAREER
Who Recruits
1. City Year
2. Apple
3. Amazon
4. JumpStart
5. Accenture

Notable Internships
1. FX Networks
2. Collins Aerospace
3. Apple

Top Industries
1. Business
2. Education
3. Operations
4. Social Services
5. Media

Top Employers
1. Kaiser Permanente
2. Los Angeles Unified School District
3. Google
4. Wells Fargo
5. Accenture

Where Alumni Work
1. Los Angeles
2. San Francisco
3. New York City
4. Seattle
5. Portland, OR

Median Earnings
College Scorecard (Early Career): $48,700
PayScale (Early Career): $57,100
PayScale (Mid-Career): $110,600

RANKINGS
Money: 518
U.S. News: 36 (T), Liberal Arts Colleges
Wall Street Journal/THE: 80 (T)
Washington Monthly: 130, Liberal Arts Colleges

COLLEGE OVERLAPS
Colorado College
Lewis & Clark College
Oberlin College
Occidental College
Whitman College

Pomona College

Claremont, California | 909-621-8134

Considered the preeminent institution among the Claremont Consortium, Pomona College in Claremont, California, is much like the elite liberal arts schools of the Northeast—Williams and Amherst—only with perfect weather, gorgeous beaches, and Disneyland in relatively close proximity. Pomona also boasts one of the lowest acceptance rates in the country, one that is on par, from a selectivity standpoint, with Yale, Columbia, Brown, and MIT. That said, if you are one of the rare individuals capable of gaining entrance, you won't find a better or more rigorous liberal arts education anywhere.

Inside the Classroom

There are forty-eight majors and minors to select from with the most popular being social sciences (20 percent), interdisciplinary studies (12 percent), mathematics (9 percent), and computer science (8 percent). More than 600 courses are on the menu at Pomona alone, but students can access any of the Claremont Consortium's 2,700 courses. Everyone begins with a critical inquiry seminar as a freshman and must complete coursework designated as writing intensive, speaking intensive, and analyzing difference. Breadth of study requirements demand that undergrads complete one course in the following six categories: criticism, analysis, and contextual study of works of the human imagination; social institutions and human behavior; history, values, ethics, and cultural studies; physical and biological sciences; mathematical and formal reasoning; and creation and performance of works of art and literature. There are literally eight ways to meet the college's foreign language requirement including AP scores, SAT Subject Tests, and passing three semesters of language, but all eight demand the demonstration of proficiency.

The school's 195 professors are dedicated to the task of undergraduate education. Pomona's 8:1 student-to-teacher ratio leads to an average class size of only fifteen students. There are only seven of 431 courses that ran in 2019-20 that contained more than forty students. Small classes also lead to the forging of student-professor bonds that help 53 percent of the undergraduate population conduct research alongside a faculty member. Each summer, 200 students remain on campus for such an endeavor. Close to 50 percent of Pomona students travel abroad to one of fifty-nine programs in thirty-four countries.

All of the college's academic offerings are highly respected by employers, graduate/professional schools, and national fellowship/scholarship competitions. Majors in economics, international relations, chemistry, and mathematics receive especially high marks. One-quarter of Pomona students apply for at least one competitive fellowship. Of the students in the Class of 2019 who applied for Fulbright Scholarships, nine were successful; thirteen won the previous year. Three captured Watson Scholarships in 2019, and a remarkable ten grads and alumni were awarded National Science Foundation Graduate Research Fellowships.

Outside the Classroom

Pomona's bustling campus is spread across 140 acres and contains fifteen residence halls and three dining halls; 98 percent of students live in campus housing. There are two co-ed fraternities on campus that student members themselves describe as "just a bunch of dorks that hang out sometimes." Pomona partners with Pitzer to field more than twenty-one varsity teams who play as the Sagehens in NCAA Division III; 20 percent of the student body are members of a varsity team, and many others participate in club and intramural athletics. Student life at Pomona is, in part, defined by the multitude of opportunities to enjoy the resources of the other Claremont Colleges—Pitzer, Scripps, Harvey Mudd, and CMC. More than 250 clubs can be accessed by students of any of the five schools. On the Loose is a popular outdoors club that organizes 150 excursions into natural settings each year. Students can tend to their own plot at an on-campus organic farm, perform for the Claremont Colleges Ballroom Dance Company, write for the Student Life newspaper, or connect with volunteer opportunities through the Draper Center for Community Partnerships. While campus itself receives rave reviews, few complain about the school's enviable location either. Less than an hour from campus, students can access all of the fun Los Angeles has to offer as well as some of the most beautiful beaches in the country.

Career Services

The Career Development Office (CDO) has seven full-time professional staff members working on grad school/career advising, employer relations, and experiential learning coordination. The CDO's 245:1 student-to-advisor ratio is better than the average college featured in our guidebook. Pomona's staff puts its resources to good use, engaging 80 percent of freshmen through lunches where the CDO's offerings are introduced. Each year, the office engages in over 1,800 one-on-one counseling appointments, more than one per enrolled undergraduate student. Two-thirds of seniors directly engage with counselors.

Pomona College

E-mail: admissions@pomona.edu | Website: www.pomona.edu

On a more global scale, Pomona students can connect with more than 8,500 employers through the school's membership in three consortia groups: the Claremont Consortium, the Career and Internship Connection, and the Liberal Arts Career Network. More than 500 employers engage in on-campus recruiting at Pomona each year, including many that attend winter break recruiting programs. Unique internship opportunities are available such as the Pomona College Internship Program (PCIP) that funds students to intern domestically in places like DC or New York or abroad in cities like Bangkok or Tokyo. Roughly 130 students are awarded PCIP positions each school year along with an additional eighty students in the summer. By senior year, 89 percent of students have participated in at least one internship, and 70 percent have completed two or more. Thanks to loads of individualized attention and ways to connect directly with top employers and graduate schools, Pomona's career services is highly regarded by our staff.

Professional Outcomes

Seventy percent of the Class of 2019 had entered the working world within six months of exiting the college. Whether entering the corporate world or a nonprofit position, employers adore Pomona grads. Overall, the largest number of Pomona alumni can be found in the offices of Google, Kaiser-Permanente, Microsoft, Amazon, and Facebook. Looking at grads from 2014-2018, many computer science majors ended up at the aforementioned tech giants. In that same time, more than one economics major landed a job at Goldman Sachs, Wells Fargo, Morgan Stanley, or Accenture. Majors in the hard sciences frequently landed at top research laboratories and hospitals. The three most popular geographical landing spots were Los Angeles, San Francisco, and New York City. Midcareer salaries are middle-of-the-pack among elite schools and are commensurate with other highly selective liberal arts schools like Williams, Middlebury, and Colby.

Of the 17 percent of Class of 2019 members who were accepted directly into graduate school, the most frequently attended institutions were a not-too-shabby list which included the University of Cambridge, Duke, Harvard, Caltech, UChicago, and Stanford. When Pomona students go to law school they attend only the best. Thirty percent of alumni were admitted into top-five law schools; nearly three-quarters were admitted into top-fourteen schools. Med school applicants were admitted at a 70 percent clip, and in recent years more than one Pomona graduate has enrolled in medical school at USC, UCLA, University of Washington, and Emory University. In short, attending Pomona as an undergraduate will put you in a direct pipeline into the world's best graduate/professional schools.

Admission

Pomona now sits among the most ultra-selective schools in the world after admitting only 7.4 percent of the 10,401 students fighting for a spot in the Class of 2023. It accepted only 6.9 percent and 8.2 percent, respectively, in the previous two cycles. The mid-50 percent ranges for enrolled students were 1410-1530 and 32-35. Students submitted SAT and ACT scores at a fairly even rate. Ninety-three percent placed in the top 10 percent of their high school class. International admits hailed from forty-seven countries, and 58 percent of admitted domestic applicants were students of color. A high yield rate of 54 percent indicates that teens who apply to Pomona are likely to attend the college if accepted.

Getting in is a genuinely holistic process that strongly weights wide-ranging factors including rigor of curriculum, GPA, class rank, standardized test scores, essays, recommendations, extracurricular activities, talent/ability, and character/personal qualities. Class of 2023 ED applicants were admitted at a rate of 15 percent, which suggests that ED does provide an admissions edge. In 1914, the school's president declared, "Let only the eager, thoughtful, and reverent enter here." Over a century later those criteria hold true with the addendum of near-perfect test scores and placement atop your high school graduating class. Like other schools with single-digit acceptance rates, there is an element of randomness that can leave valedictorians and possessors of 1600 SAT scores wondering why they were rejected.

Worth Your Money?

Pomona may have a sky-high sticker price, but it does everything in its power to make attending the school a possibility for students who otherwise could not afford it. In meeting 100 percent of the need of every eligible student, it awards an average of $55,485 per year to 51 percent of its undergraduate population. For everyone who can afford the $77k+ annual cost of attendance, that will be the actual cost because Pomona does not award merit aid. If you are offered a rare chance to attend Pomona, you should take advantage. With a superior reputation in academic and corporate circles alike, this college is definitely worth your money.

FINANCIAL
Institutional Type: Private
In-State Tuition: $56,284
Out-of-State Tuition: $56,284
Room & Board: $17,820
Required Fees: $394
Books & Supplies: $1,000

Avg. Need-Based Grant: $55,485
Avg. % of Need Met: 100%

Avg. Merit-Based Award: $0
% Receiving (All Freshmen): 0%
% Receiving (Freshmen w/o Need): 0%

Avg. Cumulative Debt: $18,829
% of Students Borrowing: 25%

CAREER
Who Recruits
1. Kaiser Permanente
2. Saatchi & Saatchi
3. UPS
4. JPMorgan Chase
5. AlphaSights

Notable Internships
1. :Los Angeles Review of Books
2. U.S. Senate
3. Spotify

Top Industries
1. Business
2. Education
3. Research
4. Media
5. Operations

Top Employers
1. Google
2. Microsoft
3. Kaiser Permanente
4. Amazon
5. Facebook

Where Alumni Work
1. Los Angeles
2. San Francisco
3. New York City
4. Seattle
5. Washington DC

Median Earnings
College Scorecard (Early Career): $58,100
PayScale (Early Career): $69,100
PayScale (Mid-Career): $137,800

RANKINGS
Money: 38
U.S. News: 4 (T), Liberal Arts Colleges
Wall Street Journal/THE: 24 (T)
Washington Monthly: 6, Liberal Arts Colleges

COLLEGE OVERLAPS
Brown University
Claremont McKenna College
Stanford University
University of Southern California
Williams College

Princeton University

Princeton, New Jersey | 609-258-3060

ADMISSION
Admission Rate: 6%
Admission Rate - Men: 5%
Admission Rate - Women: 6%
EA Admission Rate: 14%
ED Admission Rate: Not Offered
ED Admits as % of Total Admits: Not Offered
Admission Rate (5-Year Trend): -2%
% of Admits Attending (Yield): 70%
Transfer Admission Rate: 1%

SAT Reading/Writing (Middle 50%): 710-770
SAT Math (Middle 50%): 750-800
ACT Composite (Middle 50%): 33-35

% Graduated in Top 10% of HS Class: 91%
% Graduated in Top 25% of HS Class: 25%
% Graduated in Top 50% of HS Class: 100%

Demonstrated Interest: Not Considered
Legacy Status: Considered
Admission Interview Offered: Yes

ENROLLMENT
Total Undergraduate Enrollment: 5,422
% Part-Time: 2%
% Male: 50%
% Female: 50%
% Out-of-State: 82%
% Fraternity: Not Offered
% Sorority: Not Offered
% On-Campus (Freshman): 100%
% On-Campus (All Undergraduate): 96%

% African-American: 8%
% Asian: 22%
% Hispanic: 10%
% White: 39%
% Other: 5%
% Race or Ethnicity Unknown: 1%
% International: 12%
% Low-Income: 14%

ACADEMICS
Student-to-Faculty Ratio: 5 to 1
% of Classes Under 20: 75%
% of Classes 20-49: 16%
% of Classes 50 or More: 9%
% Full-Time Faculty: 77%
% Full-Time Faculty w/ Terminal Degree: 93%

Top Programs
Economics
Engineering
History
Mathematics
Philosophy
Physics
Politics
Public Policy

Retention Rate: 98%
4-Year Graduation Rate: 90%
6-Year Graduation Rate: 98%

Curricular Flexibility: Somewhat Flexible
Academic Rating: ★★★★★

#CollegesWorthYourMoney

The fourth oldest college in the United States is also an institution whose very name rings of wealth, privilege, and power—Princeton University. A charter member of the so-called Big Three alongside Harvard and Yale, Princeton has the smallest undergraduate population of that elite trio, but that doesn't stop it from churning out a dispro-portionate number of leaders and luminaries. Alumni include three current members of the US Supreme Court, eighteen Nobel Prize winners, business giants like Jeff Bezos and Steve Forbes, and countless other influential politicians, actors, writers, and scientific geniuses. We're hardly breaking new ground here—suffice to say that Princeton is Princeton.

Inside the Classroom
Once noted for its policy of grade deflation, Princeton ended that practice five years ago, and GPAs have been on the rise since, providing a source of relief to current and future undergraduates. The majority of students are required to take a freshman writing seminar, one course in each of epistemology and cognition, ethical thought and moral values, historical analysis, and quantitative reasoning as well as two courses in each of literature and the arts, social analysis, and science and technology. All students must demonstrate proficiency in a foreign language. Central to a Princeton education is the culminating senior thesis project that is developed through one-on-one mentorship with a faculty member.

An absurdly low 5:1 student to faculty ratio does, as you might expect, translate to tiny class sizes for under-graduates. Three-quarters of class sections have an enrollment of nineteen or fewer students, and 32 percent have fewer than ten students. Princeton is known for its commitment to undergraduate teaching, and students consistently rate professors as accessible and helpful. The Office of Undergraduate Research, formed in 2014, assists Tigers in locating faculty members with whom they can jointly conduct research in the summer or during a regular term. The university offers more than one hundred study abroad programs in forty-three countries; over half of its students take advantage.

As evidenced by the partial list of Princeton alumni, graduates of the university find themselves well received by the worlds of employment and top graduate schools. That goes for recipients of any degree, but the Engineering Department is widely recognized as one of the country's best as is the Woodrow Wilson School of Public and International Affairs. Prestigious scholarship programs love to go Tiger hunting. Fourteen students and alumni made off with Fulbright Scholarships in 2019, two were named Rhodes Scholars, two became Schwarzman Scholars, and so many National Science Foundation Graduate Research Fellowships were procured that four students won them from the Electrical Engineering program alone.

Outside the Classroom
An attractive and historic 500-acre campus plays home to 96 percent of Princeton undergraduates who are guaranteed housing for all four years. Freshmen and sophomores are required to live in one of six Residential College houses, each staffed by a live-in faculty member and full administrative team intent on creating a "strong sense of community, collaboration, and mutual respect, and to support individual initiative and personal growth."

Sports are serious at Princeton as the Tigers field thirty-seven varsity men's and women's squads that compete in NCAA Division I, and the school is the all-time leader in Ivy League titles. A sizable 18 percent of the undergraduate students compete at that level, and many others join one of the thirty-seven club sports teams. There are no officially recognized Greek organizations on campus, but that doesn't mean fraternities and sororities do not exist. In fact, 15-20 percent of the undergraduate population joins a Greek organization, and many more go through the "Bicker" process in an attempt to gain entry into one of the university's storied and exclusive "Eating Clubs" that are located in mansions on what is known as "The Street." The 135-member Ivy Club, immortalized by F. Scott Fitzgerald in This Side of Paradise, is Princeton's version of a Skull and Bones secret society. For everyone else, there are 300 student organizations that include popular dance troupes, singing groups, fifteen chaplaincies, the Daily Princetonian (one the oldest collegiate papers), and the 500-member American Whig-Cliosophic Society. The oldest debate team in the country, it was actually found-ed by James Madison. Princeton's location fifty-five miles from both Philadelphia and New York City means that big-city fun is always only a reasonable car or train ride away.

Career Services
The Center for Career Development at Princeton University has twenty-two professional staff members (excluding peer career advisors, and assistants) who are dedicated to tasks such as pre-law advising,

employer engagement, career advising, and alumni engagement. That 246:1 student-to-advisor ratio is superior to the average college featured in this guide. In addition to loads of individualized attention, Princeton also offers large-scale events such as the Fall HireTigers Career Fair that features one hundred top employers, and the school's online Handshake system sees over 42,000 applications for 6,500 jobs and internships each year.

An endless stream of impressive data supports the excellent work of the CCD office. In a given year, counselors engage students in 5,500 one-on-one advising sessions and attracted over 11,000 attendees at close to 400 unique career services events. Approximately 3,800 students participated in student-alumni engagement programs, and 46 percent of undergraduate participants reported that those sessions helped influence their postgraduate plans. More than 3,100 on-campus employer interviews take place each year. Highly personalized career and graduate school advising, along with ample resources and a supportive alumni base, assure graduating Tigers that a multitude of wonderful pathways await them post-commencement.

Professional Outcomes

Ninety-four percent of Princeton grads achieve post-graduation success within six months. Full-time employment was the first destination for 72.5 percent of those surveyed with professional, scientific, and technical services being the top industry, attracting 18 percent of graduates. The next most commonly entered industries were finance and insurance (13 percent), information (6 percent), and educational services (5 percent). Companies presently employing hundreds of Tiger alumni include Google, Goldman Sachs, Microsoft, McKinsey & Company, Morgan Stanley, IBM, and Facebook. The average salary reported by the 293 graduates entering the business and financial operations field was $73k while the school's 107 grads holding computer/mathematical positions averaged $107k. Those finding jobs in education, health care, or social services generally made less than $40k. The majority of grads remain in the Northeast and Mid-Atlantic regions, but 8 percent head to international destinations such as China, the United Kingdom, and South Korea.

Between 15-20 percent of graduating Tigers head directly to graduate/professional school. Princeton alumni typically choose equally prestigious graduate schools to attend. Members of one recent class flocked in the largest numbers to Stanford (21), Penn (11), Princeton (11), Harvard (11), Cambridge (11), Columbia (10), and Oxford (10). The most frequently pursued degree was a master's (40 percent) followed by a PhD (34 percent), medical school (11 percent), and law school (5 percent). In recent years, Princeton undergrads have receive acceptances into medical school 82-90 percent of the time, more than double the national average.

Admission

On the surface, Princeton's 5.7 percent acceptance rate for the Class of 2023 is extremely intimidating, as are the middle-50 percent of enrolled freshman test scores of 1470-1560 for the SAT and 33-35 for the ACT. Taking a granular look only makes things worse. The average unweighted GPA of entering first-years was 3.91 and 58 percent had a perfect 4.0. Candidates with lower than a 3.75 GPA or a 1400 SAT score were accepted only on very rare occasions.

The committee ranks nine factors as being most important in making admissions decisions: rigorous curriculum, GPA, class rank, essays, recommendations, standardized test scores, extracurricular activities, talent/ability, and character/personal qualities. Sorry, Risky Business fans, but alumni interviews are merely "considered." In 2019, single-choice early action (SCEA) applicants experienced a 14 percent acceptance rate, the lowest early-round acceptance rate in the school's history. There are a fair number of legacy admits, particularly in the early round. Overall, 14 percent of incoming freshmen in 2019-20 had Tiger lineage. Any way you slice it, getting into Princeton is a harrowing undertaking that will, more often than not, result in failure, even for some of the most accomplished applicants. Those who are successful typically have near-perfect to perfect test scores and GPAs and a "hook" to seal the deal.

Worth Your Money?

If you qualify for financial aid, your family won't pay a dime more than it can afford. That is the case for the 62 percent of current undergrads who qualify for need-based aid; they receive an annual award of $57,700. The university does not award merit aid. The average student graduates from Princeton with less than $10k in debt, less than one-third the national average. Of course, graduates also regularly walk into financially rewarding positions, so taking on any amount of debt to attend this school would absolutely be worth the sacrifice.

FINANCIAL
Institutional Type: Private
In-State Tuition: $51,870
Out-of-State Tuition: $51,870
Room & Board: $17,150
Required Fees: $930
Books & Supplies: $1,050

Avg. Need-Based Grant: $57,700
Avg. % of Need Met: 100%

Avg. Merit-Based Award: $0
% Receiving (All Freshmen): $0
% Receiving (Freshmen w/o Need): $0

Avg. Cumulative Debt: $9,445
% of Students Borrowing: 17%

CAREER
Who Recruits
1. Bain & Company
2. Schlumberger
3. MIT Lincoln Laboratory
4. Blackstone Group
5. Uber

Notable Internships
1. US Department of State
2. Jane Street
3. Bain & Company

Top Industries
1. Business
2. Education
3. Research
4. Engineering
5. Finance

Top Employers
1. Google
2. Goldman Sachs
3. Microsoft
4. McKinsey & Company
5. Facebook

Where Alumni Work
1. New York City
2. San Francisco
3. Washington DC
4. Boston
5. Philadelphia

Median Earnings
College Scorecard (Early Career): $74,700
PayScale (Early Career): $79,900
PayScale (Mid-Career): $157,200

RANKINGS
Money: 3
U.S. News: 1, National Universities
Wall Street Journal/THE: 7 (T)
Washington Monthly: 5, National Universities

COLLEGE OVERLAPS
Columbia University
Harvard University
Stanford University
University of Pennsylvania
Yale University

Purdue University — West Lafayette

West Lafayette, Indiana | 765-494-1776

After dominating Wabash College in an 1892 football contest, a newspaper reporter labeled the brutes from Purdue University as "burly boiler makers." It was intended to be derogatory—a dig at an engineering and agricultural education—but it was almost immediately embraced by not only the football team but the entire university. As the twenty-first century has progressed, Purdue University, the public STEM university in Indiana, has grown to where it now educates 33,646 undergraduates and another 10,905 graduate students and draws bright techie teens from well beyond the Hoosier State's ninety-two counties. Indiana residents comprise only 52 percent of the total undergraduate population at Purdue while 40+ percent hail from out of state, and 14 percent are international students.

Inside the Classroom
Waves of new students crash onto Purdue's West Lafayette campus each year filling up ten discipline-specific colleges in the pursuit of 200+ undergraduate majors. Yet, whether you are a member of the College of Engineering or the College of Education, you'll have to complete the same core curriculum, a thirty-credit concoction that lists among its ingredients written communication, information literacy, oral communication, science, quantitative reasoning, human behavior, and human cultures. The school's renowned Honors College welcomes 700 freshmen each fall and offers small class sizes, honors housing, and special leadership opportunities.

But class sizes are reasonable for all students, not only those in the Honors College. For a school of immense size, Purdue offers a strong 13:1 student-to-faculty ratio that leads to 42 percent of course sections having an enrollment of nineteen or fewer. You can also expect a balance of larger lectures as well as 19 percent of courses enroll more than fifty students. Undergraduate research opportunities are afforded to around 2,000 students per year. Undergrads can connect with professors on research projects during the academic year or apply to participate in a Summer Research Fellowship. A similar number, 2,400 students per year, elect to study abroad at one of 400 programs in sixty countries.

Engineering and engineering technologies majors earn 35 percent of the degrees conferred by the university. It makes sense that so many take advantage. After all, Purdue's College of Engineering cracks the top ten on almost every list of best engineering schools. The Krannert School of Management is also well regarded by employers around the country; 14 percent of degrees conferred are in business. Other popular majors include computer science (10 percent), agriculture (6 percent)—both are incredibly strong. Nationally Competitive Scholarships have been captured by recent grads of all academic backgrounds, including as many as six Fulbright Scholarships per year and a multitude of National Science Foundation Graduate Research Fellowships.

Outside the Classroom
Male-heavy to the tune of 57 percent (a typical STEM disproportionality), roughly two-fifths of the Purdue undergraduate student body lives on campus. Freshman housing is only guaranteed to those who sign a housing contract by early May; 93 percent of first-year students follow through. There are over ninety fraternity and sorority houses, and 18 percent of men and 21 percent of women partake in Greek life. Nearly 1,000 clubs and activities are available, and among those who participate, 66 percent cited their involvement as one of the major reasons they remain at the university. A hard-to-fathom 18,000 students participate in one of forty intramural sports—there are 300 flag football teams alone. There is also no shortage of big-time sports to consume as a fan. A top-ranked marching band helps cheer on the eighteen NCAA Division I squads that compete in the Big Ten Conference. Purdue has sent thirty players to the NBA, and the football team has appeared in eighteen postseason bowl games. Campus food receives favorable reviews as does the sprawling 2,000-acre campus and its proximity to traditional college town fare and basic entertainment. In addition, Indianapolis can be reached within about an hour by car, and Chicago is a nice weekend destination that is only a two-hour drive away.

Career Services
There are twenty-one professional staff members (not counting administrative assistants) occupying the offices of Purdue University's Center for Career Opportunities & Pre-Professional Advising (CCO). The majority have the title of career services consultant while others specialize in pre-professional advising. The university's overall 1,602:1 student-to-counselor ratio is quite high compared to most other schools profiled in this guidebook. Fortunately, the center is adept at organizing large-scale events, connecting with industry leaders, and facilitating experiential learning and networking opportunities for its undergraduate students.

The Industry Roundtable, held every September, is the largest student-run career fair in the United States, drawing 400 companies and 12,000+ students. A business-specific career fair attracts another 2,000 students, the Agricultural Career Fair brings one hundred companies to campus, and Purdue also offers fairs for aviation, civil engineering, hospitality/tourism, aerospace, and construction management. This robust operation brings a total of 1,400 employers to campus each year for recruiting and/or on-campus interviews. Internship numbers are equally impressive—83 percent engage in at least one internship experience during their four years of study, 27 percent complete two experiences, and 28 percent engage in three or more. Catering to the career services needs of over 33,000 undergraduates with limited staff may be a logistical battle, but it is one that Purdue's CCO is managing to win. What it lacks in the ability to hand-hold, it makes up for in the scope of offerings and the positive career results for graduates.

Professional Outcomes

Shortly after receiving their diplomas, 70 percent of members of the Class of 2019 were headed to the world of employment, 21 percent were continuing their educational journey in graduate/professional school, and a mere 4 percent were still seeking employment. The top industries entered by Purdue grads in 2019 were (1) health care, pharmaceuticals, and medical devices; (2) finance, insurance, and consulting; (3) manufacturing and machinery (4) airline, aviation, and aerospace. Companies employing the greatest number of 2019 graduates included Lockheed Martin (28), PepsiCo (27), Amazon (26), Deloitte (26), Microsoft (25), and Raytheon (24). The average starting salary was an exceptional $60,395 across all degree programs. Liberal arts and education majors earned an average salary in the neighborhood of $42k while engineering students brought home $70k. The majority of alumni remain in Indiana with Chicago, San Francisco, New York, and DC rounding out the five next most common destinations.

Purdue enjoys professional school acceptance rates that are "slightly above" the national averages. In 2019-20, the school saw 144 of its seniors apply to medical school, and many went on to attend the Indiana University School of Medicine and other Midwestern institutions including the University of Minnesota and the University of Illinois. Given the academic concentrations of many undergrads, law school is not an immensely popular choice. Interestingly, Purdue purchased an unaccredited online law school in 2017, which was recognized by the American Bar Association in 2020. Looking at all grad school applicants, 442 graduates in the Class of 2019 who continued their educations did so in state. Illinois, New York, and California all attracted forty+ graduate/professional students including top institutions like NYU, UC Berkeley, and the University of Chicago.

Admission

Purdue – West Lafayette received 54,912 applications for a spot in the Class of 2023 and admitted a friendly 60 percent of wanna-be Boilermakers. Of those who were admitted and ultimately enrolled, the median SAT score was 1330 and the median ACT score was 29. Math scores are generally stronger than reading scores—43 percent of freshmen scored above a 700 on the SAT while only 23 percent hit that same target on the reading section. Forty-nine percent placed in the top 10 percent of their high school class, and 80 percent were in the top quartile, giving a glimmer of hope to applicants with a few blemishes on their transcripts and who aren't looking to pursue either engineering or computer science. Earning entry into these majors can prove considerably more difficult.

The university's admissions staff looks foremost at the hard numbers of GPA and standardized test scores as well as the rigor of your high school curriculum. First-generation status is among the categories occupying the next rung of "important" factors. It is joined by essays, extracurricular activities, recommendations, and character/personal qualities. Women enjoyed a 66 percent acceptance rate compared to 56 percent for male applicants. There is no binding early decision option, but there is an early action round with a November 1 deadline. Acceptance rates at Purdue are definitely on the decline. In 2007, the school received approximately 20,000 applications and accepted 79 percent of the pool. Despite the rise in selectivity, Purdue remains one of the top STEM-focused universities that accepts solid-but-imperfect applicants.

Worth Your Money?

Tuition for Hoosier State residents remains a tremendous bargain at a hair under $10K. Nonresidents and international students will pay $29k in tuition which, given the graduates' employment and salary data, is still not a bad price. Like most STEM-oriented schools, Purdue is highly likely to return your investment many times over. The only person for which this school would not make complete sense is an out-of-state applicant taking loans to pursue a non-STEM/business degree.

FINANCIAL
Institutional Type: Public
In-State Tuition: $9,208
Out-of-State Tuition: $30,010
Room & Board: $10,030
Required Fees: $784
Books & Supplies: $1,160

Avg. Need-Based Grant: $12,115
Avg. % of Need Met: 77%

Avg. Merit-Based Award: $5,057
% Receiving (All Freshmen): 26%
% Receiving (Freshmen w/o Need): 12%

Avg. Cumulative Debt: $27,673
% of Students Borrowing: 51%

CAREER
Who Recruits
1. Cognex Corporation
2. Endress + Hauser
3. Lockheed Martin
4. General Motors
5. General Electric

Notable Internships
1. Caterpillar
2. Qualcomm
3. PepsiCo

Top Industries
1. Business
2. Engineering
3. Operations
4. Education
5. Sales

Top Employers
1. Amazon
2. Microsoft
3. IBM
4. Google
5. Apple

Where Alumni Work
1. Indianapolis
2. Lafayette, IN
3. Chicago
4. San Francisco
5. New York City

Median Earnings
College Scorecard (Early Career): $55,100
PayScale (Early Career): $64,400
PayScale (Mid-Career): $114,200

RANKINGS
Money: 23
U.S. News: 53 (T), National Universities
Wall Street Journal/THE: 47
Washington Monthly: 39, National Universities

COLLEGE OVERLAPS
Indiana University Bloomington
Ohio State University - Columbus
Pennsylvania State University - University Park
University of Illinois at Urbana-Champaign
University of Michigan

Reed College

Portland, Oregon | 503-777-7511

ADMISSION
Admission Rate: 39%
Admission Rate - Men: 38%
Admission Rate - Women: 40%
EA Admission Rate: NR
ED Admission Rate: 48%
ED Admits as % of Total Admits: 5%
Admission Rate (5-Year Trend): -9%
% of Admits Attending (Yield): 17%
Transfer Admission Rate: 21%

SAT Reading/Writing (Middle 50%): 670-750
SAT Math (Middle 50%): 655-770
ACT Composite (Middle 50%): 30-34

% Graduated in Top 10% of HS Class: 57%
% Graduated in Top 25% of HS Class: 72%
% Graduated in Top 50% of HS Class: 84%

Demonstrated Interest: Important
Legacy Status: Considered
Admission Interview Offered: Yes

ENROLLMENT
Total Undergraduate Enrollment: 1,457
% Part-Time: 3%
% Male: 47%
% Female: 53%
% Out-of-State: 92%
% Fraternity: Not Offered
% Sorority: Not Offered
% On-Campus (Freshman): 100%
% On-Campus (All Undergraduate): 68%

% African-American: 1%
% Asian: 8%
% Hispanic: 10%
% White: 57%
% Other: 9%
% Race or Ethnicity Unknown: 2%
% International: 12%
% Low-Income: 20%

ACADEMICS
Student-to-Faculty Ratio: 9 to 1
% of Classes Under 20: 79%
% of Classes 20-49: 16%
% of Classes 50 or More: 5%
% Full-Time Faculty: 93%
% Full-Time Faculty w/ Terminal Degree: 95%

Top Programs
Biology
Chemistry
Economics
English
History
Mathematics
Physics
Political Science

Retention Rate: 91%
4-Year Graduation Rate: 64%
6-Year Graduation Rate: 76%

Curricular Flexibility: Somewhat Flexible
Academic Rating: ★★★★

#CollegesWorthYourMoney

"A band of fierce intellectuals and the distinctive institution that nurtures them. All in for rigorous scholarship and the joy of intellectual pursuit." Thus reads the twitter profile of an elite liberal arts school of 1,457 undergraduates located in Portland, Oregon—the one-and-only Reed College. It would be difficult to create a statement that more aptly sums up this unique institution that, for many, serves primarily as a prelude to a PhD program.

Inside the Classroom
Twenty-three academic departments collectively offer forty majors, fourteen of which are interdisciplinary (e.g., history-literature or mathematics-economics). One of the most storied features of a Reed education is the mandatory, year-long freshman Humanities 110 course that comprehensively explores Greco-Roman culture and its many influences. However, in spring 2018, after a series of student-led protests over the course's "Eurocentrism," the school agreed to alter the course to include the study of other cultures. As with the aforementioned twitter statement, that anecdote also helps paint a picture of the Reed experience.

Grades at the college are, paradoxically, both (a) difficult to earn and (b) completely unknown to the students themselves. To ensure that the emphasis on the classroom remains on learning for learning's sake, grades are issued but not shared with students until graduation. The average GPA earned is 3.1, and only eleven students have graduated with a perfect 4.0 in the last three decades. The educational experience is highly personalized, and students work directly with their professors. Class sizes average seventeen students, and the student-to-faculty ratio is 9:1. Study abroad opportunities exist at fifty-two partner university programs in twenty-three countries. The college funds a number of undergraduate research opportunities for students to work alongside faculty, and all students are required to complete their own senior thesis, which is essentially a mini-dissertation under the guidance of a faculty advisor.

The areas in which the highest number of degrees are conferred are the social sciences (20 percent), biology (13 percent), foreign languages (10 percent), and the physical sciences (8 percent). All majors are viewed favorably by elite graduate programs that are fully aware of the exceptional level of rigor baked into every academic program at the college. English, math, and physics receive particularly strong praise. Competitive fellowship and scholarship programs are also acutely aware of Reed's excellence and pluck up graduates at exceptionally high rates. In its history, Reed grads have won thirty-two Rhodes Scholarships, sixty-seven Watson Fellowships, and 174 National Science Foundation Fellowships.

Outside the Classroom
Downtown Portland is only ten minutes away, making Reed's location in the southeastern corner of the city ideal for finding culture, the arts, and entertainment. Public transportation is easy to navigate, so just about anything the uber-progressive City of Roses has to offer is accessible. While 98 percent of freshmen live on campus, only 68 percent of the total student body resides in university-owned housing. Others live in affordable off-campus housing that is easy to locate in the immediate area. There are no fraternities or sororities at Reed, nor is there any semblance of highly completive athletics. There are, however, five intercollegiate club teams in which athletically-inclined students may wish to participate. While most Reedies would say their primary outside-the-classroom activity is "studying," there are ninety student-run organizations from which to choose, including KRRC, the campus radio station; Quest, the student body's independent newspaper; and typically "Reedish" groups like the Sky Appreciation Society. Renn Fayre, an annual campus-wide, weekend-long party for graduating seniors is an out-of-control event that is truly beloved by students. Notable amenities include a recently renovated ski cabin on Mt. Hood that students are free to use, and the Watzik Sports Center that boasts a pool, sauna, and climbing wall.

Career Services
The Center for Life Beyond Reed (CLBR) employs six full-time staff members giving it a 243:1 student-to-advisor ratio that is better-than-average for a college included in this guidebook. The guiding mission of the office since a 2012 rebranding is to help students "try to connect the intellectual passions they cultivate during their time here to successful careers."

On the practical side, the CLBR offers six full-day senior boot camps where students can receive help with resumes, online professional profiles, interview techniques, and helpful contacts in students' areas of interest. In recent years, it has increased engagement with freshmen and sophomores, encouraging earlier 1:1 advising sessions. Handshake and the Reed Career Network are the places online to find a job, internships, or connect with alumni. Winter Shadow internships allow current students to join alumni in their places of business. With an intense focus on preparing the next generation of academics and researchers, the campus is not swarming with corporate recruiters, yet Reed does maintain some productive relationships with employers—Microsoft, for example, contributed $500,000 toward the development of the college's computer science program. Acknowledging its immense level of success in placing students at elite graduate and professional schools, the CLBR serves its unique student population well in spite of below-average starting salaries (more on that in a moment).

Professional Outcomes

An examination of Reed's alumni database reveals that the three most common occupational pathways are business (28 percent), education (25 percent), and self-employment (19 percent). Included among the most frequent current employers are Microsoft Corporation, Kaiser Permanente, Portland Public Schools, Intel Corporation, the US Department of State, National Institutes of Health, and Apple. Because of the incredible number of students who flock to academia (more on this later), many institutions of higher education are also employers of large numbers of Reed alumni. Early-to-mid-career salary figures are generally low even by liberal arts standards. However, it is important to place that fact in proper context because that is the age when many Reed alumni may be completing an advanced degree.

Reed is rarely the final stop on a student's academic journey. In College Transitions' analysis of National Science Foundation data, Reed was the No. 2 producer of future PhD holders across all academic disciplines as determined by percentage of graduates attaining that degree. The list of the universities where the highest concentration of grads pursue their doctorates is phenomenal. Included on that list are MIT, Harvard, Stanford, Yale, Berkeley, and Princeton. MBAs were earned at institutions that include Penn, Georgetown, Columbia, and UChicago. Reedies who went the legal route obtained their JDs primarily from top-tier law schools. Recent med school applicants have enjoyed a 70 percent acceptance rate, and many have attended similarly impressive universities as those in other fields already mentioned.

Admission

Reed College's 39 percent acceptance rate does not do its level of selectivity justice, not that the college cares. Admirably, this institution has long been anti-rankings and has no interest in PR efforts to drum up more applicants for the purpose of enhancing its status. It receives fewer than 6,000 applications per year. Its students are a self-selecting crew who choose to apply to this unique liberal arts school in Portland, Oregon. The middle-50 percent range for enrolled students is right around 1325-1520 on the SATs and 30-34 on the ACTs. Grades/class rank numbers are impressive but do not automatically exclude those with an imperfect transcript; 57 percent finished in the top 10 percent of their high school class, 72 percent were in the top 25 percent, and the average GPA is a 4.0.

The Reed Admissions Office only designates three factors as being "very important" in its evaluation process: rigor of secondary school record, grades, and essays. Factors deemed "important" are standardized test scores, class rank, interview, demonstrated interest, and recommendations. This is a college that, like Wesleyan on the opposite coast, is looking for intellectual risk-takers whose passion comes through in their writing and in conversation. Applying early definitely helps as 48 percent of ED applicants are accepted (a figure that is unaffected by athletes). Teens who are destined to be Reedies are the ones who fall in love with the school in the first place. Brilliant young people with an open mind who eschew convention will be thrilled to find a home here. Of course, strong credentials will help to make that goal a reality.

Worth Your Money?

At a cost of $75,000 and little available in the way of merit aid, many pay a steep price for attending this institution. Over 50 percent of Reed students do qualify for need-based aid and receive average annual grants of $40k. Undoubtedly, the academic experience here is uniquely wonderful and a perfect fit for a certain type of budding intellectual. Yet, if you don't qualify for need-based aid and don't come from a wealthy family, you would have to make sure that the $300,000+ bill for tuition would make sense as part of your life plan. Interestingly, the average student loan debt among Reed graduates is lower than the national average.

FINANCIAL
Institutional Type: Private
In-State Tuition: $60,310
Out-of-State Tuition: $60,310
Room & Board: $15,450
Required Fees: $310
Books & Supplies: $1,050

Avg. Need-Based Grant: $40,096
Avg. % of Need Met: 100%

Avg. Merit-Based Award: $0
% Receiving (All Freshmen): 0%
% Receiving (Freshmen w/o Need): 0%

Avg. Cumulative Debt: $25,657
% of Students Borrowing: 52%

CAREER
Who Recruits
1. TerraCotta Group LLC
2. First Book
3. Cranial Technologies
4. Teach for America
5. Wayfair

Notable Internships
1. Melville House Publishing
2. RTI International
3. Whitney Museum of American Art

Top Industries
1. Business
2. Education
3. Research
4. Media
5. Operations

Top Employers
1. Google
2. Microsoft
3. Apple
4. Intel
5. Amazon

Where Alumni Work
1. Portland, OR
2. San Francisco
3. New York City
4. Seattle
5. Los Angeles

Median Earnings
College Scorecard (Early Career): $42,200
PayScale (Early Career): $60,700
PayScale (Mid-Career): $114,900

RANKINGS
Money: 551
U.S. News: 63 (T), Liberal Arts Colleges
Wall Street Journal/THE: 86 (T)
Washington Monthly: 78, Liberal Arts Colleges

COLLEGE OVERLAPS
Brown University
Carleton College
Lewis & Clark College
Swarthmore College
University of Chicago

Rensselaer Polytechnic Institute

Troy, New York | 518-276-6216

Founded almost 200 years ago, Rensselaer Polytechnic Institute is America's first technological research university and still one of its best. Fittingly situated on the eastern bank of the Hudson River in the Industrial Revolution hotspot of Troy, New York, RPI is the proud home of 6,641 of the brightest and most innovative technical undergraduate minds anywhere. This is merely perpetuating a long history of producing high achievers in the tech world. Including both faculty and alumni, Rensselaer claims eighty-five members of the National Academy of Engineering, five members of the National Inventors Hall of Fame, and a Nobel Prize winner in physics.

Inside the Classroom
There are five undergraduate schools within the larger university: The School of Architecture; the Lally School of Management; the School of Science; the School of Engineering; and the School of Humanities, Arts, and Social Sciences. All students take what is known as the HASS Core, a six course, twenty-four-credit foray into the humanities and social sciences. Beyond that, the academic programs are tailored to different schools and degree programs. There is no foreign language requirement, although the school does offer coursework in Mandarin Chinese for interested students.

The student-to-faculty ratio at RPI is 12:1, and with only about 1,300 graduate students to serve, there is plenty of time and attention left for undergraduates. Students will encounter various class sizes over the course of their four years of study. A solid 54 percent of sections contain fewer than twenty students; 10 percent will have fifty or more students. Being a research institution, RPI attracts $103 million in research funding each year, meaning that the school's 500 faculty members are constantly in the middle of projects that require student assistance. Students can participate during the academic year for credit or during the summer when select individuals receive $4,000 to work full time in a lab. International study is also encouraged at one of the school's affiliate universities in thirteen countries including Australia, Finland, and Singapore.

Engineering is the most commonly conferred degree area, accounting for 54 percent of graduates. Computer and information sciences was second (17 percent), followed by business/marketing (6 percent), engineering technology (5 percent), and biology (4 percent). The School of Engineering has a brilliant reputation with employers worldwide and is always near the top of the rankings for its programs in mechanical, aerospace, computer, electrical, and biomedical engineering. Physics, architecture, and computer science are also strong. Graduates do not apply to prestigious fellowship programs in droves, but the school does capture an occasional Fulbright or Truman Scholarship. RPI does, however, typically produce more than one annual National Science Foundation Graduate Research Fellowship winner.

Outside the Classroom
The school's 296-acre suburban campus only houses 57 percent of the student body as many upperclassmen seek off-campus apartments or join fraternities or sororities. Thirty percent of men and 16 percent of women elect to join Greek organizations. Those numbers are down after several chapters were suspended or dissolved in recent years. For a technical school, RPI boasts a highly athletic student body. Sixty-three percent of incoming freshmen participated in varsity athletics in high school, and forty-two individuals were the captains of their squads. There are twenty-three varsity men's and women's sports teams, twenty-two of which compete in NCAA Division III. The exception is men's hockey, which is one of the oldest and best teams in the entire country, having produced a long list of NHL stars over the years. Including the university's thriving intramural and club programs, 80 percent of RPI students are involved in athletics. With over 200 student organizations, students have their pick of non-sports/Greek sources of camaraderie. For example, the RPI Players has put on 300 theatrical shows over its ninety-year history, and there are nineteen service-oriented groups that serve the local community. In addition, fitness classes run by professional instructors are available just about every day at the Mueller Center. Troy itself may lack excitement, but the state capital of Albany is only ten miles away, and scenic retreats like the Berkshires or Catskills are under two hours away.

Career Services
The Center for Career and Professional Development consists of thirteen professional employees, which calculates to a student-to-advisor ratio of 480:1, a bit higher than the average school featured in this guide. However, that less-than-deal statistic is not at all representative of the exceptional work done by RPI's career services staff. Other numbers tell a different story, such as the ninety-five annual events hosted by the school that draw almost 1,900 undergrads, and the 1,900+ one-on-one counseling appointments that take place. And that doesn't even include the employer recruiting numbers that are even more eye-popping.

Rensselaer Polytechnic Institute

E-mail: admissions@rpi.edu | Website: www.rpi.edu

In a single recent school year, career fairs drew 403 employers to campus, and 102 employers conducted 1,923 on-campus interviews. Companies also hosted 132 information sessions for RPI students that same year. Companies that recruit on campus include Cisco, the Blackstone Group, Deloitte, Johnson & Johnson, and Credit Suisse. Rensselaer Alumni Connect is a platform with over 2,500 active users, 79 percent of whom are willing to introduce others to connections while 83 percent are willing to answer industry-specific questions. Internship and co-op opportunities abound, and large numbers of students land co-op positions at Hasbro (27), NASA Jet Propulsion Laboratory (10), and Walt Disney World (7). Thanks to an endless parade of recruiters flowing into campus, high starting salaries, and plenty of individualized attention, the CCPD has earned a reputation for stellar work.

Professional Outcomes

As they receive their diplomas, 55 percent of RPI grads have already landed a job, 24 percent have committed to a graduate school, and 16 percent are still seeking their next destination. The largest numbers of grads were hired by companies that included UnitedHealth (17), United Technologies (16), General Dynamics (16), Boeing (14), and IBM (12). Massive numbers of alumni hold leadership positions in corporations like Google, Pratt & Whitney, General Motors, GE, and Microsoft. Geographically, 68 percent of graduates remain in the Northeast, 10 percent head to the West—primarily to Silicon Valley—and 8 percent land in the Southeast. Recent grads enjoy starting salaries in excess of $70k.

Of the nearly one-quarter of grads who enter an advanced degree program, many headed to some of the nation's best schools. Recent grads have been accepted by the likes of Carnegie Mellon University, Duke University, Massachusetts Institute of Technology, Northwestern University, Texas A&M, and the University of Chicago. Those intent on medical school have the option to apply to RPIs seven-year BS/MD program with affiliate Albany Medical College. Recent medically-minded grads have enjoyed acceptances at the likes of Harvard Medical School and Cornell University College of Veterinary Medicine. Those intent on law school also have the option of a combined degree, in this case a BS/JD at either Albany or Columbia University.

Admission

RPI received fewer applications from Class of 2023 hopefuls than the previous year, receiving 18,635 in 2019. While the acceptance rate of 47 percent will do little to scare off prospective students, the composition of the 2019-20 freshman class was an impressive one. The median SAT score was 1440 and a solid 63 percent placed in the top 10 percent of their high school class, and 92 percent were in the top quarter. In a typical year, close to 100 students earned either valedictorian or salutatorian status. The average GPA of an entering freshman was 3.9.

There is nothing opaque about the way in which applicants are evaluated by the Rensselaer Admissions Committee. The most strongly weighted factors are GPA, test scores, class rank, and the rigor of one's high school coursework. Of secondary importance are application essays, recommendations, extracurricular activities, and character/personal qualities. Unusual for a tech school, males and females have fairly similar acceptance rates. In 2019, men were accepted at a 47 percent clip, and women were welcomed 51 percent of the time. Applying early decision provides an advantage; 65 percent of ED applicants were admitted into the Class of 2023. Rensselaer Polytechnic Institute is looking for students with GPAs above a 3.75 in most or all honors and AP courses and who scored in the 95th percentile on standardized tests. The criteria is fairly simple.

Worth Your Money?

Rensselaer's annual cost of attendance is a pretty high $75,824; the good news is that starting salaries for graduates just about matches that sum. Over one-third of entering students do get an offer of merit aid that averages almost $23k, and more than half of attendees qualify for a need-based grant with an average value of $40k. Attending a STEM-heavy school like RPI is almost always a good bet for getting an excellent return on your educational investment, even if the up-front cost is quite high.

FINANCIAL
Institutional Type: Private
In-State Tuition: $55,600
Out-of-State Tuition: $55,600
Room & Board: $15,954
Required Fees: $1,412
Books & Supplies: $1,250

Avg. Need-Based Grant: $40,272
Avg. % of Need Met: 82%

Avg. Merit-Based Award: $23,326
% Receiving (All Freshmen): 37%
% Receiving (Freshmen w/o Need): 25%

Avg. Cumulative Debt: NR
% of Students Borrowing: NR

CAREER
Who Recruits
1. U.S. Nuclear Regulatory Commission
2. Etsy
3. GlobalFoundries
4. Apprenda
5. American Airlines

Notable Internships
1. Regeneron Pharmaceuticals
2. NASA
3. Pfizer

Top Industries
1. Engineering
2. Business
3. Operations
4. Information Technology
5. Education

Top Employers
1. IBM
2. Pratt & Whitney
3. Google
4. Boeing
5. GE

Where Alumni Work
1. New York City
2. Albany, NY
3. Boston
4. San Francisco
5. Washington DC

Median Earnings
College Scorecard (Early Career): $82,000
PayScale (Early Career): $74,700
PayScale (Mid-Career): $140,800

RANKINGS
Money: 254
U.S. News: 53 (T), National Universities
Wall Street Journal/THE: 94 (T)
Washington Monthly: 82, National Universities

COLLEGE OVERLAPS
Carnegie Mellon University
Cornell University
Georgia Institute of Technology
Purdue University -- West Lafayette
Worcester Polytechnic Institute

Rhodes College

Memphis, Tennessee | 901-843-3700

ADMISSION
Admission Rate: 45%
Admission Rate - Men: 40%
Admission Rate - Women: 48%
EA Admission Rate: 55%
ED Admission Rate: 66%
ED Admits as % of Total Admits: 6%
Admission Rate (5-Year Trend): -13%
% of Admits Attending (Yield): 22%
Transfer Admission Rate: 44%

SAT Reading/Writing (Middle 50%): 620-700
SAT Math (Middle 50%): 600-730
ACT Composite (Middle 50%): 27-32

% Graduated in Top 10% of HS Class: 52%
% Graduated in Top 25% of HS Class: 83%
% Graduated in Top 50% of HS Class: 99%

Demonstrated Interest: Considered
Legacy Status: Important
Admission Interview Offered: Yes

ENROLLMENT
Total Undergraduate Enrollment: 1,973
% Part-Time: 1%
% Male: 42%
% Female: 58%
% Out-of-State: 71%
% Fraternity: 32%
% Sorority: 38%
% On-Campus (Freshman): 98%
% On-Campus (All Undergraduate): 67%

% African-American: 10%
% Asian: 6%
% Hispanic: 6%
% White: 65%
% Other: 5%
% Race or Ethnicity Unknown: 2%
% International: 6%
% Low-Income: 13%

ACADEMICS
Student-to-Faculty Ratio: 10 to 1
% of Classes Under 20: 71%
% of Classes 20-49: 29%
% of Classes 50 or More: 0%
% Full-Time Faculty: 82%
% Full-Time Faculty w/ Terminal Degree: 98%

Top Programs
Biology
Business
Chemistry
International Studies
Neuroscience
Political Science
Psychology

Retention Rate: 92%
4-Year Graduation Rate: 75%
6-Year Graduation Rate: 80%

Curricular Flexibility: Somewhat Flexible
Academic Rating: ★★★★

#CollegesWorthYourMoney

Rhodes College's Memphis location places it among the rare liberal arts schools located in an urban setting. (Occidental in Los Angeles is another such school featured in this guide.) Just four miles from the world famous Beale Street, Rhodes, founded in 1848, is one of the top colleges in the region. A progressive, service-oriented student body of 1,973 students flock to Rhodes for its small classes, awesome location, and nurturing environment that leads many on the path to top graduate and professional programs.

Inside the Classroom
The school offers fifty majors and minors and a great deal of academic autonomy along the way. The foundations requirements can be meet by roughly 400 varied courses that cover target areas such as written communication, becoming an active and engaged citizen, gaining proficiency in a second language, and understanding scientific approaches to the natural world. As part of this experience students choose between two signature courses: The Search for Values in the Light of Western Religion and History and Life: Then and Now, both of which were developed after World War II. Freshmen also must engage in the first-year experience requirement, an integrative, year-long program focused on becoming an active student-citizen as well as a first year writing seminar.

A 10:1 student-to-faculty ratio leads to an amazingly intimate average class size of only fourteen students. Only 4 percent of course sections contain more than twenty-nine students. Ninety-eight percent of the 182 full-time faculty members hold the highest degree available in their fields, so you will not be taught by TAs or adjuncts. A great deal of resources are committed to undergraduate education. For example, Rhodes puts an astounding sum of money into its physical science programs, having committed $34 million to a new science center in 2017. As a result, the school produces an incredible number of PhDs (more on this under "Professional Outcomes"). Three-quarters of students at this institution engage in some form of undergraduate research. Opportunities are plentiful in every academic discipline to collaborate with faculty on research projects, and the annual Undergraduate Research and Creativity Symposium is a chance to show off student projects. An affiliation with St. Jude's Children's Research Hospital leads to intensive summer research opportunities for those in the hard sciences. A solid 65 percent of students elect to study abroad, and the school offers many Rhodes faculty-led locations around the world.

While the sciences may be the area for which Rhodes receives the greatest recognition (biology is the most popular major), business, psychology, and international studies are also strong and attract large numbers of undergrads. In 2020 alone, seniors and alumni captured an incredible ten Fulbright Scholarships and have won Watson, Luce, and NSF Fellowships.

Outside the Classroom
This 123-acre wooded oasis in midtown Memphis is home to 67 percent of all undergraduates. Students are required to live in residence halls for their first two years. Most residence halls are intimate places of under one hundred students where everyone knows everyone. A 58/42 percent breakdown in favor of women certainly has an impact on student life. Greek life is a defining characteristic of social life at Rhodes with 38 percent of women joining a sorority and 32 percent of men pledging a fraternity. Participation in sports is also common with twenty-one men's and women's varsity teams competing in NCAA Division III athletics. The Bryan Campus Life Center offers ample facilities for recreational sports and fitness. For non-jocks, there are more than one hundred student-run organizations, and over 80 percent of students engage in community service activities. The mock trial team is exceptionally strong in national competitions. With the Lynx Lair serving as a hub for food, social events, and frequent concerts, lectures, and films there is rarely a dull moment around Rhodes. Of course, with Memphis as your backyard there are always exciting excursions for entertainment, culture, or dining. The Memphis Zoo, the Memphis Brooks Museum of Art, and the National Civil Rights Museum are only a few miles away. Campus is walker-friendly, but bikes are popular as well. The city of Memphis has over 200 miles of bike infrastructure to help ensure safety.

Career Services
The Career Services Office at Rhodes has three full-time staff members—the director, a first- and second-year counselor, and a third- and fourth-year counselor. Its 658:1 student-to-advisor ratio does not compare favorably to other liberal arts schools featured in this guide, but the push for personalized service is evident everywhere you look. The school encourages meeting one-on-one with advisors two or three times in the freshman year as well during sophomore year. Few schools promote that level of contact so early in a student's undergraduate career.

E-mail: adminfo@rhodes.edu | Website: www.rhodes.edu

Every fall, representatives from over one hundred graduate and professional schools travel to Rhodes' campus to attend the Graduate School Exposition. The 2019 Career Fair was attended by over fifty employers, including many national corporations such as AutoZone, Raymond James, and St. Jude's Research Hospital. Over 80 percent of undergraduates complete at least one internship. Those numbers are bolstered by career services partnerships with over one hundred local, national, and global employers. Many of the 13,000 alums are willing to lend a hand to a current student or recent grad seeking to network.

Professional Outcomes

Within one year of receiving their diplomas, 98 percent of Rhodes grads have found their way into the world of employment or are pursuing an advanced degree program. Among the companies employing the largest number of alumni are St. Jude's Children's Hospital, Deloitte, EY, FedEx, Raymond James, and PwC. Midcareer salaries are the second highest among any Tennessee institution, behind only Vanderbilt. Greater Memphis is where most graduates remain. Many others situate themselves in Greater Nashville, Atlanta, DC, New York, or Dallas.

A superb 86 percent of those applying to graduate school get into their top-choice institution. Medical and law school applicants are accepted at higher rates than the national average. Those with a 3.4 GPA and above the 57th percentile on the MCAT are accepted into medical school at an identical 86 percent clip and, overall, applicants enjoy a 65 percent acceptance rate. In 2019, an impressive forty-four graduates were accepted into med school. Rhodes is in the top 10 percent of science PhD-producing undergraduate schools in the country, and is ranked among the top 50 PhD producers in several social science disciplines as well, including economics, political science, and psychology. Recent graduates have been accepted into programs at elite universities including Brown, Columbia, Georgetown, Harvard Law School, New York University School of Law, and Yale Divinity School. Medical schools attended by recent grads include Tufts, Dartmouth, Boston University, Wake Forest, and UVA.

Admission

With a 45 percent acceptance rate for a place in the Class of 2023, Rhodes College is a rare school that provides an elite education without putting applicants through a harrowing admissions process with dreadfully unfavorable odds. The 5,207 hopefuls who submitted applications were a strong bunch, but those who were successful didn't have to sport a perfect transcript. The SAT mid-50 percent range was 1250-1400, although the ACT was submitted more than twice as often; 27-32 was the mid-50 percent ACT score, and just shy of half of ACT takers had a composite score above 30. Fifty-two percent of admitted freshmen held a weighted GPA of 3.75 or higher, 52 percent finished in the top decile of their high school class, and 83 percent were in the top quartile. The average GPA of incoming 2019-20 freshman was 3.7.

Rigor of secondary school record, GPA, and class rank sit atop the list of most important factors in the eyes of the admissions office. Factors considered as "important" include standardized test scores, essays, recommendations, character/personal qualities, legacy status, and racial/ethnic status. Only 22 percent of those accepted actually enrolled, thus the college values those who demonstrate interest, particularly in the form of committing through early decision. As a result, 66 percent of ED applicants were accepted in 2019. In their own words, Rhodes uses a "holistic approach to evaluate every facet of your application to get a better sense of the whole you." Obviously, the school is looking for students with strong grades in a demanding curriculum, but students do not need to have perfect test scores and grades for consideration at this fine liberal arts institution.

Worth Your Money?

Rhodes' sticker-price cost of attendance of almost $63,000 isn't particularly tough to swallow, at least when considered against the cost of many comparable institutions. Yet, Rhodes delivers merit aid packages to two-thirds of its undergrads, lowering the cost by an average of $27k per year. Further, almost 60 percent of all students receive need-based aid at an average annual total of $36k. Given the cost that most people actually pay, Rhodes College is a fairly priced option that will afford you a one-of-a-kind educational experience.

FINANCIAL
Institutional Type: Private
In-State Tuition: $48,888
Out-of-State Tuition: $48,888
Room & Board: $11,631
Required Fees: $310
Books & Supplies: $1,125

Avg. Need-Based Grant: $35,927
Avg. % of Need Met: 94%

Avg. Merit-Based Award: $26,663
% Receiving (All Freshmen): 62%
% Receiving (Freshmen w/o Need): 36%

Avg. Cumulative Debt: $26,155
% of Students Borrowing: 46%

CAREER
Who Recruits
1. St. Jude's Children's Research Hospital
2. Raymond James
3. Methodist Healthcare
4. PeaceCorps
5. Teach for America

Notable Internships
1. Graystar Real Estate
2. Christie's
3. FedEx

Top Industries
1. Business
2. Education
3. Operations
4. Social Services
5. Healthcare

Top Employers
1. St. Jude Children's Research Hospital
2. Deloitte
3. EY
4. Raymond James
5. FedEx

Where Alumni Work
1. Memphis
2. Nashville
3. Atlanta
4. Washington DC
5. New York City

Median Earnings
College Scorecard (Early Career): $53,600
PayScale (Early Career): $56,200
PayScale (Mid-Career): $115,100

RANKINGS
Money: 355
U.S. News: 54 (T), Liberal Arts Colleges
Wall Street Journal/THE: 121 (T)
Washington Monthly: 148, Liberal Arts Colleges

COLLEGE OVERLAPS
Furman University
Tulane University
The University of the South
Vanderbilt University
Wake Forest University

Rice University

Houston, Texas | 713-348-7423

ADMISSION
Admission Rate: 9%
Admission Rate - Men: 9%
Admission Rate - Women: 9%
EA Admission Rate: Not Offered
ED Admission Rate: 16%
ED Admits as % of Total Admits: 17%
Admission Rate (5-Year Trend): -8%
% of Admits Attending (Yield): 41%
Transfer Admission Rate: 7%

SAT Reading/Writing (Middle 50%): 720-770
SAT Math (Middle 50%): 750-800
ACT Composite (Middle 50%): 33-35

% Graduated in Top 10% of HS Class: 93%
% Graduated in Top 25% of HS Class: 99%
% Graduated in Top 50% of HS Class: 100%

Demonstrated Interest: Considered
Legacy Status: Considered
Admission Interview Offered: Yes

ENROLLMENT
Total Undergraduate Enrollment: 3,989
% Part-Time: 1%
% Male: 52%
% Female: 48%
% Out-of-State: 55%
% Fraternity: Not Offered
% Sorority: Not Offered
% On-Campus (Freshman): 99%
% On-Campus (All Undergraduate): 70%

% African-American: 7%
% Asian: 26%
% Hispanic: 16%
% White: 32%
% Other: 5%
% Race or Ethnicity Unknown: 1%
% International: 12%
% Low-Income: 15%

ACADEMICS
Student-to-Faculty Ratio: 6 to 1
% of Classes Under 20: 69%
% of Classes 20-49: 23%
% of Classes 50 or More: 8%
% Full-Time Faculty: 78%
% Full-Time Faculty w/ Terminal Degree: 97%

Top Programs
Architecture
Biochemistry
Biology
Cognitive Science
History
Engineering
Kinesiology
Music

Retention Rate: 97%
4-Year Graduation Rate: 84%
6-Year Graduation Rate: 93%

Curricular Flexibility: Somewhat Flexible
Academic Rating: ★★★★

#CollegesWorthYourMoney

With just shy of 4,000 undergraduates, Rice is at once a powerhouse research institution and a place where world-class instruction is the norm. The university's illustrious faculty includes multiple Nobel Prize and National Medal of Science winners as well as countless recipients of any prestigious fellowship or award that one can name. And the best news is that undergraduates have the chance to learn from that distinguished lot.

Inside the Classroom
Rice offers more than fifty majors across six broad disciplines: engineering, architecture, music, social science, humanities, and natural science. Double majoring is more common at Rice than your average university; roughly 20 percent of students graduate with a double major. Speaking of majors, there is a greater diversity of majors than one might assume at a STEM-famous school. The most commonly conferred degrees are in engineering (18 percent), the social sciences (13 percent), computer science (10 percent), parks and recreation (8 percent), biology (8 percent), and mathematics (7 percent).

Boasting a student-to-faculty ratio of 6:1, Rice offers a spectacularly intimate learning experience. Class sizes are ideally small with 69 percent containing fewer than twenty students and a median class size of only fourteen. Undergraduate research opportunities abound with 71 percent of graduates participating in academic research during their four years. Those experiences are open to freshmen through the Century Scholars Program and to all underclassmen through the Rice Undergraduate Scholars Program. Study abroad options are available in seventy countries, including collaborative programs with some of the top schools in the world including The London School of Economics, Oxford, and Cambridge; approximately 30 percent of Rice students elect to spend a semester in another country.

Programs in biology, biochemistry, cognitive science, and music are incredibly strong, while the School of Architecture and the George R. Brown School of Engineering are among the highest ranking schools in their disciplines. It is also notable that Rice is doing its part to close the STEM gender gap; the school is among the national leaders in producing female engineers, and it also boasts a 34 percent clip of female computer science majors, almost twice the national average. When it comes to procuring scholarships and fellowships upon graduation, Owls fare well, regularly producing Fulbright Scholars, Marshall Scholars, Watson Fellows, Hertz Fellows, and an occasional Rhodes Scholar (a dozen in its history).

Outside the Classroom
Central to student life at Rice is the Oxford/Cambridge-style (or more familiarly, Yale-style) residential college system. Upon matriculation, students are assigned to one of eleven residential colleges that contain their own dorms, dining halls, common areas, and faculty sponsors. Each college has its own student-run government, unique traditions, and social events. Those seeking a strong Greek life will have to look elsewhere as Rice has always operated free of fraternities and sororities. Rice does not have a particularly fervent sports culture either despite seven men's and seven women's varsity teams competing in NCAA Division I competition. The most notable squad is the baseball team that is always competing for national titles. Opportunities for intramural and club team participation are vast and include sports like aikido, badminton, and water polo. Student-run clubs are plentiful as well with over 250 to select from. The Rice Thresher, the student newspaper, is widely read and regularly wins national awards. While campus life is abuzz with activity, many venture into the city of Houston to enjoy the nightlife and cultural events in such close proximity.

Career Services
The Rice Center for Career Development (CCD) is staffed by eleven full-time professional employees, which equals a student-to-advisor ratio of 363:1, better-than-average when compared with the other institutions included in this book. Additional peer career advisors, embedded in each residential college, offer services such as resume reviews or assistance with locating internship opportunities. Internships opportunities can also be discovered at the Career and Internship Expo, which is attended by more than one hundred employers. The CCD also facilitates Owl Edge Externships, job-shadowing experiences that last from one day to a full week.

The university does a phenomenal job of facilitating on-campus interviews with 168 employers conducting interviews between 2017 and 2019. It also hosts one hundred+ events that connect students to potential employers from formal career fairs to casual events like the Chili Cook-Off. In total, 678 employers visited campus from 2017-19. The CCD does a superb job with outreach as it attracts more than 3,500 non-grad student visits per year, close to one visit per undergraduate. It's little surprise that 55 percent of graduates found their first job directly through the CCD office and 97 percent of students rate their experiences with CCD counselors positively. In short, it is hard to imagine a career services office accomplishing more for its undergraduates than the CCD does for its students at Rice.

Professional Outcomes

Six months after graduation, only 6 percent of Rice grads are still seeking employment. The overwhelming majority have found careers or a graduate school home. Companies that are known to pluck more than their fair share of employees each year from Rice's senior class include Deloitte, Capital One, JP Morgan Chase, Google, and Microsoft. Over one hundred alumni are also current employees of companies such as Shell, ExxonMobil, Chevron, Amazon, Accenture, and Facebook. Median starting salaries for Rice grads far exceed national averages. Across all majors the average starting salary is $69k. That encompasses engineering majors at the high end ($79k) and humanities majors at the low end ($52k). Texas is among the most common destinations for recent grads, but many also flock to California, New York, Wisconsin, and Washington State.

Over one-third of graduates move directly into graduate or professional school. That group fares well in gaining admission to elite graduate institutions; Harvard, Yale, Stanford, MIT, Columbia, and Berkeley are among the schools that absorb the highest number of Rice applicants. Rice is also known for producing a strong number of successful medical school applicants each year. A robust 38 percent of graduate school attendees are enrolled in medical school. Baylor College of Medicine and the med schools in the UT system are popular destinations for future doctors. Other recent grads are presently attending Harvard Medical School, Duke University School of Medicine, and Stanford Medical School.

Admission

Rice's acceptance rate for the Class of 2023 plummeted to an all-time low of 9 percent. This entrance into the single-digit club was a steep fall from the 11-17 percent acceptance rates of the last few years. The number of applications received by the university topped 27,000 for the first time, and that figure has more than doubled in the last decade. The ACT mid-50 percent range is 33-35; the SAT range is 1470-1560. Ten years ago, the 25th percentile SAT score was 130 points lower than today. This is a clear indicator that Rice's diminishing acceptance rate is, in fact, indicative of an increasingly selective student profile.

Early decision applicants, as would be expected, enjoy a better acceptance rate of 16 percent, but an applicant's bona fides still need to meet the university's sky-high standards. Rice lists more factors as being "very important" than most elite schools, granting this designation to rigor of courses, GPA, class rank, test scores, essays, recommendations, talent/ability, and character/personal qualities. An intimidating 93 percent of Rice students placed in the top 10 percent of their high school class, and 99 percent were in the top quartile. In 2018, Rice instituted an expedited system of reviewing applications; it now takes two admissions officers fewer than ten minutes to review each candidate and assign a numerical rating, a 5 being the highest. With that in mind, to have a realistic chance of getting in, the admissions staff shouldn't have to dig very deep to find reasons to say "Yes." A quality essay and glowing recommendations will help, but you'll need a sparkling academic profile and in-range test scores to make it through the first wave.

Worth Your Money?

For the 49 percent of students who qualify for need-based financial aid, Rice delivers by meeting 100 percent of every individual's demonstrated need. That equates to $47k per year, which certainly helps make the $66,000 annual cost (already a reasonable list price relative to the marketplace) of attendance more affordable. Further, 10 percent of students qualify for merit-based aid that averages $23,656. Graduates not only encounter incredibly high starting salaries, they also have less debt, on average, than the average college graduate in the United States. Needless to say, Rice is worth the cost of admissions no matter who you are or how much you have to pay.

FINANCIAL
Institutional Type: Private
In-State Tuition: $50,310
Out-of-State Tuition: $50,310
Room & Board: $14,500
Required Fees: $797
Books & Supplies: $1,250

Avg. Need-Based Grant: $46,975
Avg. % of Need Met: 100%

Avg. Merit-Based Award: $23,656
% Receiving (All Freshmen): 10%
% Receiving (Freshmen w/o Need): 5%

Avg. Cumulative Debt: $24,292
% of Students Borrowing: 25%

CAREER
Who Recruits
1. DMC, Inc.
2. INT Software
3. Quantlab
4. Oxy
5. Chevron

Notable Internships
1. The Blackstone Group
2. Jane Street
3. Houston Rockets

Top Industries
1. Business
2. Education
3. Engineering
4. Research
5. Operations

Top Employers
1. Google
2. Shell
3. ExxonMobil
4. Chevron
5. Microsoft

Where Alumni Work
1. Houston
2. San Francisco
3. Dallas
4. Austin
5. New York City

Median Earnings
College Scorecard (Early Career): $65,400
PayScale (Early Career): $74,200
PayScale (Mid-Career): $139,500

RANKINGS
Money: 18
U.S. News: 16 (T), National Universities
Wall Street Journal/THE: 15 (T)
Washington Monthly: 95, National Universities

COLLEGE OVERLAPS
Cornell University
Duke University
Northwestern University
Stanford University
The University of Texas at Austin

Rochester Institute of Technology

Rochester, New York | 585-475-6631

ADMISSION
Admission Rate: 71%
Admission Rate - Men: 68%
Admission Rate - Women: 75%
EA Admission Rate: Not Offered
ED Admission Rate: 84%
ED Admits as % of Total Admits: 8%
Admission Rate (5-Year Trend): +14%
% of Admits Attending (Yield): 19%
Transfer Admission Rate: 56%

SAT Reading/Writing (Middle 50%): 600-690
SAT Math (Middle 50%): 620-720
ACT Composite (Middle 50%): 27-32

% Graduated in Top 10% of HS Class: 39%
% Graduated in Top 25% of HS Class: 73%
% Graduated in Top 50% of HS Class: 94%

Demonstrated Interest: Considered
Legacy Status: Considered
Admission Interview Offered: Yes

ENROLLMENT
Total Undergraduate Enrollment: 13,313
% Part-Time: 3%
% Male: 67%
% Female: 33%
% Out-of-State: 48%
% Fraternity: 4%
% Sorority: 2%
% On-Campus (Freshman): 96%
% On-Campus (All Undergraduate): 49%

% African-American: 4%
% Asian: 10%
% Hispanic: 8%
% White: 65%
% Other: 4%
% Race or Ethnicity Unknown: 2%
% International: 6%
% Low-Income: 30%

ACADEMICS
Student-to-Faculty Ratio: 13 to 1
% of Classes Under 20: 48%
% of Classes 20-49: 47%
% of Classes 50 or More: 5%
% Full-Time Faculty: 73%
% Full-Time Faculty w/ Terminal Degree: 74%

Top Programs
Computer Science
Engineering
Film and Animation
Game Design and Development
Imaging Science
Management Information Systems
Photographic Arts

Retention Rate: 89%
4-Year Graduation Rate: 25%
6-Year Graduation Rate: 69%

Curricular Flexibility: Less Flexible
Academic Rating: ★★★

#CollegesWorthYourMoney

Since 1829, the Rochester Institute of Technology has been more than simply a technical school that churns out large quantities of engineers each year. With additional strengths in art and animation and design, this institution genuinely desires to "shape the future and improve the world through creativity and innovation." Even by STEM-focused school standards, the training at RIT is highly focused on career readiness and launches students into hands-on learning opportunities from the start of their freshman year. Large compared to other schools of its ilk like RPI and WPI, Rochester Institute of Technology educates 13,313 undergraduates. Half are from New York State, but students from all over the United States as well as one hundred countries brave the frigid Upstate New York weather in order to attend this accessible school that offers many standout programs and some of the best connections to industry of any school in the country.

Inside the Classroom
The co-op program is the fourth oldest in the country, and just about all students complete a one- or two-semester paid learning experience after finishing their first two years of academic study. There are nine undergraduate colleges at RIT, and while all have distinct course requirements the school's signature general education curriculum touches every single student. Students earning a bachelor's of science degree in engineering, for example, need to take sixty credit hours of general education courses—including first-year writing—and a number of perspectives courses that cover categories such as social, ethical, global, artistic, mathematics, scientific principles, and natural science inquiry. One immersion sequence that involves a three-course, deep dive into a particular topic also must be built into every undergrad's program.

RIT's 13:1 student-to-faculty ratio and a genuine commitment to undergraduate teaching leads to a respectable 48 percent of sections enrolling fewer than twenty students, and only 5 percent of courses contain more than fifty students. Additionally, RIT provides an array of undergraduate research opportunities including the Biological Sciences Research Scholars Program, the Chemistry Research Scholars Program, Economics Undergraduate Research, and the Undergraduate Research Symposium that saw 212 students give presentations in the 2018-19 academic year. Ample opportunities exist to study abroad, but few undergraduates elect to take advantage.

The most popular majors at this school are engineering, information sciences, visual and performing arts, and business. The Gleason College of Engineering and the Golisano College of Computing and Information Sciences are top-of-the-line. The latter houses RIT's game design program, which is the best on the entire East Coast. Strong film, art, and design programs also churn out successful graduates. Few pursue postgraduate fellowships, but the school does produce roughly one Fulbright Scholar and two Goldwater Scholars each cycle.

Outside the Classroom
RIT guarantees housing to freshmen and can accommodate about half the total undergraduate population in a mix of residence halls, apartments, the RIT Inn and Conference Center, Greek housing, and the global village. Like too many institutes of technology, the male-to-female ratio is heavily skewed at 2-to-1, which certainly has an impact on aspects of campus life. There are thirty fraternities and sororities on campus, but in the scope of such a large school, Greek life only draws single-digit participation. While RIT doesn't award athletic scholarships, it does field twenty-four NCAA varsity sports teams including Division I men's and women's ice hockey as well as many highly-competitive Division III teams. RIT is so competitive, in fact, rumors have swirled about a step-up to Division I. There are 300 clubs and organizations, including an extensive intramural sports program that signs up roughly half of the student body and plenty of opportunities for competitive or friendly gaming; video games are a way of life here. One of the greenest campuses around with a focus on sustainability, the 1,159 acres owned by the school offer federally designated wetlands, ample native plantings and wildlife, and a 200-acre area where most buildings are concentrated. There's enough to do on campus and in the classroom to mitigate the impact of an otherwise unexciting locale.

Career Services
The Office of Career Services and Cooperative Education (OCSCE) is staffed by twenty-seven professional staff members (not counting office assistants) who play roles such as career advisor, employer engagement and partnerships coordinator, and alumni relations coordinator. Rochester Institute of Technology's 493:1 student-to-advisor ratio is slightly higher than the average school featured in this guide, but it unquestionably has sufficient personnel to get the job done. Large-scale, university-wide career fairs are put on twice per year, drawing 726 companies and 3,500 students. Numerous boutique fairs cater to groups such as future accountants, civil engineers, and teachers. On a more personal level, the office also arranges "tailored orientations, workshops, and one-on-one advisement. It also plans and promotes events such as career fairs, workshops, and speakers from industry," and that's only the tip of the iceberg.

Rochester Institute of Technology

E-mail: admissions@rit.edu | Website: www.rit.edu

The co-op program, more than a century old, sees 2,300+ participants per year in co-op with employers from all fifty states and forty countries. The list of co-op and internship partners is incredible—Boeing, the CIA, EY, Fisher Price, Walt Disney World, SpaceX, NASA, Google, and literally dozens of other equally impressive organizations. RIT has 2,339 employer partners. The off-the-charts employer relations accomplishments do not stop there; the career services staff posts 10,000 jobs per year and facilitates 5,400 on-campus interviews, far more than the number of seniors at RIT, meaning many are interviewing with multiple companies. More than 850 companies recruit on campus every single year. In sum, the Rochester Institute of Technology offers an exceptional level of support to its undergraduates through its robust co-op program as well as all of the one-on-one attention you could desire.

Professional Outcomes

Within six months of graduation, 95.4 percent of the 2,495 members of the Class of 2017 (most recent data available) had found employment or a full-time graduate program. Major companies presently employing more 500 RIT alums include Xerox and Paychex, both with offices in Rochester. Between 200 and 450 employees of IBM, Microsoft, Apple, Intel, Amazon, Google, and Cisco were educated at RIT. Many graduates remain in the Upstate New York area while large numbers of other RIT alumni flock to New York City, Boston, DC, and San Francisco. Median income levels by midcareer are in the same neighborhood as fellow New York institutions including the University of Rochester, Fordham, and Syracuse. Starting salary figures vary greatly by major with College of Business grads landing median starting salaries between $43,000 (marketing majors) and $53,000 (finance majors), and just about all engineering grads being compensated at more than $60k. Computer science majors had a median compensation package of $83k right out of school.

In a typical year, 8-12 percent of graduates elect to pursue an advanced degree. While only a small number of RIT grads head directly to grad school, those who do typically head to some of the world's best such as Carnegie Mellon, Duke, Harvard, Johns Hopkins, MIT, Rhode Island School of Design, Penn, UVA, and the University of Michigan. The number of seniors applying to medical school has risen in recent years and is now between forty and forty-five applicants annually. Historically, the school has an 80-85 percent acceptance rate, but that number includes non-MD graduate programs in the health professions. Recent graduates have landed at top medical schools including Columbia University Vagelos College of Physicians and Surgeons, Emory University School of Medicine, Geisel School of Medicine at Dartmouth, and Georgetown University School of Medicine.

Admission

Applicants to the Rochester Institute of Technology benefit from a fairly generous acceptance rate that is typically in the mid-to-high 50-percent range; in 2019, that spiked to an even friendlier 71 percent. Students apply to individual colleges within the larger university, and standards vary somewhat from program to program. Overall, the average entering GPA was 3.7 and the average SAT score was 1309. Two-fifths placed in the top decile of their high school class, nearly three-quarters were in the top quartile, and all but 6 percent ranked in the top half.

This admissions committee looks, first and foremost, for applicants who engaged in a rigorous high school course load and achieved a solid mix of A's and B's. The four factors that make-up the second tier of admissions considerations are standardized test scores, class rank, recommendations, and the essay. It is important to note that the school is now test-optional, but only for applicants to the College of Liberal Arts. RIT's yield rate is only 19 percent, meaning that the school is eager to know if student's have genuine interest. Roughly 1,300 apply via early decision, and, in 2019, RIT rewarded their pledge of loyalty with an 84 percent ED acceptance rate.

Worth Your Money?

Yes. That's the short answer for anyone coming to RIT to study engineering or computer science. The school keeps the sticker price reasonable at a bit over $50k for tuition and under $68k total cost of attendance. Ninety-two percent of enrolled students receive some type of financial assistance each year; the average need-based grant is $30k. Those coming for liberal arts, business, or an art and design degree would have to weigh RIT's offer against their other options to find the most sensible deal.

FINANCIAL
Institutional Type: Private
In-State Tuition: $51,240
Out-of-State Tuition: $51,240
Room & Board: $13,976
Required Fees: $0
Books & Supplies: $1,082

Avg. Need-Based Grant: $29,745
Avg. % of Need Met: 87%

Avg. Merit-Based Award: $11,700
% Receiving (All Freshmen): 35%
% Receiving (Freshmen w/o Need): 12%

Avg. Cumulative Debt: $39,835
% of Students Borrowing: 75%

CAREER
Who Recruits
1. General Electric
2. Google
3. Microsoft
4. Intel
5. IBM

Notable Internships
1. GE Aviation
2. Electronic Arts
3. L.L. Bean

Top Industries
1. Engineering
2. Business
3. Operations
4. Information Technology
5. Arts & Design

Top Employers
1. Xerox
2. Paychex
3. IBM
4. Microsoft
5. Apple

Where Alumni Work
1. Rochester, NY
2. New York City
3. Boston
4. Washington DC
5. San Francisco

Median Earnings
College Scorecard (Early Career): $62,400
PayScale (Early Career): $64,800
PayScale (Mid-Career): $109,100

RANKINGS
Money: 402
U.S. News: 112 (T), National Universities
Wall Street Journal/THE: 161
Washington Monthly: 218, National Universities

COLLEGE OVERLAPS
Clarkson University
Drexel University
Rensselaer Polytechnic Institute
University at Buffalo (SUNY)
Worcester Polytechnic Institute

ADMISSION
Admission Rate: 74%
Admission Rate - Men: 73%
Admission Rate - Women: 79%
EA Admission Rate: 80%
ED Admission Rate: Not Offered
ED Admits as % of Total Admits: Not Offered
Admission Rate (5-Year Trend): +18%
% of Admits Attending (Yield): 15%
Transfer Admission Rate: 61%

SAT Reading/Writing (Middle 50%): 600-700
SAT Math (Middle 50%): 650-760
ACT Composite (Middle 50%): 27-33

% Graduated in Top 10% of HS Class: 61%
% Graduated in Top 25% of HS Class: 86%
% Graduated in Top 50% of HS Class: 100%

Demonstrated Interest: Considered
Legacy Status: Considered
Admission Interview Offered: No

ENROLLMENT
Total Undergraduate Enrollment: 2,000
% Part-Time: 1%
% Male: 76%
% Female: 24%
% Out-of-State: 65%
% Fraternity: 34%
% Sorority: 21%
% On-Campus (Freshman): 98%
% On-Campus (All Undergraduate): 57%

% African-American: 4%
% Asian: 6%
% Hispanic: 5%
% White: 64%
% Other: 5%
% Race or Ethnicity Unknown: 2%
% International: 14%
% Low-Income: 15%

ACADEMICS
Student-to-Faculty Ratio: 11 to 1
% of Classes Under 20: 53%
% of Classes 20-49: 47%
% of Classes 50 or More: 0%
% Full-Time Faculty: 95%
% Full-Time Faculty w/ Terminal Degree: 98%

Top Programs
Biomedical Engineering
Chemical Engineering
Civil Engineering
Computer Science
Electrical Engineering
Mechanical Engineering

Retention Rate: 90%
4-Year Graduation Rate: 77%
6-Year Graduation Rate: 85%

Curricular Flexibility: Less Flexible
Academic Rating: ★★★★

#CollegesWorthYourMoney

When searching for the top engineering schools you naturally encounter a number of prestigious, doctoral-granting research universities like Stanford, MIT, UC Berkeley, and Carnegie Mellon. When looking for small engineering schools, Caltech and Harvey Mudd are typically the easiest ones to locate. Likely off your radar is a small private college in Terra Haute, Indiana, that, year after year, tops the charts among engineering schools whose highest degree is a master's. The Rose-Hulman Institute of Technology offers only nineteen undergraduate degree programs to 2,000 students, mostly from the Midwest, but they go on to phenomenal postgraduate successes.

Inside the Classroom
Operating on the quarter system, courses are swift and rigorous, and pretty much everything you learn will be related to your major. Engineering students (the bulk of the student body) dive right in as first-semester freshmen by taking a heavy dose of math, science, and introductory engineering courses. The whole first year of study has room for only two electives in the realm of rhetoric/composition, the humanities, or social sciences. Foreign language is not among the requirements at this institution.

A student-to-faculty ratio of 11:1 and a minimal presence of graduate students bodes well for both class sizes and having introductory classes that are taught by full-time faculty members. The average class size is twenty, and 53 percent of sections are smaller than that. Giant lecture halls simply don't exist at Rose-Hulman as only two sections out of 410 contained greater than forty students. Undergraduate research is commonplace at this school and can be arranged through the Independent Project/Research Opportunities Program that connects you to faculty mentors and sets you on the path toward presenting your work at the End-of-Quarter Symposium. Ten-week summer research apprenticeships also are available. International opportunities can be procured through the Global E3, a consortium of sixty engineering schools of which Rose-Hulman is a member, or through participation in Engineers without Borders. This is a rare institute of technology that pushes its students to pursue an international experience; it even hosts an annual Study Abroad Fair as part of those efforts.

The engineering major accounts for 73 percent of all degrees conferred, and there's a good reason for its popularity; this program is viewed among the best by prospective employers and graduate schools, and not just in the Midwest. Rose-Hulman's reputation for excellence in engineering stretches from Silicon Valley to the East Coast. Unique undergraduate engineering programs include optical engineering and international computer science; CS, in general, is the second-most popular degree program (14 percent).

Outside the Classroom
Even more than your average STEM-focused school, the gender disparity is significant to the tune of a 76/24 split favoring males. (The school didn't become coed until 1995.) Greek life at Rose-Hulman is booming with 34 percent of men joining fraternities and 21 percent of women involved with the school's sororities. All but a handful of freshmen live on campus (it is a requirement). And 57 percent of the total undergraduate student body lives in one of ten dormitories or apartment complexes. Despite its small size, the school still fields twenty NCAA Division III sports teams, the Fightin' Engineers, who compete in the Heartland Collegiate Athletic Conference. That translates to a full quarter of the student body participating in varsity athletics. There are also ninety clubs, including a popular student newspaper, radio station, and film club plus plenty of intramural sports such as archery, ballroom dancing, scuba, and yoga. The general social hub on campus is the Mussallem Unio, with well-reviewed cuisine, a giant Connect Four board, and a lakefront view—what more can you ask for? Rose-Hulman is set on a 1,300-acre property, but the majority of campus is confined to a 200-acre tract. Terra Haute isn't exactly Midtown Manhattan, but it's not that far from a number of major Midwestern destinations with trips to Indianapolis, Chicago, Louisville, Cincinnati, or St. Louis doable on a weekend.

Career Services
The Career Services and Employer Relations Office at Rose-Hulman consists of seven professional employees, which computes to a student-to-advisor ratio of 286:1, better-than-average when compared to other schools featured in this guide. It is also notable that this career services office puts "employer relations" right in its own title, and the statistics in that area prove that this inclusion is more than warranted.

In a given year, a stunning 800-900 companies participate in events hosted by career services or had contact with students that was facilitated by career services staff in the last academic year. As a school of 2,000 undergraduates, that figure is absurdly strong. In total, almost 1,400 interviews are conducted by companies on campus annually, also a ridiculously strong number when you consider there were fewer than 500 seniors.

Rose-Hulman Institute of Technology

E-mail: admissions@rose-hulman.edu | Website: www.rose-hulman.edu

Last year, 94 percent of seniors had at least one opportunity for experiential learning via undergraduate research, co-op placement (50+ companies participate in the school's co-op program), or an internship. Three career fairs held annually in the fall, winter, and spring are extremely well attended by students as well as major hiring organizations. One recent fair drew a school record 251 companies, some of which conducted on-the-spot interviews with students. In short, thanks to the vast network of employers connected to this career services office, Rose-Hulman job-seekers are not the hunters but the hunted.

Professional Outcomes

Of the 493 graduates who strutted the stage in 2019, an enviable 98+ percent had landed at their next destination, whether employment or graduate school, within six months of exiting. Further, students in many of the school's programs enjoyed a 100 percent success rate. Top employers of Class of 2019 graduates included Boston Scientific, Cook Group, Texas Instruments, Caterpillar, Honeywell, Raytheon, and Rolls Royce. Microsoft, and Indianapolis-based pharmaceutical giant Eli Lilly also have a strong representation of Rose-Hulman-affiliated employees. The average first-year salary for the lowest-paying majors was still $62,000, and some members of the Class of 2019 took home a not-too-shabby $130,000 in first-year wages. The majority of alumni remain in Indiana with Indianapolis and Terra Haute being the two favorite destinations. Smaller pockets of graduates can be found in Chicago, Cincinnati, San Francisco, and Seattle.

Approximately 15 percent of grads immediately enroll in graduate school. They head to many of the world's most distinguished universities such as Johns Hopkins, Carnegie Mellon, Duke, Northwestern, Washington University in St. Louis, Georgia Tech, Cornell, Notre Dame, and Rice University. Only a couple of students each year head to medical school. No one from the previous two classes decided to attend law school. Clearly, and not surprisingly, the records demonstrate that students come to Rose-Hulman to enter technology/engineering fields.

Admission

Rose-Hulman's acceptance rate for membership in the Class of 2023 was an unimposing 74 percent. Compare that to other premier institutes of technology with phenomenal job placement rates and starting salaries and you might breathe a sigh of relief. Of course, the applicant pool is a self-selecting group with an affinity for STEM learning, and that leads to an impressive freshman class academic profile. The Class of 2023 had a mid-50 percent SAT range of 1260-1440 and ACT range of 27-33. Sixty-one percent of 2019-20 freshmen earned a place in the top 10 percent of their high school class while 86 percent were in the top quartile. Nearly four-fifths of students had a GPA over 3.75, and only 8 percent had under a 3.5. Suddenly, that sigh of relief feels like a distant memory. Interestingly, the school does accept a lower percentage of applicants in some cycles. Only a few years ago, the acceptance rate was under 60 percent as rates can fluctuate quite a bit at a school with a small applicant pool of under 4,500 students.

Rigor of secondary coursework and grades are the two most important factors for admission followed by standardized test scores, class rank, recommendations, and extracurricular activities. The acceptance rate for female applicants is 79 percent compared to the rate for males of 73 percent. This schools offers multiple early action application deadlines but no binding early decision option. In the admissions office's own words, successful applicants are "typically at the top of their high school graduating classes with scores in the 95th percentile on the SAT or ACT – plus they have taken a lot of high school science, math and English."

Worth Your Money?

This is a rare case where an annual cost of attendance of almost $72,000 does little to derail the financial futures of the student population. Freshmen receiving need-based aid net an average annual award of close to $34,000; average merit aid packages for those eligible neared $17,000. Even without financial aid, Rose-Hulman is definitely worth the private school cost thanks to phenomenal placement rates at top companies and extremely high starting salaries, even by STEM standards.

FINANCIAL
Institutional Type: Private
In-State Tuition: $48,507
Out-of-State Tuition: $48,507
Room & Board: $15,414
Required Fees: $1,020
Books & Supplies: $1,500

Avg. Need-Based Grant: $33,970
Avg. % of Need Met: 68%

Avg. Merit-Based Award: $16,359
% Receiving (All Freshmen): 63%
% Receiving (Freshmen w/o Need): 32%

Avg. Cumulative Debt: $47,953
% of Students Borrowing: 58%

CAREER
Who Recruits
1. Archer Daniels Midland
2. Whirlpool
3. Allegant Air
4. Kinze Manufacturing
5. Ingredion Incorporated

Notable Internships
1. Rolls-Royce
2. Halliburton
3. Tesla

Top Industries
1. Engineering
2. Operations
3. Business
4. Information Technology
5. Education

Top Employers
1. Eli Lily and Company
2. Cummins Inc.
3. Rolls-Royce
4. Caterpillar Inc.
5. Google

Where Alumni Work
1. Indianapolis
2. Terra Haute, IN
3. Chicago
4. Cincinnati
5. San Francisco

Median Earnings
College Scorecard (Early Career): $80,900
PayScale (Early Career): $78,200
PayScale (Mid-Career): $142,200

RANKINGS
Money: 449
U.S. News: Not Ranked
Wall Street Journal/THE: Not Ranked
Washington Monthly: Not Ranked

COLLEGE OVERLAPS
Case Western Reserve University
Ohio State University - Columbus
Purdue University - West Lafayette
Rensselaer Polytechnic Institute
Rochester Institute of Technology

Piscataway, New Jersey | 732-445-4636

Rutgers-New Brunswick, the flagship campus of the school's three locations (Camden and Newark being the others), is one of the oldest universities in the country. Founded in 1766 as one of nine colleges in Colonial America, the New Brunswick campus today is a top state research university that is home to 36,158 undergraduates. Garden State residents comprise 81 percent of the student body, but there has been a push in recent years to attract more out-of-staters, partially for monetary reasons. Presently, there are representatives of all fifty states and 87 countries on campus as the number of nonresidents increases each year. No matter where you're from, you'll enjoy the benefits of Rutgers' massive operation that is divided into seventeen schools and colleges, collectively offering one hundred+ undergraduate majors.

Inside the Classroom

Core requirements are variable across different programs, but members of the School of Arts & Sciences, by far the university's largest college, have a ten- to fourteen-course core. Mandates include fulfilling coursework in areas such as diversities and inequalities, our common future, natural sciences, social and historical analysis, arts and humanities, writing and communication, and quantitative and formal reasoning. In the School of Engineering, first-year coursework will look quite different as students must conquer courses that include General Chemistry for Engineers, Calculus, Analytical Physics, and Introduction to Computers for Engineers; non-STEM course-work is minimal for engineering students. A host of first-year initiatives, including Byrne Seminars and First Year Interest Group Seminars, leads to a freshman retention rate of 93 percent, a tremendous achievement for a public university.

Reasonable for a school its size and scope, Rutgers possesses a 16:1 student-to-faculty ratio. As a result, it can offer a sizable number of smaller, seminar-style courses to undergraduates. Forty-two percent of class sections have an enrollment of nineteen or fewer students compared to only 20 percent of sections that contain more than fifty undergrads. Rutgers offers 180 study abroad programs in fifty countries, but few take advantage; the participation rate is a paltry 2 percent. Undergraduate research, on the other hand, attracts more takers. T he Aresty Research Center serves as a clearinghouse that matches undergraduates with faculty members conducting research in an area of interest; there are presently 1,500 faculty partners. An annual Undergraduate Research Symposium has showcased thousands of student projects in its fifteen+ years of existence.

The areas of study in which the greatest number of degrees are conferred are business (18 percent), computer science (10 percent), engineering (10 percent), health professions (10 percent), biology (8 percent), and social sciences (8 percent). Rutgers Business School sends many majors to top Wall Street investment banks, and programs in computer science, public health, and criminal justice have a terrific national reputation. Competitive scholarship and fellowship organizations also show lots of love to Scarlet Knights. Students and alumni received twenty-six Fulbright Scholarships in 2020 and has also had Goldwater, Schwarzman, Gates-Cambridge, and Truman Scholars in recent years.

Outside the Classroom

Rutgers-New Brunswick's sprawling 2,685-acre campus is divided into five distinct, interconnected campuses. Despite one of the largest undergraduate housing operations of any school in the United States, only 43 percent of students live on campus in one of 136 residence hall buildings or university-owned apartment complexes. The Greek scene is on the rise at Rutgers as the school now has over 3,800 members of eighty+ fraternities and sororities, all of which are located off campus. The Scarlet Knights compete in NCAA Division I athletics in ten men's and fourteen women's sports. Highpoint.com Stadium is the only Division I football stadium in the NY/NJ region, but it rarely fills its 52,000-seat capacity. Rutgers students would rather play sports than watch them as a member of one of fifty-seven club teams or fifty intramural leagues. The school's five fitness and recreation centers attract more than 5,000 visitors per day; ten outdoor fields and parks also are available for student use. There are also 500+ student-run organizations, including a top-ranked Model UN team and the Rutgers University Dance Marathon that raised over one million dollars for pediatric illnesses in 2019 alone. Rutgers' excellent location makes weekend trips to Philly, New York, or the Jersey Shore a painless one-hour car ride.

Career Services

Thirty-seven professional employees staff the Rutgers University Career Services (UCS) Office in areas such as career exploration, career development, and employer relations. The university's overall student-to-counselor ratio of 927:1 is higher than the average school featured in this guidebook, but not alarmingly so when compared to other large public universities. Despite the monumental task of connecting with more than 36,000 students, the UCS has made some inroads as it currently interacts, in some form, with 56 percent of the student population each year. In 2018-19, the UCS conducted 4,817 one-on-one advising appointments.

There are plenty of large-scale offerings designed to benefit the student population. Career fair attendance is solid with 3,400 students connecting with 300 companies in the fall and 4,700 engaging with 265 employers in the spring. Another 641 unique employers visited career fairs in 2018-19. There were more than 3,400 on-campus interviews conducted with Rutgers seniors that same year. The CareerKnight online database of job and internship opportunities receives hundreds of thousands of annual hits. The Road to Wall Street mentoring program led to over 90 percent of participants landing competitive summer internships; the overall internship completion rate for graduates is an estimated 28 percent. Job search boot camps draw solid reviews as 100 percent of attendees said they have a better awareness of the next steps in the process as a result of attending. With 530,000 alumni, there is always a Scarlet Knight networking opportunity in your field of interest. Roughly two-fifths of graduates say that the Rutgers UCS contributed to their career success.

Professional Outcomes

Upon graduation, 83 percent of Rutgers students have their next stop, whether it's a first job or graduate school, squared away. Sixty-three percent of the Class of 2019 were headed directly to the world of employment where the companies hiring the largest number of grads included Amazon, Johnson & Johnson, L'Oréal, and JP Morgan Chase. Investment banks like Goldman Sachs and Citi also employ hundreds of alumni. More than 300 current employees of Verizon, Bristol-Meyers Squibb, Novartis, Amazon, Pfizer, and Google also have Scarlet Knight lineage. The median starting salary across all majors was $58,500. The median starting salary for engineering majors was $68,000 while arts and sciences grads brought home $50k. The bulk of graduates, approximately 85 percent, end up settling in New Jersey/the Greater New York area. Philadelphia, DC, and San Francisco are next in popularity.

Only 13 percent of the 2019 graduating class matriculated into full-time graduate or professional school. The most frequently attended universities were Rutgers, NYU, Columbia, Penn, and Boston University. Of the 487 graduates of the Class of 2019 who applied to medical school, 51 percent gained acceptance, a bit above the national average. Those sporting a 3.7 GPA or higher were even more successful, gaining acceptance at a 71 percent clip. Eight-seven of those accepted matriculated into one of Rutgers' two medical colleges. Recent prestigious acceptances included Duke, Georgetown, Cornell, UVA, and Stanford. Future lawyers also end up in droves at Rutgers own highly reputable law school as well as at Villanova, Fordham, and Notre Dame.

Admission

Unlike at so many other premier flagship universities around the nation, the acceptance rate at Rutgers-New Brunswick has not plummeted in recent years. Those seeking entry into the Class of 2023 were given the thumbs up 61 percent of the time. Still, the quality of the applicant pool has risen dramatically over the 2000s. Freshmen in the 2019-20 school year had an average SAT score of 1318 and an average ACT of 29. Right around two-fifths of current students placed in the top 10 percent of their high school class, and almost three-quarters landed in the top 25 percent. Five years ago, the acceptance rate at the university was a comparable 61 percent, but the SAT range was a far lower 1040-1290.

The factors deemed most important by the admissions committee are GPA, standardized test scores, and rigor of secondary curriculum. Extracurricular involvement is the lone category dubbed "important". Rutgers does offer an early action deadline of November 1, but no binding early decision plan is available. An average in the B+/A-range and standardized test scores in the 85th percentile put you firmly in play for an invitation to attend the New Brunswick campus right out of high school. Otherwise, a start at the Camden or Newark campus may be the only option. Out-of-state applicants may find slightly more relaxed admission standards, given the university's push to recruit applicants from outside New Jersey.

Worth Your Money?

Rutgers doesn't have the endowment to meet anything close to your full level of financial need, but it does award grants averaging $13,651 to 53 percent of current undergraduates. The in-state cost of attendance is $36,129, which is not a bad deal for a flagship public school in the Northeastern United States. Out-of-state students would pay close to $54k per year COA, which would be a curious move for students not receiving aid, given the likelihood that better deals would be available.

FINANCIAL
Institutional Type: Public
In-State Tuition: $12,230
Out-of-State Tuition: $29,012
Room & Board: $13,075
Required Fees: $3,177
Books & Supplies: $1,350

Avg. Need-Based Grant: $13,651
Avg. % of Need Met: 47%

Avg. Merit-Based Award: $11,936
% Receiving (All Freshmen): 21%
% Receiving (Freshmen w/o Need): 8%

Avg. Cumulative Debt: $30,829
% of Students Borrowing: 56%

CAREER
Who Recruits
1. Aerotek
2. Automatic Data
3. Enterprise Holdings
4. Insight Global
5. Robert Half

Notable Internships
1. Colgate-Palmolive
2. NBCUniversal
3. New York Giants

Top Industries
1. Business
2. Education
3. Operations
4. Healthcare
5. Sales

Top Employers
1. Johnson & Johnson
2. Verizon
3. Bristol-Myers Squibb
4. JPMorgan Chase
5. Novartis

Where Alumni Work
1. New York City
2. Philadelphia
3. Washington DC
4. San Francisco
5. Boston

Median Earnings
College Scorecard (Early Career): $57,900
PayScale (Early Career): $62,200
PayScale (Mid-Career): $121,200

RANKINGS
Money: 78
U.S. News: 63 (T), National Universities
Wall Street Journal/THE: 147 (T)
Washington Monthly: 52, National Universities

COLLEGE OVERLAPS
Boston University
New York University
Pennsylvania State University - University Park
The College of New Jersey
University of Maryland

San Diego State University

San Diego, California | 619-594-6336

They say that a rising tide lifts all boats. As the University of California system has become ultra-competitive over the past decade, the California State University system has seen many of its schools become beneficiaries of an overflow of uber-qualified applicants. San Diego State University, offering a highly affordable education in a gorgeous and temperate setting, is one such institution. A diverse school of 30,612 undergraduates, one-third of its students are Hispanic, and roughly the same percentage are first-generation students. Most hail from the Golden State, but 7 percent of the population are international students representing one of 103 countries. Don't be scared off by the low acceptance rate (34 percent); you don't need straight A's in high school to gain access to this excellent research university that boasts nearly 160 undergraduate majors, minors, and pre-professional programs.

Inside the Classroom
The general education requirements at SDSU are the breadth portion of one's education experience and will comprise approximately one-third of an undergraduate's time at the university. Forty-nine units are required, including nine units of communications and critical thinking courses; thirty-one units of foundational study in the humanities; social and behavioral sciences; and natural sciences and quantitative reasoning; and nine units in "explorations" that are upper-division courses you cannot begin until junior year. After completing sixty credits, all students must take and pass a writing placement assessment. Some majors require you to learn a language other than English while some, like engineering, do not. Lastly, there is a mandated course called American Institutions in which you must demonstrate your knowledge of California government, the US Constitution, and American history.

Like many other schools in the California State University system, cheap tuition and heavy enrollment leads to a high student-to-faculty ratio. San Diego State sports a 25:1 ratio and, consequently, classes tend to be on the large side. Thirty-one percent of course sections enroll more than forty students, and only 28 percent of sections contain fewer than twenty students. To help connect students to faculty mentors and undergraduate research opportunities, the school maintains a useful database of current professors seeking assistance. Summer research programs and an annual Undergraduate Research Symposium provide additional experiences in that realm. A solid 33 percent of recent grads reported studying abroad.

Business/marketing accounts for 22 percent of the degrees conferred, making it the school's most popular area of study. Next in line are the social sciences (9 percent), engineering (9 percent), and psychology (7 percent). You won't find the engineering or computer science programs at the top of any rankings lists, but that doesn't have much of an impact on employment, thanks to the booming local tech and startup scene. Because of its emphasis on international study, many graduates go on to win fellowships that take them all around the globe. SDSU has had as many as nine Fulbright award winners in recent years, and it often has multiple recipients of Boren, Critical Language, and Gilman Scholarships. SDSU also has had several undergraduates receive National Science Foundation Graduate Research Fellowships over the last few years.

Outside the Classroom
On-campus housing is limited, and preference is given to freshmen who take advantage at a 71 percent clip. Overall, only 23 percent of undergraduates reside in university-owned housing. However, there is plenty to bond the student body and create cohesion on campus. Fifteen percent of men and 17 percent of women belong to the university's fifty+ fraternities and sororities. In addition to Greek life, annual campus-wide events like AzFest and Homecoming Weekend unify the 30,000+ undergrads, as do basketball and football games. The Aztecs field nineteen NCAA Division I sports teams, and famous alumni athletes include Marshall Faulk (NFL), Tony Gwynn (MLB), and 2019 NBA Finals MVP Kawhi Leonard. There are 350+ student organizations including KCR College Radio that has a long history and large listenership, intramural sports that draw thousands of participants, and the Aztec Unity Project that is committed to local community service projects. Viejas Arena, where the Aztecs play basketball, doubles as a major concert venue and draws world-famous artists. San Diego weather, sunsets, and seventeen miles of coastline are all free benefits of attending SDSU. Additionally, there are multiple beaches less than ten miles from campus. The Aquaplex is, essentially, a free resort on campus for student use. It features two outdoor pools and a twenty-person spa; such is life at San Diego State.

Career Services
The main San Diego State Career Services Office employs seventeen full-time professional staff members (not counting administrative assistants) working as internship coordinators, career counselors, employer outreach specialists, and experiential learning specialists. There are an additional four staff members working out of

the Fowler College of Business, bringing the campus-wide total to twenty-one, which works out to a 1,304:1 student-to-counselor ratio, poorer than the average school profiled in this book.

SDSU offers four large-scale career fairs in the fall semester and another four fairs in the spring semester. One hundred ten employers attend the Fall Career and Internship Fair, and the Nonprofit and Education Career Fair in the spring draws thirty employers. In addition, the Graduate & Professional School Fair draws representative from ninety+ institutions. Roughly half of recent graduates reported completing at least one internship. Workshops are offered on a regular basis on useful topics such as Applying for Federal Jobs, Personal Branding Using Social Media, and Planning for Graduate School. Career counselors specialize in a variety of fields and encourage fifty-minute one-on-one career exploration sessions or fifteen-minute walk-in appointments. The Aztec Mentor Program connects juniors and seniors to alumni in their fields of interest for a minimum of eight hours of mentorship. In sum, programmatic offerings by SDSU's Career Services Office are impressive, but they do not publicize statistics on how many counseling sessions take place or how many on-campus interviews with employers occur each year.

Professional Outcomes

At the time of receiving their degrees, 72 percent of newly-minted SDSU graduates already had their next phase of life planned. Thirty-four percent of that group had secured full-time employment, 21 percent were engaged in military service/volunteer work/part-time employment, and 17 percent were entering graduate or professional school. The mean reported salary for those offered full-time employment was $53,000. Qualcomm and Wells Fargo are the two largest employers of Aztec alumni, and they are followed by Apple, Amazon, and Illumina. All of the most common geographic landing spots for alumni are within California borders; San Diego keeps a large chunk of grads while Los Angeles, San Francisco, and Orange County also have fairly strong representation.

In 2019, there were sixty-four SDSU graduates applying to medical school and, while the university lacks its own affiliated hospital/medical schools, many future physicians do remain in the state of California at universities like UC-San Diego, UC-Davis, UC-Riverside, UCLA, and Western University of Health Sciences; others move out of state to the University of Michigan, Tufts, and the University of South Carolina. Likewise, many law students remain in state at schools such as the University of San Diego School of Law, the Thomas Jefferson School of Law, Loyola Law School, Santa Clara School of Law, and UC-Davis. SDSU offers a pre-law society, mock trial team, and targeted pre-law advising to those considering a legal education.

Admission

Only 34 percent of the 69,842 applicants for a place in the Class of 2023 were accepted into the university; 22 percent of that group went on to enroll at SDSU. Despite the intimidating acceptance rate, there is plenty of room at this school for solid but less-than-perfect applicants as evidenced by the wide range of test scores and GPAs that are accepted. The mid-50 percent standardized test scores for 2019-20 freshmen were 1120-1310 on the SAT and 22-29 on the ACT. Thirty-three percent of that cohort placed within the top 10 percent of their high school class, 70 percent were in the top quartile, and 94 percent landed in top half. While 60 percent of Class of 2023 members possessed a high school GPA of 3.75 or above, 18 percent earned under a 3.5.

The admissions committee needs to work quickly to sift through the deluge of applications it receives each year. As a result, it reviews standardized test scores, GPA, rigor of courses, state residency, and literally nothing else. Soft factors like essays, recommendations, and extracurricular activities play no role in the admissions process at San Diego State. There is no early action or early decision option at SDSU, but the application deadline is quite early—December 15 last admission cycle. In spite of the low acceptance rate, students should be able to accurately gauge their odds given the relatively formulaic evaluation process. Those solidly in the middle of the wide ranges of standardized test scores can feel good about their chances.

Worth Your Money?

The process to qualify for out-of-state students to earn residency status has tightened in recent years, making it almost certain that international and non-California residents will pay roughly $42,000 per year total cost of attendance. In-state COA is estimated at $30k, with only $7,720 of that figure covering basic tuition. Thus, those living at home or commuting can attend the university at an absurdly low cost. Like the other twenty-two schools in the California State University System, SDSU is affordable and, with its excellent ties to industry, job prospects for most graduates are bright.

FINANCIAL
Institutional Type: Public
In-State Tuition: $5,742
Out-of-State Tuition: $17,622
Room & Board: $17,752
Required Fees: $1,768
Books & Supplies: $1,969

Avg. Need-Based Grant: $10,300
Avg. % of Need Met: 67%

Avg. Merit-Based Award: $3,200
% Receiving (All Freshmen): 28%
% Receiving (Freshmen w/o Need): 3%

Avg. Cumulative Debt: $21,172
% of Students Borrowing: 44%

CAREER
Who Recruits
1. Bainbridge
2. Cox Communications
3. GoSite
4. ASML
5. Marriott International

Notable Internships
1. BAE Systems
2. Cushman & Wakefield
3. U.S. Senate

Top Industries
1. Business
2. Operations
3. Education
4. Sales
5. Engineering

Top Employers
1. Qualcomm
2. Apple
3. EY
4. Amazon
5. Intuit

Where Alumni Work
1. San Diego
2. Los Angeles
3. San Francisco
4. Orange County, CA
5. Germany

Median Earnings
College Scorecard (Early Career): $51,000
PayScale (Early Career): $57,200
PayScale (Mid-Career): $107,700

RANKINGS
Money: 79
U.S. News: 143 (T), National Universities
Wall Street Journal/THE: 275
Washington Monthly: 121, National Universities

COLLEGE OVERLAPS
California Polytechnic State University, San Luis Obispo
California State University, Long Beach
University of California, Riverside
University of California, Irvine
University of California, San Diego

Santa Clara University

Santa Clara, California | 408-554-4700

ADMISSION
Admission Rate: 49%
Admission Rate - Men: 47%
Admission Rate - Women: 51%
EA Admission Rate: 61%
ED Admission Rate: 68%
ED Admits as % of Total Admits: 4%
Admission Rate (5-Year Trend): -1%
% of Admits Attending (Yield): 11%
Transfer Admission Rate: 52%

SAT Reading/Writing (Middle 50%): 630-700
SAT Math (Middle 50%): 650-740
ACT Composite (Middle 50%): 28-32

% Graduated in Top 10% of HS Class: 52%
% Graduated in Top 25% of HS Class: 88%
% Graduated in Top 50% of HS Class: 99%

Demonstrated Interest: Considered
Legacy Status: Important
Admission Interview Offered: No

ENROLLMENT
Total Undergraduate Enrollment: 5,694
% Part-Time: 2%
% Male: 50%
% Female: 50%
% Out-of-State: 4%
% Fraternity: 20%
% Sorority: 0%
% On-Campus (Freshman): 96%
% On-Campus (All Undergraduate): 58%

% African-American: 3%
% Asian: 17%
% Hispanic: 18%
% White: 47%
% Other: 8%
% Race or Ethnicity Unknown: 2%
% International: 5%
% Low-Income: 13%

ACADEMICS
Student-to-Faculty Ratio: 10 to 1
% of Classes Under 20: 55%
% of Classes 20-49: 45%
% of Classes 50 or More: 0%
% Full-Time Faculty: 62%
% Full-Time Faculty w/ Terminal Degree: 93%

Top Programs
Accounting
Bioengineering
Communication
Computer Science and Engineering
Finance
Public Health
Psychology

Retention Rate: 94%
4-Year Graduation Rate: 87%
6-Year Graduation Rate: 91%

Curricular Flexibility: Less Flexible
Academic Rating: ★★★★

#CollegesWorthYourMoney

If you were asked to name a premier university in the heart of California's Silicon Valley, chances are your immediate answer would be Stanford. Yet, those who aren't likely to be among the 5.2 percent of accepted applicants at Stanford might want to turn their attention to the Valley's second most prestigious school, one that has over ten times the acceptance rate. Santa Clara University is a Jesuit school with a growing national reputation; right now, 58 percent of undergraduates still hail from California, and major tech firms love to recruit at this excellent institution located in their own backyard.

Inside the Classroom

Students can pursue fifty degrees offered by three undergraduate colleges: the College of Arts & Sciences, the School of Engineering, and the Leavey School of Business. Santa Clara's core curriculum is designed to provide "a humanistic education that leads toward an informed, ethical engagement with the world." To accomplish that students must take (1) foundations courses in critical thinking and critical writing, cultures and ideas, a second language, mathematics, and religion, theology, and culture; (2) explorations courses in ethics, civic engagement, diversity, additional religion/theology courses, and all of the traditional prerequisites in the natural sciences, social sciences, and the arts; and (3) integrations courses in advanced writing, experiential learning for social justice, and a pathways class that requires students to make connections across disciplines. It's a tall order, involves a certain amount of religious study, and doesn't leave a ton of room for electives.

Santa Clara caters to 5,694 undergraduate students as well as another 2,975 graduate students but, thanks to a 10:1 student-to-faculty ratio, it keeps classes reasonably sized. While you won't find many single-digit enrollment seminars, 55 percent of course sections do contain fewer than twenty students. Undergraduate research opportunities are built into many academic programs, particularly in the sciences, and students can partner with willing professors for credited research study. In addition, study abroad opportunities are available on all six continents fit for human habitation, and more than 500 students take advantage each year.

The most commonly conferred degrees are in business (24 percent), the social sciences (16 percent), and engineering (14 percent). The Leavey School of Business offers highly ranked management information systems, accounting, and entrepreneurship degree programs. The engineering program is respected by employers, and computer science students fare extraordinarily well in the Silicon Valley job market, which happens to be one of the most competitive in the world. Graduates of SCU do not seek prestigious fellowships in droves, but many of those who do are successful. In 2019, six grads/alumni procured Fulbright Scholarships and the school regularly produces Udall Scholarship winners as well.

Outside the Classroom

The 106-acre campus houses only 58 percent of the undergraduate student body; however, 96 percent of first-years do reside in university-owned dorms. There are ten fraternities and six sororities at Santa Clara, and although none of them are affiliated with the university (they were dropped in 2001), Greek life still plays a significant social role. For a school of its size, athletics are surprisingly serious at SCU as the Broncos compete at the NCAA Division I level and field nineteen intercollegiate teams. Intramural sports draw an astonishing 3,800 participants every year on 500 teams in sports ranging from soccer to ping-pong. Almost every student is involved in at least one (if not two or three) of the 125 organizations presently operating. The Ruff Riders, a booster organization, is one of the largest groups of its kind with over 1,000 members. Into the Wild is another popular club that plans outdoor excursions to locations such as Big Sur, the beaches of Santa Cruz, and Lake Tahoe. World-class recreational facilities exist on campus for fitness enthusiasts such as the 45,000-square-foot Malley Fitness Center and the Sullivan Aquatic Center. The University's Silicon Valley location means that plenty of high-end cultural, dining, and entertainment options are at your fingertips, and San Francisco is only an hour away by car.

Career Services

Santa Clara's Career Center has nine full-time professional staff members working as career development specialists, employer relations specialists, and coordinators of experiential learning. The 633:1 student-to-advisor ratio is below average when compared with the other institutions featured in this guide. However, the center has many strengths, particularly its deep connections to major Silicon Valley companies. Each year, the Fall Career Fair draws many top employers (including tech companies) as well as over 1,000 undergraduates. Another STEM-specific fair in October brings in another 650 students in search of jobs. Across the school's six annual career fairs, 470 employers manned booths and spoke with SCU students.

Santa Clara University

E-mail: admission@scu.edu | Website: www.scu.edu

More than 6,000 employers recruit Santa Clara undergraduates through a mix of Career Center programs and the online job board available through the Handshake platform, and 65 percent of students utilize their account. Over 900 on-campus interviews take place each academic year. Recruiting companies include Disney, Tesla, Apple, Oracle, Cisco, Kaiser Permanente, and NBC Universal. Almost four-fifths of those completing an SCU degree completed at least one internship position during their time at the university. This school boasts an alumni network 100,000 strong, and many are willing to assist current students with finding their first job. Thanks to the strength of its employer recruiting efforts and internship program, SCU's Career Center gets high marks from our staff.

Professional Outcomes

Within six months of receiving their degrees, 89 percent of 2019 Santa Clara graduates had landed jobs, started graduate school, or committed to a full-time service program. Of those employed, the five most commonly entered industries are business development, engineering, education, entrepreneurship, and sales. The companies presently employing the greatest number of Bronco alumni are all tech giants including Cisco, Apple, Google, Oracle, Facebook, and Adobe. The median starting salary for all grads is $62,500 with engineering ($75k) majors enjoying the highest compensation, and arts & sciences grads on the low end ($51k). Roughly two-thirds of alumni remain in the Bay Area. Other West Coast destinations such as Los Angeles, Seattle, Portland, Sacramento, and San Diego also attract a fairly large number of grads.

Many graduates who continue their education at the master's or doctoral level do so at one of Santa Clara's own excellent grad programs; the same goes for law school. Over the last fifteen years, 90 percent of SCU medical school applicants with a minimum of MCAT score of 505 and a GPA of 3.5 or higher have been accepted by at least one institution. However, many fail to meet those criteria as only 40 percent of overall applicants in that period have been accepted, slightly lower than the national average. The three most frequently attended medical schools are fellow Jesuit institutions Creighton, Georgetown, and Loyola (Chicago). A look at where recent grads were pursuing additional education includes a wide range of schools that includes UCLA, Berkeley, USC, the University of Washington, and Duke University.

Admission

Growing in popularity, Santa Clara crossed the 16,000 application mark for the second straight year with the Class of 2023. A seemingly soft 49 percent of applicants were granted admission, but a glance at the profile of the average accepted applicant is more informative as to the school's level of selectivity. Of those who enrolled in the university, the middle-50 percent SAT range was a solid 1300-1420. Just a shade over 50 percent placed in the top decile of their high school class, and 88 percent finished in the top quartile. Notably, only 17 percent of admitted students went on to enroll in the freshman Class of 2019-20.

The admissions committee ranks three categories as most important: rigor of secondary school record, GPA, and essays. The list of factors ranked as "important" is far longer and includes class rank, recommendations, standardized test scores, volunteer work, racial/ethnic status, first generation status, legacy status, and extracurricular activities. Due to the aforementioned low yield rate of only 17 percent, Santa Clara is always happy to have strong applicants who are willing to commit to the school. As a result, a whopping 68 percent of early decision applicants gain admission. Santa Clara University is a school that is attracting more applicants every year as its national reputation climbs to new heights. A deceptively high acceptance rate does not do full justice to the caliber of undergraduate it currently attracts. Borderline candidates who have a strong desire to attend should definitely consider applying early decision.

Worth Your Money?

At almost $73,000 in total annual cost of attendance, Santa Clara is an expensive proposition any way you slice it. The university does dangle an average merit aid award of almost $13k to two-fifths of students to bring the price down a bit; qualifying students receive need-based grants that average close to $34,000. A Santa Clara degree won't come cheap, but that's okay for business and engineering students who will be heading to high-paying careers in Silicon Valley. Those intending to pursue majors in less immediately lucrative disciplines need to calculate whether the finances make sense for them to attend this school.

FINANCIAL
Institutional Type: Private
In-State Tuition: $54,987
Out-of-State Tuition: $54,987
Room & Board: $15,972
Required Fees: $642
Books & Supplies: $1,080

Avg. Need-Based Grant: $33,925
Avg. % of Need Met: 77%

Avg. Merit-Based Award: $12,852
% Receiving (All Freshmen): 43%
% Receiving (Freshmen w/o Need): 27%

Avg. Cumulative Debt: $26,603
% of Students Borrowing: 35%

CAREER
Who Recruits
1. Stryker Corporation
2. Gap Inc.
3. Tesla
4. Teach for America
5. Kiva

Notable Internships
1. McAfee
2. Yelp
3. Vera Wang

Top Industries
1. Business
2. Engineering
3. Education
4. Operations
5. Sales

Top Employers
1. Cisco
2. Apple
3. Google
4. Oracle
5. Facebook

Where Alumni Work
1. San Francisco
2. Los Angeles
3. Seattle
4. Sacramento
5. Portland, OR

Median Earnings
College Scorecard (Early Career): $72,600
PayScale (Early Career): $72,900
PayScale (Mid-Career): $148,600

RANKINGS
Money: 181
U.S. News: 53 (T), National Universities
Wall Street Journal/THE: 83 (T)
Washington Monthly: 143, National Universities

COLLEGE OVERLAPS
Loyola Marymount University
University of California, Davis
University of California, San Diego
University of California, Santa Barbara
University of San Diego

Scripps College

Claremont, California | 909-621-8149

ADMISSION
Admission Rate: 32%
Admission Rate - Men: Not Applicable
Admission Rate - Women: 32%
EA Admission Rate: Not Offered
ED Admission Rate: 47%
ED Admits as % of Total Admits: 12%
Admission Rate (5-Year Trend): -4%
% of Admits Attending (Yield): 29%
Transfer Admission Rate: 23%

SAT Reading/Writing (Middle 50%): 670-740
SAT Math (Middle 50%): 660-750
ACT Composite (Middle 50%): 30-33

% Graduated in Top 10% of HS Class: 78%
% Graduated in Top 25% of HS Class: 98%
% Graduated in Top 50% of HS Class: 100%

Demonstrated Interest: Not Considered
Legacy Status: Considered
Admission Interview Offered: Yes

ENROLLMENT
Total Undergraduate Enrollment: 1,089
% Part-Time: 1%
% Male: 0%
% Female: 100%
% Out-of-State: 56%
% Fraternity: Not Offered
% Sorority: Not Offered
% On-Campus (Freshman): 100%
% On-Campus (All Undergraduate): 94%

% African-American: 4%
% Asian: 16%
% Hispanic: 14%
% White: 52%
% Other: 7%
% Race or Ethnicity Unknown: 2%
% International: 5%
% Low-Income: 11%

ACADEMICS
Student-to-Faculty Ratio: 10 to 1
% of Classes Under 20: 75%
% of Classes 20-49: 25%
% of Classes 50 or More: 0%
% Full-Time Faculty: 75%
% Full-Time Faculty w/ Terminal Degree: 98%

Top Programs
Area Studies
Art
Biology
English
Media Studies
Politics
Psychology

Retention Rate: 93%
4-Year Graduation Rate: 86%
6-Year Graduation Rate: 90%

Curricular Flexibility: Somewhat Flexible
Academic Rating: ★★★★✦

#CollegesWorthYourMoney

While the East Coast is swarming with high-end women's colleges such as Wellesley, Smith, Bryn Mawr, Barnard, and Mt. Holyoke, there is only one such jewel resting closer to the Pacific Ocean. Scripps College, a member of the five-school Claremont Consortium, is the West Coast's lone elite all-female institution, making it a highly desirable destination for young women seeking a classic liberal arts education in a nurturing and supportive academic environment without the lonely, harsh winters of the Northeast.

Inside the Classroom

There are sixty-five majors available to Scripps undergrads, including some that are accessible through membership in the Consortium. Curricular requirements at Scripps are extensive, requiring a three-semester dive into interdisciplinary humanities coursework that tackles the essential question of "What makes a community?" through a combination of lecture, seminar-style discussions, and a self-designed project. All undergraduates must demonstrate competency in mathematics, foreign language, and writing. Along the way, one course must be taken in each of the four divisions: fine arts, natural sciences, letters, and social sciences. Within one's major, a minimum of eight courses must be tackled, culminating in the completion of a senior thesis, which 100 percent of graduates must complete.

A 10:1 student to faculty ratio at a school with zero grad students breeds an intimate learning atmosphere where professors are genuinely dedicated to undergraduate learning. A lack of competitiveness should not be mistaken for a lack of rigor. Scripps is loaded with driven students, 15 percent of whom elect to double major. As part of the required senior thesis, many undergraduates also have the chance to assist professors with academic/scientific research. Due to the absence of graduate students who would gobble up such positions, research opportunities are readily available for credit during the academic year as well on a full-time basis during the summer; the Scripps Undergraduate Research Fellowship is one such program. Study abroad programs in forty countries are taken advantage of by nearly two-thirds of the student body, giving Scripps one of the highest participation rates of any college in the United States.

The top three majors are: biology (22 percent); psychology (9 percent); and communication/media studies (7 percent). Each possesses a very strong reputation. Regardless of your major, however, graduate/professional schools know that earning a degree from Scripps is no small achievement. Prestigious scholarship committees also look kindly upon the school as Scripps is regularly a top twenty-five producer of Fulbright winners, taking home an incredible (considering the size of the graduating class) five awards in 2020. Recent grads have also taken home Watson Fellowships and a Davis Projects for Peace Fellowship.

Outside the Classroom

At Scripps, 94 percent of students live on the school's modestly sized 30-acre campus in one of eleven immaculately maintained dorms or in thematic housing options catering to those with goals and interests in common such as The Stem, Pre-Health Living Learning Community, and the Substance Free Community. There are no sororities at Scripps. Sports exist but are a combined effort with Harvey Mudd, and Claremont McKenna that, collectively, field eleven NCAA Division III teams. Fitness and recreational facilities are shared with Pitzer, Pomona, Harvey Mudd, and CMC. That means students have access to four swimming pools, four fitness centers, and a dozen playing fields. There are roughly thirty Scripps-only student-run organizations, but there are also more than 250 clubs that can be accessed by students of any of the five schools. One of the more notable social hubs is the Motley Coffeehouse, founded in 1974 and run entirely by Scripps students. In fact, the feminist, environmental, and social justice vibe makes its coffeehouse a perfect embodiment of the college's values and ethos. The college also boasts its own art museum, the Williamson Gallery, which contains works by many notable American artists. Of course, cultural options are hardly confined to the campus limits with Los Angeles only a forty-five minute car ride away.

Career Services

The Career Planning & Resources Office (CP&R) has four full-time professional staff members working as career counselors. Scripps' 272:1 student-to-advisor ratio is better than the average college featured in our guidebook. It may be a small office, but you won't find a more proactive group of counselors at any college in the country as the CP&R meets with 90 percent of freshmen within the students' first three weeks on campus. Larger events are typically joint affairs with the other esteemed members of the Claremont Consortium.

E-mail: admission@scrippscollege.edu | Website: www.scrippscollege.edu

Scripps takes pride in its facilitation of student internships and has the stats to prove it; 86 percent of graduates held at least one internship, and close to one-quarter completed three or more. Internship locations of note include 20th Century Fox, the California Department of Justice, and the Smithsonian. Career Treks whisk Scripps students off to metropolitan areas around the country to meet with alumni who are working in the same field of interest. Former students are always willing to lend a hand to current ones and can connect with soon-to-be grads through the Alumni Book, a compilation of student resumes. A week-long Emerging Professionals Program featuring alumni, recruiters, and CP&R counselors can be accessed for free. The office also offers a Financial Literacy Program to teach undergraduates about everything from budgeting to investing to filing taxes.

Professional Outcomes

Women land jobs at some of the world's leading companies after receiving their diplomas. The top employers of Scripps alumni include Google, Kaiser Permanente, and Amazon. Many go on to work for universities, particularly after earning additional degrees (more on this in a moment). Schools employing significant numbers of Scripps alumni include Pomona, Scripps, Stanford, UCLA, and UC-San Diego. Recent graduates also have entered positions at BlackRock, CBS, Goldman Sachs, Facebook, and Pfizer. Median salaries by midcareer are quite a bit lower than fellow Consortium member schools Pomona and Claremont McKenna, but they are comparable to other elite women's colleges such as Bryn Mawr. Most Scripps alumni remain on the West Coast with the largest percentage in Los Angeles followed by San Francisco, Seattle, Portland, San Diego, and Orange County. The most popular East Coast destinations are New York City, DC, and Boston.

An advanced degree is in the cards for most Scripps grads (12 percent of 2019 grads jumped right in), and it isn't usually too far in the future—two-thirds complete a graduate/professional program within five years of receiving their bachelor's degrees. Recent grads have pursued further study at institutions such as Caltech, Harvard, MIT, Vanderbilt, Oxford, Brown, Northwestern, and Tufts. Scripps knows what it's doing when it comes to premed, thanks to its Post-Baccalaureate Premedical Program that boasts a 98 percent+ acceptance rate; traditional undergrads also fare well above the national average. Those eyeing law school also find favorable results; recent grads have been accepted at top-tier law schools such as Emory, Georgetown, the University of Chicago, Berkeley, and the University of Michigan.

Admission

Thirty-two percent of the 3,022 women who applied for a place in the Class of 2023 were accepted. Twenty-nine percent of accepted students went on to enroll. Freshmen in 2019-20 possessed a middle-50 percent score of 1330-1470 on the SAT and 30-33 on the ACT. An impressive 78 percent came from the top decile of their high school class; 98 percent placed in the top quarter. Almost 90 percent sported a GPA of 3.75 or greater; only 4 percent earned less than a 3.5. In 2020, the school announced the implementation of a test-optional policy.

The admissions committee seeks "to build a community of curious and engaged students who are eager to contribute their diverse interests, backgrounds, and experiences to our academic and residential community." As such, they weight nine factors as being "very important" to admissions decisions: rigor of coursework, GPA, test scores, class rank, recommendations, essays, extracurricular activities, talent/ability, and character/personal qualities. Applying early decision at Scripps does yield an edge; 47 percent of ED applicants were accepted into the Class of 2023 versus 31 percent of regular round applicants. Those accepted in the early round comprised 41 percent of the incoming freshman class.

Worth Your Money?

At almost $75,000 the sticker price cost of attendance for Scripps College is undoubtedly on the high side. However, the 43 percent of undergraduates who are determined eligible for need-based aid all see 100 percent of their need met; the average grant is for $39k. Graduates leave with less than $20k in debt, far less the national average. If attending Scripps is financially feasible for your family, the quality of the educational experience and networks/resources offered by the Consortium make this school worth some level of sacrifice.

FINANCIAL
Institutional Type: Private
In-State Tuition: $56,970
Out-of-State Tuition: $56,970
Room & Board: $17,600
Required Fees: $218
Books & Supplies: $800

Avg. Need-Based Grant: $39,084
Avg. % of Need Met: 100%

Avg. Merit-Based Award: $19,547
% Receiving (All Freshmen): 13%
% Receiving (Freshmen w/o Need): 13%

Avg. Cumulative Debt: $30,150
% of Students Borrowing: 32%

CAREER
Who Recruits
1. DaVita
2. Nielsen
3. Pfizer
4. Nordstrom
5. Brancart & Brancart

Notable Internships
1. ALCU
2. Louis Vuitton
3. KPMG

Top Industries
1. Education
2. Business
3. Social Services
4. Media
5. Research

Top Employers
1. Google
2. Kaiser Permanente
3. Amazon
4. Microsoft
5. Seattle Children's

Where Alumni Work
1. Los Angeles
2. San Francisco
3. Seattle
4. New York City
5. Portland, OR

Median Earnings
College Scorecard (Early Career): $54,100
PayScale (Early Career): $58,500
PayScale (Mid-Career): $102,600

RANKINGS
Money: 182
U.S. News: 28 (T), Liberal Arts Colleges
Wall Street Journal/THE: 66 (T)
Washington Monthly: 116, Liberal Arts Colleges

COLLEGE OVERLAPS
Claremont McKenna College
Pitzer College
University of California, Los Angeles
University of Southern California
Wellesley College

Sewanee — The University of the South

Sewanee, Tennessee | 931-598-1238

ADMISSION
Admission Rate: 67%
Admission Rate - Men: 65%
Admission Rate - Women: 68%
EA Admission Rate: 82%
ED Admission Rate: 84%
ED Admits as % of Total Admits: 6%
Admission Rate (5-Year Trend): +6%
% of Admits Attending (Yield): 21%
Transfer Admission Rate: 76%

SAT Reading/Writing (Middle 50%): 580-680
SAT Math (Middle 50%): 570-660
ACT Composite (Middle 50%): 25-30

% Graduated in Top 10% of HS Class: 32%
% Graduated in Top 25% of HS Class: 60%
% Graduated in Top 50% of HS Class: 86%

Demonstrated Interest: Considered
Legacy Status: Considered
Admission Interview Offered: Yes

ENROLLMENT
Total Undergraduate Enrollment: 1,695
% Part-Time: 1%
% Male: 49%
% Female: 51%
% Out-of-State: 79%
% Fraternity: 60%
% Sorority: 74%
% On-Campus (Freshman): 100%
% On-Campus (All Undergraduate): 98%

% African-American: 4%
% Asian: 1%
% Hispanic: 5%
% White: 82%
% Other: 3%
% Race or Ethnicity Unknown: 0%
% International: 4%
% Low-Income: 20%

ACADEMICS
Student-to-Faculty Ratio: 10 to 1
% of Classes Under 20: 60%
% of Classes 20-49: 40%
% of Classes 50 or More: 1%
% Full-Time Faculty: 75%
% Full-Time Faculty w/ Terminal Degree: 93%

Top Programs
Biology
Economics
English
Environment & Sustainability
History
International & Global Studies
Politics

Retention Rate: 88%
4-Year Graduation Rate: 72%
6-Year Graduation Rate: 79%

Curricular Flexibility: Somewhat Flexible
Academic Rating: ★★★✓

#CollegesWorthYourMoney

People flying over the historic campus of the University of the South, sometimes referred to as "Sewanee" might, in a moment of panic, fret that they had accidentally hopped aboard an international flight and were passing directly over Oxford or Cambridge. This breathtaking campus that includes 13,000 acres of natural beauty known affectionately as "The Domain" is situated on Tennessee's Cumberland Plateau. The pretty packaging is not misleading; the University of the South delivers a powerful academic punch, and it isn't quite as picky as many other top schools as to who gets to step into the ring. While designated a "university," Sewanee is really more of a liberal arts college of 1,695 undergrads and fewer than one hundred graduate students.

Inside the Classroom
Offering thirty-six majors and forty-three minors, undergrads are exposed to a wide scope of liberal arts study, no matter their area of concentration. All students must complete a designated writing-intensive course by the end of their sophomore year as well as coursework fulfilling six "learning objectives." Literary analysis, understanding the arts, and seeking meaning require one course each while multiple classes are required in exploring past and present, the scientific and quantitative view, and language and global studies. Two physical education and wellness classes also must be tackled prior to graduation.

A 10:1 student-to-faculty ratio and a limited number of grad students means that undergraduate teaching remains the primary focus at Sewanee. The average class size is seventeen students, and 98 percent of course sections have an enrollment under thirty. Opportunities to conduct research with faculty members are not only plentiful, they are often funded by the university. Recent students have collaborated on fascinating research projects on topics such as Adolescent Substance Use Perception in Southern Appalachia; Synthesis of New, More Effective Anti-Cancer Metallopharmaceuticals; and Corporate Political Contributions and Stock Returns. Study abroad options that are a summer, a semester, or a full year in length are embarked upon by roughly half of all Sewanee students. European Studies and British Studies are two of the most popular global programs offered by the college.

The degrees most commonly conferred are in economics (16%), psychology (13%), political science (11%), English (10%), and biology (9%). All are strong, but Sewanee's English Department has a leading national reputation. Thanks to the Tennessee Williams Writers-in-Residence program, accomplished authors from around the globe come to teach at Sewanee, and English majors routinely continue their studies at the likes of Princeton, Yale, Duke, and the University of Chicago. The school has also historically had success in helping its students procure the most distinguished graduate fellowships. Sewanee is routinely named a top producer of Fulbright Scholars and forty-seven students have claimed Watson Scholarships since they were first made available in 1968. Incredibly, the school claims twenty-six Rhodes Scholars in its history, more than Amherst, the University of Pennsylvania, or Georgetown.

Outside the Classroom
Just about the entire student body, 98 percent to be precise, live in the dorms or in other on-campus housing. Greek life is extremely popular at Sewanee as the eleven fraternities and ten sororities attract an overwhelming 80 percent of undergraduates into rushing. When it's all said and done, 74 percent of women and 60 percent of men end up Greek affiliated. Involvement in some type of sport is also common. Eleven men's and thirteen women's Division III athletic teams are joined by 30 percent of the student population. Another eight club teams and plenty of intramural sessions draw many more. More than ninety student-run organizations are active with the most popular being the Student Government Association, the Order of Gown (focusing on campus spirit and traditions), and the Student Activity Board. If climbing, caving, hiking, biking, or canoeing is more your style, then the Sewanee Outing Program (SOP) is a must-join organization. In addition to taking outdoorsy road trips, the SOP also takes full advantage of the pristine beauty of the aforementioned Domain. With Chattanooga only an hour away and Nashville an hour-and-a-half car ride from campus, Sewanee students can access big-city fun on the weekends.

Career Services
The Career and Leadership Development Office (CLD) employs five full-time staff members, four of whom are titled director or assistant director, yet all work directly in counseling undergraduates. That equates to a student-to-staff ratio of 339:1, in the average range compared to the other institutions included in this book. The CLD does

manage to reach 97 percent of students by the time they graduate, and a hard-to-beat 99 percent report being satisfied by the guidance they receive. Events such as the annual Graduate and Professional School Fair draws reps from more than thirty-five programs including Tulane, Vanderbilt, and UGA's law schools, Wake Forest's MBA program, and Emory's School of Theology. An annual Beyond the Gates event sees close to fifty alumni from all walks of professional life spend a weekend mentoring current juniors and seniors as they ready themselves for the job search.

Via the Sewanee Pledge, the university guarantees funding for one unpaid internship or research experience for every single student. Each year, more than 200 such stipends are granted for unpaid internships alone. Over 150 Sewanee-exclusive internship opportunities are posted each year, creating a favorable environment for students to gain the inside track on desirable opportunities. Recent students have interned at Style Magazine, Accenture, the World Wildlife Fund, and the US Forest Service. The CLD at the University of the South, thanks to a high level of connection and personalized counseling, succeeds in assisting the bulk of graduates reach their next destination.

Professional Outcomes
Within six months of their commencement ceremony, 97 percent of 2019 Sewanee grads have found some form of employment or have begun their graduate studies. Seventy-one percent have obtained full-time employment with the highest number of grads entering the sectors of: business/finance (126), education (48) health care (40), and government (38). Organizations employing recent graduates include Booz Allen Hamilton, Sony Pictures, Warby Parker, BlackRock, and Massachusetts General Hospital. The largest number of total alumni can be found at Wells Fargo, Deloitte, Regions Bank, and Vanderbilt University Medical Center. Many alumni remain in the South after graduation as Nashville, Atlanta, and Chattanooga are the most frequent destinations. However, DC and New York City also contain large pockets of grads.

The majority of those in the Class of 2019 who pursued advanced degrees entered master's programs (26) followed by medical school (17), law school (8) and PhD programs (4). Elite graduate school acceptances included Johns Hopkins, Georgetown, Vanderbilt, and Washington University in St. Louis. Law schools attended included Baylor U, the College of William & Mary, and Notre Dame. Medical school acceptances in the last several years included East Carolina University and the University of Texas.

Admission
Sewanee is a rare top school that, even in 2020, still lacks a menacing acceptance rate—its 67 percent is about as friendly as you will find among top colleges. The entering Class of 2023 held strong academic credentials, sporting middle-50 percent standardized test scores of 1160-1330 on the SAT and 25-30 on the ACT (the school is test-optional). You don't need to be at the top of your high school class to gain admittance as only 32 percent placed in the top decile and 60 percent in the top quartile. The school's selectivity level is similar to that of a full decade ago.

A test-optional school, the University of the South places a strong emphasis on the rigor of one's secondary school record, GPA, and recommendations. Second billing is granted to the application essay, extracurricular activities, character/personal qualities, volunteer work, and work experience. A relatively low yield rate of 19 percent means that almost four-fifths of those accepted enroll elsewhere. While the university does not rank demonstrated interest as an important factor in admissions decisions, the committee certainly appreciates those who apply via binding early decision. In fact, 84 percent of those applying ED are accepted. A fine and distinctive education can be yours at this exceptionally beautiful Tennessee campus without the typical crucible of admissions-related stress found at many of the schools featured in this book.

Worth Your Money?
The overall cost of attendance of $60,094 represents a less-than-exorbitant sticker price in the world of small liberal arts schools. This is particularly true since 56 percent of undergrads qualify for an average merit aid award of $20k and half of all undergrads qualify for an average need-based award of $28,542. If your family has limited funds (like most), you'll want to see how much merit and need-based aid you are awarded before making a decision on whether Sewanee is the right choice for your wallet.

FINANCIAL
Institutional Type: Private
In-State Tuition: $47,708
Out-of-State Tuition: $47,708
Room & Board: $13,700
Required Fees: $272
Books & Supplies: $1,200

Avg. Need-Based Grant: $28,542
Avg. % of Need Met: 77%

Avg. Merit-Based Award: $20,258
% Receiving (All Freshmen): 56%
% Receiving (Freshmen w/o Need): 45%

Avg. Cumulative Debt: $31,737
% of Students Borrowing: 44%

CAREER
Who Recruits
1. Springbot
2. JumpCrew
3. Showtime Networks
4. Accenture
5. Harris Williams & Co.

Notable Internships
1. UBS
2. Wells Fargo
3. U.S. Senate

Top Industries
1. Business
2. Education
3. Social Services
4. Operations
5. Sales

Top Employers
1. Wells Fargo
2. Regions Bank
3. CBRE
4. Deloitte
5. Capital One

Where Alumni Work
1. Nashville
2. Atlanta
3. Chattanooga, TN
4. Washington DC
5. New York City

Median Earnings
College Scorecard (Early Career): $45,500
PayScale (Early Career): $57,000
PayScale (Mid-Career): $119,300

RANKINGS
Money: 380
U.S. News: 47 (T), Liberal Arts Colleges
Wall Street Journal/THE: 147 (T)
Washington Monthly: 105, Liberal Arts Colleges

COLLEGE OVERLAPS
Furman University
Rhodes College
University of Georgia
Wake Forest University
Washington & Lee University

Skidmore College

Saratoga Springs, New York | 518-580-5570

Founded as a women's college at the turn of the twentieth century, Skidmore still serves more women than men today, but going co-ed isn't the most notable shift that has occurred at this private liberal arts college in Upstate New York. The school's 2,662 undergrads, affectionately known as "Skiddies," have become an increasingly higher-achieving lot as the school has transformed from selective to highly selective over the past decade. What has remained is its reputation as a free-spirited institution with an extremely accessible and student-friendly faculty.

Inside the Classroom
An undergraduate-only institution, there are forty-three majors to choose from with the most popular being business, English, psychology, political science, economics, studio art, theater, biology, and environmental studies. All students begin by completing a first-year experience that is highlighted by participation in the Scribner Seminars where students begin to grasp the level of rigor that will be expected as they launch their collegiate studies. Foundations courses include Applied Quantitative Reasoning, Global Cultural Perspectives, Language Study, and Writing. Inquiry courses include Artistic Inquiry through Practice, Humanistic Inquiry and Practice, and Scientific Inquiry through Practice. It's hard to earn a diploma without completing some type of a culminating project; 75 percent complete a senior capstone, 53 percent engage in independent study, and 32 percent produce a senior thesis or advanced research project.

With no graduate students around to suck up professorial attention, undergrads reap the full benefits of the school's student-faculty ratio of 8-to-1. Skidmore's average class size is only sixteen students, and 98 percent of sections have fewer than thirty students. Twenty-two percent of sections enroll only single digits. Each year roughly 500 students, 20 percent of the student body, engage in research with a faculty mentor, including eighty students who participate in the Summer Student-Faculty Research Program. Internships and service-learning courses are a normal part of the Skidmore experience. Three-fifths of students study abroad at one of 120 programs in forty-five countries, a rate of participation that places it at the very top in the nation.

Known for its superior undergraduate teaching, a Skidmore degree will carry enough prestige to open doors to top employers and graduate schools, particularly in the aforementioned areas that are among the most popular majors. The social sciences (20 percent), business (14 percent), and the visual and performing arts (13 percent) are the most common areas of study. The school produces a surprisingly modest number of competitive postgraduate scholars and fellows. Many years it produces a finalist for a National Science Foundation, Goldwater, or Mitchell Scholarship, but it does not consistently take home the big prizes.

Outside the Classroom
Almost 90 percent of students reside in one of Skidmore's eight residence halls, which are split evenly on a North and a South campus spread over 1,000 enchanting acres. The only Greek life at Skidmore can be found in courses in the classics; there are no frats or sororities in the "Skidmore bubble." An almost 60/40 split along gender lines in favor of women certainly has an impact on social life. There are 120 active student-run clubs and nineteen Division III varsity sports teams (10 women's and 9 men's) nicknamed the Thoroughbreds. There are plenty of club sports and intramural leagues for less serious competitors. Amenities are first-class, from the apartment-style dorms to the award-winning dining services to the 150-acre North Woods oasis that can be used for anything from meditation to skiing. Saratoga Springs is a small city of 30,000, but its funky downtown is only a ten-minute walk from campus. Skidmore is located thirty minutes from Albany and three full hours from popular road trip destinations like New York City, Boston, and Montreal. Those seeking more nature-oriented recreation can easily travel to the Berkshires, Adirondacks, or Green Mountains.

Career Services
The Career Development Center (CDC) at Skidmore College is staffed by nine professionals with counseling expertise in a variety of fields. That works out to a 296:1 student-to-advisor ratio that is solidly in the average range compared to other institutions in this guidebook. The CDC hosts an annual networking event called Career Jam that is attended by hundreds of students as well as many alumni, parents, and employers. The annual Graduate and Professional School Expo attracts representatives from roughly forty-five universities to Skidmore. Students also can travel off campus to corporate destinations along the East Coast as part of the Road Trips to the Real World program.

In a single year, the CDC conducts 2,000+ one-on-one counseling sessions, brings close to 100 employers to Saratoga Springs for recruiting purposes, and facilitates more than 300 on-campus interviews. An impressive 270+ employers attend the college's job fairs. Eighty-four percent of 2019 grads participated in an internship during their time at Skidmore, and many were funded by the school. Students nab intriguing internships at places such as Tesla, The Daily Show with Trevor Noah, the NBA, Esquire Magazine, and Memorial Sloan Kettering Cancer Center. The career services staff encourages individual meetings as early as freshman year in its effort to support "all students and alumni through the creative process of integrating their liberal arts education and experiences into a satisfying career." Skidmore's CDC boasts strong internship numbers; however, with 10 percent of grads still seeking employment six months after graduation, there is room for improvement.

Professional Outcomes

Seventy-one percent of 2019 Skidmore grads were employed within six months of completing their degrees and 18 percent were enrolled in graduate school. The most frequently entered industries were education and training (17 percent); STEM (15 percent); business (15 percent); and marketing, sales, and service (13 percent). The median starting salary range for Class of 2019 grads was $40,000-$49,999. Intriguing employers of recent grads included the Metropolitan Opera, Penguin Random House, NBC Universal, Estee Lauder, and Vineyard Vines. Fairly large numbers of Skiddies can be found at major corporations including Google, Morgan Stanley, EY, Amazon, JPMorgan Chase, Fidelity Investments, and IBM. The greatest concentration of alumni can be found in Greater New York City with Boston, Albany, San Francisco, and Washington, DC, the next most popular landing spots.

Graduate acceptances procured by the Class of 2019 included Ivies like Yale, Penn, Dartmouth, and Columbia as well as other elite institutions like Johns Hopkins, Northwestern, and NYU. Skidmore students are accepted to medical school at a rate "far above the national average." Many recent med school-bound grads have attended NY-based schools like SUNY Upstate, SUNY Stony Brook, or the University of Buffalo. Over the last few years, grads have matriculated into law schools at Duke, Penn State, and the University of Miami.

Admission

For 2019-20 freshman hopefuls, only 30 percent were accepted (27.5 percent were accepted the previous year), and the average SAT was 1230-1390. It is important to note that Skidmore adopted a test-optional policy in 2016 that has led to a spike in applications. Among enrolled freshman, 53 percent submitted SAT scores, and another 22 percent submitted ACT scores, so the majority of accepted applicants are not going the test-optional route. Many students, but far from all, rank near the top of their graduating high school classes; 32 percent of members of the Class of 2023 placed in the top decile, and 62 percent earned a spot in the top quartile. Fifty-eight percent of this cohort hailed from public high schools while 32 percent were private school grads.

In the eyes of the admissions office, the rigor of secondary coursework is the only factor that rises to "most important" status. From there, class rank, GPA, essays, recommendations, extracurricular activities, talent/ability, character/personal qualities, work experience, volunteer work, and demonstrated interest are on equal footing as "important" factors. As a test-optional school, SATs and ACTs are relegated to "considered" status. In the most recent admissions cycle the acceptance rate for early decision applicants was 58 percent compared to 28 percent in the regular cycle, and ED students made up 50 percent of the freshman class. A more competitive school than in the recent past, those set on Skidmore definitely should consider applying ED and should at least go out of their way to demonstrate serious interest in the college. While test-optional, strong standardized test scores can still help you win over the admissions committee.

Worth Your Money?

Need-based grants averaging $46,800 are awarded to 51 percent of undergraduates at Skidmore. That helps defray some of the $74 in total costs each year for those with genuine financial need. Unfortunately, merit aid is only made available to 2.8 percent of the undergraduate population; thus, you are unlikely to get a significant tuition discount unless you qualify for a grant. If your parents can afford Skidmore, it is a wonderful place to spend four years learning and growing. On the other hand, we would not recommend taking on large amounts of debt in order to study theater, English, studio art, or any other popular but typically low-paying major without a clear postgraduate career and financial plan.

FINANCIAL
Institutional Type: Private
In-State Tuition: $55,136
Out-of-State Tuition: $55,136
Room & Board: $15,000
Required Fees: $1,036
Books & Supplies: $1,300

Avg. Need-Based Grant: $46,850
Avg. % of Need Met: 100%

Avg. Merit-Based Award: $15,000
% Receiving (All Freshmen): 2%
% Receiving (Freshmen w/o Need): 0%

Avg. Cumulative Debt: $31,381
% of Students Borrowing: 34%

CAREER
Who Recruits
1. New England Center for Children
2. M&T Bank
3. EY
4. NYS Department of Health
5. Carney Sandoe & Associates

Notable Internships
1. Scholastic
2. WHYY
3. Airbnb

Top Industries
1. Business
2. Education
3. Arts and Design
4. Operations
5. Media

Top Employers
1. Morgan Stanley
2. EY
3. JPMorgan Chase
4. Google
5. Fidelity Investments

Where Alumni Work
1. New York City
2. Boston
3. Albany, NY
4. San Francisco
5. Washington DC

Median Earnings
College Scorecard (Early Career): $49,700
PayScale (Early Career): $56,400
PayScale (Mid-Career): $108,600

RANKINGS
Money: 195
U.S. News: 36 (T), Liberal Arts Colleges
Wall Street Journal/THE: 98 (T)
Washington Monthly: 70, Liberal Arts Colleges

COLLEGE OVERLAPS
Bates College
Hamilton College
Tufts University
Vassar College
Wesleyan University

Smith College

Northampton, Massachusetts | 413-585-2500

You will not find a more wide-open curriculum or liberal/progressive ethos at any women's school in the country than that of Smith College; only a few coeducational institutions—perhaps Vassar or Wesleyan—can go toe-to-toe with Smith on both fronts. Its list of alumnae supports that claim with Gloria Steinem, Julia Child, and Sylvia Plath all being Smith grads (Nancy Reagan was the ideological oddball). From a Seven Sisters admissions standpoint, Smith is more selective than Mt. Holyoke but less selective than Wellesley, Bryn Mawr, or Barnard. A member of the Five College Consortium, students can cross-enroll at Mt. Holyoke, UMass, Amherst, and Hampshire. In addition to the forty-five academic departments and programs and 1,000 courses offered each academic year at Smith, an additional 4,000 courses can be accessed at partner universities.

Inside the Classroom
Smith's seven major fields of knowledge are literature, historical studies, social science, natural science, mathematics and analytical philosophy, the arts, and foreign language. Forays into each are "recommended," but the only nonnegotiable requirement is one writing-intensive course in the first or second semester of the freshman year. Otherwise, graduation requirements dictate that sixty-four credits must be taken outside of one's major. What that distribution looks like is entirely up to you. Young women seeking the ultimate level of undergraduate academic freedom will adore the Smith experience.

This college of 2,531 undergraduates boasts a student-faculty ratio of 9:1. With only a small number of graduate students to worry about, 19 percent of undergraduate sections have single-digit enrollments, and 69 percent of total class sections enroll fewer than twenty students. Each summer, eighty Smithies spend their time working side-by-side with a professor on a research project. Around 40 percent of undergrads spend a semester abroad in one of a hundred programs on six continents, including some programs taught in the native tongue for those proficient in a foreign language.

The social sciences are most popular at Smith, accounting for 22 percent of the degrees conferred, with programs in economics and government carrying very strong reputations. Next in line is biology (10 percent), health professions (9 percent), and foreign language (8 percent). Thanks to a strong decade-long push toward increasing the number of women studying such fields as engineering, mathematics, and the hard sciences, greater than two-fifths of current students are majoring in a STEM field. Smith is also the Fulbright Scholarship capital of the world producing an awe-inspiring 290 winners since 2002. Recent students also have captured Goldwater and Udall Scholarships as well as National Science Foundation Graduate Research Fellowships.

Outside the Classroom
Every freshman, and 94 percent of the total undergraduate population, lives in college-owned housing. There are thirty-seven self-governing houses, each with its own dining hall, that accommodate between ten and one hundred students; most have a mix of freshmen through seniors. No sororities operate at this school. Smith offers eleven varsity sports that compete in NCAA Division III as well as extensive intramural and club sports programs that include oddities like Quidditch and Futsal. The Outing Club is a popular way to enjoy the area's natural beauty through hikes, canoeing trips, and rock-climbing adventures. Approximately 120 student-run organizations are available with a wide selection of cultural groups, political and student government groups, and community service clubs. Each year 200+ volunteers dedicate 10,000+ hours of community service through the Jandon Center for Community Engagement. Smith's membership in the Five College Consortium leads to additional social and extracurricular opportunities on the campuses of Mt. Holyoke, UMass, Amherst, and Hampshire. Culture and relaxation can be found on campus at the Smith College Museum of Art or the school's own botanical garden. The town of Northampton is two hours west of Boston and features plenty of restaurants and an artsy vibe that meshes well with this particular college community.

Career Services
The Lazarus Center for Career Development at Smith is staffed by nine professionals, including six career advisors and internship and employer relations specialists. The 281:1 student-to-advisor ratio is better than the average school featured in this guidebook. For a small school, it puts on a fairly large Fall Career Fair that draws eighty+ companies and graduate schools. It also organizes the Spring Life Sciences, Technology & Engineering Fair that attracts thirty+ employers. In addition, Smith partners with MIT and UMass Amherst to offer access to additional off-site career fairs. Membership in the Selective Liberal Arts Consortium affords the women of Smith chances to participate in interview days with major corporations in Washington, DC, and New York City.

In a given year, 175+ companies recruit on campus, an exceptional figure for a small liberal arts school. More than 6,600 job and internship opportunities are posted each year on Handshake. Praxis grants of up to $3,500 are awarded to roughly 400 undergraduates per year to pursue unpaid internships. Current students also benefit from the network of 48,000 alumnae spread across 120 countries who are known for being generous with their time and offers of mentorship. While the school's starting salary numbers leave something to be desired, the Lazarus Center for Career Development excels in employer relations, procurement of prestigious scholarships, and offers ample individualized attention for those who seek it.

Professional Outcomes

Two years after graduating, 91 percent of Smith alumnae have found employment, and 42 percent have begun their graduate studies. More than twenty-five alumnae can be found at the US Department of State, Google, IBM, Johnson & Johnson, Accenture, Fidelity Investments, Deloitte, Microsoft, JPMorgan Chase, and Amazon. Many Smith women rise to high ranks within their respective organizations and corporations. Twenty years after graduation, 10 percent of alumnae report holding a chief executive position, and an additional 8 percent are stationed in other executive-level positions. Median career incomes are on the lower side compared to other elite schools and are comparable to those of Mt. Holyoke. Surprising given its locale, Boston is only the second-most popular destination for grads. New York City is number one with Springfield (Massachusetts), San Francisco, and DC also toward the top of the list.

Within two years of graduating, 42 percent of alumni have already entered a graduate program; within ten years of receiving their bachelor's degrees, more than three-quarters of Smith grads have earned or are working toward an advanced degree. The five most frequently attended graduate schools are Columbia, NYU, Harvard, Smith itself, and Boston University. Medical and law school acceptance rates are strong. Smith undergrads with a 3.3 GPA and a minimum of 507 on the MCAT were accepted into medical school at an 87 percent clip. The law school acceptance rate is consistently over 80 percent.

Admission

In seeking a place in the Class of 2023, almost 5,600 hopefuls applied to Smith; 32 percent were accepted, and 35 percent of that group ultimately enrolled. The college went test-optional a full decade ago, but 54 percent of the 2019-20 freshman class submitted SAT scores, and an additional 30 percent included ACT results as part of their applications. The mid-50 percent ranges on those exams were a 1330-1500 on the SAT and 30-33 on the ACT. Seventy-five percent of freshmen earned a spot in the top 10 percent of their high school class, and 96 percent placed in the top 25 percent; the average GPA was 4.0.

As stated by the committee, "Most applications are read by two members of the admission staff, and every part of your folder reveals another facet of your life." That holistic review places the greatest emphasis on five factors: rigor of coursework, GPA, recommendations, essays, and character/personal qualities. The second rung of important factors are class rank, an interview, extracurriculars, and talent/ability. Those applying through the early decision round received a boost to their admissions prospects to the tune of a 61 percent acceptance rate. Further, ED applicants accounted for 49 percent of the incoming freshman class. While not at the selectivity level of Wellesley or Barnard, Smith College has become increasingly more difficult to gain acceptance into in recent years. A sparkling high school transcript is nonnegotiable, and showing commitment through submitting an early decision application is recommended for borderline applicants who have Smith as their clear first choice.

Worth Your Money?

With a cost of attendance of $73,652, a Smith degree won't come cheap for those who do not qualify for institutional aid. The good news is that 59 percent of undergraduates do, indeed, qualify for need-based grants that average almost $52,000 annually. Merit aid awards are harder to come by and, when given, are only for a fraction of the need-based grants. Smith students have superb graduate/professional school and employment outcomes, making this school a solid choice for anyone who can afford it.

FINANCIAL
Institutional Type: Private
In-State Tuition: $55,830
Out-of-State Tuition: $55,830
Room & Board: $18,760
Required Fees: $284
Books & Supplies: $800

Avg. Need-Based Grant: $51,991
Avg. % of Need Met: 100%

Avg. Merit-Based Award: $17,907
% Receiving (All Freshmen): 9%
% Receiving (Freshmen w/o Need): 8%

Avg. Cumulative Debt: $21,460
% of Students Borrowing: 61%

CAREER
Who Recruits
1. Amazon Robotics
2. The Beacon Group
3. Woodard & Curran
4. Audible
5. Collins Aerospace

Notable Internships
1. National Institutes of Health
2. Goldman Sachs
3. Roosevelt Park Zoo

Top Industries
1. Business
2. Education
3. Healthcare
4. Social Services
5. Media

Top Employers
1. Google
2. IBM
3. Johnson & Johnson
4. Accenture
5. JPMorgan Chase

Where Alumni Work
1. New York City
2. Boston
3. Springfield, MA
4. San Francisco
5. Washington DC

Median Earnings
College Scorecard (Early Career): $46,200
PayScale (Early Career): $55,800
PayScale (Mid-Career): $113,200

RANKINGS
Money: 260
U.S. News: 15 (T), Liberal Arts Colleges
Wall Street Journal/THE: 43 (T)
Washington Monthly: 23, Liberal Arts Colleges

COLLEGE OVERLAPS
Barnard College
Bryn Mawr College
Mount Holyoke College
Scripps College
Wellesley College

Southern Methodist University

Dallas, Texas | 214-768-2058

ADMISSION
Admission Rate: 47%
Admission Rate - Men: 48%
Admission Rate - Women: 47%
EA Admission Rate: 50%
ED Admission Rate: 65%
ED Admits as % of Total Admits: 5%
Admission Rate (5-Year Trend): -3%
% of Admits Attending (Yield): 23%
Transfer Admission Rate: 57%

SAT Reading/Writing (Middle 50%): 640-720
SAT Math (Middle 50%): 660-760
ACT Composite (Middle 50%): 29-33

% Graduated in Top 10% of HS Class: 49%
% Graduated in Top 25% of HS Class: 79%
% Graduated in Top 50% of HS Class: 97%

Demonstrated Interest: Considered
Legacy Status: Considered
Admission Interview Offered: No

ENROLLMENT
Total Undergraduate Enrollment: 6,710
% Part-Time: 3%
% Male: 51%
% Female: 49%
% Out-of-State: 55%
% Fraternity: 27%
% Sorority: 36%
% On-Campus (Freshman): 98%
% On-Campus (All Undergraduate): 54%

% African-American: 4%
% Asian: 7%
% Hispanic: 12%
% White: 64%
% Other: 4%
% Race or Ethnicity Unknown: 0%
% International: 7%
% Low-Income: 12%

ACADEMICS
Student-to-Faculty Ratio: 11 to 1
% of Classes Under 20: 57%
% of Classes 20-49: 34%
% of Classes 50 or More: 10%
% Full-Time Faculty: 66%
% Full-Time Faculty w/ Terminal Degree: 85%

Top Programs
Accounting
Finance
Mathematics
Mechanical Engineering
Public Policy
Sport Management
Theatre

Retention Rate: 91%
4-Year Graduation Rate: 72%
6-Year Graduation Rate: 81%

Curricular Flexibility: Somewhat Flexible
Academic Rating: ★★★✔

#CollegesWorthYourMoney

Wealthy and moderately conservative—such is the reputation of Southern Methodist University in Dallas, Texas, a midsized private institution with a loyal alumni base and plenty of financial backing. Historically, a large percentage of the school's 6,710 undergraduates come from families earning incomes in the top 5 percent of all families in the United States. While "Methodist" is in its name, only 14 percent of students identify as affiliating with that denomination; twice as many are Catholic. Academically, the Cox School of Business has one of the most respected faculties in the world, but that is by no means the only high-profile academic department; the public policy, sports management, performing arts, music, and film programs shine almost as brightly. In total, SMU offers one hundred+ majors and eighty-five minors.

Inside the Classroom
The university's curriculum was revised in 2016 and now involves fulfilling foundation, depth, and breadth requirements. While that may sound extensive, the school offers great flexibility within those categories, and many courses within one's major will naturally fulfill some of the various mandates. Seven "proficiencies and experiences" can be met through a combination of coursework and noncredit activities that address each of human diversity, information literacy, oral communication, writing, community engagement, global engagement, and quantitative reasoning.

Thanks in part to an 11:1 student-to-faculty ratio, 57 percent of classes enroll fewer than twenty students, and fewer than 10 percent of classes enroll fifty+ undergraduates. Opportunities for personal connection and guidance extend beyond the classroom as 1,000 current SMU students have participated in undergraduate research or apprenticeships. Grants for independent research through an Engaged Learning Fellowship or a Summer Research Assistantship that pays students to work alongside faculty members for twenty-nine hours per week also are available. An annual symposium and an undergraduate-only research journal provide outlets through which you can share those valuable experiences. The 150 study abroad programs in fifty countries attract more than one-quarter of Mustangs at some point during their four years of study.

This career-minded student body gravitates toward preprofessional degrees, particularly in business (27 percent) and engineering (9 percent). SMU's Cox School of Business is top-ranked and has especially strong ties to Wall Street. Programs in engineering, sports management, and the performing arts are also very well-regarded. Most fresh SMU grads are targeting high-paying jobs or entering the graduate/professional school of their choosing, but a small number each year aim for (and win) prestigious fellowships. Mustangs are awarded between two and five Fulbright Scholarships per year, two to four Gilman Scholarships, and an occasional Goldwater or Truman Scholarship.

Outside the Classroom
Almost every freshman resides in one of the university's eleven Residential Commons (which also houses sophomores), and 54 percent of all undergraduates call the dorms home; upperclassmen occupy six separate communities. Greek life is a huge part of the social fabric at SMU with 27 percent of men joining fraternities and 36 percent of women affiliating with a sorority. Sports are also a major force as the Mustangs field seventeen teams that compete in the American Athletic Conference against Division I competition. Impressively, SMU has won eighteen conference championships in the last five years. The football tradition at SMU is strong despite a series of recruiting scandals in the '80s that led to the team being banned for the 1987 season. Now, money flows into the program legally, including the $27 million that funded a new indoor practice facility that opened in 2019. New buildings are popping up everywhere you look across campus, whether it's the 50,000-square-foot Gerald J. Ford Hall for Research and Innovation or the Crain Family Centennial Promenade running through the heart of campus. The school routinely places near the top of "most beautiful campus" lists. Those not thrilled by Greeks and sports can still choose from over 200 campus organizations or venture into Dallas as the city's downtown area is only a few miles from the school.

Career Services
The Hegi Family Career Development Center has seven full-time employees as well as two graduate assistants. Professionals fill roles such as career counselor and employer relations specialist, and the overall student-to-counselor ratio is 959:1, poorer than most midsized universities profiled in this guide. Events that take place on campus, including career fairs, draw as many as one hundred employers and 575 students. The All Majors Career Fair held in the fall of 2019 attracted fifty+ employers including heavy hitters like American Airlines, Southwest, Hershey's, Mary Kay, and Home Depot.

SMU's connected alumni base helps sustain strong school-to-employer bonds that lead to ample internship opportunities, particularly in the Dallas area. Business majors land internships at major investment firms and banks like Goldman Sachs, Citi, and JPMorgan Chase. A tremendous 90 percent of Lyle School of Engineering undergraduates complete at least one internship. Services offered by the Career Development Center include one-day externships, one-on-one career counseling that staff recommends "early and often," and the facilitation of on-campus interviews with recruiters from 160 companies, including some in the Fortune 500. Becoming a Mustang enables undergraduates of all socioeconomic backgrounds to connect to industry through networking, experiential learning opportunities, and impactful corporate relationships.

Professional Outcomes

At the moment they receive their diplomas, over two-thirds of graduates of the Class of 2019 already had their first jobs or graduate school destinations in hand. Six months after graduation, that figure rose into the mid-90s. The major corporations employing the greatest number of Mustangs are Lockheed Martin, AT&T, EY, IBM, JPMorgan Chase, Microsoft, Deloitte, American Airlines, Accenture, Oracle, Amazon, and Goldman Sachs. While close to half of SMU alums stay close to their alma mater in the Dallas-Fort Worth area, many relocate to New York City, Los Angeles, San Francisco, or DC for work. Average salaries for graduates of the Cox School of Business ranged between $52k for marketing majors to $71k for finance majors. Across all colleges and majors the average starting salary was approximately $55,000.

In a typical year, one-quarter of seniors elect to continue their education in pursuit of a graduate or professional degree. SMU itself is a popular choice, but graduates have no shortage of options, including at the nation's top universities. Of the eighty-one SMU grads applying to begin medical school in 2019, a solid 54 percent gained acceptance, better than the national average that year of 43 percent. Recent acceptances included the Baylor College of Medicine, Perelman School of Medicine at the University of Pennsylvania, University of Texas at Austin Dell Medical School, and Vanderbilt University School of Medicine. The roughly one hundred pre-law students enjoy an annual acceptance rate hovering between 70 and 85 percent. Each year, forty students enter the Pre-Law Scholars Program, which puts them on track to attend SMU's Dedman School of Law upon graduation. Other grads in recent years have entered prestigious law schools such as those at Columbia, Cornell, Duke, Penn, Stanford, and Yale.

Admission

The 13,959 applicants to the Class of 2023 was a slight increase from the previous two admissions cycles and a huge jump from the roughly 8,000 applications received in 2009. Forty-seven percent of Class of 2023 applicants were accepted, and 23 percent of those admitted chose to attend SMU. Standardized test scores have demonstrated a strong and consistent upward trend over the past decade; in 2008 the average SAT score was 1228, and the average ACT score was 27. Today, the average SAT score is 1378, and the average ACT score is a 31. Almost half finished in the top decile of their high school class, and 79 percent were at least in the top quartile. The average GPA for incoming freshmen is 3.6, and 47 percent of that group possessed a 3.75 or higher.

There are five "very important" factors given top priority by the SMU Admissions Committee: GPA, standardized test scores, rigor of coursework, recommendations, and application essays. That holistic and deep review also grants "important" status to class rank, extracurricular activities, talent/ability, and character/personal qualities. Demonstrated interest is a minor factor in the process as are first-generation and legacy status. Southern Methodist University offers an early decision option with a November 1 deadline that yields an admissions edge; ED applicants get in at a 67 percent clip. SMU also offers a second ED option with a January 15 deadline.

Worth Your Money?

Along with schools like Columbia, USC, and the University of Chicago, Southern Methodist University is near the top of the list of schools with the highest sticker prices in the country. The estimated total cost of attendance for an SMU student in 2020-21 was $79,126. So is a non-Ivy worth an Ivy price tag? Perhaps, especially after accounting for financial aid. The university is generous with merit scholarships, awarding 90 percent of students an average of $28,000 per year. Need-based aid is also disbursed freely to the point that the average cost of attendance, even for families in the highest income bracket, is $44k; families making $75k-$110k pay $32k per year, less than half the list price. Many majors within the Cox School of Business and Lyle School of Engineering start their careers with salaries that will easily cover a reasonable student loan payment.

FINANCIAL
Institutional Type: Private
In-State Tuition: $51,958
Out-of-State Tuition: $51,958
Room & Board: $17,110
Required Fees: $6,582
Books & Supplies: $800

Avg. Need-Based Grant: $21,993
Avg. % of Need Met: 85%

Avg. Merit-Based Award: $28,162
% Receiving (All Freshmen): 90%
% Receiving (Freshmen w/o Need): 65%

Avg. Cumulative Debt: $30,697
% of Students Borrowing: 28%

CAREER
Who Recruits
1. Vira Insight
2. Epsilon
3. Dell
4. Frost Bank
5. Bank of America

Notable Internships
1. Dallas Mavericks
2. Cushman & Wakefield
3. Dell

Top Industries
1. Business
2. Education
3. Operations
4. Engineering
5. Sales

Top Employers
1. Lockheed Martin
2. AT&T
3. EY
4. IBM
5. Accenture

Where Alumni Work
1. Dallas
2. India
3. Houston
4. New York City
5. Austin

Median Earnings
College Scorecard (Early Career): $60,700
PayScale (Early Career): $63,900
PayScale (Mid-Career): $125,500

RANKINGS
Money: 540
U.S. News: 66 (T), National Universities
Wall Street Journal/THE: 88
Washington Monthly: 332, National Universities

COLLEGE OVERLAPS
Baylor University
Texas A&M University - College Station
Texas Christian University
University of Texas at Austin
Vanderbilt University

St. Lawrence University

Canton, New York | 315-229-5261

Want a trivia question that is sure to stump all of your dinner party guests—or more apropos—Zoom meeting attendees? Ask them to name the oldest continuously coeducational university in the United States. The answer—St. Lawrence—is sure to surprise as its small size and Upstate New York location make it among the lesser-known liberal arts gems in the Northeast. Situated closer to Montreal than it is to Buffalo, one could argue that this 164-year old school is harder to get to than get into. While good high school grades are a must, a holistic and test-optional admissions process makes this school accessible to those with a blemish or two on their academic records.

Inside the Classroom

For a school of just 2,400 undergraduates, the size of the campus (1,000 acres) and the scope of the offerings—69 majors and 41 minors—are quite vast. Since long before freshman-exclusive courses/experiences became a fad in the higher education world, St. Lawrence has offered its first-year program, a living and learning program that lets students in the same residence hall develop the "writing, speaking, and research skills that they will need during and after college." Students are also required to take one course in the arts, humanities, social sciences, natural science with lab, quantitative literacy, and environmental literacy. Two courses that cover the category of human diversity: culture and communication are mandated; foreign language courses can count here, but there is no formal language requirement at this university.

Close faculty relationships are a true possibility at a school with an 11:1 student-to-faculty ratio and 63 percent of course sections enrolling fewer than 20 students. Only 1 percent of sections enroll more than 40 students. The average class size is just 17 students. An exceptional 82 percent of 2019 grads participated in an undergraduate research experience. Study abroad programs were taken advantage of by 64 percent of this same cohort. The Class of 2018 collectively participated in 30 off-campus programs in 20 countries.

The most popular area of study is the social sciences (28 percent), with majors in economics, political science, and psychology drawing particularly high praise. Biology is also very strong. As a whole, the quality of under-graduate teaching at SLU gets high marks across the board. However, very few graduates aim for prestigious national scholarships; 58 have won Fulbright Scholarships in the school's history, including one grad in 2019.

Outside the Classroom

You won't find a more cohesive campus environment than that of St. Lawrence where 98 percent of the undergraduate student body resides on the 1,000-acre grounds. There are 16 residence halls and 6 Greek chapters; fraternities draw in 12 percent of the male population, and sororities attract 17 percent of women. A plethora of sports options at various levels leads to a 31 percent participation rate in the 34 varsity and 25+ club and intramural teams. The Saints primarily compete against NCAA Division III competition, but the men's and women's ice hockey teams are at the Division I level. There are more than 150 student-run organizations, and 81 percent of undergrads participate in volunteer work. It's not unusual for the school to host speakers, bands, comedians, or free movie nights. Students rave about the wide-open, beautiful campus with unending greenspace and the excellent food that includes lots of local ingredients and ample vegetarian options. Canton is a town of roughly 6,500 people and is not located near any major American cities, but the Canadian border is just a half hour away, and Montreal and Ottawa make for popular road trips.

Career Services

With five professional employees who work in advising and employer engagement capacities, the St. Lawrence Career Services is able to meet the needs of this college with a 478:1 counselor-to-student ratio. There are an additional 12 upperclassmen who serve as career services interns. Personalized service and one-on-one connections are encouraged, as is participation in SLU's Signature Career Programs that include Shadow-A-Saint, LINC Mentor Program, Career Success Workshops for Sophomores, and Laurentians in Residence, a program that brings alumni and parent leaders to campus for presentations and mentoring arrangements.

Over the course of your four years at the university, you will have the option to participate in SLU Connect, a program that connects students to alumni in high-powered professions in Boston; San Francisco; Albany, New York; Burlington, Vermont; and even Big Sky, Montana. The office also provides access to micro-internships, paid 5-40-hour professional assignments that allow students to dip their toes into a corporate setting. As a result of this variety of offerings, 73 percent of graduates complete at least one internship, and 99 percent engage in some type of experiential learning. Three-fifths of all freshmen report visiting the Career Services office at least once; 75 percent visit as sophomores. Clearly, SLU does a commendable job providing counseling as well as accessible opportunities for hands-on experiences to their undergraduates.

St. Lawrence University

E-mail: admissions@stlawu.edu | Website: www.stlawu.edu

Professional Outcomes

A solid 94 percent of 2019 graduates found their way to the world of employment or a graduate/professional program within 7-10 months of leaving the university. The most common sector was finance (14 percent), followed by health services (8 percent), K-12 education (6 percent), higher education (5 percent), and research science (4 percent). More than 20 alumni can be found in the offices of Morgan Stanley, Fidelity Investments, UBS, Wells Fargo, JPMorgan Chase, Goldman Sachs, and Northwestern Mutual. The most common locations for Saints to relocate postgraduation are New York City; Boston; Utica, NY; Burlington, Vermont; and Washington, DC. The median starting salary for all graduates was $44,500 in 2018.

St. Lawrence alumni who pursue an advanced degree typically remain in the Northeast, often in the state of New York. The most commonly attended graduate schools are (in order) St Lawrence itself, Syracuse University, the University of Vermont, Boston University, and Northeastern University, along with four different SUNY campuses. Within five years of receiving their bachelor's degrees, 43 percent of graduates report engaging in further formal study. Twenty-five students who graduated between 2015 and 2019 went on to enter medical school, and 41 graduates were pursuing their law degrees in that same time frame.

Admission

St. Lawrence's acceptance rate was 42 percent of the 6,998 applicants for the Class of 2019. A decade ago, there were only approximately 4,300 applicants and a very similar acceptance rate. An early adopter of a test-optional policy (2006), the school still sees 55 percent of admitted applicants submit SAT results, and 20 percent include an ACT score with their application. The mid-50th percentile is 1170-1340 on the SAT and 24-30 on the ACT. Only 10 percent of those submitting SAT scores earned 1400 or above; 5 percent earned below 1000. Forty-two percent of 2019-20 freshmen placed in the top 10 percent of their high school class, and 77 percent landed in the top quartile. Slightly less than one quarter earned a 4.0 GPA or better, and two thirds held at least a 3.5.

When St. Lawrence assures applicants that its admissions review process is "holistic and each application is carefully reviewed," it is more than just lip service. Rigor of high school coursework, GPA, essays, recommendations, and character/personal qualities are rated as "highly important," and class rank, the interview, and extracurricular involvement are "important." Being a test-optional institution, St. Lawrence will consider SAT/ACT results along with factors like talent/ability, first-generation status, alumni relation, geographical residence, volunteer and paid work experience, and demonstrated interest. The last factor is notable because only 20 percent of those accepted to the university actually go on to enroll. Those who show their devotion through a binding early decision process are accepted at a very friendly 74 percent clip.

Worth Your Money?

With a healthy endowment of $315 million dollars, St. Lawrence is able to award some level of financial help to 99 percent of its undergraduates. The average grant to freshmen is almost $38,000, which helps to bring the $70,000+ annual cost of attendance down to a range that is competitive with many public institutions. While this liberal arts school doesn't churn out massive numbers of engineers and finance majors who typically help a school reach a high median starting salary, a St. Lawrence education, with aid, is a unique and personalized enough experience to be worth the cost for most students.

FINANCIAL
Institutional Type: Private
In-State Tuition: $58,750
Out-of-State Tuition: $58,750
Room & Board: $15,150
Required Fees: $0
Books & Supplies: $750

Avg. Need-Based Grant: $43,621
Avg. % of Need Met: 89%

Avg. Merit-Based Award: $19,522
% Receiving (All Freshmen): 40%
% Receiving (Freshmen w/o Need): 19%

Avg. Cumulative Debt: $32,390
% of Students Borrowing: 60%

CAREER
Who Recruits
1. Wayfair
2. UBS
3. Northwestern Mutual
4. Brown Brothers Harriman
5. Morgan Stanley

Notable Internships
1. Center for American Progress
2. EarthWatch Institute
3. Morgan Stanley

Top Industries
1. Business
2. Education
3. Operations
4. Sales
5. Social Services

Top Employers
1. Morgan Stanley
2. Fidelity Investments
3. Clarkson University
4. UBS
5. Wells Fargo

Where Alumni Work
1. New York City
2. Boston
3. Burlington, VT
4. Washington DC
5. Albany, NY

Median Earnings
College Scorecard (Early Career): $50,100
PayScale (Early Career): $57,900
PayScale (Mid-Career): $119,000

RANKINGS
Money: 138
U.S. News: 54 (T), Liberal Arts Colleges
Wall Street Journal/THE: 187 (T)
Washington Monthly: 99, Liberal Arts Colleges

COLLEGE OVERLAPS
Colby College
Hamilton College
Hobart and William Smith Colleges
Union College (NY)
University of Vermont

St. Olaf College

Northfield, Minnesota | 507-786-3025

ADMISSION
Admission Rate: 48%
Admission Rate - Men: 47%
Admission Rate - Women: 48%
EA Admission Rate: Not Offered
ED Admission Rate: 76%
ED Admits as % of Total Admits: 11%
Admission Rate (5-Year Trend): -12%
% of Admits Attending (Yield): 30%
Transfer Admission Rate: 35%

SAT Reading/Writing (Middle 50%): 590-710
SAT Math (Middle 50%): 600-720
ACT Composite (Middle 50%): 26-32

% Graduated in Top 10% of HS Class: 46%
% Graduated in Top 25% of HS Class: 74%
% Graduated in Top 50% of HS Class: 96%

Demonstrated Interest: Considered
Legacy Status: Considered
Admission Interview Offered: Yes

ENROLLMENT
Total Undergraduate Enrollment: 3,072
% Part-Time: 1%
% Male: 42%
% Female: 58%
% Out-of-State: 52%
% Fraternity: Not Offered
% Sorority: Not Offered
% On-Campus (Freshman): 100%
% On-Campus (All Undergraduate): 95%

% African-American: 3%
% Asian: 7%
% Hispanic: 7%
% White: 68%
% Other: 4%
% Race or Ethnicity Unknown: 0%
% International: 11%
% Low-Income: 14%

ACADEMICS
Student-to-Faculty Ratio: 12 to 1
% of Classes Under 20: 49%
% of Classes 20-49: 49%
% of Classes 50 or More: 3%
% Full-Time Faculty: 65%
% Full-Time Faculty w/ Terminal Degree: 94%

Top Programs
Area Studies
Biology
Chemistry
Economics
Exercise Science
Mathematics
Religion

Retention Rate: 91%
4-Year Graduation Rate: 81%
6-Year Graduation Rate: 86%

Curricular Flexibility: Less Flexible
Academic Rating: ★★★✔

#CollegesWorthYourMoney

Easier to gain acceptance into than neighbor/rival Carleton, St. Olaf College is a strong liberal arts school in Northfield, Minnesota, that is home to 3,072 undergraduates. Just as in 1889 when the college first opened its frost-covered doors, St. Olaf retains a strong affiliation with the Lutheran Church. Running on a 4-1-4 schedule, students take four courses during fourteen-week semesters and one course during the one month in between. Students are nicknamed Oles (pronounced OH-Leez), and they enjoy a robust academic program of eighty-five+ majors, concentrations, and pre-professional options.

Inside the Classroom
General education requirements are extensive, even by the standards of a traditional liberal arts school. This intensive regiment of coursework includes Foundation Studies, which is comprised of a first-year writing seminar, mastery of a foreign language, courses in oral communication and writing in context as well as abstract and quantitative reasoning and studies in physical movement. Freshman courses in biblical studies and theology are also mandates as well as a litany of courses across the humanities, natural sciences, and social sciences.

With a 12:1 student-to-faculty ratio and no graduate students there is ample room for mentor-mentee relationships to flourish. Forty-nine percent of all course sections contain fewer than twenty students. Graduation surveys reveal students who are immensely satisfied with the St. Olaf academic experience; 94 percent agreed that faculty made them better critical thinkers. There are multiple avenues in which students can pursue research experiences. On-campus options include applying for ten-week summer stints through the Collaborative Undergraduate Research & Inquiry program, a Steen Fellowship to encourage independent research, or an independent study conducted for credit. Studying abroad is a staple of life for Oles; three-quarters spend a semester studying off campus, the vast majority at an international locale.

The most commonly conferred degrees are in economics, biology, psychology, mathematics, and the visual and performing arts. Many departments at St. Olaf have exceptional national reputations including religion, mathematics, and chemistry. The most coveted fellowship and scholarship organizations definitely pay special attention to graduates of this institution. In fact, the college has produced an astounding five Rhodes Scholars since 1995 and Fulbright Scholarships were awarded to seven members of the Class of 2019.

Outside the Classroom
With 95 percent of students living on campus or in college-owned housing nearby, the student body functions as a fairly cohesive unit. Students remain on campus for a variety of sound reasons. For one, dining hall cuisine is regularly rated among the country's best, and for another, no Greek life exists at St. Olaf. So-called "Honor Houses" are the closest thing to frats or sororities, but they are residences based on common academic areas of study or special interests. There are twenty-one such houses at the college, including ones focused on common bonds such as Norwegian languages, Muslim identity, or the environment. The Oles field twenty-five athletic teams (13 men's, 12 women's) that compete in NCAA Division III. A hefty portion of the student body—500 undergraduates—are members of a varsity sports squad. There are more than 200 clubs active at the school. Those who enjoy the outdoor life will adore the 325 adjoining acres of woodlands, wetlands, and prairie that students can freely roam. The school's location near Carleton College opens additional chances for socialization as does the fact that Minneapolis and St. Paul are both less than fifty miles away.

Career Services
The Piper Center for Vocation and Career is staffed by thirteen professional employees serving roles such as counselor, alumni engagement, and employer relations. Additionally, the college trains 25+ peer advisors to add an extra layer of student support. Counting only professional employees, St. Olaf sports a student-to-advisor ratio of 236:1, lower than the average school included in this book. Thanks to those favorable numbers, 72 percent of undergraduates met with either a career coach or peer advisor in the 2018-19 academic year. Among graduates, more than 90 percent reported they were adequately prepared for life beyond college.

On-campus events include an annual Recruiting Showcase featuring some of the top corporate employers of Oles and a Government and Nonprofit Career Fair open to all Minnesota college students. The college also participates in the statewide Private College and Career Fair that features 260+ employers. Opportunities for experiential learning are wide ranging and taken advantage of by most students as 92 percent of 2019 percent of undergrads completed at least one internship, job-shadowing, or field experience over the course of their four years on campus. A tightknit and helpful alumni base regularly avail themselves to assist current undergrads. Alumni events like Ole Biz, which brings over a hundred graduates to Minneapolis, invites current students to learn about ten industries while networking their hearts out. The Piper Center excels in setting students up with meaningful experiences and important alumni connections, and it has a direct line to many of the region's largest corporate employers.

Professional Outcomes

In 2019, only five percent of grads were still seeking their next step six months after graduation; the rest had entered the workforce or graduate school. The great majority of alumni remain in the Greater Minneapolis-St. Paul area (more than ten times as many as relocate to second-choice destination Chicago), which impacts what companies hire the most Oles. To name names, alumni have the largest representation at Target, United-Health Group, the Mayo Clinic, Wells Fargo, Medtronic, 3M, and US Bank. Midcareer median salaries fall in the same range as other Minnesota academic powerhouses Carleton and Macalester.

While many pursuing higher education choose to stay in the Midwest, every year the college sends at least one graduate to the likes of Columbia, Yale, or Cornell to pursue an advanced degree. St. Olaf students in a premed area of concentration and who have a GPA of 3.59 or better gain acceptance to medical school at a solid 75 percent clip. The most commonly attended medical school is the University of Minnesota-Twin Cities, but recent grads have gone on to study at the University of Michigan Medical School, Washington University in St. Louis School of Medicine, and Wake Forest Medical School. Law school applicants have gone on to elite universities including Harvard, Emory, Georgetown, and UCLA. The school is also a top producer of future PhDs, placing 25th among all colleges in the percentage of graduates who go on to earn doctoral degrees in their respective fields.

Admission

Forty-eight percent of those who applied for a position in St. Olaf's Class of 2023 were granted acceptance. One decade ago, the acceptance rate was 59 percent of an applicant pool that was only one-third the size of the 2023 class. Attending freshmen in the 2019-20 school year possessed a middle-50 percent SAT range of 1220-1410 and a wide-ranging ACT composite of 26-32. The ACT was, by far, the test of choice; it was submitted by 74 percent of applicants. Just over 50 percent of freshmen boasted GPAs of over 3.75, but close to one-quarter of attendees had below a 3.5. Forty-six percent fell within the top decile of their graduating class, and 74 percent placed in the top quarter.

Rigorous coursework, GPA, and the application essay are of paramount importance to the admissions committee followed by a second tier of factors including standardized test scores, class rank, recommendations, an interview, extracurricular activities, talent/ability, and character/personal qualities. Showing a commitment to the college is rewarded on the admissions end; early decision applicants were accepted at a friendly rate of 76 percent. Overall, St. Olaf has a yield rate of 30 percent, which means that just under one-in-three accepted students actually go on to enroll. Earning admission into St. Olaf is more than a simple numbers game; a holistic approach by the committee rewards "smart, ambitious, creative people who want to be challenged." Even if you lack perfect grades or ACT scores, a candidate can still make a compelling case for acceptance into this fine Midwestern liberal arts institution.

Worth Your Money?

Total cost of attendance at St. Olaf will run you just over $65,000 per year, yet few pay that amount. Two-thirds of Oles receive some form of financial aid, and the overall value of each need-based award is $40k, ultimately making this school affordable for those with financial need. Considering the high rate of internship participation, close contact with major companies, and accessible faculty, St. Olaf is likely worth your money.

FINANCIAL
Institutional Type: Private
In-State Tuition: $51,450
Out-of-State Tuition: $51,450
Room & Board: $11,660
Required Fees: $0
Books & Supplies: $1,000

Avg. Need-Based Grant: $39,727
Avg. % of Need Met: 100%

Avg. Merit-Based Award: $18,188
% Receiving (All Freshmen): 48%
% Receiving (Freshmen w/o Need): 20%

Avg. Cumulative Debt: $28,950
% of Students Borrowing: 60%

CAREER
Who Recruits
1. Lewin Group
2. Cerner Corporation
3. Thomson Reuters
4. North Sky Capital
5. MatrixCare

Notable Internships
1. Game Informer Magazine
2. MITRE
3. 9/11 Tribute Museum

Top Industries
1. Education
2. Business
3. Operations
4. Social Services
5. Healthcare

Top Employers
1. UnitedHealth Group
2. Target
3. Mayo Clinic
4. Wells Fargo
5. U.S. Bank

Where Alumni Work
1. Minneapolis
2. Chicago
3. New York City
4. San Francisco
5. Denver

Median Earnings
College Scorecard (Early Career): $50,400
PayScale (Early Career): $57,300
PayScale (Mid-Career): $109,800

RANKINGS
Money: 100
U.S. News: 67 (T), Liberal Arts Colleges
Wall Street Journal/THE: 149 (T)
Washington Monthly: 72, Liberal Arts Colleges

COLLEGE OVERLAPS
Carleton College
Gustavus Adolphus College
Lawrence University
Macalester College
University of Minnesota - Twin Cities

Stanford, California | 650-723-2091

Fittingly situated in the heart of Silicon Valley sits one of the tech industry's top feeder schools and one of the premier research universities in the world. Among Stanford's many quantifiable boasts and brags are the lowest acceptance rate in the country, the nation's second-largest college endowment, the best all-around athletic department in the country, the second-highest total of affiliate-won Nobel Prizes, and the highest graduate starting salaries for any non-STEM-exclusive institution. At Stanford, the list of accomplishments could go longer than a vintage John Elway (an alum) deep ball.

Inside the Classroom

Just shy of 7,000 undergrads and another 10,000+ graduate students occupy this expansive campus that is the sixth largest in the nation. For perspective on its size, 19,000 bicycle parking spots can be found on university grounds. There are three undergraduate schools at Stanford: The School of Humanities & Sciences that houses the majority of the student body, the School of Engineering, and the School of Earth, Energy, and Environmental Sciences. All undergraduates must complete three courses in writing and rhetoric, one year of a foreign language, and a freshman course entitled Thinking Matters in which students choose from a full menu of courses covering a host of intellectual topics from Race in American Memory to How Does Your Brain Work? The Ways of Thinking, Ways of Doing requirement comprises eleven additional courses in ethical reasoning, applied quantitative reasoning, and aesthetic and interpretive inquiry. Further requirements are major specific. Some programs require a senior capstone, research component, practicum or, for foreign language, an oral proficiency review.

A virtually unmatched 5:1 student-to-faculty ratio sets students up for a personalized classroom experience and an incredible amount of face time with some of the leaders in their respective fields. Sixty-nine percent of classes have fewer than twenty students, and 35 percent have a single-digit enrollment. Stanford puts unmatched resources behind undergraduate research; more than $5.6 million in grant funding is allocated each year to support roughly 1,000 student research projects. Close to 900 students study abroad annually through the Bing Overseas Studies Program in eleven international cities.

The School of Engineering is one of the best in the world; all of its sub disciplines sit atop any list of best engineering programs. Programs in computer science, physics, mathematics, international relations and economics are arguably the best anywhere. In terms of sheer volume, the greatest number of degrees are conferred each year in engineering (19 percent), computer science (17 percent), interdisciplinary studies (15 percent), and the social sciences (13 percent). With ninety-six Rhodes Scholars to its credit, Stanford ranks fourth on the all-time list. In 2020, the school produced twenty-one Fulbright winners, four Schwartzman Scholars, two Truman Scholars, and in recent years has produced a multitude of winners of just about any prestigious post-grad scholarship one can name.

Outside the Classroom

Stanford is where you can receive a world-class education and experience the excitement of a typical college setting. The Cardinal have a rich sports tradition with its sixteen men's and twenty women's NCAA Division I teams. The excellence the university expects in the classroom in matched on the field; the Athletic Department has won the Directors' Cup, given to the most successful college athletic program, for twenty-four consecutive years, and at least one team has won an NCAA national championship in each of the last forty-two years. With an additional forty club teams, over 900 undergraduates compete in intercollegiate athletics. Fraternities and sororities are thriving on campus with an 18-24 percent participation rate across twenty-nine Greek organizations. Over 600 student organizations are active including sixty student-led community service organizations, the widely circulated Stanford Daily, and a vast array of ethnic/cultural groups. Ninety-two percent of undergrads live on Stanford's sprawling 8,180-acre campus in the heart of the San Francisco Peninsula. The surrounding area of Palo Alto, America's wealthiest town, is full of natural and manmade beauty and any cultural, culinary, or entertainment delight one could seek. The university itself puts its bottomless endowment to use with immaculately manicured grounds, well-maintained dorms, state-of-the-art recreational facilities, and restaurant-quality campus dining options. Simply put, the campus aesthetics at Stanford are every bit as breathtaking as the quality of its academics.

Career Services

BEAM (Bridging Education, Ambition, & Meaningful Work) is Stanford's career services office. It employs twenty-eight professional staff members who work in the Career Catalysts, Career Communities, and Career Ventures divisions. The 250:1 student-to-advisor ratio is lower than the average school featured in this guide. The three aforementioned divisions speak to the unique and comprehensive career services approach at Stanford. There is a sincere effort to get students to align their career interests with their identities and passions, cultivate a personalized network of mentors/guides, and connect directly with employers. BEAM does a fantastic job with all three phases of that process.

In a given year, the career services staff facilitated roughly 20,000 "meaningful connections" between current students and alumni/industry professionals and initiate 37,000+ "meaningful opportunities" for undergraduates to carve out a pathway toward their employment or graduate school destination. BEAM sponsors fourteen to sixteen career fairs per year, posts over 10,000 job and internship opportunities on Handshake, and runs the superb Stanford Alumni Mentoring program. Major companies recruit on campus on a constant basis because (a) of the incredible talent pool and (b) the school is located in Silicon Valley, home to most of the world's largest tech companies. Stanford facilitates internships at over 700 unique sites, and close to half of all students complete two internships as part of their undergraduate education; two-thirds complete at least one. With a robust career services department and spectacular graduate outcomes (see below), BEAM earns every ounce of its stellar reputation.

Professional Outcomes
Stanford grads entering the working world flock to three major industries in equal distribution: business/finance/consulting/retail (19 percent); computer, IT (19 percent); and public policy and service, international affairs (19 percent). Among the companies employing the largest number of recent Stanford alums are Accenture, Apple, Bain, Cisco, Facebook, Goldman Sachs, Google, McKinsey, Microsoft, and SpaceX. Other companies that employ hundreds of Cardinal alums include LinkedIn, Uber, Lyft, Salesforce, and Airbnb. California, New York, Massachusetts, Texas, DC, and Washington state were the top six destinations for recent grads. Starting salaries for Stanford grads are among the highest in the country.

Those who are graduate school bound often stay at Stanford with professors they already have a close working relationship with. The other dozen most popular universities attended by recent graduates include Oxford, Harvard, MIT, Yale, Columbia, the University of Chicago, and Johns Hopkins. You would be hard-pressed to find a top-ranked law or medical school that did not have Stanford alums among its ranks. Last year, 213 Stanford graduates applied to medical school, and acceptance rates were nearly double the national average. In sum, if you get an undergraduate degree from Stanford, your opportunities for continuing your education will be limitless.

Admission
The toughest school to get into in the United States doesn't appear to be getting less selective anytime soon. In 2019, a meager 4.3 percent of the 47,498 accomplished teens vying for a place in the Class of 2023 were offered admission. The profile of the average current student is about what you would expect at the university with the lowest acceptance rate in the country. The middle-50 percent SAT range for the Class of 2023 was 1440-1550 and 32-35 on the ACT. If you want to become a member of the Cardinal club, near-perfect grades are a prerequisite. Ninety-five percent of incoming freshmen had a GPA of a 4.0 or above in high school, although it is important to highlight that only 7 percent of applicants meeting that criterion were accepted, and only 1 percent of those with a 3.7 or lower made the cut. Almost all freshmen—96 percent—ranked in the top 10 percent of their high school class.

There are nine factors considered "very important" to the admissions office: rigor of courses, GPA, class rank, standardized test scores, essays, recommendations, extracurricular activities, talent/ability, and character/personal qualities. The last three from that list are of particular importance given that the first five will likely be similarly perfect from the bulk of those applying. First-generation status is not listed as a primary factor, but a healthy 18 percent of those admitted in 2019-20 are looking to become the first in their family to earn a degree. Stanford admissions has become the ultimate valedictorian meat grinder, now possessing a lower admission rate than Harvard. With so many top-shelf applicants for a limited number of spots, it helps to have a hook—an area in which you truly excel.

Worth Your Money?
An endowment of over $27 billion helps the school cover all of the determined need of its undergraduate students. The average need-based grant is for $55k+, which helps knock the $78,218 cost of attendance down to a manageable sum for the approximately 50 percent of students who qualify. Of course, Stanford is one of those rare universities that would be worth just about any cost.

FINANCIAL
Institutional Type: Private
In-State Tuition: $55,473
Out-of-State Tuition: $55,473
Room & Board: $17,255
Required Fees: $696
Books & Supplies: $1,290

Avg. Need-Based Grant: $55,394
Avg. % of Need Met: 100%

Avg. Merit-Based Award: $0
% Receiving (All Freshmen): 0%
% Receiving (Freshmen w/o Need): 0%

Avg. Cumulative Debt: $22,897
% of Students Borrowing: 17%

CAREER
Who Recruits
1. Masimo
2. Wealthfront
3. Calico
4. Asurion
5. Los Angeles Dodgers

Notable Internships
1. Citadel
2. SpaceX
3. United Nations

Top Industries
1. Business
2. Engineering
3. Education
4. Research
5. Operations

Top Employers
1. Google
2. Apple
3. Facebook
4. Microsoft
5. Amazon

Where Alumni Work
1. San Francisco
2. New York City
3. Los Angeles
4. Seattle
5. Boston

Median Earnings
College Scorecard (Early Career): $94,000
PayScale (Early Career): $86,800
PayScale (Mid-Career): $164,200

RANKINGS
Money: 2
U.S. News: 6 (T), National Universities
Wall Street Journal/THE: 4
Washington Monthly: 1, National Universities

COLLEGE OVERLAPS
Columbia University
Harvard University
Massachusetts Institute of Technology
Princeton University
Yale University

Stevens Institute of Technology

Hoboken, New Jersey | 201-216-5194

ADMISSION
Admission Rate: 40%
Admission Rate - Men: 38%
Admission Rate - Women: 44%
EA Admission Rate: Not Offered
ED Admission Rate: 58%
ED Admits as % of Total Admits: 9%
Admission Rate (5-Year Trend): -4%
% of Admits Attending (Yield): 23%
Transfer Admission Rate: 28%

SAT Reading/Writing (Middle 50%): 640-720
SAT Math (Middle 50%): 700-780
ACT Composite (Middle 50%): 31-34

% Graduated in Top 10% of HS Class: 74%
% Graduated in Top 25% of HS Class: 94%
% Graduated in Top 50% of HS Class: 100%

Demonstrated Interest: Considered
Legacy Status: Considered
Admission Interview Offered: Yes

ENROLLMENT
Total Undergraduate Enrollment: 3,659
% Part-Time: <1%
% Male: 71%
% Female: 29%
% Out-of-State: 38%
% Fraternity: 27%
% Sorority: 36%
% On-Campus (Freshman): 88%
% On-Campus (All Undergraduate): 51%

% African-American: 2%
% Asian: 17%
% Hispanic: 12%
% White: 62%
% Other: 0%
% Race or Ethnicity Unknown: 4%
% International: 3%
% Low-Income: 14%

ACADEMICS
Student-to-Faculty Ratio: 11 to 1
% of Classes Under 20: 46%
% of Classes 20-49: 44%
% of Classes 50 or More: 10%
% Full-Time Faculty: 67%
% Full-Time Faculty w/ Terminal Degree: 96%

Top Programs
Business & Technology
Chemical Biology
Computer Science
Cybersecurity
Engineering
Quantitative Finance

Retention Rate: 94%
4-Year Graduation Rate: 46%
6-Year Graduation Rate: 85%

Curricular Flexibility: Somewhat Flexible
Academic Rating: ★★★★

#CollegesWorthYourMoney

With the Manhattan skyline visible across the Hudson River, the Stevens Institute of Technology's Hoboken, New Jersey, campus occupies prime real estate—but the school is not merely about its breathtaking panoramic view of the Big Apple. For this small but growing private research institution with a focus on engineering and business, proximity to New York City is an asset that translates into strong corporate connections, endless internship and co-op opportunities and, ultimately, exceptional job placement rates at top companies.

Inside the Classroom

There are thirty-five undergraduate majors at Stevens across four undergraduate schools: the Schaefer School of Engineering & Science, the School of Business, the College of Arts and Letters, and the School of Systems and Enterprises. There is no core curriculum at Stevens as every set of requirements is school and major dependent. The only common academic experiences for all undergrads is a sequence of two College of Arts and Letters courses that every freshman must complete—Writing and Communications and Colloquium: Knowledge, Nature, Culture. Some engineering students complete a capstone senior design project that is often conducted in coordination with an industry sponsor.

Two-thirds of course sections have an enrollment of under thirty students, and 46 percent of sections contain fewer than twenty students. The student-to-faculty ratio is 10:1 but, of course, with over 3,400 graduate students some attention is diverted in their direction. Undergraduate research possibilities are plentiful and varied. Roughly 10 percent of each freshman class are invited to become Stevens Scholars, which guarantees a paid summer research experience with a faculty member. As a research university, the school also has close ties to industry and federally run labs that can lead to many additional research opportunities. Co-op experiences that also can involve research are embarked upon by slightly less than one-third of students. A number of study abroad programs are available with some of the most popular destinations being the United Kingdom, Belgium, Jamaica, China, Spain, Thailand, and Greece.

Engineering is, by far, the most common undergraduate major, and all programs within the Schaefer School of Engineering & Science are strong. Programs in computer science, cybersecurity, and quantitative finance also receive praise. Over 80 percent of the degrees granted at Stevens are in a STEM field, and most of the remaining grads major in business, finance, and accounting. It is uncommon for Stevens grads to pursue national fellowships or scholarships as they are traditionally focused on career or graduate school as their next step after graduation.

Outside the Classroom

A relatively low 51 percent of the undergraduate student body resides on campus in college-owned housing. Greek life is a major player on campus as fraternities and sororities attract 27 percent and 36 percent of students, respectively. Greek houses are community service oriented and work closely with charitable organizations including Big Brothers Big Sisters, the Hoboken Shelter, and the Food Bank of New Jersey. Student-athletes participate on one of twenty-six NCAA Division III varsity athletic teams known as the Ducks. There are an additional sixteen intercollegiate club sports teams and a robust intramural program featuring flag football, three-on-three basketball, and floor hockey. There are over one hundred clubs and activities to join. For the extremely adventurous, the Outdoor Adventure Program plans trips to locales like Costa Rica, Utah, and the Grand Canyon. The Stevens Honor System is taken seriously and permeates beyond academic life into the social realm. Students publish a weekly student newspaper and run campus radio and television stations. Hoboken is only one jam-packed square mile of land, making it immensely walkable. For those of age, the town holds the distinction of most bars per capita. Running alongside the Hudson is an aesthetically pleasing option and, perhaps best of all, New York City is only fifteen minutes away.

Career Services

The Stevens Career Center is made up of eight professional employees who work with undergraduate students as advisors, cooperative education coordinators, or in a director/assistant director capacity; two additional members work exclusively with the university's graduate students. The student-to-advisor ratio of 457:1, which ranks in the average range when compared against other schools featured in this guide, yet Stevens' career services offerings are as strong as they come. This is a career services office that works hard to forge corporate connections and, as a result, 80 percent of seniors have secured competitive employment prior to graduation.

In a given school year, more than 300 companies recruit on campus, a phenomenal number for a school of any size, but for a small university like Stevens, that figure is astounding. It is rare for Stevens students to not complete at least one internship over their four years of study. Ninety percent of undergrads in the School of Business land internships. The co-op track is selected by 30 percent of all students, and that entails working a forty-hour paid work week beginning in the sophomore year. Three annual career fairs in September, December, and March each attract about 900 students. The March Career Fair alone attracts 125 companies, including the likes of IBM, Verizon, and JPMorgan Chase.

Professional Outcomes

The Class of 2019 found employment or graduate school homes at a 96 percent rate within six months of receiving their degree. Engineering students entered the fields of finance (22 percent), manufacturing (14 percent), technology (14 percent), and engineering services (12 percent). Employers that hired the greatest number of Class of 2019 Stevens grads included Google, EY, Merck, Prudential, and PwC. Massive numbers of alumni (from all graduating years) can be found at major corporations including Verizon, Citi, JPMorgan Chase, Pfizer, and Johnson & Johnson. The average starting salary was $76,400. Many alumni stay local; 50 percent of 2019 graduates remained in New Jersey, and 31 percent crossed the border to New York.

Of the 21 percent of Stevens grads who immediately enroll in graduate school, 93 percent were pursuing master's or PhDs, 6 percent entered medical school, and 1 percent law school. Some enrolled in doctoral programs at prestigious institutions such as Carnegie Mellon, Georgia Tech, Penn, and Vanderbilt and master's programs at Imperial College London, Royal College of Art, Johns Hopkins, and Cornell. The school offers a three-three accelerated law option with Seton Hall University as well as a three-four accelerated med school program with Rutgers University. Recent medical school acceptances include Albert Einstein College of Medicine, Mount Sanai Medical School, and New York University School of Medicine.

Admission

There were 10,475 applications submitted for the 2019-20 freshman class, a sizable increase from the previous year. Of those hopefuls, 40 percent received an offer of acceptance compared to 50 percent a decade prior. The mid-50 percent SAT Range was 1320-1480 and the average high school GPA was 3.86. Over the last couple of years, Stevens accepted and enrolled a much greater number of students than in the past. That expansion meant that close to 1,000 freshmen enrolled into the Class of 2023 while under 700 graduated just two years ago.

In addition to strong grades and standardized test scores, the admissions committee at Stevens is looking for students with a track record of "ingenuity, inventiveness, and inspiration." The school does offer admissions interviews, including via Skype for those living more than 250 miles away. Applying early is strongly encouraged if Stevens is your top choice; the acceptance rate for ED applicants is 58 percent. The acceptance rate for women is six points higher than the acceptance rate for men, yet women still make up less than 30 percent of the student body. Stevens Institute of Technology is gaining in popularity and rapidly expanding its undergraduate enrollment. Its proximity to Manhattan, corporate connections, and stellar graduate outcomes should continue to draw larger numbers of highly qualified applicants.

Worth Your Money?

Is it good news or bad news that the average graduate's starting salary and annual cost of attendance at Stevens are nearly identical? Perhaps the adage, "You have to spend money to make money," helps answer that question. With a COA of $74k and starting salaries around the same, those paying full price will be just fine, even if they have to take out substantial loans to attend. The average need-based grant is for only $16k per year, which barely puts a dent in the tuition bill. Again, the good news is that strong career outcomes help balance the upfront costs.

FINANCIAL
Institutional Type: Private
In-State Tuition: $55,952
Out-of-State Tuition: $55,952
Room & Board: $16,244
Required Fees: $0
Books & Supplies: $1,200

Avg. Need-Based Grant: $16,113
Avg. % of Need Met: 73%

Avg. Merit-Based Award: $19,575
% Receiving (All Freshmen): 93%
% Receiving (Freshmen w/o Need): 27%

Avg. Cumulative Debt: $37,900
% of Students Borrowing: 70%

CAREER
Who Recruits
1. MThree
2. Nasdaq
3. Bristol-Meyers Squibb
4. Calgene6
5. Nielsen

Notable Internships
1. iHeartMedia
2. Merck
3. Johnson & Johnson

Top Industries
1. Engineering
2. Information Technology
3. Business
4. Operations
5. Project Management

Top Employers
1. Verizon
2. JPMorgan Chase
3. Citi
4. Johnson & JOhnson
5. Pfizer

Where Alumni Work
1. New York City
2. Philadelphia
3. San Francisco
4. Washington DC
5. Boston

Median Earnings
College Scorecard (Early Career): $89,200
PayScale (Early Career): $77,800
PayScale (Mid-Career): $147,700

RANKINGS
Money: 230
U.S. News: 80 (T), National Universities
Wall Street Journal/THE: 174
Washington Monthly: 158, National Universities

COLLEGE OVERLAPS
Lehigh University
Northeastern University
Rensselaer Polytechnic Institute
Rutgers University - New Brunswick
Worcester Polytechnic Institute

Stony Brook University (SUNY)

Stony Brook, New York | 631-632-6868

Like many schools within the SUNY system, Stony Brook University has quietly but steadily ascended into a different tier of public universities since the turn of the millennium. In fact, back in 1999 its acceptance rate was 58 percent, and the 25th percentile SAT score for accepted students was 1050; in recent years the acceptance rate has crept as low as the 30 percent, and the 25th percentile SAT score is now 1250. Shedding its "commuter school" status has been difficult, and 80 percent of undergrads still hail from in state; however, Stony Brook now also attracts students from 85 countries, which would have been an unthinkable feat when it opened as a teacher's college in 1957. In 2019-20, Stony Brook has an undergraduate enrollment of 17,909 as well as an extensive academic menu of sixty+ majors and eighty+ minors.

Inside the Classroom

There are six undergraduate colleges within the university and some, like the College of Leadership and Service or the College of Global Studies are, perhaps, unexpected options. After a two-day compulsory orientation, the journey through the Stony Brook curriculum begins. All told, that will involve checking off double-digits worth of learning objective boxes via courses in the humanities, arts, global affairs, technology, natural science, writing, human behavior, US history, and language. Additional coursework (this can be overlapping) also must fulfill mandates related to interconnectedness, deep understanding, and lifelong learning. In sum, required coursework outside of your major will take a solid three semesters to complete but, on the plus side, there is a great deal of choice within each category for you to pursue elective areas of interest.

A 19:1 student-to-faculty ratio and 8,900 graduate students isn't exactly a recipe for small classes, but undergrads will find themselves in some first-name basis classes with 41 percent of all sections containing nineteen or fewer students. However, there also will be large numbers of face-in-the-crowd experiences because one-quarter of undergraduate sections enroll fifty or more students. That type of environment is not going to spoon feed you with one-on-one faculty mentoring or the chance to participate in undergraduate research, but such experiences are available to those who show determination. In fact, more than 1,500 students have the chance to engage in undergraduate research each year. The rate of study abroad participation is low, but exciting opportunities exist for those who choose to take advantage; the school features a winter program that whisks students to Ecuador and the Galapagos.

A popular and locally well-regarded nursing program leads to the largest number of degrees being conferred in health professions (14 percent). Strong majors in biology (12 percent), engineering (9 percent), business (9 percent), and computer sciences (7 percent) also draw a sizable number of Seawolves (the school's mascot). The school's reputation in the hard sciences, particularly math, chemistry, and biomedical engineering, is aided by the affiliated Stony Brook University Hospital. With regard to prestigious postgraduate scholarships, Stony Brook students have really upped their game in recent years. In 2019, a record-tying eleven Stony Brook seniors earned National Science Foundation Graduate Research Fellowships. It also set an institutional record for the most Fulbright applicants (38), and a phenomenal ten seniors captured the coveted award. Between 2013 and 2018, seven students earned Goldwater Scholarship.

Outside the Classroom

No longer the commuter-heavy school it once was, 82 percent of freshmen and 52 percent of the total student population live on campus in one of thirty residence halls or twenty-three apartment-style buildings. Greek life is close-to-invisible but has a faint heartbeat as 3 percent of men and women join fraternities and sororities. There are approximately 550 student-athletes competing as the Seawolves on seven men's and nine women's NCAA Division I teams. There also are thirty-six club sports teams and intramural options including bowling, beach volleyball, Wiffle ball, and flag football. Over 350 clubs are on tap, including the full array of cultural, dance, charitable, and pre-professional groups. Notably strong organizations include the African Student Union, the College Democrats, and service groups like Camp Kesem and Project Sunshine. For a school without centuries of history under its belt, it does have a number of cool traditions including the annual Roth Pond Regatta where students race themed boats made of cardboard and duct tape across a campus pond. The spacious Long Island campus of 1,039 acres is located midway between Manhattan and Montauk. A train station on campus will take you the sixty miles into New York City. Parks, beaches, and shopping are all within reach, particularly for those with a car (or a friend with a car).

Career Services

The Career Center at Stony Brook University employs sixteen professional staff members who are tasked with career counseling, experiential learning, and employer relations. That translates to a 1,119:1 student-to-counselor ratio, significantly poorer than the average school featured in this guide. Fortunately, that figure does not appear to be preventing the school from reaching the entire undergraduate population. In a single school year, the center conducts 6,000 one-on-one counseling sessions, and career presentations attracted another 7,000 individuals; additionally, it facilitates 900,000 online transactions each year. It is also one of the only career centers to offer two credited courses on career development, one geared toward freshmen and sophomores and the other toward upperclassmen.

Stony Brook's staff helps facilitate roughly 1,200 undergraduate internships each year as well as 2,500 practicums and hundreds of clinical placements. Recently, it has adopted the practice of micro-internships, paid five- to forty-hour placements at companies ranging from Fortune 100 mega-corporations to small tech start-ups. Several job fairs take place each semester, including the Information Technology/Computer Science Job & Internship Fair, Engineering Job & Internship Fair, Business Job & Internship Fair, and the Healthcare, Research, & Human Services Job & Internship Fair. By drawing more than 400 regional and national companies to Stony Brook's campus, the Career Services Office provides ample opportunity for assertive students to make connections and land desirable jobs and internships in New York City and beyond. There were over 1,200 on-campus interviews conducted at the university last year.

Professional Outcomes

Based on the most recent data available, within two years of graduation, 63 percent of Stony Brook graduates are employed, 31 percent have entered graduate/professional school, and 6 percent are presently looking for their next opportunity. Graduates of the arts and sciences, social welfare, and nursing schools had the lowest reported figures of "still searching" alumni while health tech and management students had the highest. The overall median salary was $48,470 with nursing grads earning the most ($66k), followed by those who studied engineering ($60k) and business ($52k). The organizations and companies employing the greatest number of Seawolves are Northwell Health, JPMorgan Chase, Google, Amazon, Citi, Morgan Stanley, Microsoft, Apple, Bloomberg, and Facebook. Over three-quarters of alumni are settled in the Greater New York City area; sizable pockets also can be found in San Francisco, Boston, DC, and Los Angeles.

Among those pursuing further education, common choices include Stony Brook itself, other SUNY or CUNY institutions, and NYC-based powerhouses like Columbia, Fordham, and NYU. Some recent grads also have left the region to attend some of the finest schools in the world including the London School of Economics, Oxford, Caltech, Stanford, Harvard, Duke, the University of Michigan, and Yale. Traditionally, premed students with a 3.5 GPA and an MCAT in the 67th percentile gain acceptance into medical school at a 59 percent clip. The most commonly attended medical schools include Stony Brook, Downstate, Upstate, NYMC, Albany, Buffalo, Eastern Virginia, GW, Howard, Georgetown, Penn State, and Drexel. Law schools attended by recent grads include Hofstra, Boston University, Villanova, Brooklyn Law School, Wake Forest, and the Cardozo School of Law at Yeshiva University.

Admission

Members of the Class of 2023 were admitted at a 44 percent rate, a touch higher than the 39 percent of five years ago. However, the school's popularity is definitely on the rise; it attracts double the number of applicants it did fifteen years ago. Twenty-one percent of those accepted ultimately enroll, a comparable figure to past years. The caliber of freshmen Stony Brook reels in today is higher than ever. The mid-50 percent standardized test score ranges are 1250-1420 on the SAT and 26-32 on the ACT. SAT math scores were notably strong with 52 percent of this group scoring a 700 or above. Fifty-one percent of entering 2019-20 freshmen earned a spot in the top 10 percent of their high school class; 80 percent placed in the top quartile. The average high school GPA was 3.84, and 61 percent sported at least a 3.75.

There is nothing complicated about how admissions decisions are made at Stony Brook. With such a mass of applicants, the admissions committee primarily relies on the hard facts of standardized test scores and GPA within a rigorous course load with a fair number of honors and AP selections. Recommendations and the application essay also are considered "important" to the evaluation process. The application deadline for everyone is January 15 as there are no early action or early decision options.

Worth Your Money?

At $7,070 in pure tuition, students living with their parents and commuting could conceivably graduate from Stony Brook for less than the cost of one semester at NYU. To top it off, 78 percent of freshmen receive financial aid. On the other hand, out-of-staters pay $24,740 in tuition and, with living and meal costs, a degree would likely cost around $180,000 total. For the 80 percent of current undergraduates hailing from the state of New York, this university is an otherworldly bargain; for international students and Americans outside the state, the value would depend on financial aid and whether the program you would pursue would be likely to yield a solid starting salary.

FINANCIAL
Institutional Type: Public
In-State Tuition: $7,070
Out-of-State Tuition: $24,740
Room & Board: $14,278
Required Fees: $3,105
Books & Supplies: $900

Avg. Need-Based Grant: $10,477
Avg. % of Need Met: 65%

Avg. Merit-Based Award: $5,485
% Receiving (All Freshmen): 24%
% Receiving (Freshmen w/o Need): 18%

Avg. Cumulative Debt: $25,678
% of Students Borrowing: 49%

CAREER
Who Recruits
1. Travelers
2. North Atlantic Industries
3. GEICO
4. Broadbridge
5. Canon

Notable Internships
1. Moody's Analytics
2. Bank of America
3. Northrop Grumman

Top Industries
1. Business
2. Education
3. Healthcare
4. Engineering
5. Operations

Top Employers
1. Northwell Health
2. JPMorgan Chase
3. Google
4. Citi
5. Amazon

Where Alumni Work
1. New York City
2. San Francisco
3. Boston
4. Washington DC
5. Los Angeles

Median Earnings
College Scorecard (Early Career): $57,600
PayScale (Early Career): $62,000
PayScale (Mid-Career): $116,900

RANKINGS
Money: 69
U.S. News: 88 (T), National Universities
Wall Street Journal/THE: 124 (T)
Washington Monthly: 97, National Universities

COLLEGE OVERLAPS
Binghamton University (SUNY)
Rutgers University - New Brunswick
University at Albany (SUNY)
University at Buffalo (SUNY)
University of Connecticut

Swarthmore College

Swarthmore, Pennsylvania | 610-328-8300

The average person in the United States may not be fully aware that Swarthmore College, located on Philadelphia's Main Line, is one of, if not the finest liberal arts schools in the entire country. The good news is that top employers and grad schools know Swarthmore's quality well. The 1,667 undergraduate students who attend Swat are an exceptional group, having been among the 9 percent to gain acceptance. The college has never been more difficult to get into as applications have tripled since the turn of the millennium. A quick examination of the superb academics offered at this school is all it takes to fully understand the reasons for the long lines outside the gates.

Inside the Classroom
Despite its small size, the college offers forty undergraduate programs and runs 600+ courses each academic year. A member of the Tri-College Consortium with fellow top institutions Haverford and Bryn Mawr, students can cross-register at those institutions as well as at the University of Pennsylvania. Unusual for a school full of perfect-SAT/valedictorian-types, Swat also offers an honors program that involves highly independent, self-directed study that culminates with a series of oral exams. All undergrads must complete at least three courses in all three divisions: Humanities, Natural Science & Engineering, and Social Sciences. Additional requirements include three courses that are designated "writing intensive," physical education, a foreign language, and one laboratory science course.

Small, seminar-style courses are the norm at Swat—an outstanding 33 percent of sections enroll fewer than ten students, and 73 percent contain a maximum of nineteen students. Overall, the average class size is sixteen. Thanks to an 8:1 student-to-faculty ratio and zero grad students, professors are extremely available in and outside the classroom. As a result, two-thirds of graduates complete at least one undergraduate research or independent creative project, and the college sets aside $800,000 in funding for that express purpose. Forty percent of students elect to study abroad for a semester in one of 300 programs in sixty countries.

Social science degrees are the most commonly conferred, accounting for 26 percent of all 2019 graduates. Future academics and researchers would do well to look at Swat—a whopping 22 percent of graduates go on to earn PhDs. Future businessmen/women, engineers, and techies are also well positioned, given Swat's incredibly strong offerings in economics, engineering, and computer science. When it comes to prestigious scholarships, Swarthmore is winning in disproportionately large numbers. In 2020, four grads/alumni nabbed Fulbright Scholarships, four have been named Rhodes Scholars in the past decade, and undergraduates have won Gaither Fellowships, Watson Fellowships, and Luce Scholarships in recent years.

Outside the Classroom
Swarthmore is a connected and tight-knit campus community where 95 percent of students live in one of eighteen residence halls spread across the college's 425-acre grounds. Greek Life was banned in 2019. There are twenty-two sports teams competing in the NCAA Division III ranks, and roughly 20 percent of the undergraduate student body are members of one of the varsity teams. There are also plenty of intramural and club sports options, including the uber-popular ultimate Frisbee. More than one hundred campus organizations include a number of volunteer groups that attract 60 percent of the student body. The other Tri-Co member schools, Haverford College and Bryn Mawr, are in close proximity, further expanding the social scene at Swarthmore. The town itself is located on the Main Line, which means there is plenty of dining and culture available, pretty much all of which comes at a high cost. Fortunately, everything the city of Philadelphia has to offer isn't far from campus. There is a regional rail line nearby affording students access to the entire city, and West Philadelphia and University City are only about a forty-minute bike ridey.

Career Services
Career Services at Swarthmore College employs seven individuals who specialize in career education, employer relations, and internships and technology. The 238:1 student-to-advisor ratio is better than average when compared to other colleges featured in this guidebook. As a member of the Tri-College Consortium with Haverford and Bryn Mawr as well as the Fall Recruiting Consortium with schools like Brown and William & Mary, Swarthmore students are afforded innumerable opportunities to get face time with the world's leading employers; over eighty companies recruited on campus last year.

One-on-one attention is available for anyone who wishes to take advantage of it. In the 2018-19 school year Swat engaged 65 percent of the total student body, including 71 percent of seniors. The office conducted 1,140 counseling appointments with 474 unique individuals to address areas such as job search (23 percent), interview prep (19 percent), internship search (19 percent), and resume reviews (13 percent). A solid 69 percent of graduates completed at least one internship as part of the undergraduate experience; 40 percent completed one or more externships. Locations for those experiences included some of the most desirable organizations around including The World Bank, the FDA, and Capital One. Visitors to campus include more than one hundred alumni mentors per year and companies like Google, which typically spends two full days at Swat meeting with computer science students. Offering an enviable level of service to its undergraduates and producing across-the-board positive outcomes, this career services office is held in high esteem by our staff.

Professional Outcomes

Sixty-nine percent of Class of 2020 graduates had already entered the workforce shortly after graduation; 77 percent had secured a job prior to completing their degree. Popular industries included financial services (29 percent), technology/engineering (27 percent), and research (21 percent). Google is one of the leading employers of Swarthmore grads followed by Amazon, Goldman Sachs, IBM, and a number of the leading universities in the nation. The cities attracting the highest percentage of Swat alumni were Philadelphia (21 percent), DC (17 percent), New York City (20 percent), San Francisco (10 percent), and Boston (8 percent).

Three-quarters of the 2020 senior class planned to enroll in graduate school within the next five years, and approximately 20 percent do so directly after graduation. Among those pursuing advanced degrees, the most frequently attended institutions were Harvard, Penn, Yale, Princeton, Stanford, MIT, and Cornell—not a shabby top seven. PhDs were pursued by 47 percent of recent grads, while 32 percent entered master's programs, 9 percent matriculated into medical school, and 8 percent headed to law school. The medical school acceptance rate for grads and alumni typically hovers close to 85 percent, an astounding number that is roughly double the national average. The school also has an early acceptance program with Thomas Jefferson University's Sidney Kimmel Medical College. Swarthmore also sports a 97 percent acceptance rate into law schools, and the institutions attended are typically of the elite variety.

Admission

There were 11,442 applications submitted for a spot in the Class of 2023, but only 1,022 were accepted for an acceptance rate of only 9 percent. While the school's acceptance rate has decreased in the last decade (it was 16 percent ten years ago), it's unlikely that anyone will mistake Swat for anything less than one of the most selective schools in the country. Ninety percent of 2019-20 freshmen placed in the top decile of their graduating high school class. Mid-50 percent standardized test scores were 1390-1530 on the SAT and 31-35 on the ACT. For perhaps a better perspective, the median SAT score was 1470 and the median ACT score was 33.

The admissions committee ranks six factors as being of paramount importance in the admissions process: rigor of secondary coursework, class rank, GPA, application essay, recommendations, and character/personal qualities. Test scores and extracurricular activities land in the second tier, but they are serious about extra-curriculars, particularly those involving community service; 36 percent of those accepted into the Class of 2023 were involved with a community, national, or international service organization. In a typical year Swat enjoys a yield rate in excess of 40 percent, meaning that it has no trouble landing a sizable percentage of those offered admission. Legacy candidates make up 10 percent of the admitted Class of 2023 cohort while 27 percent are first generation. If Swarthmore is your top choice, applying early decision is wise; it fills over half of its class through ED, and the acceptance rate is a less cutthroat 24 percent. Unquestionably one of the best liberal arts schools anywhere, Swarthmore will continue to sport an intimidatingly low acceptance rate well into the future.

Worth Your Money?

Swarthmore has pledged to fully meet 100 percent of student need, which helps explain why the 56 percent of undergrads who are eligible receive a sizable average grant of $53k. That certainly makes the $71,110 cost of attendance more manageable for lower-income and middle- class families. On the flip side, Swat rarely awards any merit aid whatsoever, so if your parents earn a nice living, you will likely be paying the sticker price. Of course, for a chance to attend one of the best colleges in the world, that is hardly a bad choice.

FINANCIAL
Institutional Type: Private
In-State Tuition: $54,256
Out-of-State Tuition: $54,256
Room & Board: $16,088
Required Fees: $400
Books & Supplies: $1,400

Avg. Need-Based Grant: $55,233
Avg. % of Need Met: 100%

Avg. Merit-Based Award: $54,256
% Receiving (All Freshmen): 1%
% Receiving (Freshmen w/o Need): 1%

Avg. Cumulative Debt: $24,099
% of Students Borrowing: 26%

CAREER
Who Recruits
1. Foreseter Capital
2. The Brattle Group
3. Apogee Adventures
4. American Enterprise Institute
5. M&T Bank

Notable Internships
1. Salesforce
2. Deutsche Bank
3. Children's Hospital of Philadelphia

Top Industries
1. Education
2. Business
3. Research
4. Media
5. Social Services

Top Employers
1. Google
2. Amazon
3. Goldman Sachs
4. Apple
5. Facebook

Where Alumni Work
1. Philadelphia
2. New York City
3. San Francisco
4. Washington DC
5. Boston

Median Earnings
College Scorecard (Early Career): $56,700
PayScale (Early Career): $69,700
PayScale (Mid-Career): $142,300

RANKINGS
Money: 42
U.S. News: 3, Liberal Arts Colleges
Wall Street Journal/THE: 30
Washington Monthly: 15, Liberal Arts Colleges

COLLEGE OVERLAPS
Brown University
Cornell University
Princeton University
University of Chicago
Williams College

Syracuse University

Syracuse, New York | 315-443-3611

A private research university of over 15,275 undergraduates, Syracuse University has a reputation for more than just its instantly recognizable bright orange colors. The 'Cuse plays home to a diverse group of students, nationally-ranked sports teams, a devoted alumni network, and a broad array of academic offerings, including a number of standout programs.

Inside the Classroom

In total, 200+ majors and one hundred+ minors are spread across ten undergraduate schools/colleges: The School of Architecture, the College of Arts & Sciences, the School of Education, the College of Engineering & Computer Science, the Falk College of Sport & Human Dynamics, the School of Information Studies, the Whitman School of Management, the Maxwell School of Citizenship and Public Affairs, the Newhouse School of Public Communication, and the College of Visual and Performing Arts. Required courses vary significantly by school, but some common areas include two writing-intensive courses, two classes in foreign language, and a smattering of social science, math/science, and humanities selections.

Despite a high number of graduate students also studying at SU, class sizes are kept reasonably low; 59 percent contain twenty students or fewer. A student-to-faculty ratio of 15:1 does mean you are likely to receive some instruction from graduate students/adjuncts along the way. The Undergraduate Research Program runs through the College of Arts & Sciences but is open to all SU students. Willing professors extend offers for research apprenticeships to highly motivated students. Recent student-assisted, faculty-led research projects include Community Theater in Kenya, The Internet's Role in the Political Process, and Cloning of Leukemia Cells. Syracuse Abroad, the university's office of study abroad programs, arranges for 45 percent of undergrads to spend a semester in a foreign land. There are more than a hundred programs in sixty+ countries to choose from.

The most popular majors include communication/journalism (15 percent), the social sciences (14 percent, and business (10 percent). The School of Architecture, Maxwell School of Citizenship and Public Affairs, and Newhouse are all revered names that carry a good deal of weight in their respective fields. Newhouse, in particular, is dominant in the worlds of broadcasting and television/radio/film. Students of all academic backgrounds are competitive in procuring prestigious postgraduate fellowships, albeit at a modest clip. In a typical year, Orange graduates accept at least one Fulbright, Beinecke, SMART, Luce, Mitchell, and Astronaut Scholarship; ten students took home Fulbrights in 2020.

Outside the Classroom

Frigid temperatures and snowy conditions make for long, boring winters in Upstate New York. Thus, like many other institutions in the region, Syracuse receives the designation as a top (if not the top) "party school" on a fair number of lists. The sixty fraternities and sororities are at the heart of the lively social scene. Roughly one-third join a Greek organization. SU offers a big-time sports program with a rabid following. Many join the sea of orange in the Carrier Dome for football and basketball games; in total, there are seven men's and eleven women's NCAA Division I teams. Non-sports activities come in the form of 300+ student-run clubs, including a wide selection of performing arts troupes (there are seven a cappella organizations), pre-professional meet-ups, or the Daily Orange newspaper, which is one of the more widely read campus dailies in the country and a frequent award-winner. On campus, Marshall Street is home to a number of beloved eateries and bars and is rarely quiet. Likewise, the Quad is always abuzz with activity, especially when the weather is decent. The city of Syracuse may not be the most cosmopolitan locale, but it does feature Destiny USA, the nation's sixth largest shopping/entertainment complex, and it's only a short ride from campus.

Career Services

For a school of over 15,000 undergraduates, SU's Career Services Office employs a central staff of five career counseling professionals as well as smaller branch offices housed within the various colleges. Collectively, there are thirty-one full-time staff members working in career services, which equates to a 493:1 student-to-advisor ratio, higher than the average school featured in this guidebook but not all that concerning given the size of the university.

Flagship events include a Local Internship Fair, Fall Career Fair, and Spring Career Fair. Niche events are held year-round by the various colleges to cater to students in particular fields of study. Students can, at any time, utilize OrangeLink to view 6,000+ job and internship postings and keep abreast of on-campus recruiting/interviewing opportunities. Internship procurement varies greatly by school. The Whitman School of Management requires an internship for graduation, and three-quarters of them are paid positions. Many other undergrads must rely on the university's fervent alumni network comprised of about a quarter million people worldwide to land a position. Within Newhouse, companies recruiting on campus include CBS News, Hearst Television, McCann, Instagram, and NBCUniversal. The school does not publish the total number of one-on-one counseling sessions held or the number of on-campus interviews facilitated by career services.

Professional Outcomes

Six months after exiting the Carrier Dome for the final time, 65 percent of Orangemen and women have found employment (90 percent related to their career goals), 20 percent are continuing to graduate school, and 12 percent are seeking employment. The companies employing the most 'Cuse grads include major media/entertainment management companies like Conde Nast, Bloomberg, and Creative Artists Agency as well as big-name corporations like GE, KPMG, EY, Lockheed Martin, and Morgan Stanley. The average starting salary for SU undergraduates across all majors is $54k. Interestingly, due to the nature of the business for which it prepares its students, Newhouse grads earn a mean starting salary of only $47k. Those who studied at the Whitman School of Management, College of Engineering & Computer Science, or School of Information Studies averaged between $60k and $70k. Over 70 percent of graduates tend to remain in the Northeast with the South coming in a distant second, attracting 10 percent of grads.

A fair number of those headed to graduate school remain in New York state. NYU, Hofstra, Fordham, and the University of Buffalo are among the most popular destinations to pursue an advanced degree. Elite universities such as Harvard, Johns Hopkins, Columbia, and the University of Chicago also make the list of most popular graduate schools attended. Examining the past several years of law school admissions data, it is fair to say that Syracuse does not send a high number of graduates to elite law schools. The university does not publish medical school acceptance data, but a review of recent acceptances indicates a strong relationship with nearby SUNY Upstate Medical School. In that time the school also has produced some acceptances into the nation's top medical institutions.

Admission

Most colleges with national name recognition on par with the 'Cuse have experienced an uptick in selectivity since the turn of the millennium. The fact that Syracuse's numbers have held steady for a couple of decades makes it a refreshing oddity. Forty-four percent of applicants are granted acceptance, and the academic profile of the average attendee is strong but not overly intimidating. Standardized test scores do not have to be exceptional to gain acceptance into SU. The median SAT score for the Class of 2023 was 1290 and the median ACT score was 28. Last year's freshman class was comprised of 33 percent of students who finished in the top 10 percent of their high school class; 66 percent were in the top 25 percent, and 9 percent failed to crack the top 50 percent. The average GPA for all 2019-20 freshman was 3.6.

The Newhouse School of Public Communication is more selective than the university at large. The typical student admitted to Newhouse scored over 1300 on the SAT and earned a 3.8 GPA in high school. Whichever school you are applying to, early decision can work to your benefit as ED applicants got in 60 percent of the time in the most recent cycle. However, if you plan on applying ED, make sure you can afford it. While ED applicants get full consideration for financial aid, SU is on the expensive side, so having a chance to compare aid offers can be advantageous. Perfection is not expected by the SU Office of Admissions. It is a selective university that has room for those with B averages and/or non-eye-popping standardized test scores.

Worth Your Money?

With a list-price of $72,282 (annual COA), Syracuse University is not accessible to those on a budget without financial help. Those eligible for need-based grants receive an average award of $38k. Syracuse is worth spending up for if you have the opportunity to enter a top-flight program like Newhouse, and it's a solid choice if your parents are able to pay the full bill. Those on a budget who do not receive a generous aid package may find a better value elsewhere.

FINANCIAL
Institutional Type: Private
In-State Tuition: $55,926
Out-of-State Tuition: $55,926
Room & Board: $16,356
Required Fees: $0
Books & Supplies: $1,564

Avg. Need-Based Grant: $38,431
Avg. % of Need Met: 98%

Avg. Merit-Based Award: $8,990
% Receiving (All Freshmen): 33%
% Receiving (Freshmen w/o Need): 28%

Avg. Cumulative Debt: $37,563
% of Students Borrowing: 54%

CAREER
Who Recruits
1. SmartestEnergy
2. M&T Bank
3. Oppenheimer & Co.
4. City Year
5. General Electric

Notable Internships
1. Gensler
2. WeWork
3. Berksire Hathaway

Top Industries
1. Business
2. Education
3. Operations
4. Arts & Design
5. Media

Top Employers
1. IBM
2. EY
3. Microsoft
4. JPMorgan Chase
5. Amazon

Where Alumni Work
1. New York City
2. Syracuse, NY
3. Boston
4. Washington DC
5. Los Angeles

Median Earnings
College Scorecard (Early Career): $62,100
PayScale (Early Career): $60,500
PayScale (Mid-Career): $112,900

RANKINGS
Money: 239
U.S. News: 58 (T), National Universities
Wall Street Journal/THE: 124 (T)
Washington Monthly: 40, National Universities

COLLEGE OVERLAPS
Binghamton University (SUNY)
Fordham University
Pennsylvania State University - University Park
Rutgers University - New Brunswick
University of Connecticut

Temple University

Philadelphia, Pennsylvania | 215-204-7200

Back in the 1880s, in its earliest iteration, Temple University offered only evening classes for aspiring ministers. Today, it has 100 undergraduate programs spread across eight campuses, including locations in Rome and Japan, the oldest dental school in the country, as well as excellent law and medical schools. (The university health system has eight affiliated hospitals.) Like Penn State and Pitt, Temple is a "state-related university," a hybrid public/private enterprise unique to the Keystone State. The almost 29,000 undergraduate Owls are part of a growing institution that is in a perpetual state of expansion in North Philadelphia and has undergone dozens of major campus-altering renovations and new building projects in the last few years alone.

Inside the Classroom
The university's general education curriculum includes 11 courses and nine areas of learning that are divided in foundation and breadth courses. Intellectual Heritage I & II take students through ancient and modern philosophical texts that have shaped human thinking. Courses in world society, arts, human behavior, race and diversity, US society, science and technology, analytical reading and writing, and quantitative literacy round out the mandated coursework at Temple.

For a large university, a 13:1 student-to-faculty ratio translates to very reasonable class sizes and very few large lecture halls. Forty-one percent of classes have an enrollment of 19 or fewer students, and 70 percent of courses contain no more than 29 undergraduates. Undergraduate research positions are available across all 12 undergraduate schools and colleges, including a seven-month-long funded research experience called the Diamond Scholars Program. Over 200 students present at the annual Symposium for Undergraduate Research and Creativity. The school offers plenty of study abroad opportunities, including its own programs in Spain, Japan, and Italy. Overall, 11 percent of the Class of 2020 took a semester in a foreign country.

The well-regarded Fox School of Business, housed in a state-of-the-art $80 million dollar building, churns out the highest number of graduates, accounting for 26 percent of the total undergraduate degrees conferred. Communication/journalism comes in second at 12 percent, followed by visual and performing arts (7 percent), health professions (7 percent), biology (6 percent), engineering (5 percent), and psychology (5 percent). Other programs that have strong national reputations include criminal justice, public health, and kinesiology. The year 2020 marked Temple's best year ever for Fulbright Scholarships as 16 graduates/alumni captured the prestigious award. In 2017, the school produced its first Rhodes Scholar in school history.

Outside the Classroom
Once a commuter school, Temple now plays host to 79 percent of freshmen, but still just 18 percent of the overall undergraduate student body. Many students come from the city of Philadelphia or the surrounding suburbs, but 28 percent of domestic freshmen last year hailed from out of state. An additional 5 percent of the total population were international students. This diverse student body is not Greek-crazy as only 4 percent of men and 7 percent of women enter fraternities and sororities. On the athletic front, the Owls compete in 19 Division I sports that play in the American Athletic Conference. Home football games are played at Lincoln Financial Field, home of the Philadelphia Eagles. Less serious athletes can join one of the 31 active club sports teams that include fencing, equestrian, paintball, rugby, and ice hockey. More than 300 total student-run organizations make finding something in your niche area of interest quite probable. The school's location in economically disadvantaged North Philadelphia is not appealing to everyone, but the school generally creates a safe environment on campus. The annual number of incidents of robbery or burglary are on par with schools such as Cornell, BU, Duke, and Northwestern, none of which have widespread reputations as "dangerous" locales. Center City Philadelphia is a just a few miles away for those seeking all of the culture, shopping, and dining the city has to offer.

Career Services
The Career Center has 18 full-time, professional staff members, mainly with titles such as career coach, employer outreach specialist, and assistant director of internships and experiential education. There are an additional 14 employees in the Fox School of Business' Center for Student Professional Development, and additional staff members within the College of Engineering and other colleges bring the total number of career services professionals to 35, which equates to an 842:1 ratio, poorer than average when compared to other schools featured in this guide. Regardless, you can always get a same-day appointment for a resume/cover letter review, career path exploration, Handshake intro, or review of a LinkedIn profile. The Temple University Internship Program helps facilitate meaningful, paid, on-campus internships in an area of academic/career interest.

Department-specific career fairs attract many prominent local and national companies to Temple's campus. For example, the College of Science and Technology Spring 2020 Fair featured companies like GSK, Comcast NBCUniversal, Elsevier, and Eurofins Scientific. Philadelphia is home to 14 Fortune 500 Companies, all of whom recruit on campus. These include Toll Brothers, AmerisourceBergen, Campbell's Soup, DuPont, JPMorgan Chase, PwC, Aramark, Cigna, and KPMG also regularly travel to campus to meet with and interview Temple seniors. In sum, Temple has many solid connections to big-time corporate employers and offers personalized career counseling to those who take the initiative to seek it out.

Professional Outcomes

Hundreds of Owl alumni can be found at big-time companies such as Merck, Comcast, Vanguard, GlaxoSmith-Kline, Johnson & Johnson, JPMorgan Chase, and Bristol Myers Squib. The highest percentage of grads reside in Philadelphia, with New York City; Washington, DC; and Los Angeles next in popularity. Within six months of graduating, 91 percent of Fox School of Business graduates are employed or have started their business. The median salary for all graduates of that school was $57,000. According to the College Scorecard put out by the US Department of Education, salaries varied greatly across majors. For example, psychology degree earners had a median salary of $28,500 one month after graduation while computer science degree holders took home a median salary of $63,800.

In 2019-20, there were 138 Temple undergraduates who applied to medical school—the university does not release a precise acceptance rate, but many do funnel into the university's own Lewis Katz School of Medicine. In the last three years, Temple graduates have been accepted into top law schools at Yale University, Harvard University, NYU, UPenn, the University of Chicago, and Northwestern University. In sum, Temple students pursuing advanced degrees do so at a wide range of institutions, from the most selective universities to nearby state schools.

Admission

At present, Temple still accepts more students than it rejects—the admit rate was 60 percent for the Class of 2023—but the academic standards continue to rise. Last year, the average SAT score was 1238, and the average ACT was 27. The mid-50th percentile scores were 1140-1310 and 24-30. The university is test optional, but over three quarters of students submit SAT results. Another 14 percent include the ACT. Students with a B+ average fare well in the admissions process. The mean high school GPA for 2019-20 freshman was 3.54. Thirty-six percent placed in the top 10 percent of their high school class and just over three quarters placed in the top 25 percent. In total, 35,581 first-year applications were received last year, a 130+ percent increase from the turn of the millennium.

While there are holistic elements to the admissions process at Temple, the most important factors are the rigor of your high school coursework and your GPA. Class rank, test scores, the essay, recommendations, extracurriculars, talent/ability/personal qualities, alumni relation, geographical residence, state residency, volunteer work, and paid work experience are all merely "considered" during the evaluation. Getting into Temple's excellent Honors Program requires another level of credentials. For fall 2020, the average Honors student possessed a 3.94 unweighted GPA and a 1448 on the SAT.

Worth Your Money?

As with its state-related compatriots, Temple is not an eye-popping bargain like you can find with public universities in states like California, New York, North Carolina, and Florida. However, Pennsylvania residents will find the $16k in tuition costs and $12k in room and board to be reasonable, by the standards of today's marketplace. For out-of-state students, there are some situations where the $29k tuition price would be a solid value, particularly if pursuing a STEM or business degree.

FINANCIAL
Institutional Type: Public
In-State Tuition: $19,748
Out-of-State Tuition: $34,126
Room & Board: $12,188
Required Fees: $0
Books & Supplies: $1,124

Avg. Need-Based Grant: $10,829
Avg. % of Need Met: 63%

Avg. Merit-Based Award: $6,866
% Receiving (All Freshmen): 61%
% Receiving (Freshmen w/o Need): 14%

Avg. Cumulative Debt: $38,634
% of Students Borrowing: 71%

CAREER
Who Recruits
1. TJX Companies
2. Lockheed Martin
3. Comcast
4. Merck
5. Vanguard

Notable Internships
1. HelloFresh
2. Dow
3. JBT Corporation

Top Industries
1. Business
2. Education
3. Operations
4. Healthcare
5. Sales

Top Employers
1. Merck
2. Penn Medicine
3. Comcast
4. Vanguard
5. GSK

Where Alumni Work
1. Philadelphia
2. New York City
3. Washington DC
4. Los Angeles
5. Allentown, PA

Median Earnings
College Scorecard (Early Career): $50,500
PayScale (Early Career): $54,700
PayScale (Mid-Career): $98,000

RANKINGS
Money: 284
U.S. News: 103 (T), National Universities
Wall Street Journal/THE: 175 (T)
Washington Monthly: 124, National Universities

COLLEGE OVERLAPS
Drexel University
Pennsylvania State University - University Park
Rutgers University - New Brunswick
University of Delaware
University of Pittsburgh - Pittsburgh Campus

Texas A&M University — College Station

College Station, Texas | 979-845-1060

ADMISSION
Admission Rate: 58%
Admission Rate - Men: 58%
Admission Rate - Women: 57%
EA Admission Rate: Not Offered
ED Admission Rate: Not Offered
ED Admits as % of Total Admits: Not Offered
Admission Rate (5-Year Trend): -12%
% of Admits Attending (Yield): 43%
Transfer Admission Rate: 56%

SAT Reading/Writing (Middle 50%): 580-680
SAT Math (Middle 50%): 580-710
ACT Composite (Middle 50%): 26-31

% Graduated in Top 10% of HS Class: 70%
% Graduated in Top 25% of HS Class: 93%
% Graduated in Top 50% of HS Class: 99%

Demonstrated Interest: Considered
Legacy Status: Not Considered
Admission Interview Offered: No

ENROLLMENT
Total Undergraduate Enrollment: 53,791
% Part-Time: 11%
% Male: 53%
% Female: 47%
% Out-of-State: 4%
% Fraternity: 6%
% Sorority: 15%
% On-Campus (Freshman): 72%
% On-Campus (All Undergraduate): 23%

% African-American: 3%
% Asian: 8%
% Hispanic: 25%
% White: 59%
% Other: 3%
% Race or Ethnicity Unknown: 0%
% International: 1%
% Low-Income: 29%

ACADEMICS
Student-to-Faculty Ratio: 19 to 1
% of Classes Under 20: 28%
% of Classes 20-49: 48%
% of Classes 50 or More: 25%
% Full-Time Faculty: 85%
% Full-Time Faculty w/ Terminal Degree: 79%

Top Programs
Agriculture
Architecture
Business
Communication
Engineering
Kinesiology
Political Science

Retention Rate: 93%
4-Year Graduation Rate: 55%
6-Year Graduation Rate: 82%

Curricular Flexibility: Less Flexible
Academic Rating: ★★★

#CollegesWorthYourMoney

You've heard it a million times: "Everything's bigger in Texas." Perhaps the origin of that saying stems from the fact that the state is three times the size of the United Kingdom, or perhaps it was first uttered by a visitor to Texas A&M College Station's gargantuan 5,200-acre campus that is home to 53,791 undergraduates and another 14,000+ graduate and professional degree- seekers, making it one of the largest higher education operations in the United States. With nineteen schools and colleges, 130+ undergraduate degree programs, and an emphasis on agriculture, engineering, and business, this public land-grant university educates an army of future professionals who carry their Aggie pride with them for life.

Inside the Classroom
The Texas Core Curriculum dictates a good amount of the coursework underclassmen must knock out, amounting to forty-two credit hours. Mandates include three classes in life and physical sciences, two classes in each of communication, mathematics, American history, government and political science, and one class in each of language philosophy and culture, creative arts, and the social and behavioral sciences. Collectively, these courses are meant to promote six key skill areas: critical thinking, communication, empirical and quantitative, teamwork, personal responsibility, and social responsibility. Students in the university Honors College are typically required to complete a senior thesis within their departmental home.

Class sizes definitely trend large, not terribly shocking considering the 19:1 student-to-faculty ratio and a graduate school population larger than many entire universities. Only 25 percent of courses enroll fewer than twenty students at A&M, and 35 percent enroll more than forty students. In order to forge personal connections with professors, the LAUNCH program encourages students to apply to participate in undergraduate research during the school year or the summer under the mentorship of a faculty member. Some majors—chemistry, for one— require all students to complete undergraduate research as part of their bachelor's program. A&M excels in facilitating study abroad experiences, sending 5,330 students to 105 countries last year, the most of any public university in the United States.

As the name of the university implies, agriculture and engineering are at the core of what A&M does. Over 19,800 students are presently enrolled in the College of Engineering and 7,400 in the College of Agriculture and Life Sciences. Yet, the College of Liberal Arts (8,500), College of Education and Human Development (6,600), and the Mays Business School (6,300) are sizable presences on campus as well. The business, agriculture, and engineering programs all place well in national rankings and garner deep respect from major national corporations and graduate/professional schools. Considering its size, A&M does not produce a large number of prestigious postgraduate scholarship winners. In 2019, it produced twelve National Science Foundation Graduate Research Fellows, seven Gilman Scholars, and two Critical Language Scholars.

Outside the Classroom
While seventy-two percent of freshmen live on campus, just about everyone else moves into off-campus housing by sophomore year. Housing is not guaranteed to freshmen and is awarded on a first-come, first-served basis. Fortunately, nice and affordable housing in the area is ample, and the school's database, AggieSearch, helps you locate available living spaces. There are 58 Greek organizations on campus that have around a 10 percent participation rate. Athletics are huge with 650 varsity athletes competing in twenty NCAA Division I sports, and the "Twelfth Man," the fan base, is extraordinarily passionate about its teams. For non-superstar athletes, there are thirty-four club sports squads and over 12,000 students participate in intramural sports each year, making it one of the largest programs in the country. The Student Recreation Center contains 400,000 square feet of space for fun and fitness and boasts everything from an archery room to multiple pools. Texas A&M has 1,100 student organizations, making it impossible not to find your niche. An incredible 2,600 undergrads are involved in ROTC, and the Cadet Corps is the largest such group in the country. As the name implies, College Station is a happening college town, brimming with locally famous bars and eateries, particularly within the historic Northgate District. Situated in the so-called Texas Triangle in the central part of the state, major cities like Houston or Austin can be accessed easily by car for a weekend road trip.

Career Services
The Texas A&M Career Center was established in 1939, long before the term "career services" was even a concept at most schools. Including all college-specific career advisors, employer relations, and professional school advising staff members, there are thirty-nine full-time professional staff members (not including office

managers and admin assistants). That works out to a student-to-advisor ratio of 1,379:1, among the highest in this guidebook. Irrespective of that bloated ratio, the A&M career services staff does remarkable things for the second largest undergraduate student body in the United States, and it publishes the numbers to prove it.

In the 2018-19 school year, the A&M Career Center made direct contact with 20,000 students, drew 32,000 individuals to 150 outreach events, and 40,000 to 700 workshops and other career services programs. It posted 59,000 jobs and 12,000 internship opportunities on its online database and, more importantly, it enticed a stupefying 4,000 employers to actively recruit Aggie undergrads. In total, 56 percent of students had an internship, co-op, or study abroad experience while at College Station, and interns worked with 1,000 different companies. Operating on an almost unimaginable scope, Texas A&M's Career Center gets the job done.

Professional Outcomes

On graduation day 2019, a solid 54 percent of soon-to-be degree-holders had already received at least one job offer, 22 percent were heading to graduate/professional school, and 24 percent were still searching for their next career step. Texas A&M supplies a number of major oil, tech, and consulting firms with a hard-to-fathom number of employees. More than 500 Aggies presently work for companies such as ExxonMobil, Halliburton, Chevron, EY, Amazon, Microsoft, Intel, Accenture, and PWC. More than 300 alumni work for Apple, Oracle, and Google. More than 50 engineering students from the Class of 2019 alone were hired by Lockheed Martin. Starting salaries were strong with the average College of Engineering graduate making $70,500, and the average College of Liberal Arts and College of Agriculture & Life Sciences graduate netting $49,500. The vast majority of graduates remain in Texas with Houston, Dallas, College Station, Austin, and San Antonio tops in popularity. However, cities like San Fran, DC, New York, and Denver also have a notable Aggies representation.

Medical and dental school acceptance rates are far above the Texas state average. In 2018, Aggies were admitted to medical school at a 41 percent clip (state average was 32 percent) and to dental school 49 percent of the time (state average was 39 percent). Among those applicants with a 3.6 or higher GPA and a 507+ MCAT score, 77 percent were accepted to medical school. Institutions where recent graduates gained acceptance included Columbia, Cornell, Wake Forest, Yale, Vanderbilt, and Northwestern. Given the engineering focus at A&M, it may surprise you that the school is the eighth largest producer of law students in the entire country. The Class of 2019 collectively applied to 179 law schools and earned admission at 155 of them.

Admission

Texas A&M admitted a favorable 58 percent of those who applied for the 2019-20 freshman class. That group had a mid-50 percent SAT range of 1180-1390 and a 26-31 on the ACT. Texas A&M offers automatic admission for anyone in the top 10 percent of their high school class (public or private), and a hefty number of Class of 2023 members met that standard—70 percent. Overall, 93 percent finished at least in the top 25 percent. Five years ago, the acceptance rate was a more favorable 70 percent and the average applicant had lower standardized test scores and only 78 percent of students placed in the top quartile. Simply put, you'll need better academic credentials to get into A&M today than you would have in the recent past. This is especially so for engineering and business applicants who face the toughest admission odds and who will likely need to possess grades and standardized test scores at or above the 75th percentile.

The admissions office is looking primarily at class rank, standardized test scores, rigor of courses, GPA, extracurricular activities, and talent/ability. It also looks closely at geographical residence, which translates to 95 percent of undergrads presently on the College Station campus hailing from the Lone Star State. With such a large applicant pool, there are no interviews offered. There is no early action or early decision offered either; the deadline is December 1 for every applicant.

Worth Your Money?

Tuition for in-state students is under $13,000, and the total cost of attendance is less than $32k. Combine those extremely fair rates with favorable return on investment figures, and A&M is clearly one of the great values in higher education. A nonresident will pay nearly twice as much, but if you lack better in-state options close to home, a business or engineering degree from this institution will still pay for itself.

FINANCIAL
Institutional Type: Public
In-State Tuition: $7,579
Out-of-State Tuition: $34,073
Room & Board: $10,400
Required Fees: $3,652
Books & Supplies: $1,222

Avg. Need-Based Grant: $12,388
Avg. % of Need Met: 72%

Avg. Merit-Based Award: $5,177
% Receiving (All Freshmen): 19%
% Receiving (Freshmen w/o Need): 14%

Avg. Cumulative Debt: $24,590
% of Students Borrowing: 43%

CAREER
Who Recruits
1. Air Liquide
2. NBCUniversal
3. Ethos Group
4. Manhattan Associates
5. Nvidia

Notable Internships
1. Phillips 66
2. Novartis
3. CBRE

Top Industries
1. Business
2. Operations
3. Engineering
4. Education
5. Sales

Top Employers
1. Haliburton
2. Deloitte
3. EY
4. Amazon
5. Intel

Where Alumni Work
1. Houston
2. Dallas
3. College Station, TX
4. Austin
5. San Antonio

Median Earnings
College Scorecard (Early Career): $58,000
PayScale (Early Career): $62,700
PayScale (Mid-Career): $123,300

RANKINGS
Money: 11
U.S. News: 66 (T), National Universities
Wall Street Journal/THE: 83 (T)
Washington Monthly: 12, National Universities

COLLEGE OVERLAPS
Purdue University
Texas Tech University
University of Texas at Dallas
University of Houston
The University of Texas at Austin

Trinity College (CT)

Hartford, Connecticut | 860-297-2180

Established as Washington College in 1823 before being renamed in 1845, Trinity College was founded as an Episcopalian alternative to Congregationalist Yale; it is the second oldest college in the state of Connecticut. What began as a college of nine male students is today a 100-acre campus within the confines of downtown Hartford that features 2,182 full-time undergraduates, forty-one majors, and more than 900 distinct courses. Famous alumni are a disparate lot that includes both conservative voices like George Will and Tucker Carlson as well as the legendary absurdist playwright Edward Albee of *Who's Afraid of Virginia Woolf* fame.

Inside the Classroom
Freshmen learn the ropes of academic reading and writing in either a first-year seminar or via the invitation-only Gateway Program. An additional course bearing the "writing intensive" designation must be completed at some point during one's undergraduate program. All students are required to demonstrate competency as writers, quantitative thinkers, and in one foreign language. Lastly, all students must either complete a course with a global focus or participate in a study abroad program. Passing one course with a C- or better in each of the arts, humanities, natural sciences, numerical and symbolic reasoning, and the social sciences are the only other requirements in what amounts to a very open curriculum.

With a total graduate student population that doesn't even hit triple digits, the bulk of the resources are directed toward Bantam undergraduates. Thus, a student/faculty ratio of 9:1 translates to 72 percent of course sections boasting an enrollment of nineteen or fewer students, and the mean number of students in a class is seventeen. Working closely with faculty is a real possibility at this school where one hundred students conduct research each year alongside faculty through the Summer Research Program, and roughly two-thirds engage in some type of undergraduate research. Greater than 60 percent of Trinity students study abroad and have access to Trinity-exclusive programs in Shanghai and Cape Town and school-run programs in Paris, Barcelona, Rome, Vienna, and Trinidad.

Trinity College is well regarded across the board with an economics department that feeds many leading investment banks and an engineering program that is among the best you will find at a small liberal arts school. Most degrees are conferred in the social sciences, biology, and psychology. While only a small percentage of graduates pursue prestigious national fellowships, a few do typically take home Fulbrights and an occasional Watson Scholarship each year, but the school has only two Rhodes Scholars in its history.

Outside the Classroom
Eighty-six percent of Trinity undergraduates reside on campus, and 100 percent of freshmen are housed in one of seven first-year exclusive dorms. Greek life is more popular among men (29 percent join a fraternity) than women (17 percent join a sorority). Competing in the New England Small College Athletic Conference within NCAA Division III, the Bantams field twenty-eight varsity teams evenly split between men's and women's squads. Including club sports, over 40 percent of the student body participates in intercollegiate athletics. While sports and frats dominate the social scene, the Students Activities, Involvement, and Leadership Office (SAIL) oversees 150+ student-run clubs and organizations. While the school touts the "real-world" aspect of being located in downtown Hartford, the city presently has one of the highest per-capita crime rates in the United States. Affluent students, of whom there are many at Trinity, often prefer roads trips to Montreal, New York City, or Boston over their "home" city. However, the spirit of volunteerism is strong, and the Office of Community Service and Civic Engagement offers endless opportunities to work in areas such as hunger, housing, the homeless, and education.

Career Services
The Center for Student Success and Career Development features five full-time staff members who specialize in areas such as strategic partnerships, pre-law advising, and pre-health career advising. That equates to a student-to-advisor ratio of 436:1, in the average range when compared against other liberal arts colleges featured in this guide. The college is one of a dozen schools in the country that uses Stanford University's Designing Your Life approach that encourages undergraduates to shed rigid views and fears about career and, instead, use their passions, goals, and creative problem-solving skills to move toward a meaningful path. To pursue that aim, Trinity invites students to join one of six Career Communities designed for those who wish to take advantage of industry-specific career advice, internship opportunities, Career Treks, panel discussions, and Career Skills Labs.

Other perks include a Career Studio where students can stop by any time for help with tangible job search products like resumes, cover letters, or creating a LinkedIn profile. In addition, the Bantam Career Network functions like a private LinkedIn where current students can network with alumni in their fields of interest. The college does not host any large-scale career fairs, but the Career Connections Summit on parents' weekend affords undergraduates the chance to network with representatives from top corporations. Trinity has invested heavily in its career development in the last decade, and that financial commitment is starting to bear fruit. This forward-thinking center is innovating every year, and its efforts are reflected in career/graduate school outcomes, earning it top marks from our staff.

Professional Outcomes

Surveyed members of the Class of 2019 had found a positive outcome at a 97 percent clip within six months of commencement. Those entering the world of employment landed jobs at desirable organizations like the New York City Ballet, NBC Universal, and Morgan Stanley, a company with a hefty share of alumni. A large Bantam presence also can be felt in the corporate offices of Citi, Merrill Lynch, Fidelity Investments, Google, IBM, and Goldman Sachs. Finance (45 percent), science/engineering (18 percent), and health and medicine (12 percent) were the most frequently entered fields in 2019. Starting and midcareer salaries tend to be on the higher side, ranking in the top ten among highly selective private colleges alongside many engineering-heavy schools. While a fair number of graduates remain in the Hartford area, New York City and Boston occupy the one and two slots for highest alumni concentrations.

Many Trinity grads go on to prestigious graduate schools; 60 percent of alumni have entered or completed a graduate or professional program within five years. Recent graduates have matriculated into the likes of Yale Medical School, Cambridge University, and Columbia University. Medical or other health-related program applicants are successful 80 percent of the time and are presently enrolled at institutions such as Georgetown, Tufts, Penn, Cornell, and Boston University. Graduates eying law school earn an average LSAT of 160 (80th percentile) and enroll at a vast array of universities including Top Fourteen law schools like Duke, Cornell, Columbia, Stanford, and Northwestern.

Admission

The Class of 2023 saw 33 percent of applicants admitted, an acceptance rate identical to that of the previous three cycles. In Trinity's fourth year as a test-optional school, the majority of those who ultimately enrolled took advantage of the policy, not submitting an SAT or ACT score. The average scores of those who did submit standardized test results were 1366 on the SAT and 30 on the ACT. Transcripts have to be strong but not immaculate as 46 percent of attendees placed in the top decile of their high school class while 75 percent were in the top quartile.

Rigor of secondary school record, GPA, and character/personal qualities constitute the triumvirate of most important factors. The committee genuinely values intangible qualities that research has shown leads to postsecondary success such as "grit, optimism, persistence, a willingness to take risks, and an ability to overcome adversity." A supplemental essay explaining why applicants wish to attend college in an urban setting also is recommended. The college fills almost half its freshman class via two early decision rounds. The 2023 cohort was comprised of 285 ED students, which included 152 varsity athletes. ED admit rates reached 58 percent in 2018-19 cycle, and those admitted via that round comprised 52 percent of the incoming class. Trinity is a more desirable destination than ever. In 2015, only 22 percent of accepted students elected to attend, but that figure has jumped to 30 percent in recent years. Applying ED or ED II is undoubtedly a wise strategic move.

Worth Your Money?

At $76,450 in annual costs, Trinity won't come cheap. It does not offer much in the way of merit aid, instead focusing its efforts on meeting all of the demonstrated need of students eligible for financial aid. In fact, the 54 percent of current undergraduates who are need-eligible receive annual grants of over $48k per year, bringing Trinity's tuition much more within reach. As a school that helps you develop professional networks and connects you to big-time employers, Trinity can be worth taking on a reasonable amount of debt in order to attend.

FINANCIAL
Institutional Type: Private
In-State Tuition: $56,380
Out-of-State Tuition: $56,380
Room & Board: $15,300
Required Fees: $2,670
Books & Supplies: $1,000

Avg. Need-Based Grant: $48,334
Avg. % of Need Met: 100%

Avg. Merit-Based Award: $58,374
% Receiving (All Freshmen): 3%
% Receiving (Freshmen w/o Need): 1%

Avg. Cumulative Debt: $30,893
% of Students Borrowing: 44%

CAREER
Who Recruits
1. Salesforce
2. CBRE
3. UBS
4. Accenture
5. Fidelity Investments

Notable Internships
1. WeWork
2. Wayfair
3. Boston Public Health Commission

Top Industries
1. Business
2. Education
3. Operations
4. Finance
5. Sales

Top Employers
1. Morgan Stanley
2. Google
3. Citi
4. IBM
5. Merrill Lynch

Where Alumni Work
1. New York City
2. Boston
3. Hartford
4. Washington DC
5. San Francisco

Median Earnings
College Scorecard (Early Career): NR
PayScale (Early Career): $63,800
PayScale (Mid-Career): $124,200

RANKINGS
Money: 129
U.S. News: 44 (T), Liberal Arts Colleges
Wall Street Journal/THE: 92
Washington Monthly: 20, Liberal Arts Colleges

COLLEGE OVERLAPS
Boston College
Colby College
Lafayette College
Tufts University
Union College

Trinity University

San Antonio, Texas | 210-999-7207

It is rare to see a jump in selectivity on the scale of San Antonio's top school, Trinity University, which has sliced its acceptance rate in half in only a few years. The school's meteoric rise has occurred contemporaneously with its 150th anniversary, and while the school continues to be majority Texan—three-quarters of enrollees are residents—applications from out-of-staters have risen in recent years. An increasingly gifted undergraduate student body of over 2,500 enjoys the choice of forty-seven majors and a carefully crafted liberal arts core curriculum that is more demanding than the norm.

Inside the Classroom

The distinct Pathways Program guides the educational journey at Trinity and is defined by six curricular requirements that involve an overwhelming number of manufactured terminologies. First-year experience courses, capped at sixteen students, introduce freshmen to the rigors of university-level reading and writing. In order to fulfill the Approaches to Creation and Analysis pathway, students must complete one course in the humanities, the arts and creative disciplines, social and behavioral sciences, natural sciences, and quantitative disciplines. Undergrads must also check off each of the Core Capacities: (1) written, oral, and visual communication; (2) digital literacy; and (3) engaged citizenship. All must also tackle "the Interdisciplinary Clusters," three-course groupings with themes such as ecological civilization in Asia or constructing and deconstructing language. One physical education course and one academic major round out the complex labyrinth of mandated coursework at Trinity U.

Undergraduates are the primary beneficiaries of a 9:1 student-to-faculty ratio as the university only enrolls 164 graduate students. You won't encounter any adjuncts or teaching assistants at Trinity, and 95 percent of the 258 full-time faculty members hold terminal degrees in their fields. Sixty-four percent of courses enroll fewer than twenty students and only 1 percent contain more than 50. Over the summer, close to 140 students participate in intensive undergraduate research projects with faculty members. Overall, 80 percent of students engage in some type of hands-on learning, whether through research or an internship. Study abroad programs are taken advantage of by 35 percent of graduates, most of whom participate in affiliated but not Trinity-run offerings.

Trinity's well-regarded School of Business attracts the greatest percentage of students as finance, accounting, and business administration degrees account for 21 percent of the total degrees conferred. Communication, biology, foreign language, and computer science also have strong representation. The university's reputation within the state of Texas is strong, and many graduates further their education or begin their careers locally, but the national prestige of the school is growing by the year. That can be seen in the procurement of highly competitive national fellowships. They have produced multiple Goldwater Scholars and Fulbright Scholars in recent years.

Outside the Classroom

With undergraduates required to live on campus for their first three years and 74 percent of all undergraduates residing on the 117-acre grounds, the formation of a tight-knit college community is almost unavoidable. Greek life is also alive and well with roughly 25 percent participation; there are fourteen total Greek organizations on campus. Nine men's and nine women's athletic teams compete at the Division III level, and they do so with intensity; they've captured four championships in recent years. The intramural programs scoop up pretty much everyone not playing a varsity sport with roughly three-fifths of the student body participating in intramural athletics. There are also ninety-seven student-run organizations, including groups devoted to animal welfare, fantasy sports and analytics, and indigenous peoples. The spirit of service is strong as 1,600 students contribute 120,000+ volunteer hours annually. Trinity's campus is only three miles from downtown San Antonio, opening possibilities for all sorts of big-city fun, but having a car is useful. Austin is a popular weekend getaway that is roughly an hour-and-a-half drive from the university.

Career Services

The newly-created Center for Experiential Learning and Career Success (CELCS) is staffed by six full-time employees (not including administrative assistants) who specialize in areas such as career counseling, experiential learning coordination, and employer relations. That equates to a student-to-advisor ratio of 421:1, in the average range when compared against other schools in this guidebook. Fall and spring career fairs were attended by fifty-one employers in the 2018-19 academic year, including top companies like KPMG, Booz Allen Hamilton, Valero Energy, and EY. It also regularly hosts smaller-scale events such as Lunch 'n Learns, employer information sessions, and workshops on topics such as networking, interviewing, and professional dining etiquette.

ADMISSION
Admission Rate: 29%
Admission Rate - Men: 31%
Admission Rate - Women: 27%
EA Admission Rate: 63%
ED Admission Rate: 63%
ED Admits as % of Total Admits: 4%
Admission Rate (5-Year Trend): -19%
% of Admits Attending (Yield): 22%
Transfer Admission Rate: 38%

SAT Reading/Writing (Middle 50%): 650-720
SAT Math (Middle 50%): 640-730
ACT Composite (Middle 50%): 29-32

% Graduated in Top 10% of HS Class: 50%
% Graduated in Top 25% of HS Class: 82%
% Graduated in Top 50% of HS Class: 98%

Demonstrated Interest: Considered
Legacy Status: Considered
Admission Interview Offered: Yes

ENROLLMENT
Total Undergraduate Enrollment: 2,528
% Part-Time: 2%
% Male: 47%
% Female: 53%
% Out-of-State: 24%
% Fraternity: 16%
% Sorority: 28%
% On-Campus (Freshman): 100%
% On-Campus (All Undergraduate): 81%

% African-American: 4%
% Asian: 8%
% Hispanic: 21%
% White: 56%
% Other: 5%
% Race or Ethnicity Unknown: 1%
% International: 4%
% Low-Income: 14%

ACADEMICS
Student-to-Faculty Ratio: 9 to 1
% of Classes Under 20: 64%
% of Classes 20-49: 36%
% of Classes 50 or More: 1%
% Full-Time Faculty: 73%
% Full-Time Faculty w/ Terminal Degree: 95%

Top Programs
Accounting
Biology
Engineering Science
English
History
Mathematical Finance
Neuroscience

Retention Rate: 92%
4-Year Graduation Rate: 66%
6-Year Graduation Rate: 76%

Curricular Flexibility: Less Flexible
Academic Rating: ★★★⌁

#CollegesWorthYourMoney

The school switched to the Handshake platform in 2018 and presently has opportunities from 3,600 employers posted in its database. As of the 2018-19 school year, 65 percent of Trinity students participated in at least one internship during their undergraduate education. Close to 200 on-campus interviews are conducted by employers each year. There are 29,000 actively engaged Tiger alumni, and they are more than happy to provide career advice, arrange a job-shadowing experience, or offer mentorship to current students. The office also facilitates a solid number of one-on-one counseling sessions; it holds 1,000+ such appointments in a single year. The nascent CELCS is on the rise and is quickly becoming the type of career services center that the university leadership outlined in its most recent strategic plan.

Professional Outcomes

Six months after receiving their diplomas, 45 percent of Trinity grads are employed full time, and 26 percent have matriculated into graduate school; a shade under 10 percent are still seeking employment. The companies employing the largest number of alumni include USAA (a San Antonio based financial firm), PwC, EY, Deloitte, Dell, Accenture, Morgan Stanley, and Amazon. Most Trinity grads stay in the Lone Star State with San Antonio, Houston, Dallas, and Austin being the four most common landing spots. Median salaries at midcareer are solid, ranking third in the state behind Rice and Texas A&M and just in front of UT Austin. Early career salaries are estimated at $55k while median midcareer salaries are estimated at $109k.

Recent bachelor's degree-earners have been accepted into graduate school at an overall rate of 76 percent. Over the last five years, acceptance rates into medical school have consistently been above national averages, hovering between 55 percent and 75 percent, with the exception of 2017-18 when just 36 percent gained acceptance. Graduates have gone on to Dell Medical School (University of Texas), Harvard Medical School, and Tufts Medical School, among other less prestigious institutions. Law school rates have been within the 75-90 percent range in recent years. Among the most popular law schools attended by recent graduates are the University of Texas, Texas Tech, St. Mary's School of Law, and SMU.

Admission

Just five years ago, Trinity University received barely north of 4,500 applicants and admitted an unintimidating 64 percent; freshmen entering in 2019-20 faced an applicant pool of double that size and an acceptance rate of only 29 percent. Today, the mid-50 percent SAT score is 1290-1420 and the mid-50 percent ACT score is 29-32. A solid 50 percent of entering freshmen earned a place in the top 10 percent of their graduating classes, and 82 percent were in the top quartile; the average GPA was a 3.67 on a 4.0 scale. The average profile of a student beginning at Trinity only a few years ago was significantly less impressive.

Trinity may be a small school that gives each application a "thorough review," yet the meat-and-potatoes factors of GPA, class rank, test scores, and engagement in a rigorous curriculum rest atop the list of most important considerations. The next tier of factors includes an interview, essays, recommendations, extracurricular activities, talent/ability, and character/personal qualities. There would have been no reason to apply early to this university in years past, but a sharp spike in competitiveness has put this strategic option firmly in play. In 2019-20, Trinity accepted 100 of 159 early applicants for a hyper-friendly 63 percent acceptance rate. Strong test scores and B+/A- average are now prerequisites for admission to Trinity, a statement that would have been hard to believe a decade ago. If you're a borderline applicant, going the ED route makes a ton of sense.

Worth Your Money?

Amazingly, given the current landscape, a list price cost of attendance of $62,596 isn't incredibly high for a private university. Yet, the truly good news is that this sticker price is rarely what undergraduates pay. Trinity awards a merit aid discount to three-quarters of current students with an average annual value of $24,000. Further, for students meeting the criteria for need-based grant eligibility, the average annual award is $35k. With most students receiving sizable discounts, Trinity becomes a solid value, especially when you consider that its grads bring home above-average salaries at each stage of their careers. At the same time, it should be noted that Trinity grads incur an average of $43k in debt, one of the highest totals of any college high-lighted in this guide.

FINANCIAL
Institutional Type: Private
In-State Tuition: $44,064
Out-of-State Tuition: $44,064
Room & Board: $13,584
Required Fees: $616
Books & Supplies: $1,000

Avg. Need-Based Grant: $34,754
Avg. % of Need Met: 98%

Avg. Merit-Based Award: $24,124
% Receiving (All Freshmen): 76%
% Receiving (Freshmen w/o Need): 59%

Avg. Cumulative Debt: $43,005
% of Students Borrowing: 47%

CAREER
Who Recruits
1. USAA
2. AXA Advisors
3. Dell
4. Capgemini
5. KPMG

Notable Internships
1. San Antonion Spurs
2. US State Department
3. Apple

Top Industries
1. Business
2. Education
3. Operations
4. Social Services
5. Sales

Top Employers
1. USAA
2. Deloitte
3. PwC
4. EY
5. H-E-B

Where Alumni Work
1. San Antonio
2. Houston
3. Dallas
4. Austin
5. Washington DC

Median Earnings
College Scorecard (Early Career): $54,900
PayScale (Early Career): $57,700
PayScale (Mid-Career): $114,200

RANKINGS
Money: 201
U.S. News: 1, Regional Universities West
Wall Street Journal/THE: 113
Washington Monthly: 7, Master's Universities

COLLEGE OVERLAPS
Baylor University
Southern Methodist University
Texas A&M University - College Station
Texas Christian University
The University of Texas at Austin

Tufts University

Medford, Massachusetts | 617-627-3170

Quite small for being one of the nation's top research universities at just over 5,900 undergraduates, Tufts excels in delivering a highly personalized educational experience that is on par with its upper-echelon liberal arts rivals Williams and Amherst. In fact, like Amherst and Brown University, the school is notable for having no core curriculum. Instead, students are "encouraged to immerse themselves in the full expanse of course offerings, deepening existing interests while discovering new areas of study."

Inside the Classroom
Three schools serve Tufts' undergraduate population: The College of Arts & Sciences, the College of Engineering, and the School of the Museum of Fine Arts. The three schools combined offer more than ninety majors and minors; approximately one-third of all students double major, and half declare a minor. The school encourages freshmen and sophomores to "Go broad, then deep." Students who do not want to be tethered to a laundry list of required introductory courses will relish the freedom Tufts affords its undergrads.

The university prides itself on its undergraduate teaching, and it shows; 84 percent of the Class of 2019 reported feeling satisfied with their educational journey. Nearly every professor is willing to take on research assistants, and plenty of funding is available. In the College of Engineering, 60 percent of students have a chance to participate in a research project at some point during their collegiate experience. Classes are small, especially when considering the school's legitimate research university status. Eighteen percent of all courses see fewer than ten students enrolled, and 68 percent have sub-twenty enrollments. The student-to-faculty ratio is 9:1. A substantial segment of the student body, 40-45 percent, study abroad at one of eighty preapproved programs in locales such as Chile, Ghana, Hong Kong, and Madrid.

Well-regarded by industry and elite graduate/professional schools, a diploma in any discipline from Tufts will get you where you want to go. The most popular majors by volume are international relations, economics, computer science, political science, and biology—all of which receive very high marks. The university does a fantastic job helping students land nationally competitive scholarships. Tufts is a leading producer of Fulbright Scholars, hitting double digits most years, and it also has seen its fair share of Goldwater, Udall, Truman, and Astronaut Scholarships in recent memory.

Outside the Classroom
Unlike some of Tufts' graduate programs, the undergraduate schools are not located in downtown Boston. However, Medford is part of the Boston metro area and is only five miles from the city limits, which makes its location far less remote than many of its rival New England colleges. Only sixty-five percent of students live on campus in one of forty residential options ranging from traditional dorms to shared apartments. Many upperclassmen move off campus or live in fraternity or sorority houses. Close to one-quarter of the student population has traditionally gone Greek. Yet, some recent well-publicized hazing incidents led to the dissolution or suspension of many chapters that altered, at least for the time being, the influence of Greek-letter organizations on campus. Presently, only 10 percent of men and 15 percent of women are Greek affiliated. Few Tufts students are lone wolves as a staggering 94 percent join at least one of the school's 341 recognized student organizations. Opportunities for community service are plentiful. Many students are involved in athletics, whether a member of one of the twenty-nine varsity sports teams competing in NCAA Division III, twenty-two club teams, or intramural groups. Campus is attractive and full of perks, including the new 42,000-square-foot Tisch Sports & Fitness Center that features tennis courts, pools, squash courts, and dance studios. As a bonus, dining options are given rave reviews as every Tufts student has a favorite dish.

Career Services
With thirteen full-time staff members who focus on undergraduate advising, career relations, and alumni outreach, the Tufts Career Center sports a 454:1 student-to-advisor ratio, which is within the average range of schools featured in this guide. The career services staff has done an incredible job improving its outreach over the past two decades. In 1998, only 32 percent of graduates were satisfied with the university's career services, but by 2015 a healthy 83 percent expressed positive feelings, and annual interactions with students had risen to over 7,600. In 2017, they increased the number of sessions with engineering students by 41 percent from the previous year, another indicator that this is an office on the rise.

Tufts does an exceptional job of assisting undergraduates with internship procurement. A robust 68 percent of 2019 Tufts graduates completed two or more internships during their time at the university; 89 percent completed at least one. The Fall Career Fair is attended by 185+ companies, and on-campus recruiting/interviews take place throughout the academic year. Career Treks and networking events in cities like New York and San Francisco are also regular occurrences. A recent switch from the antiquated Jumbo Jobs platform to Handshake was lauded by students. As an added long-term support, alumni have lifetime access to the spectrum of career services, including one-on-one job counseling. With a solid track record in internship participation, job placement, and graduate school outcomes, Tufts career services does an exceptional job setting its undergraduates up for the next level of success.

Professional Outcomes

Six months after earning their diplomas, 98 percent of 2019 Tufts graduates were employed, attending graduate school, or otherwise productively engaged. The most commonly entered fields were health, life sciences, environmental (19 percent); engineering and technology (20 percent); finance, consulting, real estate (21 percent), and advocacy, education, and social services (14 percent). All of the leading finance, consulting, and technology companies sit atop the list of the most prolific employers of Tufts alums including Booz Allen Hamilton, JPMorgan, Facebook, Google, Deloitte, Amazon, Raytheon, Morgan Stanley, and BlackRock. The median salary at the start of what is considered midcareer is $138k, in the same ballpark as higher than Amherst, Boston College, or Harvard. Most Tufts alumni remain in the Boston area, but many also head to New York City, San Francisco, Seattle, DC, and Chicago.

Of the 17 percent of the Class of 2019 who went directly to graduate school, 86 percent were accepted into their first-choice institution. Included among the ten universities enrolling the highest number of Tufts alumni were MIT, UCLA, Penn, Carnegie Mellon, and Columbia. Law school applicants routinely gain acceptance into top-tier institutions. In recent years, alumni have been admitted into Harvard, Northwestern, University of Michigan, Penn, Duke, Brown, and Yale. Medical school applicants gained acceptance at a 75-90 percent rate, depending on the year. Those with at least a 3.5 undergraduate GPA find a med school home over 90 percent of the time.

Admission

The university's acceptance rate seems to have settled in the 14-15 percent range in recent years and held steady for the Class of 2023 despite an all-time record 22,766 applications. The vast majority of those applicants were for admittance into the School of Arts & Sciences followed by the School of Engineering with the smallest number applying to the fine arts programs. Overall, the median SAT score was 1480 and the median ACT was 33. Ninety-three percent of those accepted possessed an ACT score of 30 or above. Last year, over 80 percent of the freshman class finished in the top 10 percent of their high school class, and 95 percent were in the top quartile.

There is nothing unexpected on the list of what factors the admissions committee considers "most important." It is looking for students who achieved top grades in AP classes, scored well on standardized tests, finished in the top 10 percent of their class, come highly recommended by their high school teachers, and are capable of composing a killer essay. Like many schools in its weight class, Tufts loves to scoop up a large portion of its freshman class in the early round (although they are secretive in this regard with 2020 info)—its ED acceptance rate is historically close to four times that of the regular round— and those accepted early comprise up to 65 percent of the incoming cohort. Even though it is no longer relegated to Ivy League safety status, Tufts is still understandably eager to lock down as many top candidates as possible via ED. Like all Ivy and Ivy-equivalent schools, Tufts is looking for the best and the brightest and is competing with even bigger names to haul in the best candidates. Therefore, demonstrating commitment through ED can pay dividends for qualified applicants.

Worth Your Money?

TBoston is America's fourth-most expensive city, so perhaps it is no surprise that Tufts is on the pricey side. At $79k per year in cost of attendance, it ranks as the fifteenth most expensive school in the country. Only 40 percent of current undergrads qualify for need-based aid, and the average annual grant is for just under $47k. Of course, many in attendance don't have to worry too much about the cost because, based on historical data, a high percent of undergrads hail from wealthy families. It's no wonder that despite the high costs, graduates carry a mean amount of debt slightly lower than average (compared against all college grads). Even if you have to make an economic sacrifice to attend, Tufts is a school that will expose you to many personal and professional networks that will come in handy as you enter the world of graduate school or employment.

FINANCIAL
Institutional Type: Private
In-State Tuition: $60,862
Out-of-State Tuition: $60,862
Room & Board: $15,630
Required Fees: $0
Books & Supplies: $1,000

Avg. Need-Based Grant: $46,982
Avg. % of Need Met: 100%

Avg. Merit-Based Award: $3,000
% Receiving (All Freshmen): 4%
% Receiving (Freshmen w/o Need): 2%

Avg. Cumulative Debt: $27,006
% of Students Borrowing: 30%

CAREER
Who Recruits
1. Gelber Group
2. Cogo Labs
3. Amazon Robotics
4. Putnam Investments
5. Oppenheimer & Co.

Notable Internships
1. Deutsche Bank
2. UBS
3. Wayfair

Top Industries
1. Business
2. Education
3. Research
4. Engineering
5. Operations

Top Employers
1. Google
2. Amazon
3. Microsoft
4. Deloitte
5. Facebook

Where Alumni Work
1. Boston
2. New York City
3. San Francisco
4. Washington DC
5. Los Angeles

Median Earnings
College Scorecard (Early Career): $75,800
PayScale (Early Career): $68,300
PayScale (Mid-Career): $137,900

RANKINGS
Money: 95
U.S. News: 30 (T), National Universities
Wall Street Journal/THE: 31
Washington Monthly: 38, National Universities

COLLEGE OVERLAPS
Brown University
Boston University
Georgetown University
New York University
Washington University

ADMISSION
Admission Rate: 13%
Admission Rate - Men: 13%
Admission Rate - Women: 13%
EA Admission Rate: 17%
ED Admission Rate: 33%
ED Admits as % of Total Admits: 13%
Admission Rate (5-Year Trend): -14%
% of Admits Attending (Yield): 34%
Transfer Admission Rate: 39%

SAT Reading/Writing (Middle 50%): 660-750
SAT Math (Middle 50%): 700-770
ACT Composite (Middle 50%): 31-33

% Graduated in Top 10% of HS Class: 64%
% Graduated in Top 25% of HS Class: 88%
% Graduated in Top 50% of HS Class: 97%

Demonstrated Interest: Considered
Legacy Status: Considered
Admission Interview Offered: Yes

ENROLLMENT
Total Undergraduate Enrollment: 6,968
% Part-Time: 0%
% Male: 41%
% Female: 59%
% Out-of-State: 80%
% Fraternity: 22%
% Sorority: 51%
% On-Campus (Freshman): 98%
% On-Campus (All Undergraduate): 46%

% African-American: 5%
% Asian: 6%
% Hispanic: 7%
% White: 71%
% Other: 4%
% Race or Ethnicity Unknown: 1%
% International: 5%
% Low-Income: 10%

ACADEMICS
Student-to-Faculty Ratio: 8 to 1
% of Classes Under 20: 66%
% of Classes 20-49: 28%
% of Classes 50 or More: 6%
% Full-Time Faculty: 63%
% Full-Time Faculty w/ Terminal Degree: 95%

Top Programs
Architecture
Biology
Communication
Finance
Neuroscience
Political Science/International Relations
Sociology

Retention Rate: 93%
4-Year Graduation Rate: 77%
6-Year Graduation Rate: 86%

Curricular Flexibility: Somewhat Flexible
Academic Rating: ★★★★

#CollegesWorthYourMoney

In competition with Vanderbilt and Emory for King of the Southern Ivies status, Tulane University takes the bronze; yet, that is hardly a knock on this private, midsized university in the heart of New Orleans. Home to 6,968 undergraduates, Tulane successfully combines the benefits of a renowned research university with the friendly classroom atmosphere of a liberal arts college. In the wake of Hurricane Katrina, the school dedicated itself to community service, an attribute that is now deeply woven into the fabric of the university.

Inside the Classroom
Tulane offers seventy-five majors within five colleges, but all students, regardless of major, call Newcombe-Tulane College their home base. The school's core curriculum, which consists of thirty credits worth of courses, was redesigned in 2017 to "develop information literacy, critical thinking, and personal and social responsibility." As a result, coursework is required in the areas of writing skills, formal reasoning, foreign language, mathematics and natural sciences, social and behavioral sciences, textual and historical perspectives, aesthetics and the creative arts, and a first-year seminar called the Tulane Interdisciplinary Experience Seminar (TIDES). The TIDES courses center around engaging topics, many of which have to do with local New Orleans culture/history and involve one-on-one meetings with professors and a chance to connect with a student mentor.

Despite the presence of a significant number of graduate students, the university's enviable 8:1 student-to-faculty ratio can still be felt in the classroom. The average undergraduate class size is twenty-one students and a solid 26 percent of courses have single-digit enrollments, providing a seminar-style environment. The overwhelming majority of undergraduate courses, even introductory ones, are taught by full-time professors. Exiting student surveys indicate that this focus on undergraduate education is noted as 94 percent rated their educational experience at Tulane as either "excellent" or "good." Those aiming to engage in undergraduate research at Tulane can find it; over 200 students per year land such opportunities in the School of Science and Engineering alone. An expansive study abroad program offers more than one hundred programs in forty countries, which is taken advantage of by 600 students each year.

Business/marketing (27 percent), social science (17 percent), biology (11 percent), and health professions (8 percent) are the disciplines in which most degrees are conferred. The A.B. Freeman School of Business and programs in architecture, biology, and neuroscience enjoy strong national reputations. In its history, Tulane has produced eighteen Rhodes Scholars, one more than Emory. The university was a top producer of Fulbright Scholars in 2018 with fifteen graduates and recent alumni selected. Beinecke, Boren, Truman, and Marshall Scholarships also go to Green Wave alums with regularity.

Outside the Classroom
Fewer than half of the undergraduate population (46 percent) resides on the university's 110-acre uptown campus. Ample housing exists in the nearby community that is either within walking/biking distance of campus or accessible via the university bus system. Sororities draw in 51 percent of the female population and fraternities attract 22 percent of males. Tulane offers big-time athletics with sixteen NCAA Division I teams competing in the American Athletic Conference. An additional twenty-nine club sports teams and thirteen intramural leagues ensure that athletic participation is open to all. Over 200 student-run clubs currently are active with volunteer opportunities being among the most popular. Tulane undergrads contribute over 780,000 hours of volunteer service annually. Campus boasts thirty libraries/research centers, fifteen eateries, and the 156,000-square-foot Reily Student Recreation Center. The urban campus is located within the New Orleans city limits, only four miles from the bustling French Quarter, which provides students with all the culinary and cultural delights one can handle. The fact that classes shut down during Mardi Gras tells you all you need to know about life at Tulane.

Career Services
The Newcomb-Tulane College Career Services office is staffed by nine professionals who specialize in areas such as career advising, senior year experience coordination, pre-health advising, and pre-law advising. An additional nine career services staff members are housed within the Freeman School of Business. In total, there are 21 staff members serving undergraduates in this capacity which works out to a 332:1 student-to-counselor ratio. One of this group's greatest strengths is in organizing well-attended career and grad school fairs. The Mardi Gras Invitational Job Fair brings 145 employers to campus, the Gumbo Gathering Job Fair attracts another 134, and 118 schools are represented at the Graduate & Professional School Fair. Additionally, 11,000+ job and internship listings are posted through Tulane's Career Services Center.

Tulane University

A one-credit course entitled Majors, Internships, and Jobs teaches resume building, interview prep, and professional social media use. Many land internships through the UCAN Intern Consortium that Tulane belongs to alongside such schools as Harvard, Notre Dame, Swarthmore, and Washington University. A nationwide alumni network that is 140,000+ members strong is another great source that current undergrads can utilize to land internships or their first paid gig. Founded in 2006, post-Hurricane Katrina, The Center for Public Service ensures that all Tulane grads engage in structured volunteer work during their four years of study. At the heart of this program is a three-credit Public Internship Program that allows students to complete sixty to seventy hours with a nonprofit organization. Thanks to an emphasis on public service and large-scale networking events, the Tulane Career Center succeeds in preparing its students for the world of work and graduate school.

Professional Outcomes

Sixty-one percent of Tulane grads find employment within six months of graduation. The most popular industries were finance (17 percent), legal (17 percent), accounting (10 percent), education (6 percent), and engineering (4 percent). Significant numbers of Tulane alumni can be found working in the Louisiana-based Ochsner Health System or at corporations such as Shell, EY, Google, PwC, IBM, Morgan Stanley, Deloitte, and Accenture. Thus, it is little surprise that the school's alumni enjoy the highest salaries of any college graduates from a Louisiana-based institution. Geographically, the most popular postgraduate move is to remain in the Greater New Orleans area although New York City, DC, Houston, San Francisco, and Los Angeles attract large numbers of Green Wave alumni as well.

Seventeen percent of Tulane grads immediately enroll in graduate or professional school. The four most commonly attended graduate schools by recent grads are Tulane itself, Louisiana State University, Boston University, and Johns Hopkins University. Students applying to law and medical schools, including Tulane's own institutions, fare better than the national average. Tulane undergraduates gain acceptance to medical school 58 percent of the time, and that figure rises to 93 percent for those with at least a 3.6 GPA and a score of 509 or higher on the MCAT. Recent grads have attended Columbia, Duke, and Johns Hopkins as well as the uber-selective Tulane School of Medicine. Law school hopefuls gain acceptance at an impressive 93 percent rate including roughly seventy admits annually into Tulane's own solidly ranked law school.

Admission

Tulane received 42,185 applications for its Class of 2023 but accepted only 13 percent, part of a pattern of declining admissions rates in recent years; the Class of 2022 rate was 17 percent, and the Class of 2021 rate was 21 percent. The middle 50 percent ACT composite score range is 31-33 and the SAT range is 1370-1480. Sixty-four percent of 2019-20 freshmen had earned a place in the top decile of their high school class, and 88 percent were in the top quartile. Not everyone attending Tulane had perfect grades as 42 percent of attendees sported an unweighted high school GPA below 3.5.

With a heavy volume of applications streaming in, the Tulane Admissions Office is forced to rely on concrete factors to winnow down the pool. As a result, four factors are ranked as being most important: rigor of coursework, class rank, GPA, and standardized test scores. Essays, recommendations, and character/personal qualities receive second billing. Early decision applicants to the Class of 2023 were accepted at a 33 percent clip, while early action applicants earned admission at 17 percent rate. Unbelievably, Tulane's regular decision rate has been lower than 3 percent in back-to-back years; so, applying EA or ED is now a near-must. An institution whose heightened selectivity in recent years may go unnoticed by applicants relying on old data or the school's reputation a decade ago, Tulane has claimed its position in the realm of highly selective research universities. Successful applicants need standardized test scores above the 95th percentile to go with A's and B's in AP/honors coursework.

Worth Your Money?

Don't let the official cost of attendance of $78,000 make you think that Tulane is beyond your financial reach because a large percentage of students receive a discount in the form of merit or need-based aid that bring that sum down to a more reasonable level. Fifty-three percent of current undergrads receive an average merit aid award of $19k, and 30 percent of undergraduates are given grants averaging $37k per year. If you don't receive a sizable aid offer, the wisest move would be to evaluate (a) your other financial aid offers and (b) the amount of debt you would be likely to incur at Tulane versus the expected starting salaries for jobs related to your intended major.

FINANCIAL
Institutional Type: Private
In-State Tuition: $52,760
Out-of-State Tuition: $52,760
Room & Board: $15,774
Required Fees: $4,040
Books & Supplies: $1,200

Avg. Need-Based Grant: $37,284
Avg. % of Need Met: 94%

Avg. Merit-Based Award: $19,239
% Receiving (All Freshmen): 53%
% Receiving (Freshmen w/o Need): 43%

Avg. Cumulative Debt: $34,037
% of Students Borrowing: 34%

CAREER
Who Recruits
1. Facebook
2. Medtronic
3. Tesla
4. Starbucks
5. Amazon

Notable Internships
1. AIG
2. U.S. Senate
3. HBO

Top Industries
1. Business
2. Education
3. Operations
4. Healthcare
5. Social Services

Top Employers
1. Ochsner Health System
2. Shell
3. EY
4. PwC
5. Deloitte

Where Alumni Work
1. New Orleans
2. New York City
3. Washington DC
4. Houston
5. San Francisco

Median Earnings
College Scorecard (Early Career): $61,700
PayScale (Early Career): $59,700
PayScale (Mid-Career): $118,800

RANKINGS
Money: 527
U.S. News: 41, National Universities
Wall Street Journal/THE: 68 (T)
Washington Monthly: 244, National Universities

COLLEGE OVERLAPS
Boston University
Duke University
Emory University
University of Michigan
Vanderbilt University

Union College (NY)

Schenectady, New York | 518-388-6112

ADMISSION
Admission Rate: 43%
Admission Rate - Men: 43%
Admission Rate - Women: 42%
EA Admission Rate: Not Offered
ED Admission Rate: 61%
ED Admits as % of Total Admits: 8%
Admission Rate (5-Year Trend): +6%
% of Admits Attending (Yield): 21%
Transfer Admission Rate: 35%

SAT Reading/Writing (Middle 50%): 600-680
SAT Math (Middle 50%): 620-740
ACT Composite (Middle 50%): 27-32

% Graduated in Top 10% of HS Class: 63%
% Graduated in Top 25% of HS Class: 86%
% Graduated in Top 50% of HS Class: 98%

Demonstrated Interest: Considered
Legacy Status: Considered
Admission Interview Offered: Yes

ENROLLMENT
Total Undergraduate Enrollment: 2,189
% Part-Time: 1%
% Male: 54%
% Female: 46%
% Out-of-State: 66%
% Fraternity: 27%
% Sorority: 35%
% On-Campus (Freshman): 97%
% On-Campus (All Undergraduate): 93%

% African-American: 4%
% Asian: 5%
% Hispanic: 9%
% White: 68%
% Other: 3%
% Race or Ethnicity Unknown: 0%
% International: 10%
% Low-Income: 16%

ACADEMICS
Student-to-Faculty Ratio: 10 to 1
% of Classes Under 20: 68%
% of Classes 20-49: 31%
% of Classes 50 or More: 1%
% Full-Time Faculty: 86%
% Full-Time Faculty w/ Terminal Degree: 96%

Top Programs
Biology
Economics
Engineering
History
Mathematics
Neuroscience
Political Science
Psychology

Retention Rate: 93%
4-Year Graduation Rate: 78%
6-Year Graduation Rate: 82%

Curricular Flexibility: Less Flexible
Academic Rating: ★★★★

#CollegesWorthYourMoney

Whether intent on studying the humanities or engineering, Union College in Schenectady, New York, can perfectly meet your needs. One of the select number of schools in the country that has been in existence since the 1700s, Union, while tough to get into, has not, like many of its peer institutions, reached absurd selectivity levels in recent years. A test-optional school looking for strong but not perfect students, this rigorous, well regarded, and exclusively undergraduate institution of 2,189 students is an excellent fit for a certain subset of high schoolers. It's not a bad option considering that, in its illustrious history, Union has produced a US president, thirteen governors, 200 judges, seven cabinet secretaries, a National Book Award winner, and an Olympic Gold medalist.

Inside the Classroom
Union operates on a trimester system of ten-week terms with an extended winter break. The common curriculum is both broad and highly demanding. Students begin with a First-Year Preceptorial that seeks to sharpen skills in the areas of critical reading and thinking as well as analytical writing. The Sophomore Research Seminar mandates that students participate in structured academic research early in their collegiate career. Dutchmen also must plow through requirements in literature, natural science, quantitative and mathematical reasoning, arts and humanities, science/engineering/technology, languages and cultures, and writing across the curriculum. Union is in the exclusive club of undergraduate institutions that require all graduates to complete a senior thesis.

Class sizes at Union are favorable for creating an intimate and friendly learning environment. A 10:1 student-to-faculty ratio leads to average introductory class sizes of twenty-one and average upper-level class sizes of only fourteen. Two-thirds of course sections have an enrollment of nineteen or fewer students. Faculty-mentored research is a staple of Union's undergraduate program and is experienced by 80 percent of the student body in one form or another. During the Steinmetz Symposium, hundreds of students have the chance to showcase their research. Each year, over one hundred students conduct research with a faculty member for an entire summer. The school also takes immense pride in its popular study abroad program that sees more than 60 percent of its students from all disciplines spend a semester of study in a foreign land.

The most commonly conferred degrees are in the social sciences (24 percent), engineering (22 percent), biology (15 percent), and psychology (7 percent), with Union's engineering program having perhaps the strongest national reputation. A top producer of Fulbright Scholars, the Class of 2020 produced seven winners as well as a National Science Foundation Graduate Research Fellowship; they produced two Watson Fellows in 2019.

Outside the Classroom
Ninety-three percent of undergraduates reside in university-run dorms or one of thirteen student-run theme houses on the 120-acre grounds. The Greek influence is massive with the eighteen sororities and fraternities (ten of which are residential) attracting 27 percent of men and 35 percent of women. Regardless of Greek affiliation, every undergrad belongs to one of seven Minerva Houses, social hubs that serve to bring students and faculty together outside the classroom for social and academic activities. On the sports front, men and women's ice hockey take center stage as each battles NCAA Division I competition; the other twenty-four squads are relegated to Division III status. In total, one-third of all Union students are members of an intercollegiate sports team. Opportunities for physical fitness also exist in the form of yoga, Pilates, dance, and aerobics classes. More than 130 student-run campus clubs are on tap, including fourteen community service groups and a number of cultural, academic, political, and performance-oriented groups. Other notables include WRUC, America's first college radio station that was founded in 1920, and the Concordiensis student newspaper that launched in 1877. Schenectady's downtown is a short car ride away, and longer road trips include Saratoga Springs, a little more than half an hour away, and New York and Boston that require three-hour trips.

Career Services
The Becker Career Center is staffed by six professionals, three of whom specialize in employer relations. That works out to a 365:1 student-to-advisor ratio that falls in the average range when compared to other institutions included this guidebook. Philosophically, the staff encourages students to follow their passions by pursuing opportunities that "pique their interest and spur their enthusiasm." The staff aims to work with students early in their undergraduate careers, regularly administering tests such as the Meyers-Briggs to freshmen. Union hosts its own career fairs but also encourages participation in larger, joint efforts with other institutions. For example, Union, Swarthmore, Bard, and Connecticut College combine for the Fall Recruiting Consortium that attracts many major companies to Times Square.

E-mail: admissions@union.edu | Website: www.union.edu

Students are encouraged to connect with alumni via the Union Career Advisory Network. Alumni are eager to help current undergrads as evidenced by participation in events such as the Walk Down Wall Street that includes representatives Goldman Sachs, Barclay's Deutsche Bank, Morgan Stanley, and CITI. On-campus recruiting has doubled in the past decade and includes visits and interview opportunities with a host of desirable employers. Roughly 85 percent of Union students complete at least one internship during their four years. Overall, thanks to strong career outcomes and an influential alumni base, Becker does well for its graduates.

Professional Outcomes

Ninety-four percent of the Class of 2019 landed at their next destination within months of completing their degree with 72 percent entering full-time employment and 18 percent matriculating into graduate school. The most popular fields were engineering (17 percent), finance/banking (11 percent), healthcare (9 percent), and sales (8 percent). Of the pool of all living alumni, Union has the largest representation at IBM, GE, PwC, Morgan Stanley, Fidelity Investments, and Accenture. Location-wise, the strongest presence of Dutchmen/women can be found in New York City; Boston; Albany; Washington, DC; San Francisco; and Philadelphia. Median income figures by the start of midcareer are strong, ranking alongside other private institutions like Boston University, Trinity College, and Northeastern.

The 18 percent of students who pursue further education directly out of their undergraduate experience do so at a wide range of institutions that include many elite universities. Recent graduates have gone on to advanced business degrees at Stanford, Cornell, and UVA; advanced engineering degrees at Yale, MIT, and RPI, and science degrees at Brandeis, UCLA, and WPI. Many of those headed to medical school do so through the combined BS/MD program Union offers in conjunction with Albany Medical College, but other recent grads have gone on to study medicine at the likes of Johns Hopkins, Tufts, and Dartmouth. Likewise, many pursuing a legal education do so through the combined BA/JD program with partner Albany Law School while others have entered Harvard, Boston College, and the University of Michigan.

Admission

With an acceptance rate of 43 percent for the Class of 2023, Union College, while highly selective, offers strong students better odds of success than many others of its ilk. Still, those who ultimately enroll are often toward the top of their respective high school classes with 63 percent of 2019-20 freshmen hailing from the top decile and 86 percent from the top quartile. Of those who submit test scores (more on this in a moment), the mid-50 percent standardized test ranges are 1220-1420 on the SAT and 27-32 on the ACT.

Unless you are applying to the 3+3 Accelerated Law Program, Leadership in Medicine Program, or are a homeschooled student, Union is a test-optional institution. Yet, in the most recent admissions cycle, 59 percent submitted SAT results and 23 percent included ACT scores on their applications. Atop the list of criteria deemed "very important" in evaluating an applicant are the rigor of secondary coursework, GPA, and class rank. Soft factors like talent/ability, personal qualities, volunteer work, and extracurricular activities also play a role in evaluating candidates. If you are a student on the cusp, applying early decision is absolutely the way to go as ED applicants are given a thumbs up at a 61 percent clip. You don't need perfect grades to get into Union College—the average GPA for Class of 2023 enrollees was 3.5, and only 28 percent were over a 3.75—but you do need an area of notable strength and should be engaged in a mostly AP/honors-level high school curriculum.

Worth Your Money?

Union College sports a hefty cost of attendance of $74,085 per year. Twenty-eight percent of undergrads receive merit aid awards that average $14,500 per student, not greatly altering the high cost of the school. Where Union truly shines is with need-based aid; like the Ivies, it meets 100 percent of demonstrated need for every single student. Even with the high price tag, Union is a school that opens doors and sends many graduates directly into remunerative fields such as engineering and finance.

FINANCIAL
Institutional Type: Private
In-State Tuition: $58,956
Out-of-State Tuition: $58,956
Room & Board: $14,583
Required Fees: $471
Books & Supplies: $1,500

Avg. Need-Based Grant: $40,535
Avg. % of Need Met: 100%

Avg. Merit-Based Award: $14,500
% Receiving (All Freshmen): 28%
% Receiving (Freshmen w/o Need): 26%

Avg. Cumulative Debt: $36,921
% of Students Borrowing: 53%

CAREER
Who Recruits
1. Rapid7
2. BioSig Technologies
3. Brown Brothers Harriman
4. Northwell Health
5. Stanley Black & Decker

Notable Internships
1. Dow Jones
2. NBCUniversal
3. AIG

Top Industries
1. Business
2. Education
3. Operations
4. Engineering
5. Sales

Top Employers
1. IBM
2. GE
3. PwC
4. Morgan Stanley
5. GE Power

Where Alumni Work
1. New York City
2. Boston
3. Albany, NY
4. Washington DC
5. San Francisco

Median Earnings
College Scorecard (Early Career): $65,400
PayScale (Early Career): $66,600
PayScale (Mid-Career): $134,600

RANKINGS
Money: 128
U.S. News: 44 (T), Liberal Arts Colleges
Wall Street Journal/THE: 132
Washington Monthly: 38, Liberal Arts Colleges

COLLEGE OVERLAPS
Lafayette College
Lehigh University
Rensselaer Polytechnic Institute
Trinity College
University of Rochester

University at Buffalo (SUNY)

Buffalo, New York | 716-645-6900

ADMISSION
Admission Rate: 61%
Admission Rate - Men: 63%
Admission Rate - Women: 60%
EA Admission Rate: 77%
ED Admission Rate: Not Offered
ED Admits as % of Total Admits: Not Offered
Admission Rate (5-Year Trend): +4%
% of Admits Attending (Yield): 23%
Transfer Admission Rate: 67%

SAT Reading/Writing (Middle 50%): 570-650
SAT Math (Middle 50%): 590-690
ACT Composite (Middle 50%): 24-29

% Graduated in Top 10% of HS Class: 30%
% Graduated in Top 25% of HS Class: 65%
% Graduated in Top 50% of HS Class: 94%

Demonstrated Interest: Not Considered
Legacy Status: Not Considered
Admission Interview Offered: No

ENROLLMENT
Total Undergraduate Enrollment: 21,921
% Part-Time: 7%
% Male: 56%
% Female: 44%
% Out-of-State: 2%
% Fraternity: 1%
% Sorority: 3%
% On-Campus (Freshman): 74%
% On-Campus (All Undergraduate): 34%

% African-American: 8%
% Asian: 15%
% Hispanic: 7%
% White: 47%
% Other: 2%
% Race or Ethnicity Unknown: 5%
% International: 14%
% Low-Income: 33%

ACADEMICS
Student-to-Faculty Ratio: 14 to 1
% of Classes Under 20: 30%
% of Classes 20-49: 48%
% of Classes 50 or More: 22%
% Full-Time Faculty: 72%
% Full-Time Faculty w/ Terminal Degree: 97%

Top Programs
Business
Computer Science
English
Exercise Science
Mechanical Engineering
Public Health
Speech and Hearing Science

Retention Rate: 86%
4-Year Graduation Rate: 58%
6-Year Graduation Rate: 75%

Curricular Flexibility: Less Flexible
Academic Rating: ★★★

#CollegesWorthYourMoney

You can make all the jokes you want about the city of Buffalo (cold jokes from relatives never get old), and you can call the university bearing the city's name a "commuter school" if you want, but they don't care. SUNY University at Buffalo is the most popular destination within the colossal State University of New York system, boasting an undergraduate population of 21,921. Well-regarded and highly affordable business, engineering, and computer science programs lure an increasingly more selective group of freshmen each year. It is primarily New York residents who come to Buffalo for its robust academic offerings that include 125 undergraduate degree programs. However, the university ranks in the top twenty-five for total number of international students; there are presently 3,300 foreign students from 82 countries.

Inside the Classroom
Totaling forty credits, the UB curriculum will take the equivalent of almost three full semesters to complete. The program begins freshman year with a small seminar that emphasizes critical thinking and discussion. Next, students will knock out foundations courses in communication literacy, quantitative literacy, scientific literacy, and diversity learning followed by nine credits (each) from thematic and global pathways. Lastly, as a senior, students will complete a one-credit capstone course. Those in the university's Honors Program also must complete twenty-four credits in honors-only courses.

Despite a favorable 14:1 student-to-faculty ratio, undergraduate class sizes do tend to be rather large at the University at Buffalo. Only 30 percent of course sections enroll fewer than twenty students, and 22 percent of courses contain fifty or more students. The Center for Undergraduate Research and Creative Activity (CURCA) can help make a huge university feel a bit smaller by connecting students with faculty mentors for research endeavors. The center advertises that "100 percent of students have the opportunity to participate in research," thus, it is fair to say that procuring opportunities is simply a matter of being proactive. Likewise for those interested in spending a semester at a foreign university; UB offers 1,000 study abroad programs across all seven continents (Antarctica, anyone?).

A good number of Buffalo students flock to the school's strongest offerings with 18 percent of the degrees conferred coming from the School of Management and another 16 percent from the School of Engineering and Applied Sciences. Other commonly conferred degrees are in psychology (10 percent), biology (8 percent), and health professions (7 percent). There has been a slight uptick in recent years in undergraduates capturing prestigious postgraduate scholarships and fellowships. Five seniors/alumni won Fulbright Scholarships in 2019 while others netted Gilman and Critical Language Scholarships.

Outside the Classroom
Even though a sizable number of UB students commute from home or nearby rental homes/apartments, the school does bring 74 percent of freshmen to live in university-owned housing that features twelve residence halls and five apartment communities. Factoring in all undergrads, only 34 percent reside on campus. Greek life has only a faint heartbeat, attracting 2 percent of men and women. Want to see a big-name speaker live? The UB Speakers Series has enticed the likes of Hillary Clinton, Malcom Gladwell, and John Oliver to trek to Buffalo in recent years. There are 300+ student organizations to choose from at the university, and there are many campus-wide events that energize the Bulls community such as Fall Fest, Spring Fest, and Oozefest, which is the muddiest game of volleyball you will ever play. The sports scene is on the rise as the school now supports sixteen NCAA Division I athletic teams that compete in the Mid-American Conference. In the school's own words, the City of Good Neighbors is home to "a vibrant arts scene, quaint neighborhoods, remarkable restaurants, and an affordable cost of living." On campus, the Crossroads Culinary Center is rated the best in the entire SUNY system.

Career Services
The central Career Center at UB employs twelve professional staff members who hold titles such as career counselor, employer relations manager, and employer and alumni relationship associate. The Ciminelli Family Career Resource Center within the School of Management is staffed by nine full-time employees who work with or on behalf of undergraduate students. That translates to a 1,044:1 student-to-counselor ratio, which is significantly higher than the average school featured in this guide, but it is to be expected at a public university of Buffalo's size. The good news is that in a single academic year, almost 11,000 students utilize the Career Center through attending a job fair, a workshop, or making an individual appointment for career coaching; another 16,000 students used Bullseye, the office's online networking app.

Career Center staff could improve outreach efforts as only about 10 percent of the undergraduate student population seek direct career counseling services each year. However, the center did succeed in bringing many top employers to campus for expos such as for the STEAM Job + Internship Fair which draws one hundred+ employers and 2,000+ students each fall. The Spring Job + Internship Fair also brings out one hundred+ employers and around 1,300 students. Unfortunately, those efforts ultimately result in fewer than 500 on-campus interviews each year. Based on the most recent data available, close to 60 percent of students engage in at least one internship, co-op, or other experiential learning placement during their four years at the university. Like much else at the University of Buffalo, the career services spoils go to those who aggressively track down and utilize the available resources.

Professional Outcomes

Within six months of graduating, three-quarters of School of Management degree-holders in the Class of 2019 had found employment. The median base salary for those who found jobs was $48,000 (business grads only). UB graduates are well-represented in the corporate offices of many top finance, accounting, consulting, and technology companies. More than one hundred alumni of the school are currently employed at the likes of M&T Bank, Citi, Amazon, Microsoft, Google, JPMorgan Chase, PwC, Apple, Deloitte, and Cisco. The greatest number of alumni remain in the Buffalo area but many relocate to New York City, San Francisco, DC, and Boston.

There were 130 SUNY Buffalo graduates in 2019-20 who applied to medical school. Including those applying to osteopathic schools, a GPA of 3.5-3.7 and an MCAT score in the 505-510 range typically led to successful results. Recent graduates are currently attending medical schools at Virginia Commonwealth University and Boston University with the greatest percentage heading to the four SUNY medical training grounds at the Stony Brook, Buffalo, Upstate, and Downstate locations. Many law school attendees also stay within the SUNY system, including Buffalo's own home for legal education, but other recent grads have entered such schools as Duke, Wake Forest, and Notre Dame. That pattern is also true for those pursuing master's and doctoral degrees. Graduating with honors from UB absolutely can put elite graduate and professional schools in play, but the bulk of students select local public options.

Admission

SUNY University at Buffalo receives the largest number of applications of any school in the state system, almost 30,000; the school accepted 61 percent of those aiming to join the Class of 2023. Perfect grades aren't necessary, but you need a pretty sound transcript. Thirty percent of attending students placed in the top 10 percent of their high school class, and 65 percent finished in the top quartile. The average GPA was 3.7 and the median SAT score for a freshman in 2019-20 was a 1240, and the median ACT score was just shy of 26.

So many applicants, so little time—it's a recipe for a formulaic admissions process, and that's exactly what the University at Buffalo utilizes. At the top of the list are standardized test scores, GPA, and the rigor of one's course-work followed by the still-important factors of class rank and recommendations. In the end, 23 percent of those admitted go on to enroll. Roughly 350 students per year are admitted into the Honors College, and preference is given to those who apply earlier in the rolling process. For all applicants, we highly recommend meeting the school's priority deadline.

Worth Your Money?

Total cost of attendance for a New York resident comes to about $29,000 per year, which accounts for direct and indirect living expenses—an excellent deal for the quality of education the school provides. For those from out of state, costs climb to $46,000 per year, making attending UB a curious choice for those with more affordable options. Over 11,000 undergraduates are determined needy each year, and the school awards an average annual need-based grant of $8,861. For New York residents, SUNY Buffalo is, unequivocally and independent of circumstance, worth your money.

FINANCIAL
Institutional Type: Public
In-State Tuition: $7,070
Out-of-State Tuition: $24,740
Room & Board: $14,631
Required Fees: $3,454
Books & Supplies: $1,203

Avg. Need-Based Grant: $8,861
Avg. % of Need Met: 52%

Avg. Merit-Based Award: $3,688
% Receiving (All Freshmen): 33%
% Receiving (Freshmen w/o Need): 8%

Avg. Cumulative Debt: $25,157
% of Students Borrowing: 57%

CAREER
Who Recruits
1. ACV Auctions
2. Salesforce
3. Facebook
4. PwC
5. Apple

Notable Internships
1. Walt Disney World
2. Wegmnan's Food Markets
3. HSBC

Top Industries
1. Business
2. Education
3. Operations
4. Engineering
5. Healthcare

Top Employers
1. M&T Bank
2. Citi
3. Amazon
4. Ingram Micro
5. Microsoft

Where Alumni Work
1. Buffalo, NY
2. New York City
3. Rochester, NY
4. San Francisco
5. Singapore

Median Earnings
College Scorecard (Early Career): $52,600
PayScale (Early Career): $57,000
PayScale (Mid-Career): $103,700

RANKINGS
Money: 94
U.S. News: 88 (T), National Universities
Wall Street Journal/THE: 121 (T)
Washington Monthly: 133, National Universities

COLLEGE OVERLAPS
Binghamton University (SUNY)
Stony Brook University (SUNY)
Syracuse University
University at Albany (SUNY)
University of Pittsburgh

Tucson, Arizona | 520-621-3237

ADMISSION
Admission Rate: 85%
Admission Rate - Men: 83%
Admission Rate - Women: 86%
EA Admission Rate: Not Offered
ED Admission Rate: Not Offered
ED Admits as % of Total Admits: Not Offered
Admission Rate (5-Year Trend): +1%
% of Admits Attending (Yield): 22%
Transfer Admission Rate: 67%

SAT Reading/Writing (Middle 50%): 560-670
SAT Math (Middle 50%): 550-690
ACT Composite (Middle 50%): 21-29

% Graduated in Top 10% of HS Class: 36%
% Graduated in Top 25% of HS Class: 65%
% Graduated in Top 50% of HS Class: 88%

Demonstrated Interest: Important
Legacy Status: Not Considered
Admission Interview Offered: No

ENROLLMENT
Total Undergraduate Enrollment: 35,801
% Part-Time: 18%
% Male: 47%
% Female: 53%
% Out-of-State: 33%
% Fraternity: 10%
% Sorority: 20%
% On-Campus (Freshman): 76%
% On-Campus (All Undergraduate): 20%

% African-American: 4%
% Asian: 5%
% Hispanic: 26%
% White: 48%
% Other: 6%
% Race or Ethnicity Unknown: 5%
% International: 6%
% Low-Income: 36%

ACADEMICS
Student-to-Faculty Ratio: 15 to 1
% of Classes Under 20: 45%
% of Classes 20-49: 39%
% of Classes 50 or More: 16%
% Full-Time Faculty: 85%
% Full-Time Faculty w/ Terminal Degree: 94%

Top Programs
Business
Engineering
Geosciences
Physics
Political Science
Psychology
Public Health

Retention Rate: 83%
4-Year Graduation Rate: 47%
6-Year Graduation Rate: 65%

Curricular Flexibility: Somewhat Flexible
Academic Rating: ★★★

#CollegesWorthYourMoney

Residents of many states are lucky to have one university that (1) charges a reasonable tuition, (b) accepts the vast majority of students, even those with a B average, and (c) provides a high-quality educational and social experience for its undergraduates. Arizona is lucky to not only have Arizona State University (featured in this book), but the University of Arizona as well. A genuinely diverse school—26 percent of the undergraduate student body identifies as Hispanic, and students hail from all 50 states and 112 countries—UArizona is noted for its success in improving social mobility. It also happens to have a terrific national reputation, a status that attracts many non-residents to its exquisite Tucson campus. In fact, one-third of current Wildcats are from out of state and are willing to pay a large premium to attend the school of 35,800 undergraduates and another 10,000+ graduate students.

Inside the Classroom
The UA general education requirements entail conquering foundations courses (first-year writing, mathematics, second language), tier one courses (traditions and cultures, individuals and societies, natural sciences), tier two courses (humanities, arts, etc.), and one course that falls under the umbrella of diversity emphasis. Students in the Honors College must also complete at least 30 honors units, which includes a thesis/capstone project, prior to graduation.

A 15:1 student-to faculty ratio leads to a mix of smaller and larger course sections with 45 percent of classes having an enrollment of under 20 and 16 percent possessing 50 or more students. UArizona promotes opportunities for hands-on learning and faculty mentors through a variety of undergraduate research programs including the Summer Research Institute, Undergraduate Biology Research Program, and Collaborative Research in the Chemical Sciences. Opportunities to study abroad and earn UA credits at partner universities abound. There are 12 such programs available at locations as varied as London, Jakarta, and Phnom Penh.

Nearly doubling the number of conferred degrees in any other major, business/marketing (16 percent) is the most popular major choice at UArizona. Other common pursuits include biology (9 percent), health professions (8 percent), and engineering (8 percent). Majors within business, engineering, and the geosciences all have excellent national reputations. For those pursuing prestigious fellowships/scholarships, the university has its own Office of Nationally Competitive Scholarships. There have been years in which the school has produced double-digit numbers of Fulbright Scholars.

Outside the Classroom
This 353-acre campus is situated in a residential area of Tucson, the state's second largest city. A touch over three quarters of freshmen, but just 20 percent of the overall undergraduate student body, live in on-campus housing. Yet, in spite of this relatively low number, UArizona very much provides a quintessential big-college experience. Greek life is relatively prominent, attracting 17 percent of students, but only 26 of the 51 fraternities and sororities actually offer housing. The school is home to 500 varsity athletes who compete in 20 sports; the history of men's basketball is particularly rich and includes a 1997 NCAA title. Thirty club teams engage another 1,000 participants, and an additional 30 intramural leagues bring in thousands more. Arizona regularly garners accolades for having the nicest student recreation centers in the country. It's hard to find a Wildcat who isn't an active member of at least one organization; the school's 600 total clubs have an estimated membership of 20,000 students. Outdoor activities are accessible year-round thanks to an average annual temperature of 83 degrees. Tucson itself rates well as a fun, laid-back, bikeable city with excellent food and entertainment options.

Career Services
The Office of Student Engagement & Career Development at the University of Arizona is staffed by 18 professional employees who specialize in career education, alumni relations, employer relations, and alumni engagement. Additional career service staff members are housed with the university's various undergraduate colleges such as the College of Agriculture and Life Sciences (3) and the Eller College of Management (12), bringing the total number of staff to 33. The overall student-to-advisor ratio is 1,085:1, a high figure compared against many other institutions featured in this book.

Many large-scale events are offered by the university, including multiday, all-student career fairs in the fall and spring. Frequent employer information sessions are also offered throughout the year, as high-profile employers are more than willing to make the trek to campus to recruit UA talent. Handshake affords students access to countless job and internship opportunities, and those seeking a more personal touch can work on their resume or sales pitch with a member of the LifeLab. Job shadowing and other opportunities to connect with the 300,000 active Wildcat alumni are available to anyone who is motivated to seek them out. Within the Eller College of Management, 90 percent of undergraduates report participating in at least one internship. The school boasts a wealth of high-quality industry partners such as 3M, Honeywell, IBM, Johnson & Johnson, and Northrup Grumman.

Professional Outcomes

While across the board success rates of UArizona alumni are not published, there is enough available data for one to see the positive outcomes associated with a Wildcat education. In recent years, some of the top employers hiring Arizona grads have been Raytheon, Vanguard, PepsiCo, Amazon, KPMG, Goldman Sachs, Intel, Lockheed Martin, Nordstrom, and Texas Instruments. An astonishing 92 percent of employers rate Wildcats as coming to their first job with the skills needed to succeed; this is 66 percent higher than the national average! Graduates of the Eller College of Management enjoy a $57,606 starting salary along with an $8k signing bonus. Ninety-one percent of graduates of the College of Engineering have already secured a job or graduate school acceptance upon receiving their bachelor's diploma; this group has an average starting salary of $67,000.

Many who go on to pursue advanced degrees due so at the University of Arizona itself, which boasts a full array of graduate/professional degree programs and features the affiliated James E. Rogers College of Law and three MD-granting medical schools, including the highly regarded University of Arizona College of Medicine – Tucson. In the 2019-20 academic year, the university saw 362 undergraduates apply to medical schools, slightly more than Arizona State University. To a get a sense of the types of graduate programs one can access with a UArizona degree, recent graduates of the College of Engineering have continued their studies in master's or PhD programs at the likes of Stanford University, the University of Cambridge, Yale University, Harvard University, Carnegie Mellon University, and Georgia Tech.

Admission

Arizona continued to post unintimidating admissions numbers in the 2019-20 cycle, accepting 85 percent of the 40,854 who applied. Even better, students who struggle on standardized exams can take advantage of the school's test-optional policy. Thirty-six percent of attending students placed in the top 10 percent of their high school class while 65 percent and 88 percent were in the top 25 percent and 50 percent, respectively. Cumulative GPAs range widely, with 11 percent of students having earned a 4.0 and 20 percent having earned under a 3.0. Roughly half of applicants elect to send an ACT result, and another half send SAT scores. The mid-50 percentile ACT range is also quite wide at 21-29; on the SAT, mid-50 percentile scores were 560-670 on EBRW and 550-690 on math.

Applications to this university are reviewed on a rolling basis. The two most important factors in the eyes of the admissions committee are GPA and the rigor of one's high school courses. Items viewed as "important" are standardized test scores (if submitted), extracurricular activities, talent/ability, character/personal qualities, and the level of an applicant's demonstrated interest. It is highly unusual for the latter category to be given so much weight, however, the University of Arizona serves as a "safety school" to many applicants (the yield rate is 17 percent), and therefore, they like to know when candidates have a sincere interest in attending.

Worth Your Money?

The University of Arizona continues to be a solid deal for residents of the Grand Canyon State. Including tuition, room and board, and all fees, the estimated cost per year was $30,500 in 2020-21. An out-of-state student would expect to pay a heftier annual total of $54,500. The average need-based scholarship is $13,720, which meets an average of 67 percent of demonstrated need. Without financial aid, an out-of-state student would need to have a sound and specific reason for crossing state lines to pay $200k at a public university rather than exploring options closer to home. For the 45 percent who borrow, the average debt carried by Wildcats upon graduation is $26k.

FINANCIAL
Institutional Type: Public
In-State Tuition: $11,299
Out-of-State Tuition: $35,326
Room & Board: $13,050
Required Fees: $1,412
Books & Supplies: $800

Avg. Need-Based Grant: $13,720
Avg. % of Need Met: 67%

Avg. Merit-Based Award: $9,808
% Receiving (All Freshmen): 44%
% Receiving (Freshmen w/o Need): 34%

Avg. Cumulative Debt: $26,414
% of Students Borrowing: 45%

CAREER
Who Recruits
1. KPMG
2. Moss Adams
3. Google
4. National Securty Agency
5. JPMorgan Chase

Notable Internships
1. Arizona State Legislature
2. Arizona Public Media
3. Tucson Electric Power

Top Industries
1. Business
2. Education
3. Operations
4. Sales
5. Healthcare

Top Employers
1. Amazon
2. Intel
3. Microsoft
4. Apple
5. Honeywell

Where Alumni Work
1. Tucson
2. Phoenix
3. Los Angeles
4. San Francisco
5. New York City

Median Earnings
College Scorecard (Early Career): $47,300
PayScale (Early Career): $59,100
PayScale (Mid-Career): $106,600

RANKINGS
Money: 98
U.S. News: 97 (T), National Universities
Wall Street Journal/THE: 135 (T)
Washington Monthly: 85, National Universities

COLLEGE OVERLAPS
Arizona State University
Northern Arizona University
San Diego State University
University of Colorado Boulder
University of Oregon

University of California, Berkeley

Berkeley, California | 510-642-6000

ADMISSION
Admission Rate: 17%
Admission Rate - Men: 14%
Admission Rate - Women: 19%
EA Admission Rate: Not Offered
ED Admission Rate: Not Offered
ED Admits as % of Total Admits: Not Offered
Admission Rate (5-Year Trend): -1%
% of Admits Attending (Yield): 46%
Transfer Admission Rate: 23%

SAT Reading/Writing (Middle 50%): 640-740
SAT Math (Middle 50%): 670-790
ACT Composite (Middle 50%): 28-34

% Graduated in Top 10% of HS Class: 98%
% Graduated in Top 25% of HS Class: 100%
% Graduated in Top 50% of HS Class: 100%

Demonstrated Interest: Not Considered
Legacy Status: Not Considered
Admission Interview Offered: No

ENROLLMENT
Total Undergraduate Enrollment: 31,780
% Part-Time: 5%
% Male: 46%
% Female: 54%
% Out-of-State: 16%
% Fraternity: 3%
% Sorority: 9%
% On-Campus (Freshman): 94%
% On-Campus (All Undergraduate): 27%

% African-American: 2%
% Asian: 35%
% Hispanic: 16%
% White: 24%
% Other: 6%
% Race or Ethnicity Unknown: 4%
% International: 13%
% Low-Income: 24%

ACADEMICS
Student-to-Faculty Ratio: 19 to 1
% of Classes Under 20: 53%
% of Classes 20-49: 28%
% of Classes 50 or More: 19%
% Full-Time Faculty: 65%
% Full-Time Faculty w/ Terminal Degree: 99%

Top Programs
Biological Sciences
Business
Chemistry
Computer Science
Economics
Engineering
English
Psychology

Retention Rate: 97%
4-Year Graduation Rate: 76%
6-Year Graduation Rate: 93%

Curricular Flexibility: Somewhat Flexible
Academic Rating: ★★★★↲

#CollegesWorthYourMoney

The University of California, Berkeley, more commonly referred to as Berkeley or Cal, is the flagship university in the stellar and gargantuan UC system. Founded in 1868 with the motto "Fiat Lux" (Let there be light), the university today offers enlightenment to 31,780 undergraduate and 11,915 graduate students. The name Berkeley likely conjures up two immediate associations—academic prestige and the protests of the 1960s. While no longer a hotbed of youth unrest on the level of the Vietnam era, Berkeley remains a bastion of liberal thought and idealism. It is fitting that the school is the number one all-time producer of Peace Corps volunteers.

Inside the Classroom
More than 150 undergraduate majors and minors are available across five undergraduate schools: The College of Letters and Science, the College of Chemistry, the College of Engineering, the College of Environmental Design, and the College of Natural Resources. A sixth school, the Haas School of Business, must be applied to separately prior to one's junior year. Over two-thirds of undergrads are housed within the College of Letters and Science, which requires coursework including entry-level writing, American history and American institutions, foreign language, quantitative reasoning, and reading & composition.

Constant budget crises in the UC system haven't dented the school's reputation one iota, but the impact can be felt in measures such as student-to-faculty ratio that, at 19:1, is significantly higher than other elite flagships like UVA or Michigan. However, that doesn't translate to across-the-board large class sizes. Rather, undergrads will encounter a mix of large lectures (19 percent of sections contain more than fifty students) and tiny, single-digit enrollments in seminar-style courses (23 percent of sections contain nine or fewer students). Undergraduate research opportunities do exist despite the school's massive size; over 55 percent of students assist faculty with a research project or complete a research methods course in their time at Berkeley. Study abroad opportunities are available for those who desire them, and approximately 1,800 undergrads take a semester in a foreign country each year. Locations where Berkeley faculty deliver instruction include Taiwan, Switzerland, Serbia, Peru, and the Philippines.

Thanks to its equally esteemed graduate schools, many departments have top international reputations including computer science, engineering, chemistry, English, psychology, and economics. In a typical year, 100+ grads are awarded National Science Foundation Graduate Research Fellowships, which was more than Stanford and more than Harvard and Yale combined. In 2019, there were eight Critical Language Scholars, three Schwarzman Scholars, and two Goldwater Scholars.

Outside the Classroom
Ninety-four percent of incoming freshmen live in university-run housing, upperclassmen are generally left to fend for themselves. Housing is a challenging issue, and while the university is building new dormitories, it presently only has the capacity to house roughly one-quarter of the undergraduate population. A prominent but far from dominant Greek life attracts 9 percent of women but only 3 percent of men into sixty+ active fraternities and sororities. Cal's sports program is exceptional as the Golden Bears thirty varsity teams have won a collective eighty-seven NCAA championships in the school's history; they mostly compete in the Pac-12 Conference. With 1000+ clubs and activities, there is truly somethings for everyone, including many political and public-service organizations. Roughly 5,300 undergraduate students volunteer their time to community service projects, and the campus has a genuine focus on sustainability; 87 percent of students walk, bike, or take public transit, and the school has a goal of zero non-recycled waste by 2020. Being a few miles north of Oakland and a few miles east of San Francisco, big-city fun is never far away. Berkeley itself is replete with awesome restaurants (including, of course, many vegan options), a botanical garden, a marina, an art museum, and a 2,000-acre park.

Career Services
With thirty-three full-time employees dedicated to undergraduates, the UC Berkeley Career Center has a 963:1 student-to-counselor ratio, much higher than most of the schools featured in this guide but comparable to the other University of California institutions. What the center lacks in its ability to connect one-on-one it makes up for by putting together large-scale events that bring 350+ employers to campus every year. There are large career fairs in the fall and spring, and many industry-specific affairs are held as well including the Social Impact Career Fair, Investment Banking Forum, Law & Graduate School Fair, and the Civil & Environmental Engineering Career Fair.

A survey of employed graduates reveals that the efforts of the career center directly contributed to their job attainment. Specifically, 17 percent found their first job through on-campus recruiting, 15 percent directly from an internship, 14 percent via a career fair or information session, and 13 percent through Cal's Handshake platform. A hard-to-beat alumni network of 493,000 individuals—100,000 are dues-paying members of the alumni association— can assist you throughout your career. More than 4,500 students attend webinars and in-person events hosted by alums. The average student received two job offers. Overall, despite a high counselor-to-student ratio, Cal's career services provides plenty of opportunities for undergrads to connect with top employers, resulting in students landing positions that align with their career goals while also paying the bills.

Professional Outcomes

Upon graduating, 61 percent of Cal's Class of 2019 members had already secured employment, 19 percent were headed to graduate school, and 14 percent were still seeking their first jobs. Business was the most popular sector, attracting 59 percent of employed grads; next up were industrial (16 percent), education (12 percent) and nonprofit work (8 percent). Thousands of alumni can be found in the offices of Google, Apple, and Facebook, and 500+ Golden Bears are currently employed by Oracle, Amazon, and Microsoft. Most alumni are concentrated in the San Francisco Bay area with Los Angeles, New York, Seattle, DC, Boston, and the United Kingdom next in popularity. The average starting salary was an astonishing $75,000, across all majors.

Because almost 8,000 students earn bachelor's degrees each year, it's hard to pinpoint the most commonly attended graduate/professional schools with literally hundreds of institutions absorbing Berkeley undergrads. They range from the most selective Ivy League universities to a host of less selective institutions. For example, political science degree-holders from the Class of 2018 attended graduate schools that included Stanford, Georgetown, San Francisco State, and Eastern Michigan University. Suffice it to say that earning strong grades at Berkeley will set you up for a successful graduate application process at the nation's most elite schools. In recent years, the medical school acceptance rate has hovered in the 51-55 percent range, and law school applicants have been successful 81-89 percent of the time. Among recent grads, master's degrees were the most frequently pursued degree (719) followed by PhD (453), JD (100), and MD (94).

Admission

Berkeley received 87,398 applications for a place in the Class of 2023, but only 17 percent were offered admission. A decade prior, the university received 48,000+ applications and sported an admit rate of 22 percent. Acceptance rates fluctuate among three separate groups of candidates: California residents are usually admitted at a slightly higher rate than out-of-staters (2-3 points) and appear to have a massive advantage over international students whose acceptance rate is in the single-digits. However, the average SAT of an admitted resident is typically 100 points higher than those from the other two groups. Overall, members of the Class of 2023 possessed a mid-50 percent range of 1330-1520 on the SAT and 28-34 on the ACT. An eye-popping 97 percent placed in the top decile of their high school class, and the average unweighted GPA was 3.89.

The committee claims that the admissions review is so holistic that it "literally hugs your application." Logistically, with nearly 90,000 applications to sift through, each embrace is surely quite short. As a result, GPA, rigor of secondary school record, the essays, and standardized test scores are presently among the "very important" criteria used to winnow down the initial pool; however, all UC schools will be test-optional and then test-blind in the coming years. Becoming a Golden Bear has been highly selective process for many decades, and now it has reached its all-time high. Flawless grades in a roster of AP and honors courses is essentially a prerequisite, but there is some wiggle-room on test scores as they diminish in importance at this school.

Worth Your Money?

Paying $14,312 per year in tuition to attend one of the finest institutions in the country sounds like a pipe dream, particularly considering that some private schools charge four times that. For the one-quarter or so of the undergraduate student body from out of state, the annual cost of attendance will be $68k, a far cry from the $37k COA for Californians. For the 43 percent of students determined eligible for need-based aid, the average award is $23,767 per year, making Berkeley a genuinely accessible place for lower-income students to attend without incurring unhealthy student loan debt.

FINANCIAL
Institutional Type: Public
In-State Tuition: $14,226
Out-of-State Tuition: $42,852
Room & Board: $17,219
Required Fees: $0
Books & Supplies: $850

Avg. Need-Based Grant: $23,767
Avg. % of Need Met: 83%

Avg. Merit-Based Award: $6,464
% Receiving (All Freshmen): 7%
% Receiving (Freshmen w/o Need): 6%

Avg. Cumulative Debt: $19,773
% of Students Borrowing: 32%

CAREER
Who Recruits
1. AlphaSights
2. Fisher Investments
3. Navigant
4. Putnam Associates
5. Western Digital

Notable Internships
1. Lyft
2. WeWork
3. Airbnb

Top Industries
1. Business
2. Education
3. Engineering
4. Research
5. Operations

Top Employers
1. Google
2. Apple
3. Facebook
4. Amazon
5. Oracle

Where Alumni Work
1. San Francisco
2. Los Angeles
3. New York City
4. Seattle
5. Boston

Median Earnings
College Scorecard (Early Career): $64,700
PayScale (Early Career): $74,500
PayScale (Mid-Career): $146,700

RANKINGS
Money: 17
U.S. News: 22, National Universities
Wall Street Journal/THE: 34
Washington Monthly: 17, National Universities

COLLEGE OVERLAPS
Stanford University
University of California, Los Angeles
University of California, San Diego
University of California, Santa Barbara
University of Michigan

University of California, Davis

Davis, California | 530-752-2971

ADMISSION
Admission Rate: 39%
Admission Rate - Men: 34%
Admission Rate - Women: 43%
EA Admission Rate: Not Offered
ED Admission Rate: Not Offered
ED Admits as % of Total Admits: Not Offered
Admission Rate (5-Year Trend): -2%
% of Admits Attending (Yield): 20%
Transfer Admission Rate: 57%

SAT Reading/Writing (Middle 50%): 570-680
SAT Math (Middle 50%): 580-740
ACT Composite (Middle 50%): 25-31

% Graduated in Top 10% of HS Class: 100%
% Graduated in Top 25% of HS Class: 100%
% Graduated in Top 50% of HS Class: 100%

Demonstrated Interest: Not Considered
Legacy Status: Not Considered
Admission Interview Offered: No

ENROLLMENT
Total Undergraduate Enrollment: 30,982
% Part-Time: 3%
% Male: 39%
% Female: 61%
% Out-of-State: 5%
% Fraternity: NR
% Sorority: NR
% On-Campus (Freshman): 92%
% On-Campus (All Undergraduate): 25%

% African-American: 2%
% Asian: 28%
% Hispanic: 23%
% White: 23%
% Other: 6%
% Race or Ethnicity Unknown: 2%
% International: 17%
% Low-Income: 38%

ACADEMICS
Student-to-Faculty Ratio: 20 to 1
% of Classes Under 20: 36%
% of Classes 20-49: 34%
% of Classes 50 or More: 30%
% Full-Time Faculty: 74%
% Full-Time Faculty w/ Terminal Degree: 95%

Top Programs
Animal Science
Biological Sciences
Environmental Science
Communication
Computer Science
Engineering
English
Sociology

Retention Rate: 92%
4-Year Graduation Rate: 63%
6-Year Graduation Rate: 87%

Curricular Flexibility: Less Flexible
Academic Rating: ★★★★

#CollegesWorthYourMoney

Like so much growth in the annals of California state history, the story of UC-Davis is one of a post-World War II boom that saw the state's population increase by 53 percent from the 1940s to the 1950s. The school's rapid rise began in 1959 when Davis officially became a general campus of the University of California system. By 1962 it launched an engineering school, and its now prestigious law and medical schools opened in 1966 and 1968, respectively. One hundred years ago, Davis was known as the University Farm and offered no degree programs. Today, it is home to 30,982 undergraduates alone and offers 100+ undergraduate majors and roughly the same number of graduate programs. As with many UC campuses, the onset of the 2010s saw application numbers spike and acceptance rates plunge. The school that was once only a farm is, today, producing crops of graduates that line corporate offices at the leading tech companies in Silicon Valley.

Inside the Classroom
There are four undergraduate schools at UCD: The College of Agricultural and Environmental Sciences, the College of Biological Sciences, the College of Engineering, and the College of Letters and Science. The university has two sets of core requirements—Topical Breadth, which mandates between twelve and twenty units in each of the arts and humanities, science and engineering, and the social sciences—and Core Literacies, which include English composition; writing experience; oral skills; visual literacy; American cultures, governance, and history; domestic diversity; world cultures; quantitative literacy; and scientific literacy. All told, that adds up to eighty-seven units of required coursework, but the categories are broad, and pretty much any course you could take fits at least one, making those curricular requirements less limiting than they first appear.

A 20:1 student-to-faculty ratio isn't terribly inspiring, especially with 7,500+ graduate students stealing their share of the spotlight. While class sizes aren't small, 62 percent of sections enroll fewer than thirty students, and 71 percent of classes are kept under fifty students. There are numerous opportunities for undergraduate research through programs like the McNair Scholars Program, the Biology Undergraduate Research Program, and Sponsored Undergraduate Research programs. In 2019, a solid 42 percent of Davis seniors report having assisted a professor with research, and 50 percent engage in some type of research/creative project outside the classroom. Only 1,300 students choose to study abroad each year, but offerings do include fifty programs in thirty countries with courses taught by University of California professors.

The areas of study with the largest number of degrees awarded were psychology (9 percent), managerial economics (6 percent), economics (6 percent), neurobiology (5 percent), and human development (4 percent). Davis also attracts droves of students to programs in engineering, computer science, and animal science, all of which are nationally renowned. In recent years Davis students have begun to capture a greater number of prestigious national awards. Twelve Fulbright Scholarships were awarded to grads and alumni in 2019, and the school has had a number of Rhodes Scholarship finalists since 2010.

Outside the Classroom
At 5,300 acres, the Davis campus is one of the largest in the country, yet housing options are still expanding to keep up with enrollment increases. The housing capacity at the university is currently 11,000 students; freshmen are guaranteed on-campus housing, and 92 percent take advantage. In 2019, the school broke ground on a new housing project that will add 3,300 beds to the West Village section of the university. The gender disparity cannot be ignored at UC-Davis as women outnumber men by a 61/39 ratio. Roughly seventy Greek organizations attract 10 percent of the undergraduate population. There are approximately 800 student-run organizations, including award-winning academic teams that have captured the National Freescale Cup Autonomous Model Car Competition, the International Data Mining Cup, and the grand prize at the International Genetically Engineered Machines competition. On the subject of competition, the chance to participate in athletics exists no matter your level of skill. The Aggies field fourteen women's and nine men's Division I teams to go with twenty-seven intramural leagues and thirty-nine intercollegiate club squads. Given the school's emphasis on environmental science, it should come as no shock that it is routinely voted one of the greener campuses in the United States, and 29 percent of dining hall food is sustainably grown. Sacramento is the nearest big city, only 15 miles from campus; San Francisco is a manageable hour-long car ride away.

Career Services
The UC-Davis Internship and Career Center (ICC) has nineteen professional employees who work with or on behalf of undergraduate students, many of whom specialize in a particular discipline such as engineering and physical sciences, health and biological sciences, agricultural and environmental sciences, and liberal arts and

business. Others play roles in the areas of internship coordination, employer relations, and recruiting. Davis has a 1,631:1 student-to-staff ratio, which is among the poorest of any university profiled in this guidebook. While the staffing may be lacking for a school with close to 31,000 undergraduates, there are plenty of encouraging statistics that indicate Aggies' career prospects are in good hands.

An admirable 80 percent of undergraduates land at least one internship; 55 percent engage in two or more internships. In total, the ICC facilitates more than 10,000 internships per year. More than 500 company recruiters visit UC Davis each year looking to hire Aggies, and many major corporations attend the six large-scale career fairs that take place each year, including the Fall/Winter/Spring Internship & Career Fair, the STEM Career Fair, and the Engineering & Tech Internship & Career Fair. There are 277,000 living Aggie alumni who are embedded at many of the top companies to work for in the country. With terrific internship and recruitment statistics, the ICC overcomes its less-than-desirable staffing to be of great assistance to job-seeking graduates.

Professional Outcomes

One year after earning their BA or BS, 14 percent of Davis grads are still unemployed. Many have found homes at Silicon Valley or other California-based juggernaut employers, including about all of the world's top tech companies. The corporations employing 200 or more Aggies include Genentech, Google, Apple, Cisco, Facebook, Oracle, Amazon, Microsoft, Salesforce, Workday, and LinkedIn. More than one hundred Aggies are presently working for Adobe and rivals Uber and Lyft. The San Francisco Bay area is home to the largest concentration of Davis alumni followed by Sacramento, Los Angeles, San Diego, and Seattle. Median earnings go from $42k two years out to $107k ten years out.

Within one year of graduating, 39 percent of Aggies elect to continue their education, and 94 percent report that their undergraduate experience prepared them somewhere between adequately and "very well" for postgraduate study. The most popular degrees pursued are masters, MDs or other health doctorates, law, and MBA/MPA. The UC Davis School of Medicine, one of the best schools for primary care training in the country, tends to favor its own graduates, filling approximately 20 percent of its cohorts with homegrown students. The average undergraduate student who gained acceptance to at least one medical school possessed a 3.58 GPA and a 512 MCAT score. The UC Davis School of Law also draws heavily from its undergraduate schools, and many grads also find homes at other University of California schools. Currently, multiple Aggie alumni are enrolled at the likes of Harvard Law School, Duke University School of Law, and a host of other top-tier institutions.

Admission

Like all schools in the University of California system the Davis branch has experienced an influx of applicants in the last several years. It set a record last cycle with 77,152 freshman applications. From that pool, 41 percent were welcomed aboard to form the freshman class of 2019-20. Most had near-perfect academic transcripts as 89 percent were the proud owners of a 3.75 or higher unweighted GPA. The average SAT score was 1,277 and the average ACT was 28. A decade ago, Davis admitted 52 percent of applicants and, while grades were similarly stellar to those of the Class of 2023, standardized test scores were significantly lower.

According to admissions officers, the factors most heavily weighted in the admissions process are the rigor of one's secondary courses, GPA, and the application essay. Test scores are optional moving forward and the school will be test-blind in 2023. First-generation status is listed as a "considered" factor, but the number of students who are the first in their families to enter college suggests that this is a point of emphasis for the university. In fact, an astonishing 42 percent of current students grew up in households with parents who had not completed four-year degrees. Getting into UC-Davis is harder than it used to be and, like other University of California campuses, it requires a fairly pristine academic transcript in a rigorous curriculum, but standardized test scores can be a bit lower than at UC-San Diego and significantly lower than at Berkeley or UCLA.

Worth Your Money?

Over half of those attending UC Davis receive an average need-based grant of $21k. Considering that the estimated in-state cost of attendance is just under $38k, the majority of undergraduates are paying a reasonable price for a valuable degree. Estimated COA for nonresidents is $67k. For the 20 percent of attendees not from California, that would be an expensive venture without any financial aid, and you likely could find a better merit aid offer from a private institution.

FINANCIAL
Institutional Type: Public
In-State Tuition: $14,442
Out-of-State Tuition: $43,068
Room & Board: $14,261
Required Fees: $0
Books & Supplies: $1,136

Avg. Need-Based Grant: $21,076
Avg. % of Need Met: 82%

Avg. Merit-Based Award: $5,633
% Receiving (All Freshmen): 4%
% Receiving (Freshmen w/o Need): 3%

Avg. Cumulative Debt: $18,985
% of Students Borrowing: 46%

CAREER
Who Recruits
1. Airbnb
2. Lyft
3. Adobe
4. Linkedin
5. Cisco

Notable Internships
1. U.S. House of Representatives
2. Adidas
3. Credit Suisse

Top Industries
1. Business
2. Education
3. Operations
4. Research
5. Engineering

Top Employers
1. Kaiser Permanente
2. Genetech
3. Google
4. Apple
5. Facebook

Where Alumni Work
1. San Francisco
2. Sacramento
3. Los Angeles
4. San Diego
5. Orange County, CA

Median Earnings
College Scorecard (Early Career): $58,200
PayScale (Early Career): $64,300
PayScale (Mid-Career): $126,800

RANKINGS
Money: 10
U.S. News: 39 (T), National Universities
Wall Street Journal/THE: 38
Washington Monthly: 13, National Universities

COLLEGE OVERLAPS
University of California, Berkeley
University of California, Irvine
University of California, Los Angeles
University of California, San Diego
University of California, Santa Barbara

University of California, Irvine

Irvine, California | 949-824-6703

ADMISSION
Admission Rate: 27%
Admission Rate - Men: 25%
Admission Rate - Women: 28%
EA Admission Rate: Not Offered
ED Admission Rate: Not Offered
ED Admits as % of Total Admits: Not Offered
Admission Rate (5-Year Trend): -15%
% of Admits Attending (Yield): 24%
Transfer Admission Rate: 44%

SAT Reading/Writing (Middle 50%): 570-690
SAT Math (Middle 50%): 590-750
ACT Composite (Middle 50%): NR

% Graduated in Top 10% of HS Class: 99%
% Graduated in Top 25% of HS Class: 100%
% Graduated in Top 50% of HS Class: 100%

Demonstrated Interest: Not Considered
Legacy Status: Not Considered
Admission Interview Offered: No

ENROLLMENT
Total Undergraduate Enrollment: 30,382
% Part-Time: 2%
% Male: 48%
% Female: 52%
% Out-of-State: 2%
% Fraternity: 8%
% Sorority: 9%
% On-Campus (Freshman): 78%
% On-Campus (All Undergraduate): 41%

% African-American: 2%
% Asian: 36%
% Hispanic: 26%
% White: 13%
% Other: 4%
% Race or Ethnicity Unknown: 1%
% International: 17%
% Low-Income: 47%

ACADEMICS
Student-to-Faculty Ratio: 18 to 1
% of Classes Under 20: 52%
% of Classes 20-49: 25%
% of Classes 50 or More: 23%
% Full-Time Faculty: 82%
% Full-Time Faculty w/ Terminal Degree: 98%

Top Programs
Biological Sciences
Chemistry
Computer Science
Criminology, Law and Society
Drama
Engineering
Engish
Public Health

Retention Rate: 94%
4-Year Graduation Rate: 69%
6-Year Graduation Rate: 84%

Curricular Flexibility: Somewhat Flexible
Academic Rating: ★★★★⌐

#CollegesWorthYourMoney

A diverse school with a strong Asian and Hispanic representation that serves a phenomenally high percentage of first-generation college students, UC-Irvine is, like the other schools in the University of California system, becoming more selective every year. On the eve of the millennium as Y2K-mania reached its crescendo, Irvine was a school that accepted roughly half of its applicants and was primarily a safety school for those applying to the more prestigious UC campuses. Today, UCI is a top-of-the-list destination for 30,382 UCI undergraduate students, half of whom are California residents, and all of whom proudly call themselves Anteaters. As the third decade of the 2000s kicks off, freshmen flock to Orange County not just for the school's premier location but for the eighty stellar undergraduate academic programs the university offers at a bargain price.

Inside the Classroom
For a school with an overwhelming number of freshmen entering its gates each year, UC-Irvine takes great care to offer first-years a soft landing. The Summer Bridge Scholars Program, Freshman Edge Program, and the Freshman Seminar Series are all designed to help new students succeed, and they are effective as 93 percent of freshmen return for their sophomore year, a retention rate on par with many highly selective private institutions. All students take a liberal arts core that involves three courses in each of science and technology, arts and humanities, and the social sciences, two writing-intensive classes, and forays into foreign language, quantitative reasoning, multicultural issues, and international/global issues. Like most California publics, UCI operates on the quarter system, which means you'll need to get used to furiously paced ten-week periods of study.

At a school with an 18:1 student-to-faculty ratio and 6,526 graduate students to serve, you might expect all classes at Irvine to be held in hundred-seat lecture halls. We are pleased to report that is not the case. In fact, 52 percent of all sections enroll nineteen or fewer students, and only 23 percent of courses contain fifty+ students. The school provides a terrific number of opportunities for undergrads to participate in some type of supervised research. More than three-fifths of students have conducted a research project, and 20 percent have assisted faculty in conducting research. The Undergraduate Research Opportunities Program helps students with proposal writing, developing research plans, and presenting their results at the annual spring UCI Undergraduate Research Symposium and/or publishing their results in the UCI Undergraduate Research Journal. Most students remain on campus for all four years as only about 1,000 individuals study abroad each year.

The most degrees at Irvine are conferred in the social sciences (17 percent), business (12 percent), engineering (11 percent), and psychology (11 percent). The Samueli School of Engineering has a solid reputation as does the Bren School, the only dedicated computer science school in the University of California system. Programs in public health and biological sciences also earn very high marks. Between two and five graduates win Fulbright Scholarships each year, and Irvine has had an occasional Goldwater, Truman, or Marshall Scholar in the last few years, but winning prestigious national postgraduate scholarships is not a primary focus of Anteater alumni.

Outside the Classroom
It's hard to think of many more desirable locations for a college setting than Orange County, California. The Pacific Ocean is only five miles from campus, including the famed Laguna and Newport beaches. Los Angeles is within an hour's drive, and San Diego is about an hour and a half and, if you have a spare twenty-five minutes, you can head over to Disneyland for the afternoon. The suburban campus covers 1,474 acres, and 41 percent of students live in university housing. Freshmen are guaranteed two full years of housing should they choose to accept it but, at present, only 78 percent of freshmen live in the dorms. Six percent are members of Greek life. There are eighteen varsity sports teams and 400 total student-athletes. All-time, the school has produced 500 All-Americans and fifty-six Olympians. Currently, there are 677 registered campus organizations representing over nineteen categories. Aldrich Park, modeled after Central Park, is the beautiful centerpiece to Irvine's campus and the site of an annual spring fair. Campus-wide events like Shocktoberfest and Homecoming are well attended.

Career Services
The UCI Division of Career Pathways employs seventeen professional employees who work with or on behalf of undergraduate students as career educators, internship coordinators, or employer engagement specialists. That 1,787:1 student-to-staff ratio is among the highest of any university profiled in this guidebook. Fortunately, the school still manages to reach a significant percentage of the undergraduate population through a variety of means as evidenced by numerous impressive data points.

In the 2018-19 school year, career counselors conducted 4,523 one-on-one counseling sessions, and 450 companies attended the school's various career fairs that drew a collective student crowd of greater than 10,000. The UCI Division of Career Pathways not only hosts general fall and spring fairs but also gatherings for STEM careers, health jobs, and law school applicants. An additional 3,000 students attended Career Pathways Panels. In a single year, companies conduct on-campus interviews with 1,300+ undergraduate students. The list of on-campus recruiters included Deloitte, KPMG, Ernst and Young, PricewaterhouseCoopers, Google, Amazon, Northrop Grumman, and Johnson & Johnson. A total of 46 percent of students completed internships last year; half were noncredit internships while half were for credit. The job-shadowing program, now in its fifth year, attracted 268 student participants. Career services at UCI aren't perfect; it's simply too large an operation for fifteen people to handle, but the office possesses strong enough corporate connections to assist grads in achieving positive postgraduate outcomes.

Professional Outcomes

Accounting, aerospace, internet and software, K-12 education, real estate, and retail are among the industries attracting the greatest number of Anteaters. Companies employing the greatest number of recent grads include Boeing, the Walt Disney Company, Google, EY, and Microsoft. Many also end up with nonprofit organizations like Teach for America and City Year. Looking at alumni from all years, hundreds of individuals can be found at each of Kaiser Permanente, Facebook, Apple, Edwards Lifesciences, and Deloitte. The median salary within the first couple years of entering the working world, across all disciplines, is just under $40,000 and ten years out alumni are earning a median salary of $75k. Computer science graduates earn close to $85k right off the bat. Few grads leave the state of California; Orange County, Los Angeles, San Francisco, and San Diego soak up the vast majority.

Between 75 and 80 percent of Irvine grads plan on pursuing an advanced degree within five years of earning their bachelor's. The majority of those enrolling in graduate school do so within the state of California. Many remain at Irvine or another UC campus—Berkeley, UCLA, and San Diego are among the most popular choices. Irvine also sends graduates to Stanford and USC as well as out-of-state to the University of Washington and Georgia Tech. UC-Irvine has a strong reputation for premed. In 2020, the university produced the twenty-eighth most medical school applicants of any institution in the country, and Anteaters possessed higher MCAT scores than the national average. The prestigious UCI School of Medicine admitted seventeen of its own alumni in 2018, which accounted for more than 15 percent of the incoming class. The UC Irvine School of Law is only a decade old but has already skyrocketed toward the top of the rankings. In addition to remaining in Irvine for law school, undergrads often gain acceptance to other excellent law schools within the UC system and also have earned acceptances to the likes of Harvard, Georgetown, and the University of Michigan.

Admission

An almost incomprehensible deluge of 95,568 applications rained down on the UCI admissions staff in 2019, and its acceptance rate fell to 27 percent, a far cry from only five years prior when 41 percent of high school applicants were admitted. At the time the SAT mid-50 percent range was 1040-1290; today, it is 1190-1400, quite a metamorphosis in terms of selectivity. Getting into Irvine without placing in the top decile of your high school class is nearly impossible as 98 percent of 2019-20 freshmen earned that distinction. The average GPA for attending students was 4.0.

For a school receiving almost six-figures worth of application numbers each year, it still professes to hold seven factors as being of the highest importance: rigor of curriculum, GPA, class rank, the essay, extracurricular activities, talent/ability, work experience, and volunteer work. The school recently became test-optional and will be test-blind in Fall 2021. Interestingly, first-generation status is listed as merely "considered," yet the school's undergraduate population is comprised of an incredible 48 percent of first-generation students. While racial/ethnic status is "not considered" in admissions, one-third of the student population are underrepresented minorities.

Worth Your Money?

An annual tuition of under $16,000 for California residents helps explain the rising popularity of Irvine as well as the other UC campuses. No matter your intended major, this in-state rate represents a genuine bargain. Out-of-state residents without plans to pursue computer science or engineering should think twice before committing three times that amount in tuition costs alone. You would likely be better off pursuing options in your home state or private options with merit aid.

FINANCIAL
Institutional Type: Public
In-State Tuition: $13,727
Out-of-State Tuition: $43,481
Room & Board: $16,135
Required Fees: $0
Books & Supplies: $1,390

Avg. Need-Based Grant: $23,222
Avg. % of Need Met: 85%

Avg. Merit-Based Award: $9,384
% Receiving (All Freshmen): 2%
% Receiving (Freshmen w/o Need): 1%

Avg. Cumulative Debt: $19,597
% of Students Borrowing: 50%

CAREER
Who Recruits
1. Pacific Life
2. Edwards Life Sciences
3. Glidewell Laboratories
4. Western Digital
5. Northwestern Mutual

Notable Internships
1. Grant Thorton LLP
2. PlayStation
3. Yelp

Top Industries
1. Business
2. Engineering
3. Education
4. Operations
5. Research

Top Employers
1. Kaiser Permanente
2. Google
3. Amazon
4. Apple
5. Microsoft

Where Alumni Work
1. Orange County, CA
2. Los Angeles
3. San Francisco
4. San Diego
5. New York City

Median Earnings
College Scorecard (Early Career): $58,400
PayScale (Early Career): $62,900
PayScale (Mid-Career): $131,100

RANKINGS
Money: 13
U.S. News: 35 (T), National Universities
Wall Street Journal/THE: 80 (T)
Washington Monthly: 22, National Universities

COLLEGE OVERLAPS
University of California, Berkeley
University of California, Davis
University of California, Los Angeles
University of California, San Diego
University of California, Santa Barbara

University of California, Los Angeles

Los Angeles, California | 310-825-3101

ADMISSION
Admission Rate: 12%
Admission Rate - Men: 12%
Admission Rate - Women: 13%
EA Admission Rate: Not Offered
ED Admission Rate: Not Offered
ED Admits as % of Total Admits: Not Offered
Admission Rate (5-Year Trend): -8%
% of Admits Attending (Yield): 44%
Transfer Admission Rate: 23%

SAT Reading/Writing (Middle 50%): 640-740
SAT Math (Middle 50%): 640-790
ACT Composite (Middle 50%): 27-34

% Graduated in Top 10% of HS Class: 97%
% Graduated in Top 25% of HS Class: 100%
% Graduated in Top 50% of HS Class: 100%

Demonstrated Interest: Not Considered
Legacy Status: Not Considered
Admission Interview Offered: No

ENROLLMENT
Total Undergraduate Enrollment: 31,443
% Part-Time: 2%
% Male: 42%
% Female: 58%
% Out-of-State: 13%
% Fraternity: 11%
% Sorority: 13%
% On-Campus (Freshman): 98%
% On-Campus (All Undergraduate): 48%

% African-American: 3%
% Asian: 28%
% Hispanic: 22%
% White: 26%
% Other: 6%
% Race or Ethnicity Unknown: 3%
% International: 11%
% Low-Income: 37%

ACADEMICS
Student-to-Faculty Ratio: 18 to 1
% of Classes Under 20: 50%
% of Classes 20-49: 29%
% of Classes 50 or More: 22%
% Full-Time Faculty: 90%
% Full-Time Faculty w/ Terminal Degree: 99%

Top Programs
Computer Science
Engineering
English
Fine Arts
Mathematics
Performing Arts
Political Science
Psychology

Retention Rate: 96%
4-Year Graduation Rate: 79%
6-Year Graduation Rate: 91%

Curricular Flexibility: Somewhat Flexible
Academic Rating: ★★★★★

#CollegesWorthYourMoney

Among the most selective public universities in the country, UCLA is also the most diverse campus on the planet. The undergraduate student body is 28 percent Asian, 22 percent Hispanic, and 11 percent international, not to mention 33 percent first-generation college students, making UCLA a fascinating place to pursue one of 134 majors in 109 academic departments. More than 31,443 undergraduates enjoy a whopping 3,800 course offerings that include programs in over forty languages, many of which you won't find offered at your average university such as Armenian, Old Norse, and Sanskrit.

Inside the Classroom
The general education curriculum requires that every student explore three foundational areas: the arts and humanities, society and culture, and scientific inquiry. That entails completing ten courses. Additionally, in order to graduate you'll need to meet requirements in foreign language, writing, and diversity. The school's Capstone Initiative has sought to bring a culminating senior academic endeavor to as many students as possible. As of 2018, more than sixty majors at UCLA require a capstone experience that results in the creation of a tangible product under the mentorship of faculty members.

Close to half of classrooms contain fewer than twenty Bruins, but those taking introductory courses will find themselves in a fair number of lecture halls with a hundred or more students. Professors are given impressively high marks for a research university of UCLA's size. Over 90 percent of the graduates of the College of Letters and Science rate their professors as being both intellectually challenging and accessible. By senior year, 40 percent of undergraduates have participated in a research experience. There are multiple undergraduate research journals in which students can publish their original works as well as a Research Poster Day each May when students can present. Every year one-quarter of the undergraduate population elects to study abroad, a sharp increase from only a few years ago. UCLA has 115 partner universities in forty-two countries around the globe.

By volume, the most commonly conferred degrees are in the social sciences (26 percent), biology (14 percent), engineering (7 percent), mathematics (7 percent), and gender studies (5 percent). Departmental rankings are high across the board in areas such as computer science, engineering, film, fine and performing arts, mathematics, political science and many more. The school also produces a reasonable number of postgraduate scholarship winners—seven graduates took home Fulbright Scholarships in 2019.

Outside the Classroom
If you can't find your niche at UCLA it can hardly be blamed on the school that offers over 1,000 clubs and student organizations; 74 percent of students join at least one. There is no shortage of opportunities to volunteer in the surrounding Los Angeles community—the Volunteer Center, Center for Community Learning, and Community Programs Office offer countless avenues for civic involvement. Greek life is readily available with more than sixty fraternities and sororities on campus, but it is hardly smothering; only 11 percent of men and 13 percent of women are Greek affiliated. UCLA's sports scene boasts storied basketball and baseball teams, big-time football, and 116 all-time championships across twenty-five Division I men's and women's sports. Ninety-eight percent of freshmen reside on campus, and 48 percent of the entire student body lives in university-owned housing. As bountiful as campus life is at UCLA, the excitement that can be found in the surrounding neighborhoods is truly limitless. Within a few miles of campus undergrads can venture to Venice Beach, Santa Monica, Malibu, or Beverley Hills. In short, you won't find too many Bruins complaining of boredom.

Career Services
With twenty-seven full-time employees dedicated to undergraduates, the UCLA Career Center has a 1,165:1 student-to-counselor ratio, much higher than most of the schools featured in this guide. The university does host a number of major-specific job fairs that are attended by an impressive selection of employers. The Engineering and Technical Fair is attended by forty organizations including the CIA, Texas Instruments, Visa, and eBay. Each academic quarter the school also hosts Hire UCLA, which is well-attended by major corporations.

When it comes to finding an internship, students are not going to have their hands held throughout the entire process. The Career Center connects students with internships via Handshake, and 64 percent of undergrads do eventually land one, but the school lacks corporate partnerships that allow for a more streamlined experience. The Career Center offers services such as an online resume critique with a five-day turnaround, and students are free to schedule an appointment or drop by for career advice, a mock interview, or graduate school exploration from 9 a.m. to 4 p.m. on weekdays. Additional events are organized by the UCLA Career Center just about every day. For example, over the course of one random week in October 2020 the center hosted a resume workshop, an engineering and tech fair, a seminar on careers in biotech, and a recruiting visit from AT&T.

University of California, Los Angeles

E-mail: ugadm@saonet.ucla.edu | Website: www.ucla.edu

Professional Outcomes

UCLA grads flow most heavily into the research, finance, computer science, and engineering sectors. The employers that snatch up the highest number of recent Bruin grads include Disney, Google (where over 1,500 alumni presently work), EY, Teach for America, Amazon, and Oracle. Hundreds also can be found in the corporate offices of Uber, Microsoft, Facebook, Netflix, Salesforce, Airbnb, and LinkedIn. Internships definitely help students land jobs; students who had at least one internship found employment at double the rate of their peers who did not have such an experience. The average starting salary for full-time employment exceeds $55,000, a solid figure considering the vast array of degrees being conferred. A good number of students stay in L.A./Orange County after graduation, but the other most popular destination points include NYC, DC, Chicago, Seattle, and Boston.

Roughly one-quarter of graduates enroll directly in a graduate/professional school. The most attended grad schools are primarily other excellent California-based institutions including Stanford, Pepperdine, USC, Berkeley, and Loyola Marymount. However, Columbia, Carnegie Mellon, and NYU also make that list. UCLA students applying to medical school have experienced acceptance rates varying from 51-59 percent over recent years. The most frequently attended medical schools include Duke, Boston University, Drexel, Temple, Case Western, and NYU. Over 90 percent of Bruins applying to law school garner at least one acceptance, a clip that is roughly 15 percent better than the national average. Law schools with the highest number of UCLA grads include many of the aforementioned California universities as well Georgetown, Vanderbilt, George Washington, Duke, and American.

Admission

A decade ago, 24 percent of the roughly 50,000 applicants to UCLA received acceptance letters; today, the school receives the most applications of any college in the country with 111,322 in 2019, and the acceptance rate has fallen to 12 percent. Students from out-of-state fared better than in-state applicants and international applicants by a significant margin with out-of-staters enjoying a 16 percent acceptance rate. However, the University of California Board of Regents recently passed a measure capping out-of-state/international enrollment at 18 percent moving forward, which should curb that trend.

Those accepted straight from high school are a high-achieving bunch as a hard-to-comprehend 97 percent graduated in the top 10 percent of their high school class. The SAT 50th percentile breakdown is 1290-1510 and the ACT range is 28-34. For comparison, a decade ago, the average SAT score of an admitted student was 1330; the average ACT was 29. Thus, we can say that UCLA's shrinking acceptance rate is, indeed, indicative of increasing selectivity. It's important to note that there is more than one way through these heavily guarded gates. UCLA is extremely transfer friendly, offering admission to 5,538 such students in 2019 with the vast majority coming from California's system of community colleges. UCLA has joined the ranks of the uber-selective as the pool of top-of-their-class applicants continues to grow each year. While it does employ some semblance of a holistic process that considers personal qualities, likely contributions to campus life, and challenges overcome, applicants need to earn very high GPAs in a very rigorous high school curriculum to have a genuine shot at admission.

Worth Your Money?

The average UCLA graduate has almost $10,000 less in student loan debt than the average college graduate in the country. It helps when your in-state tuition to attend one of the finest universities around is only $12k, and the total annual cost of attendance is $36,767 for a resident but $66,521 for a nonresident. Few students receive any merit-based aid, yet over half are awarded need-based grants with a mean yearly value of roughly $21k. While they are rarely able to meet 100 percent of a student's demonstrated financial need, the school is priced so reasonably that graduates emerge with little debt and sky-high job prospects. Depending on your intended major and/or financial situation, UCLA can be worth your money even as an out-of-stater, despite the elevated price.

FINANCIAL
Institutional Type: Public
In-State Tuition: $11,994
Out-of-State Tuition: $43,188
Room & Board: $16,104
Required Fees: $1,838
Books & Supplies: $1,314

Avg. Need-Based Grant: NR
Avg. % of Need Met: NR

Avg. Merit-Based Award: $5,763
% Receiving (All Freshmen): 4%
% Receiving (Freshmen w/o Need): 3%

Avg. Cumulative Debt: $21,441
% of Students Borrowing: 40%

CAREER
Who Recruits
1. Bain & Company
2. Airbnb
3. Salesforce
4. Netflix
5. Oracle

Notable Internships
1. CBRE
2. Los Angeles Magazine
3. Northrop Grumman

Top Industries
1. Business
2. Education
3. Operations
4. Engineering
5. Media

Top Employers
1. Google
2. Apple
3. Amazon
4. Facebook
5. Microsoft

Where Alumni Work
1. Los Angeles
2. San Francisco
3. Orange County, CA
4. New York City
5. San Diego

Median Earnings
College Scorecard (Early Career): $60,700
PayScale (Early Career): $65,600
PayScale (Mid-Career): $129,400

RANKINGS
Money: 19
U.S. News: 20, National Universities
Wall Street Journal/THE: 26
Washington Monthly: 11, National Universities

COLLEGE OVERLAPS
New York University
University of California, Berkeley
University of California, San Diego
University of California, Santa Barbara
University of Southern California

University of California, Riverside

Riverside, California | 951-827-3411

ADMISSION
Admission Rate: 57%
Admission Rate - Men: 56%
Admission Rate - Women: 58%
EA Admission Rate: Not Offered
ED Admission Rate: Not Offered
ED Admits as % of Total Admits: Not Offered
Admission Rate (5-Year Trend): -1%
% of Admits Attending (Yield): 17%
Transfer Admission Rate: 39%

SAT Reading/Writing (Middle 50%): 560-650
SAT Math (Middle 50%): 550-690
ACT Composite (Middle 50%): 24-30

% Graduated in Top 10% of HS Class: 94%
% Graduated in Top 25% of HS Class: 100%
% Graduated in Top 50% of HS Class: 100%

Demonstrated Interest: Not Considered
Legacy Status: Not Considered
Admission Interview Offered: No

ENROLLMENT
Total Undergraduate Enrollment: 22,055
% Part-Time: 2%
% Male: 46%
% Female: 54%
% Out-of-State: 0%
% Fraternity: 4%
% Sorority: 6%
% On-Campus (Freshman): 70%
% On-Campus (All Undergraduate): 28%

% African-American: 3%
% Asian: 34%
% Hispanic: 42%
% White: 11%
% Other: 6%
% Race or Ethnicity Unknown: 1%
% International: 4%
% Low-Income: 55%

ACADEMICS
Student-to-Faculty Ratio: 22 to 1
% of Classes Under 20: 21%
% of Classes 20-49: 47%
% of Classes 50 or More: 32%
% Full-Time Faculty: 84%
% Full-Time Faculty w/ Terminal Degree: 98%

Top Programs
Anthropology
Business
Computer Science
Creative Writing
Engineering
Global Studies
Sociology

Retention Rate: 90%
4-Year Graduation Rate: 56%
6-Year Graduation Rate: 76%

Curricular Flexibility: Less Flexible
Academic Rating: ★★★✦

#CollegesWorthYourMoney

Ethnically and socioeconomically, the University of California – Riverside is one of the most diverse schools in the United States. Enrolling 50 percent first-generation students and more Pell Grant recipients than the entire Ivy League combined, UCR is one of the top universities in the country (if not the top) for facilitating upward mobility as well as granting financial aid. It's no wonder that this previously unheralded tentacle of the vaunted University of California system is finally beginning to get more recognition, and, in turn, become more selective; the acceptance rate has plummeted 20 points in the last decade.

Inside the Classroom
UC Riverside offers 80+ majors in five colleges: the Bourns College of Engineering; the College of Humanities, Arts, and Sciences; the College of Natural and Agricultural Sciences; the School of Business; and the School of Public Policy. Utilizing a quarter system, students most complete 180 units in order to graduate. College breadth requirements mandate that all undergrads take English composition, a foreign language, an ethnicity course, 20 units worth of natural sciences/mathematics, 20 units in the humanities, and 16 units in the social sciences.

With a 22:1 student-to-faculty ratio, you won't have the luxury of taking too many courses with a small class size. Twenty-one percent of sections enroll fewer than 20 undergrads compared to 32 percent that enroll 50 or more students. Faculty-mentored research opportunities are available for everyone, and the school has made expanding research participation to at least one fifth of the undergraduate population an institutional goal. Students can pursue mentorships with professors through an undergraduate research portal. Riverside students can also take advantage of study abroad options via the system-wide UC Education Abroad Programs that have sent students to 416 different programs in 46 countries.

There is no major at UCR that magnetically pulls in a massive chunk of the undergraduate student body. Rather, undergrads spread out to a wide array of majors with the greatest number of degrees conferred in the social sciences (19 percent), business (16 percent), biology (15 percent), psychology (10 percent), and engineering (8 percent). Students from all academic concentrations have begun to apply for prestigious national fellowship programs in recent years. Since 2013, UCR has produced 11 Goldwater Scholars, eight Fulbright Scholars, three Marshall Scholars, and two Gates-Cambridge Scholars.

Outside the Classroom
Occupying 1,900 suburban acres, UCR's campus has plenty of physical space for its undergraduates. Yet, while 70 percent of freshmen do take advantage of available dorms and campus apartments, just 28 percent of the total population reside in university-owned housing. Being unable to accommodate all students, the school does offer off-campus housing services that help undergrads locate a place to live after their first year. Greek organizations are quiet at this school, attracting just 4 percent of men and 6 percent of women. This is an extremely diverse school where only 13 percent of undergraduates are classified as White; 38 percent are Latino, and 30 percent are Asian. There are 17 Division I athletic teams, and over 300 student-athletes compete under the Highlander banner. The baseball team has produced more than a handful of major leaguers. For everyone else, there is an 80,000-square-foot recreational facility, plenty of intramural sports, and outdoor adventures arranged through the popular Outdoor Excursions Program. In total, there are 450+ student-run organizations. Riverside is a very eco-friendly campus having recently installed an additional 9,600 solar panels, and it has been recognized for its sustainability practices. Downtown Riverside is a vibrant area replete with dining, shopping, and cultural options. The Fox Performing Arts Center and the Riverside Municipal Auditorium host concerts, musicals, and comedic acts.

Career Services
The University of California Riverside Career Center employs 16 professionals with roles in the areas of career counseling (by academic discipline), industry outreach, and alumni engagement. This 1,375:1 counselor-to-student ratio may be less than desirable, but this office manages to reach a large chunk of the undergraduate student population as evidenced by the 315,542 annual website visits and 26,633 in-person student contacts made in 2018-19. Career fairs were attended by 3,860 students and 560 hiring organizations; 58 percent of seniors attended at least one job fair.

Student evaluations of the career center's planning and counseling offerings are beyond glowing; they are down-right blinding. Ninety-eight percent of workshop attendees felt that the presentation met their expectations, and 99 percent of those receiving one-on-one counseling felt better prepared to effectively complete a job or graduate school application after their visit. In 2018-19 there were 5,212 counseling appointments, including drop-ins. Over 8,500 employers connected with UCR via Handshake, and 610 students were selected for on-campus interviews with 45 unique companies. Of those that found employment, 21 percent identified the Career Center as the way in which they found the position, and 9 percent cited their internship experience, leaving little doubt the services offered at Riverside are directly leading to postgraduation student success.

Professional Outcomes

Within one year of graduation, 68 percent of Highlanders are employed, 21 percent are pursuing an advanced degree, and 10 percent are still seeking employment. Only 17 percent of the Class of 2018, left the state, with most remaining in Southern California. The most commonly entered industries were education (22 percent), business (18 percent), engineering/technology (18 percent), manufacturing/distribution (10 percent), and government (8 percent). The average starting salary for Class of 2018 graduates was $51k, with College of Engineering students earning $75k, and College of Arts & Humanities graduates averaging $37k. More than 100 alumni work for major corporations like Kaiser Permanente, Amazon, Wells Fargo, Ersi, Apple, Microsoft, Facebook, and EY. Last year's graduates also found homes with employers such as the NASA Jet Propulsion Laboratory, SPACEX, Northrop Grumman, HP, and the Walt Disney Company.

Over one fifth of all graduates began work on a graduate or advanced degree within one year of earning their bachelor's degree. The most common disciplines that grads pursue are education, physical/natural sciences, engineering/computer science, health professions, and arts/humanities. Four percent of graduates matriculate into law school, and 5 percent enroll in medical programs. In 2019, there were 216 applicants to US medical schools, and many went on to begin their studies at the UC Riverside School of Medicine, which opened its doors in 2013. Recently enrolled law students were studying at institutions such as Loyola, UCLA, UC Davis, USC, UC Irvine, and Pepperdine.

Admission

Riverside used to be one of the UC campuses you could count on to say "yes" to anyone with decent credentials; a decade ago, it accepted 76 percent of applicants. First-year students applying to enter the university in the fall of 2019 were accepted at only a 56 percent clip. The mid-50th percentile score on the SAT EBRW section was 560-650 and 550-690 on the math section. The composite ACT range was 24-30. In contrast, the ACT composite range in 2010 was 19-24. Terrific grades and a rank in the top 10 percent of one's high school class is now almost a prerequisite at Riverside. The average GPA for the Class of 2023 was 3.83, and 94 percent placed in the top decile.

The two factors that are most important to the admissions committee are GPA and the application essay. The rigor of one's postsecondary courses is "important," and test scores, talent/ability, first-generation status, and state residency are "considered." It is worth noting that all UC schools will be test blind when evaluating California residents who graduate from high school in 2021 and 2022. There is nothing particu-larly complicated about the admissions process at UC Riverside. Strong grades and well-crafted answers to the four personal insight questions should lead to a successful result.

Worth Your Money?

Like all schools in the University of California system, Riverside is worth every dollar. Tuition and fees are just $11,442 for the 2020-21 school year. Estimated total expenses for an in-state student residing in the dorms comes to almost $37,000, but that includes health insurance, transportation, and personal expenses. Nonresidents pay a sticker price of $66,431 for full cost of attendance, which is close to what you would pay at an elite private liberal arts college in New England. For that price, it would take a special set of circumstances to make this school a good value for anyone lacking residency status.

FINANCIAL
Institutional Type: Public
In-State Tuition: $13,853
Out-of-State Tuition: $43,607
Room & Board: $16,100
Required Fees: $0
Books & Supplies: $1,450

Avg. Need-Based Grant: $20,381
Avg. % of Need Met: 85%

Avg. Merit-Based Award: $8,226
% Receiving (All Freshmen): 5%
% Receiving (Freshmen w/o Need): 4%

Avg. Cumulative Debt: $20,779
% of Students Borrowing: 62%

CAREER
Who Recruits
1. Salesforce
2. Deloitte
3. AT&T
4. Amazon Web Services
5. Kaiser Permanente

Notable Internships
1. Amazon Japan
2. Kohl's
3. Blizzard Entertainment

Top Industries
1. Education
2. Business
3. Operations
4. Engineering
5. Research

Top Employers
1. Kaiser Permanente
2. Amazon
3. Google
4. Wells Fargo
5. Apple

Where Alumni Work
1. Los Angeles
2. San Francisco
3. Orange County, CA
4. San Diego
5. New York City

Median Earnings
College Scorecard (Early Career): $49,700
PayScale (Early Career): $58,700
PayScale (Mid-Career): $116,600

RANKINGS
Money: 48
U.S. News: 88 (T), National Universities
Wall Street Journal/THE: 192
Washington Monthly: 27, National Universities

COLLEGE OVERLAPS
California Polytechnic State University, San Luis Obispo
California State University, Fullerton
University of California, Davis
University of California, Irvine
University of California, Santa Cruz

University of California, San Diego

La Jolla, California | 858-534-4831

ADMISSION
Admission Rate: 32%
Admission Rate - Men: 33%
Admission Rate - Women: 32%
EA Admission Rate: Not Offered
ED Admission Rate: Not Offered
ED Admits as % of Total Admits: Not Offered
Admission Rate (5-Year Trend): -5%
% of Admits Attending (Yield): 19%
Transfer Admission Rate: 56%

SAT Reading/Writing (Middle 50%): 610-710
SAT Math (Middle 50%): 620-780
ACT Composite (Middle 50%): 24-33

% Graduated in Top 10% of HS Class: 100%
% Graduated in Top 25% of HS Class: 100%
% Graduated in Top 50% of HS Class: 100%

Demonstrated Interest: Not Considered
Legacy Status: Not Considered
Admission Interview Offered: No

ENROLLMENT
Total Undergraduate Enrollment: 30,794
% Part-Time: 2%
% Male: 50%
% Female: 50%
% Out-of-State: 7%
% Fraternity: 14%
% Sorority: 14%
% On-Campus (Freshman): 90%
% On-Campus (All Undergraduate): 38%

% African-American: 3%
% Asian: 36%
% Hispanic: 21%
% White: 19%
% Other: 0%
% Race or Ethnicity Unknown: 2%
% International: 18%
% Low-Income: 32%

ACADEMICS
Student-to-Faculty Ratio: 19 to 1
% of Classes Under 20: 47%
% of Classes 20-49: 27%
% of Classes 50 or More: 26%
% Full-Time Faculty: 84%
% Full-Time Faculty w/ Terminal Degree: 98%

Top Programs
Biological Sciences
Chemistry and Biochemistry
Cognitive Science
Communication
Computer Science
Economics
Engineering
Political Science

Retention Rate: 93%
4-Year Graduation Rate: 65%
6-Year Graduation Rate: 87%

Curricular Flexibility: Less Flexible
Academic Rating: ★★★★✦

#CollegesWorthYourMoney

Becoming a Triton used to be a disappointing consolation prize for applicants hoping to become a Bruin or a Golden Bear. While UCLA and Berkeley remain the crème de la crème of the UC system, the gap between those uber-elite jewels and UC-San Diego has closed significantly in recent years as applications have skyrocketed to the cusp of six-figures, and the profile of the average freshman has risen commensurately. In 2003, there were fewer than 20,000 undergraduates at the university; there are now in excess of 30,000. An extremely strong academic school, UCSD offers forty-two bachelor's degrees with many concentrations as well as fifty-five minors, all available for less than $12,000 per year in tuition.

Inside the Classroom
There are six undergraduate colleges at UCSD that are meant, in the Oxford and Cambridge model, not to separate by discipline but, instead, to forge flourishing small liberal arts college communities within the larger university. Core curriculum at all of the colleges includes first- year writing, advanced writing, oral communication, mathematical reasoning, quantitative reasoning, and second language. Additionally, undergrads must complete coursework in science and technological inquiry, historical inquiry, literary inquiry, social and behavioral inquiry, artistic inquiry, theological and religious inquiry, philosophical inquiry, ethical inquiry, and diversity and social justice. Two "integration" experiences in which students make connections across disciplines also must be tackled, including one during freshman year.

Over 7,600 graduate students and a 19:1 student-to-faculty ratio are two numbers that don't bode well for those hoping for an intimate classroom experience. Yet, reality is a mixed bag. While 27 percent of course sections are held in larger lecture halls and contain fifty+ students, 47 percent of undergraduate courses sport an enrollment under twenty. Sixty percent of undergrads complete at least one research project as part of their coursework, and roughly one-quarter assist a faculty member with research outside the classroom. Study abroad numbers are approaching 1,000 undergraduates per year, which is only a sliver of the total undergraduate population. Still, opportunities in forty-two countries are available for those who desire a semester of study outside of the United States.

Altogether, biology has the highest representation of all majors (20 percent) followed by the social sciences (19 percent) and mathematics (10 percent). UCSD's computer science and engineering programs have stellar reputations in the corporate and tech communities, and programs in biology, economics, and political science are among the best anywhere. In recent years nationally competitive postgraduate fellowship programs have selected a number of Tritons, and the school has produced as many as a dozen Fulbrights per year while the Biology Department alone saw four graduates capture National Science Foundation Graduate Research Fellowships last academic year.

Outside the Classroom
Ninety percent of freshmen live on the UCSD campus, but only 38 percent of the undergraduate population live in dormitories or college-owned apartments. Fraternities and sororities have a solid but not overwhelming presence on campus, drawing 14 percent of men and women. Unlike UCLA and Berkeley, San Diego doesn't offer prime-time football or basketball teams; in fact, it hasn't fielded a football team since 1968. Rather, the twenty-three Triton squads participate in NCAA Division II and fare quite well within that less competitive environment. However, plans do exist to join Division I's Big West Conference within the next few years. A diverse student body enjoys an equally diverse array of clubs. There are over 500 to choose from with many options in the areas of student government, media, and a popular intramural sports program that has a 60 percent participation rate. The 180-acre campus is situated within the wealthy beachfront town of La Jolla, a thirteen-mile highway ride from downtown San Diego. While La Jolla is not a typical college town, many students live in beachfront apartments overlooking the Pacific Ocean or Mission Bay, and few complain about the heavenly weather.

Career Services
The UC-San Diego Career Center has twenty-one full-time employees who work with or on behalf of undergraduate students, many of whom specialize in a particular discipline such as pre-law, pre-health, the social sciences, the humanities, business, or engineering. UCSD's 1,466:1 student-to-counselor ratio is toward the highest of any school featured in this guide. To compensate, it puts on a multitude of annual career fairs, many of which attract 1,000+ students. Those include large-scale fairs in the fall, winter, and spring, a Graduate School Fair, an Engineering and Computing Career Fair, and an event called Impact Career Fair: Companies for a Brighter Future. Each quarter, hundreds of companies are on campus to recruit undergraduate students.

In a single year, the school lists 8,300+ jobs/internships on Handshake, and those efforts led to roughly 80 percent of graduates having participated in an experiential learning activity—internship, research, or community service. Thirty-minute one-on-one appointments can be scheduled, but scoring one of those appointments, particularly with a "good fit" counselor can be a challenge. Students, via op-eds in the school paper, have been clamoring for an increased number of advisors to accommodate the growing number of undergraduate students at the university. Thanks to the rising prestige of the school, UCSD students have enjoyed increasingly positive post-graduation outcomes, but there is still room to increase the level of support offered.

Professional Outcomes

Employers of recent graduates included the Walt Disney Company, Tesla, NBC Universal, PwC, Northrup Grumman, and EY. More than 1,000 current Google employees are UC-San Diego alumni, and Qualcomm, Amazon, and Apple all employ 500+ each. The median early career salary is $65,000 across all majors, placing the university in the top 50 in the country. UCSD also fares well in measures of its return-on-investment potential. The bulk of grads remain in San Diego or relocate to Los Angeles or San Francisco.

UC-San Diego is a school from which you matriculate into any graduate program you desire, if you bring the requisite transcript and test scores. In 2020, there were 621 seniors applying to medical school, sixth most in the nation. Though Tritons appear to experience average to slightly below average levels of success--between 34 and 40 percent of applicants have been admitted in recent years—low acceptance rates are likely attributed to the fact that UCSD includes all undergraduate applicants in their tally, not just those who achieve a certain GPA threshold or receive an official endorsement from a pre-med advisor. Pre-law students most frequently head to California-based institutions such as the University of San Diego School of Law, California Western School of Law, Thomas Jefferson School of Law, and Santa Clara University School of Law. However, recent grads also found law school homes at the University of Chicago, Pepperdine, UCLA, Notre Dame, and Fordham.

Admission

A tsunami of 99,133 applications for a place in the Class of 2019-20 flooded the inboxes of the UC-San Diego Admissions Office, more than doubling the number of applications received a decade ago. The admit rate ten years ago was only 37 percent, not all that far from today's 32 percent. Yet, the profile of the average freshman has changed drastically in that same period. Freshmen in the Class of 2023 possessed mid-50 percent standardized test scores of a 1250-1470 on the SAT, 24-33 on the ACT, and 92 percent had a GPA higher than 3.75. A decade prior, the SAT range was 1150-1380 and "only" 84 percent had GPAs in that same range. Any way you slice it, this school has become vastly more selective in the recent past.

When you are approaching 100,000 applicants, a microscopic exploration of every application is not a realistic expectation. Thus, it makes sense that three of the four "very important" factors considered by the admissions committee are cut-and-dried: level of rigor, GPA, essays, and standardized test scores (the school will be test-blind in 2021). Class rank, interestingly, is not considered. If the person advising you on college admissions (counselor, parent, family friend) hasn't been paying close attention to the spike in applications and selectivity, UC-San Diego can easily become an institution that should be a "reach" or "target" school, but it could be mistakenly assigned the title of "safety school." In reality, a pristine academic transcript is a must for most applicants.

Worth Your Money?

For the 24 percent of undergraduates who come from outside the state, the University of California-San Diego has an annual cost of attendance of $63k. Residents, on the other hand, enjoy a COA of $33k. More than half of current students receive some level of financial aid; the average award is $20,689. Staying within the UC system is always an excellent choice for residents, and while the school is getting expensive for outsiders, it may still prove to be a degree that returns your investment, particularly if you aim to work in the tech industry.

FINANCIAL
Institutional Type: Public
In-State Tuition: $11,442
Out-of-State Tuition: $43,188
Room & Board: $14,821
Required Fees: $2,728
Books & Supplies: $1,124

Avg. Need-Based Grant: $20,689
Avg. % of Need Met: 86%

Avg. Merit-Based Award: $11,133
% Receiving (All Freshmen): 4%
% Receiving (Freshmen w/o Need): 2%

Avg. Cumulative Debt: $20,536
% of Students Borrowing: 41%

CAREER
Who Recruits
1. Nordson Corp
2. Sherwin Williams
3. IQVIA
4. Hulu
5. Netflix

Notable Internships
1. Inuit
2. Dow Jones
3. American Express

Top Industries
1. Business
2. Engineering
3. Education
4. Research
5. Operations

Top Employers
1. Google
2. Qualcomm
3. Apple
4. Amazon
5. Illumina

Where Alumni Work
1. San Diego
2. San Francisco
3. Los Angeles
4. Orange County, CA
5. New York City

Median Earnings
College Scorecard (Early Career): $59,900
PayScale (Early Career): $67,200
PayScale (Mid-Career): $136,400

RANKINGS
Money: 9
U.S. News: 35 (T), National Universities
Wall Street Journal/THE: 39
Washington Monthly: 9, National Universities

COLLEGE OVERLAPS
University of California, Berkeley
University of California, Irvine
University of California, San Diego
University of California, Santa Barbara
University of Southern California

University of California, Santa Barbara

Santa Barbara, California | 805-893-2881

When your campus is bordered on three sides by the Pacific Ocean and the weather is 70-75 degrees virtually year around, it would be easy for academics to become an afterthought. While the University of California Santa Barbara does, indeed, have a well-earned reputation as a "party school," the 23,274 undergraduate students are, today, a higher-achieving lot than ever, and they flock to UCSB for the ninety undergraduate majors and slew of top-ranked departments every bit as much as the sand and surf.

Inside the Classroom

The College of Letters and Science, the College of Engineering, and the College of Creative Studies all have different core curricular requirements. There is some crossover in terms of mandated courses in all three schools that include English, reading, and composition; literature; art; social science; and culture and thought. College of Letters and Science grads also must complete classes in foreign language and science, mathematics, and technology. Classes covering the special subject areas of European traditions, ethnicity, world cultures, and quantitative relationships are also part of some academic programs.

The student-to-faculty ratio at UC Santa Barbara is a decent 17:1, and the school does an excellent job of keeping undergraduate class sizes on the small side. In fact, more than half of sections contain fewer than twenty students, and 72 percent enroll twenty-nine or fewer. Undergraduate research opportunities definitely exist for those willing to forge relationships with faculty outside the classroom. A solid 57 percent of graduates report engaging in some type of independent study or research. It's not as easy to inspire Gauchos to leave their campus paradise for a semester in a foreign land—only around 20 percent of students participate in study abroad.

The social sciences are the most popular area of study accounting for 27 percent of the total degrees conferred. Biology (10 percent), interdisciplinary studies (8 percent), math (7 percent), and journalism (7 percent) are next in popularity. The school has highly regarded programs in communication, computer science, engineering, physics, environmental science, and the performing arts. Santa Barbara graduates do not tend to apply for prestigious postgraduate fellowships in overwhelming numbers, but the school did produce four Fulbright winners in 2020.

Outside the Classroom

Freshmen live on the UCSB campus at a 92 percent clip; overall, 39 percent of the undergraduate student population resides in university-owned housing. Santa Barbara's glorious 1,000-acre campus is set against the Pacific Ocean, and multiple beaches are literally in your backyard (you can actually hear the ocean while you're studying). Of course, keeping focused is a challenge with the perfect weather, beautiful surroundings, and the fact that, no matter what rankings list you check, UCSB is one of the top party schools in the entire country. The town of Isla Vista is almost exclusively a college town with a laid back vibe full of free spirits and free-flowing hard liquor. Fraternities and sororities have a presence but do not dominate the social scene; only 10 percent of men and 7 percent of women join Greek organizations. Just about everyone on campus is involved in athletics in some way as there are twenty-nine club sports teams and a stunning 18,000 intramural participants each year. Nineteen varsity teams compete in NCAA Division I's Big West Conference. The baseball program is, perhaps, the most notable making regular tournament appearances and having produced many MLB players in its almost one-hundred-year history. There are also over 500 student clubs and numerous campus-wide events, including the famous (or infamous) annual Halloween celebration on Isla Vista. Fifty-seven percent of students found time to engage in community service.

Career Services

USCB Career Services is run by seventeen professional employees who function as discipline-specific career counselors, employment specialists, graduate school counselors, and internship/experience managers. That 1,369:1 student-to-staff ratio is much higher than the average school in this guidebook, but that is not particularly alarming for a public university of Santa Barbara's size. Career services certainly keeps busy, hosting 284 workshops that, collectively, drew 2,454 students in 2018-19 and also meets one-on-one with 3,085 individuals through scheduled appointments and another 3,501 through drop-ins. Four job and internship fairs held over the course of the year attract 350+ employers and 4,600+ students. Additionally, staff posted 38,500 jobs on Handshake for undergraduate consumption.

ADMISSION
Admission Rate: 29%
Admission Rate - Men: 28%
Admission Rate - Women: 31%
EA Admission Rate: Not Offered
ED Admission Rate: Not Offered
ED Admits as % of Total Admits: Not Offered
Admission Rate (5-Year Trend): -10%
% of Admits Attending (Yield): 18%
Transfer Admission Rate: 51%

SAT Reading/Writing (Middle 50%): 620-720
SAT Math (Middle 50%): 620-770
ACT Composite (Middle 50%): 25-33

% Graduated in Top 10% of HS Class: 100%
% Graduated in Top 25% of HS Class: 100%
% Graduated in Top 50% of HS Class: 100%

Demonstrated Interest: Not Considered
Legacy Status: Not Considered
Admission Interview Offered: No

ENROLLMENT
Total Undergraduate Enrollment: 23,274
% Part-Time: 2%
% Male: 45%
% Female: 55%
% Out-of-State: 6%
% Fraternity: 10%
% Sorority: 7%
% On-Campus (Freshman): 92%
% On-Campus (All Undergraduate): 39%

% African-American: 2%
% Asian: 20%
% Hispanic: 26%
% White: 31%
% Other: 6%
% Race or Ethnicity Unknown: 1%
% International: 14%
% Low-Income: 36%

ACADEMICS
Student-to-Faculty Ratio: 17 to 1
% of Classes Under 20: 51%
% of Classes 20-49: 30%
% of Classes 50 or More: 19%
% Full-Time Faculty: 86%
% Full-Time Faculty w/ Terminal Degree: 100%

Top Programs
Anthropology
Communication
Computer Science
Engineering
Environmental Studies
Global and International Studies
Performing Arts
Physics

Retention Rate: 92%
4-Year Graduation Rate: 70%
6-Year Graduation Rate: 88%

Curricular Flexibility: Somewhat Flexible
Academic Rating: ★★★★✦

#CollegesWorthYourMoney

University of California, Santa Barbara

E-mail: admissions@sa.ucsb.edu | Website: www.ucsb.edu

This office is continuing to aggressively expand the number of employers who recruit on campus. Bain & Company, Goldman Sachs, US Bank, and Kaiser Permanente all have begun visiting Santa Barbara for information sessions, career fairs, and on-campus interviews. Internship experiences are supported through programs like the Intern Scholarship Program that issues $1,500 grants to help offset the costs of unpaid placements. An encouraging 45 percent of those who land an internship end up being hired by that organization on a full-time basis. Overall, this office does a nice job of bringing top employers to campus with regularity and hosts almost daily workshops on topics such as Engineering Boot Camp, Internships 101, "So You Want to be a Researcher?," and Conversations about Careers in Mental Health.

Professional Outcomes

Within six months of earning their diplomas, 84 percent of Gauchos have found employment, and only 7 percent of those seeking their first jobs have yet to nail down a position. The most popular industries entered are science/research (16 percent), engineering/computer programming (14 percent), business (13 percent) finance/accounting (11 percent), and sales (10 percent). Among the top employers of recent graduates are Google, EY, KPMG, Oracle, Amazon, IBM, and Adobe. Large numbers of UCSB alumni also can be found on the payrolls of Apple, Facebook, Microsoft, Uber, Salesforce, and Lyft. A fairly even split of Gauchos can be found in the Greater Los Angeles area and San Francisco. Many also remain in Santa Barbara or head to other Golden State locales like Sacramento, Orange County, or San Diego. Two years after graduating, UCSB alumni make an average salary of $40k, but this figure grows to an average of $93k with 15 years of experience.

Seventy-five percent of Santa Barbara grads stated they intend to pursue a graduate or professional degree at some point. Of those jumping directly into an advanced degree program, 9 percent are continuing at UCSB, 23 percent at a University of California location, 16 percent at a school within the California State University System, 22 percent at a private school in California, and 36 percent go out of state. In 2018-19, there were 174 applicants to medical schools from UCSB, and acceptance rates were in line with the national average. Recent acceptances included prestigious medical schools such as Harvard, Cornell, Tufts, Georgetown, Johns Hopkins, Dartmouth, Wake Forest, UVA, UNC-Chapel Hill, and Duke. Those applying to law school or other graduate programs also gained entrance to a wide range of schools, including the most prestigious in the country.

Admission

A line 93,457 students long formed for a place in the UC Santa Barbara Class of 2023; 30 percent were admitted, and 18 percent of those accepted ultimately enrolled in the university. Those entering the university in 2019-20 earned an average high school GPA of 4.18, and 93 percent had a GPA of over 3.75. The mid-50 percent standardized test scores were a 1260-1460 on the SAT, the more commonly submitted test, and a 25-33 on the ACT. A decade ago, Santa Barbara was a much easier university to get into. At that time the average SAT score was below 1200, and the acceptance rate was close to 50 percent. It's important that current applicants do not mistake the UCSB of ten years ago for the highly selective school it is today.

For a university approaching six figures worth of applicants, it is a bit surprising that it lists the application essay as being "very important," a designation only given to one factor: GPA. Rigor of one's high school course load is ranked as "important," and factors like work experience, extracurricular activities, state residency, and first-generation status are "considered." The entire UC system is moving toward a test-blind policy, fully removing the SATs and ACTs from the equation. As is the standard with schools in the University of California System, there is no early action or early decision; rather, the regular deadline is on the early side. You must submit your application by November 30.

Worth Your Money?

Cheap tuition (sub $13k) plus expensive California living brings the overall cost of attendance to a shade under $37,000 per year. As with all of the schools in the University of California System, even if you received zero aid, UC Santa Barbara would still be a solid investment. An out-of-state student would pay $66,372 per year in tuition, meaning that budget-conscious teens and families would likely have much better private or in-state options. The school caps nonresident enrollment at 18 percent (it currently sits below that mark), but that population has been rising in recent years, so there are many people willing to spend $268,000 on a public school education—a move that we do not recommend unless financial resources are unlimited and/or you happen to be majoring in engineering or computer science.

FINANCIAL
Institutional Type: Public
In-State Tuition: $11,994
Out-of-State Tuition: $43,188
Room & Board: $15,389
Required Fees: $3,003
Books & Supplies: $1,259

Avg. Need-Based Grant: $721,443
Avg. % of Need Met: 99%

Avg. Merit-Based Award: $10,290
% Receiving (All Freshmen): 3%
% Receiving (Freshmen w/o Need): 2%

Avg. Cumulative Debt: $18,995
% of Students Borrowing: 51%

CAREER
Who Recruits
1. Arista Networks
2. Deckers Brands
3. Peace Corps
4. Raytheon
5. West Coast Financial, LLC

Notable Internships
1. SpaceX
2. U.S. House of Representatives
3. Telsa

Top Industries
1. Business
2. Education
3. Operations
4. Sales
5. Engineering

Top Employers
1. Google
2. Apple
3. Oracle
4. Amazon
5. Microsoft

Where Alumni Work
1. Los Angeles
2. San Francisco
3. Santa Barbara, CA
4. San Diego
5. Orange County, CA

Median Earnings
College Scorecard (Early Career): $55,300
PayScale (Early Career): $62,100
PayScale (Mid-Career): $129,500

RANKINGS
Money: 55
U.S. News: 30 (T), National Universities
Wall Street Journal/THE: 74 (T)
Washington Monthly: 20, National Universities

COLLEGE OVERLAPS
University of California, Berkeley
University of California, Davis
University of California, Irvine
University of California, Los Angeles
University of California, San Diego

University of California, Santa Cruz

Santa Cruz, California | 831-459-4008

ADMISSION
Admission Rate: 51%
Admission Rate - Men: 52%
Admission Rate - Women: 51%
EA Admission Rate: Not Offered
ED Admission Rate: Not Offered
ED Admits as % of Total Admits: Not Offered
Admission Rate (5-Year Trend): -6%
% of Admits Attending (Yield): 13%
Transfer Admission Rate: 61%

SAT Reading/Writing (Middle 50%): 590-680
SAT Math (Middle 50%): 600-710
ACT Composite (Middle 50%): 24-30

% Graduated in Top 10% of HS Class: 96%
% Graduated in Top 25% of HS Class: 100%
% Graduated in Top 50% of HS Class: 100%

Demonstrated Interest: Not Considered
Legacy Status: Not Considered
Admission Interview Offered: No

ENROLLMENT
Total Undergraduate Enrollment: 17,517
% Part-Time: 3%
% Male: 52%
% Female: 48%
% Out-of-State: 4%
% Fraternity: 7%
% Sorority: 8%
% On-Campus (Freshman): 97%
% On-Campus (All Undergraduate): 50%

% African-American: 2%
% Asian: 22%
% Hispanic: 26%
% White: 31%
% Other: 8%
% Race or Ethnicity Unknown: 2%
% International: 9%
% Low-Income: 60%

ACADEMICS
Student-to-Faculty Ratio: 25 to 1
% of Classes Under 20: 20%
% of Classes 20-49: 51%
% of Classes 50 or More: 28%
% Full-Time Faculty: 72%
% Full-Time Faculty w/ Terminal Degree: 98%

Top Programs
Anthropology
Computer Science
Earth Sciences
Engineering
Environmental Studies
Film & Digital Media
Physics

Retention Rate: 89%
4-Year Graduation Rate: 59%
6-Year Graduation Rate: 89%

Curricular Flexibility: Somewhat Flexible
Academic Rating: ★★★✔

#CollegesWorthYourMoney

Along with several fellow previously unheralded UC campuses, Santa Cruz has, in recent years, gained recognition as one of the top 35 public universities in the entire country. In addition to high-level academics and an ever-increasingly accomplished pool of applicants (the average GPA of accepted students is now over 4.0), UCSC is surrounded by panoramic views of the Pacific, towering Redwoods, and is minutes away from the beaches. And, oh yeah, its athletic teams have one of the greatest nicknames in college sports—the Banana Slugs. But, don't worry, there is nothing sluggish about this often overlooked university that plays host to 17,500 bachelor's degree pursuers and 66 undergraduate majors.

Inside the Classroom
UCSC students study within one of the following academic divisions: arts, humanities, physical and biological sciences, social sciences, and the Jack Baskin School of Engineering. All first-year students take a course called College 1 their first semester that prepares students for the "styles of critical reading, thinking, and engagement that [they] will encounter throughout [their] university experience." The composition requirement is met through one or two writing courses, depending on the outcome of a placement test. In addition to these entry-level courses, students must check off a number of general education mandates in areas such as cross-cultural analysis, ethnicity and race, interpreting arts and media, math and formal reasoning, and statistical reasoning.

Santa Cruz has a student-to-faculty ratio of 25:1, one of the highest figures of any school featured in this guide. A greater percentage of classes contain 50+ students (28 percent) than under 20 students (20 percent). Fortunately, thanks in part to a relatively small number of graduate students (roughly 1,750), there are still opportunities to work side-by-side with faculty. In fact, a commendable 75 percent of undergraduates conduct research during their four years at Santa Cruz. A few years ago, the school pledged to raise the numbers of students participating in study abroad programs to 50 percent and encourage all students to take advantage of the well-established UC programs situated all around the globe.

Biology is the university's most popular major; 16 percent of all degrees conferred in 2019 were in this discipline. Fourteen percent of degrees were in the social sciences, 12 percent in psychology, and 12 percent were granted in computer and information sciences, the latter being one of UCSC's most respected programs. A notable number of Slugs volunteer with organizations like the Peace Corps and City Year following graduation. They also produce occasional winners of Fulbrights and other prestigious fellowships/scholarships; applications for Gilman Scholarships increased by 200 percent in 2020.

Outside the Classroom
Ninety-seven percent of freshmen reside in on-campus housing, but among the total undergraduate student body, that figure falls to just below 50 percent. Still, this is the highest number of any school within the University of California system. Overall, 7 percent of men and 8 percent of women enter Greek life. The UCSC campus is a vast 2,000 acres, regularly receiving praise as one of the country's most aesthetically pleasing colleges. This includes the 409-acre Natural Reserves that serve as a living laboratory for budding scientists. The Banana Slugs may have the greatest team name in college sports, but they are—unlike Cal and UCLA—light years from being an athletic powerhouse. Fifteen varsity teams complete at the NCAA Division III level. The school is home to 150+ student-run clubs covering the standard categories of politics, performance, academics, and hobbies. From beach bonfires to strolls on the boardwalk to visits to the local farmer's market, there is also plenty to do in the surrounding area. The student body is, in general, very liberal and very laid back. If you're looking for a Greek-heavy, sports-crazed campus, look elsewherer.

Career Services
The University of California Santa Cruz Career Center employs 15 professionals (including positions that are presently vacant) with roles in the areas of career counseling, employer engagement, and event planning. This 1,166:1 counselor-to-student ratio is high, but not that different from other UC branches. In a typical year, UCSC holds more than a handful of career fairs each year that are attended by as many as 50 employers and 450 students; the Graduate and Professional School Fair draws representatives from approximately 100 universities.

University of California, Santa Cruz

E-mail: admissions@ucsc.edu | Website: www.ucsc.edu

According to the most recent survey of career center utilization, 27 percent of graduates attend career fairs, 33 percent take advantage of one-on-one advising sessions, and 21 percent attend at least one workshop. The last time the center reported data on how often students came to the office for advising sessions, almost 4,000 individual appointments were made in a calendar year, and the average student satisfaction rating was 4.5 out of 5 stars. Students utilize Handshake to view tens of thousands of job and internship postings. An alumni network that is 130,000 strong can aid in this process as well.

Professional Outcomes

Within three months of earning their degree, 70 percent of UCSC grads find employment, and another 17 percent are starting graduate programs. Proximity to Silicon Valley helps open doors to companies like Google, Apple, Facebook, Genentech, and Cisco that all employ over 250 alumni. More than 100 alums can also be found in the offices of Amazon, Salesforce, Microsoft, Adobe, and LinkedIn. The majority of grads live in the San Francisco area, with large numbers also concentrated in Los Angeles, San Diego, Sacramento, and New York City.

Among those recent grads who hadn't yet started an advanced degree program, three fifths stated that they planned to do so within the next five years. In the 2019-20 academic year, 108 Slugs applied to medical school, and many have gone on to medical school, with those in the UC system being popular landing spots. Recent grads who have entered law schools have gone on to attend fellow California-based schools like Berkeley, UCLA, Santa Clara, Pepperdine, and Loyola as well as institutions like Tulane, Northeastern, and Baylor. While the quality of graduate school acceptances of Santa Cruz grads varies, many high achievers do get accepted into elite programs. For example, members of the Class of 2019 matriculated into graduate programs at Stanford, Rice, USC, and Columbia University.

Admission

Everyone knows about how selective UCLA and Berkeley are; some are catching on to the elevated admissions standards at San Diego and Santa Barbara, but few understand just how competitive admission now is for every UC branch campus, including Santa Cruz. The good news is that UCSC's acceptance rate is still 65 percent, one of the easier UC schools to gain admission into as a first-year applicant. The SAT composite middle-50 percent range was 1200-1360; the ACT range was 24-30. The average GPA for incoming 2019-20 freshmen was an unweighted 3.57. However, with weighting, the mean GPA was 3.91, and 97 percent of accepted students placed in the top decile of their graduating high school class.

Five factors are viewed as "highly important" to the admissions committee: GPA, application essays (the UC personal insight questions), state residency, the rigor of your coursework, and standardized test scores. The last factor is being phased out of UC admissions, with a test-optional policy having been adopted in the short term, and a test-blind policy slated to go into effect for those seeking to enter the university in the fall of 2023. The following factors are viewed as "important": extracurricular activities, talent/ability, character/personal qualities, first-generation status, and geographical residence. An applicant's volunteer or paid work experience is "considered." The school does not consider class rank, recommendations, legacy status, or one's level of demonstrated interest.

Worth Your Money?

One simple question to ask when determining if a school is worth your money is, "Is it in the University of California system?" If the answer is "Yes," then you are getting one of the premier bargains in the world of higher education. Sure, living in California is expensive in every other regard, but the tuition for the 2020-21 academic year is only $14,025. Those from outside the Golden State are charged an extra $29,754 nonresident tuition fee. There are circumstances where paying this amount would still be worth it (e.g., for a technology and information management degree), but in most cases this school makes the most sense for locals. Close to 70 percent of all students received some type of financial aid through the university.

FINANCIAL
Institutional Type: Public
In-State Tuition: $11,994
Out-of-State Tuition: $43,188
Room & Board: $16,641
Required Fees: $2,612
Books & Supplies: $1,162

Avg. Need-Based Grant: $20,355
Avg. % of Need Met: 82%

Avg. Merit-Based Award: $7,414
% Receiving (All Freshmen): 10%
% Receiving (Freshmen w/o Need): 9%

Avg. Cumulative Debt: $21,375
% of Students Borrowing: 56%

CAREER
Who Recruits
1. Fortinet
2. FDIC
3. Moss Adams
4. Deloitte
5. Capital Insurance Group

Notable Internships
1. Gesher Consulting Group
2. Genentech
3. Tech4Good

Top Industries
1. Business
2. Education
3. Operations
4. Engineering
5. Research

Top Employers
1. Google
2. Apple
3. Facebook
4. Amazon
5. Genentech

Where Alumni Work
1. San Francisco
2. Los Angeles
3. San Diego
4. Sacramento
5. New York City

Median Earnings
College Scorecard (Early Career): $46,900
PayScale (Early Career): $60,800
PayScale (Mid-Career): $114,700

RANKINGS
Money: 111
U.S. News: 97 (T), National Universities
Wall Street Journal/THE: 255 (T)
Washington Monthly: 91, National Universities

COLLEGE OVERLAPS
University of California, Davis
University of California, Irvine
University of California, Riverside
University of California, San Diego
University of California, Santa Barbara

University of Chicago

Chicago, Illinois | 773-702-8650

Once a bastion of uncompromising intellectuals lovingly referred to as "the place where fun comes to die," the University of Chicago has undergone a transformational rebranding over the past decade. Still a destination point for an army of 6,734 brilliant young people, it now boasts an acceptance rate in the same league with Ivies like Brown and Yale (40 percent were accepted as recently as 2005) and, while still as academically rigorous as any institution in the country, it has worked to expand its previously unidimensional appeal.

Inside the Classroom
There are fifty-one majors at the University of Chicago, but more than 50 percent of degrees conferred are in four majors: economics, biology, mathematics, and political science. Economics alone is the selection of roughly one-quarter of the undergraduate population, in large part because the university does not, for reasons of philosophy and tradition, offer a traditional business major. The University of Chicago runs on a quarter system that equates to four ten-week sessions in which students take three or four classes at a time. Given the legendarily heavy workload at the school, the truncated terms can lead to a good deal of stress and an excessive number of all-night study sessions. All undergraduates must plow through the school's common core curriculum that requires an introduction to the tools of inquiry in every discipline: math and science (6 combined courses), humanities (6 courses), and social science (3 courses). Many elect to take nothing but core courses for their entire freshman year.

A 5:1 student-to-faculty ratio means that classrooms remain fairly intimate, and face-time with the renowned faculty is a reality. More than three-quarters of UChicago undergraduate sections have an enrollment of nineteen or fewer students. Undergraduate research opportunities are ubiquitous as 80 percent of students end up working in a research capacity alongside a faculty member. A solid 48 percent of undergrads study abroad at one of the sixty-six programs offered in thirty-two cities around the world.

No matter your area of concentration, a degree from UChicago will carry a great deal of weight in the eyes of employers and graduate/professional schools alike. All of the areas previously mentioned as the most popular majors have particularly sterling reputations with a global reach. On that topic, if you name a prestigious postgraduate award or fellowship, chances are the University of Chicago is one of the most frequent producers. Perhaps most astoundingly, between faculty and alumni the UChicago boasts ninety affiliated Nobel Prizes (eight are currently on faculty) over the school's illustrious history. Lastly, it also lays claim to fifty Rhodes Scholars all time, the eighth most of any university.

Outside the Classroom
With its campus based in the Hyde Park neighborhood on Chicago's South Side, students have access to a vibrant metropolis within walking distance of their dorms. Countless museums, restaurants, bookshops, parks, and theaters are never more than a stone's throw away. Given UChicago's reputation as a haven for hardcore intellectuals, it may come as a surprise that there are nineteen official Greek organizations on campus with a participation rate of 20 percent. Athletes, nicknamed the Maroons, participate in NCAA Division III. There are twenty varsity teams that are evenly split between the genders; no athletic scholarships are offered, and athletics, in general, capture a limited degree of student attention. Yet, a hard-to-comprehend 70 percent of the student body participates in the school's extensive intramural and club sports programs. Over 400 undergraduate-run clubs are active, including a number of improv and theater groups (the university is the birthplace of modern improv), community service organizations, and publications. DOC is the nation's oldest student-run film society and screens films on a daily basis. On-campus housing consists of seven residence halls divided into thirty-nine houses designed to nurture a sense of community. Freshmen are required to participate in the university housing system, but a large percentage of upperclassmen, 48 percent of the total student body, reside in off-campus housing.

Career Services
The university pours ample resources into career services, employing fifty-eight full-time consultants who have highly specialized areas of expertise including business careers, law school planning, health-care careers, journalism, STEM, and start-ups. Boasting a student-to-advisor ratio of 116:1, UChicago has one of the absolute best ratios of any institution included in this book. It also puts its extensive staff to work on behalf of undergraduate students. To help quantify that statement, the staff engaged students in 12,409 one-on-one advising appointments in the 2018-19 school year.

An exceptional 80 percent of freshmen engage with the Career Advancement Office. Through the Metcalf Internship Program, massive numbers of students procure internship positions at top companies around the globe. In a given year, UChicago students secure more than 2,800 internships with more than 850 organizations. Undergraduates participate in excess of 500 employer site visits around the world that are known as Career Treks as well as 200 externships. The university forges strong connections with employers who are eager to conduct on-campus interviews with students; it currently has over one hundred full-time recruiting partners, including a laundry list of Fortune 1000 companies. Incredibly, 1,360 distinct employers recruited at the school during the 2018-19 academic year. Unmatched in terms of sheer personnel power and deeply committed to personalized, expert student counseling, UChicago's Career Advancement Office is a leader in the career services realm.

Professional Outcomes

On commencement day, 96 percent of recent graduates already had their next step lined up, whether that involved entering the world of employment or continuing their higher education odyssey in graduate school. Business and financial services and STEM are the two sectors that scoop up the most graduates, but public policy and consulting also were well represented. Some of the most popular employers of recent grads include Facebook, Google, JP Morgan, Goldman Sachs, McKinsey & Company, Bank of America, Citi, and Accenture. While many graduates go on to lucrative careers, average early career incomes lag a bit behind many other schools of its ilk due to the heavy number of students pursuing advanced degrees.

University of Chicago grads are highly sought after by elite graduate universities. The top seven destinations for recent graduates are Yale, Columbia, Penn, MIT, Stanford, UCLA, and Johns Hopkins. Top law schools swoon at the sight of applicants from UChicago; 83-93 percent of applicants to Top 15 institutions gain admittance. In one recent cycle, twenty-four grads were accepted by NYU, sixteen by UChicago itself, fourteen by Columbia, twelve by Harvard, and eight by Stanford. Med school applicants found similar success with 80-88 percent earning acceptance, more than double the national average. A fairly substantial 39 percent of graduates remain in the Midwest after finishing their degrees, 31 percent migrate to the Northeast, and 15 percent make the journey west.

Admission

The University of Chicago admitted a record low 6 percent of applicants for admission into the Class of 2023, placing the school in a selectivity stratosphere with Stanford, Yale, and Columbia. If you had predicted that figure at the turn of the millennium, sideways glances would have surely followed. In 2005, the university admitted 40 percent (not a typo) of applicants and still followed the beat of its own drummer, offering what was known as "The Uncommon App" and maintaining a reputation for welcoming waves of uber-serious bookworms. Changes in leadership and a decade of aggressive marketing practices (soliciting applications from unqualified students) led to a flood of new applicants and a sharp decline in the admit rate.

The average SAT score for enrolled students is now in excess of 1530, although the school announced in 2018 that it was going test-optional. Skeptics believe that one of the motivations for the policy change was to drum up even more applicants to eventually reject, further enhancing its selectivity. Interestingly, the incoming profile of a UChicago student isn't that much different from what it was when it was "easier" to get into; the average SAT score for the Class of 2008 was in the mid-1400s, the same as a decade ago, and 99 percent of incoming students finished in the top 10 percent of their high school class. In sum, UChicago still takes similarly talented academic superstars now, accepting 6 percent of applicants, as it did when it accepted almost six times that figure. The difference is that instead of attracting a self-selecting pool, it now attracts hordes of applicants, the vast majority of whom are destined for rejection.

Worth Your Money?

If you are among the roughly two-fifths of current UChicago students who qualify for financial aid, then you are in luck. The school covers 100 percent of demonstrated need, which leads to an average annual grant of $55,458. Thank goodness for that because the university has one of the highest costs of attendance of any school in the country at $80,277. Fortunately, if you need to pay back some epic loans, you should be able to do so by landing at one of the many top corporations to which the university funnels its graduates. If the University of Chicago is just a stop on the academic road, alumni do incredibly well in gaining acceptance into top graduate and professional schools. Either way, this school is worth your money, even at a relatively obscene price.

FINANCIAL
Institutional Type: Private
In-State Tuition: $60,552
Out-of-State Tuition: $60,552
Room & Board: $17,004
Required Fees: $0
Books & Supplies: $1,800

Avg. Need-Based Grant: $55,458
Avg. % of Need Met: 100%

Avg. Merit-Based Award: NR
% Receiving (All Freshmen): NR
% Receiving (Freshmen w/o Need): NR

Avg. Cumulative Debt: $26,619
% of Students Borrowing: 17%

CAREER
Who Recruits
1. Kraft Heinz
2. Nielson
3. Boston Consulting Group
4. AQR Capital Management
5. Kaufmanm Hall & Associates

Notable Internships
1. Instagram
2. The Blackstone Group
3. Jane Street

Top Industries
1. Business
2. Education
3. Research
4. Finance
5. Media

Top Employers
1. Google
2. Goldman Sachs
3. JP Morgan
4. Facebook
5. Accenture

Where Alumni Work
1. Chicago
2. New York City
3. San Francisco
4. Washington DC
5. Boston

Median Earnings
College Scorecard (Early Career): $68,100
PayScale (Early Career): $68,200
PayScale (Mid-Career): $128,800

RANKINGS
Money: 65
U.S. News: 6 (T), National Universities
Wall Street Journal/THE: 14
Washington Monthly: 24, National Universities

COLLEGE OVERLAPS
Columbia University
Harvard University
Northwestern University
Princeton University
University of Pennsylvania

University of Colorado Boulder

Boulder, Colorado | 303-492-6301

ADMISSION
Admission Rate: 78%
Admission Rate - Men: 76%
Admission Rate - Women: 80%
EA Admission Rate: 95%
ED Admission Rate: Not Offered
ED Admits as % of Total Admits: Not Offered
Admission Rate (5-Year Trend): -6%
% of Admits Attending (Yield): 22%
Transfer Admission Rate: 73%

SAT Reading/Writing (Middle 50%): 580-670
SAT Math (Middle 50%): 560-690
ACT Composite (Middle 50%): 25-31

% Graduated in Top 10% of HS Class: 26%
% Graduated in Top 25% of HS Class: 56%
% Graduated in Top 50% of HS Class: 86%

Demonstrated Interest: Not Considered
Legacy Status: Considered
Admission Interview Offered: No

ENROLLMENT
Total Undergraduate Enrollment: 31,101
% Part-Time: 7%
% Male: 55%
% Female: 45%
% Out-of-State: 42%
% Fraternity: 12%
% Sorority: 22%
% On-Campus (Freshman): 94%
% On-Campus (All Undergraduate): 28%

% African-American: 2%
% Asian: 6%
% Hispanic: 13%
% White: 67%
% Other: 6%
% Race or Ethnicity Unknown: 1%
% International: 6%
% Low-Income: 17%

ACADEMICS
Student-to-Faculty Ratio: 18 to 1
% of Classes Under 20: 44%
% of Classes 20-49: 39%
% of Classes 50 or More: 17%
% Full-Time Faculty: 72%
% Full-Time Faculty w/ Terminal Degree: 87%

Top Programs
Astronomy
Business
Computer Science
Engineering
Environmental Studies
Media Production
Physics
Psychology

Retention Rate: 87%
4-Year Graduation Rate: 46%
6-Year Graduation Rate: 69%

Curricular Flexibility: Less Flexible
Academic Rating: ★★★

#CollegesWorthYourMoney

What do you get when you place a great college town at the foothills of the Rocky Mountains and fill it with 31,100 fun-loving undergraduates? The University of Colorado Boulder is the answer to this question and a school that is now the higher education choice of more than just locals; the university draws an increasing number of out-of-state students that now comprise close to half of the total student body. It also draws thousands of international students from 100+ countries who travel to pursue one of 85 bachelor's degree programs at one of seven schools and colleges.

Inside the Classroom

In 2018, CU Boulder adopted a new set of general education requirements that takes 46 credits to fulfill. The bulk of these mandates are distributional, with Buffaloes being required to earn 12 credits in each of arts and humanities, social sciences, and natural sciences. Skills requirements include foreign language proficiency, quantitative reasoning, and written communication. Members of the Arts & Sciences Honors Program are required to write and defend an honors thesis.

An 18:1 student-to-faculty ratio suggests that small course sections would be a rarity at CU Boulder, but, in reality, class sizes are a mixed bag. Forty-four percent of classes actually have fewer than 20 students, while 18 percent of courses enroll 50 or more students. Opportunities to connect with faculty for research opportunities span all majors and fields of study. The school also offers $1,000-$2,000 grants for assistantships where students assist professors with active research and $1,500-$3,000 for original student projects. Over 1,800 students per year participate in the credit-bearing Education Abroad program that offers hundreds of destinations within 60 countries around the world. Participation in this program has almost doubled in the last decade.

Business/marketing is the discipline where the greatest number of degrees (15 percent) were conferred in 2019. Biology (13 percent), engineering (12 percent), social sciences (12 percent), and communication/journalism each account for a double-digit percentage of bachelor's degrees awarded. The College of Engineering & Applied Science and the Leeds School of Business both possess excellent national reputations. Many students pursue and capture prestigious national scholarships. In 2019, CU Boulder claimed two Goldwater Scholars, a Truman Scholar, and eight Fulbright Scholarships; it won 10 Fulbrights the previous year.

Outside the Classroom

Freshmen are required to live on campus, and pretty much everyone else lives in off-campus housing in the Boulder area. The Off-Campus Housing and Neighborhood Relations Office assists students with the search for post first-year housing. Known for their focus on Greek life, CU Boulder students join sororities in large numbers, with 22 percent of undergrads pledging; 12 percent of men join frats. The Buffs field 17 varsity sports teams that compete at the NCAA Division I level in the Pac-12 Conference. Folsom Field attracts almost 50,000 fans per game for football games, and the men's basketball squad made four appearances in March Madness in the 2010s. The university has 800+ student-run clubs with outdoor recreation-oriented organizations among the most sought after. Boulder ranks as one the very best college towns in the United States thanks to its exceptional public transportation system, bike-friendly layout, bar and restaurant scene, and the 36,000 acres of nature surrounding campus that afford opportunities for hiking, camping, skiing, snowboarding, and more. Pearl Street is rarely a dull place, offering street performers and raucous game-day pep rallies. Those looking for additional adventure can hop on US-36 and arrive in downtown Denver in a half hour.

Career Services

There are 31 professional employees working out of the Career Services office within the Division of Student Affairs. Another 16 staff members work within the Leeds School of Business as career advisors. This total of 47 career services workers equates to a 660:1 student-to-counselor ratio, not at all a bad showing for a school of CU-Boulder's immense size. This high level of support does, in fact, lead to a direct positive impact on Buffs as they move toward graduation. For Class of 2019 graduates, CU Career Services/Handshake were cited as one of the top five ways that seniors found their first jobs.

Thanks to the work of industry coaches within Leeds, nearly 80 percent of business students pursue one or more internships, and 80 companies attended 200+ on-campus engagements with undergrads. Across all departments, information sessions and career fairs are held regularly. Even in the middle of the COVID-19 pandemic, career services staff arranged a dizzying number of virtual meetups for the first month of the 2020-21 academic year featuring the likes of Bain & Company, EY, Teach for America, Deloitte, and Northwestern Mutual. There were also multiple opportunities to connect with alumni in various industries, work on personal branding, or join a Women in Finance Forum. No matter your area of academic and future career concentration, CU Boulder's career services staff will make sure you have ample chances to explore, connect, and prosper.

Professional Outcomes

Eighty-nine percent of the Class of 2019 were working or in graduate school six months after graduating from CU Boulder. The greatest number of recent Buffalo grads can be found roaming the offices of Lockheed Martin, Ball Aerospace, Deloitte, Qualcomm, Northrop Grumman, KPMG, Charles Schwab, and Boeing. More than 100 alumni can also be found at companies like Google, Oracle, Amazon, Apple, and Microsoft. Within the first five years after graduation, Boulder alumni earn an estimated median salary of $62,193. The Greater Denver area plays home to the greatest percentage of Boulder grads followed by San Francisco, New York City, Los Angeles, and Seattle.

Thirteen percent of the Class of 2019 immediately jumped into a graduate or professional degree program, and 80 percent were accepted into their first-choice school. The majority of those continuing on to an advanced degree program did so at either CU Boulder or CU Denver. The private University of Denver, the University of Washington – Seattle, Johns Hopkins, and Berkeley were the next most frequent graduate school destinations. The university produced 213 medical school applicants in 2019-20, including the University of Colorado School of Medicine.

Admission

CU Boulder is a school that offers a quality education without needing to first survive a harrowing admissions process. Those entering the university in 2019-20 encountered an acceptance rate of 76 percent. Middle-50 percent SAT composite scores of attending freshmen were 1150-1350, and the mean SAT score was 1251. Students fare equally well on each section, averaging a 625 on the EBRW section and a 626 on the math section. ACT middle-50 percent scores were 25-31 with a mean score of 27.5. In the classroom, Class of 2023 members earned an average GPA of 3.67 with 26 percent placing inside the top 10 percent of their class; 56 percent finished in the top quartile.

Academic GPA, standardized test scores, and the rigor of one's secondary school record were the three factors rated as "very important" by the University of Colorado Boulder. However, it should be noted that the school is test-optional for the Class of 2024. Factors viewed as "important" are essays, recommendations, extracurricular activities, talent/ability, character/personal qualities, and first-generation status. Legacy status, geographical residence, state residency, ethnic status, and volunteer/paid work experience are all in the "considered" category. This school is easier to get into as a resident of the Rocky Mountain State; in-staters were accepted at an 86 percent clip compared to 66 percent from out of state. Ultimately, slightly more in-state students go on to enroll in the university than those from outside of Colorado.

Worth Your Money?

The total estimated annual cost for an in-state student in 2020-21 is $28,478; non-Coloradans living in the US have a COA of $54,296, and international students have a COA of $60,156. This price makes the University of Colorado Boulder an excellent investment for anyone paying in-state tuition and, potentially, a reasonable destination for a nonresident looking for a top business or engineering program in a desirable geographic location. This school is held in enough esteem by major corporations across various industries to open doors for Buffaloes as they enter the workforce.

FINANCIAL
Institutional Type: Public
In-State Tuition: $10,728
Out-of-State Tuition: $36,546
Room & Board: $14,778
Required Fees: $1,772
Books & Supplies: $1,200

Avg. Need-Based Grant: $12,225
Avg. % of Need Met: 80%

Avg. Merit-Based Award: $9,343
% Receiving (All Freshmen): 41%
% Receiving (Freshmen w/o Need): 39%

Avg. Cumulative Debt: $27,568
% of Students Borrowing: 40%

CAREER
Who Recruits
1. NBC Universal
2. Chevron
3. Ball Aerospace
4. Zayo Group
5. Amazon Web Services

Notable Internships
1. Apple
2. Medtronic
3. Twitter

Top Industries
1. Business
2. Education
3. Operations
4. Engineering
5. Sales

Top Employers
1. Google
2. Amazon
3. Oracle
4. Apple
5. Microsoft

Where Alumni Work
1. Denver
2. San Francisco
3. New York City
4. Los Angeles
5. Seattle

Median Earnings
College Scorecard (Early Career): $50,800
PayScale (Early Career): $60,200
PayScale (Mid-Career): $119,700

RANKINGS
Money: 284
U.S. News: 103 (T), National Universities
Wall Street Journal/THE: 173
Washington Monthly: 147, National Universities

COLLEGE OVERLAPS
Colorado State University
University of Arizona
University of Denver
University of Oregon
University of Washington

University of Connecticut

Storrs, Connecticut | 860-486-3137

New England is so overflowing with superior institutions of higher education that it is genuinely a challenge to travel more than a few miles through Massachusetts or Connecticut without accidentally bumping into one of the top colleges on the planet. However, that surplus of elite universities is balanced by a notable dearth of stellar public institutions. For applicants seeking such a school, you'll have to travel to the sleepy town of Storrs, Connecticut, a half-hour east of Hartford, where you'll find a regional giant with a national reputation. The main campus of the University of Connecticut is home to 18,847 undergraduates, fourteen schools and colleges, and 115+ undergraduate majors. While 81 percent of the student body are state residents, there are also undergraduates hailing from forty-two states and 57 countries presently enrolled, and the percentage of outsiders has been on the rise in recent years.

Inside the Classroom
Whether you enter the School of Business, School of Engineering, School of Fine Arts, or other undergraduate college at Storrs you will encounter a core curriculum of basic requirements. In an effort to ensure "that a balance between professional and general education be established and maintained in which each is complementary to and compatible with the other," UConn mandates two courses in each of arts and humanities, social science, science and technology, and diversity and multiculturalism. Further, students must demonstrate competencies in information literacy, quantitative reasoning, writing, and a second language via additional coursework.

Considering the university's 16:1 student-to-faculty ratio and 8,300 graduate and professional students, one might expect all UConn courses to contain a vast sea of undergraduate faces. However, the school does a nice job of creating a balance of classroom experiences with 53 percent of sections enrolling fewer than twenty students, and only 16 percent containing more than fifty. To help forge even deeper connections with faculty, the Office of Undergraduate Research encourages students to schedule advising sessions to apply for both internal and external research posts. There are also formal programs to target including the Work-Study Research Assistant Program, the Honors Program, or the University Scholar Program that make research a centerpiece of the educational experience. Hundreds of study abroad options are on the table, and the university has taken steps to increase the rate of participation that currently sits around 15 percent.

From a sheer volume standpoint, the four most commonly conferred undergraduate degrees are in business (14 percent), engineering (12 percent), the social sciences (11 percent), and health professions/nursing (11 percent). In terms of prestige and national reputation, programs in business, pharmacy, and nursing carry a good deal of weight. Speaking of reputation, UConn's growing stature has helped its students capture an increasing number of highly competitive scholarships in 2019 including seven Fulbright Scholarships, four Goldwater Scholarships, a Udall Scholarship, and a Truman Scholarship.

Outside the Classroom
Unlike many universities of its size, a healthy 65 percent of undergraduates live on UConn's 4,100-acre campus. Freshmen are not required to live on campus, but 96 percent do. Overall, four semesters of housing are guaranteed to all entering students, and there are plenty of traditional apartments, suites, and residential learning communities available. At UConn you will be treated to one of the best college athletic programs in the country. Husky fans are a fervent bunch, and of the twenty-four varsity teams, nothing captures the attention of all of campus quite like the basketball squads. Since 1999, the men's hoops squad has captured four NCAA titles, and the women's team has won an astounding ten championships. Greek life draws 10 percent of men and 12 percent of women. In total, there are 700 student clubs and five cultural centers. Amenities include an on-campus movie theater, ice rink, and a 191,000-square-foot recreation center that opened in 2019. Volunteer spirit is strong as students contribute a collective 1.3 million hours of community service each year. Major cities like Hartford, Providence, and Boston are close enough for a weekend jaunt.

Career Services
There are twenty-four full-time employees at the University of Connecticut Center for Career Development (CCD) who serve as career consultants, corporate relations specialists, experiential learning coordinators, and operations specialists. There are an additional six career consultants who work in the School of Business and School of Engineering, bringing the total of professional staff to twenty-seven. (That does not include the career services staff members located at UConn's branch campuses.) The CCD's 785:1 student-to-advisor ratio is higher than the average school in this guidebook, but it is fairly typical for a school with close to 19,000 undergraduates.

The vast majority of Huskies utilize career services at some point in their four years, and that rate is higher among students with successful postgraduate outcomes; 79 percent of 2020 graduates took advantage of the CCD's services. Experiential learning—including internships—were completed by 80 percent of graduates. The school forges strong ties to national as well as local companies. In fact, the seventeen Fortune 500 companies located in Connecticut all recruit on the Storrs campus. There are number of career fairs throughout the year with the largest being the fall career fairs (All-University & STEM) that bring in 150 employers each per day and attract more than 2,000 students. Overall, the UConn CCD provides quality assistance to those it is able to reach, and its industry connections, particularly those with Connecticut-based companies, are strong.

Professional Outcomes

Eighty-two percent of the graduating Class of 2020 had reached a positive outcome (job, grad school, military, volunteer position) within six months of earning their degrees. Among the 58 percent that had found employment, the largest numbers landed at Aetna, Cigna, PwC, The Hartford, Travelers, and Raytheon Technologies. Historically, massive numbers of alumni also have been employed by Pratt & Whitney, Pfizer, IBM, and Deloitte. A sampling of the top job titles held by 2020 grads included financial analyst, consultant, engineer, nurse, sales consultant, and business analyst. Huskies can be found in the largest packs in New York City and Greater Hartford—73 percent who attended a Connecticut high school remain in the state post-graduation. Boston, DC, San Francisco, and Philadelphia also have their fair share of UConn alumni.

Many of the 22 percent of 2020 graduates who immediately entered a graduate or professional program did so at their home university that caters to a total of 7,000 grad students. Based on the most recent data available, UConn grads are accepted to medical school at a 65 percent clip, a far better rate than their peers. Recent acceptances include many elite medical institutions including those at the University of Pennsylvania, Georgetown, the University of Chicago, Vanderbilt, and UVA. As many as twenty-five undergraduates per year matriculate into the University of Connecticut School of Medicine. Law acceptances in the past three years include an impressive list of the nation's top institutions such as Harvard, Yale, William & Mary, Cornell, Columbia, and Boston College.

Admission

UConn accepted 49 percent of the 35,096 Class of 2023 hopefuls, representing the lowest acceptance rate in school history and quite a departure from the UConn of a generation ago. In 2000, it received one-third as many applications and admitted more than 80 percent of in-state applicants. The median SAT of freshmen arriving at the Storrs campus was 1300, and the mid-50 percent range was 1210-1420; a decade ago, a 1300 would have put you in the 75th percentile of attending students. Even with the changes to SAT in that time, that is still an indicator of a major jump in selectivity. Fifty-five percent of the entering class in 2019-20 finished in the top decile of their graduating cohort, and 88 percent placed within the top quartile. That group included an astonishing 176 valedictorians and salutatorians.

For a suddenly swamped admissions office, the most important factors in evaluating applicants are the quickest to break down: standardized test scores, GPA, class rank, and the overall rigor of one's high school curriculum. First-generation status, essays, recommendations, extracurricular activities, volunteer work, character/personal qualities, and talent/ability are secondary considerations. There are no early action or early decision options at UConn; everyone faces the same January 15 deadline, but applicants should submit by the December 1 priority deadline for their best chance at merit aid offerings.

Worth Your Money?

For Constitution State residents UConn is a rock-solid deal at $14k for tuition and a total cost of attendance hovering around $31k. Those in the other New England States can attend at a discount for under $40k, but those from other states will see an annual COA of $54k. This school is a no-brainer for state residents as it's hard to get a combination of a cheaper/better education in the Northeast. For everyone else, the value of the degree would depend on the intended area of study. However, those not eligible for a discount of some kind could very likely locate better deals within their home states.

FINANCIAL
Institutional Type: Public
In-State Tuition: $14,406
Out-of-State Tuition: $37,074
Room & Board: $13,258
Required Fees: $3,428
Books & Supplies: $950

Avg. Need-Based Grant: $13,494
Avg. % of Need Met: 59%

Avg. Merit-Based Award: $10,711
% Receiving (All Freshmen): 41%
% Receiving (Freshmen w/o Need): 17%

Avg. Cumulative Debt: $29,217
% of Students Borrowing: 56%

CAREER
Who Recruits
1. CGI Inc.
2. ScribeAmerica
3. Mercer
4. USDA
5. Fidelity Investments

Notable Internships
1. iHeartMedia
2. UBS
3. New York Yankees

Top Industries
1. Business
2. Education
3. Operations
4. Healthcare
5. Sales

Top Employers
1. Pratt & Whitney
2. Travelers
3. The Hartford
4. Aetna
5. Cigna

Where Alumni Work
1. New York City
2. Hartford, CT
3. Boston
4. Washington DC
5. San Francisco

Median Earnings
College Scorecard (Early Career): $58,400
PayScale (Early Career): $62,300
PayScale (Mid-Career): $111,400

RANKINGS
Money: 46
U.S. News: 63 (T), National Universities
Wall Street Journal/THE: 104 (T)
Washington Monthly: 87, National Universities

COLLEGE OVERLAPS
Boston University
Northeastern University
Pennsylvania State University - University Park
Syracuse University
University of Massachusetts -- Amherst

University of Delaware

Newark, Delaware | 302-831-8123

ADMISSION
Admission Rate: 68%
Admission Rate - Men: 64%
Admission Rate - Women: 71%
EA Admission Rate: NR
ED Admission Rate: Not Offered
ED Admits as % of Total Admits: Not Offered
Admission Rate (5-Year Trend): +2%
% of Admits Attending (Yield): 23%
Transfer Admission Rate: 55%

SAT Reading/Writing (Middle 50%): 590-670
SAT Math (Middle 50%): 580-690
ACT Composite (Middle 50%): 24-30

% Graduated in Top 10% of HS Class: 30%
% Graduated in Top 25% of HS Class: 64%
% Graduated in Top 50% of HS Class: 93%

Demonstrated Interest: Considered
Legacy Status: Considered
Admission Interview Offered: No

ENROLLMENT
Total Undergraduate Enrollment: 18,135
% Part-Time: 4%
% Male: 42%
% Female: 58%
% Out-of-State: 62%
% Fraternity: 18%
% Sorority: 23%
% On-Campus (Freshman): 92%
% On-Campus (All Undergraduate): 40%

% African-American: 5%
% Asian: 5%
% Hispanic: 8%
% White: 69%
% Other: 3%
% Race or Ethnicity Unknown: 3%
% International: 6%
% Low-Income: 15%

ACADEMICS
Student-to-Faculty Ratio: 12 to 1
% of Classes Under 20: 32%
% of Classes 20-49: 51%
% of Classes 50 or More: 17%
% Full-Time Faculty: 72%
% Full-Time Faculty w/ Terminal Degree: 91%

Top Programs
Chemical Engineering
Criminal Justice
Education
Exercise Science
Finance
Nutrition and Dietetics
Psychology

Retention Rate: 91%
4-Year Graduation Rate: 71%
6-Year Graduation Rate: 81%

Curricular Flexibility: Somewhat Flexible
Academic Rating: ★★★✓

#CollegesWorthYourMoney

The state of Delaware may take its share of abuse as a place with few attractions (see Wayne's World), but the state's public university is a pretty happening place. The University of Delaware's charming, almost 2,000-acre Newark campus is surrounded by one of the most lively college towns in America. Known for passionate Division I sports fans, a robust Greek life, and a number of well-regarded academic departments, the U of D is attractive to students from all over the US and the world. In fact, the majority of the school's 18,000 undergraduates come from outside of the First State, including international students from 100+ different countries.

Inside the Classroom
No matter which of the school's 140 bachelor's degree programs one pursues, there are 21 credits worth of requirements you must complete. This includes a First-Year Experience course that is a discussion-based, seminar-style class designed to provide a soft landing for freshmen, a discovery learning experience that involves an instructional venture outside of the traditional classroom, as well as one class each in the realms of multiculturalism; creative arts and humanities; history and cultural change; social and behavioral science; and mathematics, natural sciences and technology.

Even when including graduate students in the calculation, the University of Delaware's student-to-faculty ratio is only 15:1, an excellent figure for a public institution. When only counting undergraduate students and faculty, the ratio drops to an even better 12:1. Blue Hens do find themselves in an occasional larger lecture hall as 16 percent of sections enroll 50+ students, but three fifths of all courses enroll fewer than 30 students. Those who are ambitious and aggressive can unearth research opportunities at U of D; 400 students participated in the 2020 Undergraduate Research and Service Scholar Symposium. The university has the oldest study abroad program in the nation. At almost 100 years old, the program entices more than 30 percent of undergraduates to spend a semester in one of 40 foreign countries.

Nearly one third of Delaware students pursue a degree in either business or engineering, two of the school's highest-ranked departments. Nursing is also popular, with 11 percent of degrees conferred being in the health professions. Other frequently pursued majors include the social sciences (12 percent), education (6 percent), biology (6 percent), and parks and recreation (4 percent). Plenty of seniors apply for and land prestigious postgraduate fellowships; 7 Blue Hens landed Fulbright Scholarships in 2019, and students have also captured Truman, Schwarzman, and Critical Language Scholarships in recent years.

Outside the Classroom
U of D's vast campus features plenty of university-run housing in which 92 percent of freshmen and 40 percent of the entire student body reside. Fraternities attract 18 percent of the undergraduate population, and sororities draw 23 percent of all women. Greek culture is alive and well in Newark and is a significant force in the campus social scene. Out of the 21 NCAA Division I teams, the football squad is most popular and often draws crowds of close to 20,000. A full array of intramural sports and 36 club teams exist for less-gifted athletes. The club team offerings include bass fishing, figure skating, and trap and skeet. Overall, there are 300+ clubs of all varieties to choose from. The school dates back to the 1740s and is littered with iconic buildings, old and new, such as Memorial Hall, the Morris Library, and the Whitney Athletic Center. Being located halfway between Washington, DC, and New York City and right outside of Philadelphia makes the school a reasonable drive from a number of desirable urban locations.

Career Services
The Career Center at the University of Delaware has a professional staff of 22 members who work in areas such as event coordination, employer relations, and discipline-specific career advising. This works out to a 548:1 counselor-to-student ratio, better than just about every other large public university in the country. Even more importantly, the center succeeds in achieving a very high level of student engagement. In fact, approximately three quarters of all undergraduates utilized career services resources in 2018-19. In that same academic year, 12,104 students participated in 364 career readiness programs, workshops, and classroom presentations.

Of the over 11,000 students that came into the office for 1:1 career coaching or resume assistance, 99.6 percent rated the appointments positively. The center also does a stellar job connecting undergrads to internship and job opportunities, posting more than 42,000 such opportunities in a given year. Top companies flock to the 22 career fairs and meetups that take place annually in Newark; 617 unique employers visited campus in 2018-19. Companies that regularly recruit Blue Hens include Capital One, Agilent Technologies, BlackRock, Siemens, DowDuPont, Deloitte, Northrup Grumman, PwC, Intel, and Bank of America. In sum, U of D has an exceptional career services staff that is highly effective at connecting with just about every single student on campus.

Professional Outcomes

Blue Hens who strutted across the graduation stage in 2019, quickly found their next destination at a 95 percent clip. Seventy-one percent of graduates were employed, with 72 percent taking jobs at for-profit companies, 14 percent at nonprofits, 9 percent in K-12 education, and 5 percent with a government entity. The greatest number of newly minted alums were hired by ChristianaCare (51), JP Morgan Chase & Co. (51), EY (28), PwC (27), Bank of America (23), Children's Hospital of Philadelphia (19), KPMG (18), and Deloitte (18). The median starting salary for this cohort was $54,000 with a 25th percentile salary of $42,866 and a 75th percentile salary of $62,000. The top five states where Class of 2019 diploma-receivers landed were Delaware (691), New York (463), Pennsylvania (409), New Jersey (315), and Maryland (180).

Of those immediately pursuing an advanced degree, 58 percent entered master's programs, 8 percent began their doctoral studies, and nearly one quarter entered a professional program such as law, medicine, physical therapy, or pharmacy. The most frequent higher education landing spots were the U of D itself (231) followed by Thomas Jefferson University (28), Temple University (18), Widener University (17), and Wilmington University (17). More than ten individuals also matriculated into programs at elite institutions such as Columbia University, Johns Hopkins University, and NYU. The University of Delaware saw 103 seniors apply for medical school in 2019, and the most commonly attended medical schools were Philadelphia College of Osteopathic Medicine (7), Temple University (6), Thomas Jefferson University (5), Rutgers University (4), and Rowan University (4). Temple, Rutgers, Widener, and Drexel were the top law school selections for the Class of 2019, but it also sent students to Georgetown University, the College of William & Mary, and UNC Chapel Hill.

Admission

The applicant pool for the Class of 2023 was 26,500 students large, and 68 percent were ultimately granted admission. Delaware will be test optional for the Class of 2024, but it typically sees over three-quarters of applicants submit SAT scores while the rest submit ACT results. The middle-50th scores are 590-670 on the EBRW section and 580-690 on the math portion. The overall range is 1180-1340. The range for composite ACT scores is 24-30. Thirty percent of 2019-20 first-year students placed in the top ten percent of their graduating high school class, 64 percent were in the top quartile, and 93 percent were in the top half. Fifty-six percent of this group possessed high school GPAs of 3.75 or above. The average GPA for an entering freshman was 3.78.

Three factors reign supreme in the admissions process: rigor of secondary school record, GPA, and state residency. Of secondary importance are standardized test scores, application essays, recommendations, extracurricular activities, talent/ability, character/personal qualities, volunteer work, and paid work experience. "Considered" elements of one's application include class rank, first-generation status, legacy status, geographical residence, racial/ethnic status, and the level of an applicant's demonstrated interest. This school does not conduct formal interviews as part of the admissions process. Those applying to the Honors College will face additional scrutiny, with past accepted students sporting 4.0+ GPAs and SATs in the 1400s.

Worth Your Money?

With an in-state tuition of around $13k, the University of Delaware represents a solid value for residents of the First State. The full cost of attendance is close to $31,000 per year, making it comparable in price to the in-state costs of public universities in the surrounding states of Pennsylvania, New Jersey, and Maryland. Nonresidents will pay $52k per year for the privilege of becoming a Blue Hen, a price that may make sense for students with a clear postgraduation career plan and no solid in-state options of their own.

FINANCIAL
Institutional Type: Public
In-State Tuition: $12,730
Out-of-State Tuition: $34,160
Room & Board: $13,208
Required Fees: $1,550
Books & Supplies: $1,000

Avg. Need-Based Grant: $12,694
Avg. % of Need Met: 61%

Avg. Merit-Based Award: $8,543
% Receiving (All Freshmen): 30%
% Receiving (Freshmen w/o Need): 24%

Avg. Cumulative Debt: $37,447
% of Students Borrowing: 59%

CAREER
Who Recruits
1. Thomas Jefferson University Hospital
2. GlaxoSmithKline
3. BKD Leaders
4. Allan Myers
5. PwC

Notable Internships
1. Northwestern Mutual
2. Philadelphia Phillies
3. Christiana Trust

Top Industries
1. Business
2. Education
3. Operations
4. Healthcare
5. Sales

Top Employers
1. JPMorgan Chase
2. DuPont
3. Citi
4. Merck
5. Capital One

Where Alumni Work
1. Philadelphia
2. New York City
3. Washington DC
4. Baltimore
5. Boston

Median Earnings
College Scorecard (Early Career): $57,000
PayScale (Early Career): $60,800
PayScale (Mid-Career): $112,600

RANKINGS
Money: 41
U.S. News: 97 (T), National Universities
Wall Street Journal/THE: 151 (T)
Washington Monthly: 94, National Universities

COLLEGE OVERLAPS
James Madison University
Pennsylvania State University - University Park
Rutgers University - New Brunswick
University of Connecticut
University of Maryland, College Park

University of Denver

Denver, Colorado | 303-871-2036

ADMISSION
Admission Rate: 59%
Admission Rate - Men: 58%
Admission Rate - Women: 59%
EA Admission Rate: NR
ED Admission Rate: 37%
ED Admits as % of Total Admits: 1%
Admission Rate (5-Year Trend): -18%
% of Admits Attending (Yield): 11%
Transfer Admission Rate: 82%

SAT Reading/Writing (Middle 50%): 590-670
SAT Math (Middle 50%): 580-680
ACT Composite (Middle 50%): 26-31

% Graduated in Top 10% of HS Class: 39%
% Graduated in Top 25% of HS Class: 73%
% Graduated in Top 50% of HS Class: 94%

Demonstrated Interest: Considered
Legacy Status: Considered
Admission Interview Offered: No

ENROLLMENT
Total Undergraduate Enrollment: 5,774
% Part-Time: 5%
% Male: 46%
% Female: 54%
% Out-of-State: 64%
% Fraternity: 25%
% Sorority: 28%
% On-Campus (Freshman): 94%
% On-Campus (All Undergraduate): 48%

% African-American: 2%
% Asian: 4%
% Hispanic: 12%
% White: 68%
% Other: 5%
% Race or Ethnicity Unknown: 2%
% International: 6%
% Low-Income: 16%

ACADEMICS
Student-to-Faculty Ratio: 12 to 1
% of Classes Under 20: 61%
% of Classes 20-49: 33%
% of Classes 50 or More: 6%
% Full-Time Faculty: 51%
% Full-Time Faculty w/ Terminal Degree: 90%

Top Programs
Communication Studies
Finance
Hospitality Management
International Studies
Music
Psychology
Real Estate

Retention Rate: 86%
4-Year Graduation Rate: 67%
6-Year Graduation Rate: 77%

Curricular Flexibility: Somewhat Flexible
Academic Rating: ★★★

#CollegesWorthYourMoney

A midsize private university of 5,774 students, the University of Denver has a rich history by West Coast standards, having been founded a full 14 years before Colorado was even granted statehood. With over 200 total degree programs, small class sizes, and commitment to hands-on learning and international experience, DU is becoming a terrific destination point for quality students whose credentials fall short of perfection.

Inside the Classroom

Utilizing a quarter system, the university requires all undergraduate students to conquer an extensive common curriculum that ultimately comprises roughly half of one's total credits. This journey includes a first-year seminar, first-year writing and rhetoric, demonstrating proficiency in a foreign language, eight courses designated as "Ways of Knowing" and, lastly, a culminating writing-intensive advanced seminar.

Small classes are the norm at the University of Denver as 61 percent of sections contain no more than 19 students, and 83 percent enroll a maximum of 29 individuals. The student-to-faculty ratio is 12:1, allowing the school to stay committed to its mission of focusing on experiential learning. The Undergraduate Research Center helps facilitate connections between intellectually curious undergrads and faculty mentors. Three years ago, the school launched an annual Research and Scholarship Showcase to celebrate the original work of its students. You won't find many schools more committed to encouraging their undergraduates to study abroad. An astonishing 71 percent of DU students take a semester or summer in a foreign country, which has, in certain years, seen it ranked No. 1 in study abroad percentage. It offers 150 programs across 50 countries.

The Daniels College of Business is highly respected by employers and attracts the greatest number of undergraduates. Thirty-five percent of the degrees conferred in 2019 were in business/marketing, 15 percent were in the social sciences, 10 percent in biology, 7 percent in communication/journalism, 7 percent in psychology, and 6 percent in the visual and performing arts. Six students won Fulbright Scholarships in 2019, and another four captured the award in 2018; in 2020, one student was awarded a Goldwater Scholarship. Whether it's the reputation of various academic departments or the university's reputation with prestigious national fellowship organizations, DU's reputation is unquestionably on the rise.

Outside the Classroom

Ninety-four percent of freshmen and 48 percent of all undergrads reside on the University of Denver's 125-acre campus just south of downtown Denver. The buildings are a mix of nineteenth-century and new constriction, as the university splurged on building projects during the first decade of the new 2000s. Greek life has a strong heartbeat at this school with 25 percent of men joining fraternities and 28 percent of women affiliated with sororities; 22 chapters in total have houses on campus. The 17 Pioneer athletic teams all compete in NCAA Division I, with ice hockey being the most popular spectator sport with 8 all-time championships and 75+ Pioneer alumni going on to play in the National Hockey League. There are also 32 club sports teams, 23 intramural leagues, a world-class gym, the Coors Fitness Center that includes an Olympic-sized pool, racquet sports, and recreational ice skating. Over 150 other clubs exist for students to pursue their non-sports passions, including all types of performance groups; collectively, these groups put on 400+ performances per year. Few complain about this school's location just miles from the heart of Denver, one of the country's most popular cities. Whether enjoying hiking in the Rocky Mountains, enjoying the walkable urban area, or taking advantage of the campus' numerous amenities, DU students are rarely bored.

Career Services

Career & Professional Development at the University of Denver is staffed by 28 professional staff members who specialize in discipline-specific career coaching, alumni relations, and employer relations. Another 12 professionals makeup the team at the Daniels School of Business Career Services office. This total of 40 career services employees equates to a student-to-advisor ratio of 144:1, which is among the very best of any school featured in this guide, particularly for a non-liberal arts college. The impact of this exceptional level of investment in career services truly pays off, both for the university and its well-supported undergraduates. There is rarely a day when the office is not hosting a skill-building boot camp or hosting an information session with a prominent corporation. Even during the summer, in the middle of a pandemic, this office was hosting such activities daily through Zoom.

Seventy percent of DU grads participate in at least one internship during their four years; this includes 88 percent of College of Business students, 71 percent of social sciences majors, and 65 percent of engineering and computer science majors. Thirteen percent of employed Class of 2018 members landed their first jobs through an internship experience, 7 percent from a DU event, 5 percent through Pioneers Careers Online, 6 percent from a faculty member, and 2 percent from an alumni referral, meaning that the career services staff members had their hands in 33 percent of successful job hunts. By any measure, the DU career services personnel do a superb job at preparing their students for real-world success.

Professional Outcomes

Ninety percent of Pioneers have successfully entered the world of employment or graduate school within six months of earning their bachelor's degree. The 61 percent who landed their first job primarily remained in Colorado (66 percent); 9 percent headed to the West Coast, and 8 percent settled in the mid-Atlantic region. The mean starting salary of Denver grads was $49k. Those graduating from the School of Engineering and Computer Science netted an average of $69k, College of Business grads earned $54k, and arts and humanities degree-holders started at a mean salary of $43k. Top employers of the 2019 cohort included KPMG, Brown Brothers Harriman, Lockheed Martin, Epic, and Oracle. Other corporations employing 70 or more University of Denver alums include CenturyLink, Charles Schwab, Comcast, Deloitte, Amazon, Google, and Microsoft.

Eighteen percent of 2019 graduates elected to continue their education in a graduate program, including the University of Denver's own 12 schools and colleges that offer master's, doctoral, and professional degrees. This includes the Sturm College of Law that welcomes many of its own grads along with alumni of 151 other institutions. In recent years, other Pioneers have gone on to pursue legal studies at the University of Colorado, Northeastern, the University of Virginia, and the University of Minnesota. On the medical school front, there were 56 applicants from the university in the 2019-20 cycle. Unfortunately, the school does not release its annual acceptance rate.

Admission

Just a hair under 59 percent of the 21,028 applicants for a place in the 2019-20 freshman class received offers of admission. The mid-50th percentile standardized test scores were 1170-1340 on the SAT and 26-31 on the ACT; the averages were 1257 and 28, respectively. Thirteen percent scored better than 1400 on the SAT while just 2 percent scored under 1000. Thirty-nine percent of Class of 2023 members hailed from the top 10 percent of their high school class, 73 percent from the top 25 percent, and only 7 percent fell outside of the top half. The average GPA was 3.72, and 35.8 percent possessed a weighted GPA of 4.0 or higher.

The rigor of your high school coursework and your GPA are deemed the "most important" factors by UD. Test scores, essays, recommendations, talent/ability, character/personal qualities, and extracurricular activities are "important." First-generation status (15 percent of the Class of 2024 met this criteria), alumni relation, geographical residence, racial/ethnic status, volunteer work, work experience, and the level of an applicant's interest are all "considered." This school has an extraordinarily low yield rate of 11 percent, meaning that only one in ten students accepted go on to enroll. Therefore, it is undoubtedly a good idea to make it clear to the university if it is your top choice. It is a bit strange that early decision applicants were admitted at only a 37 percent clip in 2019, but it is likely that the average ED candidate was far weaker academically than the average candidate in the regular cycle.

Worth Your Money?

A full-time student living on campus will pay approximately $72,000 for the privilege in 2020-21. Unless money is no object for your family, we cannot recommend paying full price to attend this school. On the plus side, UD is generous with need-based aid, dishing out an average award of $42.9k. It offers plenty of merit aid as well. All told, 86 percent of incoming freshmen receive some type of financial aid. If you are receiving a reasonable aid package, this school can definitely be worth your money, particularly if you are pursuing a business, engineering, or computer science degree.

FINANCIAL
Institutional Type: Private
In-State Tuition: $52,596
Out-of-State Tuition: $52,596
Room & Board: $14,178
Required Fees: $1,179
Books & Supplies: $1,000

Avg. Need-Based Grant: $36,795
Avg. % of Need Met: 84%

Avg. Merit-Based Award: $21,124
% Receiving (All Freshmen): 51%
% Receiving (Freshmen w/o Need): 39%

Avg. Cumulative Debt: $27,938
% of Students Borrowing: 44%

CAREER
Who Recruits
1. Zayo Group
2. Arrow Electronics
3. U.S. Department of State
4. Google
5. Wells Fargo

Notable Internships
1. Brookings Institute
2. AARP
3. NBA

Top Industries
1. Business
2. Education
3. Operations
4. Social Services
5. information Technology

Top Employers
1. Denver Public Schools
2. Lockheed Martin
3. Walt Disney Company
4. Charles Schwab
5. Deloitte

Where Alumni Work
1. Denver
2. New York City
3. San Francisco
4. Los Angeles
5. Chicago

Median Earnings
College Scorecard (Early Career): $56,500
PayScale (Early Career): $59,000
PayScale (Mid-Career): $113,200

RANKINGS
Money: 543
U.S. News: 80 (T), National Universities
Wall Street Journal/THE: 119
Washington Monthly: 196, National Universities

COLLEGE OVERLAPS
Colorado State University
Santa Clara University
University of Colorado Boulder
University of San Diego
University of Washington

University of Florida

Gainesville, Florida | 352-392-1365

ADMISSION
Admission Rate: 37%
Admission Rate - Men: 35%
Admission Rate - Women: 38%
EA Admission Rate: Not Offered
ED Admission Rate: Not Offered
ED Admits as % of Total Admits: Not Offered
Admission Rate (5-Year Trend): -10%
% of Admits Attending (Yield): 47%
Transfer Admission Rate: 40%

SAT Reading/Writing (Middle 50%): 650-720
SAT Math (Middle 50%): 660-750
ACT Composite (Middle 50%): 28-33

% Graduated in Top 10% of HS Class: 81%
% Graduated in Top 25% of HS Class: 98%
% Graduated in Top 50% of HS Class: 100%

Demonstrated Interest: Considered
Legacy Status: Not Considered
Admission Interview Offered: No

ENROLLMENT
Total Undergraduate Enrollment: 35,405
% Part-Time: 9%
% Male: 44%
% Female: 56%
% Out-of-State: 8%
% Fraternity: 17%
% Sorority: 23%
% On-Campus (Freshman): 83%
% On-Campus (All Undergraduate): 24%

% African-American: 6%
% Asian: 9%
% Hispanic: 23%
% White: 52%
% Other: 4%
% Race or Ethnicity Unknown: 3%
% International: 3%
% Low-Income: 30%

ACADEMICS
Student-to-Faculty Ratio: 17 to 1
% of Classes Under 20: 53%
% of Classes 20-49: 37%
% of Classes 50 or More: 10%
% Full-Time Faculty: 86%
% Full-Time Faculty w/ Terminal Degree: 90%

Top Programs
Animal Science
Applied Physiology and Kinesiology
Biology
Business
Criminology
Education
Engineering
Journalism and Communication

Retention Rate: 97%
4-Year Graduation Rate: 68%
6-Year Graduation Rate: 90%

Curricular Flexibility: Somewhat Flexible
Academic Rating: ★★★★⁄

#CollegesWorthYourMoney

At a time when flagship state schools are being overrun by out-of-state and international students willing to pay full freight, the University of Florida stands strong as an almost exclusive landing spot for Sunshine State residents to the tune of 92 percent. Gator Nation could almost be its own small nation with 35,405 undergraduates, 17,000 graduate students, and roughly 400,000 living alumni. It's not hard to see why top Florida-based teens target UF as their number one choice. One of the top-ranked state universities in the U.S. can still be accessed by for an annual tuition under $7,000 at a time when many elite (and not so elite) schools are eight times higher in cost.

Inside the Classroom
With sixteen colleges and one hundred undergraduate majors to choose from, the educational experiences of UF students are exceptionally diverse. That includes one of the country's largest honors programs at 3,400 students; classes within this program are capped at twenty-five. All Gators must chomp through a blend of state and university core academic requirements that include coursework in composition, humanities, mathematics, biological and physical sciences, social and behavioral sciences, and classes with "international" and "diversity" designations.

A 17:1 student-to-faculty ratio and a massive number of graduate students leads to some fairly large undergraduate course sections. Yet, the school impressively offers 53 percent of sections with an enrollment of fewer than twenty students. The Center for Undergraduate Research offers a University Research Scholars program, summer opportunities, and it hosts its own Undergraduate Research Symposium and publishes its own UF Journal of Undergraduate Research. One-third of all 2020 grads had such an experience. The school has connections to 1,100 study abroad programs that are taken advantage of by more than 2,200 undergrads each year.

The Warrington College of Business and the Wertheim College of Engineering are highly respected, and a degree from either will yield one of the more absurd returns-on-investment in all of postsecondary education. Therefore, it's no surprise that those two programs confer the greatest percentage of degrees—13 percent and 14 percent, respectively. Biology (11 percent), the social sciences (10 percent), and communications/journalism (8 percent) are next in popularity. The procurement of highly competitive fellowships and postgraduate scholarships is not a focal point of the university, but Gators do claim their fair share. Eight graduates of the Class of 2019 won a Fulbright Scholarship, and as many as twenty-seven students have won National Science Foundation Graduate Research Fellowships in recent years.

Outside the Classroom
Not leading off with a discussion of campus life at UF with football would be an egregious case of burying the lede. The 90,000 orange-and-blue adorned fans crammed into Ben Hill Griffin Stadium, more commonly referred to as "The Swamp," captures the lifeblood of the University of Florida. And it's not only football that is a point of athletic pride in Gainesville. UF is ranked alongside Stanford and UCLA as one of the best overall sports programs in the country. Twenty of the school's twenty-one teams compete in the ultra-competitive SEC Conference, and the Gators have earned an astounding thirty-six all-time national championships. Outside of varsity sports there are 1,000 student organizations, and 76 percent of students are engaged in campus activities for a minimum of an hour per week. There are sixty intramural sports leagues, two large fitness centers, and two lakes for swimming, boating, and relaxation. Due to a dearth of school-owned housing, only 24 percent of students live on campus, almost all freshmen. Many move into Greek houses as 17 percent of men and 23 percent of women enter fraternity and sorority life. Gainesville is constructed as a Southern college town-by-numbers experience with all the requisite components of beautiful weather, an overwhelming number of restaurants, bars, and shops, plenty of parties and, of course, the sports-crazed atmosphere.

Career Services
Unlike many schools of UF's size that have a network of smaller career services offices housed within various colleges, the centralized University of Florida Career Connections Center (C3) serves more than 54,000 current students and alumni. At C3 thirty professionals are available to assist you with career counseling, internship coordination, and networking. The university's overall student-to-counselor ratio of 1,180:1 is among the poorest of any school featured in this guidebook. Still, there are many positive, measurable things occurring at this career services center.

In 2019-20, almost 19,000 students engaged with C3 through workshops, virtually, or through one-on-one sessions; that figure represents more than half of UF's undergraduate population. Staff put on 371 career planning workshops, added 42,436 job listings to Handshake, and attracted 1,488 employers and 17,194 students to career fairs. Most impressively, it facilitated over 4,600 on-campus interviews with 342 local, regional, and national employers. A solid 61 percent of 2020 graduates reported at least one non-academic internship experience during their four years of study. Twenty-three percent of employed grads reported a job fair as being a resource that helped them land their first jobs, and 10 percent cited the Career Connections Center. Despite limited staffing for individualized counseling to reach 35,000+ undergrads, UF does a nice job putting on large-scale events and bringing a vast array of companies onto campus to recruit and interview.

Professional Outcomes

At the time they received their diplomas 52 percent of the Class of 2020 had already procured a first job. The top occupational areas for 2020 graduates were engineering (9 percent), health care (9 percent), computer science (5 percent), and education (3 percent). Across the entirety of the alumni base, impressive numbers of Gators can be found at many of the nation's most desirable corporations. In fact, more than 200 UF grads are currently employed by Google, EY, Raymond James, Deloitte, Apple, Amazon, Microsoft, Oracle, PwC, and Facebook. Many graduates remain in the Gainesville area or spread out to other Florida cities including Miami, Tampa Bay, Orlando, Jacksonville, or West Palm Beach. However, substantial numbers of alumni also can be found in Atlanta, New York, DC, and San Francisco. Grads of the College of Business Administration earn median starting salaries, including bonuses, of $64k, computer science majors earn $101k, and psychology majors $40k; the average salary for all 2018 grads was $55k.

Of those seeking full-time graduate studies upon receiving their diplomas, a master's degree was the most popular pursuit (48 percent) followed by degrees in the medical field (17 percent, including 6 percent working on MDs), law school (9 percent), and PhDs (6 percent). The pre-med program is solid as UF sends the third most undergrads to medical school of any university in the country, behind only UCLA and UT Austin. Students with strong GPAs and MCAT scores feed directly into the university's own highly ranked College of Medicine. Law school applicants enjoy an 85 percent acceptance rate. The most commonly attended institution was UF's own law school where eighty-six recent graduates matriculated. Three students entered each of Harvard and the University of Chicago and two went to Yale while Columbia, NYU, and Penn all welcomed four Gators each into their prestigious law schools.

Admission

Over 38,000 students submitted applications to the University of Florida for a spot in the 2019-20 freshman class; the admit rate was 37 percent. The typical Class of 2023 admitted student possessed a 4.5 GPA, SAT score of 1380, and ACT score of 31. Students tend to rank near the top of their high school class. The latest available data from the Class of 2023 shows that 81 percent placed in the top decile of their graduating cohort, and 98 percent finished in the top 25 percent. Five years ago, the acceptance rate was a far friendlier 47 percent, and the 75th percentile SAT score was lower than the average SAT score among 2023 admits, confirmation that the sinking acceptance rate is indicative of a genuine rise in the school's level of selectivity.

With such a mammoth pile of applications to weed through, one would expect the admissions committee to place the greatest value on hard numbers like standardized test scores, GPA, and class rank. However, of those three factors, the UF Admissions Office only rates GPA as being "very important" to the process. Other considerations listed as "very important" are more in line with those of an elite liberal arts school: rigor of secondary coursework, application essay, extracurricular activities, talent/ability, character/personal qualities, and volunteer work. Grades are king for Gainesville hopefuls; 81 percent had a GPA of 3.75 or above on a 4.0 scale.

Worth Your Money?

A $6,300 annual tuition cost in the modern era of universally exorbitant tuition looks like a misprint at first glance. Amazingly, the University of Florida, even at full price—room and board and all fees—would only set you back $21k per year assuming, of course, that you qualify as a Florida resident. The sliver of students coming to Gainesville from out of state pay more than double that amount, but UF still ultimately proves a bargain. If you live in Florida and can get into the university, start packing your bags because you simply won't find a better value.

FINANCIAL
Institutional Type: Public
In-State Tuition: $6,381
Out-of-State Tuition: $28,658
Room & Board: $10,590
Required Fees: $0
Books & Supplies: $890

Avg. Need-Based Grant: $8,383
Avg. % of Need Met: 99%

Avg. Merit-Based Award: $2,832
% Receiving (All Freshmen): 44%
% Receiving (Freshmen w/o Need): 4%

Avg. Cumulative Debt: $20,388
% of Students Borrowing: 35%

CAREER
Who Recruits
1. L3 Harris Technologies
2. OMP
3. Citrix
4. Procter & Gamble
5. KPMG

Notable Internships
1. Jet Blue
2. The Walt Disney Company
3. Kellogg Company

Top Industries
1. Business
2. Education
3. Operations
4. Healthcare
5. Engineering

Top Employers
1. Amazon
2. Intel
3. Microsoft
4. Google
5. PwC

Where Alumni Work
1. Gainsville, FL
2. Miami
3. Tampa
4. Orlando
5. Jacksonville

Median Earnings
College Scorecard (Early Career): $56,000
PayScale (Early Career): $59,600
PayScale (Mid-Career): $111,000

RANKINGS
Money: 16
U.S. News: 30 (T), National Universities
Wall Street Journal/THE: 56 (T)
Washington Monthly: 15, National Universities

COLLEGE OVERLAPS
Florida State University
University of Central Florida
University of Georgia
University of Miami
University of South Florida

University of Georgia

Athens, Georgia | 706-542-8776

ADMISSION
Admission Rate: 46%
Admission Rate - Men: 42%
Admission Rate - Women: 48%
EA Admission Rate: 59%
ED Admission Rate: Not Offered
ED Admits as % of Total Admits: Not Offered
Admission Rate (5-Year Trend): -9%
% of Admits Attending (Yield): 19%
Transfer Admission Rate: 70%

SAT Reading/Writing (Middle 50%): 630-700
SAT Math (Middle 50%): 610-720
ACT Composite (Middle 50%): 27-32

% Graduated in Top 10% of HS Class: 60%
% Graduated in Top 25% of HS Class: 92%
% Graduated in Top 50% of HS Class: 99%

Demonstrated Interest: Not Considered
Legacy Status: Not Considered
Admission Interview Offered: No

ENROLLMENT
Total Undergraduate Enrollment: 29,848
% Part-Time: 6%
% Male: 43%
% Female: 57%
% Out-of-State: 12%
% Fraternity: 20%
% Sorority: 31%
% On-Campus (Freshman): 98%
% On-Campus (All Undergraduate): 32%

% African-American: 7%
% Asian: 11%
% Hispanic: 7%
% White: 69%
% Other: 4%
% Race or Ethnicity Unknown: 1%
% International: 2%
% Low-Income: 22%

ACADEMICS
Student-to-Faculty Ratio: 17 to 1
% of Classes Under 20: 48%
% of Classes 20-49: 41%
% of Classes 50 or More: 11%
% Full-Time Faculty: 88%
% Full-Time Faculty w/ Terminal Degree: 95%

Top Programs
Animal Science
Biology
Business
Exercise & Sport Science
International Affairs
Journalism & Mass Communication
Psychology
Public Health

Retention Rate: 96%
4-Year Graduation Rate: 66%
6-Year Graduation Rate: 87%

Curricular Flexibility: Somewhat Flexible
Academic Rating: ★★★★

#CollegesWorthYourMoney

Founded in 1785 as the first state-sponsored university in the country, UGA has since grown into a vast operation that boasts seventeen distinct colleges and schools that offer 143 majors. Those who make scenic Athens their undergraduate home are free to pursue concentrations in anything from the traditional disciplines to more exotic fields such as avian biology, furnishings and interiors, and turfgrass management. Becoming a Bulldog is infinitely more difficult than a generation ago, but that's an understandable marketplace adjustment for a school that is of extraordinarily high quality, about as sports conscious as any you'll come across, and that offers as low a tuition as you can hope to find anywhere in the country.

Inside the Classroom

Students cover all of the basics through the school's core curriculum that requires two or more courses in each of English, math, science, world language/culture, and social science along with one course in quantitative reasoning. Freshmen at UGA all participate in a First-Year Odyssey seminar led by a faculty member and capped at eighteen students. Within that intimate setting, students have the opportunity to explore one of 300 thought-provoking topics including Chocolate Science, Death and Dying, Pets in Modern Society, and The Psychology of Harry Potter. Freshmen also have the choice of signing up for Residential Learning Communities, a program that allows dorm residents with similar interests to take classes together. The University of Georgia is the largest undergraduate institution in the country to mandate hands-on learning for every single graduate. UGA students must fulfill that requirement by completing one from a lengthy menu of internships, service options, or research opportunities.

The school's student-to-faculty ratio is 17:1 and, with 9,000 graduate students to also serve, not all of your coursework will be conducted in a cozy setting. Still, 48 percent of sections enroll fewer than twenty students compared with 11 percent of sections that enroll fifty or more. No matter your major, UGA encourages you to conduct research with a member of the school's faculty. The Center for Undergraduate Research Opportunities (CURO) awards grants to 500 students per year, and in 2018-19 a robust 550 students presented at the CURO Symposium. Meanwhile, the Office of Global Engagement helps 2,000 students annually find which of the one hundred+ study abroad programs that are led by UGA faculty is right for them.

Business is the most commonly conferred undergraduate degree, accounting for 28 percent of diplomas earned. It is followed by social sciences (9 percent), communication & journalism (9 percent), biology (8 percent), and psychology (6 percent). Top-ranked programs include animal science, business, communications, and public and international affairs. The school has seen an increase in its number of Fulbright Scholars, producing twenty-five over the last two years. Among public institutions, UGA also has been one of the top three producers of Rhodes Scholars over the previous two decades.

Outside the Classroom

Ninety-eight percent of freshmen, but only 32 percent of the student body, reside in university-owned housing. As you would expect at a school with over 29,000 undergraduates, there is a full smorgasbord of over 800 clubs and activities from which to choose. The Center for Leadership and Service connects 12,500 students with over 228,000 volunteer hours. Fraternities and sororities have a strong presence with sixty-two Greek-letter organizations on campus that draw 20 percent of men and 31 percent of women. If you want to follow Division I athletics, UGA's perennial powerhouse football team draws 92,746 fans to Sanford Stadium each week in autumn. The school fields competitive men's and women's teams in a variety of other sports as well as a diverse selection of over seventy club and intramural teams. For non-athletic competitors, UGA's debate team has qualified for the National Debate Tournament for twenty-five consecutive years, and its chess team routinely wins state championships. The bottom line is that no matter your passion, you'll be able to find kindred spirits at UGA.

Career Services

The University of Georgia Career Center employs thirty-six full-time staff members including administrators, career consultants, and employer relations team members. That equates to a student-to-advisor ratio of 829:1, higher-than-average compared to the pool of institutions included in this book, but about average for an institution of its size. While individualized attention can occasionally be a challenge, the career center does regularly host job and internship fairs, and virtual Q&A sessions with employers are hosted on Twitter. Annually, over 1,000 companies engage in on-campus recruiting through one of the university's major-specific fairs. It's no wonder that 88 percent of 2019 grads' first jobs aligned with their career aspirations and 43 percent cited the Career Center as a most helpful resource in their successful job hunt.

Students can sign up at any time for a mock interview with a career consultant. The center also offers a more formalized series of career prep events called "Arch Ready," referencing the iconic campus landmark. Those events cover topics such as major selection, career exploration, and resume writing. The career center does engage companies to become internship partners for students, but data on the percentage of UGA undergrads that land internships is unavailable; what is known is that only 27 percent of Bulldogs who secured an internship did so through the career center. A robust alumni network will help recent grads connect with other Bulldogs anywhere in the world. Last year, 3,140 unique employers hired UGA grads, resulting in a wide-reaching alumni presence in business, government, and educational institutions.

Professional Outcomes

UGA's career outcomes rate (the percent of students employed or continuing their education six months after graduation) was 95 percent for the Class of 2019. Popular employers include Accenture, PricewaterhouseCoopers, the Walt Disney Company, and Deloitte. Seventy-one percent of 2019 grads stayed in the state of Georgia with the cities of Dallas, Houston, Chicago, DC, New York City, and San Francisco also among the top destinations. UGA does an excellent job of tracking graduates' starting salary data by school/major. That data allows prospective students to properly calibrate their financial expectations based on area of study. For instance, engineering grads in the Class of 2019 had a median starting salary of $61k while graduates of the Grady College of Journalism and Mass Communication reported a median income of $40k.

In 2019, a solid 19 percent of graduates elected to jump directly into a full-time advanced degree program. The most commonly attended graduate/professional schools included elite institutions such as Columbia, Duke, Emory, Georgia Tech, Penn, UVA, and Johns Hopkins. In a given year, roughly half of the Bulldogs applying to medical school gain acceptance. Recent graduates are currently studying medicine at local schools, such as the Mercer University School of Medicine, as well as prestigious medical training grounds like Emory, Harvard, and Washington University.

Admission

Like many flagships around the country, the University of Georgia has grown increasingly competitive in recent years. The university received 29,065 applications in 2019, more than double the number received in 2005. The acceptance rate for a place in the Class of 2023 was 46 percent. Freshmen in 2019-20 possessed an ACT mid-50 percent score of 27-32 and 1240-1400 on the SAT. A strong academic profile is also essential—60 percent of successful applicants were in the top 10 percent of their class, and 90 percent were in the top quartile. Perhaps the most intimidating statistic is that the average GPA is 4.02.

A scholarship program guaranteeing any valedictorian or salutatorian from a Georgia high school free tuition has led to 4 percent of the student body being comprised of students holding those illustrious distinctions. The UGA Admissions Office says, "More than any other single factor, the grades you earn in your high school courses play the most important role in determining your competitiveness for admission to UGA." A rigorous high school course load is a must as 96 percent of admitted students took at least one AP, IB, or dual enrollment class. In sum, this public jewel has become a destination point for the Peach State's top high school students. Knowledgeable applicants should use caution in underestimating the level of competition for spots on the picturesque Athens campus.

Worth Your Money?

You would be hard pressed to locate a better value for a college diploma from a highly respected institution than what you would get at UGA. In-state residents pay under $10k in tuition only and, thanks to cheap living in Athens, only $28k in total cost of attendance. Out-of-staters pay a not unreasonable total annual cost of $47k. The school awards an average need-based grant of $11k to 41 percent of current students. It's little wonder that the average amount of debt for a University of Georgia grad is well under the national average. In short, this school is worth the money for any type of degree; even nonresidents can find a solid value here.

FINANCIAL
Institutional Type: Public
In-State Tuition: $9,790
Out-of-State Tuition: $28,830
Room & Board: $10,328
Required Fees: $2,290
Books & Supplies: $1,052

Avg. Need-Based Grant: $11,227
Avg. % of Need Met: 79%

Avg. Merit-Based Award: $4,329
% Receiving (All Freshmen): 19%
% Receiving (Freshmen w/o Need): 2%

Avg. Cumulative Debt: $22,918
% of Students Borrowing: 41%

CAREER
Who Recruits
1. Mailchimp
2. State Farm
3. Yelp
4. Boston Consulting Group
5. Home Depot

Notable Internships
1. Anthropologie
2. Delta Air Lines
3. TJX Companies

Top Industries
1. Business
2. Education
3. Operations
4. Sales
5. Healthcare

Top Employers
1. Home Depot
2. Delta
3. EY
4. Coca Cola
5. Deloitte

Where Alumni Work
1. Atlanta
2. Athens. GA
3. New York City
4. Washington DC
5. Charlotte

Median Earnings
College Scorecard (Early Career): $50,500
PayScale (Early Career): $57,200
PayScale (Mid-Career): $107,600

RANKINGS
Money: 93
U.S. News: 47 (T), National Universities
Wall Street Journal/THE: 149 (T)
Washington Monthly: 104, National Universities

COLLEGE OVERLAPS
Clemson University
Georgia Institute of Technology
University of Florida
University of North Carolina at Chapel Hill
University of South Carolina

Chicago, Illinois | 312-996-4350

ADMISSION
Admission Rate: 73%
Admission Rate - Men: 70%
Admission Rate - Women: 75%
EA Admission Rate: 87%
ED Admission Rate: Not Offered
ED Admits as % of Total Admits: Not Offered
Admission Rate (5-Year Trend): 0%
% of Admits Attending (Yield): 27%
Transfer Admission Rate: 55%

SAT Reading/Writing (Middle 50%): 510-620
SAT Math (Middle 50%): 520-640
ACT Composite (Middle 50%): 21-28

% Graduated in Top 10% of HS Class: 28%
% Graduated in Top 25% of HS Class: 59%
% Graduated in Top 50% of HS Class: 90%

Demonstrated Interest: Considered
Legacy Status: Not Considered
Admission Interview Offered: No

ENROLLMENT
Total Undergraduate Enrollment: 21,641
% Part-Time: 7%
% Male: 48%
% Female: 52%
% Out-of-State: 3%
% Fraternity: 5%
% Sorority: 5%
% On-Campus (Freshman): 31%
% On-Campus (All Undergraduate): 14%

% African-American: 8%
% Asian: 21%
% Hispanic: 34%
% White: 26%
% Other: 3%
% Race or Ethnicity Unknown: 2%
% International: 7%
% Low-Income: 56%

ACADEMICS
Student-to-Faculty Ratio: 18 to 1
% of Classes Under 20: 35%
% of Classes 20-49: 47%
% of Classes 50 or More: 18%
% Full-Time Faculty: 74%
% Full-Time Faculty w/ Terminal Degree: 87%

Top Programs
Biology
Computer Science
Criminology
English
Engineering
Finance
Psychology

Retention Rate: 79%
4-Year Graduation Rate: 34%
6-Year Graduation Rate: 61%

Curricular Flexibility: Very Flexible
Academic Rating: ★★★

#CollegesWorthYourMoney

With no racial or ethnic majority among the student population, the University of Illinois at Chicago is one of the most genuinely diverse institutions of higher learning in the United States. It is also the largest school in the Greater Chicago area with over 21,600 undergraduates and 11,500 graduate and professional students. Undergrads pursue one of 86 bachelor's programs offered through the 11 (of 16) colleges within UIC that grant undergraduate degrees. The university, in its present form, is only 38 years old, and with its combination of desirable location and quality academics, it is sure to continue to rise up the rankings in the coming decade.

Inside the Classroom
The general education core covers six categories: analyzing the natural world, understanding the individual and society, understanding the past, understanding the creative arts, exploring world cultures, and understanding US society. Students must demonstrate proficiency as writers by either completing two English composition courses or demonstrating their skills on standardized tests. Four semesters of a foreign language is among the graduation requirements within the College of Liberal Arts and Sciences, but second language mandates vary by college. For the 1,955 students in the Honors College, at least one honors activity must be completed each semester, and an honors capstone project is required during senior year.

As would be expected at a modestly priced state school with a plethora of graduate school programs, the student-to-faculty ratio is a mediocre 18:1, and some classes, particularly those of the introductory variety, will be conducted in expansive lecture halls. Yet, while 20 percent of classes at UIC do, indeed, enroll more than 50 students, close to two thirds enroll fewer than 29. Ten percent of courses are taught by teaching assistants, but 90 percent of full-time faculty here have a PhD. Opportunities to engage in undergraduate research will not be handed to you, as at some liberal arts colleges, but the Undergraduate Research Experience, a university-wide program, does connect motivated students with faculty researchers in their field of interest. Those interested in studying abroad have access to 200+ programs in 50 countries.

The most popular majors at this school are business/marketing (15 percent), biology (14 percent), and engineering (13 percent). The next most commonly conferred degrees are in psychology (11 percent), health professions (9 percent), and the social sciences (7 percent). The business, engineering, and computer science programs all have a solid national reputation, regularly cracking "Top 100" lists in their respective disciplines. UIC is not, at this time, a prolific producer of prestigious national fellowship winners.

Outside the Classroom
One of the more diverse schools in the country by any measure, the University of Illinois at Chicago boasts large Hispanic, African American, and Asian populations as well as a sizable number of older students; 9 percent of undergrads are over the age of 25. There are a good deal of commuters and students who live in off-campus housing from the very beginning of their college journey; just one-third of freshmen and 15 percent of total undergraduates live in the dorms. Greek life is modest in size with just 6 percent of students electing to join one of the 17 sororities or 17 fraternities. Playing as the Flames, the university fields 20 NCAA Division I sports teams, and all tickets are free to students. Even with approximately half of the student body home for the weekends, there is still plenty to do on this 240-acre urban campus. There are limitless opportunities to participate in intramural sports and a 214,000-square-foot Outdoor Field Complex on which to play them. The Credit Union 1 Arena is a 9,500-seat multipurpose stadium on the university's campus that plays host to a wide range of cultural, musical, dramatic, and athletic events. Being located in the heart of one of America's most beloved cities also has many advantages. Within a couple miles of campus are sights like the Art Institute of Chicago, the Chicago Riverwalk, and, of course, plenty of world-famous pizza places.

Career Services
There are multiple career services offices within the University of Illinois at Chicago. First, there is a catch-all Career Services office staffed by eight professionals. The Engineering Career Center employs an additional four individuals. The Business Career Center offers nine career services professionals, and the College of Liberal Arts and Sciences Career Development office has another two. All told, 23 professional staff members work in career services on behalf of UIC undergraduates, equating to a less-than-ideal 939:1 student-to-advisor ratio. Still, this figure is not uncommon at a university of this size, and career services staff put on plenty of large-scale events to accommodate the heavy flow of undergraduates.

Each year, the school hosts eight major career fairs, including the UIC Graduate and Professional School Fair attended by reps from 200+ colleges and universities and the All Majors Career Fair that attracts 100+ major companies. Sixty-four percent of UIC grads report completing at least one internship during their time on campus, an impressive percentage for a public school with such high enrollment. The Engineering Career Center is always happy to discuss your career search one-on-one, review a resume, or offer useful workshops such as "Preparing for Technical Interviews with Google." The Business Career Center excels at connecting students to paid internships and on-campus interviews with some of the world's most sought-after employers.

Professional Outcomes

The Class of 2018 (most recent data available) had an 82 percent success rate six months after graduation, and 16 percent were still looking for their next opportunity. Students on the engineering, applied sciences, and public health tracks found employment or a graduate school home at the highest rates; education, architecture, and liberal arts majors had the poorest short-term outcomes. By volume, the largest employer of University of Illinois at Chicago grads are Chicago Public Schools. More than 100 alumni can also be found employed by Allstate, Amazon, Accenture, Microsoft, IBM, Google, Deloitte, and Facebook. Over 90 percent of employed 2018 grads began their careers within the state of Illinois; in the long run, the Greater Chicago area remains the most popular area of residence with San Francisco, New York City, Los Angeles, and Washington, DC, next on the list.

Recent graduates of UIC went on to enroll at top graduate schools such as Boston University, New York University, Northwestern University, and the University of Chicago. Many elected to continue their studies within the University of Illinois system at either the Urbana-Champaign or Chicago campus. In the 2019-20 school year, 245 seniors applied to medical schools around the country including the university's own University of Illinois College of Medicine. Many prelaw students matriculate into UIC's John Marshall School of Law while other recent grads have gone on to attend the University of Chicago, Boston College, Northwestern, and the University of Illinois College of Law (Urbana-Champaign).

Admission

The University of Illinois at Chicago saw 22,696 applicants in the most recent admissions cycle; 73 percent were accepted, making for a less stressful process than at many other schools featured in this guide. The SAT was the more commonly submitted of the two major standardized tests (81 percent), and the middle-50th percentile on the Reading and Writing section was 510-620, and on the math section the range was 520-640. The middle-50th percentile on the ACT was a wide-ranging 21-28. Only 28 percent of freshmen earned a place in the top 10 percent of their graduating class compared to 55 percent at the Urbana-Champaign campus. Fifty-nine percent of freshmen placed in the top quartile, and 90 percent were in the top half of their high school cohort.

Utilizing a straightforward and numbers-based admissions process, the UIC committee leans most heavily on the rigor of one's secondary school record, class rank, GPA, and standardized test scores. The only other factors that are even considered are essays, recommendations, and extracurricular activities. Applicants to the College of Engineering are held to a higher standard, as accepted students sported a middle-50 percent SAT range of 1210-1410; those admitted to the College of Education scored in the 980-1150 range. There is no early decision option at this school, but students do have the option to apply early action by November 1.

Worth Your Money?

The university rates among the best in the country for social mobility, providing the opportunity for those born into lower-income households to achieve more favorable economic standing in their adult lives. With a tuition of $10,500 for Illinois residents, the Chicago campus comes a couple thousand dollars cheaper than its Urbana-Champaign counterpart. While the school only meets 64 percent of demonstrated need, the average graduate leaves UIC only $22k in debt, significantly below the national average. Out-of-staters pay a reasonable tuition of $24,000 which, if studying within the well-regarded College of Business Administration or College of Engineering, is a price worth paying, particularly if the city of Chicago appeals to you as a postsecondary home.

FINANCIAL
Institutional Type: Public
In-State Tuition: $10,584
Out-of-State Tuition: $23,800
Room & Board: $12,479
Required Fees: $3,290
Books & Supplies: $1,400

Avg. Need-Based Grant: $13,948
Avg. % of Need Met: 64%

Avg. Merit-Based Award: $5,721
% Receiving (All Freshmen): 7%
% Receiving (Freshmen w/o Need): 4%

Avg. Cumulative Debt: $21,934
% of Students Borrowing: 58%

CAREER
Who Recruits
1. MWH Global
2. Siemens
3. Mayo Clinic
4. GrubHub
5. Allstate

Notable Internships
1. Northrop Grumman
2. Motorola
3. ScribeAmerica

Top Industries
1. Business
2. Healthcare
3. Education
4. Operations
5. Engineering

Top Employers
1. Chicago Public Schools
2. Rush University Medical Center
3. AbbVie
4. Amazon
5. JPMorgan Chase

Where Alumni Work
1. Chicago
2. San Francisco
3. New York City
4. Los Angeles
5. Washington DC

Median Earnings
College Scorecard (Early Career): $54,300
PayScale (Early Career): $59,000
PayScale (Mid-Career): $108,700

RANKINGS
Money: 64
U.S. News: 112 (T), National Universities
Wall Street Journal/THE: 89 (T)
Washington Monthly: 47, National Universities

COLLEGE OVERLAPS
DePaul University
Illinois Institute of Technology
Illinois State University
Loyola University Chicago
University of Illinois at Urbana-Champaign

University of Illinois at Urbana-Champaign

Champaign, Illinois | 217-333-0302

The University of Illinois at Urbana-Champlain, the mammoth, highly ranked research university with an iconic Midwestern campus, serves as the beloved home to 34,120 increasingly accomplished undergraduates. The university's humble beginnings as an industrial college upon its founding in 1867 are now nothing more than a distant, long-obliterated memory. Illinois' flagship institution 135 miles south of Chicago has fifteen schools and colleges, eight of which cater to undergraduate students. There are 150 academic programs including fifteen in the acclaimed Grainger College of Engineering alone.

Inside the Classroom

As at many large universities, curricular mandates vary by school. The College of Liberal Arts & Sciences, by far UIUC's largest school, has a long list of must-takes including four classes in a foreign language, two English composition courses, and two courses in each of humanities and arts, natural sciences and technology, and social and behavioral sciences. In 2019-20, three cultural studies courses were added as requirements: Western Cultures, Non-Western Cultures, and US Minority Cultures.

Illinois' student-to-faculty ratio of 20:1 is among the highest of any school in this guide, but the school still manages to keep 38 percent of sections capped at 19 students. Further, 17 percent of undergraduates work with a faculty member on a research project; another 35 percent have some type of fieldwork, practicum, or clinical experience. Unique opportunities for experiential learning abound at Research Park, an on-campus technology hub that hosts more than one hundred major corporations, and 2,100 employees who use the space as an incubator of innovation and a place to collaborate with Illinois faculty and students. Also strong, particularly for a school of UIUC's size, is the 33 percent participation rate for the school's study abroad programs that offers over 350 sites in fifty countries.

In sheer volume of degrees conferred, engineering is the leader at 20 percent followed by business/marketing (14 percent), the social sciences (9 percent), and communication/journalism (6 percent). The aforementioned Grainger College of Engineering, a top-ten school on any list, has a direct pipeline to top firms and tech companies. The Gies College of Business is also strong, particularly the Accounting Department, which is also a feeder to the world's best accounting firms. Prestigious scholarship competitions are similarly fond of Illinois grads—eleven of the forty-eight Fulbright Scholarship applicants from the university won awards, a performance comparable to elites such as Berkeley, Dartmouth, and Tufts. Seven seniors in the Class of 2019 captured National Science Foundation Graduate Research Fellowships.

Outside the Classroom

The University District is one of the only campuses in the United States better measured by miles than acres. The school's 354 buildings are contained on 3.3 square miles. Everything at UIUC is massive in scale. Twenty-four residence halls are home to half of all undergraduates, mostly freshmen, as all first-years are required to live on campus. Including private certified housing units and frat and sorority houses, approximately half of undergrads reside on campus. Student life is dominated by ninety Greek organizations that scoop up 27 percent of female and 21 percent of male undergraduates. The twenty-one NCAA Division I sports teams are also a major focal point at this school. The Fighting Illini football team plays before crowds of 60,000+ at Memorial Stadium. An unfathomable 470,000 square feet of recreational spaces offer everything from indoor tracks to a leisure pool with slide to an inline skating rink. With roughly 1,600 student-run organizations, it's hard not to find your niche somewhere. One doesn't even have to venture off university grounds to find robust cultural opportunities as the four theaters in the Krannert Center for the Performing Arts annually host more than 350 performances by students as well as touring professionals. The Krannert Art Museum boasts 10,000 original works. Those looking to road trip to a major city can reach St. Louis, Chicago, or Indianapolis in two-to-three hours by car.

Career Services

Twenty-four professional employees staff The Career Center at Illinois (TCC) with roles such as: career counselor, health-career advisor, employer relations, and professional development for international students. However, additional career services supports can be found within the Gies College of Business (three professional staff); the Grainger College of Engineering (5); the School for Information Sciences (1); the Department of Economics (1); and the College of Agricultural, Consumer & Environmental Sciences (1). All told, the University of Illinois at Urbana-Champaign possesses an overall student-to-career staff ratio of 1,004:1, which is higher than the average university featured in this book.

University of Illinois at Urbana-Champaign

E-mail: admissions@illinois.edu | Website: www.illinois.edu

Serving 34,000+ undergraduate students is a monumental task, but it's one that UIUC successfully meets by offering a wide array of services and large-group activities. The TCC served roughly one-quarter of the student population in 2018-19; 27 percent of those utilizing the office were seniors. Staff conducted 2,504 one-on-one advising sessions, completed 4,882 resume/cover letter/LinkedIn page reviews, hosted 432 employers and graduate/professional schools at career fairs, and facilitated 747 on-campus interviews. In total, 69 percent of Class of 2019 graduates completed at least one internship while at Illinois. Job shadowing, application boot camps, career fair preparation workshops, and etiquette dinners are only a small sampling of opportunities provided by the TCC to students proactive enough to take advantage. Despite the sheer numbers challenge of serving every student, UIUC Career Services provides a number of excellent programs that lead to impressive career and graduate school outcomes.

Professional Outcomes

Ninety-three percent of the members of the graduating Class of 2019 had landed at their next destination within six months of graduation. Employed (full time) graduates represented 58 percent of the total cohort, and the most popular sectors were finance, consulting, healthcare, electronics, and education. Among the corporations that landed twenty or more 2019 Illini grads were KPMG, Deloitte, Epic Systems, EY, PwC, Microsoft, and Amazon. More than fifteen newly minted grads landed at companies like Facebook, Northrup Grumman, Allstate Insurance, and Accenture. The average salary across all majors for 2019 grads was an extremely solid $63,515. Two-thirds of graduates remained in the Land of Lincoln; California, Massachusetts, Missouri, and Washington state welcomed the greatest percentages of migrating alumni.

A notably high 35 percent of Class of 2019 graduates matriculated directly into an advanced degree program with 62 percent pursuing a master's degree. More than 700 students stayed put at the University of Illinois and over twenty Class of 2019 graduates enrolled in prestigious universities such as Columbia, Cornell, Northwestern, and the University of Michigan. Fifteen+ continued their studies at Carnegie Mellon, NYU, Penn, USC, and the University of Chicago. Clearly, Illinois grads are extremely competitive candidates at all of the country's elite graduate programs. Medical school applicants fare decently with acceptance rates around 10 percent higher than the national average, and recent grads have trained at Rush University Medical College, Washington University School of Medicine in St. Louis, the University of Michigan Medical School, and Johns Hopkins. Law school applicants attend many fine institutions including the University of Illinois' own highly ranked law school.

Admission

The University of Illinois at Urbana-Champaign accepted 59 percent of the 43,509 applicants battling for a place in the Class of 2023. This is one of the gentler acceptance rates of any institution featured in this book, but don't let that figure mislead you; the Illini are a high-achieving lot. Those admitted for the 2019-20 school year had mid-50 percent standardized test scores of 1230-1460 on the SAT and 27-33 on the ACT. Fifty-five percent placed in the top decile of their graduating classes, and 86 percent hailed from the top quartile. Applicants to UIUC's Grainger College will need to possess grades and test scores well above the aforementioned averages. Standards for entry into a computer science major are similar to those encountered at an Ivy.

The admissions committee places greatest emphasis on the rigor of one's secondary school record and the GPA earned. Standardized test scores, essays, extracurricular activities, and talent/ability are considered "important" to the decision-making process. It also states that those who submit their applications by November 1 "may [have] the best chance for being admitted to our most selective programs and special attention for admission to honors programs and for merit awards." There is no reason not to apply to UIUC by the early deadline because it is a nonbinding proposition and gives you the best odds at admission.

Worth Your Money?

Almost three-quarters of undergraduates enrolled in this university are from within the state of Illinois, entitling them to an affordable education. One of the few American schools to charge different tuition rates to business/engineering majors than education/social work majors, residents enjoy an average cost of attendance between $33k and $38k per year. Nonresidents are offered a COA of $50k to $56k, lower than most private institutions, making the University of Illinois at Urbana-Champaign a viable option for some out-of-staters, particularly those planning to enter the corporate or tech world. Around half of attending undergraduates are determined eligible for need-based financial aid with an average award of $17,750.

FINANCIAL
Institutional Type: Public
In-State Tuition: $12,254
Out-of-State Tuition: $29,704
Room & Board: $12,252
Required Fees: $4,608
Books & Supplies: $1,200

Avg. Need-Based Grant: $17,750
Avg. % of Need Met: 72%

Avg. Merit-Based Award: $5,104
% Receiving (All Freshmen): 20%
% Receiving (Freshmen w/o Need): 11%

Avg. Cumulative Debt: $24,655
% of Students Borrowing: 44%

CAREER
Who Recruits
1. Micron
2. Crowe Horwath
3. Shell
4. Phillips 66
5. BP America

Notable Internships
1. Ford Motor Company
2. Uber
3. State Farm

Top Industries
1. Business
2. Education
3. Engineering
4. Operations
5. Research

Top Employers
1. Google
2. Microsoft
3. Amazon
4. EY
5. IBM

Where Alumni Work
1. Chicago
2. Urban-Champaign, IL
3. San Francisco
4. New York City
5. Los Angeles

Median Earnings
College Scorecard (Early Career): $61,500
PayScale (Early Career): $66,000
PayScale (Mid-Career): $124,400

RANKINGS
Money: 22
U.S. News: 47 (T), National Universities
Wall Street Journal/THE: 43 (T)
Washington Monthly: 18, National Universities

COLLEGE OVERLAPS
Indiana University Bloomington
Northwestern University
Purdue University - West Lafayette
University of Michigan
University of Wisconsin - Madison

University of Iowa

Iowa City, Iowa | 319-335-3847

In the classic film Field of Dreams, an Iowa farmer hears a magical voice from the depths of a cornfield delivering the cryptic message, "If you build it, he will come." Perhaps the founders of the state's flagship school heard a similar mysterious message of encouragement before the University of Iowa opened its doors in 1855. Like Kevin Costner's ghost-trodden baseball diamond in Field of Dreams, UI was a genuine original from the very start. It was the first public university in America to admit men and women on an equal basis, the first to award advanced degrees in writing, theater, and music, and it opened the first dental and law schools west of the Mississippi River. Today, Iowa ranks among the top 35 public institutions in the United States and draws undergraduates from all over the country and the world; 40 percent of the 23,000+ undergraduates hail from out of state.

Inside the Classroom
Completing the College of Liberal Arts and Sciences (CLAS) core involves a minimum of 35 credit hours plus up to four classes in a foreign language, depending on a student's level of proficiency. This includes at least one course in the following categories: rhetoric; interpretation of literature; quantitative or formal reasoning; social sciences; diversity and inclusion; historical perspectives; international and global issues; literary, visual, and performing arts; and values and culture. Two courses in the natural sciences are required. However, not all majors are required to complete the CLAS core. For example, students in the College of Engineering only have 15 mandated general education credits.

The 15:1 student-to-faculty ratio is not suggestive of an intimate learning environment, yet the University of Iowa still manages to keep half of its undergraduate sections at an enrollment of 19 or fewer students. Just 13 percent of sections enroll 50 or more undergrads. Increasing the number of undergraduate research opportunities available is part of the university's strategic plan. At present, about 30 percent of UI undergrads conduct or assist research. In 2018-19, more than 1,300 University of Iowa students studied abroad; all told, 17 percent of graduates study abroad for a semester at some point during their four years at the university.

By a wide margin, the most commonly conferred degree at UI is business (22 percent), with parks and recreation (12 percent), social sciences (9 percent), engineering (8 percent), communication & journalism (6 percent), and health professions (6 percent), next in popularity. The Tippie College of Business has a strong reputation, and the English and creative writing major allows students access to some of the same resources as the Iowa Writer's Workshop, the top-rated MFA program in the entire country. Highly competitive national postgraduate scholarships are won by Iowa grads with astonishing regularity. In 2020, there were 23 students and alumni who captured Fulbright Scholarships. Recent grads have also been awarded Boren Awards, Critical Language Scholarships, and National Science Foundation Fellowships.

Outside the Classroom
On-campus housing is primarily reserved for freshmen as 94 percent of first-years live in the dorms compared to only 28 percent of the total undergraduate student body. There is a fairly sizable Greek/party culture on campus for those who wish to partake; 17 percent of women join sororities, and 13 percent of men join fraternities. There are 27 total fraternities and 22 sorority chapters at the university. There are more women than men at this school by a 53 percent to 47 percent margin. There are plenty of big-time sports with 24 varsity teams competing in the Big Ten Conference alongside athletic powerhouses like Penn State, Ohio State, and the University of Michigan. If you are not among the 800+ athletes competing at this high level, there are countless intramural sports from archery tag to pickleball. In total, there are more than 500 student-run clubs covering every niche interest under the sun. The Campus Activities Board brings major acts to the school, typically for cheap ticket prices, and the popular Dance Marathon attracts more than 2,000 participants to help raise money to combat childhood cancers. Iowa City is safe and walkable with plenty of museums, restaurants, and natural beauty. It has, in the past, been rated the top college town in the country as well as one of the most livable cities.

Career Services
The Pomerantz Career Center employs 25 professional staff members who work in areas such as experiential education, employer relations, and career advising. This works out to a 920:1 counselor-to-student ratio, weaker than many schools in this guidebook, but not that unusual or alarming for a university of Iowa's size. In fact, in a single year, the University of Iowa managed to conduct individual counseling sessions with 5,500 students (including peer advisor sessions) and deliver career-related workshops and programs to another 7,500.

This staff does exceptional work bringing employers to campus to set-up at job fairs and even conduct on-campus job interviews. A whopping 4,600 job interviews were facilitated on the university grounds. Four major career fairs attracted 3,300 students and hundreds of companies including major corporations like Epic, Chase, BMO Financial Group, Aramark, and 3M. A testament to both the career center as well as the school's academic advising, 87 percent of Hawkeyes finding employment did so in a position that is related to their academic study. The University of Iowa is not a place where every undergraduate fully takes advantage of personalized career counseling, but there are enough supports in place to ensure that career guidance and connections are available to those who seek them out.

Professional Outcomes

Those who graduated from the University of Iowa between 2017 and 2019 found their first job or advanced degree program within six months of receiving their diploma at a 95 percent clip. Heath care is the most commonly entered industry, attracting 27 percent of employed graduates, followed by finance/insurance (16 percent), education (11 percent), marketing/PR (9 percent), information technology (9 percent), and entertainment/the arts (9 percent). Companies that presently employ hundreds of Iowa alumni include Wells Fargo, Collins Aerospace, Principal Financial Group, Amazon, Accenture, and Microsoft. While many graduates end up in Iowa City, Des Moines, and Cedar Rapids, the most popular landing spot is actually Chicago. The average median mid-career income is comparable to other Midwestern publics like Iowa State, Michigan State, and the University of Minnesota.

Twenty-seven percent of recent graduates have gone right from undergraduate to graduate school. Remaining at the University of Iowa was the most common choice, with 75 percent of grad school attendees staying put in Iowa City. Other students enrolled in the likes of Drake University, Loyola University Chicago, and DePaul University. The school saw 184 of its undergraduates apply to medical school in 2019-20, including to its own highly ranked Carver College of Medicine. Those interested in law school can elect to pursue the 3+3 program in conjunction with UI's own law school.

Admission

An 81 percent acceptance rate is about as friendly as it gets among schools included in this guide, and that's the exact percentage of applicants granted acceptance into the Class of 2023. Just 18 percent of this group elected to enroll and officially become Hawkeyes. Eighty-seven percent of 2019-20 applicants submitted an ACT score, and the mid-50th percentile range was 22-29; the SAT range was 1140-1330. Almost one third of enrolled students finished in the top 10 percent of their high school class, and 63 percent placed in the top quartile. More than half of all undergrads earned a 3.75 or above GPA while in high school.

The admissions process at the University of Iowa is about as straightforward and no frills as it gets. Rigor of high school coursework, GPA, class rank, and standardized test scores are rated as "highly important," and recommendations, talent/ability, character/personal qualities, and state residency are "considered." Applications are reviewed on a rolling basis beginning in early fall, and the final deadline for submissions isn't until May 1. In sum, applying to UIowa is not particularly stressful, the review process is transparent and predictable, and the result—the educational experience—is excellent. That's not a bad combination.

Worth Your Money?

For residents of the Hawkeye State, tuition alone at the university is under $10k, and with housing and meals the annual cost rises to over $21k. Nonresidents pay approximately $43k in total cost of attendance. There are no reciprocity agreements with nearby states. At the in-state cost, this school qualifies as a genuine bargain; at the out-of-state cost, a case can certainly be made that it is worth $170k over four years, but that would depend on one's intended major and family financial circumstances. The school does offer limited merit-based scholarships, but far more individuals qualify for need-based aid; the average package is roughly $12,500.

FINANCIAL
Institutional Type: Public
In-State Tuition: $8,073
Out-of-State Tuition: $30,036
Room & Board: $11,400
Required Fees: $1,533
Books & Supplies: $950

Avg. Need-Based Grant: $9,744
Avg. % of Need Met: 51%

Avg. Merit-Based Award: $6,677
% Receiving (All Freshmen): 49%
% Receiving (Freshmen w/o Need): 24%

Avg. Cumulative Debt: $28,328
% of Students Borrowing: 48%

CAREER
Who Recruits
1. Cottingham & Butler
2. Bristol Myers Squibb
3. State Farm
4. HNI Corporation
5. TEKsystems

Notable Internships
1. Athene
2. Principal Financial Group
3. Workiva

Top Industries
1. Business
2. Education
3. Healthcare
4. Operations
5. Sales

Top Employers
1. University of Iowa Health Center
2. Wells Fargo
3. John Deere
4. Collins Aerospace
5. Amazon

Where Alumni Work
1. Iowa City
2. Chicago
3. Des Moines
4. Cedar Rapids
5. Minneapolis

Median Earnings
College Scorecard (Early Career): $51,900
PayScale (Early Career): $56,400
PayScale (Mid-Career): $108,100

RANKINGS
Money: 118
U.S. News: 88 (T), National Universities
Wall Street Journal/THE: 162 (T)
Washington Monthly: 76, National Universities

COLLEGE OVERLAPS
Indiana University Bloomington
Iowa State University
University of Illinois at Urbana-Champaign
University of Minnesota
University of Wisconsin - Madison

University of Maryland, College Park

College Park, Maryland | 301-314-8385

It's a highly affordable research university with a respected name and a big-time sports program that, oh yeah, happens to be only minutes from Washington, DC, so it's no shock that the University of Maryland-College Park has become an increasingly popular college destination. A school that has been on the rise since it became the state's flagship campus in 1988, College Park today enrolls teens from all fifty states and international students from 59 countries, although three-quarters of the undergraduate population are residents. This university enrolls 30,511 undergraduates who can select from ninety-two majors across twelve colleges. Real Terrapins may be turtles that are hyper-aggressive carriers of salmonella, but the Maryland variety is an accomplished group of young scholars who, in overwhelming numbers, go on to do great things post-graduation.

Inside the Classroom

Depending on which college and program you are part of, the sequence and pace at which you will fill the school's general education requirements will vary. The requirements themselves will not. There are forty-one credits of required coursework that include twelve credits in communications, six in the arts and humanities, six in behavioral and social sciences, seven in biological and physical sciences, seven in interdisciplinary or emerging issues, and three in mathematics. Maryland offers one of the best Honors Colleges, and those able to gain acceptance (the average SAT is 1490) must complete three honors seminars and two additional honors courses.

Despite an 18:1 student-to-faculty ratio and a heavy concentration of graduate students, many undergraduate course sections at the University of Maryland are held in intimate classroom settings. In fact, 45 percent of sections enroll fewer than twenty students. Of course, you will also have your share of packed introductory lecture courses; 17 percent of classes enroll fifty or more students. Undergraduate research opportunities are within reach as 43 percent of graduates complete one, including 9 percent who complete a summer research experience. The Maryland Center for Undergraduate Research also facilitates numerous opportunities throughout the year and hosts an annual Undergraduate Research Day at which 350+ students make presentations. A reasonable number of students also pursue a semester overseas. Over 1,500 students elect to study abroad at one of 447 destinations.

Collectively, the social sciences account for 15 percent of degrees awarded by the University of Maryland with criminology, government and politics, and economics among the most popular majors. Engineering is next with 13 percent of undergraduate degrees conferred. It is followed by business (13 percent), computer science (13 percent), and biology (8 percent). The Robert H. Smith School of Business, the A. James Clark School of Engineering, and the Merrill College of Journalism all command respect from employers and graduate schools, as do programs in computer science and criminology. Maryland's reputation also helps its graduates win highly competitive national fellowships. In 2019, that haul included ten Boren Awards, nine Fulbrights, seven Critical Language Scholarships, four Goldwater Scholars, and a Churchill Scholarship.

Outside the Classroom

Campus is home to 92 percent of Terrapin freshmen and 39 percent of the overall undergraduate student body. Only first-year students are guaranteed housing. Greek life is prominent, attracting 19 percent of women and 14 percent of men. Major sports are a thriving enterprise at the University of Maryland as the school boasts twenty Division I teams that include a basketball team that won the NCAA tournament in 2002 and is playing in March Madness pretty much every year. There are 800+ clubs, including many in the realm of improv, comedy, and pre-professional as well as an intramural program so expansive it offers both competitive and recreational levels. Also notable are The Mighty Sound of Maryland, a big-time marching band, and the strength of the volunteering spirit that sees the U of M community contribute a collective two million hours per year. Suburban Maryland isn't the most exciting place you could hope for but, fortunately, Washington, DC, is only a short Metro ride away.

Career Services

There are twenty-six full-time staff members working out of the centralized University Career Center with sixteen undergraduate-focused employees stationed in the Robert H. Smith School of Business, five in the A. James Clark School of Engineering, and another five career counselors housed within other colleges and departments. That brings the grand total of professional career services staff members at College Park to fifty-two, equating to a 587:1 student-to-counselor ratio, below average compared to the average school in this book, but strong for a school with over 30,000 undergraduates.

A superb 83 percent of 2019 graduates reported completing at least one internship, and more than one was the norm with 32 percent completing two internships, and 33 percent completing three. Among those who desired to turn their internship into a full-time gig post-graduation, 87 percent received an offer of employment. The jobs landed by all graduates were closely aligned with student's career goals, another testament to the work of this office. To be precise, 94 percent of job-holders reported that their position either directly aligned with their career goals or was a proper stepping-stone toward their ultimate goal. The school puts on several career fairs, including a fall event that draws 3,500 students and a Computer Science Career & Internship Fair that, alone, brings 125 companies to campus. Additionally, you can turn to the 360,000 Terrapin alumni to help you open a door into just about any hiring organization you can conjure up. Terrific internship numbers, on-campus recruiting, and overall student outcomes make this a world-class career services outfit.

Professional Outcomes

Class of 2019 graduates from the University of Maryland had, within six months of graduating, successfully found their next life step 95 percent of the time. Of the 72 percent of that cohort who found employment, the companies/organizations hiring the greatest number of recent grads were Deloitte (80), Northrup Grumman (64), EY (57), Capital One (55), and KPMG (51). Taking all alumni into account, more than 200 individuals with a University of Maryland affiliation presently work for Facebook, Apple, and Google. By far the most popular landing spot for alumni is the Greater Washington, DC, area with Baltimore, New York City, San Francisco, and Philadelphia next in line. The median starting salary self-report by Class of 2019 grads was $60,570; the mid-50 percent range was $44k-$73k.

Seventeen percent of Class of 2019 members headed directly to graduate and professional school to begin work on an advanced degree. Of that contingent, 17 percent entered doctoral programs, 7 percent were on the path to becoming medical doctors, and 9 percent entered law school. By a wide margin, continuing at the University of Maryland was the top choice; 316 survey respondents reported remaining at their home institution. Other popular schools were George Washington University (30), Johns Hopkins (29), Georgetown (18), and the University of Pennsylvania (17). Medical school acceptance rates for Maryland students are excellent at over 60 percent in recent years, roughly 20 points higher than the national average. The medical schools where the largest number of alumni matriculate are the University of Maryland, George Washington University, New York Medical College, and Drexel University. Over the past few years, law school applicants earned seventy-seven acceptances to Georgetown, twenty-seven each to Michigan and Emory, twenty-six to Cornell, eighteen to Columbia, and seventeen to Harvard.

Admission

Applicants for a spot as a freshman at College Park in 2019-20 were accepted at a rate of 44 percent; a decade earlier the admit rate was 39 percent. The mid-50 percent standardized test scores for the Class of 2023 were 1290-1460 on the SAT and 29-33 on the ACT. Sixty-nine percent of enrolled students earned a spot in the top 10 percent of their high school class, and 89 percent were in the top quartile. The average weighted GPA was 4.32. Those class rank and GPA numbers are similar to those of ten years ago, but SAT scores are significantly higher today, even when accounting for post-2016 score inflation.

With 32,987 applicants, this admissions committee needs to look first at cold, hard numbers, which is why GPA, standardized tests, and the presence of a rigorous course load are ranked as "very important" factors. Class rank, the essay, recommendations, state residency, first-generation status, and talent/ability make up the next rung of "important" factors. There is no binding early decision option at Maryland; the early action deadline of November 1 will get you an answer by January 31. In sum, getting into Maryland's flagship university's main campus pretty much requires a 3.75 or higher GPA and standardized test scores above the 90th percentile.

Worth Your Money?

In-state tuition is under $11,000, and the total cost of attendance for those living on campus is $27k. Out-of-staters pay three times the tuition rate, which leads to a total cost of attendance of $53k+ to become a Terrapin. Getting literally any degree at the in-state rate is a no-brainer. For nonresidents, you would have to have a compelling reason to cross state lines to pay $200,000+. However, if you are eyeing the exceptional programs in business, engineering, or computer science, that sum may be worth the education and connections you will gain.

FINANCIAL
Institutional Type: Public
In-State Tuition: $8,824
Out-of-State Tuition: $34,936
Room & Board: $12,935
Required Fees: $1,955
Books & Supplies: $1,250

Avg. Need-Based Grant: $10,398
Avg. % of Need Met: 63%

Avg. Merit-Based Award: $7,037
% Receiving (All Freshmen): 26%
% Receiving (Freshmen w/o Need): 22%

Avg. Cumulative Debt: $29,133
% of Students Borrowing: 39%

CAREER
Who Recruits
1. AIG Retirement Services
2. Carrier Corporation
3. Corvel Corporation
4. Federal Aviation Administration
5. Lockheed Martin

Notable Internships
1. Adobe
2. Nike
3. U.S. State Department

Top Industries
1. Business
2. Education
3. Operations
4. Engineering
5. information Technology

Top Employers
1. Booz Allen Hamilton
2. Deloitte
3. IBM
4. Capital One
5. Google

Where Alumni Work
1. Washington DC
2. Baltimore
3. New York City
4. Philadelphia
5. San Francisco

Median Earnings
College Scorecard (Early Career): $62,900
PayScale (Early Career): $64,700
PayScale (Mid-Career): $117,900

RANKINGS
Money: 168
U.S. News: 58 (T), National Universities
Wall Street Journal/THE: 77 (T)
Washington Monthly: 50, National Universities

COLLEGE OVERLAPS
George Washington University
Pennsylvania State University - University Park
University of Maryland, Baltimore County
University of Michigan
Virginia Tech

Amherst, Massachusetts | 413-545-0222

ADMISSION
Admission Rate: 64%
Admission Rate - Men: 62%
Admission Rate - Women: 66%
EA Admission Rate: 75%
ED Admission Rate: Not Offered
ED Admits as % of Total Admits: Not Offered
Admission Rate (5-Year Trend): +1%
% of Admits Attending (Yield): 23%
Transfer Admission Rate: 66%

SAT Reading/Writing (Middle 50%): 590-680
SAT Math (Middle 50%): 600-710
ACT Composite (Middle 50%): 26-32

% Graduated in Top 10% of HS Class: 31%
% Graduated in Top 25% of HS Class: 70%
% Graduated in Top 50% of HS Class: 96%

Demonstrated Interest: Important
Legacy Status: Considered
Admission Interview Offered: No

ENROLLMENT
Total Undergraduate Enrollment: 24,209
% Part-Time: 7%
% Male: 50%
% Female: 50%
% Out-of-State: 17%
% Fraternity: 7%
% Sorority: 7%
% On-Campus (Freshman): 99%
% On-Campus (All Undergraduate): 63%

% African-American: 5%
% Asian: 10%
% Hispanic: 8%
% White: 61%
% Other: 3%
% Race or Ethnicity Unknown: 6%
% International: 7%
% Low-Income: 22%

ACADEMICS
Student-to-Faculty Ratio: 17 to 1
% of Classes Under 20: 50%
% of Classes 20-49: 33%
% of Classes 50 or More: 18%
% Full-Time Faculty: 82%
% Full-Time Faculty w/ Terminal Degree: 93%

Top Programs
Architecture
Business
Computer Science
Nursing
Psychology
Public Health Sciences
Sociology
Sport Management

Retention Rate: 91%
4-Year Graduation Rate: 74%
6-Year Graduation Rate: 82%

Curricular Flexibility: Somewhat Flexible
Academic Rating: ★★★✔

#CollegesWorthYourMoney

Sesame Street's iconic "One of These Things (is not like the others)" song comes to mind when examining the Five College Consortium in Western Massachusetts. The group consists of tiny, elite liberal arts schools Amherst College, Mount Holyoke, Smith, Hampshire and . . . UMass? That's right, UMass, a school that has 24,209 undergraduate students, another 7,141 graduate students, and 109 bachelor's degree programs that are offered across eight undergraduate colleges. While UMass Amherst students are free to cross-register in any course at the affiliated liberal arts havens, there is plenty to like on the grounds of the Commonwealth's flagship campus. The home of the Minutemen and Minutewomen boasts the highly ranked and affordable Isenberg School of Management as well as revered academic programs in sports management, architecture, computer science, and nursing.

Inside the Classroom
Whether you end up in the Isenberg School of Management, the College of Engineering, or the School of Public Health and Health Sciences, you will encounter the same set of general education requirements that, fortunately, are not as overbearing as at many state universities. A ten-course, thirty-credit jaunt through writing, math, analytical reasoning, the physical sciences, and social world is all it takes to knock out the full run of nonnegotiable coursework. The Commonwealth Honors College at UMass Amherst has high admissions standards (average 1386 SAT and 4.23 GPA) and even higher graduation standards, requiring additional honors coursework and the completion of a senior thesis.

The student-to-faculty ratio is 17:1, leading to undergraduate class sizes that are all over the map. You will encounter a number of smaller sections during your time at UMass as 50 percent of courses enroll fewer than twenty students; 18 percent of sections contain more than fifty students, so you also will have some larger lecture hall classes. In spite of some gigantic classes where you'll feel anonymous, a stunning 96 percent of graduates report being satisfied with their academic experience. Further, a substantial and encouraging 30 percent report engaging in some type of undergraduate research. For a large university, UMass also enjoys fairly wide participation in its study abroad program. Every year, 1,200 students spend a semester in one of more than seventy countries.

UMass has a fairly even spread of students across its various areas of concentration. Of all degrees conferred in 2019, business/marketing diplomas accounted for 15 percent. That was followed by social sciences (12 percent), biology (10 percent), health professions (9 percent), and psychology (8 percent). UMass produced an impressive number of national postgraduate scholarship winners in 2019, including six Fulbright Scholars, four Goldwater Scholars, and one grad was one of only fifteen Churchill Scholars named in the nation.

Outside the Classroom
Ninety-nine percent of freshmen live on the 1,450-acre Amherst campus, and 63 percent of the entire student body lives in university-owned housing, a relatively high figure for a state university. There are fifty-two separate residence halls. Those residing off campus typically find rentals in the surrounding towns of Amherst, Hadley, and Sunderland. Men and women both join fraternities and sororities at a 7 percent clip. Twenty-one NCAA teams compete at the Division I level, mostly within the Atlantic 10 Conference. Involvement is spread around with 38 percent of students joining at least one student-run club, 24 percent playing varsity, club, or intramural sports, and 13 percent participating in community service. There are 200+ registered student organizations, and UMass students can participate in any club or activity at the other colleges within the consortium. Amherst garners consistent praise as one the top college towns in the United States because, in its own accurate words, it offers "a perfect blend of New England natural beauty and cosmopolitan culture and energy." Even on-campus dining gets rave reviews. Road trips to Boston (90 miles) or New York City (175 miles) are possible despite the somewhat remote feel of the Western Massachusetts locale.

Career Services
There are three central career service administrators at UMass Amherst, but the majority of service providers are housed within eight career service departments in the various undergraduate colleges. Obtaining an exact count of the number of advisors was, unfortunately, not possible, but to provide some reference point for counselor availability, the business school has seven advisors and a student-to-counselor ratio of 526:1, very strong compared to the other large public universities featured in this guide. Job fair offerings are plentiful, and top employers are more than willing to make the trip to Amherst to recruit top students. Last year, the office hosted 18 career fairs and held 62 on-campus recruitment events in the fall alone.

University of Massachusetts Amherst

E-mail: mail@admissions.umass.edu | Website: www.umass.edu

Overall, Minutemen and women feel that UMass adequately prepares them for beyond graduation; 79 percent of graduates are either "very satisfied" or "somewhat satisfied" with the way the university prepared them for the world of work. Two-thirds of recent graduates had some type of practicum, internship, co-op experience, or clinical assignment. Routine internship and co-op placements include the Boston Red Sox, CNN, IBM, MTV, Disney World, the Boston Globe, Sheraton, and United Technologies. With 260,000 alumni heavily concentrated in the Boston and Springfield areas, it's hard to walk down a New England street without bumping into a UMass alum. This supportive network, coupled with respected academic programs, helps the career services staff succeed in opening doors for qualified graduates.

Professional Outcomes

Six months after graduating, 63 percent of the Class of 2019 were employed full time and 23 percent were attending graduate school part time. The most populated industries are health/medical professions (15 percent), STEM (13 percent), business (10 percent), and information technology (10 percent). Companies presently employing one hundred+ Minutemen and Minutewomen include Oracle, Mass Mutual, Amazon, IBM, Google, Intel, Microsoft, PwC, Wayfair, and Apple. Boston is the most popular landing spot for graduates; it's followed by Springfield, Massachusetts; New York City; San Francisco; Washington, DC; and Los Angeles. One-third of recent graduates earn between $50-75k per year, 57 percent earn less than that range, and 9 percent take home more than $75,000 in annual income.

If you achieve stellar grades while an undergraduate at UMass, you will have a full array of graduate/professional school options awaiting you. Medical school applicants with a 3.7 GPA and an MCAT score in at least the 79th percentile are admitted to medical school more than 75 percent of the time. That rate was even higher when you include the criteria of having clinical experience and being open to osteopathic programs. Many recent graduates have attended medical school at UMass Medical School while others have gained acceptance to medical or dental school at Harvard, the University of Chicago, the University of Michigan, and the University of Pennsylvania. Similarly, prelaw students flock to UMass' own legal training ground or other Massachusetts-based options like Suffolk Law, but recent grads also have matriculated into elite institutions like William & Mary, Northeastern, or Boston University.

Admission

Sixty-four percent of the 42,157 applicants to UMass Amherst gained entry into the Class of 2023. A popular safety school for Massachusetts residents, only 21 percent of those who were accepted ultimately enrolled in the university. The mid-50 percent scores were 1210-1370 and the equivalent ACT range was 26-32. Just shy of one-third of students hailed from the top 10 percent of their high school class, and 70 percent were in the top quartile. The university received only half as many applicants at the dawn of the new millennium. The entering Class of 2000-01 had mid-50 percent SAT scores of 1010-1240, and only 52 percent were in the top quartile of their graduating class. Clearly, admissions standards are much higher now than a generation ago.

Standardized test scores, GPA, and the level of rigor of one's coursework are the three factors weighed as "very important" by the admissions committee. Also "important" are class rank, essays, recommendations, extracurricular activities, talent/ability, character/personal qualities, first-generation status, work experience, and the level of an applicant's interest. It is rare to see a large public university even consider demonstrated interest in admissions decisions, so make sure you take advantage by reaching out to a UMass admissions officer, visiting campus, or attending an admissions event in your area.

Worth Your Money?

At full price, UMass Amherst will set a Massachusetts resident back $30k per year; an out-of-stater will pay 50k. Bay State residents are getting a terrific deal attending UMass and shouldn't hesitate to pull the trigger, regardless of their financial situation or intended academic path. With a bit of aid, it is possible to receive a four-year education at a solid institution for under six-figures in total cost of attendance. Those out of state will likely find better deals elsewhere unless they are eligible for the New England Regional Students Program that allows residents of other New England states to attend at a discount if their intended academic program is not offered by public colleges in their home state.

FINANCIAL
Institutional Type: Public
In-State Tuition: $16,389
Out-of-State Tuition: $35,710
Room & Board: $13,598
Required Fees: $0
Books & Supplies: $1,000

Avg. Need-Based Grant: $11,467
Avg. % of Need Met: 80%

Avg. Merit-Based Award: $6,313
% Receiving (All Freshmen): 36%
% Receiving (Freshmen w/o Need): 32%

Avg. Cumulative Debt: $31,755
% of Students Borrowing: 62%

CAREER
Who Recruits
1. HubSpot
2. Facebook
3. Salesforce
4. Wayfair
5. Apple

Notable Internships
1. PepsiCo
2. AIG
3. TJX Companies

Top Industries
1. Business
2. Education
3. Operations
4. Sales
5. Engineering

Top Employers
1. Oracle
2. MassMutual
3. IBM
4. Amazon
5. Google

Where Alumni Work
1. Boston
2. Springfield, MA
3. New York City
4. San Francisco
5. Washington DC

Median Earnings
College Scorecard (Early Career): $51,400
PayScale (Early Career): $60,300
PayScale (Mid-Career): $108,700

RANKINGS
Money: 72
U.S. News: 66 (T), National Universities
Wall Street Journal/THE: 151 (T)
Washington Monthly: 122, National Universities

COLLEGE OVERLAPS
Boston University
Northeastern University
Syracuse University
Pennsylvania State University - University Park
University of Connecticut

University of Miami

Coral Gables, Florida | 305-284-4323

The sunny paradise of Coral Gables, just south of Miami, is home to the University of Miami—commonly referred to as UM or "the U." It is easily identifiable by its team name, the Hurricanes, with its distinctive orange, green, and white colors. This private research institution of 11,307 undergrads, which boasts a number of top academic programs and world-renowned faculty, struggled to be taken seriously as a world-class university for many decades. Having been dubbed "Sun Tan U" in the 1940s and suffering through revelations about its morally bereft football program of the 80s and 90s was a lot to overcome, yet Miami has finally arrived as an unquestioned member of higher education's elite. More selective than ever, Miami has more than gridiron glory to brag about as we enter the third decade of the millennium.

Inside the Classroom

In an effort to ensure the acquisition of "essential intellectual skills and exposure to a range of intellectual perspectives and academic disciplines," UM mandates general education requirements via the Cognates Program. So-termed cognates are, at a minimum, three-course clusters that the faculty has determined share a focus or thematic elements. The three main areas of cognates are arts and humanities; people and society; and science, technology, engineering, and mathematics. Students fulfill one cognate through their major area of study and also must complete the other two broad areas. Hurricanes also must blow through two English composition courses and one quantitative skills class. Other than that, the core academic requirements at Miami are not prohibitive.

Students rate their teachers and their overall UM experience extremely favorably. A noteworthy 92 percent of graduates report being satisfied with their education while 82 percent were satisfied with their major. The student-to-faculty ratio is 12:1, and even though there are 6,500+ graduate students to serve, class sizes are reasonable. Fifty-one percent of all course sections contain fewer than twenty students, and only 9 percent of sections sport enrollments of more than fifty undergrads. Study abroad opportunities are vast and include university-run programs in Rome, Shanghai, India, Paris, Prague, the Galapagos, Cape Town, and Buenos Aires. Undergraduate research posts can be had, but the onus is on the student to contact a professor directly, apply for placement through the Office of Research and Community Outreach, or apply for a summer research grant.

The University of Miami confers the greatest number of degrees in business/marketing (21 percent), biology (14 percent), health professions (13 percent), engineering (10 percent), and the social sciences (9 percent). The Miami Business School and the College of Engineering enjoy solid national reputations, and programs in music, marine science, communications, and architecture sit high atop many rankings. UM graduates fared well at procuring highly competitive awards including multiple Fulbright and Goldwater Scholarship winners over the past few years.

Outside the Classroom

Eighty-nine percent of freshmen live on the University of Miami's 239-acre main campus in Coral Gables, but 63 percent of the total undergraduate student body live off campus. Fraternities attract 16 percent of male students, and sororities draw 18 percent of female students, creating a strong Greek presence within the social scene; there are close to three-dozen active Greek organizations. Of course, the U's most galvanizing force is its famous (and at times infamous) football team as well as sixteen other varsity sports squads that compete in the powerhouse Atlantic Coast Conference in NCAA Division I. Approximately 400 students participate in varsity athletics. The school is trying to move away from its "Sun Tan U" reputation, and it certainly has in terms of academic rankings, yet the South Beach atmosphere continues to earn Miami "top party school" status in many publication's rankings. For non-partiers, the school also offers 270+ clubs, thirty service organizations, an active student government, and an award-winning student-run cable channel. On-campus amenities border on luxurious with the Herbert Wellness Center being one of the finest collegiate gyms around. Students also enjoy an arboretum, the Lowe Art Museum, the Ring Theatre that launched stars like Sly Stallone and Ray Liotta, and close proximity to the beach.

Career Services

The Toppel Career Center is staffed by sixteen full-time professional employees (not counting admin assistants or office managers) who focus on employer relations, career counseling, and internship coordination. A student-to-advisor ratio of 707:1 is higher than average when set against the other institutions included in this book. Still, this office reaches the bulk of the population as 84 percent of graduates utilized Toppel at some point in their four years of study. The most utilized services were (1) resume and cover letter review, (2) career expo and fairs, (3) job and internship listing search, and (4) one-on-one career advising.

ADMISSION
Admission Rate: 27%
Admission Rate - Men: 29%
Admission Rate - Women: 25%
EA Admission Rate: 32%
ED Admission Rate: 48%
ED Admits as % of Total Admits: 7%
Admission Rate (5-Year Trend): -13%
% of Admits Attending (Yield): 21%
Transfer Admission Rate: 51%

SAT Reading/Writing (Middle 50%): 630-700
SAT Math (Middle 50%): 640-740
ACT Composite (Middle 50%): 29-32

% Graduated in Top 10% of HS Class: 59%
% Graduated in Top 25% of HS Class: 83%
% Graduated in Top 50% of HS Class: 95%

Demonstrated Interest: Considered
Legacy Status: Considered
Admission Interview Offered: No

ENROLLMENT
Total Undergraduate Enrollment: 11,307
% Part-Time: 5%
% Male: 46%
% Female: 54%
% Out-of-State: 61%
% Fraternity: 16%
% Sorority: 18%
% On-Campus (Freshman): 88%
% On-Campus (All Undergraduate): 37%

% African-American: 9%
% Asian: 4%
% Hispanic: 22%
% White: 42%
% Other: 3%
% Race or Ethnicity Unknown: 4%
% International: 14%
% Low-Income: 17%

ACADEMICS
Student-to-Faculty Ratio: 12 to 1
% of Classes Under 20: 51%
% of Classes 20-49: 41%
% of Classes 50 or More: 9%
% Full-Time Faculty: 67%
% Full-Time Faculty w/ Terminal Degree: 91%

Top Programs
Architecture
Biology
Communication
Exercise Physiology
Marine Science
Music
Sport Administration

Retention Rate: 93%
4-Year Graduation Rate: 73%
6-Year Graduation Rate: 83%

Curricular Flexibility: Very Flexible
Academic Rating: ★★★✔

#CollegesWorthYourMoney

A laundry list of impressive organizations/companies that visit Coral Gables to recruit and conduct on-campus interviews includes PepsiCo, American Airlines, Facebook, Adidas, EY, and the Miami Marlins. In a single year, 175 companies attend the annual Career Expo, nearly 47,000 jobs and internships are posted to Handshake (50 percent of 2019 grads landed one), 150+ networking events are held, 2,200+ students attend career fairs and workshops put on by Toppel staff, and close to 1,000 undergrads engage in a one-on-one career counseling session. Career services also review 2,200 resumes, conduct over 850 practice interviews, and take roughly 600 professional headshots for students to use in their job searches. That frenetic pace and strong outreach leads to mostly positive postgraduate outcomes for newly minted Hurricane alumni.

Professional Outcomes

The Hurricane Class of 2019 saw 89 percent of its members secure post-grad plans within six months with 58 percent employed full time and 34 percent in graduate school. Companies employing five or more 2018 graduates included ScribeAmerica, Citrix, NBCUniversal Bank of America, JPMorgan Chase, Citi, and Morgan Stanley. Across the entire alumni base, one hundred+ Canes also can be found in the offices of Google, IBM, PwC, Apple, and Microsoft. Average starting salaries were $54,554; those from the College of Engineering averaged $65k, business school grads took home $59k, and those from the College of Arts and Sciences enjoyed a mean income of $49k. Miami, New York, Boston, Chicago, and Los Angeles were the primary destinations of choice for 2019 grads.

The most frequently attended graduate schools included a mix of prestigious institutions, Miami itself, and other Sunshine State universities. In order, the schools of choice were Miami (186), Nova Southeastern (15), Columbia (13), NYU (12), Boston University (10), and George Washington (10). Premed students have the advantage of accumulating clinical hours within the University of Miami Health Systems or any of six other hospitals not far from campus. In a typical year, the U's own Miller School of Medicine takes forty+ of its own exiting undergraduates, and over 90 percent of "highly recommended" applicants find a medical school home somewhere in the country.

Admission

Miami received an all-time record 38,919 applications for a place in the Class of 2023. The 27 percent acceptance rate for those jockeying for a spot in the 2019-20 freshman class was significantly lower than the 40 percent acceptance rate five years prior. The middle-50 percent ranges were 1280-1420 on the SAT and 29-32 on the ACT for current freshmen. Fifty-nine percent of 2019-20 first-years earned a place in the top 10 percent of their high school class while 83 percent placed in the top quartile. The average high school GPA for attending students was 3.6.

Seven categories top the list of most important factors in making admissions decisions—GPA, rigor of coursework, class rank, standardized test scores, recommendations, application essays, and extracurricular activities, Due to the massive number of applicants, the university does not offer interviews as part of the evaluation process. The U offers an early decision round where 48 percent of applicants are let through the gates, but only about one-third of the freshman class is filled through ED. Aspiring Hurricanes will see their activities reviewed and their essays read carefully as part of a holistic process. Yet, at a school receiving so many applications, you will need to bring strong grades and within-range test scores.

Worth Your Money?

The U's cost of attendance is approaching $74,000, over three times the in-state COA for the University of Florida or Florida State. To compete for the top students, the university dishes out merit aid to half of its attending undergrads at an annual average of $26k. It also grants need-based aid to over two-fifths of students with an average annual award of almost $37,836. If your family has unlimited funds, or if you receive a solid aid package, Miami is definitely a school that can make a lot of sense from an investment standpoint. If you are on a budget, paying full freight could lead to an unpleasant financial situation early in one's adult life.

FINANCIAL
Institutional Type: Private
In-State Tuition: $52,080
Out-of-State Tuition: $52,080
Room & Board: $15,470
Required Fees: $1,602
Books & Supplies: $1,000

Avg. Need-Based Grant: $37,836
Avg. % of Need Met: 99%

Avg. Merit-Based Award: $25,539
% Receiving (All Freshmen): 46%
% Receiving (Freshmen w/o Need): 24%

Avg. Cumulative Debt: $21,000
% of Students Borrowing: 35%

CAREER
Who Recruits
1. SpaceX
2. adidas
3. Hilton
4. Ball Aerospace
5. CIA

Notable Internships
1. Lincoln Financial Group
2. Cato Institute
3. Viacom

Top Industries
1. Business
2. Education
3. Healthcare
4. Arts & Design
5. Sales

Top Employers
1. Microsoft
2. IBM
3. Citi
4. Apple
5. PwC

Where Alumni Work
1. Miami
2. New York City
3. Los Angeles
4. West Palm Beach, FL
5. Washington DC

Median Earnings
College Scorecard (Early Career): $60,100
PayScale (Early Career): $60,600
PayScale (Mid-Career): $108,600

RANKINGS
Money: 500
U.S. News: 49 (T), National Universities
Wall Street Journal/THE: 53
Washington Monthly: 199, National Universities

COLLEGE OVERLAPS
Boston University
Emory University
New York University
Tulane University
University of Florida

University of Michigan

Ann Arbor, Michigan | 734-764-7433

ADMISSION
Admission Rate: 23%
Admission Rate - Men: 21%
Admission Rate - Women: 25%
EA Admission Rate: NR
ED Admission Rate: Not Offered
ED Admits as % of Total Admits: Not Offered
Admission Rate (5-Year Trend): -10%
% of Admits Attending (Yield): 46%
Transfer Admission Rate: 42%

SAT Reading/Writing (Middle 50%): 660-740
SAT Math (Middle 50%): 680-790
ACT Composite (Middle 50%): 31-34

% Graduated in Top 10% of HS Class: 78%
% Graduated in Top 25% of HS Class: 96%
% Graduated in Top 50% of HS Class: 100%

Demonstrated Interest: Considered
Legacy Status: Considered
Admission Interview Offered: No

ENROLLMENT
Total Undergraduate Enrollment: 31,266
% Part-Time: 3%
% Male: 50%
% Female: 50%
% Out-of-State: 41%
% Fraternity: 9%
% Sorority: 19%
% On-Campus (Freshman): 97%
% On-Campus (All Undergraduate): 31%

% African-American: 4%
% Asian: 16%
% Hispanic: 7%
% White: 56%
% Other: 5%
% Race or Ethnicity Unknown: 5%
% International: 8%
% Low-Income: 14%

ACADEMICS
Student-to-Faculty Ratio: 15 to 1
% of Classes Under 20: 55%
% of Classes 20-49: 27%
% of Classes 50 or More: 18%
% Full-Time Faculty: 82%
% Full-Time Faculty w/ Terminal Degree: 92%

Top Programs
Business
Communication and Media
Computer Science
Economics
Engineering
English
Political Science
Psychology

Retention Rate: 97%
4-Year Graduation Rate: 80%
6-Year Graduation Rate: 93%

Curricular Flexibility: Somewhat Flexible
Academic Rating: ★★★★✔

#CollegesWorthYourMoney

What do you get when you combine one of the best college towns in the country, one of the premier research universities in the world, and stir in a passionate sports scene? The answer is the first public university in the Northwest Territories. Originally dubbed the "Catholepistemiad of Detroit," it is now known by the catchier name of the University of Michigan. Brilliant teens flock to Ann Arbor for 280+ undergraduate degree programs across fourteen schools and colleges, and their success can be measured in countless ways, whether you look at the 97 percent freshman retention rate or the fact that more current Fortune 100 CEOs are alums of the Ross School of Business than any other school on the planet.

Inside the Classroom
All applicants must apply to one of the fourteen schools right off the bat. The College of Literature, Science, and the Arts (LSA) serves the majority, and those accepted are held to school-specific rather than university-wide academic requirements. However, all Wolverines ultimately end up with broad academic requirements in the areas of English, foreign language, natural sciences, and social sciences. Freshmen in the LSA take a first-year seminar that is capped at eighteen students and affords an immediate opportunity to connect with a professor in an area of academic interest. LSAers also have the option to sign up for a "theme semester" in which major topics such as India in the World or Understanding Race are explored in-and-outside the classroom through activities such as museum visits, guest lectures, and film screenings.

With 31,266 undergrads, it's not surprising that undergrads will end up sitting in some large lecture halls. Michigan sports a 15:1 student-to-faculty ratio, and 18 percent of classes contain fifty or more students, but a solid 55 percent of classes offer a more intimate experience with fewer than twenty students. Opportunities to conduct independent research or work in a laboratory beside a faculty member can be found. The Undergraduate Research Opportunity Program draws in 1,300 participants each year. For students in all academic programs at Michigan, study abroad opportunities are taken advantage of at high rates. In fact, the university is fifth in the nation in the number of students it sends to study in foreign lands.

In general, the faculty is exceptional and overflowing with award-winning researchers. Michigan finds itself atop any ranking of best public research universities. The Ross School of Business offers highly rated programs in entrepreneurship, management, accounting, and finance. The College of Engineering is also one of the best in the country. By sheer numbers, the school confers more engineering degrees (16 percent) than in any other discipline. The social sciences are next (11 percent), followed by computer science which also attracts 11 percent of the student body. Graduating Wolverines are routinely awarded prestigious scholarships to continue their studies. In 2019, the school produced twenty-six Fulbright Scholars, more than any other research university in the nation.

Outside the Classroom
Ann Arbor is a prototypical college town, the type you would show to a Martian who wanted to know what a quintessential American college was like. Vibrant, stimulating, and extremely safe, the 3,200-acre campus and surrounding town are ideal places to spend four years. When your football stadium seats more than 100,000, that's a pretty solid indicator that the sports scene is thriving. Donning the iconic maize and blue jerseys, Michigan's twenty-seven Division I sports teams have enjoyed a ridiculous level of success. A substantial but not overwhelming 9 percent of men and 19 percent of women belong to one of the sixty-two fraternities and sororities on campus. A hard-to-comprehend 1,600 student organizations exist. If you can conceive it, Michigan probably already offers it, and 82 percent of the student body participates in at least one club or activity. Intramural and club sports also enjoy wide participation. The Ginsberg Center for Community and Service is popular, and 54 percent of Wolverines have engaged in volunteer experiences. Only 31 percent live on campus, almost all of whom are freshmen.

Career Services
The University of Michigan Career Center employs thirty full-time staff members (including staff working out of the engineering and business programs) as well as a handful of peer advisors. Only counting the full-time employees, UM has a student-to-advisor ratio of 1,042:1, higher than the average school featured in this guide. Thus, hand-holding is limited, but appointments with peer advisors are available for mock interviews and resume assistance. One-on-one appointments with a professional career counselor can be scheduled to discuss finding internships and jobs. The career center reaches more students through hosting workshops, putting on more than 200 per year with a total attendance exceeding 6,000 undergrads.

Staffing may be less than desired, but on the plus side, Michigan's alumni network is one of the largest and most powerful in the nation. With over half a million loyal alums spread across one hundred countries, there is always a fellow Wolverine willing to dispense advice, facilitate a job- shadowing experience or internship (77 percent landed one in 2019), or help you get your foot in the door in the industry of your choosing. Also working in the school's favor is the fact that Michigan grads are highly sought after by major employers who are happy to travel to Ann Arbor for recruiting purposes. The Ross School of Business alone arranges for hundreds of companies to recruit on campus each year, including all of the big boys: Goldman Sachs, Deutsche Bank, EY, and Morgan Stanley. At UM counselors are not going to personally hunt you down to take personality inventories and create a killer LinkedIn profile, but large-scale resources are available that will get motivated students on the right path to their next destination.

Professional Outcomes

Within three months of exiting Ann Arbor, 96 percent of the graduates of the College of Literature, Science, and the Arts are employed full time or attending graduate school. Health care, education, law, banking, research, nonprofit work, and consulting are the most popular sectors in which LSA alums launch their careers. Ross School of Business graduates fare quite well on the open market; within three months, 97 percent are employed with a median salary of $79k. The companies listed above that recruit on campus are among the top employers of recent grads along with PwC, Deloitte, and Amazon. Engineering grads have similar success with 96 percent employed or in grad school within six months for an average salary of $77k. The companies employing the greatest number of alumni across all years include General Motors, Ford, Google, Microsoft, Apple, and Facebook.

As with employers, elite graduate and professional schools also hold a Michigan diploma in high esteem. University of Michigan grads applying to law school are well prepared, averaging an LSAT score in the 80th percentile and gaining acceptance at a 92 percent clip. Those aiming for medical school average MCATs above the 85th percentile and get accepted at a 54 percent clip, a rate more than 10 percent higher than the national average. In short, if you succeed at Michigan, there isn't a graduate or professional school in existence that will be beyond your reach.

Admission

Almost 65,000 wanna-be Wolverines submitted applications last cycle. The overall acceptance rate for a place in the Class of 2023 was 23 percent, but in-state applicants fared far better, enjoying a 42 percent rate (out-of-state was 20 percent). The SAT range of current Michigan students is 1340 to 1530, and the ACT range is 31-34. For comparison, in 2014 the SAT range was 1280-1480, and the ACT range was 29-33, which tells us that admission into this popular flagship university may be a touch more difficult now than in the recent past.

The school ranks the two most important admissions factors as "rigor of secondary school record" and "GPA." Average Michigan students earned a 3.88 GPA on a 4.0 scale in the most challenging courses available to them. Standardized test scores are listed as a secondary factor alongside recommendations, personal qualities, and first-generation status. The University of Michigan has more than doubled its number of applications received in the last decade, and gaining acceptance is genuinely more challenging than ever. Top students who hail from in state will face better odds than out-of-staters who need to bring an impeccable academic record to the table to garner serious consideration.

Worth Your Money?

The average amount of debt held by a University of Michigan graduate is slightly below the national average. For residents of the Great Lakes State, the school is in the "ridiculous value" category—at least by the standards of an out-of-whack marketplace. Michigan's total cost of attendance for in-state students is $31k; the out-of-state price is over $67k. Michigan is able to meet 90 percent of qualifying students' need and the average award is $21,330. This is truly exceptional for a public institution and is only one of the many reasons this topflight university is worth your money.

FINANCIAL
Institutional Type: Private
In-State Tuition: $15,230
Out-of-State Tuition: $50,872
Room & Board: $11,996
Required Fees: $328
Books & Supplies: $1,048

Avg. Need-Based Grant: $21,330
Avg. % of Need Met: 90%

Avg. Merit-Based Award: $4,411
% Receiving (All Freshmen): 43%
% Receiving (Freshmen w/o Need): 14%

Avg. Cumulative Debt: $25,777
% of Students Borrowing: 38%

CAREER
Who Recruits
1. Hudson's Bay
2. BP America
3. Bain & Company
4. United Talent
5. News America Marketing

Notable Internships
1. Uber
2. Nike
3. Lockheed Martin

Top Industries
1. Business
2. Education
3. Engineering
4. Operations
5. Research

Top Employers
1. General Motors
2. Ford Motor Company
3. Google
4. Amazon
5. Microsoft

Where Alumni Work
1. Detroit
2. New York City
3. Chicago
4. San Francisco
5. Washington DC

Median Earnings
College Scorecard (Early Career): $63,400
PayScale (Early Career): $67,800
PayScale (Mid-Career): $121,500

RANKINGS
Money: 4
U.S. News: 24 (T), National Universities
Wall Street Journal/THE: 23
Washington Monthly: 29, National Universities

COLLEGE OVERLAPS
Cornell University
Michigan State University
Northwestern University
University of California, Berkeley
University of Pennsylvania

University of Minnesota — Twin Cities

Minneapolis, Minnesota | 612-625-2008

Home to 35,165 undergraduates, the University of Minnesota Twin Cities can easily be overshadowed by its neighboring flagships (Wisconsin, Michigan, and Illinois). Yet, UMTC deserves its fair share of the Midwestern limelight, thanks in part to a number of academic programs rising toward the top of national rankings and the university's positioning as a direct pipeline to the nineteen Fortune 500 companies located within state borders. While a 70+ percent out-of-state tuition increase over the last eight years has slowed down the tidal wave of nonresident applicants, international students and out-of-staters still make up 27 percent of the undergraduate student body. The average Gopher today boasts significantly better academic credentials than previous generations at the university. In fact, four- year graduation rates have doubled since 1997, a testament to both the improved caliber of student as well as increased institutional support.

Inside the Classroom

There are 150 majors on tap across seven freshman-admitting undergraduate colleges, but all students are subjected to the same twenty-three-credit Diversified Core as well as fifteen credits worth of Designated Themes. Those combined thirty-seven credits include forays into the art/humanities, social sciences, physical sciences, mathematics, literature, and history. More targeted topics include civic life and ethics, diversity and social justice in the US, the environment, global perspectives, and technology and society. All freshmen also must take a first-year writing course and one other course designated as "writing intensive" later in their educational journey. Students in the university's Honors Program must complete eight honors courses and a culminating senior thesis.

Despite a massive number of graduate students, this school generally keeps class sizes in check. A 17:1 student-to-faculty ratio is deployed effectively so that 64 percent of sections enroll twenty-nine or fewer students. On the other end of the spectrum, 19 percent of courses enroll fifty or more students, so you can expect some highly impersonal lecture-based introductory courses while in the Twin Cities. No matter your field of study, you can utilize UM's well-maintained database of upcoming faculty research projects as a way to connect directly with the professor of your choice; more than 250 undergraduates participate in a campus-wide undergraduate research program each summer. An outstanding 34 percent of UMTC students study abroad during their academic career with the most popular destinations being Spain, Italy, France, the United Kingdom, and Germany.

The most commonly conferred degrees at the university are in biology (11 percent), engineering (11 percent), social sciences (11 percent), business/marketing (10 percent), psychology (7 percent), and computer science (6 percent). The College of Science and Engineering and the Carlson School of Management have strong national reputations and offer top-ranked programs in accounting, business, and every branch of engineering. The quality of the chemistry, economics, psychology, and political science departments is also well-known by elite graduate schools. The school's reputation also helps those applying for prestigious postgraduate scholarships. Nine students won Fulbright Scholarships in 2019, and Minnesota also produced a number of Udall, Gilman, Critical Language, and Astronaut Scholars in recent years.

Outside the Classroom

Nine of every ten freshmen reside on the 1,200-acre Twin Cities campus in one of nine residence halls or eight apartment complexes; pretty much everyone else lives in off-campus housing as only 23 percent of the entire student body goes to sleep in university-owned domiciles. Eleven percent of undergrads participate in Greek life, so fraternities and sororities play a fairly major role in social life. The Golden Gophers compete in twenty-three varsity sports; the most successful programs are the men's and women's ice hockey teams. Over 900 student organizations are active including nine student-run cultural centers, dozens of intramural sports, and a popular Outdoors Club. Arts and culture can be found right on campus at the school's own art, design, and natural history museums as well as the nearby Minneapolis Sculpture Garden, Guthrie Theater, Walker Art Center, and Minneapolis Institute of the Arts. Natural beauty also can be enjoyed on university grounds that contain 10,000 trees in the extensive Mississippi National River and Recreation Area, an area that also features miles of bike paths. For shopping or just hanging out, the famed Mall of America is only a fifteen-minute ride away. The Minneapolis and St. Paul campuses that together form UMTC are only three miles apart, and the best of both cities can be enjoyed from that advantageous central location.

Career Services

Instead of having one centralized career services office at the Twin Cities campus, the university has smaller offices housed within each of its undergraduate colleges. The College of Liberal Arts Career Services Office leads the way with eighteen full-time professional employees from the total of sixty-five across all colleges. That 541:1 ratio is within the average range when compared to other institutions profiled in this guidebook.

However, for a school of UMTC's size, that level of support is exceptionally strong. Whether students are in the College of Science and Engineering, the Carlson School of Management, or the School of Nursing, there will be a team of experts in the areas of career counseling, graduate/professional school advising, internship coordination, and employer relations ready to work directly on your behalf.

Career fairs are similarly segmented by discipline with annual offerings targeting those entering computer science, government, business, accounting, and health management. The College of Engineering (CSE) Career Fair draws around 3,500 students in the fall and 1,700 in the spring. The spring CSE event featured 175 companies such as Dell, Hewlett Packard, Tesla, Wells Fargo, and BAE Systems. Having 485,000 living alumni, many of whom are local, is a huge advantage for carving out internships and other networking opportunities. The Carlson School of Management has a Long-Term Mentoring and Flash Mentoring program in which it will hand-pick a professional mentor from the business community to assist you. Between a sizable and friendly alumni base and a number of tight industry connections to Minnesota-based businesses, the Career Services Office at UMTC offers a wealth of opportunity to its undergraduates.

Professional Outcomes
The top seven companies snatching up the largest number of Gophers are all companies headquartered in the state of Minnesota: Medtronic (the largest medical device manufacturer in the world), Target, 3M, United Health Group, US Bank, Best Buy, and Cargill (the company with the highest revenue in the United States). Therefore, it is easy to see why roughly 70 percent of grads remain in the Greater Minneapolis-St. Paul area. San Francisco, New York, Chicago, and Seattle also attract some graduates each year, and non-Minnesota-based companies like Intel, Microsoft, Google, Apple, and Facebook all employ hundreds of Twin Cities alumni. The average starting salary for 2019 grads was $45k.

With 130 graduate programs in science, art, engineering, agriculture, medicine, and the humanities, the University of Minnesota retains many of its graduates as they pursue their next degrees. However, some of the top graduate programs in the country routinely welcome UM grads. Future doctors benefit from the BA/MD program in conjunction with the University of Minnesota Medical School. The university produces 300+ applicants to medical school every year, and many go on to study within their home state but, in recent years, Gophers also have been accepted to prestigious medical institutions like Emory, the University of Wisconsin, and Columbia University.

Admission
UMTC saw 57 percent of those seeking a place in the Class of 2023 gain acceptance. Minnesota is predominately an ACT state, and 89 percent of the 2019-20 applicants submitted results from that exam, scoring a mid-50 percent range of 26-31. Those submitting SAT scores had mid-50 percent scores of 1270-1440. Half of those attending the university placed in the top 10 percent of their high school class, and 83 percent earned spots in the top quarter. The applicant pool here has grown stronger over the last decade, but admission is only slightly more competitive now than it was a decade ago.

The only factors rated as "very important" by the admissions committee are rigor of coursework, GPA, class rank, and standardized test scores. Essays, recommendations, and interviews are not considered in the process. Freshmen accepted into the University of Minnesota Twin Cities are admitted directly into one of seven undergraduate colleges. The schools requiring the highest grades and test scores are biological sciences, management, and science and engineering (CSE). In fact, the ACT range for those admitted into the CSE is 30-34 compared with the 23-28 mid-50th range for those admitted into the College of Education and Human Development.

Worth Your Money?
In-state tuition of $15k and reasonable room-and-board fees make the list price approximately $29,000 for those from the Land of 10,000 Lakes. After financial aid, even families making over $110,000 end up paying less than $25k. That makes UMTC a strong value for Minnesota teens no matter their area of academic pursuit. While out-of-state costs will run your four-year total bill to just under $200k, the return-on-investment numbers are the strongest of any school in Minnesota. The Carlson School of Management and the College of Science and Engineering are so highly regarded that a degree from either is probably worth a private university-level price tag.

FINANCIAL
Institutional Type: Public
In-State Tuition: $15,027
Out-of-State Tuition: $33,325
Room & Board: $10,768
Required Fees:
Books & Supplies: $1,000

Avg. Need-Based Grant:
Avg. % of Need Met:

Avg. Merit-Based Award: $5,058
% Receiving (All Freshmen): 16%
% Receiving (Freshmen w/o Need): 12%

Avg. Cumulative Debt: $27,077
% of Students Borrowing: 55%

CAREER
Who Recruits
1. Enterprise Holdings
2. The Hertz Corporation
3. Aerotek
4. Thomson Reuters
5. Century Link

Notable Internships
1. Minnesota Timberwolves
2. Pratt & Whitney
3. U.S. State Department

Top Industries
1. Business
2. Education
3. Operations
4. Engineering
5. Research

Top Employers
1. Medtronic
2. Target
3. 3M
4. UnitedHealth Group
5. U.S. Bank

Where Alumni Work
1. Minneapolis
2. San Francisco
3. Chicago
4. New York City
5. Los Angeles

Median Earnings
College Scorecard (Early Career): $51,900
PayScale (Early Career): $59,900
PayScale (Mid-Career): $110,300

RANKINGS
Money: 58
U.S. News: 66 (T), National Universities
Wall Street Journal/THE: 91
Washington Monthly: 67, National Universities

COLLEGE OVERLAPS
Ohio State University - Columbus
Purdue University - West Lafayette
University of Illinois at Urbana-Champaign
University of Michigan
University of Wisconsin - Madison

University of North Carolina at Chapel Hill

Chapel Hill, North Carolina | 919-966-3621

ADMISSION
Admission Rate: 23%
Admission Rate - Men: 23%
Admission Rate - Women: 22%
EA Admission Rate: 28%
ED Admission Rate: Not Offered
ED Admits as % of Total Admits: Not Offered
Admission Rate (5-Year Trend): -4%
% of Admits Attending (Yield): 44%
Transfer Admission Rate: 49%

SAT Reading/Writing (Middle 50%): 650-730
SAT Math (Middle 50%): 650-760
ACT Composite (Middle 50%): 27-33

% Graduated in Top 10% of HS Class: 78%
% Graduated in Top 25% of HS Class: 95%
% Graduated in Top 50% of HS Class: 99%

Demonstrated Interest: Not Considered
Legacy Status: Considered
Admission Interview Offered: No

ENROLLMENT
Total Undergraduate Enrollment: 19,355
% Part-Time: 3%
% Male: 41%
% Female: 59%
% Out-of-State: 14%
% Fraternity: 18%
% Sorority: 17%
% On-Campus (Freshman): 99%
% On-Campus (All Undergraduate): 52%

% African-American: 8%
% Asian: 11%
% Hispanic: 8%
% White: 58%
% Other: 5%
% Race or Ethnicity Unknown: 4%
% International: 4%
% Low-Income: 22%

ACADEMICS
Student-to-Faculty Ratio: 13 to 1
% of Classes Under 20: 41%
% of Classes 20-49: 46%
% of Classes 50 or More: 13%
% Full-Time Faculty: 71%
% Full-Time Faculty w/ Terminal Degree: 84%

Top Programs
Area Studies
Business
Chemistry
Environmental Science and Studies
Media and Journalism
Political Science
Psychology
Public Policy

Retention Rate: 96%
4-Year Graduation Rate: 84%
6-Year Graduation Rate: 91%

Curricular Flexibility: Somewhat Flexible
Academic Rating: ★★★★

#CollegesWorthYourMoney

In 1789, a full thirty years before Thomas Jefferson founded UVA, our young nation's first public university was chartered. Four years later, the first cornerstone was laid smack dab in the middle of the new state of North Carolina, right next to a hill upon which sat New Hope Chapel. In that moment, simultaneously, the University of North Carolina and the town of Chapel Hill were born. Fast-forward 230+ years and UNC Chapel Hill is one of the most prestigious flagship public schools in the country with 329,000+ proud alumni, the vast majority of whom were born and bred in the university's home state. That fact can be attributed to a thirty-year-old state law mandating that at least 82 percent of each freshman class be comprised of in-state students.

Inside the Classroom
Massive in its scope, the lovely and affluent town of Chapel Hill is home to 19,335 undergraduates and 10,796 graduate/professional students. Undergraduates can choose from 74 bachelor's degree programs in a number of schools and colleges, the largest of which is the College of Arts & Sciences. The general education curriculum is called Making Connections and involves checking boxes in the areas of English composition and rhetoric, foreign language, quantitative reasoning, physical and life sciences, social and behavioral sciences, and the humanities and fine arts.

The student-faculty ratio is 13:1, and few courses are held in giant lecture halls; 87 percent of classes have fewer than fifty students. However, you won't have many intimate, seminar-style courses as part of your undergraduate education as only 41 percent of classes have a student enrollment under twenty. UNC sends more than one-third of graduates abroad to one of seventy countries at some point in their educational career. For a school of such massive size, an impressive 60 percent of students end up completing some type of research experience as undergraduates.

The social sciences (17 percent), media/journalism (10 percent), biology (10 percent), psychology (7 percent), business (7 percent), and parks and recreation (6 percent) are the areas in which the most degrees are conferred. The Kenan-Flager Business School is internationally renowned and requires separate admission through UNC's Assured Admission program or through an application process following freshman year. Other strong programs include those in chemistry, journalism, psychology, and political science. However, an undergraduate degree of nearly any kind from UNC will open doors in the world of employment as well as for those seeking entrance into top graduate programs around the country. In its illustrious history, UNC-Chapel Hill has produced 50+ Rhodes Scholars and thirty-eight Luce Scholars. In 2020, eleven were named Fulbright Scholars, the tenth highest total among public research universities. It also has a high rate of success in helping students procure NSF Graduate Research Fellowships.

Outside the Classroom
The University of North Carolina-Chapel Hill requires that all freshmen live in one of the school's thirty-two residence halls. However, only 52 percent of the total undergraduate population lives on campus while many others live in apartments/houses in Chapel Hill or surrounding Durham or Carrboro. Still, there are many unifying experiences that bring the campus together, none more so than UNC men's basketball. Nothing short of a local religion, it sees 22,000 pack the Dean Smith Center to root for the Tar Heels; games against rival Duke are an unforgettable experience. In sum, there are twenty-eight varsity sports teams as well as a robust network of fifty club and intramural sports. Slightly over 15 percent of UNC undergrads join a fraternity or sorority, but Greek life at UNC is unusually diverse, inclusive, and service oriented. On average, its students collectively contribute 35,000 hours of community service per year. More than 800 student activities are running on the Chapel Hill campus, highlighted by the popular twenty-four-hour UNC Dance Marathon fundraiser, an involved student government, a host of cultural and professional organizations, and the widely read Daily Tar Heel, which has a distribution of 20,000.

Career Services
UNC's University Career Services Office employs sixteen full-time staff members, excluding individuals who work as administrative assistants or in IT, who work with undergraduates. That equates to a student-to-advisor ratio of 1,210:1, significantly worse than average compared to the other institutions included in this book. Other schools within the larger university do have smaller career services offices, but they primarily serve graduate students. Despite less-than-ideal personnel numbers, the staff does create solid outcomes for graduates.

University of North Carolina at Chapel Hill

E-mail: unchelp@admissions.unc.edu | Website: www.unc.edu

Each year, career fairs draw 600+ companies to campus and almost 200 employers hold information sessions in Chapel Hill. In the 2018-19 academic year, the department held 8,499 counseling appointments and posted 46,277 jobs and internships on Handshake. The Carolina Career Partners Program helps connect local companies to undergraduate job candidates. Of those students directly entering the world of employment, 80 percent landed at least one internship while at UNC and, in one-third of those cases, the internship eventually led to a job with that same organization. All of the basic career services—resume assistance, practice interviews, 1:1 career counseling, and job and internship postings through Handshake—are available to undergraduates.

Professional Outcomes

Six months after leaving Chapel Hill, 94 percent of the Class of 2019 had entered employment, military service, or graduate school; only 6 percent were still seeking employment. Among the for-profit companies who hire the most graduates are Wells Fargo, IBM, Cisco, Deloitte, EY, Google, Microsoft, Amazon, Oracle, Facebook, McKinsey & Company, and Goldman Sachs. In the nonprofit sector, a large number of Tar Heels are snatched up by the AmeriCorps, NIH, Teach for America, and the Peace Corps. The vast majority of graduates hang their diplomas somewhere in the state of North Carolina while New York, Georgia, Texas, Florida, and Illinois also attracted 20 or more graduates in 2019. The average starting salary for members of the Class of 2019 was $56,830. A dozen years after graduating, alumni take home the fourth-highest median salary of any North Carolina institution.

In 2019, a healthy 38 percent of students enrolled directly in graduate/professional school. Some of the most commonly attended graduate schools are other Carolina-based institutions such as East Carolina University, Appalachian State, UNC-Greensboro, or—on the elite/local front—Duke and Wake Forest. Other prestigious schools frequented by UNC alums include Columbia and Harvard. UNC-Chapel Hill had 496 applicants to medical school in 2019, the eighth highest total in the nation. Recent graduates have gone on to study medicine at institutions such as Harvard Medical School, Duke University School of Medicine, UNC School of Medicine, and the Wake Forest School of Medicine.

Admission

Gaining admission into UNC-Chapel Hill is a completely different ballgame for North Carolina residents than it is for those hailing from any of the other forty-nine states or a foreign country. In-state applicants for admission into the Class of 2023 had roughly a 40 percent success rate; all others faced harsher competition as the overall acceptance rate was only 23 percent. While many other flagship state institutions such as Michigan, Wisconsin, and UVA have substantially increased their number of non-residents in recent years, UNC has does not have the authority to follow suit as out-of-state enrollment is capped at 18 percent.

Of those who enrolled, the middle 50 percent SAT range was 1300-1470 and 27-33 on the ACT. Over three-quarters of enrolled students placed in the top 10 percent of their high school class, and 15 percent were either the valedictorian or salutatorian. In addition to high grades, test scores, and placement toward the
top of your class, the UNC admissions committee considers a number of other factors to be of highest importance: test scores, essays, recommendations, extracurricular activities, talent/ability, character/personal qualities and, of course, state residency. While in-state applicants need to be strong in all of those areas, out-of-state applicants need to be exceptional, well above the mean. In sum, the fork in the residency road sends applicants down two significantly different admissions gauntlets. For out-of-staters, higher standardized test scores and/or a "hook" can help to set you apart. In-state applicants with in-range credentials have a much friendlier but still selective process awaiting them.

Worth Your Money?

One of the most incredible bargains in all of American higher education, residents of the Tar Heel State pay less than $10k in tuition and only $24,266 in annual cost of attendance. Those from out of state pay around $52k per year, not a bad price for an education at one of the premier universities in the country. UNC-Chapel Hill only grants merit aid to 28 percent of the student body, a small percentage compared to other UNC campuses (e.g., Greensboro grants aid to 60+ percent). However, UNC-Chapel Hill is, by leaps and bounds, the most generous UNC school when it comes to need-based aid. The university grants an average annual award of $15,532 to those it declares eligible, meeting 100 percent of the demonstrated need for all qualifying students. Whether you are headed to Chapel Hill as a resident or out-of-stater, you will get your money's worth at this school.

FINANCIAL
Institutional Type: Public
In-State Tuition: $7,230
Out-of-State Tuition: $35,224
Room & Board: $11,740
Required Fees: $2,002
Books & Supplies: $990

Avg. Need-Based Grant: $15,532
Avg. % of Need Met: 100%

Avg. Merit-Based Award: $11,932
% Receiving (All Freshmen): 28%
% Receiving (Freshmen w/o Need): 2%

Avg. Cumulative Debt: $21,203
% of Students Borrowing: 37%

CAREER
Who Recruits
1. Greystar
2. Lincoln Financial Group
3. PNC Bank
4. Comcast
5. Fidus Investments

Notable Internships
1. Vanguard
2. Adobe
3. The Walt Disney Company

Top Industries
1. Business
2. Education
3. Healthcare
4. Research
5. Operations

Top Employers
1. Wells Fargo
2. IBM
3. Cisco
4. Deloitte
5. EY

Where Alumni Work
1. Raleigh-Durham, NC
2. Charlotte
3. Winston-Salem, NC
4. New York City
5. Washington DC

Median Earnings
College Scorecard (Early Career): $55,600
PayScale (Early Career): $59,000
PayScale (Mid-Career): $105,400

RANKINGS
Money: 43
U.S. News: 28 (T), National Universities
Wall Street Journal/THE: 33
Washington Monthly: 19, National Universities

COLLEGE OVERLAPS
Duke University
North Carolina State University
University of Michigan
University of Virginia
Vanderbilt University

University of Notre Dame

Notre Dame, Indiana | 574-631-7505

ADMISSION
Admission Rate: 16%
Admission Rate - Men: 16%
Admission Rate - Women: 15%
EA Admission Rate: 26%
ED Admission Rate: Not Offered
ED Admits as % of Total Admits: Not Offered
Admission Rate (5-Year Trend): -6%
% of Admits Attending (Yield): 58%
Transfer Admission Rate: 30%

SAT Reading/Writing (Middle 50%): 680-760
SAT Math (Middle 50%): 620-790
ACT Composite (Middle 50%): 32-35

% Graduated in Top 10% of HS Class: 90%
% Graduated in Top 25% of HS Class: 99%
% Graduated in Top 50% of HS Class: 100%

Demonstrated Interest: Considered
Legacy Status: Considered
Admission Interview Offered: No

ENROLLMENT
Total Undergraduate Enrollment: 8,731
% Part-Time: 0%
% Male: 52%
% Female: 48%
% Out-of-State: 93%
% Fraternity: Not Offered
% Sorority: Not Offered
% On-Campus (Freshman): 100%
% On-Campus (All Undergraduate): 78%

% African-American: 4%
% Asian: 5%
% Hispanic: 11%
% White: 67%
% Other: 5%
% Race or Ethnicity Unknown: 1%
% International: 7%
% Low-Income: 11%

ACADEMICS
Student-to-Faculty Ratio: 9 to 1
% of Classes Under 20: 62%
% of Classes 20-49: 29%
% of Classes 50 or More: 9%
% Full-Time Faculty: 88%
% Full-Time Faculty w/ Terminal Degree: 90%

Top Programs
Architecture
Biological Sciences
Business
Engineering
English
Physics
Political Science
Theology

Retention Rate: 98%
4-Year Graduation Rate: 91%
6-Year Graduation Rate: 96%

Curricular Flexibility: Somewhat Flexible
Academic Rating: ★★★★★

#CollegesWorthYourMoney

As iconic for its educational quality as for its storied gridiron glory, Notre Dame is the dream destination for Catholic students with Ivy-level academic qualifications. Four-fifths of the 8,731 undergraduate students possess a Catholic religious identity, reinforcing the school's values and traditions. Academically, a robust selection of seventy-five majors are offered across six undergraduate colleges: the School of Architecture, the College of Arts and Letters, the Mendoza School of Business, the College of Engineering, the Keough School of Global Affairs, and the College of Science (that includes a premed track).

Inside the Classroom

Required coursework is comprehensive and includes four courses covering Catholic theology and philosophy. The Moreau First Year Experience is a two-semester course designed to help freshmen "integrate their academic, co-curricular, and residential experiences." Freshmen also take University Seminar, one of two writing-intensive courses mandated by the school. Six additional mandatory liberal arts courses assure that students at least dip their toes into the study of quantitative reasoning, science and technology, history, literature, and the social sciences.

A solid 62 percent of courses enroll fewer than twenty students, and 20 percent have single-digit numbers. Just 9 percent of courses have an enrollment of more than fifty undergrads. A 9:1 student-to-faculty ratio is top notch and also represents an improvement over the 12:1 ratio of a decade ago. The Center for Undergraduate Scholarly Engagement offers hundreds of opportunities for conducting research, both individually and alongside faculty; one-third of graduates ultimately partake. One of the top universities for study abroad participation, 75 percent of Notre Dame undergrads select one of seventy-six programs in twenty-nine countries; the satisfaction rate for study abroad experiences is 93 percent.

The top areas in which degrees were conferred in 2019 were: business (18 percent), the social sciences (17 percent), engineering (13 percent), and biology (8 percent). Mendoza has a reputation as one of the country's best business schools and, to a slightly lesser extent, the College of Engineering often ranks highly on "best of" lists as well. Prestigious fellowships are won by the Irish in droves. After collecting twenty-seven Fulbrights in 2020, it is one of the top producers in the whole United States. The National Science Foundation granted honors to twenty-six students and alumni in 2019. The list goes on and on with multiple Gilman, Gates Cambridge, Critical Language, and Truman Scholarships in recent years.

Outside the Classroom

Every single freshman and 78 percent of all undergrads live in one of the school's thirty residence halls. The focus of spiritual and recreational life, the residence halls serve a major role on a campus that is free of sororities and fraternities. Notre Dame also has no athletic program . . . just kidding! Sports are a way of life at the home of the Fighting Irish, whether you are a member or mere fan of one of the twenty-three NCAA Division I teams. Of course, the famed football program has a tradition unlike any other, and 81,000 pack the stands of Notre Dame Stadium each fall Saturday to cheer for the eleven-time national champions. One of the best intramural programs in the country and extensive recreational facilities ensure widespread athletic participation; the outdoor five-on-five basketball tournament draws 700 participating teams each year. If it's not sports, Irish men and women are engaged in some other meaningful activity; there are more than 500 student-run organizations active at the school. The 1,250-acre campus is as scenic as they come and includes two beautiful lakes, one famous golden dome, and all of the lush foliage one can absorb. South Bend is not a small college town but a city with a population of over 300,000. Within the immediate vicinity of campus are over fifty restaurants, seventy shops, and four museums.

Career Services

The Center for Career Development (CCD) is staffed by thirty-five professional employees who work in career advising, employer relations, or event coordination and who impact undergraduate students (additional career services branches aimed at graduate students were not included in this figure). That equates to a 249:1 student-to-advisor ratio, which is in the better-than-average range when compared with other schools featured in this guide, but it is much stronger than most schools of Notre Dame's size. In short, this office works hard on behalf of its students, bringing to mind the classic Lou Holtz line, "No one has ever drowned in sweat."

More than three-quarters of students participate in at least one internship during their undergraduate years. Career fairs are attended by 450+ employers annually, including many major corporations known for employing large numbers of Fighting Irish alumni. Overall, more than 500 companies conduct approximately 7,000 job interviews on campus each academic year. The building in which the CCD is housed features forty-five interview/meeting rooms that have seen their fair share of "welcome aboard" handshakes. An alumni base 135,000 strong, many of whom have attained leadership positions in the field, are eagerly awaiting an opportunity to help current students and graduating seniors. Having one of the most connected, passionate, and loyal alumni networks in your corner is no small advantage. Tremendous corporate connections and graduate school/employment results for recent grads led to the Notre Dame CCD receiving high marks from our staff.

Professional Outcomes

A spectacular 98 percent of Notre Dame 2019 graduates were employed within six months of completing their degrees. Of the 65 percent who directly enter the world of employment, the most common industries are financial services (17 percent), consulting (16 percent), technology (11 percent), and health services (7 percent). Massive numbers of alumni can be found in the offices of some of the nation's most desirable private employers including Deloitte, EY, PwC, IBM, Accenture, Booz Allen Hamilton, Google, Microsoft, Amazon, Goldman Sachs, JP Morgan, and McKinsey & Co. With so many entering the world's top finance & consulting firms, it isn't shocking that early career salaries tend to be high; as of 2019 the median figure was $69,000, a mark that is significantly higher than the national average for college grads. The highest concentration of alumni can be found in the Greater Chicago area followed by the Greater New York City area, South Bend itself, DC, San Francisco, and Boston.

Of the 21 percent of first-year alums who went directly into their graduate/professional studies, 19 percent were pursuing medical degrees, and 13 percent were studying law. Medical school applicants had a much higher rate of success than the national average; the Irish acceptance rate generally hovers around 80 percent. Recent grads went on to attend institutions such as Harvard Medical School, Indiana University School of Medicine, Icahn School of Medicine at Mt. Sanai, Medical College of Wisconsin, and Albert Einstein Medical College. Presently, Notre Dame graduates can be found at some of the nation's top law schools such as Columbia, Duke, Harvard, Notre Dame, Boston College, UVA, and the University of Chicago. Those attending graduate schools for other fields can be found at comparably elite institutions all over the globe.

Admission

Of the 22,200 applicants to the Class of 2023 only 3,515 were accepted, an acceptance rate of 16 percent. The yield rate—admitted applicants who enrolled—was an impressively high 58 percent. Notre Dame hopefuls will need to finish at the very top of their high school class, and we don't just mean in the top decile. A hard-to-fathom 40 percent of accepted students typically hail from the top 1 percent of the class and 90 percent of accepted students placed in the top 10 percent. The SAT mid-50 percent range has reached similarly intimidating heights; it currently sits at approximately 1400-1550. The ACT, which is submitted by 53 percent of applicants, has a mid-50 percent composite range of 32-35.

The admissions committee rates rigor of secondary coursework above all other factors. Class rank, GPA, standardized test scores, recommendations, essays, extracurricular activities, and talent/ability are all "important." Religious affiliation does matter at Notre Dame as 80 percent of admits identify as Catholic. Being a legacy applicant can help—21 percent of incoming 2019-20 freshmen were children of alumni. Both religious affiliation and legacy status are factors "considered" by the committee. In recent years, the admissions standards at Notre Dame have approached Ivy League levels. Ten years ago, the acceptance rate was a much friendlier 27 percent, and the 25th percentile SAT mark was a full eighty points lower than it is today. Those with serious ambitions to spend four years in South Bend need to be in the top 1-2 percent in both academic performance and standardized test scores. Otherwise, you'll find yourself in the Rudy Ruettiger category as a long shot.

Worth Your Money?

Notre Dame has a high cost of attendance at over $76,000 per year. However, this is a school that funnels undergrads into high-paying jobs and top professional schools, leading to high lifetime earnings and the expansion and enhancement of one's personal and professional networks. The university does grant an average of $12k in merit aid to 16 percent of the student body and meets the full financial need of close to half of all undergraduates. Those receiving need-based aid receive an average annual grant of $44,087, helping to make the school a very worthy investment and accessible to students from all socioeconomic backgrounds.

FINANCIAL
Institutional Type: Private
In-State Tuition: $57,192
Out-of-State Tuition: $57,192
Room & Board: $15,984
Required Fees: $507
Books & Supplies: $1,050

Avg. Need-Based Grant: $44,087
Avg. % of Need Met: 100%

Avg. Merit-Based Award: $12,994
% Receiving (All Freshmen): 16%
% Receiving (Freshmen w/o Need): 2%

Avg. Cumulative Debt: $27,460
% of Students Borrowing: 40%

CAREER
Who Recruits
1. Salesforce
2. Boston Consulting Group
3. Facebook
4. JPMorgan Chase
5. McKinsey & Co.

Notable Internships
1. Saks Fifth Avenue
2. Citizens Bank
3. Citadel Securities

Top Industries
1. Business
2. Education
3. Operations
4. Finance
5. Research

Top Employers
1. Deloitte
2. EY
3. PwC
4. IBM
5. Accenture

Where Alumni Work
1. Chicago
2. New York City
3. South Bend, IN
4. Washington DC
5. San Francisco

Median Earnings
College Scorecard (Early Career): $78,400
PayScale (Early Career): $70,500
PayScale (Mid-Career): $142,300

RANKINGS
Money: 60
U.S. News: 19, National Universities
Wall Street Journal/THE: 28
Washington Monthly: 23, National Universities

COLLEGE OVERLAPS
Boston College
Duke University
Georgetown University
Northwestern University
Vanderbilt University

University of Oregon

Eugene, Oregon | 541-346-3201

ADMISSION
Admission Rate: 82%
Admission Rate - Men: 78%
Admission Rate - Women: 84%
EA Admission Rate: NR
ED Admission Rate: Not Offered
ED Admits as % of Total Admits: Not Offered
Admission Rate (5-Year Trend): +7%
% of Admits Attending (Yield): 20%
Transfer Admission Rate: 62%

SAT Reading/Writing (Middle 50%): 560-660
SAT Math (Middle 50%): 540-650
ACT Composite (Middle 50%): 22-28

% Graduated in Top 10% of HS Class: 26%
% Graduated in Top 25% of HS Class: 57%
% Graduated in Top 50% of HS Class: 86%

Demonstrated Interest: Not Considered
Legacy Status: Not Considered
Admission Interview Offered: No

ENROLLMENT
Total Undergraduate Enrollment: 18,888
% Part-Time: 8%
% Male: 46%
% Female: 54%
% Out-of-State: 43%
% Fraternity: 16%
% Sorority: 18%
% On-Campus (Freshman): 93%
% On-Campus (All Undergraduate): 26%

% African-American: 2%
% Asian: 6%
% Hispanic: 13%
% White: 59%
% Other: 9%
% Race or Ethnicity Unknown: 2%
% International: 7%
% Low-Income: 24%

ACADEMICS
Student-to-Faculty Ratio: 16 to 1
% of Classes Under 20: 38%
% of Classes 20-49: 41%
% of Classes 50 or More: 21%
% Full-Time Faculty: 70%
% Full-Time Faculty w/ Terminal Degree: 95%

Top Programs
Architecture
Art and Design
Biology
Business
Education
Environmental Science
Sociology

Retention Rate: 86%
4-Year Graduation Rate: 56%
6-Year Graduation Rate: 74%

Curricular Flexibility: Somewhat Flexible
Academic Rating: ★★★

#CollegesWorthYourMoney

In 1859, as the territory of Oregon was officially granted statehood, the United States Congress instructed the state's founders that they would need to establish a public university. It took almost 15 years from that point for construction to begin on the first buildings to grace the 18-acre property that would become the University of Oregon. Today, this flagship university in the city of Eugene draws students from all over the US and even the world. In fact, 38 percent of Ducks hail from another state, and another 10 percent come from other countries. All told, 18,888 undergraduates and another 3,600 graduate students proudly wear the distinctive green and yellow color scheme that has become an unmistakable symbol of this excellent public institution.

Inside the Classroom
No matter which of the close to 80 undergraduate degrees you are pursuing, all Ducks complete coursework in the areas of arts and letters; social science; science; global perspectives; and US: difference, inequality, and agency. Those pursuing a BA degree need to demonstrate proficiency in a second language, which can be fulfilled through three semesters of coursework. Graduates of BS programs will need to demonstrate proficiency in either mathematics or computer science. First-year experience programs (FIGS) are not mandatory at the school, but they are recommended by 95 percent who have completed them.

The student-to-faculty ratio at UO is 16:1, which leads to a mix of class sizes; 53 percent contain fewer than 20 students while 21 percent of sections are larger, with 50 or more students; the median class size is 20 students. Most impressively, a healthy 73 percent of undergraduate students engage in some type of research activity. The Undergraduate Research Opportunity Program excels at connecting students to mentor professors on campus as well as external research opportunities. Ducks study abroad in 80 countries, and roughly one quarter of students do so at some point during their undergraduate years.

Students flock in large numbers to the social sciences at this university as 24 percent of undergraduate degrees conferred fall under this umbrella. The next most popular academic pursuits are business (13 percent), communication/journalism (13 percent), biology (7 percent), and the visual and performing arts (7 percent). The Lundquist College of Business and the College of Education have strong national reputations. Oregon students apply for prestigious national scholarships in droves and sport inspiring numbers of Gilman Scholars (25 in 2020) and multiple Fulbright Scholars virtually every year.

Outside the Classroom
Freshmen are pretty much the only students who live in campus housing; 93 percent of first years do so. Greek life attracts 18 percent of women into sororities and 16 percent of men into fraternities; 3,572 students participate. Enthusiasm for the athletic teams is off the charts. Eighteen Division I teams compete in the Pac-12; the men's basketball team has become a regular March Madness qualifier, and the popular Ducks football team plays before 54,000+ raucous fans. Thirty-six club and intramural sports are also available including jiujitsu, Nordic skiing, and triathlon. There are 300+ student groups and organizations in total at the university, including a strong number with an environmental theme. An environmentally conscious student body enjoys the ample natural beauty of both the 295-acre campus and the surrounding area of Eugene. Students love to ski, raft in the local rivers, and bike just about everywhere. Eugene is the third-ranked city for bicycling in the United States. Immediately surrounding campus, students can visit various farmer's markets, enjoy locally grown food, and visit museums. Portland is a road trip that be accomplished in under two hours, but many undergrads are happy to stay put in a town that sits atop national rankings for green space, clean air, and transportation options.

Career Services
There are 15 employees working out of the main University of Oregon Career Center. Another 10 professionals work within the Lundquist College of Business to bring the total number of career services workers to 25, which equates to a 756:1 student-to-counselor ratio, above average for schools included in this book, but not notably poor when compared to other large public universities. In the department's own words, "Whether you need help deciding on a profession, finding a job or internship, practicing for interviews, or writing your resume, we strive to provide guidance in all aspects of career and postgraduate life."

Career staff members at OU execute many career and graduate school fairs throughout the year. Last spring, employers in attendance included Kaiser Permanente, the US Department of Health and Human Services, Comcast, and the Portland Trailblazers. Attendance at career fairs has been rising in recent years and has increased to over 1,000 attendees; the fall fair draws 100+ companies to Eugene. The UO Alumni Association works to keep the 231,000 Duck alumni around the globe connected, which is a resource that can prove invaluable during an internship or job hunt.

Professional Outcomes

As of the publishing of this edition, the University of Oregon does not make its first-destination surveys public, nor does it offer data about where alumni land jobs or the overall placement rate of recent cohorts. Despite this dearth of data, there are many positive indicators hinting that a UO degree is quite valuable on the job market. More than 1,000 Oregon alumni work for Nike, and hundreds of others occupy offices at Intel, Amazon, Microsoft, Adidas, Google, Apple, and Salesforce. Portland and Eugene, Oregon, are the most common places to settle after graduation, but plenty of Ducks flock to San Francisco, Seattle, Los Angeles, and New York City. According to PayScale, grads with 0-5 years' experience in the workforce earn a median salary of $53k while those with 10+ years' experience are paid a median salary of $99k.

Many newfound bachelor's-holders continue their education right at OU in one of 150 degree and certificate programs, including a fair number entering the University of Oregon School of Law and the OHSU School of Medicine. A total of 122 Ducks applied to medical school last year, a comparable number to Oregon State University. The school finds itself on the list of undergraduate schools represented in the most recent Yale Law School admissions cycles. Oregon is a reputable enough public university that access to elite graduate and professional programs is certainly on the table for high achievers.

Admission

A grand total of 27,358 students applied for freshman admission, and the vast majority were let through the gates—82 percent to be precise. Starting with the fall 2021 class, the University of Oregon became a test-optional institution, but the previous year's freshmen had a middle-50 percent composite score of 1140-1340 on the SAT and 22-28 on the ACT. The majority of entering first-years possessed GPAs above a 3.5; a 4.0 GPA was achieved by 26 percent, and another 24 percent earned a 3.75-3.99. The average was a 3.65. Just over one quarter finished in the top decile of their high school class, and 57 percent earned a spot in the top quartile.

Rigor of secondary school record and GPA are the only two "very important" factors in the admissions process; standardized tests and application essays makeup the next tier of "important" categories, although it is expected that the former will fall down a tier. Oregon will consider all other "soft" factors, but it does not offer interviews or assign any weight to legacy status or demonstrated interest. Those seeking admission into the Clark Honors College must prepare for a more challenging process. The average unweighted GPA for accepted students is 3.91, and the average SAT score is 1360. Roughly 800 students are members of the Honors College.

Worth Your Money?

The annual in-state tuition of approximately $11,500 represents a reasonable deal for Beaver State residents; everyone else will pay more than triple that amount, $36,912. Financial aid is not particularly generous at this school as only an average of 55 percent of determined need is actually met. Still, students emerge with an average debt slightly below the national average at $26,500. As with most public schools, if money is an issue for your family, we recommend checking out public universities within your home state. Given the quality of the business and computer science programs, paying more to attend UO in some circumstances could be a reasonable investment.

FINANCIAL
Institutional Type: Public
In-State Tuition: $11,460
Out-of-State Tuition: $36,912
Room & Board: $12,783
Required Fees: $2,397
Books & Supplies: $1,140

Avg. Need-Based Grant: $10,512
Avg. % of Need Met: 55%

Avg. Merit-Based Award: $6,317
% Receiving (All Freshmen): 23%
% Receiving (Freshmen w/o Need): 21%

Avg. Cumulative Debt: $26,548
% of Students Borrowing: 44%

CAREER
Who Recruits
1. Apex Systems
2. Insight Global
3. Fisher Investments
4. Wayfair
5. Oracle

Notable Internships
1. Google
2. Nike
3. Bloomberg LP

Top Industries
1. Business
2. Education
3. Operations
4. Arts & Design
5. Sales

Top Employers
1. Nike
2. Intel
3. Amazon
4. Microsoft
5. adidas

Where Alumni Work
1. Portland, OR
2. Eugene, OR
3. San Francisco
4. Seattle
5. Los Angeles

Median Earnings
College Scorecard (Early Career): $44,800
PayScale (Early Career): $53,900
PayScale (Mid-Career): $101,600

RANKINGS
Money: 327
U.S. News: 103 (T), National Universities
Wall Street Journal/THE: 225 (T)
Washington Monthly: 118, National Universities

COLLEGE OVERLAPS
Arizona State University
University of Arizona
Oregon State University
University of Colorado Boulder
University of Washington

University of Pennsylvania

Philadelphia, Pennsylvania | 215-898-7507

ADMISSION
Admission Rate: 8%
Admission Rate - Men: 7%
Admission Rate - Women: 8%
EA Admission Rate: Not Offered
ED Admission Rate: 18%
ED Admits as % of Total Admits: 37%
Admission Rate (5-Year Trend): -5%
% of Admits Attending (Yield): 68%
Transfer Admission Rate: 6%

SAT Reading/Writing (Middle 50%): 700-760
SAT Math (Middle 50%): 750-800
ACT Composite (Middle 50%): 33-35

% Graduated in Top 10% of HS Class: 94%
% Graduated in Top 25% of HS Class: 98%
% Graduated in Top 50% of HS Class: 100%

Demonstrated Interest: Considered
Legacy Status: Considered
Admission Interview Offered: Yes

ENROLLMENT
Total Undergraduate Enrollment: 10,019
% Part-Time: 2%
% Male: 48%
% Female: 52%
% Out-of-State: 81%
% Fraternity: 30%
% Sorority: 28%
% On-Campus (Freshman): 100%
% On-Campus (All Undergraduate): 55%

% African-American: 10%
% Asian: 25%
% Hispanic: 11%
% White: 47%
% Other: 6%
% Race or Ethnicity Unknown: 4%
% International: 16%
% Low-Income: 14%

ACADEMICS
Student-to-Faculty Ratio: 6 to 1
% of Classes Under 20: 71%
% of Classes 20-49: 20%
% of Classes 50 or More: 9%
% Full-Time Faculty: 81%
% Full-Time Faculty w/ Terminal Degree: 100%

Top Programs
Business
Cognitive Science
Communication
Computer Science
Engineering
English
Philosophy
Political Science

Retention Rate: 98%
4-Year Graduation Rate: 86%
6-Year Graduation Rate: 96%

Curricular Flexibility: Somewhat Flexible
Academic Rating: ★★★★★

#CollegesWorthYourMoney

Once known for its insecurity over being frequently confused with Penn State and having a reputation in snooty circles as a "second-tier Ivy," the University of Pennsylvania in 2020 has long since brushed that dirt off its shoulders. Today, Penn boasts twice as many applicants as a decade ago and, with an 8 percent acceptance rate that is lower than Dartmouth's, it is now a dream destination for many of the brightest students around the world—and we mean world. 16 percent of the student body are residents of foreign countries. The 10,019 Quaker undergrads on campus in 2019-20 are pursuing ninety distinct degrees across four schools: the College of Arts & Sciences, the College of Applied Science and Engineering, the College of Nursing and, of course, arguably the top business school anywhere—Wharton.

Inside the Classroom

The Core Curriculum at UPenn is based on seven Sectors of Knowledge: society, history and tradition, arts and letters, humanities and social sciences, the living world, the physical world, and natural sciences and mathematics. In fulfilling those requirements students take mandatory courses in foreign language, writing (seminar), quantitative data analysis, formal reasoning, cross-cultural analysis, and diversity in the United States. The greatest number of students pursue degrees in business (21 percent), social sciences (14 percent), biology (10 percent), engineering (10 percent), and computer science (6 percent).

Penn has a 6:1 student-to-faculty ratio, but with a focus on research and 12,413 graduate students, not every undergraduate section is a tiny seminar. However, the university does boast an exceptional 29 percent of courses with an enrollment under ten and 71 percent with an enrollment under twenty—quite an achievement for a school of Penn's massive size. It also offers multiple ways for undergrads to conduct research, whether through independent studies or working side-by-side with faculty members. It is a testament to its focus in this area that the university publishes eleven distinct journals featuring original undergraduate research. Penn ranks first among Ivies and fourteenth among doctoral-granting institutions in study abroad participation rate; each year over 2,300 students head off to earn a semester's credit in one of eighty-five countries.

While Wharton is the ultimate name-drop, the Penn engineering program garners a more quiet respect. Outstanding programs abound throughout the university, in fields ranging from computer science to philosophy. Graduates of UPenn are, in general, met with high-paying jobs at desirable companies and entry into the best graduate and professional schools in existence. Prestigious national scholarship and fellowship programs adore Penn grads just the same. Penn grads won Rhodes Scholarships each year from 2019-21. Last year, the school produced sixteen Fulbright Scholars, two Schwarzman Scholars, two Truman Scholars, and forty-two National Science Foundation Graduate Research Fellowships.

Outside the Classroom

All freshmen, but only 55 percent of students live in university-owned housing at Penn. One reason for the lack of upperclassman interest in dorms is the popular Greek system that attracts over one-quarter of undergrads into one of fifty frat and sorority houses. The Quakers compete in thirty-three NCAA Division I sports in the Ivy League; over 1,000 members of the student body are varsity athletes. Many more participate in club and intramural athletics. There are multiple fitness centers including a 120,000-square-foot facility that includes an Olympic-size swimming pool, rock climbing wall, and sauna. The school also hosts the Penn Relays, the longest-running collegiate track meet in the country that draws 100,000 spectators annually. With 450+ student organizations active at Penn, there is a group that caters to wherever your talents and interests lie, whether that is in the performance, community service, or cultural identity realms. The school's newspaper, the Daily Pennsylvanian, has a staff of 250 students and has garnered many awards. Penn's West Philly campus is comprised of 215 buildings on 299 attached acres and contains plenty of green space. The urban setting affords students the benefits of walkability and easy trips to any part of the fifth-largest city in the United States.

Career Services

The University of Pennsylvania's Career Services Office has thirty professional staff members who are dedicated to undergraduate counseling, on-campus recruiting, and maintaining digital resources like Handshake. The 334:1 student-to-advisor ratio is average compared to other schools featured in this guide but strong for a school of Penn's size. Close to twenty annual career fairs are held, some of which are industry specific (engineering, finance, nursing) while others are themed such as the Common Good Career Fair; the Creative Career Fair; or the Startup, VC, and Data Analytics Fair.

Rising sophomores, juniors, and seniors find themselves in paid internships at some the world's top employers in droves. To quantify that, recent grads, between their junior and senior year, found positions at a 90 percent clip, including 20+ at Goldman Sachs and Morgan Stanley. Penn also excels at facilitating on-campus interviews; more than 300 companies conduct interviews on campus each year. A sizable 43 percent of 2019 grads found their position through Career Services. Ample support is also provided for those applying to medical, law, or graduate school. An equal emphasis on large-scale events such as industry-specific job fairs and one-on-one counseling leads to phenomenal graduate outcomes (more ahead).

Professional Outcomes

Seventy-seven percent of Class of 2019 Quaker grads were employed six months following degree completion, another 14 percent were in graduate school, and 5 percent were still planning their next educational/career move. Finance was the sector attracting the highest percentage of grads (30 percent) followed by consulting (18 percent), technology (16 percent), and health care (9 percent). Employers hiring the greatest number of 2019 graduates included Goldman Sachs (45), Boston Consulting Group (30), Google (30), Morgan Stanley (28), McKinsey (28), and Accenture (23). The median starting salary for all graduates is $77,500. Among elite colleges, Penn alumni enjoy the highest midcareer salaries of any school except MIT. Unsurprisingly, the Philadelphia Metro area has the strongest concentration of alumni, but New York is a close second. San Francisco and DC also have a strong Quaker presence.

For those continuing their educational journeys, the most popular move is to remain at Penn—118 members of the Class of 2019 made that decision. The next most attended graduate schools were Columbia (10), Stanford (9), and MIT (4). Students gain acceptance to medical school at a terrific rate—78 percent versus the national average of 43 percent. Medical schools that have taken more than five Penn grads since 2016-17 include Emory University, Temple University, Harvard Medical School, the Icahn School of Medicine at Mt. Sinai, and Penn's own uber-elite Perelman School of Medicine that sports a 4 percent acceptance rate. The acceptance rate into law school is 84 percent, which is made lower by the fact that the vast majority are aiming for top-tier schools. The most attended law schools is recent years are NYU School of Law, Penn Law School, Fordham University School of Law, Columbia University School of Law, and Harvard Law School.

Admission

Penn received 44,961 applications for a place in the Class of 2023, the second highest figure of any Ivy League university behind Cornell. They admitted 8 percent of that pool and the median SAT for those who went on to enroll was 1510; the median ACT was 34. A nearly unanimous 94 percent of admitted Quakers earned a place in the top decile of their graduating high school class, and the average unweighted GPA was 3.9. In the past decade, the average admitted applicant's SAT scores have increased by around fifty points, and the grades/class rank have stayed the same. Back then, the school received half as many applications, and the acceptance rate was a far more forgiving 18 percent.

According to the admissions committee, rigor of secondary school record, GPA, standardized test scores, essays, recommendations, and character/personal qualities are deemed "very important" to the evaluative process. Factors classified as "important" are class rank, the interview, extracurricular activities, and talent/ability. One in seven 2019-20 freshmen were the first in their families to attend college. Close to 1,300 students were admitted via early decision; the ED round saw an 18 percent acceptance rate, and more than half of the Class of 2023 was filled by those welcomed through a binding early acceptance. As is the case with so many top-shelf elite institutions, Penn rejects more students than ever, including thousands of teens who would have waltzed into the university a generation ago. Applying ED is a no-brainer if you want to gain a slight edge.

Worth Your Money?

Penn's total cost of attendance is $79,000+ per year and, unless you qualify for need-based financial aid, that is the price you will pay because the university does not award merit aid. It does, however, meet 100 percent of demonstrated need for all eligible students, awarding annual grants averaging $53k. Even if you are required to pay the full sticker price, Penn's starting salaries are such that even substantial loans will not be crippling to the vast majority of grads.

FINANCIAL
Institutional Type: Private
In-State Tuition: $53,166
Out-of-State Tuition: $53,166
Room & Board: $16,784
Required Fees: $6,876
Books & Supplies: $1,358

Avg. Need-Based Grant: $53,107
Avg. % of Need Met: 100%

Avg. Merit-Based Award: $0
% Receiving (All Freshmen): 0%
% Receiving (Freshmen w/o Need): 0%

Avg. Cumulative Debt: $23,009
% of Students Borrowing: 22%

CAREER
Who Recruits
1. Children's Hospital of Philadelphia
2. Teach for America
3. Facebook
4. Boston Consulting Group
5. JPMorgan Chase

Notable Internships
1. Pfizer
2. Gensler
3. HBO

Top Industries
1. Business
2. Education
3. Research
4. Operations
5. Social Services

Top Employers
1. Google
2. Amazon
3. Microsoft
4. Goldman Sachs
5. Facebook

Where Alumni Work
1. Philadelphia
2. New York City
3. San Francisco
4. Washington DC
5. Boston

Median Earnings
College Scorecard (Early Career): $85,900
PayScale (Early Career): $76,800
PayScale (Mid-Career): $152,900

RANKINGS
Money: 30
U.S. News: 8, National Universities
Wall Street Journal/THE: 13
Washington Monthly: 7, National Universities

COLLEGE OVERLAPS
Brown University
Cornell University
Columbia University
Duke University
Harvard University

University of Pittsburgh — Pittsburgh Campus

Pittsburgh, Pennsylvania | 412-624-7488

ADMISSION
Admission Rate: 57%
Admission Rate - Men: 54%
Admission Rate - Women: 59%
EA Admission Rate: Not Offered
ED Admission Rate: Not Offered
ED Admits as % of Total Admits: Not Offered
Admission Rate (5-Year Trend): +2%
% of Admits Attending (Yield): 22%
Transfer Admission Rate: 52%

SAT Reading/Writing (Middle 50%): 630-700
SAT Math (Middle 50%): 630-700
ACT Composite (Middle 50%): 28-33

% Graduated in Top 10% of HS Class: 53%
% Graduated in Top 25% of HS Class: 86%
% Graduated in Top 50% of HS Class: 98%

Demonstrated Interest: Considered
Legacy Status: Considered
Admission Interview Offered: No

ENROLLMENT
Total Undergraduate Enrollment: 19,200
% Part-Time: 4%
% Male: 47%
% Female: 53%
% Out-of-State: 29%
% Fraternity: 10%
% Sorority: 12%
% On-Campus (Freshman): 96%
% On-Campus (All Undergraduate): 42%

% African-American: 5%
% Asian: 11%
% Hispanic: 5%
% White: 68%
% Other: 4%
% Race or Ethnicity Unknown: 1%
% International: 5%
% Low-Income: 16%

ACADEMICS
Student-to-Faculty Ratio: 14 to 1
% of Classes Under 20: 45%
% of Classes 20-49: 38%
% of Classes 50 or More: 18%
% Full-Time Faculty: 78%
% Full-Time Faculty w/ Terminal Degree: 93%

Top Programs
Biology
Biomedical Engineering
Business
Chemistry
English
Neuroscience
Philosophy
Psychology

Retention Rate: 93%
4-Year Graduation Rate: 65%
6-Year Graduation Rate: 83%

Curricular Flexibility: Somewhat Flexible
Academic Rating: ★★★✦

#CollegesWorthYourMoney

A generation ago you wouldn't see many teens from outside Pennsylvania clamoring to attend the University of Pittsburgh. In fact, for everyone other than western Pennsylvania residents, Penn State was the clear number one public university in the Keystone State. Fast-forwarding to today, Pitt attracts undergraduates from all fifty states and countries around the globe. The home of the Panthers has ascended to the status of a premier public research university, and its 19,200 undergraduate students rank near the top of their respective high school classes and possess average standardized scores in the 90th percentile. Those in the Swanson School of Engineering sport SATs in the 97th percentile, and the top-ranked Honors College requires 99th percentile and above.

Inside the Classroom
The university takes great care in welcoming new students to campus and ensuring a smooth transition. First-year mentors are available to help orient new students to campus life. Academic Foundations is a one-credit course that serves as an insiders' guide to Pitt, and first-year seminar classes are centered on a theme of interest with a capped enrollment of nineteen students. Pitt admits freshmen to the Dietrich School of Arts & Sciences, the College of Business Administration, the Swanson School of Engineering, and the School of Nursing. Core coursework is mandated as follows: composition, two writing-intensive classes, algebra, quantitative and formal reasoning, two second language courses, and a class with a diversity designation. A total of nine courses in the humanities, social sciences, and natural sciences are required for all Dietrich School of Arts & Sciences students.

For a large public university, Pitt has a strong 14:1 student-to-faculty ratio and, as a result, it offers many smaller course sections to go along with some classes in large lecture halls. Forty-five percent of sections have an enrollment under twenty students while 18 percent enroll for than 50. Plenty of personal connection with professors is available to those who seek it. Undergraduate research opportunities are granted to more than half of all students. There are 350 study abroad programs in seventy-five countries, and many take advantage; the participation rate in the College of Business Administration is 55 percent.

The University of Pittsburgh is respected nationally by both top companies and prestigious graduate/professional institutions. Its engineering and business schools are rated top fifty in most rankings and are among the most commonly chosen fields of study. Pre-med offerings are also top-notch, with majors in the health professions, biology, and psychology rounding out the list of most popular majors. Pitt grads are no strangers to nationally competitive scholarships. In the last five years the school has produced forty-six Fulbright winners, seven Goldwater Scholars, two Churchill Scholars, and one Truman Scholar.

Outside the Classroom
A 132-acre urban campus houses 42 percent of the school's undergraduate student population. The Oakland neighborhood where the school is located is safe, walkable, and brimming with culture and fun. The Carnegie Museums of Art and Natural History and innumerable bars and eateries, including plenty of international options, are close by. The city, often rated as one of the "most livable in America," is truly an extension of campus, but campus itself isn't too shabby either. Pitt does guarantee housing to most students for three full years, and it is currently building dorms containing thousands of additional beds. Ten percent of men and 12 percent of women join Greek life, giving it a notable but not smothering presence. There are 400+ student organizations, and popular activities include the Pitt Dance Marathon that raised over $300,000 for the Children's Hospital of Pittsburgh. Intramural sports also are popular, and seemingly everyone participates. The university boasts an award-winning Robotics & Automation Society, Hillel Chapter, Hindu Students Council, and Society for Women Engineers. Pitt's nineteen varsity teams compete at the highest levels of NCAA Division I, and the football team shares a stadium with the Steelers and attracts over 41,000 fans per game.

Career Services
There are twenty-seven full-time employees at Pitt's Career Center, housed within the Office of Student Affairs. Members of the team serve as career consultants, employer development specialists, internship coordinators, and alumni engagement specialists. The office's 711:1 student-to-advisor ratio is greater than the average school in this guidebook but not alarming for a public university of its size. In fact, the University of Pittsburgh measures up well when it comes to the raw data in the areas of student engagement and employer relations.

In the 2018-19 school year, counselors conducted 4,573 one-on-one advising sessions and booked 402 total employers to attend their Fall Career + Internship Fair that includes separate days for engineering and computer science students. In total, 474 employers recruited at Pitt last year, and 760 on-campus interviews were held.

Companies recruiting on campus include EY, Amazon, Epic Systems, Lockheed Martin, Vanguard, Cigna, and Deloitte. Tight employer partnerships led to internships being completed by 54 percent of graduates. However, those who complete the Internship Prep Program, a combination of workshops and individual appointments hosted by the Career Center, are guaranteed an internship or comparable experiential learning activity. With well-cultivated regional and national employer connections, Pitt students are given every opportunity to secure employment at a solid median starting salary or attend a graduate school consistent with their personal and professional goals.

Professional Outcomes

Recent grads enter full-time employment at a 68 percent clip, 24 percent enter graduate or professional school on a full-time basis, and only 6 percent are still seeking employment within a few months of receiving their degrees. Engineering, nursing, business, and information sciences majors were the most likely to be employed full time upon graduation. Those majors had 73-86 percent employment rates while other majors tended to flock to graduate school in large numbers. The employers scooping up the highest number of 2018 (most recent available) graduates included the University of Pittsburgh Medical Center (170), PNC (57), BNY Mellon (36), and Deloitte (19). Actual panthers may be solitary creatures, but Pitt Panthers flock in notable quantities to major corporations. More than one hundred alumni presently work for Dick's Sporting Goods, Amazon, Google, Microsoft, and Uber. Starting salaries fluctuate across the nine undergraduate schools. The median starting salary for graduates of the Swanson School of Engineering was $65,000, College of Business Administration students earned $50,000, and Dietrich School of Arts & Sciences grads were paid just shy of $37,000. Pittsburgh, Philly, New York, and DC host the most alumni.

With so many fine graduate programs at the University of Pittsburgh itself, many newly minted grads stay put to continue their education. Among the Class of 2018, Pitt was the most popular graduate location by a wide margin, attracting 313 students. Next in popularity were Duquesne (20), Penn (17), and Temple (16). Five or more attended Columbia, UVA, Carnegie Mellon, and Boston University. Undergraduate applicants can apply to the Guaranteed Admissions Program that earns you conditional acceptance to the University of Pittsburgh School of Medicine, one of the best medical schools in the entire U.S. Recent Pitt graduates have gone on to attend law schools at George Washington University, the University of Chicago, and UVA as well as Pennsylvania-based options like Temple, Duquesne, and Pitt itself.

Admission

Pitt received 32,091 applications to join the Class of 2023 and allowed entrance to 57 percent. However, only 22 percent of accepted applicants ultimately entered the 2019-20 freshman class as many Pennsylvania residents applying to ultra-selective schools use Pitt as a safety school. However, there is nothing that comes close to screaming "safety school" when examining the academic credentials of current undergraduates. With median test scores of 1340 on the SAT and 30 on the ACT, today's Panthers are high achievers. The average GPA is 3.9 and 53 percent hailed from their graduating class' top decile, and 86 percent placed in the top quartile.

At the top of the admissions office checklist are the rigor of one's courses, GPA, and standardized test scores. The essay is the only other factor ranking at or above the "important" level. There is no early action or early decision option at Pitt, but the university does employ a rolling admission policy; so, applying early is a must if you wish to maximize your admission prospects. The Pitt Honors College has become one of the premier honors programs in the country. SAT scores for admitted honors students are generally in the 1450-1500 range and the average GPA is 4.39. The school accepts between 300 and 400 students each year. Prior to the turn of the new millennium, Pitt was a school that would admit "B" students. Twenty years ago, only 29 percent of the entering Arts & Sciences students were top-10 percent finishers, and the average SAT in the nursing program was a 1060. Today, Pitt takes "A" students who took AP courses and registered strong standardized test scores.

Worth Your Money?

Pitt's in-state tuition is just under $20,000 per year; out of state that number climbs to close to $34k. Families making over $75,000 a year are not going to receive much need-based aid and will pay somewhere near full price. Only a sliver of incoming Panther freshmen net any merit aid at all. Based on that data, it is fair to say that Pitt is worth the price of admission for any Keystone State resident, no matter what degree you may be pursuing. There is a lot to like about Pitt for out-of-state and international students, but the cost will be higher.

FINANCIAL
Institutional Type: Public
In-State Tuition: $19,718
Out-of-State Tuition: $33,746
Room & Board: $11,250
Required Fees: $0
Books & Supplies: $755

Avg. Need-Based Grant: $11,636
Avg. % of Need Met: 59%

Avg. Merit-Based Award: $11,153
% Receiving (All Freshmen): 14%
% Receiving (Freshmen w/o Need): 9%

Avg. Cumulative Debt: $39,417
% of Students Borrowing: 61%

CAREER
Who Recruits
1. American Eagle
2. Allegheny Health Network
3. FedEx
4. EPIC Systems
5. Norfolk Southern

Notable Internships
1. Boston Consulting Group
2. NASA Jet Propulsion Laboratory
3. CVS

Top Industries
1. Business
2. Education
3. Healthcare
4. Operations
5. Engineering

Top Employers
1. PNC
2. BNY Mellon
3. Deloitte
4. Dick'sSporting Goods
5. Amazon

Where Alumni Work
1. Pittsburgh
2. Philadelphia
3. New York City
4. Washington DC
5. San Francisco

Median Earnings
College Scorecard (Early Career): $53,900
PayScale (Early Career): $59,600
PayScale (Mid-Career): $104,500

RANKINGS
Money: 280
U.S. News: 58 (T), National Universities
Wall Street Journal/THE: 97
Washington Monthly: 153, National Universities

COLLEGE OVERLAPS
Boston University
New York University
Ohio State University - Columbus
Pennsylvania State University - University Park
University of Maryland

University of Richmond

Richmond, Virginia | 804-289-8640

Considering that, in 1861, many of the University of Richmond faculty went off to fight for the Confederacy whose capital was only miles from campus, it may come as a surprise that now the school is a diverse and progressive assemblage of young people from all fifty US states and more than seventy foreign countries. With 3,161 undergraduates, the school is at once modest in size and robust in its academic and student life offerings; there are over sixty undergraduate majors at the university and many standout programs, including the one-of-a-kind Jepson School of Leadership Studies as well as a host of respected pre-professional pathways.

Inside the Classroom

A distinctive general education curriculum includes a first-year seminar as well as the initial leg of a three-course wellness curriculum (the freshman course covers topics like alcohol education). From there, undergrads must demonstrate proficiency in a foreign language and then march through one course in each of historical studies, literary studies, natural sciences, social analysis, symbolic reasoning, and visual and performing arts. The list of required courses is relatively short, affording students a nice amount of academic freedom and exploration.

Don't let the "university" designation fool you; Richmond is all about undergraduate education. The student-to-faculty ratio is 8:1, the average class size is sixteen students, and not a single course is taught by a teaching assistant. Twenty-five percent of classes have single-digit enrollment numbers, and 73 percent of sections contain fewer than twenty students. Half of all Richmond students participate in an intensive research experience with a faculty member prior to graduation, and students can have those summer opportunities funded through the Richmond Guarantee that sees the university fund research apprenticeships as well as internships. More than 650 students receive such funding every summer. Going abroad is the norm at UR—59 percent take a semester or full year of study in one of seventy programs in thirty countries.

The highly regarded Robbins School of Business is responsible for granting 36 percent of the degrees conferred by the university, a staggering number that dwarfs any other field of study. The social sciences collectively attract 16 percent of the student body, and biology (premed is strong) accounts for 9 percent of degrees earned. The international relations, political science, and history departments also have excellent reputations. Applicants to prestigious fellowships fare quite well. In 2019, eight students won Fulbrights, three won Goldwater Scholarships, and one took home a Boren Scholarship.

Outside the Classroom

The University of Richmond's 350-acre campus houses 91 percent of the undergraduate population, and 99 percent of freshmen do so, creating a cohesive student body. Sixteen Greek organizations on campus rule the social scene with 27 percent of women joining sororities and 18 percent of men entering fraternity life. The Spiders compete in seventeen NCAA Division I sports within the highly competitive Atlantic Ten Conference, an astounding fact considering the size of the school's liberal arts college. There are 205 student-run organizations, including thirty club sports teams, fourteen religious groups, and seven honors societies. Intramural leagues are run out of the award-winning Weinstein Center for Recreation that contains a six-lane, twenty-five-yard swimming pool, racquetball/squash courts, and an indoor jogging track. UR's food services are regularly ranked high on lists of best college cuisine. School-run buses and shuttles make getting around a breeze. Campus is located only six miles from downtown Richmond, and longer road trips to DC (90 miles), the Atlantic Ocean, or the Blue Ridge Mountains make for an easy weekend getaway.

Career Services

The Office of Alumni and Career Services is staffed by seventeen full-time professional employees (not counting administrative coordinators) who hold positions like career advisor, employer relations coordinator, and director of experiential learning and assessment. That equates to a student-to-advisor ratio of 186:1, in the superior range when compared to the other institutions included in this book. It's no wonder that 98 percent of Richmond grads report being "generally satisfied" or "very satisfied" with their education one year after graduation, a good indicator of contentment with early career outcomes.

Richmond's career services office operates with a four-year plan that connects students to advisers during freshman year. Over three-quarters of recent grads met with an advisor during their senior year. The Spider-Connect system and alumni connections help 70 percent of UR undergraduates land at least one internship during their four years of study. There are fifty+ regional alumni groups located around the United States and abroad, creating opportunities to build bridges and find mentorships in just about any major city. Career expos on campus typically attract fifty employers, and major corporations regularly travel to Richmond to recruit and interview current seniors. Spider Road Trips and Spider Shadowing are other avenues to hands-on job exploration opportunities. With strong industry connections, more-than-adequate staffing, and a number of innovative career exploration programs, the Office of Alumni and Career Services does well for its undergraduate students.

Professional Outcomes

One year after receiving their degrees, 96 percent of 2019 Richmond grads who are seeking employment have found jobs. The most popular sectors are financial services/insurance (17 percent), accounting (7 percent), consulting (6 percent), healthcare (6 percent), teaching (6 percent), and sales/business development (6 percent). Companies where you can find at least 50 Richmond alumni employed include Capital One (which employs 300+ Spiders), Deloitte, PwC, Wells Fargo, EY, Dominion Energy, Morgan Stanley, Altria, Google, and Accenture. The average salary range one year out of school is $50,000-$55,000. The majority of students remain in the Richmond area after finishing at the university, however large pockets of alumni can be found in New York City, DC, Philadelphia, and Boston. Richmond is a school with strong connections to industry in every region of the United States.

Within a year of graduation, 23 percent of the Class of 2019 was already enrolled in a graduate or professional degree program. The school boasts an impressive list of recent acceptances into high-end law schools such as Harvard, Duke, the University of Chicago, Vanderbilt, Yale, UVA, and the University of Michigan. Even more notable is Richmond's success with helping students get accepted into medical school. From 2014-19, a phenomenal 77 percent of those who applied were accepted, a figure that blows away the national average. Medical schools attended by those students included Brown, Dartmouth, UNC, Stanford, Emory, and Harvard.

Admission

Of the 12,356 applicants for a place in the Class of 2023, only 3,500 were welcomed to the university, working out to an acceptance rate of 28 percent, an all-time low. The mid-50 percent standardized test scores also reached record levels of 1300-1450 on the SAT and 30-33 on the ACT. Fifty-nine percent of entering freshmen hailed from the top 10 percent of their high school class, and 86 percent placed in the top quartile. Unweighted GPAs ranged from a 25th percentile 3.7 and a 75th percentile of 4.0. A decade ago, 39 percent of applicants gained acceptance, and the SAT range was 1170-1370, a clear signal that Richmond has significantly increased its level of selectivity in recent years.

The admissions committee holds GPA and the rigor of one's secondary school courses as the two most important factors in evaluating an applicant. Seven categories make up the second tier of still "important" factors. Those are standardized test scores, class rank, essays, recommendations, extracurricular activities, character/personal qualities, and talent/ability. Leadership and engagement in high school is sincerely valued by this committee as the Class of 2024 included 305 athletic captains/class presidents, 73 club founders, and 251 who worked part-time or completed an internship. Applying through early decision or early action is a good idea as the school is looking for applicants for whom Richmond is a genuine top choice. The school's yield rate is 23 percent, meaning 77 percent of admitted applicants head elsewhere. Thus, it's no wonder that 42 percent of the Class of 2023 was admitted via ED and those students enjoyed a 48 percent acceptance rate compared to 19 percent in the regular round.

Worth Your Money?

Richmond's cost of attendance exceeds $72,000, making a four-year degree list price of $288,000. Unlike many private universities, it only awards merit aid to only 21 percent of the population, but those students receive a sizable discount of $32k, on average. UR focuses most of its generosity on those with true financial need, issuing average annual grants of $46,186 to 42 percent of the undergraduate student body. Further, Richmond meets 100 percent of the demonstrated need for those who qualify for financial aid. A uniquely intimate undergraduate setting and solid starting salaries (particularly for business grads) make Richmond worth your money, despite the high price tag.

FINANCIAL
Institutional Type: Private
In-State Tuition: $56,860
Out-of-State Tuition: $56,860
Room & Board: $13,430
Required Fees: $0
Books & Supplies: $1,100

Avg. Need-Based Grant: $46,186
Avg. % of Need Met: 100%

Avg. Merit-Based Award: $31,587
% Receiving (All Freshmen): 21%
% Receiving (Freshmen w/o Need): 11%

Avg. Cumulative Debt: $28,341
% of Students Borrowing: 41%

CAREER
Who Recruits
1. Baker Tilly
2. BB&T Corporation
3. Dominion Energy
4. John Hancock
5. MAXIMUS

Notable Internships
1. Cushman & Wakefield
2. The Cohen Group
3. Citi

Top Industries
1. Business
2. Education
3. Operations
4. Sales
5. Finance

Top Employers
1. Capital One
2. Deloitte
3. Wells Fargo
4. PwC
5. EY

Where Alumni Work
1. Richmond
2. New Yprk City
3. Washington DC
4. Philadelphia
5. Boston

Median Earnings
College Scorecard (Early Career): $64,500
PayScale (Early Career): $62,000
PayScale (Mid-Career): $118,200

RANKINGS
Money: 114
U.S. News: 22 (T), Liberal Arts Colleges
Wall Street Journal/THE: 59 (T)
Washington Monthly: 39, Liberal Arts Colleges

COLLEGE OVERLAPS
Boston College
College of William & Mary
Georgetown University
University of Virginia
Wake Forest University

University of Rochester

Rochester, New York | 585-275-3221

From its founding in 1850, the University of Rochester established a national reputation as a strong research university. The adoption of its Renaissance Plan in 1995 instituted a uniquely open curriculum for a STEM-focused university, smaller class sizes, and a heavy investment in modernizing campus. Paying dividends today, those changes helped the school blossom into a world-class school that is home to 6,780 undergraduates and another 5,453 graduate students. U of R's seventy-five undergraduate majors offer students a chance at a rigorous yet flexible educational experience at a small liberal arts college within a renowned research institution.

Inside the Classroom

There are literally no required subjects at the University of Rochester's College of Arts, Sciences, and Engineering. Instead, students must, over their four years of study, take one writing-focused course of their choosing and twelve-credit clusters of courses in two of the following categories (whichever two do not encompass the student's major): humanities, social sciences, and natural sciences and engineering. Those course clusters are designed to ensure "substantive and integrated study," and there are 250+ to choose from, ensuring a high degree of autonomy in selecting one's academic path. The overarching goal of the curriculum is to best reflect the school's ideals of curiosity, competence, and community.

Rochester has maintained a 10:1 student-to-faculty ratio despite graduating 500 more undergraduate students last year than a decade prior. You will encounter some large lecture halls for introductory courses, but the most common class size is ten to nineteen students; 77 percent of sections enroll fewer than twenty. An impressive 77 percent of students are involved in undergraduate research, a strong indicator that opportunities for intimate learning experiences are plentiful. Approximately one-third of students take a semester abroad in one of the forty-five+ countries the university has an affiliation with.

Excellence is everywhere you look at Rochester. The Eastman School of Music is one of the best music conservatories in the United States. The Hajim School of Engineering & Applied Sciences is a top fifty institution. Other strong majors include mathematics, economics, and political science—each will open doors in their respective fields. And graduates are no strangers to prestigious fellowship programs. In 2020, Rochester produced eleven Fulbright Scholarship winners, as well as eighteen National Science Foundation Graduate Research Fellowship recipients.

Outside the Classroom

Ninety percent of undergrads reside in university-owned housing on the school's 154-acre main campus that is nestled around a bend of the Genesee River. First-years and sophomores are required to live on campus. The school's thirty-four fraternities and sororities entice 20-26 percent of the undergraduate student body into joining. Most Greek participants—85 percent—also are engaged with other student organizations. Twenty one NCAA Division III sports teams play as the YellowJackets while the university also boasts one of the largest club sports systems with forty registered club sports and over 1,100 members. There are more than 300 clubs with which undergrads can become involved including the Campus Times, a student-run newspaper in print since 1873 and a selection of top-notch a cappella groups. There are plenty of campus-wide events such as YellowJacket Weekend, a carnival that marks the start of the academic year, and great musical acts, speakers, and activists are regularly booked to provide cultural and entertainment opportunities without straying from school grounds. Harsh weather can make for long winters, but campus is always humming with some type of appealing activity. The closest major American city is Buffalo, but for the more adventurous, Toronto, Canada, is less than three hours by car.

Career Services

The Gwen M. Green Career Center for Career Education and Connections is staffed by twenty professionals with expertise in career education and advising, employer development, and event coordination. That number does not include the many peer advisors or administrative assistants. The University of Rochester's 339:1 student-to-advisor ratio is about average for institutions featured in this guide. Still, it manages to mostly achieve its stated aim of assisting students "in achieving their individual career goals while providing them with the resources and tools they need to develop connections between their aspirations, academic pursuits, and co-curricular experiences."

The Greene Center engages more than 500 organizations annually in recruiting and career education programs. The Spring Career and Internship Fair draws forty+ employers to campus including the US

Department of State, Epic Systems, the FBI, Citi, and Johnson & Johnson. The center also offers regular events, typically multiple workshops and information sessions per week. Events in May 2019 alone included a CV and resume workshop, a night with Kraft Heinz leadership, and a virtual career conversation about innovation in the workplace. Staff is happy to meet one-on-one to help students select and secure an internship that will be meaningful to their career development process. A near-perfect 95 percent of YellowJackets complete at least one internship during their undergraduate years; 75 percent complete two or more. You can also apply for a $1,000 to $2,500 alumni grant to help fund a summer internship that might not otherwise be possible. There are a significant number of opportunities for students to engage with UR alumni through structured programs, networking, and courses offered by the Greene Center.

Professional Outcomes

Six months after receiving their diplomas, 96 percent of Class of 2019 grads had achieved positive outcomes with 56 percent employed, and a notably high 40 percent already pursuing an advanced degree. Popular industries included higher education (14 percent), healthcare (14 percent), internet and software (11 percent), and hardware (4 percent). Top employers of 2019 grads included Amazon (9), Lockheed Martin (9), EY (5), and Goldman Sachs (5). Looking across all graduating years, significant numbers of Rochester alumni also can be found in the offices of IBM, Apple, and Microsoft. The average starting salary for the most recent cohort of grads was an impressive $58,229; that figure was over $77k for graduates of the Hajim School of Engineering and close to $50k for those in the School of Arts and Sciences. Upstate New York, New York City, Boston, DC, San Francisco, and Philadelphia play home to the greatest number of alumni.

With over two-fifths of grads jumping directly into a graduate program, many continue their studies at the University of Rochester (260) or at other elite East Coast institutions such as Columbia (17), Duke (13), NYU (12), and Carnegie Mellon (10). The university has an excellent premed reputation, and acceptance rates into MD programs are significantly higher than the national average. Thanks to the Rochester Early Medical Scholars program, some premed students are already on an eight-year pathway toward the completion of a medical degree at the University's School of Medicine and Dentistry. Two years ago, Rochester's own medical school accepted four members of, neighboring SUNY Buffalo took three, and SUNY Upstate welcomed two. Students matriculated into a wide range of law schools including top tier institutions like William & Mary, Emory, Boston University, the University of Wisconsin, and Indiana University.

Admission

The fight for a place in the Class of 2023 was record setting as it was the second time in the school's history that applications exceeded 20,000 and the acceptance rate hit 30 percent. Those who enrolled possessed an average GPA of 3.7 and an average SAT score of 1394. In 2020, the university moved from test-flexible to test-optional. Undergraduate applicants to the college may now decide which exam, if any, is an accurate representation of their ability and potential for success.

Interviews are strongly recommended as part of this holistic admissions process that seeks to "identify curious, capable, and engaged students from across the globe." In addition to stellar grades in a highly rigorous academic program, the committee wants to see evidence of leadership through extracurricular involvement as well as strong character/personal qualities. An all-time high of 510 students who were freshmen in 2019-20 were accepted via early decision, and the ED acceptance rate was 33 percent, giving early applicants slightly better odds than those in the regular round. Those accepted through binding ED comprise 37 percent of the overall freshman class. In sum, Rochester has never been more difficult to get into, so there is far less room for error than there was a generation ago.

Worth Your Money?

Including tuition, fees, room and board, and other estimated expenses, the total projected cost of attendance at this school is $78,042 per year. The good news is that virtually all of those who apply for need-based aid see 100 percent of their financial need met. While a $300,000 sticker price for a bachelor's degree is steep, the majority of students receive sizable discounts via need-based or merit aid. The average net price paid by families, even those in the top income bracket, is $37,900; those in the lowest brackets paid far less. Further, significant starting salaries and corporate connections allow YellowJackets to get a running start toward financial stability. For those who know what they want from their education (i.e., certain about major and career oriented), the University of Rochester is worth your money.

FINANCIAL
Institutional Type: Private
In-State Tuition: $58,208
Out-of-State Tuition: $58,208
Room & Board: $17,130
Required Fees: $0
Books & Supplies: $1,310

Avg. Need-Based Grant: $48,013
Avg. % of Need Met: 98%

Avg. Merit-Based Award: $15,845
% Receiving (All Freshmen): 26%
% Receiving (Freshmen w/o Need): 18%

Avg. Cumulative Debt: $28,503
% of Students Borrowing: 55%

CAREER
Who Recruits
1. Instagram
2. The Martin Agency
3. Goldman Sachs
4. CarMax
5. Citi

Notable Internships
1. Wegman's Food Markets
2. Lockheed Martin
3. SpaceX

Top Industries
1. Business
2. Education
3. Research
4. Healthcare
5. Engineering

Top Employers
1. Google
2. Apple
3. IBM
4. Amazon
5. Microsoft

Where Alumni Work
1. Rochester, NY
2. New York City
3. Boston
4. Washington DC
5. San Francisco

Median Earnings
College Scorecard (Early Career): $61,200
PayScale (Early Career): $66,600
PayScale (Mid-Career): $125,100

RANKINGS
Money: 197
U.S. News: 34, National Universities
Wall Street Journal/THE: 49
Washington Monthly: 68, National Universities

COLLEGE OVERLAPS
Boston College
Carnegie Mellon University
Cornell University
Northeastern University
Tufts University

University of San Diego

San Diego, California | 619-260-4506

ADMISSION
Admission Rate: 49%
Admission Rate - Men: 45%
Admission Rate - Women: 51%
EA Admission Rate: Not Offered
ED Admission Rate: Not Offered
ED Admits as % of Total Admits: Not Offered
Admission Rate (5-Year Trend): +2%
% of Admits Attending (Yield): 17%
Transfer Admission Rate: 68%

SAT Reading/Writing (Middle 50%): 600-680
SAT Math (Middle 50%): 590-690
ACT Composite (Middle 50%): 26-31

% Graduated in Top 10% of HS Class: 33%
% Graduated in Top 25% of HS Class: 74%
% Graduated in Top 50% of HS Class: 97%

Demonstrated Interest: Considered
Legacy Status: Important
Admission Interview Offered: Yes

ENROLLMENT
Total Undergraduate Enrollment: 5,919
% Part-Time: 3%
% Male: 44%
% Female: 56%
% Out-of-State: 39%
% Fraternity: 18%
% Sorority: 32%
% On-Campus (Freshman): 95%
% On-Campus (All Undergraduate): 44%

% African-American: 3%
% Asian: 7%
% Hispanic: 21%
% White: 49%
% Other: 7%
% Race or Ethnicity Unknown: 3%
% International: 8%
% Low-Income: 19%

ACADEMICS
Student-to-Faculty Ratio: 13 to 1
% of Classes Under 20: 61%
% of Classes 20-49: 39%
% of Classes 50 or More: 0%
% Full-Time Faculty: 50%
% Full-Time Faculty w/ Terminal Degree: 94%

Top Programs
Accountancy
Business
Communication Studies
Engineering
Finance
International Relations
Psychology

Retention Rate: 92%
4-Year Graduation Rate: 66%
6-Year Graduation Rate: 81%

Curricular Flexibility: Less Flexible
Academic Rating: ★★★✦

#CollegesWorthYourMoney

To anyone outside of the Golden State, it is easy to confuse the University of California, San Diego with the University of San Diego. Not only are the names similar, but they are just a 15-minute drive away from one another. Both are excellent schools, but the latter is a private, midsized university of approximately 5,900 undergraduate students while the former is a large public institution and part of the UC system. A Catholic university, USD was founded a few years after World War II and rapidly grew into a school with eight academic divisions, including its own law school. In addition to a number of fine (and popular) departments, the school is also admired for its aesthetics—the 180-acre grounds have been named the nation's most beautiful campus by more than one major publication.

Inside the Classroom
The San Diego core constitutes 14-17 classes, a sizable portion of one's undergraduate experience. Freshmen are required to take First-Year Writing, Mathematical Reasoning, and begin work on a foreign language, which they must take up until the 201 level (as many as four courses). The school's Catholic affiliation necessitates a dive into theological and religious inquiry, philosophical inquiry, and ethical inquiry. Other explorations into areas such as artistic inquiry, scientific and technological inquiry, and literary inquiry are also required. Lastly, all students must complete an advanced integration as a senior, which takes the form of a culminating project or learning experience.

You will find nary a large lecture course anywhere in this school. In fact, 97 percent of courses at USD contain 39 or fewer students. However, only 39 percent enroll fewer than 20 students. This university's student-to-faculty ratio is 13:1. If you desire to participate in undergraduate research, there is a faculty member willing to work with you, "regardless of major or class-standing." Students can participate through a number of formal on-campus programs like the Summer Undergraduate Research Experience or the McNair Scholars Program, which provides faculty mentors and stipends as support. The 135 study abroad programs in 44 countries attract an exceptional 70 percent of Toreros. The takeaway here is that it is almost impossible to get through a USD education without engaging in at least one hands-on program.

Business and accounting are the academic programs that receive the most acclaim at USD; they also attract, by some margin, the most undergraduates. Forty-one percent of degrees conferred fall under the business umbrella. The next most popular fields are biology (12 percent), social sciences (10 percent), engineering (9 percent), and communication/journalism (8 percent). Competitive postgraduate fellowships are not a focal point of this institution, and they do not regularly produce a significant number of recipients.

Outside the Classroom
Forty-six percent of 2019-20 freshmen hailed from out of state, and all were welcomed to a campus that has a high level of first-year cohesion; 95 percent live on campus in 11 separate living areas. Looking at the undergraduate student body as a whole, only 44 percent live in school-provided housing. Greek organizations soak up a fair number of students—18 percent of men and 32 percent of women. There are 8 national fraternity chapters at the school and 9 sorority chapters. Sports at the Division I level are engaged in by 17 teams. There are also 23 club teams, and many recreational clubs, and fitness classes. Ample faith-based and community service-oriented clubs are available as are a student-run newspaper, television station, and radio station. The amenities at USD are rated as highly as the overall gorgeousness of the grounds. Campus dining nets rave reviews for its quality and diversity of cuisines—Pavilion Dining offers authentic Mexican, Thai, Vietnamese, Mediterranean, and made-to-order sushi. Famed Mission Beach, Petco Park, the San Diego Zoo, endless shopping and dining options, as well as breathtaking natural sites like La Jolla Cove are all just minutes from campus.

Career Services
The well-staffed Career Development Center (CDC) at the University of San Diego employs 20 professional employees with roles in the areas of career counseling (by academic discipline), experiential learning, employer experience coordination, and alumni engagement. This excellent 295:1 counselor-to-student ratio allows the CDC to produce great results such as 94 percent of the Class of 2019 participating in at least one experiential learning activity (e.g., internship, community service, or research opportunity).

In a single year, this office manages to hold 3,124 in-person counseling appointments and bring 302 employers and 1,532 students to job fairs and information sessions. Over 10,000 contacts are made by students with employers via Handshake; there are more than 20,000 jobs and internships posted each year. Roughly 350 students embarked on Torero Treks where undergraduates visit alumni employed by major corporations in New York, Seattle, Portland, and Los Angeles. One-on-one assistance is always available whether you are sitting down with a counselor for a Myers-Briggs assessment as a freshman, getting connected with an alum for an internship heading into the summer after sophomore year, or polishing your resume prior to a job fair senior year. The University of San Diego has notably supportive career services offerings, well-above the average of schools featured in this guide, and these efforts directly translate into positive professional outcomes.

Professional Outcomes

Half a year after being handed their diplomas, 92 percent of University of San Diego graduates have found their next destination. Seventy percent of 2019 graduates were employed at a diverse range of employers such as PwC, The Walt Disney Company, the San Diego Padres, NBC Universal, and Tesla. Large numbers of alumni are also entrenched at the likes of Apple, Google, EY, Amazon, and Salesforce. The median starting salary for a USD grad entering the job market in 2019 was a healthy $58,000. Nearly one quarter entered the world of sales, marketing, finance, or accounting. The greatest number of alumni from all years can be found clustered in San Diego, with Los Angeles, San Francisco, Orange County, and New York the top runners-up.

Of the 18 percent of 2019 grads who immediately began pursuit of an advanced degree, 35 percent were studying business, 19 percent were seeking law degrees, 13 percent were in engineering programs, and another 13 percent were in health programs. Toreros from that graduating class gained acceptances into a wide range of universities, including some of the most prestigious in the country such as Cornell, Northwestern, the University of Michigan, Yale, Columbia, Stanford, and Johns Hopkins. Medical School acceptances included the Boston University School of Medicine, Indiana University School of Medicine, and the New York University School of Medicine. Law schools attended included UCLA, the University of Chicago, and the University of Michiga.

Admission

Accepting just under half of those who apply—49 percent—the University of San Diego is one of those rare schools that hasn't become more selective in recent years; two decades ago the acceptance rate was identical. The Class of 2023 possessed mid-50th percentile test scores of 1200-1350 on the SAT and 26-31 on the ACT. Sixty-nine percent of students submitted SAT results while 43 percent included ACT results. Most SAT scores were clustered between 1000 and 1400; just 15 percent scored above a 1400. Freshmen in the 2019-20 school year earned an average weighted high school GPA of 3.93, and 48 percent achieved greater than a 4.0. One third of this group placed in the top 10 percent of their class, and just a hair short of three quarters landed in the top quartile.

When making admissions selections in 2019, this school placed the greatest emphasis on high school class rigor, GPA, and standardized test scores. However, it elected to go fully test-optional beginning in 2020, a decision that was actually independent of the coronavirus pandemic. Factors rated as "important" were as follows: class rank, essay, recommendations, extracurricular activities, talent/ability, character/personal qualities, alumni relation, religious affiliation (remember, this is a Catholic institution), and volunteer work. Showing that you have genuine interest in attending is a must as this school has only a 17 percent yield rate. It does not offer an early decision option, so if USD is your first choice, make that known through direct communication with the admissions office and by applying on or before the December regular decision deadline.

Worth Your Money?

USD does not come cheap, as the annual cost of attendance for 2020-21 is just a couple hundred bucks shy of $70k. The financial aid situation at this school is decent; 52 percent of undergraduates receive need-based aid with an annual average award of $39,172. Solid starting salaries for graduates entering certain industries can make San Diego a viable option for those receiving minimal aid. For those entering the accounting/auditing, engineering and design, finance and banking, real estate, or technology fields, remuneration is likely to be high enough to be able to comfortably pay down any educational debt accrued.

FINANCIAL
Institutional Type: Private
In-State Tuition: $52,120
Out-of-State Tuition: $52,120
Room & Board: $15,156
Required Fees: $744
Books & Supplies: $1,080

Avg. Need-Based Grant: $33,573
Avg. % of Need Met: 80%

Avg. Merit-Based Award: $20,106
% Receiving (All Freshmen): 51%
% Receiving (Freshmen w/o Need): 20%

Avg. Cumulative Debt: $30,497
% of Students Borrowing: 45%

CAREER
Who Recruits
1. NBC Universal
2. General Atomics
3. Boeing
4. PwC
5. Tesla

Notable Internships
1. Adobe
2. San Diego Padres
3. San Diego Zoo

Top Industries
1. Business
2. Education
3. Operations
4. Sales
5. Finance

Top Employers
1. US Navy
2. Northrop Grumman
3. UC San Diego
4. Qualcomm
5. Wells Fargo

Where Alumni Work
1. San Diego
2. Los Angeles
3. San Francisco
4. Orange County, CA
5. New York City

Median Earnings
College Scorecard (Early Career): $60,000
PayScale (Early Career): $61,800
PayScale (Mid-Career): $120,600

RANKINGS
Money: 399
U.S. News: 88 (T), National Universities
Wall Street Journal/THE: 156 (T)
Washington Monthly: 111, National Universities

COLLEGE OVERLAPS
Loyola Marymount University
Pepperdine University
Santa Clara University
University of San Diego
University of San Francisco

University of South Carolina

Columbia, South Carolina | 803-777-7700

ADMISSION
Admission Rate: 69%
Admission Rate - Men: 70%
Admission Rate - Women: 68%
EA Admission Rate: NR
ED Admission Rate: Not Offered
ED Admits as % of Total Admits: Not Offered
Admission Rate (5-Year Trend): +3%
% of Admits Attending (Yield): 29%
Transfer Admission Rate: 64%

SAT Reading/Writing (Middle 50%): 600-680
SAT Math (Middle 50%): 580-690
ACT Composite (Middle 50%): 25-31

% Graduated in Top 10% of HS Class: 28%
% Graduated in Top 25% of HS Class: 59%
% Graduated in Top 50% of HS Class: 90%

Demonstrated Interest: Not Considered
Legacy Status: Not Considered
Admission Interview Offered: No

ENROLLMENT
Total Undergraduate Enrollment: 27,502
% Part-Time: 4%
% Male: 46%
% Female: 54%
% Out-of-State: 39%
% Fraternity: 22%
% Sorority: 33%
% On-Campus (Freshman): 94%
% On-Campus (All Undergraduate): 27%

% African-American: 8%
% Asian: 3%
% Hispanic: 5%
% White: 75%
% Other: 4%
% Race or Ethnicity Unknown: 1%
% International: 4%
% Low-Income: 18%

ACADEMICS
Student-to-Faculty Ratio: 17 to 1
% of Classes Under 20: 38%
% of Classes 20-49: 46%
% of Classes 50 or More: 16%
% Full-Time Faculty: 70%
% Full-Time Faculty w/ Terminal Degree: 90%

Top Programs
Criminology and Criminal Justice
Exercise Science
Finance
Information Science
International Business
Public Health
Sport and Entertainment Management

Retention Rate: 89%
4-Year Graduation Rate: 64%
6-Year Graduation Rate: 77%

Curricular Flexibility: Somewhat Flexible
Academic Rating: ★★★

#CollegesWorthYourMoney

Tired of competing for the USC acronym with the University of Southern California, the University of South Carolina has adopted its own abbreviated identity: UofSC. This newfound shortened identity is attached to a school with a long and storied history, having been founded during the Jefferson administration. The 2020 version of the UofSC is a massive enterprise, enrolling 27,500 undergraduate students and operating sixteen total colleges and schools within the larger university. This includes a law school and two medical schools.

Inside the Classroom
Voted the best first-year experience of any public college, the University of South Carolina knows how to welcome freshmen to Columbia. In fact, it essentially invented the first-year experience back in the early '70s. Today, the University 101 course fosters "a sense of belonging" and "promote(s) engagement in the curricular and co-curricular life of the university." The Carolina Core makes sure that all UofSC graduates are exposed to 10 essential areas such as scientific literacy; effective, engaged, and persuasive written communication; foreign language; and information literacy. These required areas of study account for at least 36 credit hours, depending on one's foreign language proficiency when entering the university. Students can elect to take up to two "overlay" courses that fulfill two requirements at once, creating a bit more overall curricular flexibility. Honors students must take 45 credits in designated honors courses and complete a thesis. The South Carolina Honors College is extremely hard to get into (more later) and is one of the finest in the entire country.

A 17:1 student-to-faculty ratio ensures that classes with single-digit enrollment will be a rarity during one's educational journey. Still, two-thirds of all sections contain 29 or fewer students, and only 16 percent enroll more than 50 individuals. The Office of Undergraduate Research will help ambitious students locate a mentor professor in their discipline, pursue funding sources, and compete for school-based undergraduate research awards. Study abroad opportunities are also there for all who seek them; 1,742 students studied abroad in 2018-19, and UofSC runs its own programs with faculty members in Costa Rica, the Galapagos, and Tuscany, Italy.

With the superb Darla Moore School of Business available, it's no surprise that almost 30 percent of students avail themselves of the opportunity to earn a degree in the business/marketing realm. The school's international business program recently took home the top spot in the US News rankings. Other disciplines in which the greatest number of degrees are conferred include health services (11 percent), biology (11 percent), engineering (8 percent), and communication and journalism (7 percent). A top producer of Fulbright students, the university saw six students win the award in 2016; a record 40 Gamecocks applied for a Fulbright the following year, and ten were named finalists.

Outside the Classroom
Greek life and athletics are dominant forces in the culture at this 359-acre main campus in downtown Columbia. Across all varsity programs, the Gamecocks draw 1.34 million fans annually and have won 11 individual and team national championships in the last decade. One third of all undergraduate women are members of sororities, and 22 percent of men join fraternities. The vast majority of freshmen, 94 percent, reside in the dorms while only 27 percent of the overall student population remain on campus. You can certainly find a big-school party scene at UofSC, but there is much more to daily life at this school. The Leadership and Service Center supports over 500 student-run clubs in the categories of intramural sports, games, dance, academics, and more. Carolina Productions coordinates on-campus entertainment and manages to book major live acts and screenings of hit movies. Located within a mile of the statehouse, the campus is situated right in the heart of the city. Everything from art museums to escape rooms to music venues are within a short walk from the dorms.

Career Services
There are 25 professional staff members within the University of South Carolina Career Center, many of whom focus on career counseling, experiential education, and employer relations. This 1100:1 ratio is significantly higher than the average school selected for this guidebook. Fortunately, resources are plentiful to put on meaningful large-scale events like career fairs. Discipline-specific fairs in the fall of 2020 (all virtual, of course) included those focused on STEM, corporate careers, government and public service, health and wellness, and professional schools and graduate programs. Handshake can be utilized at any point in time to locate internships and begin the job hunt. On-campus interview opportunities are arranged through this platform as well.

Students have access to unique programs like the Carolina Internship Program that allows undergrads to complete an internship or co-op during the school year while maintaining full-time student status. South Carolina grads who completed an internship while at the school reported earning $7k more in annual starting salary than those who did not. The School of Business has forged partnerships with companies such as FedEx, Ipsos, Crayola, ESPN, and Coca Cola. Staff are always willing to assist with the internship/job search, prep for interviews, explore graduate school options, or help sharpen your resume. Overall, this university is not going to hold your hand through the career development process, but those who are assertive and proactive will find all the resources they need to prepare for their postgraduation launch.

Professional Outcomes

The last available outcomes data is from 2017, which reported the average starting salary for Gamecocks as $47,687. The top employers of that class included KPMG, IBM, Aramark, Bank of America, Vanguard, PwC, and Marriot. Additional companies employing 100 or more UofSC-affiliated alumni are Wells Fargo, Amazon, Colonial Life, EY, Merrill Lynch, and Microsoft. Suffice it to say, no matter at which multinational corporation you are seeking employment, you are likely to find a solid number of South Carolina alumni. While 44 percent of graduates remain in South Carolina, many also relocate to Charlotte; Atlanta; Washington, DC; and New York City.

As is the case at many large public universities, the majority of those continuing their studies in a graduate/professional degree program did so right at the University of South Carolina. Duke and Wake Forest are also frequent landing spots for those seeking an advanced degree. In 2019-20, there were 264 applicants to various med schools from the university. Seventy-two percent of honors students who apply to medical school are accepted. The most frequently attended medical school was the Medical University of South Carolina. The most commonly attended law school was the University of South Carolina Law School.

Admission

The University of South Carolina's 69 percent acceptance rate for the Class of 2023 should be encouraging for students looking for an excellent public institution that does not close its doors to students with SATs below the 90th percentile of all test takers. In fact, midrange scores are 1200-1350 on the SAT and 25-30 on the ACT. On academic performance, the school does expect a little bit closer to perfection as the mid-50th percentile range for weighted GPA is 3.78-4.50. Twenty-eight percent of 2019-20 freshmen placed in the top decile of their high school class, and 59 percent were in the top quarter. An incredible 64 percent had GPAs above 4.0, which is both impressive and raises suspicion that grade inflation is rampant in South Carolina high schools. Those admitted to the Honors College possess an average GPA of 4.71 and an SAT range of 1460-1530.

Three factors are paramount in the eyes of South Carolina admissions officers: rigor of secondary school record, GPA, and standardized test scores. If you check all three boxes, your admission is virtually assured. There are zero factors deemed "important" to the process, and "considered" factors include class rank, essays, recommendations, extracurricular activities, talent/ability, character/personal qualities, first-generation status, state residency, racial/ethnic status, and volunteer/paid work experience. The committee also states that it values factors like military experience, writing ability, and "the applicant's potential for contribution to a diverse educational environment." Students can choose to apply early action by the October 15 deadline, but there is little admissions-related advantage to doing so.

Worth Your Money?

South Carolina residents pay a total cost of attendance of slightly above $26,000 while non-residents, which make up 44 percent of the student body, pay $47,000+. The Palmetto State charges more for its public colleges than many fellow Southern states like North Carolina and Florida. Still, by nationwide standards, UofSC's price is not, by any means, out of bounds. Those who qualify for financial aid receive an average grant of roughly $6,800. If you live in a neighboring state, with a more affordable price tag, then there are limited circumstances where crossing state lines would make sense. For residents, South Carolina is a solid investment that generally leads to positive postgraduation outcomes.

FINANCIAL
Institutional Type: Public
In-State Tuition: $12,688
Out-of-State Tuition: $33,928
Room & Board: $11,006
Required Fees: $0
Books & Supplies: $1,065

Avg. Need-Based Grant: $6,767
Avg. % of Need Met: 77%

Avg. Merit-Based Award: $5,947
% Receiving (All Freshmen): 89%
% Receiving (Freshmen w/o Need): 38%

Avg. Cumulative Debt: $30,449
% of Students Borrowing: 52%

CAREER
Who Recruits
1. Collins Aerospace
2. Seibels
3. Boeing
4. Prisma Health
5. Cigna

Notable Internships
1. Becton, Dickinson and Co.
2. Enterprise Holdings
3. Sands Investment Group

Top Industries
1. Business
2. Education
3. Operations
4. Sales
5. Healthcare

Top Employers
1. Wells Fargo
2. Bank of America
3. Amazon
4. PwC
5. Boeing

Where Alumni Work
1. Columbia, SC
2. Charlotte
3. Greenville, SC
4. Charleston, SC
5. Atlanta

Median Earnings
College Scorecard (Early Career): $44,900
PayScale (Early Career): $53,800
PayScale (Mid-Career): $93,600

RANKINGS
Money: 317
U.S. News: 118 (T), National Universities
Wall Street Journal/THE: 289 (T)
Washington Monthly: 214, National Universities

COLLEGE OVERLAPS
Clemson University
College of Charleston
North Carolina State University
University of Alabama
University of Georgia

University of Southern California

Los Angeles, California | 213-740-1111

A few decades back, if you told someone in-the-know about college admissions that the University of Southern California would eventually be in the same league with UC Berkeley, they would likely have concluded that an asteroid was headed for the San Francisco Bay area. At that time, USC was stereotyped as a lily-white school for wealthy underachievers that accepted the majority of applicants. Today, the home of the Trojans is one of the premier private research universities in the country, enriched by a diverse pool of students from around the globe and sporting a lower acceptance rate than Georgetown, Tufts, Washington University in St. Louis and—to bring things full circle—Berkeley.

Inside the Classroom

There are 130 undergraduate majors and minors within the Dornslife College of Arts & Sciences alone, the University's oldest and largest school. Graduation requirements are a fairly run-of-the-mill assortment of selections across the major disciplines. By degrees conferred, the most popular areas of study are business (25 percent), social sciences (12 percent), visual and performing arts (12 percent), engineering (9 percent), and communications/journalism (8 percent).

At an institution with 20,351 undergraduates and 27,970 graduate students you would not expect to find many tiny seminar courses with single-digit enrollments, but 17 percent of classes at USC do, in fact, meet that standard. The bulk of courses offered are in the ten to nineteen range, but you also will find yourself in a fair share of large lecture halls in your time at USC. Still, there is little anonymity in a Trojan education. Aided by a favorable 8:1 student-to-faculty ratio, the school does an excellent job facilitating undergraduate research opportunities. Each school/college has a course entitled Directed Research 490 in which students work closely with a faculty supervisor and earn between two and eight credits as well as countless opportunities to get their hands dirty in academic research.

All programs within the Marshall School of Business and Viterbi School of Engineering are highly acclaimed and have far-reaching reputations with employers and elite grad schools (more on both later). Programs in communication, the cinematic arts, and the performing arts carry sterling reputations as well. Students are quite competitive in the race for elite postgraduate fellowships. In the last decade, the university has produced 100+ Fulbright Student Grant Recipients. The Class of 2019 saw four Boren winners, four Critical Language Scholarship recipients, and multiple winners of NSF awards and Gilman Scholarships.

Outside the Classroom

While most Trojans live on campus as freshmen, the majority of upperclassmen reside in the surrounding neighborhoods and commute to school. That is not entirely a matter of choice; USC offers limited university-owned housing options, only enough to accommodate 30 percent of its undergraduate population. Fortunately, the school recently opened eight new residential houses which, collectively, increased its capacity by 24 percent. Greek life is thriving at USC with a 26 percent participation rate in over sixty sororities/fraternities. The Trojans beloved football team takes center stage each fall, attracting 93,000 fans each Saturday. There are nineteen additional NCAA Division I sports teams fielded by the university as well as a massive club sports operation with 2,500+ participants. Over 1,000 student organizations are active, including popular choices like student government, cultural groups, and performance troupes. USC's LA location ensures that there is never a dearth of excitement and adventure. Within a few miles of campus are countless museums, the Staples Center, multiple theaters, and all the nightlife you could desire. Being in LA has other perks—major musical acts and guest speakers from Barack Obama to alum Will Ferrell appear at the university on a regular basis. The Visions & Voices program provides free cultural events multiple times per week that draw rave reviews from the student body.

Career Services

The University of Southern California Career Center only represents a portion of the career counseling received by Trojan undergrads as additional, more specialized experts are embedded within every undergraduate college. For example, seven professionals provide counseling only to engineering students, and six work exclusively with Annenberg students. In total, there are forty-nine full-time staff members working in counseling, employer relations, and recruiting, equating to a 415:1 student-to-counselor ratio, within the average range of institutions profiled in this book. Yet, that ratio may be the only thing that could be labelled ordinary about this highly accomplished Career Center.

On-campus recruiting at USC is extraordinary with 275 employers granting on-site interviews. In a given year, over 3,100 students participate in 5,300+ job interviews at the university. The companies recruiting on campus make for an impressive list, even if you only highlighted those that start with "A"—Adobe Systems, Accenture, Amazon, Apple, and AT&T. Outreach efforts are successful as career services engages with 6,400 students via 1:1 counseling appointments and has just shy of 10,000 attendees at workshops and other events. Large events include the Fall Career Fair that brings 200+ employers to campus, and every school has its own concentrated fairs in areas such as architecture, engineering, and pre-law. A strong alumni network of more than 437,000 is another useful resource for fresh graduates.

Professional Outcomes

USC does not release outcomes data for its graduating classes as a whole, but an examination of school-specific destinations for recent grads reveals a rosy picture. Annenberg graduates find employment at a 96-100 percent rate within six months of graduation. Alumni at the Viterbi School of Engineering are well represented at any major technology company you can name from Apple to Yahoo! and the average starting salary is $87k. The school cracked College Transitions' list of the best engineering feeder schools, sending an extremely high percentage of graduates to the most desirable employers. USC also made our list of top feeders to the tech industry alongside institutions like Caltech, MIT, and Stanford. Presently, there are between 300 and 1,500 alumni employed at each of Google, Amazon, Apple, Microsoft, Facebook, Cisco, Netflix, and Salesforce. Half of all alumni reside in the Los Angeles area while San Francisco, Orange County, and New York City are next in popularity.

Information on the graduate schools members of recent classes have attended is not published by the university (they have only recently begun to track that information). However, what can be gleaned from other sources paints a highly positive picture. College Transitions' extensive analysis of LinkedIn data revealed that the University of Southern California is one of the most prolific producers of students accepted into the T14 Law Schools. The good news doesn't stop there; the university also ranks as one of the leading producers of students accepted into top MBA programs like Wharton, Booth, and Tuck.

Admission

USC admissions (and those at several other schools) made front-page headlines for months on end in 2019 as part of the "Varsity Blues" scandal that saw famous actresses and powerful businesspeople cheating and bribing their way into the university. Interestingly, you probably wouldn't have seen people cheating their way into USC a decade ago. Admission into USC has become significantly more challenging in recent years. In 2019, of 66,198 wanna-be Trojans, only 7,558 were accepted, equating to an all-time low acceptance rate of 11 percent. The SAT range of the Class of 2023 was 1370-1520, and the ACT range was 31-34. On a 4.0 scale, the average high school GPA was 3.81. Those figures are slightly higher than in previous years.

To have a legitimate chance here, being in the top 10 percent of your high school class is likely a necessity as 88 percent of those in the freshman class held that distinction; 96 percent were in the top quartile. There are no unusual factors designated as "most important" by the admissions staff, but rigor of curriculum, grades, test scores, essays, and recommendations reign supreme. USC does not have an early action/early decision option, so all candidates are in the same boat. Legacy students, called "scions," make up a significant portion of the student body—19 percent. There is definitely an edge available for those with Trojan lineage. Those from a generation ago, including USC alumni now hoping to shepherd their own children into their alma mater, may find the current level of selectivity a complete and utter shock. For additional perspective, twenty years ago, 45 percent of applicants were accepted, and the average SAT score was over 200 points lower than it is for today's enrollees.

Worth Your Money?

At over $79,000, there is nothing shocking about the annual cost of attendance at USC; it's pretty standard these days for a private university. Where it does seem outrageously high is when you see that amount is twice the cost of any of the elite University of California schools such as Berkley or UCLA. Still, many pay less than the list price as 56 percent of current undergraduates receive merit aid awards averaging $20k per year, and 38 percent of the student population is granted need-based aid to the tune of $43k per year. Further, many USC grads go on to lucrative careers that are enhanced by the school's employer/graduate school connections as well as those of the well-connected alumni base. Those factors make this college worth your money unless, in the words of Olivia Jade Giannulli, you "don't really care about school" but "do want the experience of, like, game days, partying . . ." Sorry, couldn't resist.

FINANCIAL
Institutional Type: Private
In-State Tuition: $58,133
Out-of-State Tuition: $58,133
Room & Board: $15,916
Required Fees: $939
Books & Supplies: $1,200

Avg. Need-Based Grant: $42,820
Avg. % of Need Met: 102%

Avg. Merit-Based Award: $19,827
% Receiving (All Freshmen): 56%
% Receiving (Freshmen w/o Need): 26%

Avg. Cumulative Debt: $28,434
% of Students Borrowing: 31%

CAREER
Who Recruits
1. FTI Consulting
2. Moss Adams
3. Cornerstone Research
4. Nike
5. Universal Creative

Notable Internships
1. Dow Jones
2. Tesla
3. The Blackstone Group

Top Industries
1. Business
2. Education
3. Engineering
4. Operations
5. Media

Top Employers
1. Google
2. Amazon
3. Apple
4. Microsoft
5. Facebook

Where Alumni Work
1. Los Angeles
2. San Francisco
3. Orange County, CA
4. New York City
5. San Diego

Median Earnings
College Scorecard (Early Career): $74,000
PayScale (Early Career): $68,200
PayScale (Mid-Career): $130,800

RANKINGS
Money: 156
U.S. News: 24 (T), National Universities
Wall Street Journal/THE: 19
Washington Monthly: 53, National Universities

COLLEGE OVERLAPS
Cornell University
New York University
Stanford University
University of California, Berkeley
University of California, Los Angeles

Austin, Texas | 512-475-7399

A ridiculously affordable flagship university that also happens to be one of the top public schools in the United States, the University of Texas at Austin serves up a quality undergraduate education on a massive scale. The school's 40,163 undergraduates enjoy a dizzying 150+ distinct degree programs and 12,400+ annual course offerings. Austin itself is a progressive city that has wide appeal, even to coastal dwellers; however, thanks to the automatic admission granted to all Texas students in the top 6 percent of their high school class, the university remains 87 percent Texas residents.

Inside the Classroom

Each year 175 freshmen are admitted into the elite Plan II Honors Program, an interdisciplinary major created in 1935. One of the best honors programs in the country, Plan II students enjoy small class sizes and are required to complete a senior thesis. The school also offers its Liberal Arts Honors Program to an additional 130 students each year. All students must complete forty-two credit hours in the statewide core curriculum. That entails a first-year Signature Course in a small seminar environment, two English composition courses, one humanities course, two classes in American and Texas government, two in US history, one in the behavioral and social sciences, one in mathematics, three in the natural sciences, and one in the visual and performing arts.

An 18:1 student-to-faculty ratio and almost 11,000 graduate students on campus render across-the-board tiny class sizes an impossibility. While 37 percent of course sections enroll nineteen or fewer students, almost one-quarter of classes are filled with over fifty students. Opportunities for undergraduate research vary by school. An impressive 90 percent of engineering students conduct research or intern during their four years of study; others must compete for slots in programs such as the Freshman Research Initiative, Summer Research Scholars, or use the Eureka database to find individual professors offering research assistantships. A robust study abroad program boasts 400 offerings in 103 foreign countries; and saw 4,421 undergrads participate in a single recent year.

The Cockrell School of Engineering is one of the most heralded undergraduate engineering schools around, while The McCombs School of Business cracks just about any top ten list and dominates in the specialty areas of accounting and marketing. UT's computer science department is also top-ranked, and regularly sends graduates to the world's best tech companies (see more below). In terms of sheer volume of degrees conferred, engineering is number one (13 percent) followed by business (12 percent), social sciences (12 percent), journalism/communications (11 percent), and biology (11 percent). Prestigious fellowship organizations love UT Austin grads just as much as employers do; in 2020, the school produced an impressive 13 Fulbright Scholars.

Outside the Classroom

You won't find many schools in this book where so few undergraduates live on campus. Only 18 percent of the total student body—67 percent of freshmen—reside on the 431-acre campus. The bulk of students live in three nearby neighborhoods: Downtown Austin, East Austin, and West Campus (which is not actually part of campus). There are more than seventy Greek organizations at UT Austin with sororities attracting 17 percent of women and fraternities enlisting 13 percent of men. Sports are a way of life at this institution. Approximately 500 student athletes compete on twenty teams in NCAA Division I competition. Since 1949, the school has captured fifty-one national championships. Texas Memorial Stadium packs in 100,000+ on football Saturdays. In excess of 1,300 student organizations includes hundreds of intramural and club sports options and a sprawling media network of newspapers, magazines, television, and radio stations to ensure that no interest goes unaccounted for. The city of Austin, a liberal enclave in a conservative state, is a perennial darling of "Best Places to Live" and "Best College Towns" lists. Few complain of boredom in a city with all the live music, good food, and culture one can handle.

Career Services

There are fifteen career centers on the UT Austin campus, eleven of which cater to undergraduate students as well as the Vick Center for Strategic Advising and Career Counseling that serves undeclared students. With fifty-two full-time employees devoted to undergrads across those eleven career centers, the university offers a 772:1 student-to-counselor ratio, higher than many of the schools featured in this guide yet slightly better than average among universities close to UT's size. Some undergraduate schools offer more support than others. For example, there are twelve staff members dedicated to undergraduates in the McCombs School of Business but only two in the School of Education.

The scope of the offerings is overwhelming, as would be expected at a school with more than 40,000 under-graduates. For example, the most recent Fall Science and Technology Career Fair drew 201 employers and

2,500 students. The Spring Communication Job & Internship Fair welcomes up to eighty-five employers and 1,000 students. In a single year, the McCombs College of Business Career Expo featured 180+ corporations. Over one hundred employers engage in on-campus recruiting/interviewing with Texas Engineering students every year. Like many universities of its size, UT Austin cannot offer the hand-holding provided by many smaller liberal arts colleges, but it does provide plenty of on-campus networking opportunities for those bold enough to take advantage.

Professional Outcomes

Six months after graduating, 48 percent Longhorns are employed, 25 percent have entered graduate school, and 17 percent are still seeking their next opportunity. The for-profit sector attracts 68 percent of those employed, 18 percent pursue jobs at a nonprofit, and 14 percent enter public sector employment. At a school with nearly half a million living alumni, there is no shortage of major corporations that employ more than 500 UT Austin grads. In the tech realm Google, Facebook, Oracle, Microsoft, IBM, and Apple all meet that qualification, and giants such as Accenture, Amazon, and Uber also employ hundreds of Longhorns. Austin remains home for the largest number of graduates with the Houston, Dallas, and San Antonio areas next in popularity. Plenty of alumni also can be found in New York City and San Francisco. Starting salaries were solid and, as would be expected, fluctuated significantly by major. Business majors took home a median income of $76,000 while chemistry majors earned $46,000 and journalism majors had a median figure of $36,000.

University of Texas at Austin undergraduates go on to pursue advanced degrees in massive numbers with one-quarter electing to continue their educational journey right after completing their bachelor's. Many pursue advanced study at UT Austin itself, which offers more than one hundred graduate programs. Medical school acceptance rates hover around 55 percent, which is above the national average. The sheer volume of med school applicants is incredible; more than 900 seniors apply each year. The university's own Dell Medical School, founded in 2016, is a common destination as are other Texas-based institutions like UT-Houston, UT-San Antonio, and Baylor. Others land at premier medical schools, including Harvard, Georgetown, and UVA, each year. No matter what advanced degree you choose to pursue, an impressive UT Austin transcript can open doors to any institution in the country.

Admission

Longhorn hopefuls totaled 53,525 in the 2019 admissions cycle, almost 30,000 more than at the break of the new millennium. At that time the acceptance rate exceeded 60 percent; it is now only 32 percent. Among 2019-20 freshmen, the mid-50 percent standardized test scores were 1240-1470 on the SAT and 27-33 on the ACT. The vast majority were situated in the top 10 percent of their high school classes—87 percent earned such a distinction—and 96 percent were in the top quartile. The UT system has kept "outsiders" from making up a large percentage of the student body as 87 percent of current students hail from the Lone Star State. The school's policy of automatically accepting students from the top 6 percent of any Texas high school keeps quality homegrown freshmen pouring through the gates. There were an astounding 424 valedictorians and 284 salutatorians in the most recent cohort. Applicants to UT's business, computer science, and engineering majors will face the stiffest competition; earning entry typically requires Ivy-like credentials, especially if you're from out of state.

The university ranks pretty much every admissions factor as "very important," but it's safe to say that with such an onslaught of applications each year the hard numbers of standardized test scores, GPA, and class rank are most essential. There is no early round at UT Austin, so all applicants are in the same boat. The school has no interest in demonstrated interest on the part of applicants because it enjoys a relatively high yield rate approaching 50 percent. While the school accepts roughly 2,100 transfer students per year, that's only 28 percent of those who apply. That differs greatly from many other elite state universities where transferring is much easier than getting admitted directly out of high school. The University of Texas at Austin is the flagship school of the UT system and among the largest genuinely elite schools in the entire country. Texas residency, top-of-the-class academic performance, and solid test scores give you the best chance to get in.

Worth Your Money?

An annual in-state cost of attendance of $28k-$31k for a UT Austin degree is one of the best bargains anywhere in the country. In addition, 46 percent of undergrads qualify for need-based aid with average grants that are a hair over $10,000. Out of state, the sticker price for full COA is $55k-$63k, not an unreasonable sum for what you'll receive, particularly if you are majoring in business, engineering, or computer science. If you are a resident of Texas, there are no qualifiers—UT Austin is unquestionably worth every dollar.

FINANCIAL
Institutional Type: Public
In-State Tuition: $10,824
Out-of-State Tuition: $38,326
Room & Board: $11,812
Required Fees: $0
Books & Supplies: $700

Avg. Need-Based Grant: $9,958
Avg. % of Need Met: 74%

Avg. Merit-Based Award: $2,221
% Receiving (All Freshmen): 36%
% Receiving (Freshmen w/o Need): 2%

Avg. Cumulative Debt: $24,263
% of Students Borrowing: 40%

CAREER
Who Recruits
1. Shell
2. General Electric
3. Affigen, LLC
4. Merck
5. SnapStream

Notable Internships
1. Visa
2. Uber
3. Boeing

Top Industries
1. Business
2. Education
3. Engineering
4. Operations
5. Sales

Top Employers
1. IBM
2. Google
3. Microsoft
4. Accenture
5. Amazon

Where Alumni Work
1. Austin
2. Houston
3. Dallas
4. San Antonio
5. San Francisco

Median Earnings
College Scorecard (Early Career): $58,200
PayScale (Early Career): $63,800
PayScale (Mid-Career): $120,600

RANKINGS
Money: 29
U.S. News: 42 (T), National Universities
Wall Street Journal/THE: 61
Washington Monthly: 77, National Universities

COLLEGE OVERLAPS
Southern Methodist University
Rice University
Texas A&M University - College Station
University of Michigan
University of California, Berkeley

University of Virginia

Charlottesville, Virginia | 434-982-3200

When Thomas Jefferson helped to found the University of Virginia in 1819, our nation's third president did more than just assist in securing the funds—he also personally designed some of the campus' now famous architecture, planned the curriculum, and recruited the first faculty members. As the so-called "father" of the school, Jefferson would undoubtedly be thrilled with what his progeny has gone on to achieve. Two hundred years after its first cornerstone was laid, UVA has become one of the most iconic public universities in the United States where state residents can get an Ivy-level education at a bargain price.

Inside the Classroom
Undergrads can study within one of seven colleges/schools: the College of Arts & Sciences, the School of Engineering and Applied Science, McIntire School of Commerce, the School of Architecture, the School of Nursing, the Batten School of Leadership & Public Policy, and the Curry School of Education. Within the College of Arts & Sciences, undergraduates must complete 30 credits worth of Area Requirements broken down as follows: Natural Science and Mathematics (12), Social Sciences (6), Humanities (6), Historical Studies (3), and Non-Western Perspectives (3). Further Competency Requirements include a First Writing Requirement, Second Writing Requirement, and a Foreign Language Requirement. The 225-250 students per freshman class who are selected for the Echols Scholars Program are not bound by any competency or area requirements.

The University of Virginia sports a 14:1 student-to-faculty ratio, a very strong figure for a large public institution. As such, the school is able to offer many small classes like you would find an elite liberal arts college. In fact, 16 percent of sections boast a single-digit enrollment and 53 percent contain 19 or fewer students. Undergraduate research opportunities can be challenging to uncover at any large school where graduate students get the prime spots, yet, UVA does offer a multitude of opportunities. To cite examples, every single engineering major completes one major research project, the biology department has 230 students each semester participating research, and physics students are given the chance to get their names on published work. The classroom at UVA extends well beyond Charlottesville as one-third of the Class of 2019 took a semester abroad in one of 65 countries around the world.

The two most commonly conferred degree areas of in liberal arts/general studies (19 percent) and the social sciences (16 percent). Engineering (12 percent), business/marketing (8 percent), and biology (7 percent), are next in sheer popularity. The McIntire School of Commerce has a glowing reputation in the finance/accounting realm and the School of Engineering and Applied Science is just as highly-respected. Other notable departmental strengths include computer science, economics, and political philosophy, policy, and law. Cavaliers are extremely competitive in the pursuit of prestigious national scholarships as well. The Class of 2020 produced 22 Fulbright Scholars, five Critical Language Scholars, and a Marshall Scholar.

Outside the Classroom
Just 39 percent of all students live on UVA's campus, although 100 percent of freshman do reside on school's vast 1,682-acre grounds. Greek life is popular as 28 percent of men and 31 percent of women sign up for fraternity and sorority life. The Cavaliers compete in 27 varsity sports teams (13 men's and 14 women's) in the Atlantic Coast Conference. Approximately 2,100 students are members of 65 club sports teams and many others participate in intramural athletics. As you would expect at such a large institution, there are 1,000+ clubs available in everything from acrobatics to high powered rocketry; the process of joining some of the more competitive clubs can be fierce (i.e. the University Judiciary Committee). A cappella is a beloved pastime at the school and there are countless groups to consider. Outside of being the site of a disturbing rally in 2017, Charlottesville is generally considered to be one of the most student-friendly college towns. There is no shortage of culture, craft breweries, and outdoor recreation opportunities. Plenty of Jefferson and Madison-related history can be explored nearby and a trip to the state capital of Richmond will take you just over an hour. Those looking to fly home for the holidays will enjoy the convenience of having the Charlottesville-Albemarle Airport just eight miles from campus.

Career Services
The UVA Career Center employs 43 full-time staff members giving them a student-to-advisor ration of 396:1, which is in the average range compared to schools in this guide and a very respectable level of support for a school of the University of Virginia's size. This well-resourced office encourages one-on-one appointments, has ample drop-in hours, daily "Coffee Chats with Career Counselors," and hosts regular "Career Communities" that help students interested in a specific field like Business & Technology or Science and Sustainability."

In a typical year, over 20 percent of those finding employment are connected to their job directly by career services staff/Handshake and another 8-10 percent heard about the opportunity at a Career Services-sponsored career fair. The University hosts large scale general career fairs in the fall and spring as well many discipline-specific events. The Engineering, Science, and Technology Career Fair attracts over 2,000 students and 230 companies each year. According to the most recent statistics available, 40 percent of undergraduates land at least one paid internship and close to 50 percent have an unpaid workplace experience. There are close to a quarter of a million Cavalier alumni and many are happy to help current students find internships, employment, or offer some level of mentorship. Each year, more than 1,000 alums return to campus for this purpose.

Professional Outcomes

Sixty-seven percent of the Class of 2019 immediately joined the workforce upon receiving their degree while 15 percent headed directly to graduate school; 15 percent of graduates were still looking for their next destination. Industries attracting the greatest number of freshly-minted graduates were Internet & Software (13 percent), K-12 Education (10 percent), and Management Consulting (8 percent). The companies who scooped up the greatest number of 2019 graduates were Deloitte (55), Capital One (49), and Microsoft (29). The average starting salary for those finding employment was a robust $63k. Large numbers of recent graduates migrate to Washington DC and New York City and many others head to Boston, San Francisco, Seattle, Charlotte, and Atlanta.

Among the 2019 grads who decided to continue their education, 228 enrolled in an advanced degree program at UVA—the next most popular destinations were Virginia Commonwealth University (25), Columbia University (13), Georgetown University (13), and George Washington University (9). In recent years, medical school graduation for Cavaliers have beaten national averages. In the last six years, UVA applicants to MD programs have enjoyed between a 52-60 percent acceptance rate versus the national average range of 42-45 percent. Virginia grads head to a wide range of medical colleges including the nation's best like Johns Hopkins, Emory, Cornell, Harvard, Tufts, and Georgetown.

Admission

The University of Virginia received 40,839 applications for a place in their Class of 2023, more than double the number received in 2005. Just 24 percent of this this group were welcomed into the freshman class of 2019-20. Those that went on to attend the university possessed mid-50 percent SAT scores of 1340-1500; the ACT range was 30-34. Nine out of every ten freshman earned a place in top decile of their high school class and 98 percent landed in the top quartile. A stunning 97 percent of this cohort earned better than a 3.75 GPA and only 1 percent had less than a 3.5.

Six factors are rated by the UVA committee as being "very important" to the admissions process headlined by state residency. The school offers admission to 36 percent of locals but just 19 percent hailing from outside of the state. In seeking to maintain at least a two-thirds majority of Virginians, the student body is presently comprised of two-thirds state residents. Other highly-ranked factors included: rigor of secondary school record, class rank, GPA, recommendations, and character/personal qualities. Criteria ranked as still "important" include: standardized test scores, the application essay, extracurricular activities, and talent/ability. Early decision was just added back into the equation for the 2019-20 admissions cycle and the acceptance rate was 33 percent.

Worth Your Money?

A rare public university that meets 100 percent of all students' demonstrated financial need, UVA serves up an average of $24,625 per year to qualifying students. Roughly one-third of students take out loans and the mean amount of debt for those individuals is $26k, less than the average college graduate in the country. Residents of Virginia pay an annual cost of attendance of just $34k while out-of-state undergrads are met with a COA of almost $70,000. This school, with its sparkling national reputation and strong graduate outcomes, is worth your money either way, but the real bargain is enjoyed by those whose taxes help fund the university.

FINANCIAL
Institutional Type: Public
In-State Tuition: $15,848
Out-of-State Tuition: $49,825
Room & Board: $12,350
Required Fees: $3,120
Books & Supplies: $1,356

Avg. Need-Based Grant: $24,625
Avg. % of Need Met: 100%

Avg. Merit-Based Award: $3,726
% Receiving (All Freshmen): 1%
% Receiving (Freshmen w/o Need): 0%

Avg. Cumulative Debt: $26,023
% of Students Borrowing: 33%

CAREER
Who Recruits
1. Yext
2. Pariveda
3. Oak Hill Advisors
4. Altria
5. Harris Williams & Co.

Notable Internships
1. Strategic Investment Group
2. NBCUniversal
3. Proctor & Gamble

Top Industries
1. Business
2. Education
3. Operations
4. Research
5. Engineering

Top Employers
1. Capital One
2. Deloitte
3. EY
4. Google
5. Accenture

Where Alumni Work
1. Washington DC
2. Charlottesville, VA
3. New York City
4. Richmond, VA
5. San Francisco

Median Earnings
College Scorecard (Early Career): $61,200
PayScale (Early Career): $67,900
PayScale (Mid-Career): $131,200

RANKINGS
Money: 6
U.S. News: 26 (T), National Universities
Wall Street Journal/THE: 51
Washington Monthly: 28, National Universities

COLLEGE OVERLAPS
College of William & Mary
Duke University
University of North Carolina at Chapel Hill
University of Pennsylvania
Virginia Tech

University of Washington — Seattle

Seattle, Washington | 206-543-9686

ADMISSION
Admission Rate: 52%
Admission Rate - Men: 50%
Admission Rate - Women: 54%
EA Admission Rate: Not Offered
ED Admission Rate: Not Offered
ED Admits as % of Total Admits: Not Offered
Admission Rate (5-Year Trend): -3%
% of Admits Attending (Yield): 30%
Transfer Admission Rate: 47%

SAT Reading/Writing (Middle 50%): 600-700
SAT Math (Middle 50%): 620-770
ACT Composite (Middle 50%): 27-33

% Graduated in Top 10% of HS Class: 59%
% Graduated in Top 25% of HS Class: 89%
% Graduated in Top 50% of HS Class: 99%

Demonstrated Interest: Not Considered
Legacy Status: Not Considered
Admission Interview Offered: No

ENROLLMENT
Total Undergraduate Enrollment: 32,046
% Part-Time: 8%
% Male: 46%
% Female: 54%
% Out-of-State: 19%
% Fraternity: 14%
% Sorority: 15%
% On-Campus (Freshman): 72%
% On-Campus (All Undergraduate): 29%

% African-American: 3%
% Asian: 25%
% Hispanic: 9%
% White: 36%
% Other: 7%
% Race or Ethnicity Unknown: 4%
% International: 15%
% Low-Income: 21%

ACADEMICS
Student-to-Faculty Ratio: 21 to 1
% of Classes Under 20: 29%
% of Classes 20-49: 46%
% of Classes 50 or More: 25%
% Full-Time Faculty: 75%
% Full-Time Faculty w/ Terminal Degree: 82%

Top Programs
Biochemistry
Business
Communication
Computer Science
Engineering
Informatics
Psychology
Public Health

Retention Rate: 95%
4-Year Graduation Rate: 66%
6-Year Graduation Rate: 84%

Curricular Flexibility: Somewhat Flexible
Academic Rating: ★★★✦

#CollegesWorthYourMoney

Under the perpetually rainy skies and in the birthplace of grunge, Starbucks, and modern romantic comedies rests the flagship campus of the University of Washington system, home to 32,046 undergraduate students, only 60 percent of whom benefit from the uber-affordable in-state rate. International and out-of-state students have begun flocking to UW in recent years to enjoy the literally dozens of top-ranked academic programs and the deep connections to a handful of corporations located nearby that also happen to be some of the most desirable employers anywhere on the planet. With thirteen colleges/schools with undergraduate programs, 180+ majors, and 6,500 courses, UW can meet the needs of just about anyone.

Inside the Classroom

UDub's quarter-based academic calendar keeps students on their toes as most students take three or four classes in each of the 10-week fall, winter, and spring quarters. A strong honors program gives students access to smaller classes, but you'll likely need a 1450+ SAT score to access the program. Core curricular requirements vary by school. Some undergraduate colleges require a foreign language, but others do not. However, all students complete coursework in three Areas of Knowledge: visual, literary, and performing arts; individual societies; and the natural world. Freshmen can enroll in First-year Interest Groups or Collegium Seminars that offer small classes and engaging topics.

The university does have a relatively high 21:1 student-to-faculty ratio that makes consistently small undergraduate class sizes a logistical impossibility. One-third of sections contain forty or more students compared to 29 percent of sections that contain fewer than twenty. Still, there are opportunities for personal connections with professors as evidenced by the fact that 55 percent of graduates complete a faculty-mentored research project. The study abroad rate of participation has climbed steadily since the turn of the millennium; roughly one-fifth now spend a semester in a foreign locale.

The most commonly earned degrees at the University of Washington are in the social sciences (12 percent), biology (10 percent), engineering (10 percent), and computer science (10 percent). There are simply too many stellar majors for there to be too large a concentration in any one or two areas. The College of Engineering, which includes the revered Paul G. Allen College of Computer Science & Engineering, is one of the absolute best in the nation, but UW also boasts strong programs in everything from business to social work to environmental science. Employers adore Huskies, but so do competitive scholarship organizations. In 2019, sixteen grads and alumni were awarded Fulbrights, two won Udall Scholarships, and the school has produced thirty-five Rhodes Scholars in its illustrious history.

Outside the Classroom

A solid 83 percent of UDub students who live on campus rate the experience as "excellent." Unfortunately, only a paltry 29 percent of the undergraduate student body actually do so, and, even among freshmen, just 72 percent reside in the dorms. Some find housing in one of the school's seventy Greek organizations that boast 4,700 members. Most live in houses and apartments in the University District of the city; downtown Seattle is a short car or bus ride away. Students come together to take part in the 850+ student organizations including the Aerial Robotics Club or the Creating a Company Club. Whatever your pleasure, the Husky Union Building (HUB) is, indeed, a great place to get involved. Heck, it even has its own bowling alley. If bowling isn't athletic enough for you, enjoy the twenty-two varsity sports teams that compete in the Pac-12 Conference. Football reigns supreme as UDub boasts the largest stadium in the Pacific Northwest, and it is known to reach deafening noise levels on fall Saturdays. Recreation is aided by state-of-the-art fitness facilities that include a pool, rock-climbing wall, driving range, and Waterfront Activities Center on Lake Washington. Gear for hiking, boating, and camping can be rented from the UWild Gear Garage.

Career Services

There are eleven full-time employees at the Career and Internship Center that is housed within the Division of Student Life. Additional staff members serving undergraduate students can be found within the School of Engineering and School of Business to bring the total of career counselors to twenty-two, a relatively small number considering that they serve more than 32,000 undergraduate students. The resulting 1,457:1 student-to-advisor ratio is among the worst of any school featured in this book; however, unlike some understaffed career services offices (at schools that do make the cut for inclusion in this guide), the CIC at the University of Washington has no shortage of brag-worthy accomplishments.

UW's Career and Internship Center brings close to 400 employers to the Seattle campus each school year. In addition to the hard-to-match local corporations (chronicled in the next section), companies like Wells Fargo, Adobe Systems, Tesla, Bloomberg, Comcast, and Dell recruit and/or conduct interviews on campus. Career fairs are plentiful throughout the year and include specialty expos for data science, engineering, and business. In part due to the prime Seattle location, internships are not hard to locate; 68 percent of undergraduates complete at least one internship, 20 percent complete two, 15 percent complete three. An excellent 85 percent of 2019 grads classified their first job as being "career-related". Thanks to some extremely impressive corporate connections and an alumni base that is embedded in some of the country's most desirable employers, UW's career services successfully overcomes its numbers disadvantage.

Professional Outcomes

A few months after graduation, 61 percent of Class of 2019 graduates had found employment, 16 percent had continued their education in graduate/professional school, and 13 percent were still hunting their first job. The most popular employers of the Class of 2019 included Google, Amazon, Microsoft, and Boeing. Including all living alumni, more than 6,000 Huskies currently work for Bill Gates, and more than 4,000 work for each of Boeing and Amazon. T-Mobile, Facebook, Apple, Nordstrom, Starbucks, and Tableau Software all employ at least 500 UDub alums. The Greater Seattle area is far and away the home of choice for UW grads, followed in popularity by San Francisco, Portland, Los Angeles, and New York.

Of those headed to graduate school, just over half remain in state, mostly at the University of Washington itself to become one of the school's 15,500 graduate students. Seventy-two percent of graduate students were pursuing an MS/MA degree and 23 percent entered doctoral programs. The University of Washington has one of the best medical schools in the country, and 95 percent of accepted med students come from Washington, Wyoming, Alaska, Montana, and Idaho, thus giving UW graduates an inside track. The University of Washington School of Law is a top fifty institution that gives UW undergrads an excellent at-home option for a legal education. However, multiple graduates have also gone on to study law at Stanford, Harvard, and Fordham in recent years.

Admission

UW-Seattle admitted 52 percent of the 45,579 applicants desiring to join the Husky Class of 2023. On the SAT, the mid-50 percent range of 2019-20 freshmen was 1240-1440; the ACT range was 27-33. An impressive 72 percent of attending undergrads sported high school GPAs of 3.75 and above, and the average GPA was a 3.81. Interestingly, the admissions standards for residents, out-of-staters, and international students are similar. However, differences do exist across desired majors, with applicants to programs in engineering and computer science facing the toughest odds. Other than a rise in SAT scores, not a ton has changed at UW admissions in the past decade. Back in 2009, the acceptance rate was a somewhat comparable 61 percent, the average GPA was almost identical, but the 25th percentile SAT score was 1100 compared to 1240 today.

Predictable factors like GPA and rigor of high school coursework are designated as "very important" by the admissions committee, but so is the application essay, a surprise given the volume of applications received. Standardized test scores occupy the realm of "important" factors alongside extracurricular activities, talent/ability, first-generation status, work experience, and volunteer experience. The committee also recommends "taking full advantage of senior year, demonstrating a positive grade trend," and "exercising significant responsibility in a family, community, or employment situation or through activities."

Worth Your Money?

With an annual in-state tuition of under $11,000 and a direct pipeline to many of the world's top corporations that happen to have their headquarters in Washington state, UDub is a can't-miss option if you get the hometown discount. Many nonresidents, particularly those pursuing computer science, engineering, and business, also find a good value, even at a total cost of attendance for four years of about $225K. Students pursuing other majors may do better looking at other reputable yet less pricey options.

FINANCIAL
Institutional Type: Public
In-State Tuition: $10,370
Out-of-State Tuition: $37,071
Room & Board: $13,296
Required Fees: $1,095
Books & Supplies: $900

Avg. Need-Based Grant: $16,842
Avg. % of Need Met: 78%

Avg. Merit-Based Award: $5,217
% Receiving (All Freshmen): 8%
% Receiving (Freshmen w/o Need): 6%

Avg. Cumulative Debt: $19,198
% of Students Borrowing: 33%

CAREER
Who Recruits
1. Samsung
2. Vulcan Capital
3. Alaska Airlines
4. Liberty Mutual
5. HealthPoint

Notable Internships
1. Boeing
2. Nordstrom
3. United Nations

Top Industries
1. Business
2. Education
3. Engineering
4. Operations
5. Research

Top Employers
1. Microsoft
2. Boeing
3. Amazon
4. Google
5. T-Mobile

Where Alumni Work
1. Seattle
2. San Francisco
3. Portland, OR
4. Los Angeles
5. New York City

Median Earnings
College Scorecard (Early Career): $57,700
PayScale (Early Career): $64,800
PayScale (Mid-Career): $120,200

RANKINGS
Money: 20
U.S. News: 58 (T), National Universities
Wall Street Journal/THE: 45
Washington Monthly: 16, National Universities

COLLEGE OVERLAPS
Boston University
University of California, Berkeley
University of California, Los Angeles
University of California, San Diego
University of Southern California

ADMISSION
Admission Rate: 54%
Admission Rate - Men: 51%
Admission Rate - Women: 57%
EA Admission Rate: NR
ED Admission Rate: Not Offered
ED Admits as % of Total Admits: Not Offered
Admission Rate (5-Year Trend): +2%
% of Admits Attending (Yield): 32%
Transfer Admission Rate: 46%

SAT Reading/Writing (Middle 50%): 630-710
SAT Math (Middle 50%): 680-780
ACT Composite (Middle 50%): 27-32

% Graduated in Top 10% of HS Class: 57%
% Graduated in Top 25% of HS Class: 90%
% Graduated in Top 50% of HS Class: 100%

Demonstrated Interest: Not Considered
Legacy Status: Not Considered
Admission Interview Offered: No

ENROLLMENT
Total Undergraduate Enrollment: 33,456
% Part-Time: 10%
% Male: 48%
% Female: 52%
% Out-of-State: 38%
% Fraternity: 9%
% Sorority: 8%
% On-Campus (Freshman): 92%
% On-Campus (All Undergraduate): 26%

% African-American: 2%
% Asian: 7%
% Hispanic: 5%
% White: 69%
% Other: 3%
% Race or Ethnicity Unknown: 3%
% International: 11%
% Low-Income: 14%

ACADEMICS
Student-to-Faculty Ratio: 17 to 1
% of Classes Under 20: 44%
% of Classes 20-49: 34%
% of Classes 50 or More: 22%
% Full-Time Faculty: 83%
% Full-Time Faculty w/ Terminal Degree: 91%

Top Programs
Business
Chemistry
Communication Arts
Computer Science
Economics
Engineering
Political Science
Psychology

Retention Rate: 95%
4-Year Graduation Rate: 63%
6-Year Graduation Rate: 88%

Curricular Flexibility: Somewhat Flexible
Academic Rating: ★★★★

#CollegesWorthYourMoney

One of the country's best state institutions, the University of Wisconsin-Madison has become a coveted destination for a growing number of high-caliber teens far outside Wisconsin's seventy-two counties. In fact, the undergraduate student body of 33,456 is now comprised of 38 percent out-of-staters/foreigners. The school's over 900-acre campus is less than one mile from the Wisconsin State Capital Building and rates as one of the Midwest's most gorgeous collegiate settings. Even more attractive than the scenery are the 230+ undergraduate majors and this tough-to-match selection includes an array of renowned academic programs that rank among the best in the United States.

Inside the Classroom
There are eight schools and colleges that serve undergraduates: The College of Letters and Science, the Wisconsin School of Business, the College of Engineering, the School of Nursing, the School of Education, the School of Pharmacy, the School of Human Ecology, and the College of Agricultural and Life Sciences. Regardless of your home school, breadth is the goal of the university's general education requirements that all Badgers must complete. As a result, thirteen to fifteen credits must be spread over three areas: the natural sciences, the behavioral and social sciences, and the humanities and arts. Required courses in ethnic studies, communications, and quantitative reasoning round out the mandated portion of a Badger education.

At UW-Madison undergrads can expect a mix of large and small classes; 44 percent of sections enroll fewer than twenty students, but 28 percent contain more than forty students. The student-to-faculty ratio is 17:1, and roughly 12,000 graduate students suck up their share of attention. Undergraduate research opportunities exist, but the onus is on the student to show initiative and procure the placement. Overall, 15 percent of undergraduates participate in research with a faculty member during their four years of study. Participation is much higher when it comes to study abroad programs. Roughly 2,300 students participate each year and there are 226 programs in sixty-nine countries to choose from.

Looking for top-ranked business or engineering programs? If so, Madison is a perfect spot for you. In terms of pure percentage of degrees conferred, business (15 percent), biology (12 percent), and engineering (11 percent) are the most popular. The school's guiding principal known as "The Wisconsin Idea" is that a college education should influence lives outside the confines of the classroom. Thus, it is fitting that the university is the number one producer of Peace Corps volunteers. In 2019, a phenomenal forty students earned National Science Foundation Graduate Research Fellowships, eighteen graduates captured Fulbright Scholarships, three were named Goldwater Scholars, and one received a coveted Hertz Fellowship.

Outside the Classroom
One of the best college football towns in America, it would be wrong not to lead with the rowdy, joyous atmosphere inside Camp Randall Stadium on fall Saturdays. A sea of red fills the stadium as 80,000 fans rabidly root for the Badgers and create a quintessential Midwestern college experience. Football worship, along with the other twenty-two Division I Sports teams, unite a campus that is not exactly centralized. While 92 percent of freshmen reside in university-owned housing, only a touch over one-quarter of the total undergraduate population lives on campus. Fraternities and sororities are available but hardly dominate the scene as only 8-9 percent of Badgers join a Greek organization; still, there are sixty Greek organizations on campus with thousands of members. In excess of 900 student-run clubs and organizations are at your disposal including near-constant events hosted by the student union such as concerts, sports viewing, guest lecturers, films, and local theater productions. Nature enthusiasts don't have to travel far for hiking, boating, and birdwatching because the 300-acre Lakeshore Nature Preserve is on campus and includes four miles of shoreline along Lake Mendota. Madison is consistently ranked as one of the top college towns in the entire country because it possesses a hard-to-match combination of safety, beauty, and a booming restaurant and commercial district.

Career Services
There are ten career centers on the UW-Madison campus that, collectively, employ fifty-four professionals dedicated to career advising, internship coordination, employer relations, and other career-oriented tasks. The SuccessWorks initiative caters to students in the College of Letters & Sciences (which accounts for half of enrolled undergrads) and is the largest such office with twenty-one staff members. The Career Exploration Center (CEC) is a cross-college career services office serving those who are undecided on an area of study. Wisconsin also operates career services offices dedicated to pre-law and pre-health as well as discipline-

specific offices housed in each undergraduate school and college. Wisconsin's overall 620:1 student-to-counselor ratio is higher than average compared to many schools featured in this guide, but that figure is relatively strong for a school of its size.

There are some impressive statistics that elevate UW-Madison from run-of-the-mill status with regard to career services offerings. For one, 90 percent of graduates "agreed" or "strongly agreed" that UW-Madison prepared them for the next step on their career path. More tangibly, 82 percent reported completing at least one internship during their four years of study, and a stunningly high 23 percent completed three or more. Career fairs are sweeping enough to accommodate an undergraduate population of 30,000+. The Fall Career & Internship Fair draws 320+ employers, including many top corporations and over 3,600 students annually. Other fairs include a massive Spring Career & Internship Fair, the UW-Madison STEM Fair, and the Public Service Fair (also held in the spring). Thanks to plenty of targeted and accessible career guidance within every undergrad's home college and solid employment and grad school results, UW's career services are held in high regard by our staff.

Professional Outcomes

Sixty-seven percent of job-seeking 2019 University of Wisconsin-Madison grads had already received and/or accepted offers when they received their diplomas. The top five employers of Class of 2019 graduates were: UW-Madison, Epic, Kohl's, Oracle, and UW Health. However, across all graduating years corporations employing a minimum of 250 Badger alumni include Google, Target, Microsoft, Amazon, Apple, PwC, Accenture, and Facebook. The bulk of grads settle in the Madison area, Milwaukee, Chicago, or the Greater Minneapolis-St. Paul area. Those who leave the Midwest head to locations such as New York City, DC, San Francisco, Los Angeles, and Denver.

Of the one-quarter of the Class of 2019 who enrolled directly in graduate/professional school, 49 percent were staying at UW-Madison; more than five members of the class headed to each of the following prestigious institutions: Columbia, Northwestern, Carnegie Mellon, University of Chicago, Johns Hopkins, MIT, and Stanford. Clearly, an undergraduate degree from Wisconsin will serve you well when applying to elite graduate programs across the country. An impressive 82 members of the UW 2019 cohort matriculated in medical school, and 73 entered law school. The University of Wisconsin-Madison's own top-ranked medical school takes a high percentage of home-grown talent as does its top-thirty law school.

Admission

Fifty-four percent of the 43,921 applicants for the Class of 2023 gained entry into UW-Madison, but that figure hardly tells the tale of how selective this flagship university has become. Enrolled freshmen possessed mid-50 percent standardized test scores of 1330-1450 on the SAT and 27-32 on the ACT, 80 percent earned a GPA of greater than 3.75 on a 4.0 scale, 57 percent placed in the top decile of their graduating class, and 90 percent were in the top quartile. A handful of years ago, the SAT range was a lower 1170-1410, which is partially attributable to SAT inflation; the acceptance rate was nearly identical to the 2019-20 figure.

For a school deluged with applicants, the committee still ranks the application essay as the co-leader for most important factor considered alongside rigor of one's secondary curriculum. One's GPA, recommendations, and test scores round out the list of "important" factors. There are no admissions interviews, and demonstrated interest is not considered. It's important to point out that out-of-state applicants face significantly longer odds than in-state applicants who enjoy an acceptance rate of 68 percent. The number of out-of-state applications for this university has grown rapidly in recent years. As a result, nonresidents should have test scores closer to the 75th percentile and rank in the top 10 percent of their high school classes while applicants from Wisconsin can get away with less stellar academic profiles.

Worth Your Money?

Wisconsin residents pay less than $28k per year total cost of attendance, an incredible bargain for such a high-quality educational experience with fantastic graduate outcomes. The growing number of students who come from other states or countries help keep the UW coffers full as such students fork over $56k annually. Over one-third of students who applied for need-based aid received an average grant of $17,084. For locals, the decision to attend Wisconsin is an easy one if you are offered admission. Outsiders still can benefit from the school's stellar reputation and vast alumni networks, but they will pay a significant sum for the privilege.

FINANCIAL
Institutional Type: Public
In-State Tuition: $10,725
Out-of-State Tuition: $37,785
Room & Board: $11,558
Required Fees: $0
Books & Supplies: $1,150

Avg. Need-Based Grant: $17,084
Avg. % of Need Met: 83%

Avg. Merit-Based Award: $5,405
% Receiving (All Freshmen): 8%
% Receiving (Freshmen w/o Need): 5%

Avg. Cumulative Debt: $27,973
% of Students Borrowing: 44%

CAREER
Who Recruits
1. LInkedin
2. Facebook
3. Goldman Sachs
4. Apple
5. Accenture

Notable Internships
1. U.S. Senate
2. Ford Motor Company
3. Hasbro

Top Industries
1. Business
2. Education
3. Operations
4. Engineering
5. Research

Top Employers
1. Google
2. Target
3. Northwestern Mutual
4. Amazon
5. Microsoft

Where Alumni Work
1. Madison, WI
2. Milwaukee
3. Chicago
4. Minneapolis
5. New York City

Median Earnings
College Scorecard (Early Career): $56,200
PayScale (Early Career): $60,900
PayScale (Mid-Career): $110,000

RANKINGS
Money: 28
U.S. News: 42 (T), National Universities
Wall Street Journal/THE: 65
Washington Monthly: 21, National Universities

COLLEGE OVERLAPS
Boston University
Northwestern University
University of Illinois at Urbana-Champaign
University of Michigan
University of Minnesota - Twin Cities

Vanderbilt University

Nashville, Tennessee | 615-322-2561

With an acceptance rate that falls between Dartmouth and Cornell, Vanderbilt University in Nashville, Tennessee, has positioned itself as not only one of the South's most selective institutions but as one of the country's ultra-elite universities. Founded in 1873 by the railroad and shipping tycoon/robber baron Cornelius Vanderbilt (who had never set foot in Tennessee), this private research university is comprised of ten schools, only four of which cater to the school's 6,886 undergraduate students. Of the sixty-seven undergraduate majors, economics, politics and government, and neuroscience are among the most popular.

Inside the Classroom
Core academic requirements known as AXLE (Achieving Excellence in Liberal Arts Education) are extensive. Those in the College of Arts and Sciences must complete three or four writing-intensive courses, including a first-year writing seminar. Thirteen additional courses are mandated in foreign language, US history, social/behavioral sciences, and mathematics and natural sciences. Juniors and seniors have the option to apply to individual department's honors programs where they are then required to produce a scholarly or creative work.

With a 7:1 student-to-faculty ratio, undergraduate class sizes are kept small. In the 2019-20 school year, 25 percent of course sections contained nine or fewer students, and sixty-one contained nineteen or fewer; only 8 percent were large lecture hall affairs of more than fifty students. Undergraduate research opportunities can be found as part of the classroom curriculum, capstone experiences, or through the Vanderbilt University Summer Research Program. Two-fifths of Commodores are adventurous enough to study abroad, and 84 percent of those who do say the experience helped them build job skills. The university offers 120 programs in forty countries.

Vanderbilt alumni are quickly scooped up by many of the world's most desirable and highest-paying corporations. Elite graduate, law, and medical schools are equally fond of those with a Vandy diploma. The School of Engineering has a particularly strong national reputation as do offerings in biology, economics, education, and music. Vanderbilt has been named a Top Producer of Fulbright Scholars, having seen eight students win the award in 2019. Other recent graduates have captured Schwarzman, Boren, Critical Language, Luce, and Marshall Scholarships.

Outside the Classroom
Vanderbilt is a cohesive campus with 85 percent of all undergraduates living in the school's twenty residence halls, ten of which are exclusively for first-year students. To support its recent switch to a residential college system the school has committed $600 million to build four new facilities by 2023. The university's seventeen fraternity and fifteen sorority chapters attract 27 percent of men and 43 percent of women, making Greek life a rather dominant part of the social scene. Athletics also attract a big crowd; football games draw close to 40,000 fans, and thousands of students compete at some level. The university has ten varsity women's teams and six men's that compete in NCAA Division I. Additionally, there are more than forty intramural leagues and thirty-two club sports that offer athletic participation to all students. Overall, there are 530+ student-led organizations presently active on campus, including roughly fifty that are focused on community service. Campus is situated only a mile and a half from downtown Nashville. Music City, USA, not only offers plenty of concerts but also all of the cultural, dining, entertainment, and shopping options one could desire.

Career Services
The Vanderbilt University Career Center is staffed by fifteen full-time professionals, which equates to a student-to-advisor ratio of 459:1, in the average range compared to the liberal arts schools included in this book but quite strong for a university of Vandy's size. The center has career coaches who specialize in areas such as fellowships, STEM, economics, and the social sciences as well as three full-time staff members devoted exclusively to employer relations. The office received rave reviews from undergrads as 98 percent rated their interactions with career services staff positively, and there is plenty of evidence as to why.

In a given academic year, the office engaged in over 2,200 coaching sessions and 1,400+ twenty-minute walk-in sessions. It hosts over 500 career programs and brings 300+ employers from all over the country to Nashville to conduct 1,800+ on-campus interviews. Large scale events such as the Fall Career Fair attract 2,000+ students and recruiters from 140 companies including the likes of ExxonMobil, Merck, Boeing, and Booz Allen Hamilton. An abundance of legitimate internship opportunities are posted online on two platforms, HireADore and DoreWays. With more than 147,000 living alumni, many of whom remain actively connected

Vanderbilt University

E-mail: admissions@vanderbilt.edu | Website: www.vanderbilt.edu

to the school, Vanderbilt students have success networking with former Commodores. Overall, thanks to an exceptional record of guiding students into elite graduate/professional schools and tons of industry connections that help students launch their careers, it is not difficult to see why Vanderbilt's career services efforts are viewed so favorably by its own graduates.

Professional Outcomes

Six months after graduating from Vandy, 86 percent of the Class of 2019 were employed or in graduate school. That is an oddly low statistic as the Class of 2017 figure was 95 percent. The most commonly entered industry by recent grads were finance (18 percent) followed by technology (14 percent), consulting (11 percent), education (11 percent), and engineering (8 percent). Graduates landed jobs with every major financial firm, consulting company, and tech giant as well as with five NFL teams. Alumni across all graduating years can be found in droves at Deloitte, Google, Microsoft, EY, Morgan Stanley, Goldman Sachs, Citi, and Facebook. The greatest number of alumni in the Greater Nashville area but large pockets also assemble in New York City, Atlanta, DC, Chicago, San Francisco, and Dallas. Midcareer median salaries for Vanderbilt graduates are number one in the state by a wide margin and rank nationally alongside Northeastern powerhouses Boston College, Tufts, and Johns Hopkins.

Among 2019 graduates who went directly on to pursue advanced degrees, 16 percent were in medical school, 12 percent in law school, and 13 percent were beginning a PhD. Institutions where recent alumni are enrolled include Oxford, MIT, Stanford, Princeton, Columbia and just about every other elite university in the world. Vanderbilt undergraduates get into med school at a solid 66 percent clip, and recent acceptances included Johns Hopkins, Duke, Penn, and Yale. Those pursuing a legal education from that same graduating year landed at Vanderbilt's own excellent law school as well as UVA, Harvard, Emory, and UNC-Chapel Hill. In sum, if you succeed at Vanderbilt you will have no trouble landing at a world-class graduate or professional program.

Admission

Vanderbilt received a record 37,310 applications for a place in the Class of 2023, recording the second single-digit acceptance rate in the school's history (9 percent). For perspective, in 2000 the school received fewer than 9,000 applications and accepted 55 percent. In the 2019-20 admissions cycle the ACT was the more frequently submitted test, and the mid-50 percent range was 33-35; the range for the SAT was 1460-1560. Just a hair under 90 percent of enrolled freshmen earned places in the top 10 percent of their high school class, and 98 percent placed in the top quartile. There were 231 National Merit Scholars entering as freshmen in 2019-20. Overall, ninety-three percent of enrolled students had GPAs above 3.75 on a 4.0 scale; the average was 3.84.

Seven categories are deemed "very important" by this university's admissions committee: rigor of coursework, GPA, class rank, standardized test scores, application essay, character/personal qualities, and extracurricular involvement. Vandy is serious about its emphasis on extracurriculars; 100 percent of admitted Class of 2023 students held leadership positions in high school. Recommendations and talent/ability comprise the next tier of factors that are "important" to the process. Students applying early decision were admitted at a 20 percent clip, significantly higher than those applying via the regular round. In the last twenty years, Vandy has transformed from a school that accepted more than 50 percent of applicants to a single-digit dream crusher. The regional distinction in the "Southern Ivy" label is almost irrelevant these days. Rather, Vanderbilt is an Ivy-equivalent that happens to be located in the South, and only 33 percent of the student body hails from that region.

Worth Your Money?

The full cost of attendance at Vanderbilt is $76k, but those with financial need will pay nothing near that sum. Vandy awards an average need-based grant of $54k per year, putting it among the endlessly endowed Ivy League schools as one of the most generous colleges in the country. It is a rare school that can meet 100 percent of demonstrated need. Unlike the Ivies, those with exceptional credentials and special talents may actually be able to procure some level of merit aid as well. Twelve percent of undergraduates receive an average annual merit aid award of roughly $23k. However, even if you aren't fortunate enough to be counted among this relatively small group of merit aid recipients, Vanderbilt is still worth your money.

FINANCIAL
Institutional Type: Private
In-State Tuition: $54,158
Out-of-State Tuition: $54,158
Room & Board: $17,670
Required Fees: $0
Books & Supplies: $1,294

Avg. Need-Based Grant: $54,417
Avg. % of Need Met: 100%

Avg. Merit-Based Award: $18,722
% Receiving (All Freshmen): 12%
% Receiving (Freshmen w/o Need): 7%

Avg. Cumulative Debt: $22,727
% of Students Borrowing: 22%

CAREER
Who Recruits
1. Vineyard Vines
2. ExxonMobil
3. Teach for America
4. AllianceBernstein
5. Defense Intelligence Agency

Notable Internships
1. UBS
2. Lyft
3. Spotify

Top Industries
1. Business
2. Education
3. Research
4. Operations
5. Engineering

Top Employers
1. Deloitte
2. Google
3. Microsoft
4. EY
5. Amazon

Where Alumni Work
1. Nashville
2. New York City
3. Atlanta
4. Washington DC
5. San Francisco

Median Earnings
College Scorecard (Early Career): $69,000
PayScale (Early Career): $69,300
PayScale (Mid-Career): $129,400

RANKINGS
Money: 8
U.S. News: 14 (T), National Universities
Wall Street Journal/THE: 17
Washington Monthly: 41, National Universities

COLLEGE OVERLAPS
Duke University
Emory University
Northwestern University
Rice University
University of Michigan

Vassar College

A recent three-part Malcom Gladwell podcast was full of effusive praise for one college in Poughkeepsie, New York, that puts its money where its mouth is on the subject of making college affordable for low-income and first-generation students. Vassar deserves that type of attention for its commitment to creating a more egalitarian higher education world. Yet, this original member of the Seven Sisters that became coeducational in 1969 also has a well-deserved reputation for its exceptionally flexible and high-quality liberal education.

Inside the Classroom

Vassar's 2,441 undergraduate students have the choice of fifty-one majors and are not beholden to a core curriculum or a murderous series of freshman- and sophomore-year requirements; instead, there are only three mandates. All freshmen must take a first-year writing seminar capped at seventeen students. The second requirement is that all students must become proficient in a foreign language; among the languages offered are Korean, Hebrew, and Old English. The last is that students must take at least one course dealing with quantitative reasoning. Other than that and, of course, one's major, there is ample room to explore electives and burgeoning intellectual passions.

The college's 355 faculty members teach every single undergraduate course offered at Vassar. An 8:1 student-to-faculty ratio leads to an average class size of seventeen students, and 24 percent of all sections have an enrollment of nine or fewer. Professors are extremely available outside the classroom as 70 percent of the faculty live on or near campus, and faculty families also live within each residence hall. Opportunities to get involved in undergraduate research are taken advantage of by 300+ students each year who work side-by-side with professors on research in the sciences, social sciences, or arts and humanities. Roughly 500 students also engage in credited community-based learning in local organizations or agencies. Vassar's Undergraduate Research Summer Institute (URSI) has been operational since 1986 and offers a plethora of ten-week research experiences in everything from astronomy to computer science to psychology. Study abroad programs are taken advantage of by two-fifths of students.

In terms of number of degrees conferred, the most popular majors are in the social sciences, biology, the visual and performing arts, and psychology. The lack of a core curriculum makes it easy to double major if you desire. Many grads ultimately pursue further education and find elite graduate and professional programs that respect the rigor of a Vassar education. In 2020, Brewers landed three Fulbright Scholarships and a number of recent grads have won National Science Foundation Graduate Research Fellowships.

Outside the Classroom

Few Vassar undergraduates are eager to flee the school's idyllic 1,000-acre campus, so 97 percent of the student body remains in the residence halls all four years. Those seeking to live off campus need to request special permission. The nine traditional houses, one cooperative house, and three school-owned apartment complexes are situated on verdant grounds that have so many different tree varieties that the campus is technically branded an arboretum. Campus cohesion is further enhanced by the absence of Greek organizations. Men make up only 41 percent of the population, which can partially be attributed to the school's history as a women's college and to the realities of the demographic make-up at most liberal arts colleges. Eighteen percent of students are varsity athletes who compete as part of twenty-three NCAA Division III athletic squads. Club and intramural teams as well as facilities that include an elevated running track, a six-lane pool, a nine-hole golf course, and thirteen tennis courts ensure that opportunities for fitness are open to all. There are 145+ student-run organizations and 1,000+ annual campus events such as concerts, guest lectures, and visiting performers, so there is always something to do close to home. Poughkeepsie offers lots of natural beauty, a mall, and an array of affordable restaurants, although it won't be mistaken for a buzzing metropolis. Those seeking big-city life will have to make the two-hour trip to New York City or the three-hour ride to Boston.

Career Services

The Career Development Office (CDO) at Vassar College is staffed by eight professionals who specialize in career counseling, employer relations, law/health professions advising, and alumni outreach. That works out to a 305:1 student-to-advisor ratio, a figure superior to many schools featured in this guide. Annual events organized by this office include Career Kickoff and First Year Friday, which are designed to give freshmen an overview of the career development services available. Sophomore Career Connections and Senior Week are class-specific events intended to focus students on tasks critical to their particular place in the career development process.

ADMISSION
Admission Rate: 24%
Admission Rate - Men: 30%
Admission Rate - Women: 21%
EA Admission Rate: Not Offered
ED Admission Rate: 40%
ED Admits as % of Total Admits: 15%
Admission Rate (5-Year Trend): 0%
% of Admits Attending (Yield): 32%
Transfer Admission Rate: 11%

SAT Reading/Writing (Middle 50%): 680-750
SAT Math (Middle 50%): 690-780
ACT Composite (Middle 50%): 31-34

% Graduated in Top 10% of HS Class: 65%
% Graduated in Top 25% of HS Class: 91%
% Graduated in Top 50% of HS Class: 98%

Demonstrated Interest: Not Considered
Legacy Status: Considered
Admission Interview Offered: Yes

ENROLLMENT
Total Undergraduate Enrollment: 2,441
% Part-Time: 1%
% Male: 41%
% Female: 59%
% Out-of-State: 73%
% Fraternity: Not Offered
% Sorority: Not Offered
% On-Campus (Freshman): 100%
% On-Campus (All Undergraduate): 97%

% African-American: 4%
% Asian: 12%
% Hispanic: 11%
% White: 55%
% Other: 9%
% Race or Ethnicity Unknown: 0%
% International: 9%
% Low-Income: 28%

ACADEMICS
Student-to-Faculty Ratio: 8 to 1
% of Classes Under 20: 67%
% of Classes 20-49: 33%
% of Classes 50 or More: 0%
% Full-Time Faculty: 82%
% Full-Time Faculty w/ Terminal Degree: 89%

Top Programs
Art
Biology
Drama
Film
History
International Studies
Physics
Political Science

Retention Rate: 96%
4-Year Graduation Rate: 86%
6-Year Graduation Rate: 91%

Curricular Flexibility: Very Flexible
Academic Rating: ★★★★✔

#CollegesWorthYourMoney

In addition to hosting its own events, Vassar is a member of the Selective Liberal Arts Consortium that sponsors recruiting trips to New York City and Washington, DC. The CDO is always happy to help you with your internship, but the majority of the resources in the area are on online platforms that include Handshake. An exceptional 87 percent of Vassar grads complete at least one internship while at the college. In the 2018-19 school year the CDO conducted 3,443 one-one-one advising appointments and invited thirty-one companies to recruit on campus including NERA Economic Consulting, Teach for America, and M&T Bank. In addition to helping students find their first jobs, the CDO should be lauded for the fantastic job it does in preparing students to continue their education in medical, law, or graduate school.

Professional Outcomes

Ninety-six percent of Vassar alums enjoy positive outcomes within six months of graduation. A solid number land at highly competitive companies like Google, Facebook, EY, Deloitte, Microsoft, Citi, EY, and Amazon. Elite universities such as Harvard, Penn, NYU, and Columbia are also among the top employers of former Vassar students, many of whom earn advanced degrees and enter academia. Large contingents of Brewers can be found in the Greater New York City area as well as Boston, DC, San Francisco, Los Angeles, and Philadelphia. Average midcareer salaries are toward the bottom-of-the-pack among elite liberal arts schools, not coincidentally, in the same range as Reed, Oberlin, and Scripps that, like Vassar, produce large numbers of advanced degree earners who do not often see high remuneration early in their careers.

Within five years of graduating, the majority of Vassar alumni pursue further education, including 20 percent who enroll directly in an advanced degree program upon completing their undergraduate studies. Over the last five years medical school applicants have been admitted at an enviable 85 percent rate, twice the national average. The most commonly attended medical schools include Dartmouth, Tufts, Columbia, and Brown. Law school applicants experienced a superb 90 percent acceptance rate. Vassar ranks in the top twelve in the nation in percentage of undergraduates who go on to earn a PhD.

Admission

Vassar accepted 24 percent of the 8,961 applicants seeking to join the Class of 2023. The average SAT for admitted students was 1438, and the mean ACT was 32. Seventy-three percent were in the top decile, and 93 percent were in the top quartile. The average GPA is in the A/A- range. The number of applications has hardly increased in the past decade, and neither has the acceptance rate. (It was 25 percent in 2008-09.)

GPA and evidence of rigorous courses rests atop the list of most important factors in the eyes of the admissions committee. Standardized test scores, essays, recommendations, extracurricular activities, talent/ability, and character/personal qualities round out a holistic process as the next most important considerations. The college is extremely committed to providing need-based aid to low-income and first-generation students; nearly one-quarter of current students are Pell Grant recipients. Despite a reasonably high yield rate of 32 percent, Vassar still treasures qualified applicants who apply on a binding early-decision basis. In the 2019-20 admissions cycle, ED applicants enjoyed a 40 percent acceptance rate. Vassar deserves deep admiration for its commitment to increasing access to students from all backgrounds. It has pursued those aims at the expense of hyping application numbers and, thus, increasing the perception of selectivity. As a result, those in love with this fine liberal arts institution do not face single-digit odds as they would at many other schools of its quality.

Worth Your Money?

As a result of Vassar's mission to increase access to low-income students, it does not offer any merit aid, only need-based aid, which it offers in impressively generous quantities. The blow of the list price cost of attendance of $75,920 is softened by the fact that 56 percent of the undergraduate student population qualifies for aid, and the school meets 100 percent of the demonstrated need for all students. That translates to an average grant of over $52k, making Vassar an incredibly affordable institution for those from less advantageous economic circumstances.

FINANCIAL
Institutional Type: Private
In-State Tuition: $57,910
Out-of-State Tuition: $57,910
Room & Board: $14,220
Required Fees: $860
Books & Supplies: $900

Avg. Need-Based Grant: $51,824
Avg. % of Need Met: 100%

Avg. Merit-Based Award: $0
% Receiving (All Freshmen): 0%
% Receiving (Freshmen w/o Need): 0%

Avg. Cumulative Debt: $19,474
% of Students Borrowing: 53%

CAREER
Who Recruits
1. NERA Economic Consulting
2. Teach for America
3. Peace Corps
4. M&T Bank
5. Shearman and Sterling

Notable Internships
1. U.S. House of Representatives
2. Major League Baseball
3. YouTube

Top Industries
1. Business
2. Education
3. Media
4. Arts & Design
5. Social Services

Top Employers
1. Google
2. IBM
3. Morgan Stanley
4. Deloitte
5. Microsoft

Where Alumni Work
1. New York City
2. Boston
3. San Francisco
4. Washington DC
5. Los Angeles

Median Earnings
College Scorecard (Early Career): $54,600
PayScale (Early Career): $59,300
PayScale (Mid-Career): $118,200

RANKINGS
Money: 145
U.S. News: 13 (T), Liberal Arts Colleges
Wall Street Journal/THE: 62
Washington Monthly: 7, Liberal Arts Colleges

COLLEGE OVERLAPS
Brown University
Cornell University
Haverford College
Tufts University
Wesleyan University

Villanova University

Villanova, Pennsylvania | 610-519-4000

Positioned twelve miles outside of Philadelphia on the swanky Main Line is Villanova University, a school that, prior to winning an NCAA basketball title in 1985, possessed only a regional reputation. Thirty years later, the prestige of its powerhouse basketball program has launched an already renowned and highly desirable school into a whole new stratosphere. Today, this midsize Catholic research university is the proud home to 6,865 enthusiastic Wildcat undergraduates. For those who can conquer its suddenly highly-selective admissions process, Nova provides a world class educational experience in a spirited collegiate atmosphere.

Inside the Classroom

Students can choose one of forty-five undergraduate programs within four schools: the College of Liberal Arts & Sciences, the Villanova School of Business, the College of Engineering, and the College of Nursing. All students must conquer the school's core curriculum that is designed to ensure a "depth of study and intellectual sophistication while recognizing that learning implies different modes of inquiry." Courses in theology, ethics, and philosophy as well as the Augustine and Culture Seminar Program comprise the Core Foundational Courses. Additional requirements include all of the usual liberal arts standards (social sciences, math, foreign language, and so on) and an upper-level theology course, a writing seminar, and a senior capstone.

The university sports an 11:1 student-to-faculty ratio and offers average undergraduate classes of twenty-three students. It is possible to receive a degree from the school without ever sitting in a giant lecture hall. In fact, only 5 percent of course sections enroll forty or more students. As a consequence, professors are unusually available in and outside of the classroom. From the start of freshman year, opportunities for meaningful undergraduate research will be within your grasp. The Villanova Match Research Programs for First Year Students allows second-semester freshmen to work as research assistants alongside distinguished faculty. The Villanova Undergraduate Research Fellows Summer Program is taken advantage of by many upperclassmen. Wildcats study abroad in impressive numbers; the 37 percent participation rate places Nova among the top ten universities in the country.

Villanova's business, accounting, and engineering programs all receive a good deal of attention from ranking publications. The school's most popular degree is business with over one-quarter of all graduates majoring in it. Engineering and nursing are the second- and third-most commonly conferred degree areas. As the school's reputation reaches new heights, more students than ever are winning prestigious national awards. In 2020 alone, Villanova graduates earned seventeen Fulbright Scholarships, five Gilman Scholarships, one Goldwater Scholarships, and multiple National Science Foundation Graduate Research Fellowships.

Outside the Classroom

Over three-quarters of the undergraduate student body currently live on a 240-acre campus that is growing more beautiful and impressive by the day. Constant progress can be observed on the university's many construction projects, and we're not talking small buildings. The school is currently erecting on-campus housing for an additional 1,135 undergrads. The newly opened Finneran Pavilion and an under-construction performing arts center are emblematic of the administration's recent splurge. The school is home to twenty-four fraternities and sororities, and 21-25 percent of students participate in Greek life. Athletics, particularly basketball, are a way of life at Villanova. More than 500 student-athletes compete on the Wildcats twenty-four NCCA Division I teams, and many more participate in the forty-four club and intramural sports options. In total, there are 265 active extracurricular clubs, a fair number of which are centered on community service, which is a definite point of emphasis at Nova as students contribute a quarter million service hours annually. Radnor Township isn't cheap, but it offers tons of great hangouts and places to eat. The King of Prussia Mall, the second largest in the United States, is only a few miles away. The museums, sports, restaurants, and culture of Philly are only a straight-shot, half-hour car ride away.

Career Services

The Villanova University Career Center employs eighteen individuals who specialize in career counseling, pre-law advising, employer relations, and industry advising. The center also trains seventeen career assistants who are available to support their fellow undergraduates as well. Only counting professional employees, the office has a 381:1 student-to-counselor ratio, which is within the average range of schools profiled in this guide. However, by almost every other metric, this career center, like the university's famed basketball squad, measures up well against the competition.

Villanova University

E-mail: gotovu@villanova.edu | Website: www.villanova.edu

Including graduate students, there were 7,000 visits to the career center during the 2018-19 school year. Over 55,000 job and internship opportunities were posted online for Wildcats to explore. On campus recruiting is also strong with 400 companies making the trek to Villanova's grounds last year alone. A well-connected and passionate global network of 125,000 alumni is also available to help you make connections as you search for internships and employment. Most students are successful landing an internship as 84 percent of students complete at least one such experience at Nova. Large events like the Fall Career Fair draw 175+ employers to the Connelly Center. With a high level of personalized support, a robust Employer Relations Department, and excellent career outcomes for graduates (more in a moment), the Villanova University Career Center continues to do excellent work on behalf of its students.

Professional Outcomes

Within six months of commencement, Class of 2019 graduates had a placement rate of 97 percent with 76 percent entering the workforce and 16 percent matriculating into graduate or professional school. The most popular employers of members of the Class of 2019 were, not coincidentally, also companies with the largest Wildcat alumni representation. That list includes Vanguard, Verizon, PwC, JP Morgan Chase, Merck, Comcast, EY, Deloitte, and Morgan Stanley. The average starting salary across all colleges within the university was $62,524. Graduates of the engineering school all earned an average salary above $68,000 while the Colleges of Liberal Arts & Sciences figure was just under $53k. Remaining in the Philadelphia Metro area is the most popular move, but large numbers also migrate to New York City, DC, Boston, Chicago, San Francisco, and Los Angeles.

Class of 2019 members went on to study at a number of topflight graduate institutions. College of Engineering grads went to schools like Cornell, Stanford, and UVA. Liberal arts grads entered programs at Harvard, Tufts, UCLA, and Yale. Nova grads enjoyed a medical school admissions rate of 70-75 percent, far above the national average. Among the recent graduates applying to law school, acceptances were earned at Fordham, the University of Michigan, Northeastern, Boston College and, of course, Villanova's own Charles Widger School of Law.

Admission

The 28 percent of successful applicants who earned a place in the Class of 2023 were a particularly accomplished bunch. Those who enrolled possessed SATs in the range of 1330-1460 an ACT range of 31-34, and the average weighted GPA was 4.2. In terms of class rank, 72 percent of freshmen placed in their high school class' top decile, and 93 percent earned a spot in the top quartile. For perspective, in 2015 the university admitted 43 percent of its applicants, and the 25th percentile SAT score was an even 1200.

Rigor of coursework, GPA, class rank, and standardized test scores comprise the factors deemed most important by the committee. Essays, recommendations, extracurricular activities, work experience, and volunteer work are among the areas that receive secondary consideration. There is no interview offered as part of the admissions process. Those applying through binding early decision were accepted at a 56 percent rate, providing a solid advantage over those in the regular cycle. Villanova does advertise a holistic process, but with close to 23,000 applicants these days, your SATs, GPA, class rank, and other measurables need to be within range for serious consideration. Students (and their counselors) need to be aware of the year-by-year increases in selectivity as this school has transformed in the recent past.

Worth Your Money?

Villanova rarely covers a student's full amount of need, but 48 percent of current students do receive need-based aid that averages $38k per award; only 7 percent of undergraduates are presently receiving any merit aid. The total annual cost of attendance at Nova is a hair shy of $73k, therefore, even with aid, becoming a Wildcat is not going to come cheap. That said, starting salaries for graduates are on the higher side, making it possible to pay back the substantial loans you may need to take out in order to attend.

FINANCIAL
Institutional Type: Private
In-State Tuition: $54,550
Out-of-State Tuition: $54,550
Room & Board: $14,444
Required Fees: $880
Books & Supplies: $1,100

Avg. Need-Based Grant: $38,201
Avg. % of Need Met: 80%

Avg. Merit-Based Award: $18,712
% Receiving (All Freshmen): 7%
% Receiving (Freshmen w/o Need): 4%

Avg. Cumulative Debt: $36,716
% of Students Borrowing: 49%

CAREER
Who Recruits
1. CIA
2. KPMG
3. TD Securities
4. Boston Consulting Group
5. BNY Mellon

Notable Internships
1. QVC
2. NBC Universal
3. Pratt & Whitney

Top Industries
1. Business
2. Operations
3. Sales
4. Finance
5. information Technology

Top Employers
1. Vanguard
2. Verizon
3. PwC
4. JPMorgan Chase
5. Merck

Where Alumni Work
1. Philadelphia
2. New York City
3. Washington DC
4. Boston
5. Chicago

Median Earnings
College Scorecard (Early Career): $77,900
PayScale (Early Career): $68,300
PayScale (Mid-Career): $129,300

RANKINGS
Money: 199
U.S. News: 53 (T), National Universities
Wall Street Journal/THE: 127 (T)
Washington Monthly: 80, National Universities

COLLEGE OVERLAPS
Boston College
Fordham University
Georgetown University
Northeastern University
University of Notre Dame

Virginia Polytechnic Institute and State University

Blacksburg, Virginia | 540-231-6267

ADMISSION
Admission Rate: 70%
Admission Rate - Men: 67%
Admission Rate - Women: 75%
EA Admission Rate: 85%
ED Admission Rate: 44%
ED Admits as % of Total Admits: 6%
Admission Rate (5-Year Trend): -3%
% of Admits Attending (Yield): 34%
Transfer Admission Rate: 60%

SAT Reading/Writing (Middle 50%): 590-680
SAT Math (Middle 50%): 590-710
ACT Composite (Middle 50%): 25-31

% Graduated in Top 10% of HS Class: 29%
% Graduated in Top 25% of HS Class: 68%
% Graduated in Top 50% of HS Class: 88%

Demonstrated Interest: Not Considered
Legacy Status: Considered
Admission Interview Offered: No

ENROLLMENT
Total Undergraduate Enrollment: 29,300
% Part-Time: 2%
% Male: 57%
% Female: 43%
% Out-of-State: 25%
% Fraternity: 13%
% Sorority: 19%
% On-Campus (Freshman): 98%
% On-Campus (All Undergraduate): 35%

% African-American: 4%
% Asian: 10%
% Hispanic: 7%
% White: 64%
% Other: 5%
% Race or Ethnicity Unknown: 2%
% International: 7%
% Low-Income: 15%

ACADEMICS
Student-to-Faculty Ratio: 14 to 1
% of Classes Under 20: 29%
% of Classes 20-49: 48%
% of Classes 50 or More: 23%
% Full-Time Faculty: 90%
% Full-Time Faculty w/ Terminal Degree: 89%

Top Programs
Architecture
Animal Sciences
Business
Computer Science
Engineering
Human Nutrition, Foods, and Exercise
Industrial Design

Retention Rate: 93%
4-Year Graduation Rate: 65%
6-Year Graduation Rate: 86%

Curricular Flexibility: Somewhat Flexible
Academic Rating: ★★★✔

#CollegesWorthYourMoney

Sometimes, even the most epic debacles contain a silver lining. Such was the case when Virginia Tech admitted applicants to the Class of 2023, with an estimate that around 6,600 would enroll. When 8,000 of those admitted ended up selecting the university, the school had to offer 1,500 students financial incentives for deferring their enrollment. Logistical disaster aside, this occurrence is indicative of a positive—the ever-increasing popularity of an affordable state school that offers a world-class STEM and business education.

Inside the Classroom

Eight undergraduate colleges are housed within the larger university that collectively offer 110 distinct bachelor's degrees. The Pathways curriculum was instituted in 2015 to ensure that all students were able to participate in a general education program that followed the principles of (1) integration, (2) inclusivity, and (3) relevance. Required courses force Hokies to at least dip their toes into the worlds of discourse, quantitative and computational thinking, reasoning in the natural sciences, critique and practice in design and the arts, reasoning in the social sciences, critical thinking in the humanities, and critical analysis of identity and equity in the United States.

Classes at Virginia Tech tend be on the larger side with just 27 percent of sections containing fewer than 20 students while 32 percent enroll greater than 40 undergrads. The student-to-faculty ratio at this school is a respectable 14:1, but there are more than 7,000 graduate students to cater to. Overall, 20 percent of the Class of 2020 reported participating in some type of undergraduate research experience, but landing such opportunities is much easier for members of the Honors College. Each year, more than 1,200 students avail themselves of the chance to study abroad in locations such as Switzerland, New Zealand, France, and Scotland.

As one would expect, engineering is the area where the greatest number of degrees are conferred (23 percent), but business (21 percent) is actually a close second. Both disciplines are among the most respected at Tech, along with computer science. Other popular majors include the family and consumer sciences (9 percent), social sciences (8 percent), biology (8 percent), and agriculture (5 percent). The school set a record in 2019 for its highest number of Fulbright winners (5). It also produced Astronaut Scholars in 2017, 2018, and 2019.

Outside the Classroom

Ninety-eight percent of freshmen, but just one third of the overall student body, reside in on-campus housing on the school's sprawling 2,600-acre grounds. Roughly one quarter of current undergrads hail from out of state, so the majority of the student body are Virginia residents. There are more men than women, but the 57/43 split is not as pronounced as at some other institutes of technology. Frats attract 13 percent of males, and 19 percent of women join a sorority. More than 700 student-athletes are members of the 22 varsity sports teams that compete in the Atlantic Coast Conference at the NCAA Division I level. The Hokies' football stadium seats 66,000+ and attracts raucous crowds, so those seeking delirious football Saturdays will find VT an excellent match. Those seeking a less-competitive environment can join a club or intramural sport; there are more than 35 intramural options including activities like putt-putt, inner tube water polo, and free-throw contests. Additionally, 800 student-run organizations are presently running on campus, virtually assuring every student the chance to connect with others who share their unique interests. With large cities a few hours (or more) away, must students remain near campus on the weekends, soaking in the quintessential college town of Blacksburg, which offers a much-appreciated mix of natural beauty and restaurants, bars, and entertainment venues.

Career Services

There are 28 professional staff members within the Career and Professional Development Center (CPDC), many of whom focus on career counseling, internships/co-op coordination, and employer relations. This 993:1 ratio is higher than the average school selected for this guidebook. Regardless, this group ensures that Hokies have opportunities for career planning and connection on a grand scale, hosting 25+ career fairs per year and countless in-person and virtual workshops and employer information sessions. One glance at how employed members of the Class of 2019 found their first jobs, and it's clear that the CPDC is successfully executing its mission.

Virginia Polytechnic Institute and State University

E-mail: admissions@vt.edu | Website: www.vt.edu

Twenty-six percent of recent grads report landing their first jobs directly through a connection made at a VT career fair. The CPDC had its hand either directly or indirectly in many other positive outcomes; 6 percent of grads landed their positions through Handshake, 2 percent interviewed through the On-Campus Interviewing Program, another 2 percent were connected through a professor, and 1 percent networked at a school-sponsored employer presentation. Fifty-six percent of the Class of 2019 reported utilizing the career center to some extent, and only 16 percent stated that they "never" used any CPDC services. The majority of VT grads had some type of job-related experience during their four years in Blacksburg. Paid internships were procured by 56 percent of respondents, unpaid internships by 14 percent, and co-op placements by 5 percent. Overall, Virginia Tech's career services staff does a solid job reaching the majority of undergraduates, but there is room for improvement in terms of outreach.

Professional Outcomes

Within their first half-year in the real world, 60 percent of the Class of 2019 had found employment, 17 percent were in graduate school, and 16 percent were still looking for their next destination. The Class of 2019 sent large numbers of graduates to a variety of major corporations including Lockheed Martin (56), Deloitte (53), Capital One (53), EY (34), Booze Allen Hamilton (28), KPMG (27), and Northrop Grumman (21). The top four geographic areas where Hokies settle down are all within the same region: Washington, DC; Roanoke; Richmond; and Norfolk. The median salary for 2018-19 graduates was $61,800 with a median bonus of $5,000.

Among Class of 2018 graduates who decided to pursue an advanced degree, 268 did so right at VT, while 54 traveled a couple hundred miles east to Virginia Commonwealth University, and 13 freshly minted grads enrolled at George Mason University. Multiple members of the Class of 2019 went on to attend the likes of William & Mary, Cornell, Duke, Emory, Georgia Tech, Stanford, UC Berkeley, and UCLA. Law schools that members of this cohort are attending include Harvard, Northwestern, Washington & Lee, and Wake Forest. In the 2019-20 cycle, 124 Virginia Tech seniors applied to medical school, and acceptances included the Baylor College of Medicine and the University of Virginia as well as dental school admissions to the University of Pennsylvania and Tufts University.

Admission

The 64.8 percent acceptance rate for applicants to join the 2018-19 freshman class is not as intimidating as the admit rates at many other strong STEM institutions. This group certainly included many high achievers; the average weighted high school GPA was 4.04, and 38 percent finished in the top decile of their graduating class with 77 percent in the top quartile. Overall, 84 percent of Hokie freshmen possessed a GPA of 3.75 or better. Standardized test scores of Class of 2023 members were solid but unspectacular. The mid-50 percent ranges were 1180-1390 on the SAT and 25-31 on the ACT. The SAT is easily the more commonly submitted test, accompanying 87 percent of applications.

Virginia Tech weights four factors as having the greatest importance in admissions decisions: rigor of coursework, GPA, standardized test scores, and the application essay. While no factors are deemed "important," there are ten areas that are "considered": extracurricular activities, talent/ability, character/personal qualities, first-generation status, legacy status, geographical residence, state residency, racial/ethnic status, work experience, and volunteer work experience. While demonstrated interest is not considered, VT does appreciate students who apply either early action or early decision; three quarters of the Class of 2019 committed through these early rounds. Sixty percent of Hokies are state residents; the most nonresident students hail from Maryland, New Jersey, Pennsylvania, North Carolina, and New York. It is important to note that admissions are a bit more selective for out-of-state applicants.

Worth Your Money?

The in-state cost of attendance for those staying on campus is a relatively affordable $28,440 per year. Those coming from outside the state of Virginia will pay a COA of $48,620. At full price, this figure could give cost-conscious families pause; however, considering the median starting salary of over $60k and heavy concentration of engineering and business majors, VT will prove worth the money for many undergraduates. As with any state school of this quality, Virginia residents can rest assured that their educational investment will be well spent, regardless of one's intended major.

FINANCIAL
Institutional Type: Public
In-State Tuition: $11,420
Out-of-State Tuition: $29,960
Room & Board: $9,556
Required Fees: $2,329
Books & Supplies: $1,100

Avg. Need-Based Grant: $8,588
Avg. % of Need Met: 54%

Avg. Merit-Based Award: $3,130
% Receiving (All Freshmen): 29%
% Receiving (Freshmen w/o Need): 9%

Avg. Cumulative Debt: $33,312
% of Students Borrowing: 48%

CAREER
Who Recruits
1. Accenture
2. MITRE
3. Dominion Energy
4. Peraton
5. L3Harris

Notable Internships
1. KPMG
2. Richmond & Towers
3. Jacobs Engineering Group

Top Industries
1. Business
2. Engineering
3. Operations
4. Education
5. information Technology

Top Employers
1. Capital One
2. Booz Allen Hamilton
3. Deloitte
4. Microsoft
5. IBM

Where Alumni Work
1. Washington DC
2. Roanoke, VA
3. Richmond, VA
4. Norfolk, VA
5. New York City

Median Earnings
College Scorecard (Early Career): $62,500
PayScale (Early Career): $65,100
PayScale (Mid-Career): $122,000

RANKINGS
Money: 37
U.S. News: 74 (T), National Universities
Wall Street Journal/THE: 109 (T)
Washington Monthly: 42, National Universities

COLLEGE OVERLAPS
College of William & Mary
James Madison University
North Carolina State University
University of Maryland, College Park
University of Virginia

Wake Forest University

Winston-Salem, North Carolina | 336-758-5201

Founded as the Manual Labor Institute for Baptist preachers in 1834, Wake Forest has roots that sound exaggeratedly and humorously humble. Of course, the current vibe of the university could not be further from its modest beginnings, save the retention of its Southern charm. Today's Wake Forest is generally regarded as a bubble of conservatism and wealth—the average student's parental income is far higher than the average university—and, from an academic standpoint, this school is viewed as one of the top private research institutions outside the Northeast.

Inside the Classroom
All freshmen enter the Undergraduate College that offers forty-two majors and sixty minors. Economics, biology, psychology, finance, and communications are the areas toward which the largest number of students gravitate. Those wishing to attend the School of Business apply prior to their sophomore year. All other concentrations are open to any student. Academic requirements include a freshman seminar, a four-credit writing seminar, foreign language, physical education, and one course in both quantitative reasoning and cultural diversity.

Sporting a student-to-faculty ratio of 10:1, classes are kept on the small side with 60 percent of sections enrolling fewer than twenty students. There are a fair number of courses that have twenty to thirty-nine students, but only a minuscule number that take place in large lecture halls. Close to 60 percent of Demon Deacons have the opportunity to engage in hands-on research for academic credit. Wake's robust study abroad options feature 400 semester, summer and year-long programs in 200 cities in more than seventy countries worldwide. Undergrads participate at am 81 percent rate, good enough for the fourth highest figure among doctoral degree-granting US universities.

Wake Forest is a school with strengths across a variety of disciplines, most notably chemistry, communication, accounting, finance, and international affairs. The most frequently conferred degrees are in the social sciences (23 percent), business (18 percent), journalism (9 percent), psychology (9 percent), and biology (8 percent). Overall, the institution has an excellent reputation across the board in both employment and academic circles, and Wake Forest grads are always considered for prestigious postgraduate fellowships. Eight members of the Class of 2020 were named Fulbright Scholars and the university produces a Rhodes Scholar just about every other year.

Outside the Classroom
Greek life gets top billing when it comes to describing the social scene at Wake. Roughly half of the student body joins a fraternity or sorority, with women joining sororities at an extraordinarily high rate (59 percent). Over three-quarters of students live in university-owned housing with many off-campus upperclassmen flocking to nearby apartment complexes. The Demon Deacons are a powerhouse in NCAA Division I athletics, quite an achievement considering the university's modest size. Of the sixteen varsity sports teams that compete in the vaunted ACC, men's basketball and football draw the biggest crowds. The school is brimming with less serious but still dedicated athletes as a whopping 85 percent of the student body participates in intramural athletics. Many non-sports options also are available as there are more than 240 active student organizations on campus, including a full array of political, religious, and performing arts groups. The quaint Southern charm of campus extends into the surrounding small city of Winston-Salem, which offers its fair share of cultural, culinary, and shopping pursuits.

Career Services
The Office of Personal and Career Development (OPCD) at Wake Forest is staffed by thirty-five full-time professional employees who serve as career coaches, employer relations specialists, and counselors who work on personal and professional development with alumni. That equates to a student-to-advisor ratio of 151:1, which ranks among the best of the institutions included in this book. The OPCD is not only generously staffed; it also operates with the clear mission of readying every single Demon Deacon for a meaningful next step in life.

In a single year, career coaches met with over 4,000 members of the student body to engage in 1:1 career planning sessions and/or small workshops. Career treks took students to New York City, San Francisco, and DC to meet with alumni in their places of business. Perhaps the office's most unique feature is that it runs a sequence of for-credit College-to-Career courses. Having an actual academic program dedicated to career prep affords the OPCD the chance to teach large numbers of students about matching their personalities to fulfilling careers, finding internships, developing cover letters, considering cost-of-living issues post-graduation, and so much more. Almost one-quarter of graduates take at least one of those courses. Employer relations at Wake are also strong, and they host a number of well-attended job fairs. Additionally, more than 12,000 job and internship postings go up each year. All freshmen are introduced to the services offered via the OPCD Orientation that alerts students to the wealth of career-prep resources available to them from the moment they step on campus. Overall, Wake Forest's career services office is held in high regard, a view backed by the fact that almost every single graduate achieves a successful outcome within months of exiting campus.

Professional Outcomes

The members of the Class of 2019 didn't take long to arrive at their next destinations. Within six months of graduation, 98 percent had either landed their first professional job or were already matriculated into a graduate program. Management/Consulting, Investment Banking, and Healthcare were the top three industries. Employers landing the highest numbers of alumni included national and multinational corporations IBM, Siemens, Volvo, Goldman Sachs, Disney, Deloitte, Dell, Gucci, PepsiCo, EY, and Nike. Over 45 percent of graduates remain south of the Mason-Dixon Line; most of those who do exit the South head to the Mid-Atlantic region and the Northeast. By the start of midcareer Wake Forest alumni earn the second-highest median salary of any school in North Carolina, behind Duke but ahead of Davidson and UNC-Chapel Hill.

Just shy of 30 percent of graduates went directly from donning their caps and gowns to pursuing advanced degrees. Students attend a wide range of schools from a selectivity standpoint, but there is a strong representation of elite institutions. As one example, an examination of recent history majors shows acceptances at elite institutions including the Duke, Notre Dame, Columbia, Yale, Cornell, and Princeton. Many biology majors headed to PhD programs or into medical school at locations such as UNC, Duke, Johns Hopkins, Tufts, and Emory; Wake Forest's medical school takes in many of its own graduates. There were 125 medical school applicants in the Class of 2020 alone.

Admission

Applicants to the Class of 2023 were accepted at a 30 percent clip, a bit lower than five years prior when 36 percent of applicants were successful. However, the average profile of an admitted student has barely changed in that time. Applications may be on the rise, but the requirements for admission have stayed fairly constant. Wake Forest is a test-optional school, but among those attending students who submitted scores, the middle-50 percent ranges were 1340-1470 on the SAT and 30-33 on the ACT. Three-quarters of the freshman class finished in the top 10 percent of their high school class, and 92 percent were in the top 25 percent.

The above statistics jibe with factors that the admissions office self-reports as being "most important": rigor of curriculum, GPA, class, essay, and character/personal characteristics. If being a Demon Deacon has been your lifelong dream, then you should strongly consider applying early decision to gain an edge on your competition. However, in 2019, that advantage was less than in a typical cycle, as Wake accepted 31 percent of ED applicants compared to 29 percent in the regular round. Still, those accepted ED comprised 46 percent of the Class of 2023. Landing a spot on this gorgeous Winston-Salem campus requires passing a holistic review, perhaps made even more holistic by the university's decision to jettison standardized testing back in 2008. Nonetheless, 44 percent of applicants still submit SAT results, and 45 percent submit ACT scores. Applicants should bring stellar grades to the table, possess a robust extracurricular profile, and should use their ED card to their advantage (at least in most cycles).

Worth Your Money?

Wake Forest only awards need-based aid to 28 percent of its undergraduates, a low number compared to other top schools, but when it does offer aid, it does it right. One hundred percent see their full demonstrated need met for an average annual grant of $52,739. On the flip side, the school awards massive amounts of merit aid, an unusual practice for a school of its caliber. Over one-quarter of current undergraduates are recipients of merit-based awards that average $23k. The list price cost of attendance for Wake Forest is greater than $77,000, so those packages help make the school a bit more affordable for the non-wealthy. However, Wake grads still end up with debt loads that exceed the national average. Individuals required to take out a significant amount in loans should consider their career plans and other competing offers before deciding to attend Wake.

FINANCIAL
Institutional Type: Private
In-State Tuition: $56,722
Out-of-State Tuition: $56,722
Room & Board: $17,334
Required Fees: $1,038
Books & Supplies: $1,500

Avg. Need-Based Grant: $52,729
Avg. % of Need Met: 100%

Avg. Merit-Based Award: $23,129
% Receiving (All Freshmen): 28%
% Receiving (Freshmen w/o Need): 4%

Avg. Cumulative Debt: $34,053
% of Students Borrowing: 30%

CAREER
Who Recruits
1. MullenLowe Mediahub
2. Gap, Inc.
3. Horizon Media
4. Gartner
5. Goldman Sachs

Notable Internships
1. Bristol-Myers Squibb
2. Aramark
3. Sotheby's

Top Industries
1. Business
2. Education
3. Finance
4. Operations
5. Sales

Top Employers
1. Wells Fargo
2. EY
3. BB&T
4. PwC
5. Deloitte

Where Alumni Work
1. Winston-Salem, NC
2. New York City
3. Charlotte
4. Washington DC
5. Raleigh-Durham, NC

Median Earnings
College Scorecard (Early Career): $63,800
PayScale (Early Career): $64,800
PayScale (Mid-Career): $130,200

RANKINGS
Money: 146
U.S. News: 28 (T), National Universities
Wall Street Journal/THE: 64
Washington Monthly: 70, National Universities

COLLEGE OVERLAPS
Boston College
Emory University
University of North Carolina at Chapel Hill
University of Virginia
University of Richmond

Washington & Lee University

Lexington, Virginia | 540-458-8710

The influence of two disparate figures in American history, George Washington and Robert E. Lee (whose name the faculty recently voted to remove from the university name), helped shape a small liberal arts school known in the eighteenth century as Liberty Hall Academy and in the nineteenth century as Washington College before it evolved into Washington and Lee University that, today, is an elite liberal arts institution home to 1,860 undergraduates. Although dubbed a "university," the only postgraduate program is its law school. Set in the small town of Lexington, Virginia, Washington and Lee is one of the premier colleges of its modest size in all of the South, and it has remained highly selective for the entirety of the twenty-first century.

Inside the Classroom
W&L demands a high number of courses to fulfill its foundational and distributional requirements that collectively will take close to three full semesters to complete. Mandated coursework includes writing, foreign language, physical education, computer science, literature, fine arts, four arts and humanities classes, and two in each of the natural and social sciences. One experiential learning course that focuses on research/presentation/cultural competence rounds out the academic requirements that apply to all undergrads. The university offers thirty-seven majors and twenty-nine minors, including a fair share of interdisciplinary programs.

With an exceptionally low 8:1 student-to-faculty ratio and no graduate students to attend to, W&L undergraduates enjoy loads of attention. Over three-quarters of class sections contain nineteen or fewer students, and less than 1 percent of courses enroll more than thirty students. Instructors earn rave reviews as 98 percent of recent grads were either "very satisfied" or "satisfied" by the quality of their professors. Students can participate in research via the Summer Research Scholars that allows undergrads to collaborate with faculty in the field or lab. Studying abroad is a typical part of a Washington and Lee education with 70 percent of grads spending a semester or summer in a foreign land.

Altogether the various social science disciplines account for one-quarter of the degrees conferred at Washington and Lee, business (20 percent), biology (9 percent), and foreign language (6 percent) are next in popularity. The renowned Williams School of Commerce, Politics, and Economics offers outstanding business-oriented programs that feed many of the top corporations in the world. English, history, and W&L's Department of Journalism and Mass Communication are also highly respected. Given Washington and Lee's many strengths, a healthy number of students are encouraged to apply for prestigious fellowships, and a good number are successful. In 2020, eight undergrads were awarded Fulbrights while other recent grads have taken home Goldwater Scholarships and a William Jefferson Clinton Scholarship to study in Dubai.

Outside the Classroom
The main campus of Washington and Lee is concentrated on fifty acres, but it has an additional forty acres of playing fields and 215 acres of green space. All first-year students are required to reside in freshman-exclusive dormitories with twelve to twenty students per floor. Sophomores and juniors primarily live in dorms, apartments, and in Greek houses. To say the Greek scene dominates social life is to grossly understate its reach on campus. The school's eight sororities attract 71 percent of female students and a slightly higher 77 percent of males join the thirteen fraternities on campus. The Generals play twenty-four NCAA Division III sports, which means that varsity athletes comprise a sizable 25 percent of the student body; 40 percent play a varsity sport for at least one year. Twenty-five intramural sports, from flag football to Whiffle ball, attract three-quarters of the student body as well as many faculty members who are eligible to participate. An impressive 90 percent of surveyed undergraduates were satisfied with the school's extracurricular offerings. There are 120+ clubs and organizations presently operating, including the always popular Outing Club that camps and hikes around the neighboring wilderness on weekends. Lexington is a small town with a population around 7,000, but it does have its share of bars and restaurants. Richmond is a two-hour trip by car, and DC is a three-hour drive from campus.

Career Services
The Career and Professional Development Center (CPDC) is staffed by seven full-time professional employees serving as pre-law advisor, international advisor, assistant director of STEM programs, and assistant director of recruitment. That equates to a student-to-advisor ratio of 266:1, which is within the better-than-average range when compared to other institutions included in this book. Excellent personalized attention is provided to the tune of 960 unique student appointments (3.3 per participating student) per year. Each year, the center staff meets one-on-one with 52 percent of the student population, including two-thirds of seniors.

The CPDC brings 60+ employers to Lexington each year for information sessions, recruitment, and on-campus interviews. It also organizes six career exploration trips to DC and New York City that focused on finance, the arts, advertising, marketing, and STEM fields. Staff also host more than sixty career exploration and skill-building workshops on topics such as social media, Excel, and how to write a personal statement. A dazzling 85 percent of students complete at least one internship, fellowship, or practicum. Further, 94 percent of those completing such an experience found it "extremely helpful" or "somewhat helpful" in preparing for a career. With ample individualized attention and opportunity for hands-on experience, W&L's Career and Professional Development Center rates well in the eyes of our staff.

Professional Outcomes

Last year, 69 percent of 2019 graduates found employment within six months of saying goodbye to Lexington. The most frequently entered industries by recent grads were financial services, economics/finance, education, consulting, and real estate. With so many flocking to financial jobs, many top banks, accounting firms, and investment houses presently employ more than two dozen Generals including EY, Wells Fargo, Goldman Sachs, PwC, JP Morgan, Capital One, and Morgan Stanley. Washington and Lee is the rare college that sees the majority of its alumni relocate to cities in other states. DC, New York City, and Atlanta all draw more graduates than Roanoke or Richmond. Starting salaries for the Class of 2019 were solid with 51 percent of the cohort being paid $55,000 or more while 21 percent brought home in excess of $75,000.

Almost one-quarter of grads immediately matriculated into a graduate or professional program upon receiving their bachelor's degrees. Within five years of graduating, many attend law school (11 percent), medical schools (12 percent), and MBA Programs (7 percent). Recent physics and engineering students have gone on to graduate study at MIT, Carnegie Mellon, Stanford, and Vanderbilt. Law schools accepting recent grads included Wake Forest, Fordham, Georgetown, Vanderbilt, and W&L's own law school. Medical school acceptances included Rutgers Medical School, LSU School of Medicine in New Orleans, and University of Texas Medical Branch.

Admission

Of 6,178 applicants for a seat in the Class of 2023 only 1,147 were admitted for an acceptance rate of 19 percent; 462 ultimately enrolled. The median SAT score was 1430, and the average ACT Composite was 33. Most 2019-20 freshmen hailed from the very top of their high school class with 82 percent placing in the top decile and 96 percent in the top 25 percent. All of the admissions statistics are almost identical to those of a decade ago. In fact, the number of applicants, acceptance rate, and the achievement level of entering freshmen has remained relatively steady since the turn of the millennium.

The goal of the admissions committee is to "get to know you as well as possible through your application." The rigor of your high school curriculum is very important—96 percent of entering freshmen had an IB or AP background, and just shy of three-quarters studied four or more years of a foreign language. Only three other factors rated as "very important": class rank, extracurricular activities, and character/personal qualities. Applying early decision is a no-brainer for dedicated applicants as the acceptance rate was 43 percent versus 16 percent for those in the regular cycle. In fact, the school locks in 55 percent of its freshman class via the ED round. Washington and Lee offers a genuinely holistic admissions process. Strong grades in highly rigorous courses are nonnegotiable, but qualities like leadership and what one brings to a student community also receive strong consideration.

Worth Your Money?

While a $77k+ price tag might make cost-conscious families aggressively scratch Washington and Lee off their child's college list, it is one of the most generous schools with merit aid for exceptional students. While only 30 percent receive that form of aid, the average amount is for a difference-making sum of $54,293, with as much as 10 percent of each entering class receiving the highly coveted Johnson Scholarship, which fully covers tuition, room, and board for chosen applicants. That generosity is only trumped by the school's dedication to meeting 100 percent of financial need for every qualifying student. Thanks to that level of financial assistance and excellent graduate outcomes, Washington and Lee is worth the money for most attendees.

FINANCIAL
Institutional Type: Private
In-State Tuition: $56,170
Out-of-State Tuition: $56,170
Room & Board: $15,810
Required Fees: $1,115
Books & Supplies: $2,220

Avg. Need-Based Grant: $49,720
Avg. % of Need Met: 100%

Avg. Merit-Based Award: $54,293
% Receiving (All Freshmen): 30%
% Receiving (Freshmen w/o Need): 7%

Avg. Cumulative Debt: $22,415
% of Students Borrowing: 32%

CAREER
Who Recruits
1. Walker & Dunlap
2. Citi
3. Merrill Lynch
4. Berkeley Research Group
5. Morgan Stanley

Notable Internships
1. Estee Lauder Companies
2. Twitter
3. North Carolina Museum of Art

Top Industries
1. Business
2. Finance
3. Education
4. Legal
5. Operations

Top Employers
1. EY
2. PwC
3. Morgan Stanley
4. Wells Fargo
5. JPMorgan Chase

Where Alumni Work
1. Washington DC
2. New York City
3. Atlanta
4. Roanoke, VA
5. Richmond

Median Earnings
College Scorecard (Early Career): $76,100
PayScale (Early Career): $69,100
PayScale (Mid-Career): $145,400

RANKINGS
Money: 12
U.S. News: 9 (T), Liberal Arts Colleges
Wall Street Journal/THE: 71 (T)
Washington Monthly: 4, Liberal Arts Colleges

COLLEGE OVERLAPS
Dartmouth College
Davidson College
University of North Carolina at Chapel Hill
University of Virginia
Vanderbilt University

Washington University in St. Louis

St. Louis, Missouri | 314-935-6000

ADMISSION
Admission Rate: 15%
Admission Rate - Men: 15%
Admission Rate - Women: 15%
EA Admission Rate: Not Offered
ED Admission Rate: 42%
ED Admits as % of Total Admits: 16%
Admission Rate (5-Year Trend): -1%
% of Admits Attending (Yield): 38%
Transfer Admission Rate: 20%

SAT Reading/Writing (Middle 50%): 710-770
SAT Math (Middle 50%): 760-800
ACT Composite (Middle 50%): 32-35

% Graduated in Top 10% of HS Class: 80%
% Graduated in Top 25% of HS Class: 97%
% Graduated in Top 50% of HS Class: 99%

Demonstrated Interest: Very Important
Legacy Status: Considered
Admission Interview Offered: Yes

ENROLLMENT
Total Undergraduate Enrollment: 7,751
% Part-Time: 8%
% Male: 47%
% Female: 53%
% Out-of-State: 90%
% Fraternity: 26%
% Sorority: 38%
% On-Campus (Freshman): 100%
% On-Campus (All Undergraduate): 74%

% African-American: 9%
% Asian: 16%
% Hispanic: 9%
% White: 51%
% Other: 5%
% Race or Ethnicity Unknown: 2%
% International: 8%
% Low-Income: 6%

ACADEMICS
Student-to-Faculty Ratio: 7 to 1
% of Classes Under 20: 66%
% of Classes 20-49: 25%
% of Classes 50 or More: 10%
% Full-Time Faculty: 67%
% Full-Time Faculty w/ Terminal Degree: 93%

Top Programs
Architecture
Biology
Business
Design
Economics
Engineering
Political Science
Psychology and Brain Sciences

Retention Rate: 97%
4-Year Graduation Rate: 88%
6-Year Graduation Rate: 94%

Curricular Flexibility: Somewhat Flexible
Academic Rating: ★★★★★

#CollegesWorthYourMoney

Despite receiving consistently high rankings since U.S. News released its first college guide in 1983, Washington University in St. Louis is, perhaps, the finest institution that is not a household name across the nation. Yet, this Midwestern research and pre-professional powerhouse is one of the most respected institutions in the eyes of Fortune 500 employers and elite graduate schools alike. Catering to 7,751 undergraduates, WashU admits students into five schools: Arts & Sciences, the Olin School of Business, the School of Engineering & Applied Sciences, and the Art of Architecture programs housed within the Sam Fox School of Design and Visual Arts.

Inside the Classroom

Arts & Sciences, which claims more than half the student body, offers more than eighty majors, and all are guided by the IQ Curriculum, the school's signature liberal arts course of study. As part of the IQ Curriculum students must take courses in applied numeracy, social contrasts, writing, and an additional course that is classified as "writing intensive." WashU students also must complete coursework in the humanities, social sciences, natural sciences/math, and foreign language along with three "integrations" that can be completed via multi-semester, cross-disciplinary coursework. Engineering students are not beholden to all of those curricular mandates. Special programs include the University Scholars Program in Medicine that allows students to apply for admission to both an undergraduate degree program and medical school before entering college as well as the Beyond Boundaries Program that allows students to implement a cross-disciplinary approach with the aim of solving major global and societal problems.

The university has a 7:1 student-faculty ratio, and 66 percent of classes have fewer than twenty- students; over one-quarter have single-digit enrollments. WUSTL students are known for being more collaborative than competitive and extremely hard working as evidenced by the fact that 75 percent double major or pursue multiple degrees. The Office of Undergraduate Research helps students land opportunities to research alongside faculty, primarily in the summers. A solid 59 percent of undergraduates report participating in a research endeavor and one-third study abroad.

Nationally recognized programs are numerous: the Olin Business School, the School of Engineering & Applied Sciences, and the College of Architecture are well-respected by employers. The Biology Department prepares many successful med school candidates, including for the university's own ultra-elite medical school. The most commonly conferred degrees are in engineering (14 percent), social sciences (14 percent), biology (12 percent), business (11 percent), and psychology (8 percent). Fulbright, Gilman, Luce, and Critical Language Scholarships all have been won by WashU grads in recent years, and two students were named Rhodes finalists in 2020.

Outside the Classroom

It sounds trite, but by almost any metric one must conclude that Washington University students seem happy. Dorms, recreational facilities, and campus food are routinely rated well. The WashU atmosphere is known for being more laid-back and friendly than that at many of its elite peers. Seventy-two percent of the student body and 100 percent of freshmen reside on campus. WashU's ten fraternities and eight sororities draw roughly one-third of the student body into Greek participation. The Bears compete in NCCA Division III, fielding nine men's teams and ten women's squads. The athletically-inclined student body also has forty-one club teams, and a simply insane three-quarters of undergraduates participate in intramural sports. In excess of 380 student-run organizations are active at WUSTL, all under the purview of the Washington University Student Union, one of the most well-funded college student governments in the country. Each semester it funds a concert known as WILD (for Walk In, Lay Down) that features a big-time musical act and well-attended speaker events are also organized on a regular basis. For those inclined to explore off campus, the university is located within a few miles of the St. Louis Zoo, multiple art museums, a host of great eateries, and the gorgeous Missouri Botanical Garden.

Career Services

The Washington University in St. Louis Career Center is staffed by twenty-one full-time professional employees who specialize in employer relations, career counseling, event planning, and pre-graduate school advising. With a student-to-advisor ratio of 369:1, WUSTL compares favorably to the other institutions included in this book. Having conducted 5,112 advising sessions in the 2018-19 school year, the center staff does a superb job of engaging their undergraduate student population.

Washington University in St. Louis

E-mail: admissions@wustl.edu | Website: www.wustl.edu

Five large career fairs drew a collective audience of almost 2,334 individuals and 300 employers. The center also hosted 330 low-key employer information sessions and a number of SLAMs, miniature career fairs for a particular industry where, in a bit of a role-reversal, employers pitch their companies to students. An almost hard-to-fathom 475 employers recruit on campus each year, and close to 1,100 on-campus interviews were conducted in 2018-19. Thanks to the strong employer connections forged by career services staff, WashU students have no trouble landing internships at major companies like CBS News, Pfizer, and AT&T, and stipends are available through the university to help offset living expenses. All told, approximately 75 percent of students report completing at least one internship. With ample staffing, superior outreach, and positive student outcomes, WashU's Career Center could not be doing a better job.

Professional Outcomes

The Class of 2019 sent 74 percent of its exiting members into the workforce and 22 percent into graduate and professional schools. The thirty companies employing the highest number of WashU grads feature many of the most sought-after employers in the world including Amazon, Bain, Boeing, Deloitte, Google, IBM, Goldman Sachs, and Microsoft. Of the employed members of the Class of 2019 who reported their starting salaries, 52 percent made more than $60k. Geographically, remaining in Missouri was the favored choice among fresh alums, but a fair number also resettled in New York and California.

The universities welcoming the largest number of Bears included the prestigious institutions of Caltech, Columbia, Harvard, Penn, Princeton, and Stanford. Others were pursuing graduate degrees at non-elite schools including Case Western, Rutgers, Colorado State, and St. Louis University. In 2019, there were 61 grads accepted into med school, including at WashU's own top-ranked medical school. Baylor College of Medicine attracted a large number of future physicians; students also enjoyed acceptances into Harvard Medical School, NYU School of Medicine, and the Icahn School of Medicine at Mt. Sinai.

Admission

WashU received over 25,000 applications for a place in the Class of 2023, but it admitted only 14 percent. Eight-four percent of attending students were in the top 10 percent of their high school class, and the middle 50 percent for SATs was 1480-1570 and 33-35 for the ACTs. For historical reference, in 2010, the university accepted 21 percent of applicants, and enrolling students possessed similar standardized test scores to those being accepted today.

Even with rising application numbers, the admissions committee carefully examines each application, granting "high importance" to soft factors including character/personal qualities, extracurricular activities, talent/ability, and volunteer/work experience. Essays also grace this list, and a new supplemental essay component was added for applicants in 2019. It behooves students seriously committed to WUSTL to give serious consideration to applying early. The admission rate is 42 percent in the early round compared to only 13 percent in the regular cycle, and ED entrants comprise 43 percent of the freshman class. Formerly relegated to Ivy backup status, Washington University has stepped into the limelight as a destination point for the best and brightest from around the country. In fact, close to 65 percent of current students hail from 500+ miles away, including all fifty US states and one hundred countries. This Midwestern behemoth casts a wide net, but only brings aboard the most brag-worthy fish it can find.

Worth Your Money?

A fairly standard (in the world of elite private colleges) $75k list price cost of attendance greets WashU freshmen. Undergrads who qualify for financial aid see 100 percent of that amount met by the university, which averages out to $49k in grant money each academic year. Fourteen percent of students also receive merit aid awards averaging roughly $10,500 per year. This school has one of the wealthiest groups of students in the country (rivaled by Colorado College and Colgate) so, for many, the price tag will not break the bank. Given that reality, WUSTL can make sense for students across a wide spectrum of socioeconomic backgrounds.

FINANCIAL
Institutional Type: Private
In-State Tuition: $54,250
Out-of-State Tuition: $54,250
Room & Board: $16,900
Required Fees: $1,042
Books & Supplies: $1,126

Avg. Need-Based Grant: $48,522
Avg. % of Need Met: 100%

Avg. Merit-Based Award: $10,585
% Receiving (All Freshmen): 14%
% Receiving (Freshmen w/o Need): 10%

Avg. Cumulative Debt: $22,555
% of Students Borrowing: 27%

CAREER
Who Recruits
1. Guggenheim Investments
2. Equifax
3. Cushman & Wakefield
4. Abercrombie & Fitch
5. Chicago Trading Company

Notable Internships
1. St. Louis Post-Dispatch
2. Uber
3. BlackRock

Top Industries
1. Business
2. Education
3. Engineering
4. Research
5. Operations

Top Employers
1. Boeing
2. Google
3. Microsoft
4. Amazon
5. Mastercard

Where Alumni Work
1. St. Louis
2. New York City
3. Chicago
4. San Francisco
5. Washington DC

Median Earnings
College Scorecard (Early Career): $70,100
PayScale (Early Career): $69,300
PayScale (Mid-Career): $126,200

RANKINGS
Money: 61
U.S. News: 16 (T), National Universities
Wall Street Journal/THE: 18
Washington Monthly: 64, National Universities

COLLEGE OVERLAPS
Duke University
Northwestern University
University of Michigan
University of Pennsylvania
Vanderbilt University

Wellesley College

Wellesley, Massachusetts | 781-283-2270

ADMISSION
Admission Rate: 22%
Admission Rate - Men: Not Applicable
Admission Rate - Women: 22%
EA Admission Rate: Not Offered
ED Admission Rate: 33%
ED Admits as % of Total Admits: 16%
Admission Rate (5-Year Trend): -8%
% of Admits Attending (Yield): 44%
Transfer Admission Rate: 9%

SAT Reading/Writing (Middle 50%): 680-750
SAT Math (Middle 50%): 680-780
ACT Composite (Middle 50%): 31-34

% Graduated in Top 10% of HS Class: 79%
% Graduated in Top 25% of HS Class: 93%
% Graduated in Top 50% of HS Class: 99%

Demonstrated Interest: Considered
Legacy Status: Considered
Admission Interview Offered: Yes

ENROLLMENT
Total Undergraduate Enrollment: 2,519
% Part-Time: 5%
% Male: 2%
% Female: 98%
% Out-of-State: 86%
% Fraternity: Not Offered
% Sorority: Not Offered
% On-Campus (Freshman): 100%
% On-Campus (All Undergraduate): 97%

% African-American: 6%
% Asian: 22%
% Hispanic: 12%
% White: 35%
% Other: 7%
% Race or Ethnicity Unknown: 4%
% International: 13%
% Low-Income: 24%

ACADEMICS
Student-to-Faculty Ratio: 8 to 1
% of Classes Under 20: 66%
% of Classes 20-49: 34%
% of Classes 50 or More: 0%
% Full-Time Faculty: 88%
% Full-Time Faculty w/ Terminal Degree: 93%

Top Programs
Area Studies
Chemistry
Computer Science
Economics
English
History
Neuroscience
Political Science

Retention Rate: 95%
4-Year Graduation Rate: 84%
6-Year Graduation Rate: 91%

Curricular Flexibility: Somewhat Flexible
Academic Rating: ★★★★★

#CollegesWorthYourMoney

In 1995, the New York Times proclaimed, "More than any other college—large or small— Wellesley has groomed women who shatter the glass ceiling." Twenty five years later, Barnard has surpassed Wellesley for the lowest acceptance rate among women's colleges, but Wellesley's picture-perfect campus in suburban Boston remains the premier pipeline to the boardrooms of America's most powerful companies as well as to the highest levels of politics. Students are known to be a driven bunch as committed to full engagement with campus activities as they are to the exceptionally rigorous classroom experience.

Inside the Classroom

The college's 2,519 undergraduate students can select from fifty departmental and interdisciplinary majors, and economics, biology, and computer science are the most frequently conferred degrees. All freshmen must complete an expository writing course, and all seniors must demonstrate foreign language proficiency. In between, students are required to complete coursework in natural and physical science, mathematical modeling and problem solving, social and behavioral analysis, language and literature, art/music/theater/film/video, epistemology and cognition, historical studies, and religion/ethics/moral philosophy. There is also a multicultural and an uncredited physical education requirement.

The student-to-faculty ratio is only 8:1, leading to average class sizes in the seventeen- to twenty-student range. Twenty-one percent of course sections have single-digit enrollments while two-thirds have fewer than nineteen students. With no graduate students to compete with, opportunities for participation in research with faculty members abound. The Summer Science Research Program is cited by many graduates as the most influential part of their educational experience. Wellesley students also regularly land research positions with the National Institutes of Health, Harvard Medical School, MIT, and The Children's Hospital of Philadelphia. The Office of International Studies facilitates the overseas study of hundreds of students each year with 45 percent of juniors spending a semester in one of 160 programs worldwide.

The entire undergraduate program at Wellesley is revered by top corporations and graduate schools alike. Most programs possess sterling reputations, including chemistry, computer science, neuroscience, and political science. However, the Department of Economics appears to shine most brightly, leading many into PhD programs and high-profile careers. A large number of Wellesley graduates are awarded prestigious postgraduate scholarships each year. In 2020, the school produced three Fulbright Scholars, and have seen Gilman Scholars, Watson Fellows, Critical Languages Scholars, Princeton in Asia Fellows in recent years.

Outside the Classroom

Approximately 97 percent of undergraduates are denizens of the school's twenty-one residence halls that range in capacity from forty to 285 students. Wellesley's 500-acre campus was described by fabled architect Frederick Olmstead as possessing "a peculiar kind of intricate beauty." Thanks to Lake Waban, a golf course, an arboretum, and botanical gardens, you will never long for gorgeous landscapes and natural beauty. There are thirteen varsity athletic teams that are members of NCAA Division III as well as eight club teams in sports that include archery, equestrian, and Nordic skiing. Athletic facilities are extensive and include the Keohane Sports Center, a pool, spin rooms, dance studios, a rock climbing wall, and just about any other fitness-related amenity one can conjure up. Wellesley women have 150 student-run organizations to choose from, including a number of dance, music, and theater groups. This is a tradition-rich school with annual events like Flower Sunday and quarterly competitions like Stepsinging, a class-vs.-class singing contest on the steps of Houghton Chapel. The town of Wellesley has coffee shops, a bookstore, and a pharmacy all within a short walk. Downtown Boston is less than half an hour away by car, but most take the T, commuter trains, or a shuttle that regularly departs from campus.

Career Services

The Wellesley Career Education Office is staffed by twenty-four professionals working in career counseling, internships, fellowships, experiential learning, and employer relations. For a school with 2,500+ students, the size and scope of this office is remarkable. The 105:1 student-to-advisor ratio is unmatched by any institution in the country. It's no wonder that the National Association of Colleges and Employers named Wellesley the 2017 winner of the Career Service Excellence Award among small colleges; the department has been similarly recognized multiple times by national organizations for its superior career service offerings. Staff members regularly present at national conferences and publish on the topic of career preparation.

Wellesley College

E-mail: admission@wellesley.edu | Website: www.wellesley.edu

The office had a 98 percent satisfaction rate after in-person, one-on-one appointments; that was a dramatic improvement over the Class of 2015's satisfaction rate of 45 percent. Almost 90 percent of undergraduates complete at least one internship, including so-called Signature Internships with "leading cultural, educational, and scientific institutions; international agencies; media outlets; advocacy and community organizations; and businesses" around the globe. In the 2018-19 academic year, 81 percent of the undergraduate population engaged face-to-face with career services, and 98 percent engaged digitally. The annual total of advising sessions exceeds 6,500. There were 285 events held with a total attendance of 5,293, and thirty-four employers engaged in on-campus interviews including Google, Microsoft, Citi, and the US Department of Commerce. Unlike some of the other Seven Sister institutions, opportunities at the world's premier companies are commonplace, and salaries are higher than average. With superb resources and equally strong outcomes, the Wellesley Career Education Office deserves all of the many accolades that have been heaped upon it.

Professional Outcomes

Six months after earning their degrees, 96 percent of the Wellesley College Class of 2019 had already achieved positive outcomes. Of the three-quarters of grads who were employed, 23 percent were working in the finance/consulting/business fields, 17 percent in health care/life sciences, 15 percent in education, and 13 percent in internet and technology/engineering. The top employers included Accenture, Google, JP Morgan, Boston Children's Hospital, Goldman Sachs, and a number of top universities that included Harvard and MIT. One hundred thirty-two members of the Class of 2019 were employed in Boston, fifty-two in New York, thirty-four in California, and twenty in Washington, DC. The average starting salary was a solid $62k with an average bonus of $11k.

Wellesley grads almost universally go on to elite graduate programs. Of the 19 percent of 2019 grads who directly entered an advanced degree program, the top dozen most common schools attended included Ivies Harvard, Columbia, Brown, Penn, and Cornell and other upper-crust institutions at Stanford, MIT, Emory, NYU, Brandeis, Boston University, and the Olin College of Engineering. Medical school applicants are generally successful; from 2008-2018 an average of 72 percent of med school hopefuls were accepted by at least one university. Three or more recent grads have been accepted into medical school at Dartmouth, Tufts, Case Western, Boston University, and Northwestern. Law school acceptance rates hover in the low-to-mid 80s, a figure that is lowered by the caliber of law schools to which Wellesley grads typically apply. Law schools that accepted a minimum of three alumni in recent years include Yale, Duke, Harvard, Georgetown, Cornell, Penn, and UC Berkeley.

Admission

The 6,395 applications received for a place in the Class of 2023 was the second highest total in school history; the acceptance rate of 22 percent was two points higher than the previous cycle. Those mid-50 percent ranges of those enrolled were 1370-1510 on the SAT, 31-34 on the ACT, and 79 percent were in the top 10 percent of their class. Wellesley boasts a high yield rate of 44 percent, meaning that few apply on a whim, and nearly half of all admitted students choose to enroll in the college.

As part of its holistic review process, the admissions committee seeks "people who know that we don't know everything; who have a strong voice but listen to other voices; who have big plans but are totally open to changing them; who have taken risks, failed, and figured out a better way." As such, four factors are paramount in the evaluation process: character/personal qualities, recommendations, GPA, and rigor of one's secondary school record. The second tier of factors includes test scores, class rank, essays, talent/ability, and extracurricular activities. Applying via early decision can yield a slight advantage as 33 percent of students are accepted during the ED round. In terms of pure acceptance rate, Wellesley is the second-most selective Seven Sisters school, behind only Barnard. High grades and strong test scores are required, but many softer factors weigh heavily on admissions decisions. Applicants who are involved in their high schools and communities will fare best.

Worth Your Money?

Even at a $76,220 annual cost of attendance, Wellesley is unquestionably worth the investment. You won't receive merit aid from this school, but 58 percent of the student population does receive need-based aid, and that need is met 100 percent. That translates to an average need-based grant of $54,500. The quality of the education, mentorship, and professional networks make Wellesley, even at full price for non-STEM/business majors, the rare school that will return your money many times over.

FINANCIAL
Institutional Type: Private
In-State Tuition: $58,120
Out-of-State Tuition: $58,120
Room & Board: $17,772
Required Fees: $328
Books & Supplies: $800

Avg. Need-Based Grant: $54,500
Avg. % of Need Met: 100%

Avg. Merit-Based Award: $56,052
% Receiving (All Freshmen): 2%
% Receiving (Freshmen w/o Need): 0%

Avg. Cumulative Debt: $23,437
% of Students Borrowing: 45%

CAREER
Who Recruits
1. Boston Consulting Group
2. Teach for America
3. U.S. Federal Reserve
4. Massachusetts General Hospital
5. State Street

Notable Internships
1. Metropolitan Museum of Art
2. American Express
3. Dick Clark Productions

Top Industries
1. Business
2. Education
3. Research
4. Media
5. Social Services

Top Employers
1. Google
2. Microsoft
3. Accenture
4. Amazon
5. Facebook

Where Alumni Work
1. Boston
2. New York City
3. San Francisco
4. Washington DC
5. Los Angeles

Median Earnings
College Scorecard (Early Career): $60,800
PayScale (Early Career): $63,900
PayScale (Mid-Career): $113,700

RANKINGS
Money: 88
U.S. News: 4 (T), Liberal Arts Colleges
Wall Street Journal/THE: 29
Washington Monthly: 13, Liberal Arts Colleges

COLLEGE OVERLAPS
Barnard College
Brown University
Smith College
Tufts University
University of Pennsylvania

Wesleyan University

Middletown, Connecticut | 860-685-3000

ADMISSION
Admission Rate: 16%
Admission Rate - Men: 20%
Admission Rate - Women: 14%
EA Admission Rate: Not Offered
ED Admission Rate: 37%
ED Admits as % of Total Admits: 19%
Admission Rate (5-Year Trend): -4%
% of Admits Attending (Yield): 35%
Transfer Admission Rate: 27%

SAT Reading/Writing (Middle 50%): 650-740
SAT Math (Middle 50%): 670-770
ACT Composite (Middle 50%): 31-34

% Graduated in Top 10% of HS Class: 67%
% Graduated in Top 25% of HS Class: 86%
% Graduated in Top 50% of HS Class: 94%

Demonstrated Interest: Not Considered
Legacy Status: Considered
Admission Interview Offered: Yes

ENROLLMENT
Total Undergraduate Enrollment: 3,018
% Part-Time: 3%
% Male: 46%
% Female: 54%
% Out-of-State: 92%
% Fraternity: 4%
% Sorority: 1%
% On-Campus (Freshman): 100%
% On-Campus (All Undergraduate): 99%

% African-American: 6%
% Asian: 7%
% Hispanic: 11%
% White: 53%
% Other: 6%
% Race or Ethnicity Unknown: 3%
% International: 13%
% Low-Income: 15%

ACADEMICS
Student-to-Faculty Ratio: 8 to 1
% of Classes Under 20: 75%
% of Classes 20-49: 22%
% of Classes 50 or More: 3%
% Full-Time Faculty: 87%
% Full-Time Faculty w/ Terminal Degree: 92%

Top Programs
Area Studies
Economics
English
Film Studies
Government
Neuroscience and Behavior
Performing Arts
Sociology

Retention Rate: 97%
4-Year Graduation Rate: 88%
6-Year Graduation Rate: 92%

Curricular Flexibility: Very Flexible
Academic Rating: ★★★★✦

#CollegesWorthYourMoney

Considered one of the "Little Ivies" and officially a member of the "Little Three" alongside Amherst and Williams, Wesleyan University in Middletown, Connecticut, has much in common with its highly selective compatriots, but it also possesses a distinctively uncompromising and independent-minded student body. One telling anecdote comes from 1998 when the administration proudly unveiled the school's new slogan, "The Independent Ivy." Many young people would love for their college to associate itself with the cachet of the Ivy League, but at Wesleyan the student response was utter disgust that led to an all-out rebellion. The students launched a vocal protest, and the higher-ups quickly dropped the slogan. That's Wesleyan in a nutshell.

Inside the Classroom

At 3,018 undergraduate students, Wes is significantly larger than many of its elite liberal arts peers. With forty-five majors, seventeen minors, and over 1,000 classes running each academic year, the school truly has something for everyone. The academic requirements are relatively minimal, giving undergrads a high degree of intellectual freedom. There are two stages of general education courses: stage one sees students complete two courses each in the three divisions of Humanities & Arts, Social & Behavioral Sciences, and Natural Sciences & Math. Stage two is optional for most majors but may be required to receive departmental honors at graduation.

Just over three-quarters of class sections have fewer than twenty students, allowing for close bonds/mentorships to unfold. Students rave about the accessible faculty (the faculty-to-student ratio is 8:1), and research opportunities with professors are plentiful. The program for undergraduate Research in the Sciences funds over one hundred students per year to conduct research over the summer. The university has increased its study abroad participation in recent years to the point that almost 50 percent of students now spend a semester overseas.

There isn't one go-to major at Wes; while the social sciences (24 percent), psychology (16 percent), ethnic/gender studies (14 percent), and the visual and performing arts (12 percent) are the most popular, none represents a massive percentage of the total degrees conferred. Nearly every program at Wesleyan is respected in the employer/graduate school communities, with offerings in economics, English, film studies, and neuroscience receiving perhaps the most praise. Wesleyan was again named a top producer of Fulbright Scholars in 2018, seeing seven student and alumni winners.

Outside the Classroom

The unofficial but popular motto, "Keep Wes Weird," perfectly sums up this iconoclastic student body's vibe and helps describe life on campus. Those looking for wild frat parties and raucous football games would be highly disappointed (and confused) walking around the Wesleyan campus. Greek life attracts a minuscule 3 percent of students and, other than the one-quarter of undergraduates who comprise the rosters of the school's twenty-nine varsity sports teams, athletics are not a focal point for the average student. That being said, participation is high in intramural and club sports including ultimate Frisbee, kung fu, and WesClimb, which takes advantage of the schools own rock climbing wall. Wesleyan's other amenities include a 412-seat movie theater that screens films throughout the year, a fifty-meter swimming pool, a 7,500- square-foot gymnasium, and an ice skating rink. There are more than 250 active student-run groups with large numbers in the areas of activism/politics, identity, theater, comedy troupes, and a cappella. The Center for the Arts hosts more than 300 events each year from jazz concerts to one-person shows to art exhibitions. Middletown provides a nice enough small city environment with plenty of bars and restaurants to frequent, and Hartford is only a twenty-five minute drive. Just about everyone lives on campus.

Career Services

The Gordon Career Center is staffed by ten full-time staff who specialize in employer relations, general advising, health professions advising, STEM career advising, and business career advising. The 302:1 student-to-advisor ratio places it in the above-average range compared to other schools profiled in this guide. The school does not organize any large career expos/fairs; instead, it hosts events just about every day along the lines of a chat over coffee with Deloitte to a gathering entitled "Google at Wes: Laying the Foundation for Your Technical Career" featuring Wesleyan alumni who work for the tech giant.

Wes has partnered with a number of major employers to facilitate on-campus recruiting and interviews including Booz Allen, Lego (fun!), Pfizer, and Squarespace. Interested seniors participate in a job search boot camp known as Accelerate prior to engaging with those visiting companies. The WEShadow Externship programs allows current students the chance to spend anywhere from one day to one week at work with an alum. The Winter on Wyllys program is an intensive, two-week career development course available over the holidays. Data on internship participation rates and overall engagements with the career center is, at present, unavailable.

Professional Outcomes

By the end of calendar year 2019, the majority of those who received their diplomas in May had entered employment (68 percent). Graduate school was the next stop for 15 percent of new alums, and 9 percent were still seeking employment. Of those who landed jobs, the third highest number were in arts and entertainment, which isn't shocking when your school's alumni include the likes of Lin Manuel Miranda, Michael Bay, Joss Whedon, and countless Hollywood writers and producers. Tech/engineering/sciences and education took the silver and gold. The companies employing the highest numbers of Wesleyan Class of 2019 grads included Google, Epic, Analysis Group, Boston Medical Center, Booz Allen Hamilton, Accenture, and Capital Group. New York, Boston, San Francisco, and Hartford were the most popular post-college destinations.

Wes alumni are looked upon favorably by elite graduate and professional schools. From 2016-20 Wesleyan grads were accepted into medical school 55-77 percent of the time, much higher than the national average. Those with a 3.6 GPA or higher enjoyed a superior acceptance rate of 71-87 percent. In the same timespan law school applicants were successful 92-100 percent of the time and fared extremely well at the most prestigious universities. One year, a gasp-worthy 64 percent of law school-bound seniors found a home at a top ten law school including Yale, Harvard, Stanford, Columbia, and UChicago. Those pursuing non-professional advanced degrees enrolled in a wide range of schools from elites like MIT, Stanford, and Berkeley to state universities like Rowan, Temple, and UMass.

Admission

Wesleyan admitted 16 percent of its record-setting 13,264 applicants in 2019, a figure that has increased by more than 35 percent in the past four years. The median score on the SAT for members of the Class of 2023 was 1430 and 32 (mean) on the ACT. Interestingly, this past cycle's acceptance rate was higher than 2017's 15.4 percent clip or even that of a decade ago when the university welcomed only 15 percent of applicants. Yet, somehow that is fitting because Wesleyan's admissions, like its eclectic and talented students, is not unidimensional.

Unlike some other schools of its caliber, Wesleyan does not rule out those who finished outside of the top 10 percent of their high school class. While 67 percent of the Class of 2023 earned that distinction, 6 percent placed outside the top 50 percent. The No. 1 factor in admissions is the rigor of secondary school curriculum as it seeks young people who are "intellectual risk-takers" above all else. Standardized test scores have been made less important by Wesleyan's test-optional policy, but the vast majority of applicants submitted SAT or ACT scores in 2019. Applying early decision is definitely something you want to consider if Wesleyan is your top choice because it fills 53 percent of its freshman class via ED, and it has an admit rate more than double that of the regular cycle (37 percent versus 15 percent). Getting into Wesleyan is not as formulaic a process as it is at the majority of elite institutions. Essays, recommendations, first-generation status, ethnicity, personal characteristics, and performance in the classroom are all given genuine consideration. Possessing good stats is important to your admissions chances, but so is being an engaged and passionate learner.

Worth Your Money?

Wesleyan costs $78k-$81k annually, a price similar to its elite liberal arts kin. A tiny percentage of students receive substantial merit aid, but 98 percent receive no help of that variety. It is need-based aid that rules the day at Wes as all qualifying students have 100 percent of their demonstrated need accounted for. The average grant for those individuals is $52,000+. Not every student who goes to this school cruises into a six-figure job, but that's the aim of a Wesleyan education. This school is worth the cost because it assists you in finding a pathway that aligns with your passions, and it makes the school affordable for those in financial need.

FINANCIAL
Institutional Type: Private
In-State Tuition: $59,086
Out-of-State Tuition: $59,086
Room & Board: $16,384
Required Fees: $600
Books & Supplies: $1,200

Avg. Need-Based Grant: $52,149
Avg. % of Need Met: 100%

Avg. Merit-Based Award: $43,624
% Receiving (All Freshmen): 2%
% Receiving (Freshmen w/o Need): 0%

Avg. Cumulative Debt: $26,016
% of Students Borrowing: 36%

CAREER
Who Recruits
1. MGM Resorts International
2. Pfizer
3. Analysis Group
4. McKinsey & Co.
5. Charles River Associates

Notable Internships
1. Citadel Securities
2. ABC News
3. United Nations

Top Industries
1. Business
2. Education
3. Media
4. Research
5. Social Services

Top Employers
1. Google
2. Citi
3. JPMorgan Chase
4. Accenture
5. Morgan Stanley

Where Alumni Work
1. New York City
2. Boston
3. San Francisco
4. Hartford
5. Washington DC

Median Earnings
College Scorecard (Early Career): $54,700
PayScale (Early Career): $64,600
PayScale (Mid-Career): $134,000

RANKINGS
Money: 131
U.S. News: 20 (T), Liberal Arts Colleges
Wall Street Journal/THE: 46
Washington Monthly: 2, Liberal Arts Colleges

COLLEGE OVERLAPS
Brown University
Cornell University
Middlebury College
Tufts University
Vassar College

Whitman College

Walla Walla, Washington | 509-527-5176

ADMISSION
Admission Rate: 56%
Admission Rate - Men: 55%
Admission Rate - Women: 57%
EA Admission Rate: Not Offered
ED Admission Rate: 72%
ED Admits as % of Total Admits: 5%
Admission Rate (5-Year Trend): -1%
% of Admits Attending (Yield): 16%
Transfer Admission Rate: 49%

SAT Reading/Writing (Middle 50%): 630-710
SAT Math (Middle 50%): 610-740
ACT Composite (Middle 50%): 28-33

% Graduated in Top 10% of HS Class: 50%
% Graduated in Top 25% of HS Class: 83%
% Graduated in Top 50% of HS Class: 96%

Demonstrated Interest: Considered
Legacy Status: Considered
Admission Interview Offered: Yes

ENROLLMENT
Total Undergraduate Enrollment: 1,579
% Part-Time: 3%
% Male: 44%
% Female: 56%
% Out-of-State: 65%
% Fraternity: 35%
% Sorority: 34%
% On-Campus (Freshman): 100%
% On-Campus (All Undergraduate): 66%

% African-American: 2%
% Asian: 6%
% Hispanic: 8%
% White: 63%
% Other: 8%
% Race or Ethnicity Unknown: 4%
% International: 9%
% Low-Income: 12%

ACADEMICS
Student-to-Faculty Ratio: 9 to 1
% of Classes Under 20: NR
% of Classes 20-49: NR
% of Classes 50 or More: NR
% Full-Time Faculty: 75%
% Full-Time Faculty w/ Terminal Degree: 92%

Top Programs
Art
Biology
Chemistry
Economics
Film and Media Studies
Philosophy
Politics

Retention Rate: 89%
4-Year Graduation Rate: 79%
6-Year Graduation Rate: 90%

Curricular Flexibility: Somewhat Flexible
Academic Rating: ★★★★

#CollegesWorthYourMoney

Due to its location in Walla Walla, Washington, there are plenty of experienced high school guidance counselors around the country who have never even heard of Whitman College. Despite a lack of instant name recognition, you'll find Whitman side-by-side in the rankings with better-known West Coast liberal arts powerhouses like Colorado College, Pitzer, and Occidental. And there's a good reason for these accolades—few colleges in the Pacific Northwest offer the intimate and supportive academic and social environment available at Whitman. The 1,579 students at Whitman, all undergrads, are a collection of high school stars who possess a median SAT score of close to 1,400 and an A/A- average in a mostly AP slate of courses. With forty-nine majors and thirty-three minors, the academic offerings at this college are robust, particularly when considering its modest size.

Inside the Classroom
The Encounters Program greets freshmen with a yearlong introduction to the liberal arts. Organized around a number of themes, those courses focus on "primary sources, discussion, writing, and the construction of knowledge across academic fields." Regardless of major, all students also must pass two courses in cultural pluralism, the humanities, the social sciences, fine arts, and the sciences as well as one course in quantitative analysis. Biology, environmental studies, geology, chemistry, economics, sociology, and politics majors are all required to complete a senior research thesis.

Whitman boasts a beautifully low 9:1 student-to-faculty ratio and hosts zero graduate students, a recipe for individualized attention. The faculty has a reputation for being extremely available, attentive, and invested in undergraduate education. Undergraduate research is so embedded into the foundation of a Whitman education that the college hosts an annual Undergraduate Conference for students to present their work. Greater than 40 percent of juniors study abroad in one of eighty-eight programs in forty+ countries around the globe.

By major, the greatest number of degrees are typically conferred in the social sciences (20 percent), biology (17 percent), visual and performing arts (13 percent), physical science (9 percent), and psychology (7 percent). All degree programs have solid reputations, but the biology, politics, and economics departments all have an extra shine. Whitman also does an amazing job funneling students into the most prestigious postgraduate fellowship programs. Over the last decade Whitties have captured over sixty Fulbright Scholarships, twenty-five National Science Foundation Fellowships, a dozen Watson Fellowships, and even one Rhodes Scholarship.

Outside the Classroom
One might assume that a school with fewer than 1,500 undergraduates would house just about everyone, especially with a spacious 117-acre campus. However, only 66 percent of Whitman students reside in one of the four freshman-only dorms, four upperclassmen dorms, or the eleven Interest Houses centered around commonalities like fine arts, the environment, or Asian studies. You also might expect a West Coast liberal arts school like Whitman to be Greek free, or at least to have a minimal frat/sorority presence on campus, yet that is not at all the case. Roughly 35 percent of students join fraternities and sororities, but it is important to note that they are generally viewed as inclusive and laid-back collectives in contrast to many Greek or-ganizations at large universities. There are fifteen varsity NCAA Division III sports teams as well as ten club and sixteen intramural squads. Forty-six percent of undergrads play intramurals, and 15 percent are varsity athletes. Of the close to one hundred student organizations on campus, the Outdoor Program is one of the most popular. Many students participate in its weekend hiking, kayaking, climbing, and skiing adventures. The school also had a run of award-winning debate teams prior to 2014, although it is presently in rebuilding mode. Walla Walla is technically a city, but it's more a of quaint and charming Pacific Northwestern small town. Seattle and Portland each are over a four-hour drive.

Career Services
The Student Engagement Center (SEC) at Whitman College employs ten professional staff members and eleven undergraduate employees, many of whom serve as peer advisors. The full-time professionals serve students through career coaching, community engagement, and internship coordination. Only counting those eight professionals, the SEC still comes out with a 158:1 student-to-advisor ratio, stronger than the vast majority of colleges profiled in this guide. Thanks to that terrific level of support, Whitties can schedule up to an hour of one-on-one career counseling whenever they like. The office lays out a Four Phase Plan that, beginning freshman year, helps students begin, develop, refine, and own their stories through job shadowing, internships, alumni networking, job fairs, community service, graduate school exploration, and professional development.

E-mail: admission@whitman.edu | Website: www.whitman.edu

Community service is a major part of the Whitman experience, and the SEC facilitates experiential opportunities in Walla Walla for 320 students per week, and 70 percent of undergraduates participate each year. Many summer internships are arranged at local organizations like the Walla Walla Public Health Department, the Walla Walla Symphony, and a local minor league baseball team. The school is supportive of those wishing to spend their summers at nonprofits and funds more than 130 such internships per year. The Whitman Connect program helps link current students with the college's 16,000+ alumni, and seventy-five alumni and parents provide job-shadowing opportunities over spring break. Despite a dearth of national companies visiting campus and mediocre salary statistics, this office can be counted on to provide individualized nurturing and career guidance.

Professional Outcomes

When you confer fewer than 400 degrees each year, you don't expect to have massive pockets of graduates joining major corporations. However, it is worth noting that twenty or more alumni currently work for Microsoft, Amazon, Boeing, Starbucks, T-Mobile, and Nordstrom. In the last few years, students have taken interesting first jobs including as a paralegal at the US Department of Justice-Antitrust Division, audio archivist at the Smithsonian, and marketing assistant at Oxford University Press. The largest number of Whitties settle in Seattle, but Portland, San Francisco, Los Angeles, New York, and Denver are other common destinations. Midcareer median pay is on the lower side among elite liberal arts schools, in the same range as the aforementioned Occidental and Reed as well as Kenyon, Vassar, and Macalester. Part of the lower median pay figure may be attributable to the high number of Whitman alumni who are continuing their educations well into their late twenties and early thirties.

Over 60 percent of Whitman graduates continue their educations at a wide range of graduate and professional programs. Since 2009, the school has sent graduates to law schools such as Berkeley, the University of Washington, Columbia, Georgetown, Duke, the University of Pennsylvania, and the University of Chicago. In that same time, premed students have headed to elite medical programs at Northwestern, UVA, Dartmouth, and Stanford. A significant number of Whitman grads go on to earn PhDs; the school ranks in the top twenty nationwide in that department. While many attend elite graduate/professional programs, plenty of other grads head to West Coast publics like Colorado State University, Oregon State University, and Washington State University.

Admission

Whitman's 50 percent acceptance rate for the Class of 2023 represented an average number for the college, but it should be eye-opening for any teens looking for an elite school on the West Coast. A test-optional school since 2016, those that submit scores have a median SAT of 1380 and a 31 on the ACT. Fifty-two percent hail from the top decile of their high school class, and 83 percent placed in the top quartile. The average unweighted GPA was a 3.62, and 44 percent of applicants earned above a 3.75. Whitman is the rare elite college that has become slightly easier to get into in recent years. A decade ago, the acceptance rate was 46 percent, SAT/ACT scores were comparable, and the average GPA was actually higher.

Rigor of academic record, GPA, and the application essay form the triumvirate of "most important" factors in the eyes of the committee. Recommendations, extracurricular activities, talent/ability, and character/personal characteristics are next in order importance. In 2019, the college received 193 early decision applications and welcomed 72 percent into the fold, demonstrating a clear advantage for those willing to commit through ED. The admissions committee states that it is seeking "curious, inspired, and highly engaged students with a passion for learning and a wide and eclectic range of interests; the kind of independent-minded students who are motivated to take intellectual risks in order to become the kind of leaders who can make a difference in the world." The school's admissions practices seem to support that sentiment.

Worth Your Money?

The cost of attendance at Whitman is $70k, not an unexpected amount for a liberal arts college with such an intimate classroom and campus environment. Fortunately, approximately half of Whitman undergrads qualify for need-based aid with an average annual award of more than $43k. For those who receive a generous merit or need-based offer, Whitman can absolutely be worth your money; at full price, this may not be the best choice for families lacking the funds to pay the costs up front.

FINANCIAL
Institutional Type: Private
In-State Tuition: $55,968
Out-of-State Tuition: $55,968
Room & Board: $13,800
Required Fees: $0
Books & Supplies: $1,400

Avg. Need-Based Grant: $43,501
Avg. % of Need Met: 92%

Avg. Merit-Based Award: $13,350
% Receiving (All Freshmen): 56%
% Receiving (Freshmen w/o Need): 39%

Avg. Cumulative Debt: $18,328
% of Students Borrowing: 43%

CAREER
Who Recruits
1. The Spur Group
2. Peace Corps
3. Baker Boyer Bank
4. TFA
5. Pacific Northwest National Laboratory

Notable Internships
1. WebMD
2. U.S. House of Representatives
3. Bloomsbury USA

Top Industries
1. Business
2. Education
3. Operations
4. Social Services
5. Research

Top Employers
1. Microsoft
2. Amazon
3. Boeing
4. The Spur Group
5. T-Mobile

Where Alumni Work
1. Seattle
2. Portland, OR
3. San Francisco
4. Richland, WA
5. Los Angeles

Median Earnings
College Scorecard (Early Career): $51,300
PayScale (Early Career): $58,800
PayScale (Mid-Career): $122,100

RANKINGS
Money: 387
U.S. News: 47 (T), Liberal Arts Colleges
Wall Street Journal/THE: 98 (T)
Washington Monthly: 63, Liberal Arts Colleges

COLLEGE OVERLAPS
Colorado College
Lewis & Clark College
Macalester College
Occidental College
Pomona College

Williams College

Williamstown, Massachusetts | 413-597-2211

Massachusetts is home to many of the finest and most historic institutions of higher learning in the United States. Starting in Boston and traveling west you would encounter many schools featured in this book—MIT, Harvard, BU, BC, Northeastern, Tufts, Brandeis, Wellesley—and, eventually, the more remote campuses of Amherst and Mount Holyoke and, lastly, tucked in the Northwest corner of the state just below Vermont you would encounter the Bay State's second-oldest school and one of the most prestigious liberal arts schools in the entire country, Williams College. Set on 450 rural acres in the Berkshires, Williams educates 2,078 of the brightest and most talented undergraduates one can find. The school's twenty-five academic departments offer thirty-six majors and a number of concentrations rather than minors.

Inside the Classroom

Students only take thirty-two total courses—four per semester—as opposed to the standard five. A Winter Study session also runs for twenty-two days in January when students can dedicate all of their attention to one course. Prior to graduation students must complete three courses in each of three Divisions: Languages and the Arts, Social Studies, and Science and Mathematics. Additionally, two writing-intensive courses and one course in quantitative reasoning are required. Rare for a liberal arts school of this caliber, no foreign language is required. Instead, the option exists to take a class exploring how different cultures interact with one another. While not quite as open as the curriculum at Brown or Amherst, Williams certainly gives its students their fair share of autonomy when it comes to course selection.

The college possesses an excellent 7:1 student-faculty ratio, and 99 percent of professorial attention goes to undergrads (they only run two small graduate programs). An unparalleled 46 percent of courses have fewer than ten students enrolled. Thanks to relationships built with faculty through such small classes, one Williams student said, "Students often just need to talk to a professor to find a research opportunity." However, many formal opportunities to engage in undergraduate research exist in the summer, during a semester, or as part of one's senior honors thesis. Close to 50 percent of the junior class connects with the International Education and Study Away program to pinpoint the study abroad opportunity that is right for them. Included on that menu is the opportunity to study at Oxford for an entire year.

The greatest number of degrees are conferred in the social sciences (28 percent), math and statistics (8 percent), English (8 percent), and foreign languages (8 percent). Any degree from Williams will be viewed most favorably by graduate schools and employers, but programs in economics, English, history, math and political science are especially renowned. The college also produces a massive number of highly competitive national fellowship winners. In 2020, grads and alums won eleven Fulbright Scholarships and five NSF Graduate Research Fellowships. In the last five years, three graduates have been named Rhodes Scholars.

Outside the Classroom

For a supremely studious, tiny liberal enclave buried in the woods, Williams is unexpectedly sports-centric within the NCAA Division III. The Ephs (a shortened version of Ephraim Williams, the school's founder) compete in thirty-two varsity sports, most of which are members of the New England Small College Athletic Conference. Overall, 35 percent of the student body competes in intercollegiate sports, and many more join intramural athletic clubs. Fraternities were banished from campus more than fifty years ago, just before the school became co-educational. In the absence of Greek life, extracurriculars take on a larger social role as 96 percent of Williams undergrads are involved in at least one of the 150 outside-the-classroom organizations. Situated in the Berkshires, there is no big city that makes an easy day trip (Boston and NYC are two or three hours away), but natural beauty is ubiquitous. The largest student-run group, the Williams Outing Club, has 750 members who engage in regular hikes, campouts, and polar bear swims in the Williamstown wilderness. The vast majority of the student body—93 percent—live on campus, making the school's breathtaking residence halls the epicenter of social activity. Freshmen live together in one of two large, nearly identical residence halls that form the bustling Frosh Quad. Upperclassmen reside in one of twenty-seven more modestly sized buildings.

Career Services

The '68 Center for Career Exploration (CCE) employs thirteen full-time staff members who focus on career advising, alumni relations, and employer relations. Specialized help is available for those eying law school, a health profession, entrepreneurship, or a career in technology. The center's 160:1 student-to-advisor ratio is one of the best of any school featured in this guide. Major events hosted by the center's crew include the Fall

Job and Internship Fair that is attended by seventy employers including big names like Bain, Credit Suisse, Deloitte, Epic Systems, The New York Times, and T. Rowe Price. The Spring Job & Internship Fair is primarily focused on nonprofit employers.

Williams alumni are extremely available and willing to lend a hand to current students, and 65 percent of current students report consulting with an alum to plan their next steps after college. Additionally, alumni sponsored internships provide 143 undergraduates with a $3,800 stipend to pursue non-paying summer internships. The center also has introduced a new program of winter study internships with an alum. On-campus interviews are brokered through the CCE, but no data is available on the number of interviews taking place or about on-campus recruiting, although a fair amount of both definitely occur. The college recently identified its tracking of alumni outcomes as being an area of weakness, and it has begun making strides toward remedying the situation. Thanks to its superhuman work getting students into top graduate schools, the '68 Center for Career Exploration still has a glowing reputation.

Professional Outcomes

The top three areas of gain that Williams graduates self-report are thinking critically, writing clearly and effectively, and the ability to learn on their own. It's hard to name three traits that speak more to one's employability, so it shouldn't come as a shock that the most desirable employers adore the school's alumni. Companies/organizations that consistently snatch-up Williams graduates include Apple, Google, Goldman Sachs, McKinsey & Co., the Metropolitan Museum of Art, National Institutes of Health, and the New York Times Co. A significant number of students join the Peace Corps or are accepted into Teach for America. Business and education are the industries that attract the most students. New York City, Boston, and San Francisco are the three cities most favored by Ephs post-undergrad.

For Ephs the bachelor's degrees earned at Williams are unlikely to be their last diplomas. Approximately 75 percent pursue an advanced degree within five years of leaving the college. The most frequently attended graduate programs are a not-too-shabby trio of Harvard, Columbia, and Yale. The top business, law, and medical schools attracting grads are Harvard, Columbia, and Penn. Using LinkedIn data, we were able to determine that Williams College sends one of the highest percentages of graduates to prestigious medical schools of any institution in the country. It also ranked eighth overall on our list of the top producers of future PhDs and was third-leading producer of economics PhDs (also by percentage).

Admission

Williams' Class of 2023 admissions data looks extremely similar to that of rival Amherst. The acceptance rate was 13 percent (Amherst was 11 percent), and the average standardized test scores of enrolled students were a 1500 on the SAT and a 34 on the ACT. Only 15 percent of 2019-20 freshmen were not in the top 10 percent of their high school class. Nothing earth-shattering has occurred in Williams' admissions standards in recent years. Like many comparably ultra-selective liberal arts colleges, the admit rate has declined; in 2011, the college accepted 17 percent of the applicant pool.

The admissions office views all of the meat-and-potatoes factors as holding the most weight: rigorous schedule, test scores, class rank, and GPA, but recommendations are carefully read as well. The next tier of criteria include race/ethnicity, legacy status (7 percent of admitted students are legacies, mostly of the primary variety), first-generation status (20 percent fit that bill), and factors like volunteer and work experience. Williams seeks a racially and socioeconomically diverse group of uniquely talented students who will thrive in a close-knit academic community. However, few Hail Mary heaves end successfully here.

Worth Your Money?

The annual cost of attendance at Williams is, in the world of elite liberal arts schools in New England, priced at the slightly below average $63k (temporarily marked down for COVID), but those who aren't from wealthy backgrounds will pay far less. In fact, roughly half the student population qualifies for aid, and of that group all students have 100 percent of their financial need met with the average award being $55k. For the rich, the Williams bill won't sting too badly; for those in the lower-to-middle income brackets, the school will slice the cost significantly. For those in between, Williams is the caliber of school that is worth taking on debt in order to attend. Learning in seminar-style courses from some of the brightest minds around is worth paying for, and the connections you make (to peers and faculty) will stay with you for a lifetime.

FINANCIAL
Institutional Type: Private
In-State Tuition: $59,350
Out-of-State Tuition: $59,350
Room & Board: $15,000
Required Fees: $310
Books & Supplies: $800

Avg. Need-Based Grant: $54,973
Avg. % of Need Met: 100%

Avg. Merit-Based Award: $0
% Receiving (All Freshmen): 0%
% Receiving (Freshmen w/o Need): 0%

Avg. Cumulative Debt: $15,911
% of Students Borrowing: 33%

CAREER
Who Recruits
1. OC&C Strategy Consultants
2. Teach for America
3. M&T Bank
4. InterSystems
5. Trinity Industries

Notable Internships
1. WeWork
2. Late Night with Seth Meyers
3. Whitney Museum of American Art

Top Industries
1. Business
2. Education
3. Research
4. Finance
5. Social Services

Top Employers
1. Google
2. Goldman Sachs
3. Morgan Stanley
4. JPMorgan Chase
5. Bain & Company

Where Alumni Work
1. New York City
2. Boston
3. San Francisco
4. Washington DC
5. Albany, NY

Median Earnings
College Scorecard (Early Career): $59,000
PayScale (Early Career): $69,900
PayScale (Mid-Career): $143,400

RANKINGS
Money: 32
U.S. News: 1, Liberal Arts Colleges
Wall Street Journal/THE: 21 (T)
Washington Monthly: 10, Liberal Arts Colleges

COLLEGE OVERLAPS
Amherst College
Brown University
Cornell University
Dartmouth College
Middlebury College

Worcester Polytechnic Institute

Worcester, Massachusetts | 508-831-5286

Worcester Polytechnic Institute, commonly referred to as WPI, is a small-to-midsize private university that is one of the fastest-growing PhD-granting schools in the United States. More than 4,700 undergraduate students and an additional 2,100+ graduate students attend school in Worcester, a city roughly fifty miles, as the crow flies, from Boston. Working on a quarter schedule, students engage in three courses for seven-week sprints as they plow through one of fifty+ rigorous degree programs, primarily in engineering.

Inside the Classroom
An education at WPI is as hands-on and innovative as you will find at any university, engineering-centric or otherwise. The Interactive Qualifying Project (IPQ), often completed off campus, features work in small teams on a project that "connects science and technology with social issues and human need." The Major Qualifying Project (MQP) is a unique capstone experience in which students must identify a real-world problem and find a novel solution. A host of industry partners work with students in the MQPs. Students can participate in a four-to-eight-month paid co-op experience as part of their undergraduate experience. Core academic requirements for all undergrads also include a foray into the humanities and arts as the school seeks to produce well-rounded, team-player engineers.

With a student-to-faculty ratio of 14:1, WPI does an exceptional job keeping undergraduate classrooms cozy. In fact, a staggering 51 percent of its classes enroll fewer than ten students, creating an incredible level of academic intimacy. All students complete a minimum of two long-term research projects that are focused on solving real-world problems. That process begins freshman year, and by senior year 72 percent have engaged in off-campus research as well. Studying abroad, like most things at WPI, is not a typical experience. Many undergrads travel to one of fifty+ project centers situated on six continents where they can engage in solving real-life problems. Beginning with the Class of 2022, the school began awarding every single student $5,000 in study abroad
funding with an aim toward a 90 percent participation rate within the next few years.

The undergraduate engineering program is respected worldwide and frequently graces lists of top schools for a variety of sub-disciplines. The most popular majors are under the engineering umbrella (67 percent) and computer science (17 percent). Those completing all of those programs find favorable conditions as they approach graduate schools, potential employers, and prestigious national scholarship organizations. WPI undergrads won eleven Gilman Scholarships in 2019 and between two and five National Science Foundation Graduate Research Fellowships per year (plus many honorable mentions).

Outside the Classroom
Housing on campus is guaranteed only to freshmen; approximately three-fifths of all undergrads live on WPI's concentrated ninety-five-acre campus. Many other students reside in one of the school's nineteen fraternities and sororities; 27 percent of men and 37 percent of women go Greek. It is worth noting that women make up only 40 percent of the undergraduate student population. Twenty varsity sports teams, evenly split between men's and women's squads, compete as the Engineers in NCAA Division III. Another forty-four combined club and intramural teams and the four-floor, state-of-the-art Sports and Recreation Center that houses a pool ensure that physical activity is accessible to all. There are 225 clubs and activities that include original offerings like underwater hockey, a Rubik's Cube club, and a lock-picking club. Hey, no one would ever argue that WPI students aren't extremely creative. Of course, there are many traditional options also on the menu, including a multitude of organizations geared toward young professionals and shared academic interests. Boston is doable day trip, but there is plenty to do right in Worcester, including bustling Shrewsbury Street, museums, theaters, and loads of eateries. A growing urban area that still possesses the charm of a small-college town, Worcester can easily be navigated via public transit.

Career Services
The Career Development Center (CDC) consists of ten professional employees, which works out to a student-to-advisor ratio of 476:1, in the average range compared to other schools featured in this guide. The staff is comprised of career counselors, corporate relations specialists, and recruiting coordinators. Students at WPI report an exceptionally high rate of satisfaction with their school's career services offerings for reasons that are obvious when you examine the basic facts.

Worcester Polytechnic Institute

E-mail: admissions@wpi.edu | Website: www.wpi.edu

An extraordinary 80 percent of all undergraduates, including freshmen and sophomores, interact with the CDC in some capacity each year. Each academic year, 400+ companies recruit on WPI's campus at career fairs, networking events, or on-campus job interviews. Annually, hundreds of students participate in summer internships or co-op placements that help them expand their network of career resources; the school's many corporate partners are always willing to take on WPI interns. In addition to strongly encouraging one-on-one counseling appointments, the office provides services like corporate tours, an employer-in-residence program, corporate information sessions, panel discussions, and a robust online system that allows students to connect with alumni and potential employers. Considering its highly accessible and broad array of offerings as well as positive professional and graduate school outcomes for alumni, the Worcester Polytechnic Institute's Career Development Center receives high marks from our staff.

Professional Outcomes

Within six months of graduation, 90 percent of Class of 2019 members had progressed beyond the seeking phase and had landed jobs or enrolled full time in graduate school. Companies employing literally hundreds of WPI alumni of all ages include Raytheon, Pratt & Whitney, Dell, and BAE Systems. Recent graduates found jobs at companies that included Air BNB, DraftKings, Amazon Robotics, NASA, Harvard Medical School, the US Department of Defense, and SpaceX. The average starting salary crept above $72,000 and is currently among the highest of any in the country, impressive even for a school focused entirely on STEM disciplines. WPI graduates most frequently remain in Greater Boston, but significant numbers relocate to New York City, Hartford, San Francisco, and Providence.

Nineteen percent of recent diploma-earners elected to immediately begin work on an advanced degree. Elite graduate schools attended by Class of 2019 grads included Georgia Tech, Carnegie Mellon, Johns Hopkins, Brown, and Stanford. Premed students enjoy the university's early/assured acceptance arrangements with Tufts Veterinary School, Massachusetts College of Pharmacy & Health Sciences, and Lake Erie College of Osteopathic Medicine. Recent grads have been accepted into medical school at the likes of Dartmouth, Northwestern, and Cornell.

Admission

WPI became the first top engineering university to adopt a test-optional policy in 2007, and it remains a rare breed among STEM-focused institutions. That decision has contributed to the school now receiving over 10,600 applications versus roughly 7,000 one decade ago. The acceptance rate for a place in the 2019-20 freshman class was 49 percent. Within that cohort 63 percent finished in the top 10 percent of their high school class while 96 percent placed in the top quartile. The average GPA was 3.9, and more than four-fifths of the group possessed a GPA above a 3.75. Among those submitting standardized test scores, the mid-50 percent on the SAT was 1320-1450, and it was 29-33 on the ACT.

Rigor of secondary school record and GPA are the only two factors deemed "very important" by the Worcester Admissions Committee. Interestingly, despite being test-optional, standardized test scores are among the factors considered "important" by the school along with class rank, recommendations, extracurricular activities, and character/personal qualities. It is worth noting that, as at most engineering schools, women enjoy a higher acceptance rate than men. At WPI that disparity is more pronounced than is typical; female applicants gain acceptance 63 percent of the time, and men get in at a 44 percent clip. Valuing students who are "creative and curious," who "enjoy working together to get things done," and "feel pretty sure that they're leaders, not followers," the Worcester Polytechnic Institute Admissions Committee is looking for passionate candidates who possess strong grades in AP courses and, in many cases, superior test scores.

Worth Your Money?

If your family can afford WPI, you will likely recoup a sizable portion of the $74,300 cost of attendance. The vast majority of students do receive a merit aid package averaging $18k per year, which knocks the cost down a bit. Fortunately, with such high starting salaries for recent graduates, paying $200,000 plus for an undergraduate degree from this school is not at all an unwise investment.

FINANCIAL
Institutional Type: Private
In-State Tuition: $53,100
Out-of-State Tuition: $53,100
Room & Board: $15,680
Required Fees: $926
Books & Supplies: $1,000

Avg. Need-Based Grant: $28,153
Avg. % of Need Met: 91%

Avg. Merit-Based Award: $18,052
% Receiving (All Freshmen): 98%
% Receiving (Freshmen w/o Need): 32%

Avg. Cumulative Debt: $27,600
% of Students Borrowing: 59%

CAREER
Who Recruits
1. PepsiCo
2. BAE Systems
3. General Electric
4. Travelers
5. Raytheon

Notable Internships
1. ExxonMobil
2. Dell
3. State Street

Top Industries
1. Engineering
2. Operations
3. Business
4. Information Technology
5. Research

Top Employers
1. Raytheon
2. Pratt & Whitney
3. Dell
4. National Grid
5. Google

Where Alumni Work
1. Boston
2. New York City
3. Hartford, CT
4. San Francisco
5. Providence, RI

Median Earnings
College Scorecard (Early Career): $84,900
PayScale (Early Career): $76,500
PayScale (Mid-Career): $143,200

RANKINGS
Money: 234
U.S. News: 66 (T), National Universities
Wall Street Journal/THE: 120
Washington Monthly: 99, National Universities

COLLEGE OVERLAPS
Boston University
Clarkson University
Northeastern University
Rensselaer Polytechnic Institute
Rochester Institute of Technology

Yale University

New Haven, Connecticut | 203-432-9300

ADMISSION
Admission Rate: 6%
Admission Rate - Men: 7%
Admission Rate - Women: 6%
EA Admission Rate: Not Offered
ED Admission Rate: Not Offered
ED Admits as % of Total Admits: Not Offered
Admission Rate (5-Year Trend): -1%
% of Admits Attending (Yield): 69%
Transfer Admission Rate: 2%

SAT Reading/Writing (Middle 50%): 720-770
SAT Math (Middle 50%): 740-800
ACT Composite (Middle 50%): 33-35

% Graduated in Top 10% of HS Class: 92%
% Graduated in Top 25% of HS Class: 99%
% Graduated in Top 50% of HS Class: 100%

Demonstrated Interest: Not Considered
Legacy Status: Considered
Admission Interview Offered: Yes

ENROLLMENT
Total Undergraduate Enrollment: 6,092
% Part-Time: 0%
% Male: 49%
% Female: 51%
% Out-of-State: 92%
% Fraternity: NR
% Sorority: NR
% On-Campus (Freshman): 100%
% On-Campus (All Undergraduate): 84%

% African-American: 8%
% Asian: 20%
% Hispanic: 14%
% White: 40%
% Other: 7%
% Race or Ethnicity Unknown: 1%
% International: 10%
% Low-Income: 11%

ACADEMICS
Student-to-Faculty Ratio: 6 to 1
% of Classes Under 20: 73%
% of Classes 20-49: 18%
% of Classes 50 or More: 9%
% Full-Time Faculty: 66%
% Full-Time Faculty w/ Terminal Degree: 93%

Top Programs
Biology
Computer Science
Economics
Engineering
Global Affairs
History
Political Science
Psychology

Retention Rate: 99%
4-Year Graduation Rate: 88%
6-Year Graduation Rate: 97%

Curricular Flexibility: Somewhat Flexible
Academic Rating: ★★★★★

#CollegesWorthYourMoney

World leaders, Supreme Court justices, scores of famous actors, inventors, writers, Nobel Laureates, billionaire businessmen, even fictional billionaire businessmen like The Simpsons' Mr. Burns . . . the list of Yale alumni fills multiple volumes of history books. Founded in 1701 as a more conservative, Puritan-rooted option to Harvard, the home of the Bulldogs is today elite, even by Ivy standards, every bit as much so as its Crimson rival of over 300 years. New Haven, Connecticut, is the destination for 6,092 undergraduates and more than 7,500 graduate students yet, thanks to the nurturing Residential College housing system, the university serves as an intimate undergraduate home while still playing the role of major private research university.

Inside the Classroom
There are eighty majors and 2,000 undergraduate course offerings at Yale. The social sciences (24 percent), biology (11 percent), history (8 percent), engineering (7 percent) and computer science (7 percent) are the university's most popular areas of concentration. In aiming to strike a balance between freedom and control, the required coursework at Yale is modest and relatively broad. Students must take courses in the natural sciences, the humanities and arts, the social sciences, foreign language, quantitative reasoning, and writing. Most majors require a one-to-two semester senior capstone experience. Depending on the major, students work closely with a professor toward the completion of an essay, portfolio, or research project.

The student-to-faculty ratio of 6:1 does translate to small class sizes, even with a larger number of graduate students on campus than undergrads. Close to three-quarters of classes have an enrollment of fewer than twenty students, making for a perfect environment for teaching and learning. Undergraduate research is a staple of the Yale academic experience; 95 percent of science majors participate in research with faculty and, university-wide, undergraduate research fellowships are available to 90 percent of first-years who apply. In short, you'd have to try very hard to avoid engaging in research while an undergraduate at Yale. The number of Bulldogs electing to study abroad has skyrocketed in recent years, and 47 percent of Class of 2019 members reported having one such experience.

Many of Yale's undergraduate programs sit atop any major rankings list. Among the crème de la crème departments are biology, economics, global affairs, engineering, history, and computer science. Any degree from Yale will get your resume/application to employers or graduate schools on the top of the pile. The same goes for applications to competitive post-college scholarships, including the uber-prestigious Rhodes Scholarship. Yalies have captured the award 250+ times, second only to Harvard in the all-time rankings. In 2019, nineteen Yale students captured Fulbright Scholarships.

Outside the Classroom
With 319 years of history and a $29 billion endowment, Yale's 345-acre, tree-lined campus is a blend of beautiful stone edifices and modern amenities. Perhaps the most distinctive feature of life outside the classroom at Yale is the famed Residential College system that was imported from Oxford/Cambridge seventy years ago to facilitate a level of cohesiveness and connection typically only found at smaller liberal arts schools. Students are assigned to one of fourteen residential colleges that they will remain affiliated with for all four years. Each residence has two full-time, live-in faculty members. Greek life is not a dominant presence as only 10 percent of Yalies join a frat or sorority. So-called "secret societies," of which there are approximately forty, attract roughly half of seniors. Those include the famed Skull and Bones society, which has infiltrated American pop culture. Athletics are big-time at Yale as the Bulldogs field thirty-five NCAA Division I sports teams. An additional fifty club teams and thirty intramural sports are available for non-varsity athletes. Other student-run organizations include sixty cultural groups and fifty performance groups. Those seeking nature can canoe and camp on the 1,500 acres of the school's Outdoor Education Center or walk to the Yale Farm. Amenities and attractions include twelve dining halls, three on-campus museums, two theaters, and a library with 15 million holdings. Yale is situated in the middle of downtown New Haven, and the area is easily walkable. Boston and New York are each roughly a two-hour drive from New Haven.

Career Services
The Yale Office of Career Strategy (OCS) has fourteen professional staff members (excluding administrative assistants and counselors who only deal with graduate students) who are dedicated to tasks such as employer relations, career counseling, and summer funding opportunities. The 435:1 student-to-advisor ratio is within the average range when compared to other schools featured in this book. Still, the OCS has no shortage of brag-worthy statistics attached to its name.

For starters, in the 2018-19 academic year, the Office of Career Strategy claimed 25,277 student contacts to its credit, including over 4,800 one-on-one sessions with undergraduates. That same academic year the office hosted more than one hundred workshops and career exploration events that were attended by 8,735 students. The OCS also hosts thirteen industry-specific career fairs that attract 200 companies/organizations and close to 1,900 current students. Eighty-five top employers engaged in on-campus recruiting, and over 1,000 interviews were granted on Yale's grounds. The results are as impressive as the process—87 percent of Class of 2019 graduates reported that they were employed in an area directly related to their area of study. Yale students universally fill their summers with productive activities, often beginning immediately after their freshman year. By senior year, 38 percent have spent the previous summer at a paid internship, 15 percent at an unpaid internship, 11 percent in laboratory research, 9 percent in academic study, and 5 percent in field research.

Professional Outcomes

Shortly after graduating, 62 percent of the Yale Class of 2019 had entered the world of employment, 17 percent matriculated in graduate programs, and only 4 percent were still looking for their next destination. The most common industries entered by the newly hired were finance (16 percent), consulting (14 percent), research (9 percent), and software development (7 percent). The mean starting salary for last year's grads was $68,472; CS majors took home an average of $106k. Hundreds of Yale alums can be found at each of the world's top companies including Facebook, Google, Goldman Sachs, McKinsey & Company, Morgan Stanley, and Microsoft. Geographically, New York City has the highest concentration of alumni followed by San Francisco, Boston, DC, Los Angeles, and Chicago.

Using Class of 2019 data, among those pursuing graduate/professional programs, 18 percent were in medical school, almost one-quarter started work on a PhD, and 6 percent went directly from undergraduate studies to law school. Unsurprisingly, given the quality of the minds admitted into Yale, medical school applicants traditionally find a home 90 percent of the time, exactly twice the national average. Law school applicants do just fine as well; 87 percent were accepted into at least one school with a substantial number continuing at Yale Law School (YLS). Roughly 10 percent of YLS first-years attended Yale as undergraduates. For a complete list of where Yale alumni as a whole continue their educational journeys, simply consult a list of the best graduate/professional programs in the world.

Admission

Yale received 36,844 applications for a place in the Class of 2023, but a meager 6 percent made it through the gates. Of those admitted, 92 percent placed in the top decile of their high school graduating class. The mid-50 percent range on the SAT was 1470-1560; the ACT span was 33-35. For an even better idea of the testing mastery required to become a Bulldog, look to the fact that 83 percent had an SAT Reading score of over 700, and 90 percent had an SAT Math score over 700.

You can bet a school that rejects nearly 94 percent of applicants relies on more than a few data points. The admissions committee ranks nine factors as being "most important": rigor of secondary record, GPA, class rank, standardized test scores (SAT Subject Test scores are recommended), application essay, recommendations, extracurricular activities, talent/ability, and character/personal qualities. The committee uses two overarching questions to guide its process: "Who is likely to make the most of Yale's resources?" and "Who will contribute most significantly to the Yale community?" Yale offers a unique single-choice early action (SCEA) option with a November 1 deadline. Those going that route are not bound to attend the university if accepted, but they cannot simultaneously apply ED or EA to any other school. Of the 6,016 SCEA applicants for the 2019-20 freshman cohort, 794 were admitted, a 14 percent success rate. More 2019-20 freshmen were first-generation students (17 percent) than legacy admits (12 percent). Getting into Yale is a hard-to-predict enterprise that sees many valedictorians and salutatorians bite the dust. Fantastic numbers along with a record of special talents and accomplishments that scream "future leader" will fare best.

Worth Your Money?

Yale is one of those rare schools where the contacts and networks you create while attending will make the education worth any cost. Fortunately, thanks to a $31 billion endowment, every single student who qualifies for need-based aid sees 100 percent of that need met by the university. The average grant is for $61,067, significantly reducing the sticker price cost of attendance of almost $75,000. There is no merit aid awarded by Yale, so those not in financial need will be paying full freight, but again, that will be money well spent.

FINANCIAL
Institutional Type: Private
In-State Tuition: $57,700
Out-of-State Tuition: $57,700
Room & Board: $17,200
Required Fees: NR
Books & Supplies: $3,700

Avg. Need-Based Grant: $61,067
Avg. % of Need Met: 100%

Avg. Merit-Based Award: $0
% Receiving (All Freshmen): 0%
% Receiving (Freshmen w/o Need): 0%

Avg. Cumulative Debt: $15,379
% of Students Borrowing: 15%

CAREER
Who Recruits
1. The New York Times
2. Uber
3. Citi
4. Bain & Company
5. Boston Consulting Group

Notable Internships
1. Netflix
2. The Blackstone Group
3. United Nations

Top Industries
1. Business
2. Education
3. Research
4. Media
5. Operations

Top Employers
1. Google
2. McKinsey & Company
3. Goldman Sachs
4. Facebook
5. Morgan Stanley

Where Alumni Work
1. New York City
2. San Francisco
3. Boston
4. Washington DC
5. Los Angeles

Median Earnings
College Scorecard (Early Career): $83,200
PayScale (Early Career): $77,100
PayScale (Mid-Career): $154,600

RANKINGS
Money: 7
U.S. News: 4 (T), National Universities
Wall Street Journal/THE: 3
Washington Monthly: 4, National Universities

COLLEGE OVERLAPS
Columbia University
Dartmouth College
Harvard University
Princeton University
University of Pennsylvania

Top Colleges for America's Top Majors

Included in each school profile, we highlighted the academic programs that are among the very best on that particular campus. The next natural step is to look at top programs across all schools so that you can emerge with a bird's-eye picture of the premier American colleges in your major of interest. We included more than several dozen of the most popular areas of concentration in order to make these lists as useful and relevant to our audience as is possible.

For more useful lists, including a number of majors not covered in this book, we highly recommend visiting the College Transitions Dataverse at **www.collegetransitions.com/dataverse**. Please revisit the methodology section of this book (in the front) for an extensive explanation of how we selected the programs for inclusion.

And without further ado, we present College Transitions' Top Colleges for America's Top Majors:

Accounting
Baruch College (CUNY)
Binghamton University (SUNY)
Boston College
Brigham Young University
Bucknell University
Claremont McKenna College
Fordham University
Georgetown University
Indiana University Bloomington
Lehigh University
New York University
The Ohio State University – Columbus
Santa Clara University
University of Florida
University of Georgia
University of Illinois at Urbana-Champaign
University of Michigan
University of Notre Dame
University of Pennsylvania
University of Southern California
The University of Texas at Austin
Villanova University
Wake Forest University
Washington and Lee University
Washington University in St. Louis

Actuarial Science
Bentley University
Brigham Young University
Clemson University
Florida State University
Michigan State University
New York University
The Ohio State University – Columbus
Pennsylvania State University – University Park
Purdue University – West Lafayette
University of Notre Dame
University of California, Los Angeles
University of California, Santa Barbara
University of Florida
University of Georgia
University of Illinois at Urbana-Champaign
University of Michigan

University of Minnesota – Twin Cities
University of North Carolina at Chapel Hill
University of Pennsylvania
University of Wisconsin – Madison

Aerospace Engineering
California Institute of Technology
Case Western Reserve University
Cornell University
Georgia Institute of Technology
Massachusetts Institute of Technology
The Ohio State University – Columbus
Pennsylvania State University – University Park
Purdue University – West Lafayette
Princeton University
Rensselaer Polytechnic Institute
Stanford University
Texas A&M University – College Station
University of California, Berkeley
University of California, Los Angeles
University of Colorado Boulder
University of Illinois at Urbana-Champaign
University of Maryland, College Park
University of Michigan
University of Minnesota
University of Notre Dame
University of Southern California
The University of Texas at Austin
University of Virginia
University of Washington – Seattle
Virginia Tech

Animal Science
California Polytechnic State University, San Luis Obispo
Clemson University
Cornell University
Michigan State University
North Carolina State University
The Ohio State University – Columbus
Pennsylvania State University – University Park
Purdue University – West Lafayette
Texas A&M University – College Station
University of California, Davis
University of Connecticut

University of Florida
University of Georgia
University of Illinois at Urbana-Champaign
University of Maryland, College Park
University of Massachusetts Amherst
University of Minnesota – Twin Cities
University of Wisconsin – Madison
Virginia Tech

Architecture

California Polytechnic State University, San Luis Obispo
Carnegie Mellon University
Columbia University
The Cooper Union for the Advancement of Science and Art
Cornell University
Georgia Institute of Technology
Illinois Institute of Technology
Lehigh University
Northeastern University
Princeton University
Rensselaer Polytechnic Institute
Rice University
Syracuse University
Tulane University
University of California, Berkeley
University of Florida
University of Michigan
University of Minnesota – Twin Cities
University of Notre Dame
University of Pennsylvania
University of Southern California
The University of Texas at Austin
University of Virginia
Virginia Tech
Washington University in St. Louis

Art

Alfred University
Arizona State University
Boston University
California College of the Arts
California Institute of the Arts
Carnegie Mellon University
Columbia University
The Cooper Union for the Advancement of Science and Art
Cornell University
New York University
Pratt Institute
Princeton University
Rhode Island School of Design
Savannah College of Art and Design
School of the Art Institute of Chicago
Tufts University
University of California, Berkeley
University of California, Los Angeles
University of California, San Diego
University of Colorado Boulder
University of Michigan
University of Notre Dame
University of Pennsylvania
University of Southern California
The University of Texas at Austin
University of Washington – Seattle
University of Wisconsin – Madison

Vassar College
Virginia Commonwealth University
Washington University in St. Louis
Williams College
Yale University

Biology

Amherst College
Bowdoin College
Brandeis University
Brown University
California Institute of Technology
Carleton College
Colby College
Cornell University
Dartmouth College
Duke University
Emory University
Grinnell College
Harvard University
Haverford College
Johns Hopkins University
Macalester College
Massachusetts Institute of Technology
Pomona College
Princeton University
Reed College
Stanford University
Swarthmore College
University of California, Berkeley
University of California, Davis
University of California, Los Angeles
University of California, San Diego
University of Chicago
University of Pennsylvania
Washington University in St. Louis
Yale University

Biomedical Engineering

Boston University
Brown University
California Institute of Technology
Carnegie Mellon University
Case Western Reserve University
Columbia University
Cornell University
Duke University
Georgia Institute of Technology
Harvard University
Johns Hopkins University
Massachusetts Institute of Technology
Northwestern University
Purdue University – West Lafayette
Rice University
Stanford University
University of California, Berkeley
University of California, San Diego
University of Illinois at Urbana-Champaign
University of Michigan
University of Pennsylvania
University of Pittsburgh – Pittsburgh Campus
University of Rochester
The University of Texas at Austin
University of Washington – Seattle

University of Wisconsin – Madison
Vanderbilt University
Washington University in St. Louis
Worcester Polytechnic Institute
Yale University

Business Administration
Babson College
Bentley University
Boston College
Carnegie Mellon University
College of William & Mary
Cornell University
Emory University
Georgetown University
Georgia Institute of Technology
Indiana University Bloomington
Massachusetts Institute of Technology
New York University
Northeastern University
The Ohio State University – Columbus
Southern Methodist University
University of California, Berkeley
University of Illinois at Urbana-Champaign
University of Michigan
University of North Carolina at Chapel Hill
University of Notre Dame
University of Pennsylvania
University of Richmond
University of Southern California
The University of Texas at Austin
University of Virginia
University of Wisconsin – Madison
Villanova University
Wake Forest University
Washington and Lee University
Washington University in St. Louis

Chemical Engineering
Bucknell University
California Institute of Technology
Carnegie Mellon University
Colorado School of Mines
Columbia University
Cornell University
Georgia Institute of Technology
Johns Hopkins University
Lehigh University
Massachusetts Institute of Technology
North Carolina State University
Northwestern University
Princeton University
Purdue University – West Lafayette
Rensselaer Polytechnic Institute
Rice University
Stanford University
Tufts University
University of California, Berkeley
University of California, Santa Barbara
University of Illinois at Urbana-Champaign
University of Michigan
University of Minnesota – Twin Cities
University of Notre Dame
University of Pennsylvania

The University of Texas at Austin
University of Wisconsin – Madison
Washington University in St. Louis
Worcester Polytechnic Institute

Chemistry
Bowdoin College
Bryn Mawr College
California Institute of Technology
Carleton College
College of the Holy Cross
College of William & Mary
Columbia University
Cornell University
Grinnell College
Harvard University
Harvey Mudd College
Haverford College
Macalester College
Massachusetts Institute of Technology
Northwestern University
Pomona College
Princeton University
Reed College
Rice University
St. Olaf College
Stanford University
University of California, Berkeley
University of California, San Diego
University of Chicago
University of Illinois at Urbana-Champaign
University of Minnesota – Twin Cities
University of North Carolina at Chapel Hill
Washington University in St. Louis
Wellesley College
Williams College

Civil Engineering
Arizona State University
Bucknell University
California Institute of Technology
Carnegie Mellon University
Clarkson University
Columbia University
Cornell University
Georgia Institute of Technology
Johns Hopkins University
Lafayette College
Lehigh University
Massachusetts Institute of Technology
North Carolina State University
Northwestern University
The Ohio State University – Columbus
Pennsylvania State University – University Park
Princeton University
Purdue University – West Lafayette
Rose-Hulman Institute of Technology
Rice University
Stanford University
Texas A&M University – College Station
Tufts University
University of California, Berkeley
University of California, Davis
University of Illinois at Urbana-Champaign

University of Maryland, College Park
University of Michigan
The University of Texas at Austin
University of Wisconsin – Madison
Virginia Tech

Communication

American University
Boston College
Boston University
Cornell University
Emerson College
Fordham University
George Washington University
New York University
Northeastern University
Northwestern University
The Ohio State University – Columbus
Pennsylvania State University – University Park
Pepperdine University
Santa Clara University
Syracuse University
University of California, Berkeley
University of Florida
University of Georgia
University of Maryland, College Park
University of Miami
University of North Carolina at Chapel Hill
University of Pennsylvania
University of Southern California
The University of Texas at Austin
University of Washington – Seattle
University of Wisconsin – Madison
Vanderbilt University
Villanova University
Wake Forest University
Washington and Lee University

Computer Science

California Institute of Technology
Carleton College
Carnegie Mellon University
Columbia University
Cornell University
Duke University
Georgia Institute of Technology
Harvard University
Harvey Mudd College
Massachusetts Institute of Technology
New York University
Northeastern University
Princeton University
Purdue University – West Lafayette
Rutgers University – New Brunswick
Stanford University
Swarthmore College
University of California, Berkeley
University of California, Los Angeles
University of California, San Diego
University of Illinois at Urbana-Champaign
University of Maryland, College Park
University of Massachusetts Amherst
University of Michigan
University of Pennsylvania
University of Southern California

The University of Texas at Austin
University of Washington – Seattle
University of Wisconsin – Madison
Virginia Tech

Criminology/Criminal Justice

American University
Appalachian State University
Arizona State University
The College of New Jersey
Florida State University
George Mason University
George Washington University
Indiana University Bloomington
John Jay College of Criminal Justice (CUNY)
Marist College
Michigan State University
Northeastern University
The Ohio State University – Columbus
Pennsylvania State University – University Park
Rutgers University – New Brunswick
San Diego State University
Temple University
University of California, Irvine
University of Delaware
University of Georgia
University of Maryland, College Park
University of Miami
University of Pennsylvania
University of Pittsburgh – Pittsburgh Campus
University of South Carolina
University of Washington – Seattle

Drama and Theater Arts

Boston University
Brown University
Carnegie Mellon University
California Institute of the Arts
DePaul University
Elon University
Emerson College
Florida State University
Fordham University
The Juilliard School
Loyola Marymount University
Muhlenberg College
New York University
Northwestern University
Oberlin College
Purchase College (SUNY)
Rutgers University – New Brunswick
Southern Methodist University
Syracuse University
Temple University
University of California, Irvine
University of California, Los Angeles
University of California, San Diego
University of Miami
University of Michigan
University of North Carolina School of the Arts
University of Notre Dame
University of Southern California
Vassar College
Yale University

Economics

Amherst College
Bowdoin College
Brown University
Claremont McKenna College
Colby College
Columbia University
Cornell University
Dartmouth College
Duke University
Georgetown University
Grinnell College
Harvard University
Macalester College
Massachusetts Institute of Technology
Middlebury College
New York University
Northwestern University
Pomona College
Princeton University
Stanford University
Swarthmore College
University of California, Berkeley
University of California, San Diego
University of Chicago
University of Michigan
University of Pennsylvania
Vanderbilt University
Washington and Lee University
Williams College
Yale University

Education

Arizona State University
Boston College
Boston University
Brigham Young University
Brown University
Colgate University
College of William & Mary
Duke University
Emory University
Florida State University
Indiana University Bloomington
New York University
The Ohio State University – Columbus
Pennsylvania State University – University Park
Southern Methodist University
Swarthmore College
University of California, Irvine
University of Connecticut
University of Florida
University of Georgia
University of Illinois at Urbana-Champaign
University of Maryland, College Park
University of Michigan
University of Minnesota – Twin Cities
University of North Carolina at Chapel Hill
University of Pittsburgh – Pittsburgh Campus
The University of Texas at Austin
University of Washington – Seattle
University of Wisconsin – Madison
Vanderbilt University

Electrical Engineering

Bucknell University
California Institute of Technology
Carnegie Mellon University
Case Western Reserve University
Columbia University
Cornell University
Duke University
Franklin W. Olin College of Engineering
Georgia Institute of Technology
Massachusetts Institute of Technology
Northwestern University
The Ohio State University – Columbus
Princeton University
Purdue University – West Lafayette
Rensselaer Polytechnic Institute
Rice University
Stanford University
Texas A&M University – College Station
University of California, Berkeley
University of California, Los Angeles
University of California, San Diego
University of Illinois at Urbana-Champaign
University of Michigan
University of Maryland, College Park
University of Pennsylvania
The University of Texas at Austin
University of Washington – Seattle
University of Wisconsin – Madison
Virginia Tech
Worcester Polytechnic Institute

English

Amherst College
Barnard College
Bowdoin College
Brown University
Bryn Mawr College
College of the Holy Cross
Columbia University
Cornell University
Dartmouth College
Davidson College
Duke University
Harvard University
Haverford College
Johns Hopkins University
Kenyon College
Middlebury College
Northwestern University
Princeton University
Reed College
Stanford University
Swarthmore College
University of Michigan
University of California, Berkeley
University of California, Los Angeles
University of Chicago
University of Pennsylvania
University of Virginia
Vassar College
Williams College
Yale University

Environmental Engineering
Arizona State University
California Polytechnic State University, San Luis Obispo
California Institute of Technology
Carnegie Mellon University
Clemson University
Cornell University
Duke University
Georgia Institute of Technology
Johns Hopkins University
Massachusetts Institute of Technology
North Carolina State University
Pennsylvania State University – University Park
Purdue University – West Lafayette
Rice University
Stanford University
University at Buffalo (SUNY)
University of California, Berkeley
University of California, Davis
University of California, Riverside
University of California, San Diego
University of Colorado Boulder
University of Florida
University of Illinois at Urbana-Champaign
University of Michigan
The University of Texas at Austin
University of Washington – Seattle
University of Wisconsin – Madison
Virginia Tech
Worcester Polytechnic Institute
Yale University

Environmental Studies
Amherst College
Bates College
Bowdoin College
Carleton College
Colby College
Colorado College
Cornell University
Dartmouth College
Dickinson College
Duke University
Hamilton College
Macalester College
Middlebury College
Mount Holyoke College
Oberlin College
Pitzer College
Pomona College
Tulane University
University of California, Berkeley
University of California, Davis
University of California, Los Angeles
University of California, San Diego
University of California, Santa Barbara
University of California, Santa Cruz
University of Chicago
University of North Carolina at Chapel Hill
University of Wisconsin – Madison
Williams College
Yale University

Film
American University
Binghamton University (SUNY)
Boston University
Chapman University
Columbia University
DePaul University
Drexel University
Emerson College
Emory University
Florida State University
George Mason University
Ithaca College
Loyola Marymount University
New York University
Northwestern University
Oberlin College
Rochester Institute of Technology
Southern Methodist University
Stanford University
Syracuse University
Temple University
University of California, Irvine
University of California, Los Angeles
University of California, Santa Barbara
University of Colorado Boulder
University of Miami
University of Southern California
The University of Texas at Austin
Wesleyan University
Yale University

Finance
Arizona State University
Babson College
Baruch College (CUNY)
Bentley University
Boston College
Boston University
Carnegie Mellon University
Cornell University
Emory University
Fairfield University
Fordham University
George Washington University
Georgetown University
Indiana University Bloomington
Massachusetts Institute of Technology
New York University
The Ohio State University – Columbus
Pennsylvania State University – University Park
University of California, Berkeley
University of Illinois at Urbana-Champaign
University of Michigan
University of North Carolina at Chapel Hill
University of Notre Dame
University of Pennsylvania
University of Southern California
The University of Texas at Austin
University of Virginia
University of Washington – Seattle
University of Wisconsin – Madison
Washington University in St. Louis

Geology
Bowdoin College
Brown University
California Institute of Technology
Carleton College
College of William & Mary
Colorado School of Mines
Columbia University
Cornell University
Duke University
Lehigh University
Massachusetts Institute of Technology
Pennsylvania State University – University Park
Princeton University
Stanford University
Texas A&M University – College Station
Union College
University of California, Berkeley
University of California, Davis
University of California, Irvine
University of California, Santa Barbara
University of Florida
University of Michigan
University of Minnesota – Twin Cities
University of Pennsylvania
University of Pittsburgh – Pittsburgh Campus
The University of Texas at Austin
University of Washington – Seattle
University of Wisconsin – Madison
Whitman College
Yale University

History
Amherst College
Barnard College
Bowdoin College
Brown University
Carleton College
Colgate University
Columbia University
Cornell University
Dartmouth College
Georgetown University
Grinnell College
Harvard University
Haverford College
Johns Hopkins University
Kenyon College
Northwestern University
Oberlin College
Pomona College
Princeton University
Stanford University
Swarthmore College
University of California, Berkeley
University of California, Los Angeles
University of Chicago
University of Michigan
University of Pennsylvania
University of Wisconsin – Madison
Vanderbilt University
Williams College
Yale University

Industrial Engineering
Clarkson University
Clemson University
Columbia University
Cornell University
Georgia Institute of Technology
Lehigh University
North Carolina State University
Northeastern University
Northwestern University
The Ohio State University – Columbus
Pennsylvania State University – University Park
Purdue University – West Lafayette
Rensselaer Polytechnic Institute
Stanford University
Texas A&M University – College Station
University of California, Berkeley
University of Florida
University of Illinois at Urbana-Champaign
University of Michigan
University of Pittsburgh – Pittsburgh Campus
University of Southern California
The University of Texas at Austin
University of Wisconsin – Madison
Virginia Tech
Worcester Polytechnic Institute

Information Systems
Arizona State University
Bentley University
Brigham Young University
Carnegie Mellon University
Cornell University
Fairfield University
Georgetown University
Georgia Institute of Technology
Indiana University Bloomington
Massachusetts Institute of Technology
Miami University
New York University
Northeastern University
The Ohio State University – Columbus
Purdue University – West Lafayette
Santa Clara University
University of Arizona
University of Georgia
University of Illinois at Urbana-Champaign
University of Maryland, College Park
University of Michigan
University of Minnesota – Twin Cities
University of Pennsylvania
The University of Texas at Austin
University of Washington – Seattle
University of Wisconsin – Madison
Villanova University

International Relations
American University
Boston University
Brown University
Claremont McKenna College
Colby College
Colgate University
College of William & Mary

Columbia University
Connecticut College
Cornell University
Dartmouth College
George Washington University
Georgetown University
Harvard University
Johns Hopkins University
Mount Holyoke College
Pomona College
Princeton University
Stanford University
Swarthmore College
Tufts University
University of California, Berkeley
University of California, San Diego
University of Chicago
University of Michigan
University of Pennsylvania
University of Southern California
University of Virginia
Williams College
Yale University

Kinesiology
Boston University
Brigham Young University
Elon University
Indiana University Bloomington
Michigan State University
Northeastern University
Occidental College
Pennsylvania State University – University Park
Purdue University – West Lafayette
Rice University
Texas A&M University – College Station
University of Connecticut
University of Delaware
University of Florida
University of Georgia
University of Illinois at Urbana-Champaign
University of Maryland, College Park
University of Massachusetts Amherst
University of Miami
University of Michigan
University of Minnesota – Twin Cities
University of North Carolina at Chapel Hill
University of Pittsburgh – Pittsburgh Campus
University of South Carolina
The University of Texas at Austin
University of Virginia
University of Wisconsin – Madison
Wake Forest University

Marketing
Arizona State University
Boston College
Cornell University
Emory University
Fairfield University
Florida State University
Fordham University
George Washington University
Georgetown University

Indiana University Bloomington
New York University
The Ohio State University – Columbus
Santa Clara University
University of California, Berkeley
University of Florida
University of Illinois at Urbana-Champaign
University of Maryland, College Park
University of Michigan
University of Minnesota – Twin Cities
University of North Carolina at Chapel Hill
University of Notre Dame
University of Pennsylvania
University of Pittsburgh – Pittsburgh Campus
University of Southern California
The University of Texas at Austin
University of Virginia
University of Washington – Seattle
University of Wisconsin – Madison
Villanova University
Washington University in St. Louis

Materials Science and Engineering
California Institute of Technology
Carnegie Mellon University
Colorado School of Mines
Columbia University
Cornell University
Georgia Institute of Technology
Johns Hopkins University
Lehigh University
Massachusetts Institute of Technology
North Carolina State University
Northwestern University
The Ohio State University – Columbus
Pennsylvania State University – University Park
Purdue University – West Lafayette
Rensselaer Polytechnic Institute
Rice University
Stanford University
University of California, Berkeley
University of California, Los Angeles
University of California, Santa Barbara
University of Florida
University of Illinois at Urbana-Champaign
University of Michigan
University of Minnesota
University of Pennsylvania
The University of Texas at Austin
University of Washington – Seattle
University of Wisconsin – Madison
Virginia Tech

Mathematics
Amherst College
Bowdoin College
Brown University
California Institute of Technology
Carnegie Mellon University
Carleton College
Columbia University
Cornell University
Duke University
Harvard University

Harvey Mudd College
Johns Hopkins University
Massachusetts Institute of Technology
New York University
Northwestern University
Pomona College
Princeton University
Reed College
Rice University
Stanford University
Swarthmore College
University of California, Berkeley
University of California, Los Angeles
University of California, San Diego
University of Chicago
University of Michigan
University of Pennsylvania
University of Washington – Seattle
Williams College
Yale University

Mechanical Engineering
California Institute of Technology
Carnegie Mellon University
Case Western Reserve University
Columbia University
Cornell University
Duke University
Franklin W. Olin College of Engineering
Georgia Institute of Technology
Johns Hopkins University
Lehigh University
Massachusetts Institute of Technology
Northwestern University
The Ohio State University – Columbus
Pennsylvania State University – University Park
Princeton University
Purdue University – West Lafayette
Rensselaer Polytechnic Institute
Rice University
Rose-Hulman Institute of Technology
Stanford University
Stevens Institute of Technology
Texas A&M University – College Station
University of California, Berkeley
University of California, Los Angeles
University of Illinois at Urbana-Champaign
University of Michigan
University of Pennsylvania
The University of Texas at Austin
University of Wisconsin – Madison
Vanderbilt University
Virginia Tech
Worcester Polytechnic Institute

Music
Bard College
Belmont University
Berklee College of Music
Boston University
California Institute of the Arts
Carnegie Mellon University
Cleveland Institute of Music
Colburn School Conservatory

Curtis Institute of Music
Indiana University Bloomington
Johns Hopkins University
The Juilliard School
Lawrence University
Manhattan School of Music
New England Conservatory
New York University
Northwestern University
Oberlin College
Rice University
San Francisco Conservatory of Music
Syracuse University
University of California, Los Angeles
University of Miami
University of Michigan
University of North Texas
University of Rochester
University of Southern California
The University of Texas at Austin
Vanderbilt University
Yale University

Neuroscience
Amherst College
Barnard College
Boston University
Bowdoin College
Brandeis University
Brown University
Colgate University
College of William & Mary
Colorado College
Columbia University
Dartmouth College
Duke University
Emory University
Harvard University
Johns Hopkins University
Middlebury College
Northwestern University
Oberlin College
Pomona College
Princeton University
Tulane University
University of California, Los Angeles
University of California, San Diego
University of Pennsylvania
University of Pittsburgh – Pittsburgh Campus
University of Rochester
University of Southern California
Vanderbilt University
Washington University in St. Louis
Wellesley College
Wesleyan University

Nursing
Binghamton University (SUNY)
Boston College
Brigham Young University
Case Western Reserve University
Clemson University
The College of New Jersey
Drexel University

Emory University
Fairfield University
Georgetown University
New York University
Northeastern University
The Ohio State University – Columbus
Pennsylvania State University – University Park
Rutgers University – New Brunswick
Stony Brook University (SUNY)
University of Delaware
University of Florida
University of Massachusetts Amherst
University of Miami
University of Michigan
University of Minnesota – Twin Cities
University of North Carolina at Chapel Hill
University of Pennsylvania
University of Pittsburgh – Pittsburgh Campus
The University of Texas at Austin
University of Virginia
University of Washington – Seattle
University of Wisconsin – Madison
Villanova University

Physics
Brown University
California Institute of Technology
Carleton College
Carnegie Mellon University
Columbia University
Cornell University
Davidson College
Grinnell College
Harvard University
Harvey Mudd College
Haverford College
Johns Hopkins University
Massachusetts Institute of Technology
Pomona College
Princeton University
Reed College
Rensselaer Polytechnic Institute
Rice University
Stanford University
University of California, Berkeley
University of California, Los Angeles
University of California, Santa Barbara
University of Chicago
University of Illinois at Urbana-Champaign
University of Maryland, College Park
University of Michigan
University of Notre Dame
University of Pennsylvania
University of Rochester
Yale University

Political Science
Bowdoin College
Brown University
College of William & Mary
Columbia University
Cornell University
Dartmouth College
Duke University

Georgetown University
Hamilton College
Harvard University
Haverford College
Macalester College
Middlebury College
Northwestern University
Princeton University
Stanford University
University of California, Berkeley
University of California, Los Angeles
University of Chicago
University of Michigan
University of North Carolina at Chapel Hill
University of Notre Dame
University of Pennsylvania
University of Rochester
Vanderbilt University
Vassar College
Washington and Lee University
Wesleyan University
Williams College
Yale University

Psychology
Barnard College
Bates College
Boston College
Brown University
Claremont McKenna College
Columbia University
Dartmouth College
Duke University
Harvard University
Haverford College
Northwestern University
Pomona College
Princeton University
Stanford University
Tufts University
University of California, Berkeley
University of California, Los Angeles
University of Chicago
University of Michigan
University of Minnesota – Twin Cities
University of North Carolina at Chapel Hill
University of Pennsylvania
University of Wisconsin – Madison
Vanderbilt University
Vassar College
Washington University in St. Louis
Wellesley College
Wesleyan University
Williams College
Yale University

Statistics
Brigham Young University
Carleton College
Carnegie Mellon University
Columbia University
Cornell University
Duke University
Harvard University

Johns Hopkins University
North Carolina State University
Northwestern University
Pennsylvania State University – University Park
Purdue University – West Lafayette
Rice University
Rutgers University – New Brunswick
Stanford University
Texas A&M University – College Station
University of California, Berkeley
University of California, Los Angeles
University of California, Santa Barbara
University of Chicago
University of Connecticut
University of Florida
University of Illinois at Urbana-Champaign
University of Michigan
University of Minnesota – Twin Cities
University of North Carolina at Chapel Hill
University of Pennsylvania
University of Washington – Seattle
University of Wisconsin – Madison
Virginia Tech

Top "Feeder" Colleges

Teens eyeing highly-competitive fields (e.g. medicine, law, finance, engineering, tech, journalism, or academia), should be aware that certain undergraduate colleges serve as "feeders," annually sending a sizable number of alumni to the crème de la crème of graduate/professional programs as well as the most desirable employers. Being aware of which colleges have a direct pipeline into the advanced degree program or corporation you aim to one day target, can help put you on the path toward making that dream a reality.

The lists that follow showcase the top 30 "feeder" schools into the most highly-ranked graduate programs/ companies for a variety of disciplines/industries. The column on the left reveals the universities that send the largest raw number of graduates into top institutions (either academic or corporate). The column on the right shows the top 30 feeders when adjusted for a school's undergraduate enrollment, which allows us to highlight schools that may be smaller in size, but that still send a consistent flow of graduates to the world's premier schools/companies.

For a more detailed look at our methodology in constructing each list, please visit the College Transitions Dataverse at www.collegetransitions.com/dataverse.